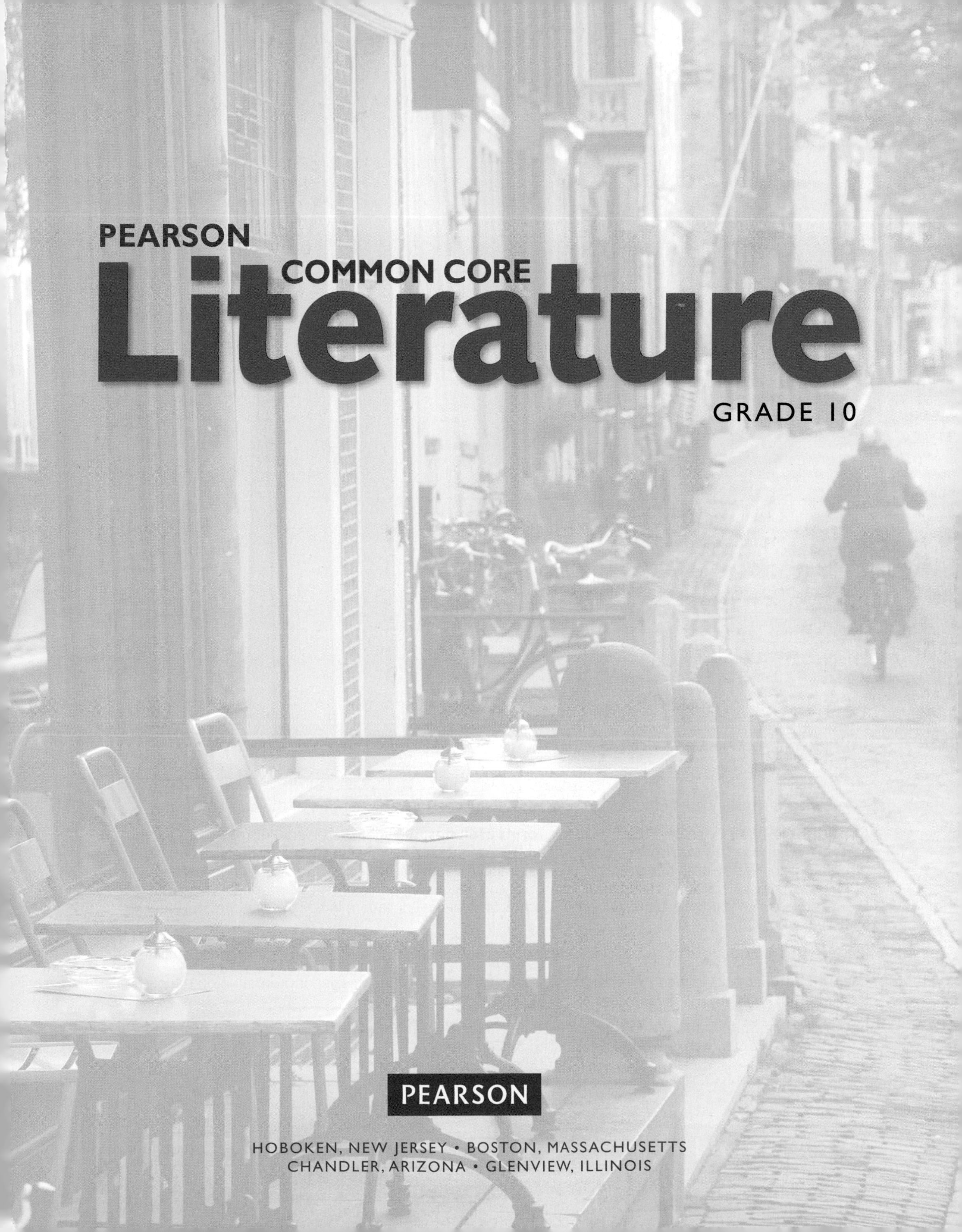

PEARSON

COMMON CORE Literature

GRADE 10

PEARSON

HOBOKEN, NEW JERSEY • BOSTON, MASSACHUSETTS
CHANDLER, ARIZONA • GLENVIEW, ILLINOIS

COVER: Tom Asz/Shutterstock.com

Acknowledgments appear in the back of this book, and constitute an extension of this copyright page.

ISBN-13: 978-0-13-326821-8
ISBN-10: 0-13-326821-7
6 7 8 9 10 11 12 13 V057 18 17 16 15 14

PEARSON COMMON CORE Literature

GRADE 10

PEARSON

HOBOKEN, NEW JERSEY • BOSTON, MASSACHUSETTS
CHANDLER, ARIZONA • GLENVIEW, ILLINOIS

Contributing Authors

The contributing authors guided the direction and philosophy of Pearson Common Core Literature. *They helped to build the pedagogical integrity of the program by contributing content expertise, knowledge of the Common Core State Standards, and support for the shifts in instruction the Common Core will bring. Their knowledge, combined with classroom and professional experience, ensures* Pearson Common Core Literature *is relevant for both teachers and students.*

William G. Brozo, Ph.D., is a Professor of Literacy in the Graduate School of Education at George Mason University in Fairfax, Virginia. He earned his bachelor's degree from the University of North Carolina and his master's and doctorate from the University of South Carolina. He has taught reading and language arts in the Carolinas and is the author of numerous articles on literacy development for children and young adults. His books include *To Be a Boy, To Be a Reader: Engaging Teen and Preteen Boys in Active Literacy; Readers, Teachers, Learners: Expanding Literacy Across the Content Areas; Content Literacy for Today's Adolescents: Honoring Diversity and Building Competence; Supporting Content Area Literacy with Technology* (Pearson); and *Setting the Pace: A Speed, Comprehension, and Study Skills Program*. His newest book is *RTI and the Adolescent Reader: Responsive Literacy Instruction in Secondary Schools*. As an international consultant, Dr. Brozo has provided technical support to teachers from the Balkans to the Middle East, and he is currently a member of a European Union research grant team developing curriculum and providing adolescent literacy professional development for teachers across Europe.

Diane Fettrow spent the majority of her teaching career in Broward County, Florida, teaching high school English courses and serving as department chair. She also worked as an adjunct instructor at Broward College, Nova Southeastern University, and Florida Atlantic University. After she left the classroom, she served as Secondary Language Arts Curriculum Supervisor for several years, working with more than 50 of the district's high schools, centers, and charter schools. During her time as curriculum supervisor, she served on numerous local and state committees; she also served as Florida's K–12 ELA content representative to the PARCC Model Content Frameworks Rapid Response Feedback Group and the PARCC K–12 and Upper Education Engagement Group. Currently she presents workshops on the Common Core State Standards and is working with Pearson on aligning materials to the CCSS.

Kelly Gallagher is a full-time English teacher at Magnolia High School in Anaheim, California, where he has taught for twenty-seven years. He is the former co-director of the South Basin Writing Project at California State University, Long Beach, and the author of *Reading Reasons: Motivational Mini-Lessons for Middle and High School; Deeper Reading: Comprehending Challenging Texts, 4–12; Teaching Adolescent Writers;* and *Readicide: How Schools Are Killing Reading and What You Can Do About It*. He is also a principal author of *Prentice Hall Writing Coach* (Pearson, 2012). Kelly's latest book is *Write Like This* (Stenhouse). Follow Kelly on Twitter @KellyGToGo, and visit him at www.kellygallagher.org.

Elfrieda "Freddy' Hiebert, Ph.D., is President and CEO of TextProject, a nonprofit organization that provides resources to support higher reading levels. She is also a research associate at the University of California, Santa Cruz. Dr. Hiebert received her Ph.D. in Educational Psychology from the University of Wisconsin-Madison. She has worked in the field of early reading acquisition for 45 years, first as a teacher's aide and teacher of primary-level students in California and, subsequently, as a teacher educator and researcher at the universities of Kentucky, Colorado-Boulder, Michigan, and California-Berkeley. Her research addresses how fluency, vocabulary, and knowledge can be fostered through appropriate texts. Professor Hiebert's research has been published in numerous scholarly journals, and she has authored or edited nine books. Professor Hiebert's model of accessible texts for beginning and struggling readers—TExT—has been used to develop numerous reading programs that are widely used in schools. Dr. Hiebert is the 2008 recipient of the William S. Gray Citation of Merit, awarded by the International Reading Association; is a member of the Reading Hall of Fame; and has chaired a group of early childhood literacy experts who served in an advisory capacity to the CCSS writers.

Donald J. Leu, Ph.D., is the John and Maria Neag Endowed Chair in Literacy and Technology and holds a joint appointment in Curriculum and Instruction and Educational Psychology in the Neag School of Education at the University of Connecticut. Don is an international authority on literacy education, especially the new skills and strategies required to read, write, and learn with Internet technologies and the best instructional practices that prepare students for these new literacies. He is a member of the Reading Hall of Fame, a Past President of the National Reading Conference, and a former member of the Board of Directors of the International Reading Association. Don is a Principal Investigator on a number of federal research grants, and his work has been funded by the U.S. Department of Education, the National Science Foundation, and the Bill and Melinda Gates Foundation, among others. He recently edited the *Handbook of Research on New Literacies* (Erlbaum, 2008).

Ernest Morrell, Ph.D., is a professor of English Education at Teachers College, Columbia University, and the president-elect of the National Council of Teachers of English (NCTE). He is also the Director of Teachers College's Harlem-based Institute for Urban and Minority Education (IUME). Dr. Morrell was an award-winning high school English teacher in California, and he now works with teachers and schools across the country to infuse multicultural literature, youth popular culture, and media production into standards-based literacy curricula and after-school programs. He is the author of nearly 100 articles and book chapters as well as five books, including *Critical Media Pedagogy: Achievement, Production, and Justice in City Schools* and *Linking Literacy and Popular Culture*. In his spare time he coaches youth sports and writes poems and plays.

Karen Wixson, Ph.D., is Dean of the School of Education at the University of North Carolina, Greensboro. She has published widely in the areas of literacy curriculum, instruction, and assessment. Dr. Wixson has been an advisor to the National Research Council and helped develop the National Assessment of Educational Progress (NAEP) reading tests. She is a former member of the IRA Board of Directors and co-chair of the IRA Commission on RTI. Recently, Dr. Wixson served on the English Language Arts Work Team that was part of the Common Core State Standards Initiative.

Grant Wiggins, Ed.D., is the President of Authentic Education in Hopewell, New Jersey. He earned his Ed.D. from Harvard University and his B.A. from St. John's College in Annapolis. Grant consults with schools, districts, and state education departments on a variety of reform matters; organizes conferences and workshops; and develops print materials and Web resources on curricular change. He is perhaps best known for being the co-author, with Jay McTighe, of *Understanding by Design* and *The Understanding by Design Handbook,* the award-winning and highly successful materials on curriculum published by ASCD.

 Contents

COMMON CORE FOUNDATIONS

COMMON CORE STATE STANDARDS

The following standards are introduced in this unit and revisited throughout the program.

Reading Literature

2. Determine a theme or central idea of a text and analyze in detail its development over the course of the text, including how it emerges and is shaped and refined by specific details; provide an objective summary of the text.

10. By the end of Grade 10, read and comprehend literature, including stories, dramas, and poems, at the high end of the grades 9–10 text complexity band independently and proficiently.

Reading Informational Text

2. Determine a central idea of a text and analyze its development over the course of the text, including how it emerges and is shaped and refined by specific details; provide an objective summary of the text.

8. Delineate and evaluate the argument and specific claims in a text, assessing whether the reasoning is valid and the evidence is relevant and sufficient; identify false statements and fallacious reasoning.

Writing

1. Write arguments to support claims in an analysis of substantive topics or texts, using valid reasoning and relevant and sufficient evidence.

2. Write informative/explanatory texts to examine and convey complex ideas, concepts, and information clearly and accurately through the effective selection, organization, and analysis of content.

5. Develop and strengthen writing as needed by planning, revising, editing, rewriting, or trying a new approach, focusing on addressing what is most significant for a specific purpose and audience.

7. Conduct short as well as more sustained research projects to answer a question (including a self-generated question) or solve a problem; narrow or broaden the inquiry when appropriate; synthesize multiple sources on the subject, demonstrating understanding of the subject under investigation.

8. Gather relevant information from multiple authoritative print and digital sources, using advanced searches effectively; assess the usefulness of each source in answering the research question; integrate information into the text selectively to maintain the flow of ideas, avoiding plagiarism and following a standard format for citation.

9. Draw evidence from literary or informational texts to support analysis, reflection, and research.

Additional standards addressed in these workshops:

Reading Informational Text
6, 9, 10;

Writing
1.a, 1.b, 1.e, 2.a–d;

Language
1, 1.b, 3, 3.a, 6

UNIT 1 Can progress be made without conflict?

PART 1
SETTING EXPECTATIONS

PART 2
TEXT ANALYSIS GUIDED EXPLORATION

CHARACTERS AND CONFLICT

PART 3
TEXT SET DEVELOPING INSIGHT

PERSEVERANCE

PART 4
DEMONSTRATING INDEPENDENCE

DIGITAL ASSETS KEY

These digital resources, as well as audio and the Online Writer's Notebook, can be found at **pearsonrealize.com**.

- Interactive Whiteboard Activities
- Virtual Tour
- Close Reading Notebook
- Video
- Close Reading Tool for Annotating Texts
- Grammar Tutorials
- Online Text Set

UNIT 1 Unit at a Glance

READ

Text Analysis
- Plot and Plot Devices
- Setting
- Theme
- Characters and Characterization
- Comparing Irony and Paradox
- Conflict
- Author's Perspective
- Dialogue
- Central Idea
- Anecdote
- Tone

Comprehension
- Make Predictions
- Make Inferences
- Draw Conclusions

Language Study
- Latin Root *-cred-*
- Latin Suffix *-ity*
- Latin Prefix *com-*
- Latin Suffix *-able*

Conventions
- Nouns
- Pronouns
- Degrees of Adjectives and Adverbs
- Verb Tenses

Language Study Workshop
- Using a Dictionary and Thesaurus

DISCUSS

Comprehension and Collaboration
- Interview
- Group Discussion

Presentation of Ideas
- Oral Reading

Responding to Text
- Group Discussion
- Panel Discussion
- Partner Discussion

Speaking and Listening Workshop
- Delivering an Oral Interpretation of a Literary Work

RESEARCH

Research and Technology
- Report on Sources

Investigate the Topic: Perseverance
- The Work Ethic
- Practicing
- Origins of the Civil Rights Movement
- Sunk Cost and Opportunity Cost
- Predictive Factors
- Futurology
- Building Skyscrapers

WRITE

Writing to Sources
- Sequel
- Letter; Literary Review
- Character Analysis
- Retellings
- Explanatory Essay
- Cause-and-Effect Essay
- Profile
- Autobiographical Narrative
- Reflective Essay
- Persuasive Essay
- Letter to the Editor
- Monologue
- Argumentative Essay

Writing Process Workshop
- Argument: Analytic Response to Literature
  - Conventions: Pronoun-Antecedent Agreement
  - Conventions: Subject-Verb Agreement

UNIT VOCABULARY

Academic Vocabulary appears in *blue*.

Introducing the Big Question *adversity, change, compromise, concession, confrontation, debate, motive, negotiate, oppose, progress, radical, reconciliation, resolve, struggle, unify*

The Monkey's Paw *grave, maligned, credulity, furtively, apathy, oppressive*

The Street of the Cañon *nonchalantly, audaciously, imperiously, disdain, plausibility, apprehension*

Civil Peace *disreputable, amenable, destitute, inaudibly, dissent, commiserate*

A Problem *pretense, candid, lofty, detestable, subdued, edifying*

Like the Sun; The Open Window *tempering, ingratiating, scrutinized, endeavored, falteringly, delusion, conduct, distortion, integrity, motive*

Contents of the Dead Man's Pocket *convoluted, reveling, interminable, convey, captures, dilemma*

***from* Swimming to Antarctica** *equilibrium, gauge, buffer, account, discern, anticipate*

Occupation: Conductorette *indignation, hypocrisy, dexterous, context, instilled, episode*

***from* The Upside of Quitting** *curdled, empirical, poignant, emphatic, anticipate, customary*

***from* The Winning Edge** *provocative, opined, tenacious, findings, factors, reviews*

Science Fiction and the Future *commencement, exploit, succumb, perspective, derive, contemporary*

***from the series* Empire State (Laying Beams), 1930–31** *vantage, plane, urban*

COMMON CORE STATE STANDARDS

For the full wording of the standards, see the standards charts following the Contents pages.

Reading Literature

RL.9-10.1, RL.9-10.2, RL.9-10.3, RL.9-10.4, RL.9-10.5, RL.9-10.6, RL.9-10.10

Reading Informational Text

RI.9-10.1, RI.9-10.2, RI.9-10.3, RI.9-10.4, RI.9-10.5, RI.9-10.6, RI.9-10.8, RI.9-10.10

Writing

W.9-10.1, W.9-10.1.a–e, W.9-10.2, W.9-10.2.a–c, W.9-10.2.e–f, W.9-10.3, W.9-10.3.a–e, W.9-10.4, W.9-10.5, W.9-10.6, W.9-10.7, W.9-10.8, W.9-10.9, W.9-10.9.a–b, W.9-10.10

Speaking and Listening

SL.9-10.1, SL.9-10.1.a–d, SL.9-10.4, SL.9-10.6

Language

L.9-10.1, L.9-10.2, L.9-10.2.a–c, L.9-10.3, L.9-10.3.a, L.9-10.4, L.9-10.4.b–d, L.9-10.5, L.9-10.6

UNIT 2 What kind of knowledge changes our lives?

PART 1
SETTING EXPECTATIONS

PART 2
TEXT ANALYSIS GUIDED EXPLORATION

SEEKING KNOWLEDGE

PART 3
TEXT SET DEVELOPING INSIGHT

VISION

PART 4
DEMONSTRATING INDEPENDENCE

DIGITAL ASSETS KEY

These digital resources, as well as audio and the Online Writer's Notebook, can be found at **pearsonrealize.com.**

- Interactive Whiteboard Activities
- Virtual Tour
- Close Reading Notebook
- Video
- Close Reading Tool for Annotating Texts
- Grammar Tutorials
- Online Text Set

UNIT 2 Unit at a Glance

READ

Text Analysis
Expository Essay
Reflective Essay
Persuasive Writing and Rhetorical Devices
Analytic and Interpretive Essays
Comparing Humorous Writing
Cultural Context
Theme
Supporting Details
Description
Diction
Similes

Comprehension
Main Idea
Evaluate Persuasion
Distinguishing Fact From Opinion

Language Study
Latin Root *-fig-*
Latin Prefix *suc-, sub-*
Latin Root *-scend-*
Greek Prefix *em-, im-*

Conventions
Action and Linking Verbs
Active and Passive Voice
Direct and Indirect Objects
Subject Complements

Language Study Workshop
Word Origins: Etymology

DISCUSS

Comprehension and Collaboration
Debate

Presentation of Ideas
Humorous Persuasive Speech
Oral Recollection

Responding to Text
Debate
Group Discussion
Partner Discussion
Small Group Discussion

Speaking and Listening Workshop
Delivering a Persuasive Speech

RESEARCH

Research and Technology
Cover Letter; Résumé

Investigate the Topic: Vision
Mass Media and "Seeing"
The Artist's Eye
The Validity of Intuition
Satellite Imaging
Vision and Meaning
Entoptic Lights and Cave Paintings
Photorealism

WRITE

Writing to Sources
Business Letter
Memoir
Letter
Critique
Explanatory Essay
Persuasive Essay
Comparison-and-Contrast Essay
Autobiographical Narrative
Informative Essay
Position Paper
Argumentative Essay

Writing Process Workshop
Argument: Persuasive Essay
Voice: Finding Your Voice
Sentence Fluency: Revising to Create Parallelism

UNIT VOCABULARY

Academic Vocabulary appears in *blue*.

Introducing the Big Question *adapt, awareness, empathy, enlighten, evolve, growth, history, ignorance, influence, insight, modified, question, reflect, revise, understanding*

***from* Longitude** *haphazardly, configuration, converge, derived, contested, impervious*

The Sun Parlor *lavished, subordinate, rejuvenation, convalesce, cajoling, succinct*

Keep Memory Alive *transcends, presumptuous, accomplices*

The American Idea *embodied, emigrants, successive, subversion*

A Toast to the Oldest Inhabitant: The Weather of New England; The Dog That Bit People *sumptuous, vagaries, incredulity, irascible, context, interpretation, manipulate, perspective*

How to React to Familiar Faces *context, expound, amiably, multitudes, overall, distortion*

***from* Magdalena Looking** *flaxen, momentous, reverence, regarded, analyses, perspective*

***from* The Statue That Didn't Look Right** *reminiscent, articulate, pastiche, fundamentally, physiological, manifest*

***from* The Shape of the World** *recurrent, obliterated, intricate, abstract, represent, aspects*

Seeing Things *auditory, neural, focal, hierarchy, precision, ornate*

How to Look at Nothing *gradients, contrived, auroras, phenomena, subjective, worldview*

***Car Reflections,* 1970 (acrylic on masonite)** *inverted, surpass*

COMMON CORE STATE STANDARDS

For the full wording of the standards, see the standards charts following the Contents pages.

Reading Literature

RL.9-10.1, RL.9-10.2, RL.9-10.3, RL.9-10.4, RL.9-10.7, RL.9-10.10

Reading Informational Text

RI.9-10.1, RI.9-10.2, RI.9-10.3, RI.9-10.4, RI.9-10.5, RI.9-10.6, RI.9-10.7, RI.9-10.8, RI.9-10.10

Writing

W.9-10.1, W.9-10.1.a–e, W.9-10.2, W.9-10.2.a, W.9-10.2.e–f, W.9-10.3, W.9-10.3.a–e, W.9-10.4, W.9-10.5, W.9-10.6, W.9-10.7, W.9-10.8, W.9-10.9, W.9-10.9.a–b, W.9-10.10

Speaking and Listening

SL.9-10.1, SL.9-10.1.a–d, SL.9-10.3, SL.9-10.4, SL.9-10.5, SL.9-10.6

Language

L.9-10.1, L.9-10.1.a, L.9-10.2, L.9-10.2.c, L.9-10.3, L.9-10.3.a, L.9-10.4, L.9-10.4.a–c, L.9-10.5, L.9-10.5.b, L.9-10.6

UNIT 3 Does all communication serve a positive purpose?

PART 1 SETTING EXPECTATIONS

PART 2 TEXT ANALYSIS GUIDED EXPLORATION

ARTFUL WORDS

DIGITAL ASSETS KEY

These digital resources, as well as audio and the Online Writer's Notebook, can be found at **pearsonrealize.com.**

- Interactive Whiteboard Activities
- Virtual Tour
- Close Reading Notebook
- Video
- Close Reading Tool for Annotating Texts
- Grammar Tutorials
- Online Text Set

UNIT 3 Unit at a Glance

READ

Text Analysis

The Speaker in Poetry
Poetic Forms
Figurative Language
Sound Devices
Comparing Theme
Personification
Dramatic Irony
Intertextuality
Memoir and Historical Writing
Expert Opinion
Diction: Technical Language

Comprehension

Read Fluently
Paraphrase

Language Study

Old English Prefix *fore-*
Latin Root *-temp-*
Latin Suffix *-ous*
Latin Suffix *-or*

Conventions

Commas and Dashes
Prepositional Phrases
Infinitives and Infinitive Phrases
Participles and Gerunds; Participle and Gerund Phrases

Language Study Workshop

Words With Multiple Meanings

DISCUSS

Comprehension and Collaboration

Poetry Reading Discussion

Presentation of Ideas

Oral Interpretation

Responding to Text

Small Group Discussion
Partner Discussion
Group Discussion
Debate

Speaking and Listening Workshop

Analyzing Media Messages

RESEARCH

Research and Technology

Literary History Report
Visual Arts Presentation

Investigate the Topic: Lost Civilizations

Myths and Ancient Civilizations
The Babylonian Captivity
The Atomic Age
Language and Culture
Stonehenge and Astronomy
Palynology
Reading the Past

WRITE

Writing to Sources

Lyric Poem
Tanka
Critical Essay; Poem
Explanatory Essay
Retelling
Argumentative Essay
Analytical Essay
Memoir
Short Story
Persuasive Essay
Informative Essay
Expository Essay

Writing Process Workshop

Explanatory Text: Cause-and-Effect Essay
Organization: Organizing a Cause-and-Effect Essay
Sentence Fluency: Revising to Combine Sentences With Verbal Phrases

UNIT VOCABULARY

Academic Vocabulary appears in *blue*.

Introducing the Big Question *confusion, connection, context, convey, discourse, emotion, explanation, interact, isolation, language, meaning, misinterpret, respond, self-expression, verbal*

Poetry Collection 1 *clenching, venerable, sullen, monotonously, foreboding, tumult*

Poetry Collection 2 *temperate, eternal, threshold, keenest*

Poetry Collection 3 *flourishes, countenance, tremulous, stance, conjured*

Poetry Collection 4 *quench, pallor, ebony, melancholy*

Hold Fast Your Dreams—and Trust Your Mistakes; All; Also All *unorthodox, idealistic, lamentation, wither, awareness, isolation, perspective, subjective*

A Tree Telling of Orpheus *rejoiced, anguish, felled, distinct, transformative, entirety*

By the Waters of Babylon *purified, nevertheless, haunches, realizations, initial, assertion*

There Will Come Soft Rains *manipulated, tremulous, oblivious, stark, social, juxtaposes*

***from* The Way to Rainy Mountain** *writhe, nomadic, tenuous, elements, demise, indigenous*

Understanding Stonehenge: Two Explanations *complex, prone, harbor, primary, theorize, align*

***from* Collapse: How Societies Choose to Fail or Succeed** *marginal, trajectory, primacy, vigorously, complexities, accessible*

Aquae Sulis, Roman Baths, 1762 *scale, attributed, excavation*

COMMON CORE STATE STANDARDS

For the full wording of the standards, see the standards charts following the Contents pages.

Reading Literature

RL.9-10.1, RL.9-10.2, RL.9-10.3, RL.9-10.4, RL.9-10.5, RL.9-10.9, RL.9-10.10

Reading Informational Text

RI.9-10.1, RI.9-10.2, RI.9-10.3, RI.9-10.4, RI.9-10.5, RI.9-10.6, RI.9-10.10

Writing

W.9-10.1, W.9-10.1.b–c, W.9-10.2, W.9-10.2.a–f, W.9-10.3, W.9-10.3.a–e, W.9-10.4, W.9-10.5, W.9-10.6, W.9-10.7, W.9-10.8, W.9-10.9, W.9-10.9.a–b, W.9-10.10

Speaking and Listening

SL.9-10.1, SL.9-10.1.a–d, SL.9-10.2, SL.9-10.3, SL.9-10.4, SL.9-10.5, SL.9-10.6

Language

L.9-10.1, L.9-10.1.b, L.9-10.2, L.9-10.3, L.9-10.3.a, L.9-10.4, L.9-10.4.a–d, L.9-10.5, L.9-10.5.a–b, L.9-10.6

UNIT 4 To what extent does experience determine what we perceive?

PART 1 SETTING EXPECTATIONS

PART 2 TEXT ANALYSIS GUIDED EXPLORATION

TRAGEDY AND SPECTACLE

PART 3

TEXT SET DEVELOPING INSIGHT

CONSCIENTIOUS OBJECTIONS

PART 4

DEMONSTRATING INDEPENDENCE

DIGITAL ASSETS KEY

These digital resources, as well as audio and the Online Writer's Notebook, can be found at **pearsonrealize.com.**

- Interactive Whiteboard Activities
- Virtual Tour
- Close Reading Notebook
- Video
- Close Reading Tool for Annotating Texts
- Grammar Tutorials
- Online Text Set

UNIT 4 Unit at a Glance

READ

Text Analysis
- Shakespeare's Tragedies
- Blank Verse
- Dramatic Speeches
- External and Internal Conflict
- Tragic Heroes
- Comparing Characters' Motivations
- Protagonist and Antagonist
- Tragic Flaw
- The Speaker in Poetry
- Rhetorical Devices
- Tone
- Expository Structure
- Technical Terms

Comprehension
- Use Text Aids
- Paraphrase
- Analyze Imagery
- Read Between the Lines
- Compare and Contrast Characters

Language Study
- Latin Suffix *-ile*
- Latin Prefix *en-*
- Latin Root *-spect-*
- Latin Root *-sum-*
- Latin Root *-stru-*

Conventions
- Absolute Adjectives and Absolute Phrases

Language Study Workshop
- Connotation and Denotation

DISCUSS

Comprehension and Collaboration
- Group Screening

Presentation of Ideas
- Dramatic Reading

Responding to Text
- Small Group Discussion
- Partner Discussion
- Panel Discussion
- Group Discussion

Speaking and Listening Workshop
- Comparing Media Coverage

RESEARCH

Research and Technology
- Women's History Report
- Advertising Poster
- Multimedia Presentation

Investigate the Topic: Conscientious Objections
- Ethics in Ancient Greece
- Conscientious Objection in U.S. History
- International PEN
- Dystopias and Utopias
- The Ethics of Research
- Conscientious Objection Around the World
- The Goddess of Liberty

WRITE

Writing to Sources
- Editorial
- Obituary
- Explanatory Essay
- Compare-and-Contrast Essay
- Narrative Reflective Essay
- Informative Reflective Essay
- Position Paper
- Definition Essay
- Argumentative Essay
- Autobiographical Narrative

Writing Process Workshop
- Narration: Autobiographical Narrative
  - Ideas: Finding an Effective Idea
  - Sentence Fluency: Revising to Combine Sentences Using Adverb Clauses

UNIT VOCABULARY

Academic Vocabulary appears in *blue*.

Introducing the Big Question *anticipate, background, bias, distortion, individual, insight, interpretation, manipulate, perspective, expectations, identity, impression, knowledge, stereotype, universal*

The Tragedy of Julius Caesar

Act I *replication, servile, spare, infirmity, portentous, prodigious*

Act II *augmented, entreated, insurrection, resolution, wrathfully, imminent*

Act III *confounded, spectacle, prophesy, strife, discourse, interred*

Act IV *legacies, condemned, chastisement, rash, mirth, presume*

Act V *fawned, presage, demeanor, disconsolate, misconstrued, meditates*

A Raisin in the Sun *looming, dignity, character, conduct, integrity, motive*

Antigone

Part 1 *sated, deflects, brazen, contradiction, principles, practical*

Part 2 *deference, contempt, piety, initial, respective, illustrate*

Conscientious Objector *flick, deliver, overcome, implicitly, absolute, resonate*

***from* Nobel Lecture** *reciprocity, inexorably, oratory, policies, laureate, awareness*

The Censors *irreproachable, ulterior, staidness, premise, reviled, regulate*

Culture of Shock *paradigm, baseline, simulation, functionary, banality, criteria*

***from* Army Regulation 600-43: Conscientious Objection** *pragmatism, expediency, demeanor, manifestation, affiliation, criteria*

Tiananmen Square "Tank Man," Beijing, China, 1989 *scale, isolation, integrity*

COMMON CORE STATE STANDARDS

For the full wording of the standards, see the standards charts following the Contents pages.

Reading Literature

RL.9-10.1, RL.9-10.2, RL.9-10.3, RL.9-10.4, RL.9-10.5, RL.9-10.6, RL.9-10.7, RL.9-10.10

Reading Informational Text

RI.9-10.1, RI.9-10.2, RI.9-10.4, RI.9-10.5, RI.9-10.6, RI.9-10.7, RI.9-10.10

Writing

W.9-10.1, W.9-10.1.a–e, W.9-10.2, W.9-10.2.a–f, W.9-10.3, W.9-10.3.a–e, W.9-10.4, W.9-10.5, W.9-10.6, W.9-10.7, W.9-10.8, W.9-10.9, W.9-10.9.a, W.9-10.10

Speaking and Listening

SL.9-10.1, SL.9-10.1.c–d, SL.9-10.3, SL.9-10.4, SL.9-10.6

Language

L.9-10.1, L.9-10.1.a–b, L.9-10.2, L.9-10.3, L.9-10.3.a, L.9-10.4, L.9-10.4.a–d, L.9-10.5.a–b, L.9-10.6

UNIT 5 Can anyone be a hero?

PART 1 SETTING EXPECTATIONS

PART 2 TEXT ANALYSIS GUIDED EXPLORATION

TIMELESS VOICES

PART 3
TEXT SET DEVELOPING INSIGHT

THE ARTHURIAN LEGEND

PART 4
DEMONSTRATING INDEPENDENCE

DIGITAL ASSETS KEY

These digital resources, as well as audio and the Online Writer's Notebook, can be found at **pearsonrealize.com.**

- Interactive Whiteboard Activities
- Virtual Tour
- Close Reading Notebook
- Video
- Close Reading Tool for Annotating Texts
- Grammar Tutorials
- Online Text Set

Unit at a Glance

READ

Text Analysis
- Myths
- Epic and Epic Hero
- Legends and Legendary Heroes
- Parody
- Comparing Archetypal Narrative Patterns
- Dialogue
- Frame Story
- Exposition
- Connotation
- Tone

Comprehension
- Analyze Cultural Context
- Analyze Worldviews
- Compare Worldviews

Language Study
- Latin Root *-dur-*
- Latin Suffix *-ive*
- Latin Suffix *-ant*
- Latin Prefix *ex-*

Conventions
- Independent and Dependent Clauses
- Sentence Types
- Fixing Common Usage Problems
- Semicolons, Colons, and Ellipsis Points

Language Study Workshop
- Idioms, Jargon, and Technical Terms

DISCUSS

Comprehension and Collaboration
- Improvised Dialogue

Presentation of Ideas
- Retelling

Responding to Text
- Panel Discussion
- Debate
- Small Group Discussion
- Partner Discussion
- Group Discussion

Speaking and Listening Workshop
- Delivering a Multimedia Presentation

RESEARCH

Research and Technology
- "Influences" Chart
- Biographical Brochure

Investigate the Topic: The Arthurian Legend
- Knighthood in Medieval Tradition
- Versions of Arthur
- Medieval Astronomy
- King Arthur and the Code of Chivalry
- Arthur as the Last Roman
- Visiting "Camelot"

WRITE

Writing to Sources
- Myth
- News Story
- Script
- Parody
- Explanatory Essay
- Literary Criticism
- Analytical Essay
- Fictional Narrative
- Persuasive Essay
- Response to Literature
- Reflective Essay
- Short Story
- Essay

Writing Process Workshop
- Informative Text: Comparison-and-Contrast Essay
  - Word Choice: Choosing Strong, Effective Words
  - Sentence Fluency: Revising to Vary Sentence Patterns

UNIT VOCABULARY

Academic Vocabulary appears in *blue*.

Introducing the Big Question *attributes, character, conduct, courage, determination, honor, inherent, integrity, legendary, persevere, principles, resolute, responsibility, sacrifice, selflessness*

Prometheus and the First People *toil, heedless, inhabit, counsel, disembarked, endure*

***from* Sundiata: An Epic of Old Mali** *fathom, innuendo, estranged, derisively, affront, efface*

Damon and Pythias *tyrant, dire, evade, impediments, serenity, composure*

***from* Don Quixote** *lucidity, affable, ingenuity, sonorous, veracious, extolled*

Cupid and Psyche; Ashputtle *adulation, allay, plague, jeered, character, context, meaning, principles*

Arthur Becomes King of Britain *skeptically, surmise, desolate, implicit, alternative, complexity*

Morte d'Arthur *bore, brandished, languid, adaptation, renditions, establish*

***from* A Connecticut Yankee in King Arthur's Court** *calamity, multitudes, conspicuous, sensibility, viewpoint, counterparts*

***from* Youth and Chivalry** *illusion, martial, stamina, unifies, integrity, interject*

***from* The Birth of Britain** *contradicted, exterminated, invincible, resistance, enduring, embodies*

***from* A Pilgrim's Search for Relics of the Once and Future King** *gullible, nostalgic, lucrative, highlight, maintain, associated*

Cartoon *from* The New Yorker *signal, privileged, relatable*

COMMON CORE STATE STANDARDS

For the full wording of the standards, see the standards charts following the Contents pages.

Reading Literature

RL.9-10.1, RL.9-10.2, RL.9-10.3, RL.9-10.4, RL.9-10.5, RL.9-10.6, RL.9-10.7, RL.9-10.10

Reading Informational Text

RI.9-10.1, RI.9-10.2, RI.9-10.3, RI.9-10.4, RI.9-10.5, RI.9-10.6, RI.9-10.7, RI.9-10.8, RI.9-10.10

Writing

W.9-10.1, W.9-10.1.a–b, W.9-10.1.e, W.9-10.2, W.9-10.2.a–d, W.9-10.2.f, W.9-10.3, W.9-10.3.a–d, W.9-10.4, W.9-10.5, W.9-10.6, W.9-10.7, W.9-10.8, W.9-10.9, W.9-10.9.a–b, W.9-10.10

Speaking and Listening

SL.9-10.1, SL.9-10.1.a–d, SL.9-10.2, SL.9-10.3, SL.9-10.4, SL.9-10.5, SL.9-10.6

Language

L.9-10.1, L.9-10.1.b, L.9-10.2, L.9-10.2.a-b, L.9-10.3, L.9-10.3.a, L.9-10.4, L.9-10.4.a, L.9-10.4.d, L.9-10.5, L.9-10.6

Range of Reading

Literature

STORIES

DRAMA

POETRY

Epics

Lyric Poems

Narrative and Dramatic Poems

Sonnets and Tanka

ONLINE LITERATURE LIBRARY

Highlighted selections are found in the **Online Literature Library** (OLL) in the Online Student Edition.

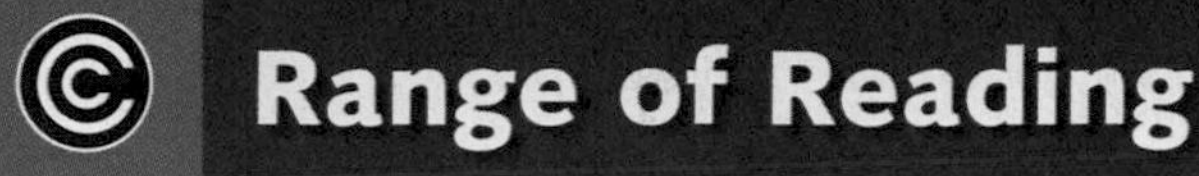

Range of Reading

Informational Text

ARGUMENTS

Opinion Pieces

Speeches

EXPOSITION

Content-Area Essays and Articles

Science Writing

ONLINE LITERATURE LIBRARY

Highlighted selections are found in the **Online Literature Library** (OLL) in the Online Student Edition.

Features and Workshops

COMPARING TEXTS

WRITING PROCESS

LANGUAGE STUDY

SPEAKING AND LISTENING

ONLINE TEXT SETS

These selections can be found in the **Online Literature Library** in the Online Student Edition

Unit 1

ESSAY **EXEMPLAR TEXT**
***from* A Quilt of a Country**
Anna Quindlen

AUTOBIOGRAPHY
***from* Desert Exile: The Uprooting of a Japanese-American Family**
Yoshiko Uchida

BIOGRAPHY
Marian Anderson: Famous Concert Singer
Langston Hughes

Unit 2

PROSE POEM
Tepeyac
Sandra Cisneros

SHORT STORY
A Visit to Grandmother
William Melvin Kelley

MEMOIR
***from* Places Left Unfinished at the Time of Creation**
John Phillip Santos

Unit 3

NONFICTION
The Marginal World
Rachel Carson

SCIENCE ARTICLE
The Spider and the Wasp
Alexander Petrunkevitch

POEM
The Kraken
Alfred, Lord Tennyson

Unit 4

REFLECTIVE ESSAY
***from* In Commemoration: One Million Volumes**
Rudolfo A. Anaya

EXPOSITORY ESSAY
Artful Research
Susan Vreeland

NOVEL EXCERPT **EXEMPLAR TEXT**
***from* Fahrenheit 451**
Ray Bradbury

Unit 5

EXPOSITORY NONFICTION
Making History With Vitamin C
Penny Le Couteur and Jay Burreson

SHORT STORY
The Masque of the Red Death
Edgar Allan Poe

SCIENCE JOURNALISM
Black Water Turns the Tide on Florida Coral
NASA News

State Standards Overview

The Common Core State Standards will prepare you to succeed in college and your future career. They are separated into four sections—Reading (Literature and Informational Text), Writing, Speaking and Listening, and Language. Beginning each section, the College and Career Readiness Anchor Standards define what you need to achieve by the end of high school. The grade-specific standards that follow define what you need to know by the end of your current grade level.

Common Core Reading Standards

College and Career Readiness Anchor Standards for Reading

Key Ideas and Details

1. Read closely to determine what the text says explicitly and to make logical inferences from it; cite specific textual evidence when writing or speaking to support conclusions drawn from the text.
2. Determine central ideas or themes of a text and analyze their development; summarize the key supporting details and ideas.
3. Analyze how and why individuals, events, and ideas develop and interact over the course of a text.

Craft and Structure

4. Interpret words and phrases as they are used in a text, including determining technical, connotative, and figurative meanings, and analyze how specific word choices shape meaning or tone.
5. Analyze the structure of texts, including how specific sentences, paragraphs, and larger portions of the text (e.g., a section, chapter, scene, or stanza) relate to each other and the whole.
6. Assess how point of view or purpose shapes the content and style of a text.

Integration of Knowledge and Ideas

7. Integrate and evaluate content presented in diverse formats and media, including visually and quantitatively, as well as in words.
8. Delineate and evaluate the argument and specific claims in a text, including the validity of the reasoning as well as the relevance and sufficiency of the evidence.
9. Analyze how two or more texts address similar themes or topics in order to build knowledge or to compare the approaches the authors take.

Range of Reading and Level of Text Complexity

10. Read and comprehend complex literary and informational texts independently and proficiently.

Grade 10 Reading Standards for Literature

Key Ideas and Details

1. Cite strong and thorough textual evidence to support analysis of what the text says explicitly as well as inferences drawn from the text.

2. Determine a theme or central idea of a text and analyze in detail its development over the course of the text, including how it emerges and is shaped and refined by specific details; provide an objective summary of the text.

3. Analyze how complex characters (e.g., those with multiple or conflicting motivations) develop over the course of a text, interact with other characters, and advance the plot or develop the theme.

Craft and Structure

4. Determine the meaning of words and phrases as they are used in the text, including figurative and connotative meanings; analyze the cumulative impact of specific word choices on meaning and tone (e.g., how the language evokes a sense of time and place; how it sets a formal or informal tone).

5. Analyze how an author's choices concerning how to structure a text, order events within it (e.g., parallel plots), and manipulate time (e.g., pacing, flashbacks) create such effects as mystery, tension, or surprise.

6. Analyze a particular point of view or cultural experience reflected in a work of literature from outside the United States, drawing on a wide reading of world literature.

Integration of Knowledge and Ideas

7. Analyze the representation of a subject or a key scene in two different artistic mediums, including what is emphasized or absent in each treatment (e.g., Auden's "Musée des Beaux Arts" and Breughel's *Landscape with the Fall of Icarus*).

8. (Not applicable to literature)

9. Analyze how an author draws on and transforms source material in a specific work (e.g., how Shakespeare treats a theme or topic from Ovid or the Bible or how a later author draws on a play by Shakespeare).

Range of Reading and Level of Text Complexity

10. By the end of grade 9, read and comprehend literature, including stories, dramas, and poems, in the grades 9–10 text complexity band proficiently, with scaffolding as needed at the high end of the range.

Grade 10 Reading Standards for Informational Text

Key Ideas and Details

1. Cite strong and thorough textual evidence to support analysis of what the text says explicitly as well as inferences drawn from the text.
2. Determine a central idea of a text and analyze its development over the course of the text, including how it emerges and is shaped and refined by specific details; provide an objective summary of the text.
3. Analyze how the author unfolds an analysis or series of ideas or events, including the order in which the points are made, how they are introduced and developed, and the connections that are drawn between them.

Craft and Structure

4. Determine the meaning of words and phrases as they are used in a text, including figurative, connotative, and technical meanings; analyze the cumulative impact of specific word choices on meaning and tone (e.g., how the language of a court opinion differs from that of a newspaper).
5. Analyze in detail how an author's ideas or claims are developed and refined by particular sentences, paragraphs, or larger portions of a text (e.g., a section or chapter).
6. Determine an author's point of view or purpose in a text and analyze how an author uses rhetoric to advance that point of view or purpose.

Integration of Knowledge and Ideas

7. Analyze various accounts of a subject told in different mediums (e.g., a person's life story in both print and multimedia), determining which details are emphasized in each account.
8. Delineate and evaluate the argument and specific claims in a text, assessing whether the reasoning is valid and the evidence is relevant and sufficient; identify false statements and fallacious reasoning.
9. Analyze seminal U.S. documents of historical and literary significance (e.g., Washington's Farewell Address, the Gettysburg Address, Roosevelt's Four Freedoms speech, King's "Letter from Birmingham Jail"), including how they address related themes and concepts.

Range of Reading and Level of Text Complexity

10. By the end of grade 9, read and comprehend literary nonfiction in the grades 9–10 text complexity band proficiently, with scaffolding as needed at the high end of the range.

b. Use narrative techniques, such as dialogue, pacing, description, reflection, and multiple plot lines, to develop experiences, events, and/or characters.
c. Use a variety of techniques to sequence events so that they build on one another to create a coherent whole.
d. Use precise words and phrases, telling details, and sensory language to convey a vivid picture of the experiences, events, setting, and/or characters.
e. Provide a conclusion that follows from and reflects on what is experienced, observed, or resolved over the course of the narrative.

Production and Distribution of Writing

4. Produce clear and coherent writing in which the development, organization, and style are appropriate to task, purpose, and audience.

5. Develop and strengthen writing as needed by planning, revising, editing, rewriting, or trying a new approach, focusing on addressing what is most significant for a specific purpose and audience.

6. Use technology, including the Internet, to produce, publish, and update individual or shared writing products, taking advantage of technology's capacity to link to other information and to display information flexibly and dynamically.

Research to Build and Present Knowledge

7. Conduct short as well as more sustained research projects to answer a question (including a self-generated question) or solve a problem; narrow or broaden the inquiry when appropriate; synthesize multiple sources on the subject, demonstrating understanding of the subject under investigation.

8. Gather relevant information from multiple authoritative print and digital sources, using advanced searches effectively; assess the usefulness of each source in answering the research question; integrate information into the text selectively to maintain the flow of ideas, avoiding plagiarism and following a standard format for citation.

9. Draw evidence from literary or informational texts to support analysis, reflection, and research.

a. Apply *grades 9–10 Reading standards* to literature (e.g., "Analyze how an author draws on and transforms source material in a specific work [e.g., how Shakespeare treats a theme or topic from Ovid or the Bible or how a later author draws on a play by Shakespeare]").
b. Apply *grades 9–10 Reading standards* to literary nonfiction (e.g., "Delineate and evaluate the argument and specific claims in a text, assessing whether the reasoning is valid and the evidence is relevant and sufficient; identify false statements and fallacious reasoning").

Range of Writing

10. Write routinely over extended time frames (time for research, reflection, and revision) and shorter time frames (a single sitting or a day or two) for a range of tasks, purposes, and audiences.

Common Core Speaking and Listening Standards

College and Career Readiness Anchor Standards for Speaking and Listening

Comprehension and Collaboration

1. Prepare for and participate effectively in a range of conversations and collaborations with diverse partners, building on others' ideas and expressing their own clearly and persuasively.
2. Integrate and evaluate information presented in diverse media and formats, including visually, quantitatively, and orally.
3. Evaluate a speaker's point of view, reasoning, and use of evidence and rhetoric.

Presentation of Knowledge and Ideas

4. Present information, findings, and supporting evidence such that listeners can follow the line of reasoning and the organization, development, and style are appropriate to task, purpose, and audience.
5. Make strategic use of digital media and visual displays of data to express information and enhance understanding of presentations.
6. Adapt speech to a variety of contexts and communicative tasks, demonstrating command of formal English when indicated or appropriate.

Grade 10 Speaking and Listening Standards

Comprehension and Collaboration

1. Initiate and participate effectively in a range of collaborative discussions (one-on-one, in groups, and teacher-led) with diverse partners on *grades 9–10 topics, texts, and issues,* building on others' ideas and expressing their own clearly and persuasively.
   a. Come to discussions prepared, having read and researched material under study; explicitly draw on that preparation by referring to evidence from texts and other research on the topic or issue to stimulate a thoughtful, well-reasoned exchange of ideas.
   b. Work with peers to set rules for collegial discussions and decision-making (e.g., informal consensus, taking votes on key issues, presentation of alternate views), clear goals and deadlines, and individual roles as needed.
   c. Propel conversations by posing and responding to questions that relate the current discussion to broader themes or larger ideas; actively incorporate others into the discussion; and clarify, verify, or challenge ideas and conclusions.
   d. Respond thoughtfully to diverse perspectives, summarize points of agreement and disagreement, and, when warranted, qualify or justify their own views and understanding and make new connections in light of the evidence and reasoning presented.
2. Integrate multiple sources of information presented in diverse media or formats (e.g., visually, quantitatively, orally) evaluating the credibility and accuracy of each source.
3. Evaluate a speaker's point of view, reasoning, and use of evidence and rhetoric, identifying any fallacious reasoning or exaggerated or distorted evidence.

Presentation of Knowledge and Ideas

4. Present information, findings, and supporting evidence clearly, concisely, and logically such that listeners can follow the line of reasoning and the organization, development, substance, and style are appropriate to purpose, audience, and task.
5. Make strategic use of digital media (e.g., textual, graphical, audio, visual, and interactive elements) in presentations to enhance understanding of findings, reasoning, and evidence and to add interest.
6. Adapt speech to a variety of contexts and tasks, demonstrating command of formal English when indicated or appropriate. (See grades 9–10 Language standards 1 and 3 for specific expectations.)

Common Core Language Standards

College and Career Readiness Anchor Standards for Reading

Conventions of Standard English

1. Demonstrate command of the conventions of standard English grammar and usage when writing or speaking.
2. Demonstrate command of the conventions of standard English capitalization, punctuation, and spelling when writing.

Knowledge of Language

3. Apply knowledge of language to understand how language functions in different contexts, to make effective choices for meaning or style, and to comprehend more fully when reading or listening.

Vocabulary Acquisition and Use

4. Determine or clarify the meaning of unknown and multiple-meaning words and phrases by using context clues, analyzing meaningful word parts, and consulting general and specialized reference materials, as appropriate.
5. Demonstrate understanding of figurative language, word relationships, and nuances in word meanings.
6. Acquire and use accurately a range of general academic and domain-specific words and phrases sufficient for reading, writing, speaking, and listening at the college and career readiness level; demonstrate independence in gathering vocabulary knowledge when considering a word or phrase important to comprehension or expression.

Grade 10 Language Standards

Conventions of Standard English

1. Demonstrate command of the conventions of standard English grammar and usage when writing or speaking.
   a. Use parallel structure.
   b. Use various types of phrases (noun, verb, adjectival, adverbial, participial, prepositional, absolute) and clauses (independent, dependent; noun, relative, adverbial) to convey specific meanings and add variety and interest to writing or presentations.

2. Demonstrate command of the conventions of standard English capitalization, punctuation, and spelling when writing.
   a. Use a semicolon (and perhaps a conjunctive adverb) to link two or more closely related independent clauses.
   b. Use a colon to introduce a list or quotation.
   c. Spell correctly.

Knowledge of Language

3. Apply knowledge of language to understand how language functions in different contexts, to make effective choices for meaning or style, and to comprehend more fully when reading or listening.
   a. Write and edit work so that it conforms to the guidelines in a style manual (e.g., *MLA Handbook, Turabian's Manual for Writers*) appropriate for the discipline and writing type.

Vocabulary Acquisition and Use

4. Determine or clarify the meaning of unknown and multiple-meaning words and phrases based on *grades 9–10 reading and content,* choosing flexibly from a range of strategies.
   a. Use context (e.g., the overall meaning of a sentence, paragraph, or text; a word's position or function in a sentence) as a clue to the meaning of a word or phrase.
   b. Identify and correctly use patterns of word changes that indicate different meanings or parts of speech (e.g., *analyze, analysis, analytical; advocate, advocacy*).
   c. Consult general and specialized reference materials (e.g., dictionaries, glossaries, thesauruses), both print and digital, to find the pronunciation of a word or determine or clarify its precise meaning, its part of speech, or its etymology.
   d. Verify the preliminary determination of the meaning of a word or phrase (e.g., by checking the inferred meaning in context or in a dictionary).

5. Demonstrate understanding of figurative language, word relationships, and nuances in word meanings.
   a. Interpret figures of speech (e.g., euphemism, oxymoron) in context and analyze their role in the text.
   b. Analyze nuances in the meaning of words with similar denotations.

6. Acquire and use accurately general academic and domain-specific words and phrases, sufficient for reading, writing, speaking, and listening at the college and career readiness level; demonstrate independence in gathering vocabulary knowledge when considering a word or phrase important to comprehension or expression.

INTRODUCTORY UNIT

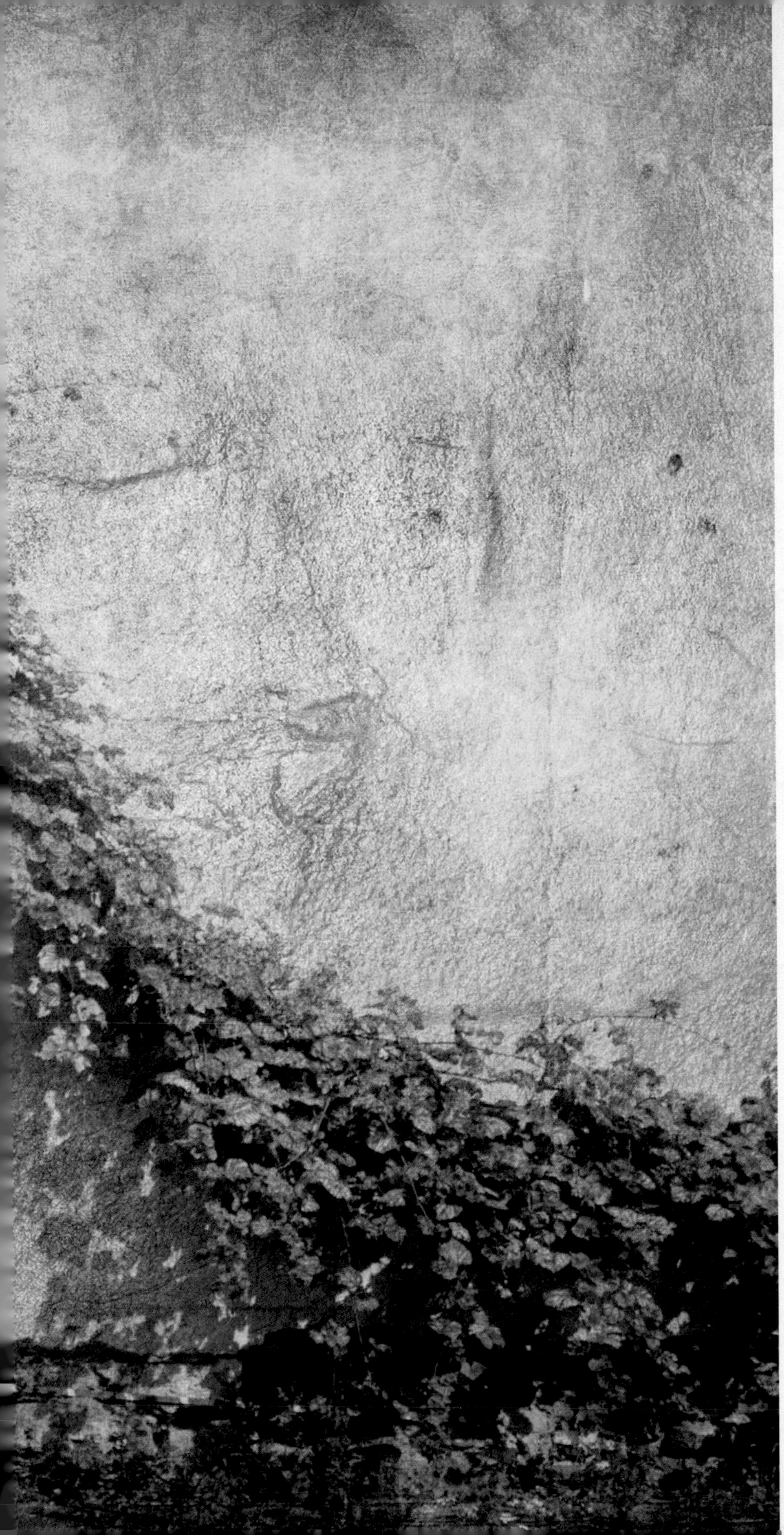

COMMON CORE WORKSHOPS

- BUILDING ACADEMIC VOCABULARY
- WRITING AN OBJECTIVE SUMMARY
- COMPREHENDING COMPLEX TEXTS
- ANALYZING ARGUMENTS
- CONDUCTING RESEARCH

Common Core State Standards

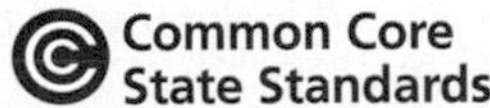

Reading Literature 2, 10
Reading Informational Text 2, 6, 8, 9, 10
Writing 1, 1a–b, 2, 2a–d, 5, 6, 7, 8, 9
Language 1, 1b, 3, 6

BUILDING ACADEMIC VOCABULARY

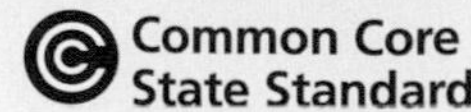

Common Core State Standards

Language

6. Acquire and use accurately general academic and domain-specific words and phrases, sufficient for reading, writing, speaking, and listening at the college and career readiness level; demonstrate independence in gathering vocabulary knowledge when considering a word or phrase important to comprehension or expression.

Academic vocabulary is the language you encounter in textbooks and on standardized tests and other assessments. Understanding these words and using them in your classroom discussions and writing will help you communicate your ideas clearly and effectively.

There are two basic types of academic vocabulary: general and domain-specific.

General academic vocabulary includes words that are not specific to any single course of study. For example, the general academic vocabulary word *analyze* is used in language arts, math, social studies, art, and so on.

Domain-specific academic vocabulary includes words that are usually encountered in the study of a specific discipline. For example, the words *factor* and *remainder* are most often used in mathematics classrooms and texts.

General Academic Vocabulary

Word	Definition	Related Words	Word in Context
adapt (uh DAPT) *v.*	change or adjust	adaptable adaptation	Remember to **adapt** your reading rate to the text.
anticipate (an TIHS uh payt) *v.*	look forward to	anticipation anticipatory	Look for clues that **anticipate** future events.
awareness (uh WAYR nihs) *n.*	having knowledge	aware unaware	The author has a great **awareness** of his readers' interests.
background (BAK grownd) *n.*	conditions that surround or come before something		An author's **background** shapes his or her writing.
bias (BY uhs) *n.*	point of view before the facts are known	biased unbiased	The speaker allowed his **bias** to show.
character (KAR ihk tuhr) *n.*	moral strength; self-discipline	characteristic characteristically	Her **character** was revealed in Act II.
comprehend (kom prih HEHND) *v.*	grasp mentally; understand	comprehension comprehensible	The side notes will help you **comprehend** new vocabulary.
conduct (KON duhkt) *n.*	way a person acts; behavior	conduct *v.* conducted	A speaker's **conduct** affects how the audience views her.
confirm (kuhn FURM) *v.*	establish the truth or correctness of something	confirmation confirmatory	**Confirm** whether the predictions are accurate.
context (KON tehkst) *n.*	circumstances that form the setting of an event	contextual	The **context** of a story may be historical.
convey (kuhn VAY) *v.*	communicate or make known	conveyed conveyance	The poet uses imagery to **convey** feelings.

Word	Definition	Related Words	Word in Context
debate (dih BAYT) *v.*	argue or discuss	debatable debater	When you **debate**, support your arguments.
differentiate (dihf uh REHN shee ayt) *v.*	distinguish between	differ different	When reading an essay, **differentiate** between fact and opinion.
discern (dih SURN) *v.*	tell the difference between two or more things; perceive	discernable discerning	Until I reached the end of the story, I couldn't **discern** the character's motives.
discourse (DIHS kawrs) *n.*	ongoing communication of ideas and information	discourse *v.*	**Discourse** in a group is an important way to hear different opinions.
distortion (dihs TAWR shuhn) *n.*	anything that shows something in an untrue way	distort distorted	Avoid using unreliable sources that exhibit a **distortion** of facts.
evaluate (ih VAL yoo ayt) *v.*	determine the worth of something	evaluation reevaluate	Rubrics help students **evaluate** their essays.
evolve (ih VOLV) *v.*	develop through gradual changes	evolution evolutionary	Dealing with conflict allows Sam to **evolve** and grow.
explanation (ehks pluh NAY shuhn) *n.*	clarifying statement	explain explanatory	A technical document provides an **explanation**.
individual (ihn duh VIHJ oo uhl) *adj.*	relating to a single person or thing	individualism individuality	Work on an **individual** response, and then discuss the question.
inherent (ihn HEHR uhnt) *adj.*	existing naturally in something	inherence inherently	Revision is an **inherent** part of the process.
insight (IHN syt) *n.*	clear idea of the nature of things	insightful insightfully	A preface provides **insight** into an author's purpose.
integrity (ihn TEHG ruh tee) *n.*	willingness to stand by moral principles		Heroes typically display great **integrity**.
interact (ihn tuhr AKT) *v.*	relate to one another; affect another	interaction interactive	The characters **interact** with one another in the play.
interpretation (ihn tur pruh TAY shuhn) *n.*	explanation of the meaning of something	interpret interpretive	Sonnets may have more than one **interpretation**.
isolation (y suh LAY shuhn) *n.*	being alone or set apart	isolate isolated	Poems address complex feelings such as **isolation**.
manipulate (muh NIHP yuh layt) *v.*	control by use of influence, often in an unfair way	manipulation manipulative	Some speakers use bias to **manipulate** their audiences.

Word	Definition	Related Words	Word in Context
meaning (MEE nihng) *n.*	significance of something	meaningful meaningfully	Break down long sentences to help determine their **meaning**.
misinterpret (mihs ihn TUR priht) *v.*	not understand correctly	interpret misinterpretation	If you **misinterpret** the instructions, you will build it wrong.
modified (MOD uh fyd) *v.*	changed; altered slightly	modification modifier	The cross-outs revealed that he had **modified** his essay.
motive (MOH tihv) *n.*	something that causes a person to act in a certain way	motivate motivation	The character's **motive** was revealed in the conclusion.
objective (uhb JEHK tihv) *adj.*	not dependent on another's point of view	objectively objectify	Critics should take an **objective** and unbiased stance.
oppose (uh POHZ) *v.*	set against; disagree with	opposing opposition	If you **oppose** another student's opinion, reply respectfully.
perspective (puhr SPEHK tihv) *n.*	way one sees things; viewpoint		I enjoy an essay more if I understand the author's **perspective**.
principles (PRIHN suh puhlz) *n.*	rules for right conduct; basics	principled unprincipled	The **principles** of spelling are simple.
radical (RAD uh kuhl) *adj.*	changed to an extreme degree	radicalism radically	Beat poetry was a **radical** departure from classic poetry.
resolute (REHZ uh loot) *adj.*	showing a fixed purpose	resolutely resolution	He is **resolute** about being honest in his article.
resolve (rih ZOLV) *v.*	reach a conclusion or decision	resolution resolved	How do the enemies **resolve** their conflicts?
respond (rih SPOND) *v.*	answer; react to	respondent response	How do you **respond** to the suspense?
responsibility (rih spon suh BIHL uh tee) *n.*	having to answer to someone; being accountable for success or failure	responsible irresponsible	It is your **responsibility** to cite your sources when writing a research report.
revise (rih VYZ) *v.*	modify	revision revisionist	**Revise** your paper by clarifying your ideas.
subjective (suhb JEHK tihv) *adj.*	based on or influenced by a person's feelings or point of view	subjectively subjectivity	It is difficult not to be **subjective** when debating.
unify (YOO nuh fy) *v.*	combine into one	unification unity	To **unify** the ideas, we should add transitions.

Ordinary Language: After reading further, I **changed** my original prediction.

Academic Language: After reading further, I **modified** my original prediction.

Ordinary Language: The author presents a unique **view** on the subject.

Academic Language: The author presents a unique **perspective** on the subject.

Practice

Examples of various kinds of domain-specific academic vocabulary appear in the charts below. On a separate piece of paper, create your own domain-specific academic vocabulary charts in which you enter new academic vocabulary words as you learn them.

Social Studies: Domain-Specific Academic Vocabulary

Word	Definition	Related Words	Word in Context
absolutism (AB suh loo tihz uhm) *n.*	principle or the exercise of complete and unrestricted power in government	absolute absolutely	The leader's **absolutism** restricted the freedom of citizens.
cartography (kahr TOG ruh fee) *n.*	design and production of maps	cartographer cartographic	The geologist studied **cartography** and made maps.
ideology (Y dee OL uh jee) *n.*	beliefs that guide individuals and groups	ideological ideologue	The communist **ideology** took hold of eastern Europe in the twentieth century.
mercantilism (MUR kuhn tihl ihz uhm) *n.*	commercialism; practice of trade and commercial activity	mercantile mercantilistic	**Mercantilism** was a large factor in the exploration of new lands.
radicalism (RAD ih kuhl ihz uhm) *n.*	favoring of drastic political, economic, or social reforms	radical radicalize	**Radicalism** in certain parts of the world has led to violence.

Create a chart for these social studies academic vocabulary words: *demobilization, democratization, nomination, resettlement,* and *reunification.*

Mathematics: Domain-Specific Academic Vocabulary

Word	Definition	Related Words	Word in Context
binary system (BY nuh ree SIHS tuhm) *n.*	system of counting or measurement based on powers of two	binary digit binaries	Computers use the **binary system.**
derivative (duh RIHV uh tihv) *n.*	rate of change of a function at any given instant	derive derived	We are going to learn about **derivatives** in advanced math.
dilation (dy LAY shuhn) *n.*	transformation that changes the size of the image in geometry	dilate dilated	We studied the **dilation** of images in our geometry class.
tangent (TAN juhnt) *n.*	line in the plane of a circle that touches the circle at only one point	tangential tangentially	We were asked to find the **tangent** of a circle.
vector (VEHK tuhr) *n.*	quantity possessing both magnitude and direction	vector *v.* vectoring	In geometry, we learned that a **vector** has both magnitude and direction.

Create a chart for these mathematics academic vocabulary words: *arc, continuity, correlation, density,* and *variance.*

Science: Domain-Specific Academic Vocabulary

Word	Definition	Related Words	Word in Context
fission (FIHSH uhn) *n.*	splitting of the nucleus of an atom or a cell	fissionable	Some organisms reproduce by **fission**.
fusion (FYOO zhuhn) *n.*	in physics, the joining of two nuclei to form one new nucleus	fuse	Nuclear fission and **fusion** are opposite processes.
genetic mutation (juh NEHT ihk myoo TAY shuhn) *n.*	any event that changes the genetic structure of an organism	genes mutate	Some **genetic mutations** lead to health problems.
isotope (Y suh tohp) *n.*	multiple forms of an element that have the same number of protons but a different number of neutrons	isotopic	There are several **isotopes** of hydrogen.
organelle (awr guh NEHL) *n.*	part of a cell that has a specialized function	organ organism	Cell walls and nuclei are examples of **organelles**.

Create a chart for these words: *catalyst, chloroplast, organic, mitochondrion,* and *semiconductor.*

Art: Domain-Specific Academic Vocabulary

Word	Definition	Related Words	Word in Context
aesthetics (ehs THEHT ihks) *n.*	study of nature, beauty, and art	aesthetic aesthetician	We studied the **aesthetics** of ancient Greek sculpture.
analogous colors (uh NAL uh guhs KUHL uhrz) *n.*	colors that are next to each other on the color wheel	analogy	The difference between **analogous** colors is small.
formalist (FAWR muhl ihst) *n.*	anyone who places importance on how well artists design their works	formal formalize	The critic, a **formalist**, liked the artists' exhibit.
radial balance (RAY dee uhl BAL uhns) *n.*	positioning objects around a central point	balanced radius	The sun is an example of an object with **radial balance**.

Create a chart for these words: *asymmetrical balance, emphasis, gradation, harmony,* and *symmetrical balance.*

Technology: Domain-Specific Academic Vocabulary

Word	Definition	Related Words	Word in Context
central processing unit (SEHN truhl PROS ehs ihng YOO niht) *n.*	component of a computer that interprets and executes programs.	CPU	The **central processing unit** is the "brain" of a computer.
local network system (LOH kuhl NEHT wurk SIHS tuhm) *n.*	system for linking computers that are close to each other	LAN	Our **local network system** allows us to share files.
microprocessor (MY kroh pros ehs uhr) *n.*	part of a computer that performs logical functions	micro processing	The information was fed into the **microprocessor**.
peripheral device (puh RIHF uhr uhl dih VYS) *n.*	device that attaches to a computer to perform a specific function	peripheral peripherally	This scanner is the newest **peripheral device** I have.
shortcut key (SHAWRT kuht kee) *n.*	key or combination of keys that executes a command	key shortcut	I used a **shortcut key** to run the spell-checker.

Create a chart for these words: *copyright violation, desktop publishing, Internet service provider, invasion of privacy,* and *operating system.*

Increasing Your Word Knowledge

Increase your word knowledge and chances of success by taking an active role in developing your vocabulary. To own a word, follow these steps:

Steps to Follow	Model
1. Learn to identify the word and its basic meaning.	The word *examine* means "to look at closely."
2. Take note of the word's spelling.	*Examine* begins and ends with an *e*.
3. Practice pronouncing the word so that you can use it in conversation.	The *e* on the end of the word *examine* is silent. Its second syllable gets the most stress.
4. Visualize the word, and illustrate its key meaning.	"When I think of the word *examine*, I visualize a doctor checking a patient's health."
5. Learn the various forms of the word and its related words.	*Examination* and *exam* are forms of the word *examine*.
6. Compare the word with similar words.	*Examine*, *peruse*, and *study* are synonyms.
7. Contrast the word with similar words.	*Examine* suggests a more detailed study than *read* or *look* at.
8. Use the word in various contexts.	"I'd like to *examine* the footprints more closely." "I will *examine* the use of imagery in this poem."

Building Your Speaking Vocabulary

Language gives us the ability to express ourselves. The more words you know, the easier it will be to get your points across. There are two main aspects of language: reading and speaking. Using the steps above will help you acquire a rich vocabulary. Follow the steps below to help you learn to use this rich vocabulary in discussions, speeches, and conversations:

Steps to Follow	Tip
1. Practice pronouncing the word.	Become familiar with pronunciation guides that allow you to sound out unfamiliar words. Listening to audio books as you read the text will help you learn pronunciations of words.
2. Learn word forms.	Dictionaries often list forms of words following the main word entry. Practice saying word families aloud: "generate," "generated," "generation," "regenerate," "generator."
3. Translate your thoughts.	Restate your own thoughts and ideas in a variety of ways—to inject formality or to change your tone, for example.
4. Hold discussions.	With a classmate, practice using academic vocabulary words in discussions about the text. Choose one term to practice at a time, and see how many statements you can create using that term.
5. Record yourself as you speak.	Analyze your word choices by listening to yourself objectively. Note places your word choice could be strengthened or changed.

WRITING AN OBJECTIVE SUMMARY

The ability to write objective summaries is key to success in college and in many careers. Writing an effective objective summary involves recording the key ideas of a text while demonstrating your understanding.

What Is an Objective Summary?

An effective objective summary is a concise, complete, accurate, and objective overview of a text. Following are key elements of an objective summary:

- A good summary focuses on the main theme or central idea of a text and specific, relevant details that support that theme or central idea. Unnecessary supporting details are left out.
- Effective summaries are brief. However, the writer must be careful not to misrepresent the text by leaving out key elements.
- A summary should accurately capture the essence of the longer text it is describing.
- Finally, the writer must remain objective, that is, refrain from inserting his or her own opinions, reactions, or personal connections into the summary.

What to Avoid in an Objective Summary

- An objective summary is not a collection of sentences or paragraphs copied from the original source.
- It is not a long recounting of every event, detail, or point in the original text.
- Finally, a good summary does not include evaluative comments, such as the reader's overall opinion of or reaction to the piece.
- An objective summary is not the reader's interpretation or critical analysis of the work.

Reading Literature

2. Determine a theme or central idea of a text and analyze in detail its development over the course of the text, including how it emerges and is shaped and refined by specific details; provide an objective summary of the text.

Reading Informational Text

2. Determine a central idea of a text and analyze its development over the course of the text, including how it emerges and is shaped and refined by specific details; provide an objective summary of the text.

INFORMATIONAL TEXT

Model Objective Summary

Note the elements of an effective objective summary that are called out in the side notes. Then, write an objective summary of a text you have recently read. Review your summary, and delete any unnecessary details, opinions, or evaluations.

Summary of "The Gift of the Magi"

"The Gift of the Magi" by O. Henry is the ~~touching~~ story of a young couple named Jim and Della and what they give up in order to buy each other the perfect Christmas gift.

The story begins with Della counting the money she has scrimped to save. To her dismay, it only adds up to one dollar and eight-seven cents.

Della is looking around their humble flat when she comes up with an idea. Catching her reflection in the mirror, she decides that she will sell her most precious possession—her long, beautiful hair. She cries only a little before putting on her coat and going to a shop where she can sell her hair.

With the twenty dollars she receives for selling her hair and a dollar of her savings, Della buys Jim a chain to go with his most precious possession—a gold watch that had belonged to his father and to his grandfather before him.

At home, Della tries to fix her short hair by curling it and begins to prepare dinner. She prays that Jim still thinks she's pretty even without her long hair.

Jim arrives home on time, ~~right around 7 o'clock. Della notes that he is always on time.~~ He does not react in any of the ways Della thought he might. She is terrified when she can't read the peculiar expression on his face. She begins to ramble about her hair growing back and tells him that she sold it for a good reason—to buy him a gift.

Finally, Jim assures Della that her cutting off her hair does not change how he feels about her, and he hands her a package. When she opens the gift, Della understands the odd expression on his face. Jim bought her the expensive hair combs she had wanted for a very long time, only now she doesn't have the hair to put them in.

Della assures him that her hair will grow back quickly, and then she presents Jim with the watch chain she bought him. ~~Jim tumbled down on the couch and put his hands under the back of his head and smiles.~~ He tells her that he sold the watch in order to buy her the combs.

The story ends with the narrator discussing the Magi—the wise men who began the tradition of giving Christmas gifts—and challenging the reader to consider whether Jim and Della were foolish or wise in their gift-giving. ~~I think most readers will agree that their gifts to each other were wise and heartfelt.~~

A one-sentence synopsis highlighting the theme or central idea of the story can be an effective start to a summary.

An adjective describing the story indicates an opinion and should not be included in an objective summary.

Relating the development of the text in chronological order makes a summary easy to follow.

Unnecessary details should be eliminated.

This sentence should be paraphrased rather than copied exactly from the story.

Key narration at the end of the story is included in the summary.

The writer's opinions should not appear in an objective summary.

COMPREHENDING COMPLEX TEXTS

Throughout your high school career, you will be required to read increasingly complex texts in preparation for college and the workplace. A complex text is a work that contains challenging vocabulary; long, complex sentences; figurative language; multiple levels of meaning; or unfamiliar settings and situations.

The selections in this textbook provide you with a range of readings, including short stories, autobiography, poetry, drama, myths, and even science and history texts. Some of these will fall within your comfort zone; others will most likely be more challenging.

Common Core State Standards

Reading Literature

10. By the end of grade 10, read and comprehend literature, including stories, dramas, and poems, at the high end of the grades 9–10 text complexity band independently and proficiently.

Reading Informational Text

9. Analyze seminal U. S. documents of historical and literary significance (e.g., Washington's Farewell Address, the Gettysburg Address, Roosevelt's Four Freedoms speech, King's "Letter from Birmingham Jail"), including how they address related themes and concepts.

10. By the end of grade 10, read and comprehend literary nonfiction at the high end of the grades 9–10 text complexity band independently and proficiently.

Strategy 1: **Multidraft Reading**

Good readers develop the habit of revisiting texts in order to comprehend them completely. Get in the habit of reading a text or portions of a text two to three times in order to get the most out of your reading experience. To fully understand a text, try this multidraft reading strategy:

First Reading

On your first reading, read to gain the basic meaning of the text. If, for example, you are reading a story, look for the basics: who does what and to whom; what conflicts arise; how conflicts are resolved. If the text is nonfiction, look for main ideas and ways in which they are presented. If you are reading a lyric poem, identify the speaker, setting, and subject.

Second Reading

During your second reading, focus on the artistry or effectiveness of the writing. Look for text structures, and think about why the author chose those organizational patterns. Then, examine the author's creative use of language and its effects. For example, does the author employ metaphor, simile, or hyperbole? If so, what effect does that use of figurative language create?

Third Reading

After your third reading, compare and contrast the text with others you have read that share an important feature. For example, once you have read Theodore Roosevelt's Inauguration Address (p. lv) and the excerpt from Dwight D. Eisenhower's speech (p. lvii), compare the way each speaker approaches the theme of national responsibility in a complex world. Evaluate the text's overall effectiveness and its central idea or theme.

INFORMATIONAL TEXT

Independent Practice

As you read this text, practice the multidraft reading strategy by completing a chart like the one below.

from Theodore Roosevelt's Inaugural Address, March 4, 1905

. . . Our relations with the other powers of the world are important; but still more important are our relations among ourselves. Such growth in wealth, in population, and in power as this nation has seen during the century and a quarter of its national life is inevitably accompanied by a like growth in the problems which are ever before every nation that rises to greatness. Power invariably means both responsibility and danger. Our forefathers faced certain perils which we have outgrown. We now face other perils, the very existence of which it was impossible that they should foresee. Modern life is both complex and intense, and the tremendous changes wrought by the extraordinary industrial development of the last half century are felt in every fiber of our social and political being. Never before have men tried so vast and formidable an experiment as that of administering the affairs of a continent under the forms of a Democratic republic. The conditions which have told for our marvelous material well-being, which have developed to a very high degree our energy, self-reliance, and individual initiative, have also brought the care and anxiety inseparable from the accumulation of great wealth in industrial centers. Upon the success of our experiment much depends, not only as regards our own welfare, but as regards the welfare of mankind. . . .

Multidraft Reading Chart

	My Understanding
First Reading Look for key ideas and details that unlock basic meaning, concepts, and themes.	
Second Reading Read for deeper meanings. Look for ways in which the author uses text structures and language to enhance meaning.	
Third Reading Read to integrate your knowledge and ideas. Connect the text to others of its kind and to your own experience.	

Strategy 2: **Close Read the Text**

To comprehend a complex text, perform a close reading—a careful analysis of the words, phrases, and sentences within the text. As you close read, use the following tips to increase your understanding:

Tips for Close Reading

1. **Break down long sentences into parts.** Look for the subject of the sentence and its verb. Then, identify which parts of the sentence modify, or give more information about, its subject.

2. **Reread passages.** When reading complex texts, reread difficult passages to make sure that you understand their meanings.

3. **Look for context clues,** such as the following:

   a. Restatement of an idea. For example, in this sentence, "wasted away" restates the verb *atrophy*.

   He exercised so that his muscles would not **atrophy,** or waste away, because of disuse.

   b. Definition of sophisticated words. In this sentence, the underlined information defines the word *monotonous*.

   The **monotonous** song was dull and unvarying.

   c. Examples of concepts and topics. In the following passage, the underlined text provides an example of the adjective *sparse*.

   The **sparse** room lacked proper furniture for guests and had no decorations on the walls.

   d. Contrasts of ideas and topics.

   Abandoning his usual **veracity,** Eli decided to fabricate a story about why he missed practice.

4. **Identify pronoun antecedents.** If long sentences or passages contain pronouns, reread the text to make sure you know to what or to whom the pronouns refer. In the following passage, the underlined pronouns all have the antecedent *love*.

   Love has been accused of many things. *It* has caused wars, and *it* has brought peace. *It* drives people to insanity, and *it* cures disease. *It* allows the dead to live on, in the broken hearts of their survivors.

5. **Look for conjunctions,** such as *and, or,* and *yet,* to understand relationships between ideas.

6. **Paraphrase,** or restate in your own words, challenging passages in order to check your understanding. Remember that a paraphrase is a word-for-word rephrasing of an original text; it is not a summary.

INFORMATIONAL TEXT

Close Reading Model

As you read President Eisenhower's Address Before the General Assembly of the United Nations on December 8, 1953, study the side notes that model ways to unlock meaning in the text.

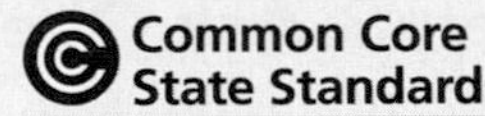

Reading Informational Text

9. Analyze seminal U.S. documents of historical and literary significance (e.g., Washington's Farewell Address, the Gettysburg Address, Roosevelt's Four Freedoms speech, King's "Letter from Birmingham Jail"), including how they address related themes and concepts.

from "Atoms for Peace" by Dwight D. Eisenhower

Madame President, Members of the General Assembly:

. . . I know that the American people share my deep belief that if a danger exists in the world, it is a danger shared by all—and equally, that if hope exists in the mind of one nation, that hope should be shared by all . . . I feel impelled to speak today in a language that in a sense is new—one which I, who have spent so much of my life in the military profession, would have preferred never to use.

That new language is the language of atomic warfare. . . .

Occasional pages of history do record the faces of the "Great Destroyers" but the whole book of history reveals mankind's never-ending quest for peace, and mankind's God-given capacity to build. It is with the book of history, and not with isolated pages, that the United States will ever wish to be identified. My country wants to be constructive, not destructive. It wants agreements, not wars, among nations. It wants itself to live in freedom, and in the confidence that the people of every other nation enjoy equally the right of choosing their own way of life.

So my country's purpose is to help us move out of the dark chamber of horrors into the light, to find a way by which the minds of men, the hopes of men, the souls of men everywhere, can move forward toward peace and happiness and well being. In this quest, I know that we must not lack patience. I know that in a world divided, such as ours today, salvation cannot be attained by one dramatic act. I know that many steps will have to be taken over many months before the world can look at itself one day and truly realize that a new climate of mutually peaceful confidence is abroad in the world. But I know, above all else, that we must start to take these steps—now.

Break down this long sentence. The speaker, *I*, is the subject, and *know* is the verb. The first phrase highlighted in green tells what the speaker knows. The last two phrases highlighted in green modify the word *belief*.

Search for context clues. The words highlighted in green can help you figure out the word highlighted in yellow.

The word "So" signals that a summarization of a key point is to come: America wants to help the world change direction.

Look for antecedents. The word "we" refers to President Eisenhower and the members of the General Assembly of the United Nations.

Strategy 3: **Ask Questions**

Be an attentive reader by asking questions as you read. Throughout this textbook, we have provided questions for you following each selection. These questions are sorted into three basic categories that build in sophistication and lead you to a deeper understanding of the texts you read.

Here is an example from this book:

Some questions are about **Key Ideas and Details** in the text. To answer these questions, you will need to locate and cite explicit information in the text or draw inferences from what you have read.

Some questions are about **Craft and Structure** in the text. To answer these questions, you will need to analyze how the author developed and structured the text. You will also look for ways in which the author artfully used language and how those word choices affected the meaning and tone of the work.

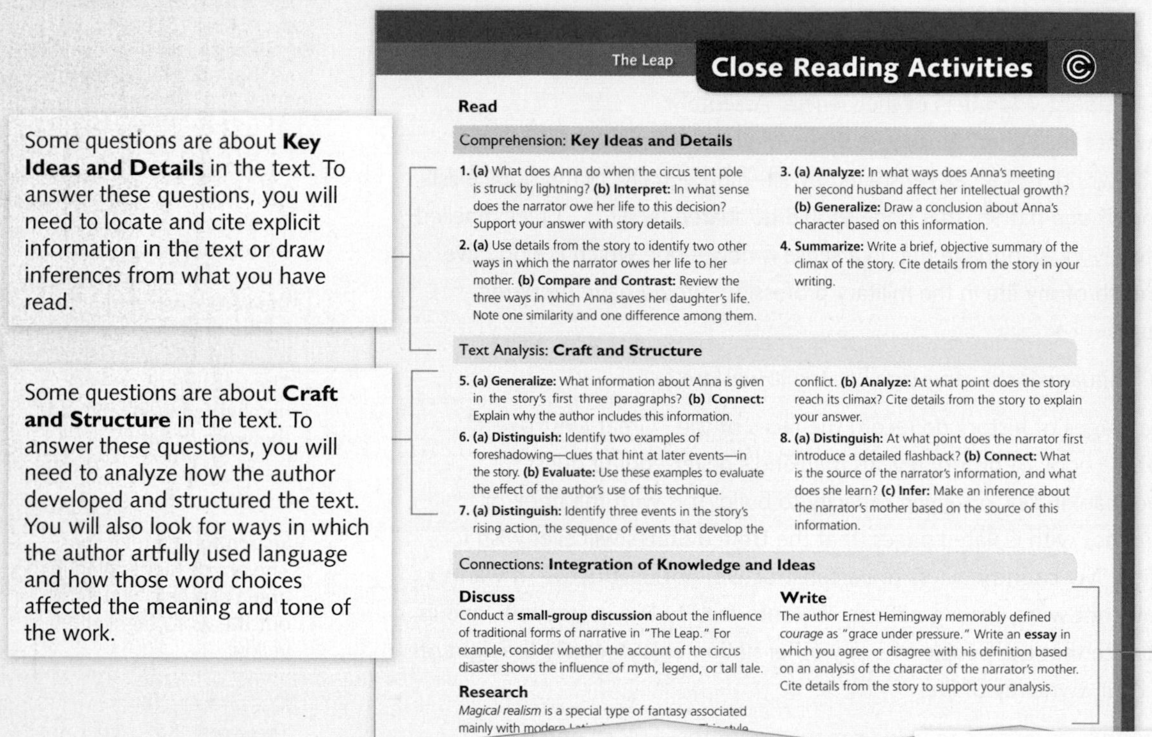

The Leap **Close Reading Activities**

Read

Comprehension: **Key Ideas and Details**

1. **(a)** What does Anna do when the circus tent pole is struck by lightning? **(b) Interpret:** In what sense does the narrator owe her life to this decision? Support your answer with story details.
2. **(a)** Use details from the story to identify two other ways in which the narrator owes her life to her mother. **(b) Compare and Contrast:** Review the three ways in which Anna saves her daughter's life. Note one similarity and one difference among them.
3. **(a) Analyze:** In what ways does Anna's meeting her second husband affect her intellectual growth? **(b) Generalize:** Draw a conclusion about Anna's character based on this information.
4. **Summarize:** Write a brief, objective summary of the climax of the story. Cite details from the story in your writing.

Text Analysis: **Craft and Structure**

5. **(a) Generalize:** What information about Anna is given in the story's first three paragraphs? **(b) Connect:** Explain why the author includes this information.
6. **(a) Distinguish:** Identify two examples of foreshadowing—clues that hint at later events—in the story. **(b) Evaluate:** Use these examples to evaluate the effect of the author's use of this technique.
7. **(a) Distinguish:** Identify three events in the story's rising action, the sequence of events that develop the conflict. **(b) Analyze:** At what point does the story reach its climax? Cite details from the story to explain your answer.
8. **(a) Distinguish:** At what point does the narrator first introduce a detailed flashback? **(b) Connect:** What is the source of the narrator's information, and what does she learn? **(c) Infer:** Make an inference about the narrator's mother based on the source of this information.

Connections: **Integration of Knowledge and Ideas**

Discuss

Conduct a **small-group discussion** about the influence of traditional forms of narrative in "The Leap." For example, consider whether the account of the circus disaster shows the influence of myth, legend, or tall tale.

Research

Magical realism is a special type of fantasy associated mainly with modern ...

Write

The author Ernest Hemingway memorably defined *courage* as "grace under pressure." Write an **essay** in which you agree or disagree with his definition based on an analysis of the character of the narrator's mother. Cite details from the story to support your analysis.

Some questions are about the **Integration of Knowledge and Ideas** in the text. These questions ask you to evaluate a text in many different ways, such as comparing texts, analyzing arguments in the text, and using many other methods to think critically about a text's ideas.

Preparing to Read Complex Texts

Attentive Reading As you read literature on your own, bring your imagination and questions to the text. The questions shown below and others that you ask as you read will help you learn and enjoy literature even more.

When reading narratives, ask yourself...

Comprehension: **Key Ideas and Details**

- Who is the story's main character? Who are the other characters, and how do they relate to the main character?
- What problems do the characters face? How do they react to these problems?
- Which characters do I like or admire? Which do I dislike? How do my reactions to the characters make me feel about the story as a whole?
- Is the setting believable and interesting? Why or why not?
- What happens in the story? Why do these events happen?

Text Analysis: **Craft and Structure**

- Who is narrating the story? Is this voice part of the story, or is it an outside observer?
- Do I find the narrator's voice interesting and engaging? Why or why not?
- Is there anything different or unusual in the way the story is structured? Do I find that structure interesting or distracting?
- Are there any passages that ... or beautiful? What ...

Common Core State Standards

Reading Literature/Informational Text

10. By the end of Grade 10, read and comprehend literature, including stories, dramas, poems, and literary nonfiction at the high end of the grades 9–10 text complexity band independently and proficiently.

As you read independently, ask similar types of questions to ensure that you fully enjoy and comprehend texts you read for both school and pleasure. We have provided sets of questions for you on the Independent Reading pages at the end of each unit.

EXEMPLAR TEXT

Model

Following is an example of a complex text. The side notes show sample questions that an attentive reader might ask while reading.

from "Classifying the Stars" by Annie J. Cannon

To the People of the State of New York:

. . . The very beginning of our knowledge of the nature of a star dates back to 1672, when Isaac Newton gave the world the results of his experiments on passing sunlight through a prism. To describe the beautiful band of rainbow tints, produced when sunlight was dispersed by his three-cornered piece of glass, he took from the Latin the word *spectrum*, meaning "an appearance."

. . . In 1814, more than a century after Newton, the spectrum of the Sun was obtained in such purity that an amazing detail was seen and studied by the German optician Fraunhofer. He saw that the multiple spectral tints, ranging from delicate violet to deep red, were crossed by hundreds of fine dark lines. In other words, there were narrow gaps in the spectrum where certain shades were wholly blotted out.

We must remember that the word *spectrum* is applied not only to sunlight, but also to the light of any glowing substance when its rays are sorted out by a prism or a grating.

Sample questions:

Key Ideas and Details
What ideas are introduced in this paragraph? What assumptions does the author make?

Craft and Structure
What organizational pattern does the writer use? How does the use of this pattern help to convey her ideas?

Integration of Knowledge and Ideas
In what ways does the information in this text expand on or contradict what I already know?

EXEMPLAR TEXT

Independent Practice

Write three to five questions you might ask yourself as you read this passage.

from "Circumference" by Nicholas Nicastro

The astrolabe . . . is a manual computing and observation device with myriad uses in astronomy, time keeping, surveying, navigation, and astrology. The principles behind the most common variety, the *planispheric* astrolabe, were first laid down in antiquity by the Greeks, who pioneered the notion of projecting three-dimensional images on flat surfaces. The device reached a high degree of refinement in the medieval Islamic world, where it was invaluable for determining prayer times and the direction of Mecca from anywhere in the Muslim world. The astrolabe was introduced to Europe by the eleventh century, where it saw wide use until the Renaissance.

ANALYZING ARGUMENTS

The ability to evaluate an argument, as well as to make one, is an important skill for success in college and in the workplace.

What Is an Argument?

In literature and writing, an **argument** is the presentation of one side of a controversial or debatable issue. Through this type of presentation, the writer logically supports a particular belief, conclusion, or point of view. A good argument is supported with strong reasoning and relevant, provable evidence.

Elements of Argument
Claim (assertion)—what the writer is trying to prove *Example: Grade point averages should be weighted.*
Grounds (evidence)—the support used to convince the reader *Example: Because difficult classes require much more work, the extra effort should be acknowledged.*
Justification—the link between the grounds and the claim; why the grounds are credible *Example: Because GPA is an indication of a student's ability to succeed in college, students who take challenging courses should be ranked above students who take easier classes even if they earn the same grade.*

Evaluating Claims

When reading or listening to an argument, critically assess the claims that are made. Analyze the argument to identify claims that are valid or can be proved true. Also evaluate evidence that supports the claims. If there is little or no reasoning or evidence provided to support the claims, the argument may not be sound. Also, be on the lookout for logical fallacies, like those listed below.

Logical Fallacies

Although they may initially seem convincing, logical fallacies involve faulty reasoning and do not support an argument.

- **False Causality:** The flawed idea that because B occurred after A, A caused B to happen
- ***Ad Hominem:*** An attack on a person's character, not on the person's position on an issue
- **Red Herring:** A provocative idea that is included in an argument to distract an audience's attention from the real issue under discussion
- **Begging the Question:** The premise or assumption that the argument is true because it is said to be true
- **Overgeneralization:** A conclusion that is based on little or no evidence

Common Core State Standards

Reading Informational Text

6. Determine an author's point of view or purpose in a text and analyze how an author uses rhetoric to advance that point of view or purpose.

8. Delineate and evaluate the argument and specific claims in a text, assessing whether the reasoning is valid and the evidence is relevant and sufficient; identify false statements and fallacious reasoning.

Language

6. Acquire and use accurately grade-appropriate general academic and domain-specific words and phrases; gather vocabulary knowledge when considering a word or phrase important to comprehension or expression.

INFORMATIONAL TEXT

Model Argument

from "Thank Heaven for Little Girls" by Rich Stearns

The lyrics to Maurice Chevalier's most enduring song describe an idyllic view of little girls and the women they become. There is much in our art and literature that romanticizes girls and women and the role they play in our culture. But sadly, in our world today, being female often means being sentenced to a life of poverty, abuse, exploitation, and deprivation.

The introduction explains the title and references a popular 1950s song to hook readers.

Compared to her male counterpart, a girl growing up in the developing world is more likely to die before her fifth birthday and less likely to go to school. She is less likely to receive adequate food or health care, less likely to receive economic opportunities, more likely to be forced to marry before the age of 16. . . .

Girls are forced to stay home from school to work. In fact, two-thirds of the nearly 800 million illiterate people in the world are women. Only one in 10 women in Niger can read. Five hundred thousand women die every year from childbirth complications—that's one woman every minute. . . .

Women are denied property rights and inheritance in many countries. Worldwide, women own only 1 percent of the world's property. They work two-thirds of all the world's labor hours but earn just 10 percent of the world's wages.

. . . Being female, in much of our world, is not "heavenly."

This paragraph describes the poverty and lack of freedoms that women face. Stearns will go on to argue that improving one (freedom) will improve the other (conditions of poverty).

And yet, in my opinion, the single-most significant thing that can be done to "cure" extreme poverty is this: protect, educate, and nurture girls and women and provide them with equal rights and opportunities—educationally, economically, and socially.

Claim: Educating women relieves poverty.

According to U.N. Secretary-General Kofi Annan: "No tool for development is more effective than the empowerment of women."

This one thing can do more to address extreme poverty than food, shelter, health care, economic development, or increased foreign assistance.

There is a saying in Ghana: "If you educate a man, you simply educate an individual, but if you educate a woman, you educate a nation." When a girl is educated, her income potential increases, maternal and infant mortality is reduced, her children are more likely to be immunized, the birth rate decreases, and HIV infection rates (especially in Africa) are lowered. She is more likely to acquire skills to improve her family's economic stability, and she is more likely to ensure that her daughters also receive an education. Educating girls pays dividend after dividend to the whole community. . . .

Grounds: The claim is supported by a quotation from U.N. Secretary-General Kofi Annan and by a Ghanaian saying. Benefits from educating girls range from reducing infant mortality to improving economic stability. These benefits are assumed to address poverty and its effects.

Unstated Justification: The evidence comes from a wide range of sources: the U.N. Secretary-General, who is an authority on international issues; an African saying; and the summarized results of implied research.

A strong conclusion does more than simply restate the claim.

THE ART OF ARGUMENT: RHETORICAL DEVICES AND PERSUASIVE TECHNIQUES

Rhetorical Devices

Rhetoric is the art of using language in order to make a point or to persuade listeners. Rhetorical devices such as the ones listed below are accepted elements of argument. Their use does not invalidate or weaken an argument. Rather, the use of rhetorical devices is regarded as a key part of an effective argument.

Rhetorical Devices	Examples
Repetition The repeated use of certain words, phrases, or sentences	Soldiers learn **true** greatness, **true** wisdom, and **true** strength.
Parallelism The repeated use of similar grammatical structures	Sports teach **the thrill of victory** and **the agony of defeat.**
Rhetorical Question Calling attention to an issue by implying an obvious answer	Isn't freedom worth fighting for?
Sound Devices The use of alliteration, assonance, rhyme, or rhythm	There are **d**ark **d**ays that lie ahead, but we will not be **d**efeated!
Simile and Metaphor Comparing two seemingly unlike things or asserting that one thing is another	**Patriotism** spread <u>like a fire</u> through the ranks of soldiers after the general's speech.

Persuasive Techniques

Persuasive techniques are often used in advertisements and in other forms of persuasion. Although techniques like the ones below may appear in formal arguments, they are less convincing than the use of logical reasoning and authoritative evidence.

Persuasive Techniques	Examples
Bandwagon Approach/Anti-Bandwagon Approach Appeals to a person's desire to belong/encourages or celebrates individuality	Come see why more people choose to shop with us/Explore your one-of-a-kind style at our unique store.
Emotional Appeal Evokes people's fear, anger, or desire	Join the army and protect our nation from those who would destroy our way of life.
Endorsement/Testimonial Employs a well-known person to promote a product or an idea	"I drink Happy Throat Tea before all of my concerts."
Loaded Language The use of words that are charged with emotion	They are suffering under a brutal dictator.
"Plain Folks" Appeal Shows a connection to everyday, ordinary people	"I grew up in a working-class neighborhood, just like this one."
Hyperbole Exaggerates to make a point	We face a thousand crises every day.

EXEMPLAR TEXT

Model Speech

The speech excerpted below includes rhetorical devices and persuasive techniques.

from "Duty, Honor, Country" by General Douglas MacArthur

Duty, Honor, Country: Those three hallowed words reverently dictate what you ought to be, what you can be, what you will be. They are your rallying points: to build courage when courage seems to fail; to regain faith when there seems to be little cause for faith; to create hope when hope becomes forlorn. Unhappily, I possess neither that eloquence of diction, that poetry of imagination, nor that brilliance of metaphor to tell you all that they mean. . . .

General MacArthur uses parallelism and repetition to emphasize the ideas of *duty, honor,* and *country.*

But these are some of the things they do. They build your basic character. They mold you for your future roles as the custodians of the nation's defense. They make you strong enough to know when you are weak, and brave enough to face yourself when you are afraid. They teach you to be proud and unbending in honest failure, but humble and gentle in success; not to substitute words for actions, not to seek the path of comfort, but to face the stress and spur of difficulty and challenge; . . . They give you a temper of the will, a quality of the imagination, a vigor of the emotions, a freshness of the deep springs of life, a temperamental predominance of courage over timidity, an appetite for adventure over love of ease. They create in your heart the sense of wonder, the unfailing hope of what next, and the joy and inspiration of life. They teach you in this way to be an officer and a gentleman.

Additional instances of parallelism clarify General MacArthur's ideas and make them more emotionally engaging.

And what sort of soldiers are those you are to lead? Are they reliable? Are they brave? Are they capable of victory? Their story is known to all of you. It is the story of the American man at arms. . . . His name and fame are the birthright of every American citizen. In his youth and strength, his love and loyalty, he gave all that mortality can give. . . .

Rhetorical questions call attention to a change in the topic.

From one end of the world to the other, he has drained deep the chalice of courage. As I listened to those songs of the glee club, in memory's eye I could see those staggering columns of the First World War, bending under soggy packs on many a weary march, from dripping dusk to drizzling dawn, slogging ankle deep through mire of shell-pocked roads; to form grimly for the attack, blue-lipped, covered with sludge and mud, chilled by the wind and rain, driving home to their objective, and for many, to the judgment seat of God.

MacArthur uses alliteration, which gives his descriptions more power.

I do not know the dignity of their birth, but I do know the glory of their death. They died unquestioning, uncomplaining, with faith in their hearts, and on their lips the hope that we would go on to victory. Always for them: Duty, Honor, Country.

Parallelism makes this phrase memorable and powerful.

Repetition of key ideas from the beginning of the speech provides a satisfying conclusion.

COMPOSING AN ARGUMENT

Choosing a Topic

When writing an argument, choose a topic that matters—to people in general and to you personally. Brainstorm for topics you would like to address, and then choose the one that most interests you.

Once you have chosen a topic, check to be sure you can make an arguable claim. Ask yourself:

1. What am I trying to prove? What ideas do I need to communicate?
2. Are there people who would disagree with my claim? What opinions might they have?
3. Do I have evidence to support my claim? Is my evidence sufficient and relevant?

If you are able to put into words what you want to prove and can answer yes to questions 2 and 3, you have an arguable claim.

Introducing the Claim and Establishing Its Significance

Before you begin writing, think about your audience and how much they already know about your topic. Then, provide only as much background information as necessary. Remember that you are not writing a summary of the issue—you are crafting an argument.

Once you have provided context for your argument, clearly state your claim, or thesis. A written argument's claim often, but not always, appears in the first paragraph.

Developing Your Claim With Reasons and Evidence

Now that you have stated your claim, support it with evidence, or grounds. A good argument should be supported with at least three solid pieces of evidence. Evidence can range from personal experience to researched data or expert opinion. Understanding your audience's knowledge level, concerns, values, and possible biases can help you decide which types of evidence will have the strongest impact. Make sure your evidence is current and comes from a credible source. Do not forget to credit your sources.

Work to address opposing ideas, or counterclaims, within the body of your argument. Consider points you have made or evidence you have provided that a reader might challenge. Decide how best to respond to these counterclaims.

Writing a Concluding Statement or Section

Restate your claim in the conclusion of your argument, and synthesize, or pull together, the evidence you have provided. Make your conclusion powerful and memorable so that your readers continue to think about your points.

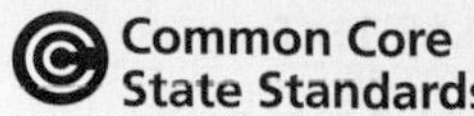

Common Core State Standards

Writing

1. Write arguments to support claims in an analysis of substantive topics or texts, using valid reasoning and relevant and sufficient evidence.

1.a. Introduce precise claim(s), distinguish the claim(s) from alternate or opposing claims, and create an organization that establishes clear relationships among claim(s), counterclaims, reasons, and evidence.

1.b. Develop claim(s) and counterclaims fairly, supplying evidence for each while pointing out the strengths and limitations of both in a manner that anticipates the audience's knowledge level and concerns.

1.e. Provide a concluding statement or section that follows from and supports the argument presented.

Practice

Complete an outline like the one below to help you plan your own argument.

Brainstorming for Topics:

____

____

The topic that most interests me is ______________________ because

____

Arguable Claim (Thesis): ______________________________

What I Already Know About the Issue: ______________________

What I Need to Find Out About the Issue:

____

Who Is My Audience, and How Much Does My Audience Know About the Issue?

____

Possible Sources of Evidence: ___________________________

Grounds to Support My Claim (at least three strong pieces of evidence):

1. ____
2. ____
3. ____

Warrants for My Grounds (why my grounds are allowed to stand as evidence):

1. ____
2. ____
3. ____

Opposing Viewpoints to Consider: ________________________

CONDUCTING RESEARCH

We are lucky to live in an age when information is plentiful. However, not all information is equally useful, or even accurate. Strong research skills will help you locate and evaluate information.

Short-Term Research

You will often need to conduct **short-term research** to answer specific questions about a text or extend your understanding of an idea. These strategies can help you find appropriate information quickly and efficiently:

Target Your Goal Decide what information you need to find before you begin your research. Drafting a specific question can help you avoid time-wasting digressions. For example, instead of simply hunting for information about Mark Twain, you might ask, "What jobs other than writing did Mark Twain have?" or, "Which of Twain's books was most popular during his lifetime?"

Use Online Search Engines Efficiently Finding information on the Internet can be both easy and challenging. Type a word or phrase into a general search engine and you will probably get hundreds—or thousands—of results. However, those results are not guaranteed to be relevant or accurate. Using quotation marks can help you focus a search. Place a phrase in quotation marks to find pages that include exactly that phrase. Add several phrases in quotation marks to narrow your results.

Scan search results before you click on them. The first result isn't always the most relevant. Read the text and consider the domain before making a choice.

Consult Multiple Sources It is always a good idea to check for answers in more than one source. This strategy helps you be sure that the information you find is accurate. Be wary if you read the exact same phrases in more than one source—there is a good chance that someone simply cut and pasted details from one site and failed to check their validity.

Common Core State Standards

Writing

5. Develop and strengthen writing as needed by planning, revising, editing, rewriting, or trying a new approach, focusing on addressing what is most significant for a specific purpose and audience.

7. Conduct short as well as more sustained research projects to answer a question (including a self-generated question) or solve a problem; narrow or broaden the inquiry when appropriate.

8. Gather relevant information from multiple authoritative print and digital sources, using advanced searches effectively; assess the usefulness of each source in answering the research question.

Evaluating Internet Domains

Not everything you read on the Internet is true, so you have to evaluate sources carefully. The last three letters of an Internet URL identify the site's domain, which can help you evaluate information on the site.

- .gov — Government sites are sponsored by a branch of the United States federal government, such as the Census Bureau, Supreme Court, or Congress. These sites are considered reliable.
- .edu — Education domains include schools from kindergartens to universities. Information from an educational research center or department is likely to be carefully checked. However, education domains can also include student pages that are not edited or monitored.
- .org — Organizations are nonprofit groups and usually maintain a high level of credibility. Keep in mind that some organizations may express strong biases.
- .com — Commercial sites exist to make a profit. Information might be biased to show a product or service in a good light. The company may be providing information to encourage sales or to promote a positive image.

Long-Term Research

Long-term research allows you to dive into a topic and conduct a detailed, comprehensive investigation. Your final goal could be a formal research report or a media presentation. An organized research plan will help you gather and synthesize information from multiple sources.

Long-term research is a flexible process—you will constantly adjust your research plan based on your findings and your growing understanding of the topic. Throughout your investigation, you might decide to return to an earlier stage to refocus your thesis, gather more information, or reflect on what you have learned.

The Research Process

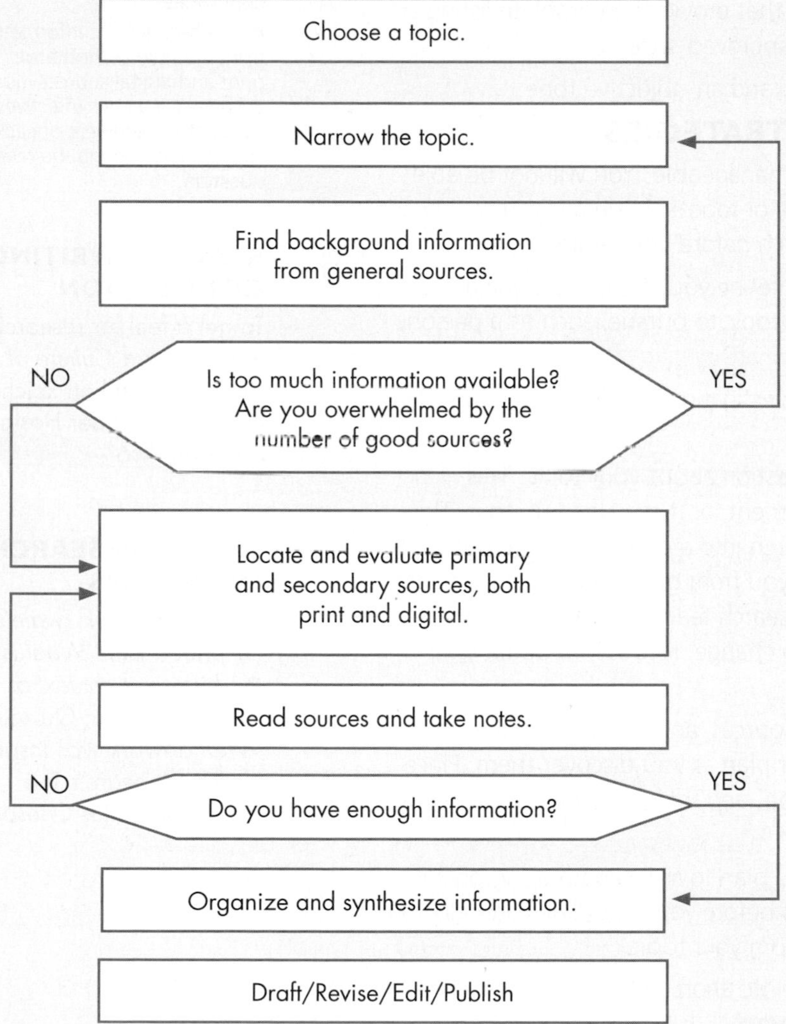

Consult the Research Process Workshop (pages lxviii–lxxiv) for more details about the steps in this flowchart.

RESEARCH PROCESS WORKSHOP

Research Writing: Research Report

A **research report** presents and interprets information gathered through the extensive study of a subject. You might use elements of a research report in writing lab reports, documentaries, annotated bibliographies, histories, and persuasive essays.

Elements of a Research Report

- a thesis statement that is clearly expressed
- factual support from a variety of reliable, credited sources
- a clear introduction, body, and conclusion
- a bibliography or Works Cited list that provides a complete listing of research sources formatted in an approved style.
- error-free grammar, a formal style, and an objective tone.

PREWRITING/PLANNING STRATEGIES

A research report needs a topic that is manageable. You will not be able to cover a broad topic, like World War II or robots, in detail. You can avoid many problems by focusing your research before you begin.

Background research can also help you refine your topic. Your initial findings can help you choose a specific topic to pursue, such as a person, an event, or a theme.

Create a research plan to guide your investigation. Your plan can include these parts:

Research Question Compose a question about your topic. This question may become your thesis statement, or it may lead up to it. The question will also help focus your research into a comprehensive but flexible search plan, as well as prevent you from gathering details that are too broad for your purpose. As your research teaches you more about your topic, you may find it necessary to change, refocus, or adapt your original question.

Source List Plan to use a variety of sources, and create a list to begin your research. Add new sources to your plan as you discover them. Place a check next to sources you have located, and then underline sources you have consulted thoroughly.

Search Terms Write down terms you plan to investigate using online search engines. Making these decisions before you go online can help you avoid digressions that take you away from your topic.

Deadlines Break a long-term project into short-term goals in order to stay on track and prevent last-minute stress.

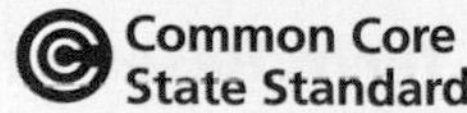

Writing

5. Develop and strengthen writing as needed by planning, revising, editing, rewriting, or trying a new approach, focusing on addressing what is most significant for a specific purpose and audience.

7. Conduct short as well as more sustained research projects to answer a question (including a self-generated question) or solve a problem; narrow or broaden the inquiry when appropriate.

8. Gather relevant information from multiple authoritative print and digital sources, using advanced searches effectively; assess the usefulness of each source in answering the research question.

READING-WRITING CONNECTION

To get a feel for research writing, read *Culture of Shock* by Stephen Reicher and S. Alexander Haslam on page 746.

SAMPLE RESEARCH QUESTIONS

What was Mark Twain's childhood like? What is the historical context of Cervantes's Don Quixote*? What artwork was inspired by Shakespeare's* The Tragedy of Julius Caesar*?*

GATHERING DETAILS THROUGH RESEARCH

Use multiple sources. An effective research project combines information from several sources, and does not rely too heavily on a single source. The creativity and originality of your research depends on how you combine ideas from many places. Plan to include a variety of these types of resources:

- **Primary and Secondary Sources:** To get a thorough view of your topic, use primary sources (firsthand or original accounts, such as interview transcripts and newspaper articles) and secondary sources (accounts that are not original, such as encyclopedia entries).
- **Print and Digital Resources:** The Internet allows fast access to data, but print resources are often edited more carefully. Plan to include both print and digital resources in order to guarantee the accuracy of your work.
- **Media Resources:** You can find valuable information in media resources such as documentaries, television programs, podcasts, and museum exhibitions. Consider attending public lectures given by experts to gain an even more in-depth view of your topic.
- **Original Research:** Depending on your topic, you may wish to conduct original research to include among your sources. For example, you might interview experts or eyewitnesses or conduct a survey of people in your community.

Locate information. You can find sources of specific information through an online search, a card catalog, or the use of more advanced tools:

- **Databases:** Access databases of information to find appropriate sources. For example, the Modern Language Association (MLA) database indexes articles on topics within the humanities.
- **Indexes:** Locate magazine or newspaper articles by consulting the *Readers' Guide to Periodical Literature.*

Sample *Readers' Guide* Entry

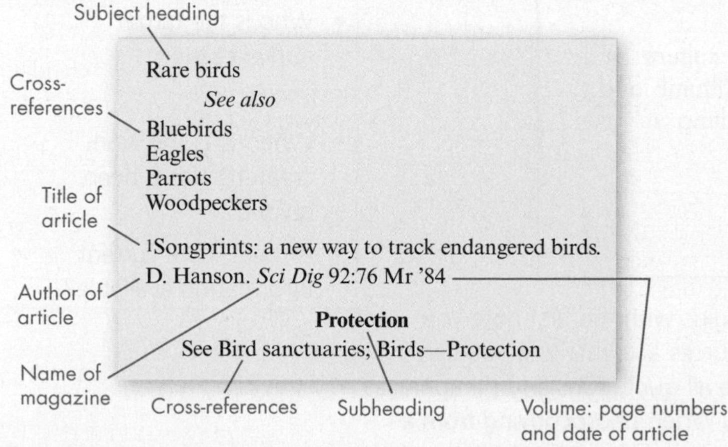

GATHERING DETAILS THROUGH RESEARCH (continued)

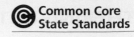

Common Core State Standards

Writing
9. Draw evidence from literary or informational texts to support analysis, reflection, and research.

Evaluate sources. Analyze and apply evaluative criteria to assess the accuracy and appropriateness of your sources for your purpose and audience. You may find the information you need to answer your research question in specialized and authoritative sources, such as almanacs (for social, cultural, and natural statistics), government publications (for law, government programs, and subjects such as agriculture), and information services. Also, consider consumer, workplace, and public documents. Consult your librarian on the best sources to use.

Record and organize information. Take notes as you locate and connect pertinent information from multiple sources, and keep a reference list of every source you use. This will help you to make distinctions between the relative value and significance of specific data, facts, and ideas.

- **Source Cards:** Create a card that identifies the author, title, publisher, city, date of publication, and page number of each source you consult.

  For Internet sources, record the name and Web address of the site and the date you accessed the information.
- **Notecards:** For each item of information, create a separate notecard that includes both the fact or idea and its source.

Source Card [A]

Marsh, Peter, M.D. *Eye to Eye: How People Interact.* Topsfield, MA: Salem House Publishers, 1988.

(p. 54)

Notecard

Gestures vary from culture to culture. The American "OK" symbol (thumb and forefinger) is considered insulting in Greece and Turkey.

Source Card: A

Reliability Checklist

Ask yourself these questions about sources you find:

AUTHORITY
- Is the author well known?
- What are the author's credentials?
- Does the author's tone win your confidence? Why or why not?

BIAS
- Does the author have any obvious biases?
- What is the author's purpose for writing?
- Who is the target audience?

CURRENCY
- When was the work created? Has it been revised?
- Is there more current information available?

Quote accurately. Responsible research begins with the first note you take. Be sure to quote and paraphrase your sources accurately so you can identify these sources later. In your notes, circle all quotations and paraphrases to distinguish them from your own comments. When photocopying from a source, include the copyright information. Also, remember to include the Web addresses of printouts from online sources.

DRAFTING STRATEGIES

W.9-10.2, W.9-10.2.a–b, W.9-10.7, W.9-10.8

[For the full standards wording, see the chart in the front of this book.]

Refine your thesis statement. Your working thesis statement should have evolved into a focused declaration as you gathered information. Now, make sure it can be proved using the facts and ideas you have compiled through research.

> **Final Thesis Statement:** Dreams make a difference in people's lives—not only to the individuals who dream them, but to society.

Organize your information. Choose an organizational strategy that matches the content and purpose of your writing. Consider using one of the strategies described in the chart below.

Synthesize ideas. Effective research writing does not merely present facts and details but synthesizes—gathers, orders, and interprets—those elements. As you draft, synthesize information into a unified whole that is driven by your original thoughts.

Use and credit sources. You may choose any of the following methods to present the ideas, facts, and examples you discover in your research. In all cases, you must credit your source.

- **Direct quotation:** Use the author's exact words when they are interesting or persuasive. Indicate any omissions with ellipsis points. Enclose direct quotations in quotation marks.
- **Paraphrase:** Restate an author's ideas in your own words.
- **Summary:** Compress a complex idea into a briefer version.
- **Facts:** If a fact is available only in one source, include documentation.

Incorporate graphic aids and visuals. Consider using illustrations, photographs, maps, graphs, or charts to clarify facts, highlight trends, or add dramatic power. You may include visuals you discover in your research materials. If so, provide full citations for them.

Organizational Strategy	Uses
Chronological Order offers information in the sequence in which it happened	historical topics; science experiments
Part-to-Whole Order examines how categories affect a larger subject	analysis of social issues; historical topics
Order of Importance presents information in order of increasing or decreasing importance	persuasive arguments; supporting a bold or challenging thesis
Comparison-and-Contrast Organization presents similarities and differences	addressing two or more subjects

REVISING STRATEGIES

Step back from your work. If possible, leave yourself time between drafting and revising. Reading your work with new energy will allow you to see it with more clarity.

Revise for conciseness. Your research report will be more effective if you avoid unnecessary complexity or wordiness. Reread your draft, circling any words that add clutter without meaning. Consider omitting those words or replacing them with better choices.

Model: Revising for Conciseness

In

~~Thus, in~~ conclusion, ~~one can see from careful observation that~~ political conflict often leads to economic change.

Revise to avoid plagiarism. To avoid plagiarism—the unethical presentation of someone else's ideas as if they were your own—you must cite sources for direct quotations, paraphrased information, or facts that are specific to a single source. Reread your draft, circling any words or ideas that are not your own. Follow the instructions on page lxxiii to correctly cite those passages.

Revise to strengthen coherence. Make sure that all of the elements in your draft follow your organizational strategy and appear in logical, or coherent, order.

- On a separate piece of paper, write the main idea of each paragraph.
- Review this list—an abbreviated version of your report—to decide whether your ideas flow logically from paragraph to paragraph.
- Check that the ideas in your introduction and conclusion match.
- Rearrange paragraphs or sections that do not build in a logical way. Consider eliminating any that stray from your thesis statement.
- Add transitional words or sentences to help readers see the connections you want to emphasize.

Peer Review

Share your draft and list of main ideas with a partner. Ask your partner to consider how well each main idea builds on the last in a logical flow. Consider moving paragraphs or sections to improve your report's coherence. Explain to your partner your reasons for specific revision choices.

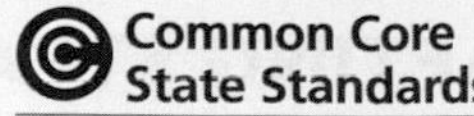

Common Core State Standards

Writing

2.c. Use appropriate and varied transitions to link the major sections of the text, create cohesion, and clarify the relationships among complex ideas and concepts.

2.d. Use precise language and domain-specific vocabulary to manage the complexity of the topic.

5. Develop and strengthen writing as needed by revising, focusing on addressing what is most significant for a specific purpose and audience.

8. Integrate information into the text selectively to maintain the flow of ideas, avoiding plagiarism and following a standard format for citation.

DOCUMENTING SOURCES

Citing Sources in the Body of a Report When citing sources in your report, follow a specific format. Modern Language Association (MLA) style calls for parenthetical citations or references. For print works, the citation usually gives the author's or editor's name followed by a page number. If the work does not have an author, use a keyword or phrase from the title. For Web sources, use the author's name if it is available, the title of the article, if any, or the title of the site itself.

Citing a Print Work: . . . men have more action-oriented dreams, while women imagine more emotional one-on-one struggles with loved ones (Van de Castle 45).

Citing a Web Source: Dreams can also bring luck, as reported by a lottery winner from Maine ("Dreaming of the Lottery").

Creating a Works Cited List or Bibliography Publication information for each source you cite must appear at the end of your report. MLA style calls for a Works Cited list, in which you list alphabetically the works you cite.

- For books, the Works Cited entry usually takes the form of the author's name, last name first, followed by the title of the work. The entry gives full publication information, including the city of publication, the name of the publisher, and the year of publication. End the citation with the medium of publication (e.g., Print).
- For articles in periodicals, the entry usually takes the form of the author's name, last name first, followed by the title of the article, then the name of the magazine. Publication information includes the date of the issue, the volume and issue number if any, and the pages on which the article appears. If the article is continued on a later, nonconsecutive page, give the number of the first page, followed by a plus sign.
- For general Web sites, give any of the following information that is available, in the order indicated: author's name, the title of the page, the title of the site, the date of last update, the medium of publication (e.g., Web), and the name of the sponsoring organization. Conclude with the date on which you consulted the site.

For more information on MLA style, see page lxxviii.

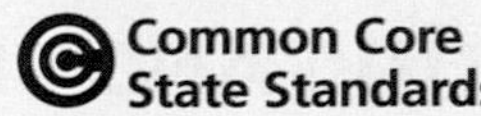

Writing

8. Gather relevant information from multiple authoritative print and digital sources, using advanced searches effectively; assess the usefulness of each source in answering the research question; integrate information into the text selectively to maintain the flow of ideas, avoiding plagiarism and following a standard format for citation.

Language

1. Demonstrate command of the conventions of standard English grammar and usage when writing or speaking.

3. Apply knowledge of language to understand how language functions in different contexts, to make effective choices for meaning or style, and to comprehend more fully when reading or listening.

3.a. Write and edit work so that it conforms to the guidelines in a style manual appropriate for the discipline and writing type.

EDITING AND PROOFREADING

Review your draft to correct factual and citation errors, as well as mistakes in format, grammar, and spelling.

Check your facts. Be sure that the facts you have included in your report are accurate. Errors sometimes occur during note-taking, drafting, and revising. To fact-check your report, place an open square next to each fact. Then, refer to your original sources to make sure you have stated each fact clearly and correctly. When you have confirmed a fact, place a check in the box and move on to the next one.

Review citations. Check that you have given credit for any ideas that are not your own. You might have unintentionally included exact phrases from one of your sources. To avoid plagiarism, you need to give credit for all of those ideas. Try reading your draft aloud. Listen for words and phrases that do not sound familiar or do not have your own voice. Chances are good that those elements came from one of your sources. Either provide an accurate citation or paraphrase to include the idea in your own words.

Focus on format. Follow the manuscript requirements by including an appropriate title page, pagination, spacing and margins, and citations. Make sure you have used the preferred system for crediting sources in your paper and for bibliographical sources at the end. Double-check all punctuation and capitalization.

Proofread. Carefully reread your draft to find and correct spelling errors. Also check to be sure that you have used quotation marks correctly and that each open quotation mark has a corresponding closing quotation mark.

Publishing and Presenting

Consider one of the following ways to share your writing:

Deliver an oral presentation. Read your research report aloud to your classmates, or consider re-creating the report as a multimedia presentation using presentation software. Add appropriate visual aids as needed, such as charts, maps, and graphs.

Organize a panel discussion. If several of your classmates have written on a similar topic, plan a discussion to compare and contrast your findings. Speakers can summarize their research before opening the panel to questions from the class.

MODEL: RESEARCH PAPER

As you read this student's completed research report, notice how she supports a thesis statement and integrates relevant research. Parenthetical citations within each paragraph refer to sources detailed in the Works Cited list at the end of the report. Marginal notes highlight elements that make this paper effective.

Student Model: Lisa Maiden, Phoenix, AZ

In Your Dreams

Ever since humans have existed, dreams have made a difference in people's lives. Julius Caesar's wife, Calpurnia, once dreamed that Caesar's statue spurted blood like a fountain while the Romans smiled and bathed in it. This nightmarish picture foreshadowed reality when Caesar was later assassinated. In 1793, Marie Antoinette had a dream of a red sun and pillar (Johnson, "Dreams"). After the sun rose, it suddenly set; this dream immediately preceded her beheading. Then, there is Robert Louis Stevenson, who believed his best stories came from dreams, including the infamous "Dr. Jekyll and Mr. Hyde." Neils Bohr dreamed of sitting on the sun with planets whizzing around him on small cords; he then developed the model of an atom. Even Genghis Khan claimed to receive his battle plans from his dream-filled nights.

Lisa begins by introducing the topic in a concise sentence.

Who were the early interpreters of dreams? Aristotle and Freud, of course, were among the scholars who labored over dream interpretation. Aristotle suggested that dreams were formed by disturbances in the body. Freud, however, believed that dreams were powerful tools for uncovering unconscious wishes. He said, "The purpose of dreams is to allow us to satisfy in fantasies the instinctual urges that society judges unacceptable" ("Dreams: History").

She correctly quotes and cites one of her sources.

Even today, creative people use their dreams to solve problems. A 1995 *Reader's Digest* article entitled "Why We Dream What We Dream" provides many examples. One such dreamer was the scientist Dmitri Ivanovich Mendeleev. He "saw" the periodic table of the elements in a dream and wrote it down the following day. Later, only one correction was needed. Screenwriter James Cameron dreamed of a robot with a red eye staring back at him. He woke up and wrote the script for *The Terminator*. Steve Allen's hit song "This Could Be the Start of Something Big" also began in a dream, as did the new way of swinging the club that allowed Jack Nicklaus to overcome his golfing problem (Kreisler 28–38).

Lisa incorporates the source of her information into the flow of her discussion.

Besides being helpful in creative work, dreams have, in many cases, foretold the future. In the weeks prior to his murder, Abraham Lincoln dreamed the White House was in mourning for an assassinated president. The film *The Secret World of Dreams* tells of a man whose dreams indicated a chronic illness even before it was diagnosed, as well as a man whose recurring nightmares of an explosion prepared him for the real thing and enabled him to save the life of a coworker. Dreams can also bring luck, as reported by a lottery winner from Maine whose dreams revealed a winning ticket ("Dreaming of the Lottery").

Lisa demonstrates the wide variety of sources she consulted in her research.

MODEL: RESEARCH PAPER (continued)

Given such cases as these, it is no mystery that modern psychology still believes in the prophetic power of dreams.

However, to understand one's dreams, one must uncover the meaning of dream symbols. Psychoanalyst Sigmund Freud said that the secret to the symbols in dreams lies within the dreamer (Bentley 4). In other words, individuals can interpret dream symbols from their own lives and the imagery around them—not just by using a dream dictionary. The Web guide "Dream Analysis and Interpretation" gives several examples of these symbols. For instance, to most dreamers, clothing symbolizes mood, attitude, or state of mind. One who wears a uniform in a dream may be influenced too much by society, while having clothes that are too short may suggest a longing for the pleasures of youth now gone. Death is also a recurring symbol. Whether the dreamer attends a funeral or is in a coffin, these pictures signify a change in one's attitude toward life or one's emotional balance. Finally, other people occur in dreams as reflections of the dreamer's own personality traits. For instance, if a dreamer is faced by the stares of others, that person may be worried about making a bad impression on other people.

Each paragraph includes a topic sentence, which is then supported in the paragraph with details.

While dreams can be interpreted according to symbols, the most common types of dreams vary throughout the human life cycle. People at different places in their lives tend to dream differently. Children's dreams reflect new impressions that they encounter each day. Bold geometric shapes are not just building blocks with which they play—they represent a fixation with family relationships. For example, a triangle would signify the relationship among the father, mother, and child. Dreams of giants indicate a child's impression of his or her own size and sense of self-worth. Naturally, everything is bigger to a child, but a child with giant proportions compared to the world around him may have an increasing self-awareness (Bentley 25). Much like a scene from *The Nutcracker,* toys come to life as the child lives out fantasies, showing developments of the young person's persona. As children become teens, they dream more about romance. Among adults, men and women dream differently. "It's biology and social conditioning," says Milton Kramer, director of the Bethesda Oak Hospital's Sleep Center in Cincinnati. Research has shown that men dream twice as often of other men as they do of women, while women tend to have an equal number of dreams of both sexes (Brown, "Dream On"). A study by Robert Van de Castle, author of *Our Dreaming Mind,* analyzed 1,000 dreams and found that men have more action-oriented dreams, while women imagine more emotional one-on-one struggles with loved ones (Van de Castle 45).

Studies are also beginning to show that a person's attitude can influence his or her dreams. University of Pennsylvania professor Aaron Beck found that angry people are the ones throwing the punches in their dream, while depressed people often find themselves the victims of rejection. However, people who have a hard time standing up for themselves are the ones likely to suffer from restless nightmares (Kreisler 36).

Through the fascinating history of dreams, the interpretation of some dream symbols, and the secret dreams of different sleepers, it is evident that dreams are important. They provide valuable insights, help solve problems, spark new thoughts and creations, and even foretell the future. Maybe people should pay more attention to their dreams. The hours one spends sleeping could be the key to a better life.

Works Cited

Bentley, Peter. *The Book of Dream Symbols*. Chronicle Books, 1995. Print.

Brown, Anna. "Dream On." *Dream News Today,* 26 April 1997: 2, 5. Dream News Publications. Web. 21 March 2015.

"Dream Analysis and Interpretation." Dream Central site. 2013. Web. 9 March 2015.

"Dreaming of the Lottery." Mystery Dreams site. 2013. Web. 11 March 2015.

"Dreams: History." ThinkQuest site. 2014. Web. 22 March 2015.

Johnson, Thomas. "Dreams Throughout the Ages." Great Moments in Dream History site. 2015. Web. 7 March 2015.

Kramer, Milton. Personal Interview. 10 March 2015.

Kreisler, Kristin V. "Why We Dream What We Dream." *Reader's Digest*. Feb. 1995: 28, 30, 34–36, 38. Print.

The Secret World of Dreams. Dir. Bruce Nash and Robyn Nash. Perf. Gerald Brodin, Scott Aguilar, Allen Perada, Stefanie Powers, and Robert R. Shafer. 1995. Questar Video, 1997. DVD.

Van de Castle, Robert L. *Our Dreaming Mind.* Ballantine, 1995. Print.

Lisa lists, in a standard format, the sources from which her information was drawn.

CITING SOURCES AND PREPARING MANUSCRIPT

In research writing, cite your sources. In the body of your paper, provide a footnote, an endnote, or a parenthetical citation, identifying the sources of facts, opinions, or quotations. At the end of your paper, provide a bibliography or a Works Cited list, a list of all the sources you cite. Follow an established format, such as Modern Language Association (MLA) Style.

Works Cited List (MLA Style)

A Works Cited list must contain accurate information sufficient to enable a reader to locate each source you cite. The basic components of an entry are as follows:

- Name of the author, editor, translator, or group responsible for the work
- Title of the work
- Place and date of publication
- Publisher

For print materials, the information required for a citation generally appears on the copyright and title pages of a work. For the format of Works Cited list entries, consult the examples at right and in the chart on page lxxix.

Parenthetical Citations (MLA Style)

A parenthetical citation briefly identifies the source from which you have taken a specific quotation, factual claim, or opinion. It refers the reader to one of the entries on your Works Cited list. A parenthetical citation has the following features:

- It appears in parentheses.
- It identifies the source by the last name of the author, editor, or translator, or by the title (for a lengthy title, list the first word only).
- It gives a page reference, identifying the page of the source on which the information cited can be found.

Punctuation A parenthetical citation generally falls outside a closing quotation mark but within the final punctuation of a clause or sentence. For a long quotation set off from the rest of your text, place the citation at the end of the excerpt without any punctuation following.

Special Cases

- If the author is an organization, use the organization's name, in a shortened version if necessary.
- If you cite more than one work by the same author, add the title or a shortened version of the title.

Sample Works Cited Lists (MLA 7th Edition)

Carwardine, Mark, Erich Hoyt, R. Ewan Fordyce, and Peter Gill. *The Nature Company Guides: Whales, Dolphins, and Porpoises*. New York: Time-Life, 1998. Print.

"Discovering Whales." *Whales on the Net*. 1998. Whales in Danger Information Service. Web. 18 Oct. 2015.

Neruda, Pablo. "Ode to Spring." *Odes to Opposites*. Trans. Ken Krabbenhoft. Ed. and illus. Ferris Cook. Boston: Little, 1995. Print.

The Saga of the Volsungs. Trans. Jesse L. Byock. London: Penguin, 1990. Print.

List an anonymous work by title.

List both the title of the work and the collection in which it is found.

Sample Parenthetical Citations

It makes sense that baleen whales such as the blue whale, the bowhead whale, the humpback whale, and the sei whale (to name just a few) grow to immense sizes (Carwardine, Hoyt, and Fordyce 19–21). The blue whale has grooves running from under its chin to partway along the length of its underbelly. As in some other whales, these grooves expand and allow even more food and water to be taken in (Ellis 18–21).

Authors' last names

Page numbers where information can be found

Works Cited List or Bibliography

Provide full source information in either a Works Cited list or a bibliography. A Works Cited list includes only those sources you paraphrased or quoted directly in your paper. By contrast, a bibliography lists all the sources you consulted during research—even those you did not cite.

MLA Style for Listing Sources

Book with one author	Pyles, Thomas. *The Origins and Development of the English Language.* 2nd ed. New York: Harcourt, 1971. Print.
Book with two or three authors	McCrum, Robert, William Cran, and Robert MacNeil. *The Story of English.* New York: Penguin, 1987. Print.
Book with an editor	Truth, Sojourner. *Narrative of Sojourner Truth.* Ed. Margaret Washington. New York: Vintage, 1993. Print.
Book with more than three authors or editors	Donald, Robert B., et al. *Writing Clear Essays.* Upper Saddle River: Prentice, 1996. Print.
Single work in an anthology	Hawthorne, Nathaniel. "Young Goodman Brown." *Literature: An Introduction to Reading and Writing.* Ed. Edgar V. Roberts and H. E. Jacobs. Upper Saddle River: Prentice, 1998. 376–385. Print. [Indicate pages for the entire selection.]
Introduction to a work in a published edition	Washington, Margaret. Introduction. *Narrative of Sojourner Truth.* By Sojourner Truth. Ed. Washington. New York: Vintage, 1993. v–xi. Print.
Signed article from an encyclopedia	Askeland, Donald R. "Welding." *World Book Encyclopedia.* 1991 ed. Print.
Signed article in a weekly magazine	Wallace, Charles. "A Vodacious Deal." *Time* 14 Feb. 2000: 63. Print.
Signed article in a monthly magazine	Gustaitis, Joseph. "The Sticky History of Chewing Gum." *American History* Oct. 1998: 30–38. Print.
Newspaper	Thurow, Roger. "South Africans Who Fought for Sanctions Now Scrap for Investors." *Wall Street Journal* 11 Feb. 2000: A1+. Print. [For a multipage article that does not appear on consecutive pages, write only the first page number on which it appears, followed by the plus sign.]
Unsigned editorial or story	"Selective Silence." Editorial. *Wall Street Journal* 11 Feb. 2000: A14. Print. [If the editorial or story is signed, begin with the author's name.]
Signed pamphlet or brochure	[Treat the pamphlet as though it were a book.]
Work from a library subscription service	Ertman, Earl L. "Nefertiti's Eyes." *Archaeology* Mar.–Apr. 2008: 28–32. *Kids Search.* EBSCO. New York Public Library. Web. 18 June 2008. [Indicate the date you accessed the information.]
Filmstrips, slide programs, videocassettes, DVDs, and other audiovisual media	*The Diary of Anne Frank.* Dir. George Stevens. Perf. Millie Perkins, Shelley Winters, Joseph Schildkraut, Lou Jacobi, and Richard Beymer. 1959. Twentieth Century Fox, 2004. DVD.
CD-ROM (with multiple publishers)	Simms, James, ed. *Romeo and Juliet.* By William Shakespeare. Oxford: Attica Cybernetics; London: BBC Education; London: Harper, 1995. CD-ROM.
Radio or television program transcript	"Washington's Crossing of the Delaware." *Weekend Edition Sunday.* Natl. Public Radio. WNYC, New York. 23 Dec. 2013. Print. Transcript.
Internet Web page	"Fun Facts About Gum." NACGM site. 1999. National Association of Chewing Gum Manufacturers. Web. 19 Dec. 2015. [Indicate the date you accessed the information.]
Personal interview	Smith, Jane. Personal interview. 10 Feb. 2015.

All examples follow the style given in the *MLA Handbook for Writers of Research Papers,* seventh edition, by Joseph Gibaldi.

UNIT 1

THE BIG ? Can progress be made without conflict?

UNIT PATHWAY

PART 1
SETTING EXPECTATIONS

- INTRODUCING THE BIG QUESTION
- CLOSE READING WORKSHOP

PART 2
TEXT ANALYSIS
GUIDED EXPLORATION

CHARACTERS AND CONFLICT

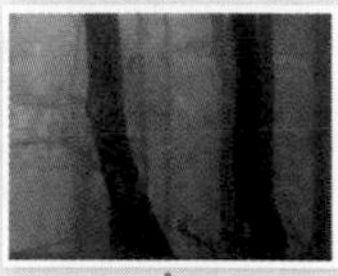

PART 3
TEXT SET
DEVELOPING INSIGHT

PERSEVERANCE

PART 4
DEMONSTRATING INDEPENDENCE

- INDEPENDENT READING
- ONLINE TEXT SET

CLOSE READING TOOL

Use this tool to practice the close reading strategies you learn.

STUDENT eTEXT

Bring learning to life with audio, video, and interactive tools.

ONLINE WRITER'S NOTEBOOK

Easily capture notes and complete assignments online.

Find all Digital Resources at **pearsonrealize.com**

Introducing the Big Question

Can progress be made without conflict?

In literature, a conflict is a struggle between two or more opposing forces. In real life, conflicts may arise between people who have different hopes or visions for the future. They may agree in general that they want a better future, but they may not agree about what "better" means or how to achieve it. Such differences may spark confrontations or even hostility. In most cases, people on opposite sides of a conflict eventually compromise in order to resolve differences and move forward. The questions arise: Was conflict an important part of the process that finally brought the groups to a resolution? Did conflict help both parties better understand their goals or fine tune their plans? Can true progress be made without conflict?

Exploring the Big Question

Collaboration: Group Discussion Start thinking about the Big Question by considering different ways people can make progress in their lives. List situations in which you or someone else has made progress. Give an example of each of the following circumstances that may lead to progress.

- Someone overcomes adversity in an athletic or academic competition.
- A change is made after an argument.
- A concession is offered for the sake of achieving a common goal.
- Internal conflict, a struggle within oneself, leads to personal progress.
- A change to a situation ends up causing a conflict.

Share your examples with a small group of classmates. Talk about whether progress was achieved and if there was any conflict involved. Listen carefully to group members' examples, and try to build on their ideas.

Connecting to the Literature The readings in this unit will help you think about different types of conflict and the ways in which people either make progress, or fail to do so. As you read, consider the types of problems characters face and how—or even whether—they resolve them.

Vocabulary

Speaking and Listening

1. Initiate and participate effectively in a range of collaborative discussions with diverse partners on grades 9–10 topics, texts, and issues, building on others' ideas and expressing their own clearly and persuasively.

Language

6. Acquire and use accurately general academic and domain-specific words and phrases, sufficient for reading, writing, speaking, and listening at the college and career readiness level; demonstrate independence in gathering vocabulary knowledge when considering a word or phrase important to comprehension or expression.

4.d. Verify the preliminary determination of the meaning of a word or phrase.

Acquire and Use Academic Vocabulary The term "academic vocabulary" refers to words you typically encounter in scholarly and literary texts and in technical and business writing. It is the language that helps to express complex ideas. Review the definitions of these academic vocabulary words that relate to this unit's Big Question.

debate (dē bāt′) *v.* argue or discuss

motive (mōt′ iv) *n.* something that causes a person to act a certain way

oppose (ə pōz′) *v.* set against

radical (rad′ i kəl) *adj.* tending to make extreme changes in existing views, conditions, or institutions

resolve (ri zälv′, -zôlv) *v.* reach a conclusion or decision

unify (yo͞o′ nə fi′) *v.* combine into one

Use these words as you complete Big Question activities in this unit that involve reading, writing, speaking, and listening. Because they are related to the themes of progress and conflict, they will help you to express your thoughts effectively.

Gather Vocabulary Knowledge Additional words related to progress and conflict are listed below. Categorize the words by deciding whether you know each one well, know it a little bit, or do not know it at all.

adversity	**concession**	**progress**
change	**confrontation**	**reconciliation**
compromise	**negotiate**	**struggle**

Then, complete the following steps:

1. Write the definitions of the words you know.
2. Using a print or an online dictionary, look up the meanings of the words you do not know. Then, write the meanings.
3. If you think you know a word's meaning, write it down. Consult a dictionary to confirm the word's meaning. Revise your original definition if necessary.
4. If you are not sure of a word's meaning, consult a dictionary. Then, record the meaning.
5. Use all the words in a paragraph about progress and conflict.

Close Reading Workshop

In this workshop, you will learn an approach to reading that will deepen your understanding of literature and will help you better appreciate the author's craft. The workshop includes models for the close reading, discussion, research, and writing activities you will complete as you study the texts in this unit. After you have reviewed the strategies and models, practice your skills with the Independent Practice selection.

Common Core State Standards

RL.9-10.1, RL.9-10.2, RL.9-10.3, RL.9-10.4, RL.9-10.5, SL.9-10.1, SL.9-10.4, W.9-10.8, W.9-10.9, W.9-10.10

[For full standards wording, see the chart in the front of this book.]

CLOSE READING: SHORT STORY

In Part 2 of this unit, you will focus on reading various short stories. Use these strategies as you read the texts:

Comprehension: Key Ideas and Details

- Read first to unlock basic meaning.
- Use context clues to help you determine the meanings of unfamiliar words. Consult a dictionary, if necessary.
- Note unfamiliar details that you might need to clarify through research.
- Distinguish between ideas that are stated directly and those you must infer.

Ask yourself questions such as these:

- Who are the main characters?
- When and where does the action take place?
- What conflicts do the characters face? How does each character respond to those conflicts?

Text Analysis: Craft and Structure

- Think about the genre of the work and how the author presents ideas.
- Analyze the features that contribute to the author's style. Notice the author's diction (word choice), syntax (arrangement of words in sentences), and tone (attitude toward the audience and subject).
- Take note of how the author uses imagery and description to create a distinct mood.
- Consider the story's narrative structure, including the use of exposition and dialogue to convey information and build irony.

Ask yourself questions such as these:

- How does the setting of the story (both the time and the place) affect the characters and events?
- By the end of the story, how do the characters change? What do these changes suggest about the story's deeper meaning?

Connections: Integration of Knowledge and Ideas

- Look for relationships among key ideas. Identify causes and effects, and comparisons and contrasts.
- Look for important images and symbols, and analyze their deeper meanings. Then, synthesize to determine the theme or central insight conveyed by the author.
- Compare and contrast this work with other works you have read, either by the same author or different authors.

Ask yourself questions such as these:

- How has this work increased my knowledge of a subject, an author, or a theme?
- In what ways is this story special, unique, or worthy of reading?

Read

As you read this short story, take note of the annotations that model ways to closely read the text.

Reading Model

"Early Autumn"[1] by Langston Hughes

When Bill was very young, they had been in love. Many nights they had spent walking, talking together. Then something not very important had come between them, and they didn't speak. Impulsively, she had married a man she thought she loved. Bill went away, bitter about women.[2]

Yesterday, walking across Washington Square, she saw him for the first time in years.

"Bill Walker," she said.

He stopped. At first he did not recognize her, to him she looked so old.

"Mary! Where did you come from?"

Unconsciously, she lifted her face as though wanting a kiss, but he held out his hand. She took it.

"I live in New York now," she said.

"Oh"—smiling politely. Then a little frown came quickly between his eyes.[3]

"Always wondered what happened to you, Bill."

"I'm a lawyer. Nice firm, way downtown."

"Married yet?"

"Sure. Two kids."[4]

"Oh," she said.

A great many people went past them through the park. People they didn't know. It was late afternoon. Nearly sunset. Cold.[5]

"And your husband?" he asked her.

"We have three children. I work in the bursar's office at Columbia."

"You're looking very . . ." (he wanted to say *old*) ". . . well," he said.

Key Ideas and Details

1 The title suggests that the story will address an ending that comes "early," or too soon. The poetic word "autumn," rather than its more ordinary synonym "fall," adds to the title's emotional quality.

Craft and Structure

2 The first paragraph provides compact exposition about the characters' shared past. The idea that Mary married a man she only "*thought* she loved" suggests that she regrets her choices.

Key Ideas and Details

3 Bill's "polite smile" is replaced by a "little frown." The first expression suggests Bill's indifference, while the latter suggests something more complex—perhaps a memory of the bitterness Mary caused him.

Craft and Structure

4 The characters rarely speak in full sentences. The clipped quality of the dialogue suggests that powerful emotions, not openly admitted, flow beneath the surface of this meeting.

Craft and Structure

5 The park is "cold" and full of "people they didn't know." These details paint a picture of a world without warmth or connection and reflect the characters' emotional distance from one another.

She understood. Under the trees in Washington Square, she found herself desperately[6] reaching back into the past. She had been older than he then in Ohio. Now she was not young at all. Bill was still young.

"We live on Central Park West," she said. "Come and see us sometime."

"Sure," he replied. "You and your husband must have dinner with my family some night. Any night. Lucille and I'd love to have you."

The leaves fell slowly from the trees in the Square. Fell without wind. Autumn dusk. She felt a little sick.[7]

"We'd love it," she answered.

"You ought to see my kids." He grinned.

Suddenly the lights came on up the whole length of Fifth Avenue, chains of misty brilliance in the blue air.

"There's my bus," she said.

He held out his hand. "Good-bye."

"When . . ." she wanted to say, but the bus was ready to pull off. The lights on the avenue blurred, twinkled, blurred. And she was afraid to open her mouth as she entered the bus. Afraid it would be impossible to utter a word.[8]

Suddenly she shrieked very loudly. "Good-bye!" But the bus door had closed.

The bus started. People came between them outside, people crossing the street, people they didn't know. Space and people. She lost sight of Bill. Then she remembered she had forgotten to give him her address—or to ask him for his—or tell him that her youngest boy was named Bill, too.[9]

Craft and Structure

6 Tucked into the narration, the word "desperately" expresses the depth of Mary's feelings, which she cannot openly show.

Integration of Knowledge and Ideas

7 Descriptive details reflect Mary's feelings and emphasize the story's themes of ending and loss. The leaves fall "without wind" as though they are simply giving up.

Craft and Structure

8 The lights, "blurred, twinkled, blurred" because Mary's eyes are full of tears. The author omits the conjunction "and" after "twinkled," but he adds it to the next sentence and ends with a fragment. The syntax reflects the disorder and intensity of Mary's emotions.

Integration of Knowledge and Ideas

9 The phrase "people they didn't know" echoes the earlier passage and emphasizes Mary's isolation. She is separated from Bill by "space and people" and by her inability to say what she feels. The detail about her son suggests her continued love for Bill and the depth of her regret.

Discuss

Sharing your own ideas and listening to the ideas of others can deepen your understanding of a text and help you look at a topic in a whole new way. As you participate in collaborative discussions, work to have a genuine exchange in which classmates build upon one another's ideas. Support your points with evidence and ask meaningful questions.

Discussion Model

Student 1: One thing I notice about this story is how specific the setting is. Hughes doesn't just set it in a park, but in a specific park—Washington Square in New York City. And he mentions other specific places, like Central Park West. I think that makes the story seem more authentic.

Student 2: Yes, and the narrator also mentions Ohio, but not until later in the story. It seems that Ohio was where Mary and Bill met. I thought it was interesting that Mary tells Bill "I live here now," meaning New York. Bill frowns when she says that, but why? It made me think that the "not very important" reason they broke up might have been her not wanting to leave Ohio. So, maybe he's realizing she left Ohio anyway.

Student 3: I agree about the importance of the setting. I wonder why Hughes chose New York City and even Ohio as key places in this story. Do you think he had some special connection to either place?

Research

Targeted research can clarify unfamiliar details and shed light on various aspects of a text. Consider questions that arise in your mind as you read, and use those questions as the basis for research.

Research Model

Questions: *Why did Langston Hughes set this story in New York City?*

Key Words for Internet Search: Langston Hughes + New York City

Result: Poetry Foundation, Langston Hughes biography

What I Learned: Langston Hughes was born in Missouri, but later lived in New York City, where he ultimately died. He is the leading literary figure of the Harlem Renaissance, an artistic movement associated with Harlem, a predominately African American neighborhood in New York City. The story "Early Autumn" is not typical of Hughes's work, which usually celebrates African American culture. However, it does show Hughes's affection for his adopted city.

Write

Writing about a text will deepen your understanding of it and will also allow you to share your ideas more formally with others. The following model essay evaluates Langston Hughes's use of setting and cites evidence to support the main ideas.

Writing Model: Argument

Langston Hughes's Use of Setting in "Early Autumn"

The seasons of the year are traditional symbols for the stages of human life. Spring connects with childhood, summer with youth, autumn with middle age, and winter with death. Langston Hughes sets his short story "Early Autumn" in the late afternoon of a fall day. This symbolic use of setting is the story's most important quality. More than any other element, the setting helps to create a sad portrait of characters feeling the loss of love and youth.

The writer states the claim of the essay in the first paragraph. This is an effective strategy for a short essay.

Hughes emphasizes the season by placing it in the story's title, so the reader immediately wonders if autumn means just the time of the story or if it also symbolizes a stage of life. The season's link to the coming of old age is reinforced by the time of day, sunset, which is also a traditional symbol of loss. In addition, an urban location filled with anonymous commuters forms the place of the story. This place combines with the autumn sunset to create a somber setting for Hughes's characters.

By choosing to explore the symbolism of the setting, the writer shows an awareness of the author's craft.

Hughes develops this brief narrative through dialogue between the two characters. Bill and Mary, once romantically linked, meet accidentally after a long separation. However, Hughes interrupts this conversation with details of setting that build up the sense of loss: "A great many people went past them through the park. People they didn't know. It was late afternoon. Nearly sunset. Cold." These short sentences feel distant and cold, like Bill and Mary's current relationship.

The writer supports claims with specific details from the story.

With Mary, Hughes clearly links symbolic setting and fading youth: "Under the trees in Washington Square, she found herself desperately reaching back into the past. She had been older than he then in Ohio. Now she was not young at all." Hughes reinforces the link between autumn and Mary's sudden, anxious feeling that she has grown old, or that Bill's feelings for her have just died out as time has passed: "The leaves fell slowly from the trees in the Square. Fell without wind. Autumn dusk. She felt a little sick."

Attention to key elements of the author's craft—characterization and setting—help to reinforce the focus of the essay.

As a writer of fiction, Hughes is best known for warm, sometimes funny tales of Harlem life. By contrast, Bill and Mary's world is cold and impersonal: "People came between them outside, people crossing the street, people they didn't know. Space and people. She lost sight of Bill." Effectively combining autumn, sunset, and city streets, Hughes uses the setting to give the reader a melancholy glimpse of the end of love and youth.

The writer pulls in research to provide context for a point.

As you read the following story, apply the close reading strategies you have learned. You may need to read the story multiple times to fully explore its plot, characters, and theme.

The Leap

by Louise Erdrich

My mother is the surviving half of a blindfold trapeze act, not a fact I think about much even now that she is sightless, the result of **encroaching** and stubborn cataracts. She walks slowly through her house here in New Hampshire, lightly touching her way along walls and running her hands over knickknacks, books, the drift of a grown child's belongings and castoffs. She has never upset an object or as much as brushed a magazine onto the floor. She has never lost her balance or bumped into a closet door left carelessly open.

It has occurred to me that the catlike precision of her movements in old age might be the result of her early training, but she shows so little of the drama or flair one might expect from a performer that I tend to forget the Flying Avalons. She has kept no sequined costume, no photographs, no fliers or posters from that part of her youth. I would, in fact, tend to think that all memory of double somersaults and heart-stopping catches had left her arms and legs were it not for the fact that sometimes, as I sit sewing in the room of the rebuilt house in which I slept as a child, I hear the crackle, catch a whiff of smoke from the stove downstairs, and suddenly the room goes dark, the stitches burn beneath my fingers, and I am sewing with a needle of hot silver, a thread of fire.

I owe her my existence three times. The first was when she saved herself. In the town square a replica tent pole, cracked and splintered, now stands cast in concrete. It **commemorates** the disaster that put our town smack on the front page of the Boston and New York tabloids. It is from those old newspapers, now historical records, that I get my information. Not from my mother, Anna of the Flying Avalons, nor from any of her in-laws, nor certainly from the other half of her particular act, Harold Avalon, her first husband. In one news account it says, "The day was mildly overcast, but nothing in the air or temperature gave any hint of the sudden force with which the deadly gale would strike."

Meet the Author

Award-winning novelist, poet, and short story writer **Louise Erdrich** (b. 1954) combines traditional storytelling with experimental narrative techniques. Born to a German American father and a French-Native American mother, Erdrich writes from the complex perspective of two distinct cultures.

◀ Vocabulary

encroaching (en krōch´ iŋ) *adj.* intruding on, especially in a gradual way

commemorates (kə mem´ ə rāts) *v.* honors a memory

CLOSE READING TOOL

Read and respond to this selection online using the **Close Reading Tool.**

I have lived in the West, where you can see the weather coming for miles, and it is true that out here we are at something of a disadvantage. When extremes of temperature collide, a hot and cold front, winds generate instantaneously behind a hill and crash upon you without warning. That, I think, was the likely situation on that day in June. People probably commented on the pleasant air, grateful that no hot sun beat upon the striped tent that stretched over the entire center green. They bought their tickets and surrendered them in anticipation. They sat. They ate caramelized popcorn and roasted peanuts. There was time, before the storm, for three acts. The White Arabians[1] of Ali-Khazar rose on their hind legs and waltzed. The Mysterious Bernie folded himself into a painted cracker tin, and the Lady of the Mists made herself appear and disappear in surprising places. As the clouds gathered outside, unnoticed, the ringmaster cracked his whip, shouted his introduction, and pointed to the ceiling of the tent, where the Flying Avalons were perched.

They loved to drop gracefully from nowhere, like two sparkling birds, and blow kisses as they threw off their plumed helmets and high-collared capes. They laughed and flirted openly as they beat their way up again on the trapeze bars. In the final vignette of their act, they actually would kiss in midair, pausing, almost hovering as they swooped past one another. On the ground, between bows, Harry Avalon would skip quickly to the front rows and point out the smear of my mother's lipstick, just off the edge of his mouth. They made a romantic pair all right, especially in the blindfold sequence.

That afternoon, as the anticipation increased, as Mr. and Mrs. Avalon tied sparkling strips of cloth onto each other's face and as they puckered their lips in mock kisses, lips destined "never again to meet," as one long breathless article put it, the wind rose, miles off, wrapped itself into a cone, and howled. There came a rumble of electrical energy, drowned out by the sudden roll of drums. One detail not mentioned by the press, perhaps unknown—Anna was pregnant at the time, seven months and hardly showing, her stomach muscles were that strong. It seems incredible that she would work high above the ground when any fall could be so dangerous, but the explanation—I know from watching her go blind—is that my mother lives comfortably in extreme elements. She is one with the constant dark now, just as the air was her home, familiar to her, safe, before the storm that afternoon.

From opposite ends of the tent they waved, blind and smiling, to the crowd below. The ringmaster removed his hat and called for silence, so that the two above could concentrate. They rubbed their hands in chalky powder, then Harry launched himself and swung, once, twice, in huge calibrated beats across space. He hung from his knees and on the third swing stretched wide his arms, held his hands out to receive his pregnant wife as she dove from her shining bar.

---

1. **Arabians** horses of the Arabian breed.

It was while the two were in midair, their hands about to meet, that lightning struck the main pole and sizzled down the guy wires, filling the air with a blue radiance that Harry Avalon must certainly have seen through the cloth of his blindfold as the tent buckled and the edifice[2] toppled him forward, the swing continuing and not returning in its sweep, and Harry going down, down into the crowd with his last thought, perhaps, just a prickle of surprise at his empty hands.

My mother once said that I'd be amazed at how many things a person can do within the act of falling. Perhaps, at the time, she was teaching me to dive off a board at the town pool, for I associate the idea with midair somersaults. But I also think she meant that even in that awful doomed second one could think, for she certainly did. When her hands did not meet her husband's, my mother tore her blindfold away. As he swept past her on the wrong side, she could have grasped his ankle, the toe-end of his tights, and gone down clutching him. Instead, she changed direction. Her body twisted toward a heavy wire and she managed to hang on to the braided metal, still hot from the lightning strike. Her palms were burned so terribly that once healed they bore no lines, only the blank scar tissue of a quieter future. She was lowered, gently, to the sawdust ring just underneath the dome of the canvas roof, which did not entirely settle but was held up on one end and jabbed through, torn, and still on fire in places from the giant spark, though rain and men's jackets soon put that out.

Three people died, but except for her hands my mother was not seriously harmed until an overeager rescuer broke her arm in **extricating** her and also, in the process, collapsed a portion of the tent bearing a huge buckle that knocked her unconscious. She was taken to the town hospital, and there she must have hemorrhaged,[3] for they kept her, confined to her bed, a month and a half before her baby was born without life.

◀ **Vocabulary**
extricating (eks´ tri kāt iŋ) *n.* the action of setting free or removing from a difficult situation

Harry Avalon had wanted to be buried in the circus cemetery next to the original Avalon, his uncle, so she sent him back with his brothers. The child, however, is buried around the corner, beyond this house and just down the highway. Sometimes I used to walk there just to sit. She was a girl, but I rarely thought of her as a sister or even as a separate person really. I suppose you could call it the egocentrism[4] of a child, of all young children, but I considered her a less finished version of myself.

When the snow falls, throwing shadows among the stones, I can easily pick hers out from the road, for it is bigger than the others and in the shape of a lamb at rest, its legs curled beneath. The carved lamb looms larger as the years pass, though it is probably only my eyes, the vision shifting, as what is close to me blurs and distances sharpen. In odd moments, I think it is the edge drawing near, the edge of everything, the unseen horizon we do not really speak of in the eastern woods. And it also seems to me, although this is probably an idle fantasy, that the statue is growing more sharply

2. **edifice** (ed´ i fis) *n.* large structure or building.
3. **hemorrhaged** (hem´ ər ij'd´) *v.* bled heavily.
4. **egocentrism** (ē´ gō sen´ triz əm) *n.* self-centeredness; inability to distinguish one's own needs and interests from those of others.

etched, as if, instead of weathering itself into a porous mass, it is hardening on the hillside with each snowfall, perfecting itself.

It was during her confinement in the hospital that my mother met my father. He was called in to look at the set of her arm, which was complicated. He stayed, sitting at her bedside, for he was something of an armchair traveler and had spent his war quietly, at an air force training grounds, where he became a specialist in arms and legs broken during parachute training exercises. Anna Avalon had been to many of the places he longed to visit—Venice, Rome, Mexico, all through France and Spain. She had no family of her own and was taken in by the Avalons, trained to perform from a very young age. They toured Europe before the war, then based themselves in New York. She was illiterate.

It was in the hospital that she finally learned to read and write, as a way of overcoming the boredom and depression of those weeks, and it was my father who insisted on teaching her. In return for stories of her adventures, he graded her first exercises. He bought her her first book, and over her bold letters, which the pale guides of the penmanship pads could not contain, they fell in love.

I wonder if my father calculated the exchange he offered: one form of flight for another. For after that, and for as long as I can remember, my mother has never been without a book. Until now, that is, and it remains the greatest difficulty of her blindness. Since my father's recent death, there is no one to read to her, which is why I returned, in fact, from my failed life where the land is flat. I came home to read to my mother, to read out loud, to read long into the dark if I must, to read all night.

Once my father and mother married, they moved onto the old farm he had inherited but didn't care much for. Though he'd been thinking of moving to a larger city, he settled down and broadened his practice in this valley. It still seems odd to me, when they could have gone anywhere else, that they chose to stay in the town where the disaster had occurred, and which my father in the first place had found so **constricting**. It was my mother who insisted upon it, after her child did not survive. And then, too, she loved the sagging farmhouse with its scrap of what was left of a vast acreage of woods and hidden hay fields that stretched to the game park.

Vocabulary ▶
constricting (kən strikt′ iŋ) *adj.* preventing freedom of movement; limiting

I owe my existence, the second time then, to the two of them and the hospital that brought them together. That is the debt we take for granted since none of us asks for life. It is only once we have it that we hang on so dearly.

I was seven the year the house caught fire, probably from standing ash. It can rekindle, and my father, forgetful around the house and **perpetually** exhausted from night hours on call, often emptied what he thought were ashes from cold stoves into wooden or cardboard containers. The fire could have started from a flaming box, or perhaps a buildup of creosote inside the chimney was the culprit. It started right around the stove, and the heart of the house was gutted. The baby-sitter, fallen asleep in my father's den on the

perpetually (pər pech′ o͞o əl ē) *adv.* continuing forever; constantly first floor, woke to find the stairway to my upstairs room cut off by flames. She used the phone, then ran outside to stand beneath my window.

When my parents arrived, the town volunteers had drawn water from the fire pond and were spraying the outside of the house, preparing to go inside after me, not knowing at the time that there was only one staircase and that it was lost. On the other side of the house, the superannuated[5] extension ladder broke in half. Perhaps the clatter of it falling against the walls woke me, for I'd been asleep up to that point.

As soon as I awakened, in the small room that I now use for sewing, I smelled the smoke. I followed things by the letter then, was good at memorizing instructions, and so I did exactly what was taught in the second-grade home fire drill. I got up, I touched the back of my door before opening it. Finding it hot, I left it closed and stuffed my rolled-up rug beneath the crack. I did not hide under my bed or crawl into my closet. I put on my flannel robe, and then I sat down to wait.

Outside, my mother stood below my dark window and saw clearly that there was no rescue. Flames had pierced one side wall, and the glare of the fire lighted the massive limbs and trunk of the vigorous old elm that had probably been planted the year the house was built, a hundred years ago at least. No leaf touched the wall, and just one thin branch scraped the roof. From below, it looked as though even a squirrel would have had trouble jumping from the tree onto the house, for the breadth of that small branch was no bigger than my mother's wrist.

Standing there, beside Father, who was preparing to rush back around to the front of the house, my mother asked him to unzip her dress. When he wouldn't be bothered, she made him understand. He couldn't make his hands work, so she finally tore it off and stood there in her pearls and stockings. She directed one of the men to lean the broken half of the extension ladder up against the trunk of the tree. In surprise, he complied. She ascended. She vanished. Then she could be seen among the leafless branches of late November as she made her way up and, along her stomach, inched the length of a bough that curved above the branch that brushed the roof.

Once there, swaying, she stood and balanced. There were plenty of people in the crowd and many who still remember, or think they do, my mother's leap through the ice-dark air toward that thinnest extension, and how she broke the branch falling so that it cracked in her hands, cracked louder than the flames as she vaulted with it toward the edge of the roof, and how it hurtled down end over end without her, and their eyes went up, again, to see where she had flown.

I didn't see her leap through air, only heard the sudden thump and looked out my window. She was hanging by the backs of her heels from the new gutter we had put in that year, and she was smiling. I was not surprised to see her, she was so matter-of-fact. She tapped on the window. I remember how she did it, too. It was the friendliest tap, a bit **tentative**, as if she was

◀ **Vocabulary**
tentative (ten´ tə tiv) *adj.* hesitant; not confident

---

5. **superannuated** (so͞o´ pər an´ yo͞o āt´ əd) *adj.* too old to be usable.

afraid she had arrived too early at a friend's house. Then she gestured at the latch, and when I opened the window she told me to raise it wider and prop it up with the stick so it wouldn't crush her fingers. She swung down, caught the ledge, and crawled through the opening. Once she was in my room, I realized she had on only underclothing, a bra of the heavy stitched cotton women used to wear and step-in, lace-trimmed drawers. I remember feeling light-headed, of course, terribly relieved, and then embarrassed for her to be seen by the crowd undressed.

I was still embarrassed as we flew out the window, toward earth, me in her lap, her toes pointed as we skimmed toward the painted target of the fire fighter's net.

I know that she's right. I knew it even then. As you fall there is time to think. Curled as I was, against her stomach, I was not startled by the cries of the crowd or the looming faces. The wind roared and beat its hot breath at our back, the flames whistled. I slowly wondered what would happen if we missed the circle or bounced out of it. Then I wrapped my hands around my mother's hands. I felt the brush of her lips and heard the beat of her heart in my ears, loud as thunder, long as the roll of drums.

Close Reading Activities

Read

Comprehension: **Key Ideas and Details**

1. **(a)** What does Anna do when the circus tent pole is struck by lightning? **(b) Interpret:** In what sense does the narrator owe her life to this decision? Support your answer with story details.
2. **(a)** Use details from the story to identify two other ways in which the narrator owes her life to her mother. **(b) Compare and Contrast:** Review the three ways in which Anna saves her daughter's life. Note one similarity and one difference among them.
3. **(a) Analyze:** In what ways does Anna's meeting her second husband affect her intellectual growth? **(b) Generalize:** Draw a conclusion about Anna's character based on this information.
4. **Summarize:** Write a brief, objective summary of the climax of the story. Cite details from the story in your writing.

Text Analysis: **Craft and Structure**

5. **(a) Generalize:** What information about Anna is given in the story's first three paragraphs? **(b) Connect:** Explain why the author includes this information.
6. **(a) Distinguish:** Identify two examples of foreshadowing—clues that hint at later events—in the story. **(b) Evaluate:** Use these examples to evaluate the effect of the author's use of this technique.
7. **(a) Distinguish:** Identify three events in the story's rising action, the sequence of events that develop the conflict. **(b) Analyze:** At what point does the story reach its climax? Cite details from the story to explain your answer.
8. **(a) Distinguish:** At what point does the narrator first introduce a detailed flashback? **(b) Connect:** What is the source of the narrator's information, and what does she learn? **(c) Infer:** Make an inference about the narrator's mother based on the source of this information.

Connections: **Integration of Knowledge and Ideas**

Discuss

Conduct a **small-group discussion** about the influence of traditional forms of narrative in "The Leap." For example, consider whether the account of the circus disaster shows the influence of myth, legend, or tall tale.

Research

Magical realism is a special type of fantasy associated mainly with modern Latin American writers. This style of writing combines realistic events and details with contrasting elements of myth, magic, and the world of dreams. Briefly research magical realism and evaluate its possible influence on Erdrich's writing, particularly this story. Consider the following story events:

a. the circus disaster **b.** the rescue

Take notes as you perform your research. Then, write a brief **explanation** of magical realism and assess its influence on Erdrich's writing.

Write

The author Ernest Hemingway memorably defined *courage* as "grace under pressure." Write an **essay** in which you agree or disagree with his definition based on an analysis of the character of the narrator's mother. Cite details from the story to support your analysis.

Can progress be made without conflict?

Consider what the narrator comes to understand as she is being rescued from the fire by her mother. Does the narrator grow as a result of what she has learned? Explain your answer.

"It's loss and regret and misery and yearning that drive **the story forward.**"

—Margaret Atwood

PART 2

TEXT ANALYSIS GUIDED EXPLORATION

CHARACTERS AND CONFLICT

Each day, we are faced with conflicts. From minor disagreements to major arguments, from clashes with friends to internal struggles, conflict is a constant presence in our lives. While we may find ourselves wishing conflict away, there are other ways to think about it—for example, as a vehicle for change or growth. As you read the texts in this section, consider the role conflict plays in each one. Then, think about how characters' differing reactions to the problems they face relate to the Big Question for this unit: **Can progress be made without conflict?**

◀ CRITICAL VIEWING What mood do the details of this photograph suggest? Is this mood one most people would associate with conflict? Why or why not?

READINGS IN PART 2

CLOSE READING TOOL

Use the **Close Reading Tool** to practice the strategies you learn in this unit.

Focus on Craft and Structure

Elements of a Short Story

A short story is a brief work of fiction. Like all fiction, short stories focus on **characters** in **conflict**.

A **short story** is a brief work of fiction that can usually be read in one sitting. Because short stories are compact, writers usually limit the number of characters, the range of settings, and the scope of the action.

Characters are the personalities that take part in the action of a story. An author portrays characters by using a set of techniques that are collectively called **characterization**, or **character development**. Descriptive details, dialogue, and other literary elements help readers understand characters' qualities, including their feelings, thoughts, motivations, and behavior.

The characters in a story interact within a **setting,** or a particular time and place. In some stories, the setting is simply a backdrop for the action. In other stories, the setting exerts a strong influence on characters, shaping their personalities and motivations.

In every story, characters face a **conflict** that sets the plot in motion. The **plot** is the sequence of interrelated events that make up the action. As events unfold, the plot develops to a **climax,** or high point of tension. The tension subsides as the plot reaches the **resolution,** when events come to a close.

All of the elements of a short story work together to suggest a theme, or central insight about life. A **theme** is not a summary of a story's events. Instead, it is a generalization about what the events mean. A theme may be stated explicitly, but more often it is implied. The reader must examine the relationships among the story's elements to arrive at an interpretation of its theme.

All of the elements of a short story contribute to its deeper meaning, or theme.

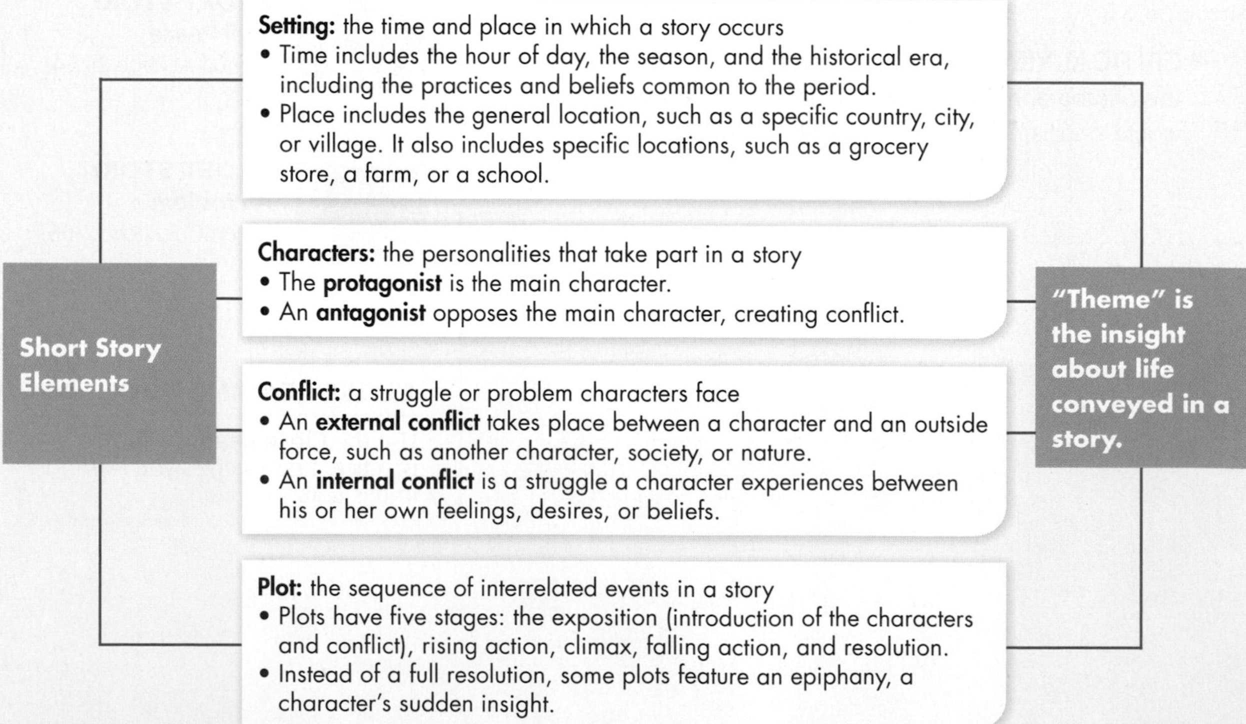

Short Story Elements
Setting: the time and place in which a story occurs
• Time includes the hour of day, the season, and the historical era, including the practices and beliefs common to the period.
• Place includes the general location, such as a specific country, city, or village. It also includes specific locations, such as a grocery store, a farm, or a school.
Characters: the personalities that take part in a story
• The **protagonist** is the main character.
• An **antagonist** opposes the main character, creating conflict.
Conflict: a struggle or problem characters face
• An **external conflict** takes place between a character and an outside force, such as another character, society, or nature.
• An **internal conflict** is a struggle a character experiences between his or her own feelings, desires, or beliefs.
Plot: the sequence of interrelated events in a story
• Plots have five stages: the exposition (introduction of the characters and conflict), rising action, climax, falling action, and resolution.
• Instead of a full resolution, some plots feature an epiphany, a character's sudden insight.
"Theme" is the insight about life conveyed in a story.

Genre and Structure A **genre** is a classification of literary works that share certain elements, such as character types and common plot patterns. Mysteries, fantasy, and realistic fiction are types of fictional genres. Short stories appear in all fictional genres, from traditional tales with formulaic plots, to online experiments in which the reader decides who the characters are and what they do.

A story's **structure** is the way in which the events of the plot unfold and the reader learns about characters and situations. A story's structure is shaped, in part, by the story's genre. For example, a mystery story is usually structured around an intriguing problem and a protagonist who seeks to solve it. The plot usually involves many twists and turns that finally arrive at a logical, but surprising, resolution. A mystery writer is not obliged to follow that pattern and may break from the genre conventions. Some mystery writers, for instance, are as interested in developing complex characters as they are in relating complex plots. In general, however, a story's genre helps shape its structure.

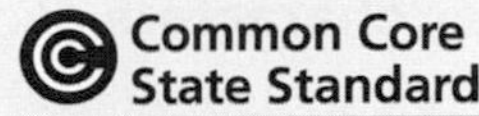

Reading Literature

3. Analyze how complex characters develop over the course of a text, interact with other characters, and advance the plot or develop the theme.

5. Analyze how an author's choices concerning how to structure a text, order events within it, and manipulate time create such effects as mystery, tension, or surprise.

Common Genres of Fiction

Realistic	A story that portrays believable characters facing a true-to-life conflict in a realistic setting **Example:** A high-school athlete changes her priorities in life after an injury keeps her from playing sports.
Speculative (Science Fiction)	A story, often set in the future, in which actual or imagined science and technology play a central role **Example:** In the year 2090, humans declare war on androids after the machines attempt to overthrow the government.
Historical	A story set in the past that combines fictional characters with historical figures or events **Example:** A young man assists the Wright brothers at Kitty Hawk as they test various versions of their airplane.
Humorous	A story with comical characters and situations intended to amuse readers **Example:** Home alone, a bloodhound and a terrier join forces to track down and open a hidden bag of pet food.
Parody	An imitation of another story or writing style, intended to comment on or poke fun at the original **Example:** A retelling of a fairy tale in which characters are terrified, rather than delighted, by magical events.

Analyzing Character and Structure in Short Stories

Complex **characters** and effective **structures** are at the heart of most short stories.

Analyzing Characters

Characters provide the moving force in most short stories. Their conflicts set off the plot, and their actions and reactions keep it going. Characters can be classified according to the manner in which they are portrayed.

Types of Characters	
Flat, or Stock, Characters	Have just one or two traits
Round, or Complex, Characters	Have many traits, including both faults and virtues
Static Characters	Do not change during the story
Dynamic Characters	Change as a result of the experiences they undergo in the story

The main characters in most literary fiction are complex because they exhibit many different traits. Like real human beings, their personalities cannot be summed up in a word or simple phrase. However, complex characters may or may not be dynamic. For example, a complex character who undergoes a crisis may not change as a result.

All characters have **motivations,** or reasons for feeling and behaving as they do. Complex characters may have multiple or even **conflicting motivations.** For example, a character who desires to be true to his or her values may also want to fit in with a clique. Those two motivations conflict. They may cause the character to be confused, or to take actions that complicate his or her situation in unexpected ways.

Characterization is the method by which an author develops a character. In **direct characterization,** the **narrator**—the character or voice telling the story—directly states a character's traits.

Example: Direct Characterization

Lauren was always the first to volunteer to help, but then she never stopped reminding everyone about her good deeds. That was one of her greatest faults.

In **indirect characterization,** the narrator reveals a character's personality by describing a character's appearance, feelings, behavior, and thoughts, as well as his or her interactions with other characters. **Dialogue,** the words that characters speak, is one of the key tools an author uses to reveal character traits. The ways in which characters speak—their use of sarcasm, humor, or anger—can be just as revealing as the statements they make. In the example shown below, dialogue reveals what the characters are like as well as what they think.

Example: Indirect Characterization

Matt stared at the huge pile of envelopes that he had to stuff for the fundraiser. "How will we finish in time?" he asked wearily.

"Lauren said she'd be here to help," LaTise mumbled, rolling her eyes.

Sarah added, "Then she'll spend the entire fundraiser announcing how she did it all by herself."

Just then, Lauren walked in. "Never fear! I'm here to save the day!"

Structuring a Text

The foundation of a story's **structure** is its plot—the series of interrelated events that unfold as characters face a conflict. The order in which the author arranges events is an important part of that structure.

Chronological order, in which events unfold in a sequence from beginning to end, is the most common structure. However, authors may vary that basic structure to create effects such as mystery, tension, or surprise. Consider the following narrative techniques.

Flashbacks interrupt the flow of a chronological sequence to describe earlier events. Flashbacks may take the form of a memory, a dream, or an actual relocation of the story into the past. Flashbacks may provide information about a character's past or insights into his or her motivations.

Flashback in a Chronological Sequence

Sequence	Event
First	Felicia waits for Nathan.
Second	Nathan arrives.
Third	They go to dinner.
Fourth	At dinner, Nathan asks Felicia to marry him.
Flashback	Felicia recalls the first time they met.
Fifth	Felicia says yes.

Parallel plots occur when an author develops two distinct storylines, with two sets of characters, in a single work. Parallel plots often explore similar conflicts among different groups of people. Often, these separate storylines ultimately join into a single, unified tale.

Pacing, the speed or rhythm of the writing, influences how readers experience a story. Slow pacing can create tension or suspense by delaying an anticipated event. Authors may slow the pace of events by adding detailed descriptions of the action or of a character's thoughts and feelings.

Example: Slow Pacing

Luis nervously stared at the clock. The hand trudged from one second to the next as though it were moving through mud. He counted along with each tick, dragging out the name of each number to match the sluggish twitches of the hand. "One . . . two . . . three . . ."

His heart slowed, but his mind raced. If Jim arrived before the 3 o'clock train and found him, the whole scheme would fall apart.

By contrast, fast pacing creates a sense of energy and excitement. Short and even fragmented sentences and rapid cutting from detail to detail increase the story's pace.

Example: Fast Pacing

Luis stared at the clock. 2:55.

He peered down the platform. A man in a suit was walking toward him. 2:56. He looked down the track. No train.

The man drew closer. Was it Jim?

Luis's heart pounded in his ears. 2:57. If Jim found him first the scheme would fail.

The man was getting closer. Luis pulled down his hat. 2:58. Was that a train whistle? Time was running out.

Building Knowledge

Meet the Author

W. W. Jacobs (1863–1943) As a boy, William Wymark Jacobs traveled far and wide in his imagination. He lived in London, England, in a house near the docks, and he listened eagerly to the tales of adventure told by sailors whom he met there. These tales shaped the stories he wrote as an adult—stories in which everyday life is disrupted by strange and fantastic events. "The Monkey's Paw" is his most famous tale of the supernatural.

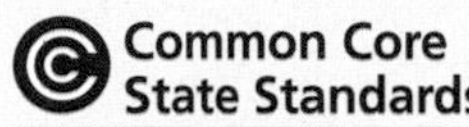

Common Core State Standards

Reading Literature

1. Cite strong and thorough textual evidence to support analysis of what the text says explicitly as well as inferences drawn from the text.

5. Analyze how an author's choices concerning how to structure a text, order events within it, and manipulate time create such effects as mystery, tension, or surprise.

Can progress be made without conflict?

Explore the Big Question as you read "The Monkey's Paw." Take notes on how the characters deal with the conflict between what they want and reality.

CLOSE READING FOCUS

Key Ideas and Details: **Make Predictions**

Predictions are logical guesses you make about what will happen later in a narrative. To make predictions, notice key details in a story and consider the outcomes they lead you to expect. As you read on, you may revise your predictions. At the end of a story, verify your predictions by comparing your expectations to the actual outcome.

Craft and Structure: **Plot and Plot Devices**

A **plot** is the sequence of related events in a story. A typical plot revolves around a **conflict**—a struggle between opposing forces—and follows a structure, or pattern:

- **Exposition:** The characters, setting, and basic situation are introduced.
- **Rising Action:** The central conflict begins and develops.
- **Climax:** The conflict reaches its highest point of tension.
- **Falling Action:** The tension in the story decreases.
- **Resolution:** The conflict ends and any remaining issues are resolved.

Writers use various devices to add tension to a plot. One device is **foreshadowing**, or the use of details that hint at later events. Authors may also add tension—as well as provide information—through the use of **flashback,** a technique that involves a switch from the present time of the narrative to a past time. Flashbacks may take the form of memories, dreams, or other sequences that interrupt the main story.

Vocabulary

The words below are critical to understanding the text that follows. Copy the words into your notebook. For each word, write down another word that is in the same family (for example: *credulity; credulous*).

grave	**maligned**	**credulity**
furtively	**apathy**	**oppressive**

CLOSE READING MODEL

The passage below is from W. W. Jacobs's short story "The Monkey's Paw." The annotations to the right of the passage show ways in which you can use close reading skills to make predictions and to analyze the author's use of plot devices.

from "The Monkey's Paw"

He took something out of his pocket and proffered it. Mrs. White drew back with a grimace, but her son, taking it, examined it curiously.[1]

"And what is there special about it?" inquired Mr. White as he took it from his son, and having examined it, placed it upon the table.

"It had a spell put on it by an old fakir," said the sergeant major, "a very holy man. He wanted to show that fate ruled people's lives, and that those who interfered with it did so to their sorrow.[2] He put a spell on it so that three separate men could each have three wishes from it."

His manner was so impressive that his hearers were conscious that their light laughter jarred somewhat. "Well, why don't you have three, sir?" said Herbert White, cleverly.

The soldier regarded him in the way that middle age is wont to regard presumptuous youth. "I have," he said, quietly, and his blotchy face whitened.[3]

"And did you really have the three wishes granted?" asked Mrs. White.

"I did," said the sergeant major, and his glass tapped against his strong teeth.[3]

Make Predictions

1 Mrs. White reacts with a "grimace"—an expression of disgust—when she sees the object that the sergeant pulls from his pocket. Her son then examines it closely. These details tell you that the object is, at the very least, unusual. They also suggest that it will play an important role in the story.

Plot and Plot Devices

2 The sergeant major says that those who "interfered" with the object "did so to their sorrow." Note that he does not say "peril" or "doom." This detail is a clue that interacting with the object may result in loss or grief.

Plot and Plot Devices

3 The sergeant major fails to hide his distress as he discusses the object. His face "whitened"; his glass "tapped" against his teeth, a detail that suggests he is trembling. He speaks "quietly" in short phrases, as though the subject is too painful to discuss. These are all examples of foreshadowing, or hints of events to come.

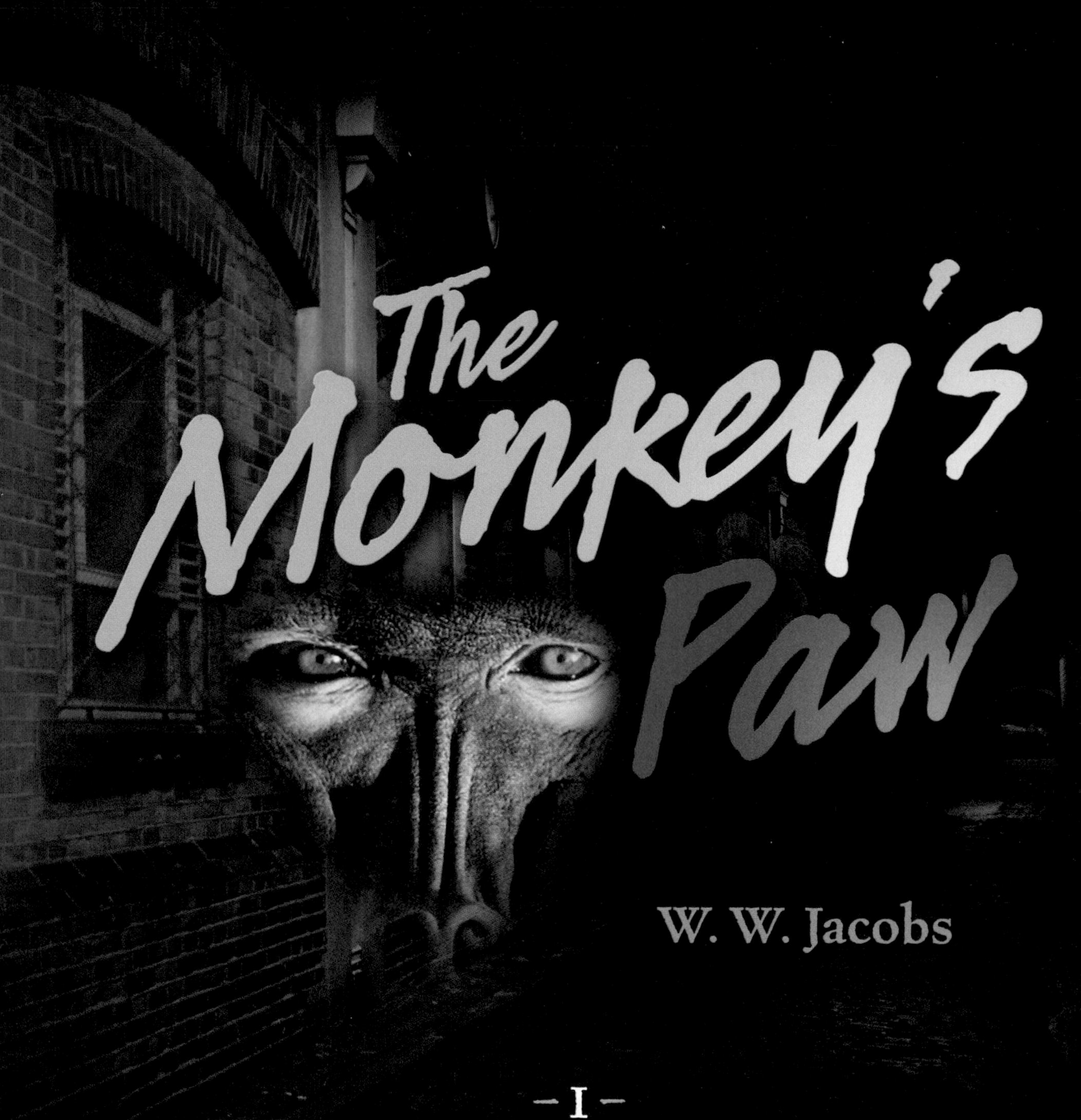

The Monkey's Paw

W. W. Jacobs

– I –

Without, the night was cold and wet, but in the small parlor of Laburnam Villa the blinds were drawn and the fire burned brightly. Father and son were at chess, the former, who possessed ideas about the game involving radical changes, putting his king into such sharp and unnecessary perils that it even provoked comment from the white-haired old lady knitting placidly by the fire.

"Hark at the wind," said Mr. White, who, having seen a fatal mistake after it was too late, was amiably desirous of preventing his son from seeing it.

"I'm listening," said the latter, grimly surveying the board as he stretched out his hand. "Check."

"I should hardly think that he'd come tonight," said his father, with his hand poised over the board.

"Mate,"[1] replied the son.

"That's the worst of living so far out," bawled Mr. White, with sudden and unlooked-for violence; "of all the beastly, slushy, out-of-the-way places to live in, this is the worst. Pathway's a bog, and the road's a torrent. I don't know what people are thinking about. I suppose because only two houses on the road are let, they think it doesn't matter."

"Never mind, dear," said his wife, soothingly; "perhaps you'll win the next one."

Mr. White looked up sharply, just in time to intercept a knowing glance between mother and son. The words died away on his lips, and he hid a guilty grin in his thin gray beard.

"There he is," said Herbert White, as the gate banged to loudly and heavy footsteps came toward the door.

The old man rose with hospitable haste, and opening the door, was heard condoling with the new arrival. The new arrival also condoled with himself, so that Mrs. White said, "Tut, tut!" and coughed gently as her husband entered the room, followed by a tall, burly man, beady of eye and rubicund of visage.[2]

"Sergeant Major Morris," he said, introducing him.

The sergeant major shook hands, and taking the proffered seat by the fire, watched contentedly while his host got out tumblers and stood a small copper kettle on the fire.

At the third glass his eyes got brighter, and he began to talk, the little family circle regarding with eager interest this visitor from distant parts, as he squared his broad shoulders in the chair and spoke of wild scenes and doughty[3] deeds; of wars and plagues and strange peoples.

"Twenty-one years of it," said Mr. White, nodding at his wife and son. "When he went away he was a slip of a youth in the warehouse. Now look at him."

"He don't look to have taken much harm," said Mrs. White, politely.

Plot
What important background information about the characters and their home is given in the exposition of this story?

Comprehension
Who has arrived at the Whites' house?

1. **mate** *n.* checkmate, a chess move that prevents the opponent's king from escaping capture and so ends the game.
2. **rubicund** (ro͞o´ bə kund´) **of visage** (viz´ ij) having a red face.
3. **doughty** (dout´ ē) *adj.* brave.

"I'd like to go to India myself," said the old man, "just to look round a bit, you know."

"Better where you are," said the sergeant major, shaking his head. He put down the empty glass, and sighing softly, shook it again.

"I should like to see those old temples and fakirs and jugglers," said the old man. "What was that you started telling me the other day about a monkey's paw or something, Morris?"

"Nothing," said the soldier, hastily. "Leastways nothing worth hearing."

"Monkey's paw?" said Mrs. White, curiously.

"Well, it's just a bit of what you might call magic, perhaps," said the sergeant major, offhandedly.

His three listeners leaned forward eagerly. The visitor absent-mindedly put his empty glass to his lips and then set it down again. His host filled it for him.

"To look at," said the sergeant major, fumbling in his pocket, "it's just an ordinary little paw, dried to a mummy."

▼ Critical Viewing
What details of this man's appearance might make you think that he is "a very holy man"?

He took something out of his pocket and proffered it. Mrs. White drew back with a grimace, but her son, taking it, examined it curiously.

"And what is there special about it?" inquired Mr. White as he took it from his son, and having examined it, placed it upon the table.

"It had a spell put on it by an old fakir," said the sergeant major, "a very holy man. He wanted to show that fate ruled people's lives, and that those who interfered with it did so to their sorrow. He put a spell on it so that three separate men could each have three wishes from it."

His manner was so impressive that his hearers were conscious that their light laughter jarred somewhat.

"Well, why don't you have three, sir?" said Herbert White, cleverly.

The soldier regarded him in the way that middle age is wont to regard presumptuous youth. "I have," he said, quietly, and his blotchy face whitened.

"And did you really have the three wishes granted?" asked Mrs. White.

"I did," said the sergeant major, and his glass tapped against his strong teeth.

"And has anybody else wished?" persisted the old lady.

"The first man had his three wishes, yes," was the reply; "I don't know what the first two were, but the third was for death. That's how I got the paw."

His tones were so **grave** that a hush fell upon the group.

"If you've had your three wishes, it's no good to you now, then, Morris," said the old man at last. "What do you keep it for?"

The soldier shook his head. "Fancy, I suppose," he said, slowly. "I did have some idea of selling it, but I don't think I will. It has caused enough mischief already. Besides, people won't buy. They think it's a fairy tale, some of them, and those who do think anything of it want to try it first and pay me afterward."

"If you could have another three wishes," said the old man, eyeing him keenly, "would you have them?"

"I don't know," said the other. "I don't know."

He took the paw, and dangling it between his forefinger and thumb, suddenly threw it upon the fire. White, with a slight cry, stooped down and snatched it off.

"Better let it burn," said the soldier, solemnly.

"If you don't want it, Morris," said the other, "give it to me."

"I won't," said his friend doggedly. "I threw it on the fire. If you keep it, don't blame me for what happens. Pitch it on the fire again, like a sensible man."

The other shook his head and examined his new possession closely. "How do you do it?" he inquired.

"Hold it up in your right hand and wish aloud," said the sergeant major, "but I warn you of the consequences."

"Sounds like the *Arabian Nights*,"[4] said Mrs. White, as she rose and began to set the supper. "Don't you think you might wish for four pairs of hands for me?"

Her husband drew the talisman from his pocket, and then all three burst into laughter as the sergeant major, with a look of alarm on his face, caught him by the arm. "If you must wish," he said, gruffly, "wish for something sensible."

Mr. White dropped it back in his pocket, and placing chairs, motioned his friend to the table. In the business of supper the talisman was partly forgotten, and afterward the three sat listening in an enthralled fashion to a second installment of the soldier's adventures in India.

"If the tale about the monkey's paw is not more truthful than those he has been telling us," said Herbert, as the door closed behind their guest, just in time for him to catch the last train, "we shan't make much out of it."

"Did you give him anything for it, Father?" inquired Mrs. White,

Spiral Review
THEME What theme does Morris's story suggest to readers that the characters do not seem to perceive?

◀ **Vocabulary**
grave (grāv) *adj.* very serious and worrying

Plot
How does the information about the previous wishers foreshadow danger for the Whites?

Comprehension
According to the sergeant major, what is special about the monkey's paw?

4. ***Arabian Nights*** collection of stories from the ancient Near East telling of fantastical adventures and supernatural beings.

regarding her husband closely.

"A trifle," said he, coloring slightly. "He didn't want it, but I made him take it. And he pressed me again to throw it away."

"Likely," said Herbert, with pretended horror. "Why, we're going to be rich, and famous and happy. Wish to be an emperor, Father, to begin with; then you can't be bossed around."

Vocabulary ▶
maligned (mə līnd′) *adj.* spoken ill of

credulity (krə do͞o′ lə tē) *n.* tendency to believe too readily

He darted round the table, pursued by the **maligned** Mrs. White armed with an antimacassar.[5]

Mr. White took the paw from his pocket and eyed it dubiously. "I don't know what to wish for, and that's a fact," he said, slowly. "It seems to me I've got all I want."

"If you only cleared the house, you'd be quite happy, wouldn't you?" said Herbert, with his hand on his shoulder. "Well, wish for two hundred pounds,[6] then; that'll just do it."

His father, smiling shamefacedly at his own **credulity**, held up the talisman, as his son, with a solemn face somewhat marred by a wink at his mother, sat down at the piano and struck a few impressive chords.

"I wish for two hundred pounds," said the old man distinctly.

A fine crash from the piano greeted the words, interrupted by a shuddering cry from the old man. His wife and son ran toward him.

"It moved," he cried, with a glance of disgust at the object as it lay on the floor. "As I wished it twisted in my hand like a snake."

"Well, I don't see the money," said his son as he picked it up and placed it on the table, "and I bet I never shall."

"It must have been your fancy, Father," said his wife, regarding him anxiously.

He shook his head. "Never mind, though; there's no harm done, but it gave me a shock all the same."

They sat down by the fire again while the two men finished their pipes. Outside, the wind was higher than ever, and the old man started nervously at the sound of a door banging upstairs. A silence unusual and depressing settled upon all three, which lasted until the old couple rose to retire for the night.

Make Predictions
What do characters in stories about wishes usually learn? Predict the results of Mr. White's wish.

"I expect you'll find the cash tied up in a big bag in the middle of your bed," said Herbert, as he bade them good night, "and something horrible squatting up on top of the wardrobe watching you as you pocket your ill-gotten gains."

Herbert sat alone in the darkness, gazing at the dying fire, and seeing faces in it. The last face was so horrible and so simian[7] that he gazed at it in amazement. It got so vivid that, with a little uneasy

---

5. **antimacassar** (an′ ti mə kas′ ər) *n.* small cover for the arms or back of a chair or sofa.
6. **pounds** *n.* units of English currency, roughly comparable to dollars.
7. **simian** (sim′ ē ən) *adj.* monkeylike.

laugh, he felt on the table for a glass containing a little water to throw over it. His hand grasped the monkey's paw, and with a little shiver he wiped his hand on his coat and went up to bed.

–II–

In the brightness of the wintry sun next morning as it streamed over the breakfast table Herbert laughed at his fears. There was an air of prosaic wholesomeness about the room which it had lacked on the previous night, and the dirty, shriveled little paw was pitched on the sideboard with a carelessness which betokened no great belief in its virtues.

"I suppose all old soldiers are the same," said Mrs. White. "The idea of our listening to such nonsense! How could wishes be granted in these days? And if they could, how could two hundred pounds hurt you, Father?"

"Might drop on his head from the sky," said the frivolous Herbert.

"Morris said the things happened so naturally," said his father, "that you might if you so wished attribute it to coincidence."

"Well, don't break into the money before I come back," said Herbert, as he rose from the table. "I'm afraid it'll turn you into a mean, avaricious[8] man, and we shall have to disown you."

His mother laughed, and following him to the door, watched him down the road, and, returning to the breakfast table, was very happy at the expense of her husband's credulity. All of which did not prevent her from scurrying to the door at the postman's knock, nor prevent her from referring somewhat shortly to retired sergeant majors of bibulous habits when she found that the post brought a tailor's bill.

"Herbert will have some more of his funny remarks, I expect, when he comes home," she said, as they sat at dinner.

"I dare say," said Mr. White, "but for all that, the thing moved in my hand; that I'll swear to."

"You thought it did," said the old lady soothingly.

"I say it did," replied the other. "There was no thought about it; I had just—What's the matter?"

His wife made no reply. She was watching the mysterious movements of a man outside, who, peering in an undecided fashion at the house, appeared to be trying to make up his mind to enter. In mental connection with the two hundred pounds, she noticed that the stranger was well dressed, and wore a silk hat of glossy newness. Three times he paused at the gate, and then walked on

Plot
How does the conversation about the money foreshadow a problem?

Comprehension
For what does Mr. White wish?

8. **avaricious** (av′ ə rish′ əs) *adj.* greedy for wealth.

again. The fourth time he stood with his hand upon it, and then with sudden resolution flung it open and walked up the path. Mrs. White at the same moment placed her hands behind her, and hurriedly unfastening the strings of her apron, put that useful article of apparel beneath the cushion of her chair.

Vocabulary ▶
furtively (fur´ tiv lē) *adv.* secretively; sneakily; stealthily

She brought the stranger, who seemed ill at ease, into the room. He gazed at her **furtively**, and listened in a preoccupied fashion as the old lady apologized for the appearance of the room, and her husband's coat, a garment which he usually reserved for the garden. She then waited patiently for him to broach his business, but he was at first strangely silent.

"I—was asked to call," he said at last, and stooped and picked a piece of cotton from his trousers. "I come from 'Maw and Meggins.'"

The old lady started. "Is anything the matter?" she asked, breathlessly. "Has anything happened to Herbert? What is it? What is it?"

Her husband interposed. "There, there, mother," he said, hastily. "Sit down, and don't jump to conclusions. You've not brought bad news, I'm sure, sir," and he eyed the other wistfully.

"I'm sorry—" began the visitor.

"Is he hurt?" demanded the mother, wildly.

Plot
In what way does the stranger's answer increase the tension of the rising action?

The visitor bowed in assent. "Badly hurt," he said quietly, "but he is not in any pain."

"Oh, thank God!" said the old woman, clasping her hands. "Thank God for that! Thank—"

She broke off suddenly as the sinister meaning of the assurance dawned upon her and she saw the awful confirmation of her fears in the other's averted face. She caught her breath, and turning to her husband, laid her trembling old hand upon his. There was a long silence.

"He was caught in the machinery," said the visitor at length, in a low voice.

"Caught in the machinery," repeated Mr. White, in a dazed fashion, "yes."

He sat staring blankly out at the window, and taking his wife's hand between his own, pressed it as he had been wont to do in their old courting days nearly forty years before.

"He was the only one left to us," he said, turning gently to the visitor. "It is hard."

The other coughed, and, rising, walked slowly to the window. "The firm wished me to convey their sincere sympathy with you in your great loss," he said, without looking round. "I beg that you will understand I am only their servant and merely obeying orders."

There was no reply; the old woman's face was white, her eyes staring, and her breath inaudible; on the husband's face was a look such as his friend the sergeant might have carried into his first action.

"I was to say that Maw and Meggins disclaim all responsibility," continued the other. "They admit no liability at all, but in consideration of your son's services they wish to present you with a certain sum as compensation."

Mr. White dropped his wife's hand, and rising to his feet, gazed with a look of horror at his visitor. His dry lips shaped the words, "How much?"

"Two hundred pounds," was the answer.

Unconscious of his wife's shriek, the old man smiled faintly, put out his hands like a sightless man, and dropped, a senseless heap, to the floor.

–III–

In the huge new cemetery, some two miles distant, the old people buried their dead, and came back to a house steeped in shadow and silence. It was all over so quickly that at first they could hardly realize it, and remained in a state of expectation as though of something else to happen—something else which was to lighten this load, too heavy for old hearts to bear.

Make Predictions
Do you think the Whites will make another wish? Why or why not?

But the days passed, and expectation gave place to resignation—the hopeless resignation of the old, sometimes miscalled **apathy**. Sometimes they hardly exchanged a word, for now they had nothing to talk about, and their days were long to weariness.

◀ **Vocabulary**
apathy (ap´ə thē) *n.* lack of interest or emotion

It was about a week after that the old man, waking suddenly in the night, stretched out his hand and found himself alone. The room was in darkness, and the sound of subdued weeping came from the window. He raised himself in bed and listened.

"Come back," he said, tenderly. "You will be cold."

"It is colder for my son," said the old woman, and wept afresh.

The sound of her sobs died away on his ears. The bed was warm, and his eyes heavy with sleep. He dozed fitfully, and then slept until a sudden wild cry from his wife awoke him with a start.

"*The paw!*" she cried wildly. "The monkey's paw!"

He started up in alarm. "Where? Where is it? What's the matter?"

She came stumbling across the room toward him. "I want it," she said quietly. "You've not destroyed it?"

"It's in the parlor, on the bracket," he replied, marveling. "Why?"

She cried and laughed together, and bending over, kissed his cheek.

Comprehension
How do the Whites get their money?

"I only just thought of it," she said hysterically. "Why didn't I think of it before? Why didn't *you* think of it?"

"Think of what?" he questioned.

"The other two wishes," she replied rapidly. "We've only had one."

"Was not that enough?" he demanded, fiercely.

"No," she cried triumphantly; "we'll have one more. Go down and get it quickly, and wish our boy alive again."

The man sat up in bed and flung the bedclothes from his quaking limbs. "You are mad!" he cried, aghast.

"Get it," she panted; "get it quickly, and wish—Oh, my boy, my boy!"

Her husband struck a match and lit the candle. "Get back to bed," he said unsteadily. "You don't know what you are saying."

"We had the first wish granted," said the old woman feverishly; "why not the second?"

"A coincidence," stammered the old man.

"Go and get it and wish," cried his wife, quivering with excitement.

The old man turned and regarded her, and his voice shook. "He has been dead ten days, and besides he—I would not tell you else, but—I could only recognize him by his clothing. If he was too terrible for you to see then, how now?"

"Bring him back," cried the old woman, and dragged him toward the door. "Do you think I fear the child I have nursed?"

He went down in the darkness, and felt his way to the parlor, and then to the mantelpiece. The talisman was in its place, and a horrible fear that the unspoken wish might bring his mutilated son before him ere he could escape from the room seized upon him, and he caught his breath as he found that he had lost the direction of the door. His brow cold with sweat, he felt his way round the table, and groped along the wall until he found himself in the small passage with the unwholesome thing in his hand.

"The other two wishes," she replied rapidly. "We've only had one."

Even his wife's face seemed changed as he entered the room. It was white and expectant, and to his fears seemed to have an unnatural look upon it. He was afraid of her.

"*Wish!*" she cried, in a strong voice.

"It is foolish and wicked," he faltered.

"*Wish!*" repeated his wife.

He raised his hand. "I wish my son alive again."

Plot
In what way does this new wish increase the tension of the story?

The talisman fell to the floor, and he regarded it fearfully. Then he sank trembling into a chair as the old woman, with burning eyes, walked to the window and raised the blind.

He sat until he was chilled with the cold, glancing occasionally at the figure of the old woman peering through the window. The candle-end, which had burned below the rim of the china candlestick, was throwing pulsating shadows on the ceiling and walls, until, with a flicker larger than the rest, it expired. The old man, with an unspeakable sense of relief at the failure of the talisman, crept back to his bed, and a minute or two afterward the old woman came silently and apathetically beside him.

Neither spoke, but lay silently listening to the ticking of the clock. A stair creaked, and a squeaky mouse scurried noisily through the wall. The darkness was **oppressive**, and after lying for some time screwing up his courage, he took the box of matches, and striking one, went downstairs for a candle.

◀ **Vocabulary**
oppressive (ə pres´ iv) *adj.* causing great discomfort; distressing

At the foot of the stairs the match went out, and he paused to strike another; and at the same moment a knock, so quiet and stealthy as to be scarcely audible, sounded on the front door.

The matches fell from his hand and spilled in the passage. He stood motionless, his breath suspended until the knock was repeated. Then he turned and fled swiftly back to his room, and closed the door behind him. A third knock sounded through the house.

"*What's that?*" cried the old woman, starting up.

"A rat," said the old man in shaking tones—"a rat. It passed me on the stairs."

His wife sat up in bed listening. A loud knock resounded through the house.

"It's Herbert!" she screamed. "It's Herbert!"

She ran to the door, but her husband was before her, and catching her by the arm, held her tightly.

"What are you going to do?" he whispered hoarsely.

"It's my boy; it's Herbert!" she cried, struggling mechanically. "I forgot it was two miles away. What are you holding me for? Let go. I must open the door."

"Don't let it in," cried the old man, trembling.

"You're afraid of your own son," she cried, struggling. "Let me go. I'm coming, Herbert, I'm coming."

There was another knock, and another. The old woman with a sudden wrench broke free and ran from the room. Her husband followed to the landing, and called after her appealingly as she hurried downstairs. He heard the chain rattle back and the bottom bolt drawn slowly and stiffly from the socket. Then the old woman's voice, strained and panting.

"The bolt," she cried, loudly. "Come down. I can't reach it."

But her husband was on his hands and knees groping wildly on

Comprehension
Why is Mr. White afraid?

Plot
How does the difference between what Mr. and Mrs. White are trying to do bring events to a climax?

the floor in search of the paw. If he could only find it before the thing outside got in. A perfect fusillade[9] of knocks reverberated through the house, and he heard the scraping of a chair as his wife put it down in the passage against the door. He heard the creaking of the bolt as it came slowly back, and at the same moment he found the monkey's paw, and frantically breathed his third and last wish.

The knocking ceased suddenly, although the echoes of it were still in the house. He heard the chair drawn back and the door opened. A cold wind rushed up the staircase, and a long loud wail of disappointment and misery from his wife gave him courage to run down to her side, and then to the gate beyond. The street lamp flickering opposite shone on a quiet and deserted road.

9. **fusillade** (fyo͞o´ sə lād´) *n.* rapid firing, as of gunshots.

Language Study

Vocabulary An **analogy** shows the relationship between pairs of words. The words shown in blue below appear in "The Monkey's Paw." Use one word from the list to complete each numbered analogy. Your choice should create a word pair that matches the relationship between the first two words given. Explain the relationship in each analogy.

grave **maligned** **furtively** **apathy** **oppressive**

1. ran : rapidly :: snuck :
2. kindness : cruelty :: passion :
3. nourished : starved :: praised :
4. lighthearted : cheerful :: serious :
5. cautious : reckless :: pleasant :

WORD STUDY
The **Latin root *-cred-*** means "believe." In this story, a character must monitor his **credulity**, or readiness to believe, as he hears a wild story about a supernatural object.

Word Study

Part A Explain how the **Latin root *-cred-*** contributes to the meanings of *credence, credo,* and *discredit.* Consult a dictionary if necessary.

Part B Use the context of the sentences and what you know about the Latin root *-cred-* to explain your answer to each question.

1. Would you believe an *incredible* rumor?
2. Does someone who usually tells lies have *credibility*?

Close Reading Activities

Literary Analysis

Key Ideas and Details

1. **(a)** How does each of the Whites react when first hearing the legend of the monkey's paw? **(b) Compare and Contrast:** At the end of the story, how have Mr. and Mrs. White's feelings about the talisman changed?
2. **(a)** According to Sergeant Major Morris, what lesson does the fakir want to teach? **(b) Interpret:** Does the fakir succeed? Cite evidence to support your answer.

Craft and Structure

3. **Plot** Complete a plot diagram like the one shown. **(a)** Describe three events in the rising action. **(b)** Identify the point at which the story reaches its climax. **(c)** Identify one event in the falling action.
4. **Plot and Plot Devices** Sergeant Major Morris's advice to Mr. White is to "wish for something sensible." How does this advice foreshadow later events? Cite details from the text to support your answer.

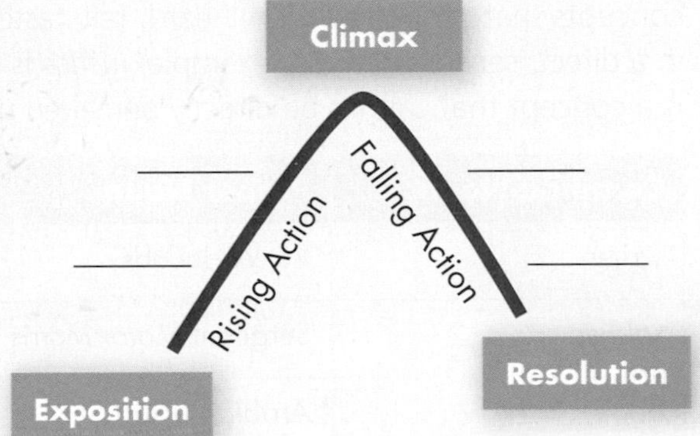

5. **(a)** How does Mr. White word his first wish? **(b) Analyze:** How might he have reworded that wish for better effect? **(c) Make a Judgment:** Would any version of the wish be foolproof? Cite story details to support your answer.
6. **(a) Interpret:** Why do you think the author chose to omit the specific wording of Mr. White's final wish? **(b) Connect:** Which details convey the content of the last wish? Explain.

Integration of Knowledge and Ideas

7. **(a) Compare and Contrast:** In what way is this story similar to and different from other stories you know that involve three wishes? **(b) Interpret:** What overall insight or theme is revealed in this story? Cite details to support your response.
8. THE BIG ? **Can progress be made without conflict? (a)** Identify three different conflicts that arise for the Whites after they are introduced to the monkey's paw. **(b)** As each conflict is resolved, are the Whites in better or worse condition than they were before? Explain. **(c)** Would a wish to eliminate all conflict have improved the Whites' lives? Cite details from the story to explain your answers.

ACADEMIC VOCABULARY

As you write and speak about "The Monkey's Paw," use the words related to conflict that you explored on page 3 of this book.

Conventions: Nouns

A **noun** is a word that names a person, a place, or a thing. Nouns can also be ideas or concepts.

A **common noun** refers to any one of a certain kind of person, place, thing, or idea; for example, *nation*. A **proper noun** refers to a specific person, place, thing, or idea; for example, *India*. Proper nouns always begin with capital letters.

Common nouns can be further categorized as concrete or abstract. **Concrete nouns** name things that can be directly experienced or perceived by the senses. *Airplane* is a concrete noun because it is something you can see, feel, and hear. **Abstract nouns** name ideas or concepts that cannot be seen, heard, felt, tasted, smelled, or experienced in a direct, sensory way. For example, *justice* is an abstract noun because it is a concept that cannot be directly perceived using your senses.

Common Nouns	Proper Nouns	Concrete Nouns	Abstract Nouns
writer	W. W. Jacobs	factory	courage
soldier	Sergeant Major Morris	paw	luck
book	*Arabian Nights*	train	superstition
road	River Road	monkey	fear

Practice A

Identify the underlined word in each sentence as either a proper or a common noun.

1. Until Mr. White made his first wish, he lived an uneventful life.
2. The Whites had an unexpected visitor.
3. The author of the story grew up in England.
4. The cursed paw was a source of grief.

Reading Application Find three concrete nouns and three abstract nouns in "The Monkey's Paw."

Practice B

Label each noun as concrete or abstract. Then, use each word in a sentence.

1. sorrow
2. door
3. coincidence
4. talisman
5. determination

Writing Application Using this sentence as a model, write two sentences that each contain both a concrete and an abstract noun: *Today is a basket of joy*.

Writing to Sources

Narrative Write a **sequel** to "The Monkey's Paw." A sequel is an episode that occurs after the end of a story. It often addresses issues left open by the original story or reveals the outcome of an unresolved ending. For example, a sequel to "The Monkey's Paw" could show what happens after Mr. White rushes out to the deserted street at the story's end.

- Use a plot diagram to plan your sequel. Identify details to include in each stage of the plot and the event that will serve as the climax.
- Try to reflect W. W. Jacobs's writing style. Use vivid details to describe events, and create a mood appropriate to the characters, setting, and action of your sequel.
- Use foreshadowing to build suspense.
- Consider adding a flashback to help explain the characters' present actions. Likewise, recall events from "The Monkey's Paw" to connect the stories across time.

Grammar Application As you write, pay attention to your use of proper nouns, and be sure to capitalize them.

Speaking and Listening

Comprehension and Collaboration In a small group, conduct an **interview** between a skeptical journalist and the Whites after the tragedy. Prepare questions that will allow Mr. and Mrs. White to share their story. Follow these steps to plan and present the interview:

- Choose roles and set rules about how to ask and respond to questions appropriately.
- As the journalist, prepare questions that demonstrate knowledge of the story but also express reasonable doubts about the events.
- As the Whites, stay in character as you respond to questions and use the types of words such an older couple would find natural. You may also use direct quotations from the story in your responses.

After the interview, evaluate the presentation. Discuss which questions and responses were most effective, using language that conveys maturity and respect. Summarize points of agreement and disagreement. Then, compile your responses in a brief report.

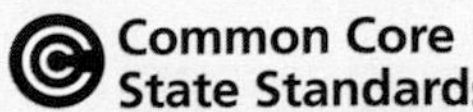

Writing

3. Write narratives to develop real or imagined experiences or events using effective technique, well-chosen details, and well-structured event sequences.

3.b. Use narrative techniques, such as dialogue, pacing, description, reflection, and multiple plot lines, to develop experiences, events, and/or characters.

3.c. Use a variety of techniques to sequence events so that they build on one another to create a coherent whole.

3.d. Use precise words and phrases, telling details, and sensory language to convey a vivid picture of the experiences, events, setting, and/or characters.

Speaking and Listening

1.a. Come to discussions prepared, having read and researched material under study; explicitly draw on that preparation by referring to evidence from texts and other research on the topic or issue to stimulate a thoughtful, well-reasoned exchange of ideas.

1.b. Work with peers to set rules for collegial discussions.

Language

2. Demonstrate command of the conventions of standard English when writing.

5. Demonstrate understanding of figurative language, word relationships, and nuances in word meanings.

Building Knowledge

Can progress be made without conflict?

Explore the Big Question as you read "The Street of the Cañon." Take notes on the story's portrayal of the relationship between progress and conflict.

CLOSE READING FOCUS

Key Ideas and Details: **Make Inferences**

An **inference** is a logical guess about information that is not directly stated in a literary work. When making an inference, you consider information that is stated in the text along with your knowledge about people and the world in general. For instance, if a writer does not name a setting but describes igloos and extreme cold, you can infer that the story is set in the Arctic. After you make an inference, read on to find additional support for it. If new details contradict your inference, modify it.

Craft and Structure: **Setting**

Setting is the time and place in which the events of a story unfold. To establish a setting, writers may use **description,** creating word pictures that show what the physical location is like. They may also provide information about less visible aspects of the setting, such as the characters' culture, values, and beliefs.

- Setting may affect a story's plot. In a story set in the Arctic wilderness, for example, characters will face challenges not found in a tropical resort hotel.
- Setting helps readers understand the action in a story. For example, in a story set in medieval times, a knight may be concerned about his honor. In a story set in World War II Europe, a family might be concerned about their very survival.

Vocabulary

The words below are critical to understanding the text that follows. Copy the words into your notebook. Which word means the opposite of *timidly*?

nonchalantly	**imperiously**	**plausibility**
audaciously	**disdain**	**apprehension**

Meet the Author

Josephina Niggli (1910–1983) was born in Monterrey, Mexico, but grew up on both sides of the border between Mexico and the United States. Niggli's work includes poetry, short stories, plays, and radio and television scripts. She found theater thrilling, writing, "Once you have experienced the emotion of having a play produced, you are forever lost to the ordinary world." Niggli is best known for *Mexican Village*, a collection of ten stories that capture the rich local color of Mexico.

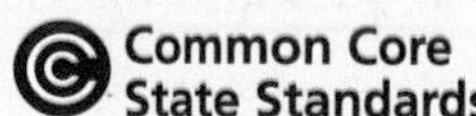

Common Core State Standards

Reading Literature

1. Cite strong and thorough textual evidence to support analysis of what the text says explicitly as well as inferences drawn from the text.

4. Determine the meaning of words and phrases as they are used in the text, including figurative and connotative meanings.

Language

4. Determine or clarify the meaning of unknown and multiple-meaning words and phrases based on grades 9–10 reading and content.

CLOSE READING MODEL

The passage below is from Josephina Niggli's short story "The Street of the Cañon." The annotations to the right of the passage show ways in which you can use close reading skills to make inferences and analyze setting.

from "The Street of the Cañon"

Carefully adjusting[1] his flat package so that it was not too prominent,[1] he squared his shoulders and walked jauntily across the street to the laughter-filled house.[2] Little boys packed in the doorway made way for him, smiling and nodding to him. The long, narrow room with the orchestra at one end was filled with whirling dancers. Rigid-backed chaperones were gossiping together, seated in their straight chairs against the plaster walls. Over the scene was the yellow glow of kerosene lanterns,[2] and the air was hot with the too-sweet perfume of gardenias, tuberoses, and the pungent scent of close-packed humanity.

The man in the doorway, while trying to appear at ease, was carefully examining every smiling face. If just one person recognized him, the room would turn on him like a den of snarling mountain cats,[3] but so far all the laughter-dancing eyes were friendly.

Make Inferences

1 Phrases such as "carefully adjusting," and "not too prominent" suggest that the man is eager to hide the package he is carrying.

Setting

2 Details of the "laughter-filled house" and "whirling dancers" tell you that the setting is a party. The mention of "kerosene lanterns" is a clue to the time setting—an era before the widespread use of electricity.

Make Inferences

3 Phrases such as "trying to appear at ease" and "carefully examining every smiling face" suggest that the man is nervous. The following sentence confirms that he is afraid of being recognized. You can infer that the man has an unpleasant history with this town.

Dance in Tehuantepec, 1935. Diego Rivera. Los Angeles County Museum of Art.

The Street of the Cañon

Josephina Niggli

▲ **Critical Viewing** What does this painting suggest about the setting of the story?

It was May, the flowering thorn was sweet in the air, and the village of San Juan Iglesias in the Valley of the Three Marys was celebrating. The long dark streets were empty because all of the people, from the lowest-paid cowboy to the mayor, were helping Don Roméo Calderón celebrate his daughter's eighteenth birthday.

On the other side of the town, where the Cañon Road led across the mountains to the Sabinas Valley, a tall slender man, a package clutched tightly against his side, slipped from shadow to shadow.

Once a dog barked, and the man's black suit merged into the blackness of a wall. But no voice called out, and after a moment he slid into the narrow, dirt-packed street again.

The moonlight touched his shoulder and spilled across his narrow hips. He was young, no more than twenty-five, and his black curly head was bare. He walked swiftly along, heading always for the distant sound of guitar and flute. If he met anyone now, who could say from which direction he had come? He might be a trader from Monterrey, or a buyer of cow's milk from farther north in the Valley of the Three Marys. Who would guess that an Hidalgo man dared to walk alone in the moonlit streets of San Juan Iglesias?

Make Inferences
Make an inference about the towns of Hidalgo and San Juan Iglesias. What kinds of details might confirm your inference?

Carefully adjusting his flat package so that it was not too prominent, he squared his shoulders and walked jauntily across the street to the laughter-filled house. Little boys packed in the doorway made way for him, smiling and nodding to him. The long, narrow room with the orchestra at one end was filled with whirling dancers. Rigid-backed chaperones[1] were gossiping together, seated in their straight chairs against the plaster walls. Over the scene was the yellow glow of kerosene lanterns, and the air was hot with the too-sweet perfume of gardenias, tuberoses,[2] and the pungent scent of close-packed humanity.

Setting
To which senses does this description of the setting appeal?

The man in the doorway, while trying to appear at ease, was carefully examining every smiling face. If just one person recognized him, the room would turn on him like a den of snarling mountain cats, but so far all the laughter-dancing eyes were friendly.

Suddenly a plump, officious little man, his round cheeks glistening with perspiration, pushed his way through the crowd. His voice, many times too large for his small body, boomed at the man in the doorway. "Welcome, stranger, welcome to our house." Thrusting his arm through the stranger's, and almost dislodging the package, he started to lead the way through the maze of dancers. "Come and drink a toast to my daughter—to my beautiful Sarita. She is eighteen this night."

In the square patio the gentle breeze ruffled the pink and white oleander bushes. A long table set up on sawhorses held loaves of flaky crusted French bread, stacks of thin, delicate tortillas, plates of barbecued beef, and long red rolls of spicy sausages. But most of all there were cheeses, for the Three Marys was a cheese-eating valley. There were yellow cheese and white cheese and curded

Comprehension
What occasion is the village of San Juan Iglesias celebrating?

1. **chaperones** (shap′ ər ōnz′) older or married women who accompany and supervise the behavior of young people in public.
2. **gardenias** (gär dēn′ yəz), **tuberoses** (to͞ob′ rōz′ əs) two types of plants with especially sweet-smelling flowers.

LITERATURE IN CONTEXT

Language Connection

Spanish Vocabulary

Set in Mexico, the story contains several Spanish words and terms, including

- **cañon** canyon; a narrow valley between high cliffs
- **tío** uncle
- **hola** Spanish exclamation meaning "hi"
- **don** title of respect meaning "sir"; often placed before a man's name
- **parada** literally, "parade"; a dance in which partners stride around together

Connect to the Literature

Why do you think Niggli included these terms in the story? **[Interpret]**

cheese from cow's milk. There was even a flat white cake of goat cheese from distant Linares, a delicacy too expensive for any but feast days.

To set off this feast were bottles of beer floating in ice-filled tin tubs, and another table was covered with bottles of mescal, of tequila, of maguey wine.

Don Roméo Calderón thrust a glass of tequila into the stranger's hand. "Drink, friend, to the prettiest girl in San Juan. As pretty as my fine fighting cocks, she is. On her wedding day she takes to her man, and may she find him soon, the best fighter in my flock. Drink deep, friend. Even the rivers flow with wine."

The Hidalgo man laughed and raised his glass high. "May the earth be always fertile beneath her feet."

Someone called to Don Roméo that more guests were arriving, and with a final delighted pat on the stranger's shoulder, the little man scurried away. As the young fellow smiled after his retreating host, his eyes caught and held another pair of eyes—laughing black eyes set in a young girl's face. The last time he had seen that face it had been white and tense with rage, and the lips clenched tight to prevent an outgushing stream of angry words. That had been in February, and she had worn a white lace shawl over her hair. Now it was May, and a gardenia was a splash of white in the glossy dark braids. The moonlight had mottled his face that February night, and he knew that she did not recognize him. He grinned impudently[3] back at her, and her eyes widened, then slid sideways to one of the chaperones. The fan in her small hand snapped shut. She tapped its parchment tip against her mouth and slipped away to join the dancing couples in the front room. The gestures of a fan translate into a coded language on the frontier. The stranger raised one eyebrow as he interpreted the signal.

But he did not move toward her at once. Instead, he inched slowly back against the table. No one was behind him, and his hands quickly unfastened the package he had been guarding so long. Then he **nonchalantly** walked into the front room.

Vocabulary ▶ nonchalantly (nän′ shə länt′ lē) *adv.* casually; indifferently

The girl was sitting close to a chaperone. As he came up to her he swerved slightly toward the bushy-browed old lady.

"Your servant, señora. I kiss your hands and feet."

The chaperone stared at him in astonishment. Such fine manners were not common to the town of San Juan Iglesias.

"Eh, you're a stranger," she said. "I thought so."

3. **impudently** (im′ pyo͞o dənt lē) *adv.* in a shamelessly bold or provocative way.

"But a stranger no longer, señora, now that I have met you." He bent over her, so close she could smell the faint fragrance of talcum on his freshly shaven cheek.

"Will you dance the *parada* with me?"

This request startled her eyes into popping open beneath the heavy brows. "So, my young rooster, would you flirt with me, and I old enough to be your grandmother?"

"Can you show me a prettier woman to flirt with in the Valley of the Three Marys?" he asked **audaciously**.

She grinned at him and turned toward the girl at her side. "This young fool wants to meet you, my child."

The girl blushed to the roots of her hair and shyly lowered her white lids. The old woman laughed aloud.

"Go out and dance, the two of you. A man clever enough to pat the sheep has a right to play with the lamb."

The next moment they had joined the circle of dancers and Sarita was trying to control her laughter.

"She is the worst dragon in San Juan. And how easily you won her!"

"What is a dragon," he asked **imperiously**, "when I longed to dance with you?"

"Ay," she retorted, "you have a quick tongue. I think you are a dangerous man."

In answer he drew her closer to him, and turned her toward the orchestra. As he reached the chief violinist he called out, "Play the *Virgencita*, 'The Shy Young Maiden.'"

The violinist's mouth opened in soundless surprise. The girl in his arms said sharply, "You heard him, the *Borachita*, 'The Little Drunken Girl.'"

◀ **Vocabulary**
audaciously (ô dā′ shəs lē) *adv.* in a bold manner

imperiously (im pir′ ē əs lē) *adv.* arrogantly

Comprehension
Why does the stranger ask the girl's chaperone to dance?

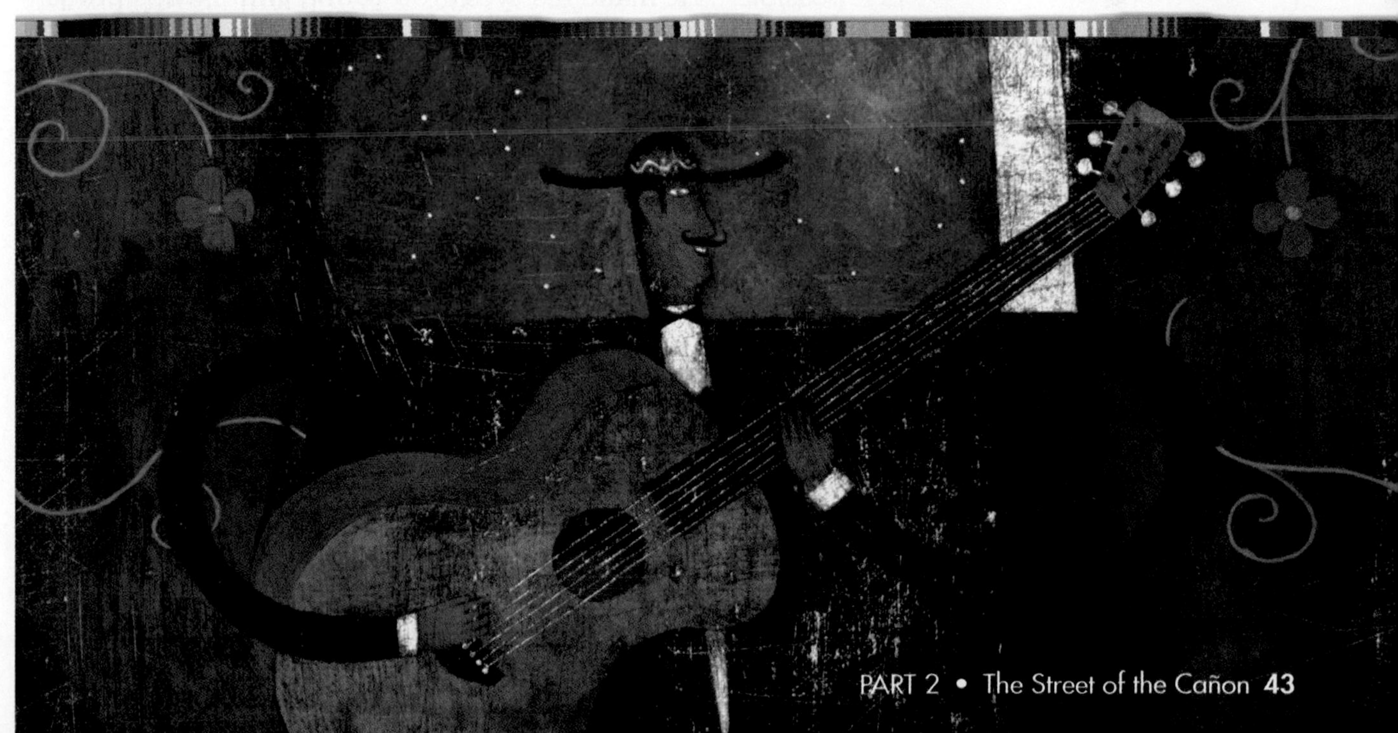

With a relieved grin, the violinist tapped his music stand with his bow, and the music swung into the sad farewell of a man to his sweetheart:

Farewell, my little drunken one,
I must go to the capital
To serve the master
Who makes me weep for my return.

Spiral Review
PLOT What conflict does the stranger's cold reaction to the song help develop?

The stranger frowned down at her. "Is this a joke, señorita?" he asked coldly.

"No," she whispered, looking about her quickly to see if the incident had been observed. "But the *Virgencita* is the favorite song of Hidalgo, a village on the other side of the mountains in the next valley. The people of Hidalgo and San Juan Iglesias do not speak."

"That is a stupid thing," said the man from Hidalgo as he swung her around in a large turn. "Is not music free as air? Why should one town own the rights to a song?"

The girl shuddered slightly. "Those people from Hidalgo—they are wicked monsters. Can you guess what they did not six months since?"

The man started to point out that the space of time from February to May was three months, but he thought it better not to appear too wise. "Did these Hidalgo monsters frighten you, señorita? If they did, I personally will kill them all."

She moved closer against him and tilted her face until her mouth was close to his ear. "They attempted to steal the bones of Don Rómolo Balderas."

Vocabulary ▶
disdain (dis dān´) *n.* a feeling or a show of a lack of respect

plausibility (plô´ zə bil´ i tē) *n.* believability; seeming truth

"Is it possible?" He made his eyes grow round and his lips purse up in **disdain**. "Surely not that! Why, all the world knows that Don Rómolo Balderas was the greatest historian in the entire Republic. Every school child reads his books. Wise men from Quintana Roo to the Río Bravo bow their heads in admiration to his name. What a wicked thing to do!" He hoped his virtuous tone was not too virtuous for **plausibility**, but she did not seem to notice.

"It is true! In the night they came. Three devils!"

"Young devils, I hope."

"Young or old, who cares? They were devils. The blacksmith surprised them even as they were opening the grave. He raised such a shout that all of San Juan rushed to his aid, for they were fighting, I can tell you. Especially one of them—their leader."

"And who was he?"

"You have heard of him doubtless. A proper wild one named Pepé Gonzalez."

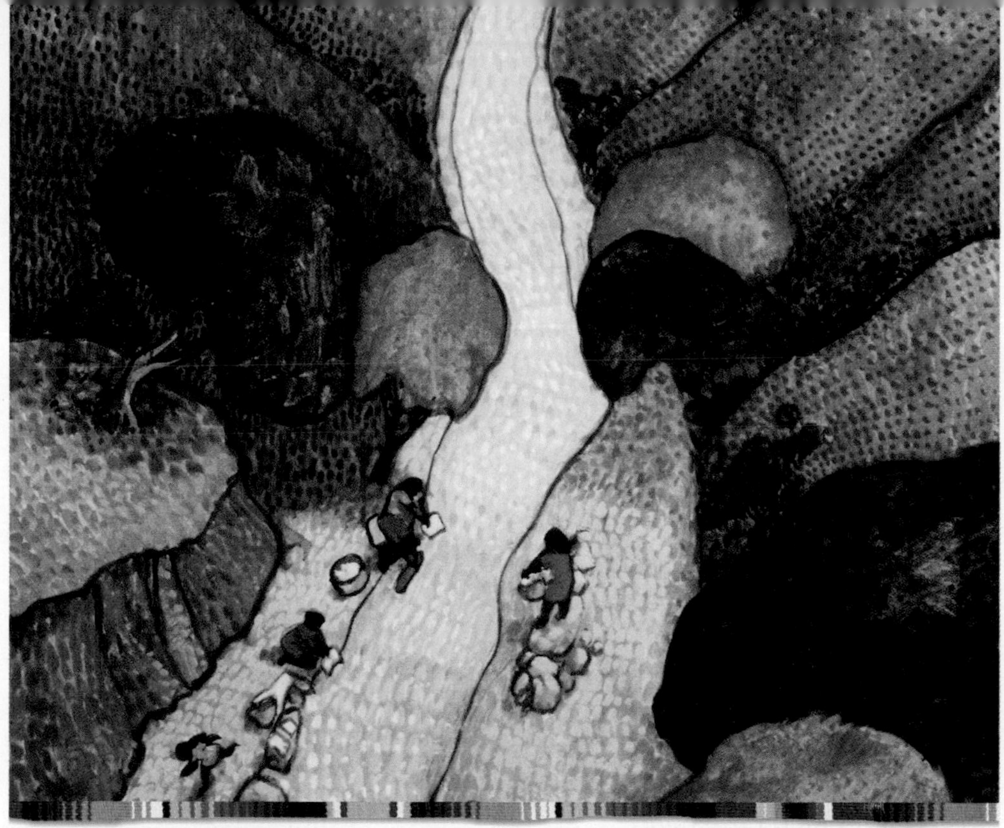

◀ **Critical Viewing**
Compare the mood of this painting with the mood of the story.

"And what happened to them?"

"They had horses and got away, but one, I think, was hurt."

The Hidalgo man twisted his mouth remembering how Rubén the candymaker had ridden across the whitewashed line high on the cañon trail that marked the division between the Three Marys' and the Sabinas' sides of the mountains, and then had fallen in a faint from his saddle because his left arm was broken. There was no candy in Hidalgo for six weeks, and the entire Sabinas Valley resented that broken arm as fiercely as did Rubén.

The stranger tightened his arm in reflexed anger about Sarita's waist as she said, "All the world knows that the men of Hidalgo are sons of the mountain witches."

"But even devils are shy of disturbing the honored dead," he said gravely.

"'Don Rómolo was born in our village,' Hidalgo says. 'His bones belong to us.' Well, anyone in the valley can tell you he died in San Juan Iglesias, and here his bones will stay! Is that not proper? Is that not right?"

To keep from answering, he guided her through an intricate dance pattern that led them past the patio door. Over her head he could see two men and a woman staring with amazement at the open package on the table.

Make Inferences
Make an inference about the stranger's connection to the men who tried to raid the grave.

Comprehension
What did three men from Hidalgo try to do a few months earlier?

His eyes on the patio, he asked blandly, "You say the leader was one Pepé Gonzalez? The name seems to have a familiar sound."

"But naturally. He has a talent." She tossed her head and stepped away from him as the music stopped. It was a dance of two *paradas*. He slipped his hand through her arm and guided her into place in the large oval of parading couples. Twice around the room and the orchestra would play again.

"A talent?" he prompted.

"For doing the impossible. When all the world says a thing cannot be done, he does it to prove the world wrong. Why, he climbed to the top of the Prow, and not even the long vanished Joaquín Castillo had ever climbed that mountain before. And this same Pepé caught a mountain lion with nothing to aid him but a rope and his two bare hands."

"He doesn't sound such a bad friend," protested the stranger, slipping his arm around her waist as the music began to play the merry song of the soap bubbles:

Pretty bubbles of a thousand colors
That ride on the wind
And break as swiftly
As a lover's heart.

The events in the patio were claiming his attention. Little by little he edged her closer to the door. The group at the table had considerably enlarged. There was a low murmur of excitement from the crowd.

"What has happened?" asked Sarita, attracted by the noise.

"There seems to be something wrong at the table," he answered, while trying to peer over the heads of the people in front of him. Realizing that this might be the last moment of peace he would have that evening, he bent toward her.

"If I come back on Sunday, will you walk around the plaza with me?"

She was startled into exclaiming, "Ay, no!"

"Please. Just once around."

"And you think I'd walk more than once with you, señor, even if you were no stranger? In San Juan Iglesias, to walk around the plaza with a girl means a wedding."

"Ha, and you think that is common to San Juan alone? Even the devils of Hidalgo respect that law," he added hastily at her puzzled upward glance. "And so they do in all the villages." To cover his lapse[4] he said softly, "I don't even know your name."

Setting
How does the time and place of the story affect the way Sarita responds to the stranger?

4. **lapse** (laps) *n.* slip; error.

A mischievous grin crinkled the corners of her eyes. "Nor do I know yours, señor. Strangers do not often walk the streets of San Juan."

Before he could answer, the chattering in the patio swelled to louder proportions. Don Roméo's voice lay on top, like thick cream on milk. "I tell you it is a jewel of a cheese. Such flavor, such texture, such whiteness. It is a jewel of a cheese."

"What has happened?" Sarita asked of a woman at her elbow.

"A fine goat's cheese appeared as if by magic on the table. No one knows where it came from."

"Probably an extra one from Linares," snorted a fat bald man on the right.

"Linares never made such a cheese as this," said the woman decisively.

"Silence!" roared Don Roméo. "Old Tío Daniel would speak a word to us."

A great hand of silence closed down over the mouths of the people. The girl was standing on tiptoe trying vainly to see what was happening. She was hardly aware of the stranger's whispering voice although she remembered the words that he said. "Sunday night—once around the plaza."

She did not realize that he had moved away, leaving a gap that was quickly filled by the blacksmith.

Old Tío Daniel's voice was a shrill squeak, and his thin, stringy neck jutted forth from his body like a turtle's from its shell. "This is no cheese from Linares," he said with authority, his mouth sucking in over his toothless gums between his sentences. "Years ago, when the great Don Rómolo Balderas was still alive, we had such cheese as this—ay, in those days we had it. But after he died and was buried in our own sainted ground, as was right and proper . . ."

"Yes, yes," muttered voices in the crowd. He glared at the interruption. As soon as there was silence again, he continued:

"After he died, we had it no more. Shall I tell you why?"

"Tell us, Tío Daniel," said the voices humbly.

"Because it is made in Hidalgo!"

The sound of a waterfall, the sound of a wind in a narrow cañon, and the sound of an angry crowd are much the same. There were no distinct words, but the sound was enough.

"Are you certain, Tío?" boomed Don Roméo.

"As certain as I am that a donkey has long ears. The people of Hidalgo have been famous for generations for making cheese like this—especially that wicked one, that owner of a cheese factory,

Comprehension
What has appeared on the table on the patio?

Make Inferences
Do details here support your inference about the stranger's link with Hidalgo? Explain.

Vocabulary ▶
apprehension
(ap′ rē hen′ shən) *n.* anxious feeling; fear

Timotéo Gonzalez, father to Pepé, the wild one, whom we have good cause to remember."

"We do, we do," came the sigh of assurance.

"But on the whole northern frontier there are no vats like his to produce so fine a product. Ask the people of Chihuahua, of Sonora. Ask the man on the bridge at Laredo, or the man in his boat at Tampico, '*Hola*, friend, who makes the finest goat cheese?' And the answer will always be the same, 'Don Timotéo of Hidalgo.'"

It was the blacksmith who asked the great question. "Then where did that cheese come from, and we haters of Hidalgo these ten long years?"

No voice said, "The stranger," but with one fluid movement every head in the patio turned toward the girl in the doorway. She also turned, her eyes wide with something that she realized to her own amazement was more **apprehension** than anger.

But the stranger was not in the room. When the angry, muttering men pushed through to the street, the stranger was not on the plaza. He was not anywhere in sight. A few of the more religious crossed themselves for fear that the Devil had walked in their midst. "Who was he?" one voice asked another. But Sarita, who was meekly listening to a lecture from Don Roméo on the propriety of dancing with strangers, did not have to ask. She had a strong suspicion that she had danced that night within the circling arm of Pepé Gonzalez.

Language Study

Vocabulary The words listed below appear in "The Street of the Cañon." Match each statement that follows with a word from the list. Explain each choice.

nonchalantly audaciously imperiously disdain apprehension

1. A conceited individual might act this way.
2. A nervous person may have difficulty behaving this way.
3. People with many fears often feel a sense of this.
4. A captain who treated officers with this attitude would often be disliked.
5. Extreme situations may call for people to act this way.

WORD STUDY
The **Latin suffix *-ity*** means "quality of or state of being." In this story, a man hopes the tone he uses has **plausibility**, or the quality of being plausible, or believable.

Word Study

Part A Explain how the **Latin suffix *-ity*** contributes to the meanings of the words *accessibility, activity*, and *responsibility.* Consult a dictionary if necessary.

Part B Use the context of the sentences and what you know about the Latin suffix *-ity* to explain your answer to each question.

1. Could you easily read a letter that lacked *legibility*?
2. Is a movie that is known for its *complexity* usually easy to understand?

Close Reading Activities

Literary Analysis

Key Ideas and Details

1. **Make Inferences (a)** What descriptive words does the author use to tell how the Hidalgo man walks into the village? **(b)** What does the man wish to prevent others from learning?
2. **(a)** Whom does the Hidalgo man first ask to dance? **(b) Interpret:** Why does he ask her? Cite story details to support your response.
3. **Make Inferences (a)** Based on the information in the first three paragraphs of the story, what two inferences could you make about the stranger's plans? **(b)** For each inference, note at least one detail later in the story that either confirms it or disproves it. Record your answers in a chart like the one shown.
4. **Make Inferences (a)** Make an inference concerning Sarita's feelings about the stranger at the end of the story. **(b)** Cite three details to support your inference.

Inference	
Confirming Details	**Disproving Details**

Craft and Structure

5. **Setting (a)** Identify these aspects of the story's setting: the country, the town, and the historical period. **(b)** For each aspect, give an example of a description that helps make the setting vivid for readers.
6. **Setting (a)** According to details in the text, what dangers does the man from Hidalgo face? **(b)** Explain why these types of dangers might not apply in a story set in a different town or time.

Integration of Knowledge and Ideas

7. **Draw Conclusions:** Why are the towns quarreling? Explain how you know, basing your answer on evidence from the text.
8. **Hypothesize:** What might the villagers have done to the stranger if they had discovered his identity? Explain, citing details from the story to support your answer.

9. THE BIG ? **Can progress be made without conflict?** Why does the stranger risk danger to dance with Sarita and leave the gift? Do you think he hopes to ease the conflict that has existed between the two villages, or does he have some other motivation? Explain your response using details from the story.

ACADEMIC VOCABULARY

As you write and speak about "The Street of the Cañon," use the words related to conflict that you explored on page 3 of this book.

Conventions: Pronouns

Pronouns are words that are used in place of nouns, other pronouns, or groups of words serving as nouns. The words that pronouns replace are called antecedents.

A **personal pronoun** refers to the person speaking (first person); the person spoken to (second person); or the person, place, or thing spoken about (third person). **Possessive pronouns** show ownership: The toy is *his*.

Personal Pronouns	Singular	Plural
First Person	I, me, my, mine	we, us, our, ours
Second Person	you, your, yours	you, your, yours
Third Person	he, him, his, she, her, hers, it, its	they, them, their, theirs

A **relative pronoun** is a pronoun that begins a dependent clause. It relates the information in the clause to a noun or pronoun in the sentence. The relative pronouns in these sentences are underlined.

- This is the flower <u>that</u> Sarita wore.
- The stranger leaves a package, <u>which</u> contains cheese.
- He approaches the woman <u>who</u> is sitting with Sarita.
- Sarita is the girl with <u>whom</u> the stranger dances.
- The candymaker, <u>whose</u> arm was broken, fell from his saddle.

Practice A

Identify the pronoun in each sentence, and tell whether it is a regular personal pronoun or a possessive pronoun. Then, classify the pronoun as first person, second person, or third person.

1. The village of Hidalgo claims Don Rómolo because he was born there.
2. The men failed in their attempt.
3. Do you think the stranger is in danger?
4. Sarita did not say, "Welcome to my party."

Reading Application In "The Street of the Cañon," find four sentences that contain pronouns. For each, write the pronoun and tell what type it is—personal, possessive, or relative.

Practice B

Complete the items using a relative pronoun and a clause that relates to the underlined noun.

1. Don Roméo Calderón is the <u>man</u> ___________.
2. The stranger noticed the fine <u>foods</u> ___________.
3. The <u>cheese</u> from Linares, ___________, was purchased only for feast days.
4. Don Rómolo was a <u>historian</u> ___________.
5. The <u>package</u> ___________ draws attention.

Writing Application Write three sentences about "The Street of the Cañon." Use a different type of pronoun in each sentence.

Writing to Sources

Argument Write a **letter** to a friend in which you express and defend a claim about "The Street of the Cañon." Then, rewrite the letter as a **literary review** for a newspaper.

- In the letter, include a summary of the story, a statement expressing a claim about the story, and details to support your position. Use an informal approach and familiar language suitable for a friendly letter.
- To rewrite your letter as a literary review, refine the structure of your argument and replace informal language with more formal diction appropriate to the new audience and purpose.
- Clearly state and defend your claim. Support your argument using details and examples from the text.
- Exclude any information or opinions from your original letter that are irrelevant for a newspaper piece.

In both versions of your argument, include valid reasoning and sufficient evidence to support your claims.

Grammar Application As you write, use personal pronouns and relative pronouns correctly.

Speaking and Listening

Presentation of Ideas Locate a copy of Alfred Noyes's poem "The Highwayman." With a partner, read the poem, comparing and contrasting it with the story "The Street of the Cañon." Then, present an **oral reading** of "The Highwayman," followed by a discussion of the similarities and differences between the poem and the story.

- As you read the poem, use a dictionary to look up the definitions and pronunciations of any words you do not know.
- Take careful notes about the similarities and differences between the poem and Niggli's story. Cite specific details from both texts to support your interpretations and ideas.
- Practice your oral reading in front of a mirror, or ask friends or family members to listen to your reading and offer suggestions.
- Vary your tone of voice to reflect the poem's meaning. In addition, try different pacing to best capture the emotion and rhythm.

After you deliver your reading, lead a discussion to compare the poem and the story. Present the ideas from your notes, and then invite classmates to ask questions and contribute their own ideas.

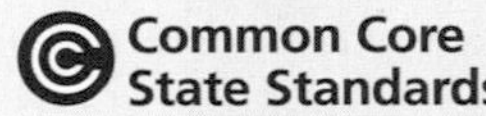

Writing
1. Write arguments to support claims in an analysis of substantive topics or texts, using valid reasoning.
4. Produce clear and coherent writing in which the development, organization, and style are appropriate to task, purpose, and audience.

Speaking and Listening
6. Adapt speech to a variety of contexts and tasks, demonstrating command of formal English when indicated or appropriate.

Language
1. Demonstrate command of the conventions of standard English grammar and usage when writing or speaking.

Building Knowledge

Meet the Author

Chinua (chin yōō ä) **Achebe** (ä chā bā) (1930–2013), is renowned for novels and stories that explore the conflicts of modern Africans. Achebe was born into the Ibo tribe of Nigeria. According to one critic, "In the English language, he is the founding father of modern African literature." Achebe's first and most celebrated novel, *Things Fall Apart* (1958), portrays the disruption of Ibo tribal society by Western colonial rule.

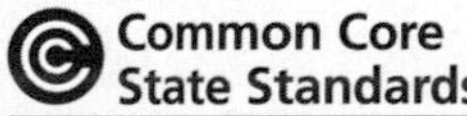

Reading Literature

1. Cite strong and thorough textual evidence to support analysis of what the text says explicitly as well as inferences drawn from the text.

2. Determine a theme or central idea of a text and analyze in detail its development over the course of the text, including how it emerges and is shaped and refined by specific details; provide an objective summary of the text.

6. Analyze a particular point of view or cultural experience reflected in a work of literature from outside the United States, drawing on a wide reading of world literature.

Can progress be made without conflict?

Explore the Big Question as you read "Civil Peace." Take notes about the conflicts that characters continue to face after a bitter war.

CLOSE READING FOCUS

Key Ideas and Details: **Draw Conclusions**

A **conclusion** is a decision or an opinion a reader reaches based on information in a text. To draw conclusions about a story's theme, or deeper meaning, identify important details in the text and consider what they suggest about issues in the characters' lives, in the world of the story, or in the real world. Also, think about what characters experience and learn, and what those lessons suggest about larger ideas. Use that information to draw conclusions about a story's theme.

Craft and Structure: **Theme**

The **theme** of a literary work is the central idea it communicates about life. For example, a story might convey the theme "Suffering cannot be justified." Often, the themes a writer explores spring from the *historical context* of a work, the web of social and cultural influences that are part of a story's setting. In some works, the historical context of the setting and the author's life are one and the same. The author's word choice often reflects that historical context and contributes to the expression of a story's theme. To convey a theme, a writer may:

- Have the narrator or another character directly state the theme.
- Suggest the theme through patterns of story elements—for instance, by repeating certain types of images or phrases.

In many cases, the theme of a work reflects a **philosophical assumption**—the writer's basic beliefs about life. For instance, a writer may believe that being generous leads to happiness and may explore that idea in his or her writing.

Vocabulary

The words below are critical to understanding the text that follows. Copy the words into your notebook. Which word is an antonym for *wealthy*?

disreputable	**amenable**	**destitute**
inaudibly	**dissent**	**commiserate**

CLOSE READING MODEL

The passage below is from Chinua Achebe's short story "Civil Peace." The annotations to the right of the passage show ways in which you can use close reading skills to draw conclusions and explore theme.

from "Civil Peace"

Jonathan Iwegbu counted himself extraordinarily lucky. "Happy survival!" meant so much more to him[1] than just a current fashion of greeting old friends in the first hazy days of peace. It went deep to his heart.[1] He had come out of the war with five inestimable blessings—his head, his wife Maria's head and the heads of three out of their four children.[2] As a bonus he also had his old bicycle—a miracle too but naturally not to be compared to the safety of five human heads.

The bicycle had a little history of its own. One day at the height of the war it was commandeered "for urgent military action."[3] Hard as its loss would have been to him he would still have let it go without a thought[4] had he not had some doubts about the genuineness of the officer. It wasn't his disreputable rags, nor the toes peeping out of one blue and one brown canvas shoe, nor yet the two stars of his rank done obviously in a hurry in biro, that troubled Jonathan; many good and heroic soldiers looked the same or worse.

Theme
1 In this first paragraph of the story, the narrator points directly to Jonathan's unusual sense of luck and gratitude. This attitude toward adversity may prove to be part of the story's theme.

Draw Conclusions
2 Jonathan is grateful "three out of their four children" survived the war. This detail, subtly tucked into the story, lets you draw the conclusion that the war was a long, terrible conflict that took the lives of many innocents.

Draw Conclusions
3 The idea that a bicycle would be needed for "urgent military action" lets you draw the conclusion that the war was not a well-funded, high-tech affair. Instead, it was a conflict most likely fought by poor and desperate people.

Theme
4 Jonathan's willingness to part with his bicycle—to "let it go without a thought"—adds to his portrayal as a man of unusual calm and acceptance. This quality in Jonathan may play a role in the story's plot and in its theme.

Civil Peace

Chinua Achebe

Jonathan Iwegbu counted himself extraordinarily lucky. "Happy survival!" meant so much more to him than just a current fashion of greeting old friends in the first hazy days of peace. It went deep to his heart. He had come out of the war with five inestimable blessings—his head, his wife Maria's head and the heads of three out of their four children. As a bonus he also had his old bicycle—a miracle too but naturally not to be compared to the safety of five human heads.

The bicycle had a little history of its own. One day at the height of the war it was commandeered "for urgent military action." Hard as its loss would have been to him he would still have let it go without a thought had he not had some doubts about the genuineness of the officer. It wasn't his **disreputable** rags, nor the toes peeping out of one blue and one brown canvas shoe, nor yet the two stars of his rank done obviously in a hurry in biro,[1] that troubled Jonathan; many good and heroic soldiers looked the same or worse. It was rather a certain lack of grip and firmness in his manner. So Jonathan, suspecting he might be **amenable** to influence, rummaged in his raffia bag and produced the two pounds with which he had been going to buy firewood which his wife, Maria, retailed to camp officials for extra stock-fish and corn meal, and got his bicycle back. That night he buried it in the little clearing in the bush where the dead of the camp, including his own youngest son, were buried. When he dug it up again a year later after the surrender all it needed was a little palm-oil greasing. "Nothing puzzles God," he said in wonder.

◀ **Vocabulary**
disreputable (dis rep´ yo͞o tə bəl) *adj.* not respectable; having or deserving a bad reputation

amenable (ə mē´ nə bəl) *adj.* responsive; open

He put it to immediate use as a taxi and accumulated a small pile of Biafran[2] money ferrying camp officials and their families across the four-mile stretch to the nearest tarred road. His standard charge per trip was six pounds and those who had the money were only glad to be rid of some of it in this way. At the end of a fortnight[3] he had made a small fortune of one hundred and fifteen pounds.

Theme
What do these stories of Jonathan's "blessings" have in common?

Then he made the journey to Enugu and found another miracle waiting for him. It was unbelievable. He rubbed his eyes and looked again and it was still standing there before him. But, needless to say, even that monumental blessing must be accounted also totally inferior to the five heads in the family. This newest miracle was his little house in Ogui Overside. Indeed nothing puzzles God! Only two houses away a huge concrete edifice some wealthy contractor had put up just before the war was a mountain of rubble. And here was Jonathan's little zinc house of no regrets built with mud blocks quite intact! Of course the doors and windows were missing and five sheets off the roof. But what was that? And anyhow he had returned to Enugu early enough to pick up bits of old zinc and wood and soggy sheets of cardboard lying around the neighborhood before thousands more came out of their forest holes looking for

Comprehension
What are the five blessings for which Jonathan is grateful?

1. **biro** (bī´ rō) *n.* British expression for "ballpoint pen."
2. **Biafran** (bē äf´ rən) *adj.* of the rebellious southeastern region of Nigeria, which declared itself the independent Republic of Biafra in the civil war of 1967.
3. **fortnight** (fôrt´ nīt´) *n.* British English for "two weeks."

Vocabulary ▶
destitute (des′ tə to͞ot′) *adj.* lacking the basic necessities of life; poverty-stricken

▼ Critical Viewing
Does the expression on this man's face suggest he has a personality similar to Jonathan's? Explain.

the same things. He got a **destitute** carpenter with one old hammer, a blunt plane and a few bent and rusty nails in his tool bag to turn this assortment of wood, paper and metal into door and window shutters for five Nigerian shillings or fifty Biafran pounds. He paid the pounds, and moved in with his overjoyed family carrying five heads on their shoulders.

His children picked mangoes near the military cemetery and sold them to soldiers' wives for a few pennies—real pennies this time—and his wife started making breakfast akara balls[4] for neighbors in a hurry to start life again. With his family earnings he took his bicycle to the villages around and bought fresh palm-wine which he mixed generously in his rooms with the water which had recently started running again in the public tap down the road, and opened up a bar for soldiers and other lucky people with good money.

At first he went daily, then every other day and finally once a week, to the offices of the Coal Corporation where he used to be a miner, to find out what was what. The only thing he did find out in the end was that that little house of his was even a greater blessing than he had thought. Some of his fellow ex-miners who had nowhere to return at the end of the day's waiting just slept outside the doors of the offices and cooked what meal they could scrounge together in Bournvita tins. As the weeks lengthened and still nobody could say what was what Jonathan discontinued his weekly visits altogether and faced his palm-wine bar.

But nothing puzzles God. Came the day of the windfall when

4. **akara** (ə kär′ ə) **balls** *n.* deep-fried balls of ground beans.

after five days of endless scuffles in queues[5] and counterqueues in the sun outside the Treasury he had twenty pounds counted into his palms as ex-gratia[6] award for the rebel money he had turned in. It was like Christmas for him and for many others like him when the payments began. They called it (since few could manage its proper official name) *egg-rasher.*

As soon as the pound notes were placed in his palm Jonathan simply closed it tight over them and buried fist and money inside his trouser pocket. He had to be extra careful because he had seen a man a couple of days earlier collapse into near-madness in an instant before that oceanic crowd because no sooner had he got his twenty pounds than some heartless ruffian picked it off him. Though it was not right that a man in such an extremity of agony should be blamed yet many in the queues that day were able to remark quietly at the victim's carelessness, especially after he pulled out the innards of his pocket and revealed a hole in it big enough to pass a thief's head. But of course he had insisted that the money had been in the other pocket, pulling it out too to show

Draw Conclusions What conclusion can you draw about Jonathan's attitude toward good and bad events? Explain.

Comprehension What does Jonathan get in exchange for the rebel money he has saved?

5. **queues** (kyo͞oz) *n.* British English for "lines."
6. **ex-gratia** (eks grā´ shē ə) as a favor (Latin).

LITERATURE IN CONTEXT

Geography Connection

Nigerian Civil War

Jonathan is delighted that his home in Enugu still stands—and for good reason. Enugu was at the center of the civil war that broke out in Nigeria in 1967. The war began when the eastern region of Nigeria declared itself the independent Republic of Biafra, with Enugu as its capital. The city was invaded by Nigerian federal troops just five months after independence. The war resulted in horrific famine as well as violence. It ended in 1970 with the defeat of Biafra and the reunification of Nigeria.

Connect to the Literature

Which of Jonathan's experiences can you connect to events of the Nigerian Civil War? Explain.

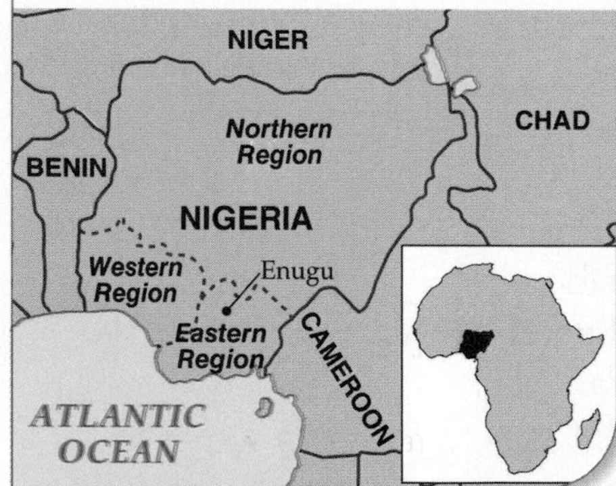

its comparative wholeness. So one had to be careful.

Jonathan soon transferred the money to his left hand and pocket so as to leave his right free for shaking hands should the need arise, though by fixing his gaze at such an elevation as to miss all approaching human faces he made sure that the need did not arise, until he got home. ●

He was normally a heavy sleeper but that night he heard all the neighborhood noises die down one after another. Even the night watchman who knocked the hour on some metal somewhere in the distance had fallen silent after knocking one o'clock. That must have been the last thought in Jonathan's mind before he was finally carried away himself. He couldn't have been gone for long, though, when he was violently awakened again.

"Who is knocking?" whispered his wife lying beside him on the floor.

"I don't know," he whispered back breathlessly.

The second time the knocking came it was so loud and imperious that the rickety old door could have fallen down.

"Who is knocking?" he asked them, his voice parched and trembling.

"Na tief-man and him people," came the cool reply. "Make you hopen de door."[7] This was followed by the heaviest knocking of all.

Maria was the first to raise the alarm, then he followed and all their children.

"Police-o! Thieves-o! Neighbors-o! Police-o! We are lost! We are dead! Neighbors, are you asleep? Wake up! Police-o!"

This went on for a long time and then stopped suddenly. Perhaps they had scared the thief away. There was total silence. But only for a short while.

"You done finish?" asked the voice outside. "Make we help you small. Oya, everybody!"

"Police-o! Tief-man-so! Neighbors-o! we done loss-o! Police-o! . . ."

There were at least five other voices besides the leader's.

Jonathan and his family were now completely paralyzed by terror. Maria and the children sobbed **inaudibly** like lost souls. Jonathan groaned continuously.

Vocabulary ▶
inaudibly (in ô′ də blē) *adv.* in a way that cannot be heard

The silence that followed the thieves' alarm vibrated horribly. Jonathan all but begged their leader to speak again and be done with it.

7. **"Na tief-man . . . hopen de door"** (dialect) "I am a thief with my accomplices. Open the door."

"My frien," said he at long last, "we don try our best for call dem but I tink say dem all done sleep-o . . . So wetin we go do now? Sometaim you wan call soja? Or you wan make we call dem for you? Soja better pass police. No be so?"

"Na so!" replied his men. Jonathan thought he heard even more voices now than before and groaned heavily. His legs were sagging under him and his throat felt like sandpaper.

"My frien, why you no de talk again. I de ask you say you wan make we call soja?"

"No."

"Awrighto. Now make we talk business. We no be bad tief. We no like for make trouble. Trouble done finish. War done finish and all the katakata wey de for inside. No Civil War again. This time na Civil Peace. No be so?"

"Na so!" answered the horrible chorus.

"What do you want from me? I am a poor man. Everything I had went with this war. Why do you come to me? You know people who have money. We . . ."

"Awright! We know say you no get plenty money. But we sef no get even anini. So derefore make you open dis window and give us one hundred pound and we go commot. Orderwise we de come for inside now to show you guitar-boy like dis . . ."

A volley of automatic fire rang through the sky. Maria and the children began to weep aloud again.

"Ah, missisi de cry again. No need for dat. We done talk say we na good tief. We just take our small money and go nwayorly. No molest. Abi we de molest?"

"At all!" sang the chorus.

"My friends," began Jonathan hoarsely. "I hear what you say and I thank you. If I had one hundred pounds . . ."

"Lookia my frien, no be play we come play for your house. If we make mistake and step for inside you no go like am-o. So derefore . . ."

"To God who made me; if you come inside and find one hundred pounds, take it and shoot me and shoot my wife and children. I swear to God. The only money I have in this life is this twenty-pounds *egg-rasher* they gave me today . . ."

"Ok. Time de go. Make you open dis window and bring the twenty pound. We go manage am like dat."

There were now loud murmurs of **dissent** among the chorus: "Na lie de man de lie; e get plenty money . . . Make we go inside and search properly well . . . Wetin be twenty pound? . . ."

"Shurrup!" rang the leader's voice like a lone shot in the sky and silenced the murmuring at once. "Are you dere? Bring the money quick!"

◀ **Vocabulary**
dissent (di sent′)
n. disagreement; refusal to accept a common opinion

Comprehension
Who are the people at Jonathan's door, and what do they want?

Vocabulary ▶
commiserate
(kə miz′ ər āt′) *v.*
sympathize with or show sorrow for

"I am coming," said Jonathan fumbling in the darkness with the key of the small wooden box he kept by his side on the mat.

At the first sign of light as neighbors and others assembled to **commiserate** with him he was already strapping his five-gallon demijohn[8] to his bicycle carrier and his wife, sweating in the open fire, was turning over akara balls in a wide clay bowl of boiling oil. In the corner his eldest son was rinsing out dregs of yesterday's palm-wine from old beer bottles.

"I count it as nothing," he told his sympathizers, his eyes on the rope he was tying. "What is *egg-rasher*? Did I depend on it last week? Or is it greater than other things that went with the war? I say, let *egg-rasher* perish in the flames! Let it go where everything else has gone. Nothing puzzles God."

Spiral Review
PLOT What pattern from earlier in the story is repeated here, and what role does the phrase "Nothing puzzles God" play in that pattern?

8. **demijohn** (dem′ i jän′) *n.* large glass or earthenware bottle with a wicker cover.

Language Study

Vocabulary The words listed below appear in "Civil Peace." For each sentence, replace the word in italics with its **antonym,** or word of opposite meaning, from the list. Then, explain which version makes more sense.

disreputable **amenable** **destitute** **inaudibly** **dissent**

1. We should not give charity to the most *wealthy*.
2. People go to this bank because it is *respectable*.
3. Ellen is *resistant* to trading bicycles with me because she likes hers.
4. His dog howled *audibly*, and the loud noise scared the cats away.
5. If there is *agreement* about going to the concert, I will buy a ticket.

WORD STUDY

The **Latin prefix *com-*** means "together" or "with." In this story, a character and his neighbors **commiserate**, or feel sorrow together, after he and his family are robbed.

Word Study

Part A Explain how the **Latin prefix *com-*** contributes to the meanings of *compassion, compare,* and *comfort*. Consult a dictionary if necessary.

Part B Use the context of the sentences and what you know about the prefix *com-* to explain your answer to each question.

1. What would happen to an uncooked egg under *compression*?
2. What effect would a *compromise* have on warring factions?

Close Reading Activities 

Literary Analysis

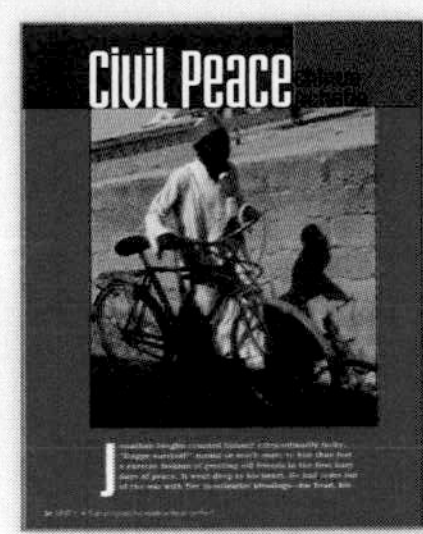

Key Ideas and Details

1. **(a)** What are the "five inestimable blessings" for which Jonathan is grateful? **(b) Infer:** In what sense has the war enhanced Jonathan's appreciation for his life?
2. **(a)** How does Jonathan react to the damage to his house? **(b) Connect:** Considering the situation in his country, does his reaction make sense? Explain your answer, citing details from the story.
3. **Draw Conclusions (a)** Draw a conclusion about the thieves' response to the losses of war based on what they say and do. **(b)** What key details in the story support your conclusion?

Craft and Structure

4. **Theme (a)** Identify the three events in the story that prompt Jonathan to use the expression "Nothing puzzles God." **(b)** Judging from the circumstances of each event, explain what you think Jonathan means by this expression.
5. **Theme (a)** Using a chart like the one shown, analyze three episodes that spark a strong response in Jonathan. **(b)** How are these episodes related? **(c)** What do Jonathan's responses suggest about the story's theme? Explain.

Episode
Jonathan's Response
Reason for the Response

Integration of Knowledge and Ideas

6. **Interpret:** In this story, Achebe makes the philosophical assumption that we must be able to let go of what we have lost in order to survive. If Jonathan had refused to let go, how might he have behaved after the theft? Cite details from the story to support your answer.
7. **(a) Compare and Contrast:** In what ways is the period the thieves call "civil peace" similar to and different from a civil war? **(b) Connect:** Why do you think the author chose the term "Civil Peace" as the story's title? Explain your reasoning, using details from the story.

8. THE BIG ? **Can progress be made without conflict? (a)** How does Jonathan change as he experiences the conflicts in his life? **(b)** Does he undergo these changes because of or in spite of the conflicts he experiences? Explain, citing details from the story.

ACADEMIC VOCABULARY

As you write and speak about "Civil Peace," use the words related to conflict that you explored on page 3 of this text.

Conventions: Degrees of Adjectives and Adverbs

An **adjective** is a word that describes a noun or a pronoun. An **adverb** is a word that modifies a verb, an adjective, or another adverb.

Most adjectives and adverbs have three different forms, called degrees of comparison—the *positive*, the *comparative*, and the *superlative*. Use the positive form when no comparison is involved. Use the comparative to compare two items or groups of items. Use the superlative to compare more than two. For most one-syllable adjectives and adverbs, add *-er* to form the comparative and *-est* to form the superlative. For most longer words, use *more* or *most*. A few adjectives and adverbs, such as *good* and *well,* have irregular comparative and superlative forms.

Comparing with Adjectives			Comparing with Adverbs		
Positive	**Comparative**	**Superlative**	**Positive**	**Comparative**	**Superlative**
brave	braver	bravest	soon	sooner	soonest
alert	more alert	most alert	happily	more happily	most happily
good	better	best	well	better	best

Practice A

In each sentence, underline the adjective or adverb used to compare. State whether it expresses comparative or superlative degree.

1. Of all the survivors, Jonathan was the most grateful.
2. Jonathan had to be more alert than the man whose money was stolen.
3. The most terrifying moment came when thieves knocked on the door, demanding money.
4. Jonathan always believed he was luckier than others.

Reading Application In "Civil Peace," find one example of each degree of comparison and identify the part of speech and degree.

Practice B

Write the comparative and superlative form of each adjective or adverb below.

1. important
2. good
3. unhappily
4. stark

Writing Application Write a brief paragraph about Jonathan's experience. Include one example each of a positive, a comparative, and a superlative adjective or adverb.

Writing to Sources

Explanatory Text The fate of the main character in "Civil Peace" is determined in large part by his personality. Write a brief **character analysis** of Jonathan. In your analysis, identify Jonathan's main character traits, including his strengths and weaknesses.

- First, review the story to analyze the character in detail. Using a two-column chart, list Jonathan's strengths and weaknesses.
- Identify specific examples in the story that demonstrate each trait.
- Consulting your list, select the main ideas you want to convey and the order in which you will express them.
- As you draft, introduce ideas and support them with examples of incidents and descriptions from the story that show Jonathan's traits.
- Use phrases such as *for example* to link supporting details to your main idea. Include transitions such as *instead* to connect ideas.
- End with a conclusion that logically follows from and completes the ideas you developed in the body of your essay.

Grammar Application As you write, use comparative and superlative adjectives and adverbs to show both what Jonathan does and what he is like.

Speaking and Listening

Comprehension and Collaboration Hold a **group discussion** about the theme expressed in Chinua Achebe's story. Work to come to an agreement about the story's deeper meaning and Achebe's likely purpose in writing it. In addition, consider ways in which the theme applies to your life or the lives of people today. To aid the discussion, follow these tips:

- Begin by having each group member offer an interpretation of the story's theme. Then, compare and discuss these ideas.
- Add to others' ideas and support your own viewpoints with details from the story. Include quotations that support your points.
- Express your ideas clearly and without offending others. Allow your position to be challenged and, when appropriate, adjust your ideas in light of strong evidence others present.
- Clarify, illustrate, or verify a response when asked to do so. Ask other students follow-up questions to help members of the group clarify their own positions and make new connections among ideas.

As a group, decide on a single interpretation of the story's theme to share with the class.

Common Core State Standards

Writing

2.a. Introduce a topic; organize complex ideas, concepts, and information to make important connections and distinctions.

2.b. Develop the topic with well-chosen, relevant, and sufficient facts, extended definitions, concrete details, quotations, or other information and examples appropriate to the audience's knowledge of the topic.

2.c. Use appropriate and varied transitions to link the major sections of the text, create cohesion, and clarify the relationships among complex ideas and concepts.

2.f. Provide a concluding statement or section that follows from and supports the information or explanation presented.

Speaking and Listening

1.c. Propel conversations by posing and responding to questions that relate the current discussion to broader themes or larger ideas; actively incorporate others into the discussion; and clarify, verify, or challenge ideas and conclusions.

1.d. Respond thoughtfully to diverse perspectives, summarize points of agreement and disagreement, and, when warranted, qualify or justify their own views and understanding and make new connections in light of the evidence and reasoning presented.

Language

1. Demonstrate command of the conventions of standard English grammar and usage when writing or speaking.

Building Knowledge

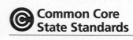

Anton Chekhov (1860–1904) trained as a doctor, but devoted himself to writing. The Russian author once said that a writer is not an entertainer, but "a man who has signed a contract with his conscience and his sense of duty." Some of Chekhov's works show how Russian society trapped people into unproductive lives. Others humorously reveal universal human weaknesses. Today, Chekhov is regarded as one of the greatest modern writers and one of the most important dramatists of all time.

Common Core State Standards

Reading Literature

1. Cite strong and thorough textual evidence to support analysis of what the text says explicitly as well as inferences drawn from the text.

3. Analyze how complex characters develop over the course of a text, interact with other characters, and advance the plot or develop the theme.

Language

4. Determine or clarify the meaning of unknown and multiple-meaning words and phrases based on grades 9–10 reading and content, choosing flexibly from a range of strategies.

Can progress be made without conflict?

Explore the Big Question as you read "A Problem." Take notes on the differing attitudes characters express toward Sasha's problems and his future prospects.

CLOSE READING FOCUS

Key Ideas and Details: **Make Inferences**

An **inference** is a logical assumption a reader makes based on details in a story. Making inferences can help you understand characters' actions and motivations—what they do and why they do it. To make inferences about characters, relate them to your own experience. For example, if a character avoids eye contact, think of people you may know who act this way. You might infer that the character is shy, or that he or she is hiding something.

- As you read, look for ways in which characters and situations in a story seem familiar to your own experiences.
- Think about what your observations suggest about the story's events.

Craft and Structure: **Characters and Characterization**

Characters are the people, animals, or even objects who perform the actions and experience the events of a narrative. Writers use two main types of **characterization** to bring characters to life.

- **Direct Characterization:** Through the narrator, the writer tells readers what a character is like; for example, "Hugo is generous to a fault."
- **Indirect Characterization:** The writer reveals a character's traits through dialogue (the character's words), the character's actions and thoughts, and the interactions between the character and others.

As you read, take note of **character development**—changes a character undergoes in a story.

Vocabulary

You will encounter the following words in this story. Decide whether you know each word well, know it a little bit, or do not know it at all. After you have read the selection, see how your knowledge of each word has increased.

pretense	**candid**	**lofty**
detestable	**subdued**	**edifying**

CLOSE READING MODEL

The passage below is from Anton Chekhov's short story "A Problem." The annotations to the right of the passage show ways in which you can use close reading skills to make inferences and analyze characterization.

from "A Problem"

Sasha Uskov sat at the door and listened. He felt neither terror, shame, nor depression, but only weariness and inward emptiness. It seemed to him that it made absolutely no difference to him whether they forgave him or not;[1] he had come here to hear his sentence and to explain himself simply because kind-hearted Ivan Markovitch had begged him to do so.[2] He was not afraid of the future. It made no difference to him where he was: here in the hall, in prison, or in Siberia.

"If Siberia, then let it be Siberia, damn it all!"[3]

He was sick of life and found it insufferably hard. He was inextricably involved in debt; he had not a farthing in his pocket; his family had become detestable to him; he would have to part from his friends and his women sooner or later, as they had begun to be too contemptuous of his sponging on them.[4] The future looked black.

Make Inferences

1 Sasha feels no "terror, shame" or "depression." Instead, he feels an "inward emptiness" and is unconcerned with forgiveness. You can infer that he has done something wrong but feels no remorse.

Characterization

2 "Kind-hearted" Ivan Markovitch had "begged" Sasha to "explain himself," which tells you that Sasha did not want to do so. These details portray Markovitch as caring and concerned, and Sasha as indifferent to others' feelings.

Make Inferences

3 Sasha's intense reaction to the thought of going to Siberia tells you it must be a bleak place. His angry outburst also suggests that his indifference about his fate may not be real.

Characterization

4 Sasha is "sick of life" and "inextricably involved in debt." He finds his family "detestable," and has abused his friends by "sponging" on them. These details portray Sasha as a troubled, unethical person.

A Problem

ANTON CHEKHOV

•

TRANSLATED BY CONSTANCE GARNETT

The strictest measures were taken that the Uskovs' family secret might not leak out and become generally known. Half of the servants were sent off to the theater or the circus; the other half were sitting in the kitchen and not allowed to leave it. Orders were given that no one was to be admitted. The wife of the Colonel, her sister, and the governess, though they had been initiated into the secret, kept up a **pretense** of knowing nothing; they sat in the dining room and did not show themselves in the drawing room or the hall.

Sasha Uskov, the young man of twenty-five who was the cause of all the commotion, had arrived some time before, and by the advice of kind-hearted Ivan Markovitch, his uncle, who was taking his part, he sat meekly in the hall by the door leading to the study, and prepared himself to make an open, **candid** explanation.

The other side of the door, in the study, a family council was being held. The subject under discussion was an exceedingly disagreeable and delicate one. Sasha Uskov had cashed at one of the banks a false promissory note,[1] and it had become due for payment three days before, and now his two paternal uncles and Ivan Markovitch, the brother of his dead mother, were deciding the question whether they should pay the money and save the family honor, or wash their hands of it and leave the case to go to trial.

To outsiders who have no personal interest in the matter such questions seem simple; for those who are so unfortunate as to have to decide them in earnest they are extremely difficult. The uncles had been talking for a long time, but the problem seemed no nearer decision.

"My friends!" said the uncle who was a colonel, and there was a note of exhaustion and bitterness in his voice. "Who says that family honor is a mere convention? I don't say that at all. I am only warning you against a false view; I am pointing out the possibility of an unpardonable mistake. How can you fail to see it? I am not speaking Chinese; I am speaking Russian!"

"My dear fellow, we do understand," Ivan Markovitch protested mildly.

"How can you understand if you say that I don't believe in family honor? I repeat once more; fa-mil-y ho-nor false-ly un-der-stood is a prejudice! Falsely understood! That's what I say: whatever may be the motives for screening a scoundrel, whoever he may be, and helping him to escape punishment, it is contrary to law and unworthy of a gentleman. It's not saving the family honor; it's civic cowardice! Take the army, for instance. . . . The honor of the army is more precious to us than any other honor, yet we don't screen

◀ Critical Viewing
Based on this painting, what do you expect the mood of the story will be?

◀ Vocabulary
pretense (prē tens´) *n.* a pretending; a false show of something

candid (kan´ did) *adj.* honest; direct

Comprehension
Why is Sasha in trouble?

1. **promissory note** written promise to pay a specified sum on demand; an IOU.

Character and Characterization Contrast the Colonel's position with Ivan Markovitch's. What does this contrast indirectly reveal about the two?

our guilty members, but condemn them. And does the honor of the army suffer in consequence? Quite the opposite!"

The other paternal uncle, an official in the Treasury, a taciturn, dull-witted, and rheumatic man, sat silent, or spoke only of the fact that the Uskovs' name would get into the newspapers if the case went for trial. His opinion was that the case ought to be hushed up from the first and not become public property; but, apart from publicity in the newspapers, he advanced no other argument in support of this opinion.

The maternal uncle, kind-hearted Ivan Markovitch, spoke smoothly, softly, and with a tremor in his voice. He began with saying that youth has its rights and its peculiar temptations. Which of us has not been young, and who has not been led astray? To say nothing of ordinary mortals, even great men have not escaped errors and mistakes in their youth. Take, for instance, the biography of great writers. Did not every one of them gamble, drink, and draw down upon himself the anger of right-thinking people in his young days? If Sasha's error bordered upon crime, they must remember that Sasha had received practically no education; he had been expelled from the high school in the fifth class; he had lost his parents in early childhood, and so had been left at the tenderest age without guidance and good, benevolent influences. He was nervous, excitable, had no firm ground under his feet, and, above all, he had been unlucky. Even if he were guilty, anyway he deserved indulgence[2] and the sympathy of all compassionate souls. He ought, of course, to be punished, but he was punished as it was by his conscience and the agonies he was enduring now while awaiting the sentence of his relations. The comparison with the army made by the Colonel was delightful, and did credit to his **lofty** intelligence; his appeal to their feeling of public duty spoke for the chivalry of his soul, but they must not forget that in each individual the citizen is closely linked with the Christian. . . .

Vocabulary ▶
lofty (lôf′ tē) *adj.* elevated in character; noble

"Shall we be false to civic duty," Ivan Markovitch exclaimed passionately, "if instead of punishing an erring boy we hold out to him a helping hand?"

Ivan Markovitch talked further of family honor. He had not the honor to belong to the Uskov family himself, but he knew their distinguished family went back to the thirteenth century; he did

2. **indulgence** (in dul′ jəns) *n.* forgiveness; tolerance.

not forget for a minute, either, that his precious, beloved sister had been the wife of one of the representatives of that name. In short, the family was dear to him for many reasons, and he refused to admit the idea that, for the sake of a paltry fifteen hundred rubles,[3] a blot should be cast on the escutcheon[4] that was beyond all price. If all the motives he had brought forward were not sufficiently convincing, he, Ivan Markovitch, in conclusion, begged his listeners to ask themselves what was meant by crime? Crime is an immoral act founded upon ill-will. But is the will of man free? Philosophy has not yet given a positive answer to that question. Different views were held by the learned. The latest school of Lombroso,[5] for instance, denies the freedom of the will, and considers every crime as the product of the purely anatomical peculiarities of the individual.

"Ivan Markovitch," said the Colonel, in a voice of entreaty, "we are talking seriously about an important matter, and you bring in Lombroso, you clever fellow. Think a little, what are you saying all this for? Can you imagine that all your thunderings and rhetoric will furnish an answer to the question?"

Sasha Uskov sat at the door and listened. He felt neither terror, shame, nor depression, but only weariness and inward emptiness. It seemed to him that it made absolutely no difference to him whether they forgave him or not; he had come here to hear his sentence and to explain himself simply because kind-hearted Ivan Markovitch had begged him to do so. He was not afraid of the future. It made no difference to him where he was: here in the hall, in prison, or in Siberia.

"If Siberia, then let it be Siberia, damn it all!"

He was sick of life and found it insufferably hard. He was inextricably involved in debt; he had not a farthing[6] in his pocket; his family had become **detestable** to him; he would have to part from his friends and his women sooner or later, as they had begun to be too contemptuous of his sponging on them. The future looked black.

Sasha was indifferent, and was only disturbed by one circumstance; the other side of the door they were calling him a scoundrel and a criminal. Every minute he was on the point of jumping up, bursting into the study and shouting in answer to the detestable metallic voice of the Colonel:

"You are lying!"

Make Inferences
Based on Sasha's thoughts, what can you infer about how mature he is?

◀ Vocabulary
detestable (dē tes´ tə bəl) *adj.* deserving hate or scorn; offensive

Comprehension
What is one reason Ivan Markovitch wants to help Sasha?

---

3. **rubles** (ro͞o´ bəlz) *n.* A ruble is the basic unit of Russian currency.
4. **escutcheon** (e skuch´ ən) *n.* shield displaying a family's coat of arms, symbol of its nobility.
5. **Lombroso** Cesare Lombroso (1835–1909), an Italian criminologist who believed that criminals were of a distinct human type and were led to crime by hereditary, inborn characteristics.
6. **farthing** (fär´ thiŋ) *n.* coin of little value.

Critical Viewing ▶
How is the painting similar to or different from your mental image of the Uskovs' home?

Character and Characterization
How do Sasha's thoughts about himself compare with what you have learned about his character?

"Criminal" is a dreadful word—that is what murderers, thieves, robbers are; in fact, wicked and morally hopeless people. And Sasha was very far from being all that. . . . It was true he owed a great deal and did not pay his debts. But debt is not a crime, and it is unusual for a man not to be in debt. The Colonel and Ivan Markovitch were both in debt. . . .

"What have I done wrong besides?" Sasha wondered.

He had discounted a forged note. But all the young men he knew did the same. Handrikov and Von Burst always forged IOU's from their parents or friends when their allowances were not paid at the regular time, and then when they got their money from home they redeemed them before they became due. Sasha had done the same, but had not redeemed the IOU because he had not got the money which Handrikov had promised to lend him. He was not to blame; it was the fault of circumstances. It was true that the use of another person's signature was considered reprehensible; but, still, it was not a crime but a generally accepted dodge, an ugly formality which injured no one and was quite harmless, for in forging the Colonel's signature Sasha had had no intention of causing anybody damage or loss.

"No, it doesn't mean that I am a criminal . . ." thought Sasha. "And it's not in my character to bring myself to commit a crime. I am soft, emotional. . . . When I have the money I help the poor. . . ."

Sasha was musing after this fashion while they went on talking the other side of the door.

"But, my friends, this is endless," the Colonel declared, getting excited. "Suppose we were to forgive him and pay the money. You know he would not give up leading a dissipated life, squandering money, making debts, going to our tailors and ordering suits in our names! Can you guarantee that this will be his last prank? As far as I am concerned, I have no faith whatever in his reforming!"

The official of the Treasury muttered something in reply; after him Ivan Markovitch began talking blandly and suavely again. The Colonel moved his chair impatiently and drowned the other's words with his detestable metallic voice. At last the door opened and Ivan Markovitch came out of the study; there were patches of red on his cleanshaven face.

"Come along," he said, taking Sasha by the hand. "Come and speak frankly from your heart. Without pride, my dear boy, humbly and from your heart."

Sasha went into the study. The official of the Treasury was sitting down; the Colonel was standing before the table with one hand in his pocket and one knee on a chair. It was smoky and stifling in the study. Sasha did not look at the official or the Colonel; he felt

suddenly ashamed and uncomfortable. He looked uneasily at Ivan Markovitch and muttered:

"I'll pay it . . . I'll give it back. . . ."

"What did you expect when you discounted the IOU?" he heard a metallic voice.

"I . . . Handrikov promised to lend me the money before now."

Spiral Review
PLOT What conflict are readers suddenly aware of in this scene?

Sasha could say no more. He went out of the study and sat down again on the chair near the door. He would have been glad to go away altogether at once, but he was choking with hatred and he awfully wanted to remain, to tear the Colonel to pieces, to say something rude to him. He sat trying to think of something violent and effective to say to his hated uncle, and at that moment a woman's figure, shrouded in the twilight, appeared at the drawing room door. It was the Colonel's wife. She beckoned Sasha to her, and, wringing her hands, said, weeping:

"*Alexandre*, I know you don't like me, but . . . listen to me; listen, I beg you. . . . But, my dear, how can this have happened? Why, it's awful, awful! For goodness' sake, beg them, defend yourself, entreat them."

Character and Characterization
How does the writer reveal without directly stating it that Sasha is not sorry?

Sasha looked at her quivering shoulders, at the big tears that were rolling down her cheeks, heard behind his back the hollow, nervous voices of worried and exhausted people, and shrugged his shoulders. He had not in the least expected that his aristocratic relations would raise such a tempest over a paltry fifteen hundred rubles! He could not understand her tears nor the quiver of their voices.

An hour later he heard that the Colonel was getting the best of it; the uncles were finally inclining to let the case go for trial.

"The matter's settled," said the Colonel, sighing. "Enough."

After this decision all the uncles, even the emphatic Colonel, became noticeably depressed. A silence followed.

"Merciful Heavens!" sighed Ivan Markovitch. "My poor sister!"

Vocabulary ▶
subdued (səb do͞od′)
adj. quiet; lacking energy

And he began saying in a **subdued** voice that most likely his sister, Sasha's mother, was present unseen in the study at that moment. He felt in his soul how the unhappy, saintly woman was weeping, grieving, and begging for her boy. For the sake of her peace beyond the grave, they ought to spare Sasha.

Make Inferences
Based on Ivan's response and your knowledge of families, make an inference about the uncles' feelings for Sasha's mother.

The sound of a muffled sob was heard. Ivan Markovitch was weeping and muttering something which it was impossible to catch through the door. The Colonel got up and paced from corner to corner. The long conversation began over again.

But then the clock in the drawing room struck two. The family council was over. To avoid seeing the person who had moved him to such wrath, the Colonel went from the study, not into the hall, but into the vestibule. . . . Ivan Markovitch came out into the hall. . . . He was agitated and rubbing his hands joyfully. His tear-stained eyes looked good-humored and his mouth was twisted into a smile.

"Capital," he said to Sasha. "Thank God! You can go home, my dear, and sleep tranquilly. We have decided to pay the sum, but on condition that you repent and come with me tomorrow into the country and set to work."

A minute later Ivan Markovitch and Sasha in their greatcoats and caps were going down the stairs. The uncle was muttering something **edifying**. Sasha did not listen, but felt as though some uneasy weight were gradually slipping off his shoulders. They had forgiven him; he was free! A gust of joy sprang up within him and sent a sweet chill to his heart. He longed to breathe, to move swiftly, to live! Glancing at the street lamps and the black sky, he remembered that Von Burst was celebrating his name day[7] that evening at the "Bear," and again a rush of joy flooded his soul. . . .

◀ **Vocabulary**
edifying (ed´ i fī´ iŋ) *adj.* instructive in such a way as to improve morally or intellectually

They had forgiven him; he was free! A gust of joy sprang up within him and sent a sweet chill to his heart. He longed to breathe, to move swiftly, to live!

"I am going!" he decided.

But then he remembered he had not a farthing, that the companions he was going to would despise him at once for his empty pockets. He must get hold of some money, come what may!

"Uncle, lend me a hundred rubles," he said to Ivan Markovitch.

His uncle, surprised, looked into his face and backed against a lamppost.

"Give it to me," said Sasha, shifting impatiently from one foot to the other and beginning to pant. "Uncle, I entreat you, give me a hundred rubles."

Comprehension
What decision do the uncles come to regarding Sasha?

7. **name day** feast day of the saint after whom a person is named.

His face worked; he trembled, and seemed on the point of attacking his uncle. . . .

"Won't you?" he kept asking, seeing that his uncle was still amazed and did not understand. "Listen. If you don't, I'll give myself up tomorrow! I won't let you pay the IOU! I'll present another false note tomorrow!"

Petrified, muttering something incoherent in his horror, Ivan Markovitch took a hundred-ruble note out of his pocketbook and gave it to Sasha. The young man took it and walked rapidly away from him. . . .

Character and Characterization
In what way does Sasha's character develop at the end of the story?

Taking a sledge, Sasha grew calmer, and felt a rush of joy within him again. The "rights of youth" of which kind-hearted Ivan Markovitch had spoken at the family council woke up and asserted themselves. Sasha pictured the drinking party before him, and, among the bottles, the women, and his friends, the thought flashed through his mind:

"Now I see that I am a criminal; yes, I am a criminal."

Language Study

Vocabulary The words listed below appear in "A Problem." Answer each question that follows. Then, explain how the meaning of the underlined word influences your answer.

candid **subdued** **pretense** **lofty** **edifying**

1. Why might you expect a candid answer from a good friend?
2. When might it be a good idea to keep your conversation subdued?
3. Is someone who displays a pretense of wealth actually rich?
4. What lofty goals might an aspiring leader have?
5. When might a child expect an edifying speech from an adult?

WORD STUDY
The **Latin suffix *-able*** means "worthy of; capable of being." In this story, Sasha finds the Colonel's voice **detestable**, or worthy of being hated.

Word Study

Part A Explain how the **Latin suffix *-able*** contributes to the meanings of these words: *admirable, calculable,* and *negotiable*. Consult a dictionary if necessary.

Part B Use the context of the sentences and what you know about the Latin suffix *-able* to explain your answer to each question.

1. If you have a *curable* disease, is it likely that you will eventually feel better?
2. When an athlete makes a *remarkable* play, do spectators usually cheer?

Close Reading Activities

Literary Analysis

Key Ideas and Details

1. **(a)** Why is Sasha in trouble? **(b) Compare and Contrast:** Use details from the story to compare or contrast the position each uncle takes toward Sasha's problem.
2. **Make Inferences** How does Sasha feel about having been caught doing wrong? On which story details is your inference based?
3. **Make Inferences (a)** How does Sasha see himself at the end of the story? **(b)** How does he arrive at this perception? Support your answer with story details.

Craft and Structure

4. **Characterization** Citing details from the story, compare and contrast the characters of Ivan Markovitch and the Colonel.
5. **Characterization (a)** Using a chart like the one shown, cite three examples of indirect characterization used to portray Sasha. Choose one from the beginning, one from the middle, and one from the end of the story. **(b)** With what aspects of life is Sasha primarily concerned? Explain. **(c)** In what ways, if any, does the character of Sasha develop over the course of the story? Explain.
6. **Characterization (a)** Cite two examples of dialogue from Sasha and two from Ivan. **(b)** What does each example reveal about the two characters' differences? Explain.

What He Says
What He Does
What Others Say About Him

Integration of Knowledge and Ideas

7. **Draw Conclusions:** What can you conclude about the view of human nature portrayed in this story? Support your answer with details about the characters of Sasha, the Colonel, and Ivan Markovitch.
8. **(a) Evaluate:** Does Ivan Markovitch's attitude help or harm Sasha? Explain. **(b) Take a Position:** Would it have been better for Sasha if the family had chosen to send him to prison? Explain your response.

9. THE BIG ? **Can progress be made without conflict? (a)** In his support for Sasha, how does Ivan Markovitch define progress? Explain. **(b)** Did Ivan Markovitch make progress with the other uncles in his fight for Sasha? Why or why not? **(c)** Explain why Sasha did or did not learn his lesson after being given a second chance. Cite text evidence to support your answer.

ACADEMIC VOCABULARY

As you write and speak about "A Problem," use the words related to conflict that you explored on page 3 of this textbook.

Close Reading Activities Continued

Conventions: Verb Tenses

A **verb** is a word that expresses existence, action, or occurrence. A **tense** is a form of a verb that indicates when an action or a condition occurs in time. All verbs have six basic tenses: present, past, future, present perfect, past perfect, and future perfect.

Six Basic Verb Tenses			
Present	He *arrives* today.	**Present Perfect**	He *has arrived* already.
Past	He *arrived* yesterday.	**Past Perfect**	He *had arrived* earlier than expected.
Future	He *will arrive* tomorrow.	**Future Perfect**	He *will have arrived* by next week.

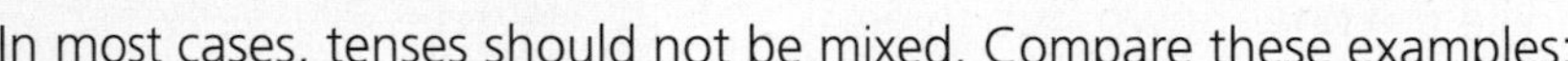

In most cases, tenses should not be mixed. Compare these examples:

Mixed Tenses: Kei *has knocked* and *waited* patiently at the door. Nothing *happens*. Kei *had decided* to leave.

Consistent Tense: Kei *knocked* and *waited* patiently at the door. Nothing *happened*. Kei *decided* to leave.

Mixing tenses is correct only when a sentence refers to actions occurring at two different times: Kei *had waited* for ten minutes before the door *opened*.

Practice A

Revise the sentences to correct mixed tenses.

1. Until Sasha's friends complained, he will live a quiet, uneventful life.
2. In the past, Sasha sponged money from friends who start to get angry.
3. After the uncles make their decision, Sasha will have felt better.
4. Sasha's uncles have gone easy on him and he returned to his old ways.

Reading Application Find two sentences in "A Problem" that contain correct use of mixed tenses. For each sentence, write down the verbs, and identify the tense each one represents.

Practice B

State whether the use of mixed tenses in the following sentences is correct. If incorrect, revise the sentence.

1. After he decides to go to the party, Sasha had demanded money from his uncle.
2. Sasha avoided punishment when Ivan Markovitch defends him to the others.
3. Sasha had escaped punishment before his uncles learned the truth.
4. As Ivan Markovitch pleaded for Sasha, the Colonel will change his mind.

Writing Application Write down three reasons why the Colonel thought Sasha should be punished. Use verb tenses correctly.

Writing to Sources

Narrative Write two brief **retellings** of "A Problem." First, retell the story from the point of view of the Colonel and then from the point of view of Ivan Markovitch.

- List the story's main events, and plan the order in which you will retell them. Aim for a smooth progression that flows logically.
- Identify details that highlight specific ways in which each character sees Sasha's behavior, his effects on others, and his prospects for the future. Incorporate these distinctions into each retelling.
- Review the story for dialogue, descriptions, and other elements that help to convey characters' attitudes and emotions. Consider how the Colonel and Ivan Markovitch may have interpreted what they heard and saw in different ways. Incorporate those elements into each retelling.
- Write each retelling in the first-person point of view. Use the pronoun *I* and relate events from the perspective of the character telling the story.
- When you have completed a first draft, evaluate your use of language and replace any weak or vague words with more precise or vivid choices.

Grammar Application Review your use of verbs to ensure that you have not incorrectly mixed tenses.

Research and Technology

Build and Present Knowledge Write a **report on sources** for a research project about nineteenth-century Russian society. Use the following question to focus your research: How might Sasha's place in Russian society have affected his behavior and expectations? Follow these steps to complete the assignment:

- Find three to four sources of varied types, including books, online material, and videos or other media.
- Evaluate the reliability of each source. Consider the date it was published, the author's credentials, and its accuracy.
- Write a summary of your findings, including a reason for or against using each source. Refer to a style manual to make sure you cite publication information for each source correctly.
- Then, write a preliminary answer to the focus question. List further research steps you would take to more fully answer the question.
- Present your summary and citations, preliminary answer to the focus question, and plan for further research in a slide presentation, poster, or essay form.

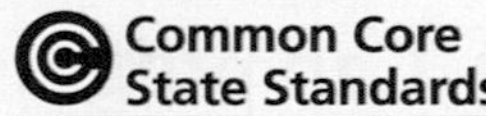

Writing

3.a. Engage and orient the reader by setting out a problem, situation, or observation, establishing one or multiple point(s) of view, and introducing a narrator and/or characters; create a smooth progression of experiences or events.

3.b. Use narrative techniques, such as dialogue, pacing, description, reflection, and multiple plot lines, to develop experiences, events, and/or characters.

3.d. Use precise words and phrases, telling details, and sensory language to convey a vivid picture of the experiences, events, setting, and/or characters.

8. Gather relevant information from multiple authoritative print and digital sources; assess the usefulness of each source in answering the research question; integrate information into the text selectively to maintain the flow of ideas, avoiding plagiarism and following a standard format for citation.

Language

1. Demonstrate command of the conventions of standard English grammar and usage when writing or speaking.

Comparing Texts

Can progress be made without conflict?

Explore the Big Question as you read these stories. Take notes about the ways in which each story portrays conflict. Then, compare and contrast how the conflict in each story affects the characters.

READING TO COMPARE IRONY AND PARADOX

Authors R. K. Narayan and Saki both use irony and paradox in their work. As you read each story, consider how each writer employs these literary devices to explore ideas about honesty and deceit. After you have read both stories, compare the roles that irony and paradox play in each one.

SHORT STORY

SHORT STORY

"Like the Sun"

R. K. Narayan (1906–2001)
Indian author R. K. Narayan was a native Tamil speaker but wrote in English, becoming one of his country's most celebrated authors. In addition to novels and short stories, he wrote a memoir, *My Days*, and English translations of the ancient Sanskrit epics the *Ramayana* and the *Mahabharata*. Many of the ideas for his stories were inspired by different elements of his own life.

"The Open Window"

Saki (1870–1916)
Saki is the pen name of Hector Hugh Munro. Born to British parents in Burma (also known as Myanmar), Saki lived in England for most of his life. He began his career writing political satires for newspapers and later turned to fiction. Today, Saki is best known for his witty, sometimes cruel, short stories, many of which feature humorous surprise endings.

Comparing Irony and Paradox

Irony is the effect created when a writer sets up contrasts between readers' or characters' expectations and reality. Irony may involve a discrepancy between appearance and reality, between expectation and outcome, or between stated meaning and intended meaning. A writer's use of irony often adds emotional intensity to a story or creates a sense of surprise when readers learn that a situation or a character has a different truth.

There are three main types of irony:

- In **situational irony,** an event directly contradicts strong expectations. *Example: In a story in which two companions hide from an enemy, one of the two turns out to be an enemy operative.*
- In **verbal irony,** a character says the opposite of what he or she really means.
  Example: After the enemy operative gives up his companion, the one betrayed says, "I'm glad I trusted you."
- In **dramatic irony,** the reader knows something a character does not. *Example: During the whole story, readers know that the operative is actually a long-lost brother of the one he betrays—but neither character is aware of this.*

In addition to irony, writers may use **paradox**—a statement that seems contradictory but actually reveals a deeper truth. For example, consider the following statement: "One must sometimes be cruel to be kind." At first, the statement seems impossible—how can cruelty be kind? However, the statement makes sense when you consider that seemingly unkind words or actions can actually help someone face a painful truth or develop stronger skills.

In "Like the Sun" and "The Open Window," the writers use irony and paradox to explore contradictory ideas of honesty and deceit. As you read, use a diagram like the one shown to note examples of irony and paradox in these stories.

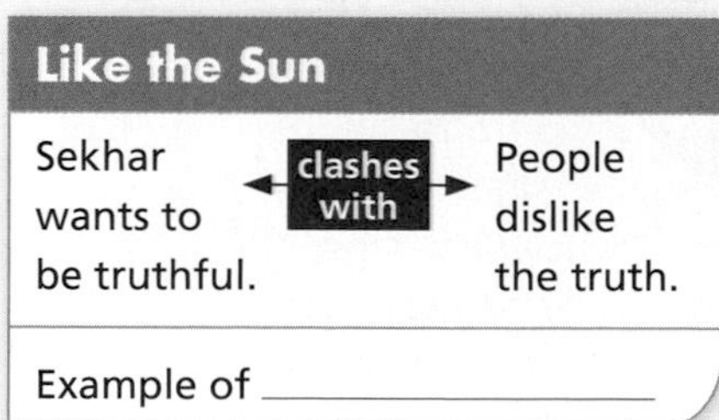

Like the Sun
Sekhar wants to be truthful.
clashes with
People dislike the truth.
Example of ______________

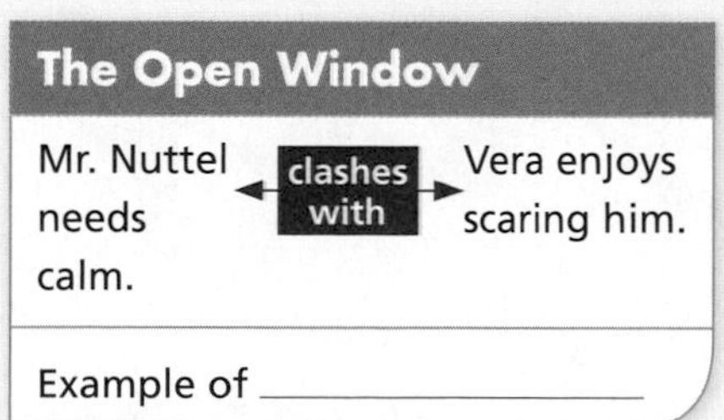

The Open Window
Mr. Nuttel needs calm.
clashes with
Vera enjoys scaring him.
Example of ______________

Common Core State Standards

Reading Literature

5. Analyze how an author's choices concerning how to structure a text, order events within it, and manipulate time create such effects as mystery, tension, or surprise.

Writing

2. Write informative/explanatory texts to examine and convey complex ideas, concepts, and information clearly and accurately through the effective selection, organization, and analysis of content.

2.b. Develop the topic with well-chosen, relevant, and sufficient facts, extended definitions, concrete details, quotations, or other information and examples appropriate to the audience's knowledge of the topic.

10. Write routinely over extended time frames and shorter time frames for a range of tasks, purposes, and audiences.

Like the Sun

R. K. Narayan

Truth, Sekhar reflected, is like the sun. I suppose no human being can ever look it straight in the face without blinking or being dazed.

He realized that, morning till night, the essence of human relationships consisted in tempering truth so that it might not shock. This day he set apart as a unique day—at least one day in the year we must give and take absolute Truth whatever may happen. Otherwise life is not worth living. The day ahead seemed to him full of possibilities. He told no one of his experiment. It was a quiet resolve, a secret pact between him and eternity.

◀ **Vocabulary**
tempering (tem´ pər iŋ) *n.* changing to make more suitable, usually by mixing with something

The very first test came while his wife served him his morning meal. He showed hesitation over a tidbit, which she had thought was her culinary masterpiece. She asked, "Why, isn't it good?" At other times he would have said, considering her feelings in the matter, "I feel full up, that's all." But today he said, "It isn't good. I'm unable to swallow it." He saw her wince and said to himself, Can't be helped. Truth is like the sun.

Spiral Review
THEME Based on the first two paragraphs, what thematic ideas do you think the author is developing? Explain.

His next trial was in the common room when one of his colleagues came up and said, "Did you hear of the death of so-and-so? Don't you think it a pity?" "No," Sekhar answered. "He was such a fine man—" the other began. But Sekhar cut him short with: "Far from it. He always struck me as a mean and selfish brute."

During the last period when he was teaching geography for Third Form A,[1] Sekhar received a note from the headmaster: "Please see me before you go home." Sekhar said to himself: It must be about these horrible test papers. A hundred papers in the boys' scrawls; he had shirked this work for weeks, feeling all the time as if a sword were hanging over his head.

The bell rang and the boys burst out of the class.

Sekhar paused for a moment outside the headmaster's room to button up his coat; that was another subject the headmaster always sermonized about.

He stepped in with a very polite "Good evening, sir."

The headmaster looked up at him in a very friendly manner and asked, "Are you free this evening?"

Sekhar replied, "Just some outing which I have promised the children at home—"

"Well, you can take them out another day. Come home with me now."

"Oh . . . yes, sir, certainly. . ." And then he added timidly, "Anything special, sir?"

"Yes," replied the headmaster, smiling to himself. . . ."You didn't know my weakness for music?"

"Oh, yes, sir. . ."

"I've been learning and practicing secretly, and now I want you to hear me this evening. I've engaged a drummer and a violinist to accompany me—this is the first time I'm doing it full-dress and I want your opinion. I know it will be valuable."

Irony and Paradox Is the headmaster's request for Sehkar's feedback an example of irony? Why or why not?

Sekhar's taste in music was well known. He was one of the most dreaded music critics in the town. But he never anticipated his musical inclinations would lead him to this trial. . . . "Rather a surprise for you, isn't it?" asked the headmaster. "I've spent a fortune on it behind closed doors. . . ." They started for the headmaster's house. "God hasn't given me a child, but at least let him not deny me the consolation of music," the headmaster said, pathetically, as they walked. He incessantly chattered about music: how he began one day out of sheer boredom; how his teacher at first laughed at him, and then gave him hope; how his ambition in life was to forget himself in music.

Vocabulary ▶
ingratiating (in grā′ shē āt′ iŋ) *adj.* acting in a way intended to win someone's favor

At home the headmaster proved very **ingratiating**. He sat Sekhar on a red silk carpet, set before him several dishes of delicacies, and fussed over him as if he were a son-in-law of the house. He even

1. **Third Form A** in British-style schools, an advanced class roughly equivalent to eighth grade in the United States school system.

said, “Well, you must listen with a free mind. Don’t worry about these test papers.” He added half humorously, “I will give you a week’s time.”

“Make it ten days, sir,” Sekhar pleaded.

“All right, granted,” the headmaster said generously. Sekhar felt really relieved now—he would attack them at the rate of ten a day and get rid of the nuisance.

The headmaster lighted incense sticks. “Just to create the right atmosphere,” he explained. A drummer and a violinist, already seated on a Rangoon mat, were waiting for him. The headmaster sat down between them like a professional at a concert, cleared his throat and began an alapana[2], and paused to ask, “Isn’t it good Kalyani[3]?” Sekhar pretended not to have heard the question. The headmaster went on to sing a full song composed by Thyagaraja[4] and followed it with two more. All the time the headmaster was singing, Sekhar went on commenting within himself, He croaks like a dozen frogs. He is bellowing like a buffalo. Now he sounds like loose window shutters in a storm.

The incense sticks burnt low. Sekhar’s head throbbed with the medley of sounds that had assailed his eardrums for a couple of hours now. He felt half stupefied. The headmaster had gone nearly hoarse, when he paused to ask, “Shall I go on?” Sekhar replied, “Please don’t, sir; I think this will do. . . .” The headmaster looked stunned. His face was beaded with perspiration. Sekhar felt the greatest pity for him. But he felt he could not help it. No judge delivering a sentence felt more pained and helpless. Sekhar noticed that the headmaster’s wife peeped in from the kitchen, with eager curiosity. The drummer and the violinist put away their burdens with an air of relief. The headmaster removed his spectacles, mopped his brow, and asked, “Now, come out with your opinion.”

“Can’t I give it tomorrow, sir?” Sekhar asked tentatively.

“No. I want it immediately—your frank opinion. Was it good?”

“No, sir. . . .” Sekhar replied.

“Oh! . . . Is there any use continuing my lessons?”

“Absolutely none, sir. . . .” Sekhar said with his voice trembling. He felt very unhappy that he could not speak more soothingly. Truth, he reflected, required as much strength to give as to receive. All the way home he felt worried. He felt that his official life was not going to be smooth sailing hereafter. There were questions of increment

▲ Critical Viewing
What can you conclude about the sitar (si tär′), a traditional Indian instrument, based on this image? Explain.

Comprehension
What does the headmaster request that Sekhar do that evening?

2. **alapana** (äl ä′ pä nä) in classical Indian music, an improvisational exploration of a melody, without a defined beat, and intended to showcase the talent of a singer.
3. **Kalyani** (käl yä′ nē) traditional Indian folk songs.
4. **Thyagaraja** (tē ä′ gä rä′ jä) (1767–1847) revered composer of Indian devotional songs.

and confirmation[5] and so on, all depending upon the headmaster's goodwill. All kinds of worries seemed to be in store for him. . . . Did not Harishchandra[6] lose his throne, wife, child, because he would speak nothing less than the absolute Truth whatever happened?

At home his wife served him with a sullen face. He knew she was still angry with him for his remark of the morning. Two casualties for today, Sekhar said to himself. If I practice it for a week, I don't think I shall have a single friend left.

He received a call from the headmaster in his classroom next day. He went up apprehensively.

"Your suggestion was useful. I have paid off the music master. No one would tell me the truth about my music all these days. Why such antics at my age! Thank you. By the way, what about those test papers?"

Irony and Paradox
How does Sekhar's experience contradict the idea that "honesty is the best policy"?

"You gave me ten days, sir, for correcting them."

"Oh, I've reconsidered it. I must positively have them here tomorrow. . . ." A hundred papers in a day! That meant all night's sitting up! "Give me a couple of days, sir. . . ."

"No. I must have them tomorrow morning. And remember, every paper must be thoroughly **scrutinized**."

Vocabulary ▶ scrutinized
(skro͞ot´ 'n īzd)
v. examined carefully

"Yes, sir," Sekhar said, feeling that sitting up all night with a hundred test papers was a small price to pay for the luxury of practicing Truth.

5. **increment and confirmation** salary increase and job security.
6. **Harishchandra** (he rish chen´ dra) legendary Hindu king who was the subject of many Indian stories. His name has come to symbolize truth and integrity.

Critical Thinking

1. **Key Ideas and Details: (a)** What experiment does Sekhar plan at the beginning of the story? **(b) Connect:** What conflict does this create for him?
2. **Key Ideas and Details:** Is the headmaster pleased or angry that Sekhar has told him the truth about his music? Explain your inference.
3. **Key Ideas and Details: (a)** Are there any benefits to Sekhar's truth telling? **(b) Support:** Cite story details and logical reasons to support your conclusion.
4. **Integration of Knowledge and Ideas:** Based on the results of Sekhar's experiment, do you think people prefer to avoid conflicts by avoiding truth? Explain. ***[Connect to the Big Question: Can progress be made without conflict?]***

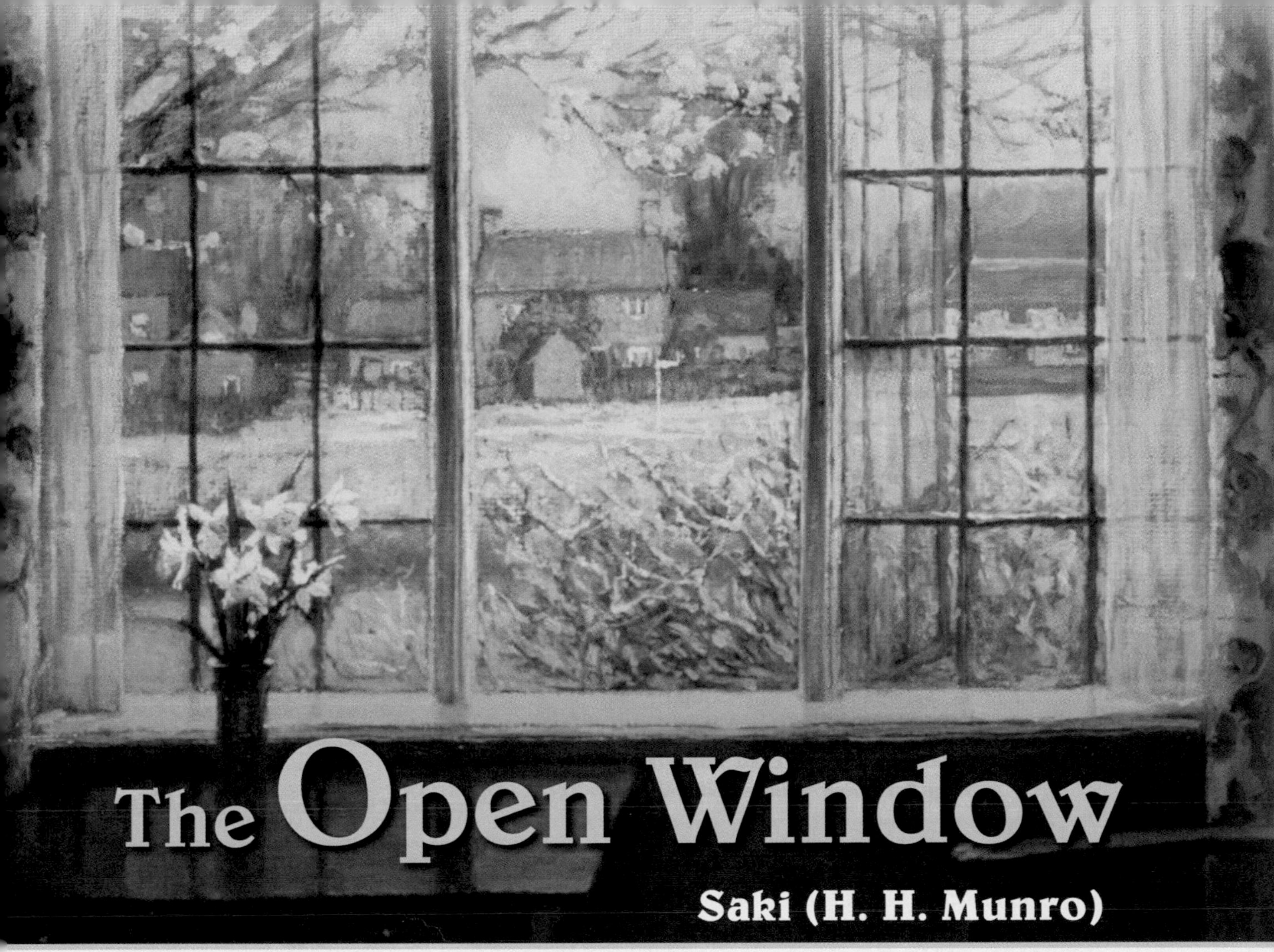

The Open Window

Saki (H. H. Munro)

"My aunt will be down presently, Mr. Nuttel," said a very self-possessed young lady of fifteen; "in the meantime you must try and put up with me."

Framton Nuttel endeavored to say the correct something that should duly flatter the niece of the moment without unduly discounting the aunt that was to come. Privately he doubted more than ever whether these formal visits on a succession of total strangers would do much towards helping the nerve cure which he was supposed to be undergoing.

"I know how it will be," his sister had said when he was preparing to migrate to this rural retreat; "you will bury yourself down there and not speak to a living soul, and your nerves will be worse than ever from moping. I shall just give you letters of introduction[1] to all the people I know there. Some of them, as far as I can remember, were quite nice."

◀ **Vocabulary**
endeavored (en dev´ ərd) *v.* tried to achieve a set goal

1. **letters of introduction** letters introducing two strangers, written by someone who knows them both. The person to whom such a letter is written is obliged to provide hospitality to the person carrying the letter.

Framton wondered whether Mrs. Sappleton, the lady to whom he was presenting one of the letters of introduction, came into the nice division.

"Do you know many of the people round here?" asked the niece, when she judged that they had had sufficient silent communion.

"Hardly a soul," said Framton. "My sister was staying here, at the rectory, you know, some four years ago, and she gave me letters of introduction to some of the people here."

He made the last statement in a tone of distinct regret.

Spiral Review
THEME Why is Vera's question, in which she seeks confirmation of Mr. Nuttel's ignorance, important?

"Then you know practically nothing about my aunt?" pursued the self-possessed young lady.

"Only her name and address," admitted the caller. He was wondering whether Mrs. Sappleton was in the married or widowed state. An undefinable something about the room seemed to suggest masculine habitation.

"Her great tragedy happened just three years ago," said the child; "that would be since your sister's time."

"Her tragedy?" asked Framton; somehow in this restful country spot tragedies seemed out of place.

An undefinable something about the room seemed to suggest masculine habitation.

"You may wonder why we keep that window wide open on an October afternoon," said the niece, indicating a large French window that opened on to a lawn.

"It is quite warm for the time of the year," said Framton; "but has that window got anything to do with the tragedy?"

"Out through that window, three years ago to a day, her husband and her two young brothers went off for their day's shooting. They never came back. In crossing the moor to their favorite snipe-shooting ground[2] they were all three engulfed in a treacherous piece of bog.[3] It had been that dreadful wet summer, you know, and places that were safe in other years gave way suddenly without warning. Their bodies were never recovered. That was the dreadful part of it." Here the child's voice lost its self-possessed note and became **falteringly** human. "Poor aunt always thinks that they will come back some day, they and the little brown spaniel that was lost with them, and walk in at that window just as they used to do. That is why the window is kept open every evening till it is quite

Vocabulary ▶
falteringly (fôl′ tər iŋ lē) *adv.* spoken hesitatingly or with a wavering voice

2. **snipe-shooting ground** area for hunting snipe—wading birds that live chiefly in marshy places and have long, flexible bills.
3. **bog** small swamp; wet, spongy ground.

dusk. Poor dear aunt, she has often told me how they went out, her husband with his white waterproof coat over his arm, and Ronnie, her youngest brother, singing, 'Bertie, why do you bound?' as he always did to tease her, because she said it got on her nerves. Do you know, sometimes on still, quiet evenings like this, I almost get a creepy feeling that they will walk in through that window—"

She broke off with a little shudder. It was a relief to Framton when the aunt bustled into the room with a whirl of apologies for being late in making her appearance.

"I hope Vera has been amusing you?" she said.

"She has been very interesting," said Framton.

"I hope you don't mind the open window," said Mrs. Sappleton briskly; "my husband and brothers will be home directly from shooting, and they always come in this way. They've been out for snipe in the marshes today, so they'll make a fine mess over my poor carpets. So like you menfolk, isn't it?"

She rattled on cheerfully about the shooting and the scarcity of birds, and the prospects for duck in the winter. To Framton, it was all purely horrible. He made a desperate but only partially successful effort to turn the talk on to a less ghastly topic; he was conscious that his hostess was giving him only a fragment of her attention, and her eyes were constantly straying past him to the open window and the lawn beyond. It was certainly an unfortunate coincidence that he should have paid his visit on this tragic anniversary.

Irony and Paradox
What kind of irony is involved when Mrs. Sappleton does not know about the tall tale Vera told Mr. Nuttel?

"The doctors agree in ordering me complete rest, an absence of mental excitement, and avoidance of anything in the nature of violent physical exercise," announced Framton, who labored under the tolerably widespread **delusion** that total strangers and chance acquaintances are hungry for the least detail of one's ailments and infirmities, their cause and cure. "On the matter of diet they are not so much in agreement," he continued.

◀ **Vocabulary**
delusion (di lo͞o′ zhan) *n.* erroneous belief that is held despite evidence to the contrary

"No?" said Mrs. Sappleton, in a voice which only replaced a yawn at the last moment. Then she suddenly brightened into alert attention—but not to what Framton was saying.

"Here they are at last!" she cried. "Just in time for tea, and don't they look as if they were muddy up to the eyes!"

Framton shivered slightly and turned towards the niece with a look intended to convey sympathetic comprehension. The child was staring out through the open window with dazed horror in her eyes. In a chill shock of nameless fear Framton swung round in his seat and looked in the same direction.

Comprehension
What does Vera say is her aunt's great tragedy?

In the deepening twilight three figures were walking across the lawn towards the window; they all carried guns under their arms, and one of them was additionally burdened with a white coat hung over his shoulders. A tired brown spaniel kept close at their heels. Noiselessly they neared the house, and then a hoarse young voice chanted out of the dusk: "I said, Bertie, why do you bound?"

Framton grabbed wildly at his stick and hat; the hall door, the gravel drive, and the front gate were dimly noted stages in his headlong retreat. A cyclist coming along the road had to run into the hedge to avoid imminent collision.

"Here we are, my dear," said the bearer of the white mackintosh,[4] coming in through the window; "fairly muddy, but most of it's dry. Who was that who bolted out as we came up?"

"A most extraordinary man, a Mr. Nuttel," said Mrs. Sappleton; "could only talk about his illnesses, and dashed off without a word of goodbye or apology when you arrived. One would think he had seen a ghost."

"I expect it was the spaniel," said the niece calmly; "he told me he had a horror of dogs. He was once hunted into a cemetery somewhere on the banks of the Ganges[5] by a pack of pariah dogs, and had to spend the night in a newly dug grave with the creatures snarling and grinning and foaming just above him. Enough to make anyone lose their nerve."

Romance at short notice was her specialty.

---

4. **mackintosh** (mak′ in täsh′) *n.* waterproof raincoat.
5. **Ganges** (gan′ jēz) river in northern India and Bangladesh.

Critical Thinking

1. **Key Ideas and Details: (a)** Why is Mr. Nuttel visiting the country? **(b) Interpret:** Why is this detail critical to the story?
2. **Key Ideas and Details: (a)** Why does Vera tell Mr. Nuttel the story about the hunters' deaths? **(b) Connect:** Is it unusual for her to tell such stories? Explain.
3. **Key Ideas and Details:** How are Mr. Nuttel and Vera similar and how are they different? Use details from the story to support your answer.
4. **Integration of Knowledge and Ideas: (a)** What motivates Vera to create conflict where none exists? **(b)** Do you think she is satisfied by the results? **(c)** Does Vera's behavior prevent progress, or does it somehow promote it? Explain, citing details from the story to support your response. ***[Connect to the Big Question: Can progress be made without conflict?]***

Comparing Irony and Paradox

1. **Craft and Structure (a)** Analyze one example of **irony** in each story. For each example, identify and explain the elements that contrast with one another. **(b)** Did you identify situational, verbal, or dramatic irony? Explain.
2. **Craft and Structure** Explain how each story explores a **paradox:** **(a)** "Like the Sun": Telling the truth is a virtue that leads to punishment. **(b)** "The Open Window": The cure for Mr. Nuttel's illness makes him worse.
3. **Craft and Structure** Complete a diagram like this one to show how irony and paradox are used in each story. Consider whether these devices simply add humor or whether they emphasize the impossible dilemmas facing a character.

Like the Sun	The Open Window
Effect of Irony and Paradox:	Effect of Irony and Paradox:

Timed Writing

Explanatory Text: Essay

Both Narayan and Saki use irony or paradox to explore ideas. In an essay, compare and contrast how the authors present the concepts of truth and deception in these stories. Provide evidence from the texts to support your understanding. **(30 minutes)**

5-Minute Planner

1. Read the prompt carefully and completely.
2. Identify a few examples of irony or paradox in each story.
3. Draw a conclusion about the message each writer is expressing about truth, deception, and honesty.
4. Take notes on how the use of irony and paradox helps each writer express his message. Find quotations from the text that you can include to support your ideas.
5. Reread the prompt, and then draft your essay.

USE ACADEMIC VOCABULARY

As you write, use academic language, including the following words or their related forms:

conduct
distortion
integrity
motive

For more information about academic vocabulary, see the Introductory Unit.

Language Study

Using a Dictionary and Thesaurus

A **dictionary** is an alphabetical listing of words. It provides a variety of information about words, including their definitions, parts of speech, etymologies, and more. Notice the information given in this dictionary entry.

Part of Speech · Related Words · Etymology · Definition

> **narrate** (nar′āt; na rāt′, nə-) *vt., vi.* **-rat′ed, -rat′ing** [< L *narratus*, pp. of *narrare*, to tell, akin to *gnarus*, acquainted with < IE **gnoro-* < base **gen-*, to KNOW] **1.** to tell (a story) in writing or speech **2.** to give an account of (happenings, etc.)

In addition to information about the word, a dictionary includes a guide to pronunciation. Most dictionaries provide a key to the symbols at the bottom of the page or in the front of the dictionary.

Dictionaries also provide information about the related forms of words. Related forms are new words created by adding prefixes or suffixes to a base word. For example, the entry above shows that the words *narrated* and *narrating* can be formed by adding suffixes to the word *narrate.*

A **thesaurus** is a reference book that lists synonyms, or words with similar meanings. You can use a thesaurus to increase your vocabulary or to find alternative words to express your meaning. Here is an example of a thesaurus entry:

> **entertainer** *n.* **1.** entertainer, performer, artist, dancer, hoofer **2.** actor, actress, player, thespian, mime, villain, character *v.* entertain, act, perform, dramatize, dance, play

Both dictionaries and thesauruses are available in print, in computer programs, and on the Internet.

Practice A

Look up each word in a thesaurus. For each, write two words that have almost the same meaning.

1. disapproval
2. patience
3. talk
4. repeatedly
5. remember
6. joke

Common Core State Standards

Language

4. Determine or clarify the meaning of unknown and multiple-meaning words and phrases based on grades 9–10 reading and content, choosing flexibly from a range of strategies.

4.b. Identify and correctly use patterns of word changes that indicate different meanings or parts of speech.

4.c. Consult general and specialized reference materials, both print and digital, to find the pronunciation of a word or determine or clarify its precise meaning, its part of speech, or its etymology.

4.d. Verify the preliminary determination of the meaning of a word or phrase.

Practice B

Use a dictionary to answer questions 1–7 and a thesaurus to respond to questions 8 and 9.

1. Some words have more than one dictionary definition. **(a)** What is the definition of *idle* in the following sentence? *Eliot sat idle all afternoon.* **(b)** What is another definition for *idle*?
2. **(a)** What is the adverb form of the word *sleepy*? **(b)** Use the adverb form of the word *sleepy* in a sentence.
3. What is the meaning of the word *cuff* when used as a verb?
4. If a situation is *fraught* with danger, is it safe? Explain.
5. Which dictionary definition is correct for *sorry* as it is used in the following sentence? *In Aunt Sarah's opinion, I was one sorry entertainer.*
6. **(a)** Note two words that are related to the verb *revise*. **(b)** Define each word and identify its part of speech.
7. How many definitions does your dictionary give for the word *frost*?
8. Find three synonyms for *deadly.*
9. Rewrite this sentence twice using synonyms for *genuine*: *The painting turned out to be a genuine Van Gogh.*

Activity Create a notecard like the one shown for each of these words:

allay unkempt linear quandary naive

Word:
Definition:
Pronunciation:
Sentence:

Read your sentences aloud. Then, in a group, trade cards and read one another's sentences. Check one another's pronunciation and usage. Refer to a dictionary if you disagree on the pronunciation or word meaning.

Comprehension and Collaboration

Look up the following words in a dictionary or reliable online source. Find the earliest usage of each word and its definition. Then, locate a more modern definition of each word. Talk with a group about how the meaning of each word has changed over the years. Is the original meaning still used?

- **flaunt**
- **cab**
- **fragile**
- **vandal**

Speaking and Listening

Delivering an Oral Interpretation of a Literary Work

You can share your ideas about a poem—or anything else you read—by delivering an oral interpretation for an audience. To do so, combine a careful analysis of the work with an expressive reading or performance that reveals your understanding and demonstrates your sensitivity to the author's choices.

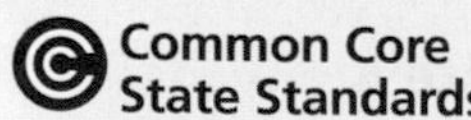

Common Core State Standards

Speaking and Listening

1. Initiate and participate effectively in a range of collaborative discussions with diverse partners on grades 9–10 topics, texts, and issues, building on others' ideas and expressing their own clearly and persuasively.

1.b. Work with peers to set rules for collegial discussions and decision-making, clear goals and deadlines, and individual roles as needed.

6. Adapt speech to a variety of contexts and tasks, demonstrating command of formal English when indicated or appropriate.

Learn the Skills

Use the following strategies to complete the activity on page 93.

Advance a judgment about significant ideas. Clearly state the main ideas expressed in the literary work. Discuss ways in which the author presents and develops those ideas and why they are powerful or important. Present a thesis statement that clearly reflects your interpretation and evaluation of the work.

Support ideas and viewpoints. Your views will carry more weight if you support them with details from the text. Read excerpts from the work to share the writer's style and tone with your audience. Choose sections that illustrate key ideas and are pleasing or powerful when read aloud.

Pose questions. Poets and fiction writers rarely state their themes or central ideas directly. Rather, they suggest meaning through characterization, plot, imagery, figurative language, and details. They may also purposely leave some aspects of a story or poem ambiguous, or unexplained. Introduce some of the unstated themes or complexities of a work by asking a question and then answering it using examples from the works.

Prepare your delivery. Preparation is the key to feeling relaxed in front of an audience. These techniques can help you deliver a confident and effective presentation:

- **Organize your ideas.** Write each key idea on a separate note card. As you rehearse, experiment with the order of the cards. Then, number the cards in the best order.
- **Communicate with your voice.** Speak clearly and comfortably without rushing. Use the tone and pitch of your voice to add variety.
- **Use effective body language.** Your gestures and posture send a signal to your audience. Energetic body language shows that you think your subject is important. Maintain eye contact to keep your audience's attention.

Practice the Skills

Presentation of Knowledge and Ideas Use what you have learned in this workshop to perform the following task.

ACTIVITY: **Deliver an Oral Interpretation**

Select a poem, short story, or piece of nonfiction. Prepare a three-minute presentation in which you interpret this work. Develop your interpretation by answering the following questions:

- How would you summarize your interpretation of the work? What is your thesis or claim?
- Which details from the work most clearly explain and support your interpretation?
- Why are these details powerful and meaningful?
- What questions should your classmates ask themselves about the work?
- What examples from the work help answer those questions?

As your classmates deliver their presentations, listen attentively. Use the Presentation Evaluation Guide below to analyze their presentations.

Presentation Evaluation Guide

Rate each statement on a scale of 1 (not accurate) to 5 (completely accurate). Explain your ratings.

____ The presentation was focused around a clear claim or thesis.
____ The claim was sufficiently supported with details from the text.
____ The presentation analyzed subtleties in the text.
____ The presentation was logically organized.
____ The presenter spoke clearly and expressively.
____ The speaker used a variety of speaking tones and pitches.
____ The speaker used effective gestures and other body language.

What was most effective about this presentation?

____

Comprehension and Collaboration With a group of classmates, discuss which presentations were easiest to follow and why. To keep your conversation focused, set a time limit, and choose roles, such as discussion leader, timekeeper, summarizer, and clarifier. Together, decide what rules you will follow. For example, determine whether listeners may interrupt a speaker to ask questions or whether they should hold questions until the speaker is finished.

Write an Argument

Analytic Response to Literature

Defining the Form An **analytic response to literature** is a form of essay in which a reader presents a critical interpretation of a literary work. The essay may focus on an entire literary work or may zero in on a particular aspect of the work. You might use elements of this type of writing in book reviews, articles, and readers' journals.

Assignment Write an analytic response to a favorite piece of literature. Analyze a poem, a play, a story, or a screenplay. Include these elements:

- ✓ an opening that introduces the topic and contains a *thesis statement* that clearly presents your position on an aspect of the work
- ✓ *references* to specific aspects of the work, such as its theme or style, expressed in literary terms appropriate for the audience
- ✓ well-chosen, relevant *evidence* from the literary work or other texts
- ✓ a formal writing *style* and use of precise literary language
- ✓ consideration of *alternate interpretations* and use of convincing reasons and evidence to support your own
- ✓ logical *organization* that clarifies the relationships among ideas
- ✓ error-free grammar, including *correct pronoun-antecedent agreement and correct subject-verb agreement*
- ✓ a *conclusion* that summarizes the thesis statement and follows logically from the ideas discussed in the body paragraphs

To preview the criteria on which your analytic response to literature may be judged, see the rubric on page 101.

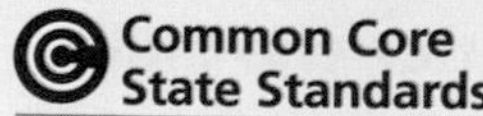

Common Core State Standards

Writing

1. Write arguments to support claims in an analysis of substantive topics or texts, using valid reasoning and relevant and sufficient evidence.

1.a. Introduce precise claim(s), distinguish the claim(s) from alternate or opposing claims, and create an organization that establishes clear relationships among claim(s), counterclaims, reasons, and evidence.

1.b. Develop claim(s) and counterclaims fairly, supplying evidence for each while pointing out the strengths and limitations of both in a manner that anticipates the audience's knowledge level and concerns.

1.c. Use words, phrases, and clauses to link the major sections of the text, create cohesion, and clarify the relationships between claim(s) and reasons, between reasons and evidence, and between claim(s) and counterclaims.

1.d. Establish and maintain a formal style and objective tone while attending to the norms and conventions of the discipline in which they are writing.

1.e. Provide a concluding statement or section that follows from and supports the argument presented.

9. Draw evidence from literary or informational texts to support analysis, reflection, and research.

FOCUS ON RESEARCH

When you write analytic responses to literature, you might perform research to

- learn more about the author of the work and the types of subjects that he or she often explores.
- read critical articles or essays about the work you are analyzing.
- learn more about the historical or cultural background of the work you are analyzing.

Smoothly integrate information from research into your writing, and cite all sources accurately and thoroughly. See the Citing Sources pages in the Introductory Unit of this textbook for additional guidance.

READING-WRITING CONNECTION

For an example of critical writing, read "The American Idea" by Theodore H. White on page 242.

Prewriting/Planning Strategies

Use these strategies to find a topic:

Hold a group discussion. With a small group, discuss the literary works that have provoked strong feelings in you. For each item, briefly describe any memorable details about the work or your experience reading it. Review your ideas and choose one work as your topic.

Ask your own questions. Decide which aspects of the literary work interest you, bother you, or raise questions. For example, the actions or personality of one character may seem ambiguous or confusing. The complexity of the plot and characters may cause you to wonder how each character's actions affect the others or how the actions of a particular character affect the plot. Jot down two or three questions that you hope to answer by writing your analytical response.

Example Questions

- In *Julius Caesar*, why do Antony and Cassius meet different fates?
- Does Sasha learn a lesson in "A Problem"?
- Why does Shakespeare choose to compare his subject's beauty to a summer's day in Sonnet 18?

Consider your audience. Identify your audience and assess their knowledge of your topic. If you need to cover subjects that are unfamiliar to your readers, plan to include details that will help them understand. Use a chart like the one shown to organize your response.

My Topic and Audience

Topic: "Civil Peace" by Chinua Achebe
Audience: classmates
What they know: They are familiar with the story because we read it in class.
What they do not know: They may not be familiar with the social upheavals in Nigeria during Achebe's lifetime.

Go back to the source. Find the information you need by rereading the work and identifying details and examples that relate to your topic. For additional insight, research what critics have said about the work. Write each detail or quotation on a separate index card. Then, organize the cards into general categories.

Consider counterclaims. Rich literary works may be open to a variety of interpretations. Gather information about viewpoints that differ from your own. Develop reasons and evidence to show why these viewpoints are less convincing than yours.

Drafting Strategies

Write a thesis statement that clearly expresses your claim. Review your notes and consider the main point you want to make about the literary work. Write a statement that expresses that point. Include this thesis in your introduction and use it to direct the rest of your essay.

Organize your response. A compelling response to literature can be organized into three parts: the introduction; the body, in which you analyze key elements; and the conclusion, in which you summarize and explain why your ideas are important. Each part of the essay should build on the part that came before, and every point you make should connect directly to your thesis.

Use information from the text in various ways. For every major idea in your essay, provide evidence from the literary work or another relevant source. Consider these options:

- Use **exact quotations** to show a character's personality, a poet's use of imagery, or a writer's style. Identify all quotations clearly and use quotation marks. Use a colon to introduce exact quotations. Check a reliable style manual to make sure you follow proper form for all quotations and citations.
- Use **paraphrases**—your own restatement of ideas—in the text to clarify a conflict, to present a writer's theme, or to include key concepts. Be sure that your paraphrase accurately reflects the original text and that you cite sources for any ideas that are not your own.
- Use **summaries** to provide an overview of a writer's opinion or to explain a series of events.

Using Information From the Text	
Exact Quotation	BRUTUS. Into what dangers would you lead me, Cassius, That you would have me seek into myself For that which is not in me? *(Julius Caesar, Act I, sc. ii, ll. 63–65)*
Paraphrase	What dangerous situation are you leading me into, Cassius, by telling me I have greatness in me when I do not?
Summary	Brutus wonders what dangers Cassius is trying to draw him into through flattery.

Whatever format you use to integrate evidence, use transitional words and phrases to explain the link between the literature and your thesis.

Address alternate viewpoints. Introduce other interpretations of the work. Explain why these alternate viewpoints may be interesting but are ultimately less convincing or useful than yours.

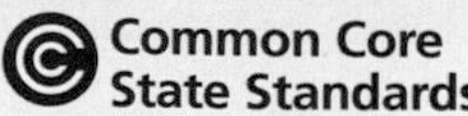

Writing

1. Write arguments to support claims in an analysis of substantive topics or texts, using valid reasoning and relevant and sufficient evidence.

1.a. Introduce precise claim(s), distinguish the claim(s) from alternate or opposing claims, and create an organization that establishes clear relationships among claim(s), counterclaims, reasons, and evidence.

1.b. Develop claim(s) and counterclaims fairly, supplying evidence for each while pointing out the strengths and limitations of both in a manner that anticipates the audience's knowledge level and concerns.

1.c. Use words, phrases, and clauses to link the major sections of the text, create cohesion, and clarify the relationships between claim(s) and reasons, between reasons and evidence, and between claim(s) and counterclaims.

1.e Provide a concluding statement or section that follows from and supports the argument presented.

9. Draw evidence from literary or informational texts to support analysis, reflection, and research.

Language

2.b. Use a colon to introduce a list or quotation.

3.a. Write and edit work so that it conforms to the guidelines in a style manual.

Pronoun-Antecedent Agreement

Antecedents are the nouns or other pronouns for which pronouns stand. A pronoun must agree with its antecedent in number, person, and gender.

Identifying Incorrect Pronoun-Antecedent Agreement In your writing, check each pronoun to make sure it agrees with its antecedent. Ask three things about the antecedent:

- *Number:* Is it singular or plural?
- *Person:* Is it first person (the one speaking), second person (the one being spoken to), or third person (the one spoken about)?
- *Gender:* Is it masculine, feminine, or neuter?

In the example sentences shown below, the antecedents are underlined with a single rule and the pronouns are underlined with a double rule.

Examples: Pronoun-Antecedent Agreement
Marie Curie is known for her work with radium.
My father and I saw the experiment. We were amazed.
The experiment was important. It contributed greatly to science.

Special Problems With Agreement Use a plural pronoun for a compound antecedent joined by *and*.

Lewis and Clark described the expedition in their journal.

Use a singular pronoun for a compound antecedent in which singular words are joined by *or* or *nor*.

Neither Lewis nor Clark regretted his journey.

Fixing Agreement Errors To fix a pronoun and antecedent that do not agree, choose the pronoun that has the correct number, person, and gender.

1. Describe the number, person, and gender of the antecedent.
2. Choose a pronoun with the same number, person, and gender.

Grammar in Your Writing

Circle the pronouns in two paragraphs of your draft. Draw an arrow to the antecedent for each pronoun. Evaluate whether or not the pronoun and antecedent agree. Replace any incorrect pronouns.

Revising Strategies

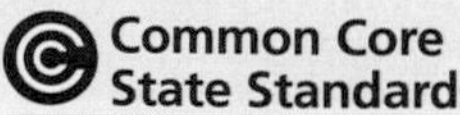

Use specific terms. The correct use of formal or specialized terms can help you express shades of meaning and add a sense of serious scholarship to your work. Use a dictionary and/or a thesaurus to locate the words with the precise meaning you want to express. Formal terminology may include literary terms, the names of literary movements, references to periods in history, or place names. Review your use of such terms to make sure they are correct.

Nonspecific: the old system of government

Specific: the ancient Roman republic

Clarify connections among ideas. Make sure you help readers follow your ideas by providing clear directions in the form of transitional expressions. For example, if you wish to show a contrast between ideas, you might use the words *however* or *conversely*. Check your draft and add transitional expressions as needed.

Cut excess writing. When revising, one of your most important goals is to delete words, phrases, sentences, and even paragraphs that do not add meaning or depth to your essay. As you review your draft, look for these types of unnecessary material:

- **Repeated Ideas:** Extend important ideas with fresh information, but cut repetitions that add nothing new.
- **Unrelated Details:** Be sure that every detail relates directly to your thesis. Eliminate material that seems off target, or revise to show its relationship to your thesis.
- **Inconsistencies:** Make sure that every sentence and every paragraph clearly relates to those that precede and follow.

Peer Review

Exchange drafts with a partner. Highlight passages that include ineffective repetition, unclear transitions, unrelated details, or inconsistent statements. Discuss how to modify the highlighted material. Then, revise your draft, cutting unnecessary details or adding clarifying language.

Model: Eliminating Unnecessary Writing

In Act I, Scene ii, Cassius shows his careful attention to others' moods and intentions. Cassius tells Brutus that he senses Brutus has something on his mind. ~~Cassius sees that something is bothering Brutus.~~ Brutus assures Cassius that what is troubling him has nothing to do with Cassius, who is one of his good friends. ~~He is not upset with Cassius.~~

This writer deletes repeated ideas to make this paragraph more effective.

Common Core State Standards

Writing

1.c. Use words, phrases, and clauses to link the major sections of the text, create cohesion, and clarify the relationships between claim(s) and reasons, between reasons and evidence, and between claim(s) and counterclaims.

1.d. Establish and maintain a formal style and objective tone while attending to the norms and conventions of the discipline in which they are writing.

5. Develop and strengthen writing as needed by planning, revising, editing, rewriting, or trying a new approach, focusing on addressing what is most significant for a specific purpose and audience.

Language

1. Demonstrate command of the conventions of standard English grammar and usage when writing or speaking.

Subject-Verb Agreement

Every complete sentence contains a subject and a verb, or predicate. The subject is what the sentence is about, while the verb tells what the subject is or does. For a sentence to be correct, both the subject and verb must be singular or plural.

Identifying Errors Errors in agreement can occur when the subject and verb are separated by other words, phrases, or clauses. In the examples below, subjects are underlined, and verbs are set in italic type.

Singular Subject and Verb

Incorrect: The <u>decision</u> of the board members *are* final.

Correct: The <u>decision</u> of the board members *is* final.

Plural Subject and Verb

Incorrect: <u>Students</u> who park here seldom *follows* the rules.

Correct: <u>Students</u> who park here seldom *follow* the rules.

Agreement errors also occur with compound subjects and with indefinite pronouns serving as subjects.

Identifying Indefinite Pronouns These are the most common indefinite pronouns categorized by number:

Singular: anybody, anyone, each, either, every, everybody, neither, nobody, nothing, somebody, something

Plural: both, few, many, others, several

Singular or Plural: all, any, more, most, none, some

Singular Indefinite Pronoun and Verb

Incorrect: <u>Everybody</u> who lives here *go* to the annual town picnic.

Correct: <u>Everybody</u> who lives here *goes* to the annual town picnic.

Fixing Errors To correct mismatched subjects and verbs, follow these steps:

1. Identify the subject and determine whether it is singular or plural.
2. Select the verb that matches the subject.
   - For compound subjects joined by *and,* use the plural form.
   - For singular subjects joined by *or* or *nor,* use the singular form.
   - When the subject is an indefinite pronoun, use the appropriate form of the verb.

Grammar in Your Writing

Circle all the subjects in two paragraphs of your draft. For each subject, draw an arrow to the verb that tells what it does. Make sure that you have used the form of the verb that agrees with the subject.

STUDENT MODEL: **Christopher Rich, Omaha, Nebraska**

Response to *The Tragedy of Julius Caesar*

In all tales, modern or ancient, characters at odds often differ in obvious ways. One may be likable and honest—a natural leader. The other may be unpleasant and sneaky. However, sometimes enemies are actually very similar. No exception to this rule, Shakespeare's Antony and Cassius of *The Tragedy of Julius Caesar* share many characteristics but come to very different ends.

Christopher includes a clear thesis statement in his introduction.

Marcus Antonius and Caius Cassius, both patricians and warriors, are presented as two of Rome's most noble citizens. Both are seen by plebians as noble and honest, if humanly flawed, men. In truth, they are among the most manipulative characters in the play. Cassius is the first to exploit his power to manipulate, using it to coerce Brutus onto the side of the conspirators. Flattering Brutus, ("I know that virtue to be in you, Brutus, / As well as I do know your outward favor") (I, ii, 90–91) and challenging his honor as a Roman, Cassius wins the support of his brother-in-law. Antony, however, shows his ability in a far less conspicuous way. After the assassination of Caesar in Act III, Antony cleverly manipulates the commoners. His subtle and smooth way of controlling the crowd with a pause in his voice reflects his manipulative ability.

Christopher accurately quotes significant passages from the text.

Despite their powers of persuasion, these two show great allegiance to their loved ones. Over Caesar's body, in Act III, Scene i, Antony says he is willing to throw his country into civil war. Later, Cassius kills himself when he thinks that his best friend has been killed, taking loyalty to the extreme.

Though people may have many similarities, it is the differences that separate warriors and politicians. Always at the beck and call of the dictator who would be king, Antony is known by the common folk to be a possible successor to the "coronet." Cassius, however, is opposed to Caesar, not only politically but also personally, and is one of Caesar's least favorite people: "Yond Cassius has a lean and hungry look" (I, ii, 194). Cassius himself admits to his own dislike of Caesar by telling a story from their youth, in Act I, Scene ii, lines 97–131. It is their differences that determine the eventual fate of the characters.

A point-by-point plan of organization focuses first on similarities and then moves onto differences.

In the end, the obvious similarities of these characters are not as important as their differences. The fate that each meets—Cassius commits suicide and Antony becomes part of the triumvirate that rules Rome—is determined by how each uses his personality traits.

In his conclusion, Christopher restates his thesis and provides an insight that takes the analysis further.

Common Core State Standards

Language
2.c. Spell correctly.

Editing and Proofreading

Review your draft to correct errors in grammar, spelling, and punctuation.

Focus on spelling. Endings that sound the same or almost the same, such as *-ize, -ise,* and *-yze,* can be tricky to spell. Usually, *-ize* is added to another word to make a verb, such as *civilize* or *characterize*. For *-ise* and *-yze,* there are no dependable rules. Memorize the spellings or refer to a dictionary if you are unsure of the spelling.

Spiral Review
Earlier in this unit, you learned about **pronouns** (p. 50) Review your response to literature to be sure you have correctly used personal and relative pronouns.

Publishing and Presenting

Consider one of the following ways to share your writing:

Present your response to a book club. Share your response to literature with members of a book club. Invite a group of students, friends, or family members to read the work of literature you will address. Set a meeting time and give a brief introduction to the work. Then, read your essay aloud. Follow your reading with a general discussion to share ideas and responses. As you discuss the literature and your analysis, be open to the ideas of others rather than simply defending your own.

Publish an online review. Post a literary review on a student or bookstore Web site. Remember to check each site for specific submission requirements. Then, follow the correct procedures to retrieve and reproduce your document across platforms.

Reflecting on Your Writing

Writer's Journal Jot down your answers to this question:
How did writing about the work help you better understand it?

Self-Evaluation Rubric

Use the following criteria to evaluate the effectiveness of your essay.

Criteria	Rating Scale
PURPOSE/FOCUS Introduces a precise claim and distinguishes the claim from (implied) alternate or opposing claims; provides a concluding section that follows from and supports the argument presented	*not very.........very* 1 2 3 4
ORGANIZATION Establishes a logical organization; uses words, phrases and clauses to link the major sections of the text, create cohesion, and clarify relationships among claims, reasons, and evidence, and between claims and counterclaims	1 2 3 4
DEVELOPMENT OF IDEAS/ELABORATION Develops the claim and counterclaims fairly, supplying evidence for each while pointing out the strengths and limitations of both	1 2 3 4
LANGUAGE Establishes and maintains a formal style and objective tone	1 2 3 4
CONVENTIONS Attends to the norms and conventions of the discipline	1 2 3 4

Assessment: Skills

SELECTED RESPONSE

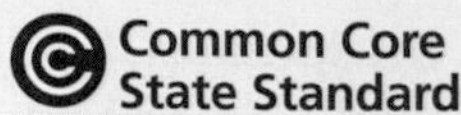

RL.9-10.1, RL.9-10.2. RL.9-10.3, RL.9-10.4, RL.9-10.5; W.9-10.3
[For the full wording of the standards, see the standards chart in the front of your textbook.]

I. Reading Literature

Directions: *Read the excerpt from "The Masque of the Red Death" by Edgar Allan Poe. Then, answer each question that follows.*

The "Red Death" had long devastated the country. No pestilence had ever been so fatal, or so hideous. Blood was its Avatar and its seal—the redness and the horror of blood. There were sharp pains, and sudden dizziness, and then profuse bleeding at the pores, with dissolution. The scarlet stains upon the body and especially upon the face of the victim, were the pest ban which shut him out from the aid and from the sympathy of his fellow men. And the whole seizure, progress and termination of the disease, were the incidents of half an hour.

But the Prince Prospero was happy and dauntless and sagacious. When his dominions were half depopulated, he summoned to his presence a thousand hale and lighthearted friends from among the knights and dames of his court, and with these retired to the deep seclusion of one of his castellated abbeys. This was an extensive and magnificent structure, the creation of the prince's own eccentric yet <u>august</u> taste. A strong and lofty wall girdled it in. This wall had gates of iron. The courtiers, having entered, brought furnaces and massy hammers and welded the bolts. They resolved to leave means neither of ingress or egress to the sudden impulses of despair or frenzy from within. The abbey was amply provisioned. With such precautions the courtiers might bid defiance to contagion. The external world could take care of itself. In the meantime it was folly to grieve, or to think. The prince had provided all the appliances of pleasure. There were buffoons, there were improvisatori, there were ballet dancers, there were musicians, there was Beauty, there was wine. All these and security were within. Without was the "Red Death."

It was toward the close of the fifth or sixth month of his seclusion, and while the pestilence raged most furiously abroad, that the Prince Prospero entertained his thousand friends at a masked ball of the most unusual magnificence.

It was a voluptuous scene, that masquerade. But first let me tell of the rooms in which it was held.

1. **Part A** What does the reader learn about Prince Prospero through **direct characterization?**

A. He is dangerous. **C.** He is sincere.
B. He is scared. **D.** He is happy.

Part B Which sentence from the passage directly characterizes the Prince?

A. "The prince had provided all the appliances of pleasure."
B. "But the Prince Prospero was happy and dauntless and sagacious."
C. "...the Prince Prospero entertained his thousand friends at a masked ball of the most unusual magnificence."
D. "No pestilence had ever been so fatal, or so hideous."

2. What is the **setting** of this excerpt?

A. a very poor countryside
B. the king's lavish castle
C. Prince Prospero's abbey
D. a secluded, underground room

3. Which part of the story's **plot** does this excerpt represent?

A. exposition
B. climax
C. falling action
D. resolution

4. This excerpt uses all of the following techniques *except*—

A. indirect characterization.
B. dialogue.
C. narration.
D. description.

5. Who reveals details about the **characters** in this excerpt from the story?

A. the courtiers
B. Prince Prospero
C. a narrator
D. Prince Prospero's friends

6. Which of the following phrases provides the best clue to the time **setting** of the story?

A. "had long devastated the country"
B. "among the knights and dames of his court"
C. "resolved to leave means neither of ingress or egress"
D. "while the pestilence raged most furiously abroad"

7. **Part A** Which answer choice best defines the underlined word *august* as it is used in the excerpt?

A. impressive, majestic
B. unusual, bizarre
C. plain, boring
D. thrifty, practical

Part B Which context clues help you to infer the meaning of *august?*

A. deep seclusion
B. hale and lighthearted
C. castellated
D. extensive and magnificent

Timed Writing

8. Write an original narrative to continue the story begun in the excerpt on page 102. Your narrative should include either an example of **foreshadowing** or an example of **irony.** Be sure to use what you have learned about the characters and situation so far as you tell what happens next.

GO ON

II. Reading Informational Text

Directions: *Read the passage. Then, answer each question that follows.*

RI.9-10.1; W.9-10.5; L.9-10.1, L.9-10.4.a

[For full standards wording, see the chart in the front of this book.]

Association Football

In the United States, tens of thousands of kids play a game called *soccer*. Elsewhere, the same ball game is called *association football*, or, in some countries, *futbol*. Around the world, about 40 million players are registered, plus there are thousands of others who play pickup games in streets, parks, school yards, and vacant lots, and even on beaches.

The game is played with two teams of eleven players each. The ultimate objective is to move the ball into the opposing team's goal net, without using the hands or arms. Players may bump the ball with their heads, hips, or knees, or they may kick the ball, but only the goalie, who stands in front of the goal, can touch the ball with his or her hands. The rules are simple, and the game can be played almost anywhere. This may be one reason soccer is the most popular game in the world, not only for players but for spectators as well.

1. According to the article, all of the following are names for the game described *except*—

A. soccer.
B. association football.
C. *futbol.*
D. kickball.

2. Judging from its context, what is the best definition of the underlined word *ultimate?*

A. eventual
B. secondary
C. excellent
D. lowest

3. Part A According to the article, which of the following statements is true of the game?

A. One must be registered in order to play.
B. Rules require all players to use only their feet.
C. It is the most popular game in the world.
D. It is played with twenty-two players on each team.

Part B Which detail from the passage best supports the answer to Part A?

A. "Players may bump the ball with their heads, hips, or knees..."
B. "The ultimate objective is to move the ball into the opposing team's goal net..."
C. "Around the world, about 40 million players are registered, plus there are thousands of others who play pickup games..."
D. "The game is played with two teams of eleven players each."

III. Writing and Language Conventions

Directions: *Read the passage. Then, answer each question that follows.*

(1) The air lock doors opened with a hiss. (2) As Mark stepped outside, he could feel the icy winds, even through his protective suit. (3) The blackness of the sky was broken by the glow at the horizon—the sun setting on Mars.

(4) "This is it, Joey," he is saying, looking down at the limp, furry, black body in his arms.

(5) He walked swiftly—bounced, really, in the thin gravity—away from the glowing glass dome of the city. (6) Carefully, Mark placed his body in a shallow hole, kicking dirt back over it and mounding the grave with rocks. (7) Mark felt tears in his eyes, tears he couldn't wipe through his helmet. (8) He had been a good dog. (9) Joey had been his first pet, brought to Mars when Mark's family moves there years earlier. (10) Losing him meant that his last tie to his old life on Earth was gone. (11) Mark was now completely Martian.

1. Which **possessive proper noun** should replace the **possessive pronoun** *his* in sentence 6 for clarity?
   A. its
   B. Mark's
   C. Joey's
   D. Dog's

2. Which **degree of adjective** is the word *good* in sentence 8?
   A. comparative
   B. superlative
   C. negative
   D. positive

3. How should the phrase *is saying* in sentence 4 be revised so that the **verb tense** is consistent in the story?
   A. says
   B. said
   C. has said
   D. keep as is

4. Which of the following describes the **personal pronoun** *he* in Sentence 8?
   A. first person
   B. second person
   C. first and second person
   D. third person

5. How should sentence 9 be revised so that the **verb tense** in the sentence is consistent?
   A. Joey had been his first pet, brought to Mars when Mark's family moved there years earlier.
   B. Joey had been his first pet, brought to Mars when Mark's family did move there years earlier.
   C. Joey had been his first pet he brings to Mars when Mark's family had moved there years earlier.
   D. Joey had been his first pet, brought to Mars when Mark's family will move there.

CONSTRUCTED RESPONSE

Directions: *Follow the instructions to complete the tasks below as required by your teacher.*

As you work on each task, incorporate both general academic vocabulary and literary terms you learned in Parts 1 and 2 of this unit.

RL.9-10.2, RL.9-10.3, RL.9-10.4; W.9-10.2 W.9-10.7, W.9-10.8, W.9-10.9.a; SL.9-10.1.d, SL.9-10.4; L.9-10.1

[For full standards wording, see the chart in the front of this book.]

Writing

TASK 1 Literature [RL.9-10.3; W.9-10.2, W.9-10.9.a; L.9-10.1]

Analyze the Development of Complex Characters

Choose two stories from Part 2 of this unit that each feature characters with conflicting motivations. Write an essay in which you analyze and then compare and contrast the two characters.

- Identify the characters you will analyze, and explain the reasons for your choices.
- Explain what motivates each character to behave as he or she does. Discuss specific similarities and differences in the ways each character experiences conflicting motivations.
- Compare and contrast the changes each character undergoes as a result of his or her experiences.
- Cite evidence from the texts, including relevant details and direct quotations, to support your analysis.
- Correct any errors you find in subject-verb agreement.

TASK 2 Literature [RL.9-10.4; W.9-10.2, W.9-10.9.a; L.9-10.1]

Analyze Setting

Write an essay analyzing how descriptions in a story from Part 2 of this unit evoke a sense of time and place.

- Identify the time and place in which the story is set.
- Quote vivid descriptions of the setting from the story, including those that appeal to the senses.
- Evaluate the significance of setting in the story. For example, you might explain whether the setting helps shape the conflicts that characters experience.
- Use conventions of standard English in your essay.

TASK 3 Literature [RL.9-10.2; W.9-10.2, W.9-10.9.a; L.9-10.1]

Analyze the Theme of a Story

Write an essay in which you analyze the development of the theme of a story from Part 2 of this unit.

Part 1

- As you review the story, take notes.
- Use your notes to write a short summary in which you briefly identify the main characters and describe key events in the story's plot.
- Answer the following questions:
  What is the theme of the story?
  Does the narrator or a character state the theme directly, or is the theme implied through story details and events?

Part 2

- Write an essay in which you describe how the theme is first presented in the story and how it is shaped and refined over the course of the story.
- Cite details and examples from the story to support your analysis.
- Avoid mixing verb tenses unnecessarily.

Speaking and Listening

TASK 4 Literature [RL.9-10.3; SL.9-10.1.d]

Present Dialogue

Work with a partner to select and present a portion of dialogue from a story in Part 2 of this unit.

- Select a passage of dialogue that gives readers insight into two or more characters' personalities.
- Work together to determine how the dialogue should be spoken. Your presentation should clearly reflect the characters' traits.
- Reread the text and practice delivering the dialogue. Then, present the dialogue to the class.
- After your presentation, explain how you arrived at your interpretation of the characters. Cite specific details from the text that support your choices.
- Encourage your classmates to ask questions about the characters, the dialogue, and your interpretation.
- Respond thoughtfully to your classmates' ideas, summarize points of agreement and disagreement, and make new connections in light of the reasoning they present.

TASK 5 Literature [RL.9-10.5; SL.9-10.4]

Analyze Plot

Prepare and deliver an oral presentation in which you analyze the plot of a story from Part 2 of this unit.

- Select a story with a plot that contains at least one instance of foreshadowing.
- As you analyze the story, create a plot diagram to show the sequence of events.
- Use the following labels in your diagram: exposition, rising action, climax, falling action, resolution. Also note in the diagram where the author uses foreshadowing to hint at upcoming events.
- Draw a conclusion about the way the author crafted the plot and how techniques like foreshadowing add tension to a story.
- Use the diagram you created to present your information clearly and logically. Read portions of the text aloud to demonstrate your ideas.

Research

TASK 6 Literature [RL.9-10.2; W.9-10.2, W.9-10.7, W.9-10.8, W.9-10.9.a]

Can progress be made without conflict?

In Part 2 of this unit, you have read texts related to progress and conflict. Now, you will conduct a short research project on progress and conflict as these ideas relate to a social issue. Choose a social issue that is meaningful to you—it could be one you would like to see move toward positive change, or one that has already done so. Review the following guidelines before you begin your research:

- Focus your research on one social issue.
- Gather information from at least two reliable sources. Your sources may be print or digital.
- Take notes as you investigate the issue and the conflict surrounding it.
- Cite your sources.

When you have completed your research, write an essay in response to this unit's Big Question. As part of your response, discuss how your initial ideas have changed or been reinforced. Support your position with examples from texts you have read in Part 2 and those you discovered through research.

"Every **struggle** is a **victory**."

—**Helen Keller**

PART 3

TEXT SET DEVELOPING INSIGHT

PERSEVERANCE

The readings in this section explore concepts of perseverance, or "grit." Society generally sees perseverance as a virtue that lets us solve problems and achieve goals. Our regard for perseverance is connected to our notions of achievement—successful entrepreneurs never stop trying and heroes do not give up. However, there are other ways of looking at perseverance. As you read these selections, ask yourself: Should we always be persistent? Is quitting ever the right thing to do? Then, consider how ideas of perseverance relate to the Big Question for this unit: **Can progress be made without conflict?**

◀ CRITICAL VIEWING Consider the endeavor depicted in this image. What personal qualities must the person pictured here possess in order to continue her pursuit?

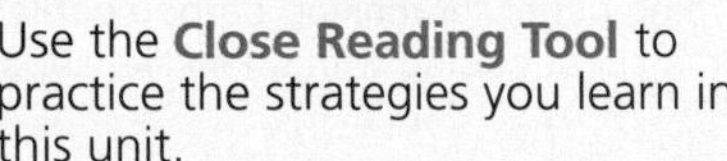

CLOSE READING TOOL

Use the **Close Reading Tool** to practice the strategies you learn in this unit.

READINGS IN PART 3

Contents of the Dead Man's Pocket

Jack Finney

At the little living-room desk Tom Benecke rolled two sheets of flimsy[1] and a heavier top sheet, carbon paper sandwiched between them, into his portable. Interoffice Memo, the top sheet was headed, and he typed tomorrow's date just below this; then he glanced at a creased yellow sheet, covered with his own handwriting, beside the typewriter. "Hot in here," he muttered to himself. Then, from the short hallway at his back, he heard the muffled clang of wire coat hangers in the bedroom closet,

1. **flimsy** (flim′ zē) *n.* thin typing paper for making carbon copies. Carbon copies are created by placing carbon paper, a sheet coated with an inklike substance, between two pieces of typing paper.

and at this reminder of what his wife was doing he thought: Hot, no—guilty conscience.

He got up, shoving his hands into the back pockets of his gray wash slacks, stepped to the living-room window beside the desk and stood breathing on the glass, watching the expanding circle of mist, staring down through the autumn night at Lexington Avenue, eleven stories below. He was a tall, lean, dark-haired young man in a pullover sweater, who looked as though he had played not football, probably, but basketball in college. Now he placed the heels of his hands against the top edge of the lower window frame and shoved upward. But as usual the window didn't budge, and he had to lower his hands and then shoot them hard upward to jolt the window open a few inches. He dusted his hands, muttering.

But still he didn't begin his work. He crossed the room to the hallway entrance and, leaning against the doorjamb, hands shoved into his back pockets again, he called, "Clare?" When his wife answered, he said, "Sure you don't mind going alone?"

"No." Her voice was muffled, and he knew her head and shoulders were in the bedroom closet. Then the tap of her high heels sounded on the wood floor and she appeared at the end of the little hallway, wearing a slip, both hands raised to one ear, clipping on an earring. She smiled at him—a slender, very pretty girl with light brown, almost blonde, hair—her prettiness emphasized by the pleasant nature that showed in her face. "It's just that I hate you to miss this movie; you wanted to see it too."

"Yeah, I know." He ran his fingers through his hair. "Got to get this done though."

She nodded, accepting this. Then, glancing at the desk across the living room, she said, "You work too much, though, Tom—and too hard."

He smiled. "You won't mind though, will you, when the money comes rolling in and I'm known as the Boy Wizard of Wholesale Groceries?"

"I guess not." She smiled and turned back toward the bedroom.

At his desk again, Tom lighted a cigarette, then a few moments later as Clare appeared, dressed and ready to leave, he set it on the rim of the ash tray. "Just after seven," she said. "I can make the beginning of the first feature."

He walked to the front-door closet to help her on with her coat. He kissed her then and, for an instant, holding her close, smelling the perfume she had used, he was tempted to go with her; it was not actually true that he had to work tonight, though he very much wanted to. This was his own project, unannounced as yet in his office, and it could be postponed. But then they won't see it till Monday, he thought once again, and if I give it to the boss tomorrow he might read it over the weekend . . . "Have a good time," he said aloud. He gave his wife a little swat and opened the door for her, feeling the air from the building hallway, smelling faintly of floor wax, stream gently past his face.

He watched her walk down the hall, flicked a hand in response as she waved, and then he started to close the door, but it resisted for a moment. As the door opening narrowed, the current of warm air from the hallway, channeled through this smaller opening now, suddenly rushed past him with accelerated force. Behind him he heard the slap of the window curtains against the wall and the sound of paper fluttering from his desk, and he had to push to close the door.

Turning, he saw a sheet of white paper drifting to the floor in a series of arcs, and another sheet, yellow, moving toward the window, caught in the dying current flowing through the narrow opening. As he watched, the paper struck the bottom edge of the window and hung there for an instant, plastered against the glass and wood. Then as the moving air stilled completely, the curtains swinging back from the wall to hang free again, he saw the yellow sheet drop to the window ledge and slide over out of sight.

He ran across the room, grasped the bottom edge of the window and tugged, staring through the glass. He saw the yellow sheet, dimly now in the darkness outside, lying on the ornamental ledge a yard below the window. Even as he watched, it was moving, scraping slowly along the ledge, pushed by the breeze that pressed steadily against the building wall. He heaved on the window with all his strength and it shot open with a bang, the window weight rattling in the casing. But the paper was past his reach and, leaning out into the night, he watched it scud steadily along the ledge to the south, half plastered against the building wall. Above the muffled sound of the street traffic far below, he could hear the dry scrape of its movement, like a leaf on the pavement.

The living room of the next apartment to the south projected a yard or more farther out toward the street than this one; because of this the Beneckes paid seven and a half dollars less rent than their neighbors. And now the yellow sheet, sliding along the stone ledge, nearly invisible in the night, was stopped by the projecting blank wall of the next apartment. It lay motionless, then, in the corner formed by the two walls—a good five yards away, pressed firmly against the ornate corner ornament of the ledge, by the breeze that moved past Tom Benecke's face.

He knelt at the window and stared at the yellow paper for a full minute or more, waiting for it to move, to slide off the ledge and fall, hoping he could follow its course to the street, and then hurry down in the elevator and retrieve it. But it didn't move, and then he saw that the paper was caught firmly between a projection of the **convoluted** corner ornament and the ledge. He thought about the poker from the fireplace, then the broom, then the mop—discarding each thought as it occurred to him. There was nothing in the apartment long enough to reach that paper.

◀ **convoluted** (kän′ və lo͞ot′ id) *adj.* twisted in a complicated way

It was hard for him to understand that he actually had to abandon it—it was ridiculous—and he began to curse. Of all the papers on his desk, why did it have to be this one in particular! On four long Saturday afternoons he had stood in supermarkets counting the people who passed certain displays, and the results were scribbled on that yellow sheet. From stacks of trade publications, gone over page by page in snatched half hours at work and during evenings at home, he had copied facts, quotations, and figures onto that sheet. And he had carried it with him to the Public Library on Fifth Avenue, where he'd spent a dozen lunch hours and early evenings adding more. All were needed to support and lend authority to his idea for a new grocery-store display method; without them his idea was a mere opinion. And there they all lay, in his own improvised shorthand—countless hours of work—out there on the ledge.

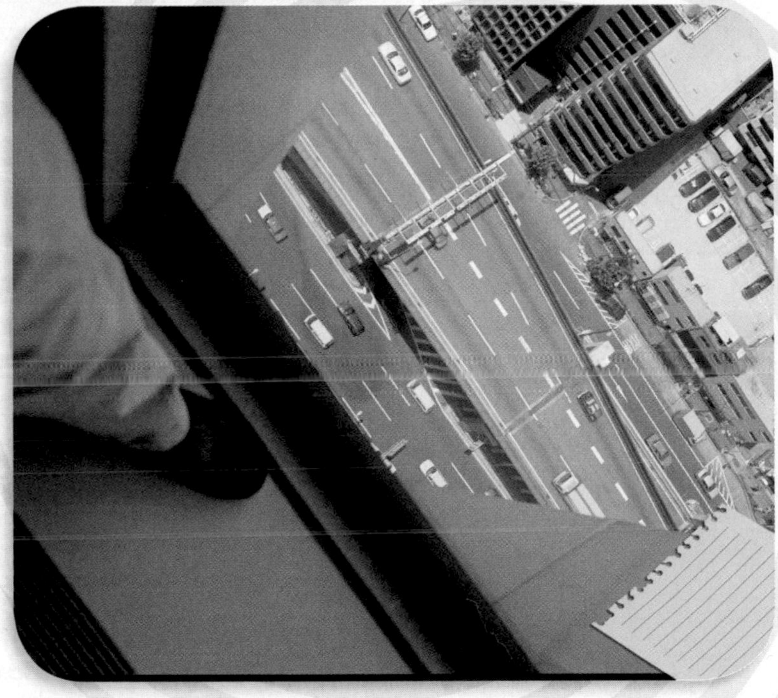

For many seconds he believed he was going to abandon the yellow sheet, that there was nothing else to do. The work could be duplicated. But it would take two months, and the time to present this idea . . . was *now*, for use in the spring displays. He struck his fist on the window ledge. Then he shrugged. Even if his plan were adopted, he told himself, it wouldn't bring him a raise in pay—not immediately, anyway, or as a direct result. It won't bring me a promotion either, he argued—not of itself.

But just the same, and he couldn't escape the thought, this and other independent projects, some already done and others planned for the future, would gradually mark him out from the score of other young men in his company. They were the way to change from a name on the payroll to a name in the minds of the company officials. They were the beginning of the long, long climb to where he was determined to be, at the very top. And he knew he was going out there in the darkness, after the yellow sheet fifteen feet beyond his reach.

By a kind of instinct, he instantly began making his intention acceptable to himself by laughing at it. The mental picture of himself sidling along the ledge outside was absurd—it was actually comical—and he smiled. He imagined himself describing it; it would make a good story at the office and, it occurred to him, would add a special interest and importance to his memorandum, which would do it no harm at all.

To simply go out and get his paper was an easy task—he could be back here with it in less than two minutes—and he knew he wasn't deceiving himself. The ledge, he saw, measuring it with his eye, was about as wide as the length of his shoe, and perfectly flat. And every fifth row of brick in the face of the building, he remembered—leaning out, he verified this—was indented half an inch, enough for the tips of his fingers, enough to maintain balance easily. It occurred to him that if this ledge and wall were only a yard above ground—as he knelt at the window staring out, this thought was the final confirmation of his intention—he could move along the ledge indefinitely.

On a sudden impulse, he got to his feet, walked to the front closet and took out an old tweed jacket; it would be cold outside. He put it on and buttoned it as he crossed the room rapidly toward the open window. In the back of his mind he knew he'd better hurry and get this over with before he thought too much, and at the window he didn't allow himself to hesitate.

He swung a leg over the sill, then felt for and found the ledge a yard below the window with his foot. Gripping the bottom of the window frame very tightly and carefully, he slowly ducked his head under it, feeling on his face the sudden change from the warm air of the room to the chill outside. With infinite care he brought out his other leg, his mind concentrating on what he was doing. Then he slowly stood erect. Most of the putty, dried out and brittle, had dropped off the bottom edging of the window frame, he found, and the flat wooden edging provided a good gripping surface, a half inch or more deep, for the tips of his fingers.

Now, balanced easily and firmly, he stood on the ledge outside in the slight, chill breeze, eleven stories above the street, staring into his own lighted apartment, odd and different-seeming now.

First his right hand, then his left, he carefully shifted his fingertip grip from the puttyless window edging to an indented row of bricks directly to his right. It was hard to take the first shuffling sideways step then—to make himself move—and the fear stirred in his stomach, but he did it, again by not allowing himself time to think. And now—with his chest, stomach, and the left side of his face pressed against the rough cold brick—his lighted apartment was suddenly gone, and it was much darker out here than he had thought.

Without pause he continued—right foot, left foot, right foot, left—his shoe soles shuffling and scraping along the rough stone, never lifting from it, fingers sliding along the exposed edging of brick. He moved on the balls of his feet, heels lifted slightly; the ledge was not quite as wide as he'd expected. But leaning slightly inward toward the face of the building and pressed against it, he could feel his balance firm and secure, and moving along the ledge was quite as easy as he had thought it would be. He could hear the buttons of his jacket scraping steadily along the rough bricks and feel them catch momentarily, tugging a little, at each mortared crack. He simply did not permit himself to look down, though the compulsion to do so never left him; nor did he allow himself actually to think. Mechanically—right foot, left foot, over and again—he shuffled along crabwise, watching the projecting wall ahead loom steadily closer . . .

He simply did not permit himself to look down, though the compulsion to do so never left him...

Then he reached it, and, at the corner—he'd decided how he was going to pick up the paper—he lifted his right foot and placed it carefully on the ledge that ran along the projecting wall at a right angle to the ledge on which his other foot rested. And now, facing the building, he stood in the corner formed by the two walls, one foot on the ledging of each, a hand on the shoulder-high indentation of each wall. His forehead was pressed directly into the corner against the cold bricks, and now he carefully lowered first one hand, then the other, perhaps a foot farther down, to the next indentation in the rows of bricks.

Very slowly, sliding his forehead down the trough of the brick corner and bending his knees, he lowered his body toward the paper lying between his outstretched feet. Again he lowered his fingerholds another foot and bent his knees still more, thigh muscles taut, his forehead sliding and bumping down the brick V. Half squatting now, he dropped his left hand to the next indentation and then slowly reached with his right hand toward the paper between his feet.

He couldn't quite touch it, and his knees now were pressed against the wall; he could bend them no farther. But by ducking his head another inch lower, the top of his head now pressed against the bricks, he lowered his right shoulder and his fingers had the paper by a corner, pulling it loose. At the same instant he saw, between his legs and far below, Lexington Avenue stretched out for miles ahead.

He saw, in that instant, the Loew's theater sign, blocks ahead past Fiftieth Street; the miles of traffic signals, all green now; the lights of cars and street lamps; countless neon signs; and the moving black dots of people. And a violent instantaneous explosion of absolute terror roared through him. For a motionless instant he saw himself externally—bent practically double, balanced on this narrow ledge, nearly half his body projecting out above the street far below—and he began to tremble violently, panic flaring through his mind and muscles, and he felt the blood rush from the surface of his skin.

In the fractional moment before horror paralyzed him, as he stared between his legs at that terrible length of street far beneath him, a fragment of his mind raised his body in a spasmodic jerk to an upright position again, but so violently that his head scraped hard against the wall, bouncing off it, and his body swayed outward to the knife edge of balance, and he very nearly plunged backward and fell. Then he was leaning far into the corner again, squeezing and pushing into it, not only his face but his chest and stomach, his back arching; and his fingertips clung with all the pressure of his pulling arms to the shoulder-high half-inch indentation in the bricks.

He was more than trembling now; his whole body was racked with a violent shuddering beyond control, his eyes squeezed so tightly shut it was painful, though he was past awareness of that. His teeth were exposed in a frozen grimace, the strength draining like water from his knees and calves. It was extremely likely, he knew, that he would faint, to slump down along the wall, his face scraping, and then drop backward, a limp weight, out into nothing. And to save his life he concentrated on holding onto consciousness, drawing deliberate deep breaths of cold air into his lungs, fighting to keep his senses aware.

Then he knew that he would not faint, but he could neither stop shaking nor open his eyes. He stood where he was, breathing deeply, trying to hold back the terror of the glimpse he had had of what lay below him; and he knew he had made a mistake in not making himself stare down at the street, getting used to it and accepting it, when he had first stepped out onto the ledge.

It was impossible to walk back. He simply could not do it. He couldn't bring himself to make the slightest movement. The strength was gone from his legs; his shivering hands—numb, cold and desperately rigid—had lost all deftness; his easy ability to move and balance was gone. Within a step or two, if he tried to move, he knew that he would stumble clumsily and fall.

Seconds passed, with the chill faint wind pressing the side of his face, and he could hear the toned-down volume of the street traffic far beneath him. Again and again it slowed and then stopped, almost to silence; then presently, even this high, he would hear the click of the traffic signals and the subdued roar of the cars starting up again. During a lull in the street sounds, he called out. Then he was shouting "*Help!*" so loudly it rasped his throat. But he felt the steady pressure of the wind, moving between his face and the blank wall, snatch up his cries as he uttered them, and he knew they must sound directionless and distant. And he remembered how habitually, here in New York, he himself heard and ignored shouts in the night. If anyone heard him, there was no sign of it, and presently Tom Benecke knew he had to try moving; there was nothing else he could do.

Eyes squeezed shut, he watched scenes in his mind like scraps of motion-picture film—he could not stop them. He saw himself stumbling suddenly sideways as he crept along the ledge and saw his upper body arc outward, arms flailing. He saw a dangling shoestring caught between the ledge and the sole of his other shoe, saw a foot start to move, to be stopped with a jerk, and felt his balance leaving him. He saw himself falling with a terrible speed as his body revolved in the air, knees clutched tight to his chest, eyes squeezed shut, moaning softly.

Out of utter necessity, knowing that any of these thoughts might be reality in the very next seconds, he was slowly able to shut his mind against every thought but what he now began to do. With fear-soaked slowness, he slid his left foot an inch or two toward his own impossibly distant window. Then he slid the fingers of his shivering left hand a corresponding distance. For a moment he could not bring himself to lift his right foot from one ledge to the other; then he did it, and became aware of the harsh exhalation of air from his throat and realized that he was panting. As his right hand, then, began to slide along the brick edging, he was astonished to feel the yellow paper pressed to the bricks underneath his stiff fingers, and he uttered a terrible, abrupt bark that might have been a laugh or a moan. He opened his mouth and took the paper in his teeth, pulling it out from under his fingers.

By a kind of trick—by concentrating his entire mind on first his left foot, then his left hand, then the other foot, then the other hand—he was able to move, almost imperceptibly, trembling steadily, very nearly without thought. But he could feel the terrible strength of the pent-up horror on just the other side of the flimsy barrier he had erected in his mind; and he knew that if it broke through he would lose this thin artificial control of his body.

During one slow step he tried keeping his eyes closed; it made him feel safer, shutting him off a little from the fearful reality of where he was. Then a sudden rush of giddiness swept over him and he had to open his eyes wide, staring sideways at the cold rough brick and angled lines of mortar, his cheek tight against the building. He kept his eyes open then, knowing that if he once let them flick outward, to stare for an instant at the lighted windows across the street, he would be past help.

He didn't know how many dozens of tiny sidling steps he had taken, his chest, belly, and face pressed to the wall; but he knew the slender hold he was keeping on his mind and body was going to break. He had a sudden mental picture of his apartment on just the other side of this wall—warm, cheerful, incredibly spacious. And he saw himself striding through it, lying down on the floor on his back, arms spread wide, **reveling** in its unbelievable security. The impossible remoteness of this utter safety, the contrast between it and where he now stood, was more than he could bear. And the barrier broke then, and the fear of the awful height he stood on coursed through his nerves and muscles.

reveling ▶ (rev´ əl iŋ) *v.* taking great pleasure or delight

A fraction of his mind knew he was going to fall, and he began taking rapid blind steps with no feeling of what he was doing, sidling with a clumsy desperate swiftness, fingers scrabbling along the brick, almost hopelessly resigned to the sudden backward pull and swift motion outward and down. Then his moving left hand slid onto not brick but sheer emptiness, an impossible gap in the face of the wall, and he stumbled.

His right foot smashed into his left anklebone; he staggered sideways, began falling, and the claw of his hand cracked against glass and wood, slid down it, and his fingertips were pressed hard on the puttyless edging of his window. His right hand smacked gropingly beside it as he fell to his knees; and, under the full weight and direct downward pull of his sagging body, the open window dropped shudderingly in its frame till it closed and his wrists struck the sill and were jarred off.

For a single moment he knelt, knee bones against stone on the very edge of the ledge, body swaying and touching nowhere else, fighting for balance. Then he lost it, his shoulders plunging backward, and he flung his arms forward, his hands smashing against the window casing on either side; and—his body moving backward—his fingers clutched the narrow wood stripping of the upper pane.

The impossible remoteness of this utter safety, the contrast between it and where he now stood, was more than he could bear.

For an instant he hung suspended between balance and falling, his fingertips pressed onto the quarter-inch wood strips. Then, with utmost delicacy, with a focused concentration of all his senses, he increased even further the strain on his fingertips hooked to these slim edgings of wood. Elbows slowly bending, he began to draw the full weight of his upper body forward, knowing that the instant his fingers slipped off these quarter-inch strips he'd plunge backward and be falling. Elbows imperceptibly bending, body shaking with the strain, the sweat starting from his forehead in great sudden drops, he pulled, his entire being and thought concentrated in his fingertips. Then suddenly, the strain slackened and ended, his chest touching the window sill, and he was kneeling on the ledge, his forehead pressed to the glass of the closed window.

Dropping his palms to the sill, he stared into his living room—at the red-brown davenport[2] across the room, and a magazine he had left there; at the pictures on the walls and the gray rug; the entrance to the hallway; and at his papers, typewriter and desk, not two feet

2. **davenport** (dav′ ən pôrt′) *n.* large couch.

from his nose. A movement from his desk caught his eye and he saw that it was a thin curl of blue smoke; his cigarette, the ash long, was still burning in the ash tray where he'd left it—this was past all belief—only a few minutes before.

His head moved, and in faint reflection from the glass before him he saw the yellow paper clenched in his front teeth. Lifting a hand from the sill he took it from his mouth; the moistened corner parted from the paper, and he spat it out.

For a moment, in the light from the living room, he stared wonderingly at the yellow sheet in his hand and then crushed it into the side pocket of his jacket.

He couldn't open the window. It had been pulled not completely closed, but its lower edge was below the level of the outside sill; there was no room to get his fingers underneath it. Between the upper sash and the lower was a gap not wide enough—reaching up, he tried—to get his fingers into; he couldn't push it open. The upper window panel, he knew from long experience, was impossible to move, frozen tight with dried paint.

Very carefully observing his balance, the fingertips of his left hand again hooked to the narrow stripping of the window casing, he drew back his right hand, palm facing the glass, and then struck the glass with the heel of his hand.

His arm rebounded from the pane, his body tottering, and he knew he didn't dare strike a harder blow.

His arm rebounded from the pane, his body tottering, and he knew he didn't dare strike a harder blow.

But in the security and relief of his new position, he simply smiled; with only a sheet of glass between him and the room just before him, it was not possible that there wasn't a way past it. Eyes narrowing, he thought for a few moments about what to do. Then his eyes widened, for nothing occurred to him. But still he felt calm: the trembling, he realized, had stopped. At the back of his mind there still lay the thought that once he was again in his home, he could give release to his feelings. He actually would lie on the floor, rolling, clenching tufts of the rug in his hands. He would literally run across the room, free to move as he liked, jumping on the floor, testing and reveling in its absolute security, letting the relief flood through him, draining the fear from his mind and body. His yearning for this was astonishingly intense, and somehow he understood that he had better keep this feeling at bay.

He took a half dollar from his pocket and struck it against the pane, but without any hope that the glass would break and with very little disappointment when it did not. After a few moments of thought he drew his leg up onto the ledge and picked loose the knot of his shoelace. He slipped off the shoe and, holding it across the instep, drew back his arm as far as he dared and struck the leather heel against the glass. The pane rattled, but he knew he'd been a long way from breaking it. His foot was cold and he slipped the shoe back on. He shouted again experimentally, and then once more, but there was no answer.

The realization suddenly struck him that he might have to wait here till Clare came home, and for a moment the thought was funny. He could see Clare opening the front door, withdrawing her key from the lock, closing the door behind her, and then glancing up to see him crouched on the other side of the window. He could see her rush across the room, face astounded and frightened, and hear himself shouting instructions: "Never mind how I got here! Just open the wind—" She couldn't open it, he remembered, she'd never been able to; she'd always had to call him. She'd have to get the building superintendent or a neighbor, and he pictured himself smiling and answering their questions as he climbed in. "I just wanted to get a breath of fresh air, so—"

He couldn't possibly wait here till Clare came home. It was the second feature she'd wanted to see, and she'd left in time to see the first. She'd be another three hours or—He glanced at his watch; Clare had been gone eight minutes. It wasn't possible, but only eight minutes ago he had kissed his wife goodbye. She wasn't even at the theater yet!

It would be four hours before she could possibly be home, and he tried to picture himself kneeling out here, fingertips hooked to these narrow strippings, while first one movie, preceded by a slow listing of credits, began, developed, reached its climax and then finally ended. There'd be a newsreel next, maybe, and then an animated cartoon, and then **interminable** scenes from coming pictures. And then, once more, the beginning of a full-length picture—while all the time he hung out here in the night.

◀ **interminable** (in tʉr′ mi nə bəl) *adj.* endless or seemingly endless

He might possibly get to his feet, but he was afraid to try. Already his legs were cramped, his thigh muscles tired; his knees hurt, his feet felt numb and his hands were stiff. He couldn't possibly stay out here for four hours, or anywhere near it. Long before that his legs and arms would give out; he would be forced to try changing his position often—stiffly, clumsily, his coordination and strength gone—and he would fall. Quite realistically, he knew that he would fall; no one could stay out here on this ledge for four hours.

A dozen windows in the apartment building across the street were lighted. Looking over his shoulder, he could see the top of a man's head behind the newspaper he was reading; in another window he saw the blue-gray flicker of a television screen. No more than twenty-odd yards from his back were scores of people, and if just one of them would walk idly to his window and glance out. . . . For some moments he stared over his shoulder at the lighted rectangles, waiting. But no one appeared. The man reading his paper turned a page and then continued his reading. A figure passed another of the windows and was immediately gone.

In the inside pocket of his jacket he found a little sheaf of papers, and he pulled one out and looked at it in the light from the living room. It was an old letter, an advertisement of some sort; his name and address, in purple ink, were on a label pasted to the envelope. Gripping one end of the envelope in his teeth, he twisted it into a tight curl. From his shirt pocket he brought out a book of matches. He didn't dare let go the casing with both hands, but, with the twist of paper in his teeth, he opened the matchbook with his free hand; then he bent one of the matches in two without tearing it from the folder, its red-tipped end now touching the striking surface. With his thumb, he rubbed the red tip across the striking area.

He did it again, then again, and still again, pressing harder each time, and the match suddenly flared, burning his thumb. But he kept it alight, cupping the matchbook in his hand and shielding it with his body. He held the flame to the paper in his mouth till it caught. Then he snuffed out the match flame with his thumb and forefinger, careless of the burn, and replaced the book in his pocket. Taking the paper twist in his hand, he held it flame down, watching the flame crawl up the paper, till it flared bright. Then he held it behind him over the street, moving it from side to side, watching it over his shoulder, the flame flickering and guttering in the wind.

There were three letters in his pocket and he lighted each of them, holding each till the flame touched his hand and then dropping it to the street below. At one point, watching over his shoulder while the last of the letters burned, he saw the man across the street put down his paper and stand—even seeming, to Tom, to glance toward his window. But when he moved, it was only to walk across the room and disappear from sight.

There were a dozen coins in Tom Benecke's pocket and he dropped them, three or four at a time. But if they struck anyone, or if anyone noticed their falling, no one connected them with their source, and no one glanced upward.

His arms had begun to tremble from the steady strain of clinging to this narrow perch, and he did not know what to do now and was terribly frightened. Clinging to the window stripping with one hand, he again searched his pockets. But now—he had left his wallet on his dresser when he'd changed clothes—there was nothing left but the yellow sheet. It occurred to him irrelevantly that his death on the sidewalk below would be an eternal mystery; the window closed—why, how, and from where could he have fallen? No one would be able to identify his body for a time, either—the thought was somehow unbearable and increased his fear. All they'd find in his pockets would be the yellow sheet. *Contents of the dead man's pockets*, he thought, *one sheet of paper bearing penciled notations—incomprehensible.*

He understood fully that he might actually be going to die; his arms, maintaining his balance on the ledge, were trembling steadily now. And it occurred to him then with all the force of a revelation that, if he fell, all he was ever going to have out of life he would then, abruptly, have had. Nothing, then, could ever be changed; and nothing more—no least experience or pleasure—could ever be added to his life. He wished, then, that he had not allowed his wife to go off by herself tonight—and on similar nights. He thought of all the evenings he had spent away from her, working; and he regretted them. He thought wonderingly of his fierce ambition and of the direction his life had taken; he thought of the hours he'd spent by himself, filling the yellow sheet that had brought him out here. *Contents of the dead man's pockets*, he thought with sudden fierce anger, *a wasted life.*

He was simply not going to cling here till he slipped and fell; he told himself that now. There was one last thing he could try; he had been aware of it for some moments, refusing to think about it, but now he faced it. Kneeling here on the ledge, the fingertips of one hand pressed to the narrow strip of wood, he could, he knew, draw his other hand back a yard perhaps, fist clenched tight, doing it very slowly till he sensed the outer limit of balance, then, as hard as he was able from the distance, he could drive his fist forward against the glass. If it broke, his fist smashing through, he was safe; he might cut himself badly, and probably would, but with his arm inside the room, he would be secure. But if the glass did not break, the rebound, flinging his arm back, would topple him off the ledge. He was certain of that.

He tested his plan. The fingers of his left hand clawlike on the little stripping, he drew back his other fist until his body began teetering backward. But he had no leverage now—he could feel that there would be no force to his swing—and he moved his fist

slowly forward till he rocked forward on his knees again and could sense that his swing would carry its greatest force. Glancing down, however, measuring the distance from his fist to the glass, he saw that it was less than two feet.

It occurred to him that he could raise his arm over his head, to bring it down against the glass. But, experimenting in slow motion, he knew it would be an awkward . . . blow without the force of a driving punch, and not nearly enough to break the glass.

Facing the window, he had to drive a blow from the shoulder, he knew now, at a distance of less than two feet; and he did not know whether it would break through the heavy glass. It might; he could picture it happening, he could feel it in the nerves of his arm. And it might not; he could feel that too—feel his fist striking this glass and being instantaneously flung back by the unbreaking pane, feel the fingers of his other hand breaking loose, nails scraping along the casing as he fell.

He waited, arm drawn back, fist balled, but in no hurry to strike; this pause, he knew, might be an extension of his life. And to live even a few seconds longer, he felt, even out here on this ledge in the night, was infinitely better than to die a moment earlier than he had to. His arm grew tired, and he brought it down and rested it.

He waited, arm drawn back, fist balled, but in no hurry to strike; this pause, he knew, might be an extension of his life.

Then he knew that it was time to make the attempt. He could not kneel here hesitating indefinitely till he lost all courage to act, waiting till he slipped off the ledge. Again he drew back his arm, knowing this time that he would not bring it down till he struck. His elbow protruding over Lexington Avenue far below, the fingers of his other hand pressed down bloodlessly tight against the narrow stripping, he waited, feeling the sick tenseness and terrible excitement building. It grew and swelled toward the moment of action, his nerves tautening. He thought of Clare—just a wordless, yearning thought—and then drew his arm back just a bit more, fist so tight his fingers pained him, and knowing he was going to do it. Then with full power, with every last scrap of strength he could bring to bear, he shot his arm forward toward the glass, and he said, "*Clare!*"

He heard the sound, felt the blow, felt himself falling forward, and his hand closed on the living-room curtains, the shards and fragments of glass showering onto the floor. And then, kneeling there on the ledge, an arm thrust into the room up to the shoulder, he began picking away the protruding slivers and great wedges of glass from the window frame, tossing them in onto the rug. And, as he grasped the edges of the empty window frame and climbed into his home, he was grinning in triumph.

He did not lie down on the floor or run through the apartment, as he had promised himself; even in the first few moments it seemed to him natural and normal that he should be where he was. He simply turned to his desk, pulled the crumpled yellow sheet from his pocket and laid it down where it had been, smoothing it out; then he absently laid a pencil across it to weight it down. He shook his head wonderingly, and turned to walk toward the closet.

There he got out his topcoat and hat and, without waiting to put them on, opened the front door and stepped out, to go find his wife. He turned to pull the door closed and the warm air from the hall rushed through the narrow opening again. As he saw the yellow paper, the pencil flying, scooped off the desk and, unimpeded by the glassless window, sail out into the night and out of his life, Tom Benecke burst into laughter and then closed the door behind him.

ABOUT THE AUTHOR

Jack Finney (1911–1995)

While working at an advertising agency, Jack Finney dreamed of becoming a writer. He realized his dream when he entered his first short story in a contest sponsored by a magazine—and won. Finney went on to become a hugely successful author of thrillers and science fiction. His novel *The Invasion of the Body Snatchers*, first published in 1955, has been the source of four major film adaptations. Two of his novels, *Time and Again* and *From Time to Time,* are tales of time travel in which the hero escapes the present for a simpler and calmer time in the past. Unlike his hero, Finney was happy to live in the present. "There's no past time I'd like to stay in," he said. "I want to stay here permanently."

Close Reading Activities

READ

Comprehension

Reread all or part of the text to help you answer the following questions.

1. Why does Tom choose to stay home?
2. What causes Tom to go out on the ledge?
3. How does Tom finally succeed in reentering his apartment?
4. What happens again after Tom gets back into the apartment, and how does he respond?

Research: Clarify Details This story may include references that are unfamiliar to you. Choose at least one unfamiliar detail and briefly research it. Then, explain how the information you learned from research sheds light on an aspect of the story.

Summarize Write an objective summary of the story. Remember that an objective summary is free from opinion and evaluation.

Language Study

Selection Vocabulary The following passages appear in the story. Define each boldfaced word. Then, write a paragraph in which you use all three words in a logical way.

- … the paper was caught firmly between a projection of the **convoluted** corner ornament and the ledge.
- And he saw himself striding through it, lying down on the floor on his back, arms spread wide, **reveling** in its unbelievable security.
- … then an animated cartoon, and then **interminable** scenes from coming pictures.

Diction and Style Study the sentence from the story that appears below. Then, answer the questions.

> With fear-soaked slowness, he slid his left foot an inch or two toward his own impossibly distant window.

1. **(a)** What does the adjective *fear-soaked* mean in this sentence? **(b)** Identify at least three synonyms for this term that Finney could have used.
2. What image of Tom's physical and emotional state does the adjective *fear-soaked* convey that the synonyms you chose would not? Explain.

Conventions Read this passage from the story and identify two adverbs in the comparative degree. For each adverb, state the verb it modifies in the passage. Then, write down its positive and superlative forms. Explain how the two adverbs add to the portrayal of Tom's situation.

> He waited, arm drawn back, fist balled, but in no hurry to strike; this pause, he knew, might be an extension of his life. And to live even a few seconds longer, he felt, even out here on this ledge in the night, was infinitely better than to die a moment earlier than he had to.

Academic Vocabulary

The following words appear in blue in the instructions and questions on the facing page.

convey **captures** **dilemma**

Categorize the words by deciding whether you know each one well, know it a little bit, or do not know it at all. Then, use a print or online dictionary to look up the definitions of the words you are unsure of or do not know at all.

Literary Analysis

Reread the identified passages. Then, respond to the questions that follow.

Focus Passage 1 *(pp. 114–115)*
He swung a leg … than he had thought.

Key Ideas and Details

1. **(a) Contrast:** Contrast the words the author uses to describe how Tom moves each of his legs onto the ledge. **(b) Interpret:** What does this contrast **convey** about Tom's situation?

Craft and Structure

2. **(a)** Identify details in the passage that relate to heat and cold. Note other details related to light and dark. **(b) Connect:** Explain how each set of images **captures** the physical realities of Tom's actions. **(c) Analyze:** In what ways might each set of images also be symbolic? Explain.
3. **Analyze:** How does the choppy syntax, or structure, of the sentence beginning, "It was hard to take the first shuffling sideways step" reflect Tom's struggle between his fear and his goal? Explain.

Integration of Knowledge and Ideas

4. **(a)** What mental strategy does Tom use to get himself to move along the ledge? **(b) Connect:** How does this strategy relate to the larger lesson Tom learns in the story?

Focus Passage 2 *(pp. 122–123)*
There were a dozen coins … *a wasted life.*

Key Ideas and Details

1. **(a)** Which two of Tom's qualities are described as "fierce"? **(b) Connect:** Explain how these two qualities are linked to Tom's **dilemma**.

Craft and Structure

2. **(a) Describe:** How does Tom's attitude change in this passage? **(b) Interpret:** How does the author use repetition to reveal this change? Explain.
3. **(a) Generalize:** Tom thinks "wonderingly" about his past. What does the word "wonderingly" suggest about Tom's understanding of his previous choices? Explain. **(b) Analyze:** How does Tom's changed understanding foreshadow, or hint at, the plot's resolution?
4. **Connect:** Explain the connection between this passage and the story's title. What aspect of Tom's experience does the title emphasize?

Integration of Knowledge and Ideas

5. **(a)** What occurs to Tom "with all the force of a revelation"? **(b) Connect:** How does this revelation relate to the larger meaning of the story?

Conflict

A **conflict** is a struggle between opposing forces. An external conflict is a struggle between a character and an outside force. An internal conflict is a struggle within a character. Reread the selection, and take notes on the conflicts Tom faces.

1. How does the main external conflict in this story change Tom? Explain.
2. **(a)** What is Tom's main internal conflict? **(b)** How does this conflict appear to be resolved at the end of the story? **(c)** Describe an alternative resolution the story might have had.
3. **Perseverance:** How does Tom's perseverance both create and resolve his conflicts? Explain, citing details from the story to support your thinking.

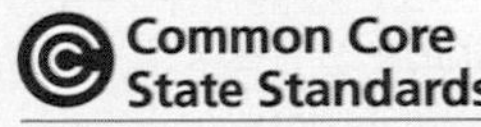

Common Core State Standards

RL.9-10.1, RL.9-10.2, RL.9-10.3, RL.9-10.4, RL.9-10.5; L.9-10.3, L.9-10.4, L.9-10.6
[For full standards wording, see the chart in the front of this book.]

DISCUSS

From Text to Topic **Group Discussion**

Discuss the following passage with a group of classmates. Take notes during the discussion. Contribute your own ideas, and support them with examples from the text.

> He thought wonderingly of his fierce ambition and of the direction his life had taken; he thought of the hours he'd spent by himself, filling the yellow sheet that had brought him out here. *Contents of the dead man's pockets,* he thought with sudden fierce anger, *a wasted life*.

QUESTIONS FOR DISCUSSION:

1. How has perseverance affected Tom's life?
2. Why does Tom now question the perseverance he brought to the pursuit of success?
3. What ideas about the values that make life meaningful are implied by this passage and by the story as a whole?

WRITE

Writing to Sources **Informative Text**

Assignment

Write a **cause-and-effect essay** in which you analyze the development of Tom's predicament in this story. In particular, discuss how Tom's perseverance both causes his situation and helps him escape it.

Prewriting and Planning Reread the story, looking for details that show how Tom's perseverance contributes to both the creation and the resolution of his problems. Record your notes in a chart or diagram that shows the chain of causes and effects that leads Tom to his resolution.

Drafting Choose an organizational structure that will help you express your ideas clearly.

- Use **chronological order** to show a flow of related causes and effects. Describe the sequence of events in time order, discussing how each cause leads to an effect.
- Use **root cause analysis** to show how one cause has many effects. Explain the initial cause and then discuss the separate effects.

In your draft, cite specific examples from the story to support your points.

Revising Reread your essay, making sure you have fully explained causes and effects. Connect your ideas by using transitional expressions, such as those listed below, that clarify these relationships.

therefore *as a result* *consequently* *for this reason*

Editing and Proofreading Make sure that the transitional words and phrases you have used accurately define relationships among your ideas. In addition, make sure you have correctly punctuated sentences containing transitions.

CONVENTIONS

When you join two closely related independent clauses with a transitional word or phrase, use a semicolon before the transition and a comma after it.

RESEARCH

Research **Investigate the Topic**

The Work Ethic At the beginning of "Contents of the Dead Man's Pocket," Tom perceives the effort reflected in the yellow paper as "the beginning of the long, long climb to where he was determined to be, at the very top." His attitude reflects what is often described as the "work ethic," a cultural view that sees a moral value in hard work.

Assignment

Conduct research to find out about the historical origins of the traditional American work ethic. Consult both primary and secondary sources. Take clear notes, and carefully identify your sources so that you can easily access the information later. Share your findings in a **presentation** for the class.

PREPARATION FOR ESSAY

You may use the results of this research project in an essay you will write at the end of this section.

Gather Sources Locate authoritative print and electronic sources. Secondary sources (such as history texts or articles in newspapers or magazines) will give you a broad overview of the topic and provide historical and cultural background. Such texts often cite primary sources (such as letters, journals, diaries, and memoirs) as references.

Take Notes Take notes on each source, either electronically or on notecards. Use an organized note-taking strategy.

- Label each note with a main idea. You may have several notes for each main idea.
- Clearly identify any text that is a direction quotation rather than a paraphrase. Use quotation marks to indicate direct quotations.
- Paraphrase ideas that are important but that you do not plan to quote word for word. Make sure to gather source information for paraphrased ideas just as carefully as you do for direct quotations.
- Thoroughly record source information to use in citations.

Synthesize Multiple Sources Gather data from both your primary and secondary sources and review it carefully. Draw a meaningful conclusion about the topic that makes sense of all the evidence, including data that might be contradictory. Use this conclusion to create a focus for your presentation. Then, organize your information and examples into a clear, logical sequence. You may write an outline, construct a script, or simply arrange your notecards in the order in which you will present ideas. End by creating a Works Cited list. See the Citing Sources pages in the Introductory Unit of this textbook for additional guidance.

Organize and Present Ideas Review your outline or sequence of ideas and practice delivering your presentation. After you deliver your presentation, accept questions from the audience and respond thoughtfully.

Common Core State Standards

W.9-10.2, W.9-10.4, W.9-10.5, W.9-10.7, W.9-10.8, W.9-10.9.a, W.9-10.10; SL.9-10.1, SL.9-10.4, SL.9-10.6; L.9-10.2.a

[For full standards wording, see the chart in the front of this book.]

In 2002, swimmer Lynne Cox attempted an ambitious feat—swimming a mile in the frigid waters of Antarctica. Cox sailed on the ship Orlova *with a team of seven friends, including team leader Barry Binder and her physicians, Susan Sklar, Gabriella Miotta, and Laura King. Martha Kaplan, Cox's agent, would scout for danger as Cox swam, while Dan Cohen stood by as a rescue swimmer. Scott Pelley, a television producer, also came. The ship's crew included Dr. Anthony Block and expedition leader Susan Adie.*

from Swimming to Antarctica

Lynne Cox

When I returned to my cabin, I thought for a long time about what I was about to attempt.

I had mixed feelings about the test swim. In some ways, it had given me confidence: I now knew that I could swim for twenty-two minutes in thirty-three-degree water. But it had also made me feel uncertain. It had been the most difficult and probably the most dangerous swim I had ever done. Part of me wanted to be satisfied with it. Part of me didn't want to attempt the mile. I was afraid.

The water temperature on the big swim would be a degree colder. Thirty-two degrees. That was a magic number, the temperature at which freshwater froze. I wondered if in thirty-two-degree water the water in my cells would freeze, if my body's tissues would become permanently damaged. I wondered if my mind would function better this time, if I would be able to be more aware of what was happening, or if it would be further dulled by the cold. Would my core temperature drop faster, more quickly than I could recognize? Would I be able to tell if I needed to get out? Did I really want to risk my life for this? Or did I want to risk failure?

The other part of me wanted to try, wanted to do what I had trained for, wanted to explore and reach beyond what I had done. That part of me was excited about venturing into the unknown. That part of me knew I would have felt a tremendous letdown if I didn't get a chance to try. I wanted to do it now.

The next morning, on December 15, 2002, Susan called me up to the bridge. She pointed out Water Boat Point. The tiny gray beach between steep glaciers was completely blocked by icebergs and brash ice.[1] There was no place to land.

We continued sailing south through the Gerlache Strait, past mountain-high glaciers and by ship-sized icebergs ranging in shades of blue from juniper berry to robin's-egg to light powder blue. In the protection of the Antarctic Peninsula, the wind dropped off and the sea grew calmer. When we reached Neko Harbor, about an hour later, Susan called me up to the bridge. She was excited. The beach was free of icebergs and brash ice. A landing was possible.

Now I would have a chance to swim the first Antarctic mile. I was thrilled and scared, but I tried to remain calm; I knew that the weather could suddenly change and the swim would be off. I met with Barry Binder, who said, "I'll get the crew into the Zodiacs[2] and come and get you when everything's set."

I walked to the ship's library, drank four eight-ounce cups of hot water, and ate two small croissants for breakfast—they were high in fat and carbohydrates, two sources of energy I would need for the swim. Then I started through the hallway to my cabin, where many of the *Orlova's* passengers were waiting, eager to find out if I was going to swim. They wished me luck and said they would wait for me at the finish. I stopped by Dan's cabin to ask him if he would jump into the water with me at the end of the swim. He was already in his

1. **brash ice** *n.* floating fragments of ice.
2. **Zodiacs** *n.* speedboats.

dry suit, prepared to go. Everyone was doing what we had practiced. All I could do was to go back to my room and wait. Gabriella came in to take a core temperature; it was up to 100.4 degrees. Knowing I was venturing into unknown waters, I must have psyched myself up so much that I increased my body temperature. Gabriella left me alone while I put on my swimsuit and sweats. I rubbed sunscreen on my face, but not on my arms or legs; it could make my skin slippery, and if my crew needed me to get out of the water quickly, that would create a problem. The night before, three of the crew had spotted a pod of eight killer whales swimming into the Gerlache Strait. They hadn't been moving fast. I hoped they were still north of us.

I stared out the window at the brown crescent-shaped beach. There were snow-covered hills directly above the beach, and massive glaciers on either side. I picked out landmarks, places I could aim for, so I'd know if I was on or off course.

Dr. Block caught me at the top of the stairs, just before we stepped out the door and onto the ramp, and asked if I would sit down on a step so he could trace two veins on my hands with a blue Magic Marker. It was just a precaution, he said, in case I needed emergency assistance; this way he would easily be able to find a vein to start an IV. I gave him my right hand and watched him draw the blue lines for the television camera. It gave me the creeps. Why did he have to do this now, right before I swam? Didn't he realize this kind of stuff psychs people out? *I know the swim is dangerous, but he could have done this hours ago, not just before I swam. Get over it,* I told myself. *Shake it off. Take a deep breath. Refocus. Take another breath. Good. Now think about the swim.* I smiled. *I'm so ready for this.*

Walking to the door, I peeked out and felt a blast of icy wind hit my face from the northwest. It was blowing in off the glaciers in gusts to twenty-five knots,[3] and the air temperature was thirty-two degrees. I felt the hair rising on my arms and my jaw tighten to suppress a shiver. I was much more nervous than I had been during my first swim. I had greater expectations of myself now. I wanted to swim the first Antarctic mile, and I knew I would be very disappointed if I didn't succeed.

I stared across the icy water at Neko Harbor's beach and felt excitement building within me. Quickly, before I could lose my chance, I pulled off my sweat suit and shoes and stuck them in a corner of the ship, climbed down the gangway, sat on the platform, and dangled my feet in the water. Surprisingly, it didn't feel any colder than it had two days before. I didn't realize then that the nerves on my skin's surface had been damaged from the first swim. I didn't know that the nerves that signaled danger weren't firing.

---

3. **knots** (näts) *n.* a rate of speed. One knot equals one nautical mile (6,076.12 feet) per hour.

I wasn't aware that my first line of defense was gone. I had no idea that prolonged exposure in thirty-two-degree water could cause permanent nerve and muscle damage. And I didn't know then that when an untrained person is immersed in water colder than forty degrees, their nerves are cooled down so they can't fire at the neuromuscular level. After only seven or eight minutes the person's body seizes up and [he or she] can't move. It was a good thing I didn't know any of this. All I knew was that I was ready. I took a deep breath, leaned back, and threw myself forward into the thirty-two-degree water.

When I hit the water, I went all the way under. I hadn't intended to do that; I hadn't wanted to immerse my head, which could over-stimulate my vagus nerve[4] and cause my heart to stop beating. Dog-paddling as quickly as I could, I popped up in the water, gasping for air. I couldn't catch my breath. I was swimming with my head up, hyperventilating.[5] I kept spinning my arms, trying to get warm, but I couldn't get enough air. I felt like I had a corset tightening around my chest. I told myself to relax, take a deep breath, but I couldn't slow my breath. And I couldn't get enough air in. I tried again. My body wanted air, and it wanted it now. I had to override that reaction of hyperventilating. I had to concentrate on my breath, to press my chest out against the cold water and draw the icy air into my lungs.

My body resisted it. The air was too cold. My body didn't want to draw the cold air deep into my lungs and cool myself from the inside. It wanted to take short breaths so the cold air would be warmed in my mouth before it reached my lungs. I was fighting against myself.

I noticed my arms. They were bright red, and I felt like I was swimming through slush. My arms were thirty two degrees, as cold as the sea. They were going numb, and so were my legs. I pulled my hands right under my chest so that I was swimming on the upper inches of the sea, trying to minimize my contact with the water. I was swimming fast and it was hard to get enough air. I began to notice that the cold was pressurizing my body like a giant tourniquet. It was squeezing the blood from the exterior part of my body and pushing it into the core. Everything felt tight. *Focus on your breath,* I told myself. *Slow it down. Let it fill your lungs. You're not going to be able to make it if you keep going at this rate.*

My arms were thirty-two degrees, as cold as the sea. They were going numb, and so were my legs.

It wasn't working. I was laboring for breath harder than on the test swim. I was in oxygen debt,[6] panting, gasping. My breath was inefficient, and the oxygen debt was compounding. In an attempt to create heat, I was spinning my arms wildly, faster than I'd ever

---

4. **vagus** (vāg´ əs) **nerve** *n.* either of a pair of nerves running from the brain to the heart that regulate the heartbeat.
5. **hyperventilating** *v.* breathing so rapidly or deeply as to cause dizziness or fainting.
6. **oxygen debt** *n.* an increased need for oxygen in the body brought on by intensive activity.

turned them over before. Laura later told me that I was swimming at a rate of ninety strokes per minute, thirty strokes per minute quicker than my normal rate. My body was demanding more oxygen, but I couldn't slow down. Not for a nanosecond. Or I would freeze up and the swim would be over.

An icy wave slapped my face: I choked and felt a wave of panic rise within me. My throat tightened. I tried to clear my throat and breathe. My breath didn't come out. I couldn't get enough air in to clear my throat. I glanced at the crew. They couldn't tell I was in trouble. If I stopped, Dan would jump in and pull me out. I still couldn't get a good breath. I thought of rolling on my back to give myself time to breathe, but I couldn't. It was too cold. I closed my mouth, overrode everything my body was telling me to do, held my breath, and gasped, coughed, cleared my windpipe, and relaxed just a little, just enough to let my guard down and catch another wave in the face. I choked again. I put my face down into the water, hoping this time I could slow my heart rate down. I held my face in the water for two strokes and told myself, *Relax, just turn your head and breathe.*

It was easier to breathe in a more horizontal position. I thought it might be helping. I drew in a deep breath and put my face down again. I knew I couldn't do this for long. I was losing too much heat through my face. The intensity of the cold was as sharp as broken glass. I'd thought that swimming across the Bering Strait[7] in thirty-eight-degree water had been tough, but there was a world of difference between thirty-eight degrees and thirty-two. In a few seconds, the cold pierced my skin and penetrated into my muscles. It felt like freezer burn, like touching wet fingers to frozen metal.

The intensity of the cold was as sharp as broken glass.

Finally I was able to gain control of my breath. I was inhaling and exhaling so deeply I could hear the breath moving in and out of my mouth even though I was wearing earplugs. I kept thinking about breathing, working on keeping it deep and even; that way I didn't have time to think about the cold.

My brain wasn't working as it normally did. It wasn't flowing freely from one idea to another—it was moving mechanically, as if my awareness came from somewhere deep inside my brain. Maybe it was because my body was being assaulted with so many sensations, too different and too complex to recognize. Or maybe it was because my blood and oxygen were going out to the working muscles. I didn't know.

For the next five or six minutes, I continued swimming, telling myself that I was doing well, telling myself that this was what I

7. **Bering Strait** (berʹ iŋ strāt) *n.* the body of water between Russia and Alaska, joining the Pacific and Arctic oceans.

had trained for. Then something clicked, as if my body had gained **equilibrium**. It had fully closed down the blood flow in my skin and fingers and toes. My arms and legs were as cold as the water, but I could feel the heat radiating deep within my torso and head, and this gave me confidence. I knew that my body was protecting my brain and vital organs. Staring through the clear, silver-blue water, I examined my fingers; they were red and swollen. They were different than when I'd been swimming in the Bering Strait, when they'd looked like the fingers of a dead person. They looked healthy, and I thought their swollenness would give me more surface area, more to pull with.

◀ **equilibrium** (ē´ kwi lib´ rē əm) *n.* state of balance

I smiled and looked up at the crew, who were in the Zodiacs on either side of me. Each of them was leaning forward, willing me ahead. Their faces were filled with tension. Gabriella, Barry, Dan, and Scott were leaning so far over the Zodiac's pontoon I felt as if they were swimming right beside me. I was sprinting faster than I ever had before, moving faster than the Zodiac, and I was getting fatigued quickly. The water was thicker than on the test swim, and it took more force to pull through on each stroke. My arms ached. I didn't feel right; I couldn't seem to get into any kind of a rhythm. Then I sensed that something was wrong.

We were heading to the left, toward some glaciers. This didn't make sense; we couldn't land there. It was too dangerous. The glaciers could calve[8] and kill us.

"Barry, where are we going?" I shouted, using air I needed for breathing.

He pointed out our direction—right toward the glaciers. I didn't understand. I didn't want to go that way. I wanted to aim for the beach. I was confused. I was moving my arms as fast as they would go, and it was taking all I had. From each moment to the next, I had to tell myself to keep going. The water felt so much colder than on the test swim. It had already worked its way deep into my muscles. My arms and legs were stiff. My strokes were short and choppy. But I kept going, telling myself to trust the crew and focus on the glaciers to watch the outcropping of rocks that was growing larger. I couldn't get into any kind of pace.

Abruptly the Zodiacs zagged to the right. I looked up and thought, *Wow, okay; we're heading for the beach now.* For a moment, I started to feel better. I was able to extend my reach farther, and I could see passengers from the *Orlova* walking along the snowbanks. In the distance, their clothes lost their color and they looked black, like giant penguins. I saw smaller black figures, too—real penguins nesting near the edge of the shore. For a few moments, I felt like I

---

8. **calve** (käv) *v.* give birth to young; used here to refer to the "birth" of a new ice mass when a piece of a glacier splits off.

was going to be okay, like I was going to make it in to shore, but then the Zodiacs abruptly turned farther to the right, and we were headed past the beach for another range of glaciers.

Finally, it occurred to me that the *Orlova* had anchored too close to shore for me to swim a mile, so Barry was adding distance by altering the course. And the ship's captain was on the bridge monitoring our course on his GPS[9] and radioing our Zodiacs, updating them on the distance we had traveled. One of the passengers, Mrs. Stokie, who was on the bridge with him, told me later, "The captain was watching you and he was shaking his head. He was an older man, and he had experienced everything. And now he was seeing something new. It was good for him. Still, I think he couldn't believe it."

We continued on right past the beach, toward more glaciers.

"How long have I been swimming?" I asked.

"Fifteen minutes," Barry said.

I had swum a little more than half a mile. I looked up at the shore. If I turned left, I could make it in. I could reach the shore. This struggle could be over. But I wouldn't complete the mile. I had swum farther two days before. But I was tired now, and this was so much harder. I just didn't feel right. I couldn't figure out what the problem was. I kept talking to myself, coaching myself to keep going. Then I felt it; it was the water pressure, and it was increasing on my back. It meant there was a strong current behind me. I looked at the glaciers onshore, using the fixed points to **gauge** how fast the current was flowing. It was flowing at over a knot. I wondered if I would have enough strength to fight it when we turned around and headed back for the beach. It would cut my speed by half and could cause me to lose heat more rapidly.

gauge ▶ (gāj) *v.* measure something's size, amount, extent or capacity

Barry and the crew in the Zodiacs couldn't feel what was happening. They had no idea we were moving into a risky area. If the current grew any stronger, it could cost us the swim. Barry motioned for me to swim past a peninsula and across a narrow channel. I lifted my head and pulled my hands directly under my chest, to gain more lift, so I could look across the bay and see if we had any other options for landing. There were no alternatives. This made me very uncomfortable. Chances were good that there would be a strong current flowing into or out of the narrow bay. And if we got caught in that current, all would be lost.

We started across the inlet, and within a moment I could feel that second current, slamming into our right side at two knots, pushing us into the inlet. Without any explanation, I spun around, put my head down, dug my arms into the water, and crabbed[10] into the current.

---

9. **GPS** "Global Positioning System," referring here to a portable device that provides information about the bearer's location and speed.
10. **crabbed** *v.* moved sideways or diagonally.

I focused on repositioning myself so I could parallel shore again and head toward Neko Harbor. Barry knew I knew what I was doing. But the abrupt course change caught the Zodiac drivers by surprise. They scattered in different directions, trying to avoid ramming into each other and trying to catch up with me. The motor on the lead Zodiac on my left sputtered and stopped. The second Zodiac immediately pulled up beside me. I sprinted against the current.

"How long have I been swimming?"

"Twenty-one minutes," Barry said. He and all the crew were watching me intently, their faces filled with tension and concern.

I put my head down, and something suddenly clicked. Maybe it was because I knew shore was within reach, or maybe because I got a second wind; I don't know. But I was finally swimming strongly, stretching out and moving fluidly. My arms and legs were as cold as the sea, but I felt the heat within my head and contained in my torso and I thrilled to it, knowing my body had carried me to places no one else had been in only a bathing suit. I looked down into the water; it was a bright blue-gray and so clear that it appeared as if I were swimming through air. The viscosity of the water was different, too; it was thicker than any I had ever swum in. It felt like I was swimming through gelato. And I got more push out of each arm stroke than I ever had before. I looked at the crew. They were leaning so far over the pontoons, as if they were right there with me. I needed to let them know I was okay.

I lifted my head, took a big breath, and shouted, "Barry, I'm swimming to Antarctica!"

I saw the smiles, heard the cheers and laughs, and I felt their energy lift me. They were as thrilled as I was. I swam faster, extending my arms, pulling more strongly, reaching for the shores of Antarctica. Now I knew we were almost there.

The crew was shouting warnings about ice. I swerved around two icebergs. Some chunks looked sharp, but I was too tired to care. I swam into whatever was in my path. It hurt, but all I wanted now was to finish.

As we neared shore, I lifted my head and saw the other passengers from the *Orlova*, in their bright red and yellow hats and parkas, tromping down the snowbanks, spreading their feet and arms wide for balance, racing to the water's edge to meet us. I lifted my foot and waved and saw my crew break into bigger smiles.

I'm almost done, I thought. *I feel okay. I feel strong. I feel warm inside. My arms and legs are thirty-two degrees. But I feel good. I can stretch out my strokes and put my face in the water. Maybe I can go a little farther. Maybe I can see what more I can do. Maybe I can swim five or ten more minutes. Or maybe I should be happy with what I've done. My skin is so cold I can't feel it, and when I stop swimming, I don't know how far my temperature's going to drop.* I looked at my watch. Twenty-three minutes. I'd been in a minute longer than two days before. *How much difference would a minute make? I asked myself. How much difference is there between thirty-two-degree and thirty-three-degree water? Remember what Dr. Keatinge*[11] *said: once your temperature starts to drop, it will drop very fast. If you continue swimming, you're going to cool down even more. Remember how hard you shivered last time? Remember how much work it was? Remember how uncomfortable you were? This is the place where people make mistakes, when they're tired and cold and they push too far into the unknown. You could really hurt yourself. Finish now. You've done a good job. Be satisfied with what you've done. Go celebrate with your friends.*

Turning in toward shore, I again lifted my foot and waved it, and my friends waved back and cheered. One hundred yards from shore, I saw chinstrap penguins sliding headfirst, like tiny black toboggans, down a steep snowbank. When they reached the base of the hill, they used their bristly tails like brakes, sticking them into the snow to stop their momentum. They waddled across the beach at full tilt, holding their wings out at their sides for balance. Reaching the water, they dove in headfirst, then porpoised across it, clearing it by one or two feet with each surface dive. They tucked their wings back by their sides so they would be more aerodynamic. When they neared the Zodiacs, they dove and flapped their wings under the water as if they were flying through air. It was amazing to think this was the only place they would fly. They zoomed under me in bursts of speed, and their bubbles exploded like white fireworks. More penguins joined in. One cannonballed off a ledge, another slipped on some ice and belly flopped, and three penguins swam within inches of my hands. I reached out to touch one, but he swerved and flapped his wings, so he moved just beyond my fingertips. I had no idea why they were swimming with me, but I knew it was a good sign; it meant there were no killer whales or leopard seals in the area.

When I reached knee-deep water, Dan jumped in, ran through the water, looped his arm through mine, and helped me stand. "Are you okay?" he asked.

"Yes. We made it!" I said.

Everyone around me was crying. Susan Adie helped Dan pull me up the incline. Martha wrapped a towel around my shoulders. Barry hugged me tightly. Laura and Susan began drying me off. I was so cold I was already starting to shiver hard. My legs were stiffer than after the other swim. The crew helped me into the Zodiac and I flopped onto the floor. Laura and Susan piled on top of me to protect

---

11. **Dr. Keatinge** Cox's doctor on her swim across the Bering Strait.

me from the wind, and we pounded across the water, my head slamming into the Zodiac's floor. I managed to lift my head so that someone could place a hand under it to **buffer** the impact. I was so cold and stiff and shaking harder than before.

◀ **buffer**
(buf´ ər) *v.* lessen a shock; cushion

When we reached the *Orlova*, it took me a minute to stand, to gain my balance, and as I climbed the ramp's steps I clung to the railing and pulled myself up, shaking hard. By the time I reached the top of the ramp, my teeth were chattering and I was breathing harder and faster than when I had been swimming. I didn't like being so cold. I didn't like my body having to work so hard. My temperature had dropped to 95.5 degrees, and I couldn't control my shaking. I just let go, and my body bounced up and down with shakes and shivers.

Quickly Martha and Dan and the three doctors huddled around me like emperor penguins, and their combined comfort and body heat began to warm me. It seemed as if I would never stop shaking, and I was completely exhausted. Within half an hour my shivering had subsided to small body shudders. Once I was able to stand and maintain my balance, the doctors helped me pull on a special top and pants that had been designed by a friend. She had sewn pockets under the arms, in the groin area, and into a scarf and had placed chemical packs that emitted heat inside the pockets. Their placement in the clothing warmed the major blood-flow areas of my body so that I was heated from the inside out. It was effective, and within an hour my temperature was back to normal.

That night we celebrated with everyone aboard the *Orlova*. I had swum the first Antarctic mile—a distance of 1.06 miles, in fact—in thirty-two-degree water in twenty-five minutes. I had been able to do what had seemed impossible because I'd had a crew who believed in me and in what we as human beings were capable of. It was a great dream, swimming to Antarctica.

ABOUT THE AUTHOR

Lynne Cox (b.1957)

Raised in California, Lynne Cox started breaking swimming records when she was young. At age fourteen, she swam twenty-six miles from Catalina Island to the California coast. The next year, she broke the men's and the women's records swimming the English Channel.

Cox's ability to swim so well is due in part to her natural build. She has a high percentage of body fat, evenly distributed around her body. This fat helps her float and provides insulation. Her unique body has allowed her to swim in waters ranging from the Bering Strait to Antarctica. Today, Lynne Cox stands as the most successful cold-water long-distance swimmer ever.

Close Reading Activities

READ

Comprehension

Reread all or part of the text to help you answer the following questions.

1. What is Cox's goal in this swim?
2. What physical challenges does Cox face when she starts her swim?
3. What changes for Cox after she shifts her breathing strategy?
4. What is the outcome of Cox's attempt?

Research: Clarify Details This memoir may include references to concepts that are unfamiliar to you. Choose at least one of these concepts and briefly research it. Then, write a paragraph in which you explain how the information you learned helps you better understand an aspect of the text.

Summarize Write an objective summary of the text, one that is free of opinion or evaluation.

Language Study

Selection Vocabulary: Technical Terms The following phrases appear in the memoir. Define each boldfaced word as it is used in the text. Then, identify a technical meaning for each word.

- gained **equilibrium**
- **gauge** how fast
- **buffer** the impact

Literary Analysis

Reread the identified passage. Then, respond to the questions that follow.

Focus Passage *(pp. 137–138)*

The crew was shouting … *your friends.*

Key Ideas and Details

1. **(a)** What does the crew warn Cox about? **(b)** How does Cox respond? **(c) Interpret:** What does Cox's response show about her character?
2. **(a)** How does Cox describe the passengers from the *Orlova?* **(b) Interpret:** How does this description affect the mood of her **account**?

Craft and Structure

3. **(a)** Identify two examples of repeated grammatical patterns in the italicized sentences. **(b) Connect:** What does her use of parallel structure reveal about Cox's thought process?

Integration of Knowledge and Ideas

4. **(a)** What types of information appear in the sentences beginning with "Remember"? **(b) Interpret:** What do these sentences help you **discern** about Cox's attitude toward her goals? Explain.

Author's Perspective

An **author's perspective** includes the judgments, attitudes, and experiences he or she brings to the subject. Reread the excerpt and note details that suggest Cox's perspective.

1. **(a)** What potential danger does Dr. Block **anticipate**? **(b)** How do the doctor's precautionary steps affect Cox's thinking? **(c)** What does Cox's reaction reveal about her perspective?
2. **Perseverance: (a)** List two ways in which Cox's story would be different if told by a reporter. **(b)** How might such a change affect the presentation of Cox's determination?

DISCUSS • RESEARCH • WRITE

From Text to Topic **Panel Discussion**

Use the following passage as the subject for a panel discussion. Take notes during the discussion. Contribute your own ideas, and support them with examples from the text.

> That night we celebrated with everyone aboard the *Orlova*. I had swum the first Antarctic mile—a distance of 1.06 miles, in fact—in thirty-two-degree water in twenty-five minutes. I had been able to do what had seemed impossible because I'd had a crew who believed in me and in what we as human beings were capable of. It was a great dream, swimming to Antarctica.

QUESTIONS FOR DISCUSSION

1. What attitude does Cox show toward her achievement?
2. In Cox's view, what role does her team have in the success of her swim?
3. Why do people set themselves "impossible" goals, such as Cox's Antarctic swim?

Research **Investigate the Topic**

Practicing Lynne Cox excels as a cold-water swimmer, in part, because of her unique combination of physical traits. She also excels because she has prepared, trained, and practiced for most of her life.

Assignment

Research different theories about how people learn and master challenging skills. Find information about the relationship between practice, effort, and talent in achieving excellence in an academic, athletic, or artistic pursuit. Share your findings in an **informal speech or presentation**.

PREPARATION FOR ESSAY

You may use the results of this research in an essay you will write at the end of this section.

Writing to Sources **Informative Text**

In *Swimming to Antarctica,* Lynne Cox describes how a combination of physical, intellectual, and emotional qualities help her achieve her dream.

Assignment

Write a **profile,** or biographical sketch, of Lynne Cox. Describe her athletic and emotional attributes, and explain how she was able to achieve her goals. Follow these steps:

- Introduce Cox's combination of traits.
- Cite examples from the memoir that show how these different characteristics contribute to Cox's achievements.
- Use vivid, descriptive words that make Cox's journey, including its preparation and aftermath, come alive for readers.

ACADEMIC VOCABULARY

Academic terms appear in blue on these pages. If these words are not familiar to you, use a dictionary to find their definitions. Then, use them as you speak and write about the text.

Common Core State Standards

RI.9-10.1, RI.9-10.2, RI.9-10.4, RI.9-10.5; W.9-10.2, W.9-10.4, W.9-10.7, W.9-10.9, W.9-10.10; SL.9-10.1, SL.9-10.4, SL.9-10.6; L.9-10.1, L.9-10.4, L.9-10.6

[For full standards wording, see the chart in the front of this book.]

Occupation: Conductorette

from

I Know Why the Caged Bird Sings

Maya Angelou

I had it. The answer came to me with the suddenness of a collision. I would go to work. Mother wouldn't be difficult to convince; after all, in school I was a year ahead of my grade and Mother was a firm believer in self-sufficiency. In fact, she'd be pleased to think that I had that much gumption, that much of her in my character. (She liked to speak of herself as the original "do-it-yourself girl.")

Once I had settled on getting a job, all that remained was to decide which kind of job I was most fitted for. My intellectual pride had kept me from selecting typing, shorthand or filing as subjects in school, so office work was ruled out. War plants and shipyards demanded birth certificates, and mine would reveal me to be fifteen, and ineligible for work. So the well-paying defense jobs were also out. Women had replaced men on the streetcars as conductors and motormen, and the thought of sailing up and down the hills of San Francisco in a dark-blue uniform, with a money changer at my belt, caught my fancy.

Mother was as easy as I had anticipated. The world was moving so fast, so much money was being made, so many people were dying in Guam, and Germany,[1] that hordes of strangers became good friends overnight. Life was cheap and death entirely free. How could she have the time to think about my academic career?

To her question of what I planned to do, I replied that I would get a job on the streetcars. She rejected the proposal with: "They don't accept colored people on the streetcars."

I would like to claim an immediate fury which was followed by the noble determination to break the restricting tradition. But the truth is, my first reaction was one of disappointment. I'd pictured myself, dressed in a neat blue serge suit, my money changer swinging jauntily at my waist, and a cheery smile for the passengers which would make their own work day brighter.

From disappointment, I gradually ascended the emotional ladder to haughty **indignation**, and finally to that state of stubbornness where the mind is locked like the jaws of an enraged bulldog.

◀ **indignation** (in´ dig nā´ shən) *n.* anger that is a reaction to injustice or meanness

I would go to work on the streetcars and wear a blue serge suit. Mother gave me her support with one of her usual terse asides, "That's what you want to do? Then nothing beats a trial but a failure. Give it everything you've got. I've told you many times, 'Can't do is like Don't Care.' Neither of them have a home."

1. **Guam** (gwäm), **and Germany** places where World War II (1939–1945) was fought. Guam is an island in the Pacific Ocean.

Translated, that meant there was nothing a person can't do, and there should be nothing a human being didn't care about. It was the most positive encouragement I could have hoped for.

In the offices of the Market Street Railway Company, the receptionist seemed as surprised to see me there as I was surprised to find the interior dingy and the décor drab. Somehow I had expected waxed surfaces and carpeted floors. If I had met no resistance, I might have decided against working for such a poor-mouth-looking concern. As it was, I explained that I had come to see about a job. She asked, was I sent by an agency, and when I replied that I was not, she told me they were only accepting applicants from agencies.

The classified pages of the morning papers had listed advertisements for motorettes and conductorettes and I reminded her of that. She gave me a face full of astonishment that my suspicious nature would not accept.

"I am applying for the job listed in this morning's *Chronicle* and I'd like to be presented to your personnel manager." While I spoke in supercilious accents, and looked at the room as if I had an oil well in my own backyard, my armpits were being pricked by millions of hot pointed needles. She saw her escape and dived into it.

"He's out. He's out for the day. You might call tomorrow and if he's in, I'm sure you can see him." Then she swiveled her chair around on its rusty screws and with that I was supposed to be dismissed.

"May I ask his name?"

She half turned, acting surprised to find me still there.

"His name? Whose name?"

"Your personnel manager."

hypocrisy ▶ (hi päk′ rə sē) *n.* the act of saying one thing but doing another

We were firmly joined in the **hypocrisy** to play out the scene.

"The personnel manager? Oh, he's Mr. Cooper, but I'm not sure you'll find him here tomorrow. He's . . . Oh, but you can try."

"Thank you."

"You're welcome."

And I was out of the musty room and into the even mustier lobby. In the street I saw the receptionist and myself going faithfully through paces that were stale with familiarity, although I had never encountered that kind of situation before and, probably, neither had she. We were like actors who, knowing the play by heart, were still able to cry afresh over the old tragedies and laugh spontaneously at the comic situations.

The miserable little encounter had nothing to do with me, the me of me, any more than it had to do with that silly clerk. The incident was a recurring dream, concocted years before by stupid whites and it eternally came back to haunt us all. The secretary and I were like Hamlet and Laertes[2] in the final scene, where, because of harm done by one ancestor to another, we were bound to duel to the death. Also because the play must end somewhere.

I went further than forgiving the clerk, I accepted her as a fellow victim of the same puppeteer.

On the streetcar, I put my fare into the box and the conductorette looked at me with the usual hard eyes of white contempt. "Move into the car, please move on in the car." She patted her money changer.

Her Southern nasal accent sliced my meditation and I looked deep into my thoughts. All lies, all comfortable lies. The receptionist was not innocent and neither was I. The whole charade we had played out in that crummy waiting room had directly to do with me, Black, and her, white.

I wouldn't move into the streetcar but stood on the ledge over the conductor, glaring. My mind shouted so energetically that the announcement made my veins stand out, and my mouth tighten into a prune.

I WOULD HAVE THE JOB. I WOULD BE A CONDUCTORETTE AND SLING A FULL MONEY CHANGER FROM MY BELT. I WOULD.

The next three weeks were a honeycomb[3] of determination with apertures for the days to go in and out. The Negro organizations to whom I appealed for support bounced me back and forth like a shuttlecock on a badminton court. Why did I insist on that particular job? Openings were going begging that paid nearly twice the money. The minor officials with whom I was able to win an audience thought me mad. Possibly I was.

The minor officials with whom I was able to win an audience thought me mad. Possibly I was.

Downtown San Francisco became alien and cold, and the streets I had loved in a personal familiarity were unknown lanes that twisted with malicious intent. Old buildings, whose gray rococo façades[4] housed my memories of the Forty-Niners, and Diamond Lil, Robert Service, Sutter and Jack London,[5] were then imposing structures viciously joined to keep me out. My trips to the streetcar office were of the frequency of a person on salary. The struggle expanded. I was no longer in conflict only with the Market Street Railway but with the marble lobby of the building which housed its offices, and elevators and their operators.

2. **Hamlet and Laertes** (lā ʉr′ tēz) characters in William Shakespeare's tragedy *Hamlet* who duel at the end of the play. Hamlet held an ancestral grudge against Fortinbras, the son of his father's enemy. Hamlet's duel with Laertes at the end of the play resolves a different conflict.
3. **honeycomb** (hun′ ē kōm′) *n.* wax structure, filled with holes, that bees build to store honey.
4. **rococo façades** (rə kō′ kō fə sädz′) elaborately designed building fronts.
5. **the Forty-Niners...Jack London** The author refers to figures associated with the gold rushes of the 1800s. Forty-Niners were prospectors who came to San Francisco during the California Gold Rush of 1849; Diamond Lil was a flashy entertainer; Robert Service was a Canadian poet who portrayed Yukon Gold Rush miners of the 1890s; John Sutter owned the land where gold was first discovered in California; Jack London was a writer who re-created his experiences in the Yukon Gold Rush in his stories.

During this period of strain Mother and I began our first steps on the long path toward mutual adult admiration. She never asked for reports and I didn't offer any details. But every morning she made breakfast, gave me carfare and lunch money, as if I were going to work. She comprehended the perversity of life, that in the struggle lies the joy. That I was no glory seeker was obvious to her, and that I had to exhaust every possibility before giving in was also clear.

On my way out of the house one morning she said, "Life is going to give you just what you put in it. Put your whole heart in everything you do, and pray, then you can wait." Another time she reminded me that "God helps those who help themselves." She had a store of aphorisms which she dished out as the occasion demanded. Strangely, as bored as I was with clichés, her inflection gave them something new, and set me thinking for a little while at least. Later when asked how I got my job, I was never able to say exactly. I only knew that one day, which was tiresomely like all the others before it, I sat in the Railway office, ostensibly waiting to be interviewed. The receptionist called me to her desk and shuffled a bundle of papers to me. They were job application forms. She said they had to be filled in triplicate. I had little time to wonder if I had won or not, for the standard questions reminded me of the necessity for **dexterous** lying. How old was I? List my previous jobs, starting from the last held and go backward to the first. How much money did I earn, and why did I leave the position? Give two references (not relatives).

dexterous ▶ (deks′ tər əs) *adj.* having or showing mental skill

Sitting at a side table my mind and I wove a cat's ladder of near truths and total lies. I kept my face blank (an old art) and wrote quickly the fable of Marguerite Johnson, aged nineteen, former companion and driver for Mrs. Annie Henderson (a White Lady) in Stamps, Arkansas.

I was given blood tests, aptitude tests, physical coordination tests, and Rorschachs,[6] then on a blissful day I was hired as the first Negro on the San Francisco streetcars.

---

6. **Rorschachs** (rôr′ shäks′) The Rorschach test uses abstract images to measure an individual's personality traits.

Mother gave me the money to have my blue serge suit tailored, and I learned to fill out work cards, operate the money changer and punch transfers. The time crowded together and at an End of Days I was swinging on the back of the rackety trolley, smiling sweetly and persuading my charges to "step forward in the car, please."

For one whole semester the street cars and I shimmied up and scooted down the sheer hills of San Francisco. I lost some of my need for the Black ghetto's shielding-sponge quality, as I clanged and cleared my way down Market Street, with its honky-tonk homes for homeless sailors, past the quiet retreat of Golden Gate Park and along closed undwelled-in-looking dwellings of the Sunset District.

My work shifts were split so haphazardly that it was easy to believe that my superiors had chosen them maliciously. Upon mentioning my suspicions to Mother, she said, "Don't worry about it. You ask for what you want, and you pay for what you get. And I'm going to show you that it ain't no trouble when you pack double."

She stayed awake to drive me out to the car barn at four thirty in the mornings, or to pick me up when I was relieved just before dawn. Her awareness of life's perils convinced her that while I would be safe on the public conveyances, she "wasn't about to trust a taxi driver with her baby."

When the spring classes began, I resumed my commitment with formal education. I was so much wiser and older, so much more independent, with a bank account and clothes that I had bought for myself, that I was sure that I had learned and earned the magic formula which would make me a part of the gay life my contemporaries led.

ABOUT THE AUTHOR

Maya Angelou (b. 1928)

Maya Angelou was born Marguerite Johnson in St. Louis, Missouri. Some of the communities in which she grew up were segregated. African Americans were excluded from facilities—such as hotels, restaurants, public transportation, and schools—used by whites. However, Angelou rejects bitterness, asserting, "The honorary duty of a human being is to love." In 1940, as the United States prepared for World War II, Angelou moved with her mother to San Francisco, California. She later spent several years in Africa and worked with Martin Luther King, Jr., during the civil rights movement. Her literary success came in 1970 with the publication of *I Know Why the Caged Bird Sings,* the first book of her multi-volume autobiography.

Close Reading Activities

READ

Comprehension

Reread all or part of the text to help you answer the following questions.

1. Why does Angelou decide to seek work as a streetcar conductorette?
2. What is the main obstacle Angelou must overcome?
3. How does Angelou's job quest affect her relationship with her mother?

Research: Clarify Details This selection may include references that are unfamiliar to you. Choose at least one unfamiliar detail and briefly research it. Then, explain how the information you learned helps you better understand the text.

Summarize Write an objective summary of the selection, one that is free from opinion and evaluation.

Language Study

Selection Vocabulary The following sentences appear in "Occupation: Conductorette." Define each boldfaced word. Then, write a description of a person or a situation that displays the qualities associated with each word.

- From disappointment, I gradually ascended the emotional ladder to haughty **indignation** ...
- We were firmly joined in the **hypocrisy** ...
- ... the standard questions reminded me of the necessity for **dexterous** lying.

Literary Analysis

Reread the identified passage. Then, respond to the questions that follow.

Focus Passage *(pp. 144–145)*

We were firmly joined ... I WOULD.

Key Ideas and Details

1. **(a)** To what does Angelou compare her argument with the receptionist? **(b) Interpret:** How does this comparison reflect the social **context**, or cultural barriers, Angelou is facing?

Craft and Structure

2. **(a) Distinguish:** In the sentence beginning "The incident," identify two words that relate to states that are not quite real. **(b) Interpret:** What does Angelou's diction suggest about her attitude toward prejudice? Explain.
3. **(a)** Which words does the author repeat in the last paragraph? **(b) Evaluate:** What does this repetition suggest about Angelou's mindset?

Integration of Knowledge and Ideas

4. **(a) Infer:** Why does Angelou refuse to move into the streetcar when prompted by the conductorette? **(b) Synthesize:** In what way does her refusal symbolize the goal she sets for herself at the end of the passage?

Dialogue

Dialogue is conversation between characters. Reread the selection, and take notes on Angelou's use of dialogue.

1. **(a)** The author quotes her mother, but merely implies her own side of the conversation. Write down two sentences that fill out the daughter's part in that dialogue. **(b)** What does the mother's statement tell you about the values she **instilled** in her daughter? Explain.
2. **Perseverance: (a)** Cite a passage of dialogue that shows the author's determination to get a job. **(b)** How do Angelou's questions during the conversation illustrate her perseverance?

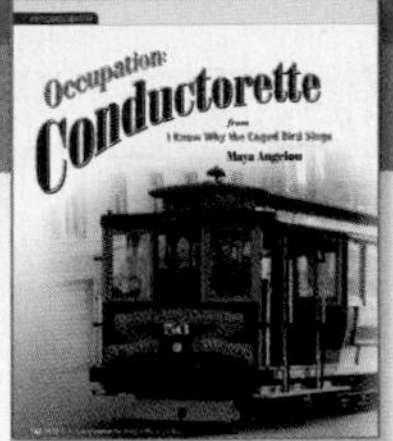

DISCUSS • RESEARCH • WRITE

From Text to Topic **Group Discussion**

Discuss the following passage with a group of classmates. Take notes during the discussion. Contribute your own ideas, and support them with examples from the text.

> The next three weeks were a honeycomb of determination with apertures for the days to go in and out. The Negro organizations to whom I appealed for support bounced me back and forth like a shuttlecock on a badminton court. Why did I insist on that particular job? Openings were going begging that paid nearly twice the money. The minor officials with whom I was able to win an audience thought me mad. Possibly I was.

QUESTIONS FOR DISCUSSION

1. Why do the people around Angelou fail to understand her determination to be a conductorette?
2. Why might Angelou think that her youthful self was in some sense "mad"?

Research **Investigate the Topic**

Origins of the Civil Rights Movement This **episode** from Angelou's youth took place in 1943, when she was fifteen years old. At that time, the civil rights movement was about a decade away.

Assignment

Conduct research on the origins of the civil rights movement in the late 1940s. Find out what conditions were like for many African Americans at that time and research the first pieces of legislation that would lead to change. Based on this information, draw conclusions about the relationship between perseverance and social change. Take clear notes and carefully identify your sources. Share your findings in an **oral presentation** for the class.

PREPARATION FOR ESSAY

You may use the results of this research in an essay you will write at the end of this section.

Writing to Sources **Narrative**

In this excerpt, Maya Angelou looks back at her stubborn pursuit of a youthful ambition. Others questioned her goal, but the experience shaped her character.

Assignment

Write an **autobiographical narrative** in which you describe a goal that you once pursued intensely and which you feel has shaped who you are. Follow these steps:

- Introduce the goal and explain your enthusiasm for it.
- Clearly describe the steps you took to pursue that goal.
- Clarify differences between your perspectives on the goal then and now.
- Provide a conclusion in which you refer to both your experience and Angelou's to draw a conclusion about the value of youthful persistence.

ACADEMIC VOCABULARY

Academic terms appear in blue on these pages. If these words are not familiar to you, use a dictionary to find their definitions. Then, use them as you speak and write about the text.

Common Core State Standards

RI.9-10.1, RI.9-10.2, RI.9-10.3, RI.9-10.4, RI.9-10.5; W.9-10.3, W.9-10.4, W.9-10.7, W.9-10.9, W.9-10.10; SL.9-10.1, SL.9-10.4, SL.9-10.6; L.9-10.1, L.9-10.4, L.9-10.6

[For full standards wording, see the chart in the front of this book.]

Robert Reich

Stephen J. Dubner

from

The Upside of Quitting

Freakonomics Radio

09/30/2011 | 11:31 AM

Stephen J. DUBNER: I'd like you to stop whatever you're doing right now. No, no, I don't mean stop so you can give your full attention to this radio show. Honestly, radio is the perfect medium for multitasking—unless maybe you're using a chainsaw or something. What I mean is Stop. Whatever. You're. Doing. As in, doing with your life. Maybe it's your job. Maybe it's a relationship that's **curdled**. Maybe there's some dream project you've been working on so long that you can't even remember what got you all heated up about it in the first place. I want to encourage you to just quit. Or at least think about quitting. Why? Well, because everybody else is always saying the opposite. It's become so ingrained that we don't even think about it any more. You know: "A quitter never wins and a winner never quits." You know what I think when I hear people say that? I think: "Are you sure?"

◀ **curdled** (kurd′ 'ld) *v.* spoiled or soured

ANNOUNCER: From WNYC and APM: American Public Media, this is Freakonomics Radio. Today: "The Upside of Quitting." Here's your host, Stephen Dubner.

DUBNER: So I hang out with a lot of economists. (I know, you're envious.) But there are two things they love to talk about that will help us understand quitting. One is called "sunk cost" and the other is "opportunity cost." "Sunk cost" is about the past—it's the time, or money, or sweat equity[1] that you've put into something, which makes it hard to abandon. "Opportunity cost" is about the future. It means that for every hour or dollar you spend on one thing, you're giving up the opportunity to spend that hour or dollar on something else—something that might make your life better. If only you weren't so worried about the sunk cost. If only you could quit. . . . First, here's someone who made headlines when he quit.

Robert REICH: *Well, this was long in coming—I was feeling more and more miserable about not seeing my kids; it was weighing on me to a greater extent. I made the decision that shortly after the election I would leave. And then one day I went into the Oval Office[2] and explained to the president that I just felt that I had no choice. He was very understanding about it.*

DUBNER: That's Robert Reich. He was the U.S. Secretary of Labor during President Clinton's first term. He helped put in place the

1. **sweat equity** familiar expression for labor invested in a project.
2. **Oval Office** U.S. president's office in the White House.

Family and Medical Leave Act; he raised the minimum wage. On his watch, unemployment fell below 5 percent—the lowest it had been in 20 years! Now it's hard to say how effective any one person in Washington really is, but *Time* magazine named Reich one of the 10 best Cabinet members of the twentieth century. And then Reich quit.

REICH: *The question for me was, "How do I alert my employees and the segment of the public that feel that they are relying on me in some way?" How did I handle it publicly? It's a delicate matter. I decided that I would write an op-ed*[3] *for* The New York Times, *"My Personal Family Leave Act." I had been responsible for implementing the Family and Medical Leave Act that actually was passed years before. And it seems to me important to say to men as well as women that it is okay to leave your job.*

DUBNER: Here, as Reich wrote it, was his dilemma: "You love your job and you love your family, and you desperately want more of both." His wife and two teenage sons were back in Cambridge, Massachusetts. And he was—well, he could have been anywhere. . . .

The funny thing is no one believed Reich quit because he actually wanted to spend more time with his family. That's what CEOs[4] say when they're booted. But people—especially male people—don't quit White House jobs to do that. But Reich really meant it! As he saw it, there was a big upside to quitting.

REICH: *It was exactly the right move. I think if I had not done it I would have regretted it all my life. The boys then would have gone off to college, off to their careers. I just wouldn't have had those years. At the same time, I think I was fooling myself a little bit in thinking that young teenage boys would drop everything when their father came home and say, "Oh, Dad, it's great to have you. Let's play!" No, they were very happy to have me there, but they said, "But, Dad, we're going off with our friends." So, I kind of would trail around after them a little bit with my metaphoric tail between my legs and try to say, "Wouldn't you like to play? How about going to a baseball game?"*

You get a phone call that says, "How's it feel to be the next member of the Houston Astros?" It's a dream come true.

DUBNER: Robert Reich quit what was, for him, a dream job: running the Department of Labor of the United States. But tell me the truth—when you were a kid, did you dream of running the Department of Labor? Or did you have a dream that sounded more like this?

Justin HUMPHRIES: *You get a phone call that says, "How's it feel to be the next member of the Houston Astros?" It's a dream come true. So I ended up signing. I got some money to pay for school, and went straight to Martinsville at 18.*

---

3. **op-ed** article on a page of special features often appearing opposite the editorial page of a newspaper.
4. **CEOs** abbreviation for "Chief Executive Officers," officials who exercise chief decision-making powers in a business or other organization.

DUBNER: That's Justin Humphries. Not long ago, he was considered one of the best young baseball players in the country—a big power-hitter from a suburb of Houston. Getting drafted by the hometown Astros was especially sweet—and they threw in some money for education, for later. But Humphries wasn't thinking about that. He had one goal: to make the majors. So he went off to the Astros' minor-league team in Martinsville, Virginia. And then more teams in Kentucky, Louisiana, Florida, New Jersey. But not, you may have noticed, Houston. He hit pretty well—but he hurt his wrist, and then his knee, and in 2009, at the ripe age of 27, Humphries quit baseball. Now, only 11 percent of the kids who get drafted each year make the majors; but, probably close to 100 percent of them think they will. Humphries, even before he quit for good, started back in school, at a junior college in Texas. He wound up transferring to Columbia University, where he took a sociology course with a professor named Sudhir Venkatesh. . . .

Sudhir VENKATESH: *I'm interested in quitting for a number of reasons, not the least of which is that it's hard for me to do it. But I also think it's just really, really hard the older you get, especially when you start identifying yourself with a job.*

DUBNER: *All right, so you actually looked in a fairly systematic,* empirical *way at baseball players.*

◀ **empirical** (em pir′ i kəl) *adj.* based on observation or experience

VENKATESH: *I actually never thought I would be interested in looking at baseball from the standpoint of a job, but one of my students, Justin Humphries, used to play baseball for the Houston Astros organization.*

HUMPHRIES: *So, I was sitting in his classroom, and I started thinking about all the issues that I had seen in independent baseball and affiliated baseball:*[5] *guys living check-to-check, struggling with whether they should go back to school, family life, issues at home. And I thought I could use some of the things that we were learning in class, talk to some of these guys, and find out whether the stories and things that I was seeing and hearing would be reflected in the numbers.*

VENKATESH: *We followed a sample of the draft class of 2001—that's about 10 years—and so we thought that would help us understand what happens to these folks. . . . I think one of the most curious things that we find is how much ten years matter. If you take two people, let's say one played baseball and one didn't, the person who plays baseball is making about forty percent less on average ten years after he enters the game than the person who just wanted a regular career. . . .*

---

5. **affiliated baseball** minor-league baseball teams linked to major-league teams and serving to prepare players for the major leagues; also known as "farm teams."

DUBNER: *So, Sudhir, you went down to Camden not long ago, right? To talk to some of these ballplayers? Camden is in the Atlantic League. That's an independent league, meaning there's no direct path to a big-league team. A lot of the guys on a team like this have already been through the minor leagues and either topped out in talent or aged out, right?*

VENKATESH: *Most of the guys on the Camden Riversharks are probably in their late twenties, and so they've actually had careers in the Minor League system. It didn't happen for them. And so they come into the Atlantic League thinking that they're still going to be able to make it. You want to be able to tell them, "Hey, do you know that it's really unlikely that you're going to make it?" We learned that very few people, if any, around them are telling them this. So, they're not really prepared to talk about it, except some. Noah Hall was a really, really interesting person because he actually was thinking that this may be the end.*

Noah HALL: *It's probably not happening. It's probably not happening, but I'm still going to prepare the same way I would, regardless. I mean, in the back of my mind it's still there. I feel like sometimes if I have a good start to this year, I could get picked up. It could happen.*

VENKATESH: *Noah is 34. Noah has been playing 16 seasons including this one. When you look at him, you probably don't think that he is a baseball player. He looks like a running back. This is a guy who really looks like he's never, ever going to stop playing.*

HALL: *Some guys just see the writing on the wall. And I just try to ignore the writing on the wall. I don't want to look back and say I didn't give it everything I could. I think I could still play another 5, 10 years.*

Sudhir Venkatesh

VENKATESH: *Noah's from Northern California, and he was raised by his mom, a nurse. Noah has a wife, Kelly—and they have a lovely son, Isaiah. Kelly and Isaiah follow Noah around to whatever team he ends up playing for that season—and let me tell you, he's played on a lot of teams over the years.*

Kelly HALL: *I'm the one who's there when he has a good game or when he has a bad game. I go through that emotional roller coaster with him.*

VENKATESH: *One of the strange things we found out when we spoke to baseball players is that they have their own language for quitting. They actually quit. They just don't call it that. They don't call it quitting. They don't call it giving up. But, they say, "You know what? I'm just going to shut it down for a while."*

VENKATESH: *So, what does it mean to be a quitter as opposed to a "shutter downer"?*

HALL: *Probably the same thing. It just sounds better when you say, "I'm just shutting down." It's like you're not really doing it, but you are.*

VENKATESH: *Have you ever wanted to tell him, but you had to hold yourself back?*

Kelly HALL: *To shut it down? All the time. Especially in the last couple of years. We've actually fought over it. Because it's so hard. I understand that it's got to be really hard, because I do know how much he loves the game.*

DUBNER: *Wow, that's particularly* **poignant** *in my view because baseball's one of those rare sports that doesn't have a clock; no game is ever out of reach. I mean, you could be behind a thousand runs in the bottom of the ninth and theoretically still come back and win. So, part of the ethic of baseball is "Never, never, never quit." Quitting is not an option.*

◀ **poignant** (poin´ yənt) *adj.* emotionally affecting; touching, moving

VENKATESH: *Quitting is usually not an option. But Justin is trying to make it easier on players to quit and to make that transition. He's been working on building an organization that could help players to get out of baseball when the time is right and to join the world in which the rest of us live.*

HUMPHRIES: *Well, when you're 25, playing independent ball, making less than $2,000 a month, living off your parents because you can't financially sustain yourself, at some point, you have to tell yourself, "I can't do this to myself. I can't do this to my parents. And I can't continue when I know that there is untapped potential to do other things."*

So, part of the ethic of baseball is "Never, never, never quit." Quitting is not an option.

DUBNER: So, Justin Humphries stared right into the dark heart of his sunk costs, all those years he spent pursuing his dream—and he made the big quit. . . . "A quitter never wins and a winner never quits." In 1937, a self-help pundit named Napoleon Hill included that phrase in his very popular book *Think and Grow Rich*. Hill was inspired in part by the rags-to-riches industrialist Andrew Carnegie. These days the phrase is often attributed to Vince Lombardi, the legendarily tough football coach. What a lineage! And it does make a lot of sense, doesn't it? Of course it takes tremendous amounts of time and effort and, for lack of a more scientific word, stick-to-itiveness, to make any real progress in the world. But time and effort and even stick-to-itiveness are not in infinite supply. Remember the opportunity cost: every hour, every ounce of effort you spend here cannot be spent there. So, let me counter Napoleon Hill's phrase with another one, certainly not as well known. It's something that Stella Adler, the great acting coach, used to say: Your choice is your talent. So, if you realize that you've made a wrong choice—even if already you've sunk way too much cost into it—well, I've got one word to say to you, my friend. Quit.

Close Reading Activities

READ

Comprehension

Reread all or part of the text to help you answer the following questions.

1. What does Dubner first ask his audience to think about?
2. Why did Robert Reich resign as U.S. Secretary of Labor?
3. How did Sudhir Venkatesh study the issues involved in athletes' decisions to quit baseball?

Research: Clarify Details This transcript may include references that are unfamiliar to you. Choose at least one unfamiliar detail and briefly research it. Then, explain how the information you learned from research sheds light on an aspect of the transcript.

Summarize Write an objective summary of the text. Remember that an objective summary is free from opinion and evaluation.

Language Study

Selection Vocabulary The following passages appear in "The Upside of Quitting." Identify at least one synonym and one antonym for each boldfaced word. Then, use each word in a sentence of your own.

- Maybe it's a relationship that's **curdled**.
- All right, so you actually looked in a fairly systematic, **empirical** way at baseball players.
- Wow, that's particularly **poignant** in my view…

Literary Analysis

Reread the identified passage. Then, respond to the questions that follow.

Focus Passage *(p. 151)*

I'd like you to stop … when he quit.

Key Ideas and Details

1. **(a) Define:** What are "sunk cost" and "opportunity cost"? **(b) Analyze:** Why might people's worries about sunk costs prevent them from quitting something?

Craft and Structure

2. **(a)** What demand does Dubner make of his audience in the first sentence? **(b) Connect:** How does he repeat this demand, using a different grammatical structure, later in the paragraph? **(c) Interpret:** How does the changed grammar make Dubner's demand more **emphatic**? Explain.
3. **(a)** Identify two passages that reflect the spoken nature of this text. **(b) Interpret:** Explain how each passage you chose "sounds" like speech. **(c) Revise:** For each example, write a revision that would be more typical of a written text.

Integration of Knowledge and Ideas

4. **Analyze:** How does the decision to focus an entire radio broadcast on the topic of quitting automatically establish a main idea? Explain.

Central Idea

A **central idea** is an author's key message or insight. Reread the text, and take notes on ways in which Dubner develops a central idea.

1. What might a reader **anticipate** about the central idea of the selection from its title? Explain.
2. How do the experiences of Reich, Humphries, and Hall illustrate a central idea?
3. **Perseverance:** How does the central idea of this text challenge people's **customary** thinking about perseverance? Cite textual details in your answer.

DISCUSS • RESEARCH • WRITE

From Text to Topic **Partner Discussion**

Discuss the following passage with a partner. Take notes during the discussion. Contribute your own ideas, and support them with examples from the text.

> Of course it takes tremendous amounts of time and effort and, for lack of a more scientific word, stick-to-itiveness, to make any real progress in the world. But time and effort and even stick-to-itiveness are not in infinite supply. Remember the opportunity cost: every hour, every ounce of effort you spend here cannot be spent there.

QUESTIONS FOR DISCUSSION

1. Why does Dubner remind listeners that there is a link between perseverance and progress?
2. How might the existence of this link create conflicts for people?

Research **Investigate the Topic**

Sunk Cost and Opportunity Cost Stephen Dubner introduces two concepts from economics: "sunk cost" and "opportunity cost." He stresses that people's decisions to quit are affected by both concepts, but that a consideration of "opportunity cost" is critical.

Assignment
Conduct research into the economic concept of "opportunity cost." Consult a variety of authoritative sources, including economics reference works. Take clear notes, and carefully identify your sources. Write an **annotated outline** in which you identify your sources and findings.

PREPARATION FOR ESSAY

You may use the results of this research in an essay you will write at the end of this section.

Writing to Sources **Informative Text**

Stephen Dubner uses economic analysis to examine real-world human behavior. Adopt his approach in examining your own experience.

Assignment
Write a **reflective essay** in which you evaluate a decision you made in the past in terms of its "opportunity cost" and its "sunk cost." Follow these steps:

- Introduce the decision and its "opportunity cost."
- Provide transitions to mark the progression of events.
- Use description to create a vivid picture of your experience, including both progress made and the "sunk cost" associated with it.
- Conclude by linking an insight gained from your experience to the ideas in "The Upside of Quitting."

ACADEMIC VOCABULARY

Academic terms appear in blue on these pages. If these words are not familiar to you, use a dictionary to find their definitions. Then, use them as you speak and write about the text.

Common Core State Standards

RI.9-10.1, RI.9-10.2, RI.9-10.4, RI.9-10.5, RI.9-10.6; W.9-10.3, W.9-10.4, W.9-10.7, W.9-10.8, W.9-10.9, W.9-10.10; SL.9-10.1, SL.9-10.6; L.9-10.4, L.9-10.6
[For full standards wording, see the chart in the front of this book.]

from

The Winning Edge

by Peter Doskoch

In the summer of 1994, in the tallest of Princeton University's ivory towers,[1] Andrew Wiles was completing one of the most extraordinary odysseys in the history of math. For more than three decades, Wiles had been obsessed with Fermat's Last Theorem, a seemingly simple problem that had stumped mathematicians for 350 years. French mathematician Pierre de Fermat had noted that although there are plenty of solutions to the equation $X^2 + Y^2 = Z^2$ (for example, $3^2 + 4^2 = 5^2$), there is no corresponding solution if the numbers are cubed instead of squared. In fact, Fermat scribbled in the margin of a book that he had "truly marvelous" proof that the equation $X^n + Y^n = Z^n$ has no solution if n is any number greater than 2. Unfortunately, he never put his proof on paper.

Wiles was 10 years old when he encountered the theorem. "It looked so simple, and yet all the great mathematicians in history couldn't solve it. I knew from that moment that I had to." When classmates were flocking to rock concerts, he was studying how geniuses of prior eras approached the problem. He abandoned the quest after college in order to focus on his budding academic career, but his obsession was rekindled in 1986, when a fellow mathematician showed that proving a certain mathematical hypothesis—this one unsolved for a mere 30 years—would also prove Fermat's theorem. He set aside all but the few classes he was teaching—and revealed his quest to no one but his wife. To disguise his single-mindedness, he rationed the publication of previously completed work.

Despite long hours of focus—his only source of relaxation was playing with his two young children—the next few years produced little concrete progress. "I wasn't going to give up. It was just a question of which method would work," says Wiles. In 1993, after

1. **ivory towers** familiar expression for places of learning.

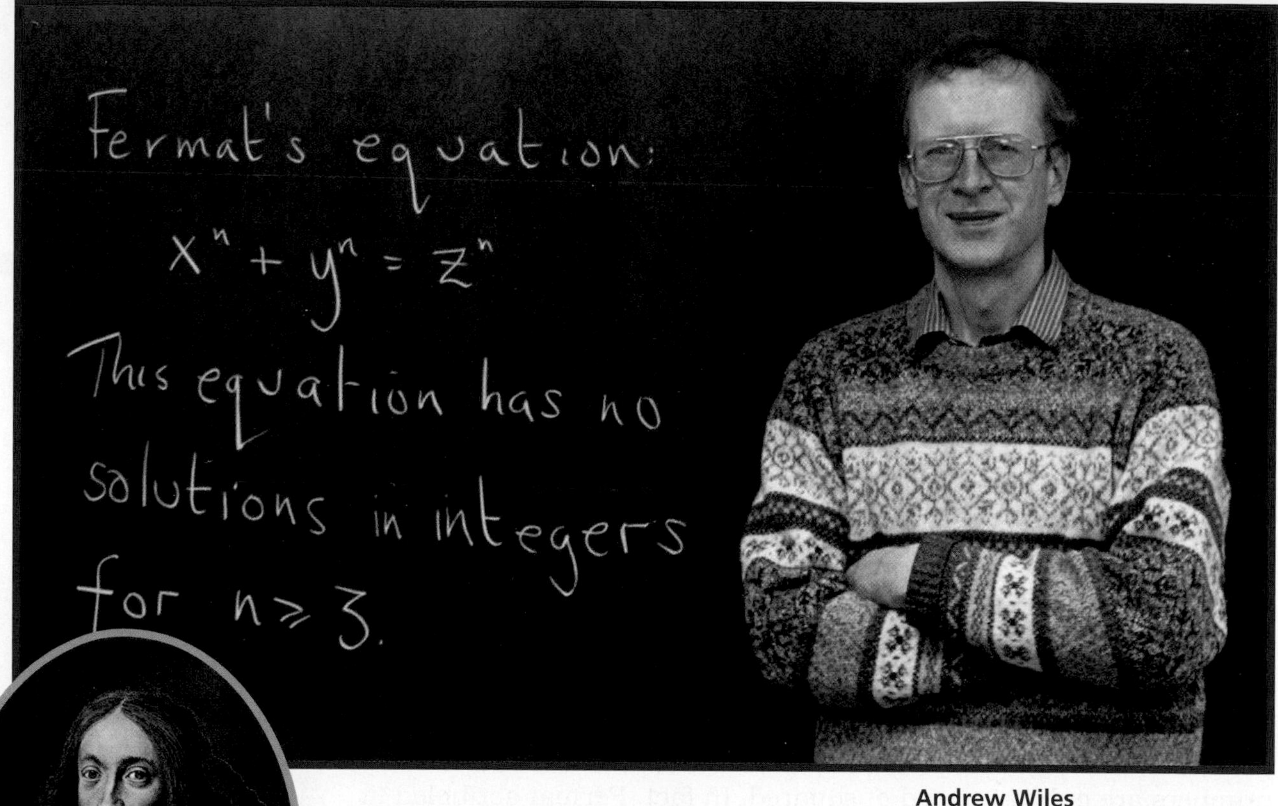

Fermat's equation:
$x^n + y^n = z^n$
This equation has no
solutions in integers
for n ≥ 3.

Andrew Wiles

Pierre de Fermat

seven straight years of intense work—more than 15,000 hours—Wiles stepped up to the podium at a conference in England and, over the course of three lectures, presented his completed proof of Fermat's Last Theorem.

A media frenzy followed. The shy mathematician found himself named one of *People* magazine's 25 Most Intriguing People of the Year, alongside Oprah and Princess Diana. But a handful of peer reviewers poring over the 200-page proof found several small errors. Wiles set to work addressing them. After a full year of frustrating struggle, Wiles had the insight that allowed him to fix them.

Wiles's intellect is inarguably impressive; one of his colleagues told *The New York Times* that only 1 in 1,000 professional mathematicians were capable of understanding Wiles's work. However, the Princeton professor himself attributes his accomplishment not to his brains but to his persistence. "For me, it was the main thing," he says.

It is likely that somewhere, at this very moment, a parent or coach is declaring to a discouraged child that "quitters never win." But perseverance has come to seem like quaint lip service against the tide of interest in talent and aptitude, flashier gifts that nature, or genes, seem to inarguably confer.

And yet grit may turn out to be at least as good a gauge of future success as talent itself. In a series of **provocative** new studies at the University of Pennsylvania, researchers find that the gritty are more likely to achieve success in school, work and other pursuits—perhaps because their passion and commitment help them endure the inevitable setbacks that occur in any long-term undertaking. In other words, it's not just talent that matters but also character. "Unless you're a genius, I don't think that you can ever do better than your competitors without a quality like grit," says Martin E. P. Seligman, director of the university's Positive Psychology Center.

◀ **provocative** (prə väk′ə tiv) *adj.* exciting; stimulating

Indeed, experts often speak of the "10-year rule"—that it takes at least a decade of hard work or practice to become highly successful in most endeavors, from managing a hardware store to writing sitcoms—and the ability to persist in the face of obstacles is almost always an essential ingredient in major achievements. The good news: Perhaps even more than talent, grit can be cultivated and strengthened.

How Much Does Talent Count?

"Many of life's failures are people who did not realize how close they were to success when they gave up," **opined** Thomas Edison, a man almost as famous for lauding perspiration as he is for inventing the lightbulb. If effort is the bedrock of success, what role do intelligence and other abilities play? "IQ counts for different amounts depending on the task and situation," emphasizes intelligence expert Robert Sternberg, dean of arts and sciences at Tufts University.

◀ **opined** (ō pīnd′) *v.* stated an opinion

Many large-scale analyses, however, suggest that a mere 25 percent of the differences between individuals in job performance—and a third of the difference in grade point average—can be attributed to IQ (personality factors, creativity and luck are said to contribute to the other 75 percent). Angela Duckworth, a graduate student at Penn who, together with Seligman, has conducted several key studies on grit, argues that the precise number isn't as important as knowing that intelligence accounts for only a fraction of success.

If 25 percent seems surprisingly low, that's partly because the hard work and determination that go into accomplishing Something Important are overshadowed by those rare but delightful lightning strikes of inspiration, mythologized as the visit of the Muse.[2] "Unfortunately, no one comes in my window and whispers poems to me," laments David Baker, director of creative writing at Denison University and author of seven books of poetry, including *Midwest*

2. **Muse** one of nine goddesses in classical mythology who were believed to inspire poets, artists, and thinkers.

Eclogue. "Poets work hard. I may work on a single poem for weeks or months and write 60 or 70 drafts—only to decide that draft 22 was the good one."

Such persistence is vital even for an indisputable genius. Mozart's diaries, for example, contain an oft-cited passage in which the composer reports that an entire symphony appeared, supposedly intact, in his head. "But no one ever quotes the next paragraph, where he talks about how he refined the work for months," notes Jonathan Plucker, an educational psychologist at Indiana University.

Angela Duckworth had studied neurobiology in college and eventually went on to teach. . . "It became pretty obvious to me that IQ didn't explain why so many of the kids had reading skills that were four grade levels below their average," she says. "The failure of kids to reach their potential was almost hitting me over the head." Already in her 30s and with a young child, Duckworth was intrigued enough to return to school for a Ph.D.

She approached Seligman, best known for his groundbreaking work on optimism, and together, they began identifying high achievers in various fields, interviewing them, and describing the characteristics that distinguished them.

"There were certainly a fair number of people who were brilliant, ambitious and persevering," Duckworth reports. "But there were also a lot who were not a genius in any way but were really **tenacious**." They began referring to this tenacity as grit—the determination to accomplish an ambitious, long-term goal despite the inevitable obstacles. Grit clearly resides in the same psychological neighborhood as motivation and self-discipline, but it's on a distinct property—and no one had ever knocked on its front door before.

tenacious ▶ (tə nā′shəs) *adj.* persistent in seeking a goal

Altogether Different

Not that researchers have ignored it altogether. Louis Terman, the legendary psychologist who followed a group of gifted boys from childhood to middle age, reported that "persistence in the accomplishment of ends" was one of the factors that distinguished the most successful men from the least successful. And in the most-cited paper in the giftedness literature, University of Connecticut psychologist Joseph Renzulli, director of the National Research Center on the Gifted and Talented, argued that "task commitment"—perseverance, endurance and hard work—is one of the three essential components of giftedness (along with ability and creativity). Indeed, Renzulli says, the evidence that these nonintellectual factors are critical to giftedness is "nothing short of overwhelming."

For the 95 percent of humanity that isn't recognized as gifted, Duckworth and Seligman have an egalitarian finding: Grit has value for people at all levels of ability.

In fact, their initial studies show that grit and intelligence are completely independent traits. Both enhance the likelihood of success, but the brightest among us are no more likely than the dimmest to be gritty. "I would be surprised if grit only matters for the upper echelons,"[3] Duckworth says. "One could argue that if you don't have a lot of raw ability, it's doubly important to be focused, hardworking and able to bounce back from setbacks."

The Penn researchers have already found that grit is valuable in a variety of real-world academic settings—such as middle school spelling bees. And they're looking at its real-world value among real estate agents and Wharton Business School grads.

They've proved that grit is the premier attribute for surviving the grueling first summer of training at West Point ("Beast Barracks"), when as many as 5 percent of new cadets typically drop out. "West Point costs hundreds of thousands of dollars per student, so the military has a keen interest in predicting attrition," Duckworth explains. A grit questionnaire administered to all 1,223 cadets entering the class of 2008 showed that grit is the single best yardstick for predicting who will survive the academy's punishing first weeks. It bested such highly touted measures as high school class rank, SAT scores, athletic experience, and faculty appraisal scores. "Sticking with West Point doesn't have as much to do with how smart you are as your character does," Duckworth concludes.

The Power of Passion

Certainly character was a tremendous asset to Andrew Wiles, who says he has a "single-mindedness that I don't see in most other people." But he also had "a special passion" for Fermat's Last Theorem. It is this sort of fervor and fascination that might just be the cornerstone of grit. . . .

Although extremely persistent people are usually passionate about their work, that doesn't mean that the passion always comes first. Perseverance, notes Duckworth, can itself foster passion. Often the most fascinating aspects of a topic (particularly a highly complex one) become apparent only after deep immersion, to a level "where you understand it and are enlivened by it."

Such is the case with Duckworth herself, who says that she decided on graduate school after a string of job stints in neuroscience research, management consulting and teaching spawned a desire to stick with one thing long enough to become an expert in it. "I *decided* to be persevering," she

"Sticking with West Point doesn't have as much to do with how smart you are as your character does. . ."

3. **echelons** (esh′ə länz) *n.* levels or grades in an organization or area of activity.

says. Although she had always been interested in education and achievement, her passion for exploring grit fully emerged only after she had been pursuing it for a while.

For others, persistence may grow from a desire to test one's limits, to see how far one can go—sometimes literally. Think of endurance athletes, for whom challenge isn't merely an obstacle to accomplishing something but often the spur to action in the first place. Duckworth points to athletes who spend months or years training for a marathon not because they love the act of running long distances but because they want the personal satisfaction or public glory of *having run* a marathon. . . .

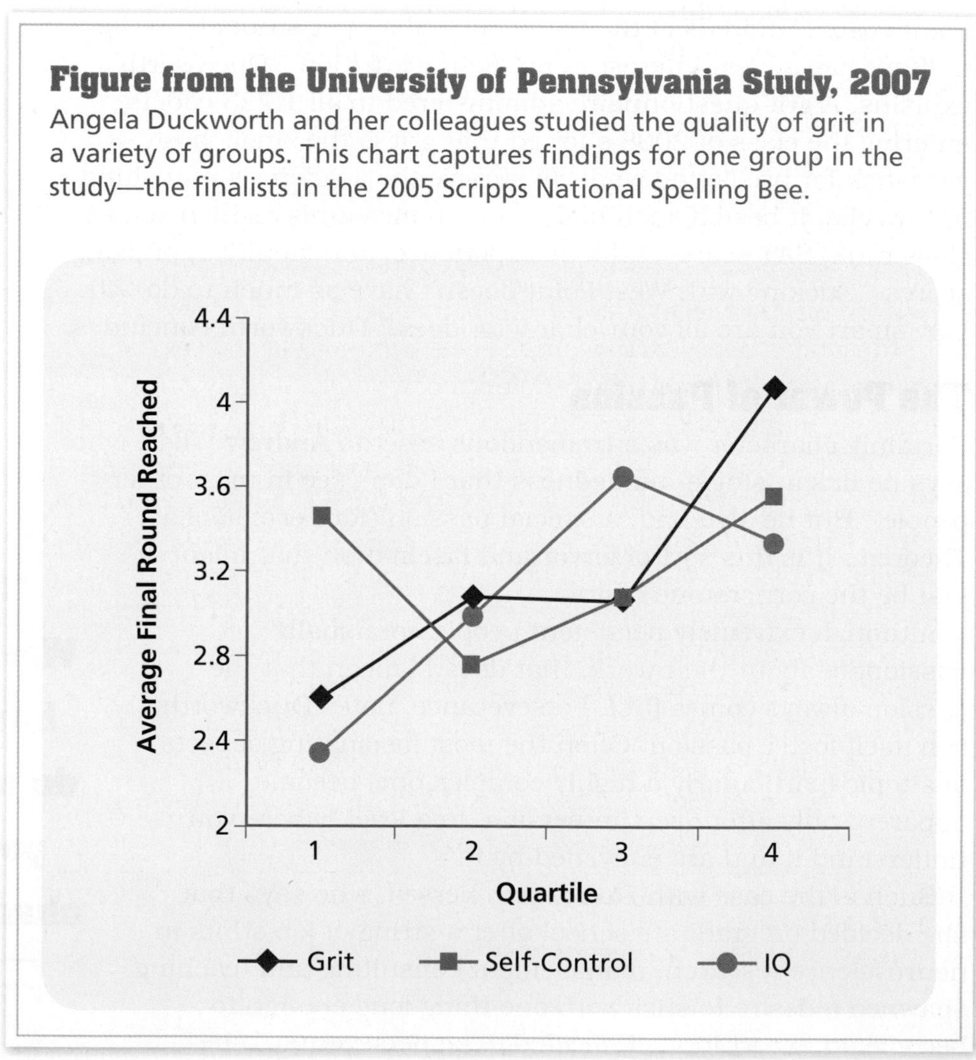

Figure from the University of Pennsylvania Study, 2007

Angela Duckworth and her colleagues studied the quality of grit in a variety of groups. This chart captures findings for one group in the study—the finalists in the 2005 Scripps National Spelling Bee.

Also in the Mix

Passion may be the linchpin[4] of grit, but it's not the only element. Ambition is right on its heels. For some of us, vowing to organize our closet next weekend may represent the height of our ambition. Truly gritty people, however, tend to set especially challenging long-term goals; one of Duckworth's students confidently stated that he planned to become a U.S. Senator. . . .

Then there's optimism, a trait that Dean Keith Simonton of the University of California at Davis finds is extremely common among high achievers. "It helps them hang in there in times when they have to overcome all of these obstacles," he observes. "They just really believe in the end that they're going to win, and until they do, they're just going to keep on pushing, keep on making the phone calls, writing the letters, whatever they have to do."

... one of Duckworth's students confidently stated that he planned to become a U.S. Senator.

It's this optimism, most likely, that helped Chester Carlson convince someone that the technology he had invented was worthwhile, even after more than 20 companies and the National Inventors Council rejected his work. Carlson called his new process electrophotography; today it's known as photocopying. . . .

The need for grit is generally hidden from the young until they head off to college or enter the workforce. That's when it first becomes necessary to chart one's own course and set one's own goals. Before then, achievement hinges largely on doing your homework—and that's chosen by others and assigned to you. Nonetheless, says Duckworth, perseverance clearly matters for kids. Gritty youngsters get better grades than their peers. And, as a study of participants in the National Spelling Bee revealed, kids who ranked high in grit were more likely to reach the final round of the competition, for the simple reason that they had worked harder than their rivals to prepare for the event. . . .

Despite instant messaging, speed dating, and immediate gratification, the idea that perseverance pays off big-time is slowly gathering steam. It augurs[5] a far more democratic vision than a culture of achievement that recognizes only talent. No wonder grit is on its way to becoming The Next Big Thing.

4. **linchpin** familiar expression for an element that holds a structure together and is critical to its function.
5. **augurs** (ô´gərz) *v.* hints at promise of something.

Close Reading Activities

READ

Comprehension

Reread all or part of the text to help you answer the following questions.

1. What decision did Andrew Wiles make when he was ten years old?
2. In addition to perseverance, what other assets does Andrew Wiles credit for his success?
3. According to Joseph Renzulli, what are the three essential components of giftedness?

Research: Clarify Details This article may include references that are unfamiliar to you. Choose at least one unfamiliar detail and briefly research it. Then, explain how the information you learned from research sheds light on an aspect of the article.

Summarize Write an objective summary of the article. Remember that an objective summary is free from opinion and evaluation.

Language Study

Selection Vocabulary The phrases at right appear in the article. Define each boldfaced word. Then, use the word in a new sentence.

- a series of **provocative** new studies
- **opined** Thomas Edison
- were really **tenacious**

Literary Analysis

Reread the identified passage. Then, respond to the questions that follow.

Focus Passage *(pp. 162–163)*
Not that researchers ... from setbacks.

Key Ideas and Details

1. **Interpret:** According to the author, are gifted people always gritty? Explain.
2. **Paraphrase:** What is "task commitment"?

Craft and Structure

3. **(a) Summarize:** Summarize the main idea of each paragraph in this passage. **(b) Classify:** For each idea, state the types of evidence used to support it.
4. **Analyze:** How does the word *egalitarian*, used to describe Duckworth and Seligman's **findings**, connect to the statistic about "95 percent of humanity"? Explain.
5. **(a) Distinguish:** Identify two synonyms for *perseverance* in this passage. **(b) Define:** What connotation does each synonym have? **(c) Analyze:** How does the use of these varied terms enrich the analysis? Explain.

Integration of Knowledge and Ideas

6. **Analyze:** After reading this passage, define a "winning edge." Explain your response.

Anecdote

An **anecdote** is a brief story told to make a point. Reread the article and take notes on anecdotes the author uses to develop and support ideas.

1. **(a)** Why is the discussion of Andrew Wiles an anecdote while the quotations from David Baker, Thomas Edison, and others are merely examples? **(b)** In addition to the one about Wiles, what other anecdote appears in this article? Explain.
2. **Perseverance:** How does the author's use of anecdotes support his ideas about perseverance? Cite specific examples from the article in your response.

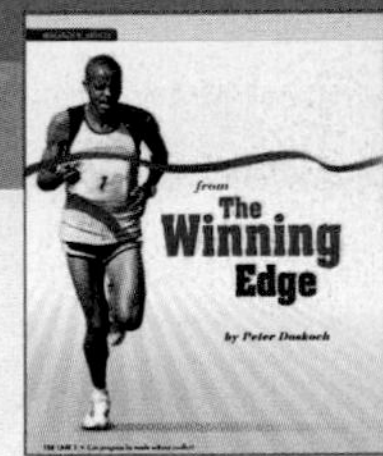

DISCUSS • RESEARCH • WRITE

From Text to Topic **Group Discussion**

Discuss the following passage with a small group. Take notes during the discussion. Contribute your own ideas, and support them with details from the text.

> They've proved that grit is the premier attribute for surviving the grueling first summer of training at West Point ("Beast Barracks"), when as many as 5 percent of new cadets typically drop out. "West Point costs hundreds of thousands of dollars per student, so the military has a keen interest in predicting attrition," Duckworth explains. A grit questionnaire administered to all 1,223 cadets entering the class of 2008 showed that grit is the single best yardstick for predicting who will survive the academy's punishing first weeks.

QUESTIONS FOR DISCUSSION

1. Why is grit such a good indicator of which cadets will complete summer training at West Point?
2. Is someone's grittiness the best indicator of his or her potential to be a strong military officer? Why or why not?

Research **Investigate the Topic**

Predictive Factors West Point is one of many schools that assess a variety of achievement and personality **factors**, including a candidate's "grit" level, to predict the potential success of incoming students.

PREPARATION FOR ESSAY

You may use the results of this research in an essay you will write at the end of this section.

Assignment

Conduct research to find out what factors are commonly used to predict success in college and which factors are the best predictors. Take organized notes, and identify your sources so you can cite them accurately. Share your findings in a **blog post** or **brief report.**

ACADEMIC VOCABULARY

Academic terms appear in blue on these pages. If these words are not familiar to you, use a dictionary to find their definitions. Then, use them as you speak and write about the text.

Writing to Sources **Argument**

In "The Winning Edge," the author **reviews** the body of research that suggests perseverance may be even more important than talent or intelligence in achievement. He praises these findings as being "a far more democratic vision than a culture of achievement that recognizes only talent."

Assignment

Write a **persuasive essay** in which you state and defend a position about what this research suggests for American education. Consider these questions: Should children be educated about developing perseverance? Students are honored for displaying talent; should they also be honored for displaying grit? Follow these steps:

- Support your arguments with evidence from "The Winning Edge."
- Clearly connect your arguments and evidence.
- Use vivid, persuasive language to convince your audience.

Common Core State Standards

RI.9-10.1, RI.9-10.2, RI.9-10.3, RI.9-10.4, RI.9-10.5, RI.9-10.8; W.9-10.1, W.9-10.4, W.9-10.6, W.9-10.7; SL.9-10.1; L.9-10.3, L.9-10.4, L.9-10.6

[For full standards wording, see the chart in the front of this book.]

Science Fiction and the Future

Ursula K. Le Guin

We know where the future is. It's in front of us. Right? It lies before us—a great future lies before us—we stride forward confidently into it, every **commencement**, every election year. And we know where the past is. Behind us, right? So that we have to turn around to see it, and that interrupts our progress ever forward into the future, so we don't really much like to do it.

◀ **commencement** (kə mens′ mənt) *n.* ceremony marking school graduation and conferring of degrees

It seems that the Quechua-speaking[1] peoples of the Andes see all this rather differently. They figure that because the past is what you know, you can see it—it's in front of you, under your nose. This is a mode of perception rather than action, of awareness rather than progress. Since they're quite as logical as we are, they say that the future lies behind—behind your back, over your shoulder. The future is what you can't see, unless you turn around and kind of snatch a glimpse. And then sometimes you wish you hadn't, because you've glimpsed what's sneaking up on you from behind... So, as we drag the Andean peoples into our world of progress, pollution, soap operas, and satellites, they are coming backwards—looking over their shoulders to find out where they're going.

I find this an intelligent and appropriate attitude. At least it reminds us that our talk about "going forward into the future" is a metaphor, a piece of mythic thinking taken literally, perhaps even a bluff, based on our macho fear of ever being inactive, receptive, open, quiet, still. Our unquiet clocks make us think that we make time, that we control it. We plug in the timer and make time happen. But in fact the future comes, or is there, whether we rush forward to meet it in supersonic jets with nuclear warheads, or sit on a peak and watch the llamas[2] graze. Morning comes whether you set the alarm or not.

1. **Quechua** (kech′ wä) **-speaking** using one of a family of languages spoken by Native American peoples of the Andean region of South America; the ancient Incas spoke Quechua.
2. **llamas** (lä′ məz) grazing animals of the Andes domesticated by the Incas.

The future is not mere space. This is where I part company with a whole variety of science fiction, the imperialistic[3] kind, as seen in all the Space Wars and Star Wars novels and films and the whole branch of SF[4] that reduces technology to hi-tech. In such fictions, space and the future are synonymous: they are a place we are going to get to, invade, colonize, **exploit**, and suburbanize.

exploit ▶ (eks ploit′) *v.* take advantage of

If we do "get to" space, it's not unlikely that that's how we'll behave there. It is possible that we will "conquer" space. But it is not possible that we will "conquer" the future, because there is no way we can get there. The future is the part of the space-time continuum[5] from which—in the body and in ordinary states of consciousness— we are excluded. We can't even see it. Except for little glimpses over the shoulder.

It is possible that we will "conquer" space. But it is not possible that we will "conquer" the future, because there is no way we can get there.

When we look at what we can't see, what we do see is the stuff inside our heads. Our thoughts and our dreams, the good ones and the bad ones. And it seems to me that when science fiction is really doing its job that's exactly what it's dealing with. Not "the future." It's when we confuse our dreams and ideas with the non-dream world that we're in trouble, when we think the future is a place we own.

3. **imperialistic** (im pir′ē ə lis′ tik) *adj.* focused on empires.
4. **SF** abbreviation for "science fiction."
5. **space-time continuum** four-dimensional space defined by three spatial coordinates (length, width, and breadth) and one temporal coordinate (time).

Then we **succumb** to wishful thinking and escapism,[6] and our science fiction gets megalomania,[7] and thinks that instead of being fiction it's prediction, and the Pentagon and the White House begin to *believe* it, and we get True Believers conquering the future by means of SDI.[8]

◀ **succumb** (sə kum′) *v.* yield to

As a science-fiction writer I personally prefer to stand still for long periods, like the Quechua, and look at what is, in fact, in front of me: the earth; my fellow beings on it; and the stars.

---

6. **escapism** (e skāp′ iz′ əm) *n.* use of imagination as an escape from reality.
7. **megalomania** (me gə lō mā′nē ə) *n.* mental disorder characterized by delusions of personal grandeur.
8. **SDI** abbreviation for "Strategic Defense Initiative," ground and space-based missile defense system proposed by U.S. president Ronald Reagan in the 1980s but never implemented; popularly known as "Star Wars."

ABOUT THE AUTHOR

Ursula K. Le Guin (b. 1929)

The child of anthropologists and writers Alfred and Theodora Kroeber, Ursula K. Le Guin became one of the most admired and influential science fiction and fantasy writers of the contemporary period. The influence of her parents' work with Native American cultures can often be seen in Le Guin's writing, such as her novella *The Word for World Is Forest* (1972), in which she presents a sympathetic account of alien peoples whose environment and way of life are threatened by modern technological civilization. Le Guin has made major contributions to science fiction's utopian tradition, including the novel *The Dispossessed: An Ambiguous Utopia* (1974) and her classic anti-utopian fable "The Ones Who Walk Away from Omelas." Another important element in Le Guin's science fiction has been a feminist view of gender relations. Notably, in her novel *The Left Hand of Darkness* (1969) she describes an alien world inhabited by people who, at different periods of their lives, may be either male or female. Le Guin's critical writing is collected in the volumes *Language of the Night* (1979) and *Dancing at the Edge of the World* (1989).

Close Reading Activities

READ

Comprehension

Reread all or part of the text to help you answer the following questions.

1. According to Le Guin, how do the Quechua-speaking peoples perceive the past and future?
2. In Le Guin's view, how does our typical understanding of the future lead to specific attitudes about progress and conquest?
3. How does Le Guin see customary attitudes toward the future played out in science fiction writing?

Research: Clarify Details This speech may include references that are unfamiliar to you. Choose at least one unfamiliar detail and briefly research it. Then, explain how the information you learned from research sheds light on an aspect of the speech.

Summarize Write an objective summary of the speech. Remember that an objective summary is free from opinion and evaluation.

Language Study

Selection Vocabulary The following passages appear in the speech. Define each boldface word. Then, use each word in a sentence of your own.

- … a great future lies before us—we stride forward confidently into it, every **commencement** …
- … they are a place we are going to get to, invade, colonize, **exploit,** and suburbanize.
- Then we **succumb** to wishful thinking …

Literary Analysis

Reread the identified passage. Then, respond to the questions that follow.

Focus Passage *(p. 169)*

It seems that the Quechua…alarm or not.

Key Ideas and Details

1. **(a)** How does Le Guin feel about the Quechua attitude toward the future? Explain. **(b) Interpret:** What **perspective** on the future does she **derive** from this attitude? Explain.

Craft and Structure

2. The author defines "our world" as being one of "progress, pollution, soap operas, and satellites." **(a) Generalize:** What vision of **contemporary** life do these words suggest? Explain. **(b) Analyze:** How does the use of alliteration in this word series add to its effect? Explain.
3. **(a) Interpret:** What are the "unquiet clocks"? **(b) Analyze:** According to Le Guin, how do these clocks affect our perceptions? Explain.

Integration of Knowledge and Ideas

4. **(a)** In the last two sentences, what images illustrate contrasting visions of the future? **(b) Analyze:** How do these images highlight the differences Le Guin sees between "perception rather than action" and "awareness rather than progress"?

Tone

In literature, **tone** is the author's attitude toward the subject or audience. Reread the speech, and take notes about the author's tone.

1. Le Guin refers to the future as a place to "invade, colonize, exploit, and suburbanize." What tone does this passage convey? Explain.
2. **Perseverance: (a)** Describe Le Guin's tone in the final paragraph of the speech. **(b)** Do you think Le Guin feels perseverance is admirable? Explain.

Science Fiction and the Future
Ursula K. Le Guin

DISCUSS • RESEARCH • WRITE

From Text to Topic **Group Discussion**

Discuss the following passage with a small group. Take notes during the discussion. Contribute your own ideas, and support them with examples from the text.

> The future is not mere space. This is where I part company with a whole variety of science fiction, the imperialistic kind … and the whole branch of SF that reduces technology to hi-tech. In such fictions, space and the future are synonymous: They are a place we are going to get to, invade, colonize, exploit, and suburbanize.

QUESTIONS FOR DISCUSSION

1. Why does Le Guin object to science fiction of the "imperialistic" and "hi-tech" kinds? What do those terms mean?
2. What does Le Guin mean when she says, "In such fictions, space and the future are synonymous"?

Research **Investigate the Topic**

Futurology Le Guin objects to science fiction in which "space and the future are synonymous." Futurologists are social scientists who study current trends in order to forecast future developments.

PREPARATION FOR ESSAY

You may use the results of this research in an essay you will write at the end of this section.

Assignment

Conduct research to determine what futurologists are predicting about space travel, technology, and the attitudes that will shape life in the future. Do futurologists believe most people will continue to value goal-oriented persistence? Take careful notes, including source information. Write a **short essay** in which you explain your findings.

Writing to Sources **Argument**

In "Science Fiction and the Future," Ursula K. Le Guin expresses her views about certain aspects of both contemporary society and science fiction. If this speech appeared in a newspaper, her ideas would prompt responses.

Assignment

Write a **letter to the editor** in which you argue for or against the message Le Guin expresses in her speech. Follow these steps:

- Introduce and explain your position about the ideas Le Guin explores.
- Provide strong evidence, including quotations from Le Guin's essay, to support your position.
- Use formal, polite language that builds a respectful tone.
- Provide a conclusion that summarizes your position and provides a final reflection on the ideas in Le Guin's speech.

ACADEMIC VOCABULARY

Academic terms appear in blue on these pages. If these words are not familiar to you, use a dictionary to find their definitions. Then, use them as you speak and write about the text.

Common Core State Standards

RI.9-10.1, RI.9-10.2, RI.9-10.4, RI.9-10.5, RI.9-10.6; W.9-10.1, W.9-10.4, W.9-10.7, W.9-10.9, W.9-10.10; SL.9-10.1, SL.9-10.6; L.9-10.4, L.9-10.6

[For full standards wording, see the chart in the front of this book.]

from the series Empire State (Laying Beams), 1930–31

ABOUT THE PHOTOGRAPHER

Lewis Wickes Hine (1874–1940) was a sociologist and photographer who used his camera as a tool for social reform. In particular, his photographs of child workers succeeded in getting protective laws passed in the United States. Hine also took numerous photographs of American workers. This photograph is from a series of shots of workers constructing the Empire State Building in New York City. The building was completed in 1931.

READ • RESEARCH • WRITE

Common Core State Standards

W.9-10.3; W.9-10.7.
[For full standards wording, see the chart in the front of this book.]

Comprehension

Look at the photograph closely. Then, answer the following questions.

1. Where are the workers, and what are they doing in this photograph?
2. From what **vantage** point or position does it appear the photographer is standing to shoot the photograph? Explain.

Critical Analysis

Key Ideas and Details

1. (a) Interpret: Do the workers in the photo seem concerned or anxious? **(b) Analyze:** Which details in their postures and expressions support your interpretation? Explain.

Craft and Structure

2. (a) Analyze: How does the photographer use the building's structure to divide the **plane** of the image into a foreground and a background? **(b) Connect:** What information does the background of the photograph provide to the viewer?

3. (a) Deduce: Why is it significant that the viewer can see the street through the space below the workers? Explain. **(b) Analyze:** How do both the distant line of the horizon and the expanse of sky behind the workers add to the viewer's understanding and to the feeling of the image?

Integration of Knowledge and Ideas

4. Perseverance: (a) What does this photograph demonstrate about people's ambitions in New York City during the early 1930s? Explain. **(b)** What does this image suggest about the power of perseverance? Explain.

ACADEMIC VOCABULARY

Academic terms appear in blue on these pages. If these words are not familiar to you, use a dictionary to find their definitions. Then, use them as you speak and write about the text.

Research **Investigate the Topic**

Building Skyscrapers Conduct research about the construction of skyscrapers in the United States beginning in the late 1800s. Consult reliable secondary sources, including **urban** histories, as well as interesting primary sources, such as newspapers of the era and oral histories by workers. Gather information to explain how people of the era felt about these structures and what such tall buildings came to symbolize.

Writing to Sources **Narrative Text**

Write a **monologue** in the voice of a construction worker in this photograph. Imagine the man's daily routine and the thoughts, feelings, and effort he brings to his work. Include a description of the moment captured in the photograph.

Assessment: Synthesis

Speaking and Listening: Group Discussion

Perseverance and Conflict The texts in this section vary in genre, length, style, and perspective. However, all of them address the idea of perseverance. Some voices offer examples of feats that require intense commitment, suggesting that success is founded on persistence. Other voices wonder if perseverance and forward progress are, perhaps, neither so connected nor so important. Questions about the value of perseverance—the conflicts it may create for individuals and for society as a whole—are fundamentally related to the Big Question addressed in this unit: **Can progress be made without conflict?**

▲ Refer to the selections you read in Part 3 as you complete the activities on this assessment.

Assignment

Conduct discussions. With a small group, conduct a discussion about the values of perseverance and progress. Refer to the texts in this section, other texts you have read, and your personal experience and knowledge to support your ideas. Begin your discussion by addressing the following questions:

- What is the relationship between perseverance and progress?
- Does the emphasis that society in general places on persistence and progress affect the way individuals think and behave? If so, how?
- Under what circumstances might perseverance create conflicts for an individual? For a society?
- Is quitting always wrong? Are there any circumstances in which quitting is the right thing to do?

Summarize and present your ideas. After you have fully explored the topic, summarize your discussion and present your findings to the class as a whole.

Criteria for Success

✓ **Organizes the group effectively**
Appoint a group leader and a timekeeper. The group leader should start off the discussion questions and ask follow-up questions. The timekeeper should ensure the discussion as a whole lasts 20 minutes.

✓ **Maintains focus of discussion**
As a group, stay on topic and avoid straying into other subject areas.

✓ **Involves all participants equally and fully**
Everyone in the group should take turns speaking and contributing ideas.

✓ **Follows the rules for collegial discussion**
As each group member speaks, others should listen carefully. Each participant should relate his or her ideas to those of others and support opinions with sound reasoning and evidence. Express disagreement with respect.

USE NEW VOCABULARY

As you speak and share ideas, work to use the vocabulary words you have learned in this unit. The more you use new words, the more comfortable you will become with them.

Writing: **Narrative**

Perseverance and Conflict Whether it is fiction or nonfiction, a narrative requires conflict to engage readers' imaginations. The conflicts we read about in narratives often mirror the conflicts that we encounter in real life and may prompt us to overcome our own challenges and problems. These conflicts often require a decision about whether or not we should persist in a course of action.

Common Core State Standards

W.9-10.3.a–d, W.9-10.4, W.9-10.5; SL.9-10.1.a–d, SL.9-10.4, SL.9–10.6

[For full standards wording, see the chart in the front of this book.]

Assignment

Write an **autobiographical narrative,** or true story of your own life, that illustrates one of two possible experiences: (1) You persevere in a course of action, overcoming conflicts to achieve personal progress; or (2) You face too much conflict and choose to stop pursuing a goal. Relate this experience to the texts that you have read in this section. Remember that an effective autobiographical narrative does not just present a series of events but explores the significance of an episode in the writer's life.

Criteria for Success

Purpose/Focus

✓ **Connects specific incidents with larger ideas**
Make meaningful connections between your experiences and the texts you have read in this section.

✓ **Clearly conveys the significance of the story**
Provide a conclusion in which you reflect on what you experienced.

Organization

✓ **Sequences events logically**
Structure your narrative so that individual events build on one another to create a coherent whole.

Development of Ideas/Elaboration

✓ **Supports insights**
Include both personal examples and details from the texts in this section.

✓ **Uses narrative techniques effectively**
Even though an autobiographical narrative is nonfiction, it may include storytelling elements like those found in fiction. Consider using plot devices, such as flashback and foreshadowing.

Language

✓ **Uses literary devices effectively**
Use descriptive details, imagery, and figurative language to paint word pictures that help readers see settings and characters.

Conventions

✓ **Does not have errors**
Check your narrative to eliminate errors in grammar, spelling, and punctuation.

WRITE TO EXPLORE

Writing helps you figure out what you know, feel, and think about a topic. As you work, recognize that your ideas might change. Be ready to make adjustments to your plan.

Writing to Sources: **Argument**

Perseverance, Progress, and Conflict The related readings in this section raise questions, such as the following, about the values of perseverance and progress:

- What is progress? How do people measure it? Is progress the same for everyone?
- What kinds of conflicts arise when people do not define progress in the same way?
- When is perseverance most valuable? When is it least valuable?
- Should a society as a whole share the same general ideas about progress and perseverance?
- When are other traits—such as judgment, insight, or the ability to compromise—more valuable or less valuable than perseverance?

Focus on the question that intrigues you the most, and then complete the following assignment.

Assignment

Write an **argumentative essay** in which you state and defend a claim about the value of perseverance, or working toward a goal, in the face of conflict. Build evidence for your claim by analyzing the relationship between perseverance and progress in two or more texts from this section. Clearly present, develop, and support your ideas with examples and details from the texts.

INCORPORATE RESEARCH

Strengthen your position by pulling in facts, quotations, and data you gathered while conducting research related to the readings in this section. Make sure to cite your sources correctly.

Prewriting and Planning

Choose texts. Review the texts in the section to decide which ones you will cite in your essay. Select at least two that will provide strong material to support your position.

Gather details and craft a working thesis, or claim. Use a chart like the one shown to develop your claim. Though you may refine or change your ideas as you write, the working version will establish a clear direction.

Focus Question: Is progress the same for everyone?

Text	Passage	Notes
"Science Fiction and the Future"	Morning comes whether you set the alarm or not.	author notes that the usual ideas about progress and the future are not universal
from "The Upside of Quitting"	Remember the opportunity cost: every hour, every ounce of effort you spend here cannot be spent there.	author says that progress is, in part, a matter of choices
Example Claim: There is more than one way to measure progress, to pursue one's goals, and to define success.		

Prepare counterarguments. For each point you intend to make, identify a possible objection. Plan to include the strongest of these counterclaims in your essay: Introduce and provide evidence to refute them.

Drafting

Sequence your ideas and evidence. Organize your ideas in a logical sequence. Select details from your chart that correlate with each point, and be sure to provide evidence that directly supports the ideas you want to express.

Address counterclaims. The strongest arguments take counterclaims, or opposing ideas, into account and provide evidence that shows they are not convincing. As you order your ideas, explain opposing claims, interpretations, or opinions. Then, write a logical response that refutes each counterclaim.

Introduce, develop, and connect ideas. Write an engaging introduction. Consider beginning with a compelling quotation or a detail. Use words, phrases, and clauses to link the sections of your essay and clarify the relationships between your claims and evidence. Then, write a strong conclusion that ends your essay with a clear, memorable statement.

W.9-10.1a–e, W.9-10.4, W.9-10.5, W.9-10.9, W.9-10.10; L.9-10.2

[For full standards wording, see the chart in the front of this textbook.]

Revising and Editing

Review content. Make sure that your position is clearly stated and that you have supported it with strong evidence from both the texts and your research. Add more evidence if necessary.

Review style. Check to be sure you have found the clearest, simplest way to communicate your ideas. Revise your word choice, where necessary, to maintain an objective tone. Replace flat or dull words with more vivid choices.

CITE RESEARCH CORRECTLY

See the Citing Sources pages in the Introductory Unit of this textbook for information on how to format parenthetical citations within your essay.

Self-Evaluation Rubric

Use the following criteria to evaluate the effectiveness of your essay.

Criteria	Rating Scale
Purpose/Focus Introduces a precise claim and distinguishes the claim from (implied) alternate or opposing claims; provides a concluding section that follows from and supports the argument presented	*not very.......very* 1 2 3 4
Organization Establishes a logical organization; uses words, phrases and clauses to link the major sections of the text, create cohesion, and clarify relationships among claims, reasons, and evidence, and between claims and counterclaims	1 2 3 4
Development of Ideas/Elaboration Develops the claim and counterclaims fairly, supplying evidence for each while pointing out the strengths and limitations of both	1 2 3 4
Language Establishes and maintains a formal style and objective tone	1 2 3 4
Conventions Attends to the norms and conventions of the discipline	1 2 3 4

Independent Reading

Titles for Extended Reading

In this unit, you have read texts in a variety of genres. Continue to read on your own. Select works that you enjoy, but challenge yourself to explore new authors and works of increasing depth and complexity. The titles suggested below will help you get started.

INFORMATIONAL TEXT

Biography of an Atom
by Jacob Bronowski and Millicent Selsam

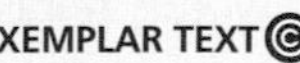

This **nonfiction** book by Millicent Selsam, a biologist and former science teacher, and Jacob Bronowski, an expert in both literature and science, explains atoms in a friendly, engaging way.

Up From Slavery
by Booker T. Washington — Signet, 2000

During his life, Booker T. Washington was a slave, an educator, an orator, and the founder of Tuskegee University. In this **autobiography**, Washington tells the remarkable story of his rise from houseboy to activist for social change.

The Illustrated Book of Great Composers
by Wendy Thompson — EXEMPLAR TEXT

In this beautifully illustrated **reference book,** pianist, violinist, and radio producer Wendy Thompson describes the lives and achievements of more than 100 renowned composers.

Euclid's Elements
by Euclid
Translated by Thomas L. Heath — EXEMPLAR TEXT

When the mathematician Euclid wrote this **treatise** in the third century B.C., he might as well have been planning a modern high school geometry course. Geometry students still learn the same axioms and proofs that Euclid proposed so many centuries ago. This translation includes all thirteen books written by this Greek "Father of Geometry."

LITERATURE

Anton Chekhov: Selected Stories
by Anton Chekhov

Against the backdrop of Russia's bustling cities and rugged countryside, Chekhov brings vivid characters to life. This collection of his renowned **short stories** shows everyday struggles portrayed with honesty and humor.

The Prince and the Pauper
by Mark Twain — Signet, 1980

The sixteenth-century royal court and the boisterous London streets spring to life in this **novel** about a poor boy who exchanges identities with Edward Tudor, the prince of England.

The Collected Short Fiction of C. J. Cherryh
by C. J. Cherryh — Daw Books, 2008

From stories of an alien world threatened by a cooling sun to a tale of a woman cursed with unbelievable visions, this collection of **short stories** introduces readers to Cherryh's boundless imagination.

ONLINE TEXT SET

ESSAY
***from* A Quilt of a Country**
Anna Quindlen

AUTOBIOGRAPHY
***from* Desert Exile: The Uprooting of a Japanese-American Family**
Yoshiko Uchida

BIOGRAPHY
Marian Anderson: Famous Concert Singer Langston Hughes

Preparing to Read Complex Texts

Attentive Reading As you read literature on your own, bring your imagination and questions to the text. The questions shown below and others that you ask as you read will help you learn and enjoy literature even more.

Reading Literature/ Informational Text
10. By the end of Grade 10, read and comprehend literature, including stories, dramas, poems, and literary nonfiction at the high end of the grades 9–10 text complexity band independently and proficiently.

When reading narratives, ask yourself...

Comprehension: **Key Ideas and Details**

- Who is the story's main character? Who are the other characters, and how do they relate to the main character?
- What problems do the characters face? How do they react to these problems?
- Which characters do I like or admire? Which do I dislike? How do my reactions to the characters make me feel about the story as a whole?
- Is the setting believable and interesting? Why or why not?
- What happens in the story? Why do these events happen?

Text Analysis: **Craft and Structure**

- Who is narrating the story? Is this voice part of the story, or is it an outside observer?
- Do I find the narrator's voice interesting and engaging? Why or why not?
- Is there anything different or unusual in the way the story is structured? Do I find that structure interesting or distracting?
- Are there any passages that I find especially strong or beautiful? What qualities make them so?
- Do I understand why characters act and feel as they do? Do their thoughts and actions seem real? Why or why not?

Connections: **Integration of Ideas**

- What does this story mean to me? Does it convey a theme or an insight that I find important and true? Why or why not?
- Does the story remind me of others I have read? If so, how?
- Have I gained new knowledge from reading this story? If so, what have I learned?
- Would I recommend this story to others? If so, to whom?
- Would I like to read other stories by this author? Why or why not?

UNIT 2

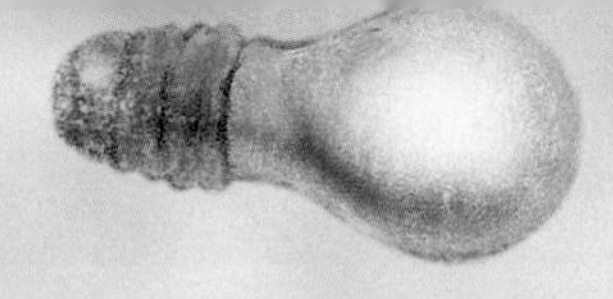

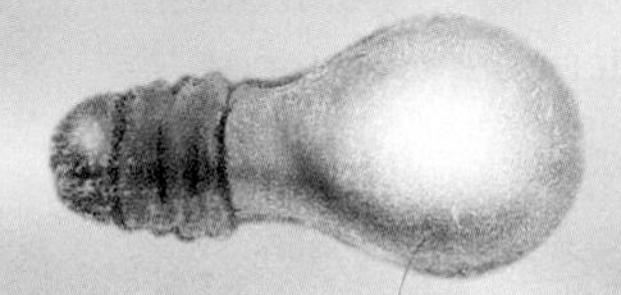

THE BIG ?

What kind of knowledge changes our lives?

UNIT PATHWAY

PART 1
SETTING EXPECTATIONS

- INTRODUCING THE BIG QUESTION
- CLOSE READING WORKSHOP

PART 2
TEXT ANALYSIS
GUIDED EXPLORATION

SEEKING KNOWLEDGE

PART 3
TEXT SET
DEVELOPING INSIGHT

VISION

PART 4
DEMONSTRATING INDEPENDENCE

- INDEPENDENT READING
- ONLINE TEXT SET

CLOSE READING TOOL

Use this tool to practice the close reading strategies you learn.

STUDENT eTEXT

Bring learning to life with audio, video, and interactive tools.

ONLINE WRITER'S NOTEBOOK

Easily capture notes and complete assignments online.

Find all Digital Resources at **pearsonrealize.com**

Introducing the Big Question

What kind of knowledge changes our lives?

One aspect of knowledge is the mastering of a body of facts or a range of information about a topic. As we learn, we may also develop insight into a problem or arrive at a deeper awareness and understanding of the world around us. When we gain real knowledge, we leave ignorance behind, question old attitudes, and revise ideas that are outdated or wrong. While not all information may cause such a noticeable difference in our lives, some knowledge can transform the ways in which we perceive ourselves and relate to one another. What type of knowledge has that power? What kind of knowledge changes our lives?

Exploring the Big Question

Collaboration: Group Discussion Start thinking about the Big Question by considering the different types of knowledge people gain throughout their lives. List the people, ideas, and subjects about which you have gained important knowledge. Describe one specific example of each of the following categories:

- discovering something new about someone that caused you to view that person differently
- a time you put a new skill to use
- a historical event, invention, or philosophy that changed the way people live
- an essay or a book that altered how you view the world
- a problem or conflict that made you take action

Share your examples with others in a small group. Participate effectively in the group discussion by building on teammates' ideas and by presenting your own relevant ideas clearly and persuasively.

Connecting to the Literature Each reading in this unit will give you insight into the Big Question. After you read each selection, pause to consider what you learned. Then, think about how that new knowledge changes your understanding of the world around you.

Vocabulary

Speaking and Listening
1. Initiate and participate effectively in a range of collaborative discussions with diverse partners on grades 9–10 topics, texts, and issues, building on others' ideas and expressing their own clearly and persuasively.

Language
4.d. Verify the preliminary determination of the meaning of a word or phrase.

6. Acquire and use accurately general academic and domain-specific words and phrases, sufficient for reading, writing, speaking, and listening at the college and career readiness level; demonstrate independence in gathering vocabulary knowledge when considering a word or phrase important to comprehension or expression.

Acquire and Use Academic Vocabulary The term "academic vocabulary" refers to words you typically encounter in scholarly and literary texts and in technical and business writing. It is the language that helps to express complex ideas. Review the definitions of these academic vocabulary words.

adapt (ə dapt′) *v.* change or adjust

awareness (ə wer′ nis) *n.* having knowledge

evolve (ē välv′, -vôlv′) *v.* develop through gradual changes

insight (in′ sīt′) *n.* clear idea about the true nature of something

modified (mäd′ ə fīd′) *v.* changed or altered slightly

revise (ri vīz′) *v.* reconsider and modify

Use these words as you complete Big Question activities in this unit that involve reading, writing, speaking, and listening.

Gather Vocabulary Knowledge Additional words related to knowledge and change are listed below. Categorize the words by deciding whether you know each one well, know it a little bit, or do not know it at all.

empathy	**history**	**question**
enlighten	**ignorance**	**reflect**
growth	**influence**	**understanding**

Then, complete the following steps:

1. Write the definitions of the words you know.
2. Using a print or an online dictionary, look up the meanings of the words you do not know. Then, write the meanings.
3. If you think you know a word's meaning but are not certain, write your idea of the word's definition. Consult a dictionary to confirm the word's meaning. Revise your original definition if necessary.
4. If a word sounds familiar but you do not know its meaning, consult a dictionary. Then, record the meaning.
5. Use all of the words in a paragraph about knowledge and change.

Close Reading Workshop

In this workshop, you will learn an approach to reading that will deepen your understanding of literature and will help you better appreciate the author's craft. The workshop includes models for the close reading, discussion, research, and writing activities you will complete as you study the texts in this unit. After you have reviewed the strategies and models, practice your skills with the Independent Practice selection.

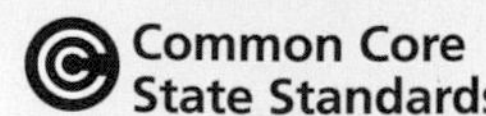

Common Core State Standards

RI.9-10.1, RI.9-10.2, RI.9-10.3, RI.9-10.4, RI.9-10.6; W.9-10.2, W.9-10.7, W.9-10.9.b; SL.9-10.1

[For full standards wording, see the chart in the front of this book.]

CLOSE READING: **NONFICTION**

In Part 2 of this unit, you will focus on reading various works of nonfiction. Use these strategies as you read the texts.

Comprehension: **Key Ideas and Details**

- Read first to get a basic understanding of the main ideas.
- Clarify the meanings of unfamiliar words. To do so, use context clues or consult a dictionary.
- Identify references that are unfamiliar to you and briefly research them.
- Distinguish between directly stated ideas and those that are suggested through details.

Ask yourself questions such as these:

- What is the author's most important point?
- What is the author's perspective or point of view on the topic?
- How does the author support his or her ideas?

Text Analysis: **Craft and Structure**

- Think about how the genre of the work fits the topic.
- Determine the author's purpose and how his or her word choice and tone support it.
- Notice how the author organizes ideas and how various sections of the text connect.

Ask yourself questions such as these:

- Who is the author's intended audience and how does the author interest or engage those readers?
- What literary techniques or rhetorical devices does the author use? How do those devices affect what I learn or feel about the topic?
- What evidence does the author use to support claims or illustrate ideas? Is that evidence varied, valid, and convincing?
- How does the author order and connect ideas and evidence?

Connections: **Integration of Knowledge and Ideas**

- Look for relationships among ideas. Identify causes and effects, problems and solutions, or comparisons and contrasts.
- Look for ideas the author restates and the examples used to support them.
- Compare and contrast this text with other works that you have read.

Ask yourself questions such as these:

- How has this work increased my knowledge?
- How does this work relate to others on a similar topic?
- How is this work important, unique, or worthy of reading?

Read

As you read this excerpt from a speech, take note of the annotations that model ways to closely read the text.

Reading Model

from "Address to Students at Moscow State University" by Ronald Reagan

But progress is not foreordained. The key is freedom—freedom of thought, freedom of information, freedom of communication.[1] The renowned scientist, scholar, and founding father of this university, Mikhail Lomonosov, knew that. "It is common knowledge," he said, "that the achievements of science are considerable and rapid, particularly once the yoke of slavery is cast off and replaced by the freedom of philosophy."...

The explorers of the modern era are the entrepreneurs, men with vision, with the courage to take risks and faith enough to brave the unknown.[2] These entrepreneurs and their small enterprises are responsible for almost all the economic growth in the United States. They are the prime movers of the technological revolution. In fact, one of the largest personal computer firms in the United States was started by two college students, no older than you, in the garage behind their home.[3] Some people, even in my own country, look at the riot of experiment that is the free market and see only waste. What of all the entrepreneurs that fail? Well, many do, particularly the successful ones; often several times. And if you ask them the secret of their success, they'll tell you it's all that they learned in their struggles along the way; yes, it's what they learned from failing. Like an athlete in competition or a scholar in pursuit of the truth, experience is the greatest teacher. . . .

We are seeing the power of economic freedom spreading around the world. Places such as the Republic of Korea, Singapore, Taiwan have vaulted into the technological era, barely pausing in the industrial age along the way. Low-tax agricultural policies in the subcontinent mean that in some years India is now a net exporter of food. Perhaps most exciting are the winds of change that are blowing over the People's Republic of China, where one-quarter of the world's population is now getting its first taste of economic freedom. At the same time, the growth of democracy has become one of the most powerful political movements of our age.[4] In Latin America in the 1970s, only a third of the population lived under democratic government; today over 90 percent does. In the Philippines, in the Republic of Korea, free, contested, democratic elections are the order of the day. Throughout the world, free markets are the model for growth. Democracy is the standard by which governments are measured.

Key Ideas and Details

1 President Reagan states his central idea: Freedom is key to progress of all kinds. His use of repetition creates a driving rhythm that emphasizes this point.

Craft and Structure

2 In dramatic language (*men with vision, courage, faith, brave*) Reagan implies that, like the explorers of old, entrepreneurs are visionaries who change the world. He then supports this point of view with evidence.

Craft and Structure

3 Reagan appeals directly to his audience with an example of students "no older than you." His mention of a "garage behind their home" suggests that in a free market even people of modest means can be successful.

Key Ideas and Details

4 This sentence marks a turning point in the speech. The president was speaking about economic freedom but now turns to a new idea: political freedom.

We Americans make no secret of our belief in freedom. In fact, it's something of a national pastime. Every 4 years the American people choose a new president, and 1988 is one of those years. At one point there were 13 major candidates running in the two major parties, not to mention all the others, including he Socialist and Libertarian candidates—all trying to get my job. About 1,000 local television stations, 8,500 radio stations, and 1,700 daily newspapers—each one an independent, private enterprise, fiercely independent of the Government[5] —report on the candidates, grill them in interviews, and bring them together for debates. In the end, the people vote; they decide who will be the next president. But freedom doesn't begin or end with elections.

Go to any American town,[6] to take just an example, and you'll see dozens of churches, representing many different beliefs—in many places, synagogues and mosques—and you'll see families of every conceivable nationality worshiping together. Go into any schoolroom,[6] and there you will see children being taught the Declaration of Independence, that they are endowed by their Creator with certain unalienable rights—among them life, liberty, and the pursuit of happiness—that no government can justly deny; the guarantees in their Constitution for freedom of speech, freedom of assembly, and freedom of religion. Go into any courtroom,[6] and there will preside an independent judge, beholden to no government power. There every defendant has the right to a trial by a jury of his peers, usually 12 men and women—common citizens; they are the ones, the only ones, who weigh the evidence and decide on guilt or innocence. In that court, the accused is innocent until proven guilty, and the word of a policeman or any official has no greater legal standing than the word of the accused. Go to any university campus,[6] and there you'll find an open, sometimes heated discussion of the problems in American society and what can be done to correct them. Turn on the television, and you'll see the legislature conducting the business of government right there before the camera, debating and voting on the legislation that will become the law of the land. March in any demonstration, and there are many of them; the people's right of assembly is guaranteed in the Constitution and protected by the police. Go into any union hall,[6] where the members know their right to strike is protected by law. . . .

Craft and Structure

5 Reagan mentions many different types of candidates to show the diversity of political expression in America. Data about American media develops this idea. Reagan's audience would have recognized the dramatic contrast to their own system of state-controlled politics and media.

Craft and Structure

6 Reagan repeats the phrases "go into any / go to any" to point out the variety of ways in which people experience political freedom in America. The repetition adds a rhythm that emphasizes the importance of the ideas.

But freedom is more even than this. Freedom is the right to question and change the established way of doing things. It is the continuing revolution of the marketplace. It is the understanding that allows us to recognize shortcomings and seek solutions. It is the right to put forth an idea, scoffed at by the experts, and watch it catch fire among the people. It is the right to dream—to follow your dream or stick to your conscience, even if you're the only one in a sea of doubters. Freedom is the recognition that no single person, no single authority or government has a monopoly on the truth, but that every individual life is infinitely precious, that every one of us put on this world has been put there for a reason and has something to offer.[7] ...

Your generation is living in one of the most exciting, hopeful times in Soviet history. It is a time when the first breath of freedom stirs the air and the heart beats to the accelerated rhythm of hope, when the accumulated spiritual energies of a long silence yearn to break free. I am reminded of the famous passage near the end of Gogol's *Dead Souls*. Comparing his nation to a speeding troika, Gogol asks what will be its destination. But he writes, "There was no answer save the bell pouring forth marvelous sound."[8]

We do not know what the conclusion will be of this journey, but we're hopeful that the promise of reform will be fulfilled. In this Moscow spring, this May 1988, we may be allowed that hope: that freedom, like the fresh green sapling planted over Tolstoy's grave, will blossom forth at last in the rich fertile soil of your people and culture.[9] We may be allowed to hope that the marvelous sound of a new openness will keep rising through, ringing through, leading to a new world of reconciliation, friendship, and peace. . . .

Integration of Knowledge and Ideas

7 In this paragraph, the president brings listeners full circle. Using repetition ("Freedom is..."; "It is..."), parallelism, and emotional language he sums up and explains the significance of his central idea.

Craft and Structure

8 You might research Nikolai Gogol to discover that he was a nineteenth century Russian author who criticized Russian bureaucracy. Reagan uses this allusion to connect to his audience and their history.

Integration of Knowledge and Ideas

9 In a simile, Reagan likens the growth of a young tree to the blossoming forth of freedom, thus ending his speech with an emotional appeal framed in a powerful visual image.

Discuss

Sharing your own ideas and listening to the ideas of others can deepen your understanding of a text and help you look at a topic in a whole new way. As you participate in collaborative discussions, work to have a genuine exchange in which classmates build upon one another's ideas. Support your points with evidence and ask meaningful questions.

Discussion Model

Student 1: I am surprised the Soviet government allowed President Reagan to speak to students in Moscow. I thought the U.S. and the Soviet Union were enemies, so I wonder why they let him do this. President Reagan argues for freedom in his speech, but his tone seems to be understanding rather than harsh.

Student 2: I noticed that he sometimes spoke formally and at other times it was like he was having a conversation with the students. Sometimes, he sounds like a teacher explaining how government works.

Student 3: Yes, and he didn't say anything bad about the Soviet Union. He just talked about why life in the United States was good. He talked about how Americans experience freedom all the time.

Research

Targeted research can clarify unfamiliar details and shed light on various aspects of a text. Consider questions that arise in your mind as you read, and use those questions as the basis for research.

Research Model

Questions: *How did relations between the United States and the Soviet Union change in the late 1980s?*

Key Words for Internet Search: U.S.-Soviet relations and Ronald Reagan

Result: Mikhail Gorbachev, The Ronald Reagan Presidential Foundation

What I Learned: Ronald Reagan was the fortieth president of the United States, serving from 1981 to 1989. Mikhail Gorbachev became the leader of the Soviet Union in 1985. Together, Reagan and Gorbachev built a positive relationship between their two countries. Among other initiatives, the two leaders successfully negotiated nuclear arms treaties. This was a major change from the strong hostility that had existed between the United States and the Soviet Union since the 1950s.

Write

Writing about a text will deepen your understanding of it and will also allow you to share your ideas more formally with others. The following model essay examines President Reagan's arguments in his speech to the students at Moscow University.

Writing Model: Argument

Ronald Reagan's Argument in Favor of the U.S. System of Government

In his speech at Moscow State University in 1988, President Ronald Reagan explained his belief that freedom has two main parts: economics and politics. For Reagan, economic freedom is the foundation for political freedom and the two components are what make the American system superior. At the time of the speech, the Soviet Union was becoming more open as leader Mikhail Gorbachev worked for reform. Reagan hoped to influence the direction that the Soviet Union would take during its period of change. In this speech, the president clearly assumes that his audience does not know very much about freedom and needs to learn. He takes on the role of a teacher instructing his listeners.

The writer includes background information from research. This effort shows a consideration of the audience, because readers may be unfamiliar with the historical context of Reagan's speech.

The writer states a claim—a specific interpretation of the Reagan speech. This interpretation will be defended in examples and details throughout the essay.

The excerpt from the speech begins with a focus on economic freedom. Reagan explains his belief that economic freedom allows Americans to become entrepreneurs, which fuels economic growth in their country. Reagan mentions that entrepreneurs can be as young as the college students in his audience. He says that entrepreneurs need not fear failure, as "experience is the greatest teacher."

Reagan also points out that economic freedom includes allowing other countries to achieve economic success. He applauds the "spreading around the world" of economic freedom. He seems to be suggesting that he wants the Soviet Union to be a part of this change.

The writer consistently and effectively cites evidence from the speech.

Reagan shifts his emphasis from economic freedom to political freedom in the next part of the excerpt. He highlights the importance of the ability of the people in the United States to choose their leaders freely through open elections. He continues with other examples of political freedom, including freedom of speech and the right to a fair trial. Reagan lives up to his reputation as a great orator with the words, "Freedom is the recognition that no single person, no single authority or government has a monopoly on the truth, but that every individual life is infinitely precious."

The writer follows through on the idea, first presented in the introduction, that Reagan is concerned with both economic and political freedom.

The president concludes by telling his audience that the Soviet Union has the opportunity to enjoy the same freedoms that the United States enjoys. He says, "It is a time when the first breath of freedom stirs the air." In effect, Reagan uses this speech to lay out a plan for the Soviet reform movement. This was a striking change from previous U.S.-Soviet relations—and previous speeches of Reagan's—which were very hostile. In this speech, the president became a teacher, welcoming students to a new era and a new understanding of the possibilities the future might hold.

The writer ends the essay with a powerful conclusion by indicating the importance of the speech in both American and world history.

As you read the following work of nonfiction, apply the close reading strategies you have learned. You may need to read the work multiple times to fully explore the sequence of events, identify descriptive details, and consider the author's insights.

Meet the Author

In 2001, **Erik Weihenmayer** (b. 1968) became the first blind person to climb to the summit of Mount Everest. This excerpt is taken from his memoir of that achievement.

Vocabulary ▶

apprehension (ap´ rē hen´ shən) *n.* anxiety

sparse (spärs) *adj.* thinly spread; not plentiful

CLOSE READING TOOL

Read and respond to this selection online using the **Close Reading Tool.**

Everest *from* Touch the Top of the World

by Erik Weihenmayer

We left our tents a little before 9:00 p.m. on May 24. Because of our twenty-four-hour delay and the **apprehension** of other expeditions to share a summit day with me, we moved across the South Col with only one other team behind us. We had no worries of the typical horde clogging the fixed lines but could direct our full focus toward the mountain. The wind was blowing so loudly through the col that I couldn't hear the bells jingling from Chris's ice axe. Chris and I expected this, so for the first two hours he clanked his metal axe against rocks he passed. Finally, we worked our way around to the mountain's leeward[1] side, where Everest itself protected us from the wind. Chris had lost his voice, so his verbal directions were **sparse**. At each anchor, he'd hold the new line with his hand, so I could locate it and clip in. Chris was moving in front of me at his usual rock-solid pace, and I was right on his heels. We were making unbelievable time.

As we got higher up the mountain, four distinct changes had begun to work in my favor. Earlier, in the icefall, each step was very specific, but the terrain above the South Col consisted of steep forty-five-degree snow faces a hundred yards wide, intermingled with ten-to-fifty-foot crumbly rock steps. I could stay in the kicked boot holes of Chris or kick my own steps. Where I stepped had become less important than maintaining internal balance. I could breathe, scan my ice axe, and count on the next step. The slope was often so steep that I could lean forward and feel the rock or snow steps with my gloved hands, and I had trained myself long ago to save energy by landing my feet in the same holds my hands had just left. Finally, when I needed it most, the mountain had given me a pattern.

The thin oxygen of extreme altitude reduced us to a crawl. It was like moving through a bizarre atmosphere of syrup mixed with a narcotic. My team, struggling just to put one foot in front of the other, moved so slowly, it gave me more time to scan my axe across the snow and feel my way forward. The third equalizer was the darkness. With just a trickle of light produced

---

1. **leeward** (lē´ wərd´) *adj.* away from the wind.

by headlamps, my sighted team could only see a few feet in front of them. Bulky goggles blocked their side vision, and oxygen masks covered much of their visual field. Also, the pure oxygen trickling through their masks would flow up and freeze the lenses of their goggles so that they constantly had to remove them to wipe the lenses clean. Those brief moments when eyes are exposed to the elements, corneas will freeze, and the intense rays of the sun reflecting off the snow cause instant snow blindness. Not once did I ever have to worry about these complications.

In addition, my teammates had chosen smaller masks that rode low and tight across their cheeks and hung mostly below their chins. This allowed climbers to see better and prevented pure oxygen from seeping into their lenses, but also allowed plenty of pure oxygen to escape into the wind. I, on the other hand, had the luxury of choosing the largest mask I could find and wore it high on my face, getting the most benefit from the oxygen flow and the **ambient** air around the mask. I'm sure I made a freakish sight with my gigantic mask covering my goggles, like a day long ago in wrestling practice when I had put my sweatshirt on backward, with the hood covering my face, and chased the terrified freshmen around the mat. The consistent terrain, the altitude, the mask, and the darkness were great equalizers. I wouldn't go so far as to claim these gave me an advantage, but it was a matter of perspective. The mountain had gotten desperately harder for everyone else, while it had gotten slightly easier for me.

◀ **Vocabulary**
ambient (am′ bē ənt) *adj.* surrounding; on all sides

For two and a half months, all the decisions, the logistics, the backup safety plans had been implemented and executed by PV, and now, somewhere below the Balcony, the exhausting burden of leadership finally took its toll. Suddenly feeling listless and unable to catch his breath even with his oxygen bottle at full flow, PV had **arduously** turned back. He managed to convince Brad and Sherm, next to him, that he was strong enough to descend alone, in retrospect, a ploy that might have turned deadly, but PV's weary brain had never stopped calculating the big picture. He had refused to divert any energy from the team's summit effort. Through periodic radio checks as PV dropped altitude, I could hear his characteristically hyper voice growing flat, and just below a steep ice bulge, only an hour from Camp Four, PV sat down in the snow.

◀ **Vocabulary**
arduously (är′ jo͞o əs lē) *adv.* with great difficulty; laboriously

"I'm very tired," he said. "I don't know if I can make it. I might need some assistance." PV's one warning before we left the tent was "If you sit down, you'll stay there." So, beginning to panic, I ripped my radio out of my pocket. "Is anyone near PV who can help him down?" I asked. "Is anyone reading me?" I repeated myself several times to empty static.

A few weeks earlier, Dr. Gipe had received the sad news that a close family friend had been killed in a skiing accident; a three-thousand-foot day in the Death Zone just didn't seem fair to his family, so that night, he had never left his tent. His decision was a tough one to make, but extremely fortunate for PV's sake. "This is Gipe at the South Col," finally came over the radio. "I'm strapping on my crampons right now. I'm going out to get PV." Dr. Gipe met PV about a half an hour from camp, up again and staggering slowly toward the tents.

With the first crisis of the night averted, Chris and I plodded up a steep gully, which led us to the Balcony, a flat snow platform, ten feet wide. Michael Brown arrived first at about 2:00 a.m., with Chris and me right behind. All night, the weather had remained clear, with high clouds to the southeast and distant lightning flashes illuminating the sky, but at the Balcony, our luck suddenly ran out. We walked into a blasting storm. Wind and horizontal snow raked our down suits and covered us with a layer of ice. The lightning strikes were now on top of us, exploding like a pyrotechnic[2] show. Chris later said he couldn't see his feet through the blowing snow, which stopped us short, since the southeast ridge above narrowed to fifteen feet wide. Mike O.'s and Didrik's headlamps had simultaneously flickered out, and one of Didrik's crampons had popped off. "Someone come and help us," Mike yelled over the radio. Charley headed back and found them sitting in the snow only twenty feet away.

Chris and I huddled together in the wind, waiting for the others to arrive. "What do you think, Big E?" he asked. "It's lookin' pretty grim." When the others trickled in, Sherm wanted to go on; Charley wanted to turn back, and Erie thought we should wait. For forty-five minutes, we waited, periodic arguments breaking out whether to go on or descend. I was beginning to shiver and forced myself to bounce up and down, and to windmill my arms. We were so close, and I was feeling strong. Turning back was a crushing proposition, but I also wasn't willing to go bullheadedly forward and throw my life away. My mind was starting to settle on the possibility of turning back, when Kevin's voice from Base Camp crackled over my radio. Throughout the expedition, Kevin had been learning to read the satellite weather reports we received every few days over the Internet. From the weather map, it appeared the storm was moving rapidly to the northeast toward Bhutan, and where we stood on the Balcony, we were directly northeast of Base Camp. "Hey you guys, don't quit yet," his voice sounded urgent. "The storm's cleared down here. It just might pass over you."

"Weather is also clearing here," Kami said from Camp Two below. Chris glanced over at me. Beyond my right hip, shining through the storm clouds, he could see a star. "Let's see if this thing breaks up," he said. Sherm must have felt good tidings, too, because he pushed on. Chris and I followed.

Following the narrow exposed southeast shoulder, I felt the first warmth of the sun about 4:00 a.m.; so high up, no other mountain blocked the sunrise. The weather had thankfully turned spectacular.

---

2. **pyrotechnic** (pī´ rə tek´ nik) *adj.* of or pertaining to fireworks; here, brilliant; dazzling.

Still hours below the South Summit, we were stalled out again. The fixed lines, running up the steepest slope yet, had been frozen over by a hard windswept crust of snow. Jeff and Brad moved ahead, pulling the lines free, an exhausting job at twenty-eight thousand feet. The job was quickly wearing Jeff down, but he said later that with each gasping breath as he heaved the rope free, he envisioned the two of us standing on top together. Soon he was beginning to feel faint and dizzy. As he knelt in the snow, Brad, behind him, examined his oxygen equipment and assessed that his regulator, connecting the long tube of his mask to his bottle, had malfunctioned. The internal valves responsible for regulating flow were notoriously prone to freezing shut. "Who's got an extra regulator?" Brad called out over the radio, but tired bodies and brains could not recall who had thrown in the extras in the presummit shuffle. "My day's finished if I can't find the extra," Jeff yelled testily.

It may not have been PV's time to summit, but he wasn't through benefiting the team. "Calm down," he advised, lying weakly on his back in his tent. "Everyone take a deep breath. Ang Pasang and Sherm are carrying the extra regulators." Luckily, Ang Pasang was only a hundred feet behind. Together, Brad and Ang Pasang screwed on Jeff's new regulator.

By 8:00 a.m., we had struggled on to the South Summit, 28,700 feet. After a short rest, Chris took off for the summit, cranking it into "Morris gear," and Luis took over in front of me. From the South Summit, the true summit is still at least two hours away across the three-hundred-foot-long knife-edge ridge, up the fifty-foot vertical Hillary Step, and finally traversing up a long slightly broader ridge to the summit.

Jeff, exhausted from his two-hour struggle pulling lines, stopped short in front of me. "I'm wasted. I've gotta go down," he said reluctantly. "This'll have to be my summit."

For a moment I wanted to goad him on the way we had done each other on winter training climbs of Colorado fourteeners. "If you wanna turn back, just say the word," we'd jab. "Of course, I'll have to tell everyone you were a whiney little crybaby." But 28,700 feet above sea level wasn't the place to motivate with bravado or ego, so assessing that he was strong enough to get down, I rested a hand on Jeff's shoulder and wished him a safe descent. Jeff had been with me from the beginning, practically introducing me to the mountains. He had shown extraordinary patience as I stumbled along experimenting with brand-new trekking poles. We had even stood together on the summit of Denali[3] and El Capitan,[4] so I knew that reaching the summit of Mt. Everest without him wouldn't feel complete. Suddenly, a wave of heavy exhaustion passed over me, and I felt weary and crumpled. "Maybe I'll go down too," I readied my lips to say, but then Luis was crunching through the snow in front of me, and I forced myself to revive.

---

3. **Denali** (di nä′ lē) name of the National Park in which Mt. McKinley is located.
4. **El Capitan** (el′ ka′ pē tan′) a peak in the Sierra Nevada mountain range in the Yosemite Valley of central California.

Down-climbing the twenty-foot vertical snow face on the backside of the South Summit leading onto the knife-edge ridge went against my survival instinct. The ridge is the width of a picnic table and always heavily corniced[5] with snow. To the left is an eight-thousand-foot drop into Nepal, and on the right, a twelve-thousand-foot drop into Tibet. PV had told me that while crossing the ridge on his 1998 attempt, he had driven his ice axe into the snow and, after withdrawing it, had stared through the small hole into the early morning light of Tibet. In 1995, on Brad's second attempt, a climber in front of him had taken his first step onto the ridge just before the entire right half of it dropped away. The climber jumped back to safety, but a second later he would have ridden the cornice into Tibet. This year, the ridge was drier and more stable. Frozen boot steps traversed along the lefthand side. I'd scan my pole until it dropped into a boot mark, then cautiously lower my foot. I knew I couldn't make a mistake here: six hard steady breaths, another solid step, and a relaxed, focused mind like clear water.

Climbing the Hillary Step, I felt I was in my element, feeling the rock under my gloves. I stuck the crampon points of my right foot tenuously into a tiny crack and the left points into a cornice of snow, slid my ascender as high as it would go on the rope, and stood up and quickly reached for the next knob of rock. At the top, I awkwardly belly-flopped onto a flat ledge, slowly pulled myself to my feet, and began traversing the last slope to the summit. For forty minutes I trudged upward. My heavy sluggish muscles felt as if they were pushing through wet cement. With each step closer, the real possibility of standing on top began to trickle through my focused brain. I had speculated success in a conceptual way and as a way to motivate myself when I was down, but it was dangerous to believe it as a fact. A team could be turned back for so many reasons at any time. Just keep moving, I thought. You're not there yet.

Then a body moved down the slope toward me and I felt thin wiry arms beneath a puffy down suit wrapping around me. "Big E!" The voice rasped, so hollow and wispy, I had trouble recognizing it as Chris. His voice tried to say more, but his quaking words dissipated in the wind. Then he leaned in against my ear. "Big E"—his voice gave way to tears, then struggled out in an immense effort—"you're about to stand on top of the world." Then he quickly let go and hurriedly moved down the slope.

Luis and I linked our arms, and in a few steps, the earth flattened and the massive sky closed around me on all sides. "This is Erik, Luis, and Ang Pasang," I said over the radio. "We're on the top. I can't believe it; we're on the top."

"You're the best, Big E!" Kevin yelled from Base Camp. "I love you guys." I could hear the entire Base Camp crew cheering behind him.

"You're the strongest man in the world," PV said.

---

5. **corniced** (kôr′ nist) *adj.* in architecture, having a projecting decorative strip atop a wall or building; here, characterized by overhanging masses of snow or ice.

I turned around, surprised to hear more crampons moving up behind me. "I wasn't gonna let you stand on top and hear about it the rest of my life," Jeff said, with a little pep left in his voice. One of the greatest joys of my summit was that Jeff hadn't turned back at all. From the South Summit, he had watched us down-climb onto the knife-edge ridge and move toward the Hillary Step. Later he told me, "I simply had to follow." Behind Jeff came Erie, Michael B., Didrik, Charley, and Mike O. Sherm had been the first on the team to summit, becoming the oldest man in history to stand on the top of the world, but better than his record was the fact that his son, Brad, had stepped onto the summit right behind him. Nineteen team members made it to the summit: eleven Westerners and eight Sherpas, the most from one team to reach the top in a single day. So it was a crowded summit as we all stood together, hugging and crying on a snow platform the size of a single-car garage.

Another storm was rolling in from the north. "Weather's changing fast," PV called up on the radio. "You guys need to go down immediately." I turned to head down with Erie, when Jeff said, "Wait a second, Big E. You'll only be here once in your life. Look around. Think about where you are and what you've done." So I suspended my nerves for a moment, reached down and touched the snow through my gloved hand, listened to the Sherpa prayer flags flapping in the wind, and heard the infinite sound of space around me, as on my first rock climb. After I had gone blind almost twenty years ago, I would have been proud to find the bathroom, so I said a quick prayer and thanked God for giving me so much. Then it was time to go down.

We descended through heavy snowfall but, thankfully, little wind. Erie took over guiding me, down the Hillary Step, across the knife edge, and contrary to his fears that he wouldn't be strong enough to make the top, he was stronger and more lucid on the way down from Everest's summit than most were on the top of a peak in Colorado. Reaching our tents at about 3:00 p.m., I hugged Erie. "Today," I said, "you were my guardian angel. I'm glad you're here."

That night, Kevin radioed up to report that he had called Ellie on the sat phone with the news. "She screamed loud enough to break the neighbors' windows." He laughed. The next days were exhausting as we fought our way through the screaming wind of the South Col, down the Lhotse Face—where my rubbery legs refused to obey my brain—and finally one last trip through the icefall. At the bottom, in Superman's Palace, of course, the whole team was waiting, and the party lasted long after the sun had sunk below Pumori.

Despite our success, plenty of **detractors** voiced their opinions on Internet chat rooms and in letters to the editor. I've heard all the ridiculous assumptions.

"Now that a blind guy's climbed it, everyone's going to want to climb it. They're going to think it's easy. People will probably get hurt."

◀ **Vocabulary**
detractors (dē trak′ tors) *n.* those who discredit someone's accomplishments

"Why are people thinking this is such a big deal? Anyone can be short-roped to the top by nineteen seeing-eye guides."

My teammates constantly come to my rescue with carefully crafted comebacks like "Before you start spouting a bunch of lies over a public forum, get your facts straight, dude!"

"Don't let 'em get to you," Chris Morris said after I shared with him their comments. "You climbed every inch of that mountain, and then some."

I knew he was right. There were some who would never be convinced, others who still had no idea what to think, but many others for whom the climb forced a higher expectation of their own possibilities. I don't climb mountains to prove to anyone that blind people can do this or that. I climb for the same reason an artist paints a picture: because it brings me great joy. But I'd be lying if I didn't admit my secret satisfaction in facing those cynics and blowing through their doubts, destroying their negative stereotypes, taking their very narrow parameters of what's possible and what's not, and shattering them into a million pieces.

Vocabulary ▶
parameters (pə ram′ ət ərz) *n.* boundaries or limits

When those **parameters** are rebuilt, thousands and thousands of people will live with fewer barriers placed before them, and if my climbs can play a small role in opening doors of opportunity and hope for those who will come after us, then I am very proud of what we were able to achieve . . .

Close Reading Activities

Read

Comprehension: **Key Ideas and Details**

1. (a) Identify at least two challenges that high altitude presents to the climbers. **(b) Connect:** According to the author, in what ways is his blindness a benefit in meeting those challenges? Explain.

2. (a) Classify: Identify at least one example of each of the following types of aid the team receives: technical assistance, emotional support, communications assistance. **(b) Generalize:** Explain how others' actions help the author and his team reach the summit.

3. (a) Interpret: How do some critics respond to Weihenmayer's success in reaching the summit of Everest? **(b) Analyze:** Judging from the details in this memoir, how would you answer those critics?

4. Summarize: Write a brief, objective summary of the memoir. Cite textual details in your writing.

Text Analysis: **Craft and Structure**

5. (a) Distinguish: Cite at least one passage in which the author uses description to paint a picture of the setting. **(b) Analyze:** How does his presentation of the setting increase the suspense of the narrative? Explain.

6. (a) Distinguish: Note two examples of figurative language the author uses to capture the physical discomfort of high-altitude exertion. **(b) Connect:** For each example, explain how it clarifies the physical challenges the team must overcome.

7. (a) Distinguish: At what point does the author interrupt the forward flow of the narrative with discussion of an earlier event? Explain. **(b) Interpret:** What information does the author provide with this flashback?

8. (a) Summarize: The author states that high altitude is no place to "motivate with bravado or ego." Explain his point. **(b) Compare and Contrast:** Cite examples from the memoir that illustrate better types of motivation in such a dangerous endeavor.

Connections: **Integration of Knowledge and Ideas**

Discuss

Conduct a **partner discussion** about the ways in which Weihenmayer uses his other senses to make up for his lack of sight during the climb. Summarize your discussion and share your ideas with the class as a whole.

Research

Briefly research the dangers posed by extreme altitude and the measures climbers take to overcome those dangers. Consider the following:

a. the physical challenges of extreme altitude

b. the psychological challenges of high altitude

c. the history of climbing equipment and the role technology plays in climbing today

Take notes as you perform your research. Then, write a **report** in which you analyze how Weinhenmayer and his team prepared for their Everest climb and assess whether their preparations were adequate.

Write

Consider how the account of Weihenmayer's climb would have been different if it had been written in the third person. Write an **essay** in which you analyze how the author's first-person point of view shapes the story. Cite details from the work to support your analysis.

What kind of knowledge changes our lives?

Erik Weihenmayer accomplished amazing things after he became blind at age thirteen. Does he have knowledge that many others lack? If so, what is that knowledge, and how has it helped him live a full life?

"**New knowledge** is the most **valuable** commodity on earth."

—**Kurt Vonnegut, Jr.**

PART 2

TEXT ANALYSIS GUIDED EXPLORATION

SEEKING KNOWLEDGE

Most people are flooded with information every day. We watch videos and movies, read the news, and receive messages through our mobile devices. While some of this information-gathering activity is important, it is not the same as the focused pursuit of knowledge that happens through reading, research, and reflection. As you read the texts in this section, think about how the knowledge each author shares adds to your understanding of the world. Then, consider how each selection contributes to your thinking about the Big Question for this unit: **What kind of knowledge changes our lives?**

◀ CRITICAL VIEWING What do the illustration and quotation suggest about the nature of curiosity and the desire for understanding?

READINGS IN PART 2

CLOSE READING TOOL

Use the **Close Reading Tool** to practice the strategies you learn in this unit.

Focus on Craft and Structure

Elements of Essays and Speeches

Essays and speeches express an author's **point of view** about a single topic.

An **essay** is a short nonfiction work that conveys a central idea or key concept about a specific topic. It also expresses its author's **point of view,** or perspective, on the topic.

A **speech** is a nonfiction work that a speaker delivers to an audience. Like an essay, a speech usually presents a central idea and expresses the speaker's point of view on a topic.

Whether an author is writing an essay or a speech, he or she always has a **purpose,** or reason, for writing. A writer chooses details to include in an essay or speech based on his or her purpose. For example, a writer who wishes to warn of the dangers of pollution might include facts about its impact on health. Certain types of writing lend themselves to specific purposes:

- Expository writing **informs or explains.**
- Argumentative writing **persuades,** or convinces readers to believe or to do something.
- Narrative writing **entertains** by telling a story.

An author may have more than one purpose in a single work. For example, he or she might inform by telling an entertaining story about a topic. Usually, however, an author has one overriding purpose.

Effective essays and speeches employ the following elements in ways that suit the material, the circumstances of the writing, and the audience.

Elements of Essays and Speeches

Element	Definition
Author's Purpose	The author's main reason for writing
Central Idea	The author's main, or central, point
Point of View	The author's overall stance on the subject; an author's point of view reflects his or her beliefs, experiences, and values.
Structure	The organizational pattern the author uses to develop and present his or her ideas
Style	The author's distinct approach to writing; stylistic elements include the author's **syntax** (sentence structure, length, and variety) and **diction** (word choice).
Rhetorical Devices	Patterns of word choice, syntax, and meaning used to emphasize ideas, including *parallelism,* the use of similar grammatical structures to express related ideas
Tone	The author's emotional attitude toward his or her subject and audience

Types of Essays

Essays are often categorized by their general purposes.

- An **expository essay** explains a topic by providing information about it or by exploring an idea related to it.
- A **persuasive essay, or argument,** attempts to convince readers to accept the writer's point of view on an issue or to take a particular course of action.
- A **reflective essay** presents experiences that inspired the writer's thoughts or feelings about a topic.
- A **narrative essay** tells the story of real events or experiences.
- A **descriptive essay** provides specific details to create an impression of a person, an object, or an experience.

An author may combine elements of different types of essays in order to fulfill a purpose. For example, in an argumentative essay persuading readers to exercise, an author might narrate a story about personal experiences with an exercise program.

Types of Speeches

When developing a speech, a writer must consider several factors: his or her purpose for writing, the occasion or event at which the speech will be delivered, and the audience. Imagine, for example, the differences between a speech for a school graduation ceremony and a speech for a surprise birthday party. The chart below shows possible occasions and audiences for several common types of speeches.

Common Core State Standards

Reading Informational Text

3. Analyze how the author unfolds an analysis or series of ideas or events, including the order in which the points are made, how they are introduced and developed, and the connections that are drawn between them.

4. Determine the meaning of words and phrases as they are used in a text, including figurative, connotative, and technical meanings; analyze the cumulative impact of specific word choices on meaning and tone.

5. Analyze in detail how an author's ideas or claims are developed and refined by particular sentences, paragraphs, or larger portions of a text.

6. Determine an author's point of view or purpose in a text and analyze how an author uses rhetoric to advance that point of view or purpose.

Type of Speech	Possible Occasion and Audience
Address: a formal, prepared speech that is usually delivered by someone of importance	A graduation speech, delivered by a principal to an audience of parents, faculty, staff, and students
Lecture: a prepared, often formal speech that informs or instructs an audience	A speech explaining a medical discovery, delivered by a scientist to doctors at a medical convention
Talk: an informal speech delivered in a conversational style	A report on a fundraiser, delivered by a student to other members of a volunteer club
Sermon: a prepared, often formal speech intended to teach or inspire	A speech about a religious figure, delivered by a pastor to the congregation of a church
Presentation: a prepared speech about a topic; may include visual aids	A multimedia presentation about a historical event, delivered by a student to a history class
Extemporaneous Speech: a speech delivered without preparation, usually in a conversational style	A toast at a wedding, delivered by a wedding guest to the bride and groom

Analyzing the Development of Ideas

Writers use a variety of techniques to develop, refine, and support the **central ideas** in their essays and speeches.

A writer will employ several different elements to fulfill his or her purpose and to develop the key ideas in an essay or speech. These elements include support for his or her claims; a specific organizational structure; rhetorical devices; imagery and figurative language; and effective word choice.

Types of Support Supporting a claim means giving readers valid reasons to believe it is true. Here are some types of support:

- **Facts,** or statements that can be proved true
- **Statistics,** or numerical data that presents important information on a subject
- **Descriptions,** or details that tell what something looks like, sounds like, and so on
- **Examples,** or specific cases that illustrate an idea
- **Reasons,** or statements that justify or explain a belief
- **Expert opinions,** or statements made by people who have special knowledge of a topic

The methods an author uses to support a claim depend upon his or her purpose and audience. Notice, for example, how the author relies on description in this persuasive speech to potential vacationers.

Example: Description

Leave Winter Behind!
Take off those heavy boots and warm your feet on a soft, sandy beach. Listen to the call of the gulls as you gaze at aqua waves lapping a golden shore.

Organization of Ideas Authors organize ideas to emphasize the connections among them. In an effective essay or speech, key ideas are introduced, developed, and refined at all levels of the work. For example, a work may be divided into **sections** that introduce central ideas. **Paragraphs** develop and support those ideas, and **sentences** within the paragraphs present supporting details and connect one idea to another.

An author chooses the overall organizational structure that best fits his or her topic. In a long work, an author may employ several different methods of organization. The following are some common organizational patterns.

Example: Organizational Structures

- **Chronological order** presents events in the order in which they happen.
- **Spatial order** presents details from left to right, bottom to top, near to far, and so on.
- **List organization** presents connected details consecutively or sorts them into categories.
- **Comparison-and-contrast organization** groups ideas according to their similarities and differences.
- **Cause-and-effect organization** shows how one event causes another.
- **Problem-and-solution organization** identifies a problem, and then presents ways to solve it.

Rhetorical Devices Rhetorical devices are language techniques that an author uses to support and emphasize central ideas, create rhythm, and make a work memorable. Although rhetorical devices by themselves are not sufficient to support a claim, they add force and appeal to a writer's work and aid readers in grasping, retaining, and accepting a writer's ideas. Some common rhetorical devices are listed below.

- **Repetition** is the reuse of a key word, phrase, or idea.
  Example: We will play with pride. We will play with sportsmanship. We will play to win.
- **Parallel structure** is the use of similar grammatical structures to express related ideas.
  Example: They will walk out of the darkness, into the light, beyond limitations.
- **Restatement** is the expression of the same idea in different words to strengthen a point.
  Example: We won't give up. Quitting is not an option.
- **Rhetorical questions** are inquiries that have obvious answers and that are asked for effect.
  Example: Do you really need to talk on your cell phone while you drive? Can't that call wait?
- **Analogies** are comparisons that show similarities between things that are otherwise not alike.
  Example: Our belief in this mission is a fire that keeps us warm.

Imagery and Figurative Language In addition to rhetorical devices, authors use other creative methods to invigorate their writing. **Imagery** includes vivid details that appeal to the five senses of sight, sound, touch, taste, and smell. **Figurative language** is writing or speech that is not meant to be interpreted literally. It includes **figures of speech** that make unexpected comparisons or describe and explain in fresh, imaginative ways. Three common figures of speech are simile, metaphor, and personification.

- A **simile** is a direct comparison that contains the word *like* or *as: My little brother is as annoying and tenacious as a swarm of mosquitoes.*
- A **metaphor** describes one thing as if it were another: *Each day is a gift.*
- **Personification** assigns human characteristics to a nonhuman subject: *The old car coughed, wheezed, and refused to move.*

Tone and Word Choice The tone of an essay or speech is the author's attitude toward his or her subject and audience. An author's tone may be formal or informal, ironic, amused, angry, sarcastic, or anything in between. Tone is revealed through an author's choice of words as well as the devices he or she uses. The **connotations,** or emotional associations, of words play a key part in creating tone.

Example: Humorous Tone

Finally, I finished writing my first draft. I admit it was a little rough. Well, maybe more than a little rough. To be honest, it was so rough you could sand wood with it.

 Building Knowledge

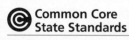

Dava Sobel (b. 1947) attended the Bronx High School of Science and went on to become an award-winning science reporter for *The New York Times.* While researching the history of longitude, she stumbled onto the topic of her next book: Italian Renaissance astronomer Galileo and his daughter. Sobel wrote about their relationship in *Galileo's Daughter*.

Common Core State Standards

Reading Informational Text

1. Cite strong and thorough textual evidence to support analysis of what the text says explicitly as well as inferences drawn from the text.

2. Determine a central idea of a text and analyze its development over the course of the text, including how it emerges and is shaped and refined by specific details; provide an objective summary of the text.

4. Determine the meaning of words and phrases as they are used in a text, including figurative, connotative, and technical meanings; analyze the cumulative impact of specific word choices on meaning and tone.

5. Analyze in detail how an author's ideas or claims are developed and refined by particular sentences, paragraphs, or larger portions of a text.

What kind of knowledge changes our lives?

Explore the Big Question as you read this excerpt from *Longitude*. Take notes on how discovery and invention expand society's understanding of the world.

CLOSE READING FOCUS

Key Ideas and Details: **Main Idea**

To fully understand an essay, identify its **main, or central, idea** and the **supporting details** that explain or illustrate it. To analyze how the author develops, supports, and refines a main idea, pause after key sentences, paragraphs, or sections of the text to **summarize** the points expressed in that section. Then, consider how each idea connects to those that precede and follow it. When you summarize, you briefly restate the most important idea and key details of a text.

Craft and Structure: **Expository Essay**

An **expository essay** is a brief nonfiction work in which an author informs the reader by explaining, defining, or interpreting an idea. Often, the writer reaches a conclusion through reasoning, or logic.

Diction, or the author's word choice, sets one expository essay off from another. Diction may be formal, informal, sophisticated, or slangy. It may include technical language, such as scientific terms. **Tone** is the author's attitude toward the subject or audience. An author's tone may be critical, serious, silly, or a combination of qualities. A writer's diction contributes to both the meaning and tone of an essay.

Vocabulary

You will encounter the following words in this essay. Decide whether you know each word well, know it a little bit, or do not know it at all. After you have read the selection, see how your knowledge of each word has increased.

haphazardly **configuration** **converge**
derived **contested** **impervious**

CLOSE READING MODEL

The passage below is from Dava Sobel's book-length essay *Longitude*. The annotations to the right of the passage show ways in which you can use close reading skills to analyze main ideas and expository essays.

from *Longitude*

Any sailor worth his salt[1] can gauge his latitude well enough by the length of the day, or by the height of the sun or known guide stars above the horizon. Christopher Columbus followed a straight path across the Atlantic when he "sailed the parallel" on his 1492 journey, and the technique would doubtless have carried him to the Indies had not the Americas intervened.[2]

The measurement of longitude meridians, in comparison, is tempered by time.[3] To learn one's longitude at sea, one needs to know what time it is aboard ship and also the time at the home port or another place of known longitude—at that very same moment. The two clock times enable the navigator to convert the hour difference into a geographical separation. Since the Earth takes twenty-four hours to complete one full revolution of three hundred sixty degrees, one hour marks one twenty-fourth of a spin, or fifteen degrees. And so each hour's time difference between the ship and the starting point marks a progress of fifteen degrees of longitude to the east or west.[4]

Expository Essay

1 *Worth his salt* is an idiom that means "worth one's pay," or "capable." Some scholars think the phrase comes from the Roman era when sailors were paid partly in salt. Sobel could have written "Any capable sailor." Instead, she mixes in an idiom that reflects her nautical topic.

Main Idea

2 Sobel uses the example of Columbus to support her point. The reference is one most readers will know. It is also dramatic—Columbus sailed across an entire ocean even though he did not know exactly where he was.

Expository Essay

3 *Tempered* means "changed by the addition of something else"—in this case, by time. Sobel is playing with words, because *temper* shares origins with time-related terms, such as *tempo* and *temporary*. Her diction, and the tone it creates, is both playful and subtle.

Expository Essay

4 In order to make sure her point about the challenge of measuring longitude is clear, Sobel gives basic information about Earth's rotation.

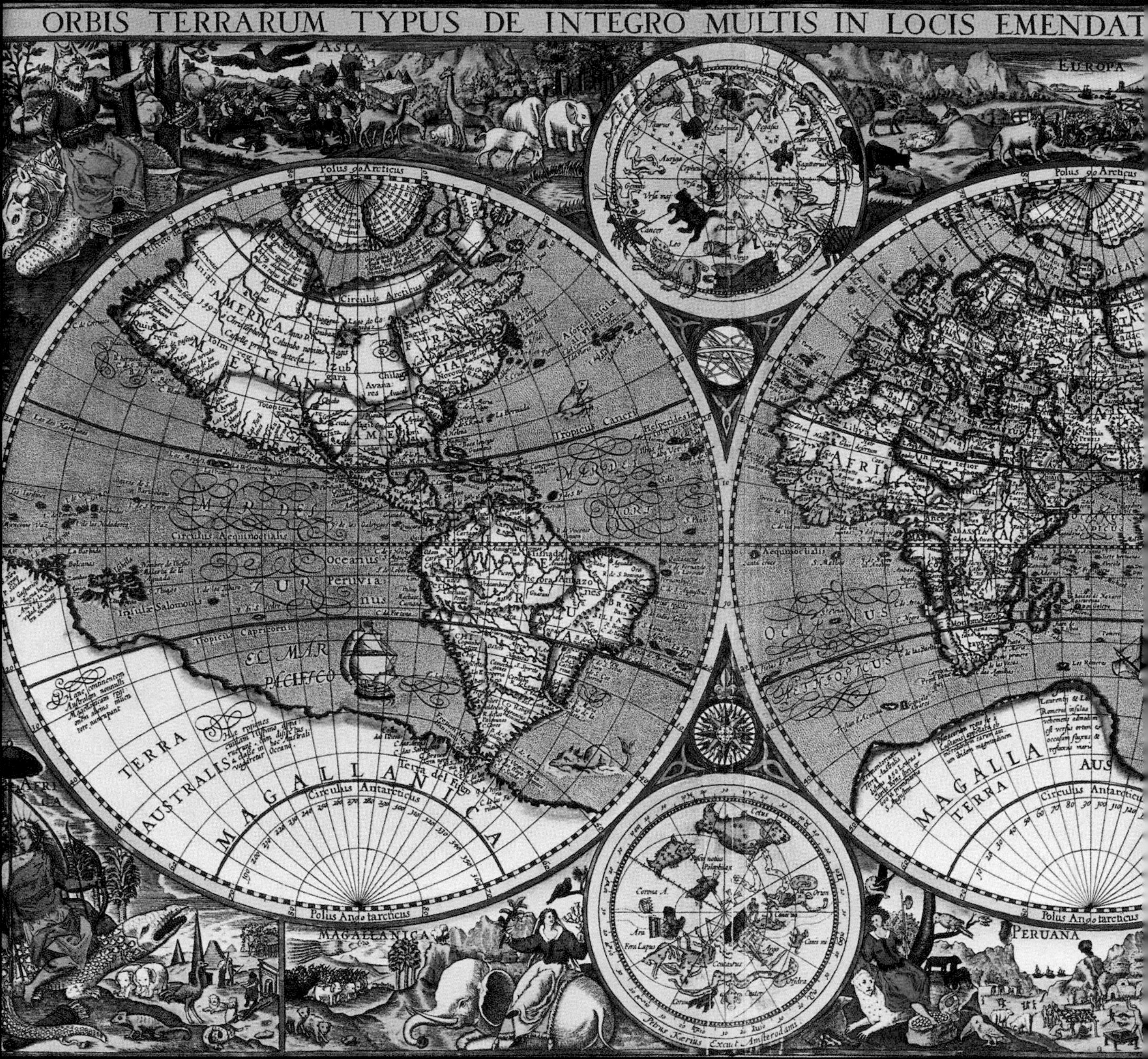
ORBIS TERRARUM TYPUS DE INTEGRO MULTIS IN LOCIS EMENDAT
ASIA
EUROPA
Polus Arcticus
Circulus Arcticus
AMERICA
Tropicus Cancri
Circulus Aequinoctialis
Oceanus
Peruvia
Tropicus Capricorni
EL MAR PACIFICO
TERRA AUSTRALIS MAGALLANICA
Circulus Antarcticus
Polus Antarcticus
MAGALLANICA
PERUANA
Terra del Fogo
Petrus Kaerius Excud. Amsterodami

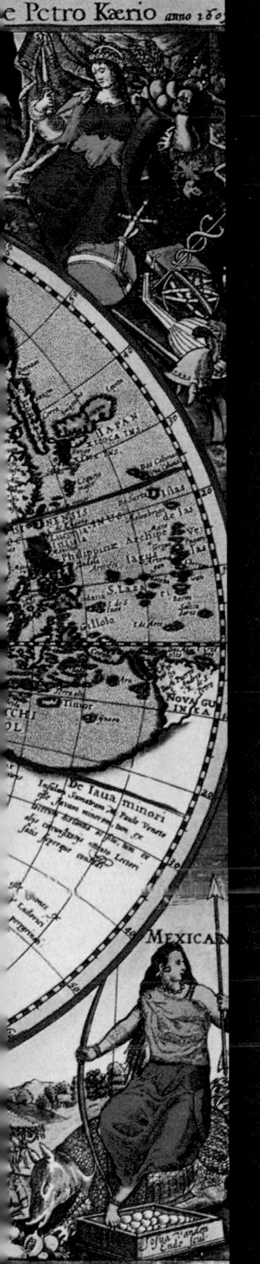

from Longitude

DAVA SOBEL

"When I'm playful
I use the meridians of
longitude and parallels
of latitude for a seine,
and drag the Atlantic Ocean
for whales."

~Mark Twain
Life on the Mississippi

Once on a Wednesday excursion when I was a little girl, my father bought me a beaded wire ball that I loved. At a touch, I could collapse the toy into a flat coil between my palms, or pop it open to make a hollow sphere. Rounded out, it resembled a tiny Earth, because its hinged wires traced the same pattern

Vocabulary ▶
haphazardly (hap′ haz′ ərd lē) *adv.* in an unplanned or a disorganized way

configuration (kən fig′ yə rā′ shən) *n.* arrangement of parts; pattern

converge (kən vʉrj′) *v.* to come together

▼ **Critical Viewing**
How does this image convey the endurance of the system of longitude and latitude?

of intersecting circles that I had seen on the globe in my schoolroom—the thin black lines of latitude and longitude. The few colored beads slid along the wire paths **haphazardly**, like ships on the high seas.

My father strode up Fifth Avenue to Rockefeller Center with me on his shoulders, and we stopped to stare at the statue of Atlas,[1] carrying Heaven and Earth on his.

The bronze orb that Atlas held aloft, like the wire toy in my hands, was a see-through world, defined by imaginary lines. The Equator. The Ecliptic. The Tropic of Cancer. The Tropic of Capricorn. The Arctic Circle. The prime meridian. Even then I could recognize, in the graph-paper grid imposed on the globe, a powerful symbol of all the real lands and waters on the planet.

Today, the latitude and longitude lines govern with more authority than I could have imagined forty-odd years ago, for they stay fixed as the world changes its **configuration** underneath them—with continents adrift across a widening sea, and national boundaries repeatedly redrawn by war or peace.

As a child, I learned the trick for remembering the difference between latitude and longitude. The latitude lines, the *parallels*, really do stay parallel to each other as they girdle the globe from the Equator to the poles in a series of shrinking concentric[2] rings. The meridians of longitude go the other way: They loop from the North Pole to the South and back again in great circles of the same size, so they all **converge** at the ends of the Earth.

Lines of latitude and longitude began crisscrossing our worldview in ancient times, at least three centuries before the birth of Christ. By A.D. 150, the cartographer and astronomer Ptolemy had plotted them on the twenty-seven maps of his first world atlas. Also for this landmark volume, Ptolemy listed all the place names in an index, in alphabetical order, with the latitude and longitude of each—as well as he could gauge them from travelers' reports. Ptolemy himself had only an armchair appreciation of the wider world. A common misconception of

1. **Fifth Avenue . . . Rockefeller Center . . . Atlas** landmarks in the borough of Manhattan of New York City. Rockefeller Center features a statue of Atlas, the Greek giant condemned to carry the heavens on his shoulders.
2. **concentric** (kən sen′ trik) *adj.* having a center in common.

his day held that anyone living below the Equator would melt into deformity from the horrible heat.

The Equator marked the zero-degree parallel of latitude for Ptolemy. He did not choose it arbitrarily but took it on higher authority from his predecessors, who had **derived** it from nature while observing the motions of the heavenly bodies. The sun, moon, and planets pass almost directly overhead at the Equator. Likewise the Tropic of Cancer and the Tropic of Capricorn, two other famous parallels, assume their positions at the sun's command. They mark the northern and southern boundaries of the sun's apparent motion over the course of the year.

◀ **Vocabulary**
derived (di rīvd′) *v.* reached by reasoning

Ptolemy was free, however, to lay his prime meridian, the zero-degree longitude line, wherever he liked. He chose to run it through the Fortunate Islands (now called the Canary and Madeira Islands) off the northwest coast of Africa. Later mapmakers moved the prime meridian to the Azores and to the Cape Verde Islands,[3] as well as to Rome, Copenhagen, Jerusalem, St. Petersburg, Pisa, Paris, and Philadelphia, among other places, before it settled down at last in London. As the world turns, any line drawn from pole to pole may serve as well as any other for a starting line of reference. The placement of the prime meridian is a purely political decision.

Main Idea
What main idea does the writer support using examples like Rome and Copenhagen?

Here lies the real, hard-core difference between latitude and longitude—beyond the superficial difference in line direction that any child can see: The zero-degree parallel of latitude is fixed by the laws of nature, while the zero-degree meridian of longitude shifts like the sands of time. This difference makes finding latitude child's play, and turns the determination of longitude, especially at sea, into an adult dilemma—one that stumped the wisest minds of the world for the better part of human history.

A common misconception of his day held that anyone living below the Equator would melt into deformity from the horrible heat.

Any sailor worth his salt can gauge his latitude well enough by the length of the day, or by the height of the sun or known guide stars above the horizon. Christopher Columbus followed a straight path across the Atlantic when he "sailed the parallel" on his 1492 journey, and the technique would doubtless have carried him to the Indies had not the Americas intervened.

The measurement of longitude meridians, in comparison, is tempered by time. To learn one's longitude at sea, one needs to know what time it is aboard ship and also the time at the home

Comprehension
Name an important contribution made to science or navigation by Ptolemy.

3. **Azores** (ā′ zôrz′) . . . **Cape Verde** (vurd) **Islands** two island groups in the Atlantic Ocean; the Azores are off Portugal and the Cape Verde Islands are off the westernmost point of Africa.

LITERATURE IN CONTEXT

Science Connection

Longitude and Latitude
The lines of longitude and latitude form an imaginary grid that can be used to name the exact location of any place on Earth.

- The **equator** is the line of latitude on which all points are the same distance from the North and South poles. The sun appears directly overhead at the equator on March 21 and September 21 of each year.
- The **Tropic of Cancer** is 23° 27′ north of the equator. It marks the northernmost latitude at which the sun can appear directly overhead—an event that occurs at noon on June 20 or 21.
- The **Tropic of Capricorn**, at 23° 27′ south, is the southernmost latitude at which the sun can appear directly overhead. The sun reaches its highest position at this tropic at noon on December 20 or 21.
- The prime meridian is the line of longitude chosen as the 0° line.

Connect to the Literature

What does this information indicate about how sailors determine latitude by the sun?

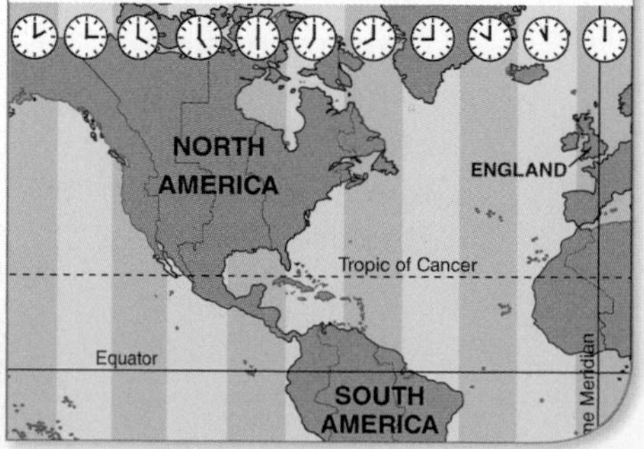

port or another place of known longitude—at that very same moment. The two clock times enable the navigator[4] to convert the hour difference into a geographical separation. Since the Earth takes twenty-four hours to complete one full revolution of three hundred sixty degrees, one hour marks one twenty-fourth of a spin, or fifteen degrees. And so each hour's time difference between the ship and the starting point marks a progress of fifteen degrees of longitude to the east or west. Every day at sea, when the navigator resets his ship's clock to local noon when the sun reaches its highest point in the sky, and then consults the home-port clock, every hour's discrepancy between them translates into another fifteen degrees of longitude.

Those same fifteen degrees of longitude also correspond to a distance traveled. At the Equator, where the girth of the Earth is greatest, fifteen degrees stretch fully one thousand miles. North or south of that line, however, the mileage value of each degree decreases. One degree of longitude equals four minutes of time the world over, but in terms of distance, one degree shrinks from sixty-eight miles at the Equator to virtually nothing at the poles.

Precise knowledge of the hour in two different places at once—a longitude prerequisite so easily accessible today from any pair of cheap wristwatches—was utterly unattainable up to and including the era of pendulum clocks.[5] On the deck of a rolling ship, such clocks would slow down, or speed up, or stop running altogether. Normal changes in temperature encountered en route from a cold country of origin to a tropical trade zone thinned or thickened a clock's lubricating oil and made its metal parts expand or contract with equally disastrous results. A rise or fall in barometric pressure, or the subtle variations in the Earth's gravity from one latitude to another, could also cause a clock to gain or lose time.

For lack of a practical method of determining longitude, every great captain in the Age of Exploration[6]

---

4. **navigator** (nav′ ə gāt′ ər) *n.* a person skilled in locating the position and plotting the course of a ship or an aircraft.
5. **pendulum** (pen′ dyo͞o ləm) **clocks** clocks whose timekeeping movement is regulated by a pendulum, a weight swinging freely from a fixed point.
6. **Age of Exploration** the period from about 1450 to about 1700, when European navigators sailed to new territories and founded colonies in Africa, the Americas, and Asia.

became lost at sea despite the best available charts and compasses. From Vasco da Gama to Vasco Núñez de Balboa, from Ferdinand Magellan to Sir Francis Drake[7]—they all got where they were going willy-nilly, by forces attributed to good luck or the grace of God.

As more and more sailing vessels set out to conquer or explore new territories, to wage war, or to ferry gold and commodities between foreign lands, the wealth of nations floated upon the oceans. And still no ship owned a reliable means for establishing her whereabouts. In consequence, untold numbers of sailors died when their destinations suddenly loomed out of the sea and took them by surprise. In a single such accident, on October 22, 1707, at the Scilly Isles near the southwestern tip of England, four homebound British warships ran aground and nearly two thousand men lost their lives. •

Main Idea
Which detail in this paragraph supports Sobel's idea that not knowing one's longitude was dangerous?

Comprehension
What key technical problem prevented sailors from measuring longitude accurately?

7. **Vasco da Gama** (väs′ kô də gä′ mə) . . . **Vasco Núñez de Balboa** (väs′ kô no͞o′ nyeth *th*e bal bō′ ə) . . . **Ferdinand Magellan** (mə jel′ ən) . . . **Sir Francis Drake** famous explorers of the fifteenth and sixteenth centuries.

Expository Essay
How do the details in this paragraph contribute to the author's tone?

The active quest for a solution to the problem of longitude persisted over four centuries and across the whole continent of Europe. Most crowned heads of state eventually played a part in the longitude story, notably King George III of England and King Louis XIV of France. Seafaring men such as Captain William Bligh of the *Bounty* and the great circumnavigator Captain James Cook, who made three long voyages of exploration and experimentation before his violent death in Hawaii, took the more promising methods to sea to test their accuracy and practicability.

Renowned astronomers approached the longitude challenge by appealing to the clockwork universe: Galileo Galilei, Jean Dominique Cassini, Christiaan Huygens, Sir Isaac Newton, and Edmond Halley,[8] of comet fame, all entreated the moon and stars for help. Palatial observatories were founded at Paris, London, and Berlin for the express purpose of determining longitude by the heavens. Meanwhile, lesser minds devised schemes that depended on the yelps of wounded dogs, or the cannon blasts of signal ships strategically anchored—somehow—on the open ocean.

In the course of their struggle to find longitude, scientists struck upon other discoveries that changed their view of the universe. These include the first accurate determinations of the weight of the Earth, the distance to the stars, and the speed of light.

▲ King George III

As time passed and no method proved successful, the search for a solution to the longitude problem assumed legendary proportions, on a par with discovering the Fountain of Youth, the secret of perpetual motion, or the formula for transforming lead into gold.[9] The governments of the great maritime nations—including Spain, the Netherlands, and certain city-states of Italy—periodically roiled the fervor by offering jackpot purses for a workable method. The British Parliament, in its famed Longitude Act of 1714, set the highest bounty of all, naming a prize equal to a king's ransom (several million dollars in today's currency) for a "Practicable and Useful" means of determining longitude.

8. **Galileo Galilei** (gal´ ə lā´ ō gal´ ə lā ē) . . . **Jean-Dominique Cassini** (zhän dō mi nēk´ kä sē´ nē) . . . **Christiaan Huygens** (hī´ gənz) . . . **Sir Isaac Newton . . . Edmond Halley** (hal´ ē) pioneering astronomers and scientists of the sixteenth through the eighteenth centuries. Their work redefined people's picture of the universe, replacing traditional views with modern ones.

English clockmaker John Harrison, a mechanical genius who pioneered the science of portable precision timekeeping, devoted his life to this quest. He accomplished what Newton had feared was impossible: He invented a clock that would carry the true time from the home port, like an eternal flame, to any remote corner of the world.

Harrison, a man of simple birth and high intelligence, crossed swords with the leading lights of his day. He made a special enemy of the Reverend Nevil Maskelyne, the fifth astronomer royal, who **contested** his claim to the coveted prize money, and whose tactics at certain junctures can only be described as foul play.

With no formal education or apprenticeship to any watchmaker, Harrison nevertheless constructed a series of virtually friction-free clocks that required no lubrication and no cleaning, that were made from materials **impervious** to rust, and that kept their moving parts perfectly balanced in relation to one another, regardless of how the world pitched or tossed about them. He did away with the pendulum, and he combined different metals inside his works in such a way that when one component expanded or contracted with changes in temperature, the other counteracted the change and kept the clock's rate constant.

◀ **Vocabulary**
contested (kən test′ əd) *v.* tried to disprove or invalidate something; disputed

impervious (im pʉr′ vē əs) *adj.* not affected by

Comprehension
What important device did Harrison invent?

Note, the Distance between the two Lines a, b, is right in this Draught, but is somewhat too great in the Draughts to which this belongs: And it is to be observ'd that one of the Pillars must be plac'd a little farther from the end of the Ballance spring. ~~But it is to be noted~~ ~~see below~~

But it is to be noted, that what I thought of gaining, as in this Draught &c. [viz. from the Ballance being transfer'd to the other side of a Watch] I afterwards consider'd would be nothing, or at least very immaterial; hence, as in common the most proper.

◀ **Critical Viewing**
Does the appearance of Harrison's marine watch reflect its world-altering importance? Explain.

---

9. **Fountain of Youth . . . lead into gold** three imaginary goals seriously pursued by inquirers. The Fountain of Youth was supposed to restore youth. Perpetual motion would allow people to generate power endlessly without consuming fuel. A formula to turn the cheap metal lead into the precious metal gold was sought for centuries by alchemists.

Spiral Review
SERIES OF IDEAS In what way does this paragraph develop the drama of Sobel's account? What point about science does it support?

His every success, however, was parried by members of the scientific elite, who distrusted Harrison's magic box. The commissioners charged with awarding the longitude prize—Nevil Maskelyne among them—changed the contest rules whenever they saw fit, so as to favor the chances of astronomers over the likes of Harrison and his fellow "mechanics."[10] But the utility and accuracy of Harrison's approach triumphed in the end. His followers shepherded Harrison's intricate, exquisite invention through the design modifications that enabled it to be mass produced and enjoy wide use.

An aged, exhausted Harrison, taken under the wing of King George III, ultimately claimed his rightful monetary reward in 1773—after forty struggling years of political intrigue, international warfare, academic backbiting, scientific revolution, and economic upheaval.

All these threads, and more, entwine in the lines of longitude. To unravel them now—to retrace their story in an age when a network of orbiting satellites can nail down a ship's position within a few feet in just a moment or two—is to see the globe anew.

---

10. **"mechanics"** skilled workers and tradesmen, of a lower class than merchants or aristocrats.

Language Study

Vocabulary The underlined words in each question appear in the excerpt from *Longitude.* Write an answer to each question. Then, explain how the meaning of the underlined word helped you do so.

1. What might a room look like if it is haphazardly decorated?
2. Has he derived a correct conclusion if he was missing information?
3. Do you think anyone is truly impervious to criticism?
4. How could you determine if two streets converge?
5. What tone would you find at a debate over a contested election?

WORD STUDY
The **Latin root *-fig-*** means "form" or "shape." In this essay, the author explains that the world changes its **configuration**, its contours and *forms*. Nevertheless, the lines of latitude and longitude stay fixed.

Word Study

Part A Explain how the **Latin root *-fig-*** contributes to the meanings of these words: *effigy, figment,* and *figurine.* Consult a dictionary if necessary.

Part B Use the context of the sentences and what you know about the Latin root *-fig-* to explain your answer to each question.

1. If a room becomes *transfigured*, will it look different?
2. What are you doing if you *reconfigure* a chart?

Close Reading Activities

Literary Analysis

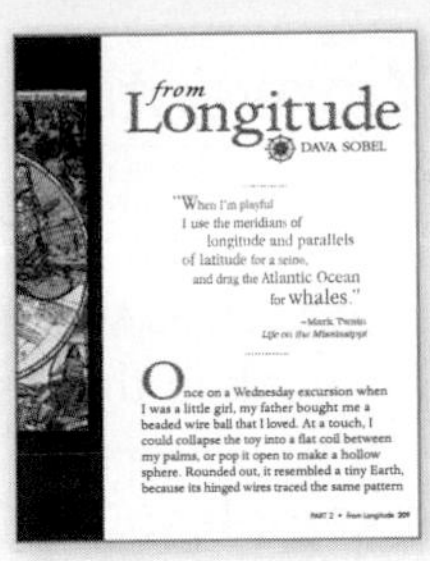

Key Ideas and Details

1. **(a)** According to Sobel, what are two methods sailors can use to estimate latitude? **(b) Apply:** Using one of these methods, explain how you could tell whether you were at the equator—the zero-degree latitude.
2. **Analyze:** Briefly explain why the invention of an accurate clock was crucial to solving the problem of determining longitude.
3. **Main Idea** Using a chart like the one shown, state the main ideas Sobel expresses in this essay. Identify two supporting details for each idea you cite.
4. **Main Idea** Write a summary of the essay.

Problem of Longitude
Importance of Longitude
Harrison's Invention

Craft and Structure

5. **Expository Essay (a)** Note three facts Sobel includes about astronomy or navigation. **(b)** What idea, action, or event does each fact help Sobel explain?
6. **Expository Essay (a)** Identify three examples of technical diction, one example of scholarly diction, and one example of informal diction in this essay. **(b)** For each, explain your choice.
7. **Expository Essay (a)** Describe the overall tone of this essay. **(b)** Explain how Sobel's diction contributes to that tone. Cite specific examples from the essay to support your response.

Integration of Knowledge and Ideas

8. **(a) Analyze Cause and Effect:** Why did Harrison have difficulty getting his solution to the problem of measuring longitude recognized? **(b) Extend:** What do his difficulties say about the role of class in his society? Explain.
9. **Analyze:** The beginning and ending of the essay are set in the modern world, but the body focuses on the 18th century. What point is Sobel making by bookending the essay in this way? Explain, citing details from the text.

10. THE BIG ? **What kind of knowledge changes our lives? (a)** How would the world be different today without Harrison's clock? **(b)** Is the ability to measure longitude life-changing knowledge? Explain, using details from Sobel's essay to support your position.

ACADEMIC VOCABULARY

As you write and speak about *Longitude,* use the words related to knowledge and understanding that you explored on page 185 of this textbook.

Conventions: Action and Linking Verbs

An **action verb** is a verb that shows physical or mental action. A **linking verb** expresses state of being or tells what the subject is by linking it to one or more words in the predicate.

Examples:

Action Verb: Europeans *explored* faraway lands. (shows physical action)

Linking Verb: The navigator *is* a good mathematician. (links *navigator* to *mathematician*)

The most common linking verb is *be* in one of its forms—*is, are, was, were,* and so on. Other linking verbs include *feel* when used in a sentence such as "I feel ill" and *grew* when used in a sentence such as "He grew tall." *Become* and *seem* can also be linking verbs. To tell whether a verb is functioning as a linking verb, replace it with the appropriate form of *be*. If the sentence still makes sense, then the verb is a linking verb.

Testing Verbs to See if They Are Linking Verbs:

Action Verb: I *smelled* the salt air. (cannot replace with a form of *be*)

Linking Verb: The sea *smelled* salty. (can replace with *was*)

Practice A

State whether the underlined word in each sentence is an action verb or a linking verb.

1. Columbus used lines of latitude to cross the Atlantic.
2. It once seemed impossible to measure longitude.
3. At first, some sailors might feel seasick.
4. John Harrison invented an instrument to measure longitude.
5. Dava Sobel researched this complex topic.

Reading Application In the excerpt from *Longitude*, find two sentences with action verbs and two sentences with linking verbs.

Practice B

For each word, write a sentence using the word as a linking verb and another sentence using the word as an action verb.

1. look
2. grow
3. smell
4. feel

Writing Application Use this sentence as a model to write two sentences that contain both action and linking verbs: *Navigators know that longitude is wider at the equator than at the pole.*

Writing to Sources

Explanatory Text Write a **business letter** in which you imagine that you are John Harrison explaining your invention to King George III. Maintain an objective style and formal tone appropriate for a business letter and for your audience and purpose.

- Reread the excerpt from *Longitude* and gather details about Harrison's invention to include in your letter.
- Include a heading, address, and greeting.
- Write an opening paragraph in which you convey respect and the desire to help the king solve a problem.
- Explain that your clock is the solution to the navigation problems sailors face. Support your claim with the details you gathered from Sobel's essay.
- Mention the resistance you have met from the Royal Society. Use persuasive techniques, formally and politely stated, to convince the King to side with you.
- Restate the importance of your claim in your conclusion. End with a polite closing.

Grammar Application As you write, use linking verbs correctly and action verbs effectively.

Speaking and Listening

Presentation of Ideas Deliver a **humorous persuasive speech** in which you propose moving the prime meridian to your hometown.

- Plan humorous approaches to meet your audience's knowledge and interests.
- Formulate a clear thesis—the main idea you want to get across.
- Support your ideas with facts and examples, including details from *Longitude*.
- Address specific concerns your audience may have, anticipating and answering any objections.
- Choose appropriate language. Slang might seem contemporary, but formal language might command respect. Figurative language such as similes, metaphors, or imagery can make your message vivid.

After you have delivered your speech, invite and answer questions from the audience.

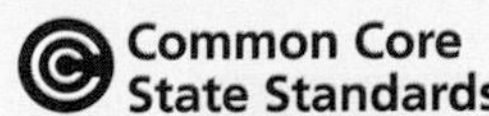

Common Core State Standards

Writing

2.e. Establish and maintain a formal style and objective tone while attending to the norms and conventions of the discipline.

Speaking and Listening

4. Present information, findings, and supporting evidence clearly, concisely, and logically such that listeners can follow the line of reasoning and the organization, development, substance, and style are appropriate to purpose, audience, and task.

6. Adapt speech to a variety of contexts and tasks, demonstrating command of formal English when indicated or appropriate.

Building Knowledge

Meet the Author

By the age of fourteen, **Dorothy West** (1907–1998) was winning writing competitions in Boston, where she grew up. In 1926, she moved to New York City, which was at the time the center of an outpouring of African American creativity called the Harlem Renaissance. West's fiction and essays earned her recognition as a significant voice of the era.

What kind of knowledge changes our lives?

Explore the Big Question as you read "The Sun Parlor." Take notes on how the author gains new insights into her family's history and values.

CLOSE READING FOCUS

Key Ideas and Details: **Main Idea**

As you read nonfiction, **analyze main ideas and supporting details** in the text. To do so, recognize the most important points the writer makes and identify the information that explains or illustrates them. To aid your analysis, ask questions like the following:

- What is the topic of this passage?
- What key idea does the author explore in this passage?
- Which details in the text relate to the key idea?
- How does each idea connect to the one that precedes and follows it?

Craft and Structure: **Reflective Essay**

In a **reflective essay,** a writer presents the experiences that shape his or her thoughts on a topic. The author also weaves connections between personal experiences and a point of general interest, such as an insight about life. The writer may reflect on any number of topics, including the following:

- an event, a time period, or a person from his or her own life
- a specific scene, an occasion, a place, or an idea
- a work of art, literature, or music

Most reflective essays use informal language that suits the personal, reflective purpose. They may also include dialogue, images, description, and other literary elements you are used to seeing in fiction. As you read, look for these characteristics of reflective essays.

Vocabulary

The words below are critical to understanding the text that follows. Copy the words into your notebook. Which word is an antonym for *long-winded*?

lavished	**subordinate**	**rejuvenation**
convalesce	**cajoling**	**succinct**

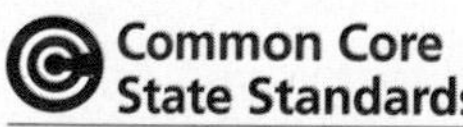

Common Core State Standards

Reading Informational Text

3. Analyze how the author unfolds an analysis or series of ideas or events, including the order in which the points are made, how they are introduced and developed, and the connections that are drawn between them.

6. Determine an author's point of view or purpose in a text and analyze how an author uses rhetoric to advance that point of view or purpose.

Language

6. Acquire and use accurately general academic and domain specific words and phrases, sufficient for reading and writing at the college and career readiness level.

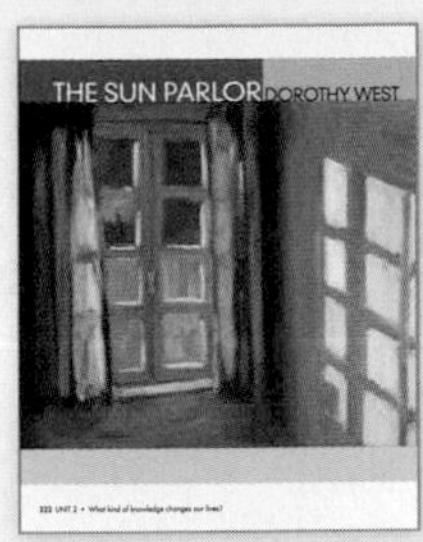

CLOSE READING MODEL

The passage below is from Dorothy West's essay "The Sun Parlor." The annotations to the right of the passage show ways in which you can use close reading skills to analyze main ideas in reflective essays.

from "The Sun Parlor"

School vacation began, and Sis arrived for the long holiday, the car pulling up at the edge of the brick walk, and Sis streaking into the house for a round of hugs, then turning to tear upstairs to take off her travel clothes and put on her play clothes, and suddenly her flying feet braking[1] to a stop in front of the sun parlor, its open door inviting inspection.

She who was always in motion, she who never took time for a second look at anything, or cared whether her bed was smooth or crumpled, or noticed what was on her plate as long as it was something to eat[2]—she, in the awakening that came when was eight, in her first awareness of something outside herself, stood in the doorway of the sun parlor, her face filled with the joy of her discovery, and said in a voice on the edge of tears, "It's the most beautiful room I ever saw in my whole life."[3]

I did not hear her. I did not really hear her. I did not recognize the magnitude of that moment.[4]

Main Idea

1 West begins in the past tense, but then switches to the past progressive *(pulling, streaking)*, which shows continuing action. This choice helps the author convey a main idea—that Sis never stops moving.

Main Idea

2 The author says that Sis "was always in motion," and then adds details to support that point. The idea that Sis is usually excited and unaware of her surroundings is a key idea.

Reflective Essay

3 West refers to Sis's "awakening" and repeats that idea in various ways. Sis is experiencing an abrupt change in how she sees the world. That change is part of the larger topic of the essay.

Reflective Essay

4 West repeats the idea that she did not hear Sis: "did not really hear… did not recognize." The real focus of West's reflection is not a room but a lost moment, or a failure of some kind.

THE SUN PARLOR

DOROTHY WEST

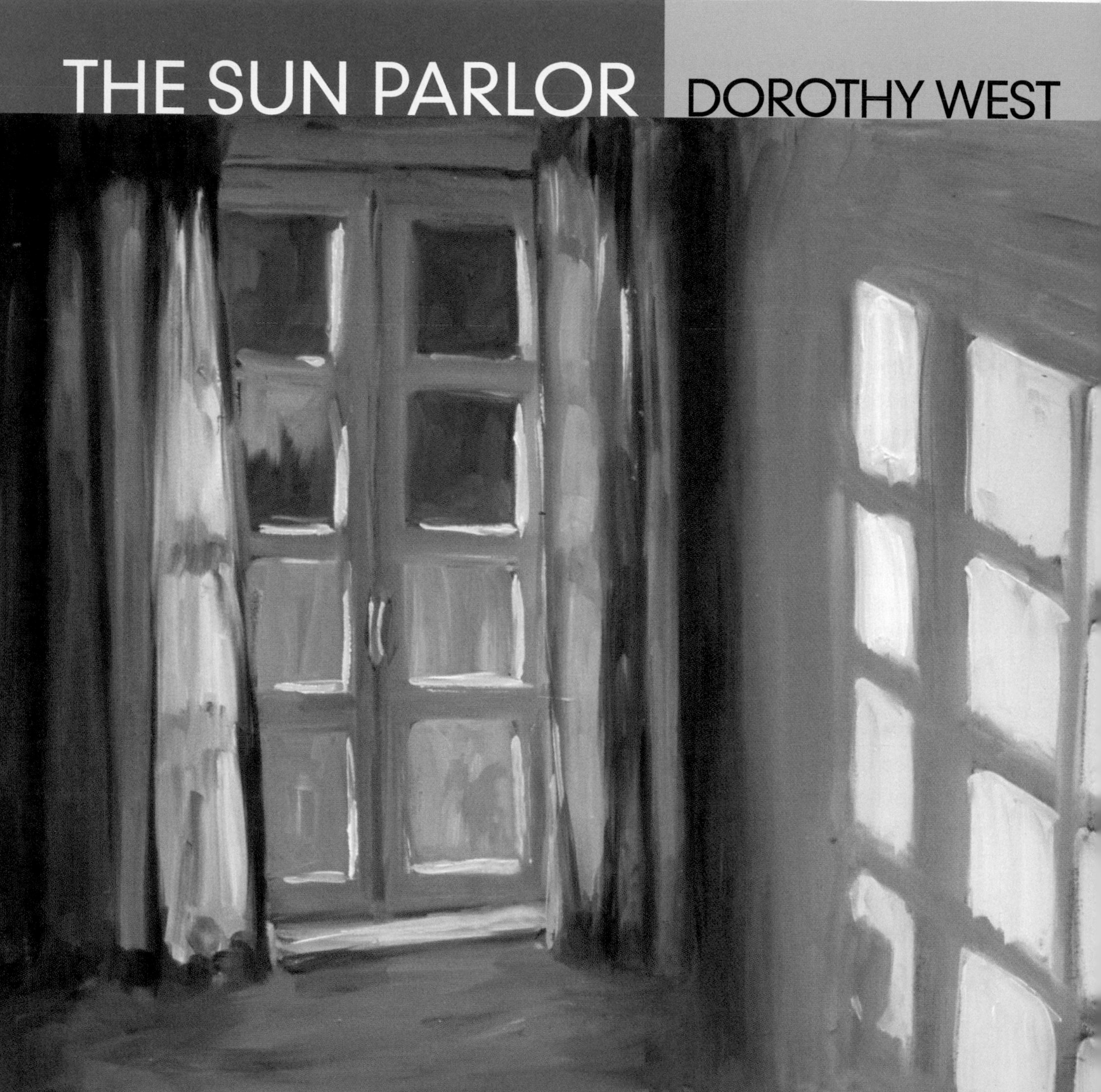

This is a tale with a moral. I will try not to tax your attention too long. But I have to go way back to begin because it begins with my childhood. It is about houses and children, and which came first.

There were four of us children, well-schooled in good manners, well-behaved almost all of the time, and obedient to the commands of grown-ups, the power people who could make or break us.

We lived in a beautiful house. The reason I knew that is because all my mother's friends said so, and brought their other friends to see it. On the day appointed for the tour, which included inspection of every room on every floor, my mother would gather us around her and say in her gentlest voice, "I'm sorry, children, but Mrs. So-and-so is coming today and bringing a friend to see our house. You children keep clean and play quietly while they're here. It's not a real visit. They won't stay long. It'll be over before you can say Jack Robinson."

Most often a first-time caller, having **lavished** praise on everything she saw, including us, proceeded out without any further remarks. But there were others who, when they saw four children good as gold, did not see beyond their size, and asked my mother in outspoken horror, "How can you bear to let children loose in a lovely house like this?"

Every time it happened we were terrified. What would happen to us if my mother decided her house was too good for us and she hated the sight of us? What would we do, where would we go, would we starve?

My mother looked at our stricken faces, and her own face softened and her eyes filled with love. Then she would say to her inquisitor, though she did not say it rudely, "The children don't belong to the house. The house belongs to the children. No room says, *Do not enter.*"

I did not know I could ever forget those sentiments. But once, to my lasting regret, I did. With the passage of years I took my place with grown-ups, and there was another generation, among them the little girl, Sis, who was my mother's treasure. The summer she was eight was the one time I forgot that a child is not **subordinate** to a house.

We had a cottage in the Highlands of Oak Bluffs of unimpressive size and appearance. My mother loved it for its easy care. It couldn't even stand in the shade of our city house, and there certainly were no special rules for children. No one had ever looked aghast at a child on its premises.

Except me, the summer I painted the sun parlor. I am not a painter, but I am a perfectionist. I threw my whole soul into the project, and worked with such diligence and painstaking care

◀ **Critical Viewing**
Based on this painting, what feelings do you think will be described in the essay?

◀ **Vocabulary**
lavished (lav′ isht) *v.* gave with extreme generosity

subordinate (sə bôrd′ 'n it) *adj.* below another in importance or rank

Spiral Review
DEVELOPMENT OF IDEAS What central idea does the author introduce in her opening paragraphs? What is its connection to the rest of the essay?

Comprehension
What does the author say she regrets forgetting?

that when the uncounted hours ended I felt that I had painted the Sistine Chapel.[1]

School vacation began, and Sis arrived for the long holiday, the car pulling up at the edge of the brick walk, and Sis streaking into the house for a round of hugs, then turning to tear upstairs to take off her travel clothes and put on her play clothes, and suddenly her flying feet braking to a stop in front of the sun parlor, its open door inviting inspection.

Main Idea
Which details support the idea that Sis's reaction is exceptional?

She who was always in motion, she who never took time for a second look at anything, or cared whether her bed was smooth or crumpled, or noticed what was on her plate as long as it was something to eat—she, in the awakening that came when she was eight, in her first awareness of something outside herself, stood in the doorway of the sun parlor, her face filled with the joy of her discovery, and said in a voice on the edge of tears, "It's the most beautiful room I ever saw in my whole life."

I did not hear her. I did not really hear her. I did not recognize the magnitude of that moment. I let it sink to some low level of my subconscious. All I saw was that her foot was poised to cross the threshold of my chapel.

Reflective Essay
How is this experience connected to the lesson that the author learned from her mother?

I let out a little cry of pain. "Sis," I said, "please don't go in the sun parlor. There's nothing in there to interest a child. It's not a place for children to play in. It's a place for grown-ups to sit in. Go and change. Summer is outside waiting for you to come and play wherever you please."

In a little while the sounds of Sis's soaring laughter were mingling with the happy sounds of other vacationing children. They kept any doubt I might have had from surfacing. Sis was surely more herself running free than squirming on a chair in the sun parlor.

All the same I monitored that room, looking for smudges and streaks, scanning the floor for signs of scuffing. The room bore no scars, and Sis showed no trace of frustration.

The summer flowed. My friends admired the room, though they did it without superlatives. To them it was a room I had talked about redoing for a long time. Now I had done it. So much for that.

The summer waned, and Sis went home for school's reopening, as did the other summer children, taking so much life and laughter with them that the ensuing days recovered slowly.

Vocabulary ▶ rejuvenation
(ri jo͞o′ və nā′ shən)
n. the act of making new, youthful, or energetic again

Then my mother's sister, my favorite aunt, arrived from New York for her usual stay at summer's end. She looked ten years younger than her actual years. She seemed to bounce with energy, as if she had gone through some process of **rejuvenation**. We asked her for the secret.

1. **the Sistine Chapel** (sis′ tēn′ chap′ əl) place of worship in the Vatican, Rome, the Pope's residence. The chapel is famed for scenes painted on its walls and ceiling by Michelangelo.

There was no way for us to know in the brimful days that followed that there really was a secret she was keeping from us. She had had a heart attack some months before, and she had been ordered to follow a strict set of rules: plenty of rest during the day, early to bed at night, take her medicine faithfully, carefully watch her diet.

She was my mother's younger sister. My mother had been her babysitter. She didn't want my mother to know that she was back to being a baby again, needing to be watched over, having to be put down for a nap, having to be spoon-fed pap. She kept herself busy around the clock, walking, lifting, sitting up late, eating her favorite foods and forgetting her medicine.

▼ Critical Viewing
Do you think this painting reflects the author's description of the summer children? Why or why not?

Comprehension
What is the matter with West's aunt?

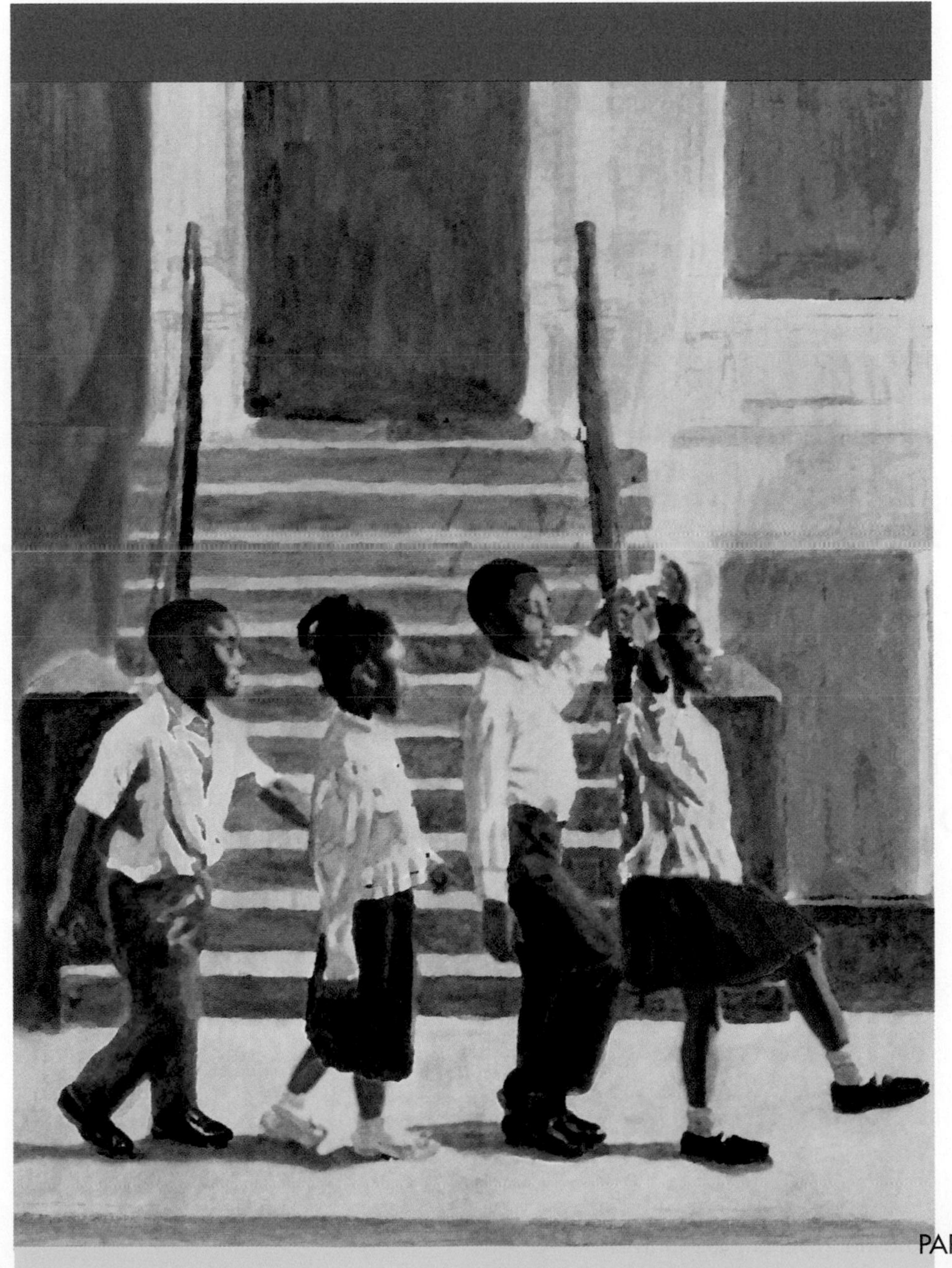

Critical Viewing ▶
In what way does this painting suggest a room apart from the rest of the house, like the sun parlor?

Main Idea
What main idea do these details about the aunt's stay in the sun parlor suggest?

Vocabulary ▶
convalesce (kän′ və les′) *v.* regain strength and health

cajoling (kə jōl′ iŋ) *n.* coaxing with flattery

succinct (sək siŋkt′) *adj.* clearly and briefly stated

And then one day standing over the stove involved in the making of a meal that a master chef might envy, she collapsed, and the doctor was called, and the doctor called the ambulance.

She was in the hospital ten days. When she was ready to come home to **convalesce**, we turned the sun parlor into a sickroom, for the stairs to the upper story were forbidden to her. At night we who, when she slept upstairs, would talk family talk back and forth from our beds far into the night, without her we were now quiet, not wanting our voices to wake her if she was asleep, knowing her recovery depended on rest and quiet.

But at night she slept fitfully. The sleeping house and separation from the flock were unbearable. She was afraid of the sun parlor, seeing it as an abnormal offshoot from the main part of the house, its seven long windows giving access to so many imagined terrors. She did not know if we would hear her if she called. She did not know if she would ever get well.

She did not get well. She went back to the hospital, and for our sakes was brave in her last days, comforting us more than we comforted her.

When it was over, we took the sickbed away and restored the sun parlor to its natural look. But it did not look natural. The sadness resisted the sun's **cajoling**. It had settled in every corner. The seven long windows streaming light did not help. I closed the door and locked it.

My mother saw the closed door and the key in my hand. She said as a simple statement of fact, "A little girl wanted to love that room, and you wouldn't let her. We learn so many lessons as we go through life."

"I know that now," I said. "I wish I had known it then."

Another summer came, and with it Sis. The sun parlor door was open again, the room full of light with the sadness trying to hide itself whenever she passed. I did not know how to say to her, "You can go in the sun parlor if you want to." I did not know whether she knew it had been a sickroom, and might say, "Take your sun parlor and you-know-what," though in less **succinct** phrasing. I did not know if she yet knew that nothing can be the same once it has been different.

"We learn so many lessons as we go through life."

Other summers passed, older family members died, and mine became the oldest generation. I was living on the Island year-round in the winterized cottage. The sun parlor was just another everyday room, its seven long windows reduced to three of standard size, most of the furniture replaced for sturdier sitting.

Sis was married, a mother, coming to visit when she could—coming, I think, to look for bits and pieces of my mother in me, wanting to see her ways, hear her words through me.

It was a year ago that I asked her the question that had been on my mind, it seems, forever. A dozen times I had bitten it off my tongue because I did not know what she might answer.

"Sis," I said, "do you remember the summer I painted the sun parlor and acted as if I thought more of it than I thought of you? I'm not asking you to forgive me. All I want to know is if sometimes my mother said to you when I went out, 'She's gone.'" My mother always referred to me as "she" when she was annoyed with me. "'She said she'd be gone awhile. You go play in that sun parlor if you want to. There's nothing in there you can hurt. Nothing in that room is worth as much as a child.'"

I saw her lips beginning to part. And I felt my heart trembling.

"I don't want to know the answer. Please don't tell me the answer. I had to ask the question. It's enough for me that you listened."

She smiled.

Reflective Essay
What lesson about life has the author learned?

Language Study

Vocabulary The words listed below appear in "The Sun Parlor." For each sentence that follows, write a new sentence using a word from the list. Base your sentence on the pattern and meaning of the original sentence.

lavished **subordinate** **rejuvenation** **convalesce** **cajoling**

1. I gave in to my brother's wheedling and lent him my new game.
2. The junior counselors did not have the same privileges but they also did not have the same responsibilities.
3. They showered praise on us for our successful fund drive.
4. A month's vacation will help rebuild Alice's strength and energy.
5. After she broke her leg, my sister had to stay home for a month to regain her strength.

WORD STUDY
The **Latin prefix *suc-*** is another spelling of the prefix ***sub-*,** meaning "under," "less or lower than," or "following after." In this essay, the author imagines how something could be said in a more **succinct** way, using fewer words.

Word Study

Part A Explain how the **Latin prefix *suc-*** contributes to the meanings of the words *succeed*, *successor*, and *succor*. Consult a dictionary if necessary.

Part B Use the context of the sentences and what you know about the Latin prefix *suc-* to explain your answer to each question.

1. If books you requested from the library arrive in *succession,* will you receive them all at the same time?
2. Will a person with strong willpower easily *succumb* to others?

Close Reading Activities

Literary Analysis

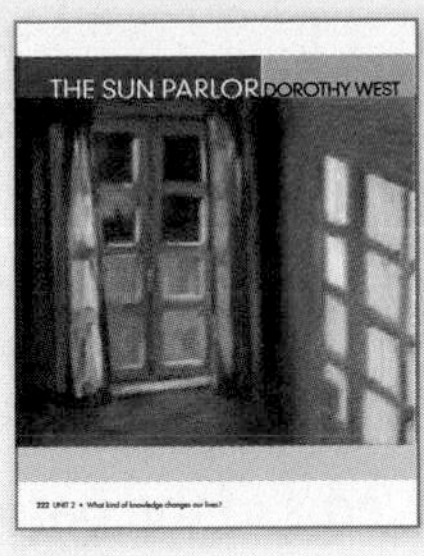

Key Ideas and Details

1. **Main Idea** Reread the first six paragraphs. **(a)** What is the main idea of this section? **(b)** Which details from the text support that idea? Explain.
2. **Main Idea (a)** What is the next main idea you find in the essay? **(b)** Identify three supporting details from the essay that develop this idea. **(c)** Explain the purpose or function of each detail—what new information or quality does it add?
3. **(a)** What project does West undertake to improve the sun parlor? **(b) Infer:** Why does she tell Sis to stay out of the room? **(c) Connect:** Does West's response to Sis reflect what her mother taught her? Explain, citing evidence from the text.

Craft and Structure

4. **Reflective Essay (a)** Using a chart like the one shown, list details West includes that show her feelings about the sun parlor. Then, list other details that describe facts about the room or events that took place there. **(b)** Using these details as support, explain how the topic of the sun parlor allows West to reflect on larger, more important ideas about life.
5. **Reflective Essay (a)** What transition in the narrative occurs with the paragraph beginning "Other summers passed"? **(b)** How does this transition reinforce the enduring importance of the lesson West learned through her experience with Sis and the sun parlor? Explain.

Feelings

Events and Facts

Insights

Integration of Knowledge and Ideas

6. **(a) Compare and Contrast:** Using details from the selection, contrast Sis's first reaction to the parlor with her reactions to other events as described in the selection. **(b) Interpret:** What does West mean by calling Sis's reaction to the parlor part of an "awakening"?

7. THE BIG ? **What kind of knowledge changes our lives?** With a small group, discuss the following questions: **(a)** What does West mean when she says to Sis, "It's enough for me that you listened"? **(b)** In what ways might that statement also indicate a reason West wrote this essay? **(c)** Why it is important to West that people "listen"? Work together to develop your responses to the questions, and then present your interpretation to the class.

ACADEMIC VOCABULARY

As you write and speak about "The Sun Parlor," use the words related to knowledge and understanding that you explored on page 185 of this textbook.

Close Reading Activities Continued

Conventions: Active and Passive Voice

A verb is in the **active voice** when the subject performs the action. A verb is in the **passive voice** when the action is performed on the subject.

Verbs in the passive voice consist of a form of *be* followed by the past participle of the main verb. Active voice is usually the best choice to use in your writing because it is more concise and direct. However, passive voice is appropriate when the writer wants to emphasize the recipient of the action. Passive voice is also correct when the subject performing the action is unknown or unimportant.

Active Voice: The student *answered* the question.
Passive Voice: The question *was answered* by the student.

Active Voice: Jeremy *ate* the last cookie.
Passive Voice: The last cookie *was eaten* by Jeremy.

Active Voice: Someone *found* the puppies at a nearby park.
Passive Voice: The puppies *were found* at a nearby park.

Practice A

Identify each verb or verb phrase as active or passive.

1. Their house was toured frequently by friends and acquaintances.
2. The children behaved well during the visits.
3. Sometimes important lessons are forgotten over the years.
4. The sun parlor was painted with great care.
5. Sis came to a sudden stop at the door to the room.

Reading Application Choose four sentences from "The Sun Parlor." For each sentence, identify the verb or verb phrase and label it as active or passive. If a sentence has more than one verb or verb phrase, label them all.

Practice B

Change the following sentences from passive voice to active voice. You may need to add words to indicate who performed the action.

1. Young children were respected by West's mother.
2. Sis was told to stay out of the sun parlor.
3. The house was admired by the visitors.
4. The aunt had been given instructions by the doctor.
5. Some of the furniture was replaced in later years.

Writing Application Write two sentences in the passive voice describing incidents or situations from the essay. Then, rewrite each sentence in the active voice.

Writing to Sources

Narrative A **memoir** is a type of autobiographical writing in which an author relates a memory and reflects on its meaning. West's reflective essay displays some of the qualities of a memoir. Imagine that the sun parlor itself is able to tell its own story. Write a memoir in the voice of the room in which you describe the events West notes in her essay. Explain what the author's painting of its walls, Sis's visit, and the aunt's ordeal mean to the "life" of the sun parlor.

- Write in the first person, using the pronoun *I* to speak as the voice of the room.
- Use precise words and phrases and concrete sensory details to paint vivid images of the room's experiences.
- Write in a style that creates a believable voice for the room.
- Reflect the events and ideas West describes in her essays. Organize ideas in a logical order.
- Write a conclusion that follows from the observations you made earlier in the memoir. In your conclusion, share your insights with readers and reveal why the events from the life of the room are important.

Grammar Application As you write, use active and passive voice appropriately and effectively.

Speaking and Listening

Presentation of Ideas Prepare an **oral recollection.** Focus on someone you know who is interesting and important to you or on a group with which you have been involved.

- Provide key details to develop your subject. Organize them logically, and build toward a central insight.
- Clearly establish your point of view and your relationship with the subject of your recollection.
- Include sensory details and concrete images.
- Make connections between the types of experiences West describes in her essay and those you are recalling.
- First, present your recollection to a classmate. Then, revise your draft based on feedback from your partner. Make sure the reasoning you use to connect details to your central insight is clear and that the style of your presentation is appropriate for your audience and purpose.
- Present a revised version of your recollection to the class.

Writing

3.a. Engage and orient the reader by setting out a problem, situation, or observation, establishing one or multiple point(s) of view, and introducing a narrator and/or characters; create a smooth progression of experiences or events.

3.d. Use precise words and phrases, telling details, and sensory language to convey a vivid picture of the experiences, events, setting, and/or characters.

3.e. Provide a conclusion that follows from and reflects on what is experienced, observed, or resolved over the course of the narrative.

Speaking and Listening

4. Present information, findings, and supporting evidence clearly, concisely, and logically such that listeners can follow the line of reasoning and the organization, development, substance, and style are appropriate to purpose, audience, and task.

Language

3. Apply knowledge of language to understand how language functions in different contexts, to make effective choices for meaning or style, and to comprehend more fully when reading or listening.

Building Knowledge

Meet the Author

The Romanian-born teacher, philosopher, and writer **Elie Wiesel** (b. 1928) was deported to the Nazi death camp at Auschwitz at age fifteen. His parents and sister all perished at the hands of the Nazis. In 1955, Wiesel published an account of his experiences, *And the World Kept Silent.* The English adaptation of the work, *Night*, was published in 1960. Wiesel says, "I wrote it for the other survivors who found it difficult to speak. And I wanted really to tell them, 'Look, you must speak . . . we must try.'"

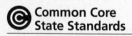

Common Core State Standards

Reading Informational Text

6. Determine an author's point of view or purpose in a text and analyze how an author uses rhetoric to advance that point of view or purpose.

8. Delineate and evaluate the argument and specific claims in a text, assessing whether the reasoning is valid and the evidence is relevant and sufficient; identify false statements and fallacious reasoning.

What kind of knowledge changes our lives?

Explore the Big Question as you read "Keep Memory Alive." Take notes on how Wiesel's experiences during the Holocaust shape his adult understanding of the world.

CLOSE READING FOCUS

Key Ideas and Details: **Evaluate Persuasion**

When reading persuasive writing, **evaluate the writer's argument.** Consider whether the writer supports claims with sound evidence and logical reasoning. In addition, determine whether **persuasive techniques,** such as emotional language or the rhetorical devices described below, are effectively used to enhance the impact of the argument. Conversely, recognize when they are used to cover up a lack of logical reasoning or strong evidence.

Craft and Structure: **Persuasive Writing and Rhetorical Devices**

Persuasive writing is nonfiction that is intended to convince people to take a particular action or position. Persuasive writers present and defend their claims and ideas in an **argument,** or a logically linked series of points that build to a conclusion. They also use **rhetorical devices,** or verbal techniques, that create emphasis and appeal to emotions. While rhetorical devices cannot replace strong arguments, they can move readers, helping them to understand, remember, and accept a writer's ideas. Here are some common rhetorical devices:

- **repetition:** reuse of a key word or idea for emphasis
- **parallelism:** similar grammatical structures expressing related ideas
- **restatement:** expression of the same idea in different words

Note that a given passage might display more than one rhetorical quality. For example, an instance of restatement may also involve parallelism.

Vocabulary

The words below are critical to understanding the text that follows. Decide whether you know the word well, know it a little bit, or do not know it at all. After you read, see how your knowledge of each word has increased.

transcends **presumptuous** **accomplices**

CLOSE READING MODEL

The passage below is from Elie Wiesel's speech, "Keep Memory Alive." The annotations to the right of the passage show ways in which you can use close reading skills to evaluate persuasive writing and rhetorical devices.

from "Keep Memory Alive"

It is with a profound sense of humility that I accept the honor you have chosen to bestow upon me. I know: your choice transcends me. This both frightens and pleases me.[1]

It frightens me[1] because I wonder: do I have the right to represent the multitudes who have perished? Do I have the right to accept this great honor on their behalf?[2] I do not.[3] That would be presumptuous. No one may speak for the dead, no one may interpret their mutilated dreams and visions.[3]

It pleases me[1] because I may say that this honor belongs to all the survivors and their children, and through us, to the Jewish people with whose destiny I have always identified.

I remember: it happened yesterday or eternities ago. A young Jewish boy discovered the kingdom of night. I remember his bewilderment. I remember his anguish. It all happened so fast.

Persuasive Writing

1 Wiesel says that the honor he is receiving "both frightens and pleases me." In the next paragraph he explains why it frightens him and then, in a second paragraph, why it pleases him. Even though Wiesel addresses an emotional topic, he does so with clear logic and organization.

Persuasive Writing and Rhetorical Devices

2 Wiesel asks whether he has the right to accept an honor on behalf of "multitudes" and then whether he has the right to accept "on their behalf." An example of restatement and repetition, this language tells you that this question refers to a key idea.

Evaluate Persuasion

3 Wiesel answers the questions he posed earlier: "I do not. That would be presumptuous. No one may speak for the dead." Even though his subject is profoundly emotional, this response shows logical reasoning and is, therefore, persuasive.

Keep Memory Alive

ELIE WIESEL

It is with a profound sense of humility that I accept the honor you have chosen to bestow upon me. I know: your choice **transcends** me. This both frightens and pleases me.

It frightens me because I wonder: do I have the right to represent the multitudes who have perished? Do I have the right to accept this great honor on their behalf? I do not. That would be **presumptuous**. No one may speak for the dead, no one may interpret their mutilated dreams and visions.

It pleases me because I may say that this honor belongs to all the survivors and their children, and through us, to the Jewish people with whose destiny I have always identified.

I remember: it happened yesterday or eternities ago. A young Jewish boy discovered the kingdom of night. I remember his bewilderment, I remember his anguish. It all happened so fast. The ghetto.[1] The deportation. The sealed cattle car. The fiery altar upon which the history of our people and the future of mankind were meant to be sacrificed.

◀ **Vocabulary**
transcends (tran sendz´) *v.* goes beyond the limits of; exceeds

presumptuous (prē zump´ cho͞o əs) *adj.* overstepping appropriate bounds; too bold

Persuasive Writing
Identify two examples of parallelism in the second paragraph.

1. **The ghetto** (get´ ō) During the Second World War, the Nazis forced Jews in European cities to live in crowded, restricted neighborhoods, or ghettos.

◀ **Critical Viewing**
How does this image of children being sent to a Nazi concentration camp add force to Wiesel's point about the necessity of remembering? Explain.

I remember: he asked his father: "Can this be true? This is the 20th century, not the Middle Ages. Who would allow such crimes to be committed? How could the world remain silent?"

And now the boy is turning to me: "Tell me," he asks. "What have you done with my future? What have you done with your life?"

And I tell him that I have tried. That I have tried to keep memory alive, that I have tried to fight those who would forget. Because if we forget, we are guilty, we are **accomplices**.

Vocabulary ▶
accomplices (ə käm′ plis iz) *n.* people who help another person commit a crime

And then I explained to him how naive we were, that the world did know and remain silent. And that is why I swore never to be silent whenever and wherever human beings endure suffering and humiliation. We must always take sides. Neutrality[2] helps the oppressor, never the victim. Silence encourages the tormentor, never the tormented.

---

2. **Neutrality** (no͞o tral′ ə tē) *n.* state of not taking sides in a conflict; quality of being unbiased.

Language Study

Vocabulary Words that have similar meanings are called **synonyms.** Words that have opposite meanings are called **antonyms.** The italicized words in each numbered item below appear in "Keep Memory Alive." Explain whether each word pair contains synonyms or antonyms. Then, write a sentence in which you use both words correctly.

1. *presumptuous,* modest
2. *transcends,* exceeds
3. *accomplices,* collaborators

WORD STUDY

The **Latin root *-scend-*** means "climb." In this speech, the author talks about receiving an honor that **transcends**, or climbs and goes beyond, him as an individual.

Word Study

Part A Explain how the **Latin root *-scend-*** contributes to the meanings of *transcendental, ascendant,* and *condescend*. Consult a dictionary if necessary.

Part B Use the context of the sentences and what you know about the Latin root *-scend-* to explain your answer to each question.

1. Are you going uphill or downhill as you *ascend* a mountain?
2. If someone is a *descendant* of a mayor, are the two people related?

Close Reading Activities 

Literary Analysis

Key Ideas and Details

1. **Evaluate Persuasion** What central argument does Wiesel present in this speech? Explain, citing details from the speech.
2. **Evaluate Persuasion (a)** What questions does the young Wiesel ask his father? **(b)** How do these questions support Wiesel's central argument?
3. **Evaluate Persuasion** Wiesel writes, "Because if we forget, we are guilty, we are accomplices." **(a)** Explain Wiesel's point: Why would forgetting make people "accomplices"? **(b)** Identify the support Wiesel provides for this claim. **(c)** Is the claim logical? Explain, citing evidence from the text to support your thinking.

Craft and Structure

4. **Persuasive Writing and Rhetorical Devices** Complete a chart like the one shown, listing examples of the rhetorical devices Wiesel uses and analyzing their likely effects on listeners.

	Repetition	Parallelism	Restatement
Example			
Effect			

5. **Persuasive Writing (a)** What does the child Wiesel ask the adult Wiesel in paragraph six? **(b)** What explanation does the adult Wiesel provide about the world's silence? **(c)** What do these questions tell you about the choices Wiesel made in his adult life? Explain.
6. **Persuasive Writing and Rhetorical Devices** At the end of the speech, Wiesel includes three statements about taking sides, neutrality, and silence. **(a)** Explain how the meaning of each statement is both similar and different. **(b)** Are these three sentences examples of restatement? Explain.

Integration of Knowledge and Ideas

7. **(a) Draw Conclusions:** Judging by his argument in "Keep Memory Alive," why does Wiesel believe the honor he is receiving belongs to the people who died in the Holocaust? **(b) Analyze:** Why does he say that receiving the award both "frightens and pleases" him?

8. THE BIG ? **What kind of knowledge changes our lives?** During the Holocaust, Wiesel and millions of other children gained horrible knowledge about the human capacity for evil. With a small group, discuss Wiesel's response to this knowledge, basing your answers on this speech. Consider whether Wiesel's response is most likely typical of those who suffered at the hands of the Nazis.

ACADEMIC VOCABULARY

As you write and speak about "Keep Memory Alive," use the words related to knowledge and understanding that you explored on page 185 of this book.

Conventions: Direct and Indirect Objects

A **direct object** is a noun or pronoun that receives the action of an action verb. An **indirect object** is used with a direct object and names the person or thing that something is given to or done for.

To find the direct object of a verb, answer the question "[verb] *whom?*" or "[verb] *what?*"

Example: Sam threw Fred the ball.

Threw what? ANSWER: the ball (direct object)

To find the indirect object of a verb, answer the question "[verb] *to or for whom?*" or "[verb] *to or for what?*"

Example: Sam threw Fred the ball.

Threw to whom? ANSWER: Fred (indirect object)

Indirect objects may appear only between verbs and direct objects in sentences.

Practice A

Identify the verb and direct object in each sentence. Then, identify any indirect objects the sentence may contain.

1. The Nobel committee gave Wiesel an important award.
2. Wiesel asked his father questions.
3. History teaches the world valuable lessons.
4. In *Night,* the author's father gives him guidance.
5. The audience offered Wiesel applause.

Reading Application In "Keep Memory Alive" find two sentences that have direct objects. Identify and label the verb and the object in each sentence.

Practice B

Identify the action verb and direct object in each sentence below. Then, rewrite each sentence, adding an indirect object, if possible.

1. The author's father taught a lesson.
2. The award recipients showed their medals.
3. The King of Sweden presented a prize.
4. The Nobel committee granted the prize money.
5. Documentaries tell historical accounts.

Writing Application Write two sentences about Wiesel's speech using the following grammatical order: subject, action verb, indirect object, direct object.

Writing to Sources

Argument Write a **letter** to Wiesel in which you respond to his claim in "Keep Memory Alive" that forgetting makes people accomplices to crimes or atrocities. Follow these tips:

- State the general meaning of the word "accomplice." Then, explain to Wiesel how you interpret that word in the context of his speech.
- Express your opinion about the role of memory in society. Explain why you think a society should or should not remember the past, including painful moments or terrible actions.
- Use examples from your own observations, other reading, and Wiesel's text to support your position.

As you draft, use rhetorical devices thoughtfully to emphasize or clarify your ideas. Likewise, use formal, respectful language appropriate to the purpose and audience of your letter. For example, in this type of letter, the formal term *impressive* would be more appropriate than the informal word *awesome*.

Grammar Application Direct and indirect objects always follow action verbs. As you draft, use action verbs, followed by direct and indirect objects, whenever possible to make your writing more precise.

Speaking and Listening

Comprehension and Collaboration With a group of classmates, hold a **debate** about the following paraphrased claim from Wiesel's speech:

People who do not speak up against injustice are accomplices.

Choose a notetaker and moderator, and divide the group into teams to argue for and against this claim.

- Present your point of view and support it with evidence.
- Use persuasive language and rhetorical devices that convey your ideas clearly and powerfully.
- During the debate, listen closely to the arguments from the opposing team and respond accurately. Point out any instances of the opposing team's use of exaggerated evidence or faulty reasoning.
- Conclude your presentation by summarizing your position.

After the debate, as a group review the notes and identify the ideas that were expressed most persuasively.

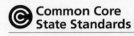

Writing

1.d. Establish and maintain a formal style and objective tone while attending to the norms and conventions of the discipline in which they are writing.

Speaking and Listening

3. Evaluate a speaker's point of view, reasoning, and use of evidence and rhetoric, identifying any fallacious reasoning or exaggerated or distorted evidence.

Language

5. Demonstrate understanding of figurative language, word relationships, and nuances in word meanings.

Building Knowledge

Theodore H. White (1915–1986) worked as a newsboy for the *Boston Globe* to help pay for his education at Harvard University. After he graduated, Henry Luce, founder of *Time* magazine, hired White as the magazine's correspondent in eastern Asia. White later earned fame for his book about the election of John F. Kennedy: *The Making of the President*. Today, he is viewed as one of the finest political reporters of the twentieth century.

What kind of knowledge changes our lives?

Explore the Big Question as you read "The American Idea." Take notes about the ideals upon which the author says the country was founded and consider how those ideals have changed people's lives.

CLOSE READING FOCUS

Key Ideas and Details: **Distinguishing Fact from Opinion**

Essay writers seek both to explain ideas and to persuade readers of their points of view. To be effective, a writer should present facts and evidence rather than unsupported opinions. Therefore, it is important to evaluate the content of essays by **distinguishing between fact and opinion.**

- A statement of **fact** can be proved true.
- A statement of **opinion** expresses a belief or a viewpoint and must be supported by facts, reasons, and logic.

As you read, identify statements of opinion and note the evidence the author uses to support them. Consider whether the development of ideas is effective because opinions are supported with sound reasoning and relevant facts.

Craft and Structure: **Analytic and Interpretive Essays**

In an **analytic essay,** a writer explores an idea by breaking it into parts. In an **interpretive essay,** a writer presents his or her understanding of an issue or topic. A single essay may combine features of both types. To bring readers to accept an analysis or interpretation, a writer may develop it with varied types of appeals:

- **Appeals to Authority:** calls upon the opinions of experts
- **Appeals to Reason:** calls upon logic
- **Appeals to Emotions:** calls upon feelings like fear, sympathy, or pride
- **Appeals to Shared Values:** calls upon shared beliefs about what is good, right, or fair

Vocabulary

The words below are key to understanding the text that follows. Copy the words into your notebook. Which one is a synonym for *sequential?*

embodied **emigrants** **successive** **subversion**

Common Core State Standards

Reading Informational Text

1. Cite strong and thorough textual evidence to support analysis of what the text says explicitly as well as inferences drawn from the text.

3. Analyze how the author unfolds an analysis or series of ideas or events, including the order in which the points are made, how they are introduced and developed, and the connections that are drawn between them.

5. Analyze in detail how an author's ideas or claims are developed and refined by particular sentences, paragraphs, or larger portions of a text.

CLOSE READING MODEL

The passage below is from Theodore White's essay "The American Idea." The annotations to the right of the passage show ways in which you can use close reading skills to analyze essays and distinguish between facts and opinions.

from "The American Idea"

Some of the first European Americans had come to the new continent to worship God in their own way, others to seek their fortunes. But over a century-and-a-half, the new world changed those Europeans,[1] above all the Englishmen who had come to North America. Neither King nor Court nor church could stretch over the ocean to the wild continent. To survive, the first emigrants had to learn to govern themselves. But the freedom of the wilderness whetted their appetites for more freedoms.[2] By the time Jefferson drafted his call, men were in the field fighting for those new-learned freedoms, killing and being killed by English soldiers, the best-trained troops in the world, supplied by the world's greatest navy.[3] Only something worth dying for could unite American volunteers and keep them in the field—a stated cause, a flag, a nation they could call their own.[4]

Distinguishing Fact from Opinion

1 In the first sentence, White states a fact. In the next sentence, he states an opinion: "the new world changed those Europeans." White must supply evidence to support that opinion.

Analytic and Interpretive Essays

2 White sets up an interpretation based on logic: Distance kept British institutions from maintaining power in the colonies. The colonists stepped into the void, asserted their own power, and grew to like it.

Distinguishing Fact from Opinion

3 Facts about British military might support White's interpretation of events, especially his point about the low odds of success faced by American volunteers.

Analytic and Interpretive Essays

4 White expresses an opinion, as it may or may not be true that "only something worth dying for" could unite the volunteers. He also appeals to readers' emotions by referring to American ideals: "a flag, a nation they could call their own."

The American Idea

Theodore H. White

The idea was there at the very beginning, well before Thomas Jefferson put it into words—and the idea rang the call.

Jefferson himself could not have imagined the reach of his call across the world in time to come when he wrote:

"We hold these truths to be self-evident, that all men are created equal, that they are endowed by their Creator with certain unalienable rights, that among these are life, liberty, and the pursuit of happiness."

But over the next two centuries the call would reach the potato patches of Ireland, the ghettoes of Europe, the paddyfields of China, stirring farmers to leave their lands and townsmen their trades and thus unsettling all traditional civilizations.

It is the call from Thomas Jefferson, **embodied** in the great statue that looks down the Narrows of New York Harbor,[1] and in the immigrants who answered the call, that we now celebrate.

Some of the first European Americans had come to the new continent to worship God in their own way, others to seek their fortunes. But, over a century-and-a-half, the new world changed those Europeans, above all the Englishmen who had come to North America. Neither King nor Court nor Church could stretch over the ocean to the wild continent. To survive, the first **emigrants** had to learn to govern themselves. But the freedom of the

Analytic and Interpretive Essays
What emotional appeals does White use in the opening paragraphs of this essay?

◀ **Vocabulary**
embodied (em bäd′ ēd) *v.* gave form to; made concrete

emigrants (em′ i grənts) *n.* people who leave their country or region to settle elsewhere

Comprehension
According to Thomas Jefferson, what three rights do all men have?

1. **the great statue that looks down the Narrows of New York Harbor** Statue of Liberty.

wilderness whetted their appetites for more freedoms. By the time Jefferson drafted his call, men were in the field fighting for those new-learned freedoms, killing and being killed by English soldiers, the best-trained troops in the world, supplied by the world's greatest navy. . . . Only something worth dying for could unite American volunteers and keep them in the field—a stated cause, a flag, a nation they could call their own.

When, on the Fourth of July, 1776, the colonial leaders who had been meeting as a Continental Congress in Philadelphia voted to approve Jefferson's Declaration of Independence, it was not puffed-up rhetoric for them to pledge to each other "our lives, our fortunes and our sacred honor." Unless their new "United States of America" won the war, the Congressmen would be judged traitors as relentlessly as would the irregulars-under-arms in the field. . . .

The new Americans were tough men fighting for a very tough idea. How they won their battles is a story for the schoolbooks, studied by scholars, wrapped in myths by historians and poets. But what is most important is the story of the idea that made them into a nation, the idea that had an explosive power undreamed of in 1776.

The new Americans were tough men fighting for a very tough idea.

All other nations had come into being among people whose families had lived for time out of mind on the same land where they were born. . . . Englishmen are English, Frenchmen are French, Chinese are Chinese, while their governments come and go; their national states can be torn apart and remade without losing their nationhood. But Americans are a nation born of an idea; not the place, but the idea, created the United States Government.

The story we celebrate is the story of how this idea worked itself out, how it stretched and changed and how the call for "life, liberty and the pursuit of happiness" does still, as it did in the beginning, mean different things to different people.

Distinguishing Fact from Opinion
Identify one fact and one opinion expressed in the essay so far.

▲ Thomas Jefferson ▲ John Adams

The debate began with the drafting of the Declaration of Independence. That task was left to Jefferson of Virginia, who spent two weeks in an upstairs room in a Philadelphia boarding house penning a draft, while John Adams and Benjamin Franklin questioned, edited, hardened his phrases. By the end of that hot and muggy June, the three had reached agreement: the Declaration contained the ringing universal theme Jefferson strove for and, at the same time, voiced American grievances toughly enough to please the feisty Adams and the pragmatic Franklin. After brief debate, Congress passed it.

As the years wore on, the great debate expanded between Jefferson and Adams. The young nation flourished and Jefferson chose to think of America's promise as a call to all the world, its promises universal. A few weeks before he died, he wrote, "May it be to the world, what I believe it will be (to some parts sooner, to others later, but finally to all), the signal of arousing men to burst their chains." To Adams, the call meant something else—it was the call for *American* independence, the cornerstone of an *American* state.

Their argument ran through their **successive** Administrations. Adams, the second President, suspected the French Revolutionaries; Alien and Sedition Acts[2] were passed during his term of office to protect the American state and its liberties

2. Alien and Sedition Acts laws passed by Congress in 1798 restricting immigration and regulating the expression of criticism of the government.

LITERATURE IN CONTEXT

History Connection

The American Revolution
White makes a number of references to the era of the American Revolution.

- **The Declaration of Independence** Written by Thomas Jefferson, the Declaration announced the colonies' decision in 1776 to break away from Great Britain. In the opening paragraph, Jefferson refers to the phrase *unalienable* **(un āl´ yən ə bəl)** rights—those rights that cannot be taken or given away.
- **Irregulars-Under-Arms** The colonists who fought the British in the Revolution could be considered irregulars-under-arms. As rebels, they did not belong to a regularly established army.

Connect to the Literature

What contrasting views of the American idea are represented by Jefferson's "unalienable rights" and by Adams's views on immigration?

◀ **Vocabulary**
successive (sək ses´ iv) *adj.* following one after another in sequence

Comprehension
What document did the Founders draft to present their ideals?

Vocabulary ▶
subversion (səb vʉr′ zhən) *n.* activity meant to overthrow something established

against French **subversion**. But Jefferson, the third President, welcomed the French. The two men, once close friends, became archrivals. Still, as they grew old, their rivalry faded; there was glory enough to share in what they had made; in 1812, they began a correspondence that has since become classic, remembering and taking comfort in the triumphs of their youth.

Spiral Review
SERIES OF IDEAS Why does White conclude with this story of Jefferson's and Adams's deaths?

Adams and Jefferson lived long lives and died on the same day—the Fourth of July, 1826, 50 years to the day from the Continental Congress's approval of the Declaration. Legend has it that Adams breathed on his death bed, "Thomas Jefferson still survives." As couriers set out from Braintree[3] carrying the news of Adams's death, couriers were riding north from Virginia with the news of Jefferson's death. The couriers met in Philadelphia. Horace Greeley,[4] then a youth in Vermont, later remembered: ". . . When we learned . . . that Thomas Jefferson and John Adams, the author and the great champion, respectively, of the Declaration, had both died on that day, and that the messengers bearing South and North, respectively, the tidings of their decease, had met in Philadelphia, under the shadow of that Hall in which our independence was declared, it seemed that a Divine attestation had solemnly hallowed and sanctified the great anniversary by the impressive ministration of Death."

3. **Braintree** town in Massachusetts (now called Quincy) where John Adams lived and died.
4. **Horace Greeley** famous American newspaper publisher.

Language Study

Vocabulary Word **analogies** match the relationship in one pair of words with that in another. The italicized words in each numbered item below appear in "The American Idea." For each item, choose the word from the lettered choices that follow to correctly complete each analogy.

1. immigrants : enter :: *emigrants* : (a) leave (b) stay (c) build

2. entertainment : comedian :: *subversion* : (a) film (b) spy (c) ship

3. many : few :: *successive* : (a) logical (b) interrupted (c) finished

WORD STUDY
The **Greek prefix *em-*** or ***im-*** means "in" or "into." In this essay, the author explains that Jefferson's ideas about liberty are **embodied**, or put into concrete form, in the Statue of Liberty.

Word Study

Part A Explain how the **Greek prefix *em-*** contributes to the meanings of *empathy, emphasize,* and *empower.* Consult a dictionary if necessary.

Part B Use the context of the sentences and what you know about the Greek prefix *em-* to explain your answer to each question.

1. Would a person most likely feel *embittered* after winning a lottery?

2. Does someone who is *emboldened* become courageous or fearful?

Close Reading Activities

Literary Analysis

Key Ideas and Details

1. (a) Identify three groups that White says heard the call of the American idea. **(b) Infer:** How did the call of the American idea affect each of them? Cite details from the text in your answer.

2. Compare and Contrast: What differences does White see between early American settlers and people living in other lands at that time? Explain.

3. Distinguish between Fact and Opinion (a) List two opinions that White includes about people or events. **(b)** Note specific facts he uses to support each opinion.

4. Distinguish between Fact and Opinion Cite the evidence White uses to support the following opinion: "The new Americans were tough men fighting for a very tough idea."

Craft and Structure

5. Analytic and Interpretive Essays (a) Use a chart like the one shown to identify the positions and details White includes in the analytic sections of the essay. **(b)** Explain how the story about Adams and Jefferson, along with other details and varied types of appeals, strengthens White's presentation of an "American idea."

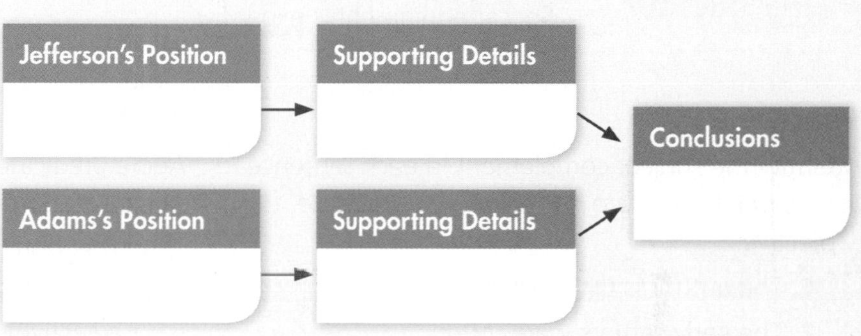

Integration of Knowledge and Ideas

6. Evaluate: Do you agree with White that the phrase "life, liberty, and the pursuit of happiness" means different things to different people? Cite evidence from the text to support your answer.

7. Draw Conclusions: What does White mean when he writes, "Americans are a nation born of an idea"? Explain, citing details from the text.

8. THE BIG ? **What kind of knowledge changes our lives?** Both Adams and Jefferson witnessed the birth of the American nation. According to White, how did knowledge of that experience change their lives? Use details from the text to support your answer.

ACADEMIC VOCABULARY

As you write and speak about "The American Idea," use the words related to knowledge and understanding that you explored on page 185 of this textbook.

Close Reading Activities Continued

Conventions: Subject Complements

Predicate nominatives and **predicate adjectives** are **subject complements.** They appear after a linking verb such as *be, is,* or *seem,* and they rename, identify, or describe the subject of the sentence.

A subject and a predicate nominative both name the same person, place, or thing. The linking verb joins them and makes them equal. In the examples, the subject is underlined once and the predicate nominative is underlined twice.

Examples: Their first choice was you.
Our vacation destination is the beach.

A predicate adjective appears after a linking verb and describes the subject of the sentence. In the examples, the subject is underlined once and the predicate adjective is underlined twice.

Examples: Roses are red.
Soccer equipment is expensive.

Practice A

Identify the subject complement in each sentence and label it *predicate nominative* or *predicate adjective.*

1. The author is the speaker.
2. The early settlers were tough.
3. The author, Theodore H. White, seems knowledgeable.
4. The American idea is alive and well.
5. During his lifetime, John Adams was Thomas Jefferson's rival.

Reading Application In "The American Idea," find and copy one sentence that has a predicate nominative and one sentence that has a predicate adjective. In each example you find, label the complement, underline the subject, and circle the linking verb.

Practice B

Add a predicate nominative or predicate adjective, as indicated, to complete each sentence.

1. Theodore H. White is (predicate nominative).
2. The early Americans were (predicate adjective).
3. The coincidence that Adams and Jefferson died on the same day seemed (predicate adjective).
4. The Declaration of Independence is (predicate nominative).
5. The history of the nation is (predicate adjective).

Writing Application Write a brief paragraph about the writing of the Declaration of Independence. Include at least two predicate adjectives and at least two predicate nominatives. After you draft, identify the subject complements you have included.

Writing to Sources

Argument Write a **critique**, or critical evaluation, of White's essay. Identify one of the central claims in the essay, and assess the quality of the evidence White uses to support it.

- Before you draft, gather examples of the evidence White uses. For each piece of evidence, note whether it is effective.
- Consider discussing each piece of evidence in a separate paragraph. Use details from the selection to support your opinions.
- Identify any ambiguities, or unclear concepts, in the text by looking for sections that confused you. Decide whether White clarified those ideas for you and, if so, how.
- Conclude with a statement that evaluates the overall strength of White's evidence, making sure to note whether he supports all opinions with sound reasoning and facts.
- Present your evaluation to the class. Ask whether listeners agree with your ideas and discuss any differences.

Grammar Application As you write your critique, be aware of your use of subject complements.

Research and Technology

Build and Present Knowledge Use multiple reliable sources to research one of the historical figures White discusses in this essay. For example, you might learn more about Thomas Jefferson or John Adams. Then, write a **cover letter** and **résumé** that the person you chose might have submitted for the job of "Founder of the Republic."

- Conduct research to identify the education and experience that make your subject suitable for the job.
- Consult reference works to find a suitable format for cover letters and résumés.
- In the cover letter, weave in details from White's essay to present an overview of your subject's effectiveness and importance as a leader in the American cause. In the resume, cite specific details about the subject's education or training, experiences, and achievements.
- Use action verbs and vivid descriptions to make your writing engaging.

Submit your letter and résumé to peers for review. Then, compare the materials written by other classmates and come to an agreement about which applicant is best qualified for the job of "Founder of the Republic."

Writing

1. Write arguments to support claims in an analysis of substantive topics or texts, using valid reasoning and relevant and sufficient evidence.

1.e. Provide a concluding statement or section that follows from and supports the argument presented.

7. Conduct research projects to answer a question or solve a problem; narrow or broaden the inquiry; and synthesize multiple sources on a subject.

Language

1. Demonstrate command of the conventions of standard English grammar and usage when writing or speaking.

Comparing Texts

What kind of knowledge changes our lives?

Explore the Big Question as you read this humorous speech and essay. Take notes on the ways in which each work transforms the speaker's or narrator's knowledge about a bad situation into humor.

READING TO COMPARE HUMOROUS WRITING

Authors Mark Twain and James Thurber used the tools of comedy in different ways. As you read, compare the two authors' topics, styles, and use of literary devices to create classic works of American humor.

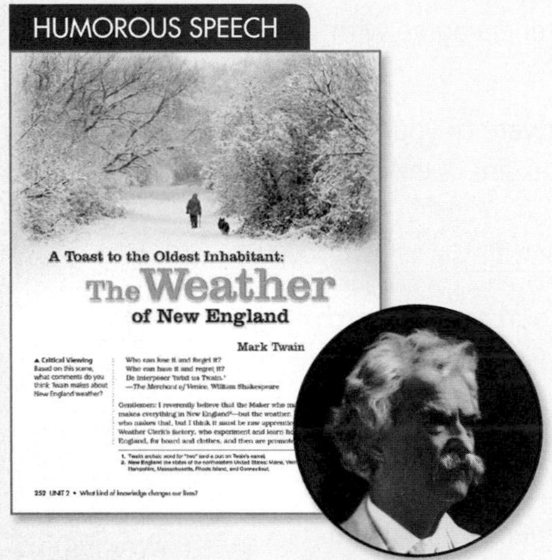

HUMOROUS SPEECH

A Toast to the Oldest Inhabitant: The Weather of New England

Mark Twain

HUMOROUS ESSAY

The Dog That Bit People

James Thurber

"A Toast to the Oldest Inhabitant"

Mark Twain (1835–1910)
Mark Twain is the pen name of Samuel Langhorne Clemens, one of America's greatest writers. He is most famous for two classic novels: *The Adventures of Tom Sawyer* (1876) and *The Adventures of Huckleberry Finn* (1884). Later in his life, Mark Twain became a sought-after, highly paid public speaker. His speeches, like his stories, display his powers of observation and his unmatched ability to find humor in real life.

"The Dog that Bit People"

James Thurber (1894–1961)
A native of Columbus, Ohio, James Thurber went to work for the U.S. State Department after college. Soon afterward, however, he found his true calling: He became a humorist, writing essays and drawing cartoons for *The New Yorker*, a famous magazine. Thurber won fame for his whimsical depictions of human (and animal) silliness.

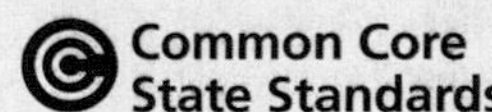

Comparing Humorous Writing

In a **humorous essay** or **speech,** a writer presents a subject in an unexpected, amusing way. The writer may treat a serious situation lightly or a ridiculous situation seriously. Techniques for creating humor include the following.

- Using **hyperbole,** or exaggeration, a writer describes people, things, or events as if they were much more important than they are—for instance, calling the discovery of a missing sock a "joyous reunion."
- Using **understatement,** a writer speaks of people, things, or events as if they were less important than they are—for instance, saying that "the weather was less than ideal" after a violent storm carries off picnic tables.

When a writer uses humor to point out the foolishness of a particular type of human behavior or of a particular institution, the result is called **satire.**

Mark Twain's speech "A Toast to the Oldest Inhabitant . . ." and James Thurber's essay "The Dog That Bit People" use humor, but their comic techniques are different. Use a chart like the one shown to compare the elements that make these selections humorous.

	Hyperbole	Understatement	Satire
Twain			
Thurber			

Diction, or word choice, is another literary element that contributes to humor. Authors try to select words that precisely convey the meaning they intend. To do so, they consider a word's **connotation**—the set of ideas associated with it—as well as the word's denotation, or definition. For example, the words *house* and *home* both mean "place to live," but the word *home* is associated with ideas like family and comfort. The word *house* does not have these connotations. As you read the selections, consider the connotations of the authors' diction and analyze how precise word choices contribute to both humorous meaning and **tone,** or the expression of the writer's attitude toward his or her subject and reader.

Common Core State Standards

Reading Informational Text

4. Determine the meaning of words and phrases as they are used in a text, including figurative, connotative, and technical meanings; analyze the cumulative impact of specific word choices on meaning and tone.

6. Determine an author's point of view or purpose in a text and analyze how an author uses rhetoric to advance that point of view or purpose.

7. Analyze various accounts of a subject told in different mediums, determining which details are emphasized in each account.

Writing

2. Write informative/explanatory texts to examine and convey complex ideas, concepts, and information clearly and accurately through the effective selection, organization, and analysis of content.

2.a. Introduce a topic; organize complex ideas, concepts, and information to make important connections and distinctions.

10. Write routinely over extended time frames and shorter time frames for a range of tasks, purposes, and audiences.

Language

5.b. Analyze nuances in the meaning of words with similar denotations.

A Toast to the Oldest Inhabitant: The Weather of New England

Mark Twain

▲ **Critical Viewing** Based on this scene, what comments do you think Twain makes about New England weather?

Who can lose it and forget it?
Who can have it and regret it?
Be interposer 'twixt us Twain.[1]
—*The Merchant of Venice*, William Shakespeare

Gentlemen: I reverently believe that the Maker who made us all, makes everything in New England[2]—but the weather. I don't know who makes that, but I think it must be raw apprentices in the Weather Clerk's factory, who experiment and learn how in New England, for board and clothes, and then are promoted to make

1. **Twain** archaic word for "two" (and a pun on Twain's name).
2. **New England** the states of the northeastern United States: Maine, Vermont, New Hampshire, Massachusetts, Rhode Island, and Connecticut.

weather for countries that require a good article, and will take their custom elsewhere if they don't get it. There is a **sumptuous** variety about the New England weather that compels the stranger's admiration—and regret. The weather is always doing something there; always attending strictly to business; always getting up new designs and trying them on the people to see how they will go. But it gets through more business in spring than in any other season. In the spring I have counted one hundred and thirty-six different kinds of weather inside of four and twenty hours. It was I that made the fame and fortune of that man that had that marvelous collection of weather on exhibition at the Centennial[3] that so astounded the foreigners. He was going to travel all over the world and get specimens from all the climes. I said, "Don't you do it; you come to New England on a favorable spring day." I told him what we could do, in the way of style, variety, and quantity. Well, he came, and he made his collection in four days. As to variety—why, he confessed that he got hundreds of kinds of weather that he had never heard of before. And as to quantity—well, after he had picked out and discarded all that was blemished in any way, he not only had weather enough, but weather to spare; weather to hire out; weather to sell; to deposit; weather to invest; weather to give to the poor.

◀ **Vocabulary**
sumptuous (sump´ cho͞o əs) *adj.* lavish

Humorous Writing
What hyperbole does Twain use here to make his point about New England weather?

Comprehension
What is the main characteristic of New England weather according to Twain?

3. **Centennial** international trade fair held in 1876 in Philadelphia to mark the hundredth anniversary of the Declaration of Independence. The fair featured scientific and technological marvels of the day.

▼ **Critical Viewing**
Are you surprised there is such a wide variety of weather in such a small area of the United States? Why or why not?

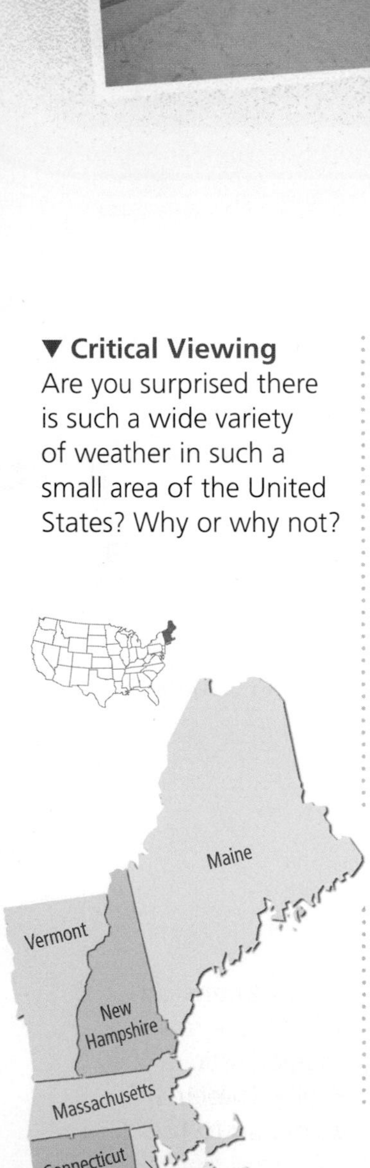

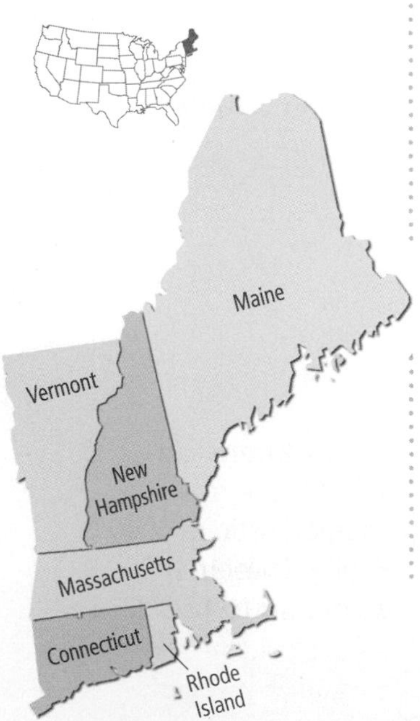

The people of New England are by nature patient and forbearing; but there are some things which they will not stand. Every year they kill a lot of poets for writing about "Beautiful Spring." These are generally casual visitors, who bring their notions of spring from somewhere else, and cannot, of course, know how the natives feel about spring. And so, the first thing they know, the opportunity to inquire how they feel has permanently gone by.

Old Probabilities has a mighty reputation for accurate prophecy, and thoroughly well deserves it. You take up the papers and observe how crisply and confidently he checks off what today's weather is going to be on the Pacific, down South, in the Middle States, in the Wisconsin region; see him sail along in the joy and pride of his power till he gets to New England, and then—see his tail drop. *He* doesn't know what the weather is going to be like in New England. He can't any more tell than he can tell how many Presidents of the United States there's going to be next year.[4] Well, he mulls over it, and by and by he gets out something about like this: Probable nor'-east to sou'-west winds, varying to the southard and westard and eastard and points between; high and low barometer, swapping around from place to place; probable areas of rain, snow, hail, and drought, succeeded or preceded by earthquakes, with thunder and lightning.

4. **how many Presidents of the United States there's going to be next year** The United States presidential election of 1876 was one of the most disputed, with two declared "winners" when Twain gave this speech. Rutherford B. Hayes was declared the final victor on March 2, 1877.

Then he jots down this postscript from his wandering mind, to cover accidents: "But it is possible that the program may be wholly changed in the meantime."

Yes, one of the brightest gems in the New England weather is the dazzling uncertainty of it. There is only one thing certain about it, you are certain there is going to be plenty of weather—a perfect grand review; but you never can tell which end of the procession is going to move first. You fix up for the drought; you leave your umbrella in the house and sally out with your sprinkling pot, and ten to one you get drowned. You make up your mind that the earthquake is due; you stand from under, and take hold of something to steady yourself, and the first thing you know, you get struck by lightning. These are great disappointments. But they can't be helped. The lightning there is peculiar; it is so convincing! When it strikes a thing, it doesn't leave enough of that thing behind for you to tell whether—well, you'd think it was something valuable, and a Congressman had been there.

Humorous Writing How does Twain use understatement here to add humor?

Humorous Writing What does Twain satirically imply about congressmen in this paragraph?

And the thunder. When the thunder commences to merely tune up, and scrape, and saw, and key up the instruments for the performance, strangers say, "Why, what awful thunder you have here!" But when the baton is raised and the real concert begins, you'll find that stranger down in the cellar, with his head in the ash barrel.

Now, as to the size of the weather in New England—lengthways, I mean. It is utterly disproportioned to the size of that little country. Half the time, when it is packed as full as it can stick, you will see that New England weather sticking out beyond the edges and projecting around hundreds and hundreds of miles over the neighboring states. She can't hold a tenth part of her weather. You can see cracks all about, where she has strained herself trying to do it.

Yes, one of the brightest gems in the New England weather is the dazzling uncertainty of it.

I could speak volumes about the inhuman perversity of the New England weather, but I will give but a single specimen. I like to hear rain on a tin roof, so I covered part of my roof with tin, with an eye to that luxury. Well, sir, do you think it ever rains on the tin? No, sir; skips it every time.

Mind, in this speech I have been trying merely to do honor to the New England weather—no language could do it justice. But, after all, there are at least one or two things about that weather (or, if you please, effects produced by it) which we residents would not like to part with. If we hadn't our bewitching autumn foliage, we should still have to credit the weather with one feature which compensates for

Comprehension According to Twain, how easy is it to predict New England weather?

Vocabulary ▶
vagaries (vā′ gər ēz) *n.* erratic or unpredictable actions

Humorous Writing
What makes this paragraph different from the rest of the essay?

all its bullying **vagaries**—the ice storm—when a leafless tree is clothed with ice from the bottom to the top—ice that is as bright and clear as crystal; when every bough and twig is strung with ice beads, frozen dewdrops, and the whole tree sparkles, cold and white, like the Shah[5] of Persia's diamond plume. Then the wind waves the branches, and the sun comes out and turns all those myriads of beads and drops to prisms, that glow and burn and flash with all manner of colored fires, which change and change again, with inconceivable rapidity, from blue to red, from red to green, and green to gold—the tree becomes a spraying fountain, a very explosion of dazzling jewels; and it stands there the acme, the climax, the supremest possibility in art or nature, of bewildering, intoxicating, intolerable magnificence! One cannot make the words too strong.

Month after month I lay up my hate and grudge against the New England weather; but when the ice storm comes at last, I say: "There—I forgive you, now—the books are square between us, you don't owe me a cent; go, and sin no more; your little faults and foibles count for nothing—you are the most enchanting weather in the world!"

5. Shah (shä) *n.* formerly, the title of the ruler of Persia (now Iran).

Critical Thinking

1. **Key Ideas and Details: (a)** According to Twain, what quality or feature of New England weather "compels the stranger's admiration"? **(b) Connect:** What point does Twain support with the story of the man who collected and exhibited weather?
2. **Key Ideas and Details: (a)** What is the profession of "Old Probabilities"? **(b) Interpret:** What point is Twain making in the anecdote about this character? Explain.
3. **Craft and Structure:** Twain describes New England weather as having "inhuman perversity." **(a) Interpret:** Is the connotation of these words positive or negative? **(b) Analyze:** How does the connotation affect the tone of the writing? Explain.
4. **Integration of Knowledge and Ideas:** What knowledge allows Twain to appreciate New England's tumultuous weather? *[Connect to the Big Question: What kind of knowledge changes our lives?]*

The Dog That Bit People

Nobody Knew Exactly What Was the Matter with Him, James Thurber

James Thurber

Probably no one man should have as many dogs in his life as I have had, but there was more pleasure than distress in them for me except in the case of an Airedale named Muggs. He gave me more trouble than all the other fifty-four or -five put together, although my moment of keenest embarrassment was the time a Scotch terrier named Jeannie, who had just had six puppies in the clothes closet of a fourth floor apartment in New York, had the unexpected seventh and last at the corner of Eleventh Street and Fifth Avenue during a walk she had insisted on taking. Then, too, there was the prize winning French poodle, a great big black poodle—none of your little, untroublesome white miniatures—who got sick riding in the rumble seat[1] of a car with me on her way to the Greenwich Dog Show. She had a red rubber bib tucked around her throat and, since a rain storm came up when we were halfway through the Bronx, I had to hold over her a small green umbrella, really more of a parasol. The rain beat down fearfully and suddenly the driver of the car drove into a big garage, filled with mechanics. It happened so quickly that I forgot to put the umbrella down and I will always remember, with sickening distress, the look of **incredulity** mixed with hatred that came over the face of the particular hardened garage man that came over to see what we

▲ Analyze Representations
Which elements of this drawing by Thurber suggest that Muggs has a difficult personality?

◀ Vocabulary
incredulity
(in´ krə dōō´ lə tē) *n.*
unwillingness to believe

Comprehension
What does Thurber say was his most embarrassing moment?

1. **rumble seat** *n.* in some early automobiles, an open seat in the rear, behind the roofed seat, which could be folded shut when not in use.

wanted, when he took a look at me and the poodle. All garage men, and people of that intolerant stripe, hate poodles with their curious hair cut, especially the pom-poms that you got to leave on their hips if you expect the dogs to win a prize.

But the Airedale, as I have said, was the worst of all my dogs. He really wasn't my dog, as a matter of fact: I came home from a vacation one summer to find that my brother Roy had bought him while I was away. A big, burly, choleric dog, he always acted as if he thought I wasn't one of the family. There was a slight advantage in being one of the family, for he didn't bite the family as often as he bit strangers. Still, in the years that we had him he bit everybody but mother, and he made a pass at her once but missed. That was during the month when we suddenly had mice, and Muggs refused to do anything about them. Nobody ever had mice exactly like the mice we had that month. They acted like pet mice, almost like mice somebody had trained. They were so friendly that one night when mother entertained at dinner the Friraliras, a club she and my father had belonged to for twenty years, she put down a lot of little dishes with food in them on the pantry floor so that the mice would be satisfied with that and wouldn't come into the dining room. Muggs stayed out in the pantry with the mice, lying on the floor, growling to himself—not at the mice, but about all the people in the next room that he would have liked to get at. Mother slipped out into the pantry once to see how everything was going. Everything was going fine. It made her so mad to see Muggs lying there, oblivious of the mice—they came running up to her—that she slapped him and he slashed at her, but didn't make it. He was sorry immediately, mother said. He was always sorry, she said, after he bit someone, but we could not understand how she figured this out. He didn't act sorry.

Humorous Writing
Explain how Thurber uses understatement when comparing Muggs's treatment of family and strangers.

Mother used to send a box of candy every Christmas to the people the Airedale bit. The list finally contained forty or more names. Nobody could understand why we didn't get rid of the dog. I didn't understand it very well myself, but we didn't get rid of him. I think that one or two people tried to poison Muggs—he acted poisoned once in a while—and old Major Moberly fired at him once with his service revolver near the Seneca Hotel in East Broad Street—but Muggs lived to be almost eleven years old and even when he could hardly get around he bit a Congressman who had called to see my father on business. My mother had never liked the Congressman—she said the signs of his horoscope showed he couldn't be trusted (he was Saturn with the moon in Virgo)—but she sent him a box of candy that Christmas. He sent it right back, probably because he suspected it was trick candy. Mother

Humorous Writing
Which details in this paragraph seem to be hyperboles?

persuaded herself it was all for the best that the dog had bitten him, even though father lost an important business association because of it. "I wouldn't be associated with such a man," mother said, "Muggs could read him like a book."

We used to take turns feeding Muggs to be on his good side, but that didn't always work. He was never in a very good humor, even after a meal. Nobody knew exactly what was the matter with him, but whatever it was it made him **irascible**, especially in the mornings. Roy never felt very well in the morning, either, especially before breakfast, and once when he came downstairs and found that Muggs had moodily chewed up the morning paper he hit him in the face with a grapefruit and then jumped up on the dining room table, scattering dishes and silverware and spilling the coffee. Muggs' first free leap carried him all the way across the table and into a brass fire screen in front of the gas grate but he was back on his feet in a moment and in the end he got Roy and gave him a pretty vicious bite in the leg. Then he was all over it; he never bit anyone more than once at a time. Mother always mentioned that as an argument in his favor; she said he had a quick temper but that he didn't hold a grudge. She was forever defending him. I think she liked him because he wasn't well. "He's not strong," she would say, pityingly, but that was inaccurate; he may not have been well but he was terribly strong.

◀ **Vocabulary**
irascible (i ras´ ə bəl) *adj.* quick tempered

One time my mother went to the Chittenden Hotel to call on a woman mental healer who was lecturing in Columbus on the subject of "Harmonious Vibrations." She wanted to find out if it was possible to get harmonious vibrations into a dog. "He's a large tan-colored Airedale," mother explained. The woman said that she had never treated a dog but she advised my mother to hold the thought that he did not bite and would not bite. Mother was holding the thought the very next morning when Muggs got the iceman but she blamed that slip-up on the iceman. "If you didn't think he would bite you, he wouldn't," mother told him. He stomped out of the house in a terrible jangle of vibrations.

Spiral Review
SERIES OF IDEAS
Explain what the story of "harmonious vibrations" adds to your understanding of the mother.

One morning when Muggs bit me slightly, more or less in passing, I reached down and grabbed his short stumpy tail and hoisted him into the air. It was a foolhardy thing to do and the last time I saw my mother, about six months ago, she said she didn't know what possessed me. I don't either, except that I was pretty mad. As long as I held the dog off the floor by his tail he couldn't get at me, but he twisted and jerked so, snarling all the time, that I realized I couldn't hold him that way very long. I carried him to the kitchen and flung him onto the floor and shut the door on him just as he crashed against it. But I forgot about the backstairs.

Comprehension
How does Muggs generally respond to people?

Muggs at His Meals Was an Unusual Sight, James Thurber

▲ **Analyze Representations**
How does this drawing of Muggs compare and contrast with the behavior described in the essay?

Muggs went up the backstairs and down the frontstairs and had me cornered in the living room. I managed to get up onto the mantelpiece above the fireplace, but it gave way and came down with a tremendous crash throwing a large marble clock, several vases, and myself heavily to the floor. Muggs was so alarmed by the racket that when I picked myself up he had disappeared. We couldn't find him anywhere, although we whistled and shouted, until old Mrs. Detweiler called after dinner that night. Muggs had bitten her once, in the leg, and she came into the living room only after we assured her that Muggs had run away. She had just seated herself when, with a great growling and scratching of claws, Muggs emerged from under a davenport where he had been quietly hiding all the time, and bit her again. Mother examined the bite and put arnica[2] on it and told Mrs. Detweiler that it was only a bruise. "He just bumped you," she said. But Mrs. Detweiler left the house in a nasty state of mind.

Lots of people reported our Airedale to the police but my father held a municipal office at the time and was on friendly terms with the police. Even so, the cops had been out a couple of times—once when Muggs bit Mrs. Rufus Sturtevant and again when he bit Lieutenant-Governor Malloy—but mother told them that it hadn't been Muggs' fault but the fault of the people who were bitten. "When he starts for them, they scream," she explained, "and that excites him." The cops suggested that it might be a good idea to tie the dog up, but mother said that it mortified him to be tied up and that he wouldn't eat when he was tied up.

Humorous Writing
Which details here suggest that Thurber is satirizing pet owners?

Muggs at his meals was an unusual sight. Because of the fact that if you reached toward the floor he would bite you, we usually put his food plate on top of an old kitchen table with a bench alongside the table. Muggs would stand on the bench and eat. I remember that my mother's Uncle Horatio, who boasted that he was the third man up Missionary Ridge,[3] was splutteringly indignant when he found out that we fed the dog on a table because we were afraid to put his plate on the floor. He said he wasn't afraid of any dog that ever lived and that he would put the dog's plate on the floor if we would give it to him. Roy said that if Uncle Horatio had fed Muggs on the ground just before the battle he would have been the first man up Missionary Ridge. Uncle Horatio was furious. "Bring him in! Bring him in now!" he shouted. "I'll feed the — on the floor!" Roy was all for giving him a chance, but my father wouldn't hear of it. He said that Muggs had already been fed. "I'll feed him again!" bawled Uncle Horatio. We had quite a time quieting him.

In his last year Muggs used to spend practically all of his time outdoors. He didn't like to stay in the house for some reason or other—perhaps it held too many unpleasant memories for him. Anyway, it was hard to get him to come in and as a result the garbage man, the iceman, and the laundryman wouldn't come near the house. We had to haul the garbage down to the corner, take the laundry out and bring it back, and meet the iceman a block from home. After this had gone on for some time we hit on an ingenious arrangement for getting the dog in the house so that we could lock him up while the gas meter was read, and so on. Muggs was afraid of only one thing, an electrical storm. Thunder and lightning frightened him out of his senses (I think he thought a storm had broken the day the mantelpiece fell). He would rush into the house and hide under

Comprehension
Why does Uncle Horatio get angry?

2. **arnica** (är′ ni kə) *n.* preparation once used for treating bruises.
3. **Missionary Ridge** hill near Chattanooga, Tennessee, that was the site of a Civil War battle.

Humorous Writing Why is this anecdote about the thunder machine an example both of hyperbole and of understatement?

a bed or in a clothes closet. So we fixed up a thunder machine out of a long narrow piece of sheet iron with a wooden handle on one end. Mother would shake this vigorously when she wanted to get Muggs into the house. It made an excellent imitation of thunder, but I suppose it was the most roundabout system for running a household that was ever devised. It took a lot out of mother.

A few months before Muggs died, he got to "seeing things." He would rise slowly from the floor, growling low, and stalk stiff-legged and menacing toward nothing at all. Sometimes the Thing would be just a little to the right or left of a visitor. Once a Fuller Brush salesman[4] got hysterics. Muggs came wandering into the room like Hamlet[5] following his father's ghost. His eyes were fixed on a spot just to the left of the Fuller Brush man, who stood it until Muggs was about three slow, creeping paces from him. Then he shouted. Muggs wavered on past him into the hallway grumbling to himself but the Fuller man went on shouting. I think mother had to throw a pan of cold water on him before he stopped. That was the way she used to stop us boys when we got into fights.

Muggs died quite suddenly one night. Mother wanted to bury him in the family lot under a marble stone with some such inscription as "Flights of angels sing thee to thy rest" but we persuaded her it was against the law. In the end we just put up a smooth board above his grave along a lonely road. On the board I wrote with an indelible pencil "Cave Canem."[6] Mother was quite pleased with the simple classic dignity of the old Latin epitaph.

4. **Fuller Brush salesman** salesman for the Fuller Brush Company who went door-to-door demonstrating cleaning equipment; a figure celebrated in comic strips and movies of the 1920s through the 1940s.
5. **Hamlet** the main character of William Shakespeare's play *Hamlet*; in the play, he is visited by the ghost of his murdered father.
6. **"Cave Canem"** (kä´ vä kä´ nem´) Latin for "Beware of the dog."

Critical Thinking

1. **Key Ideas and Details: (a)** Which event was Thurber's "foolhardy" experience with Muggs? **(b) Analyze:** List reactions you expect the family to have to this experience and explain which are missing in the essay.
2. **Key Ideas and Details:** What do other people think of the family's tolerance for Muggs's behavior? Explain.
3. **Craft and Structure: (a)** Is the connotation of Muggs's epitaph positive or negative? **(b)** Is the connotation appropriate? Explain.
4. **Integration of Knowledge and Ideas:** Why does the family keep Muggs despite their knowledge of his bad nature? ***[Connect to the Big Question: What kind of knowledge changes our lives?]***

Comparing Humorous Writing

1. **Craft and Structure (a)** Find an example of **hyperbole** in each work. **(b)** Find an example of **understatement** in each work. **(c)** Compare Twain's and Thurber's use of these devices, explaining which device each writer uses most.
2. **Craft and Structure (a)** Which author treats a potentially serious subject lightly? **(b)** Which treats an ordinary subject with exaggerated seriousness? **(c)** How do the forms—essay and speech—shape the way ideas are presented? Give examples.
3. **Integration of Knowledge and Ideas (a)** Find an example of **satire** in each essay. **(b)** Identify the type of person satirized in each. Do you think satirizing such people is fair or justified? Explain.

A Toast to the Oldest Inhabitant:
The Weather of New England
Mark Twain

The Dog That Bit People
James Thurber

Timed Writing

Explanatory Text: Essay

In an essay, compare how Twain and Thurber use conflict to develop their humorous writing. Analyze how they use hyperbole, understatement, and precise diction to portray those conflicts and make them funny. **(30 minutes)**

5-Minute Planner

1. Read the prompt carefully and completely.
2. Before you write, complete a chart like the one shown to identify each conflict and the comic details that depict it.

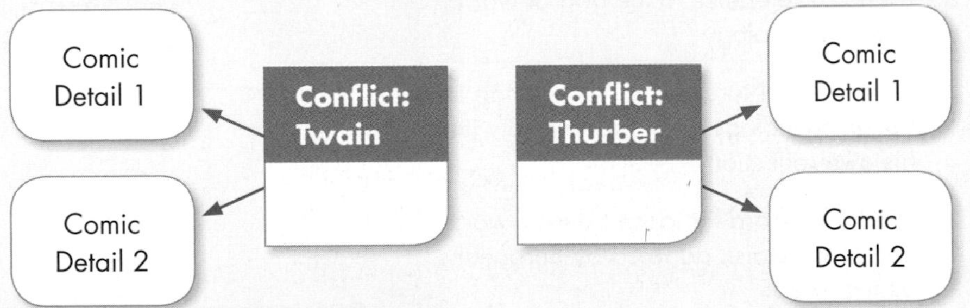

3. Analyze the authors' diction, tone, and use of hyperbole and understatement. Take notes on specific details that support your analysis.
4. Develop an outline logically organizing your points.
5. Reread the prompt, and then draft your essay.

USE ACADEMIC VOCABULARY

As you write, use academic language, including the following words or their related forms:

context
interpretation
manipulate
perspective

For more information about academic vocabulary, see page xlvi.

Language Study

Word Origins: Etymology

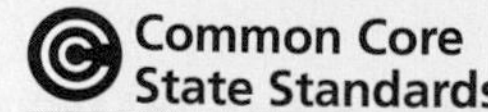

Common Core State Standards

Language

4.c. Consult general and specialized reference materials, both print and digital, to find the pronunciation of a word or determine or clarify its precise meaning, its part of speech, or its etymology.

Words enter the English language from many sources. The **etymology**, or history of a word, can often be traced back through the centuries to its origin in an ancient language. A word's etymology identifies that language of origin and tells how the word's spelling and meaning have changed over time.

English as a language dates back to about the year 500, when Germanic tribes including Angles, Saxons, and Jutes settled in England. This first form of English is known as Old English. In the years following 1066, English changed dramatically as a result of the Norman invasion, which brought Old French to England and produced what we now call Middle English. During a period known as the Renaissance, roughly between 1300 and 1500, there was a renewed interest in the classical languages of Greek and Latin that greatly influenced the English language. As a result, grammar, spelling, and pronunciation changed and Modern English emerged.

Through the centuries, words from other languages continue to be incorporated into English. In some cases, the meanings of these **borrowed words** stay the same as they cross into English. In other cases, they change to take on new meanings.

This chart shows how a few words first entered the English language.

Word	Definition	Origin
Thursday	the fifth day of the week	Old Norse word *Thorsdagr,* which means "Thor's day," a reference to the god of thunder in Norse mythology
martial	of or suitable for war	Latin word *martialis,* which means "of Mars," a reference to the god of war in Roman mythology
narcissistic	showing excessive self-love	reference to Narcissus, a young man in Greek mythology who falls in love with his own reflection
pajamas	night clothes	Hindi; the word for loose trousers worn tied at the waist, adopted by Europeans as nightwear
sleuth	person who follows a trail; detective	Old Norse, from the word for "trail"

Practice A

Look up each of the following words in a print or an online dictionary. Define each word and explain its origin.

1. psyche
2. algebra
3. tycoon
4. anger
5. banjo
6. theater

Practice B

Each numbered question contains a word that has come into the English language from Greek, Latin, or Old Norse. Use a dictionary to find each italicized word's origin and meaning. Then, use that information to answer the question.

1. How did the word *tantalizing* come to mean "tempting" or "enticing"?
2. What qualities does something *titanic* share with the Titans in Greek mythology?
3. What kind of day was the word *dismal* originally used to describe?
4. For which Norse god is *Wednesday* named?
5. What kind of journey is an *odyssey,* and which hero of Greek mythology took this kind of journey?
6. Why is the word *mercurial* used to describe someone who is lively and quick-witted?
7. What does it mean to be part of a *clique*? From where does this term derive?

Activity Use a print or an online dictionary to identify the source of each of the following English words. Then, use a graphic organizer like the one shown to explain how the English word and its source word are related. The first item has been completed as an example.

1. consequence **2.** agony **3.** detour **4.** thespian **5.** pendant

Source Word	Connection	English Word
the Latin word *consequi,* which means "to follow after"	A consequence is a result that follows after a cause.	consequence, which means "outcome or effect"

Comprehension and Collaboration

With a partner, research these words, all of which derive from ancient Greek theater. In writing, explain how each word's theatrical meaning relates to its everyday meaning.

- **catastrophe**
- **antagonist**
- **chorus**

Speaking and Listening

Delivering a Persuasive Speech

A convincing persuasive speech depends on two key elements: strong writing and a powerful delivery. Your words and presentation style must connect with your audience, so use language that is appropriate for your purpose and will engage your listeners.

Common Core State Standards

Writing

1. Write arguments to support claims in an analysis of substantive topics or texts, using valid reasoning and relevant and sufficient evidence.

Speaking and Listening

3. Evaluate a speaker's point of view, reasoning, and use of evidence and rhetoric, identifying any fallacious reasoning or exaggerated or distorted evidence.

4. Present information, findings, and supporting evidence clearly, concisely, and logically such that listeners can follow the line of reasoning and the organization, development, substance, and style are appropriate to purpose, audience, and task.

6. Adapt speech to a variety of contexts and tasks, demonstrating command of formal English when indicated or appropriate.

Learn the Skills

Support your opinion. In a persuasive speech you define and support a claim—your position, or point of view on a topic. Gather supporting evidence, such as facts, expert opinions, expressions of commonly accepted beliefs, and relevant anecdotes. Evaluate your evidence from your audience's point of view. Ensure that your line of reasoning is free of hidden biases, unsupported leaps of logic, too many generalizations, or vague connections.

Consider your purpose. Think about your general purpose—to persuade—as well as your specific goals. For example, you might want to persuade your audience to take a particular action as well as to share your position. Organize your speech in a way that will make it easy for your audience to follow your reasoning.

Use rhetorical devices. Strengthen your argument by using rhetorical devices, such as repetition and parallel structure. Choose words carefully, paying attention to both their sounds and connotations. Work to appeal to your audience's emotions and beliefs while using formal English to maintain their respect.

SAMPLE READER'S SCRIPT

start gradually
The plans for the new park at Elm Street call for a baseball field,‖a playground,‖and a big lawn. It sounds great, but it could be **energetic** better.

There is one thing missing:‖dogs!‖We need a dog run. We do not have a **slower** single public dog run in our city.

‖ = pause

Focus on your opening and closing. Grab your audience's attention in your introduction, and summarize your points in a memorable way in your conclusion.

Prepare a reader's script. Once you have written your speech, plan how you will present it. Mark a copy of your speech to show words you will emphasize and places you will pause, as modeled in the sample reader's script above. Use effective pacing. Slow down to stress key statements; speed up to emphasize emotion. Use a casual tone when telling a personal anecdote. Use a serious tone when quoting an expert.

Establish eye contact. Keep your audience interested by making frequent eye contact. Practice your speech so that it is familiar to you.

Practice the Skills

Presentation of Knowledge and Ideas Use what you have learned in this workshop to perform the following task.

ACTIVITY: **Deliver a Persuasive Speech**

Choose a topic that has two sides. Organize a presentation in which you take a stand. Practice delivering your speech for a classmate. Based on the feedback you receive, revise your presentation. Then, deliver the speech for the full class. Consider the following questions as you develop your speech:

- How clear is the position, point of view, or claim?
- Is the position supported by varied and convincing evidence?
- Is the evidence logically and clearly organized?
- Is the line of reasoning easy for listeners to follow?

As your classmates present their speeches, listen carefully. Use a Presentation Checklist like the one shown to analyze and evaluate their presentations. Then, invite your classmates to use a similar checklist to analyze and evaluate your presentation.

Presentation Checklist

Presentation Content

Did the presentation meet all the requirements of the activity? Check all that apply.

❏ Its organization and style supported the purpose and task.
❏ It did not contain poor logic or hidden biases; the reasoning was logical.
❏ It met all of the criteria listed in the activity assignment.

Presentation Delivery

Did the speaker effectively deliver the speech? Check all that apply.

❏ The speaker used appropriate grammar and language.
❏ The speaker used effective pacing.
❏ The speaker made frequent eye contact with the audience.

Comprehension and Collaboration After all the class members have delivered their speeches, discuss which ones were the most effective and why. Offer positive suggestions for approaches or techniques that will help each student strengthen his or her speaking skills.

Writing Process

Write an Argument

Writing

1. Write arguments to support claims in an analysis of substantive topics or texts, using valid reasoning and relevant and sufficient evidence.

1.a. Introduce precise claim(s), distinguish the claim(s) from alternate or opposing claims, and create an organization that establishes clear relationships among claim(s), counterclaims, reasons, and evidence.

5. Develop and strengthen writing as needed by planning, focusing on addressing what is most significant for a specific purpose and audience.

7. Conduct short as well as more sustained research projects to answer a question or solve a problem; narrow or broaden the inquiry when appropriate; synthesize multiple sources on the subject.

Persuasive Essay

Defining the Form Persuasion is a part of daily life. For example, you might use persuasion to convince a friend to try a new food or volunteer for a cause. To make your case, you might use logic, appeals to your friend's emotions, and evidence that supports your position. When writing persuasively, you apply the same principles, but more formally. In a **persuasive essay,** such as the one you will write in this assignment, a writer tries to convince readers to accept a particular point of view or take a specific action. Other types of persuasive writing include editorials, position papers, letters to the editor, and proposals.

Assignment Write a persuasive essay supporting your position on a current issue that matters to you. Include these elements:

- ✓ a clear description of the issue and a clear, precise *thesis statement that asserts your position, or claim,* about the issue
- ✓ reliable and varied *evidence* that supports and helps to develop your position, or claim
- ✓ *arguments* that acknowledge and refute opposing claims
- ✓ vivid, *persuasive language* that sets a formal *tone* and appeals to your audience
- ✓ a logical *organization* that shows the relationship among claims, counterclaims, and evidence
- ✓ error-free grammar, including *correct use of parallel structures*

To preview the criteria on which your persuasive essay may be judged, see the rubric on page 275.

FOCUS ON RESEARCH

When you write persuasive essays, you might perform research to

- strengthen your claims with reliable facts and data.
- support your position with quotations from experts.
- incorporate more precise and thorough background information that will help readers understand the issue.

Be sure to note all resources you use in your research, and to credit those sources in your final draft. See the Citing Sources pages in the Introductory Unit of this textbook for additional guidance.

READING-WRITING CONNECTION

To get a feel for persuasive writing, read the excerpt from Alexander Solzhenitsyn's "Nobel Lecture" on page 734.

Prewriting/Planning Strategies

Brainstorm and freewrite. Think about topics that cause you and others to argue. Using a chart like the one shown, make a list of the subjects and issues that have prompted debate and circle the one that most intrigues you. Then, freewrite for three minutes about that topic. Review what you have written and circle any strong opinions or clear claims that have emerged. Select the subject with the clearest statement and use it as the starting point for your essay.

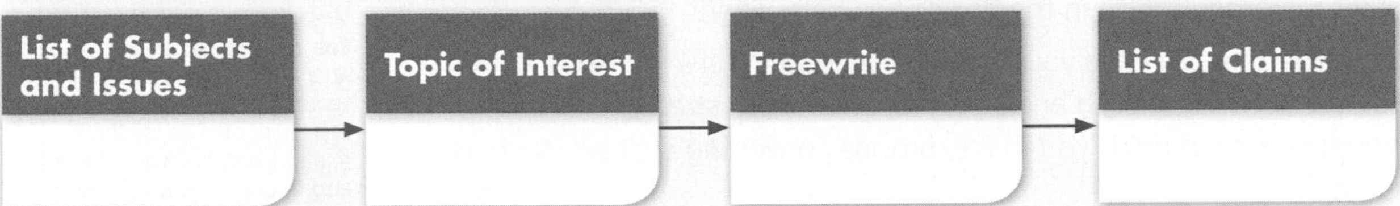

Narrow your inquiry. You may not have enough details about your topic to focus your ideas. More information can help you break the topic into meaningful parts. For example, freedom of speech is far too broad to discuss in a brief essay. However, after you learn more about it, you may choose to narrow your inquiry and research questions and write about balanced reporting in television news. Before you begin your first draft, identify an aspect of the topic that is manageable in the space of your essay.

Look at both sides of the issue. An effective persuasive essay anticipates and addresses differing opinions. It considers the knowledge level and concerns of readers and addresses their expectations. Use a pro-and-con chart like the one shown to identify counterarguments. In the left-hand column, list arguments that support your claim. In the right-hand column, list opposing arguments. Use the chart to brainstorm for ideas, reasons, and evidence that counter the opposing claims.

Pro-and-Con Chart	
Topic: Honor Students Should Be Rewarded	
Supporting	**Opposing**
• Honor-roll students are responsible and dedicated. • They know the material.	• It is unfair to other students. • There would be inequality.

Drafting Strategies

Evaluate your arguments. Write each idea on a separate notecard. Then, consider whether your reasoning is valid and persuasive to your intended audience. Delete cards with faulty ideas that may not persuade readers. Then, organize the cards in order of persuasiveness.

Emphasize your strongest argument. Introduce your topic and state your claim in a precisely worded *thesis statement*. In the body of your essay, support your thesis with arguments and reasons. Use transitions to show the relationships between claims, reasons, and counterclaims and to create cohesion. Finish with a conclusion that urges readers to act. Consider the organization in the box shown below right.

Offer evidence. Develop your claim and counterclaims fairly by providing evidence for each and by pointing out their strengths and limitations. For each point you make, provide convincing *support*, such as these types of evidence:

- **Facts:** information that can be proved true
- **Statistics:** numerical evidence
- **Expert Opinion:** information or quotations from experts
- **Case Studies:** analyses of examples that illustrate your opinions
- **Anecdotes:** relevant experiences or examples that help support your claim

Model: Supporting Opinion With Evidence

Final exams are meant to test students' overall grasp of the course material. However, honor-roll students have already shown that they have mastered the course. School records show over 95% of honor-roll students have a straight "A" average.

Convincing statistical evidence supports the writer's opinion.

Identify your sources. The inclusion of *reliable sources* strengthens your arguments. When you present a fact or detail from your research, use a style guide to correctly provide the source of the information. If you quote someone, use quotation marks. When you use expert opinion, identify the expert and his or her qualifications. In addition, make sure to build a strong link between the quotation and your argument.

Writing

1.a. Introduce precise claim(s), distinguish the claim(s) from alternate or opposing claims, and create an organization that establishes clear relationships among claim(s), counterclaims, reasons, and evidence.

1.b. Develop claim(s) and counterclaims fairly, supplying evidence for each while pointing out the strengths and limitations of both in a manner that anticipates the audience's knowledge level and concerns.

1.c. Use words, phrases, and clauses to link the major sections of the text, create cohesion, and clarify the relationships between claim(s) and reasons, between reasons and evidence, and between claim(s) and counterclaims.

1.e. Provide a concluding statement or section that follows from and supports the argument presented.

Organizing a Persuasive Essay

- Begin with a precise statement of your claim.
- Explain your second-best argument.
- Present and argue against a counterclaim.
- Organize the rest of your arguments in order of persuasiveness.
- End with your best argument.
- Wrap up with a concluding statement that follows from and supports the argument.

Finding Your Voice

Voice is the writer's distinctive "sound" or way of "speaking" on the page. It is created through elements such as word choice, sentence structure, and tone. Voice, in its written form, can be described in the same way the spoken word is described—fast, slow, blunt, and so on. Use the following tips to help you find the appropriate voice for your persuasive essay.

Choose effective words. Before you begin your essay, think about how you want to sound; for example, impassioned, concerned, reasonable, or detached. Your choice of words and the structure of your sentences communicate your voice. Try saying a few sentences aloud. You might tape-record your voice, or have a friend listen to you speak. Then, decide whether the sound of your voice is what you wish to convey on the page. Use a chart like the following to record words or phrases that reflect your voice.

Voice and/or Tone	Words and Phrases
impassioned	*We urgently need...; So much is at stake...*
concerned	*I am concerned...; The problem is serious...*
reasonable	*We all will benefit from...; We have the resources to...; Some people may disagree with me...*

Consider your audience and tone. Employ a voice that is true to who are and that you feel will reach your audience and help to promote your message. Be respectful to those whose opinions may differ. When writing a persuasive essay, your goal is to promote your views with both logic and evidence, so your voice should be thoughtful and respectful. Even if you are passionate about the subject, maintain a reasonable tone.

Revise to create appropriate formality. Check that your tone is polite and your style is appropriately formal. Replace casual language with formal language that still reflects your voice in an authentic way.

Casual: The park's a big old mess.
More Formal: The park is littered with trash.

Revising Strategies

Test your support. Every paragraph in your essay should play a clear role in *supporting your argument*. Use these steps to test each paragraph:

- Underline the sentence that states the main idea of the paragraph. If a topic sentence is missing, consider adding one.
- Put a star next to each sentence that supports the main idea. If a sentence is not starred, consider modifying or deleting it.
- If a topic sentence has fewer than two supporting details, add more evidence or reconsider whether the point is worth including.

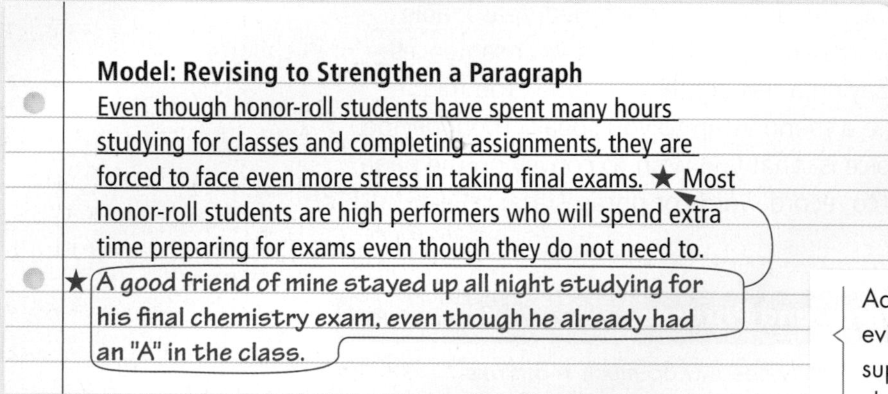

Model: Revising to Strengthen a Paragraph
Even though honor-roll students have spent many hours studying for classes and completing assignments, they are forced to face even more stress in taking final exams. ★ Most honor-roll students are high performers who will spend extra time preparing for exams even though they do not need to.
★ A good friend of mine stayed up all night studying for his final chemistry exam, even though he already had an "A" in the class.

Additional anecdotal evidence helps to support the writer's claim.

Choose powerful words. Clear, strong language will help make your ideas memorable. Consider these options:

- **Comparatives and Superlatives** Comparative adjectives, such as *sharper* and *bolder*, clarify your ideas. Avoid overuse of predictable or subjective superlatives, such as *best*, *smartest*, *strongest*, or *bravest*.
- **Action Verbs** Strong verbs make your ideas more compelling.

  Linking verb: The policy *is* unfair. (weak)

  Action verb: The policy *cheats* us all. (strong)
- **Connotation** Be aware of **connotations**, the emotions a word sparks. Positive connotations can support ideas. Negative connotations can stress drawbacks of opposing arguments, but being overly negative can backfire. A neutral, objective tone shows fair-mindedness.

  Objective: We can look into this problem.

  Positive: We can rise to meet this challenge.

  Negative: We can attempt to approach this impossible task.

Peer Review

Review a classmate's work. Circle ten weak words in your partner's essay. In a peer conference, discuss possible replacements.

Common Core State Standards

Writing

1. Write arguments to support claims in an analysis of substantive topics or texts, using valid reasoning and relevant and sufficient evidence.

1.d. Establish and maintain a formal style and objective tone while attending to the norms and conventions of the discipline.

5. Develop and strengthen writing as needed by planning, revising, editing, rewriting, or trying a new approach, focusing on addressing what is most significant for a specific purpose and audience.

Language

1.a. Use parallel structure.

3. Apply knowledge of language to understand how language functions in different contexts, to make effective choices for meaning or style, and to comprehend more fully when reading or listening.

Revising to Create Parallelism

Parallelism is the use of similar grammatical forms or patterns to express similar ideas. Effective use of parallelism can connect your ideas and make them memorable.

Example: We like running, biking, and playing soccer.

Identifying Faulty Parallelism Parallel constructions place equal ideas in words, phrases, or clauses of similar types. Ideas are not parallel if the grammatical structure shifts.

	Nonparallel	Parallel
use of verb forms	We want to be learning, growing, and to succeed.	We want to learn, to grow, and to succeed.
use of objects	Students benefit from limits that are respectful, reasonable freedoms, and being inspired by classes.	Students benefit from respectful limits, reasonable freedoms, and inspiring classes.

Fixing Errors Follow these steps to revise nonparallel constructions:

1. **Identify similar or equivalent ideas within a sentence.**
2. **Identify the form in which the ideas are expressed.** Then, read the sentence aloud to hear changes in rhythm or pattern.
3. **Rewrite the sentence so that all the elements match the stronger pattern.** Choose forms that produce the smoothest rhythm or require the fewest words. Look at these examples:

   Nouns: hand, heart, and mind

   Verb Forms: to seek, to question, and to learn

   Phrases: defining the borders, preserving our resources, securing the future

   Adverb clauses: wherever we go, whatever we do

   Adjective clauses: who commits, who practices, who focuses
4. **Punctuate correctly.** Use commas to separate three or more words, phrases, or clauses in a parallel series.

Grammar in Your Writing

Review three paragraphs in your essay, circling sentences that present a series of equivalent ideas. If they have varying grammatical structures, revise them to build parallelism.

STUDENT MODEL: **Esther Herrera, Hialeah, FL**

True Reward for Our Achievements

Straight-A students have been rewarded in different ways for their hard work. They have been given the chance to eat breakfast with the principal, they have received gifts and certificates, and they have been publicly acknowledged. Schools hope that these policies will not only serve as a reward to students but also as an inspiration to others to do well in their classes. However, these honor-roll students show little interest in the awards; they want something else. These students should be exempt from taking the final exam because they have demonstrated responsibility and dedication, they know the material, and most importantly they feel that other students will likely be inspired to achieve the ultimate honor-roll goal.

Esther clearly states her opinion on the issue.

Primarily, honor-roll students should be exempt from taking the final exam because they are responsible and dedicated. These students have stayed on task throughout the year, going out of their way to turn in a job well done. Sometimes, they sacrificed by staying up late to finish homework assignments. As one honor student recalled, "One time, I stayed up, literally, all night so that I could finish a project. The problem was not finishing it but making sure that it would come out perfect; it did."

The writer states the argument and then supports it with valid evidence.

In addition, teachers should not have to give these students the final examination. Because they got A's in the first, second, third, and fourth quarters, it is clear that the students know the material very well. Furthermore, the final exam is added stress, because students worry and get nervous taking tests.

On the other hand, eleven out of twenty-five students whom I interviewed believe that such an exemption policy would not be fair to the other students. However, all students were given the same opportunity to get A's. The striking thing about this survey is that many students who were in favor of an exemption policy were not honor students. Instead, they were students who might work harder to earn the privilege of not taking the final exam. What I say to the first eleven students is: Accept the challenge.

By referring to a survey she conducted, Esther shows her research and writes with authority.

Here, the writer addresses those who oppose her ideas.

In conclusion, honor-roll students should be exempt from taking the final exam because they have already proved themselves. These students deserve a true reward: the knowledge that their efforts have been recognized.

Esther restates her opinion in her conclusion.

Common Core State Standards

Writing
6. Use technology, including the Internet, to produce, publish, and update individual or shared writing products, taking advantage of technology's capacity to link to other information and to display information flexibly and dynamically.

Language
2.c. Spell correctly.

Editing and Proofreading

Review your draft to correct errors in grammar, spelling, capitalization, and punctuation.

Focus on spelling. Some vowel sounds in words are silent, which can make correct spelling difficult. Generally, two vowels are used to spell a sound that usually takes only one vowel, as in the final syllable of *porcelain*. If a word gives you problems, create a memory aid to remember the spelling. For example, you may say, "*u* hides in *camouflage*."

Spiral Review
Earlier in the unit, you learned about **active and passive voice** (p. 230). Check your essay to be sure you have used passive voice only when the subject of the sentence receives the action or the performer of an action is unknown.

Publishing and Presenting

Consider one of the following ways to share your writing:

Publish for an audience. If your topic relates to a school or community issue, submit your essay to a school or local newspaper, or post it on a class Web site. If you post on a Web site, create links to relevant information. Update the links when new information becomes available.

Deliver a speech. Use your persuasive essay as the basis for an in-class speech followed by a question-and-answer session. Survey your audience before and after your speech to see if you have changed their minds about your topic. Encourage the entire class to join in the question-and-answer period and clarify, verify, or challenge ideas.

Reflecting on Your Writing

Writer's Journal Jot down your answers to this question:

How did writing about an issue help you better understand it?

Self-Evaluation Rubric

Use the following criteria to evaluate the effectiveness of your essay.

Criteria	Rating Scale
PURPOSE/FOCUS Introduces a precise claim and distinguishes the claim from (implied) alternate or opposing claims; provides a concluding section that follows from and supports the argument presented	*not very* .... *very* 1 2 3 4
ORGANIZATION Establishes a logical organization; uses words, phrases and clauses to link the major sections of the text, create cohesion, and clarify relationships among claims, reasons, and evidence, and between claims and counterclaims	1 2 3 4
DEVELOPMENT OF IDEAS/ELABORATION Develops the claim and counterclaims fairly, supplying evidence for each while pointing out the strengths and limitations of both	1 2 3 4
LANGUAGE Establishes and maintains a formal style and objective tone	1 2 3 4
CONVENTIONS: Attends to the norms and conventions of the discipline	1 2 3 4

Assessment: Skills

SELECTED RESPONSE

Common Core State Standards

RI.9-10.1, RI.9-10.2, RI.9-10.4, RI.9-10.6; W.9-10.5, W.9-10.10; L.9-10.4.a

[For full standards wording, see the chart in the front of this book.]

I. Reading Literature/Informational Text

Directions: *Read the excerpt from "Editorial on the Anniversary of the Fall of the Berlin Wall" from* The New York Times, *November 10, 1999. Then, answer each question that follows.*

The Berlin Wall was bound to fall eventually. But that it came down as bloodlessly as it did 10 years ago this week is largely a tribute to one leader. Today Mikhail Gorbachev is a political pariah in Russia and increasingly forgotten in the West. But history will remember him generously for his crucial role in ending the cold war and pulling back the Iron Curtain that Stalin drew across Europe in 1945.

Liquidating the Soviet empire was not what Mr. Gorbachev had in mind when he came to power in 1985. He was shrewd enough to recognize that radical changes were urgently needed to stave off economic and political bankruptcy in Russia and its European satellites....

Once Mr. Gorbachev lifted the lid with the openness of glasnost and the attempted economic restructuring of perestroika, change took on a dynamic of its own. Similar energies were unleashed in the once-captive nations of Eastern Europe as it became clear that he would not send Soviet tanks to bail out the unpopular client regimes that had held sway there since World War II.

As political pressures began to build in the late 1980's, Mr. Gorbachev was left with two options. He could hurtle ahead toward full political and economic freedom. Or he could reverse course and crack down, as so many previous Soviet leaders had done. He chose to do neither. He was too much a creature of his Soviet Communist upbringing to subject his own power to the test of electoral democracy. But he was too enlightened to unleash the kind of thorough repression that might have preserved the Soviet empire for a few more years.

Others stepped in to accelerate the transformations Mr. Gorbachev had begun, and in 1989 the fixtures of the Soviet empire began to crumble....

Through it all, Mr. Gorbachev and his like-minded foreign minister, Eduard Shevardnadze, stayed their hand, reflecting not only their idealism about reshaping East-West relations but also a pragmatic calculation that the Soviet Union could no longer afford an empire. For permitting its dissolution, Mr. Gorbachev paid a high price. Within two years he had been pushed from power in Moscow....

History has passed Mr. Gorbachev by. But this week, especially, he deserves to be remembered for what he did and, perhaps more important, what he refused to do. With a wisdom and decency that is sadly rare in international power politics, he chose not to defend a dying system with a final, futile spasm of murderous force.

1. **Part A** Which of the following statements is a **claim** made in the excerpt?

   A. Gorbachev did not play an important role in the fall of the Berlin Wall.
   B. Gorbachev was disliked as a leader and will not be remembered.
   C. Gorbachev should be celebrated for what he did while in power.
   D. Gorbachev's greatest achievement was preserving the Soviet empire.

   Part B What evidence is used to support the claim?

   A. statistics on the number of people who disliked Gorbachev
   B. examples of Gorbachev's contributions
   C. reasons why the Berlin Wall would have fallen without Gorbachev's involvement
   D. expert opinions on Gorbachev's achievements

2. Which word best describes the **tone** of this passage?

   A. uncertain
   B. amused
   C. angry
   D. scholarly

3. Which answer choice most accurately describes the organizational structure of the editorial?

   A. chronological order
   B. comparison-and-contrast organization
   C. list organization
   D. problem-and-solution organization

4. Which **rhetorical device** is used in the following passage from the editorial?

   > ...he deserves to be remembered for what he did and, perhaps most important, what he refused to do.

   A. a slogan
   B. a rhetorical question
   C. repetition
   D. parallelism

5. What is the main **purpose** of this passage?

   A. to analyze a text
   B. to tell a story
   C. to persuade
   D. to entertain

6. Which words best describe the **diction**, or word choice, used in the passage?

   A. basic, elementary
   B. vague, unclear
   C. colloquial, slangy
   D. formal, sophisticated

7. **Part A** Which is the best definition of the underlined word *regimes* as it is used in the text?

   A. natural borders of countries
   B. often oppressive systems of government
   C. classic examples of architecture
   D. healthy types of routines

   Part B Which answer choice lists the context clues that best clarify the meaning of *regimes*?

   A. once-captive nations; held sway
   B. economic; perestroika
   C. similar energies; unleashed
   D. bail out; since World War II

Timed Writing

8. Write a response to the editorial in which you use **rhetorical devices.** Define the rhetorical devices you use and describe how they create emphasis or appeal to emotions. Be sure to follow the conventions of standard English.

II. Reading Functional Texts

Directions: *Read the passage. Then, answer each question that follows.*

Common Core State Standards

RI.9-10.1, RI.9-10.4; W.9-10.5; L.9-10.1, L.9-10.4.a

[For full standards wording, see the chart in the front of this book.]

Using the Easy Smoothie Maker

Now create a nutritious, energy-packed smoothie in just a few seconds.

Read Safety Precautions Before Operation

- Do not immerse cord or base in water.
- Operate only on a clean, flat surface.
- Handle the cutting blade assembly carefully to avoid injury.

Before beginning—

- Wash the blade assembly and Smoothie Cup in warm soapy water before using.
- Firmly place the four rubber suction cups on the feet of the base.

To create your own delicious smoothie—

1) Place the base on the counter, pressing firmly to secure the suction cups.
   - Make sure the counter is free of water or grease.
   - Do NOT plug in the Easy Smoothie Maker until it is completely assembled.
2) Place ingredients in the Smoothie Cup and screw on the cutting blade assembly.
   - Place the solid ingredients in the Smoothie Cup, and then add milk or yogurt.
   - Screw the cutting blade assembly on top of the filled Smoothie Cup.
3) Set the filled Smoothie Cup on the base and engage the motor.
   - Turn the Smoothie Cup over and place on the base, clicking it into place.
   - Plug in the base and press the "on" button for 10 seconds.
   - Remove the Smoothie Cup from the base, unscrew the blade assembly, and enjoy!

1. According to the directions, which of the following items should you handle carefully?

A. the base
B. the blade assembly
C. milk or yogurt
D. the suction cups

2. Which answer choice is the best definition of the underlined word *assembly* as it is used in the passage?

A. a collection of parts put together
B. a protective cover
C. a bundle of electrical wires
D. a box used to store small pieces

3. According to the directions, when should the Smoothie Maker be plugged in?

A. before adding the ingredients
B. after unscrewing the blade assembly
C. before screwing on the cutting blade
D. after placing the filled cup on the base

III. Writing and Language Conventions

Directions: *Read the passage. Then, answer each question that follows.*

(1) My dad and I had looked forward to our camping trip in the mountains for weeks. (2) Charlie, the family's black Labrador pup, was going along. (3) It was our first visit to the mountains.

(4) Our campsite was lined with fragrant green pines. (5) The scenery impressed me. (6) I inhaled the fresh mountain air. (7) Then, I grabbed my fishing tackle, and I strolled down the path to the lake with my dog. (8) Charlie ran after me, ready for fun.

(9) "Watch out for bears, Joe," Dad called.

(10) "Thanks for the reminder!" I said. (11) As I rounded a bend, though, right in front of me was a small black bear ambling along the path. (12) Charlie's fur bristled, his senses on full predator alert. (13) The bear stopped cold and stared hard. (14) I froze. (15) I held my breath until the bear finally turned and hurried off down the path.

(16) A lot of camping has been done since then, but the excitement of that first trip will never be forgotten.

1. Which of the following sentences contains a **linking verb?**
   - **A.** sentence 3
   - **B.** sentence 5
   - **C.** sentence 8
   - **D.** sentence 9

2. Which revision of sentence 5 contains a **subject complement?**
   - **A.** Impressive scenery surrounded me.
   - **B.** The scenery was impressive.
   - **C.** The scenery impressed me.
   - **D.** I saw impressive scenery.

3. Which type of **verb** is used in sentence 6?
   - **A.** linking
   - **B.** active
   - **C.** future tense
   - **D.** present tense

4. Which of the following statements is the *best* way to rewrite sentence 16 in the **active voice?**
   - **A.** Camping has been done a lot since then, but the excitement of that first trip is never forgotten.
   - **B.** Since then, a lot of camping has been done, but the excitement of the first trip will be remembered.
   - **C.** I've done a lot of camping since then, but I'll never forget the excitement of that first trip.
   - **D.** The excitement of that first trip is still remembered even though so much camping has happened since then.

5. Which sentence uses the **passive voice?**
   - **A.** sentence 1
   - **B.** sentence 2
   - **C.** sentence 3
   - **D.** sentence 4

CONSTRUCTED RESPONSE

Directions: *Follow the instructions to complete the tasks below as required by your teacher.*

As you work on each task, incorporate both general academic vocabulary and literary terms you learned in Parts 1 and 2 of this unit.

RI.9-10.2, RI.9-10.3, RI.9-10.4, RI.9-10.5, RI.9-10.6, RI.9-10.8; W.9-10.7, W.9-10.8, W.9-10.9.b; SL.9-10.4; L.9-10.1.a, L.9-10.2.c
[For full standards wording, see the chart in the front of this book.]

Writing

TASK 1 Informational Text [RI.9-10.6; L.9-10.2.c.]

Determine an Author's Point of View and Analyze Use of Rhetorical Devices

Write an essay in which you determine an author's point of view and analyze his or her use of rhetorical devices in an essay from Part 2 of this unit.

- Describe the author's point of view and explain how it affects his or her discussion of the topic.
- Discuss specific ways in which the author's use of rhetorical devices advances his or her point of view.
- Cite specific examples from the text to support your analysis.
- Edit your essay for correct capitalization and punctuation. Ensure that words are spelled correctly.

TASK 2 Informational Text [RI.9-10.8]

Analyze an Argument

Write an essay in which you evaluate the argument in a persuasive work from Part 2 of this unit.

- Present the author's argument, delineating both his or her specific claims and supporting evidence.
- Determine whether the author's argument is sound, the reasoning valid, and the evidence both relevant and sufficient.
- Identify any faulty reasoning or fallacious arguments in the work. Explain your position and provide evidence from the text to support your ideas.
- Follow your class style guide when quoting sentences or short paragraphs from the text.

TASK 3 Informational Text [RI.9-10.3, RI.9-10.5]

Analyze the Organization of Ideas

Write an essay in which you analyze the organization of ideas in a nonfiction work from this unit.

Part 1

- Review and evaluate the order of ideas in an informational text from this unit.
- As you are reviewing the text, make notes on the overall structure of the work, including the order in which supporting ideas are introduced.
- Answer the following questions:
  What specific structural choices does the writer make?
  How does the writer connect ideas?

Part 2

- Write an essay in which you explain how the writer organizes sections, paragraphs, and individual sentences to develop key points and establish a logical flow of ideas.
- Maintain a consistent style and formal tone throughout your essay.
- Be sure to cite specific and relevant examples from the text.

Speaking and Listening

TASK 4 Informational Text [RI.9-10.6; SL.9-10.4]

Analyze an Author's Purpose

Deliver a speech in which you analyze an author's purpose in one work from Part 2 of this unit.

- Provide both a brief summary of the work and basic information about the author, including the era in which he or she wrote and his or her style and customary topics.
- Describe the author's purpose for writing this work. Explain specific concepts, attitudes, or feelings you think the author wanted to convey. Cite details from the work to support your thinking.
- Note specific ways in which the author uses rhetoric to support his or her purpose, and evaluate its effectiveness.
- Present your findings and supporting evidence clearly so that your audience can follow your reasoning.

TASK 5 Informational Text [RI.9-10.4; SL.9-10.4; L.9-10.1.a]

Analyze the Effect of Word Choice on Tone

Deliver an oral presentation in which you analyze the effect of word choice on tone in two works from Part 2 of this unit.

- Choose two works that offer clear and distinct tones. Explain your choices, describing how the tones of the two works differ.
- Identify specific word choices from each work and explain how these choices affect both meaning and tone.
- Use a graphic organizer to show how the tones of the two works differ.
- Present your ideas clearly and concisely so that your listeners can follow your reasoning.
- Use parallel structures to help engage your listeners.

Research

TASK 6 Informational Text [RI.9-10.2; W.9-10.7, W.9-10.8, W.9-10.9.b]

What kind of knowledge changes our lives?

In Part 2 of this unit, you have read texts that explore the importance of knowledge. Now you will conduct a short research project on the knowledge you will need to be successful in a career. Choose a field that interests you and learn what sort of training and knowledge that career requires. Use the texts you have read in Part 2 of this unit as well as your research to reflect on and write about this unit's Big Question. Review the following guidelines before you begin your research:

- Focus your research on one career and the knowledge needed to be successful in that life path.
- Gather information from at least two reliable sources. Your sources may be print or digital.
- Take notes as you investigate the knowledge requirements for the particular career you chose.
- Cite your sources.

When you have completed your research, write a brief essay in response to the Big Question. Present your information and then discuss how your initial ideas have either changed or been reinforced. Refer to at least one example from a text you have read in Part 2 of this unit and one example from your research.

"At the **moment** of vision,
the eye sees **nothing**."
—William Golding

PART 3
TEXT SET DEVELOPING INSIGHT

VISION

The readings in this section raise questions about what we really see when we look at the world. Ranging from explanations of physical sight to discussions about maps, media, painting, and sculpture, these texts explore the connections between seeing and interpreting. As you read these selections, consider what they suggest about vision and perception. Then, think about how vision and perception relate to the Big Question for this unit: **What kind of knowledge changes our lives?** What are the connections between what we see, what we perceive, and what we know?

◀ CRITICAL VIEWING In what ways does this photograph trick the eye? How many different perspectives does it capture?

CLOSE READING TOOL

Use the **Close Reading Tool** to practice the strategies you learn in this unit.

READINGS IN PART 3

Marilyn Monroe, Andy Warhol. © Andy Warhol Foundation.

Marilyn Monroe, Andy Warhol. © Andy Warhol Foundation.

HOW TO REACT to FAMILIAR FACES

Umberto Eco

A few months ago, as I was strolling in New York, I saw, at a distance, a man I knew very well heading in my direction. The trouble was that I couldn't remember his name or where I had met him. This is one of those sensations you encounter especially when, in a foreign city, you run into someone you met back home, or vice versa. A face out of **context** creates confusion. Still, that face was so familiar that, I felt, I should certainly stop, greet him, converse; perhaps he would immediately respond, "My dear Umberto, how are you?" or "Were you able to do that thing you were telling me about?" And I would be at a total loss. It was too late to flee. He was still looking at the opposite side of the street, but now he was beginning to turn his eyes towards me. I might as well make the first move; I would wave and then, from his voice, his first remarks, I would try to guess his identity.

We were now only a few feet from each other, I was just about to break into a broad, radiant smile, when suddenly I recognized him. It was Anthony Quinn.[1] Naturally, I had never met him in my life, nor he me. In a thousandth of a second I was able to check myself, and I walked past him, my eyes staring into space.

Afterwards, reflecting on this incident, I realized how totally normal it was. Once before, in a restaurant, I had glimpsed Charlton Heston[2] and had felt an impulse to say hello. These faces inhabit our memory; watching the screen, we spend so many hours with them that they are as familiar to us as our relatives', even more so. You can be a student of mass communication, debate the effects of reality, or the confusion between the real and the imagined, and **expound** the way some people fall permanently into this confusion; but still you are not immune to the syndrome.[3] And there is worse.

context (kän′ tekst′) *n.* situation in which something is found

expound (ek spound′) *v.* explain in detail

1. **Anthony Quinn** (1915–2001) was a film actor who won two Academy Awards.
2. **Charlton Heston** (1923–2008) was a film actor who won an Academy Award for his role in the film *Ben-Hur.*
3. **syndrome** (sin′ drōm′) *n.* set of symptoms or characteristics occurring together and defining a disease or condition.

Close Reading Activities

READ

Comprehension

Reread all or part of the text to help you answer the following questions.

1. What mistaken impression does the author have when he first sees Anthony Quinn?
2. According to Eco, why do people feel they know someone they have seen on TV or in movies?
3. What complaint does Eco hear from people who appear often on television?
4. According to Eco, how does the "reality" of TV change how people see the everyday world?

Research: Clarify Details This essay may include references that are unfamiliar to you. Choose at least one of these details and briefly research it. Then, write a paragraph in which you explain how the information you learned from research sheds light on an aspect of the essay.

Summarize Write an objective summary of the essay. Remember that an objective summary is free from opinion and evaluation.

Language Study

Selection Vocabulary The following passages appear in this essay. Explain the meaning of each boldfaced word and identify a synonym. Then, use the word in a sentence of your own.

- A face out of **context** creates confusion.
- You can be a student of mass communication, debate the... confusion between the real and imagined, and **expound** the way some people fall permanently into this confusion...
- And they continue their conversation **amiably**...

Diction and Style Study the following sentence from the essay. Then, answer the questions.

> I have received confidences from people who, appearing fairly frequently on TV, have been subjected to the mass media over a certain period of time.

1. **(a)** What does *confidences* mean in this sentence? **(b)** Identify two other words Eco might have chosen instead of *confidences*. **(c)** How would those other choices affect the meaning of the passage? Explain.
2. What does Eco's use of the word *subjected* tell you about his attitude toward media? Explain.

Conventions Read this sentence from the selection. Identify the part of the sentence that displays parallelism, and the part that does not. Explain how parallelism helps to clarify Eco's meaning and how the part that is not parallel creates emphasis.

> You can be a student of mass communication, debate the effects of reality, or the confusion between the real and the imagined, and expound the way some people fall permanently into this confusion; but still you are not immune to the syndrome.

Academic Vocabulary

The following words appear in blue in the instructions and questions on the facing page.

multitudes **overall** **distortion**

Copy the words into your notebook. Use a dictionary to identify the meaning of each word. Then, use each word in a sentence.

Literary Analysis

Reread the identified passages. Then, respond to the questions that follow.

Focus Passage 1 *(p. 285)*
A few months ago . . . staring into space.

Key Ideas and Details

1. **(a) Connect:** To what "sensation" is Eco referring in the third sentence? **(b) Interpret:** According to Eco, why is this "sensation" a problem when it is experienced "out of context"?
2. **Infer:** Why did Eco choose to turn away rather than greet the person he recognized? Explain.

Craft and Structure

3. This entire passage can be considered an anecdote, or brief story that makes a point. **(a) Interpret:** What is Eco's main point in this passage? **(b) Analyze:** Explain why Eco's use of an anecdote is an effective way to make that point.
4. **Interpret:** Eco includes an imagined conversation in this anecdote. How does this use of dialogue make his confusion clearer for the reader?

Integration of Knowledge and Ideas

5. **Connect:** Eco includes himself among the **multitudes** who are sometimes affected by a confusion between media and reality. Explain why this approach to the topic is effective.

Focus Passage 2 *(p. 286)*
Such people . . . about my business.)

Key Ideas and Details

1. What is the "world of images" Eco describes?
2. **(a)** According to Eco, how does the "mass media's imaginary world" relate to "real life"? **(b) Connect:** In Eco's view, how does that relationship contribute to the reactions people have when they encounter celebrities? Explain.

Craft and Structure

3. **(a) Interpret:** In what context is the word "protagonist" usually used? Explain. **(b) Analyze:** How does this word choice contribute to Eco's central idea?
4. **Analyze:** Eco describes an imaginary scene, including dialogue: "And you know something? He seems real!" How does this little scene both add humor and clarify Eco's **overall** point?

Integration of Knowledge and Ideas

5. **Summarize:** According to the author, what causes the **distortion** in people's perceptions when a face familiar from media appears in the real world?

Cultural Context

Cultural context refers to the traditions, beliefs, and history of the society from which an author hails or within which a literary work is set. The author's cultural context shapes his or her approach to a topic and the reader's cultural context influences his or her perceptions of a work. Reread the selection, and take notes on details that reveal the cultural context.

1. Cite at least two details in this essay that show its modern, urban cultural context.
2. **(a)** What types of cultural experience must a reader have in order to appreciate this essay? **(b)** Does the author expect readers to share his cultural context? Explain, citing details from the essay.
3. **Vision:** Based on your interpretation of the essay, explain how cultural context affects what people perceive as either real or imaginary.

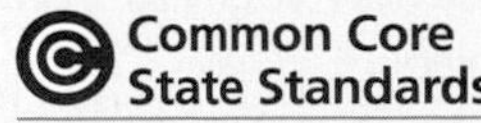

Common Core State Standards

RI.9-10.1, RI.9-10.2, RI.9-10.3, RI.9-10.4, RI.9-10.5, RI.9-10.6; L.9-10.1.a, L.9-10.4, L.9-10.5, L.9-10.6
[For full standards wording, see the chart in the front of this book.]

DISCUSS

From Text to Topic **Debate**

Debate the following passage with a group of classmates. Come to an agreement about the mass media's portrayal of reality.

> The mass media first convinced us that the imaginary was real, and now they are convincing us that the real is imaginary; and the more reality the TV screen shows us, the more cinematic our everyday world becomes.

QUESTIONS FOR DISCUSSION:

1. Are most people unable to distinguish what is real from what is imaginary on TV?
2. Why might it be a bad idea to deal with serious issues as they are dealt with on TV?
3. Does "reality TV" influence the way we see reality itself?

WRITE

Writing to Sources **Argumentative Text**

Assignment

Write a **persuasive essay** about the effects of media on viewers' perceptions of reality. Support your stance with details from Eco's essay and with your own observations and examples from current media.

Prewriting and Planning Reread the selection, looking for details that Eco uses to support his argument. Take careful notes of your observations.

Drafting Consider using either chronological order or order of importance organization to structure your ideas.

- With **chronological order** you describe the sequence of events that lead to a situation or result. This structure can clarify causes and effects.
- With **order of importance organization** you state your least important claim first and end with your most important claim.

Regardless of the organizational structure you choose, weave in details and examples to support every claim.

Revising Circle the claim you make in each paragraph and underline the details that support it. If your support is insufficient or weak, add stronger evidence. In addition, use transitions, such as the following words and phrases, to connect your claims and evidence.

for example	*as an illustration*	*for instance*	*in particular*
to clarify	*thus*	*in other words*	*specifically*

Editing and Proofreading Review your draft and change any inappropriate uses of passive voice to active voice.

Passive Voice: Entertainment magazines are read by many people.
Active Voice: Many people read entertainment magazines.

CONVENTIONS

Passive voice is appropriate only when the subject receives the action of the verb or is unknown. If the subject is actually doing something, use active voice.

RESEARCH

Research **Investigate the Topic**

Mass Media and "Seeing" Eco makes the point that mass media influences our interpretation of what we see in everyday life. For example, events that occur during a competitive reality show may alter people's perception of what is fair or honest behavior. Products used by characters in the movies or on TV may be seen as preferable to similar products. Some studies suggest that violence in mass media may desensitize people to violence in real life.

Assignment

Conduct research to learn what social scientists have to say about the influence of media on people's perceptions. Consult scholarly journals, university Web sites, and reliable magazines. Take clear notes and carefully record your sources so that you can easily access the information later. Share your findings in a **multimedia presentation**.

PREPARATION FOR ESSAY

You may use the knowledge you gain during this research assignment in an essay you will write at the end of this section.

Gather Sources Locate authoritative sources, both print and electronic. Scholarly articles and research reports by social scientists are very precise and detailed. You may also consult secondary sources, such as popular magazine articles, that summarize expert findings. Look for sources that feature experts and current information. Locate video or audio selections that will enhance your topic.

Take Notes Take notes on each source, either electronically or on note cards. Use an organized note-taking strategy.

- Write the main idea at the top of each card or note. Create a new note for each new idea, even if it is from the same source.
- Copy relevant quotes that you can use in your presentation. Be sure to use quotation marks and carefully document the source of each quote.
- Electronically save photographs, audio clips, or video clips you might include in your presentation. Write the source information on a separate list.
- Use an accepted style for citations to record all source information

Synthesize Multiple Sources Assemble data from your sources and use it to draw conclusions about how mass media influences the way people view the world. Use your notes to write an outline for your presentation. Decide where you will include photos, video, or audio clips to add interest and support your ideas. Create a Works Cited list and convert the list to a slide to include at the end of your presentation. See the Citing Sources pages in the Introductory Unit of this textbook for additional guidance.

Organize and Present Ideas Obtain whatever equipment you need for your presentation in advance. Review your outline and practice delivering your presentation. Be ready to answer questions from your audience.

Common Core State Standards

W.9-10.1.a, W.9-10.1.c, W.9-10.4, W.9-10.5, W.9-10.6, W.9-10.7, W.9-10.8; SL.9-10.1, SL.9-10.4, SL.9-10.5; L.9-10.3, L.9-10.3.a

[For full standards wording, see the chart in the front of this book.]

NOVEL EXCERPT

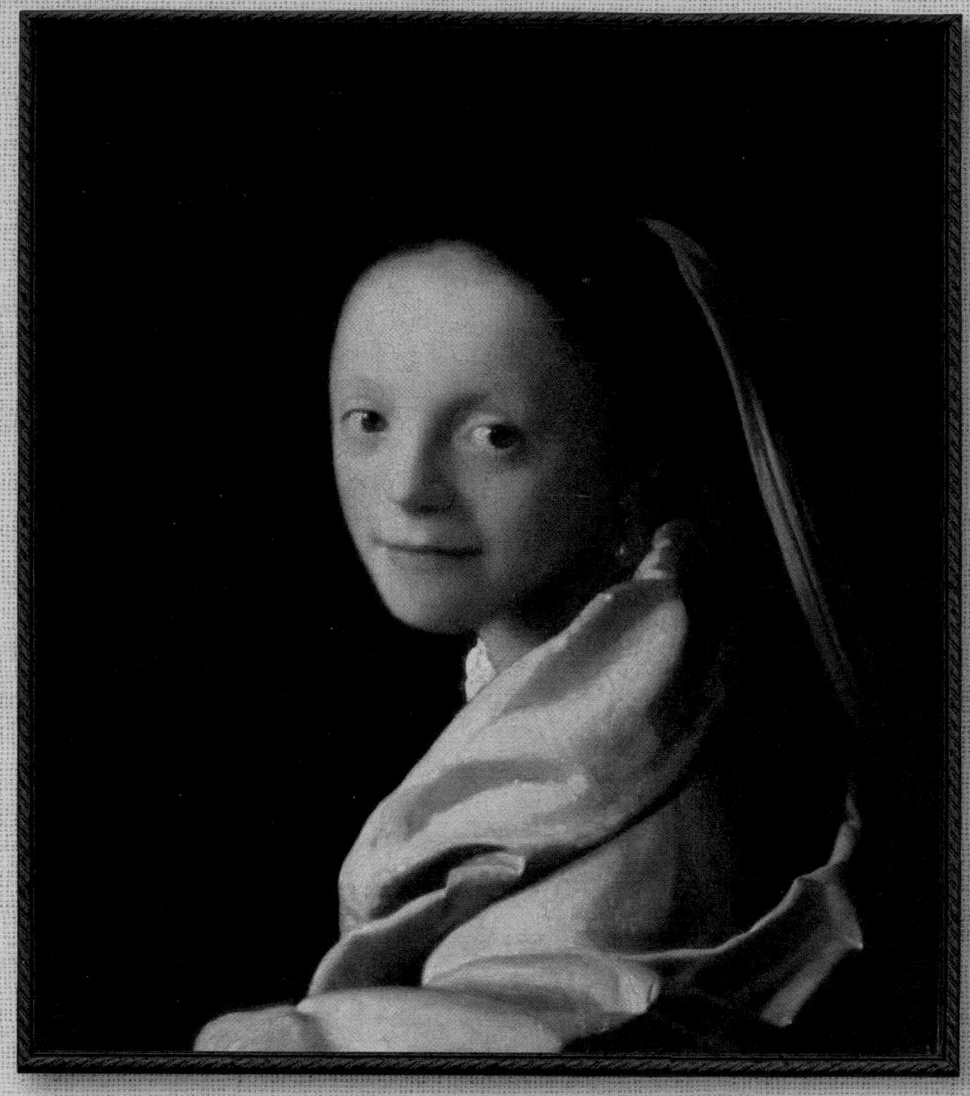

from Magdalena Looking

by Susan Vreeland

This selection is an excerpt from the novel* Girl in Hyacinth Blue*, a work of historical fiction. The main character is Magdalena, the fictional daughter of artist Johannes Vermeer. Vermeer (1632–1675) was a real person—a famous painter who lived in Delft, a city in the Netherlands.

Late one afternoon when Magdalena finished the clothes washing and her mother let her go out, she ran from their house by the Nieuwe Kerk across the market square, past van Buyten's bakery, over two cobbled bridges across the canals, past the blacksmith's all the way to Kethelstraat and the town wall where she climbed up and up the ochre stone steps, each one as high as her knee, to her favorite spot in all of Delft,[1] the round sentry post. From that great height, oh, what she could see. If only she could paint it. In one direction Schiedam Gate and beyond it the twin towers of Rotterdam Gate, and ships with odd-shaped sails the color of brown eggshells coming up the great Schie River from the sea, and in another direction strips of potato fields with wooden plows casting shadows over the soil like long fingers, and orchards, rows of rounded green as ordered as Mother wished their eleven young lives to be, and the smoke of the potteries and brickeries, and beyond that, she didn't know. She didn't know.

She stood there looking, looking, and behind her she heard the creak and thrum of the south windmill turning like her heart in the sea wind, and she breathed the brine[2] that had washed here from other shores. Below her the Schie lay like a pale yellow ribbon along the town wall. The longer she looked, the more it seemed to borrow its color from the sky. In the wind, the boats along the Schie docks with their fasteners clanking and their hollow bellies nudging one

1. **Nieuwe Kerk** (nü´ e kārk) **. . . van Buyten's** (fän bī ´ tens) **. . . Kethelstraat** (kā´ tel strät) **. . . Delft . . .** Nieuwe *Kerk* means "New Church"; Kethelstraat is a street in the city; Delft is a manufacturing city on the Schie River in the Netherlands.
2. **brine** (brīn) *saltwater.*

◀ *Portrait of a Young Woman* (also known as *Study of a Young Woman*, or *Girl with a Veil)* by Johannes Vermeer; oil on canvas; c. 1665–67 another made a kind of low rattling music she loved. It wasn't just today. She loved the sentry post in every kind of weather. To see rain pocking the gray sea and shimmering the stone bridge, to feel its cold strings of water on her face and hands, filled her to bursting.

She moved to a notch in the wall and just then a gust of wind lifted her skirts. The men on the bridge waiting with their bundles to go to sea shouted something in words she did not understand. She'd never tell Mother. Mother did not want her going there. The sentry post was full of guards smoking tobacco, Mother had said. There was some dark thing in her voice, as though she thought Magdalena should be afraid, but Magdalena did not know how to feel that then, or there.

Up there, high up above the town, she had longings no one in the family knew. No one would ever know them, she thought, unless perhaps a soul would read her face or she herself would have soul enough to speak of them. Wishes had the power to knock the breath out of her. Some were large and throbbing and persistent, some mere pinpricks of golden light, short-lived as fireflies but keenly felt. She wished for her chores to be done so she'd have time to race to the town wall every day before supper, or to the Oude Kerk[3] to lift the fallen leaves from her brother's grave. She wished her baby sisters wouldn't cry so, and the boys wouldn't quarrel and wrestle underfoot or run shouting through the house. Father wished that too, she knew. She wished there were not so many bowls to wash, thirteen each meal. She wished her hair shone **flaxen** in the sunlight of the market square like little Geertruida's.[4] She wished she could travel in a carriage across borders to all the lands drawn on her father's map.

flaxen ▶
(flak′ sən) *adj.*
light yellow

She wished the grocer wouldn't treat her so gruffly when he saw her hand open out to offer four guilders,[5] all that her mother gave her to pay the grocery bill that was mounting into the hundreds, as far as she could tell. She wished he wouldn't shout; it sent his garlic breath straight into her nostrils. The baker, Hendrick van Buyten, was kinder. Two times so far he let Father pay with a painting so they could start over. Sometimes he gave her a still-warm bun to eat while walking home. And sometimes he put a curl of honey on it. She wished the grocer was like him.

She wished Father would take the iceboat to the Schie more often. He'd bought a fine one with a tall ivory sail. "Eighty guilders," Mother grumbled. "Better a winter's worth of bread and meat." On winter Sundays if the weather was clear, and if he was between paintings, it whisked them skimming across the white glass of the canal. She'd never known such speed. The sharp cold air blew life and hope and excitement into her ears and open mouth.

---

3. **Oude Kerk** (ou′ de kärk) *Oude Kerk* means "Old Church."
4. **Geertruida's** (kher trī′ das)
5. **guilders** (gil′ dərz) *n.* The guilder is the basic unit of Dutch currency.

She remembered wishing, one particular morning when Father mixed lead white with the smallest dot of lead-tin yellow[6] for the goose quill in a painting of Mother writing a letter, that she might someday have someone to write to, that she could write at the end of a letter full of love and news, "As ever, your loving Magdalena Elisabeth."

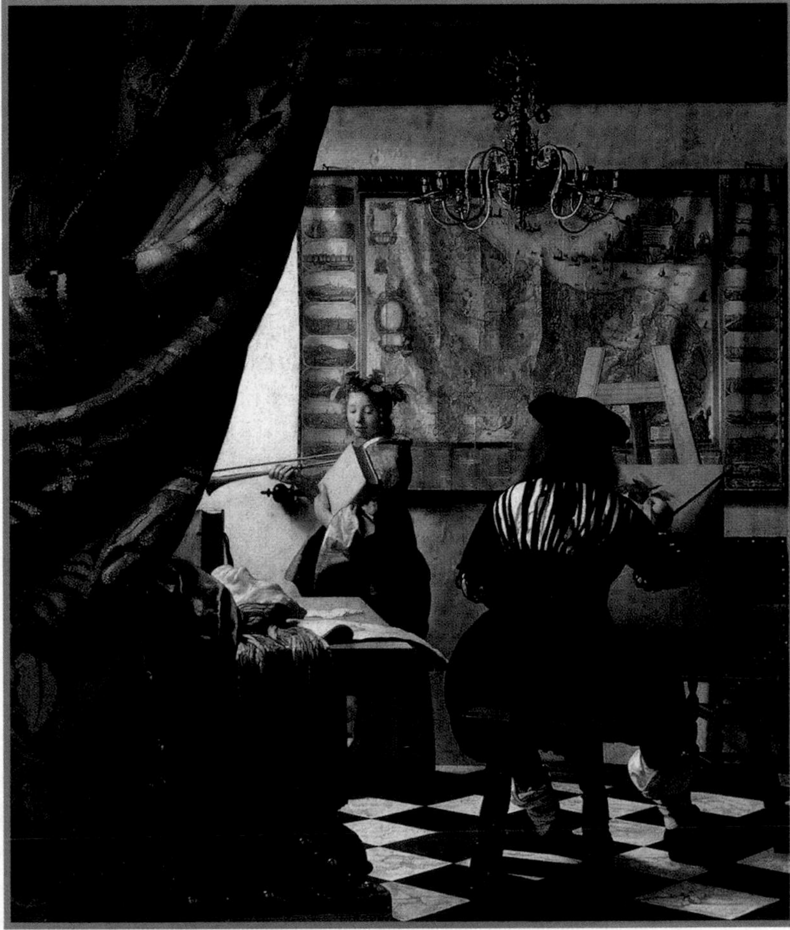

The Art of Painting (also known as *The Allegory of Painting)* by Johannes Vermeer; oil on canvas; c. 1666

He painted Mother often, and Maria he painted once, draped her head in a golden mantle and her shoulders in a white satin shawl. She was older, fifteen, though only by eleven months. It might be fun to dress up like Maria did, and wear pearl earrings and have Father position her just so, but the only part she really wished for was that he would look and look and pay attention.

More than all those wishes, she had one pulsing wish that outshone all the others. She wished to paint. Yes, me, she thought, leaning out over the stone wall. I want to paint. This and everything. The world from that vantage point stretched so grandly. Up there, beauty was more than color and shapes, but openness, light, the air itself, and because of that, it seemed untouchable. If only the act of wishing would make her able. Father only smiled queerly when she told him she wanted to paint, just as if she'd said she wanted to sail the seas, which, of course, she also wished, in order to paint what she would see. When she said so, that she wished to paint, Mother thrust into her hands the basket of mending to do.

Often from the edge of the room, she'd watch him work. Because he was always asking for quiet, with the little ones running through the room laughing or shouting, she didn't ask him many questions. He rarely answered anyway. Still, she studied how much linseed oil he used to thin the ultramarine,[7] and watched him apply it over a

6. **lead white . . . lead-tin yellow** references to pigments made from lead and tin and mixed with oil to produce paints of various colors.
7. **linseed oil . . . ultramarine** Linseed oil, made from the seed of the flax plant, can be used as the base for oil paint. Ultramarine is a rich blue.

glassy layer of reddish brown. By magic, it made the dress he painted warmer than the blue on the palette. He would not let her go with him to the attic where he ground lead-tin yellow to powder, but he did send her to the apothecary[8] for the small bricks of it, and for linseed oil. Always there was money for that, but she didn't know what to answer when the apothecary demanded the guilders for her brother's potions still owed after he died.

If only she could have colors of her own, and brushes. She wouldn't just paint pictures of women inside cramped little rooms. She'd paint them out in marketplaces, bending in the potato fields, talking in doorways in the sunlight, in boats on the Schie, or praying in the Oude Kerk. Or she'd paint people skating, fathers teaching their children on the frozen Schie.

Fathers teaching their children. The thought stopped her.

Looking from the sentry tower at a cloud darkening the river, she knew, just as she knew she'd always have washing and mending to do, that it would not be so. She'd worn herself out with wishing, and turned to go. She had to be home to help with supper.

On a spring day that began in no special way, except that she had climbed the town wall the afternoon before, and all over Delft lime trees lining the canals had burst into chartreuse[9] leaves, and light shone through them and made them yellower except where one leaf crossed over another and so was darker—on that spring-certain day, out of some unknown, unborn place came that scream. "I hate to mend," she shouted to the walls, to Mother, to anyone. "It's not making anything."

Father stepped into the room, looked at Mother and then scowled at Magdalena. It had been her job to keep her little brothers quiet for him, or shoo them out of doors, and here she was, the noisy one.

No one moved. Even the boys were still. At first she looked only at Father's hand smeared with ultramarine powder, not in his eyes, too surprised by the echo of her voice to fling out any additional defiance. She loved him, loved what he did with that hand, and even, she suspected, loved what he loved, though they had not spoken of it. When that thought lifted her face to his, she saw his cheeks grow softer, as if he noticed her in his house for the first time. He drew her over to the table by the window, brought the sewing basket, placed on her lap her brother's shirt that needed buttons, adjusted the chair, opened the window, a little more, then less, and discovered that at a certain angle, it reflected her face. "If you sit here mending, I will paint you, Magdalena. But only if you stop that shouting."

---

8. **apothecary** (ə päth′ ə ker′ ē) *n.* historical term for a pharmacist; a dealer in medicines and various other preparations and chemicals.
9. **chartreuse** (shär tro͞oz′) pale, yellowish green.

He positioned her shoulders, and his hands resting a moment were warm through the muslin[10] of her smock and seemed to settle her.

Mother rushed over to take away Geertruida's glass of milk.

"No, leave it, Catharina. Right there in the light."

For days she sat there, still as she could for Father, and yet sewing a few stitches every so often to satisfy Mother. In that mood of stillness, all the things within her line of vision touched her deeply. The tapestry laid across the table, the sewing basket, the same glass repoured each day to the same level, the amber-toned map of the world on the wall—it plucked a lute string in her heart that these things she'd touched, grown as familiar to her as her own skin, would be looked at, marveled at, maybe even loved by viewers of his painting.

... she saw his cheeks grow softer, as if he noticed her in his house for the first time.

On sunny days the panes of window glass glistened before her. Like jewels melted into flat squares, she thought. Each one was slightly different in its pale transparent color—ivory, parchment, the lightest of wines and the palest of tulips. She wondered how glass was made, but she didn't ask. It would disturb him.

Outside the window the market chattered with the selling of apples and lard and brooms and wooden buckets. She liked the cheese porters in their flat-brimmed red hats and stark white clothes. Their curved yellow carrying platforms stacked neatly with cheese rounds were suspended on ropes between pairs of them, casting brown shadows on the paving stones. Two platforms diagonally placed in the midground between their carriers would make a nice composition with the repeated shapes of those bulging cheese rounds. She'd put a delivery boy wheeling his cart of silver cod in the background against the guild hall, and maybe in the foreground a couple of lavender gray pigeons pecking crumbs. The carillon[11] from Nieuwe Kerk ringing out the hour sounded something profound in her chest. All of it is ordinary to everyone but me, she thought.

All that month she did not speak, the occasion too **momentous** to dislodge it with words. He said he'd paint her as long as she didn't shout, and so she did not speak a word. Her chest ached like a dull wound when she realized that her silence did not cause him a moment's reflection or curiosity. When she looked out the corner of her eye at him, she could not tell what she meant to him. Slowly, she came to understand that he looked at her with the same interest he gave to the glass of milk.

◀ **momentous** (mō men′təs) *adj.* important; of great significance

Maybe it was because she wasn't pretty like Maria. She knew her jaws protruded and her watery, pale eyes were too widely set. She had a mole on her forehead that she always tried to hide by tugging

10. muslin (muz′ lin) *n.* strong, plain cotton cloth.
11. carillon (kar′ ə län′) *n.* a set of tuned church bells.

at her cap. What if no one would want the painting? What then? It might be her fault, because she wasn't pretty. She wished he'd say something about her, but all he said, not to her directly, more to himself, was how the sunlight whitened her cap at the forehead, how the shadow at the nape of her neck reflected blue from her collar, or how the sienna of her skirt deepened to Venetian red[12] in the folds. It was never her, she cried to herself, only something surrounding her that she did not make or even contribute to knowingly. Another wish that never would come true, she saw then, even if she lived forever, was that he, that someone, would look at her not as an artistic study, but with love. If two people love the same thing, she reasoned, then they must love each other, at least a little, even if they never say it. Nevertheless, because he painted with such studied concentration, and because she held him in awe, she practiced looking calm for him as she looked out the window, but when she saw the canvas, what she intended as calm looked more like wistfulness.[13]

The painting was not bought by the brewer, Pieter Claesz van Ruijven,[14] who bought most of her father's work. He saw it, but passed over it for another. Disgrace seared her so that she could not speak that night. The painting hung without a frame in the outer kitchen where the younger children slept. Eventually the family had to give up their lodgings at Mechelen on the square, and take smaller rooms with Grandmother Maria on the Oude Langendijck.[15] Her father stopped taking the iceboat out to the Schie, sold it, in fact. He rarely painted, the rooms were so cramped and dark, the younger children boisterous, and a few years later, he died.

When she washed him in his bed that last time, his fingers already cold, she had a thought, the shame of which prevented her from uttering: It would make a fine painting, a memorial, the daughter with towel and blue-figured washing bowl at bedside, her hand covering his, the wife exhausted on the Spanish chair clutching a crucifix, the father-husband, eyes glazed, looking to another landscape. While he painted everyone else, no one was there to paint him, to make him remembered. She yearned to do it, but the task was too fearsome. She lacked the skill, and the one to teach her had never offered.

Even though she asked for them, Mother sold his paints and brushes to the Guild of St. Luke. It helped to pay a debt. When Mother became sick with worry, Magdalena had the idea to take the painting to Hendrick van Buyten, the baker, because she knew he

---

12. **sienna** (sē en´ ə) . . . **Venetian** (və nē´ shən) **red** colors; sienna is a reddish or yellowish brown, and Venetian red is a brownish red.
13. **wistfulness** *n.* a mood of wishfulness or vague longing.
14. **Pieter Claesz van Ruijven** (pē ter kläs fän rī fen)
15. **Mechelen** (me´ khe len) . . . **Oude Langendijck** (ou´ de läŋ en dīk) The Mechelen was an inn owned by the Vermeer family. The Oude Langendijck is a canal in Delft.

liked her. And he accepted it, along with one of a lady playing a guitar, for the debt of six hundred seventeen guilders, six stuivers,[16] more than two years' worth of bread. He smiled at her and gave her a bun.

Within a year, she married a saddlemaker named Nicolaes, the first man to notice her, a hard worker whose pores smelled of leather and grease, who taught her a pleasure not of the eyes, but, she soon realized, a man utterly without imagination. They moved to Amsterdam and she didn't see the painting again for twenty years.

Young Woman with a Water Jug (also known as *Young Woman with a Water Pitcher*) by Johannes Vermeer; oil on canvas; c. 1660–1662

In 1696, just after their only living child, Magritte, damp with fever, stopped breathing in her arms, Magdalena read in the Amsterdamsche Courant of a public auction of one hundred thirty-four paintings by various artists. "Several outstandingly artful paintings," the notice said, "including twenty-one works most powerfully and splendidly painted by the late J. Vermeer of Delft, will be auctioned May 16, 1:00, at the Oude Heeren Logement."[17] Only a week away. She thought of Hendrick. Of course he couldn't be expected to keep those paintings forever. Hers might be there. The possibility kept her awake nights.

Entering the auction gallery, she was struck again by that keenest of childhood wishes—to make a record not only of what she saw, but how. The distance she'd come from that, and not even a child to show for it! She shocked herself by asking, involuntarily, what had been the point of having lived? Wishing had not been enough. Was it a mistake that she didn't beg him to teach her? Maybe not. If she'd seen that eventually, with help, she could paint, it might have made the years of birthing and dying harder. But then the birthing and dying would have been painted and the pain given. It would have served a purpose. Would that have been enough—to tell a truth in art?

She didn't know.

---

16. **stuivers** (stī´ fers) *n.* coins worth a fraction of a guilder; roughly, a dime.

17. **Oude Heeren Logement** (ou´ de her´ en lōzh mōn) *Oude Heeren Logement* means "Old Gentlemen's Inn."

reverence ▶ (rev′ ə rəns) *n.* respect or honor that is shown

To see again so many of Father's paintings was like walking down an avenue of her childhood. The honey-colored window, the Spanish chair, the map she'd stared at, dreaming, hanging on the wall, Grandmother Maria's golden water pitcher, Mother's pearls and yellow satin jacket—they commanded such a **reverence** for her now that she felt they all had souls.

And suddenly there she was on canvas, framed. Her knees went weak.

Hendrick hadn't kept it. Even though he liked her, he hadn't kept it.

Almost a child she was, it seemed to her, gazing out the window instead of doing her mending, as if by the mere act of looking she could send her spirit out into the world. And those shoes! She had forgotten. How she loved the buckles, and thought they made her such a lady. Eventually she'd worn the soles right through, but now, brand-new, the buckles glinted on the canvas, each with a point of golden light. A bubble of joy surged upward right through her.

No, she wasn't beautiful, she owned, but there was a simplicity in her young face that she knew the years had eroded, a stilled longing in the forward lean of her body, a wishing in the intensity of her eyes. The painting showed she did not yet know that lives end abruptly, that much of living is repetition and separation, that buttons forever need resewing no matter how ferociously one works the thread, that nice things almost happen. Still a woman overcome with wishes, she wished Nicolaes would have come with her to see her in the days of her sentry post wonder when life and hope were new and full of possibility, but he had seen no reason to close up the shop on such a whim.

She stood on tiptoe and didn't breathe when her painting was announced. Her hand in her pocket closed tight around the twenty-four guilders, some of it borrowed from two neighbor women, some of it taken secretly from the box where Nicolaes kept money for leather supplies. It was all she could find, and she didn't dare ask for more. He would have thought it foolish.

"Twenty," said a man in front of her.

"Twenty-two," said another.

"Twenty-four," she said so loud and fast the auctioneer was startled. Did he see something similar in her face? He didn't call for another bid. The painting was hers!

"Twenty-five."

Her heart cracked.

The rest was a blur of sound. It finally went to a man who kept conferring with his wife, which she took as a good sign that it was going to a nice family. Forty-seven guilders. Most of the paintings sold for much more, but forty-seven was fine, she thought. In fact, it filled her momentarily with what she'd been taught was the sin of pride. Then she thought of Hendrick and a pain lashed through her. Forty-seven guilders minus the auctioneer's fee didn't come close to what her family had owed him.

She followed the couple out into the drizzle of Herengracht,[18] wanting to make herself known to them, just to have a few words, but then dropped back. She had such bad teeth now, and they were people of means. The woman wore stockings. What would she say to them? She didn't want them to think she wanted anything.

She walked away slowly along a wet stone wall that shone iridescent, and the wetness of the street reflected back the blue of her best dress. Water spots appeared fast, turning the cerulean[19] to deep ultramarine, Father's favorite blue. Light rain pricked the charcoal green canal water into delicate, dark lace, and she wondered if it had ever been painted just that way, or if the life of something as inconsequential as a water drop could be arrested and given to the world in a painting, or if the world would care.

She thought of all the people in all the paintings she had seen that day, not just Father's, in all the paintings of the world, in fact. Their eyes, the particular turn of a head, their loneliness or suffering or grief was borrowed by an artist to be seen by other people throughout the years who would never see them face to face. People who would be that close to her, she thought, a matter of a few arms' lengths, looking, looking, and they would never know her.

---

18. **Herengracht** (her´ en khräkht) the "Gentleman's Canal"; one of the three main canals in the center of the city of Amsterdam.
19. **cerulean** (sə ro͞o´ lē ən) *adj.* sky blue.

ABOUT THE AUTHOR

Susan Vreeland (b. 1946)

Best-selling novelist Susan Vreeland was a high school English teacher in California for thirty years. Most of her fiction, including her seven novels, focuses on characters whose lives are deeply intertwined with—and affected by—great works of art. As Vreeland notes: "Thanks to art, instead of seeing only one world and time period, our own, we see it multiplied and can peer into other times, other worlds which offer windows to other lives."

Close Reading Activities

READ

Comprehension

Reread all or part of the text to help you answer the following questions.

1. What does Magdalena's father do for a living?
2. What does Magdalena's father agree to do for her?
3. Why does Magdalena believe that her father has no interest in her?
4. Where does Magdalena later see her portrait?

Research: Clarify Details This selection may include references that are unfamiliar to you. Choose at least one unfamiliar reference, and briefly research it. Then, explain how the information you learned helps you better understand the selection.

Summarize Write an objective summary of the selection, one that is free from opinion and evaluation.

Language Study

Selection Vocabulary The following sentences appear in the selection. Define each boldface word. Then, use the word in a new sentence.

- She wished her hair shown **flaxen** in the sunlight of the market square like little Geertruida's.
- All that month she did not speak, the occasion too **momentous** to dislodge it with words.
- ... they commanded such a **reverence** for her now that she felt they all had souls.

Literary Analysis

Reread the identified passage. Then, respond to the questions that follow.

Focus Passage *(pp. 297–298)*

All that month . . . more like wistfulness.

Key Ideas and Details

1. **(a)** What is the "momentous" occasion Magdalena does not want to "dislodge"? **(b) Interpret:** Why does Magdalena avoid speaking for a month?

Craft and Structure

2. **(a) Compare and Contrast:** Explain how Magdalena's emotions and thoughts differ from her outward behavior. **(b) Support:** Which details show that difference? Explain.
3. **(a) Distinguish:** What words does the father use to identify various colors? **(b) Analyze:** How does this word choice support the characterization of the father as a master artist?

Integration of Knowledge and Ideas

4. **(a) Compare and Contrast:** What does Magdalena's father see as he paints his daughter and what does Magdalena wish he would see? **(b) Make a Judgment:** Does the father truly see Magdalena? Explain your answer.

Theme

A **theme** is the central message or insight expressed in a literary work. Reread the selection, and take notes about details that suggest the story's theme.

1. **(a)** What is Magdalena's "one pulsing wish"? **(b)** What obstacles keep her from fulfilling her wish? **(c)** What theme does Magdalena's conflict suggest? Explain.
2. **Vision: (a)** How does this selection explore differences between "seeing" and "knowing"? Explain. **(b)** What theme does this selection express about what art can and cannot achieve?

DISCUSS • RESEARCH • WRITE

From Text to Topic **Partner Discussion**

Discuss the following passage with a partner. Take notes during the discussion. Contribute your own ideas, and support them with examples from the text. Then, join with other groups to share your ideas.

> If only she could have colors of her own, and brushes. She wouldn't just paint pictures of women inside cramped little rooms. She'd paint them out in marketplaces, bending in the potato fields, talking in doorways in the sunlight, in boats on the Schie, or praying in the Oude Kirk. Or she'd paint people skating, fathers teaching their children on the frozen Schie.

QUESTIONS FOR DISCUSSION

1. What does this passage show about ways in which Magdalena's vision of the world differs from her father's?
2. Is Magdalena's vision more realistic than her father's?

Research **Investigate the Topic**

The Artist's Eye "Magdalena Looking" is a fictional story in which the real figure of Johannes Vermeer plays a major role. Vermeer almost always painted interiors and re-used the same props in painting after painting. Nevertheless, his work is now **regarded** as one of the greatest achievements of the Dutch Golden Age.

Assignment

Conduct research on Vermeer. Consult biographies, art history texts, and critical **analyses** of Vermeer's work. Draw conclusions about the vision of life captured in Vermeer's paintings. Include several paintings as examples and share your ideas in an **oral presentation**.

PREPARATION FOR ESSAY

You may use the results of this research in an essay you will write at the end of this section.

Writing to Sources **Informative Text**

Both writers and painters portray characters and scenes, but the tools they use to do so are quite different.

Assignment

Write a **comparison-and-contrast essay** in which you analyze Vreeland's use of words to create a setting and compare it with a painter's use of color, line, and **perspective** to create a scene on canvas. Follow these steps:

- Choose a scene from "Magdalena Looking" to analyze. Explain why you chose it.
- Locate a painting, such as one by Vermeer, to use as a comparison. Choose a painting that portrays a scene similar to the one Vreeland describes.
- Explain how Vreeland uses language to create images in the reader's mind. Compare these examples to the painter's tools of color and line.
- Provide a conclusion in which you summarize your analysis.

ACADEMIC VOCABULARY

Academic terms appear in blue on these pages. If these words are not familiar to you, use a dictionary to find their definitions. Then, use them as you speak and write about the text.

Common Core State Standards

RL.9-10.1, RL.9-10.2, RL.9-10.3, RL.9-10.4, RL.9-10.7; W.9-10.2, W.9-10.4, W.9-10.7, W.9-10.9; SL.9-10.1, SL.9-10.4; L.9-10.6

[For full standards wording, see the chart in the front of this book.]

from The Statue That Didn't Look Right

from

Blink: The Power of Thinking Without Thinking

Malcolm Gladwell

In September of 1983, an art dealer by the name of Gianfranco Becchina approached the J. Paul Getty Museum in California. He had in his possession, he said, a marble statue dating from the sixth century BC. It was what is known as a kouros— a sculpture of a nude male youth standing with his left leg forward and his arms at his sides. There are only about two hundred kouroi in existence, and most have been recovered badly damaged or in fragments from gravesites or archeological digs. But this one was almost perfectly preserved. It stood close to seven feet tall. It had a kind of light-colored glow that set it apart from other ancient works. It was an extraordinary find. Becchina's asking price was just under $10 million.

The Getty moved cautiously. It took the kouros on loan and began a thorough investigation. Was the statue consistent with other known kouroi? The answer appeared to be yes. The style of the sculpture seemed reminiscent of the Anavyssos kouros in the National Archaeological Museum of Athens, meaning that it seemed to fit with a particular time and place. Where and when had the statue been found? No one knew precisely, but Becchina gave the Getty's legal department a sheaf of documents relating to its more recent history. The kouros, the records stated, had been in the private collection of a Swiss physician named Lauffenberger since the 1930s, and he in turn had acquired it from a well-known Greek art dealer named Roussos.

◀ **reminiscent** (rem′ ə nis′ ənt) *adj.* tending to remind; suggesting

A geologist from the University of California named Stanley Margolis came to the museum and spent two days examining the surface of the statue with a high-resolution stereomicroscope.[1] He then removed a core sample measuring one centimeter in diameter and two centimeters in length from just below the right knee and

1. **stereomicroscope** (ster′ ē ō′ mī ′ krə skōp′) *n.* microscope that makes an object appear three-dimensional.

analyzed it using an electron microscope, electron microprobe, mass spectrometry, X-ray diffraction, and X-ray fluorescence. The statue was made of dolomite marble from the ancient Cape Vathy quarry on the island of Thasos, Margolis concluded, and the surface of the statue was covered in a thin layer of calcite—which was significant, Margolis told the Getty because dolomite can turn into calcite only over the course of hundreds, if not thousands, of years. In other words, the statue was old. It wasn't some contemporary fake.

The Getty was satisfied. Fourteen months after their investigation of the kouros began, they agreed to buy the statue. In the fall of 1986, it went on display for the first time....

The kouros, however, had a problem. It didn't look right. The first to point this out was an Italian art historian named Federico Zeri, who served on the Getty's board of trustees. When Zeri was taken down to the museum's restoration studio to see the kouros in December of 1983, he found himself staring at the sculpture's fingernails. In a way he couldn't immediately **articulate**, they seemed wrong to him. Evelyn Harrison was next. She was one of the world's foremost experts on Greek sculpture, and she was in Los Angeles visiting the Getty just before the museum finalized the deal with Becchina. "Arthur Houghton, who was then the curator, took us down to see it," Harrison remembers. "He just swished a cloth off the top of it and said, 'Well, it isn't ours yet, but it will be in a couple of weeks.' And I said, 'I'm sorry to hear that.'" What did Harrison see? She didn't know. In that very first moment, when Houghton swished off the cloth, all Harrison had was a hunch, an instinctive sense that something was amiss. A few months later, Houghton took Thomas Hoving, the former director of the Metropolitan Museum of Art in New York, down to the Getty's conservation studio to see the statue as well. Hoving always makes a note of the first word that goes through his head when he sees something new, and he'll never forget what that word was when he first saw the kouros. "It was 'fresh' —'fresh,'" Hoving recalls. And "fresh" was not the right reaction to have to a two-thousand-year-old statue. Later, thinking back on that moment, Hoving realized why that thought had popped into his mind: "I had dug in Sicily, where we found bits and pieces of these things. They just don't come out looking like that. The kouros looked like it had been dipped in the very best caffè latte. . . ."[2]

articulate ▶ (är tik′ yo͞o lāt′) *v.* say clearly

Hoving turned to Houghton. "Have you paid for this?"

Houghton, Hoving remembers, looked stunned.

"If you have, try to get your money back," Hoving said. "If you haven't, don't."

---

2. **caffè latte** (kä fā lä′ tā) *n.* Italian for "coffee with milk."

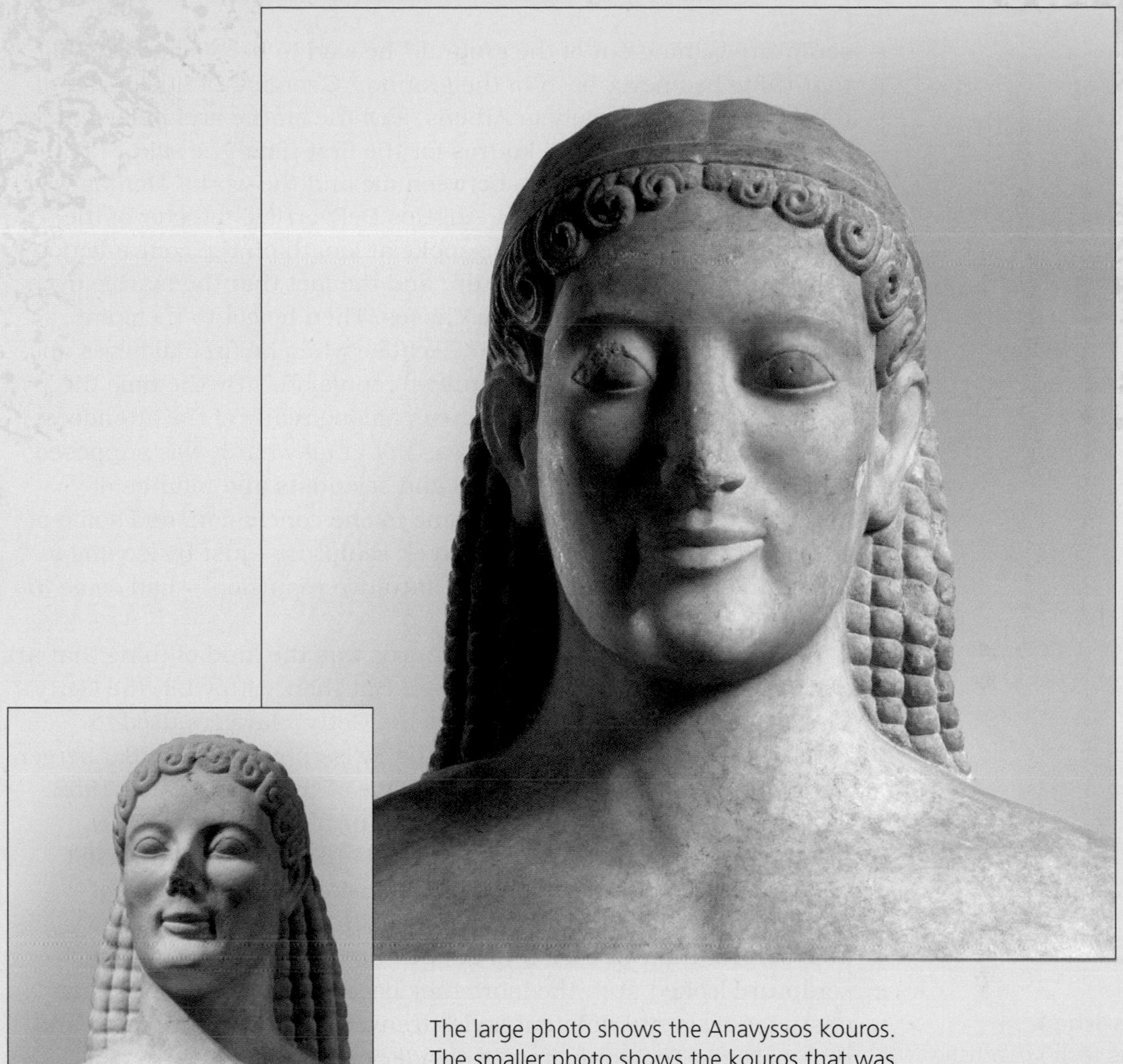

The large photo shows the Anavyssos kouros. The smaller photo shows the kouros that was purchased by the Getty.

The Getty was getting worried, so they convened a special symposium on the kouros in Greece. They wrapped the statue up, shipped it to Athens, and invited the country's most senior sculpture experts. This time the chorus of dismay was even louder.

Harrison, at one point, was standing next to a man named George Despinis, the head of the Acropolis Museum in Athens. He took one look at the kouros and blanched. "Anyone who has ever seen a sculpture coming out of the ground," he said to her, "could tell that that thing has never been in the ground." Georgios Dontas, head of the Archeological Society in Athens, saw the statue and immediately felt cold. "When I saw the kouros for the first time," he said, "I felt as though there was a glass between me and the work." Dontas was followed in the symposium by Angelos Delivorrias, director of the Benaki Museum in Athens. He spoke at length on the contradiction between the style of the sculpture and the fact that the marble from which it was carved came from Thasos. Then he got to the point. Why did he think it was a fake? Because when he first laid eyes on it, he said, he felt a wave of "intuitive repulsion."[3] By the time the symposium was over, the consensus among many of the attendees appeared to be that the kouros was not at all what it was supposed to be. The Getty, with its lawyers and scientists and months of painstaking investigation, had come to one conclusion, and some of the world's foremost experts in Greek sculpture—just by looking at the statue and sensing their own "intuitive repulsion"—had come to another. Who was right?

For a time it wasn't clear. The kouros was the kind of thing that art experts argued about at conferences. But then, bit by bit, the Getty's case began to fall apart. The letters the Getty's lawyers used to carefully trace the kouros back to the Swiss physician Lauffenberger, for instance, turned out to be fakes. One of the letters dated 1952 had a postal code on it that didn't exist until twenty years later. Another letter dated 1955 referred to a bank account that wasn't opened until 1963. Originally the conclusion of long months of research was that the Getty kouros was in the style of the Anavyssos kouros. But that, too, fell into doubt: the closer experts in Greek sculpture looked at it, the more they began to see it as a puzzling **pastiche** of several different styles from several different places and time periods. The young man's slender proportions looked a lot like those of the Tenea kouros, which is in a museum in Munich, and his stylized, beaded hair was a lot like that of the kouros in the Metropolitan Museum in New York. His feet, meanwhile, were, if anything, modern. The kouros it most resembled, it turned out, was a smaller, fragmentary statue that was found by a British art historian in Switzerland in 1990. The two statues were cut from similar marble and sculpted in quite similar ways. But the Swiss kouros didn't come from ancient Greece. It came from a forger's workshop in Rome in the early 1980s. And what of the scientific analysis that said that the surface of the Getty kouros could only have aged over many hundreds or thousands of years? Well, it turns

pastiche ▶ (pas tēsh´) *n.* artistic work made up of parts taken from different sources

3. **intuitive repulsion** (in´ to͞o´ i tiv ri pul´ shən) *n.* sudden feeling of dislike, as if by instinct.

out things weren't that cut and dried. Upon further analysis, another geologist concluded that it might be possible to "age" the surface of a dolomite marble statue in a couple of months using potato mold. In the Getty's catalogue, there is a picture of the kouros, with the notation "About 530 BC, or modern forgery."

When Federico Zeri and Evelyn Harrison and Thomas Hoving and Georgios Dontas—and all the others—looked at the kouros and felt an "intuitive repulsion," they were absolutely right. In the first two seconds of looking—in a single glance—they were able to understand more about the essence of the statue than the team at the Getty was able to understand after fourteen months.

ABOUT THE AUTHOR

Malcolm Gladwell (b. 1963)

Born in England and educated in Canada, Malcolm Gladwell began his career as a business and science reporter for *The Washington Post*. Since 1996, he has been a regular contributor to *The New Yorker* magazine. Gladwell's gift for making new ideas in the sciences and social sciences both understandable and valuable to general audiences has earned him many honors. His books include *The Tipping Point: How Little Things Make a Big Difference* (2000), *Blink: The Power of Thinking Without Thinking* (2005), and *Outliers: The Story of Success* (2008); all reached number one on *The New York Times* Best Sellers list.

Gladwell's success lies in his ability to interest readers in what may be complex or obscure subjects. "Good writing does not succeed or fail on the strength of its ability to persuade," he declares. "It succeeds or fails on the strength of its ability to engage you, to make you think, to give you a glimpse into someone else's head."

Close Reading Activities

READ

Comprehension

Reread all or part of the text to help you answer the following questions.

1. For what two main reasons was the Getty Museum kouros initially considered "extraordinary"?
2. What did art historians Federico Zeri and Evelyn Harrison first perceive about the statue?
3. What two pieces of evidence suggested that the letters provided with the statue were fakes?

Research: Clarify Details This selection may include references that are unfamiliar to you. Choose at least one of those references, and briefly research it. Then, explain how the information you learned helps you better understand the selection.

Summarize Write an objective summary of the text. Remember that an objective summary is free from opinion and evaluation.

Language Study

Selection Vocabulary The following passages appear in the text. Define each boldface word. Then, write a paragraph in which you use all three words logically.

- The style of the sculpture seemed **reminiscent** of the Anavyssos kouros...
- In a way he couldn't immediately **articulate**, they seemed wrong to him.
- The closer experts in Greek sculpture looked at it, the more they began to see it as a puzzling **pastiche** of several different styles

Literary Analysis

Reread the identified passage. Then, respond to the questions that follow.

Focus Passage *(pp. 307–308)*
The Getty was getting worried... Who was right?

Key Ideas and Details

1. **Compare and Contrast:** How did the findings of the symposium differ from those reached by scientists after months of study?

Craft and Structure

2. **Interpret:** What does the phrase "chorus of dismay" suggest about the manner in which the symposium members voiced their opinions?
3. **(a) Distinguish:** Identify details that describe the historians' first reactions to the statue. **(b) Analyze:** How does this language connect to the idea of intuition or a "gut reaction"? Explain.

Integration of Knowledge and Ideas

4. **Draw Conclusions:** Judging from this passage, what does the word "right" mean in the title? Explain.

Supporting Details

A **supporting detail** is a fact or example that adds information. Reread the text, and note the types of supporting details Gladwell uses.

1. **(a)** Cite two scientific details that "proved" the statue's authenticity. **(b)** How are the scientific details **fundamentally** different from those that describe the experts' reactions? Explain.
2. **Vision:** Gladwell includes numerous quotations from experts. Why are quotations a particularly effective type of supporting detail in a text about intuition and perception?

DISCUSS • RESEARCH • WRITE

From Text to Topic **Group Discussion**

Discuss the following passage with a group of classmates. Take notes during the discussion. Contribute your own ideas, and support them with examples from the text.

> When Federico Zeri and Evelyn Harrison and Thomas Hoving and Georgios Dontas—and all the others—looked at the kouros and felt an "intuitive repulsion," they were absolutely right. In the first two seconds of looking—in a single glance—they were able to understand more about the essence of the statue than the team at the Getty was able to understand after fourteen months.

QUESTIONS FOR DISCUSSION

1. Why might expert art historians describe their reaction to a fake as "repulsion"?
2. Without knowing anything about the statue, how might a non-expert, casual observer "see" it?

Research **Investigate the Topic**

The Validity of Intuition Intuition is understanding that comes through an immediate feeling rather than through conscious reasoning.

Assignment
Conduct research about the **physiological** and psychological aspects of "intuition." Use a variety of print and electronic sources that discuss intuition, "gut feelings," and hunches. Find out about the causes for such reactions and how they **manifest** themselves. Take careful notes and identify your sources so that you can defend your findings. Share your research in a **panel discussion** with other class members.

PREPARATION FOR ESSAY

You may use the results of this research in an essay you will write at the end of this section.

ACADEMIC VOCABULARY

Academic terms appear in blue on these pages. If these words are not familiar to you, use a dictionary to find their definitions. Then, use them as you speak and write about the text.

Writing to Sources **Narrative**

"The Statue That Didn't Look Right" discusses how experts' educated perceptions and intuition may have been more accurate than scientific analysis.

Assignment
Write an **autobiographical narrative** in which you describe how intuition or a hunch influenced a decision you made, and how that decision worked out. Follow these steps:

- Clearly introduce the situation.
- Describe your responses to the situation, the elements that influenced your thinking, and how you arrived at your final decision.
- Use vivid, descriptive details.
- Provide a conclusion in which you compare and contrast your experience to the experts' reactions as described in Gladwell's text.

 **Common Core State Standards**

RI.9-10.1, RI.9-10.2, RI.9-10.4, RI.9-10.5; W.9-10.3, W.9-10.4, W.9-10.7, W.9-10.9; SL.9-10.1, SL.9-10.4; L.9-10.4, L.9-10.6
[For full standards wording, see the chart in the front of this book.]

from The Shape of the World

from Life by the Numbers

Keith Devlin

recurrent ▶ (ri kʉr′ ənt) *adj.* happening again and again

obliterated ▶ (ə blit′ ər āt′ id) *adj.* destroyed; wiped out

In years when the rains were particularly hard, the ancient Egyptians living in the Nile Valley faced a **recurrent** problem. The river would burst its banks and flood the surrounding plains, washing away the markers that the farmers used to indicate the boundaries of their land. To overcome this problem, they needed a way to accurately reconstruct the **obliterated** boundary lines. That meant taking measurements of the earth's surface and recording them in the form of a map. Thus was geometry born—or so the story goes. In any event the word *geometry* comes from the two Greek words *geo*, meaning earth, and *metros*, meaning measurement.

From its beginnings five thousand years ago in ancient Egypt, geometry developed into a rich and powerful branch of mathematics, having many applications.

From those same beginnings, modern mapmaking—the official term is *cartography*—developed, as people sought ever more reliable ways to answer the questions, Where am I? and How do I get where I want to go?

Those questions came down to knowing the shape of the earth—the shapes of the landmasses, the shapes of the different regions and countries, the positions and shapes of the rivers, where the mountain ranges are, the layout of the roads, and so on.

Today, mapmakers are still making use of geometry to draw maps. Nigel Holmes is a present-day mapmaker. His maps appear every week in newspapers and magazines such as *The New York Times*, *Time*, and *Sports Illustrated*. The maps he draws show readers where the explosion happened, where the plane crashed, where the armed conflict is.

In drawing his maps, Holmes faces the same geometry problem that all mapmakers have faced throughout the ages. It's a two-part problem, often made more difficult because one part can affect the other. The first part is scale. A mapmaker may have to represent anything from a city block to an entire country, or even the whole world, on a map measuring a few inches across. To do this, the map has to be drawn to scale, with, say, one inch on the map corresponding to a quarter of a mile of city streets or a thousand miles of the earth's surface.

In the case of a map of a city, or even a small country, drawing a map "to scale" is not difficult. You just multiply all measurements taken on the ground by a fixed "scale factor." The hard question is to decide what details to include in the map and what to leave out. That's not a mathematical question; it depends on the purpose to which the map will be put.

It's when the map covers a significant portion of the earth's surface that things get tricky. That's when you face the second part of the mapmaker's problem: the earth's curvature. How do you represent features of a curved surface on the flat surface of a map?

Holmes likes to explain the problem by using an orange to represent the earth. To obtain a map of the earth's surface, the most obvious approach is to remove the peel and lay it flat. But no matter how hard you try, the orange peel stays curved. It is in order to overcome the orange-peel problem that mapmakers turn to mathematics.

The challenge facing the cartographer, then, is to represent the curved surface of the earth, or a portion of it, on a flat sheet of paper. Mathematicians call such a representation a "projection"—they say the earth's surface is projected onto a flat plane. Ideally, a cartographer wants to represent accurately those geographic features that are important in a map—direction, shape, scaled distance, and scaled surface area. In other words, to be really useful, a map should tell you which direction to go to get from *A* to *B*, what is the shape of a particular region *C* (state, country, topographic region, etc.), how far it is from *A* to *B*, and how big is region *C*. However, because of the orange peel problem, it is not possible to find a projection that preserves all four of these features at once. The cartographer has to make a choice, depending on the purpose the map is intended to serve. Once that choice has been made, the mapmaker then turns to geometry to find the appropriate projection—a formula that translates points from one geometric shape to another, from a sphere to a flat plane.

A familiar example of a projection, found in many school atlases in Europe and North America, is the Mercator projection, introduced by the Flemish[1] geographer Gerardus Mercator in 1569 in order to provide sailors with a reliable navigational tool.

Back in the sixteenth century, long before the days of modern electronic navigational aids, if you were a sailor, the most important feature in a map was compass direction. It was even more important than distance. Accordingly, Mercator drew his map so that it was accurate in terms of direction: if a sailor drew a straight line on the map from, say, Gibraltar[2] in the Mediterranean to Boston in the New World, then the line represented the path from Gibraltar to Boston that followed a constant compass bearing. What is more, at any point on the line, indeed at any point on Mercator's map, north is directly above the point and south directly below.

How did Mercator draw such a map? The key to drawing any map is the grid system: how you represent on the map the lines of latitude and longitude that curve around the globe. Once you have drawn the grid system, all that remains is to transfer the details within each grid region of the globe to the corresponding grid region of the map. The grid system determines both the scale and the degree of distortion that will arise because of the orange-peel problem.

Mercator's map uses a rectangular grid: lines of longitude are drawn vertically; lines of latitude are drawn horizontally. For town

1. **Flemish** (flem´ ish) *adj.* from the region of Flanders, which is now part of Belgium.
2. **Gibraltar** (jə brôl´ tər) *n.* island that lies at the entrance of the Mediterranean Sea and that is a territory of Great Britain.

plans and maps that represent at most a few hundred miles, rectangular grid maps are perfectly adequate in all respects. But for a map of the world, they present a significant problem: they distort shape. The further you get from the equator, the greater the distortion, as small regions near the poles get stretched out farther and farther across the width of the map. For example, on the Mercator map, Greenland appears to be a huge continent, very wide at the top, but in reality it has the same surface area as Mexico, which looks fairly tiny on the map.

To obtain a rectangular map that was true to compass bearings, and thus could be used by navigators, Mercator compensated for the increasing horizontal stretching that occurs the farther you get from the equator by steadily increasing the vertical distance between the lines of latitude. "I have gradually extended the degrees of latitude in the directions of both Poles in the same proportion in which the parallels of latitude increase in their relation to the equator," he wrote. Though it would have been possible to draw his grid system

Mercator projection

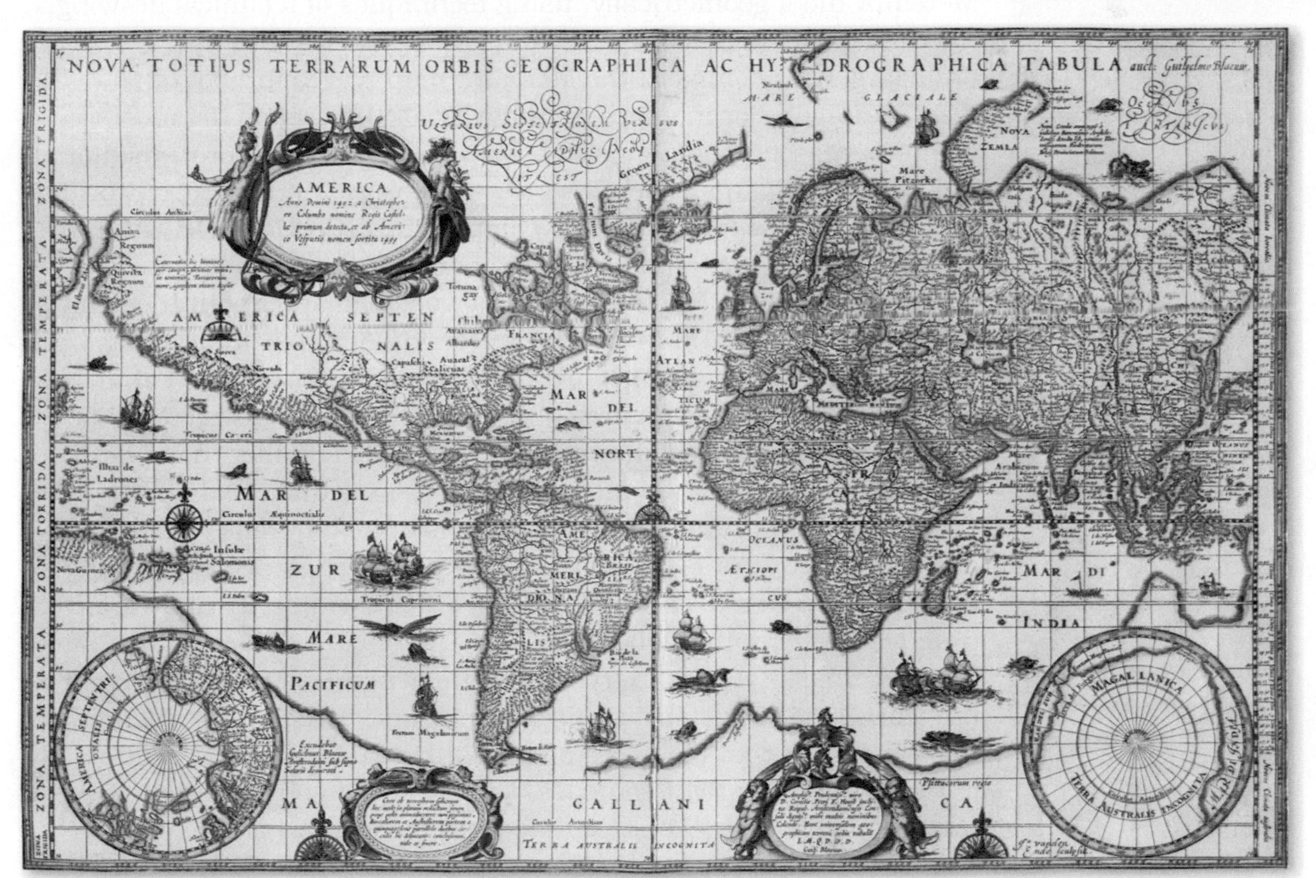

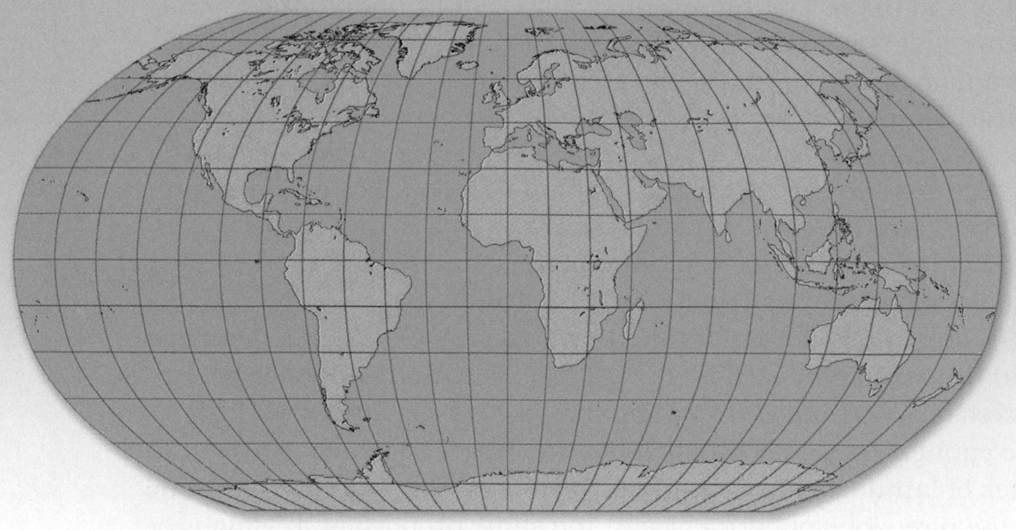

Robinson projection

by calculating the different distances between the lines of latitude, Mercator did it geometrically, using techniques of technical drawing.

While useful for sailors in the days when navigation was done largely by compass, the Mercator map has a number of disadvantages. For instance, in today's world, perhaps the most common reason people consult a map of the world is not navigational but social—to gain an overall sense of the world and to locate world events. For those kinds of uses, compass direction is irrelevant, but shape and area are arguably very important.

For example, the Mercator map shows Greenland about the same size as the African continent. But in reality, Africa, with an area of 30 million square kilometers, is nearly fifteen times larger than Greenland, which has an area of 2.1 million square kilometers. The Mercator map also shows Africa as slightly smaller than North America, giving the impression that the two continents are of comparable size. But again, the reality is quite different. The area of North America is 19 million square kilometers. Africa is half as big again![3] In fact, a glance at a globe will show that Africa dwarfs practically every other landmass!

Thus, when it comes to trying to get a general sense of the size of the world, the Mercator map is extremely misleading. In particular, the distortions that result from the mathematics Mercator used in order to get the right compass bearing tend to obscure the huge problems that can arise in feeding the peoples of the African continent.

---

3. **half as big again** one-and-a-half times larger.

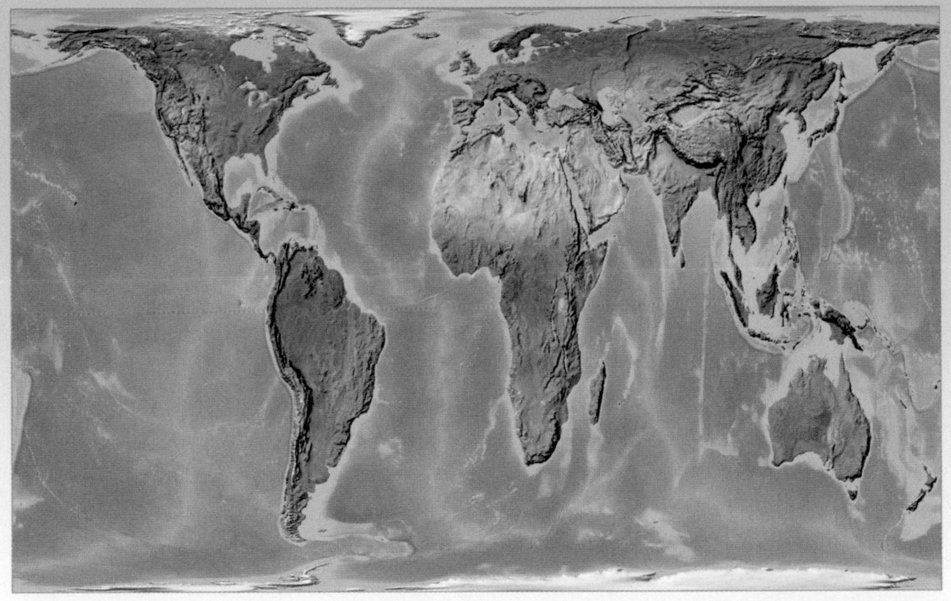

Peters projection

This was precisely the point made by the German cartographer Arno Peters, who, in 1983, produced a rectangular-grid map of the world that is faithful to land area. These days, argued Peters, the most important feature to preserve in a global map is land area. Next comes shape. Forget compass bearings altogether. The Peters map distorts shape and distance (and compass direction), but is accurate in terms of surface area. To obtain his map, Peters had to resort to some fairly **intricate** mathematics—there is no simple geometric projection that will produce a map representing area accurately.

◀ **intricate**
(in′ tri kit) *adj.* having many parts; complex

The introduction of the Peters map highlighted a feature of mathematics that professionals are well aware of but that outsiders sometimes overlook. Mathematics is completely accurate and precise. It does for us exactly what we tell it to do. But if we forget the assumptions we make before we start to use the mathematics, if we forget what features we decided to ignore, then the result can be misleading.

Because of the orange-peel problem, in order to represent the round earth on a flat surface, the cartographer has to decide what features to preserve, and then use the appropriate mathematical transformation. The resulting map gives a view of the world shaped by that mathematical transformation, and that view can affect the way people approach the world's problems. Mercator's map was highly reliable for the ocean navigator. But it is woefully inadequate for giving any sense of how big the different continents and countries are.

Close Reading Activities

READ

Comprehension

Reread all or part of the text to help you answer the following questions.

1. Why was it especially important for the ancient Egyptians to mark the boundaries of their land?
2. What are the origins of the word *geometry*?
3. What is the two-part problem that mapmakers face?

Research: Clarify Details Choose at least one unfamiliar detail from this selection and briefly research it. Then, explain how the information you learned helps you better understand the text.

Summarize Write an objective summary of the selection. Remember that an objective summary is free from opinion and evaluation.

Language Study

Selection Vocabulary The following passages appear in "The Shape of the World." Identify one synonym and one antonym for each boldfaced word. Then, use each word in a sentence of your own.

- . . . the ancient Egyptians living in the Nile Valley faced a **recurrent** problem.
- . . . they needed a way to accurately reconstruct the **obliterated** boundary lines.
- To obtain his map, Peters had to resort to some fairly **intricate** mathematics...

Literary Analysis

Reread the identified passage. Then, respond to the questions that follow.

Focus Passage *(pp. 313–314)*

It's when the map . . . sphere to a flat plane.

Key Ideas and Details

1. Under what circumstances does the making of an accurate map get "tricky"?

Craft and Structure

2. **(a)** What problem is summarized by the question the author poses in the first paragraph? **(b) Analyze:** How does the second paragraph relate to the first? Explain.
3. **(a)** What analogy, or comparison, does Devlin use to illustrate the problem stated in the first paragraph? **(b) Evaluate:** Does this analogy effectively clarify a complex topic? Explain.

Integration of Knowledge and Ideas

4. **(a)** What criteria does a cartographer use to choose a projection for a map? **(b) Infer:** What does this suggest about the ways in which maps represent reality? Support your answer with textual details.

Description

Description is the use of sensory details to create a word picture or mental image. Writers often use description to help explain **abstract** ideas. Reread the text, and note how Devlin uses description.

1. **(a)** What aspects of the Mercator map does Devlin describe? **(b)** How does this description clarify the Mercator map's "disadvantages"?
2. **Vision:** Cite another example of description in the selection that helps readers understand the limitations of maps and the reasons for those limitations. Explain your choice.

DISCUSS • RESEARCH • WRITE

From Text to Topic **Partner Discussion**

Discuss the following passage with a partner. Take notes during the discussion. Contribute your own ideas, and support them with examples from the text.

> Because of the orange-peel problem, in order to represent the round earth on a flat surface, the cartographer has to decide what features to preserve, and then use the appropriate mathematical transformation. The resulting map gives a view of the world shaped by that mathematical transformation, and that view can affect the way people approach the world's problems.

QUESTIONS FOR DISCUSSION

1. Are maps accurate representations of reality?
2. In what specific ways might people's perceptions of geography affect how they deal with issues?

Research **Investigate the Topic**

Satellite Imaging Maps, such as the one invented by Mercator, once changed how people view and navigate the world. Today, satellite imaging is again providing people with new perspectives on our world.

Assignment

Conduct research to learn about satellite imaging. Find information about the history, technology, uses, and effects of satellite imaging. Carefully consider the reliability of your sources and gather information for citation. Share your findings in a short **report** that includes visual images as examples.

PREPARATION FOR ESSAY

You may use the results of this research in an essay you will write at the end of this section.

Writing to Sources **Informative Text**

"The Shape of the World" describes how cartographers handle geometrical distortions when attempting to **represent** Earth in two dimensions. It also explains how the user's needs help a cartographer choose the factors to show on a map.

Assignment

Write an **essay** in which you explain how different types of maps help us see different **aspects** of the world. Consider Devlin's discussion of the Mercator and Peters maps, as well as the reasons people use maps today.

- Write a clear statement of purpose.
- Discuss at least two types of maps and the reasons people use them today. Organize information to reflect that focus.
- Connect your personal observations and experience with information from Devlin's text, making sure to correctly cite or attribute that information.

ACADEMIC VOCABULARY

Academic terms appear in blue on these pages. If these words are not familiar to you, use a dictionary to find their definitions. Then, use them as you speak and write about the text.

Common Core State Standards

RI.9-10.1, RI.9-10.2, RI.9-10.4, RI.9-10.5, RI.9-10.6; W.9-10.2, W.9-10.4, W.9-10.7, W.9-10.9.b; SL.9-10.1; L.9-10.4, L.9-10.6

[For full standards wording, see the chart in the front of this book.]

SCIENCE WRITING

Seeing Things

from

How the Brain Works

John McCrone

Lift your eyes and look around. It is so easy. The world just floods in, an instant panorama. Nothing is missed, nothing is invented, and nothing is incoherent. OK, now forget all the evidence of your eyes, because seeing the world is not like that at all.

How do your brain pathways process what you experience in a single moment? Well, let's imagine what happens in your brain as you round a street corner and are confronted by a rhinoceros blocking your way.

First, your brain has to take in the raw sensations. The rhinoceros and every other object in the field of view reflects light of various intensities and wavelengths. This light hits the back of your eyeballs, where it is picked up by a layer of pigmented nerve cells, the retina. The scene is then relayed to the occipital lobe[1] at the back of your head. A map of what you are seeing is projected (upside down) onto the primary visual cortex—a palm-sized, ½-in (2-millimeter) thick sheet of about half a billion densely interconnected neurons.

Eyeball

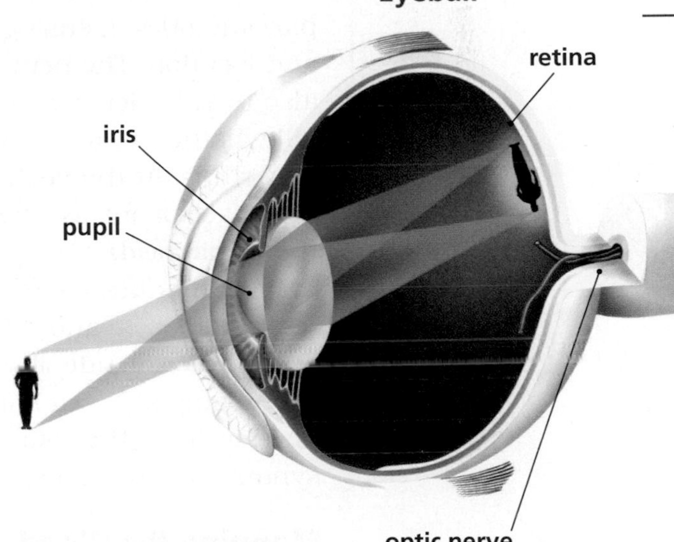

optic nerve
The optic nerve transmits visual information from the retina to the brain.

Are you aware of anything yet? No, even though there has been some initial sharpening and tidying up of the picture. The primary visual cortex, or V1, is simply the first staging post. The serious analysis is to follow.

The human cortex has about 30 modules devoted to extracting the detail of visual experiences. Physically, the cortex is a single continuous sheet. Logically, however, it is broken into a mosaic of processing areas, with each patch of processing connected to the next patch, which builds to form an ever-rising stack of activity.

1. **occipital lobe** (äk si´ pə təl lōb) *n.* structure at the back of the brain that has a form like a three-sided pyramid.

So you round the corner. A pattern of information is splashed across the primary visual cortex. A hierarchy of visual modules then starts to make sense of this pattern. The very next level, V2, is important for highlighting the boundaries and contours of what you are seeing. Like a heavy black marker, it draws around edges so that the shape of the object stands out from the shapes of the background. Next, there is V3, which takes the analysis of shape and perspective a step further, while V4 takes the wavelength information and turns it into an experience of color. As the analysis continues, each level feeds the activity of the next to extract increasingly precise details. The brain cannot swallow the visual scene at one time, so it pulls it to pieces, distilling the information progressively. Sight is actually a bundle of senses—for color, motion, form, and so on—all "flying in formation."[2]

Branching Pathways

Rather early on in the visual process, a fork appears in the visual hierarchy. One branch heads up the back of the skull toward the parietal lobes, focusing on "where is it?" questions to do with motion and location. The neurons are tuned to pick up shifts of position and also to subtract our own motion from the emerging picture so we can tell whether we are moving toward an object or the object is moving toward us. At the peak of this brain path emerges a general feel for the space about us—how near or distant are the many elements of the visual field.

The other branch of analysis runs down the brain toward the temporal lobes, and this focuses on "what is it?" questions. Driven by a gathering tide of sensory details—a distinctive silhouette, a horny gray hide, an impression of great bulk—these areas can put an identity to the visual object. Using the memories etched into their synaptic connections, they will splutter the answer "rhinoceros!"

Mapping the World

Yet at this stage the visual pathway is still busy mapping and recognizing everything in the field of view. As you turn a corner, you must take in the whole scene before you can zero in on any of its parts. Other neurons will be energetically signaling people, houses, cars, trees. Somehow the "rhinoceros" neurons need to make themselves heard over the general hubbub of activity.

So far we have been talking about the back half of the brain, the sensory cortex. Each of the senses—touch, taste, hearing, balance, and sight—has its own corner of this sheet. And each follows the same hierarchical logic. With hearing, for example, a pattern of

2. **flying in formation** moving as one unit, as with a group of military aircraft.

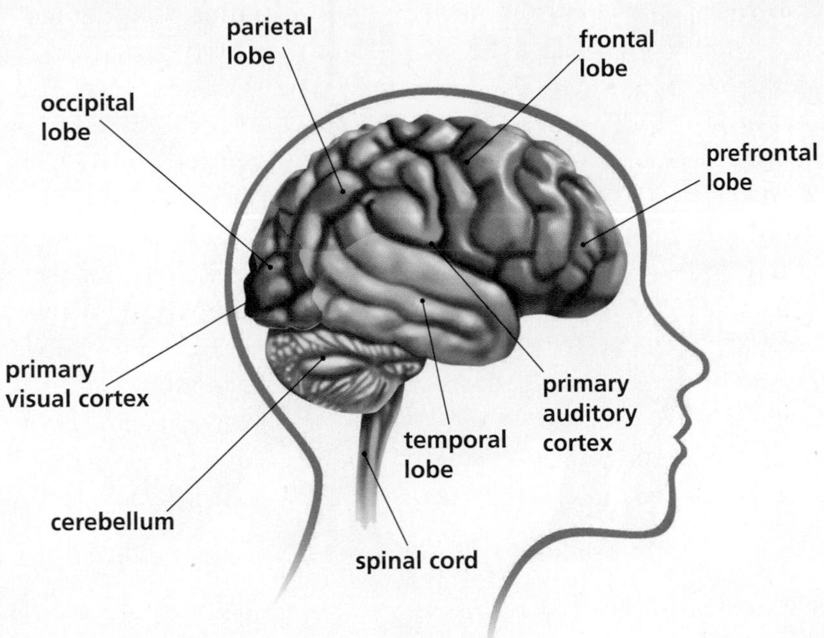

raw frequencies is mapped onto the primary **auditory** cortex. Then further stages of processing identify and locate the sounds. The next phase of brain activity must draw in the frontal cortex.

◀ **auditory** (ô′ də tôr′ ē) *adj.* related to hearing or the organs of hearing

Memory Snapshots

For the sake of completeness, we should mention that as the sensory hierarchies reach a peak, they also being to converge. In special "multi-modal" areas such as the entorhinal cortex and especially the hippocampus,[3] neurons start to fire in response to combinations of noises, visions, smells, and other sensations. The many strands of sensory activity are tied together. This does not mean the hippocampus suddenly lights up with miniature sensory images. But a pattern of activity forms that "points back" to a stack of other **neural** patterns. The hippocampus reflects the fact that certain details exist, spread across the rest of the sensory cortex circuitry.

◀ **neural** (no͝or′ əl) *adj.* related to nerves or the nervous system

Among other things, this allows the hippocampus to be a memory organ. A snapshot of neural activity at the level of the hippocampus can be used later to cause firing to follow a reverse path back down the sensory hierarchy, recreating the feel of the original experience. Memory is a general property of brains, as every synaptic connection is shaped by experience. But the hippocampus is positioned to capture specific memories, to trap a neural template of a particular sensory state, and then to use that template hours or even years later to reconstruct that moment.

---

3. **hippocampus** (hip′ ō kam′ pəs) *n.* curved structure that sits below the middle of the brain and helps with navigation and memory.

Interpretation

Anyway, getting back to our rhinoceros example, first the sensory half of the brain maps everything—all the details. Next, the frontal lobes need to kick in. The sensory picture has to be focused by a frontal act of attention that then leaves the brain in a state of intention—knowing both what is happening and what it wants to do about it.

The very highest levels of the brain are the dozen or so processing areas that make up the prefrontal lobes. These areas are not interested in what is routine about any moment, just what is significant and worthy of closer examination. It is when news of a rhinoceros-shaped patch of visual activity hits this part of the brain that a sharp conscious experience can start to dawn.

Acting in concert with the arousal and emotion centers of the lower brain, with which they have intimate connections, the prefrontal lobes organize a state of attention. The paying of attention has the effect of actually defining the sensory experience. The sensory cortex begins by responding to the full panorama—the rhinoceros—but also everything else. Attention goes back over this to create contrast. It turns up the volume of the neurons representing the rhinoceros, pushing irrelevant details such as the presence of people, houses, cars, and trees into the dim fringes of that moment's awareness.

This is one of the advantages of the brain being an organic network of connections rather than a strict input-output device. The "output" areas can reach back down to alter their own inputs. Any input actually starts as more of a suggestion—"hey, I might be important." Many inputs are analyzed, and eventually there is feedback to say, "yes, you were the bit that mattered." The brain's pathways actually evolve a response.

Mounting a Response

A second obvious effect of paying attention to a particular aspect of a moment is that it unleashes a flood of thought, emotions, and associations. The whole of the brain is prompted to respond to the **focal** event with whatever resources are available. So noting the sight of a rhinoceros will bring any stored mental associations to the surface. Even as we are recognizing the animal, relevant thoughts will be bubbling up in us. Has it seen us? Is there a zoo nearby? Should we freeze or run? Could this be a practical joke or maybe even a dream? Our arousal centers will be making decisions about whether to relax or whether to pump up the body for action. Our motor areas, behind the prefrontal regions on the frontal cortex sheet, will be gearing up to execute any intentions beginning to form. And even our language areas may start to organize a suitable (or suitably strangled) vocal response.

◂ **focal**
(fō´ kəl) *adj.* at the center of activity or attention

The brain thus takes in the whole of each moment and extracts, and responds to, its core aspect. A lamppost or parked car may have been clearly visible alongside the rhino. But it is unlikely we would have any thoughts or feelings about them. The brain's mission is to find out what matters most and then to respond to that in as full and as coherent a way as possible.

It is when news of a rhinoceros-shaped patch of visual activity hits this part of the brain that a sharp conscious experience can start to dawn.

So now lift your eyes again. Isn't it amazing that so much mapping and analyzing must be taking place for you to have any kind of sensory panorama? It may appear to happen almost instantaneously, but in fact it doesn't. It takes time, and that's another problem that brains have to overcome.

Close Reading Activities

READ

Comprehension

Reread all or part of the text to help you answer the following questions.

1. What is the retina?
2. What does the V2 layer of the visual cortex do?
3. What part of the brain "points back" to the look and feel of a previous experience?
4. According to the author, what is the brain's mission?

Research: Clarify Details This text may include references that are unfamiliar to you. Choose at least one of these details and briefly research it. Then, explain how the information you learned helps you better understand the selection.

Summarize Write an objective summary of the text, one that is free from opinion and evaluation.

Language Study

Selection Vocabulary: Science The following passages appear in "Seeing Things." Define each boldfaced word. Then, for each word, identify its root and at least one other word that shares that root.

- But a pattern of activity forms that "points back" to a stack of other **neural** patterns.
- The whole of the brain is prompted to respond to the **focal** event…
- With hearing, for example, a pattern of raw frequencies is mapped onto the primary **auditory** cortex.

Literary Analysis

Reread the identified passage. Then, respond to the questions that follow.

Focus Passage *(p. 322)*
Rather early on…splutter the answer "rhinoceros!"

Key Ideas and Details

1. **(a)** At what point do two branches appear in the brain's visual **hierarchy**? **(b) Classify:** What types of visual information do the two parts of the brain handle?

Craft and Structure

2. **Analyze:** What does the word "tuned" suggest about the **precision** of neural activity? Explain.
3. **Analyze:** How does the word "splutter" connect the biological process the author is describing with the surprise someone might feel upon seeing a rhino on a city street? Explain.

Integration of Knowledge and Ideas

4. **Synthesize:** What role does memory play in the neurological function of seeing?

Diction

Diction is a writer's word choice. It may be described in many ways, including formal, informal, **ornate**, familiar, technical, and so on. Reread the text, and take notes on the author's diction.

1. Cite three examples of technical or scientific diction and three examples of informal, familiar diction. Explain each choice.
2. How does the author's diction suit both his subject and intended audience? Explain.

DISCUSS • RESEARCH • WRITE

From Text to Topic **Small Group Discussion**

Discuss the following passage with a small group of classmates. Take notes during the discussion. Contribute your own ideas and support them with details from the text.

> The brain thus takes in the whole of each moment and extracts, and responds to, its core aspect. A lamppost or parked car may have been clearly visible alongside the rhino. But it is unlikely we would have any thoughts or feelings about them. The brain's mission is to find out what matters most and then to respond to that in as full and as coherent a way as possible.

QUESTIONS FOR DISCUSSION

1. Is it surprising that our brains automatically dismiss so much?
2. What does this suggest about how personal experience affects what we see at any given moment?

Research **Investigate the Topic**

Vision and Meaning "Seeing Things" explains that visual information must be interpreted by the brain before it enters our awareness and serves as a basis for action.

PREPARATION FOR ESSAY

You may use the results of this research in an essay you will write at the end of this section.

Assignment

Conduct research to learn more about the factors that shape what and how we see. Use an online search engine and key words such as "vision," "perception," and "interpretation." Select high-quality educational and scientific sites for materials. Take clear notes and document your sources. Then, write several **paragraphs** in which you explain your findings.

ACADEMIC VOCABULARY

Academic terms appear in blue on these pages. If these words are not familiar to you, use a dictionary to find their definitions. Then, use them as you speak and write about the text.

Writing to Sources **Narrative**

In "Seeing Things" we learn that what we see—and how we react to those sights—is the result of interpretations our brains make.

Assignment

Write an **autobiographical narrative** in which you describe a time you witnessed a surprising, confusing, or unusual sight. Explain what was happening both in your brain and in the world as you took in the sight. Follow these steps:

- Use vivid, colorful language to describe details.
- Narrate your reaction by going through the basics of the neurological process, illustrating each step with a detail about what you saw. Incorporate information from McCrone's text.
- Conclude by describing your reaction to what you saw and any actions that you took as a result.

Common Core State Standards

RI.9-10.1, RI.9-10.2, RI.9-10.3, RI.9-10.4, RI.9-10.6; W.9-10.2, W.9-10.3, W.9-10.4, W.9-10.7, W.9-10.9; SL.9-10.1; L.9-10.4, L.9-10.5, L.9-10.6

[For full standards wording, see the chart in the front of this book.]

How to Look at Nothing

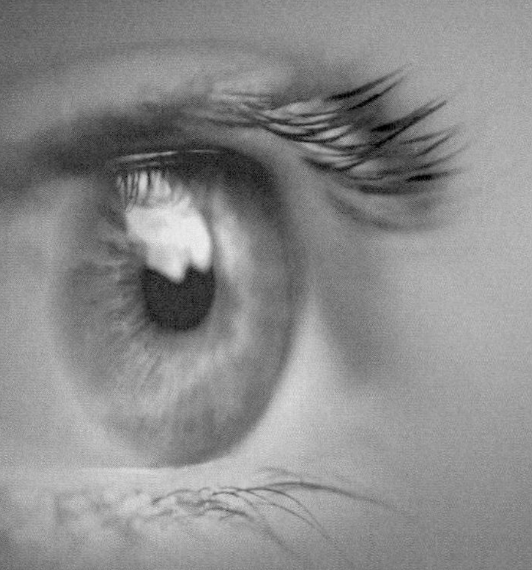

from **How to Use Your Eyes**

James Elkins

Is it possible to see absolutely nothing? Or do you always see something, even if it is nothing more than a blur or the insides of your own eyelids?

This question has been well investigated. In the 1930s, a psychologist named Wolfgang Metzger designed an experiment to show that if you have nothing to look at, your eyes will stop functioning. Metzger put volunteers in rooms that were lit very carefully so there was no shadow and no **gradients** from light to dark. The walls were polished, so it was impossible to tell how far away they were. After a few minutes in an environment like that, the volunteers reported "gray clouds" and darkness descending over their visual field. Some experienced an intense fear and felt as though they were going blind. Others were sure that dim shapes were drifting by, and they tried to reach out and grab them. Later it was found that if the room is illuminated with a bright color, within a few minutes it will seem to turn dull gray. Even a bright red or green will seem to turn gray.

◄ **gradients** (grā´ dē ənts) *n.* series of gradual changes that go across a unit in a single direction

Apparently the eye cannot stand to see nothing, and when it is faced with nothing, it slowly and automatically shuts down. You can simulate these experiments at home by cutting ping-pong balls in half and cupping them lightly over your eyes. Since you can't focus that close, your eye has no detail to latch on to, and if you're sitting in a place with fairly even illumination, you won't have any shadows or highlights to watch. After a few minutes, you will begin to feel what the people in those experiments experienced. For me, it is a slow creeping claustrophobia and an anxiety about what I'm seeing—or even *if* I am seeing. If I use a red light bulb instead of a white one, the color slowly drains out until it looks for all the world as if the light were an ordinary white bulb.

(This experiment won't work, by the way, if you close your eyes. The slight pressure of your eyelids on your corneas and the tiny flicker of your eye muscles will produce hallucinations, called entoptic lights, which will give you something to look at. The only drawback to using ping-pong balls is that your eyelashes get in the way. The experimenters recommend using "a light coating of nonirritating, easily removed, latex-based surgical adhesive" to fasten the eyelashes to the upper lid—but it's probably better to get along without it.)

These experiments are interesting but they are also artificial. It takes something as **contrived** as a polished white wall, or halves of

◄ **contrived** (kən trīvd´) *adj.* created from a plan; not happening naturally a ping-pong ball, to create a wholly uniform visual field.[1] There is another way to see nothing that I like much better, and that is trying to see something in pitch darkness. In recent decades scientists have figured out that it takes only between five to fifteen photons[2] entering the eye before we register a tiny flash of light. That is an unimaginably tiny quantity, millions of times fainter than a faint green flash from a lightning bug. Unless you have been in a cave or a sealed basement room, you have never experienced anything that dark. And yet the eye is prepared for it.

It takes at least five photons to produce the sensation of light, instead of just one, because there is a chemical in the eye that is continuously breaking down, and each time a molecule breaks, it emits a photon. If we registered every photon, our eyes would register light continuously, even if there were no light in the world outside our own eyes. The chemical that emits the light is rhodopsin, which is the same chemical that enables us to see in dim light to begin with. So as far as our visual system is concerned, there is no way to distinguish between a molecule of rhodopsin that has broken down spontaneously and one that broke down because it was hit by a photon. If we saw a flash every time a rhodopsin molecule decomposed, we would be seeing fireworks forever, so our retinas are designed to *start* seeing only when there is a little more light.

Unless you have been in a cave or a sealed basement room, you have never experienced anything that dark. And yet the eye is prepared for it.

Five to fifteen photons is an estimate and there is no way to make it exact, but the reason why it can't be exact is itself exact. It has to do with quantum mechanics, the branch of physics that deals with particles like photons. According to quantum physics, the action of photons can be known only statistically and not with utter precision. The precise theory shows that the answer is imprecise. There is also a second reason why we can never know exactly how little light we can see. The human visual system is "noisy"—it is not efficient and it fails a certain percentage of the time. Only cave explorers and volunteers in vision experiments have ever experienced perfect darkness, and even then they see spots of light. Those are "false positives," reports that there is light when there isn't. We see light when we shouldn't and we fail to see light when, by the laws of physics, we should. Also, the two eyes take in different photons and so they never work in perfect harmony. In extremely low light, a report of light from one eye might be overruled by a report of darkness from the other. Many things can happen along the complicated pathway from the rhodopsin in the retina to the centers of visual processing.

These phenomena of false positives are called by the wonderful name "dark noise" and the not-so-wonderful technical term "equivalent Poisson noise." Then there's light generated inside the eye

1. **visual field** entire area visible at a particular moment.
2. **photons** (fō′ tänz) *n.* units that quantify the intensity of light.

itself, called the "dark light of the eye." It may have a photochemical origin, such as the light from rhodopsin; wherever it comes from, it contributes to the sensation of light.

Entoptic light, the dark noise, the dark light of the eye—this is the end of seeing. But they are wonderful phenomena. To see them, you have to find a perfectly dark spot—a windowless basement room or a hallway that can be entirely closed off and then you have to spend at least a half hour acclimatizing to the dark. Where I live, in the city, it is impossible to find real darkness. There is a bathroom in our apartment that opens onto an interior hallway, but even if I close all the curtains, close off the hallway, and shut the bathroom door behind me, light still comes in under the doorway. I don't see it at first, but after ten minutes my eyes pick out a faint glow. Real darkness is elusive.

In the end, when there is nothing left to see, the eye and the brain invent lights. The dark room begins to shimmer with entoptic auroras. They seem to mirror my state of mind—if I am tired I see more of them, and if I rub my eyes they flower into bright colors. In total darkness, entoptic displays can seem as bright as daylight, and it takes several minutes for them to subside. Looking at them, it is easy to be sympathetic with anthropologists who think that all picture-making began with hallucinations. Some entoptic displays are as lovely and evanescent as auroras, and others as silky and seductive as a ghost. Pure dark, in the absence of entoptic colors, is still alive with dark noise. If I try to fix my gaze on some invisible object—say my hand held up in front of me—then my visual field starts to sparkle with small flashes of dark noise, the sign that my neurons are trying to process signals that aren't really there. They can also become quite strong, like the sparks that come off bedsheets on a cold winter night. I can also try to erase all sense of illumination by letting my eyes rest or wander wherever they want. When I do that, I am still aware of the sensation of light—really it is too dim to be called light; it is more the memory of light. Perhaps that is the "dark light of the eye," the chemicals splitting and reforming in the eye in the normal processes of molecular life.

◀ **auroras**
(ə rōr´ əz) *n.* patterns of light arranged in streams or arcs

So I am left with this strange thought: even though we overlook so many things and see so little of what passes in front of us, our eyes will not stop seeing, even when they have to invent the world from nothing. Perhaps the only moments when we truly see nothing are the blank, mindless stretches of time that pass unnoticed between our dreams. But maybe death is the only name for real blindness. At every other moment our eyes are taking in light or inventing lights of their own: it is only a matter of learning how to see what our eyes are bringing us.

Close Reading Activities

READ

Comprehension

Reread all or part of the text to help you answer the following questions.

1. What happens to the eye when it is "faced with nothing"?
2. What are entoptic light, dark noise, and dark light of the eye?
3. For what reason does the human eye *not* register every photon?

Research: Clarify Details This text may include references that are unfamiliar to you. Choose at least one unfamiliar detail and briefly research it. Then, explain how the information you learned from research sheds light on an aspect of the text.

Summarize Write an objective summary of the text. Remember that an objective summary is free from opinion and evaluation.

Language Study

Selection Vocabulary The following sentences appear in the selection. Define each boldfaced word. Then, use each word in a new sentence.

- ... there was no shadow and no **gradients** from light to dark.
- It takes something as **contrived** as a polished white wall ... to create a wholly uniform visual field.
- The dark room begins to shimmer with entoptic **auroras.**

Literary Analysis

Reread the identified passage. Then, respond to the questions that follow.

Focus Passage *(p. 331)*
Entoptic light, the dark noise ... molecular life.

Key Ideas and Details

1. **(a)** For the author, what is "the end of seeing"? **(b) Interpret:** Why is this term appropriate for the **phenomena** he describes? Explain, citing details from the focus passage.

Craft and Structure

2. **Interpret:** Identify at least two words in this passage that give entoptic lights and dark noise magical qualities. Explain each choice.
3. **Analyze:** How does the author's use of the first-person point of view affect what he is able to share about the subject? Explain.

Integration of Knowledge and Ideas

4. **Distinguish:** What is the difference, in the author's point of view, between the "end of seeing" and "real blindness"?

Similes

A **simile** is a figure of speech that uses the words *like, as,* or *than* to draw a comparison between two apparently unlike things. Reread the article and note the author's use of similes.

1. **(a)** Choose two similes from the selection. **(b)** For each choice, explain what two unlike things the author compares.
2. **Vision:** How does the author use similes to clarify information and to describe the personal, **subjective** experience of "seeing nothing"?

DISCUSS • RESEARCH • WRITE

From Text to Topic **Group Discussion**

Discuss the following passage with a group of classmates. Take notes during the discussion. Listen carefully to others and contribute your own ideas, supporting each one with examples from the text.

> So I am left with this strange thought: even though we overlook so many things and see so little of what passes in front of us, our eyes will not stop seeing, even when they have to invent the world from nothing.

QUESTIONS FOR DISCUSSION

1. How does what we "see" in the dark differ from what we "see" in the light?
2. Would the world "invented" by the eye be the same for everyone? Why or why not?

Research **Investigate the Topic**

Entoptic Lights and Cave Paintings According to Elkins, some archaeologists believe that "picture-making," such as prehistoric cave paintings, may have begun with the "hallucinations" of entoptic lights.

Assignment

Conduct research to learn about Paleolithic cave paintings, such as those in southwestern France. Consult books, journals, and Web sites. If possible, you may also watch a documentary about the discovery of the caves and the art they contain. In addition to facts about the paintings, find theories about their origins, purposes, and the **worldview** they express. Take careful notes and identify your sources for citation. Share your findings in an **oral presentation**.

PREPARATION FOR ESSAY

You may use the results of this research in an essay you will write at the end of this section.

ACADEMIC VOCABULARY

Academic terms appear in blue on these pages. If these words are not familiar to you, use a dictionary to find their definitions. Then, use them as you speak and write about the text.

Writing to Sources **Argument**

"How to Look at Nothing" suggests that what we "see" is not necessarily produced by external forces. What does this say about our ability to judge what is real and the decisions we make based on those judgments?

Assignment

Write a **position paper** in which you defend a claim about the relationship between people's perceptions, opinions, and actions. Follow these steps:

- Write a thesis statement in which you express a clear position.
- Use the first person point of view, as Elkins does, but support your ideas and claims with facts and clearly described experiences.
- Cite information from Elkins's article to support your ideas.
- Use similes to clarify your ideas.

RI.9-10.1, RI.9-10.2, RI.9-10.4, RI.9-10.5, RI.9-10.6; W.9-10.1, W.9-10.4, W.9-10.5, W.9-10.7; SL.9-10.1, SL.9-10.4; L.9-10.4, L.9-10.5, L.9-10.6

[For full standards wording, see the chart in the front of this book.]

Car Reflections, 1970 (acrylic on masonite) by Richard Estes

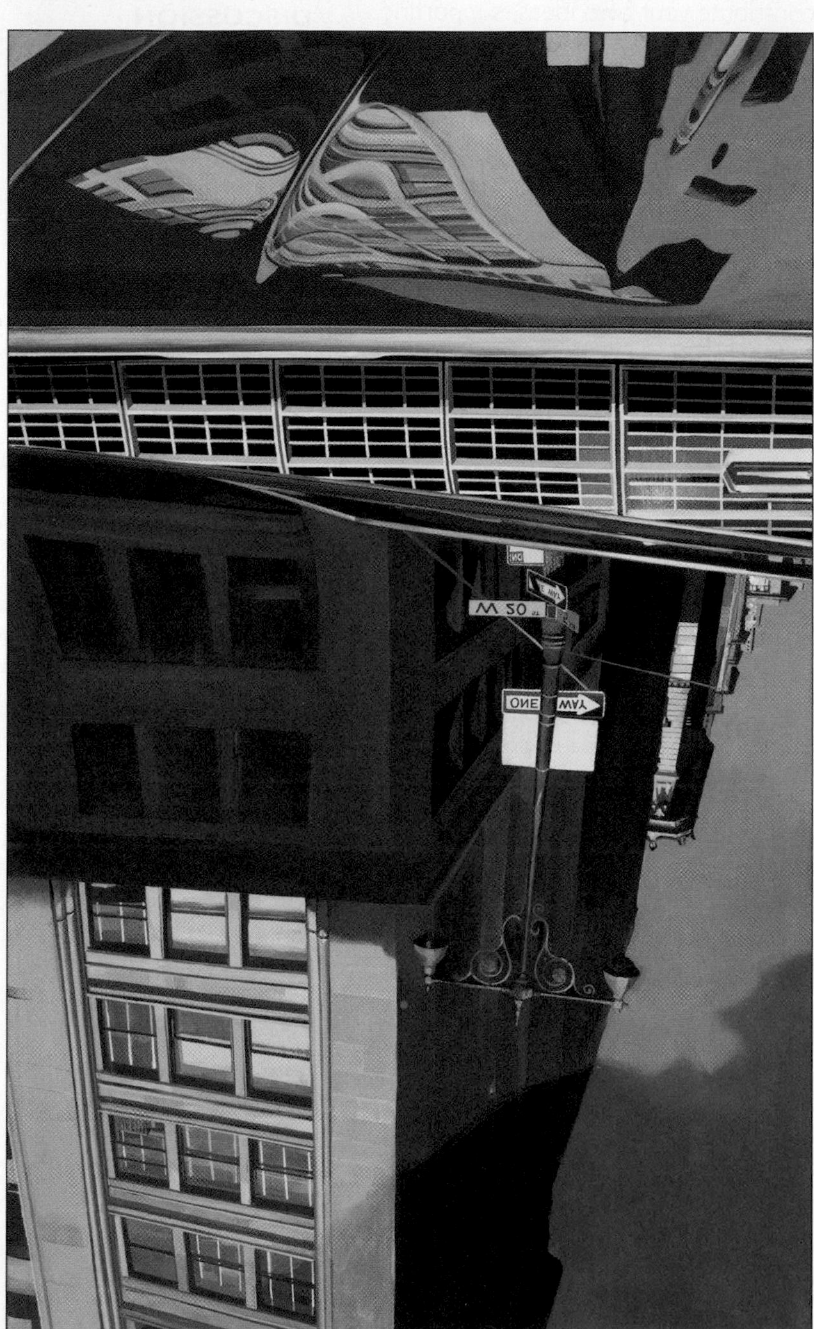

ABOUT THE ARTIST

Richard Estes (b. 1936)

Richard Estes is one of the foremost practitioners of a type of painting called photorealism, which began in the 1960s. As the name suggests, photorealism was inspired by photography. Photorealists like Estes work to create super-real images that rival photos in their clarity and focus. Photorealists also seek to reinvent the types of subject matter traditionally seen as acceptable for art, and so they paint everyday objects and scenes, such as cars, streets, stores, and factories.

READ • RESEARCH

Common Core State Standards

W.9-10.2., W.9-10.7
[For full standards wording, see the chart in the front of this book.]

Comprehension

Look at the painting closely. Then, answer the questions that follow.

1. How does the title of the painting relate to the image?
2. Where is the viewer standing in relationship to the cars? Explain.

Critical Analysis

Key Ideas and Details

1. (a) Interpret: Which parts of the cars does this painting portray?
(b) Analyze: Which details help you identify these parts of the cars? Explain.

2. (a) What objects do the reflections show? **(b)** Why do some of the reflections appear **inverted**? **(c) Connect:** How do the details of the top reflection relate to the details of the bottom reflection? Explain.

3. Infer: What do the reflections suggest about the location of the cars—where are they parked?

Craft and Structure

4. (a) Analyze: How does the use of blue in the bottom portion of the painting help to trick the viewer's eye? **(b) Interpret:** In what other ways does the use of color affect how the viewer sees the image? Explain.

Integration of Knowledge and Ideas

5. Evaluate: How is this painting both like and not like a photograph? Explain.

6. Synthesize: In what ways does this painting challenge the viewer's ability to "see" reality? Explain.

ACADEMIC VOCABULARY

Academic terms appear in blue on these pages. If these words are not familiar to you, use a dictionary to find their definitions. Then, use them as you speak and write about the text.

Research

Photorealism This painting is an example of photorealism. Photorealist artists use specific techniques to create super-realistic images that rival or **surpass** photography in their precision and clarity. These paintings challenge notions of how people see and perceive what is real.

Assignment

Conduct research about an important photorealist painter, such as Richard Estes, Audrey Flack, or Chuck Close. Gather information about the artist's subject matter, painting techniques, and beliefs about art. Consult reliable online and print sources. Share your findings in an **annotated slide presentation.**

Assessment: Synthesis

Speaking and Listening: Group Discussion

Vision and Knowledge The texts in this section vary in genre, length, style, and perspective. However, all of them comment in some way on how people see and perceive the world. Our interpretations of what we see influence what we know and understand and how we act as a result. This idea is fundamentally related to the Big Question addressed in this unit: **What kind of knowledge changes our lives?**

▲ Refer to the selections you read in Part 3 as you complete the activities on this assessment.

Assignment

Conduct discussions. With a small group, conduct a discussion about what it means to "see" and to "know." Refer to the texts in this section, other texts you have read, and your personal experience to support your ideas. Begin your discussion by addressing the following questions:

- What is a basic difference between physical vision and "seeing" in the sense of perception or interpretation?
- What aspects of "seeing" are based on human physiology and what aspects are based on a person's "worldview" produced over time by experience?
- To what extent is our knowledge of the world based on our interpretations?
- How do new interpretations lead to new understandings and, in turn, to new interpretations?
- Does knowledge change us?

Summarize and present your ideas. After you have fully explored the topic, summarize your discussion and present your findings to the class as a whole.

Criteria for Success

✓ **Organizes the group effectively**
Appoint a group leader and a timekeeper. The group leader should introduce the topic and questions and keep the discussion organized. The timekeeper should make sure the discussion takes no longer than 20 minutes.

✓ **Maintains focus of discussion**
As a group, stay disciplined and focus on the topic at hand.

✓ **Involves all participants equally and fully**
Work to create a forum in which everyone participates and no one person dominates the conversation.

✓ **Follows the rules for collegial discussion**
Listen carefully to one another and respond thoughtfully. Address one another with respect. Add to one another's ideas and support your ideas persuasively with convincing, appropriate evidence.

USE NEW VOCABULARY

As you speak and share ideas, work to use the vocabulary words you have learned in this unit. The more you use new words, the more you will "own" them.

Writing: Narrative

Common Core State Standards

W.9-10.3.a–e, W.9-10.4, W.9-10.5; SL.9-10.1.a–d, SL.9-10.4, SL.9-10.6

[For full standards wording, see the chart in the front of this book.]

Vision and Knowledge The word *vision* refers to both the physical ability to see and to the ability to perceive, understand, and imagine. We *see* scenery, but we also *see*, or perceive, situations. That second meaning often plays an important role in stories, both fictional and true.

Assignment

Write a **nonfiction narrative**, or true story, about a conflict you either experienced or witnessed that was caused by people's differing perceptions of a situation. Relate this experience to ideas you have read about and researched in this section. Keep in mind that creative nonfiction often uses literary elements, such as dialogue and figurative language, to make factually accurate information more interesting and vivid.

Criteria for Success

Purpose/Focus

✓ **Connects specific incidents with larger ideas**
Make meaningful connections between your story and the texts you have read in this section.

✓ **Clearly conveys the significance of the story**
Provide a conclusion in which you reflect on the relationship between perceptions, knowledge, and behavior.

Organization

✓ **Sequences events logically**
Structure your narrative so that individual events build on one another to create a coherent whole.

Development of Ideas/Elaboration

✓ **Supports insights**
Include examples and details from both your own experiences and from the texts you have read in this section.

✓ **Uses literary techniques effectively**
Use literary elements such as dialogue, pacing, and reflection to engage the reader.

Language

✓ **Uses language precisely and effectively**
Use sensory details or figurative language to bring scenes and settings to life.

Conventions

✓ **Does not have errors**
Check your narrative to eliminate errors in grammar, spelling, and punctuation.

WRITE TO EXPLORE

As you write, you may find the ideas from a text to be less relevant than you had first thought. Allow for such changes in your thinking. You may even be able to include a discussion of your changing opinion in your narrative.

Writing to Sources: **Argument**

Vision and Knowledge The readings in this section present ideas about vision, perception, and knowledge. They raise questions, such as the following, about what it means to see and what it means to know.

- What role does perception play in an individual's understanding of other people and the world around them?
- How much of what we see and perceive is conscious and how much is unconscious?
- In what ways does experience, training, or artistic ability influence what a person "sees"?
- What is the relationship between the world "out there" and the world as it is represented in the mind of the individual?

Focus on the question that intrigues you the most, and then complete the following assignment.

Assignment

Write an **argumentative essay** in which you state and defend a claim about the connections between people's perceptions, knowledge, and actions. Support your claim by citing information, examples, and details from two or more texts in this section.

INCORPORATE RESEARCH

Strengthen your position by pulling in facts, quotations, and data you gathered while conducting research related to the readings in this section. Make sure to cite your sources correctly.

Prewriting and Planning

Choose texts. Review the texts in the section to decide which ones you will cite in your essay. Select at least two that clearly relate to your topic and position.

Gather details and develop your argument. Use a chart like the one shown to identify specific claims that support your argument. Though you may refine or change your ideas as you write, the working version will establish a clear direction.

Focus Question: In what ways does experience, training, or artistic ability influence what a person "sees"?

Text	Passage	Notes
"The Statue that Didn't Look Right"	He [Zeri] found himself staring at the sculpture's fingernails. In a way he couldn't immediately articulate, they seemed wrong to him.	Zeri is a trained art historian, so he sees details that others may not.
"Seeing Things"	It is when news of a rhinoceros-shaped patch of visual activity hits this part of the brain that a sharp conscious experience can start to dawn.	The brain decides what is important based on prior experience.
Example Claim: Experience teaches, so someone with a "trained" eye sees more than others.		

Plan to discuss counterarguments. For each point you plan to make to support your argument, note a possible objection. Include a discussion of these counterclaims in your essay and show why they are not convincing.

Drafting

Sequence your ideas and evidence. Organize your ideas in a logical sequence. Select details from your chart that correlate with each point, and be sure to provide evidence that directly supports the ideas you want to express.

Address counterclaims. As you organize your ideas, introduce opposing opinions or differing interpretations. Show you have considered those other views but also explain why your claims are stronger. Support your ideas with strong evidence from both the texts and your research.

Introduce, develop, and connect ideas. Write an introduction in which you clearly state your main idea or argument. Develop that idea through your body paragraphs, making sure to connect and clarify your ideas by using appropriate transitional words, phrases, and clauses. Conclude with a strong, memorable paragraph in which you restate your argument.

Revising and Editing

Review content. Make sure that your main argument and supporting claims are clearly stated and that you have supported them with convincing textual evidence. Elaborate on your ideas or add more proof as needed.

Review style. Reread your work and make sure you have used varied sentence types to add interest to your writing. Check that you have punctuated all sentences correctly.

Common Core State Standards

W.9-10.1.a–e, W.9-10.5, W.9-10.9; L.9-10.1

[For full standards wording, see the chart in the front of this book.]

PARAPHRASE CORRECTLY

Be sure to use your own words when describing ideas presented in other works, and always provide proper citations for paraphrased material.

Self-Evaluation Rubric

Use the following criteria to evaluate the effectiveness of your essay.

Criteria	Rating Scale
PURPOSE/FOCUS Introduces a precise claim and distinguishes the claim from (implied) alternative or opposing claims; provides a concluding section that follows from and supports the argument presented	*not very .... very* 1 2 3 4
ORGANIZATION Establishes a logical organization; uses words, phrases, and clauses to link the major sections of the text, create cohesion, and clarify relationships among claims, reasons, and evidence, and between claims and counterclaims	1 2 3 4
DEVELOPMENT OF IDEAS/ELABORATION Develops the claim and counterclaims fairly, supplying evidence for each while pointing out the strengths and limitations of both	1 2 3 4
LANGUAGE Establishes and maintains a formal style and objective tone	1 2 3 4
CONVENTIONS Attends to the norms and conventions of the discipline	1 2 3 4

Independent Reading

Titles for Extended Reading

In this unit, you have read texts in a variety of genres. Continue to read on your own. Select works that you enjoy, but challenge yourself to explore new topics, new authors, and works of increasing depth and complexity. The titles suggested below will help you get started.

INFORMATIONAL TEXT

Night
by Elie Wiesel

During World War II, approximately 6 million European Jews were killed in concentration camps set up by the Nazi regime. *Night* is a **memoir** that describes the author's experiences as a 15-year-old boy who survived the camps but was tormented by what he had seen and experienced.

Touch the Top of the World
by Erik Weihenmayer
Signet, 1999

Erik Weihenmayer had already climbed five of the world's highest peaks when he decided to climb Mount Everest—the "top of the world." Despite having lost his eyesight when he was a child, Weihenmayer achieved his goal. In this **memoir,** he recounts the challenges he faced and the fulfillment he experienced on his high-altitude adventure.

The Longitude Prize
by Joan Dash
Farrar, Straus and Giroux, 2000

EXEMPLAR TEXT

During the eighteenth century, the British government offered a large monetary prize to the first person to develop a method for measuring longitude at sea. The government hoped to reduce the losses of both sailors and ships. This work of **historical nonfiction** tells the story of clockmaker John Harrison, who invented a creative answer to a national problem.

Roughing It
by Mark Twain

In this **semi-autobiographical account,** Twain recounts his years in the American West, when vigilantes ruled the land and gold prospecting was the rage. A unique mixture of true account and tall tale, this book is humorous and wildly entertaining.

LITERATURE

In the Time of the Butterflies
by Julia Alvarez
Algonquin Books, 2010

EXEMPLAR TEXT

This **novel** is set in the Dominican Republic during the mid-twentieth century. It is based on the real-life stories of the Mirabal sisters, who took part in a plot to topple their oppressive government. Beginning with their childhoods, the author gives life to these courageous sisters.

Lord of the Flies
by William Golding
Berkley Publishing Group, 1954

In this **novel,** a plane crash leaves a group of boys stranded without adults on a deserted island. A dark influence soon casts a shadow over the young survivors, and life turns dangerous and deadly.

Animal Farm
by George Orwell

With idealism and stirring slogans, mistreated animals take over a farm and try to create a paradise of progress, justice, and equality. As the **novel** progresses, however, the reality of the situation points to far different truths. A mix of fable and political satire, this book takes aim at totalitarianism in all its forms.

ONLINE TEXT SET

PROSE POEM
Tepeyac Sandra Cisneros

SHORT STORY
A Visit to Grandmother
William Melvin Kelley

MEMOIR
***from* Places Left Unfinished at the Time of Creation** John Phillip Santos

Preparing to Read Complex Texts

Attentive Reading As you read on your own, bring your imagination and questions to the text. The questions shown below and others that you ask as you read will help you learn and enjoy reading even more.

Reading Literature/ Informational Text

10. By the end of grade 10, read and comprehend literature, including stories, dramas, and poems, and literary nonfiction at the high end of the grades 9–10 text complexity band independently and proficiently.

When reading nonfiction, ask yourself…

Comprehension: **Key Ideas and Details**

- Who is the author? Why did he or she write the work?
- Is the author an expert on the topic? How do I know?
- Are the ideas the author conveys important? Do they merit my attention? If not, why?
- Does any one idea strike me as being the most important? Why?
- Do any particular details strike me as being more important than others? If so, why?
- Does the author state his or her position directly? If not, how does he or she communicate a particular perspective on the topic?

Text Analysis: **Craft and Structure**

- Does the author organize ideas so that I can follow them? If not, what is wrong with the way the text is ordered?
- Does the author give me a new way of looking at a topic? If so, how? If not, why?
- What do I notice about the author's style—his or her use of language?
- Does the author use strong evidence? Do I find any of the evidence unconvincing? If so, why?

Connections: **Integration of Ideas**

- Do the attitudes of a particular time or place affect the author's ideas? If so, how?
- Do I agree or disagree with the author's basic premise? Why?
- How does this work relate to others I have read about this or a related topic?
- How would I write about a similar topic? Would I follow an approach similar to the author's, or would I handle the topic differently?
- What have I learned from this text?

UNIT 3

Does all communication serve a positive purpose?

UNIT PATHWAY

PART 1
SETTING EXPECTATIONS

- INTRODUCING THE BIG QUESTION
- CLOSE READING WORKSHOP

PART 2
TEXT ANALYSIS
GUIDED EXPLORATION

ARTFUL WORDS

PART 3
TEXT SET
DEVELOPING INSIGHT

LOST CIVILIZATIONS

PART 4
DEMONSTRATING INDEPENDENCE

- INDEPENDENT READING
- ONLINE TEXT SET

CLOSE READING TOOL

Use this tool to practice the close reading strategies you learn.

STUDENT eTEXT

Bring learning to life with audio, video, and interactive tools.

ONLINE WRITER'S NOTEBOOK

Easily capture notes and complete assignments online.

Find all Digital Resources at **pearsonrealize.com**

Introducing the Big Question

Does all communication serve a positive purpose?

Communication, the act of exchanging information and ideas, can take many forms. Some, like traffic signs, are basic and straightforward. Others, like art, music, and literature, are multi-faceted and complex. In addition, human beings are constantly finding new methods for our communications—from nonverbal gestures to poems, from handwritten notes to satellite transmissions. Some forms of communication are private, meant only for one other person or even just for the self, while others are public and meant for everyone. Given the energy we put into communicating, questions arise: Are there any negatives to all the activity surrounding the sharing of thoughts, feelings, and information? How do we deal with misunderstandings, misinterpretations, or even bad intentions? Does all communication serve a positive purpose?

Exploring the Big Question

Collaboration: Group Discussion Start thinking about the Big Question by identifying why people communicate with each other. Give a specific example of each of the following categories:

- Informing people of a problem or an important issue
- Using art or music as a form of self-expression
- Clearing up a misunderstanding
- Understanding the feelings and experiences of others
- Passing along the latest gossip to a friend
- Telling a current news story or explaining historical events

Discuss why someone would communicate in each situation and whether the communication would have a positive or negative effect.

Before you begin the discussion, set rules that will help you share ideas as a group. For example, you might have each group member write down his or her ideas and then take turns reading them aloud. After that, you might open up the discussion to general contributions. As you conduct your discussion, use the words related to communication listed on the page at right.

Connecting to the Literature Each reading in this unit will give you additional insight into the Big Question. After you read each selection, pause to consider the ideas it communicates.

Vocabulary

Speaking and Listening

1. Initiate and participate effectively in a range of collaborative discussions with diverse partners on grades 9–10 topics, texts, and issues, building on others' ideas and expressing their own clearly and persuasively.

1.b. Work with peers to set rules for collegial discussions and decision-making, clear goals and deadlines, and individual roles as needed.

Language

6. Acquire and use accurately general academic and domain-specific words and phrases, sufficient for reading, writing, speaking, and listening at the college and career readiness level; demonstrate independence in gathering vocabulary knowledge when considering a word or phrase important to comprehension or expression.

Acquire and Use Academic Vocabulary

Acquire and Use Academic Vocabulary The term "academic vocabulary" refers to words you typically encounter in scholarly and literary texts and in technical and business writing. It is the language that helps to express complex ideas. Review the definitions of these academic vocabulary words.

context (kän´ tekst´) *n.* circumstances that form an event's setting

convey (kən vā´) *v.* communicate, express, or make known

discourse (dis´ kors) *n.* ongoing communication of ideas and information

explanation (eks´ plə nā´ shən) *n.* clarifying statement

interact (in´ tər akt´) *v.* relate to one another; affect another

isolation (ī´sə lā´ shən) *n.* state of aloneness or separation

meaning (mē´ niŋ) *n.* ideas that are indicated or expressed; significance

misinterpret (mis´ in tʉr´ prit) *v.* understand incorrectly

respond (ri spänd´) *v.* answer

Use these words as you complete Big Question activities in this unit that involve reading, writing, speaking, and listening.

Gather Vocabulary Knowledge Additional words related to communication are listed below. Categorize the words by deciding whether you know each one well, know it a little bit, or do not know it at all.

confusion	connection	emotion
language	self-expression	verbal

Then, complete the following steps:

1. Write the definitions of the words you know.
2. Consult a print or an online dictionary to confirm the definitions of the words you know. Revise your original definitions if necessary.
3. Use the dictionary to look up the meanings of the words you do not know. Then, write the meanings.
4. Use all the words in a paragraph about communication.

Close Reading Workshop

In this workshop, you will learn an approach to reading that will deepen your understanding of literature and will help you better appreciate the writer's craft. The workshop includes models for the close reading, discussion, research, and writing activities you will complete as you study the texts in this unit. After you have reviewed the strategies and models, practice your skills with the Independent Practice selection.

Common Core State Standards

RL.9-10.1, RL.9-10.2, RL.9-10.4, RL.9-10.5; W.9-10.1, W.9-10.7, W.9-10.9; SL.9-10.1; L.9-10.3, L.9-10.5

[For full standards wording, see the chart in the front of this book.]

CLOSE READING: **POETRY**

In Part 2 of this unit, you will focus on reading various poems. Use these strategies as you read the texts:

Comprehension: **Key Ideas and Details**

- Read first to understand basic meaning.
- Consult a dictionary or analyze context clues to define unfamiliar words in the poem.
- Notice references to events, people, or ideas that are unfamiliar to you and research them.
- Read to enjoy the musicality, imagery, and figurative language of the poem.

Ask yourself questions such as these:

- Who is the speaker of the poem?
- Is the poem telling a story, presenting an idea, or describing a moment in time?
- Which details help me understand the poem?
- How do specific words and images help me draw inferences about the poem's meaning?

Text Analysis: **Craft and Structure**

- Notice the poem's overall form, including the types of stanzas and the lengths of lines.
- Consider other structural elements of the poem, such as the presence or absence of rhyme, repetition, and meter.
- Analyze imagery and figures of speech and evaluate how these contribute to the poem's tone and meaning.
- Take note of how the poet uses language and structure to express layers of meaning.

Ask yourself questions such as these:

- What figurative language does the poet use, and how does that language contribute to the poem's meaning?
- How is the poem structured and how does the structure affect how I read it?
- How do sound devices influence my understanding of the poem?

Connections: **Integration of Knowledge and Ideas**

- Look for images, sound devices, and ideas that repeat throughout the poem.
- Look for symbols and analyze what they mean within the world of the poem.
- Synthesize your observations to determine the theme or central insight.
- Compare and contrast this poem with other poems.

Ask yourself questions such as these:

- How has this poem increased my understanding of an idea, a poet, or poetry in general?
- In what ways is this poem special or unique?

Read

As you read this poem, note the annotations that model ways to closely read the text.

Reading Model

"I Am Offering this Poem" by Jimmy Santiago Baca

I am offering this poem to you,
since I have nothing else to give.[1]
Keep it like a warm coat[2]
when winter comes to cover you,[3]
or like a pair of thick socks[2]
the cold cannot bite through,[3]
I love you,[4]

I have nothing else to give you,
so it is a pot full of yellow corn
to warm your belly in winter,
it is a scarf for your head, to wear
over your hair, to tie up around your face,
I love you,[4]

Keep it, treasure this as you would
if you were lost, needing direction,
in the wilderness[5] life becomes when mature;
and in the corner of your drawer,
tucked away like a cabin or hogan[4]
in dense trees,[5] come knocking,
and I will answer, give you directions,
and let you warm yourself by this fire,
rest by this fire, and make you feel safe
I love you,[4]

It's all I have to give,
and all anyone needs to live,[4]
and to go on living inside,
when the world outside
no longer cares if you live or die;[5]
remember,
I love you.[4]

Key Ideas and Details

1 The speaker uses the word "offering" instead of a synonym such as "giving." In its noun form, "offering" has a sacred connotation. That connotation suggests the speaker is offering a holy gift—this poem—to the reader.

Craft and Structure

2 Two similes compare the poem to a coat and thick socks—items that offer protection and warmth. Images in later stanzas will restate this connection between the poem and warmth.

Integration of Knowledge and Ideas

3 The personification of "winter" as able to "cover," and "cold" as able to "bite" makes the outside world a hostile force. This contrasts with the warmth the poem offers.

Craft and Structure

4 The speaker repeats "I love you" at the end of each stanza. One interpretation is that the words "I love you" are the poem being offered. In the last two stanzas, the poem, love, or both becomes a kind of home—"a cabin or hogan"—and safe haven that is all "anyone needs to live."

Integration of Knowledge and Ideas

5 Throughout the poem, the speaker distinguishes between a warm inner world of love and a cold outside world. In this poem, things *outside* the safe haven love creates are a "wilderness." Ultimately, the speaker claims that if love is present *inside* the reader, nothing *outside* matters.

Discuss

Sharing your own ideas and listening to the ideas of others can deepen your understanding. As you discuss a text, work to have a genuine exchange in which you build upon one another's ideas and ask meaningful questions.

Discussion Model

Student 1: This is a love poem but there's nothing in it about the person who is loved. It is about love, but not about romance. I also think it might be about the power of a poem to build a world for the reader.

Student 2: That's interesting. The speaker says the "offering" is the poem itself. The reader isn't given a real warm coat or thick socks. The reader is being given words for those things, but not the things themselves.

Student 3: Yes, but you don't get the sense that the speaker wishes there was more to give. The poem is enough. I think there is something here about the power of words themselves to affect people and I wonder if that's something Baca writes about a lot.

Research

Consider questions that arise in your mind as you read. Use those questions as the basis for targeted research that will help you better understand a text.

Research Model

Question: Key Words for Internet Search: Jimmy Santiago Baca poetry

Result: The Poetry Foundation

What I Learned: Baca spent time in prison but experienced a major shift in his life after reading poetry by Chilean poet Pablo Neruda and Spanish poet Federico García Lorca. In his work he explores his roots in the American Southwest as well as issues of social justice. He also writes about the power of language itself, noting: "I approach language as if it will contain who I am as a person."

Write

Writing about a text will deepen your understanding of it and will also allow you to share your ideas more formally with others. The following model essay evaluates Baca's use of imagery and cites evidence to support the main idea.

Writing Model: Explanatory Essay

Figurative Language in "I Am Offering this Poem"

In "I Am Offering this Poem," poet Jimmy Santiago Baca uses figurative language to say that love can protect, nourish, and sustain. In the first stanza, the speaker states that he has "nothing else to give" besides the poem. In place of other gifts, the poem is an "offering." The speaker establishes that the poem is a protective and comforting force with similes and metaphors such as "like a warm coat," "a pair of thick socks," and "warm your belly in winter." The speaker also compares the poem to such objects as a map or a sock that can be hidden and kept safe.

The writer expresses a clear position in the first paragraph.

The writer immediately introduces evidence that supports the claim.

The speaker also contrasts the harshest elements of nature to the warmth of the offered poem. In the first stanza, "winter" can "cover" and "cold" can "bite." This use of personification establishes nature as an enemy, and allows the reader to visualize the brutality of a world in which love is absent. In the third stanza, the speaker says, "if you were lost, needing direction, / in the wilderness life becomes when mature." The speaker repeats, almost as a protective charm, "I love you." Baca's use of repetition drives home the message and adds a musical quality to the poem's rhythm.

Baca uses sensory details, such as "thick socks" and "yellow corn," throughout the poem. His precise diction and details complement the speaker's sincerity and engage the reader's senses.

Many of Baca's other poems also use natural imagery and strong sensory details. The poet grew up in the American Southwest, where he had a difficult childhood. His understanding of the importance of love and the danger of its absence is evident in the poem. By repeating "I love you" at the end of every stanza, and using metaphors and similes to compare love to comfort, Baca suggests that his "offering" is not only the poem, but love itself: "all anyone needs to live, / and to go on living."

Frequent and thoughtful quotations from the text support the writer's interpretation of the poem.

The writer establishes and then analyzes the poet's use of figurative language and sound devices.

In the concluding paragraph, the writer restates the thesis and revisits some of the evidence presented in the essay.

INDEPENDENT PRACTICE

As you read the following poems, apply the close reading strategies you have learned. You may need to read the poems multiple times.

The Poetic Interpretation of the Twist

by Cornelius Eady

I know what you're expecting to hear.
You think to yourself: Here's a guy who must understand what
the twist was all about.
Look at the knuckles of his hands,
Look at his plain, blue shirt hanging out of the back
of his trousers.
The twist must have been the equivalent of
the high sign
In a secret cult.

I know
I know
I know

Meet the Author

Cornelius Eady (b. 1954) is the author of numerous books of poetry, including *Brutal Imagination*, which was a finalist for the 2001 National Book Award, and *Victims of the Latest Dance Craze*, which won the 1985 Lamont Poetry Prize.

CLOSE READING TOOL

Read and respond to this selection online using the **Close Reading Tool.**

But listen: I am still confused by the mini-skirt
As well as the deep meaning of vinyl on everything.
The twist was just a children's game to us.
I know you expect there ought to be more to this,
The reason the whole world decided to uncouple,

But why should I lie to you? Let me pull up a chair
And in as few words as possible,
Re-create my sister,
Who was renowned for running like a giraffe.
Let me re-create my neighborhood,
A dead-end street next to the railroad tracks.
Let me re-create
My father, who would escape the house by bicycle
And do all the grocery shopping by himself.

Let's not forget the pool hall and the barbershop,
Each with their strange flavors of men,
And while we're on the subject,
I must not **slight** the ragweed,
The true rose of the street.

Vocabulary ▶
slight (slīt) *v.* treat with disrespect or indifference

All this will still not give you the twist.

Forgive me for running on like this.
Your question has set an expectation
That is impossible to meet

Your question has put on my shoulders
A troublesome responsibility

Because the twist is gone.
It is the foundation of a bridge
That has made way for a housing project

And I am sorry to admit
You have come to the wrong person.
I recall the twist
The way we recall meeting a distant aunt as a baby
Or the afternoons spent in homeroom
Waiting for the last bell.

My head hurts.
I am tired of remembering.
Perhaps you can refresh my memory
And tell me
How we got on this topic?
As a favor to me,
Let's not talk anymore about old dances.

I have an entire world on the tip of my tongue.

The Empty Dance Shoes

by Cornelius Eady

My friends,
As it has been proven in the laboratory,
An empty pair of dance shoes
Will sit on the floor like a wart
Until it is given a reason to move.

Those of us who study inertia
(Those of us covered with wild hair and sleep)
Can state this without fear:
The energy in a pair of shoes at rest
Is about the same as that of a clown

Knocked flat by a sandbag.
This you can tell your friends with certainty:
A clown, flat on his back,
Is a lot like an empty pair of
    dancing shoes.

An empty pair of dancing shoes
Is also a lot like a leaf
Pressed in a book.
And now you know a simple truth:

A leaf pressed in, say, *The Colossus*
by Sylvia Plath,[1]
Is no different from an empty pair of dance shoes

Even if those shoes are in the middle of the Stardust Ballroom
With all the lights on, and hot music shakes the windows
   up and down the block.
This is the secret of inertia:
The shoes run on their own sense of the world.
They are in sympathy with the rock the kid skips
   over the lake
After it settles to the mud.
Not with the ripples,
But with the rock.

Vocabulary ▶
application
(ap′ li kā′ shən) *n.* act of putting something to use

A practical and personal **application** of inertia
Can be found in the question:
Whose Turn Is It
To Take Out The Garbage?
An empty pair of dance shoes
Is a lot like the answer to this question,
As well as book-length poems
Set in the Midwest.

To sum up:
An empty pair of dance shoes
Is a lot like the sand the 98-pound weakling
   brushes from his cheeks
As the bully tows away his girlfriend.
Later,

When he spies the coupon at the back of the comic book,
He is about to act upon a different set of scientific principles.
He is ready to dance.

---

1. ***The Colossus* by Sylvia Plath** volume of poetry by American poet Sylvia Plath (1932–1963).

Close Reading Activities

Read

Comprehension: **Key Ideas and Details**

1. **(a)** In "The Poetic Interpretation of the Twist," what memories does the speaker mention as he tries to remember the twist? **(b) Infer:** From what stage of the speaker's life do those memories come? Cite details that support your inference.
2. **(a) Analyze:** What is the speaker saying about the passage of time and the difficulty of remembering the past? **(b) Interpret:** Explain the meaning of the poem's last line.
3. **(a) Connect:** In "The Empty Dance Shoes," note three examples the speaker uses to illustrate the principle of inertia. **(b) Deduce:** What does the speaker mean by *inertia* in this poem? Explain.
4. **Summarize:** Write a brief, objective summary of each poem.

Text Analysis: **Craft and Structure**

5. **Analyze:** Examine the line structure of each poem. How does the structure affect each poem's rhythm?
6. **(a) Distinguish:** Which poem borrows language from physics? **(b) Evaluate:** What tone, or attitude, does that scientific language help to create? Explain.
7. **(a) Summarize:** What happens to the "98-pound weakling" at the end of "The Empty Dance Shoes"? **(b) Draw Conclusions:** What are the new "scientific principles" that will now guide his actions and how are they different from those of inertia? Explain.
8. **(a)** What common topic connects the two poems? Explain. **(b) Interpret:** What other thematic elements appear in both poems? Cite textual details that support your interpretation.

Connections: **Integration of Knowledge and Ideas**

Discuss

Conduct a **small-group discussion** about regret as a theme in both poems. Consider the ways the poet uses music, family relationships, and memory to illustrate this idea.

Research

Eady's work is deeply influenced by music, especially jazz. Briefly research another poet who was influenced by jazz. Choose a specific poem by that poet and analyze how it presents the following elements:

a. a sense of rhythm and movement conveyed through sound devices and figurative language

b. references to specific social behaviors and attitudes

c. a clear tone or attitude toward the topic

Take notes as you research and analyze the poem. Then, write a brief **analysis** in which you compare and contrast the poem you researched with one of the poems by Cornelius Eady. Cite textual details from both poems to support your ideas.

Write

"Dancing is a positive form of personal and social expression." Write an **essay** from the point of view of one of Eady's speakers in which you agree or disagree with that statement. Cite details from each poem to support your position.

Does all communication serve a positive purpose?

Consider the ways in which the speaker in "The Poetic Interpretation of the Twist" communicates with the reader. From the speaker's point of view, is the result of the communication positive, negative, or ambiguous? Use evidence from the poem to support your answer.

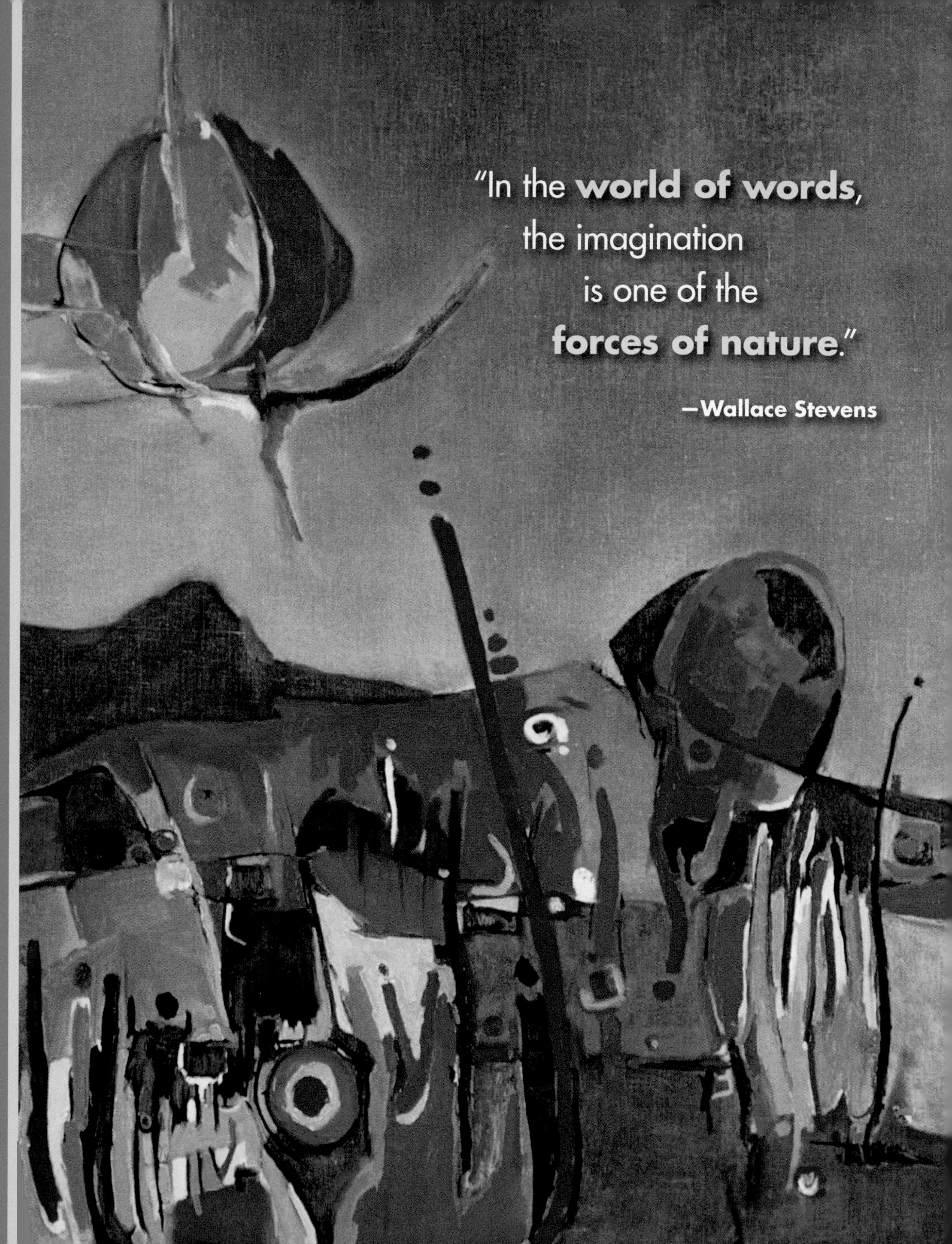
"In the **world of words,**
the imagination
is one of the
forces of nature."
—Wallace Stevens

PART 2

TEXT ANALYSIS GUIDED EXPLORATION

ARTFUL WORDS

Language is both a means of communicating basic information and a powerful creative medium. Skilled writers use words the way artists use paint—to tell stories, conjure images, engage the senses, and stir the imagination. As you read the poems in this section, notice the ways in which the lyrical, artful quality of words enhances the expression of feeling and thought. Then, consider how these texts relate to the Big Question for this unit: **Does all communication serve a positive purpose?**

◀ CRITICAL VIEWING How does the exercise of imagination help the viewer discover meaning in this painting? Explain.

READINGS IN PART 2

CLOSE READING TOOL

Use the **Close Reading Tool** to practice the strategies you learn in this unit.

Focus on Craft and Structure

Elements of Poetry

Poetry combines structural elements with **concise, musical, and emotionally charged language** to express multiple layers of meaning.

Poetry is a musical form of literature in which words may suggest multiple layers of meaning. These layers emerge through the structure of the poem, the sounds and meanings of words, and the speaker's voice.

Structure and Meter Poems consist of lines that may be organized into groups called **stanzas. Meter** is the rhythmic pattern established by stresses, or beats, within each line of a poem. Meter is measured in units called **feet.**

Readers identify meter by **scanning** each line of a poem, or marking each stressed syllable with an accent (´) and each unstressed syllable with a horseshoe symbol (˘). Vertical lines (|) are used to divide each line into feet. Most metrical feet consist of one stressed and one or more unstressed syllables.

Types of Metrical Feet

Name	Symbol	Example
iamb	˘ ´	*begin*
trochee	´ ˘	*catching*
anapest	˘ ˘ ´	*understand*
dactyl	´ ˘ ˘	*bicycle*
spondee	´ ´	*heartthrob*

By counting the number of feet in each line, readers can identify metrical patterns. One classic pattern is **iambic tetrameter,** which contains eight syllables—four iambic feet.

Example: Iambic Tetrameter

Wĕ wéar | thĕ másk | thăt grins | ănd liés,
from "We Wear the Mask," Paul Laurence Dunbar

Another classic pattern is **iambic pentameter,** which contains ten syllables—five iambic feet—as in the following example.

Example: Iambic Pentameter

Ănd súm|mĕr's léase|hăth áll|tŏo shórt|ă dáte:
from Sonnet 18, William Shakespeare

Enjambment To maintain a metrical pattern, a poet may carry a thought over from one line to the next. When a line breaks before completing a grammatical unit that can stand on its own, the line is said to be **enjambed.** In the following example, lines 2–4 are enjambed.

Example: Enjambment

It is a beauteous evening, calm and free,
The holy time is quiet as a Nun
Breathless with adoration; the broad sun
Is sinking down in its tranquillity.
from "It Is a Beauteous Evening," William Wordsworth

Though line 2—"The holy time is quiet as a Nun"—appears to make sense by itself, line 3—"Breathless with adoration; the broad sun"— does not. Line 2 is enjambed with line 3. Similarly, line 3 is enjambed with line 4. Enjambment allows Wordsworth to maintain five strong beats per line, as shown in this example.

Example: Enjambment and Meter

Thĕ hó | lỳ time | ĭs qúi | ĕt ás | ă Nún Bréathlĕss |
wĭth ád | ŏ rá | tiŏn; thé | brŏad sún

Sound in Poetry

Meter is just one element of rhythm in poetry, and not all poems make use of it. For example, poems written in **free verse** do not follow regular metrical patterns. They do, however, include rhythmic elements that are often created through the combinations of word sounds. Sound devices are forms of repetition. Poets may repeat words and phrases to emphasize important ideas. They may also employ more sophisticated sound devices to add meaning and music to their work.

Rhyme and Rhyme Scheme

Rhyme is the repetition of vowel and consonant sounds at the ends of words, as in the words *proud* and *allowed*. Rhymes at the end of lines are called **end rhymes.** Rhymes that appear within lines are called **internal rhymes.**

Exact rhymes can sometimes be heavy or predictable. Poets may employ **slant rhyme,** which uses words with similar, but not exact, end sounds, as in *gill* and *shell* or *understand* and *find*.

Rhyme scheme is the pattern of end rhymes in a poem. Readers identify a rhyme scheme by assigning a letter of the alphabet to each line. When two end words rhyme, the lines are marked with the same letter, as in the following example.

Example: Rhyme Scheme

The bride hath paced into the hall, **a**
Red as a rose is she; **b**
Nodding their heads before
her goes **c**
The merry minstrelsy. **b**

from "Rime of the Ancient Mariner," Samuel Taylor Coleridge

A **couplet** is a pair of rhyming lines, usually of the same meter and length. A couplet usually expresses a single idea and often functions as a complete stanza.

Example: Couplet

So long as men can breathe, or eyes
can see,
So long lives this, and this gives life
to thee.

from Sonnet 18, William Shakespeare

Other Sound Devices

Poets may also use sound devices other than rhyme. Like rhyme, these devices emphasize key ideas, create connections among words, and elicit emotional responses. The chart that follows defines and provides examples of sound devices often used in poetry.

Example: Poetic Sound Devices

Alliteration is the repetition of initial consonant sounds.

Example: Loquacious locals like to talk to the town.

Assonance is the repetition of vowel sounds within stressed syllables that end in different consonant sounds.

Example: We dully trudged along the dusty tunnel.

Consonance is the repetition of final consonant sounds in stressed syllables that have different vowel sounds.

Example: The nervous move at every living sound.

Onomatopoeia is an actual or invented word that imitates the sound of what it names or describes.

Example: The galumphing runner huffed and puffed.

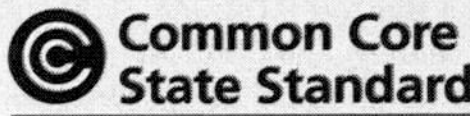

Common Core State Standards

Reading Literature

4. Determine the meaning of words and phrases as they are used in the text, including figurative and connotative meanings; analyze the cumulative impact of specific word choices on meaning and tone.

5. Analyze how an author's choices concerning how to structure a text, order events within it, and manipulate time create such effects as mystery, tension, or surprise.

Language

5.a. Interpret figures of speech in context and analyze their role in the text.

5.b. Analyze nuances in the meaning of words with similar denotations.

Determining Poetic Meaning

To fully understand a poem, consider the voice of the **speaker** as well as the literal and **figurative** meanings of words.

Speaker and Tone

While structural elements support a poem's message, poetic meaning is largely determined by voice, tone, and language.

Voice emerges from a poem's **speaker,** who serves the same function as the narrator in a story. Even in a personal poem in which the speaker uses the first-person pronoun *I*, the speaker is not the poet but rather an imaginary voice created by the poet to tell the poem.

Tone is the attitude projected toward the subject and the audience. Tone is supported by meter and sound devices, but it is primarily established through word choice. A *formal tone* features standard English and formal grammar, as in the following example.

Example: Formal Tone

Tears, idle tears, I know not what they mean,
Tears from the depth of some divine despair
Rise in the heart, and gather to the eyes,
In looking on the happy Autumn-fields,
And thinking of the days that are no more.

from "Tears, Idle Tears," Alfred, Lord Tennyson

An *informal tone* may feature colloquial language—local idioms and slang expressions—as in the example below.

Example: Informal Tone

"I'm dreadin' what I've got to watch," the
Color-Sergeant said.

from "Danny Deever," Rudyard Kipling

Kinds of Poetic Language

Poets combine literal and figurative language to generate layers of meaning or to invite a deeper understanding of a subject.

Denotation is a word's definition. Poems benefit from the use of specific words and phrases. For example, the word *store* communicates a general concept, but the phrase *lumber warehouse* conjures up a particular image.

Connotations are the emotional associations a word evokes. For example, the word *car* is a neutral word. However, *junker* suggests an old, broken-down vehicle, while *classic* implies a car worthy of showing off.

Sensory details, which appeal to sight, sound, hearing, taste, and touch, create imagery in the mind of the reader and evoke emotional associations. For example, the phrase "crispy, tart green apple" evokes sense memories about how apples sound, taste, and look.

Figurative Language is not meant to be taken literally. These words and phrases draw comparisons between ideas or images.

- **Similes** make direct comparisons between unlike things using *as* or *like*: *Her glance hit me like a spear*.
- **Metaphors** make direct comparisons by stating that one thing is another: *Her glance was a spear*.
- **Personification** gives human qualities to nonhuman things: *The lights in the window winked at me*.
- **Hyperbole** is an extreme exaggeration: *After three eons, I saw him again*.

Forms and Types of Poetry

A poem's form can help convey its message and tone.

Free verse may use rhyme, sound devices, meter, and varied stanzas, but does not follow a fixed pattern. In the following free verse poem, the repetition of words and phrases emphasizes ideas and creates a rhythm.

Example: Free Verse

A noiseless patient spider,
I mark'd, where, on a little promontory, it
stood, isolated;
Mark'd how, to explore the vacant, vast
surrounding,
It launch'd forth filament, filament, filament,
out of itself;
Ever unreeling them—ever tirelessly speeding
them.

from "A Noiseless, Patient Spider,"
Walt Whitman

Formal verse follows established patterns. Each standard poetic form has specific requirements regarding rhyme scheme, meter, and line or stanza structure.

Types of Poetry

Though poems employ many different formats, most poems fall into one of three categories: narrative poems, dramatic poems, and lyric poems.

Narrative poetry tells a story and has a plot, characters, and a setting. Two common types of narrative poems are epic poems and ballads. An **epic poem** is a long narrative poem about gods or heroes. A **ballad** is a shorter poem that describes a single event and may be set to music. Most ballads include short stanzas and a refrain that repeats several times, like the chorus in a song.

Dramatic poetry, which tells a story using a character's own thoughts or spoken statements, is a component of many classical plays. In these plays, noble characters may deliver rhythmic, poetic speeches, while lower-class characters speak in regular prose. The term *dramatic poetry* is also used to refer to poems in which one or more characters speak.

Lyric poetry expresses the feelings of a single speaker, using melodic language, imagery, rhythm, and sound devices to express emotions. Lyric is the most common category of poetry in modern literature. Common lyric forms include the ode, elegy, sonnet, haiku, and tanka.

- **Odes** are poems of praise that often exhibit complex metrical patterns, specific rhyme schemes, and stanzas of ten or more lines each.
- **Elegies** are poems of loss that express both praise for the dead and an element of consolation.
- **Sonnets** are fourteen-line poems in which each line consists of five iambic feet (iambic pentameter). In a **Petrarchan sonnet,** an eight-line stanza with an *abbaabba* rhyme scheme is followed by a six-line stanza with a *cdecde* rhyme scheme. In a **Shakespearean sonnet,** three stanzas of four lines apiece have an *abab/cdcd/efef* rhyme scheme, followed by a two-line stanza with a *gg* rhyme scheme.
- A **haiku** is a form of Japanese poetry that consists of three unrhymed lines of five, seven, and five syllables. A **tanka** is a form of Japanese poetry that has five unrhymed lines consisting of five, seven, five, seven, and seven syllables. Both forms often describe a scene from nature and use imagery to convey a single vivid emotion or impression.

Example: Haiku

A crusty snowdrift,
sooty from a week's traffic:
Oh, for a warm day!

Example: Tanka

The sun is blinding.
Glaring on the frozen lake,
It's fire without warmth.
Beneath the ice, the fish swim,
Oblivious to season.

Building Knowledge

Does all communication serve a positive purpose?

Explore the Big Question as you read these poems. Take notes on the types of communication—both verbal and non-verbal—that are portrayed in these poems.

CLOSE READING FOCUS

Key Ideas and Details: **Read Fluently**

Reading fluently means reading with expression and understanding. When reading poetry, you can improve your fluency by reading aloud, modifying your reading rate to appreciate different aspects of the poem.

- First, read the poem aloud slowly. Follow the punctuation and group words for clarity. Focus on understanding the basic meaning.
- Read the poem again, pausing briefly at the ends of lines to hear how line breaks affect the meaning. Listen for the musical qualities of the poem and slow down or speed up to emphasize those qualities.
- Reread the poem again with full expression, emphasizing ideas, images, and sounds. Listen for the mood the words create.

Craft and Structure: **The Speaker in Poetry**

The **speaker** is the imaginary voice that is speaking in a poem. Often, the speaker bears a close resemblance to the poet. However, it is wrong to assume that the poet and the speaker are identical. The speaker is a persona, or an assumed, imagined voice.

- In a **narrative poem,** the speaker tells a story from a particular point of view. Narrative poems feature all the storytelling elements of narrative prose, including settings, characters, conflict, and plot.
- In a **lyric** poem, the speaker explores a distinct moment in time.

In both types of poem, the speaker expresses a particular **tone,** or attitude toward the subject. In addition, all forms of poetry may contain **imagery**—language that appeals to the senses—as well as **figurative language,** or words used imaginatively rather than literally.

Vocabulary

The following words appear in these poems. Copy the words into your notebook and note which ones are adjectives. Explain how you know.

foreboding	**tumult**	**monotonously**
venerable	**sullen**	**clenching**

Common Core State Standards

Reading Literature

1. Cite strong and thorough textual evidence to support analysis of what the text says explicitly as well as inferences drawn from the text.

4. Determine the meaning of words and phrases as they are used in a text, including figurative and connotative meanings; analyze the cumulative impact of specific word choices on meaning and tone.

CLOSE READING MODEL

The passages below are from two poems in Poetry Collection 1. The annotations to the right of the passages show ways in which you can read fluently and apply interpretation skills to understand the speaker in poetry.

from "The Fish" by Elizabeth Bishop

I caught a tremendous fish
and held him beside the boat[1]
half out of water, with my hook
fast in a corner of his mouth.
He didn't fight.
He hadn't fought at all.[2]
He hung a grunting weight,
battered and venerable
and homely.[3]

The Speaker in Poetry

1 The speaker simply tells the reader what happened: "I caught a tremendous fish." The speaker's tone seems neutral but has an underlying excitement.

Read Fluently

2 Read these lines aloud to hear how they add to the speaker's calm but urgent tone. The repetition of the idea of fighting suggests that something important is going on—the fish did not fight.

The Speaker in Poetry

3 Precise adjectives describe the fish. *Battered* suggests the fish has experienced many battles. *Venerable* suggests age and wisdom. *Homely* means unattractive or ugly. The speaker sees the fish as a powerful creature with a long history.

from "The Guitar" by Federico García Lorca

Now begins the cry
Of the guitar,
Breaking the vaults
Of dawn.
Now begins the cry
Of the guitar.[4]
Useless
To still it.

Read Fluently

4 If you stop at the end of each line, its meaning may be difficult to grasp. However, if you read these lines in sentences, following the punctuation, the image of a mournful guitar heard early in the morning becomes clear.

Meet the Poets

"Making a Fist"
Naomi Shihab Nye (b. 1952)
Poet and author Naomi Shihab Nye has won many awards for her works for both adults and young people. Her poetry often draws inspiration from the places where she has lived—St. Louis, Missouri, and Jerusaleum in Israel, as well as her current home of San Antonio, Texas.

"The Fish"
Elizabeth Bishop (1911–1979)
In 1945, Elizabeth Bishop won a poetry contest, leading to the publication of her first poetry collection, *North and South,* which included "The Fish." Her work is noted for its precise images, wit, and unsentimental insights. During her lifetime Bishop was often regarded as a "poet's poet" without appeal for a larger readership. However, toward the end of her life she was recognized as a major voice in twentieth century literature.

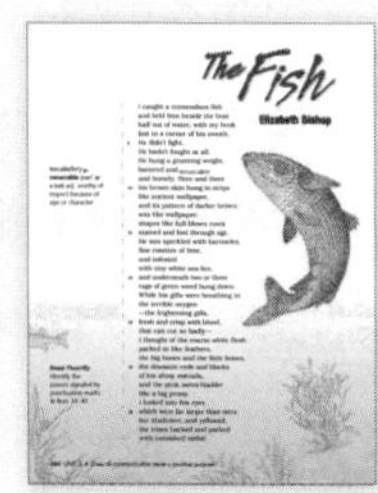

"The Guitar"
Federico García Lorca (1898–1936)
Poet and playwright Federico García Lorca is considered one of the greatest Spanish writers. A native of rural Andalusia, García Lorca wrote many of his poems shortly after World War I. Lorca was killed by Nationalist forces—those supporting the military dictator Francisco Franco—at the outbreak of the Spanish Civil War.

"The Bridegroom"
Alexander Pushkin (1799–1837)
Alexander Pushkin is considered the father of modern Russian literature. Though a nobleman, he had great sympathy for poor Russian peasants. In literature, too, he was a rebel, drawing on folklore to express his democratic ideas. Like many of Pushkin's works, his poem "The Bridegroom" is based on a folk tale. This particular tale has many versions in Russian, German, English, and even American folk literature.

Making a Fist

Naomi Shihab Nye

For the first time, on the road north of Tampico,[1]
I felt the life sliding out of me,
a drum in the desert, harder and harder to hear.
I was seven, I lay in the car
watching palm trees swirl a sickening pattern
past the glass.
My stomach was a melon split wide inside my skin.

"How do you know if you are going to die?"
I begged my mother.
We had been traveling for days.
With strange confidence she answered,
"When you can no longer make a fist."

Years later I smile to think of that journey,
the borders we must cross separately,
stamped with our unanswerable woes.
I who did not die, who am still living,
still lying in the backseat behind all my questions,
clenching and opening one small hand.

The Speaker in Poetry
Identify one detail the poet uses to tell a story and one she uses to present an image or convey a feeling.

◀ **Vocabulary**
clenching (klench′ iŋ) *v.* closing or holding tightly

1. **Tampico** (täm pē′ kō) seaport in eastern Mexico.

The Fish

Elizabeth Bishop

I caught a tremendous fish
and held him beside the boat
half out of water, with my hook
fast in a corner of his mouth.
He didn't fight.
He hadn't fought at all.
He hung a grunting weight,
battered and **venerable**
and homely. Here and there
his brown skin hung in strips
like ancient wallpaper,
and its pattern of darker brown
was like wallpaper:
shapes like full-blown roses
stained and lost through age.
He was speckled with barnacles,
fine rosettes of lime,
and infested
with tiny white sea-lice,
and underneath two or three
rags of green weed hung down.
While his gills were breathing in
the terrible oxygen
—the frightening gills,
fresh and crisp with blood,
that can cut so badly—
I thought of the coarse white flesh
packed in like feathers,
the big bones and the little bones,
the dramatic reds and blacks
of his shiny entrails,
and the pink swim-bladder
like a big peony.
I looked into his eyes
which were far larger than mine
but shallower, and yellowed,
the irises backed and packed
with tarnished tinfoil

Vocabulary ▶
venerable (ven´ ər ə bəl) *adj.* worthy of respect because of age or character

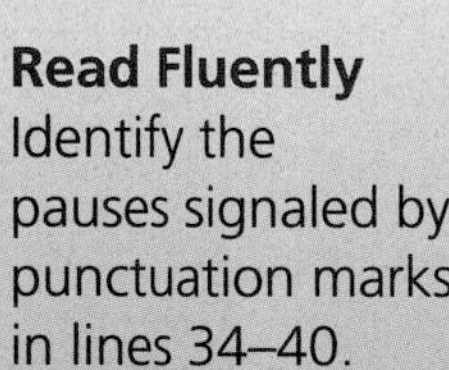

Read Fluently
Identify the pauses signaled by punctuation marks in lines 34–40.

seen through the lenses
of old scratched isinglass.[1]
They shifted a little, but not
to return my stare.
—It was more like the tipping
of an object toward the light.
I admired his **sullen** face,
the mechanism of his jaw,
and then I saw
that from his lower lip
—if you could call it a lip—
grim, wet, and weaponlike,
hung five old pieces of fish-line,
or four and a wire leader
with the swivel still attached,
with all their five big hooks
grown firmly in his mouth.
A green line, frayed at the end
where he broke it, two heavier lines,
and a fine black thread
still crimped from the strain and snap
when it broke and he got away.
Like medals with their ribbons
frayed and wavering,
a five-haired beard of wisdom
trailing from his aching jaw.
I stared and stared
and victory filled up
the little rented boat,
from the pool of bilge
where oil had spread a rainbow
around the rusted engine
to the bailer rusted orange,
the sun-cracked thwarts[2]
the oarlocks on their strings,
the gunnels[3]—until everything
was rainbow, rainbow, rainbow!
And I let the fish go.

◀ **Vocabulary**
sullen (sul′ ən) *adj.* gloomy and showing resentment

◀ **Critical Viewing**
Does this fish look like the "venerable" old warrior described in the poem? Explain.

The Speaker in Poetry
What details in the speaker's conclusion provide a dramatic insight and a surprising action?

---

1. **isinglass** (ī′ zin glas′) *n.* transparent material once used in windows.
2. **thwarts** (*th*wôrtz) *n.* seats in a boat for rowers.
3. **gunnels** (gun′ əlz) *n.* upper edges of the sides of a ship or boat.

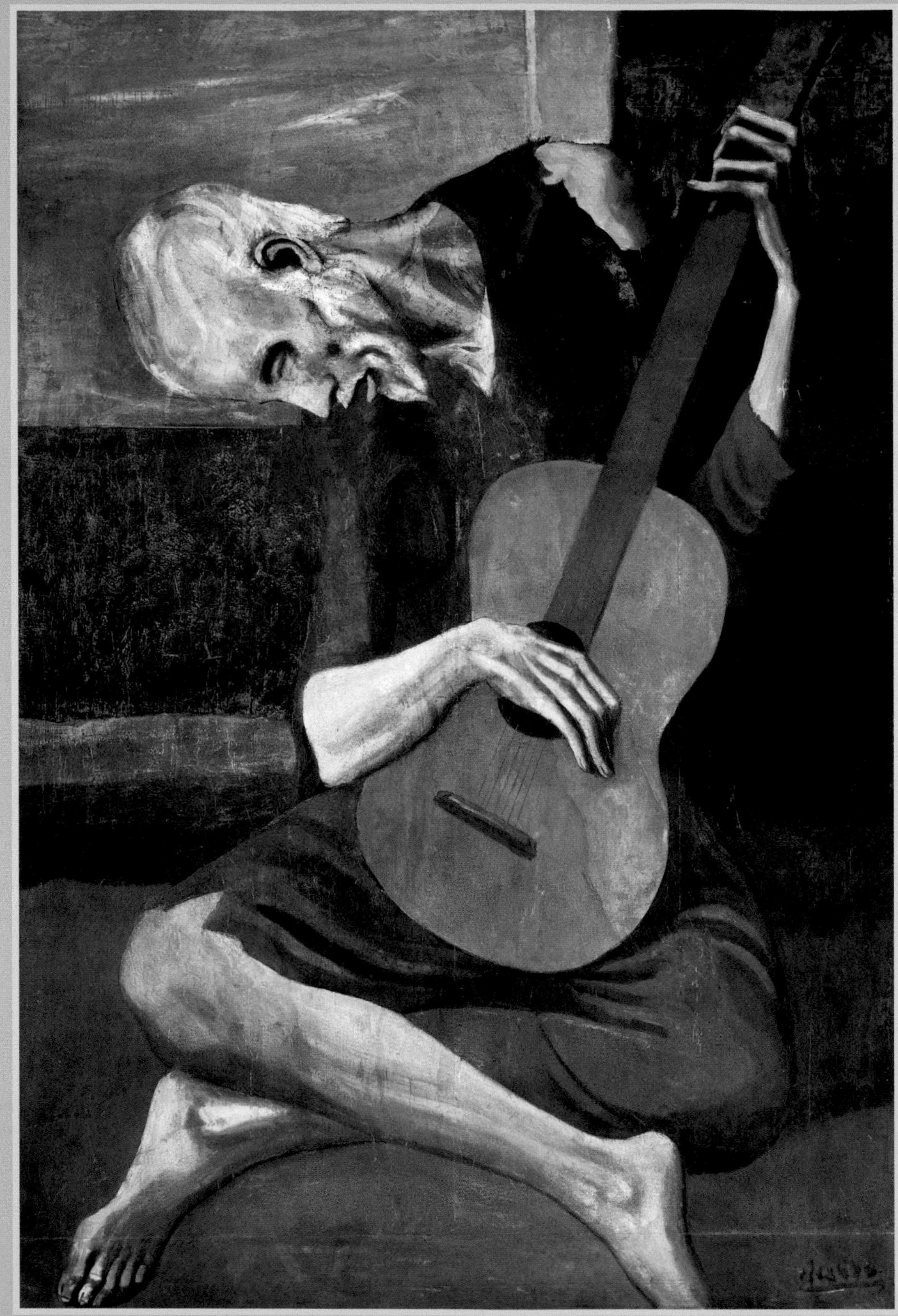

The Old Guitarist, 1903, Pablo Picasso. The Art Institute of Chicago.™ ©2004 Estate of Pablo Picasso/Artists Rights Society (ARS), New York.

The Guitar

Federico García Lorca

translated by Elizabeth du Gué Trapier

Now begins the cry
Of the guitar,
Breaking the vaults
Of dawn.
Now begins the cry
Of the guitar.
Useless
To still it.
Impossible
To still it.
It weeps **monotonously**
As weeps the water,
As weeps the wind
Over snow.
Impossible
To still it.
It weeps
For distant things,
Warm southern sands
Desiring white camellias.
It mourns the arrow without a target,
The evening without morning.
And the first bird dead
Upon a branch.
O guitar!
A wounded heart,
Wounded by five swords.

◀ **Vocabulary**
monotonously (mə nät′ ′n əs lē) *adv.* in a dull, unvarying way

The Speaker in Poetry
What feelings do the speaker's use of images in lines 19–24 convey?

The Bridegroom

Alexander Pushkin

translated by D.M. Thomas

▲ **Critical Viewing**
Which details in this painting suggest that a single marriage is significant to the whole world?

For three days Natasha,
The merchant's daughter,
Was missing. The third night,
She ran in, distraught.
Her father and mother
Plied her with questions.
She did not hear them,
She could hardly breathe.

Stricken with **foreboding**
They pleaded, got angry,
But still she was silent;
At last they gave up.
Natasha's cheeks regained
Their rosy color.
And cheerfully again
She sat with her sisters.

Once at the shingle-gate
She sat with her friends
—And a swift troika[1]
Flashed by before them;
A handsome young man
Stood driving the horses;
Snow and mud went flying,
Splashing the girls.

He gazed as he flew past,
And Natasha gazed.
He flew on. Natasha froze.
Headlong she ran home.
"It was he! It was he!"
She cried. "I know it!
I recognized him! Papa,
Mama, save me from him!"

Full of grief and fear,
They shake their heads, sighing.
Her father says: "My child,
Tell me everything.
If someone has harmed you,
Tell us . . . even a hint."
She weeps again and
Her lips remain sealed.

◀ **Vocabulary**
foreboding (fôr bōd′ iŋ) *n.* a feeling that something bad will happen

The Speaker in Poetry
Which details in this stanza does the speaker use to tell a story?

Comprehension
Why do Natasha's mother and father question her?

1. **troika** (troi′ kə) *n.* Russian carriage or sleigh drawn by a team of three horses.

The next morning, the old
Matchmaking woman
Unexpectedly calls and
Sings the girl's praises;
Says to the father: "You
Have the goods and I
A buyer for them:
A handsome young man.

"He bows low to no one,
He lives like a lord
With no debts nor worries;
He's rich and he's generous,
Says he will give his bride,
On their wedding-day,
A fox-fur coat, a pearl,
Gold rings, brocaded[2] dresses,

"Yesterday, out driving,
He saw your Natasha;
Shall we shake hands
And get her to church?"
The woman starts to eat
A pie, and talks in riddles,
While the poor girl
Does not know where to look.

"Agreed," says her father;
"Go in happiness
To the altar, Natasha;
It's dull for you here;
A swallow should not spend
All its time singing,
It's time for you to build
A nest for your children."

Natasha leaned against
The wall and tried
To speak—but found herself
Sobbing; she was shuddering
And laughing. The matchmaker
Poured out a cup of water,
Gave her some to drink,
Splashed some in her face.

Read Fluently
How many sentences are there in this stanza of eight lines?

Spiral Review
TONE Identify the metaphor in lines 65–72. What does the comparison suggest about the father's attitude toward Natasha?

2. **brocaded** (brō kād′ əd) *adj.* with raised designs woven into the cloth.

Her parents are distressed.
Then Natasha recovered,
And calmly she said:
"Your will be done. Call
My bridegroom to the feast,
Bake loaves for the whole world,
Brew sweet mead[3] and call
The law to the feast."

"Of course, Natasha, angel!
You know we'd give our lives
To make you happy!"
They bake and they brew;
The worthy guests come,
The bride is led to the feast,
Her maids sing and weep;
Then horses and a sledge[4]

With the groom—and all sit.
The glasses ring and clatter,
The toasting-cup is passed
From hand to hand in **tumult**,
The guests are drunk.

BRIDEGROOM
"Friends, why is my fair bride
Sad, why is she not
Feasting and serving?"

The bride answers the groom:
"I will tell you why
As best I can. My soul
Knows no rest, day and night
I weep; an evil dream
Oppresses me." Her father
Says: "My dear child, tell us
What your dream is."

"I dreamed," she says, "that I
Went into a forest,
It was late and dark;

◀ **Vocabulary**
tumult (to͞o′ mult) *n.* noisy commotion

Comprehension
What plans does Natasha's father make for her?

3. **mead** (mēd) *n.* drink made of fermented honey and water.
4. **sledge** (slej) *n.* sleigh.

The moon was faintly
Shining behind a cloud;
I strayed from the path;
Nothing stirred except
The tops of the pine-trees.

"And suddenly, as if
I was awake, I saw
A hut. I approach the hut
And knock at the door
—Silence. A prayer on my lips
I open the door and enter.
A candle burns. All
Is silver and gold."

BRIDEGROOM
"What is bad about that?
It promises wealth."

BRIDE
"Wait, sir, I've not finished.
Silently I gazed
On the silver and gold,
The cloths, the rugs, the silks
From Novgorod,[5] and I
Was lost in wonder.

"Then I heard a shout
And a clatter of hoofs . . .
Someone has driven up
To the porch. Quickly
I slammed the door and hid
Behind the stove. Now
I hear many voices . . .
Twelve young men come in,

5. **Novgorod** (näv′ gə räd′) city in northwestern Russia.

"And with them is a girl,
Pure and beautiful.
They've taken no notice
Of the ikons,[6] they sit
To the table without
Praying or taking off
Their hats. At the head,
The eldest brother,

At his right, the youngest;
At his left, the girl.
Shouts, laughs, drunken clamor . . . "

BRIDEGROOM
"That betokens merriment."

BRIDE
"Wait, sir, I've not finished.
The drunken din goes on
And grows louder still.
Only the girl is sad.

"She sits silent, neither
Eating nor drinking;
But sheds tears in plenty;
The eldest brother
Takes his knife and, whistling,
Sharpens it; seizing her by
The hair he kills her
And cuts off her right hand."

"Why," says the groom, "this
Is nonsense! Believe me,
My love, your dream is not evil."
She looks him in the eyes.
"And from whose hand
Does this ring come?"
The bride said. The whole throng
Rose in the silence.

The Speaker in Poetry
What details help the bride's narrative grow in excitement?

6. **ikons** (ī′ känz′) *n.* sacred religious images.

With a clatter the ring
Falls, and rolls along
The floor. The groom blanches,
Trembles. Confusion . . .
"Seize him!" the law commands.
He's bound, judged, put to death.
Natasha is famous!
Our song at an end.

Language Study

Vocabulary The words listed in blue appear in Poetry Collection 1. Write a sentence about the situation described in the numbered items that follow. Use one word from the list in each sentence. Make sure to use each word only once.

venerable **monotonously** **tumult** **clenching** **sullen**

1. a visit with an elderly, much-admired musician
2. a dripping faucet
3. a loud and crowded city council meeting
4. gripping a pencil tightly before a test.
5. a rainy day causes someone to feel gloomy and sad

WORD STUDY

The Old English prefix ***fore-*** means "before," "in front," or "beforehand." In "The Bridegroom," when a young woman arrives home distraught, her parents are filled with **foreboding**, sensing something bad before it actually happens.

Word Study

Part A The **Old English prefix *fore-*** means "before," "in front," or "beforehand." Explain how the prefix *fore-* contributes to the meanings of these words: *forerunner, foreshadow,* and *foretell.* Consult a dictionary if necessary.

Part B Use the context of the sentences and what you know about the Old English prefix *fore-* to explain your answer to each question.

1. Why is it a good idea to check the weather *forecast* before going on a hike?
2. Would you *forewarn* a friend if you thought she was in danger?

Close Reading Activities

Literary Analysis

Key Ideas and Details

1. **(a) Interpret:** At the end of "Making a Fist," in what sense is the speaker still a child? **(b) Analyze:** What are the borders that the speaker says one "must cross separately"? Explain.
2. **(a)** What decision does the speaker of "The Fish" make at the end of the poem? **(b) Analyze:** What realization about the fish motivates this decision? Support your answer with details from the poem.
3. **(a)** At the end of "The Guitar," what are the "five swords" that "wound" the guitar? **(b) Interpret:** Explain the meaning of the figurative language in the last three lines of the poem.
4. **(a)** In "The Bridegroom," how does Natasha react during the matchmaker's visit? **(b) Interpret:** Explain what her "dream" reveals about the reasons for her reaction.
5. **Read Fluently** Choose one poem from this collection and identify specific lines in which you changed your reading rate as you read the poem aloud. Explain the qualities in those lines that led you to make those adjustments.

Craft and Structure

6. **The Speaker in Poetry (a)** Compare the speakers in "The Guitar" and "The Fish." In your response, explain whether each speaker is a character in a story or another type of persona. **(b)** Compare the emotional attitude each speaker expresses.
7. **The Speaker in Poetry (a)** Which poem in this collection is most clearly a story told by a narrator? **(b)** Which poem is most clearly a lyric in which the speaker's persona closely resembles that of the poet? Explain your reasoning, citing details from the poems.

Integration of Knowledge and Ideas

8. **Analyze:** In what ways do both "Making a Fist" and "The Fish" fit the definition of a narrative poem and in what ways do they fit the definition of a lyric poem? Explain your answer, citing details from the poems.

9. THE BIG ? **Does all communication serve a positive purpose?** **(a)** Choose one of the poems from this collection and explain how it presents a subject in a unique way. How does this fresh perspective change your understanding of the subject? **(b)** Based on your answer, explain the type of communication poetry can achieve that, perhaps, other forms of writing or art cannot. **(c)** Evaluate whether that type of communication is positive and, if so, for whom.

ACADEMIC VOCABULARY

As you write and speak about Poetry Collection 1, use the words related to communication that you explored on page 345 of this book.

Close Reading Activities Continued

Conventions: Commas and Dashes

Commas are used to separate or join similar sentence elements and to show the relationship between ideas. **Dashes** are used to create longer, more emphatic pauses than commas.

- Use commas to separate three or more words or phrases in a series.
- Use a comma and a coordinating conjunction (*and, but, or, nor, for, so,* and *yet*) to link two independent clauses in a compound sentence.
- Use commas to set off introductory, parenthetical, and nonessential words, phrases, and clauses.
- Use dashes to indicate an abrupt change of thought, a dramatic interrupting idea, or a summary statement.

Commas: Natasha, a reluctant bride, had witnessed a terrible crime. *(used to set off a nonessential phrase)*

Dashes: There are many versions of the story—like most folk tales—because it was retold in different ways at different times. *(used to indicate an interrupting idea)*

Practice A

Rewrite each sentence, inserting dashes or commas where necessary. Then, explain what function the additional punctuation serves.

1. Natasha was anxious unhappy and afraid.
2. A humble creature an old battered fish gives the speaker a new way of thinking about life.
3. Natasha seems to accept her fate but she is not as meek as she seems.
4. The instrument a guitar makes a sad sound.

Reading Application Find an example of commas and an example of dashes in one of the poems in Poetry Collection 1. For each example, explain how the punctuation marks are used.

Practice B

Rewrite the following sentences, correcting any errors with commas or dashes. If no corrections are necessary, write *correct*.

1. The guitar seems to weep for everything camellias birds and memories.
2. Natasha does not like her groom and she will do what it takes to escape the marriage.
3. A battle-scarred fish—trailing fish hooks and old lines—earns the speaker's admiration.
4. The speaker who ultimately views her childhood fears with amusement learns to accept her questions.

Writing Application Write a brief summary of "The Fish." Use commas and dashes to set off pieces of information where appropriate.

Writing to Sources

Poem Write your own **lyric poem** in response to any of the poems in Poetry Collection 1.

- Choose one of the poems from the collection. Briefly, write an explanation of why you chose it and identify qualities it presents that you find appealing.
- List figurative language and imagery you find in the poem. Refer to these examples as you create your own poetic style.
- Remember your purpose. Review your draft to ensure that your writing expresses an insight gained in a distinct moment of time.
- Note ideas in your poem that might be deepened by the use of an allusion, or reference, to the work you chose. Add an allusion to the original poem if appropriate.
- Read your draft aloud to a partner, and ask whether any ideas are unclear. Use your partner's answers to guide you in revising your poem.

Grammar Application If you have included commas and dashes in your poem, make sure you have used them correctly to show relationships among your ideas.

Speaking and Listening

Presentation of Ideas Present an **oral interpretation** of the Pushkin poem "The Bridegroom." Go online or use library resources to locate and study the source material upon which Pushkin based the poem. Write an introduction in which you analyze how the poet modified the source material to create a new work. Answer these questions in your introduction:

- Which elements from the source material appear in the newer work?
- Which elements from the source material have been changed in the newer work?
- Do the source material and the newer work share a common theme?

After you have written your introduction, prepare your oral interpretation. To do so, practice reading the poem aloud with fluency. Convey the poem's key emotions and ideas by changing the speed and volume of your voice. Deliver your interpretation, starting with your introduction. Then, invite and answer questions about the poem and the choices you made in your presentation.

Common Core State Standards

Reading Literature
9. Analyze how an author draws on and transforms source material in a specific work.

Writing
4. Produce clear and coherent writing in which the development, organization, and style are appropriate to task, purpose, and audience.
5. Develop and strengthen writing as needed by planning, revising, editing, rewriting, or trying a new approach, focusing on addressing what is most significant for a specific purpose and audience.
9.a. Apply *grades 9–10 Reading standards* to literature.

Speaking and Listening
6. Adapt speech to a variety of contexts and tasks, demonstrating command of formal English when indicated or appropriate.

Language
1.b. Use various types of phrases and clauses to convey specific meanings and add variety and interest to writing or presentations.
2. Demonstrate command of the conventions of standard English capitalization, punctuation, and spelling when writing.
5. Demonstrate understanding of figurative language, word relationships, and nuances in word meanings.

Building Knowledge

Does all communication serve a positive purpose?

Explore the Big Question as you read Poetry Collection 2. Take notes on how the poets communicate their insights about people and relationships.

CLOSE READING FOCUS

Key Ideas and Details: **Read Fluently**

When you **read fluently,** you read smoothly and with understanding, placing emphasis appropriately and pausing where necessary. To increase your fluency when reading a poem, preview the work by looking over the text in advance. This will give you a broad sense of what the poem is about and will allow you to watch for specific details as you read the text more thoroughly.

- Use footnotes and other text aids to learn unfamiliar words.
- Determine where each sentence in the poem begins and ends. If you notice that a sentence stretches over more than one line, prepare to read it through the end of each line, pausing only when the punctuation indicates you should. If you are reading aloud, come to a full stop at a period and pause slightly at a comma. If there is a semicolon or a colon, come to a full stop but raise your voice slightly to indicate that a closely related idea follows.
- Form a rough idea of the topic and mood of the work. A quick look at the type of words and images used in the poem may show you whether the mood is sad or happy, serious or humorous.
- Read the poem with its mood in mind. If you are reading aloud, change the tone of your voice by either speaking more quietly or more loudly. Read at a quicker pace if the action is exciting, or at a slower pace if the mood is suspenseful.

Vocabulary

The words below appear in the poems that follow. Copy the words into your notebook. Which word is a synonym for *everlasting*?

threshold	**keenest**
temperate	**eternal**

Common Core State Standards

Reading Literature

1. Cite strong and thorough textual evidence to support analysis of what the text says explicitly as well as inferences drawn from the text.

5. Analyze how an author's choices concerning how to structure a text, order events within it, and manipulate time create such effects as mystery, tension, or surprise.

Language

6. Acquire and use accurately general academic and domain-specific words and phrases, sufficient for reading, writing, speaking, and listening at the college and career readiness level; demonstrate independence in gathering vocabulary knowledge when considering a word or phrase important to comprehension or expression.

Craft and Structure: **Poetic Forms**

To unify sounds and ideas in a poem, a poet may follow a **poetic form,** or defined structure. Each poetic form uses a set number of lines and a distinctive **meter** and pattern of **rhymes.** (For more on these elements, see pp. 356–359) The following are some traditional poetic forms.

Tanka is a five-line, unrhymed Japanese form.

- The first and third lines of tanka contain five syllables. The second, fourth, and fifth lines have seven syllables. (The number of syllables can vary when a tanka is translated into English.) Thus, the syllable pattern is 5-7-5-7-7.

  Example: The flowing river (5)
  Twists and turns and runs away (7)
  Thinking of the sea (5)
  Through the forests light and dark (7)
  At last kissing salty waves. (7)

- The author's choice of form is related to the effect that he or she wishes to create. The tanka's brief and concise structure, for example, helps the poet express a strong feeling, a powerful thought, or a focused image or idea. In the above example, the poet concentrates on a river's journey through varied landscapes as it flows toward and empties into the ocean.

A **sonnet** is a fourteen-line form with a specific line count, rhyme scheme, and rhythmic pattern. In a **Shakespearean sonnet,** the lines are grouped into three **quatrains** (groups of four lines) and a **couplet,** a pair of rhymed lines. The rhyme scheme is *abab, cdcd, efef, gg*. This form is so common in English poetry and was so identified with William Shakespeare and the time period during which he lived that these sonnets are also called *English sonnets* or *Elizabethan sonnets*.

- In a Shakespearean sonnet, the first quatrain introduces a situation or a topic to be considered, identifies a problem, or presents a question.
- The second and third quatrains develop the issue introduced in the first quatrain.
- Often, at the beginning of the third quatrain or in the couplet, the writer presents a turning point in which the situation is explained, the problem is solved, or the question is answered.
- The couplet often provides a final commentary on or summary of the ideas explored in the first twelve lines.

Craft and Structure: **Poetic Forms**

- Beyond their specific rhyme scheme and formula for content, Shakespearean sonnets also follow a strict rhythmic pattern called *iambic pentameter.* An *iamb* is a metrical foot with one unstressed syllable followed by a stressed syllable, as in the word *again*. *Pentameter* is verse written in five-foot lines. Therefore, in a sonnet, each line contains five metrical feet in which the first syllable is unaccented and the second syllable is accented. The pattern sounds like this: "da-DUM, da-DUM, da-DUM, da-DUM, da-DUM."

Another common sonnet form is known as the **Italian sonnet,** or the **Petrarchan sonnet,** named for the Italian poet Petrarch, who lived from 1304 to 1374. In this format, the sonnet's fourteen lines are split into an *octet*, or a group of eight lines, and a *sestet*, or a group of six lines. The octet follows a set rhyme scheme of *abba abba*, but the sestet may vary in its rhyme scheme. For example, it might have a pattern of *cdecde*, or *ccddee*, or *cddcdd*.

A **villanelle** is a nineteen-line form with a pattern of repeated lines and a specific rhyme scheme.

- The lines of a villanelle are grouped into five three-line stanzas and one four-line stanza. The lines rhyme *aba, aba, aba, aba, aba, abaa.*
- Line 1 is repeated in lines 6, 12, and 18. Line 3 is repeated in lines 9, 15, and 19.
- This deliberate repetition can create a chanting effect—such as "I wake to sleep, and take my waking slow" in "The Waking," a villanelle by Theodore Roethke. It can also suggest intense emotion.

CLOSE READING MODEL

Two poems from Poetry Collection 2 appear below: a tanka by Ono Komachi and Sonnet 18 by William Shakespeare. The annotations to the right of each poem show ways in which you can use close reading skills to study the structure of a poem and to read more fluently.

Tanka

Was it that I went to sleep
Thinking of him,
That he came in my dreams?[1]
Had I known it a dream
I should not have wakened.

Read Fluently

1 The first three lines are all one sentence. You would not pause after the first line when reading the poem. The comma after the second line marks a slight pause, and the question mark at the end of line three indicates a more solid stop.

Sonnet 18

Shall I compare thee to a summer's day?
Thou art more lovely and more temperate:
Rough winds do shake the darling buds of May,
And summer's lease hath all too short a date:[2]
Sometime too hot the eye of heaven shines,
And often is his gold complexion dimmed;
And every fair from fair sometime declines,
By chance or nature's changing course untrimmed;
But thy eternal summer shall not fade,
Nor lose possession of that fair thou owest;
Nor shall Death brag thou wander'st in his shade,
When in eternal lines to time thou grow'st:
So long as men can breathe, or eyes can see,
So long lives this, and this gives life to thee.[3]

Poetic Forms

2 This is a classic Elizabethan, or Shakespearean, sonnet. It has three quatrains, or stanzas of four lines. In each quatrain, the first and third lines rhyme, and the second and fourth lines also rhyme. This first quatrain introduces a question, which the rest of the poem explores.

Poetic Forms

3 An Elizabethan sonnet ends with a couplet, or pair of lines. In Shakespeare's sonnets, that final couplet usually presents a twist or shift in perspective on the topic the sonnet addresses.

Building Knowledge Continued

Meet the Poets

Sonnet 18
William Shakespeare (1564–1616)
Even though he is most famous as a playwright, Shakespeare also wrote brilliant sonnets. Today, the English sonnet, which he perfected, is also known as the Shakespearean sonnet. (For more about Shakespeare and his career, see pages 540–541.)

Sonnet 18

William Shakespeare

"Do Not Go Gentle into That Good Night"
Dylan Thomas (1914–1953)
Born in Wales, in Great Britain, Dylan Thomas fell in love with words early in life. Poems poured out of him, and by the age of twenty, he had written most of the poems for which he is famous today.

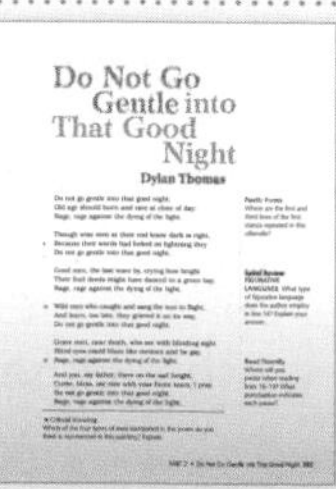

Do Not Go Gentle into That Good Night

Dylan Thomas

"My City"
James Weldon Johnson (1871–1938)
Born in Jacksonville, Florida, James Weldon Johnson became the first African American allowed to practice law in Florida. Johnson also published a newspaper and was a leader in civil rights work.

My City

"One cannot ask loneliness..."
Priest Jakuren (1139–1202)
Priest Jakuren was a Buddhist priest whose poems are filled with beautiful yet melancholy imagery. After entering the priesthood at the age of twenty-three, he traveled the Japanese countryside.

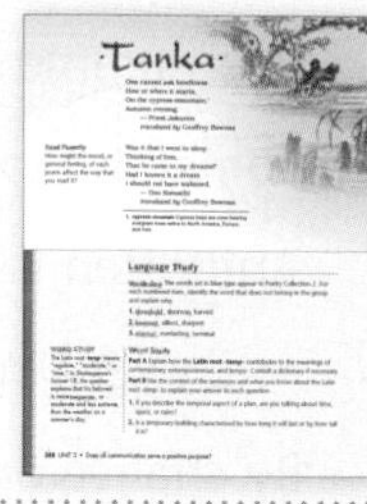

Tanka

"Was it that I went to sleep..."
Ono Komachi (active ca. 833–857)
A celebrated beauty with a strong personality, Ono Komachi was an early Japanese tanka poet. Her poems are marked by passion and energy. The few details known about her life have inspired many legends.

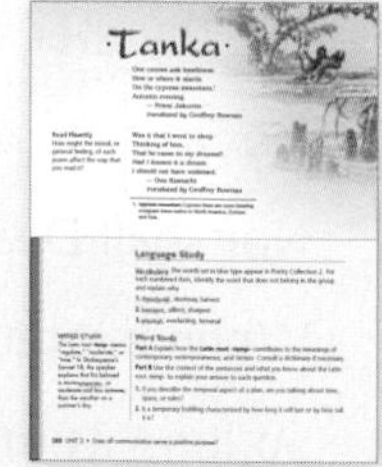

Tanka

Sonnet 18

William Shakespeare

Shall I compare thee to a summer's day?
Thou art more lovely and more **temperate**:
Rough winds do shake the darling buds of May,
And summer's lease hath all too short a date:
Sometime too hot the eye of heaven shines,
And often is his gold complexion dimmed;
And every fair from fair sometime declines,
By chance or nature's changing course untrimmed;[1]
But thy **eternal** summer shall not fade,
Nor lose possession of that fair thou owest;[2]
Nor shall Death brag thou wander'st in his shade,
When in eternal lines to time thou grow'st:
    So long as men can breathe, or eyes can see,
    So long lives this, and this gives life to thee.

◀ **Vocabulary**

temperate (tem′ pər it) *adj.* mild; kept within limits

eternal (ē tur′ nəl) *adj.* without beginning or end; everlasting

Poetic Forms

In what way does the couplet at the conclusion summarize the main idea of the poem?

1. **untrimmed** *adj.* stripped of ornaments or beautiful features.
2. **owest** (ō′ ist) *v.* own.

Do Not Go Gentle into That Good Night

Dylan Thomas

Do not go gentle into that good night,
Old age should burn and rave at close of day;
Rage, rage against the dying of the light.

Though wise men at their end know dark is right,
Because their words had forked no lightning they
Do not go gentle into that good night.

Good men, the last wave by, crying how bright
Their frail deeds might have danced in a green bay,
Rage, rage against the dying of the light.

Wild men who caught and sang the sun in flight,
And learn, too late, they grieved it on its way,
Do not go gentle into that good night.

Grave men, near death, who see with blinding sight
Blind eyes could blaze like meteors and be gay,
Rage, rage against the dying of the light.

And you, my father, there on the sad height,
Curse, bless, me now with your fierce tears, I pray.
Do not go gentle into that good night.
Rage, rage against the dying of the light.

Poetic Forms
Where are the first and third lines of the first stanza repeated in this villanelle?

Spiral Review
FIGURATIVE LANGUAGE What type of figurative language does the author employ in line 14? Explain your answer.

Read Fluently
Where will you pause when reading lines 16–19? What punctuation indicates each pause?

◀ Critical Viewing
Which of the four types of men mentioned in the poem do you think is represented in this painting? Explain.

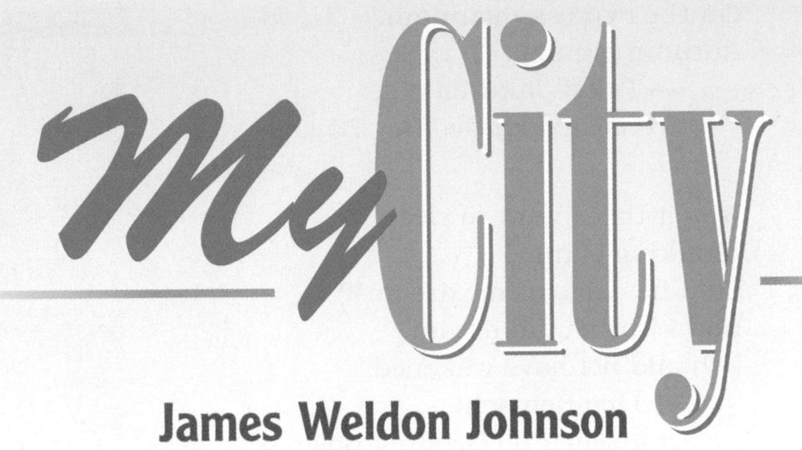

My City

James Weldon Johnson

When I come down to sleep death's endless night,
The **threshold** of the unknown dark to cross,
What to me then will be the **keenest** loss,
When this bright world blurs on my fading sight?
Will it be that no more I shall see the trees
Or smell the flowers or hear the singing birds
Or watch the flashing streams or patient herds?
No, I am sure it will be none of these.
But, ah! Manhattan's sights and sounds, her smells,
Her crowds, her throbbing force, the thrill that comes
From being of her a part, her subtile spells,
Her shining towers, her avenues, her slums—
O God! the stark, unutterable pity,
To be dead, and never again behold my city!

◀ Vocabulary
threshold (thresh´ ōld´) *n.* the bottom of a doorway; entrance or a point of beginning

keenest (kēn´ ist) *adj.* sharpest; most cutting

Poetic Forms
Which syllables are stressed in the iambic pentameter of line 9?

◀ Critical Viewing
Which lines in the poem does this painting best illustrate? Explain.

·Tanka·

One cannot ask loneliness
How or where it starts.
On the cypress-mountain,[1]
Autumn evening.
— Priest Jakuren
translated by Geoffrey Bownas

Read Fluently
Do these poems convey similar moods? Explain.

Was it that I went to sleep
Thinking of him,
That he came in my dreams?
Had I known it a dream
I should not have wakened.
— Ono Komachi
translated by Geoffrey Bownas

1. **cypress-mountain** Cypress trees are cone-bearing evergreen trees native to North America, Europe, and Asia.

Language Study

Vocabulary The words set in blue type appear in Poetry Collection 2. For each numbered item, identify the word that does not belong in the group and explain why.

1. **threshold**, doorway, harvest
2. **keenest**, silliest, sharpest
3. **eternal**, everlasting, terminal

WORD STUDY
The Latin root ***-temp-*** means "regulate," "moderate," or "time." In Shakespeare's Sonnet 18, the speaker explains that his beloved is more **temperate**, or moderate and less extreme, than the weather on a summer's day.

Word Study

Part A Explain how the **Latin root *-temp-*** contributes to the meanings of *contemporary, extemporaneous,* and *tempo*. Consult a dictionary if necessary.

Part B Use the context of the sentences and what you know about the Latin root *-temp-* to explain your answer to each question.

1. If you describe the *temporal* aspect of a plan, are you talking about time, space, or rules?
2. Is a *temporary* building characterized by how long it will last or by how tall it is?

Close Reading Activities

Literary Analysis

Key Ideas and Details

1. **(a) Analyze:** In Sonnet 18, identify three ways in which the speaker says a summer day may become less than perfect. **(b) Infer:** What is the speaker's main reason for saying the beloved is superior to a summer's day?
2. **Interpret:** In "Do Not Go Gentle Into That Good Night," to what do the phrases "that good night," "close of day," and "dying of the light" refer? Explain.
3. **(a)** To whom does the speaker of "Do Not Go Gentle…" speak directly? **(b) Infer:** What is the speaker asking of this person, and why? Explain, citing details from the poem.
4. **(a)** In "My City," what question does the speaker ask and answer? **(b) Analyze:** In what way does the speaker's answer challenge customary notions about the world's beauty? CIte details from the poem in your response.
5. **(a)** What question cannot be asked in "One cannot ask loneliness…"? **(b) Connect:** How does the image of the mountain relate to the speaker's thoughts about loneliness? Explain.

Craft and Structure

6. **Poetic Forms (a)** Identify the repeated lines in the villanelle "Do Not Go Gentle into That Good Night." **(b)** What ideas does the repetition of these lines reinforce? Explain, citing details from the poem.
7. **Poetic Forms** Explain how "One cannot ask loneliness…" and "Was it that I went to sleep…" fulfill the definition of tanka in both form and content. Cite details from the poems in your response.
8. **Poetic Forms** Using a chart like the one shown, analyze how the poets use the sonnet structure to build meaning in both Sonnet 18 and "My City."

Message of Quatrain 1
Connection: Quatrains 1 and 2
Connection: Quatrains 2 and 3
Connection: Couplet to Quatrains

Integration of Knowledge and Ideas

9. THE BIG ? **Does all communication serve a positive purpose?** These poems address complex and sometimes difficult subject matter, including isolation, loneliness, the pain of loss, and the fear of dying. Does the exploration of such negative feelings and ideas in poetry serve a positive purpose? Explain your position, citing details from these poems as support.

ACADEMIC VOCABULARY

As you write and speak about Poetry Collection 2, use the words related to communication that you explored on page 345 of this textbook.

Conventions: Prepositional Phrases

A **prepositional phrase** is made up of a preposition, the object of the preposition, and any modifiers of the object. A prepositional phrase modifies other words by functioning either as an adjective or as an adverb within sentences.

In the examples below, the prepositions are underlined and the objects of the prepositions are in boldface.

in the big **city**	during Ono's **time**	at the **end** of his **life**
from the first **stanza**	on the **streets** of **London**	before the last two **lines**

A prepositional phrase that serves as an adjective is called an **adjective phrase.** It modifies a noun or pronoun and tells *what kind* or *which one.*

Adjective Phrase: The subject *of the first tanka* is loneliness.

The phrase *of the first tanka* modifies the noun *subject* by telling *which one.*

A prepositional phrase that serves as an adverb is called an **adverb phrase.** It modifies a verb and tells *where, when, in what way,* or *to what extent.*

Adverb Phrase: The students analyzed the poems *with great care.*

The phrase *with great care* modifies the verb *analyzed* by telling *in what way.*

Practice A

Identify the prepositional phrase in each sentence and tell whether it is an adjective phrase or an adverb phrase. Then, tell which word it modifies

1. Other poets of the time inspired Johnson.
2. The speaker compares the beloved to a mild summer day.
3. The language of the poem is enthusiastic.
4. The couplet at the end of the sonnet often summarizes the main idea.

Reading Application Find two examples of prepositional phrases in the poems in Poetry Collection 2. Identify each phrase as either an adjective phrase or an adverb phrase.

Practice B

Add a prepositional phrase to the blank in each item. The phrase should act as an adjective or adverb and give additional information.

1. The speaker of "My City" loves the sights and sounds __________.
2. In "Do Not Go Gentle..." the speaker pleads __________.
3. One poem __________ is Sonnet 18.
4. To read poetry more fluently, practice __________.

Writing Application Look at the model sentence and identify the adjective phrase and the adverb phrase. Then, following the model, write two sentences of your own.

The woman in the poem wakens from her dream.

Writing to Sources

Poetry Write your own **tanka,** following the traditional Japanese form. Follow these steps:

- Review the definition of a tanka on page 379.
- Think of a subject for your tanka. Focus on a single strong image or idea.
- As you draft, choose words that will allow you to follow the prescribed syllable pattern for each line.
- After you draft, read your tanka aloud to make sure it fits the form. If necessary, you may invert normal word order as long as your meaning remains clear.

As you work on your poem, think about your purpose for writing. Make sure you use the structure of the tanka to express a strong feeling, a powerful thought, or a focused image or idea.

Grammar Application As you write, use prepositional phrases correctly to modify other words in the poem.

Speaking and Listening

Comprehension and Collaboration In a small group, listen several times to a recording of either Dylan Thomas reading "Do Not Go Gentle into That Good Night" or someone reading Shakespeare's Sonnet 18. Afterward, hold a **poetry reading discussion** in which you explore what the reading added to your understanding and appreciation of the poem. Answer the following questions as you hold your discussion, building on each other's ideas.

- Does the reader speed up at certain parts of the poem? Does he or she slow down at other parts?
- Does the reader put emphasis on certain words? Are there similarities in the words that the reader emphasizes?
- Does the reader emphasize the rhythm?
- Does the reader convey a specific emotion or mood?
- Did hearing the poem read aloud improve your understanding and enjoyment of it?

After the discussion, have several people in your group read the poem aloud. Assess how the different readings affect listeners.

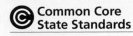

Writing

4. Produce clear and coherent writing in which the development, organization, and style are appropriate to task, purpose, and audience.

Speaking and Listening

1. Initiate and participate effectively in a range of collaborative discussions with diverse partners.

Language

1. Demonstrate command of the conventions of standard English grammar and usage when writing or speaking.

1.b. Use various types of phrases and clauses to convey specific meanings and add variety and interest to writing or presentations.

Building Knowledge

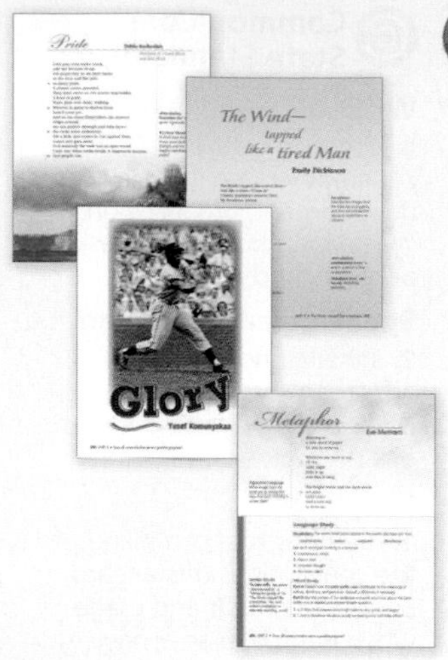

Does all communication serve a positive purpose?

Explore the Big Question as you read these poems. Take notes on how the poets communicate the extraordinary nature of seemingly ordinary moments.

CLOSE READING FOCUS

Key Ideas and Details: **Paraphrase**

To understand a poem's central idea, **paraphrase** it, or restate the meaning in your own words.

- Begin by picturing the imagery and actions described in the poem. Try to form clear pictures of the descriptive details.
- Then, keeping that mental picture of the poem in mind, restate the lines, capturing their essential meaning but using your own words.

Craft and Structure: **Figurative Language**

Figurative language is not meant to be taken literally. Poets often use the following **figures of speech**, or types of figurative language, to convey ideas in fresh and innovative ways. Each of these figures of speech compares two things that are alike in certain respects but not in others.

- **Simile:** compares unlike things using the word *like* or as. *Example:* He runs like a cheetah.
- **Metaphor:** one thing is spoken about as if it were something else. *Example:* During the holidays, the stores are zoos.
- **Personification:** an object, animal, or idea is spoken of as if it were human. *Example:* The trees danced in the wind.

Because figurative language often uses sensory details and expresses meaning in concrete terms, it is an important source of **imagery,** or word-pictures, in poetry.

Vocabulary

The words below are critical to understanding the poems that follow. Copy the words into your notebook. Decide whether you know each word well, know it a little bit, or do not know it at all. After you read, see how your knowledge of each word has increased.

countenance **tremulous** **stance** **conjured** **flourishes**

Common Core State Standards

Reading Literature

1. Cite strong and thorough textual evidence to support analysis of what the text says explicitly as well as inferences drawn from the text.

2. Determine a theme or central idea of a text.

4. Determine the meaning of words and phrases as they are used in a text, including figurative and connotative meanings; analyze the cumulative impact of specific word choices on meaning and tone.

CLOSE READING MODEL

The passages below are from the poems "Glory" by Yusef Komunyakaa and "The Wind…" by Emily Dickinson. The annotations to the right of each passage show ways in which you can use close reading skills to paraphrase and analyze figurative language.

from "Glory"

Most were married teenagers
Working knockout shifts daybreak
To sunset six days a week—
Already old men playing ball
In a field between a row of shotgun houses
& the Magazine Lumber Company.[1]
They were all Jackie Robinson
& Willie Mays, a touch of
Josh Gibson & Satchell Paige[2]
In each stance & swing, a promise
Like a hesitation pitch always
At the edge of their lives,
Arms sharp as rifles.

Paraphrase

1 The opening details present vivid images of the baseball players and their field. A reader might restate the lines in this way: *The ballplayers are just teens but work long hours six days a week, making them old before their time. Their field is stuck between a row of low-rent houses and a lumberyard.*

Figurative Language

2 The poet uses a metaphor, comparing the players to some of the greatest baseball stars in history. The metaphor suggests that the men imagine themselves to be as graceful and gifted as their heroes.

from "The Wind—tapped like a tired Man"

The Wind—tapped like a tired Man—[3]
And like a Host—"Come in"
I boldly answered—entered then
My Residence within

A Rapid—footless Guest—
To offer whom a Chair
Were as impossible as hand
A Sofa to the Air—[4]

Figurative Language

3 The poem begins with a simile that compares the wind to a tired man. The line is also an example of personification since the wind is given the human ability to tap on a house to come in. Together, these figures of speech portray the wind as a humanlike visitor.

Paraphrase

4 A reader might paraphrase the stanza in this way: *The wind has no body; it moves quickly and cannot be made to stop.*

Meet the Poets

"Pride"

Dahlia Ravikovitch (1936–2005)

Israeli poet Dahlia Ravikovitch was born in a town near Tel Aviv and was raised on a kibbutz, a cooperative settlement. Her father's death in an accident when she was six was a powerful influence on her life and work. Her intensely personal poems are charged with images from nature, history, and religion.

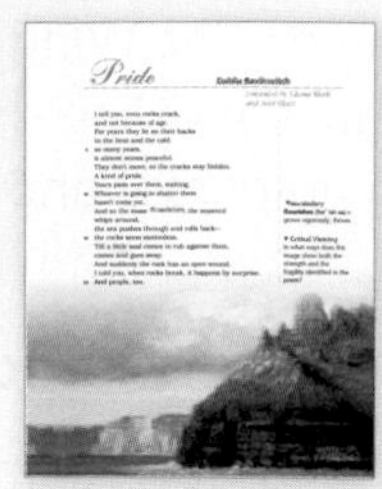

"The Wind—tapped like a tired Man"

Emily Dickinson (1830–1886)

Now regarded as one of America's greatest poets, Emily Dickinson was scarcely known during her own era. She spent almost her entire life in her parents' home, and rarely left her house. Although she wrote more than a thousand poems, only seven were published during her lifetime—and those were published anonymously.

"Glory"

Yusef Komunyakaa (b. 1947)

Yusef Komunyakaa was born in the small rural town of Bogalusa, Louisiana. He is now a creative writing professor at Princeton University in New Jersey. Komunyakaa's collection *Neon Vernacular* earned him a Pulitzer Prize in 1994. He has said that "the writer has to get down to the guts of the thing...."

"Metaphor"

Eve Merriam (1916–1992)

Eve Merriam developed a fascination with poetry at an early age. Although she also wrote plays and picture books, she believed poetry to be the most immediate and richest form of communication. Her body of work includes poetry for both adults and children.

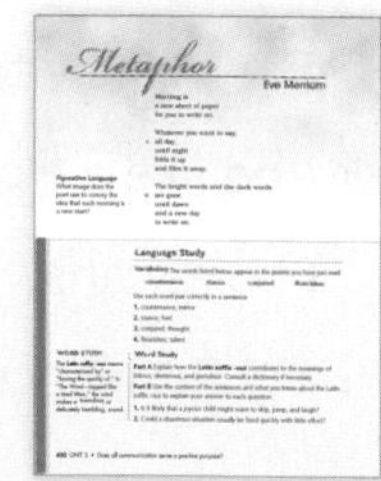

Pride

Dahlia Ravikovitch

translated by Chana Bloch and Ariel Bloch

I tell you, even rocks crack,
and not because of age.
For years they lie on their backs
in the heat and the cold,
so many years,
it almost seems peaceful.
They don't move, so the cracks stay hidden.
A kind of pride.
Years pass over them, waiting.
Whoever is going to shatter them
hasn't come yet.
And so the moss **flourishes**, the seaweed
whips around,
the sea pushes through and rolls back—
the rocks seem motionless.
Till a little seal comes to rub against them,
comes and goes away.
And suddenly the rock has an open wound.
I told you, when rocks break, it happens by surprise.
And people, too.

◀ **Vocabulary**
flourishes (flur´ ish əs) *v.* grows vigorously; thrives

▼ **Critical Viewing**
In what ways does this image show both the strength and the fragility identified in the poem?

The Wind—tapped like a tired Man

Emily Dickinson

The Wind—tapped like a tired Man—
And like a Host—"Come in"
I boldly answered—entered then
My Residence within

A Rapid—footless Guest—
To offer whom a Chair
Were as impossible as hand
A Sofa to the Air—

No Bone had He to bind Him—
His Speech was like the Push
Of numerous Humming Birds at once
From a superior Bush—

His **Countenance**—a Billow—
His Fingers, as He passed
Let go a music—as of tunes
Blown **tremulous** in Glass—

He visited—still flitting—
Then like a timid Man
Again, He tapped—'twas flurriedly—
And I became alone—

Paraphrase
Describe two images that the third stanza suggests, and then paraphrase the stanza to understand its content.

◀ Vocabulary

countenance (kount´'n əns) *n.* a person's face or expression

tremulous (trem´ yo͞o ləs) *adj.* trembling; quivering

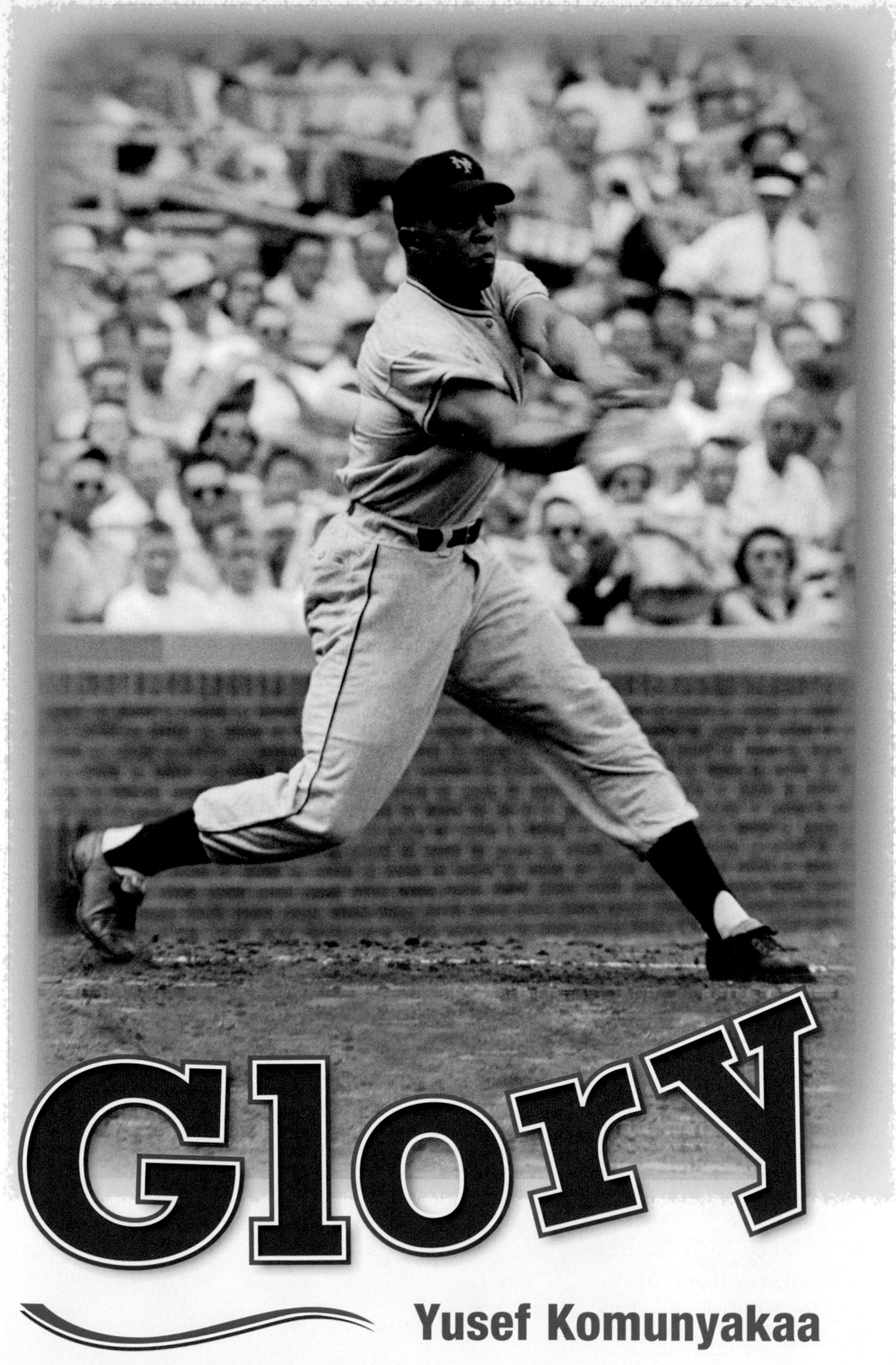

Glory

Yusef Komunyakaa

Most were married teenagers
Working knockout shifts daybreak
To sunset six days a week—
Already old men playing ball
In a field between a row of shotgun houses
& the Magazine Lumber Company.
They were all Jackie Robinson
& Willie Mays, a touch of
Josh Gibson & Satchell Paige[1]
In each **stance** & swing, a promise
Like a hesitation pitch always
At the edge of their lives,
Arms sharp as rifles.
The Sunday afternoon heat
Flared like thin flowered skirts
As children & wives cheered.
The men were like cats
Running backwards to snag
Pop-ups & high-flies off
Fences, stealing each other's glory.
The old deacons & raconteurs[2]
Who umpired made an *Out* or *Safe*
Into a song & dance routine.
Runners hit the dirt
& slid into homeplate,
Cleats catching light,
As they **conjured** escapes, outfoxing
Double plays. In the few seconds
It took a man to eye a woman
Upon the makeshift bleachers,
A stolen base or homerun
Would help another man
Survive the new week.

◀ **Vocabulary**
stance (stans) *n.* the way one stands, especially the placement of the feet

conjured (kän′ jərd) *v.* performed tricks in which things seem to appear, disappear, or change as if by magic

1. **Jackie Robinson / & Willie Mays . . . / Josh Gibson & Satchell Paige** African American baseball stars of the 1920s through the 1970s.
2. **deacons & raconteurs** (rak′ än tʉrz′) assistant officers of a church and skilled storytellers.

Metaphor

Eve Merriam

Morning is
a new sheet of paper
for you to write on.

Whatever you want to say,
all day,
until night
folds it up
and files it away.

The bright words and the dark words
are gone
until dawn
and a new day
to write on.

Figurative Language
What image does the poet use to convey the idea that each morning is a new start?

Language Study

Vocabulary The words listed below appear in the poems you have just read.

countenance **stance** **conjured** **flourishes**

Use each word pair correctly in a sentence

1. countenance; mirror
2. stance; feet
3. conjured; thought
4. flourishes; talent

WORD STUDY
The **Latin suffix *-ous*** means "characterized by" or "having the quality of." In "The Wind—tapped like a tired Man," the wind makes a **tremulous**, or delicately trembling, sound.

Word Study

Part A Explain how the **Latin suffix *-ous*** contributes to the meanings of *bilious, dexterous,* and *garrulous*. Consult a dictionary if necessary.

Part B Use the context of the sentences and what you know about the Latin suffix *-ous* to explain your answer to each question.

1. Is it likely that a *joyous* child might want to skip, jump, and laugh?
2. Could a *disastrous* situation usually be fixed quickly with little effort?

Close Reading Activities

Literary Analysis

Key Ideas and Details

1. **(a) Interpret:** According to the speaker in "Pride," why do rocks crack? **(b) Draw Conclusions:** What does the poem suggest about differences between how things seem and how they really are? Explain, citing details from the text.
2. **(a)** Who is the guest in "The Wind—tapped like a tired Man"? **(b)** Identify three details in the poem that show how this guest is unlike any other.
3. **(a)** In "Glory," state three important things you learn about the men in the first three lines. **(b) Interpret:** How do these details support the idea, stated in line 4, that they are "already old men"? Explain. **(c) Connect:** How do the ideas introduced in the first four lines relate to those stated in the last three lines? Explain.
4. **Paraphrase (a)** Paraphrase the poem "Metaphor." **(b)** Compare your paraphrase to the original. What qualities does the poem have that the paraphrase does not? Explain, citing details from the poem.
5. **Paraphrase (a)** Describe the image you picture when reading the third stanza of "The Wind—tapped like a tired Man." **(b)** Paraphrase this stanza. **(c)** How does paraphrasing this stanza help you better understand its central idea?

Craft and Structure

6. **Figurative Language** Use a chart like the one shown to complete the following activity: **(a)** Find at least one example each of a simile, a metaphor, and personification in the poems from Poetry Collection 3. **(b)** For each example, explain what similarities in otherwise unlike things the figure of speech suggests and evaluate its effectiveness in doing so. **(c)** Discuss your evaluations with a partner. Then, explain whether your discussion changed your appreciation of the poems and, if so, in what ways.

Poem
Device
Explanation
First Evaluation
Final Evaluation

Integration of Knowledge and Ideas

7. **Analyze:** How do both "Pride" and "Glory" attempt to define abstract ideas, or make them concrete? Explain, citing details from both poems.

8. THE BIG ? **Does all communication serve a positive purpose?** **(a)** Identify three ordinary events described in these poems and explain how the poets present these events in a new light. **(b)** Judging from your answers, explain how poetry can transform one's perceptions. **(c)** Is that sort of change positive, negative, or neutral? Explain your position, citing details from the poems to support your ideas.

ACADEMIC VOCABULARY

As you write and speak about Poetry Collection 3, use the words related to communication that you explored on page 345 of this textbook.

Conventions: **Infinitives and Infinitive Phrases**

An **infinitive** is a form of the verb that generally appears with the word *to* and acts as a noun, an adjective, or an adverb.

Examples:

Infinitive (*noun*): Last year, my friend Ana learned *to drive*.

Infinitive (*adjective*): She was motivated by a desire *to succeed*.

Infinitive (*adverb*): Unfortunately, I am still unable *to drive*.

An **infinitive phrase** consists of an infinitive along with any modifiers, objects, or complements, all acting together as a single part of speech. In standard English, the word *to* should not be split or separated from its verb—its modifiers follow the verb.

Infinitive phrase: He tried *to answer decisively*. (*Decisively* modifies the infinitive *to answer*.)

Notice that an infinitive phrase includes *to* and a verb, as in *to remember*. When *to* is used in a prepositional phrase, it is followed by a noun or pronoun, as in *to the store*.

Practice A

Identify the infinitive or infinitive phrase in each sentence and tell whether it acts as a noun, an adjective, or an adverb.

1. The player's goal was to hit a home run.
2. Another player tried to snag a pop-up hit.
3. To welcome the wind was the host's plan.
4. Today is a blank sheet upon which to write.
5. The rocks seem able to lie on their backs.

Reading Application Identify two lines from the poems in Poetry Collection 3 that include examples of infinitives or infinitive phrases.

Practice B

Identify the infinitive or infinitive phrase in each sentence. Then, use the same infinitive or infinitive phrase in an original sentence.

1. Are rocks able to hide their flaws?
2. The poem seems to compare rocks and people.
3. The players like to imagine heroic feats.
4. For them, it is a glory to play.

Writing Application Choose one illustration from Poetry Collection 3 and write three sentences about this image. In each sentence, include an infinitive or infinitive phrase that functions as a noun, an adjective, or an adverb.

Writing to Sources

Argument Write a **critical essay** in which you reflect on the language techniques used in the four poems in this collection and discuss those you found most effective.

- Decide on the criteria you will use in your evaluation. For example, you might choose to judge the cleverness, originality, or beauty of the language.
- Review the poems carefully, using your criteria as a guide. For additional insight, research other critics' commentaries about the language techniques used by the poet.
- Identify specific words, lines, or sections of the poem that still raise questions in your mind. To clarify the text, find unfamiliar words in a dictionary, paraphrase the lines, describe the image, or discuss possible interpretations with a partner.
- As you draft your essay, present your positions clearly and concisely. Then, support each claim with relevant quotations from the poems.

Grammar Application In your draft, vary your sentences by beginning at least one with an infinitive phrase.

Research and Technology

Build and Present Knowledge Write a brief **literary history report** about one of the following topics:

- Explain how Emily Dickinson's poems were eventually published.
- Describe Eve Merriam's career.
- Discuss Yusef Komunyakaa's career and the subject matter for which he is most famous.

Follow these guidelines to conduct your research:

- Use a variety of sources, including biographical encyclopedias and reliable Web sites.
- Check the claims in one source against the claims in the others. Consider and assess the reliability of each source.
- Choose significant information, such as specific facts and dates. Omit details that do not support your purpose.
- Integrate the information from your sources into your report.

Post your report on a class Web site or blog and invite discussion about the information you have gathered. In particular, consider how the information you learned sheds light on an aspect of the poet's work.

Writing

1. Write arguments to support claims in an analysis of substantive topics or texts, using valid reasoning and relevant and sufficient evidence.

6. Use technology, including the Internet, to produce, publish, and update individual or shared writing products, taking advantage of technology's capacity to link to other information and to display information flexibly and dynamically.

9. Draw evidence from literary or informational texts to support analysis, reflection, and research.

Language

1.b. Use various types of phrases and clauses to convey specific meanings and add variety and interest to writing or presentations.

4.c. Consult general and specialized reference materials, both print and digital, to find the pronunciation of a word or determine or clarify its precise meaning, its part of speech, or its etymology.

5.a. Interpret figures of speech in context and analyze their role in the text.

Building Knowledge

Does all communication serve a positive purpose?

Explore the Big Question as you read these poems. Take notes about types of communication each poem describes.

CLOSE READING FOCUS

Key Ideas and Details: **Paraphrase**

To better understand a poem, **paraphrase** it, restating the ideas in your own words. First, break down long sentences into parts. Identify the main actions and who or what performs them. Next, identify details that show when, where, how, or why each action is performed. Then, write a paraphrase in your own words.

Original Text: When fighting for his country, he lost an arm and was suddenly afraid: "From now on, I shall only be able to do things by halves . . ." *from* "A Man," by Nina Cassian

Paraphrase: He lost his arm fighting in a war and was afraid of what his life would now be like.

Craft and Structure: **Sound Devices**

To tap the music in words, poets use a variety of **sound devices**, or patterns of word sounds. These devices include the following:

- **Alliteration:** repetition of consonant sounds at the beginnings of nearby words, as in "silent song"
- **Assonance:** repetition of vowel sounds in nearby stressed syllables, as in "deep and dreamless." Unlike rhyming syllables, assonant syllables end in different consonants.
- **Consonance:** repetition of consonant sounds at the ends of nearby stressed syllables with different vowel sounds, as in "heat lightning"
- **Onomatopoeia:** use of words to imitate actual sounds, such as *buzz, tap,* or *splash*

Sound devices may add to a poem's mood or deepen its meaning.

Vocabulary

The words below are key to understanding the text that follows. Copy the words into your notebook. For each word, write down an antonym.

pallor **ebony** **melancholy** **quench**

Common Core State Standards

Reading Literature

2. Determine a theme or central idea of a text.

4. Determine the meaning of words and analyze the impact of specific word choices on meaning and tone.

Language

6. Acquire and use academic and domain-specific words and phrases.

CLOSE READING MODEL

The passages below are taken from two poems in Poetry Collection 4. The annotations to the right of each passage show ways in which you can use close reading skills to paraphrase and to analyze sound devices.

"Reapers"

Black reapers with the sound of steel on stones
Are sharpening scythes. I see them place the hones
In their hip-pockets as a thing that's done,
And start their silent swinging, one by one.[1]
Black horses drive a mower through the weeds,
And there, a field rat, startled, squealing bleeds,
His belly close to ground. I see the blade,
Blood-stained, continue cutting weeds and shade.

Paraphrase
1 These lines describe a series of simple, connected actions. A paraphrase could read: *The reapers sharpen their scythes and then, one by one, start mowing the field.*

from "Jazz Fantasia"

Drum on your drums, batter on your banjoes,
sob on the long cool winding saxophones.
Go to it, O jazzmen.

Sling your knuckles on the bottoms of the happy
tin pans, let your trombones ooze, and go husha-
husha-hush with the slippery sand-paper.[2]

Moan like an autumn wind high in the lonesome treetops,
moan soft like you wanted somebody terrible, cry like a
racing car slipping away from a motorcycle cop,
bang-bang! you jazzmen, bang altogether drums, traps,
banjoes, horns, tin cans[3]—make two people fight on the
top of a stairway and scratch each other's eyes in a
clinch tumbling down the stairs.

Sound Devices
2 This line repeats the /h/ and /s/ sounds at the beginning of words, and /sh/ sound near the ends of others. These uses of alliteration and consonance suggest the rhythmic brushing sounds common in jazz percussion.

Sound Devices
3 In this passage, the words *bang-bang* imitate drum rhythms—an example of onomatopoeia. The device is continued when the speaker lists the instrument names in a drum-like percussive sequence: "drums, traps, / banjoes, and tin cans."

Meet the Poets

"Jazz Fantasia"

Carl Sandburg (1878–1967)
Carl Sandburg once observed that some poetry was perfect only in form: "All dressed up with nowhere to go." In contrast, his own poetry dresses in blue jeans, going everywhere and speaking in the voices of everyday people. Born in Galesburg, Illinois, Sandburg settled for a time in Chicago.

"Meeting at Night"

Robert Browning (1812–1889)
During his lifetime, Robert Browning was not as famous as his wife, poet Elizabeth Barrett Browning. Today, though, it is Robert who is considered the more innovative poet. He is admired especially for his dramatic monologues, poems in which characters speak directly to readers or other characters.

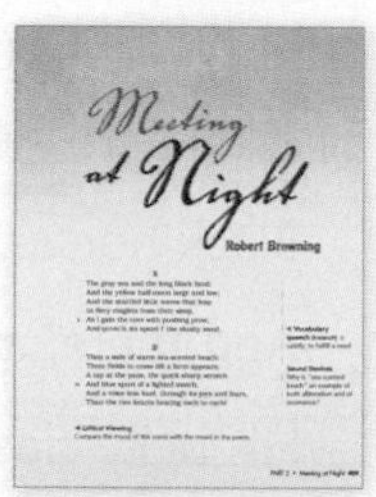

"The Weary Blues"

Langston Hughes (1902–1967)
As a young man, Langston Hughes moved from Missouri to Kansas to Illinois to Cleveland, Ohio, where he was voted class poet in high school. Later, he became one of the major voices of the Harlem Renaissance, a flowering of African American artistic activity in New York City during the 1920s and 1930s.

"Reapers"

Jean Toomer (1894–1967)
"My position in America has been a curious one," Jean Toomer once observed. Reflecting on his diverse ethnic background—French, Dutch, German, and Native American, as well as African American—Toomer called himself the "human race."

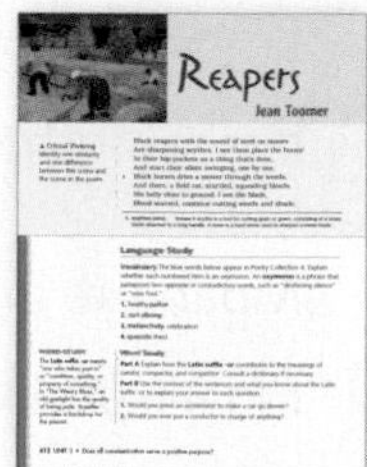

Jazz Fantasia

Carl Sandburg

Drum on your drums, batter on your banjoes,
sob on the long cool winding saxophones.
Go to it, O jazzmen.

Sling your knuckles on the bottoms of the happy
tin pans, let your trombones ooze, and go husha-
husha-hush with the slippery sand-paper.

Moan like an autumn wind high in the lonesome treetops,
moan soft like you wanted somebody terrible, cry like a
racing car slipping away from a motorcycle cop,
bang-bang! you jazzmen, bang altogether drums, traps,
banjoes, horns, tin cans—make two people fight on the
top of a stairway and scratch each other's eyes in a
clinch[1] tumbling down the stairs.

Can[2] the rough stuff . . . now a Mississippi steamboat
pushes up the night river with a hoo-hoo-hoo-oo . . . and
the green lanterns calling to the high soft stars . . . a red
moon rides on the humps of the low river hills . . . go to it,
O jazzmen.

Spiral Review
WORD CHOICE What is the effect of using the verb *batter* to refer to playing the banjo?

Paraphrase
Who or what performs the main action in this stanza?

1. **clinch** *n.* in boxing, the act of gripping the opponent's body with the arms.
2. **Can** *v.* slang for "stop" or "cease."

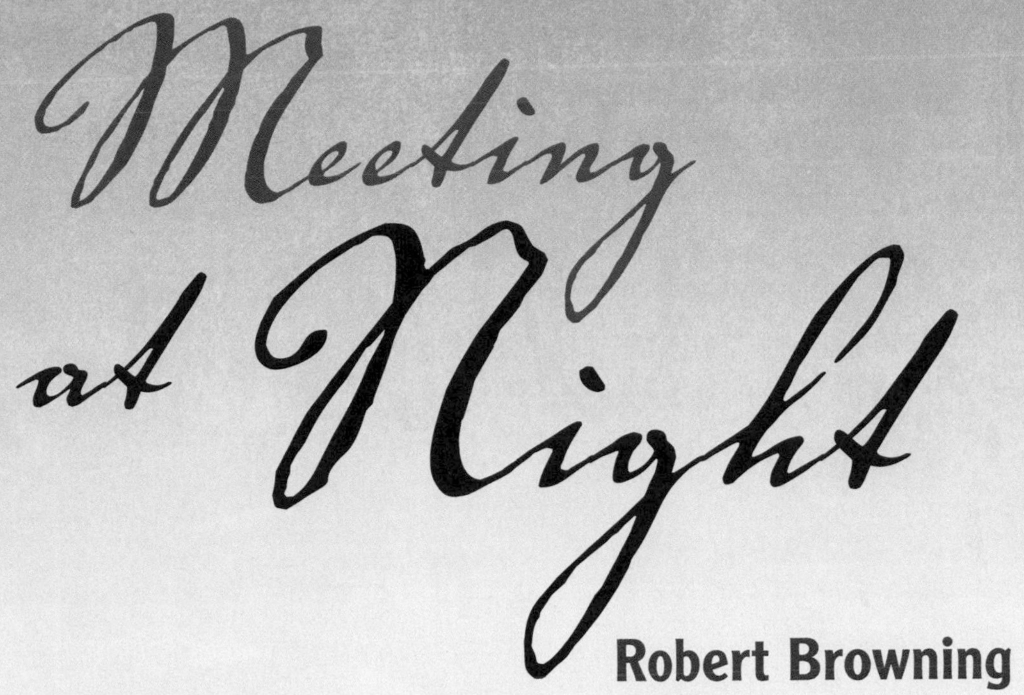

Meeting at Night

Robert Browning

1

The gray sea and the long black land;
And the yellow half-moon large and low;
And the startled little waves that leap
In fiery ringlets from their sleep,
As I gain the cove with pushing prow,
And **quench** its speed i' the slushy sand.

2

Then a mile of warm sea-scented beach;
Three fields to cross till a farm appears;
A tap at the pane, the quick sharp scratch
And blue spurt of a lighted match,
And a voice less loud, through its joys and fears,
Than the two hearts beating each to each!

◀ **Vocabulary**
quench (kwench) *v.* satisfy; to fulfill a need

Sound Devices
Why is "sea-scented beach" an example of both alliteration and of assonance?

◀ **Critical Viewing**
Compare the mood of this scene with the mood in the poem.

The Weary Blues

Langston Hughes

Droning a drowsy syncopated[1] tune,
Rocking back and forth to a mellow croon,
    I heard a Negro play.
Down on Lenox Avenue[2] the other night
By the pale dull **pallor** of an old gas light
    He did a lazy sway. . . .
    He did a lazy sway. . . .
To the tune o' those Weary Blues.
With his **ebony** hands on each ivory key
He made that poor piano moan with melody.
    O Blues!
Swaying to and fro on his rickety stool
He played that sad raggy tune like a musical fool.
    Sweet Blues!
Coming from a black man's soul.
    O Blues!
In a deep song voice with a **melancholy** tone
I heard that Negro sing, that old piano moan—
    "Ain't got nobody in all this world,
    Ain't got nobody but ma self.
    I's gwine to quit ma frownin'
    And put ma troubles on the shelf."
Thump, thump, thump, went his foot on the floor.
He played a few chords then he sang some more—
    "I got the Weary Blues
    And I can't be satisfied.
    Got the Weary Blues
    And can't be satisfied—
    I ain't happy no mo'
    And I wish that I had died."
And far into the night he crooned that tune.
The stars went out and so did the moon.
The singer stopped playing and went to bed
While the Weary Blues echoed through his head.
He slept like a rock or a man that's dead.

◀ **Vocabulary**

pallor (pal′ ər) *n.* lack of color; unnatural paleness

ebony (eb′ ə nē) *adj.* black

melancholy (mel′ ən käl′ ē) *adj.* sad

Sound Devices
Why is "thump, thump, thump" an example of onomatopoeia?

1. **syncopated** (siŋ′ kə pāt′ id) *adj.* with a catchy or an emphatic rhythm created by accenting beats that are usually unaccented.
2. **Lenox Avenue** street in Harlem, a historic African American neighborhood in New York City.

◀ **Critical Viewing**
Does this painting express the same mood as Hughes's poem? Explain.

Reapers

Jean Toomer

▲ **Critical Viewing** Identify one similarity and one difference between this scene and the scene in the poem.

Black reapers with the sound of steel on stones
Are sharpening scythes. I see them place the hones[1]
In their hip-pockets as a thing that's done,
And start their silent swinging, one by one.
Black horses drive a mower through the weeds,
And there, a field rat, startled, squealing bleeds,
His belly close to ground. I see the blade,
Blood-stained, continue cutting weeds and shade.

1. **scythes** (sīthz) . . . **hones** A scythe is a tool for cutting grain or grass, consisting of a sharp blade attached to a long handle. A hone is a hard stone used to sharpen a metal blade.

Language Study

Vocabulary The blue words below appear in Poetry Collection 4. Explain whether each numbered item is an oxymoron. An **oxymoron** is a phrase that juxtaposes two opposite or contradictory words, such as "deafening silence" or "wise fool."

1. healthy **pallor**
2. dark **ebony**
3. **melancholy** celebration
4. **quench** thirst

WORD STUDY

The **Latin suffix *-or*** means "one who takes part in" or "condition, quality, or property of something." In "The Weary Blues," an old gaslight has the quality of being pale. Its **pallor** provides a backdrop for the pianist.

Word Study

Part A Explain how the **Latin suffix *-or*** contributes to the meanings of *candor, compactor,* and *competitor*. Consult a dictionary if necessary.

Part B Use the context of the sentences and what you know about the Latin suffix *-or* to explain your answer to each question.

1. Would you press an *accelerator* to make a car go slower?
2. Would you ever put a *conductor* in charge of anything?

Close Reading Activities

Literary Analysis

Key Ideas and Details

1. **(a) Contrast:** Contrast three of the musical moods described in the third and fourth stanzas of "Jazz Fantasia." **(b) Analyze:** What do these changing moods suggest about the power of jazz to capture human experience? Explain.
2. **(a)** Identify the series of colors named or suggested in "Meeting at Night." **(b) Analyze:** How might this color series reflect the speaker's emotional and physical journey? Explain, citing details from the poem.
3. **(a)** List four adjectives that Hughes uses to describe the music in "The Weary Blues." **(b) Interpret:** Why do you think he uses the verb "moan" rather than "play"? **(c) Infer:** What mood do the adjectives, verb, and song lyrics create? Explain.
4. **Interpret:** In the poem "Reapers," what perception of farm labor does the final image convey? Explain, citing details from the poem.
5. **Paraphrase (a)** In the first stanza of "Meeting at Night," what action is performed and who or what performs it? **(b)** Write a paraphrase of the first stanza.
6. **Paraphrase** Paraphrase the third stanza of "Jazz Fantasia."

Craft and Structure

7. **Sound Devices (a)** Using a chart like the one shown, identify examples of sound devices in "The Weary Blues" and "Jazz Fantasia." **(b)** Explain what each example adds to the poem.
8. **Sound Devices (a)** Compare the effects of sound devices in "Meeting at Night" with those in another poem from Poetry Collection 4. **(b)** Discuss your answers with a partner. Then, with your partner, draw conclusions about how poets use sound. Support your conclusions with examples from the poems. **(c)** Present your conclusions to the class.

Alliteration
Consonance
Assonance
Onomatopoeia

Integration of Knowledge and Ideas

9. THE BIG ? **Does all communication serve a positive purpose?** Hughes's "The Weary Blues" and Sandburg's "Jazz Fantasia" celebrate musical forms—the blues and jazz—that have their roots in the music of enslaved Africans. Research the history of those musical forms. Identify the different types of communication that had to occur in order for the music to evolve. Categorize each one as negative, positive, or neutral. In what ways, if any, are those types of communication echoed in these poems? Write a summary of your findings.

ACADEMIC VOCABULARY

As you write and speak about Poetry Collection 4, use the words related to communication that you explored on page 345 of this textbook.

Conventions: **Participles and Gerunds; Participial and Gerund Phrases**

A **participle** is a verb form used as an adjective to modify a noun or pronoun. A **gerund** is a verb form ending in *-ing* that acts as a noun.

Examples: *a <u>creaking</u> floor* (present participle)

a <u>fried</u> egg (past participle)

<u>Dancing</u> is my favorite pastime. (gerund—noun as subject)

I enjoy <u>singing</u>. (gerund—noun as direct object)

A **participial phrase** consists of a participle and any modifiers, object, or complement. A **gerund phrase** includes a gerund with any modifiers, object, or complement. In these examples, the participial and gerund phrases are underlined.

Examples: *a dress <u>designed by her aunt</u>* (participial phrase, modifies "dress")

<u>Limping badly</u>, the hiker continued down the slope. (participial phrase, modifies "hiker")

David was incapable of <u>reciting the poem.</u> (gerund phrase—noun as object of a preposition)

<u>Quickly gathering details</u> is important. (gerund phrase—noun as subject)

Practice A

Underline and identify the participle, participial phrase, gerund, or gerund phrase in each sentence.

1. Writing brought the poet a deep sense of satisfaction and success.
2. Through their work, artists like Hughes created a changed culture.
3. Copying jazz and blues rhythms, Hughes created a new kind of poetry.
4. The artist enjoyed touring the nation with her exhibit.

Reading Application Identify and label two participles and two gerunds in the poems from Poetry Collection 4.

Practice B

Combine each pair of sentences by using a participial or gerund phrase.

1. The jazzman sings. He draws the attention of his audience.
2. A reaper surveys the field. She looks at the hay she has cut.
3. The drummer bangs his drum. He marches in the parade.
4. The musician was accepted into the band. This was the best thing to happen to him.

Writing Application Write a brief paragraph about watching a musical performance. Include at least one participial phrase and one gerund phrase in your paragraph.

Writing to Sources

Informative Text Write a **critical essay** in which you analyze the use of sound devices in one of the poems from Poetry Collection 4. Consider how sound devices contribute to the mood, make the language memorable, or add to the meaning of the poem. Follow these guidelines as you write:

- Support and clarify your ideas by using concrete details, quotations, and examples from the texts.
- Use varied transitions to make the relationships between ideas and examples clear.
- End with a conclusion that supports the ideas you presented earlier.

After you have completed your essay, write a **poem** in which you use sound devices in ways that are similar to the poem you analyzed in your critical essay.

Grammar Application Vary your sentences by using participles, gerunds, and both participial and gerund phrases.

Research and Technology

Build and Present Knowledge Choose a visual artist associated with the Harlem Renaissance. Research the artist and his or her work, identifying elements of both style and content that make it distinctive. Then, compare the art to a poem by one of the Harlem Renaissance poets in this collection—Jean Toomer or Langston Hughes. Prepare a **visual arts presentation** in which you present your comparison of the visual art and the poem. Follow these guidelines:

- Research artists of the Harlem Renaissance and choose a famous work for your comparison.
- Analyze the image for its content and style, drawing on information you gather from research. Consider how the poem displays similar or different content and style.
- Summarize your ideas in a short essay and use visual aids to clarify your ideas and enhance the appeal of your presentation.
- After you have delivered your presentation, publish your work on a class or school Web site and provide links to sites that display work by Harlem Renaissance artists.

Common Core State Standards

Writing

2. Write informative texts.

4. Produce clear and coherent writing in which the development, organization, and style are appropriate to task, purpose, and audience.

6. Use technology to produce and publish writing products, taking advantage of technology's capacity to display information flexibly and dynamically.

7. Conduct short as well as more sustained research projects to answer a question or solve a problem; synthesize multiple sources on the subject.

Language

1. Demonstrate command of the conventions of standard English grammar.

1.b. Use various types of phrases and clauses to convey specific meanings and add variety and interest to writing or presentations.

Comparing Texts

Does all communication serve a positive purpose?

Explore the Big Question as you read these texts. Take notes on the ways in which each author responds to experiences or messages of disappointment.

READING TO COMPARE THEME

Author Billy Joel and poets Bei Dao and Shu Ting communicate about topics that are at once personal and universal. As you read these selections, consider how each author uses language to express similar ideas but does so in unique ways. After you have read all three texts, compare and contrast the insights they convey.

"Hold Fast Your Dreams—and Trust Your Mistakes"
Billy Joel (b. 1949)
Famed musician Billy Joel grew up in the suburbs of New York City. He studied classical music as a child but went on to make rock and roll history as one of the most successful recording acts of his generation. To date, he has sold more than 100 million records worldwide. Joel was inducted into the Rock and Roll Hall of Fame in 1999.

Hold Fast Your Dreams—
and Trust Your Mistakes
Billy Joel

"All"
Bei Dao (b. 1949)
In the 1970s, Bei Dao's poems became rallying cries for those Chinese who wanted their country to become more democratic. Since 1989, when Chinese government troops brutally suppressed dissent, Bei Dao has lived abroad.

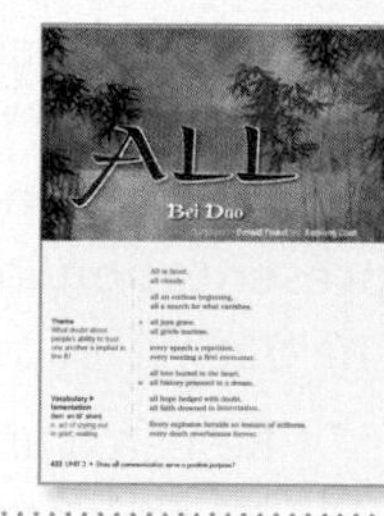
ALL
Bei Dao

"Also All"
Shu Ting (b. 1952)
As a teenager, Shu Ting (the pen name of Gong Peiyu) suffered harsh treatment from the Chinese government because of her father's nonconformist beliefs. She gained fame as a poet while still in her twenties, winning China's National Poetry Award in 1981 and 1983.

Also
ALL
Shu Ting

Comparing Theme

A **theme** is the essential idea that all the elements of a literary work combine to express. An author's *diction*, or choice of words, is one key ingredient in the expression of a theme. The events or situations an author describes are another key element in the expression of a theme. For example, the authors of this collection of texts dramatize the contradictions, conflicts, and complications of life by exploring the following types of situations.

- By pursuing their dreams, people make their lives meaningful—yet if their plans fail, their lives may seem empty.
- People strive for what they desire—yet they may long most intensely for what they have lost or can never have.

In presenting such contradictions or conflicts, each of these writers asks a similar question: How we are to find meaning in our lives, even in the face of personal disappointment or failure? Each author's specific answer—his or her thematic insight—is unique.

Writers' unique expressions of similar themes come through in a variety of ways. For example, one writer may use familiar settings and informal diction, while another may use symbols and formal diction. The types of details and the language each author uses are clues to his or her distinct viewpoint on an idea. As you read, use a chart like the one shown to note how the three writers in this collection use language and details to express thematic messages in their own unique ways.

Key Word / Phrase / Detail	Relationship to Message / Theme

Common Core State Standards

Reading Literature

2. Determine a theme or central idea of a text and analyze in detail its development over the course of the text, including how it emerges and is shaped and refined by specific details.

4. Determine the meaning of words and phrases as they are used in the text, including figurative and connotative meanings; analyze the cumulative impact of specific word choices on meaning and tone.

Writing

2. Write informative/explanatory texts to examine and convey complex ideas, concepts, and information clearly and accurately.

2.a. Introduce a topic; organize complex ideas, concepts, and information to make important connections and distinctions; include formatting, graphics, and multimedia when useful to aiding comprehension.

2.b. Develop the topic with well-chosen, relevant, and sufficient facts, extended definitions, concrete details, quotations, or other information and examples.

10. Write routinely over extended time frames and shorter time frames for a range of tasks, purposes, and audiences.

The Stranger album, 1977

Billy Joel performing during rehearsals, 2003

Hold Fast Your Dreams—and Trust Your Mistakes

Billy Joel

Commencement Speech at Fairfield University
Fairfield, Connecticut, May 19, 1991

When I was first asked to speak to the graduating class of Fairfield University, my initial reaction was not too dissimilar to a certain philosophy professor who is a member of the faculty here. I had to ask myself, What makes me qualified to do this? What relevance do I have to the future lives of these young people? After all, I did not even go to college, and I did write a song called "Only the Good Die Young." So, why me?

After meeting with a group of Fairfield students, I realized what I might be able to share with you from my perspective. I have lived what many would consider to be an **unorthodox** life, but it has always been an interesting one.

It is true that I did not graduate from high school; but like you, I did spend years majoring in my own area of study. I am a graduate of the University of Rock and Roll, Class of 1970. My diploma was a check—a week's worth of wages earned from playing long nights in smoky, crowded clubs in the New York area. Through the years, I have been given platinum albums, Grammys, keys to cities, and many other awards which are considered prestigious in my profession. But the greatest award I have ever received was that check—my diploma—made out to Billy Joel in 1970. This particular check was enough to cover my rent and my expenses. It was also enough to convince me that I no longer needed to work in a factory or be a short-order cook or pump gas or paint houses or do any of the other day jobs I had done in order to make ends meet. That check meant that I was now able to make a living solely by doing

◀ **Vocabulary**
unorthodox (un ôr′ thə däks′) *adj.* not traditional

Spiral Review
IMAGERY How does Joel describe the clubs where he played? What effect does the description create?

Comprehension
What does Joel say was his area of study?

Vocabulary ▶
idealistic (ī´dē ə lis´ tik) *adj.* thinking or acting based on how things should be rather than how they are

Theme
What does Joel's imagined relationship with his 21-year-old self reveal about his lifelong hopes and dreams?

Theme
What does the use of words "flubs" and "foul-ups" show about Joel's attitude towards mistakes?"

the thing that I loved most—making music. It meant that I had become self-reliant as a musician. I will never forget that day. I consider it to be one of the most important days in my life.

I also remember the twenty-one-year-old Billy Joel and I often wonder what it would be like if we could, somehow, meet each other. Here I am, forty-two, exactly twice his age. What would I think of him? Would I find him to be naive, arrogant, simplistic, crude, noble, hopelessly **idealistic**? Perhaps all of these things. But more important, what would he think of me? Have I fulfilled his dream? Have I created the kind of music he would have wanted to have written? Have I compromised any of his ideals? Have I broken any of the promises I made to him? Have I lost the desire to be the best he could be? Would he be disappointed in me? Would he even like me?

That twenty-one-year-old has been the biggest pain in the neck I have had to endure in my life. Yet he has had more influence on the work I have done than anyone else for the last twenty-one years. He has been my greatest teacher, my deepest conscience, my toughest editor, and my harshest critic. He has significantly shaped my life. I can say to you today that what you are at this moment in your lives you will always be in your hearts.

When I met with your fellow students, they asked me what is the most powerful lesson I have learned. After eleven years of classical training, I learned to play the piano, but I realized that I was not destined to be another Van Cliburn. I learned to write songs, although what I really wanted to write were symphonies like Beethoven. I have learned to perform, but somehow I knew I would never be able to move like Michael Jackson or sing like Ray Charles.

Out of respect for things that I was never destined to do, I have learned that my strengths are a result of my weaknesses, my success is due to my failures, and my style is directly related to my limitations. You see, the only original things I have ever done have been accidents, mistakes, flubs, foul-ups, and their attendant solutions. I have an inherent talent for stumbling onto something. I am an expert at making bad choices and illogical decisions. I have discovered that after all those years of musical instruction, after all that practice to be perfect, after all that hard work trying to compose the right notes, I am gifted with the knack of hitting exactly the wrong notes at precisely the right time.

This is the secret of originality. Think about it. You may have learned all there is to know about reproducing the art of someone else, but only you can commit a colossal blunder in your own exquisite style. This is what makes you unique. But then you are faced with solving the problem. This is what makes you inventive. Commit enough blunders and you become an artist. Solve all the problems you have created and they will call you a genius.

Only you can commit a colossal blunder in your own exquisite style.

I have learned that no matter how successful or proficient or accomplished I might think I am, I am always going to make mistakes. I will always have to face some difficulties. I am always going to have to deal with the possibility of failure, and I will always be able to utilize these things in my work. So I am no longer afraid of becoming lost, because the journey back always reveals to me something new about my life and about my own humanity, and that is, ultimately, good for the artist.

Theme
Why does Joel no longer fear "becoming lost"?

Critical Thinking

1. **Key Ideas and Details: (a)** What was Joel's "college diploma"? **(b) Infer:** How did getting it change his life? Explain.
2. **Key Ideas and Details: (a)** Why do you think Joel says that his younger self has been "the biggest pain in [his] neck"? **(b)** What four roles has his younger self played in his life? **(c)** What effect does Joel create by listing the roles in a series? Explain, citing details from the text in your response.
3. **Craft and Structure: (a)** What does Joel say is the source of his strengths? His success? **(b)** What is the impact of Joel's use of antonyms to identify the sources? Explain, supporting your ideas with textual details.
4. **Integration of Knowledge and Ideas: (a)** What positive effects might Joel's speech have on his audience? Explain. **(b)** In what ways could giving this speech serve a positive purpose in Joel's life? Explain. *[Connect to the Big Question: Does all communication serve a positive purpose?]*

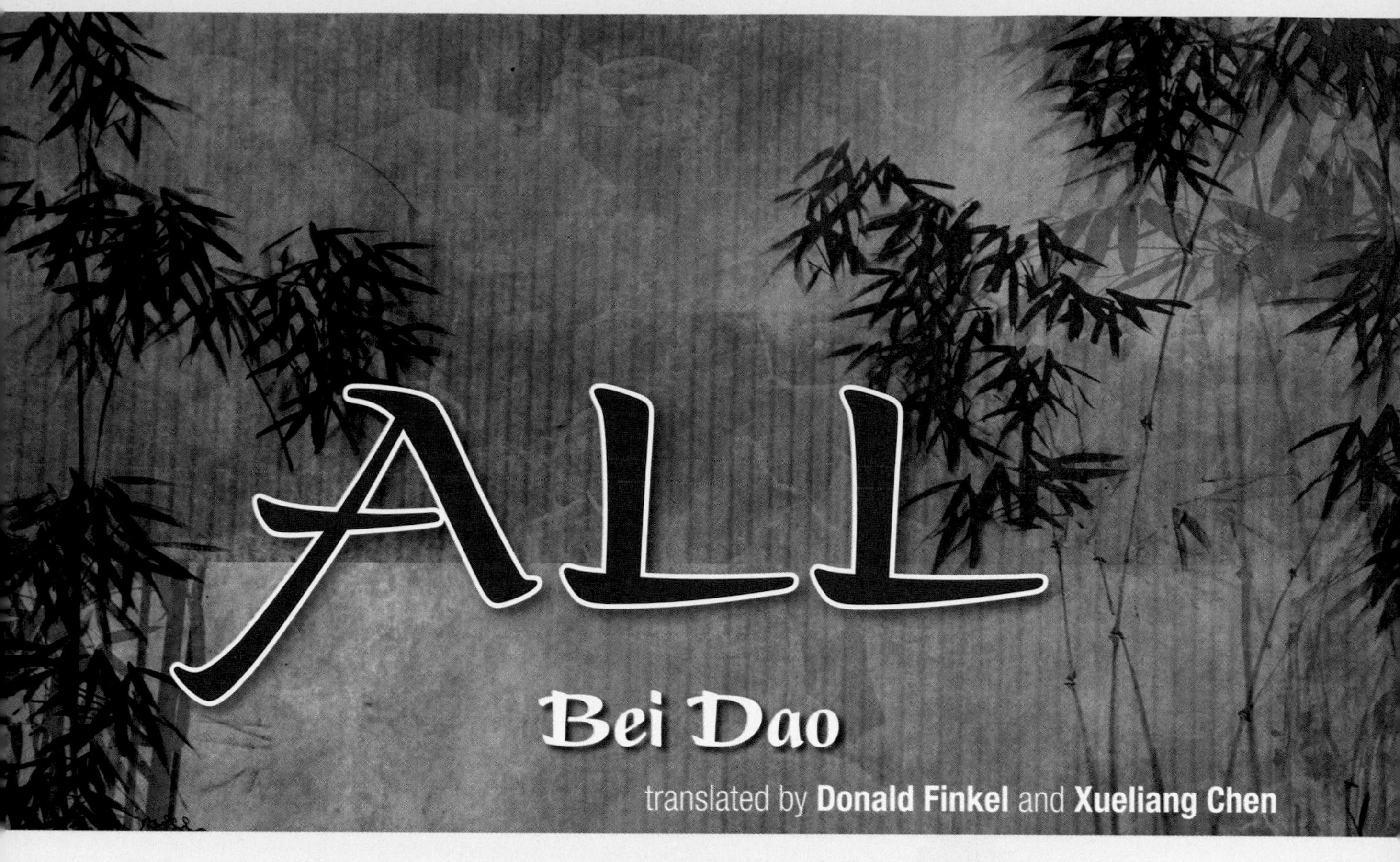

ALL

Bei Dao

translated by **Donald Finkel** and **Xueliang Chen**

All is fated,
all cloudy,

all an endless beginning,
all a search for what vanishes,

all joys grave,
all griefs tearless,

every speech a repetition,
every meeting a first encounter,

all love buried in the heart,
all history prisoned in a dream,

all hope hedged with doubt,
all faith drowned in **lamentation**.

Every explosion heralds an instant of stillness,
every death reverberates forever.

Theme
What doubt about people's ability to trust one another is implied in line 8?

Vocabulary ▶ lamentation
(lam′ ən tā′ shən)
n. act of crying out in grief; wailing

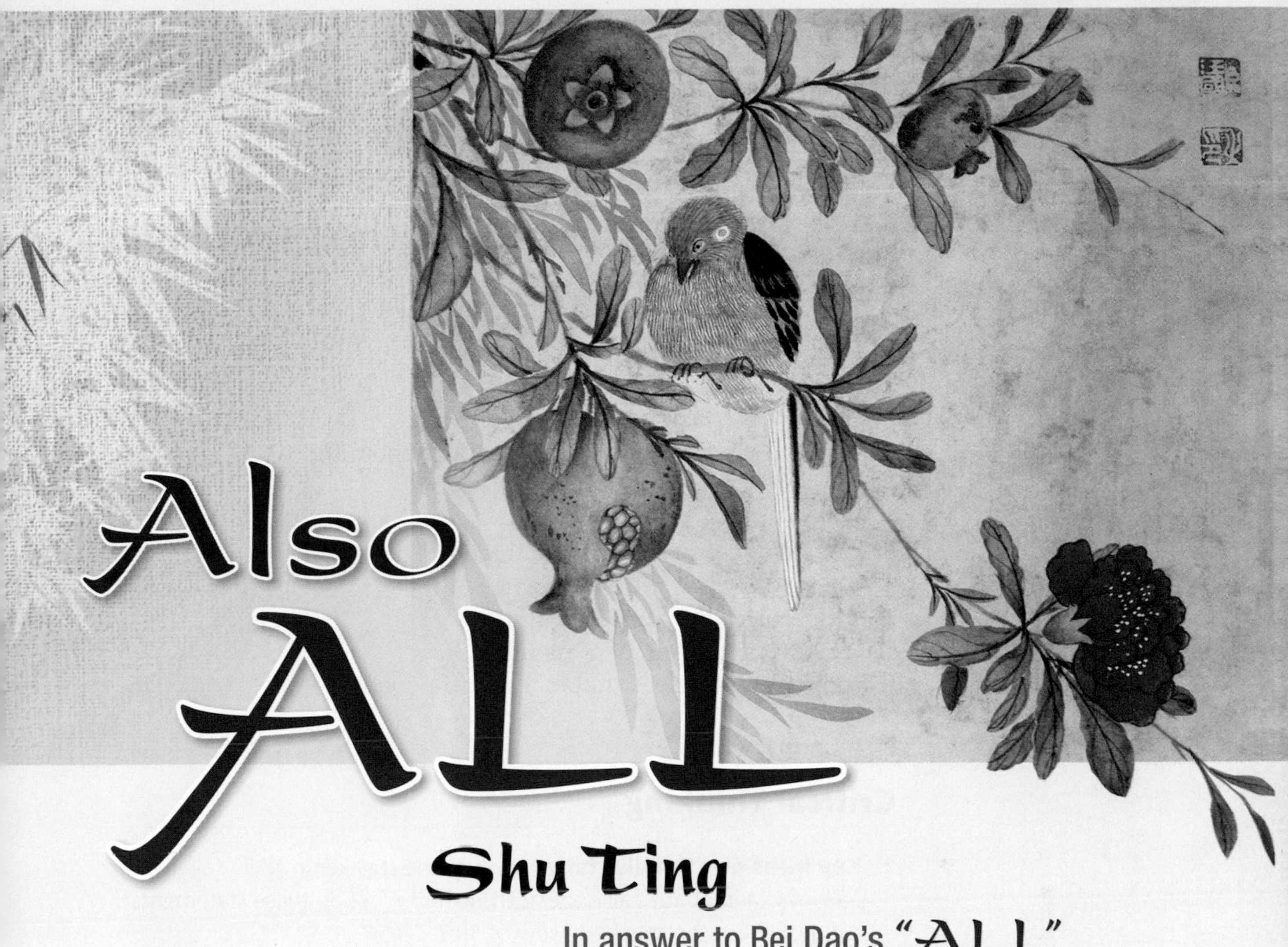

Also ALL

Shu Ting

In answer to Bei Dao's "ALL"

Background Bei Dao and Shu Ting both belonged to a group of Chinese writers known as the Misty Poets. Influenced by Western poets and breaking with Chinese tradition, the Misty Poets used vivid imagery and expressed strong personal emotions. By speaking up for individual feelings, they expressed a quiet opposition to the government of China. In "Also All," Shu Ting answers Bei Dao's poem "All."

Not all trees are felled by storms.
Not every seed finds barren soil.
Not all the wings of dream are broken,
nor is all affection doomed
to **wither** in a desolate heart.

◀ **Vocabulary**
wither (with́ ər) *v.* shrivel from loss of moisture

No, not all is as you say.

Not all flames consume themselves,
shedding no light on other lives.
Not all stars announce the night
and never dawn. Not every song
will drift past every ear and heart.

No, not all is as you say.

Not every cry for help is silenced,
nor every loss beyond recall.
Not every chasm spells disaster.
Not only the weak will be brought to their knees,
nor every soul be trodden under.

It won't all end in tears and blood.
Today is heavy with tomorrow—
the future was planted yesterday.
Hope is a burden all of us shoulder
though we might stumble under the load.

Critical Thinking

1. **Key Ideas and Details: (a)** What does the speaker in "All" say about "all joys" and about "all hope"? **(b) Infer:** What do these statements suggest about the speaker's view of life?
2. **Craft and Structure: (a)** What words does the speaker of "All" repeat at the beginning of lines? **(b)** What is the impact of the repetition in expressing main ideas in the poem? Cite textual details in your response.
3. **Key Ideas and Details: (a)** What does the speaker in "Also All" point out about the effect of a storm on trees? **(b) Infer:** Is her viewpoint basically optimistic or pessimistic? Support your answer with details from the poem.
4. **Key Ideas and Details: (a)** In what way does "Also All" answer the speaker's points in "All"? **(b) Speculate:** How might the speaker in "All" answer the point in the last two lines of "Also All"?
5. **Integration of Knowledge and Ideas: (a)** What is Bei Dao's attitude about life and the future? **(b)** What is Shu Ting's attitude about the present and the future? **(c)** Do both poems serve a positive purpose? Explain. *[Connect to the Big Question: Does all communication serve a positive purpose?]*

Writing to Sources

Comparing Theme

1. **Craft and Structure (a)** Sum up the central insights in "Hold Fast Your Dreams . . . ." **(b)** Would you view the central insights differently if Joel had used more formal diction? Explain, citing details from the text.
2. **Craft and Structure (a)** Sum up the insights expressed in each poem. **(b)** List three phrases in each poem that help reveal these insights. Explain your answers.
3. **Key Ideas and Details** What reaction might the speaker in "All" have to Joel's speech? Explain, using details from the selections.
4. **Key Ideas and Details (a)** The diagram lists four possible responses to disappointment and failure. Copy the diagram, and list details from the selections that reflect these responses. **(b)** Use your analysis to compare the insights into success and failure the authors express in these selections.

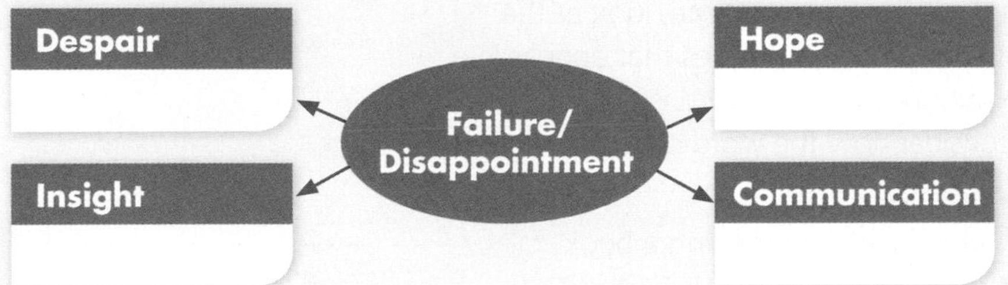

Timed Writing

Explanatory Text: Essay

In an essay, compare each writer's insights about success. Consider how each writer's diction and choices of details help convey this message. **(35 minutes)**

5-Minute Planner

1. Read the prompt carefully and completely.
2. Consider the theme or central message of each work. Gather your ideas by jotting down answers to these questions:
   - What is each author's attitude toward hope and success?
   - How does each writer's word choice help reveal this attitude?
   - Which details in each selection support its theme most strongly?
3. Choose an organizing structure appropriate to your purpose. Note that the prompt requires you to compare the selections.
4. Reread the prompt, and then draft your essay.

USE ACADEMIC VOCABULARY

As you write, use academic language, including the following words or their related forms:

awareness
isolation
perspective
subjective

For more information about academic vocabulary, see page xlvi.

Language Study

Words With Multiple Meanings

Many words in English have **multiple meanings.** Consider this dictionary entry for *coast*:

Dictionary

The first part of the entry gives meanings for the noun *coast.*

The second part of the entry gives meanings for the verb *coast.*

coast (kōst) *n.* [ME *coste*, coast < OFr, a rib, hill, shore, coast < L *costa*, a rib, side] **1.** land alongside the sea; seashore **2.** [Obs] frontier borderland **3.** a slide or ride, as on a sled going down an incline by the force of gravity— ***vi.*** **1.** to sail along or near a coast, esp. from port to port **2.** to go down an incline, as on a sled **3.** to continue in motion on momentum or by the force of gravity after propelling power has stopped **4.** to continue without serious effort, letting one's past efforts carry one along

This means "obsolete," or no longer in use.

Common Core State Standards

Language

4. Determine or clarify the meaning of unknown and multiple-meaning words and phrases based on grades 9–10 reading and content.

4.a. Use context as a clue to the meaning of a word or phrase.

4.c. Consult general and specialized reference materials, both print and digital, to find the pronunciation of a word or determine or clarify its precise meaning, its part of speech, or its etymology.

4.d. Verify the preliminary determination of the meaning of a word or phrase.

To determine which meaning a writer is using in a sentence, look at the **context clues.** Context clues are other words and phrases that appear in a text. They can shed light on how a multiple-meaning word is being used in a particular passage. For example, consider how the word *coast* is used in the following sentence:

My brother coasted through law school without opening a book.

The sentence presents a variety of context clues. First, *coast* is used as a verb. Second, the phrase *without opening a book* suggests "without much effort." To confirm the meaning, try each of the four definitions for verbs in the sentence. The definition that fits is 4—"to continue without serious effort, letting one's past efforts carry one along."

Practice A

Read each sentence. Choose the multiple-meaning word that makes sense in each sentence pair: *vacuum, break, negative, police.*

1. **(a)** His _______ attitude kept him from succeeding in school.
   (b) The _______ of a photograph shows light and dark in reverse.
2. **(a)** I need to _______ the rug before company arrives.
   (b) The absence of air creates a _______.
3. **(a)** We must _______ the campus for litter.
   (b) My older sister went to the _______ academy when she was twenty.
4. **(a)** We definitely wanted to _______ free of our routine.
   (b) The sun shone through a _______ in the clouds.

Practice B

Using context clues, write your own definition for the underlined word in each sentence. With a partner, discuss which context clues helped you to determine the meaning of the word. Then, look up the word in a dictionary to confirm or correct your definition.

1. The map didn't show the <u>cardinal</u> directions!
2. A cold <u>draft</u> came in under the door and through cracks around the window.
3. She didn't seem to <u>harbor</u> any hard feelings over what I'd said.
4. The <u>launch</u> sped across the choppy bay.
5. How can you <u>gauge</u> someone's interest in the drama?
6. To prepare for the long Alaskan winter, Andrew stocked his cabin with flour, cereal, potatoes, and other <u>staples</u>.
7. The truck bounced its way across the sandy <u>wash</u>.
8. Their <u>plot</u> to avoid the extra work failed completely.
9. Don't <u>force</u> the lock or you may break the key off.
10. The sailor could hardly stay on his feet as he walked across the heaving <u>deck</u> of the ship.

Activity Look in a dictionary to find the multiple definitions of these words: *litter, fan, coat, pump*, and *contract*. Write each word on a separate notecard like the one shown. Fill in the middle column of the notecard according to one of the word's meanings. Fill in the right column according to another of the word's meanings. Then, trade notecards with a partner and discuss the different meanings and uses of the words that each of you found.

Word	First Meaning	Second Meaning

Comprehension and Collaboration

Find each of these words in a dictionary: *craft, switch, exhaust*. Select one of the meanings for each and write a sentence in which the context clearly illustrates the meaning. Trade sentences with a partner. Identify the definition of the word in each of your partner's sentences.

Speaking and Listening

Analyzing Media Messages

Common Core State Standards

Speaking and Listening
3. Evaluate a speaker's point of view, reasoning, and use of evidence and rhetoric, identifying any fallacious reasoning or exaggerated or distorted evidence.

Some television, radio, and Internet sources are truthful, thorough, and objective. Others offer information that is inaccurate, incomplete, or reported in a biased way. To evaluate media messages, stay alert and analyze claims critically.

Learn the Skills

Use the strategies to complete the activity on page 429.

Evaluate the content of the message. Carefully consider and evaluate what the message says.

- **Look for support for claims.** Note facts, statistics, quotations, and other evidence. If no support is provided, decide whether you have any reason to accept the claims in the message.
- **Consider bias.** People quoted in media may present biased, or one-sided, evidence. Consider the reasons a source might have to favor one version of events over another or to exaggerate or distort evidence. Note whether opposing viewpoints have been left out and why a speaker might omit them.
- **Look for faulty reasoning.** Ask yourself whether the claims made are contradictory or vague. Look for logical fallacies, such as insisting something is correct because most people think it is.
- **Look for illegal statements.** There are laws to protect people from libel (false written statements) and slander (false spoken statements). Be alert to accusations that are not supported by facts.

Evaluate the style of the message. Once you understand a message's content, consider its delivery. Some media techniques sway viewers or misrepresent ideas.

- **Be aware of stereotypes.** Watch for stereotypes, or oversimplified ideas about a group of people. Many stereotypes are negative images based on race, gender, age, occupation, or social role.
- **Detect cultural assumptions.** Media presentations can reflect basic assumptions about what is important or good. Think about whether you agree with such value judgments.
- **Be alert to charged or emotional language.** Listen for words and phrases that are meant to manipulate or affect your emotions.
- **Consider the impact of the medium.** Background music, images, and graphics may capture your attention. If they have been added only to stir emotions, they are not evidence.

Practice the Skills

Presentation of Knowledge and Ideas Use what you have learned in this workshop to perform the following task.

ACTIVITY: **Analyze a Media Message**

Using the Analysis Checklist below as a guide, analyze a television newscast or advertisement. Then, share your analysis in a group discussion.

- Watch the newscast or advertisement multiple times and observe it carefully.
- As you watch, refer often to the Analysis Checklist.
- Take notes on your observations.
- Use your checklist and notes to present your ideas to a small group of classmates.

Analysis Checklist

Rating Scale (Use the rating scale to evaluate the media message.)

Poor Excellent

1 2 3 4 5

Message Purpose

What is the main purpose of the message?

____

____

Use of Facts and Evidence

______ Relevant Support ______ Complete Support

______ Unbiased Support ______ Sound Reasoning

Message Style

______ Relevance of Graphics or Images ______ Avoidance of Charged Language

______ Relevance of Music ______ Avoidance of Stereotypes

Conclusions

Was the message trustworthy?

____

____

Did the message fulfill its purpose?

____

____

Comprehension and Collaboration After you present your analysis of the media message to a small group, lead a brief discussion. Ask group members whether your observations are similar to or different from theirs. Make sure that everyone participates in the discussion.

Writing Process

Write an Explanatory Text

Exposition: Cause-and-Effect Essay

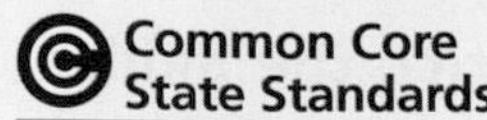

Writing

2. Write informative/explanatory texts to examine and convey complex ideas, concepts, and information clearly and accurately through the effective selection, organization, and analysis of content.

5. Develop and strengthen writing as needed by planning, revising, editing, rewriting, or trying a new approach, focusing on addressing what is most significant for a specific purpose and audience.

7. Conduct short as well as more sustained research projects to answer a question or solve a problem; narrow or broaden the inquiry when appropriate.

Defining the Form Whenever something unusual happens, the first question most people ask is, "Why?" A **cause-and-effect essay** can satisfy a reader's curiosity. It might explain why a weird new fashion fad began or what happened as a result of a groundbreaking court decision. You might use elements of this form in research papers, informative articles, and reflective essays.

Assignment Write an essay in which you explain a cause-and-effect relationship. Include these elements:

✓ a *thesis statement* in which you clearly state the cause-and-effect relationships you will explore

✓ an effective and *logical method of organization* that allows you to explain complex ideas clearly and thoroughly

✓ well-chosen, relevant *supporting evidence* and examples that develop your topic and suit your audience and purpose

✓ *transitions* that smoothly and clearly connect your ideas

✓ definitions and careful *use of language* appropriate for your topic and audience

✓ error-free grammar, including *correct use of verbal phrases*

To preview the criteria on which your cause-and-effect essay may be judged, see the rubric on page 437.

FOCUS ON RESEARCH

When you write explanatory essays, you might perform research to

- learn more about a process or situation in order to provide clearer background information.
- clarify explanations and ideas with precise information, including facts and data.
- confirm that all of your information is thorough and accurate.
- locate specific examples to illustrate your points.

Be sure to take careful notes, noting down all the information you will need to accurately credit your sources. See the Citing Sources pages in the Introductory Unit of this textbook for additional guidance.

READING-WRITING CONNECTION

To get a feel for cause-and-effect essays, read the excerpt from *Collapse: How Societies Choose to Fail or Succeed* by Jared Diamond on page 496.

Prewriting/Planning Strategies

Choose one of the following strategies to find a topic and focus for your essay.

Make a list. Brainstorm for a list of scientific phenomena, historic events, or popular trends that you find interesting, important, or surprising. Look over your list to choose a topic you would like to explore in an essay.

Scan a newspaper or magazine. Review print or online articles, looking for ideas that make you ask, "Why?" Identify possible topics and then conduct short research projects to learn more about the subjects that spark your interest. Review your research notes and choose a topic to address.

Narrow your topic. Once you have a topic, make sure that you can discuss it fully in your essay. If your topic is too broad, you may need to focus it. For example, you might not be able to answer "Why did the Great Depression happen?" in a short essay. Instead, you could focus your inquiry on why the stock market crashed in October of 1929.

Make a cause-and-effect chart. Organizing your ideas and details in a cause-and-effect chart can help you form a clear picture of the relationships you will discuss. One chart shown here presents three possible causes of one effect. The other chart classifies the possible effects of one cause.

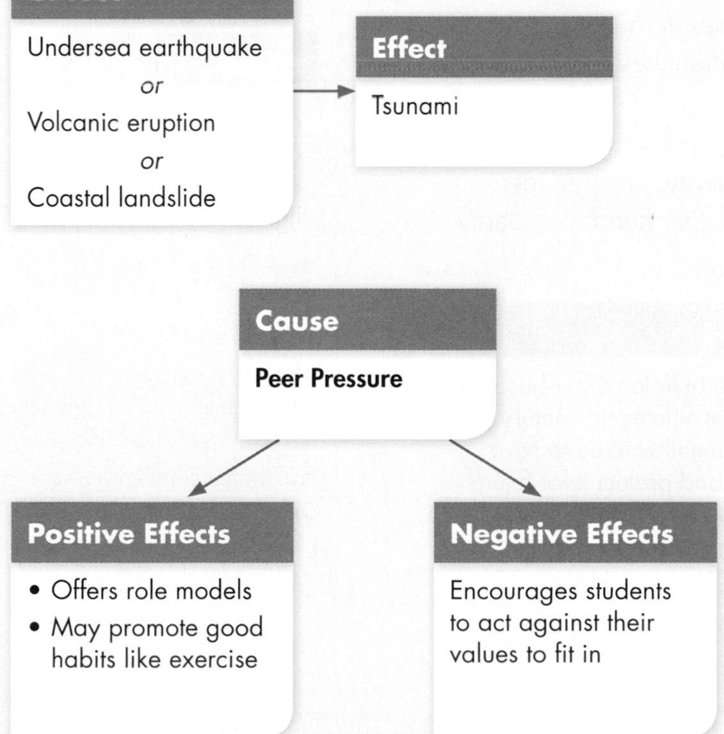

Drafting Strategies

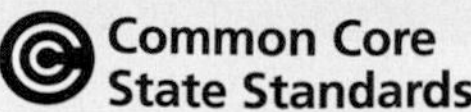

Writing

2.a. Introduce a topic, organize complex ideas, concepts, and information to make important connections and distinctions.

2.c. Use appropriate and varied transitions to link the major sections of the text, create cohesion, and clarify the relationships among complex ideas and concepts.

2.d. Use precise language and domain-specific vocabulary to manage the complexity of the topic.

2.f. Provide a concluding statement or section that follows from and supports the information or explanation presented.

Clarify your analysis. Even if you are describing a complicated chain of effects, you will need a clear and direct introduction. Prepare a simplified cause-and-effect chart like the one shown below right to organize your prewriting ideas. It can show you which ideas are most essential to your topic.

Consider your audience. As you draft your essay, keep your audience, or readers, in mind.

- **Include background information.** Cause-and-effect essays may include information that is unfamiliar or obscure to many readers. To help your audience understand your ideas, use precise words and provide full explanations. For instance, if you are writing about pollution from traffic, you might explain the differences between diesel fuel and regular gasoline. In addition, make sure to define unfamiliar words or phrases. You may do so in the body of your essay or in footnotes. For example, an essay on air pollution might include footnotes for terms such as *carbon footprint*.
- **Use a respectful tone.** As you draft, be respectful of differing viewpoints. For example, if you are describing how industry contributes to air pollution, remember that factories provide jobs and are often vital parts of local economies. Present pros and cons, but always maintain a respectful tone.

Cause

Bicycles are built using new, stronger materials.

↓

Effect

New bicycles are faster, more comfortable, and lighter.

Use clear transitions. Specific words and phrases, called transitions or transitional expressions, can help you introduce causes and effects. For example, use *therefore, consequently, as a result,* or *for that reason* to introduce effects. Refer to causes with transitional expressions such as *because, since, as,* or *for the reason that.*

Also consider phrases that help you connect, contrast, and compare ideas. You might use *not only . . . but also* to join two related ideas. Other transitions, such as *however* and *on the other hand,* can clarify contrasting ideas.

Using Transitions	
The buffalo nearly became extinct in the nineteenth century. George Grinnell worked to save the animal and protect it for future generations. Today, several herds are thriving in the wild.	*Because* the buffalo nearly became extinct in the nineteenth century, George Grinnell worked to save the animal and protect it for future generations. *As a result,* several herds are thriving in the wild today.

Organizing a Cause-and-Effect Essay

Organization is the order in which you present your ideas. A thoughtful, logical organization can help you present your ideas and the ways in which they are connected more effectively.

Choose a logical organization. The structure you choose for a cause-and-effect essay depends on the ideas you are trying to convey and the kind of information you are using as evidence.

- **Chronological Order** Writing about causes and effects in time sequence makes sense for many essays, especially those in which a single cause leads to multiple effects. You might start by discussing the cause. Then, present the various effects in sequence. Alternatively, you can start with an effect and then work back to its causes one at a time.

  Example: The sinking of the *Titanic* led to new marine regulations for ocean-going vessels. New regulations included these mandates: constant radio contact between ships and sufficient lifeboats for every passenger on board.

- **Order-of-Importance Organization** If you are writing about a topic in which many causes contribute to a single effect, consider presenting your ideas in order of importance. You might begin with your most important cause or save the most important cause for last.

  Example: The tragic disaster of the *Titanic's* maiden voyage was the result of many factors. Chief among them was the obvious failure of the crew to navigate around an iceberg. The resulting damage to the ship's hull made the sinking inevitable.

  Another contributing factor was the lack of adequate lifeboats for all passengers. Nor were the passengers and crew familiar with safety procedures. The ship's manufacturer and owners were so certain the ship was "unsinkable" they simply ignored the most basic precautions.

Check your organization. As you review your overall organization, make sure that you have presented your ideas in logical order and have established clear relationships among them. Include an introduction, a body, and a conclusion that supports your analysis. To make sure your organization is logical and consistent, underline the main idea you state in your introduction. Then, review your body paragraphs and conclusion, circling the sentences that develop or restate your main idea. All the items you circle should show clear, logical relationships.

Revising Strategies

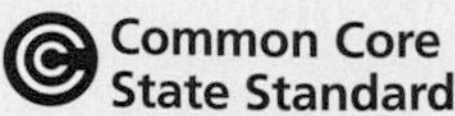

Look for careless repetition. Effective use of repetition helps to emphasize key ideas and create a memorable impact. Sloppy repetition, however, weakens your writing. Look for words that appear too often or too close together. Use a thesaurus to find words with related meanings or use a pronoun to replace a noun that you have used many times.

Too Much Repetition: Bees *buzz* as a result of beating their wings *rapidly*. When an intruder approaches, bees beat their wings even more *rapidly*. As a result, *the bees' buzzing* grows louder.

More Effective: Bees *buzz* as a result of beating their wings *rapidly*. When an intruder approaches, bees beat their wings *faster* and their *buzzing* grows louder.

Consider your style and tone. Use language that will further your purpose for writing. A formal style that is free of slang words and that creates a serious, objective tone is appropriate for cause-and-effect essays.

Color-code to identify related details. Each paragraph in your essay should have a strong, single focus. First, circle the topic sentence of each paragraph. If you cannot find a topic sentence, consider adding one. Then, underline sentences that contain details that support the topic of the paragraph.

Peer Review

After identifying topic sentences and supporting details, look at the sentences that are neither circled nor underlined. With a partner, discuss whether to rewrite or delete these sentences. You might also consider moving those sentences to a paragraph where they support the topic more effectively. After revising, explain your decisions to your partner.

Model: Revising to Strengthen Focus

Ice storms caused devastation throughout the Northeast. Power lines were downed by the heavy coating of ice, causing widespread electric outages. ~~People became bored without access to television.~~ Roads coated with ice became impassable.

The writer deleted a sentence that offered useful information but did not relate to the topic of the paragraph.

Writing

2.e. Establish and maintain a formal style and objective tone while attending to the norms and conventions of the discipline in which they are writing.

5. Develop and strengthen writing as needed by planning, revising, editing, rewriting, or trying a new approach, focusing on addressing what is most significant for a specific purpose and audience.

Language

1. Demonstrate command of the conventions of standard English grammar and usage when writing or speaking.

1.b. Use various types of phrases and clauses to convey specific meanings and add variety and interest to writing or presentations.

Revising to Combine Sentences With Verbal Phrases

The repetition of too many sentences with the same structure can create choppy, uninteresting writing. Use verbal phrases to combine a series of short, choppy sentences into longer, more flowing ones.

Identifying Verbal Phrases Verbal phrases use verbs but act as nouns, adjectives, or adverbs.

The Three Types of Verbal Phrases

Participial Phrase	Gerund Phrase	Infinitive Phrase
a participle—a form of a verb that can act as an **adjective**—and any modifiers, object, or complement	a gerund—a verb ending in *-ing* that functions as a **noun**—and any modifiers, object, or complement	an infinitive—a form of verb that appears after the word *to* and acts as a **noun,** an **adjective,** or an **adverb**—and any modifiers, object, or complement
Walking by herself, Sara felt peaceful. *(modifies Sara)*	*Speaking in public* is scary. *(acts as subject)*	Her advice was *to start small. (acts as predicate nominative)*

A verbal phrase serving as a modifier should be close to the word it modifies.

Misplaced: *Eating fish,* the scientists saw a baby seal.

Correct: The scientists saw a baby seal *eating fish.*

Combining Sentences Using Verbal Phrases Use verbal phrases to combine choppy sentences. Follow these steps:

1. **Express the ideas from a short sentence as a verbal phrase.**
2. **Insert the phrase into a new sentence, locating it near the word or words being modified.**
3. **Punctuate the new sentence correctly.** Look at this example:

   Choppy sentences: The cheetah moves silently. It stalks its prey.

   Combined into one sentence: Stalking its prey, the cheetah moves silently.

Grammar in Your Writing

Review your essay, looking for short sentences that might be combined using verbal phrases. Be sure to avoid misplaced modifiers.

STUDENT MODEL: **Andrew Vanover, Raleigh, NC**

Hurricane: Causes and Effects

Everyone dreads the hurricane season. When that time of year comes around, we all lock down and get ready for the harsh winds and power outages. The 2004 season started out with a bang. Large parts of the coast were torn apart as storms rolled in, one after another.

Causes of Hurricanes

Hurricanes form when weather patterns of different temperatures run into each other and start spinning. When a cold front out in the ocean, moving in one direction, comes in contact with a warm front moving in the opposite direction, winds start. These winds start moving in circular motions. As they spin, they pick up speed. These large areas of fast-moving winds generate tornadoes that pull water up into the storm. Hurricanes have high winds with tornadoes and carry large amounts of water.

Andrew uses subheads to clearly organize the information. This paragraph explains what causes hurricanes.

When it starts, the storm is classified as a tropical depression. As it becomes stronger, it is called a tropical storm. If the wind speeds get high enough, the tropical storm is categorized as a hurricane.

Effects of Hurricanes: Damage to Property

When the storm hits land, it dumps all its water, and that is when it becomes the most destructive. Some of the water soaks into the ground, but often there is more water than the land can absorb. As a result, the water quickly runs off to lower areas. These run-offs are called flash floods. Flash floods can wash away land and possessions or destroy them by filling them with water. At the same time, hurricane winds can blow over trees and power lines. With the power out, repairs are hard to make quickly. This means power can be out for a week or longer. Hurricanes also bring lightning, which can cause fires in trees or houses.

Andrew breaks his discussion of the effects of hurricanes into two sections.

Effects of Hurricanes: Damage to Business

During the late summer and fall of 2004, the state of Florida was hit by four major hurricanes: Charley, Frances, Ivan, and Jeanne. Each hurricane caused so much damage that it could not be repaired before the next storm hit. The damage was so bad that President Bush asked Congress for 7.1 billion dollars for repairs in Florida. Many people had to board up stores and wait in line for electric generators. In addition, relief workers were sent down to Florida to help deliver meals, water, and ice.

These storms not only caused trouble for the insurance companies, but also affected the citrus and tourism industries. The citrus growers in Florida lost about half of their grapefruit crop during Hurricane Frances. Tourism was also hurt because people do not want to travel into a disaster zone.

Andrew uses a specific detail to support his broader claims.

Conclusion

The hurricane season of 2004 was more intense than previous years. This is said to be from warm temperatures in the Atlantic Ocean and a decrease in wind shear. We hope that in the future we will better be able to predict and prepare for these hurricanes.

Editing and Proofreading

Review your draft to correct errors in grammar, spelling, capitalization, and punctuation.

Focus on usage errors. Check your writing for commonly confused words. Remember that *then* refers to time and *than* is used for comparisons. Use *since* to refer to a previous time, not to mean "because." If you are unsure about a word, consult a dictionary or usage guide.

Spiral Review
Earlier in this unit, you learned about **commas and dashes** (p. 376). Review your draft carefully to be sure you have used these punctuation marks correctly.

Publishing and Presenting

Consider one of the following ways to share your writing:

Give a class presentation. Use your essay as the basis of a presentation. Use photographs, charts, maps, or diagrams to make your cause-and-effect relationships clear. Practice combining visuals with your writing, deciding when you will show each visual as you share the ideas from your essay.

Use e-mail. Share your writing electronically. Type your essay using word-processing software. Attach the file to an e-mail to a friend or relative. Save printouts of the essay and any responses in your writing portfolio.

Reflecting on Your Writing

Writer's Journal Jot down your answers to this question:
How did writing about your topic help you to understand it?

Self-Evaluation Rubric

Use the following criteria to evaluate the effectiveness of your essay.

Criteria	Rating Scale
Purpose/Focus Introduces a specific topic; provides a concluding section that follows from and supports the information or explanation presented	*not very* .... *very* 1 2 3 4
Organization Organizes complex ideas, concepts, and information to make important connections and distinctions; uses appropriate and varied transitions to link the major sections, create cohesion, and clarify relationships among ideas	1 2 3 4
Development of Ideas/Elaboration Develops the topic with well-chosen, relevant and sufficient facts, extended definitions, concrete details, quotations or other information and examples appropriate to the audience's knowledge of the topic	1 2 3 4
Language Uses precise language and domain-specific vocabulary to manage the complexity of the topic; establishes and maintains a formal style and objective tone	1 2 3 4
Conventions Attends to the norms and conventions of the discipline	1 2 3 4

SELECTED RESPONSE

RL.9-10.4, RL.9-10.5; W.9-10.10; L.9-10.4.a
[For full standards wording, see the chart in the front of this book.]

I. Reading Literature

Directions: *Read "Mowing" by Robert Frost. Then, answer each question that follows.*

There was never a sound beside the wood but one,
And that was my long scythe* whispering to the ground.
What was it it whispered? I knew not well myself;
Perhaps it was something about the heat of the sun,
Something, perhaps, about the lack of sound—
And that was why it whispered and did not speak.
It was no dream of the gift of <u>idle</u> hours,
Or easy gold at the hand of fay or elf:
Anything more than the truth would have seemed too weak
To the earnest love that laid the swale in rows,
Not without feeble-pointed spikes of flowers
(Pale orchises), and scared a bright green snake.
The fact is the sweetest dream that labor knows.
My long scythe whispered and left the hay to make.

* scythe (sī*th*) *n.* long, curved blade set on a pole-like handle used in cutting hay by hand

1. **Part A** "Mowing" most clearly resembles which **poetic form?**

   A. sonnet
   B. tanka
   C. free verse
   D. villanelle

   Part B Which aspect of the poem indicates its form?

   A. The lines of the poem do not follow a fixed pattern.
   B. The poem features repeated lines.
   C. The poem contains fourteen lines.
   D. The poem has five lines that do not rhyme.

2. Which answer choice best identifies the **speaker** in this poem?

   A. scythe
   B. whisperer
   C. father
   D. farmer

3. **Part A** Which answer choice is a type of **sound device?**

   A. stanza
   B. consonance
   C. enjambment
   D. couplet

   Part B Which passage from the poem best represents the sound device of **alliteration?**

   A. "It was no dream of the gift of idle hours"
   B. "left the hay to make"
   C. "was why it whispered"
   D. "sound beside the wood"

4. Which answer choice best describes the **tone** of the poem?

   A. deeply appreciative
   B. lightly playful
   C. confused and frustrated
   D. dark and bitter

5. Which answer choice is a type of **figurative language?**

   A. rhyme scheme
   B. connotation
   C. meter
   D. metaphor

6. Which passage from the poem is an example of **personification?**

   A. "feeble-pointed spikes of flowers"
   B. "my long scythe whispering"
   C. "easy gold at the hand of fay or elf"
   D. "something about the heat of the sun"

7. Which is the best definition of the underlined word *idle* as it is used in the poem?

   A. lazy
   B. tired
   C. motionless
   D. hazardous

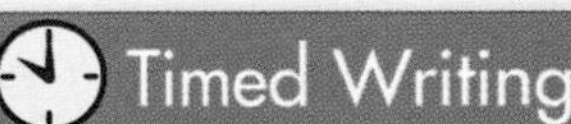

Timed Writing

8. Reread "Mowing" and write a **paraphrase** of the poem's first six lines. Then, briefly explain the process you used to develop your paraphrase.

GO ON

II. Reading Informational Text

Directions: *Read the article. Then, answer each question that follows.*

Common Core State Standards

RI.9-10.2, RI.9-10.3; L.9-10.1, L.9-10.1.b, L.9-10.2

[For full standards wording, see the chart in the front of this book.]

The Bees

Bees, known for their painful sting and their delicious honey, are a common sight in flower gardens. Blossoms provide bees with their food—pollen and nectar. Bees have specialized adaptations for collecting food, including hairy bodies, pollen baskets, and special tongues for gathering nectar.

Honeybees

Honeybees, the most commonly known type of bee, are organized social insects. Honeybees live in complex colonies in which large numbers of individuals act together nearly as a single organism. The bee colony consists of specialized individuals: the queen bee, worker bees, and drones.

Queen bee. The queen bee is a fully developed female. Her only job is to lay eggs. When summer flowers begin blooming, the queen begins to lay her eggs, numbering a thousand or more per day.

Worker bees. Worker bees are undeveloped females. A colony can have up to 60,000 female bees. They collect nectar and pollen, convert it into honey, raise the young, and build their honeycomb. As they collect pollen, some clings to the hairs on their bodies. Flying from blossom to blossom, the bees pollinate flowers, fruit trees, and vegetable plants.

Drones. The drones are male bees. Their only job is to mate with the queen. When fall arrives, drones are driven out of the hive to die. Some of the eggs the queen lays are unfertilized. These develop into adult drones. This process of producing life from unfertilized eggs is known as *parthenogenesis.*

1. If the topic you wanted to learn about was dangerous insects, what would you do after scanning this article?

A. reread the article
B. move on to another source
C. skim the article
D. look for more information on honeybees

2. Which sentence accurately states a fact presented in the article?

A. Worker bees are more important than drones.
B. Queen bees, worker bees, and drones all have special functions.
C. Parthenogenisis happens when drone eggs are fertilized.
D. The life cycle of worker bees is short.

3. **Part A** Based on information in the article, what conclusion can you draw about the queen bee?

A. She has an easy life.
B. The worker bees are jealous of her.
C. The colony would die without her.
D. The other bees are more important than she is.

Part B What piece of evidence about the queen bee is implied rather than directly stated?

A. She lays a great number of eggs.
B. She has only one job.
C. She is the only member of the colony that can lay eggs.
D. She can lay unfertilized eggs that produce drones.

III. Writing and Language Conventions

Directions: *Read the passage. Then, answer each question that follows.*

(1) The crunching of the leaves make me aware of my dad, who is walking about ten feet ahead of me. (2) I struggle to keep up with him during our hike. (3) Although I was born and raised in the city, my dad is determined to make me appreciate what he calls "the great outdoors."

(4) Each November he and I drive miles from the city to a state park. (5) When I was younger, I begged not to go—really begged—but he refused to listen. (6) Walking now behind my dad, the air seems sweet. (7) The trees around me are as tall as city skyscrapers, and just as impressive in their own way. (8) Light is dancing across the floor of the forest, flickering here and there. (9) The forest is quiet; you can actually hear the breeze as it whispers. (10) For the first time, I will walk the forest, listen to its music and acknowledge its exquisiteness.

1. Which of these groups of words from the passage is a **gerund phrase?**

A. flickering here and there (sentence 8)
B. is dancing across the floor (sentence 8)
C. the crunching of the leaves (sentence 1)
D. during our hike (sentence 2)

2. Which revision to sentence 9 includes a **present participle?**

A. The forest is quiet; you can actually hear the whispering breeze.
B. The forest is quiet; you can actually hear the breeze start whispering.
C. The forest is growing quiet; you can actually hear the breeze.
D. The forest is quiet; you can actually hear the whispered breeze.

3. Which revision to sentence 6 shows the correct placement of a **verbal phrase** used as a modifier?

A. Walking now behind my dad, a sweetness fills the air.
B. Walking now behind my dad, I find the air sweet.
C. The air seems sweet, walking now behind my dad.
D. Walking now, the air behind my dad seems sweet.

4. Which of these sentences contain **infinitive phrases?**

A. sentences 2 and 3
B. sentences 3 and 4
C. sentences 4 and 5
D. sentences 5 and 8

5. Which of the following suggestions shows correct use of **commas** and **dashes?**

A. Remove the comma in sentence 3.
B. Change the dashes to commas in sentence 5.
C. Add a comma after *music* in sentence 10.
D. Change the comma to a dash in sentence 8.

6. Which of the **prepositional phrases** in sentence 1 is used as an adjective?

A. about ten feet ahead
B. of me
C. of my dad
D. of the leaves

CONSTRUCTED RESPONSE

Directions: *Follow the instructions to complete the tasks below as required by your teacher.*

As you work on each task, incorporate both general academic vocabulary and literary terms you learned in Parts 1 and 2 of this unit.

RL.9-10.2, RL.9-10.4, RL.9-10.5; W.9-10.2, W.9-10.4, W.9-10.7, W.9-10.9, W.9-10.9.a; SL.9-10.1.c, SL.9-10.6

[For full standards wording, see the chart in the front of this book.]

Writing

TASK 1 Literature [RL.9-10.2; W.9-10.4]

Analyze Speaker and Theme

Write an essay in which you analyze how a poem's speaker helps to develop and convey a theme.

- Select a poem from Part 2 of this unit and describe the speaker.
- Use details from the poem to support your description.
- Explain how the speaker is important to the theme of the poem. For example, the speaker may reveal information, attitudes, feelings, or impressions that contribute to the theme.
- Use precise language in your essay, and be sure to correctly punctuate any direct quotations from the poem.
- Provide a concluding statement that follows from and supports the information in your essay.

TASK 2 Literature [RL.9-10.4; W.9-10.2]

Analyze Figurative Language

Write an essay in which you analyze the poet's use of figurative language in a poem.

- Select a poem from Part 2 of this unit that contains striking examples of figurative language, such as metaphors, similes, or personification.
- Cite the examples of figurative language and interpret them. Explain what the poet is expressing through the use of figurative language.
- Analyze the effect of figurative language on the poem's meaning.
- Cite specific examples from the text to support your analysis.
- Make sure you use correct capitalization and punctuation in your writing.

TASK 3 Literature [RL.9-10.4; W.9-10.2]

Analyze Imagery

Write an essay in which you compare and contrast the use of imagery in two poems from Part 2 of this unit.

Part 1

- Select two poems from Part 2 of this unit that are noteworthy for their uses of imagery and sensory language.
- Explain the role imagery and sensory language play in each poem. Cite examples of specific images and discuss how they contribute to the meaning of each poem.
- Discuss similarities and differences in each poet's use of imagery.

Part 2

- Write an explanation of the role imagery plays in poetry.
- Discuss at least two main reasons a poet would choose to use rich imagery and sensory language.
- Support your ideas with details and examples from the poems.
- Be sure to use proper language conventions in your writing.

Speaking and Listening

TASK 4 Literature [RL.9-10.4; SL.9-10.6]

Analyze Sound Devices

Prepare and deliver an oral presentation in which you analyze the use of sound devices in a poem from Part 2 of this unit.

- Select a poem that makes interesting and significant use of sound devices, such as alliteration, assonance, consonance, and onomatopoeia.
- Identify the sound devices and analyze the effect that they have on the meaning of the poem, as well as how they contribute to the mood of the poem.
- As you present your analysis, read key passages aloud to demonstrate the effects of the sound devices.
- Draw conclusions about the role of sound devices in poetry.
- Present your ideas in a clear and logical way.

TASK 5 Literature [RL.9-10.5; SL.9-10.1.c, SL.9-10.6]

Compare Poetic Structures

Prepare and give an oral presentation in which you compare the effect of structure in two poems.

- Select two poems from Part 2 of this unit that are recognized poetic forms, such as a sonnet, villanelle, or tanka. Identify the poems and forms you will be discussing.
- Analyze the relationship between form and meaning. Determine what the form of each poem contributes to its meaning. For example, you may decide that repetition in a villanelle has an impact on meaning, or that a sonnet presents a logical argument.
- Compare the different effects of each structure. Use details from the poems to support your ideas.
- During your oral presentation, use formal English, appropriate volume, and clear pronunciation.
- Invite questions after your presentation. Respond with further elaboration, referring back to the poems.

Research

TASK 6 Literature [RL.9-10.5; W.9-10.7, W.9-10.9.a]

Does all communication serve a positive purpose?

In Part 2 of this unit, you have read poetry that communicates on many different levels. Now you will conduct a short research project on one form of communication, which can be verbal, visual, or auditory. Use the literature you have read in Part 2 of this unit as well as your research to reflect upon and write about this unit's Big Question. Review the following guidelines before you begin your research:

- Focus your research on one form of communication and its positive or negative effects.
- Gather your information from at least two reliable sources. Your sources may be print or digital.
- Take careful notes as you conduct your research.
- Cite your sources.

When you have completed your research, write a brief essay in response to the Big Question. Discuss how your initial ideas about communication have changed or been reinforced. Support your response with details from the literature you read and from the information you discovered through research.

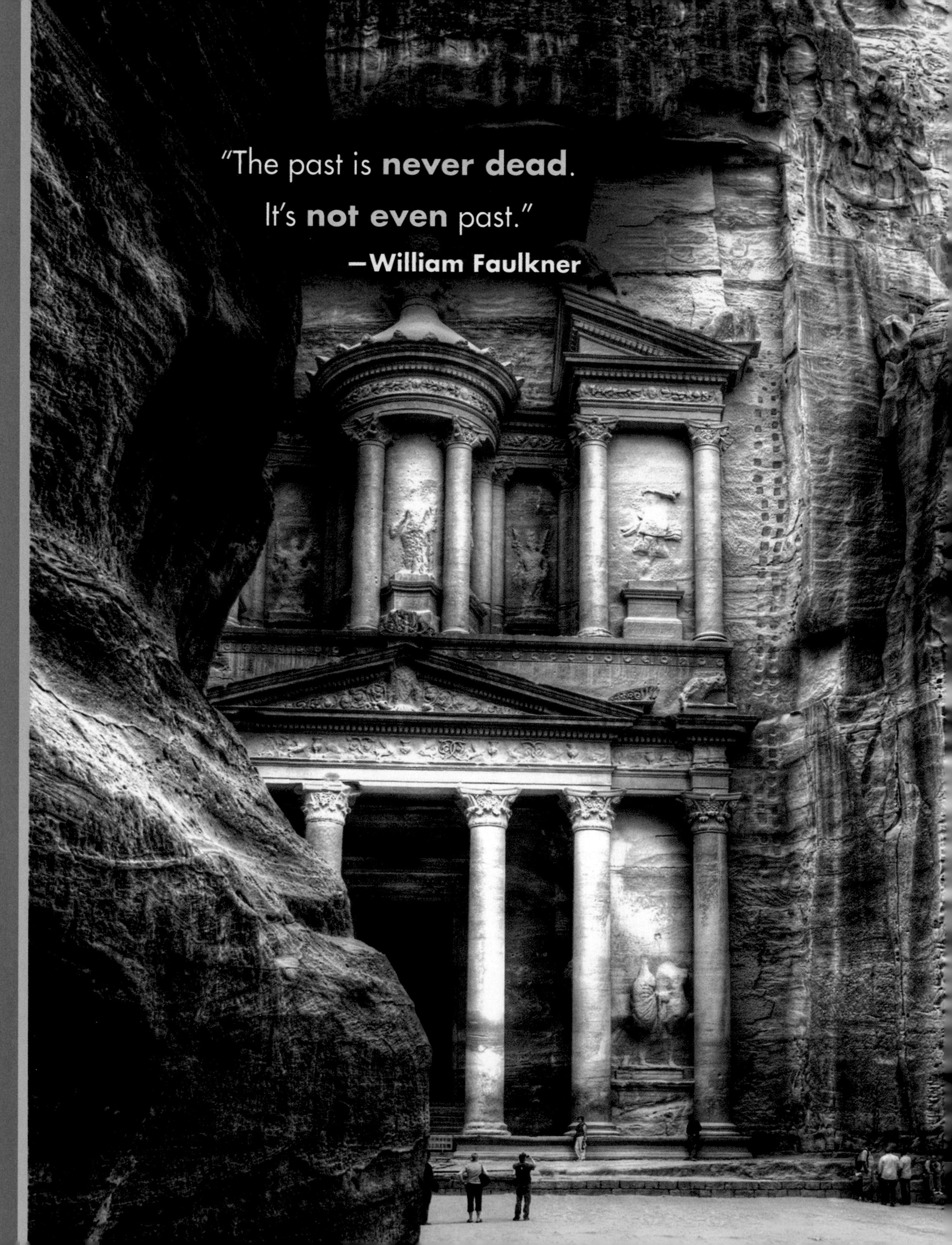
"The past is **never dead**.
It's **not even** past."
—William Faulkner

PART 3

TEXT SET DEVELOPING INSIGHT

LOST CIVILIZATIONS

The readings in this section explore lost civilizations, both real and imaginary. Ancient cultures live on through artifacts, ruins, myths, and legends. Scholars examine the remnants of lost civilizations, hoping to solve their mysteries. Fiction writers and poets mine ancient cultures for stories that still move readers. These texts raise important questions: By understanding lost civilizations can we make a better future for our own? What can we learn from the past? After reading these selections, consider the answers each suggests to the Big Question for this unit: **Does all communication serve a positive purpose?**

◀ CRITICAL VIEWING Imagine you are one of the tourists pictured in this photograph. What observations, reflections, and questions might you have in this setting?

READINGS IN PART 3

CLOSE READING TOOL

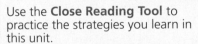

Use the **Close Reading Tool** to practice the strategies you learn in this unit.

A Tree Telling of Orpheus

Denise Levertov

White dawn. Stillness. When the rippling began
I took it for sea-wind, coming to our valley with rumors
of salt, of treeless horizons. But the white fog
didn't stir; the leaves of my brothers remained outstretched,
unmoving.
Yet the rippling drew nearer—and then
my own outermost branches began to tingle, almost as if
fire had been lit below them, too close, and their twig-tips
were drying and curling.
Yet I was not afraid, only
deeply alert.

I was the first to see him, for I grew
out on the pasture slope, beyond the forest.
He was a man, it seemed: the two
moving stems, the short trunk, the two
arm-branches, flexible, each with five leafless
twigs at their ends,
and the head that's crowned by brown or gold grass,
bearing a face not like the beaked face of a bird,
more like a flower's.
He carried a burden made of
some cut branch bent while it was green,
strands of a vine tight-stretched across it. From this,
when he touched it, and from his voice
which unlike the wind's voice had no need of our
leaves and branches to complete its sound,
came the ripple,
But it was now no longer a ripple (he had come near and
stopped in my first shadow) it was a wave that bathed me
as if rain
rose from below and around me
instead of falling.
And what I felt was no longer a dry tingling:

I seemed to be singing as he sang, I seemed to know
what the lark knows; all my sap
was mounting towards the sun that by now
had risen, the mist was rising, the grass

was drying, yet my roots felt music moisten them
deep under earth.

He came still closer, leaned on my trunk:
the bark thrilled like a leaf still-folded.
Music! There was no twig of me not
trembling with joy and fear.

Then as he sang
it was no longer sounds only that made the music:
he spoke, and as no tree listens I listened, and language
came into my roots
out of the earth,
into my bark
out of the air,
into the pores of my greenest shoots
gently as dew
and there was no word he sang but I knew its meaning.
He told of journeys,
of where sun and moon go while we stand in dark,
of an earth-journey he dreamed he would take some day
deeper than roots . . .
He told of the dreams of man, wars, passions, griefs,
and I, a tree, understood words—ah, it seemed
my thick bark would split like a sapling's that
grew too fast in the spring
when a late frost wounds it.

Fire he sang,
that trees fear, and I, a tree, **rejoiced** in its flames.
New buds broke forth from me though it was full summer.
As though his lyre (now I knew its name)
were both frost and fire, its chords flamed
up to the crown of me.
I was seed again.
I was fern in the swamp.
I was coal.

rejoiced ▶
(ri joist′) *v.* showed happiness

And at the heart of my wood
(so close I was to becoming man or a god)
there was a kind of silence, a kind of sickness,
something akin to what men call boredom,
something

(the poem descended a scale, a stream over stones)
that gives to a candle a coldness
in the midst of its burning, he said.

It was then,
when in the blaze of his power that
reached me and changed me
I thought I should fall my length,
that the singer began
to leave me. Slowly
moved from my noon shadow
to open light,
words leaping and dancing over his shoulders
back to me
rivery sweep of lyre-tones becoming
slowly again
ripple.

And I
in terror
but not in doubt of
what I must do
in **anguish**, in haste,
wrenched from the earth root after root,
the soil heaving and cracking, the moss tearing asunder—
and behind me the others: my brothers
forgotten since dawn. In the forest
they too had heard,
and were pulling their roots in pain
out of a thousand years' layers of dead leaves,
rolling the rocks away,
breaking themselves
out of
their depths.

◀ **anguish**
(aŋ´ gwish) *n.* extreme suffering, as from grief or pain

You would have thought we would lose the sound of the lyre,
of the singing
so dreadful the storm-sounds were, where there was no storm,
no wind but the rush of our
branches moving, our trunks breasting the air.
But the music!
The music reached us.

Clumsily,
stumbling over our own roots,
rustling our leaves
in answer,
we moved, we followed.

All day we followed, up hill and down.
We learned to dance,
for he would stop, where the ground was flat,
and words he said
taught us to leap and to wind in and out
around one another   in figures   the lyre's measure designed.
The singer
laughed till he wept to see us, he was so glad.
At sunset
we came to this place I stand in, this knoll[1]
with its ancient grove that was bare grass then.
In the last light of the day his song became
farewell.
He stilled our longing.
He sang our sun-dried roots back into earth,
watered them: all-night rain of music so quiet
we could almost
not hear it in the
moonless dark.
By dawn he was gone.
We have stood here since,
in our new life.
We have waited.

1. **knoll** (nōl) *n.* small hill.

He does not return.
It is said he made his earth-journey, and lost
what he sought.
It is said they **felled** him
and cut up his limbs for firewood.
And it is said
his head still sang and was swept out to sea singing.
Perhaps he will not return.
But what we have lived
comes back to us.
We see more.
We feel, as our rings increase,
something that lifts our branches, that stretches our furthest
leaf-tips
further.
The wind, the birds,
do not sound poorer but clearer,
recalling our agony, and the way we danced.
The music!

◀ **felled**
(feld) *v.* cut or knocked down

ABOUT THE AUTHOR

Denise Levertov (1923–1997)

At the age of twelve, English-born Denise Levertov sent some of her poems to the famous poet T. S. Eliot. Eliot replied with two pages of what Levertov called "excellent advice." Five years later, her first poem was published in *Poetry Quarterly*.

In 1948, Levertov moved with her new husband to the United States, where she became acquainted with the experimental work of Ezra Pound and William Carlos Williams, two poets of the Imagist school. While Levertov was influenced by the Imagists, she developed her own style. Her first books, published in the 1950s, established her as an important American writer.

Over the course of her prolific career, Levertov published more than twenty volumes of poetry and four books of prose. She wrote about themes as varied as nature, love, politics, and faith. From 1982 to 1993, she taught at Stanford University. She spent the last decade of her life in Seattle, Washington, during which time she published five more volumes of poetry. Her final book, *This Great Unknowing: Last Poems,* was published posthumously in 1999.

Close Reading Activities

READ

Comprehension

Reread all or part of the text to help you answer the following questions.

1. Who or what is speaking in this poem?
2. As the speaker listens to the singer, what does it start to hear that changes its basic comprehension of the world?
3. What do the speaker and its neighbors do when the singer begins to leave?
4. After their experience with the singer, how do the wind and birds sound to the speaker and its neighbors?

Research: Clarify Details This poem may include references to concepts that are unfamiliar to you. Choose at least one of these concepts and briefly research it. Then, write a paragraph in which you explain how the information you learned from research sheds light on an aspect of the poem.

Summarize Write an objective summary of the poem. Remember that an objective summary is free from opinion and evaluation.

Language Study

Selection Vocabulary The following passages appear in "A Tree Telling of Orpheus." Define each boldfaced word. Use a dictionary, if necessary. Then, write a description of a situation that displays the qualities associated with each word.

- Fire, he sang, / that trees fear, and I, a tree, **rejoiced** in its flames.
- And I / in terror / but not in doubt of what I must do / in **anguish,** in haste, wrenched from the earth root after root.
- It is said they **felled** him / and cut up his limbs for firewood.

Diction and Style Study the first sentences of the poem, which appear below. Then, answer the questions that follow.

White dawn. Stillness. When the rippling began / I took it for sea-wind, coming to our valley with rumors / of salt, of treeless horizons.

1. **(a)** What synonym could replace *rumors*? **(b)** Explain how the quality of the line would change if you were to replace *rumors* with the synonym.
2. The first two sentences of the poem are fragments. **(a)** Rewrite those fragments as a single, complete sentence, adding whatever words are necessary. **(b)** Explain which version is more powerful and why.

Conventions Read this passage from the poem. Identify prepositional phrases that describe the action. Then, explain how the poet's use of prepositional phrases enhances the effect of the passage.

he spoke, and as no tree listens I listened, and language / came into my roots / out of the earth, / into my bark / out of the air, / into the pores of my greenest shoots

Academic Vocabulary

The following words appear in blue in the instructions and questions on the facing page.

distinct **transformative** **entirety**

Copy the words into your notebook. Find the meaning of each word and note its part of speech.

Literary Analysis

Reread the identified passages. Then, respond to the questions that follow.

Focus Passage 1 *(p. 447)*

I was the first … a dry tingling:

Key Ideas and Details

1. **Infer:** What is the "burden" the man carries? Cite specific details that help you make this inference.
2. **(a) Infer:** What is the "ripple" that becomes a "wave"? **(b) Interpret:** How does this wave affect the speaker? Explain.

Craft and Structure

3. **(a) Infer:** What is the speaker describing in the image of "the head that's crowned by brown or gold grass"? **(b) Analyze:** What other details in the passage show the **distinct** way in which the speaker sees the world? Explain.
4. **Analyze:** Which details in this passage suggest that the speaker does not yet know the words for many of the concepts the singer brings? Explain, citing details from the passage.

Integration of Knowledge and Ideas

5. **Generalize:** In the focus passage, a transformation begins in the speaker that is completed by the end of the poem. What is this transformation? Use details from the poem to support your explanation.

Focus Passage 2 *(pp. 450–451)*

He sang our … back to us.

Key Ideas and Details

1. **Infer:** What actions does the speaker describe in the first five lines of the passage?
2. **Interpret:** What does the speaker mean in saying Orpheus "made his earth-journey"? Explain.

Craft and Structure

3. **(a) Interpret:** What type of song does the image of an "all-night rain of music so quiet" suggest? **(b) Analyze:** What does this image tell you about the emotional bond between the speaker and the singer? Explain.
4. **(a) Evaluate:** What is the effect of the series of short, simple sentences in lines 140 to 144? **(b) Modify:** How would the mood of this section change if these short sentences were combined into one longer thought? Explain.

Integration of Knowledge and Ideas

5. **Interpret:** Which clues in the passage suggest a deeper meaning to the line "We have stood here since, / in our new life"?
6. **Synthesize:** What does this poem say about the **transformative** power of art? Explain.

Personification

Personification is a form of figurative language in which human qualities are given to nonhuman things. This poem retells the myth of Orpheus, extending the use of personification present in the original story. Reread the poem and take notes on ways in which the poet uses personification.

1. How is the poem in its **entirety** an example of personification? Explain.
2. **(a)** Note specific details in the poem that reflect the personified speaker's way of understanding Orpheus, music, and the world in general. Explain each choice. **(b)** Over the course of the poem, how does that understanding change but remain true to the speaker's perspective? Explain.

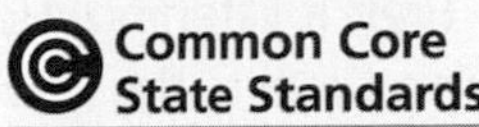

Common Core State Standards

RL.9-10.1, RL.9-10.2, RL.9-10.4, RL.9-10.5, RL.9-10.9; L.9-10.3, L.9-10.4, L.9-10.4.d, L.9-10.5, L.9-10.1b, L.9-10.6

[For full standards wording, see the chart in the front of this book.]

DISCUSS

From Text to Topic **Small Group Discussion**

Discuss the following passage with a small group. Contribute your own ideas, supporting them with examples from the text, and constructively comment on classmates' ideas. Take notes for later use.

> … as no tree listens I listened, and language / came into my roots / out of the earth, / into my bark / out of the air, / into the pores of my greenest shoots / gently as dew / and there was no word he sang but I knew its meaning.

QUESTIONS FOR DISCUSSION:

1. How does Orpheus' music change the speaker?
2. What does this poem suggest about the power of language and stories?
3. Is a "lost" civilization truly lost if its stories continue?

WRITE

Writing to Sources **Narrative Text**

Assignment

Write a **retelling** of the story of Orpheus and the trees from the point of view of Orpheus. Accurately reflect both the events the poem describes, and the quality of the singer's interactions with the trees. Just as Levertov creates a believable voice and perspective for the speaker in her poem, you should create a believable voice for Orpheus.

Prewriting and Planning Reread the poem, identifying the sequence of events it describes. Write an outline that captures that information. Then, for each item on your outline, identify details that convey the qualities of the scene. Take notes about how Orpheus would experience those events.

Drafting Follow your outline as you draft. Use the first-person point of view and incorporate sensory details and figurative language that help to convey what Orpheus saw, did, thought, felt, and said. In addition, vary your sentence structures so that your writing flows smoothly and reflects the way a musician like Orpheus might hear language.

- **Without Sentence Variety or Figurative Language:** I came up the hill. I was singing. Then, I saw the first one. I thought it seemed old. I thought it heard me. I could tell because little things gave it away.
- **With Sentence Variety and Figurative Language:** I came up the hill, strumming and singing, and saw the first one. It was as gnarled and patient as a very old man. I felt it listening. How can you tell a tree is listening? Though there is no breeze, the leaves move.

Revising Make sure you have fully conveyed Orpheus' unique way of seeing—and of hearing—the world. Replace any vague words with more vivid choices.

Editing and Proofreading Reread your narrative several times, checking each time for spelling, punctuation, and capitalization errors. Fix any errors you find.

CONVENTIONS

Use a variety of types of phrases, clauses, and sentences to add interest to your writing. Make sure to use commas correctly to set off dependent clauses.

RESEARCH

Research **Investigate the Topic**

Myths and Ancient Civilizations Orpheus is a character from Greek mythology. A myth is a tale that explains the actions of gods (and the human heroes who interact with them) or the causes of natural phenomena. Originally religious in nature, myths express the central values of the people who created them.

> **Assignment**
> Conduct research to learn about similarities and differences in myths from a variety of ancient civilizations. Choose three civilizations from different parts of the world, including Europe, Africa, Asia, the Middle East, or the Americas. Consult both books and digital sources. Take careful notes and identify your sources for citation. Share your findings in a **multimedia presentation** for the class.

PREPARATION FOR ESSAY

You may use the knowledge you gain during this research assignment to support your claims in an essay you will write at the end of this section.

Gather Sources Locate authoritative print and electronic sources. Primary sources might include translations of myths from various world cultures. You may also use secondary sources, such as scholarly articles and even documentaries. Evaluate the credibility of the sources you find, and use only those that provide reliable, well-written, and accurate information.

Take Notes Take careful notes from each source, identifying key ideas and supporting details. Use an organized note-taking strategy.

- Use spreadsheet or note-taking software to set up categories of information. For example, you might collect information about different myths in one column or section and scholarly or critical information in another.
- Organize specific pieces of information into the categories you established. As you work, you might find the need to combine, add, or delete categories of data. That is part of the process of learning through research.
- Gather multimedia sources, including audio, video, and images, to incorporate into your presentation.
- Carefully record source information for use in your citations.

Synthesize Multiple Sources Assemble data from your sources and organize it logically so that it flows as a cohesive presentation. Use your notes to outline your presentation into sections focusing on the myths themselves, their similarities, and their differences. Indicate in your outline where you will include images, audio, and other media in your presentation. Create a Works Cited list. For additional guidance in doing so, see the Citing Sources pages in the Introductory Unit of this textbook.

Organize and Present Ideas Review your outline, ensuring that your presentation accurately reflects your research. Obtain whatever equipment you need ahead of time and practice delivering your presentation. Be ready to answer questions from your audience.

RL.9-10.1; W.9-10.3.a–e, W.9-10.4, W.9-10.5, W.9-10.6, W.9-10.7, W.9-10.8, W.9-10.9.a; SL.9-10.1, SL.9-10.2, SL.9-10.4, SL.9-10.5; L.9-10.1.b, L.9-10.2, L.9-10.3.a

[For full standards wording, see the chart in the front of this book.]

By the Waters of Babylon

STEPHEN VINCENT BENÉT

The north and the west and the south are good hunting ground, but it is forbidden to go east. It is forbidden to go to any of the Dead Places except to search for metal, and then he who touches the metal must be a priest or the son of a priest. Afterwards, both the man and the metal must be **purified**! These are the rules and the laws: they are well made. It is forbidden to cross the great river and look upon the place that was the Place of the Gods—this is most strictly forbidden. We do not even say its name though we know its name. It is there that spirits live, and demons—it is there that there are the ashes of the Great Burning. These things are forbidden—they have been forbidden since the beginning of time.

◀ **purified** (pyoor´ ə fīd´) *v.* rid of impurities or pollution; made pure

My father is a priest; I am the son of a priest. I have been in the Dead Places near us, with my father—at first, I was afraid. When my father went into the house to search for the metal, I stood by the door and my heart felt small and weak. It was a dead man's house, a spirit house. It did not have the smell of man, though there were old bones in a corner. But it is not fitting that a priest's son should show fear. I looked at the bones in the shadow and kept my voice still.

Then my father came out with the metal—a good, strong piece. He looked at me with both eyes but I had not run away. He gave me the metal to hold—I took it and did not die. So he knew that I was truly his son and would be a priest in my time. That was when I was very young—**nevertheless**, my brothers would not have done it, though they are good hunters. After that, they gave me the good piece of meat and the warm corner by the fire. My father watched over me—he was glad that I should be a priest. But when I boasted or wept without a reason, he punished me more strictly than my brothers. That was right.

◀ **nevertheless** (nev´ ər *thə* les´) *adv.* in spite of that; however

After a time, I myself was allowed to go into the dead houses and search for metal. So I learned the ways of those houses—and if I saw bones, I was no longer afraid. The bones are light and old—sometimes they will fall into dust if you touch them. But that is a great sin.

I was taught the chants and the spells—I was taught how to stop the running of blood from a wound and many secrets. A priest must know many secrets—that was what my father said. If the hunters think we do all things by chants and spells, they may believe so—it does not hurt them. I was taught how to read in the old books and how to make the old writings—that was hard and took a long time. My knowledge made me happy—it was like a fire in my heart. Most of all, I liked to hear of the Old Days and the stories of the gods. I asked myself many questions that I could not answer, but it was good to ask them. At night, I would lie awake and listen to the wind—it seemed to me that it was the voice of the gods as they flew through the air.

We are not ignorant like the Forest People—our women spin wool on the wheel, our priests wear a white robe. We do not eat grubs from the tree, we have not forgotten the old writings, although they are hard to understand. Nevertheless, my knowledge and my lack of knowledge burned in me—I wished to know more. When I was a man at last, I came to my father and said, "It is time for me to go on my journey. Give me your leave."

He looked at me for a long time, stroking his beard, then he said at last, "Yes. It is time." That night, in the house of the priesthood, I asked for and received purification. My body hurt but my spirit was a cool stone. It was my father himself who questioned me about my dreams.

He bade me look into the smoke of the fire and see—I saw and told what I saw. It was what I have always seen—a river, and, beyond it, a great Dead Place and in it the gods walking. I have always thought about that. His eyes were stern when I told him—he was no longer my father but a priest. He said, "This is a strong dream."

> He bade me look into the smoke of the fire and see—I saw and told what I saw.

"It is mine," I said, while the smoke waved and my head felt light. They were singing the Star song in the outer chamber and it was like the buzzing of bees in my head.

He asked me how the gods were dressed and I told him how they were dressed. We know how they were dressed from the book, but I saw them as if they were before me. When I had finished, he threw the sticks three times and studied them as they fell.

"This is a very strong dream," he said. "It may eat you up."

"I am not afraid," I said and looked at him with both eyes. My voice sounded thin in my ears but that was because of the smoke.

He touched me on the breast and the forehead. He gave me the bow and the three arrows.

"Take them," he said. "It is forbidden to travel east. It is forbidden to cross the river. It is forbidden to go to the Place of the Gods. All these things are forbidden."

"All these things are forbidden," I said, but it was my voice that spoke and not my spirit. He looked at me again.

"My son," he said. "Once I had young dreams. If your dreams do not eat you up, you may be a great priest. If they eat you, you are still my son. Now go on your journey."

I went fasting, as is the law. My body hurt but not my heart. When the dawn came, I was out of sight of the village. I prayed and purified myself, waiting for a sign. The sign was an eagle. It flew east.

Sometimes signs are sent by bad spirits. I waited again on the flat rock, fasting, taking no food. I was very still—I could feel the sky above me and the earth beneath. I waited till the sun was beginning to sink. Then three deer passed in the valley, going east—they did not wind me or see me. There was a white fawn with them—a very great sign.

I followed them, at a distance, waiting for what would happen. My heart was troubled about going east, yet I knew that I must go. My head hummed with my fasting—I did not even see the panther spring upon the white fawn. But, before I knew it, the bow was in my hand. I shouted and the panther lifted his head from the fawn. It is not easy to kill a panther with one arrow but the arrow went through his eye and into his brain. He died as he tried to spring—he rolled over, tearing at the ground. Then I knew I was meant to go east—I knew that was my journey. When the night came, I made my fire and roasted meat.

It is eight suns' journey to the east and a man passes by many Dead Places. The Forest People are afraid of them but I am not. Once I made my fire on the edge of a Dead Place at night and, next morning, in the dead house, I found a good knife, little rusted. That was small to what came afterward, but it made my heart feel big. Always when I looked for game, it was in front of my arrow, and twice I passed hunting parties of the Forest People without their knowing. So I knew my magic was strong and my journey clean, in spite of the law.

Toward the setting of the eighth sun, I came to the banks of the great river. It was half-a-day's journey after I had left the god-road—we do not use the god-roads now for they are falling apart into great blocks of stone, and the forest is safer going. A long way off, I had seen the water through trees but the trees were thick. At last, I came out upon an open place at the top of a cliff. There was the great river below, like a giant in the sun. It is very long, very wide. It could eat all the streams we know and still be thirsty. Its name is Ou-dis-sun, the Sacred, the Long. No man of my tribe had seen it, not even my father, the priest. It was magic and I prayed.

Then I raised my eyes and looked south. It was there, the Place of the Gods.

How can I tell what it was like—you do not know. It was there, in the red light, and they were too big to be houses. It was there with the red light upon it, mighty and ruined. I knew that in another moment the gods would see me. I covered my eyes with my hands and crept back into the forest.

Surely, that was enough to do, and live. Surely it was enough to spend the night upon the cliff. The Forest People themselves do not come near. Yet, all through the night, I knew that I should have to cross the river and walk in the places of the gods, although the gods ate me up. My magic did not help me at all and yet there was a fire in my bowels, a fire in my mind. When the sun rose, I thought, "My journey has been clean. Now I will go home from my journey." But, even as I thought so, I knew I could not. If I went to the place of the gods, I would surely die, but, if I did not go, I could never be at peace with my spirit again. It is better to lose one's life than one's spirit, if one is a priest and the son of a priest.

Nevertheless, as I made the raft, the tears ran out of my eyes. The Forest People could have killed me without fight, if they had come upon me then, but they did not come. When the raft was made, I said the sayings for the dead and painted myself for death. My heart was cold as a frog and my knees like water, but the burning in my mind would not let me have peace. As I pushed the raft from the shore, I began my death song—I had the right. It was a fine song.

> "I am John, son of John," I sang. "My people are the Hill People. They are the men.
> I go into the Dead Places but I am not slain.
> I take the metal from the Dead Places but I am not blasted.
> I travel upon the god-roads and am not afraid. E-yah! I have killed the panther, I have killed the fawn!
> E-yah! I have come to the great river. No man has come there before.
> It is forbidden to go east, but I have gone, forbidden to go on the great river, but I am there.
> Open your hearts, you spirits, and hear my song.
> Now I go to the Place of the Gods, I shall not return.
> My body is painted for death and my limbs weak, but my heart is big as I go to the Place of the Gods!"

All the same, when I came to the Place of the Gods, I was afraid, afraid. The current of the great river is very strong—it gripped my raft with its hands. That was magic, for the river itself is wide and calm. I could feel evil spirits about me, in the bright morning; I could feel their breath on my neck as I was swept down the stream. Never have I been so much alone—I tried to think of my knowledge, but it was a squirrel's heap of winter nuts. There was no strength in my knowledge any more, and I felt small and naked as a new-hatched bird—alone upon the great river, the servant of the gods.

Yet, after a while, my eyes were opened and I saw. I saw both banks of the river—I saw that once there had been god-roads across it, though now they were broken and fallen like broken vines. Very great they were, and wonderful and broken—broken in the time of the Great Burning when the fire fell out of the sky. And always the current took me nearer to the Place of the Gods, and the huge ruins rose before my eyes.

I do not know the customs of rivers—we are the People of the Hills. I tried to guide my raft with the pole but it spun around. I thought the river meant to take me past the Place of the Gods and out into the Bitter Water of the legends. I grew angry then—my heart felt strong. I said aloud, "I am a priest and the son of a priest!" The gods heard me—they showed me how to paddle with the pole on one side of the raft. The current changed itself—I drew near to the Place of the Gods.

When I was very near, my raft struck and turned over. I can swim in our lakes—I swam to the shore. There was a great spike of rusted metal sticking out into the river—I hauled myself up upon it and sat there, panting. I had saved my bow and two arrows and the knife I found in the Dead Place but that was all. My raft went whirling downstream toward the Bitter Water. I looked after it, and thought if it had trod me under, at least I would be safely dead. Nevertheless, when I had dried my bow-string and restrung it, I walked forward to the Place of the Gods.

It felt like ground underfoot; it did not burn me. It is not true what some of the tales say, that the ground there burns forever, for I have been there. Here and there were the marks and stains of the Great Burning, on the ruins, that is true. But they were old marks and old stains. It is not true either, what some of our priests say, that it is an island covered with fogs and enchantments. It is not. It is a great Dead Place—greater than any Dead Place we know. Everywhere in it there are god-roads, though most are cracked and broken. Everywhere there are the ruins of the high towers of the gods.

How shall I tell what I saw? I went carefully, my strung bow in my hand, my skin ready for danger. There should have been the wailings of spirits and the shrieks of demons, but there were not. It was very silent and sunny where I had landed—the wind and the rain and the birds that drop seeds had done their work—the grass grew in the cracks of the broken stone. It is a fair island—no wonder the gods built there. If I had come there, a god, I also would have built.

How shall I tell what I saw? The towers are not all broken—here and there one still stands, like a great tree in a forest, and the birds nest high. But the towers themselves look blind, for the gods are gone. I saw a fish-hawk, catching fish in the river. I saw a little dance of white butterflies over a great heap of broken stones and columns. I went there and looked about me—there was a carved stone with cut-letters, broken in half. I can read letters but I could not understand these. They said UBTREAS. There was also the shattered image of a man or a god. It had been made of white stone and he wore his hair tied back like a woman's. His name was ASHING, as I read on the cracked half of a stone. I thought it wise to pray to ASHING, though I do not know that god.

How shall I tell what I saw? There was no smell of man left, on stone or metal. Nor were there many trees in that wilderness of stone. There are many pigeons, nesting and dropping in the towers—the gods must have loved them, or, perhaps, they used them for sacrifices. There are wild cats that roam the god-roads, green-eyed, unafraid of man. At night they wail like demons, but they are not demons. The wild dogs are more dangerous, for they hunt in a pack, but them I did not meet till later. Everywhere there are the carved stones carved with magical numbers or words.

I went North—I did not try to hide myself. When a god or a demon saw me, then I would die, but meanwhile I was no longer afraid. My hunger for knowledge burned in me—there was so much that I could not understand. After a while, I knew that my belly was hungry. I could have hunted for my meat, but I did not hunt. It is known that the gods did not hunt as we do—they got their food from enchanted boxes and jars. Sometimes these are still found in the Dead Places—once, when I was a child and foolish, I opened such a jar and tasted it and found the food sweet. But my father found out and punished me for it strictly, for, often, that food is death. Now, though, I had long gone past what was forbidden, and I entered the likeliest towers, looking for the food of the gods.

I found it at last in the ruins of a great temple in the mid-city. A mighty temple it must have been, for the roof was painted like the sky at night with its stars—that much I could see, though the colors were faint and dim. It went down into great caves and tunnels—perhaps they kept their slaves there. But when I started to climb down, I heard the squeaking of rats, so I did not go—rats are unclean, and there must have been many tribes of them, from the squeaking. But near there, I found food, in the heart of a ruin, behind a door that still opened. I ate only the fruits from the jars—they had a very sweet taste. There was drink, too, in bottles of glass—the drink of the gods was strong and made my head swim. After I had eaten and drunk, I slept on the top of a stone, my bow at my side.

When I woke, the sun was low. Looking down from where I lay, I saw a dog sitting on his **haunches**. His tongue was hanging out of his mouth; he looked as if he were laughing. He was a big dog, with a gray-brown coat, as big as a wolf. I sprang up and shouted at him but he did not move—he just sat there as if he were laughing. I did not like that. When I reached for a stone to throw, he moved swiftly out of the way of the stone. He was not afraid of me; he looked at me as if I were meat. No doubt I could have killed him with an arrow, but I did not know if there were others. Moreover, night was falling.

◀ **haunches** (hänch′ əz) *n.* hind pair of legs on a four-legged animal

I looked about me—not far away there was a great, broken god-road, leading North. The towers were high enough, but not so high, and while many of the dead-houses were wrecked, there were some that stood. I went toward this god-road, keeping to the heights of the ruins, while the dog followed. When I had reached the god-road, I saw that there were others behind him. If I had slept later, they would have come upon me asleep and torn out my throat. As it was, they were sure enough of me; they did not hurry. When I went into the dead-house, they kept watch at the entrance—doubtless they thought they would have a fine hunt. But a dog cannot open a door and I knew, from the books, that the gods did not like to live on the ground but on high.

I had just found a door I could open when the dogs decided to rush. Ha! They were surprised when I shut the door in their faces—it was a good door, of strong metal. I could hear their foolish baying beyond it, but I did not stop to answer them. I was in darkness—I found stairs and climbed. There were many stairs, turning around till my head was dizzy. At the top was another door—I found the knob and opened it. I was in a long small chamber—on one side of it was a bronze door that could not be opened, for it had no handle. Perhaps there was a magic word to open it, but I did not have the word. I turned to the door in the opposite side of the wall. The lock of it was broken and I opened it and went in.

I went toward this god-road, keeping to the heights of the ruins, while the dog followed.

Within, there was a place of great riches. The god who lived there must have been a powerful god. The first room was a small anteroom—I waited there for some time, telling the spirits of the place that I came in peace and not as a robber. When it seemed to me that they had had time to hear me, I went on. Ah, what riches! Few, even, of the windows had been broken—it was all as it had been. The great windows that looked over the city had not been broken at all though they were dusty and streaked with many years. There were coverings on the floors, the colors not greatly faded, and the chairs were soft and deep. There were pictures upon the walls, very strange, very wonderful—I remember one of a bunch of flowers in a jar—if you came close to it, you could see nothing but bits of color, but if you stood away from it, the flowers might have been picked yesterday. It made my heart feel strange to look at this picture—and to look at the figure of a bird, in some hard clay, on a table and see it so like our birds. Everywhere there were books and writings, many in tongues that I could not read. The god who lived there must have been a wise god and full of knowledge. I felt I had right there, as I sought knowledge also.

> **Everywhere there were lights—lines of light—circles and blurs of light—ten thousand torches would not have been the same.**

Nevertheless, it was strange. There was a washing-place but no water—perhaps the gods washed in air. There was a cooking-place but no wood, and though there was a machine to cook food, there was no place to put fire in it. Nor were there candles or lamps—there were things that looked like lamps but they had neither oil nor wick. All these things were magic, but I touched them and lived—the magic had gone out of them. Let me tell one thing to show. In the washing-place, a thing said "Hot" but it was not hot to the touch—another thing said "Cold" but it was not cold. This must have been a strong magic but the magic was gone. I do not understand—they had ways—I wish that I knew.

It was close and dry and dusty in their house of the gods. I have said the magic was gone but that is not true—it had gone from the magic things but it had not gone from the place. I felt the spirits about me, weighing upon me. Nor had I ever slept in a Dead Place before—and yet, tonight, I must sleep there. When I thought of it, my tongue felt dry in my throat, in spite of my wish for knowledge. Almost I would have gone down again and faced the dogs, but I did not.

I had not gone through all the rooms when the darkness fell. When it fell, I went back to the big room looking over the city and made fire. There was a place to make fire and a box with wood in it, though I do not think they cooked there. I wrapped myself in a floor-covering and slept in front of the fire—I was very tired.

Now I tell what is very strong magic. I woke in the midst of the night. When I woke, the fire had gone out and I was cold. It seemed to me that all around me there were whisperings and voices. I closed my eyes to shut them out. Some will say that I slept again, but I do not think that I slept. I could feel the spirits drawing my spirit out of my body as a fish is drawn on a line.

Why should I lie about it? I am a priest and the son of a priest. If there are spirits, as they say, in the small Dead Places near us, what spirits must there not be in that great Place of the Gods? And would not they wish to speak? After such long years? I know that I felt myself drawn as a fish is drawn on a line. I had stepped out of my body—I could see my body asleep in front of the cold fire, but it was not I. I was drawn to look out upon the city of the gods.

It should have been dark, for it was night, but it was not dark. Everywhere there were lights—lines of light—circles and blurs of light—ten thousand torches would not have been the same. The sky itself was alight—you could barely see the stars for the glow in the sky. I thought to myself "This is strong magic" and trembled. There was a roaring in my ears like the rushing of rivers. Then my eyes grew used to the light and my ears to the sound. I knew that I was seeing the city as it had been when the gods were alive.

That was a sight indeed—yes, that was a sight: I could not have seen it in the body—my body would have died. Everywhere went the gods, on foot and in chariots—there were gods beyond number and counting and their chariots blocked the streets. They had turned night to day for their pleasure—they did not sleep with the sun. The noise of their coming and going was the noise of many waters. It was magic what they could do—it was magic what they did.

I looked out of another window—the great vines of their bridges were mended and the god-roads went East and West. Restless, restless, were the gods and always in motion! They burrowed tunnels under rivers—they flew in the air. With unbelievable tools they did giant works—no part of the earth was safe from them, for, if they wished for a thing, they summoned it from the other side of the world. And always, as they labored and rested, as they feasted and made love, there was a drum in their ears—the pulse of the giant city, beating and beating like a man's heart.

Were they happy? What is happiness to the gods? They were great, they were mighty, they were wonderful and terrible. As I looked upon them and their magic, I felt like a child—but a little more, it seemed to me, and they would pull down the moon from the sky. I saw them with wisdom beyond wisdom and knowledge beyond knowledge. And yet not all they did was well done—even I could see that—and yet their wisdom could not but grow until all was peace.

Then I saw their fate come upon them and that was terrible past speech. It came upon them as they walked the streets of their city. I have been in the fights with the Forest People—I have seen men die. But this was not like that. When gods war with gods, they use weapons we do not know. It was fire falling out of the sky and a mist that poisoned. It was the time of the Great Burning and the Destruction. They ran about like ants in the streets of their city—poor gods, poor gods! Then the towers began to fall. A few escaped—yes, a few. The legends tell it. But, even after the city had become a Dead Place, for many years the poison was still in the ground. I saw it happen, I saw the last of them die. It was darkness over the broken city, and I wept.

All this, I saw. I saw it as I have told it, though not in the body. When I woke in the morning, I was hungry, but I did not think first of my hunger, for my heart was perplexed and confused. I knew the reason for the Dead Places but I did not see why it had happened. It seemed to me it should not have happened, with all the magic they had. I went through the house looking for an answer. There was so much in the house I could not understand—and yet I am a priest and the son of a priest. It was like being on one side of the great river, at night, with no light to show the way.

Then I saw the dead god. He was sitting in his chair, by the window, in a room I had not entered before and, for the first moment, I thought that he was alive. Then I saw the skin on the back of his hand—it was like dry leather. The room was shut, hot and dry—no doubt that had kept him as he was. At first I was afraid to approach him—then the fear left me. He was sitting looking out over the city—he was dressed in the clothes of the gods. His age was neither young nor old—I could not tell his age. But there was wisdom in his face and great sadness. You could see that he would have not run away. He had sat at his window, watching his city die—then he himself had died. But it is better to lose one's life than one's spirit—and you could see from the face that his spirit had not been lost. I knew that, if I touched him, he would fall into dust—and yet, there was something unconquered in the face.

That is all of my story, for then I knew he was a man—I knew then that they had been men, neither gods nor demons. It is a great knowledge, hard to tell and believe. They were men—they went a dark road, but they were men. I had no fear after that—I had no fear going home, though twice I fought off the dogs and once I was hunted for two days by the Forest People. When I saw my father again, I prayed and was purified. He touched my lips and my breast, he said, "You went away a boy. You come back a man and a priest."

I said, "Father, they were men! I have been in the Place of the Gods and seen it! Now slay me, if it is the law—but still I know they were men."

He looked at me out of both eyes. He said, "The law is not always the same shape—you have done what you have done. I could not have done it in my time but you come after me. Tell!"

I told and he listened. After that, I wished to tell all the people but he showed me otherwise. He said, "Truth is a hard deer to hunt. If you eat too much truth at once, you may die of the truth. It was not idly that our fathers forbade the Dead Places." He was right—it is better the truth should come little by little. I have learned that, being a priest. Perhaps, in the old days, they ate knowledge too fast.

Nevertheless, we make a beginning. It is not for the metal alone we go to the Dead Places now—there are the books and the writings. They are hard to learn. And the magic tools are broken—but we can look at them and wonder. At least, we make a beginning. And, when I am chief priest we shall go beyond the great river. We shall go to the Place of the Gods—the place newyork—not one man but a company. We shall look for the images of the gods and find the god ASHING and the others—the gods Lincoln and Biltmore[1] and Moses.[2] But they were men who built the city, not gods or demons. They were men. I remember the dead man's face. They were men who were here before us. We must build again.

---

1. **Biltmore** hotel in New York City.
2. **Moses** Robert Moses (1888–1981), former New York City municipal official who oversaw many large construction projects.

ABOUT THE AUTHOR

Stephen Vincent Benét (1898–1943)

Stephen Vincent Benét was born into a military family in Bethlehem, Pennsylvania. His father, a colonel in the army, loved literature and read aloud to his family in the evenings. These literary evenings clearly influenced Stephen and his two siblings, as all of them grew up to become writers.

Much of Benét's work centers on American history and folklore, including his most famous story, "The Devil and Daniel Webster," and his epic poem of the Civil War, *John Brown's Body*. The latter work won the Pulitzer Prize in 1929. Toward the end of his life, Benét was working on an epic poem, entitled *Western Star*, based on American history. Benét had planned to write a narrative that would span five books, but only completed the first volume before his death. That first book was published in 1944 and won its author a second, posthumous Pulitzer Prize.

Close Reading Activities

READ

Comprehension

Reread all or part of the text to help you answer the following questions.

1. Why are the narrator and his father allowed to touch metal from the Dead Places?
2. What did the narrator do that was "forbidden"?
3. What is the connection between the narrator's people and the gods of the Dead Places?

Research: Clarify Details This story may include references that are unfamiliar to you. Choose at least one unfamiliar detail and briefly research it. Then, explain how the information you learned from research sheds light on an aspect of the story.

Summarize Write an objective summary of the story. Remember that an objective summary is free from opinion and evaluation.

Language Study

Selection Vocabulary The following passages appear in the story. Define each boldfaced word. Then, use the word in a sentence of your own.

- … both the man and the metal must be **purified.**
- … **nevertheless,** my brothers would not have done it…
- … I saw a dog sitting on his **haunches.**

Literary Analysis

Reread the identified passage. Then, respond to the questions that follow.

Focus Passage *(pp. 466–467)*

Then I saw … still I know they were men."

Key Ideas and Details

1. **(a) Summarize:** What does John, the narrator, observe about the "dead god"? **(b) Analyze:** Why do these observations free him from fear?

Craft and Structure

2. **(a) Distinguish:** What phrase does John repeat in the beginning of the second paragraph? **(b) Interpret:** What does this repetition suggest about his **realizations** in that moment? Explain.
3. **Interpret:** How does the author's use of dashes hint at John's behavior and emotions as he observes the room? Explain.

Integration of Knowledge and Idea

4. **Connect:** In this passage John repeats an idea from earlier in the story: It is "better to lose one's life than one's spirit." How does he demonstrate that value throughout the story? Explain.

Dramatic Irony

Dramatic irony involves a contrast between what a character thinks to be true and what the reader knows to be true. Reread the story, and take notes on how it employs dramatic irony.

1. **(a)** What American city is the "Place of the Gods"? **(b)** What destroyed the city? **(c)** Who are the "gods"? **(d)** When is the story set?
2. **(a)** For items b and c in question 1, explain the **initial** contrast between John's understanding and the reader's. **(b)** At what point in the story does John's understanding catch up to the reader's? Explain.
3. **Lost Civilizations:** How does the use of dramatic irony in this story suggest the loss of knowledge that may happen when a civilization fails? Explain.

DISCUSS • RESEARCH • WRITE

From Text to Topic **Partner Discussion**

Discuss the following passage with a partner. Take notes during the discussion. Listen carefully to your partner's arguments and add your own points of both agreement and disagreement.

> After that, I wished to tell all the people but he showed me otherwise. He said, "Truth is a hard deer to hunt. If you eat too much truth at once, you may die of the truth. It was not idly that our fathers forbade the Dead Places." He was right—it is better the truth should come little by little. I have learned that, being a priest. Perhaps, in the old days, they ate knowledge too fast.

QUESTIONS FOR DISCUSSION

1. Is John's interpretation of his father's warning a comment on life today—do we "eat knowledge" too fast?
2. Is access to knowledge the reason the civilization in the story failed?

Research **Investigate the Topic**

The Babylonian Captivity The title "By the Waters of Babylon" is an allusion, or reference, to a Biblical psalm. The psalm itself is an allusion to the Babylonian Captivity. Authors often use allusions to add richness and symbolism to a literary work.

Assignment
Conduct research to learn about the Babylonian Captivity. Consult Psalm 137 in the Hebrew or Christian Bible, as well as analyses of the historical event. Take clear notes so that you can easily access the information later. Draw connections between the psalm, the historical event, and Benét's story. Share your findings in an **oral report.**

PREPARATION FOR ESSAY

You may use the results of this research in an essay you will write at the end of this section.

Writing to Sources **Argument**

"By the Waters of Babylon" describes a post-apocalyptic world in which people have lost the knowledge possessed by their ancestors. In such a circumstance, should the past remain a mystery—as in the "Dead Places" of Benét's tale—or should it be taught and discussed?

Assignment
Write an **argumentative essay** in which you state and defend a position on whether a culture should try to keep the memory of its past, including its failures, alive. Follow these steps:

- Clearly state your claim or **assertion** about the issue. Use Benét's story as evidence. You may also cite actual historical events.
- Use clear transitions to connect your claims and evidence.
- Anticipate and address potential counterarguments.

ACADEMIC VOCABULARY

Academic terms appear in blue on these pages. Use a dictionary to find their definitions. Then, use them as you speak and write about the text.

Common Core State Standards

RL.9-10.1, RL.9-10.2, RL.9-10.3, RL.9-10.4, RL.9-10.5, RL.9-10.9; W.9-10.1, W.9-10.1.b–c, W.9-10.4, W.9-10.7, W.9-10.9.a; SL.9-10.1, SL.9-10.4; L.9-10.4, L.9-10.6
[For full standards wording, see the chart in the front of this book.]

The Body of a House, #1 of 8. © Robert Beckmann, 1993. Collection, Nevada Museum of Art, Reno

There Will Come Soft Rains

Ray Bradbury

In the living room the voice-clock sang,

Tick-tock, seven o'clock, time to get up, time to get up, seven o'clock! as if it were afraid that nobody would. The morning house lay empty. The clock ticked on, repeating and repeating its sounds into the emptiness. *Seven-nine, breakfast time, seven-nine*!

In the kitchen the breakfast stove gave a hissing sigh and ejected from its warm interior eight pieces of perfectly browned toast, eight eggs sunnyside up, sixteen slices of bacon, two coffees, and two cool glasses of milk.

"Today is August 4, 2026," said a second voice from the kitchen ceiling, "in the city of Allendale, California." It repeated the date three times for memory's sake. "Today is Mr. Featherstone's birthday Today is the anniversary of Tilita's marriage. Insurance is payable, as are the water, gas, and light bills."

Somewhere in the walls, relays clicked, memory tapes glided under electric eyes.

Eight-one, tick-tock, eight-one o'clock, off to school, off to work, run, run, eight-one! But no doors slammed, no carpets took the soft tread of rubber heels. It was raining outside. The weather box on the front door sang quietly: "Rain, rain, go away; rubbers, raincoats for today . . ." And the rain tapped on the empty house, echoing.

Outside, the garage chimed and lifted its door to reveal the waiting car. After a long wait the door swung down again.

At eight-thirty the eggs were shriveled and the toast was like stone. An aluminum wedge scraped them into the sink, where hot water whirled them down a metal throat which digested and flushed them away to the distant sea. The dirty dishes were dropped into a hot washer and emerged twinkling dry.

Nine-fifteen, sang the clock, *time to clean.*

Out of warrens in the wall, tiny robot mice darted. The rooms were acrawl with the small cleaning animals, all rubber and metal. They thudded against chairs, whirling their mustached runners, kneading the rug nap, sucking gently at hidden dust. Then, like mysterious invaders, they popped into their burrows. Their pink electric eyes faded. The house was clean.

Ten o'clock. The sun came out from behind the rain. The house stood alone in a city of rubble and ashes. This was the one house left standing. At night the ruined city gave off a radioactive glow which could be seen for miles.

It quivered at each sound, the house did. If a sparrow brushed a window, the shade snapped up. The bird, startled, flew off!

Ten-fifteen. The garden sprinklers whirled up in golden founts, filling the soft morning air with scatterings of brightness. The water pelted windowpanes, running down the charred west side where the house had been burned evenly free of its white paint. The entire west face of the house was black, save for five places. Here the silhouette[1] in paint of a man mowing a lawn. Here, as in a photograph, a woman bent to pick flowers. Still farther over, their images burned on wood in one titanic instant, a small boy, hands flung into the air; higher up, the image of a thrown ball, and opposite him a girl, hands raised to catch a ball which never came down.

The five spots of paint—the man, the woman, the children, the ball—remained. The rest was a thin charcoaled layer.

The gentle-sprinkler rain filled the garden with falling light.

Until this day, how well the house had kept its peace. How carefully it had inquired, "Who goes there? What's the password?" and, getting no answer from lonely foxes and whining cats, it had shut up its windows and drawn shades in an old-maidenly preoccupation with self-protection which bordered on a mechanical paranoia.

It quivered at each sound, the house did. If a sparrow brushed a window, the shade snapped up. The bird, startled, flew off! No, not even a bird must touch the house!

1. **silhouette** (sil′ ə wet′) *n.* outline of a figure, filled in with a solid color.

The house was an altar with ten thousand attendants, big, small, servicing, attending, in choirs. But the gods had gone away, and the ritual of the religion continued senselessly, uselessly.

Twelve noon.

A dog whined, shivering, on the front porch.

The front door recognized the dog voice and opened. The dog, once huge and fleshy, but now gone to bone and covered with sores, moved in and through the house, tracking mud. Behind it whirred angry mice, angry at having to pick up mud, angry at inconvenience.

For not a leaf fragment blew under the door but what the wall panels flipped open and the copper scrap rats flashed swiftly out. The offending dust, hair, or paper, seized in miniature steel jaws, was raced back to the burrows. There, down tubes which fed into the cellar, it was dropped into the sighing vent of an incinerator which sat like evil Baal[2] in a dark corner.

The dog ran upstairs, hysterically yelping to each door, at last realizing, as the house realized, that only silence was here.

It sniffed the air and scratched the kitchen door. Behind the door, the stove was making pancakes which filled the house with a rich baked odor and the scent of maple syrup.

The dog frothed at the mouth, lying at the door, sniffing, its eyes turned to fire. It ran wildly in circles, biting at its tail, spun in a frenzy, and died. It lay in the parlor for an hour.

Two o'clock, sang a voice.

Delicately sensing decay at last, the regiments of mice hummed out as softly as blown gray leaves in an electrical wind.

Two-fifteen.

The dog was gone.

In the cellar, the incinerator glowed suddenly and a whirl of sparks leaped up the chimney.

Two thirty-five.

Bridge tables sprouted from patio walls. Playing cards fluttered onto pads in a shower of pips. Glasses manifested on an oaken bench with egg-salad sandwiches. Music played.

But the tables were silent and the cards untouched.

At four o'clock the tables folded like great butterflies back through the paneled walls.

Four-thirty.

---

2. **Baal** (bā´ əl) *n.* ancient Near Eastern deity, later associated with evil.

The nursery walls glowed.

Animals took shape: yellow giraffes, blue lions, pink antelopes, lilac panthers cavorting in crystal substance. The walls were glass. They looked out upon color and fantasy. Hidden films clocked through well-oiled sprockets, and the walls lived. The nursery floor was woven to resemble a crisp, cereal meadow. Over this ran aluminum roaches and iron crickets, and in the hot still air butterflies of delicate red tissue wavered among the sharp aroma of animal spoors![3] There was the sound like a great matted yellow hive of bees within a dark bellows, the lazy bumble of a purring lion. And there was the patter of okapi[4] feet and the murmur of a fresh jungle rain, like other hoofs, falling upon the summer-starched grass. Now the walls dissolved into distances of parched weed, mile on mile, and warm endless sky. The animals drew away into thorn brakes and water holes.

It was the children's hour.

Five o'clock. The bath filled with clear hot water.

manipulated ▶ (mə nip′ yo͞o lāt′ id) *v.* managed or controlled through clever moves

Six, seven, eight o'clock. The dinner dishes **manipulated** like magic tricks, and in the study a click. In the hearth a fire now blazed up warmly.

Nine o'clock. The beds warmed their hidden circuits, for nights were cool here.

Nine-five. A voice spoke from the study ceiling:

"Mrs. McClellan, which poem would you like this evening?"

The house was silent.

The voice said at last, "Since you express no preference, I shall select a poem at random." Quiet music rose to back the voice. "Sara Teasdale. As I recall, your favorite. . . .

There will come soft rains and the smell of the ground,
And swallows circling with their shimmering sound;

And frogs in the pools singing at night,
And wild plum trees in **tremulous** *white;*

tremulous ▶ (trem′ yo͞o ləs) *adj.* trembling; quivering; timid; fearful

Robins will wear their feathery fire,
Whistling their whims on a low fence-wire;

And not one will know of the war, not one
Will care at last when it is done.

---

3. **spoors** (spo͝orz) *n.* droppings of wild animals.
4. **okapi** (ō kä′ pē) *n.* African animal related to the giraffe but with a much shorter neck.

Not one would mind, neither bird nor tree,
If mankind perished utterly;

And Spring herself, when she woke at dawn
Would scarcely know that we were gone."

The fire burned on the stone hearth. The empty chairs faced each other between the silent walls, and the music played.

At ten o'clock the house began to die.

The wind blew. A falling tree bough crashed through the kitchen window. Cleaning solvent, bottled, shattered over the stove. The room was ablaze in an instant!

"Fire!" screamed a voice. The house lights flashed, water pumps shot water from the ceilings. But the solvent spread on the linoleum, licking, eating, under the kitchen door, while the voices took it up in chorus: "Fire, fire, fire!"

The house tried to save itself. Doors sprang tightly shut, but the windows were broken by the heat and the wind blew and sucked upon the fire.

At ten o'clock the house began to die.

The house gave ground as the fire in ten billion angry sparks moved with flaming ease from room to room and then up the stairs. While scurrying water rats squeaked from the walls, pistoled their water, and ran for more. And the wall sprays let down showers of mechanical rain.

But too late. Somewhere, sighing, a pump shrugged to a stop. The quenching rain ceased. The reserve water supply which had filled baths and washed dishes for many quiet days was gone.

The fire crackled up the stairs. It fed upon Picassos and Matisses[5] in the upper halls, like delicacies, baking off the oily flesh, tenderly crisping the canvases into black shavings.

Now the fire lay in beds, stood in windows, changed the colors of drapes!

And then, reinforcements.

From attic trapdoors, blind robot faces peered down with faucet mouths gushing green chemical.

---

5. **Picassos** (pi kä´ sōz) **and Matisses** (mä tēs´ əz) paintings by the celebrated modern painters Pablo Picasso (1881–1973) and Henri Matisse (1869–1954).

The fire backed off, as even an elephant must at the sight of a dead snake. Now there were twenty snakes whipping over the floor, killing the fire with a clear cold venom of green froth.

But the fire was clever. It had sent flame outside the house, up through the attic to the pumps there. An explosion! The attic brain which directed the pumps was shattered into bronze shrapnel on the beams.

The fire rushed back into every closet and felt of the clothes hung there.

The house shuddered, oak bone on bone, its bared skeleton cringing from the heat, its wire, its nerves revealed as if a surgeon had torn the skin off to let the red veins and capillaries quiver in the scalded air. Help, help! Fire! Run, run! Heat snapped mirrors like the first brittle winter ice. And the voices wailed Fire, fire, run, run, like a tragic nursery rhyme, a dozen voices, high, low, like children dying in a forest, alone, alone. And the voices fading as the wires popped their sheathings like hot chestnuts. One, two, three, four, five voices died.

Help, help! Fire! Run, run! Heat snapped mirrors like the first brittle winter ice. And the voices wailed Fire, fire, run, run, like a tragic nursery rhyme.

In the nursery the jungle burned. Blue lions roared, purple giraffes bounded off. The panthers ran in circles, changing color, and ten million animals, running before the fire, vanished off toward a distant steaming river. . . .

Ten more voices died. In the last instant under the fire avalanche, other choruses, **oblivious**, could be heard announcing the time, playing music, cutting the lawn by remote-control mower, or setting an umbrella frantically out and in the slamming and opening front door, a thousand things happening, like a clock shop when each clock strikes the hour insanely before or after the other, a scene of maniac confusion, yet unity; singing, screaming, a few last cleaning mice darting bravely out to carry the horrid ashes away! And one voice, with sublime disregard for the situation, read poetry aloud in the fiery study, until all the film spools burned, until all the wires withered and the circuits cracked.

oblivious ▶ (ə bliv′ ē əs) *adj.* unaware

The fire burst the house and let it slam flat down, puffing out skirts of spark and smoke.

In the kitchen, an instant before the rain of fire and timber, the stove could be seen making breakfasts at a psychopathic rate, ten dozen eggs, six loaves of toast, twenty dozen bacon strips, which, eaten by fire, started the stove working again, hysterically hissing!

The crash. The attic smashing into kitchen and parlor. The parlor into cellar, cellar into subcellar. Deep freeze, armchair, film tapes, circuits, beds, and all like skeletons thrown in a cluttered mound deep under.

Smoke and silence. A great quantity of smoke.

Dawn showed faintly in the east. Among the ruins, one wall stood alone. Within the wall, a last voice said, over and over again and again, even as the sun rose to shine upon the heaped rubble and steam:

"Today is August 5, 2026, today is August 5, 2026, today is . . ."

ABOUT THE AUTHOR

Ray Bradbury (1920–2012)

Ray Bradbury, one of the world's most celebrated writers of science fiction and fantasy, was born in Waukegan, Illinois. As a child, he was influenced by the stories of Edgar Allan Poe and Jules Verne, and developed a fascination with horror movies and futuristic fantasy. Bradbury decided to become a writer as a teenager, later saying that he wanted to use fiction to "live forever." Bradbury considered most of his work fantasy rather than science fiction, explaining, "Science fiction is the art of the possible. Fantasy is the art of the impossible."

Bradbury published his first novel, *The Martian Chronicles*, in 1950. His novel *Fahrenheit 451*, published in 1953, became an instant best seller and is still his most famous work. Throughout his entire life, Bradbury wrote for several hours every day, producing more than thirty books, hundreds of short stories, poems, essays, and screenplays. He won a special Pulitzer Prize in 2007 "for his distinguished, prolific, and deeply influential career as an unmatched author of science fiction and fantasy." Bradbury died in 2012 at the age of 91.

Close Reading Activities

READ

Comprehension

Reread all or part of the text to help you answer the following questions.

1. What is the daily routine of the automated house?
2. What has happened to the rest of the houses?
3. What are the five spots of paint on the exterior of the house?
4. By the end of the story, what happens to the house?

Research: Clarify Details This story may include references that are unfamiliar to you. Choose at least one unfamiliar detail, and briefly research it. Then, explain how the information you learned from research sheds light on an aspect of the story.

Summarize Write an objective summary of the story. Remember that an objective summary is free from opinion and evaluation.

Language Study

Selection Vocabulary The passages at right appear in the story. Identify the root of each boldface word. Explain what the root means and how that meaning is evident in the word. Then, identify another word that shares the same root.

- The dinner dishes **manipulated** like magic tricks, and in the study a click.
- *And frogs in the pools singing at night,*
  And wild plum trees in ***tremulous*** *white;*
- … other choruses, **oblivious,** could be heard …

Literary Analysis

Reread the identified passage. Then, respond to the questions that follow:

Focus Passage *(pp. 472–473)*
Until this day … senselessly, uselessly.

Key Ideas and Details

1. **(a)** Who are the "gods" who have gone away? **(b) Interpret:** How does the house react to this abandonment? Explain.
2. **Contrast:** What **stark** contrast does this passage set up between the house's behavior and the new reality?

Craft and Structure

3. **(a) Interpret:** Cite details that portray the house as a fussy person. **(b) Analyze:** How does this use of personification add to the emotional quality of both the passage and the story as a whole?

Integration of Knowledge and Idea

4. **Connect:** How does the idea that the house continues its routine "senselessly, uselessly" foreshadow, or hint at, the house's behavior at the end of the story? Explain, citing story details.

Intertextuality

Intertextuality is a term that refers to relationships among literary works. Allusions to and retellings of older works are two types of intertextuality. Reread the story and analyze the relationship between the poem it quotes and the story itself.

1. Do the poem and the story express similar messages? Cite details from both works in your explanation.
2. Is the story a "retelling" of the poem? Explain.
3. **Lost Civilizations:** What does the story and the poem it contains suggest about humanity's responsibility toward civilization and nature? Explain.

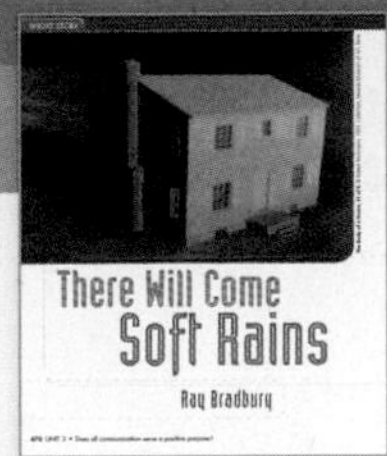

DISCUSS • RESEARCH • WRITE

From Text to Topic **Group Discussion**

Discuss the following passage with a group of classmates. As you share ideas, record your notes and observations. Cite details from the text to support your ideas.

> The entire west face of the house was black, save for five places. Here the silhouette in paint of a man mowing a lawn. Here, as in a photograph, a woman bent to pick flowers. Still farther over, their images burned on wood in one titanic instant, a small boy, hands flung into the air; higher up, the image of a thrown ball, and opposite him a girl, hands raised to catch a ball which never came down.

QUESTIONS FOR DISCUSSION

1. How does this passage reflect realities associated with nuclear war?
2. What does this passage tell you about the war that has just occurred?
3. Based on this passage, what kind of civilization is now lost?

Research **Investigate the Topic**

The Atomic Age Bradbury wrote this story in 1950, five years after the United States dropped the first atomic bombs on Japan, and one year before the Soviet Union successfully tested its own atomic device.

Assignment
Conduct research to learn about the atom bomb and its first use by the United States at the end of World War II. Find out how fears of nuclear war led to **social** and political consequences, including the rise of the Cold War. Write an **annotated bibliography** in which you provide detailed information about the sources you locate.

PREPARATION FOR ESSAY

You may use the results of this research in an essay you will write at the end of this section.

Writing to Sources **Informative Text**

"There Will Come Soft Rains" describes "life" after a nuclear attack. Authors have chosen many ways to present this topic. Consider the qualities that make Bradbury's story unique and worth reading.

Assignment
Write an **analytical essay** in which you discuss how Bradbury **juxtaposes** the ordinary elements of daily life with the horror of disaster. Consider his uses of figurative language, including personification, metaphor, and simile, and other literary devices to create a striking portrayal. Follow these steps:

- Clearly state your purpose for writing and include a summary of the story.
- Follow an organized structure that lays out your ideas in a logical progression.
- Cite passages from the story to support your explanations and interpretations.

ACADEMIC VOCABULARY

Academic terms appear in blue on these pages. If these words are not familiar to you, use a dictionary to find their definitions. Then, use them as you speak and write about the text.

Common Core State Standards

RL.9-10.1, RL.9-10.2, RL.9-10.4, RL.9-10.5; W.9-10.2, W.9-10.7, W.9-10.9; SL.9-10.1; L.9-10.4.b, L.9-10.5, L.9-10.6
[For full standards wording, see the chart in the front of this book.]

from The Way to Rainy Mountain

N. Scott Momaday

A single knoll rises out of the plain in Oklahoma, north and west of the Wichita Range.[1] For my people, the Kiowas, it is an old landmark, and they gave it the name Rainy Mountain. The hardest weather in the world is there. Winter brings blizzards, hot tornadic winds arise in the spring, and in summer the prairie is an anvil's edge. The grass turns brittle and brown, and it cracks beneath your feet. There are green belts along the rivers and creeks, linear groves of hickory and pecan, willow and witch hazel. At a distance in July or August the steaming foliage seems almost to **writhe** in fire. Great green and yellow grasshoppers are everywhere in the tall grass, popping up like corn to sting the flesh, and tortoises crawl about on the red earth, going nowhere in the plenty of time. Loneliness is an aspect of the land. All things in the plain are isolate; there is no confusion of objects in the eye, but one hill or one tree or one man. To look upon that landscape in the early morning, with the sun at your back, is to lose the sense of proportion. Your imagination comes to life, and this, you think, is where Creation was begun.

◀ **writhe** (rīth) *v.* make twisting or turning movements as from pain

I returned to Rainy Mountain in July. My grandmother had died in the spring, and I wanted to be at her grave. She had lived to be very old and at last infirm. Her only living daughter was with her when she died, and I was told that in death her face was that of a child.

I like to think of her as a child. When she was born, the Kiowas were living the last great moment of their history. For more than a hundred years they had controlled the open range from the Smoky Hill River to the Red, from the headwaters of the Canadian to the fork of the Arkansas and Cimarron.[2] In alliance with the Comanches,[3] they had ruled the whole of the southern Plains. War was their sacred business, and they were among the finest horsemen the world has ever known. But warfare for the Kiowas was preeminently a matter of disposition rather than of survival, and they never understood the grim, unrelenting advance of the

1. **Wichita** (wich′ ə tô′) **Range** mountain range in southwestern Oklahoma.
2. **Smoky Hill River . . . Cimarron** (sim′ ə rän′) these rivers all run through or near Oklahoma. The area Momaday is defining stretches from central Kansas south through Oklahoma and from the Texas panhandle east to Tulsa, Oklahoma.
3. **Comanches** (kə man′ chēz) *n.* a Native American people of the southern Great Plains, known for their horse-riding ability.

U.S. Cavalry. When at last, divided and ill-provisioned, they were driven onto the Staked Plains in the cold rains of autumn, they fell into panic. In Palo Duro Canyon they abandoned their crucial stores to pillage and had nothing then but their lives. In order to save themselves, they surrendered to the soldiers at Fort Sill[4] and were imprisoned in the old stone corral that now stands as a military museum. My grandmother was spared the humiliation of those high gray walls by eight or ten years, but she must have known from birth the affliction of defeat, the dark brooding of old warriors.

Although my grandmother lived out her long life in the shadow of Rainy Mountain, the immense landscape of the continental interior lay like memory in her blood.

Her name was Aho, and she belonged to the last culture to evolve in North America. Her forebears came down from the high country in western Montana nearly three centuries ago. They were a mountain people, a mysterious tribe of hunters whose language has never been positively classified in any major group. In the late seventeenth century they began a long migration to the south and east.

nomadic ▶ (nō mad′ ik) *adj.* moving from place to place; without a permanent home

It was a journey toward the dawn, and it led to a golden age. Along the way the Kiowas were befriended by the Crows,[5] who gave them the culture and religion of the Plains. They acquired horses, and their ancient **nomadic** spirit was suddenly free of the ground. They acquired Tai-me, the sacred Sun Dance doll, from that moment the object and symbol of their worship, and so shared in the divinity of the sun. Not least, they acquired the sense of destiny, therefore courage and pride. When they entered upon the southern Plains they had been transformed. No longer were they slaves to the simple necessity of survival; they were a lordly and dangerous society of fighters and thieves, hunters and priests of the sun. According to their origin myth, they entered the world through a hollow log. From one point of view, their migration was the fruit of an old prophecy, for indeed they emerged from a sunless world.

Although my grandmother lived out her long life in the shadow of Rainy Mountain, the immense landscape of the continental interior lay like memory in her blood. She could tell of the Crows, whom she had never seen, and of the Black Hills,[6] where she had never been. I wanted to see in reality what she had seen more perfectly in the

4. **Fort Sill** fort established by the United States government in 1869 as a base of military operations during U.S. Army battles with Native Americans of the southern plains.
5. **Crows** members of a Native American tribe of the northern Plains; like other Plains tribes, they hunted buffalo.
6. **Black Hills** mountain range running from southwestern South Dakota to northeastern Wyoming.

mind's eye, and traveled fifteen hundred miles to begin my pilgrimage.

Yellowstone,[7] it seemed to me, was the top of the world, a region of deep lakes and dark timber, canyons and waterfalls. But, beautiful as it is, one might have the sense of confinement there. The skyline in all directions is close at hand, the high wall of the woods and deep cleavages of shade. There is a perfect freedom in the mountains, but it belongs to the eagle and the elk, the badger and the bear. The Kiowas reckoned their stature by the distance they could see, and they were bent and blind in the wilderness.

Descending eastward, the highland meadows are a stairway to the plain. In July the inland slope of the Rockies is luxuriant with flax and buckwheat, stonecrop and larkspur.[8] The earth unfolds and the limit of the land recedes. Clusters of trees, and animals grazing far in the distance, cause the vision to reach away and wonder to build upon the mind. The sun follows a longer course in the day, and the sky is immense beyond all comparison. The great billowing clouds that sail upon it are shadows that move upon the brain like water, dividing light. Farther down, in the land of the Crows and Blackfeet,[9] the plain is yellow. Sweet clover takes hold of the hills and bends upon itself to cover and seal the soil. There the Kiowas paused on their way; they had come to the place where they must change their lives. The sun is at home on the plains. Precisely there does it have the certain character of a god. When the Kiowas came to the land of the Crows, they could see the dark lees of the hills at dawn across the Bighorn River, the profusion of light on the grain shelves, the oldest deity ranging after the solstices. Not yet would they veer southward to the caldron[10] of the land that lay below; they must wean their blood from the northern

▼ Chief Sa-tan-ta of the Kiowas

7. **Yellowstone** Yellowstone National Park, lying mostly in Wyoming but including strips in southern Montana and eastern Idaho.
8. **flax and buckwheat, stonecrop and larkspur** various types of plants.
9. **Blackfeet** tribe of the region that includes present-day Montana and parts of Canada.
10. **caldron** (kôl′ drən) *n.* pot for boiling liquids; large kettle.

winter and hold the mountains a while longer in their view. They bore Tai-me in procession to the east.

A dark mist lay over the Black Hills, and the land was like iron. At the top of a ridge I caught sight of Devil's Tower upthrust against the gray sky as if in the birth of time the core of the earth had broken through its crust and the motion of the world was begun. There are things in nature that engender an awful quiet in the heart of man; Devil's Tower is one of them. Two centuries ago, because they could not do otherwise, the Kiowas made a legend at the base of the rock. My grandmother said:

▼ The Devil's Tower in northeastern Wyoming

Eight children were there at play, seven sisters and their brother. Suddenly the boy was struck dumb; he trembled and began to run upon his hands and feet. His fingers became claws, and his body was covered with fur. Directly there was a bear where the boy had been. The sisters were terrified; they ran, and the bear after them. They came to the stump of a great tree, and the tree spoke to them. It bade them climb upon it, and as they did so it began to rise in the air. The bear came to kill them, but they were just beyond its reach. It reared against the tree and scored the bark all around with its claws. The seven sisters were borne into the sky, and they became the stars of the Big Dipper.

From that moment, and so long as the legend lives, the Kiowas have kinsmen in the night sky. Whatever they were in the mountains, they could be no more. However **tenuous** their well-being, however much they had suffered and would suffer again, they had found a way out of the wilderness.

tenuous ▶
(ten′ yo͞o əs) *adj.*
flimsy; not strong

My grandmother had a reverence for the sun, a holy regard that now is all but gone out of mankind. There was a wariness in her, and an ancient awe. She was a Christian in her later years, but she had come a long way about, and she never forgot her birthright. As a child she had been to the Sun Dances; she had taken part in those annual rites, and by them she had learned the restoration of her people in the presence of Tai-me. She was about seven when the last Kiowa Sun Dance was held in 1887 on the Washita River above Rainy Mountain Creek. The buffalo were gone. In order to consummate the ancient sacrifice—to impale the head of a buffalo bull upon the medicine tree—a delegation of old men journeyed into Texas, there to beg and barter for an animal from the Goodnight herd. She was ten when the Kiowas came together for the last time as a living Sun Dance culture. They could find no buffalo; they had to hang an old hide from the sacred tree. Before the dance could begin, a company of soldiers rode out from Fort Sill under orders to disperse the tribe. Forbidden without cause the essential act of their faith, having seen the wild herds slaughtered and left to rot upon the ground, the Kiowas backed away forever from the medicine tree. That was July 20, 1890, at the great bend of the Washita. My grandmother was there. Without bitterness, and for as long as she lived, she bore a vision of deicide.[11]

Now that I can have her only in memory, I see my grandmother in the several postures that were peculiar to her: standing at the wood stove on a winter morning and turning meat in a great iron skillet; sitting at the south window, bent above her beadwork, and afterwards, when her vision failed, looking down for a long time into the fold of her hands; going out upon a cane, very slowly as she did when the weight of age came upon her; praying. I remember her most often at prayer. She made long, rambling prayers out of suffering and hope, having seen many things. I was never sure that I had the right to hear, so exclusive were they of all mere custom and company. The last time I saw her she prayed standing by the side of her bed at night, naked to the waist, the light of a kerosene lamp moving upon her dark skin. Her long, black hair, always drawn and braided in the day, lay upon her shoulders and against her breasts like a shawl. I do not speak Kiowa, and I never understood her prayers, but there was something inherently sad in the sound, some merest hesitation upon the syllables of sorrow. She began in a high and descending pitch, exhausting her breath to silence; then again and again—and always the same intensity of effort, of something that is, and is not, like urgency in the human voice. Transported so in the dancing light among the shadows of her room, she seemed beyond

Transported so in the dancing light among the shadows of her room, she seemed beyond the reach of time. But that was illusion; I think I knew then that I should not see her again.

11. **deicide** (dē′ ə sīd′) *n.* killing of a god.

the reach of time. But that was illusion; I think I knew then that I should not see her again.

Houses are like sentinels in the plain, old keepers of the weather watch. There, in a very little while, wood takes on the appearance of great age. All colors wear soon away in the wind and rain, and then the wood is burned gray and the grain appears and the nails turn red with rust. The windowpanes are black and opaque; you imagine there is nothing within, and indeed there are many ghosts, bones given up to the land. They stand here and there against the sky, and you approach them for a longer time than you expect. They belong in the distance; it is their domain.

Once there was a lot of sound in my grandmother's house, a lot of coming and going, feasting and talk. The summers there were full of excitement and reunion. The Kiowas are a summer people; they abide the cold and keep to themselves, but when the season turns and the land becomes warm and vital they cannot hold still; an old love of going returns upon them. The aged visitors who came to my grandmother's house when I was a child were made of lean and leather, and they bore themselves upright. They wore great black hats and bright ample shirts that shook in the wind. They rubbed fat upon their hair and wound their braids with strips of colored cloth. Some of them painted their faces and carried the scars of old and cherished enmities. They were an old council of warlords, come to remind and be reminded of who they were. Their wives and daughters served them well. The women might indulge themselves; gossip was at once the mark and compensation of their servitude. They made loud and elaborate talk among themselves, full of jest and gesture, fright and false alarm. They went abroad in fringed and flowered shawls, bright beadwork and German silver. They were at home in the kitchen, and they prepared meals that were banquets.

There were frequent prayer meetings, and great nocturnal feasts. When I was a child I played with my cousins outside, where the lamplight fell upon the ground and the singing of the old people rose up around us and carried away into the darkness. There were a lot of good things to eat, a lot of laughter and surprise. And afterwards, when the quiet returned, I lay down with my grandmother and could hear the frogs away by the river and feel the motion of the air.

Now there is a funeral silence in the rooms, the endless wake of some final word. The walls have closed in upon my grandmother's house. When I returned to it in mourning, I saw for the first time in my life how small it was. It was late at night, and there was a white moon, nearly full. I sat for a long time on the stone steps by the kitchen door. From there I could see out across the land; I could see the long row of trees by the creek, the low light upon the rolling plains, and the stars of the Big Dipper. Once I looked at the moon and caught sight of a strange thing. A cricket had perched upon the handrail, only a few inches away from me. My line of vision was such that the creature filled the moon like a fossil. It had gone there, I thought, to live and die, for there, of all places, was its small definition made whole and eternal. A warm wind rose up and purled like the longing within me.

The next morning I awoke at dawn and went out on the dirt road to Rainy Mountain. It was already hot, and the grasshoppers began to fill the air. Still, it was early in the morning, and the birds sang out of the shadows. The long yellow grass on the mountain shone in the bright light, and a scissortail hied above the land. There, where it ought to be, at the end of a long and legendary way, was my grandmother's grave. Here and there on the dark stones were ancestral names. Looking back once, I saw the mountain and came away.

ABOUT THE AUTHOR

N. Scott Momaday (b. 1934)

As a child growing up on the Native American reservations where his parents taught, N. Scott Momaday learned the traditions of his father's Kiowa culture as well as those of the Navajo, Apache, and Pueblo Indians. At the same time, the author received a modern education. "I grew up in two worlds and straddle both those worlds even now," he says. "It has made for confusion and a richness in my life."

Momaday has made much of this richness, celebrating Native American traditions in novels, essays, and poetry. In his three autobiographical works, including *The Way to Rainy Mountain,* the author combines his family history with Kiowa stories. His first novel, *House Made of Dawn,* established Momaday as a prominent author and was awarded the Pulitzer Prize for Fiction in 1969.

Close Reading Activities

READ

Comprehension

Reread all or part of the text to help you answer the following questions.

1. What is Rainy Mountain and where is it located?
2. Why did the author make a "pilgrimage" to Rainy Mountain?
3. What happened at the last Kiowa Sun Dance that changed Kiowa culture?

Research: Clarify Details This text may include references that are unfamiliar to you. Choose at least one unfamiliar detail and briefly research it. Then, explain how the information you learned from research sheds light on an aspect of the text.

Summarize Write an objective summary of the text. Remember that an objective summary is free from opinion and evaluation.

Language Study

Selection Vocabulary The following sentences appear in the text. Define each boldfaced word. Then, for each, identify one synonym and one antonym.

- At a distance in July or August the steaming foliage seems almost to **writhe** in fire.
- They acquired horses, and their ancient **nomadic** spirit was suddenly free of the ground.
- However **tenuous** their well-being, however much they had suffered and would suffer again, they had found a way out of the wilderness.

Literary Analysis

Reread the identified passage. Then, respond to the questions that follow.

Focus Passage *(p. 486)*

Houses are like … meals that were banquets.

Key Ideas and Details

1. **Connect:** How do the events at the grandmother's home reflect a lost way of life?

Craft and Structure

2. **(a) Interpret:** Explain the simile in the first sentence. **(b) Connect:** How does the simile relate to the "old council of warlords" mentioned in the second paragraph? Explain.
3. **Interpret:** What does the author mean when he describes the visitors as being "made of lean and leather"? Explain, citing additional textual details.

Integration of Knowledge and Idea

4. **(a) Analyze:** Why would old warlords "cherish" ancient "enmities"? **(b) Synthesize:** How does this passage connect to the idea, stated earlier in the text, that the Kiowa were a warrior people? Explain.

Memoir and Historical Writing

A **memoir** is a type of autobiography. **Historical writing** is nonfiction about past events and their effects on groups of people. Reread the story, and note how it combines **elements** of both genres.

1. Explain how Momaday interweaves discussion of his personal journey with historical information.
2. **Lost Civilizations:** Cite specific ways in which the combination of memoir and history in this text paints a clear picture of how a culture was lost and how that loss affects later generations.

from
The Way to
Rainy
Mountain
N. Scott Momaday

DISCUSS • RESEARCH • WRITE

From Text to Topic **Partner Discussion**

Discuss the following passage with a partner. Take notes during your discussion, summarize your ideas, and share them with the class.

> A cricket had perched upon the handrail, only a few inches away from me. My line of vision was such that the creature filled the moon like a fossil. It had gone there, I thought, to live and die, for there, of all places, was its small definition made whole and eternal. A warm wind rose up and purled like the longing within me.

QUESTIONS FOR DISCUSSION

1. How does the image of the cricket in the moon relate to the author's longing?
2. What does this passage say about the loss Momaday feels over his grandmother's death and the **demise** of her culture?

Research **Investigate the Topic**

Language and Culture Many **indigenous** peoples, such as the Kiowa, still exist, but their languages are being lost.

Assignment
Conduct research to find out how the loss of their languages is affecting indigenous peoples in North America and what efforts are being made to fight this trend. Consult publications from the United Nations and the Administration for Native Americans. Identify your sources accurately for later confirmation and citation. Share your findings in a **slide presentation** for the class.

PREPARATION FOR ESSAY

You may use the results of this research in an essay you will write at the end of this section.

Writing to Sources **Narrative**

"The Way to Rainy Mountain" describes the personal journey the author undertakes as he seeks to pay tribute to his grandmother and his culture.

Assignment
Write a **memoir** in which you describe how the personal or cultural history of a relative or other influential adult in your life helped you gain a valuable insight. Follow these steps:

- Use Momaday's writing as a model for your memoir by incorporating both personal details and historical information.
- Use figurative language, images, and description to convey a vivid picture of people, events, and ideas.
- Summarize the insights that you gained from your experiences and observations.

ACADEMIC VOCABULARY

Academic terms appear in blue on these pages. If these words are not familiar to you, use a dictionary to find their definitions. Then, use them as you speak and write about the text.

Common Core State Standards

RI.9-10.1, RI.9-10.2, RI.9-10.4, RI.9-10.5; W.9-10.3, W.9-10.3.d, W.9-10.4, W.9-10.7; SL.9-10.1, SL.9-10.4, SL.9-10.5; L.9-10.4, L.9-10.5.a–b, L.9-10.6
[For full standards wording, see the chart in the front of this book.]

JOURNALISM

Understanding Stonehenge

Two Explanations • Rossella Lorenzi

Was the prehistoric monument built to unite a land or as a destination to heal the sick? Recent research supports both ideas.

After centuries of puzzling over the meaning of Stonehenge, laser-equipped researchers have concluded that the prehistoric monument was built to show off the solstices.[1]

Apart from revealing 71 new images of Bronze Age[2] axeheads, which bring the number of this type of carvings known at Stonehenge to 115, the English Heritage groundbreaking analysis showed that the stones were shaped and crafted differently in various parts of the stone circle.

In particular, the stones first seen when approaching the monument from the northeast were completely "pick dressed." Stonehenge workers removed their brown and grey surface crust to show a bright, grey-white surface that would glisten at sunset on the shortest day of the year and in the dawn light on the longest day.

According to the researchers, this provides an almost definitive proof that it was the intent of Stonehenge's builders to align the monument with the two solstices along a northeast/southwest axis.

Located in the county of Wiltshire, at the center of England's densest **complex** of Neolithic[3] and Bronze Age monuments, Stonehenge has been the subject of myth, legend and—more recently—scientific research for more than eight centuries.

◄ **complex** (käm′ pleks) *n.* assemblage of units, such as houses or other buildings, that together form a single section or group

The mysterious circle of large standing stones has been interpreted in the most disparate ways—as a temple for sun worship, a temple of the ancient druids, a healing center, a burial site and a huge calendar.

The new laser findings appear to be compatible with two main theories taking shape in recent years to explain the monument's purpose.

According to archaeologist Mike Parker Pearson, head of the Stonehenge Riverside Project, the iconic monument was built as a grand act of union after a long period of conflict between east and west Britain.

Another theory, posed by archaeologists Geoff Wainwright and Timothy Darvill, says Stonehenge was a destination to which the sick traveled from around Europe to be healed by its magical powers.

"The scanning work at Stonehenge is really important and has

1. **solstices** (säl′ stis əz) in the Northern Hemisphere, June 21—the summer solstice—marks the day with the longest period of daylight, and December 21—the winter solstice—marks the day with the shortest period of daylight.
2. **Bronze Age** prehistoric period that began in Britain in about 1900 B.C. and during which British peoples first starting making tools from metal.
3. **Neolithic** (nē′ ō lith′ ik) *adj.* relating to prehistoric period that began in Britain in about 4000 B.C. and during which British peoples made tools from polished stone.

opened our eyes to many new aspects of Neolithic technology," Darvill, professor of archaeology in the School of Applied Sciences at Bournemouth University, England, told Discovery News.

Darvill and Wainwright made one of the most significant findings in 2005, when they located the quarry where the bluestones, which form Stonehenge's inner circle, were cut around 2500 B.C.

The archaeologists discovered a "small crag-edged promontory with a stone bank across its neck" at one of the highest points of Carn Menyn, a mountain in the Preseli Hills of Pembrokeshire, in southwest Wales.

prone ▶ (prōn) *adj.* lying or leaning face downward

The site, which measures less than half a hectare, is characterized by numerous **prone** pillar stones with clear signs of working. Darvill described it as "a veritable Aladdin's Cave[4] of made-to-measure pillars for aspiring circle builders."

The bluestones weighed about four tons and were between six and nine feet in height and would have been transported 240 miles to the famous site at Salisbury Plain in Wiltshire.

According to Darvill, the color and the presence of distinctive white spots made the Preseli Hills stones very pleasing aesthetically.

"Importantly, the methods of working the bluestones seems to be the same as for the central Trilithons[5] and serves to support the idea I put forward some time ago that these two components of the monument were contemporary and somehow linked," Darvill said.

harbor ▶ (här′ bər) *v.* house or shelter; be the place where something belongs

According to the archaeologist, the huge stones were taken on such a journey from their Welsh location because they were believed to **harbor** great powers.

In 2008, Darvill and Wainwright excavated a small patch of earth at Stonehenge. The dig unearthed about 100 pieces of organic material from the original bluestone sockets and provided the most accurate dating for their erection, pinpointing the bluestone construction to 2300 B.C. It also produced a large number of bluestone chippings, as if people flaked them off to create little amulet bits.

The presence of a large number of human remains in tombs near Stonehenge showing physical injury and disease and analysis of teeth reveal that around half of the corpses were not native to the Stonehenge area and suggested Stonehenge served as a center for healing, said the archaeologists.

Attracted by the powers of the bluestones, the sick and injured would have come to the site from far away.

---

4. **Aladdin's** (ə la′ dinz) **Cave** place full of amazing things that seem magical; the idiom refers to the cave full of treasure discovered by Aladdin in a story from *The Thousand and One Nights*.
5. **Trilithons** (tri′ li thänz) *n.* groups of three stones; in each group, two stones serve as posts supporting a third stone set horizontally on top.

"The new work indirectly supports the healing hypothesis as it shows the importance of the stones from Wales," Darvill said.

"It also shows that most of them have had bits chipped off them and some have been reduced to stumps by removals exactly as we suggested was the case," he added.

But according to Mike Parker Pearson, the enigmatic stone circle had nothing to do with sickness and diseases. On the contrary, it was built as a grand act of union after a long period of conflict between east and west Britain.

"Stonehenge itself was a massive undertaking, requiring the labor of thousands to move stones from as far away as west Wales, shaping them and erecting them. Just the work itself, requiring everyone literally to pull together, would have been an act of unification," Parker Pearson said.

Because of Stonehenge's solstice-aligned avenue, prehistoric people would have seen the spot as nothing less than the "center of the world."

According to Parker Pearson, the discovery of the winter sunset axis at Stonehenge by the laser scan project supports his previous findings.

"Our study of seasonal culling of animals eaten at feasts at Durrington Walls, from the time when the sarsens were put up around 2500 B.C., shows that they were killed at two times of the year, most in the midwinter period and the rest in the summer," Parker Pearson said.

The midwinter solstice was the most important time for these ceremonial gatherings, presumably the beginning and end of their year.

"We have isotope evidence for people bringing their animals from all over Britain, tying in with the theme of unification. You could call it the Neolithic version of Christmas and New Year," Parker Pearson said.

Tags: Archaeologist, Archaeology, Europe, Laser, Prehistoric

Close Reading Activities

READ

Comprehension

Reread all or part of the text to help you answer the following questions.

1. What are the two main theories about Stonehenge?
2. What discoveries about Stonehenge have researchers made using lasers?
3. What is the "almost definitive proof" that the builders of Stonehenge attempted to align the monument with the solstices?

Research: Clarify Details This article may include references that are unfamiliar to you. Choose at least one unfamiliar detail, and briefly research it. Then, explain how the information you learned from research sheds light on an aspect of the article.

Summarize Write an objective summary of the article. Remember that an objective summary is free from opinion and evaluation.

Language Study

Selection Vocabulary: Archaeology The following passages appear in the text. Define each boldface word as it is used in the article. Then, identify at least two other meanings for each word.

- Located in the county of Wiltshire, at the center of England's densest **complex** of Neolithic and Bronze Age monuments …
- The site … is characterized by numerous **prone** pillar stones with clear signs of working.
- … they were believed to **harbor** great powers.

Literary Analysis

Reread the identified passage. Then, respond to the questions that follow.

Focus Passage *(pp. 492–493)*
In 2008 … "center of the world."

Key Ideas and Details

1. **(a) Deduce:** According to the author, what **primary** piece of evidence leads some scientists to **theorize** that Stonehenge was a center for healing? **(b) Compare:** How does archaeologist Parker Pearson interpret the same evidence differently? Explain.

Craft and Structure

2. **(a) Summarize:** Summarize the first paragraph. **(b)** What information does the author provide in paragraphs 2 through 5 and how does it relate to the first paragraph? **(c)** What transition occurs in paragraph 6? Explain your answers.

Integration of Knowledge and Idea

3. **Analyze:** Why does the author describe Stonehenge as "enigmatic"?

Expert Opinion

An **expert opinion** is a statement made by someone with special knowledge of a topic. Nonfiction authors often cite expert opinions as evidence. Reread the article, and take notes on the author's use of expert opinion.

1. **(a)** Identify two examples of expert opinion in the article. **(b)** Does each example present reliable expert information? Explain.
2. **(a)** Would Lorenzi's own statements also be considered "expert opinion"? Why or why not?

DISCUSS • RESEARCH • WRITE

From Text to Topic **Debate**

Read the following passage. Then, hold a class debate in which you discuss the value of conducting research on ancient sites like Stonehenge. Use information from the article to support your positions.

> After centuries of puzzling over the meaning of Stonehenge, laser-equipped researchers have concluded that the prehistoric monument was built to show off the solstices.
>
> Apart from revealing 71 new images of Bronze Age axeheads ... the English Heritage groundbreaking analysis showed that the stones were shaped and crafted differently in various parts of the stone circle.

QUESTIONS FOR DISCUSSION

1. Are research efforts, like those that have been done at Stonehenge for centuries, valuable to humanity?
2. Is it important that people living today understand Bronze Age cultures?

Research **Investigate the Topic**

Stonehenge and Astronomy One theory about Stonehenge is that the builders used the positions of the sun and other celestial objects to **align** the stones along the axis of the solstice.

Assignment

Conduct research to learn about theories involving the relationship between Stonehenge and astronomy. Consult scholarly books and articles as well as documentary films and Web sites. Take clear notes and carefully identify your sources so that you can easily access the information later. Share your findings in a magazine-style **article.**

PREPARATION FOR ESSAY

You may use the results of this research in an essay you will write at the end of this section.

Writing to Sources **Narrative**

"Understanding Stonehenge" explains several theories about why Stonehenge was built and provides evidence supporting each theory. Consider what it might have been like for a person who was involved in building the monument.

Assignment

Write a **short story** in which you describe a day in the life of a person involved in the building of Stonehenge. Include information and details from Lorenzi's article. Follow these tips:

- Choose a character and point of view.
- Decide which theory presented in the article your character's actions will represent.
- Draw a plot diagram to outline your story.
- Vary your sentence types and use literary devices thoughtfully.

ACADEMIC VOCABULARY

Academic terms appear in blue on these pages. Use a dictionary to find their definitions. Then, use them as you speak and write about the text.

Common Core State Standards

RI.9-10.1, RI.9-10.2, RI.9-10.3, RI.9-10.4, RI.9-10.5, RI.9-10.6; W.9-10.3, W.9-10.3.a, W.9-10.3.c, W.9-10.4, W.9-10.6, W.9-10.7; SL.9-10.1, SL.9-10.3; L.9-10.4.a, L.9-10.6

[For full standards wording, see the chart in the front of this book.]

EXPOSITORY NONFICTION

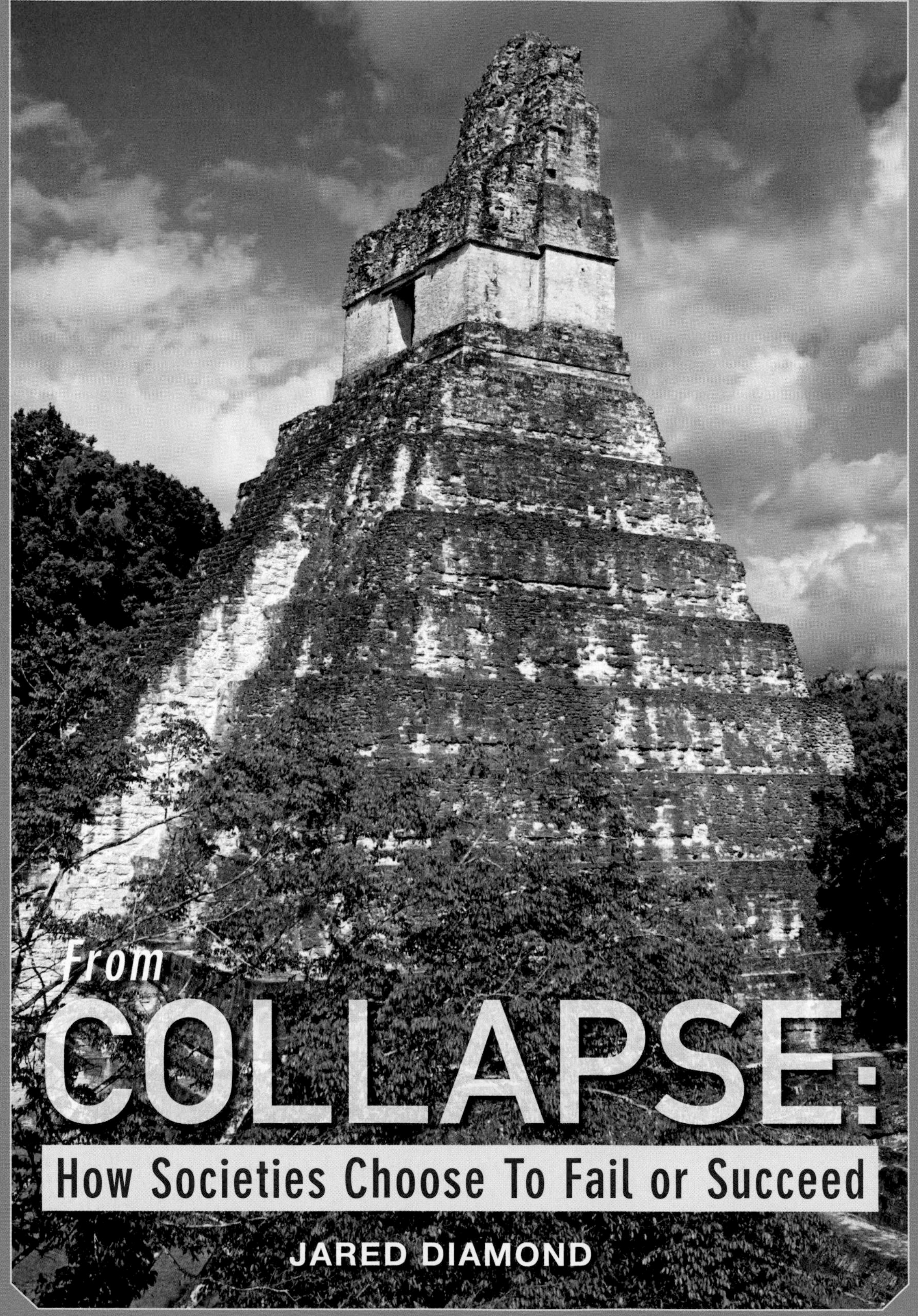

From COLLAPSE: How Societies Choose To Fail or Succeed

JARED DIAMOND

The monumental ruins left behind by past societies hold a romantic fascination for all of us. We marvel at them when as children we first learn of them through pictures. When we grow up, many of us plan vacations in order to experience them at firsthand as tourists. We feel drawn to their often spectacular and haunting beauty, and also to the mysteries that they pose. The scales of the ruins testify to the former wealth and power of their builders—they boast "Look on my works, ye mighty, and despair!"[1] in Shelley's words. Yet the builders vanished, abandoning the great structures that they had created at such effort. How could a society that was once so mighty end up collapsing? What were the fates of its individual citizens?—did they move away, and (if so) why, or did they die there in some unpleasant way? Lurking behind this romantic mystery is the nagging thought: might such a fate eventually befall our own wealthy society? Will tourists someday stare mystified at the rusting hulks of New York's skyscrapers, much as we stare today at the jungle-overgrown ruins of Maya cities?

◀ The photograph at left shows the ruins of Tikal Temple, part of an ancient Mayan city located in what is now northern Guatemala.

It has long been suspected that many of those mysterious abandonments were at least partly triggered by ecological problems: people inadvertently destroying the environmental resources on which their societies depended. This suspicion of unintended ecological suicide—ecocide—has been confirmed by discoveries made in recent decades by archaeologists, climatologists, historians, paleontologists and palynologists (pollen scientists). The processes through which past societies have undermined themselves by damaging their environments fall into eight categories, whose relative importance differs from case to case: deforestation and habitat destruction, soil problems (erosion, salinization, and soil fertility losses), water management problems, overhunting, overfishing, effects of introduced species on native species, human population growth, and increased per capita impact of people.

Those past collapses tended to follow somewhat similar courses constituting variations on a theme. Population growth forced people to adopt intensified means of agricultural production (such as irrigation, double-cropping, or terracing), and to expand farming

1. **"look on . . . and despair!"** line from the poem "Ozymandias" by the British poet Percy Bysshe Shelley. The poem concerns ancient Egyptian ruins.

marginal ▶ (mär′ jə nəl) *adj.* borderline; between good enough and not good enough

from the prime lands first chosen onto more **marginal** land, in order to feed the growing number of hungry mouths. Unsustainable practices led to environmental damage of one or more of the eight types just listed, resulting in agriculturally marginal lands having to be abandoned again. Consequences for society included food shortages, starvation, wars among too many people fighting for too few resources, and overthrows of governing elites by disillusioned masses. Eventually, population decreased through starvation, war, or disease, and society lost some of the political, economic, and cultural complexity that it had developed at its peak. Writers find it tempting to draw analogies between those trajectories of human societies and the trajectories of individual human lives—to talk of a society's birth, growth, peak, senescence, and death—and to assume that the long period of senescence that most of us traverse between our peak years and our deaths also applies to societies. But that metaphor proves erroneous for many past societies (and for the modern Soviet Union): they declined rapidly after reaching peak numbers and power, and those rapid declines must have come as a surprise and shock to their citizens. In the worst cases of complete collapse, everybody in the society emigrated or died. Obviously, though, this grim **trajectory** is not one that all past societies followed unvaryingly to completion: different societies collapsed to different degrees and in somewhat different ways, while many societies didn't collapse at all.

trajectory ▶ (trə jek′ tə rē) *n.* curve or surface that follows a particular path

The risk of such collapses today is now a matter of increasing concern; indeed, collapses have already materialized for Somalia, Rwanda,[2] and some other Third World countries. Many people fear that ecocide has now come to overshadow nuclear war and emerging diseases as a threat to global civilization. The environmental problems facing us today include the same eight that undermined past societies, plus four new ones: human-caused climate change, buildup of toxic chemicals in the environment, energy shortages, and full human utilization of the Earth's photosynthetic capacity.[3] Most of these 12 threats, it is claimed, will become globally critical within the next few decades: either we solve the problems by then, or the problems will undermine not just Somalia but also First World societies. Much more likely than a doomsday scenario

---

2. **Somalia** (sō mä′ lē ə), **Rwanda** (ro͞o än′ də) two countries in east Africa that experienced disastrous civil wars in the 1990s.
3. **photosynthetic capacity** (fō tō′ sin thet′ ik kə pas′ i tē) maximum rate at which leaves can remove carbon dioxide from the air during photosynthesis.

involving human extinction or an apocalyptic collapse of industrial civilization would be "just" a future of significantly lower living standards, chronically higher risks, and the undermining of what we now consider some of our key values. Such a collapse could assume various forms, such as the worldwide spread of diseases or else of wars, triggered ultimately by scarcity of environmental resources. If this reasoning is correct, then our efforts today will determine the state of the world in which the current generation of children and young adults lives out their middle and late years.

But the seriousness of these current environmental problems is vigorously debated. Are the risks greatly exaggerated, or conversely are they underestimated? Does it stand to reason that today's human population of almost seven billion, with our potent modern technology, is causing our environment to crumble globally at a much more rapid rate than a mere few million people with stone and wooden tools already made it crumble locally in the past? Will modern technology solve our problems, or is it creating new problems faster than it solves old ones? When we deplete one resource (e.g., wood, oil, or ocean fish), can we count on being able to substitute some new resource (e.g., plastics, wind and solar energy, or farmed fish)? Isn't the rate of human population growth declining, such that we're already on course for the world's population to level off at some manageable number of people?

All of these questions illustrate why those famous collapses of past civilizations have taken on more meaning than just that of a romantic mystery. Perhaps there are some practical lessons that we could learn from all those past collapses. We know that some past societies collapsed while others didn't: what made certain societies especially vulnerable? What, exactly, were the processes by which past societies committed ecocide? Why did some past societies fail to see the messes that they were getting into, and that (one would think in retrospect) must have been obvious? Which were the solutions that succeeded in the past? If we could answer these questions, we might be able to identify which societies are now most at risk, and what measures could best help them, without waiting for more Somalia-like collapses.

But there are also differences between the modern world and its problems, and those past societies and their problems. We shouldn't be so naïve as to think that study of the past will yield simple solutions, directly transferable to our societies today. We differ from past societies in some respects that put us at lower risk than them; some of those respects often mentioned include our powerful technology (i.e., its beneficial effects), globalization, modern medicine, and greater knowledge of past societies and of distant modern societies. We also differ from past societies in some respects that put us at greater risk than them: mentioned in that connection are, again, our potent technology (i.e., its unintended destructive effects), globalization (such that now a collapse even in remote Somalia affects the U.S. and Europe), the dependence of millions (and, soon, billions) of us on modern medicine for our survival, and our much larger human population. Perhaps we can still learn from the past, but only if we think carefully about its lessons. . . .

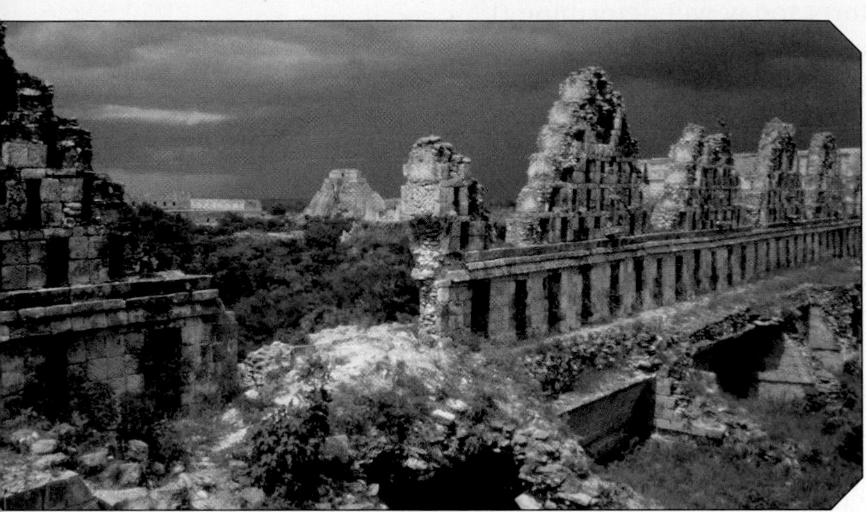

▲ The photograph above shows part of the ruins of Uxmal, the site of an ancient Mayan city located in what is now Mexico.

I don't know of any case in which a society's collapse can be attributed solely to environmental damage: there are always other contributing factors. When I began to plan this book, I didn't appreciate those complications, and I naïvely thought that the book would just be about environmental damage. Eventually, I arrived at a five-point framework of possible contributing factors that I now consider in trying to understand any putative environmental collapse. Four of those sets of factors—environmental damage, climate change, hostile neighbors, and friendly trade partners—may or may not prove significant for a particular society. The fifth set of factors—the society's responses to its environmental problems—always proves significant. Let's consider these five sets of factors one by one, in a sequence not implying any **primacy** of cause but just convenience of presentation.

primacy ▶ (prī´ mə sē) *n.* state of being first in time, order, rank, etc.

A first set of factors involves damage that people inadvertently inflict on their environment, as already discussed. The extent and reversibility of that damage depend partly on properties of people (e.g., how many trees they cut down per acre per year), and partly on properties of the environment (e.g., properties determining how many seedlings germinate per acre, and how rapidly saplings grow, per year). Those environmental properties are referred to either as fragility (susceptibility to damage) or as resilience (potential for recovery from damage), and one can talk separately of the fragility or resilience of an area's forests, its soils, its fish populations and so on. Hence the reasons why only certain societies suffered environmental collapses might in principle involve either exceptional imprudence of their people, exceptional fragility of some aspects of their environment, or both.

A next consideration in my five-point framework is climate change, a term that today we tend to associate with global warming caused by humans. In fact, climate may become hotter or colder, wetter or drier, or more or less variable between months or between years, because of changes in natural forces that drive climate and that have nothing to do with humans. Examples of such forces include changes in the heat put out by the sun, volcanic eruptions that inject dust into the atmosphere, changes in the orientation of the Earth's axis with respect to its orbit, and changes in the distribution of land and ocean over the face of the Earth. Frequently discussed cases of natural climate change include the advance and retreat of continental ice sheets during the Ice Ages beginning over two million years ago, the so-called Little Ice Age from about A.D. 1400 to 1800, and the global cooling following the enormous volcanic eruption of Indonesia's Mt. Tambora on April 5, 1815. That eruption injected so much dust into the upper atmosphere that the amount of sunlight reaching the ground decreased until the dust settled out, causing widespread famines even in North America and Europe due to cold temperatures and reduced crop yields in the summer of 1816 ("the year without a summer"). . . .

Eventually, population decreased through starvation, war, or disease, and society lost some of the political, economic, and cultural complexity that it had developed at its peak.

Natural climate changes may make conditions either better or worse for any particular human society, and may benefit one society while hurting another society. (For example, we shall see that the Little Ice Age was bad for the Greenland Norse but good for the Greenland Inuit.[4]) In many historical cases, a society that was depleting its environmental resources could absorb the losses

4. **Greenland Norse . . . Greenland Inuit** (in′ o͞o it) During the 10th century, the Norse came from Europe to settle in Greenland; the Inuit had lived in Greenland since ancient times. The Greenland Norse lived mainly in cities while Greenland Inuit lived in rural areas.

as long as the climate was benign, but was then driven over the brink of collapse when the climate became drier, colder, hotter, wetter, or more variable. Should one then say that the collapse was caused by human environmental impact, or by climate change? Neither of those simple alternatives is correct. Instead, if the society hadn't already partly depleted its environmental resources, it might have survived the resource depletion caused by climate change. Conversely, it was able to survive its self-inflicted resource depletion until climate change produced further resource depletion. It was neither factor taken alone, but the combination of environmental impact and climate change, that proved fatal.

A third consideration is hostile neighbors. All but a few historical societies have been geographically close enough to some other societies to have had at least some contact with them. Relations with neighboring societies may be intermittently or chronically hostile. A society may be able to hold off its enemies as long as it is strong, only to succumb when it becomes weakened for any reason, including environmental damage. The proximate cause of the collapse will then be military conquest, but the ultimate cause—the factor whose change led to the collapse—will have been the factor that caused the weakening. Hence collapses for ecological or other reasons often masquerade as military defeats . . .

The fourth set of factors is the converse of the third set: decreased support by friendly neighbors, as opposed to increased attacks by hostile neighbors. All but a few historical societies have had friendly trade partners as well as neighboring enemies. Often, the partner and the enemy are one and the same neighbor, whose behavior shifts back and forth between friendly and hostile. Most societies depend to some extent on friendly neighbors, either for imports of essential trade goods (like U.S. imports of oil, and Japanese imports of oil, wood, and seafood, today), or else for cultural ties that lend cohesion to the society (such as Australia's cultural identity imported from Britain until recently). Hence the risk arises that, if your trade partner becomes weakened for any reason (including environmental damage) and can no longer supply the essential import or the cultural tie, your own society may become weakened as a result. This is a familiar problem today because of the First World's dependence on oil from ecologically fragile and politically troubled Third World countries that imposed an oil embargo in 1973. Similar problems arose in the past for the Greenland Norse, Pitcairn Islanders, and other societies.

The last set of factors in my five-point framework involves the ubiquitous question of the society's responses to its problems, whether those problems are environmental or not. Different societies respond differently to similar problems. For instance, problems of deforestation arose for many past societies, among which Highland New Guinea, Japan, Tikopia, and Tonga developed successful forest management and continued to prosper, while Easter Island, Mangareva, and Norse Greenland failed to develop successful forest management and collapsed as a result. How can we understand such differing outcomes? A society's responses depend on its political, economic, and social institutions and on its cultural values. Those institutions and values affect whether the society solves (or even tries to solve) its problems.

ABOUT THE AUTHOR

Jared Diamond (b. 1937)

Jared Diamond is a Pulitzer Prize-winning author as well as an ecologist, biologist, and professor of geography and physiology at the University of California, Los Angeles. He speaks twelve languages and has made more than twenty expeditions to New Guinea and neighboring islands to study the ecology of birds. Diamond is a recipient of a fellowship from the MacArthur Foundation—often called the "Genius" grant.

Diamond believes that recognizing a problem paves the way to solving it. "Our biggest threat is not an asteroid about to crash into us, something we can do nothing about. Instead, all the major threats facing us today are problems entirely of our own making. And since we made the problems, we can also solve the problems."

Close Reading Activities

READ

Comprehension

Reread all or part of the text to help you answer the following questions.

1. What are the eight types of environmental damage listed by Diamond?
2. What four new types of environmental problems have occurred in more recent times?
3. What are the five factors that Diamond believes contribute to the collapse of a society?

Research: Clarify Details This text may include references that are unfamiliar to you. Choose at least one unfamiliar detail and briefly research it. Then, explain how the information you learned from research sheds light on an aspect of the text.

Summarize Write an objective summary of the text. Remember that an objective summary is free from opinion and evaluation.

Language Study

Selection Vocabulary: Sociology The following passages appear in the excerpt. Define each boldfaced term. Then, use the word in a sentence of your own.

- Let's consider these five sets of factors one by one, … not implying any **primacy** of cause …
- …to expand farming from the prime lands…onto more **marginal** land...
- Obviously, though, this grim **trajectory** is not one that all past societies followed unvaryingly…

Literary Analysis

Reread the identified passage. Then, respond to the questions that follow.

Focus Passage *(p. 499)*

But the seriousness … Somalia-like collapses.

Key Ideas and Details

1. **(a)** According to the author, what aspect of the world's current environmental problems is being **vigorously** debated? **(b) Compare:** How do comparisons with the past complicate this debate? Explain, citing details from the text.

Craft and Structure

2. **Interpret:** How does Diamond's use of questions work to both introduce his topic and to hint at its **complexities**? Explain.
3. **Analyze:** What other purpose might the author have for presenting information in a series of questions? Explain your thinking.

Integration of Knowledge and Idea

4. **Generalize:** Does Diamond believe that people can control the forces that affect the survival of civilizations? Explain, citing details from the text.

Diction: Technical Language

Technical language is a type of diction, or word choice. It includes words and phrases experts use to describe specific concepts. Reread the excerpt, and take notes on Diamond's use of technical terms.

1. **(a)** Identify two examples of technical language in the text and explain what each term means. **(b)** How does Diamond make the meanings of technical terms **accessible** to the general reader?
2. Based on your reading of this selection, explain why technical language is an important aspect of expository texts. Cite examples from the text to support your answer.

DISCUSS • RESEARCH • WRITE

From Text to Topic **Small Group Discussion**

Discuss the following passage with a small group. Take notes during the discussion. Contribute your own ideas, and support them with examples from the text. Discuss any ideas on which you disagree.

> We differ from past societies in some respects that put us at lower risk than them; some of those respects often mentioned include our powerful technology ... We also differ from past societies in some respects that put us at greater risk than them: mentioned in that connection are, again, our potent technology ... Perhaps we can still learn from the past, but only if we think carefully about its lessons.

QUESTIONS FOR DISCUSSION

1. How can the same factor—powerful technology—put our society at both a lower and a greater risk of collapse?
2. Why is globalization both a positive and negative factor to a society's survival?

Research **Investigate the Topic**

Palynology Palynologists, or pollen scientists, can help us recreate environmental factors in ancient societies.

Assignment

Conduct research to find out more about the methods used by palynologists to study older civilizations. Select scholarly journals, popular science magazines, and academic or scientific Web sites that describe what palynologists do. Explain how the discoveries of palynologists often have far-reaching consequences. Take clear notes and identify your sources. Write up your findings in a research **summary.**

PREPARATION FOR ESSAY

You may use the results of this research in an essay you will write at the end of this section.

Writing to Sources **Argument**

The excerpt from *Collapse* explores the factors that contributed to the failure of past societies. Diamond argues that an understanding of why ancient societies fell may help protect our society from a similar fate.

Assignment

Write a **persuasive essay** in which you state and defend a position about Diamond's argument. Do you agree that it is important to understand the collapse of past societies? Should we invest money, time, and energy into doing so, or should we focus resources on the future? Follow these steps:

- Write a clear statement of your thesis.
- Choose a text structure that allows you to (1) provide reasons why your position is correct, and (2) include supporting examples and details from Diamond's text.
- Consider posing questions to the reader as you explain your points.

ACADEMIC VOCABULARY

Academic terms appear in blue on these pages. Use a dictionary to find their definitions. Then, use them as you speak and write about the text.

Common Core State Standards

RI.9-10.1, RI.9-10.2, RI.9-10.3, RI.9-10.4, RI.9-10.5; W.9-10.1, W.9-10.4, W.9-10.7, W.9-10.9.b; SL.9-10.1; L.9-10.3, L.9-10.4, L.9-10.4.c–d, L.9-10.6

[For full standards wording, see the chart in the front of this book.]

Aquae Sulis, Roman Baths, 1762

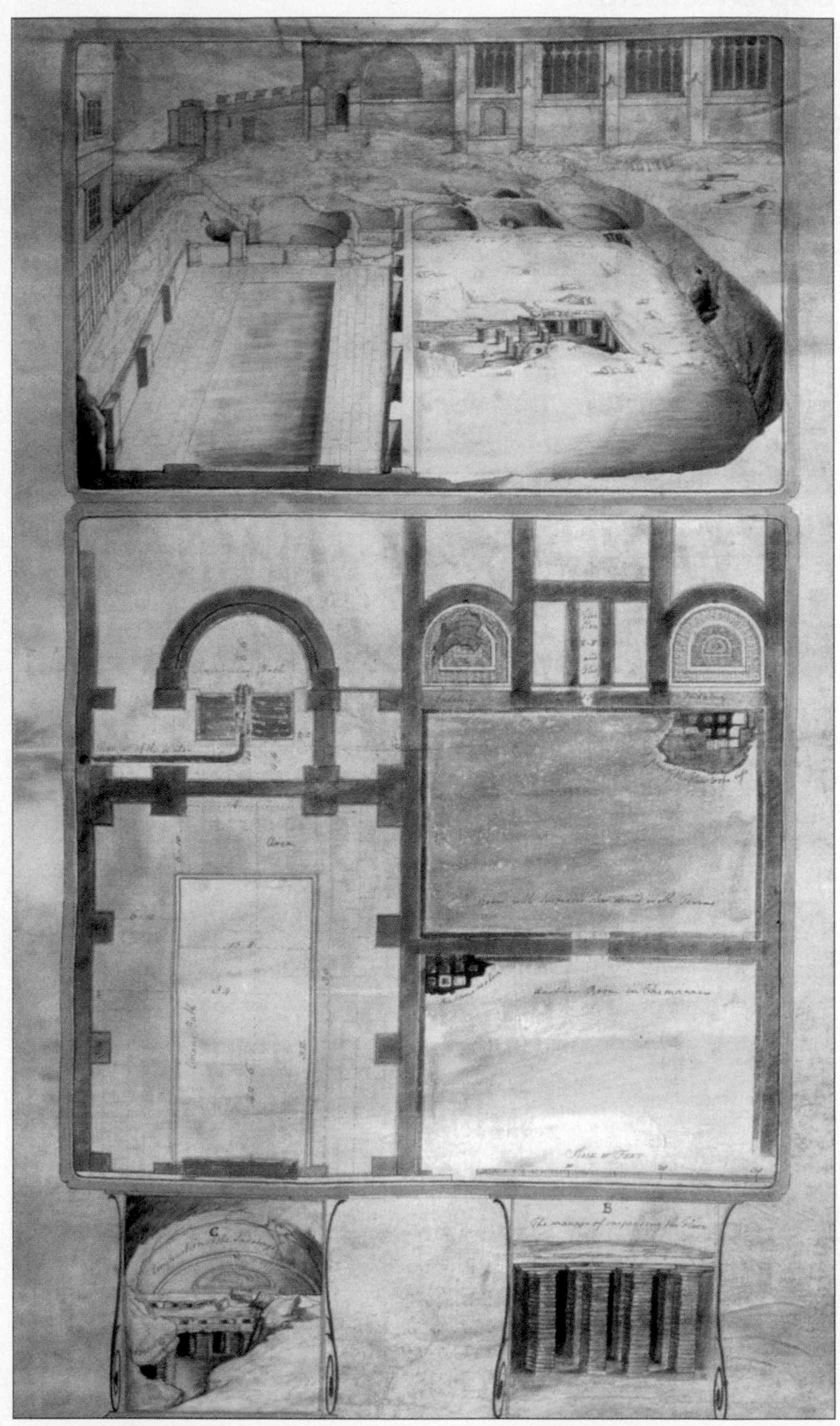

ABOUT THE DRAWING

This pen and ink drawing with watercolor was made in 1762. It captures the excavation of the Roman Baths in Aquae Sulis, once a small town in the Roman province of Britannia that today is known as Bath. The baths were originally built starting in and around 54 AD. Excavations began in 1755.

READ • RESEARCH • WRITE

Comprehension

Look at the image closely. Then, answer the following questions.

1. What does the top section of the drawing depict?

2. What do the other sections of the drawing show?

Critical Analysis

Key Ideas and Details

1. (a) Interpret: Which details in the drawing suggest what the exterior of the structure might look like? **(b) Deduce:** What does this drawing tell viewers about the style of ancient Roman architecture? Explain your answers.

Craft and Structure

2. (a) Interpret: Describe the view of the bathhouse captured in each section of the drawing. **(b) Connect:** How do the multiple views included in this drawing create a complete picture of the structure? **(c) Connect:** Why might eighteenth century archaeologists have wanted multiple drawings of the structure in a single document? Explain.

3. Analyze: Which details in the drawing suggest a sense of **scale** and of the ways in which people might have moved around the building? Explain.

Integration of Knowledge and Ideas

4. Synthesize: What do the architectural details captured in the drawing suggest about the importance the ancient Romans **attributed** to this type of structure? Explain.

Research/Write **Informative Text**

Reading the Past Briefly conduct research into the **excavation** of ancient buildings and learn how archaeologists make meaning from such findings. Then, write an **informative essay** in which you discuss what can be learned about lost civilizations from the study of ancient buildings. Consider how buildings provide information about a culture's social organization and values, its successes, and its failures.

Common Core State Standards

W.9-10.2; W.9-10.7

[For full standards wording, see the chart in the front of this book.]

ACADEMIC VOCABULARY

Academic terms appear in blue on these pages. If these words are not familiar to you, use a dictionary to find their definitions. Then, use them as you speak and write about the text.

PREPARATION FOR ESSAY

You may use the results of this research in an essay you will write at the end of this section.

Assessment: Synthesis

Speaking and Listening: Group Discussion

Lost Civilizations and Communication The texts in this section vary in genre, length, style, and perspective. All of them, however, deal in some way with the cultures or histories of lost civilizations. This information is communicated in genres ranging from poetry to apocalyptic fiction, and from reflections on one's heritage to an analysis of why societies collapse. All are fundamentally related to the Big Question addressed in this unit: **Does all communication serve a positive purpose?**

▲ Refer to the selections you read in Part 3 as you complete the activities on this assessment.

Assignment

Conduct discussions. With a small group of classmates, conduct a discussion about lost civilizations and communication. Refer to the texts in this section, other texts you have read, and your personal experience and knowledge to support your ideas. Begin your discussion by addressing the following questions:

- What role does communication play in the success or failure of a civilization?
- In what ways are artifacts of past civilizations—literature, works of art, everyday objects, and even buildings—a form of communication?
- How do various types of communication help us understand different aspects of lost civilizations?
- What, in your opinion, is the most promising use of communication in helping a civilization to thrive?

Summarize and present your ideas. After you have fully explored the topic, summarize your discussion and present your findings to the class as a whole.

Criteria for Success

✓ **Organizes the group effectively**
Appoint a group leader and a timekeeper. The group leader should present the discussion questions. The timekeeper should make sure the discussion takes no longer than 20 minutes.

✓ **Maintains focus of discussion**
As a group, stay on topic and avoid straying into other subject areas.

✓ **Involves all participants equally and fully**
Make sure all group members have equal opportunities to contribute ideas.

✓ **Follows the rules for collegial discussion**
Conduct a genuine discussion in which you share your ideas and genuinely listen to those of others. Support your ideas and opinions with evidence. Express differing viewpoints with courtesy.

USE NEW VOCABULARY

As you speak and share ideas, work to use the vocabulary words you have learned in this unit. The more you use new words, the more you will "own" them.

Writing: **Narrative**

Lost Civilizations and Communication Communication serves a positive purpose when it allows people to explain or clear up a source of confusion, or to engage in dialogue that might help to solve a problem. Communication can serve a negative purpose, however, if it leads to arguments or misunderstanding.

Common Core State Standards

W.9-10.3a–e, W.9-10.4, W.9-10.5; SL.9-10.1.a–d, SL.9-10.4; L.9-10.2

[For full standards wording, see the chart in the front of this book.]

Assignment

Write a **story** in which you tell a fictionalized account of a real historical event. Draw on the research you have completed in this section to gather ideas. Incorporate several characters in your narrative and use dialogue to demonstrate the role communication played in the events. Your narrative should not only describe the event but also suggest its significance.

Criteria for Success

Purpose/Focus

✓ **Connects specific incidents with larger ideas**
Make meaningful connections between the characters and events you describe and the research you have conducted in this section.

✓ **Clearly conveys the significance of the story**
Through dialogue and description, demonstrate how the events you relate in the story affect character's lives.

Organization

✓ **Sequences events logically**
Structure your narrative so that events are ignited by a conflict and progress through the stages of a plot.

Development of Ideas/Elaboration

✓ **Supports insights**
Incorporate details from the texts you have read and the research you have conducted in this section to add authenticity and meaning to your story.

✓ **Uses narrative techniques effectively**
Develop realistic, expressive dialogue among characters to add interest and information to your story.

Language

✓ **Uses descriptive language effectively**
Use sensory details, images, and figurative language to paint word pictures that help readers understand settings and characters.

Conventions

✓ **Does not have errors**
Check your story to eliminate errors in grammar, spelling, and punctuation.

WRITE TO EXPLORE

Remember that effective writing requires revision. An outline can guide your first draft, but add new ideas that occur to you as you write. When you revise again, make sure these ideas connect.

Writing to Sources: **Explanatory Text**

Lost Civilizations and Communication The related readings in this section present a range of ideas about lost civilizations and communication. They raise questions, such as the following:

- In what ways can lost civilizations communicate to the future?
- Are painful events of the past important to communicate or should we allow them to be forgotten?
- How does an author's purpose influence the choices he or she uses to communicate information about a lost civilization?
- What positive and/or negative effect might information about lost civilizations have on the reader?

Focus on the question that intrigues you the most, and then complete the following assignment.

Assignment

Write an **expository essay** in which you explain, describe, and discuss one or more aspects of your chosen question. Build evidence for each of your points by analyzing how the topic is communicated in two or more texts from this section. Clearly present, develop, and support your ideas with examples and details from the texts.

INCORPORATE RESEARCH

Strengthen your essay by pulling in facts, quotations, and data you gathered while conducting research related to the readings in this section. Make sure to cite your sources correctly.

Prewriting and Planning

Choose texts. Review the texts in this section to determine which ones you will cite in your essay. Select at least two that will provide strong material to support your explanation.

Gather details. Use a chart like the one shown to identify details that you might use in your essay.

Focus Question: In what ways can lost civilizations communicate to the future?

Text	Passage	Notes
"By the Waters of Babylon"	It is not for the metal alone we go to the Dead Places now—there are books and the writings. They are hard to learn.	Benét's story suggests the power of writing to communicate all that people once knew.
"There Will Come Soft Rains"	The house stood alone in a city of rubble and ashes. This was the one house left standing.	Bradbury's story suggests that the future can be destroyed, so the past communicates nothing.
Example Topic: A lost civilization may not be truly lost as long as some piece of its culture remains.		

Drafting

Sequence ideas and identify evidence. Organize your ideas in a logical sequence. Select details from your chart that correlate with each point you wish to make. Provide specific evidence that directly supports your ideas.

Develop your Ideas. Fully explain your ideas so that a reader can follow your logic. Anticipate questions readers might have and include reasons and convincing evidence to answer them.

Introduce, develop, and connect ideas. In your introduction, explain your topic and purpose, and note which texts you will explore in your essay. In your body paragraphs, follow through on the idea you stated in the introduction. Carefully use transitions to lead the reader through your thought process, linking your paragraphs logically and clarifying the connections between your examples and your ideas. In your conclusion, restate your main idea.

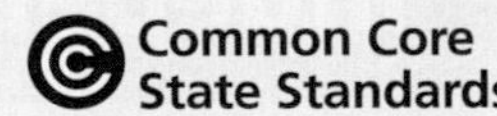

W.9-10.2.a–f, W.9-10.4, W.9-10.5, W.9-10.9; L.9-10.3.a
[For full standards wording, see the chart in the front of this book.]

Revising and Editing

Review content. Make sure that your purpose for writing is clearly stated and that you have analyzed the texts accurately. Check that you have used textual evidence or researched information to support all of your ideas. Add examples or explanations as needed.

Review style. Make sure you have used language that is appropriate for an academic purpose and that your tone is properly formal.

USING QUOTATIONS

When quoting directly from a text, remember to set the author's words with quotation marks and cite the information properly. See the Research Workshop in the Introductory Unit for additional guidance.

Self-Evaluation Rubric

Use the following criteria to evaluate the effectiveness of your essay.

Criteria	Rating Scale
PURPOSE/FOCUS Introduces a specific topic; provides a concluding section that follows from and supports the information or explanation presented.	*not very .... very* 1 2 3 4
ORGANIZATION Organizes complex ideas, concepts, and information to make important connections and distinctions; uses appropriate and varied transitions to link the major sections, create cohesion, and clarify relationships among ideas	1 2 3 4
DEVELOPMENT OF IDEAS/ELABORATION Develops the topic with well-chosen, relevant and sufficient facts, extended definitions, concrete details, quotations, or other information and examples appropriate to the audience's knowledge of the topic	1 2 3 4
LANGUAGE Uses precise language and domain-specific vocabulary to manage the complexity of the topic; establishes and maintains a formal style and objective tone	1 2 3 4
CONVENTIONS Attends to the norms and conventions of the discipline	1 2 3 4

Independent Reading

Titles for Extended Reading

In this unit, you have read texts in a wide variety of genres. Continue to read on your own. Select works that you enjoy, but challenge yourself to explore new authors and works of increasing depth and complexity. The titles suggested below will help you get started.

INFORMATIONAL TEXT

The Story of Art: A Pocket Edition
by E. H. Gombrich
EXEMPLAR TEXT

This **nonfiction history** traces the development of art, from prehistoric cave painting to the twentieth century. The director of the famous Louvre Museum wrote about this book, "Almost as well known as the *Mona Lisa, ... The Story of Art* unites learning and pleasure."

Ancient Rome: Voyages Through Time
by Peter Ackroyd

Spanning centuries of war and conquest, this work of **historical nonfiction** brings the reader face to face with famous and infamous Roman rulers, along with the architectural marvels of their age—aqueducts, amphitheaters, spectacular temples, and the Circus Maximus.

Before Columbus: The Americas of 1491
by Charles C. Mann
Atheneum, 2009
EXEMPLAR TEXT

In this **nonfiction** book, the author vividly describes life in the Americas before Columbus. He tells how natives accomplished such feats as producing genetically engineered corn and building enormous pyramids.

Immigrant Voices: Twenty Four Narratives on Becoming an American
Edited by Gordon Hutner
Signet, 1999

This collection of **autobiographical narratives** and **essays** explores the experience of becoming American from many different points of view, including those of a female doctor from Germany forbidden to practice and a man from India struggling to become a writer.

LITERATURE

The Song of the Lark
by Willa Cather

This **novel** tells the story of a small-town girl who sets herself apart due to her musical abilities. It is a lonely, isolated path she chooses as she pursues a career as an opera singer and dedicates herself to her art.

Victims of the Latest Dance Craze
by Cornelius Eady
Carnegie Mellon University Press, 1997

The **poems** in this collection invite readers to experience the world as a rhythmic place alive with sound and motion. Inventive language is woven throughout.

Lift Every Voice and Sing
by James Weldon Johnson
EXEMPLAR TEXT

Johnson wrote the title poem of this **poetry** collection in 1900 for a Lincoln birthday celebration. Its dual message, acknowledging past suffering while expressing hope for the future, has moved and inspired generations of African Americans.

ONLINE TEXT SET

NONFICTION
The Marginal World Rachel Carson

SCIENCE ARTICLE
The Spider and The Wasp Alexander Petrunkevitch

POEM
The Kraken
Alfred, Lord Tennyson

Preparing to Read Complex Texts

Attentive Reading As you read literature on your own, bring your imagination and questions to the text. The questions shown below and others that you ask as you read will help you learn and enjoy literature even more.

Reading Literature/ Informational Text

10. By the end of Grade 10, read and comprehend literature, including stories, dramas, poems, and literary nonfiction at the high end of the grades 9–10 text complexity band independently and proficiently.

When reading poetry, ask yourself...

Comprehension: **Key Ideas and Details**

- What do I understand about the poem from its title?
- Who is the speaker of the poem? What is the speaker telling me?
- What subject matter does the poem address?
- Is the poem telling a story? If so, who are the characters, and what are they doing?
- Is the poem exploring a single moment in time? If so, what is that moment and what emotions are connected to it?

Text Analysis: **Craft and Structure**

- How does the poem's structure and appearance affect the way I read it?
- Is the poem an example of a particular form? If so, how does the form affect what I understand and feel about the poem?
- Does the poet use repetition, rhyme, or other sound devices? If so, what effect do these devices create?
- Does the poem use symbols, figurative language, or imagery? If so, how do these devices add to the poem's deeper meaning?

Connections: **Integration of Ideas**

- What theme, meaning, or insight, does the poem express? Does any one line or section simply state that theme? If so, which one? If not, which details help me understand the poem's deeper meaning?
- Has the poem helped me understand something in a new way? If so, how?
- In what ways is this poem similar to others I have read? In what ways is it different from others I have read?
- Would I like to read more poems by this poet? Why or why not?
- Could this poem serve as an inspiration to other writers, artists, or musicians? Why or why not?

UNIT 4

THE BIG ?

To what extent does experience determine what we perceive?

UNIT PATHWAY

PART 1
SETTING EXPECTATIONS
- INTRODUCING THE BIG QUESTION
- CLOSE READING WORKSHOP

PART 2
TEXT ANALYSIS
GUIDED EXPLORATION

TRAGEDY AND SPECTACLE

PART 3
TEXT SET
DEVELOPING INSIGHT

CONSCIENTIOUS OBJECTIONS

PART 4
DEMONSTRATING INDEPENDENCE
- INDEPENDENT READING
- ONLINE TEXT SET

CLOSE READING TOOL

Use this tool to practice the close reading strategies you learn.

STUDENT eTEXT

Bring learning to life with audio, video, and interactive tools.

ONLINE WRITER'S NOTEBOOK

Easily capture notes and complete assignments online.

Find all Digital Resources at **pearsonrealize.com**

Introducing the Big Question

To what extent does experience determine what we perceive?

A person's experience is everything he or she has lived through, seen, read, or heard about. It is the background that shapes his or her perspective, or point of view, about the world.

This suggests that our perceptions of the world are unique—ours and ours alone. After all, even if we have common or shared moments, we are individuals who experience life separately. At the same time, we do share some experiences, find common ground, and participate in moments that affect us in similar ways. Such moments may involve families, communities, and even entire nations. Can such shared experiences lead us to perceive things in the same ways? If so, do we still hold on to our individual perceptions? To what extent does experience determine what we perceive?

Exploring the Big Question

Collaboration: Small Group Discussion Start thinking about the Big Question by working with a small group of classmates to describe how different background experiences might affect two people's perceptions of a similar situation. Consider the situations listed below.

- moving to a new city or town and having to attend a new school
- deciding whether or not someone is being truthful about a situation
- persuading someone to do the right thing
- trying to get a person of another generation to understand your point of view
- attempting a new sport that requires a high level of athletic ability
- encountering an emergency situation that requires a quick response

Discuss how each person's experiences might affect his or her point of view. Present your ideas clearly and persuasively, and work together to build on one another's ideas.

Connecting to the Literature Each reading in this unit will give you additional insight into the Big Question. After you read each selection, pause to consider what it suggests about the ways in which our experiences shape our perceptions of other people, situations, and ourselves.

Vocabulary

Speaking and Listening

1. Initiate and participate effectively in a range of collaborative discussions with diverse partners on grades 9–10 topics, texts, and issues, building on others' ideas and expressing their own clearly and persuasively.

Language

6. Acquire and use accurately general academic and domain-specific words and phrases, sufficient for reading, writing, speaking, and listening at the college and career readiness level; demonstrate independence in gathering vocabulary knowledge when considering a word or phrase important to comprehension or expression.

Acquire and Use Academic Vocabulary The term "academic vocabulary" refers to words you typically encounter in scholarly and literary texts and in technical and business writing. It is the language that helps to express complex ideas. Review the definitions of these academic vocabulary words.

anticipate (an tis´ ə pāt´) *v.* look forward to

background (bak´ ground´) *n.* all of a person's education, training, and experience

bias (bī´ əs) *n.* preference for one thing, person, or group, often in a way considered unfair

distortion (di stôr´ shən) *n.* anything that shows something in an untrue way

individual (in´ də vij´ o͞o əl) *adj.* relating to a single person or thing

insight (in´ sīt´) *n.* clear idea of the nature of things

interpretation (in tur´ prə tā´ shən) *n.* someone's perception or explanation of the meaning of something

manipulate (mə nip´ yo͞o lāt´) *v.* control by use of influence, often in an unfair way

perspective (pər´ spek´ tiv) *n.* how one sees things; viewpoint

Use these words as you complete Big Question activities in this unit that involve reading, writing, speaking, and listening.

Gather Vocabulary Knowledge Additional words related to experience and perception are listed below. Categorize the words by deciding whether you know each one well, know it a little bit, or do not know it at all.

expectations	**impression**	**stereotype**
identity	**knowledge**	**universal**

Then, complete the following steps:

1. Write the definitions of the words you know.
2. Consult a print or an online dictionary to confirm the definitions of the words you know. Revise your original definitions if necessary.
3. Use the dictionary to look up the meanings of the words you do not know. Then, write the definitions.
4. Use all the words in a paragraph in which you describe how life experience has changed the way you perceive something or someone.

Close Reading Workshop

In this workshop, you will learn an approach to reading that will deepen your understanding of literature and will help you better appreciate the author's craft. The workshop includes models for the close reading, discussion, research, and writing activities you will complete as you study literature in this unit. After you have reviewed the strategies and models, practice your skills with the Independent Practice selection.

Common Core State Standards

RL.9-10.1, RL.9-10.2, RL.9-10.3, RL.9-10.5, RL.9-10.6; W.9-10.1, W.9-10.7, W.9-10.9; SL.9-10.1

[For full standards wording, see the chart in the front of this book.]

CLOSE READING: **DRAMA**

In Part 2 of this unit, you will focus on reading various dramas. Use these strategies as you read the texts:

Comprehension: **Key Ideas and Details**

- Read first to understand the characters, situation, and setting.
- Use context clues to help you determine the meanings of unfamiliar words. Consult a dictionary, if necessary.
- Identify unfamiliar details that you might need to clarify through research.
- Distinguish between what characters state directly and what audiences must infer.

Ask yourself questions such as these:

- Who are the main characters, and what are their relationships?
- When and where does the action take place?
- What problems do characters face, and how do they respond?

Text Analysis: **Craft and Structure**

- Consider the genre of the play—whether it is a comedy or a tragedy—and how that shapes the portrayal of characters and events.
- Notice how the playwright develops characters through both dialogue and stage directions.
- Pay attention to the playwright's use of figurative language as well as special types of speeches.
- Analyze how the playwright develops one or more conflicts through the sequence of events and characters' responses to those events.

Ask yourself questions such as these:

- What do the dialogue and stage directions tell me about each character's background, attitudes, and motivations?
- How are the characters' personal qualities reflected in the way they speak?

Connections: **Integration of Knowledge and Ideas**

- Look for relationships among key ideas. Identify causes, effects, comparisons, and contrasts.
- Analyze the deeper meanings of events. Then, synthesize to determine the theme or central insight the playwright conveys.
- Compare and contrast this work with other works you have read, either by the same author or by different authors.

Ask yourself questions such as these:

- How has this work increased my knowledge of drama or a particular playwright?
- What does this play contribute to my understanding of people and their relationships?

Read

As you read this excerpt from a play, take note of the annotations that model ways to closely read the text. The Norwegian playwright Henrik Ibsen finished *A Doll House* in 1879. The play is set in that same year, in the Helmer family's middle-class Norwegian home. Torvald Helmer has recently been hired as a banker, a great relief to the family, which has experienced financial difficulties. In this scene, Torvald's wife, Nora, has just returned from Christmas shopping.

Reading Model

from *A Doll House* by Henrik Ibsen (translated by Rolf Fjelde)

HELMER. *(In his room.)* Is that my lark twittering[1] there?

NORA. *(Busy opening some of her parcels.)* Yes, it is.

HELMER. Is it the squirrel frisking[1] around?

NORA. Yes!

HELMER. When did the squirrel get home?

NORA. Just this minute. *(Hides the bag of macaroons in her pocket and wipes her mouth.)*[2] Come here, Torvald, and see what I've been buying.

HELMER. Don't interrupt me. (*A little later he opens the door and looks in, pen in hand.*) Buying, did you say? What! All that? Has my little spendthrift been making the money fly again?[3]

NORA. Why, Torvald, surely we can afford to launch out a little now. It's the first Christmas we haven't had to pinch.

HELMER. Come come; we can't afford to squander money.

NORA. Oh yes, Torvald, do let us squander a little, now[4]—just the least little bit! You know you'll soon be earning heaps of money.

HELMER. Yes, from New Year's Day. But there's a whole quarter before my first salary is due.

Craft and Structure

1 Torvald's nicknames for Nora demonstrate his affection, but also show that he views her as a small, silly creature whose pursuits in life are unimportant.

Craft and Structure

2 The stage directions show that Nora feels the need to hide her actions from her husband. This detail suggests she may be hiding other, perhaps more significant, aspects of herself, as well.

Key Ideas and Details

3 Torvald's words and actions demonstrate his controlling behavior and condescending attitude toward Nora.

Craft and Structure

4 This dialogue reveals that Torvald wishes to control the family budget. His viewpoint clashes with Nora's need for cheer and freedom. This section of dialogue reveals the underlying conflict between these two characters.

Nora. Never mind; we can borrow in the meantime.

Helmer. Nora! (*He goes up to her and takes her playfully by the ear.*) Still my little featherbrain![5] Supposing I borrowed a thousand crowns today, and you made ducks and drakes of them during Christmas week, and then on New Year's Eve a tile blew off the roof and knocked my brains out.

Nora. *(Laying her hand on his mouth.)* Hush! How can you talk so horridly?

Helmer. But supposing it were to happen—what then?

Nora. If anything so dreadful happened, it would be all the same to me whether I was in debt or not.

Helmer. But what about the creditors?

Nora. They! Who cares for them? They're only strangers.

Helmer. Nora, Nora! What a woman you are! But seriously, Nora, you know my principles on these points. No debts! No borrowing! Home life ceases to be free and beautiful as soon as it is founded on borrowing and debt. We two have held out bravely till now, and we are not going to give in at the last.

Nora. *(Going to the fireplace.)* Very well—as you please, Torvald.[6]

Integration of Knowledge and Ideas

5 Nora's proposal causes Torvald to tug at her ear. Ibsen notes that Torvald does this "playfully," but the gesture adds to the portrayal of the imbalance in their marriage. Torvald treats Nora like a child and—at this point in the play—she behaves like one.

Integration of Knowledge and Ideas

6 This passage of dialogue highlights key aspects of the two characters' personalities, behavior, and conflicts: Nora lacks experience with the world and the realities of debt. Torvald is dismissive of Nora, and—apparently—anxious and controlling about money. In the final line of this passage, Nora walks over to the fireplace as she voices agreement to her husband's statement. Readers are left to wonder if Nora really means what she says.

Discuss

Sharing your own ideas and listening to the ideas of others can deepen your understanding of a text and help you look at a topic in a whole new way. As you participate in collaborative discussions, work to have a genuine exchange in which classmates build upon one another's ideas. Support your points with evidence and ask meaningful questions.

Discussion Model

Student 1: It bothers me that Torvald Helmer doesn't want Nora to waste money, but he talks to her as if she couldn't possibly have anything worthwhile to do. He calls her a lark and a squirrel and a featherbrain. Why would he be surprised that she wants to go shopping?

Student 2: I see what you mean, but she has been spending money they don't have—yet. Nora isn't being very considerate of her husband. Also, the fact that she hides the macaroons makes her seem immature. It doesn't surprise me that Torvald treats her like a child. It's as if he's being kind instead of angry, because she won't react to anger in an adult way.

Student 3: Yes, but at the end, they both seem to care about their marriage. Nora seems genuinely horrified at the thought that Torvald could die, and Torvald talks about how the two of them held out bravely, as if dealing with a lack of money has been a team effort. Torvald does seem very focused on money, though. Does his phrase "make ducks and drakes" have something to do with spending money?

Research

Targeted research can clarify unfamiliar details and shed light on various aspects of a text. Consider questions that arise in your mind as you read, and use those questions as the basis for research.

Research Model

Question: *What does it mean to "make ducks and drakes" of something?*

Key Words for Internet Search: make ducks and drakes

Result: Dictionary Web sites

What I Learned: *Ducks and Drakes* is the Old English name for a game of skipping or skimming stones across a water surface. The phrase "make ducks and drakes" is an idiom, derived from the game, that means "behave recklessly" or "squander one's wealth."

Write

Writing about a text will deepen your understanding of it and will also allow you to share your ideas more formally with others. The following model essay examines the relationship between Torvald and Nora Helmer as portrayed in the scene from *A Doll House*.

Writing Model: Argument

An Obstacle to Communication in *A Doll House* by Henrik Ibsen

In *A Doll House*, the conversation between Torvald and Nora Helmer reveals a pattern in their relationship that interferes with their ability to communicate. The husband, Torvald, does not take his wife, Nora, seriously, and this attitude stifles her responses.

Critical writing is a form of argument in which the writer's interpretation of a text is the main claim. Here, the writer states a claim in the opening paragraph.

Ibsen uses dialogue and stage directions (such as Torvald taking Nora by the ear) to establish this pattern. In this scene, the couple argue over spending money. Helmer repeatedly refers to Nora's spending as wasteful. He calls her a spendthrift, which is someone who wastes money. He asks her not to squander, which means spending wastefully. When he says, "Supposing I borrowed a thousand crowns today, and you made ducks and drakes of them ..." he means Nora would waste the money, or use it recklessly.

The writer refers to Ibsen's use of elements of drama and then quotes dialogue to show just how the playwright uses the techniques.

Nora does not disagree. Nevertheless, she tries reasoning with Torvald about "wasting" money. She says, "Oh yes, Torvald, do let us squander a little, now—just the least little bit!"

It is the holiday season. Torvald has just taken a new job and will be earning money. Nora wants to spend money in anticipation of having enough, while Torvald wants to wait until his pay increases. The husband's point of view is reasonable. An observer could expect the couple to negotiate a compromise. But Torvald's tone gets in the way of a reasonable discussion. His words belittle Nora. He calls her "my lark," "the squirrel," "my little featherbrain," and "my little spendthrift." These pet names imply that he sees Nora as a little being who is helpless, weak, and incapable of rational thinking. When Nora expresses horror at the thought of his death and says she would not care about creditors, he says, "What a woman you are!"

With organization and logic, the writer makes connections to clarify relationships among ideas.

Again, the writer identifies a literary technique and gives examples that show how Ibsen uses it.

Torvald rejects Nora's suggestion that they go into debt temporarily. As his reason, he says, "you know my principles on these points." His principles are as reasonable as his point of view. Still, when he tells Nora that the two of them have lived up to his principles so far, "and we are not going to give in at the last," it is hard to reconcile this responsible version of Nora with the featherbrain. Ironically, this is when Nora does give in. She says, "Very well—as you please, Torvald," and stops communicating.

The writer shows an understanding of irony in this compact concluding statement. This observation reinforces the claim that was introduced in the first paragraph of this essay.

As you read the following excerpt from a play, apply the close reading strategies you have learned. You may need to read the excerpt multiple times.

from *An Enemy of the People*

by Henrik Ibsen (translated by Rolf Fjelde)

Background At the opening of the play, the future looks good for Dr. Thomas Stockmann's hometown. The town has finally opened a health resort for visitors, who come to drink and bathe in the local water, which is said to have healthful effects. Just when the town is beginning to benefit from the new business, however, Dr. Stockmann makes an alarming discovery. Sewage from a nearby industrial town is polluting the water. As Dr. Stockmann explains to his wife, his oldest child, Petra, and a few friends, the town will have to relocate the pipes that feed the baths in order to prevent the spread of disease. He has sent a report on the problem to his brother Peter, mayor of the town. The next morning, Peter pays him a visit.

Mayor Stockmann. (*Entering from the hall.*) Good morning.

Dr. Stockmann. Good to see you, Peter!

Mrs. Stockmann. Morning, Peter. How's everything with you?

Mayor Stockmann. Just so-so, thank you. (*To the* DOCTOR.) Yesterday, after office hours, I received a report from you, discussing the condition of the water at the baths.

Dr. Stockmann. Yes. Have you read it?

Mayor Stockmann. I have.

Dr. Stockmann. What have you got to say about it?

Mayor Stockmann. (*Glancing at the others.*) Hm—

Mrs. Stockmann. Come along, Petra.

(*She and* PETRA *go into the room on the left.*)

Mayor Stockmann. (*After a moment.*) Was it necessary to press all these investigations behind my back?

Dr. Stockmann. Well, as long as I didn't have absolute proof, then—

Mayor Stockmann. And now you think you do?

Dr. Stockmann. You must be convinced of that yourself.

Mayor Stockmann. Is it your object to put this document before the board of directors by way of an official recommendation?

Dr. Stockmann. Of course. Something has to be done about this. And fast.

Meet the Author

Norwegian playwright **Henrik Ibsen,** born in 1828, left Oslo in 1864 out of frustration with the country's theatrical culture. He spent 27 years writing plays in Italy and Germany. During that time, he gained an international reputation for his work. He died in Oslo in 1906.

CLOSE READING TOOL

Read and respond to this selection online using the **Close Reading Tool.**

Mayor Stockmann. As usual, in your report you let your language get out of hand. You say, among other things, that what we're offering our summer visitors is guaranteed poison.

Dr. Stockmann. But, Peter, how else can you describe it? You've got to realize—this water is poison for internal or external use! And it's foisted on poor, suffering creatures who turn to us in good faith and pay us exorbitant fees to gain their health back again!

Vocabulary ▶
exorbitant (eg zôr′ bi tənt) *adj.* excessive.

Mayor Stockmann. And then you arrive at the conclusion, by your line of reasoning, that we have to build a sewer to drain off these so-called impurities from Mølledal,[1] and that all the water mains have to be relaid.

Dr. Stockmann. Well, do you see any other way out? I don't.

Mayor Stockmann. I invented a little business this morning down at the town engineer's office. And in a half-joking way, I brought up these proposals as something we perhaps ought to take under advisement[2] at some time in the future.

Dr. Stockmann. Some time in the future!

Mayor Stockmann. He smiled at my whimsical extravagance—naturally. Have you gone to the trouble of estimating just what these proposed changes would cost? From the information I received, the expenditure would probably run up into several hundred thousand crowns.[3]

Dr. Stockmann. As high as that?

Mayor Stockmann. Yes. But that's not the worst. The work would extend over at least two years.

Dr. Stockmann. Two years? Two full years?

Mayor Stockmann. At the least. And meanwhile what do we do with the baths? Shut them down? Yes, we'll have to. Do you really think anyone would make the effort to come all the distance here if the rumor got out that the water was contaminated?

Dr. Stockmann. Yes, but Peter, that's what it is.

Mayor Stockmann. And then all this happens now—just now, when the baths were being recognized. Other towns in this area have the same resources for development as health resorts. Don't you think they'll leap at the chance to attract the whole flow of tourists to them? No question of it. And there we are, left stranded. We'll most likely have to abandon the whole costly enterprise; and then you'll have ruined the town you were born in.

Dr. Stockmann. I—ruined—!

---

1. **Mølledal** (möl′ ə däl′) fictional Norwegian town.
2. **to take under advisement** to think over carefully.
3. **crowns** *n.* A crown is the Norwegian unit of currency; krone (krō′ nə).

Mayor Stockmann. It's through the baths alone that this town has any future to speak of. You can see that just as plain as I can.

Dr. Stockmann. But then what do you think ought to be done?

Mayor Stockmann. From your report I'm unable to persuade myself that the condition of the baths is as critical as you claim.

Dr. Stockmann. Look, if anything, it's worse! Or it'll be that by summer, when the warm weather comes.

Mayor Stockmann. Once again. I think you're exaggerating considerably. A capable doctor must know the right steps to take—he should be able to control toxic[4] elements, and to treat them if they make their presence too obvious.

Dr. Stockmann. And then—? What else—?

Mayor Stockmann. The water system for the baths as it now stands is simply a fact and clearly has to be accepted as such. But in time the directors will more than likely agree to take under consideration to what extent—depending on the funds available—they can institute certain improvements.

Dr. Stockmann. And you can think I'd play along with that kind of trickery!

Mayor Stockmann. Trickery?

Dr. Stockmann. Yes, it's a trick—a deception, a lie, an out-and-out crime against the public and society at large!

Mayor Stockmann. As I've already observed, I've not yet persuaded myself that there's any real **impending** danger here.

◀ **Vocabulary**
impending (im pend´ iŋ) *adj.* about to happen.

Dr. Stockmann. Yes, you have! There's no alternative. My report is perfectly accurate, I know that! And you're very much aware of it, Peter, but you won't admit it. You're the one who got the baths and the water system laid out where they are today; and it's *this*—it's this hellish miscalculation that you won't concede. Pah! You don't think I can see right through you?

Mayor Stockmann. And even if it were true? Even if I seem a bit overanxious about my reputation, it's all for the good of the town. Without moral authority I could hardly guide and direct affairs in the way I believe serves the general welfare. For this reason—among many others—it strikes me as imperative[5] that your report not be submitted to the board of directors. It has to be withheld for the common good. Then, later, I'll bring the matter up for discussion, and we'll do the very best we can, as quietly as possible. But nothing—not the slightest word of this catastrophe must leak out to the public.

Dr. Stockmann. My dear Peter, there's no stopping it now.

---

4. **toxic** (täk´ sik) *adj.* poisonous.
5. **imperative** (im per´ ə tiv) *adj.* absolutely necessary; urgent.

Mayor Stockmann. It must and it will be stopped.

Dr. Stockmann. I'm telling you, it's no use. Too many people know already.

Mayor Stockmann. Know already! Who? Not those fellows from the *Courier*—?

Dr. Stockmann. Why, of course they know. The independent liberal press is going to see that you do your duty.

Mayor Stockmann (*After a short pause.*) You're an exceptionally thoughtless man, Thomas. Haven't you considered the consequences that can follow for you?

Dr. Stockmann. Consequences? For me?

Mayor Stockmann. For you and your family as well.

Dr. Stockmann. What the devil does *that* mean?

Mayor Stockmann. I think, over the years, I've proved a helpful and accommodating brother to you.

Dr. Stockmann. Yes, you have, and I'm thankful to you for that.

Mayor Stockmann. I'm not after thanks. Because, in part, I was forced into it—for my own sake. I always hoped I could keep you in check somewhat if I helped better your economic status.

Dr. Stockmann. What? Just for your own sake—!

Mayor Stockmann. In part, I said. It's embarrassing for a public servant when his closest relative goes and compromises himself again and again.

Dr. Stockmann. And that's what you think I do?

Mayor Stockmann. Yes, unfortunately you do, without your knowing it. You have a restless, unruly, combative nature. And then this unhappy knack[6] of bursting into print on all kinds of likely and unlikely subjects. You're no sooner struck by an idea than right away you have to scribble a newspaper article on it, or a whole pamphlet even.

Dr. Stockmann. Well, but isn't it a citizen's duty to inform the public if he comes on a new idea?

Mayor Stockmann. Oh, the public doesn't need new ideas. The public is served best by the good, old, time-tested ideas it's always had.

Dr. Stockmann. That's putting it plainly!

Vocabulary ▶
impetuosity (im pech´ o͞o äs´ i tē) *n.* sudden action with little thought.

Mayor Stockmann. I have to talk to you plainly for once. Up till now I've always tried to avoid that because I know how irritable you are; but now I'm telling you the truth, Thomas. You have no conception how much you injure yourself with your **impetuosity**. You complain about the authorities and, yes, the government; you rail against them—and insist

6. **knack** (nak) *n.* trick; particular skill.

you're being passed over and persecuted. But what can you expect—someone as troublesome as you.

Dr. Stockmann. Ah—so I'm troublesome, too?

Mayor Stockmann. Yes, Thomas, you're a very troublesome man to work with. I know from experience. You show no consideration at all. You seem to forget completely that I'm the one you can thank for your post here as staff physician at the baths—

Dr. Stockmann. I was the inevitable[7] choice—I and nobody else! I was the first to see that this town could become a flourishing spa;[8] and I was the *only* one who could see it then. I stood alone fighting for that idea for years; and I wrote and wrote—

Mayor Stockmann. Unquestionably. But the right moment hadn't arrived yet. Of course you couldn't judge that from up there in the wilds. But when the opportune time came, and I—and a few others—took the matter in hand—

Dr. Stockmann. Yes, and bungled the whole magnificent plan. Oh yes, it's really coming out now what a brilliant crew you've been!

Mayor Stockmann. All that's coming out, to my mind, is your usual hunger for a good fight. You want to attack your superiors—it's your old pattern. You can't stand any authority over you; you resent anyone in a higher position and regard him as a personal enemy—and then one weapon's as good as another to use. But now I've acquainted you with the vital interests at stake here for this whole town—and, naturally, for me as well. And so I'm warning you, Thomas, I'll be **adamant** about the demand I am going to make of you.

◀ **Vocabulary**
adamant (ad´ ə mənt) *adj.* firm.

Dr. Stockmann. What demand?

Mayor Stockmann. Since you've been so indiscreet as to discuss this delicate issue with outsiders, even though it should have been kept secret among the directors, it of course can't be hushed up now. All kinds of rumors will go flying around, and the maliciously inclined will dress them up with trimmings of their own. It'll therefore be necessary that you publicly deny these rumors.

Dr. Stockmann. I! How? I don't understand.

Mayor Stockmann. We can expect that, after further investigation, you'll arrive at the conclusion that things are far from being as critical or dangerous as you'd first imagined.

Dr. Stockmann. Ah—you expect that!

Mayor Stockmann. Moreover, we expect that you'll support and publicly affirm your confidence in the present directors to take thorough and conscientious measures, as necessary, to remedy any possible defects.

---

7. **inevitable** (in ev´ i tə bəl) *adj.* certain to happen; that which cannot be avoided.
8. **spa** (spä) *n.* health resort where people drink and bathe in mineral waters.

Dr. Stockmann. But that's utterly out of the question for me, as long as they try to get by with patchwork. I'm telling you that, Peter; and it's my unqualified opinion—!

Mayor Stockmann. As a member of the staff, you're not entitled to any personal opinions.

Dr. Stockmann. (*Stunned.*) Not entitled—?

Mayor Stockmann. As a staff member, I said. As a private person—why, that's another matter. But as a subordinate official at the baths, you're not entitled to express any opinions that contradict your superiors.

Dr. Stockmann. That's going too far! I, as a doctor, a man of science, aren't entitled to—!

Mayor Stockmann. What's involved here isn't a purely scientific problem. It's a mixture of both technical and economic considerations.

Dr. Stockmann. I don't care what the hell it is! I want the freedom to express myself on any problem under the sun!

Mayor Stockmann. Anything you like—except for the baths. We forbid you that.

Dr. Stockmann (*Shouting.*) You forbid—! You! A crowd of—!

Mayor Stockmann. *I* forbid it—*I*, your supervisor. And when I forbid you, then you obey.

Close Reading Activities

Read

Comprehension: **Key Ideas and Details**

1. **(a)** What problem does Dr. Stockmann report to the mayor? **(b)** What solution does Dr. Stockmann propose? **(c) Summarize:** How does the mayor react to this proposal? Explain.
2. **(a)** What information does the mayor acquire from an engineer about the proposed solution? **(b) Infer:** How does this information contribute to his reaction? Explain.
3. **(a) Draw Conclusions:** What is the mayor's goal with regard to the problem? Explain his reasons. **(b) Connect:** What is the mayor willing to risk to achieve this goal? Explain.
4. **Summarize:** Write a brief, objective summary of the excerpt. Cite specific details from the excerpt in your writing.

Text Analysis: **Craft and Structure**

5. **(a)** Skim the dialogue looking for exclamation marks. Which character's speeches contain more? **(b) Interpret:** What does this suggest about the character's emotions, speech patterns, and overall personality? Explain.
6. **(a)** What event causes the mayor to call his brother "an exceptionally thoughtless man"? **(b) Infer:** What previous experiences and judgments underlie the mayor's statement? Cite specific details.
7. **(a) Compare and Contrast:** How does Dr. Stockmann's description of his own character differ from the mayor's perceptions of him? Explain, citing specific details. **(b) Generalize:** What conflict does this create between the brothers? Explain.
8. **(a) Evaluate:** Which brother does Ibsen present as being more vulnerable? Explain. **(b) Synthesize:** What theme about morality and power is suggested by the situation portrayed in this scene? Explain.

Connections: **Integration of Knowledge and Ideas**

Discuss

Conduct a **small-group discussion** about the tactics the two men use to argue. Do they "fight fair"? Consider how each man describes his own character and compares himself to his sibling.

Research

The economic catastrophe Mayor Stockmann wants to avoid hinges on the town's ability to attract "health tourists" to its waters. Find out what is at stake. Briefly research spas and their popularity in 1880s Europe. In particular, locate the following information:

a. the reasons that people "took the waters" in spa towns
b. the advertised health benefits of mineral springs
c. the impact successful spas had on their local economies

Take notes as you perform your research. Then, write a brief **description** of what visitors to the Stockmanns' town might be seeking from the baths.

Write

Which brother do you think is the real "enemy of the people" of the play's title? Write an **essay** in which you introduce a claim and support it with details from the play. Include specific details about each brother's position on the issue over which they disagree.

To what extent does experience determine what we perceive?

Consider the role their family relationship plays in the argument between the brothers. Are their perceptions of each other as adult men accurate? Explain your answer.

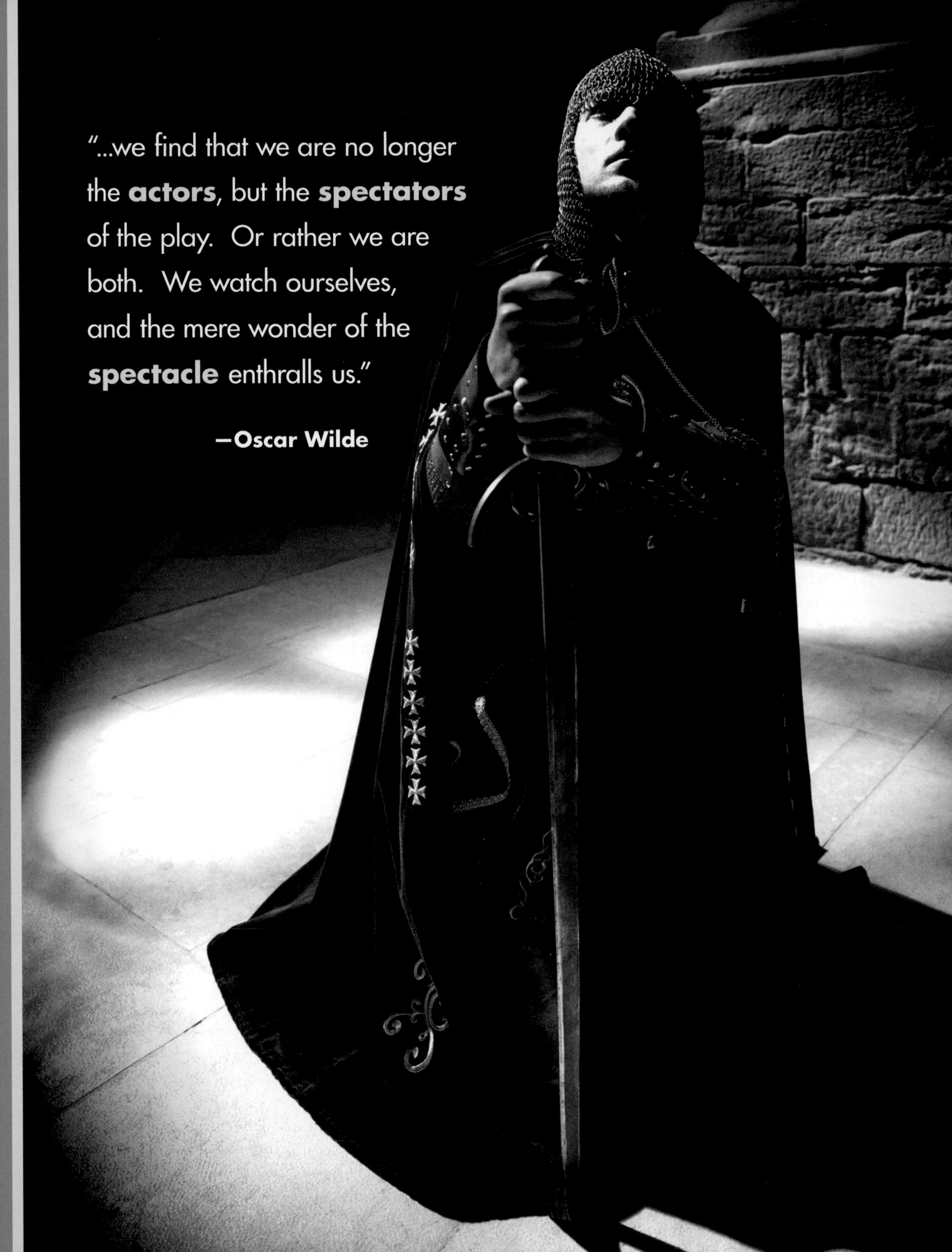

"...we find that we are no longer the **actors**, but the **spectators** of the play. Or rather we are both. We watch ourselves, and the mere wonder of the **spectacle** enthralls us."

—Oscar Wilde

PART 2

TEXT ANALYSIS GUIDED EXPLORATION

TRAGEDY AND SPECTACLE

If a drama is successful, we relate to the struggles and triumphs of the characters whose lives unfold before our eyes. Those lives may be very different from our own, but through the spectacle of the play we understand them. In Shakespeare's *The Tragedy of Julius Caesar,* the title character is a military leader, and other key characters are people of power. However, one need not be a general or person of noble birth to understand the conflicts these characters face. As you read the play, consider the truths it explores about human nature, including our struggles over power, identity, dignity, and honor.

◀ CRITICAL VIEWING What does this image suggest about drama as a vehicle for powerful emotional and artistic expression?

READINGS IN PART 2

CLOSE READING TOOL

Use the **Close Reading Tool** to practice the strategies you learn in this unit.

Focus on Craft and Structure

Elements of Drama

Drama is **storytelling** brought to life through **performance.**

Drama is a story that is written as a script and intended for performance by actors.

Like other narratives, a drama portrays characters caught up in conflict. The struggles that characters face in a drama spark a sequence of events, called the **plot,** which eventually reaches a **climax,** the point of highest intensity in the action. The **resolution,** or settling of the conflict, allows the story to wind down and leads to the drama's conclusion.

Character and conflict work together in a drama, or play, to engage readers or viewers. As events unfold, characters react and change, revealing their personalities and motives.

In performance, the various elements of drama combine to produce the illusion of reality known as **dramatic effect.** Through this effect, the author, or **playwright,** explores a **theme**—an insight or a message about life. The example in the next column explains how elements in a play create dramatic effect.

Example: Dramatic Effect

In *The Tragedy of Romeo and Juliet*, two lovers cannot marry because their families are sworn enemies. The play retains its dramatic effect, even centuries after it was first performed, because its key ideas are timeless. The **characters** of two people in love, the **conflict** of circumstances that keep the lovers apart, and **themes** about the power, difficulties, and danger of love, are concepts that still have relevance in the modern world.

A playwright divides a **script** into basic units called **acts.** Within acts, there may be further divisions known as **scenes.** Scenes often serve to shift the action's setting or time or to introduce new characters. Characters' speech is called **dialogue,** and notes in the script on how the play should be performed are called **stage directions.** The chart below further defines and explains these basic elements of drama.

The Elements of Drama

Acts and Scenes	Acts and scenes are the basic divisions of drama. Dramas may contain a varying number of acts, each of which may contain a number of scenes.
Stage Directions	Stage directions are notes that tell how a play should be performed or staged. They may appear in italics or be set off by brackets or parentheses. Stage directions may include the following information: • Background about the setting or characters • Instructions that tell how actors should move and speak • Abbreviations such as *O.S.* (offstage), *D.S.* (downstage, or closer to the audience), and *U.S.* (upstage, or farther from the audience) • Details about scenery, lighting, and costumes
Sets	Sets define the area in which the play's action occurs. They include the physical elements placed on the stage. A set may be realistic and look like an actual place, or it may be more abstract.
Props	A prop is a movable object, such as a book, a pen, or a flashlight. Props add realism to the action in a play.

Dramatic Forms

The ancient Greeks, who developed drama as an organized literary form, created two basic types of plays. These broad categories still define drama today.

Tragedy

A **tragedy** traces the downfall of the main character, or **protagonist,** who is often called the **tragic hero.**

- In classic drama, the tragic hero is an important person, such as a general or a king.
- The hero is admirable but is defeated by a **tragic flaw,** a mistake or character defect.

Comedy

A **comedy** has a happy ending for the protagonist.

- Comedies often feature events in which the world's order or balance is disrupted.
- The ending restores order and may reward the hero.

Comedies are often funny, but they can make a serious point. The main distinction between tragedy and comedy is how the story ends: Tragedies end in death, defeat, or exile; comedies end in weddings or other joyful events.

Dramatic Structures Classic dramas, such as most ancient Greek and Shakespearean works, take place in five acts and thus are called **five-act plays.** The acts typically follow this plot structure:

Act 1: introduction/exposition;
Act 2: rising action;
Act 3: climax;
Act 4: falling action;
Act 5: resolution.

In most dramatic works, the five segments of plot are compressed into fewer acts. Many **screenplays, teleplays,** and **operas** are framed in three acts. Act 1 introduces main characters and sets the conflict in motion. Act 2 escalates the conflict and increases tension for the protagonist. Act 3 takes the conflict to a climax and reveals the outcome in a resolution.

Shorter dramatic works may consist of only a single act. **One-act plays** may be divided into several scenes.

Dramatic Dialogue In most dramatic works, dialogue is the playwright's main tool. Many ancient Greek plays also employ the convention of the **chorus,** a group of actors onstage who observe the action but do not participate in it. The members of the chorus would most often sing their lines, but sometimes their lines were spoken aloud in unison instead. The chorus provides background information and reacts to events. Some modern plays feature a chorus.

In other modern dramas, a **narrator** may replace the chorus. In certain films, for example, the voice of an unseen narrator may introduce the story, set up a scene, or tell viewers about a character.

Playwrights may use other types of dramatic speeches to advance plot and reveal character.

- A **monologue** is a long speech that one character delivers to other characters onstage.
- A **soliloquy** is a speech in which a character, alone on stage, "thinks aloud," revealing private thoughts.
- An **aside** is a remark that a character makes to the audience but that other characters do not hear.

Reading Literature

3. Analyze how complex characters develop over the course of a text, interact with other characters, and advance the plot or develop the theme.

Analyzing Complex Characters

The ways in which **complex characters** react to **conflict** help develop the **theme** in a dramatic work.

Characters in Conflict

In both tragedies and comedies, characters face **conflict,** a struggle between opposing forces. There are two main types of conflict:

- **External Conflict:** An external conflict is a struggle against an outside force, such as nature, another character, or the pressures of society. For example, a character who faces pressure from bullies at school experiences an external conflict.
- **Internal Conflict:** An internal conflict is a struggle within the mind of a character. For example, a character who struggles with his desire to support his family while following his dream to become an actor experiences an internal conflict.

The most interesting dramatic works feature conflicts that engage the audience. For tragic characters, the conflict may be life threatening. For comedic characters, the threat may be perceived. For example, a character in a romantic comedy may think that a coworker is trying to win over the woman he loves, when in reality, the coworker is not interested in the woman.

Protagonist and Antagonist Most plays and movies focus on a single main character—the **protagonist.** The character who opposes the main character and either creates or intensifies the conflict is called the **antagonist.**

Characterization and Motivation Through the use of **characterization**—the dialogue and actions that reveal a character's personality—a playwright provides clues about the human qualities of a character as well as clues about the character's **motivation,** or reasons for behaving a certain way. It is up to the reader or audience to infer what these clues mean.

Clues	Motivation
A young, thin boy eyes a loaf of bread; then he steals it.	The child is hungry.
A policeman detains the child; then he lets him go.	The policeman feels sorry for the child.

Complex Characters Great dramas present interesting protagonists and antagonists. Such characters are referred to as *complex*, which means they have strengths and weaknesses and experience mixed emotions. Complex characters have **multiple motivations,** or a variety of reasons for behaving as they do. In literary terms, complex characters are **round,** rather than flat, and **dynamic,** rather than static. **Flat** or **static** characters often represent stereotypes and do not change or develop over the course of a play. The arch-villain and the selfless best friend are two examples of flat or static characters.

Complex Characters	Limited Characters
• **Round:** multidimensional; possess more than one motivation; display many qualities, including strengths and weaknesses • **Dynamic:** undergo change during the course of play; grow in terms of improvement or self-realization	• **Flat:** one-dimensional; have only one motivation; display only one quality or trait • **Static:** remain the same throughout the play; resist or are unable to adjust to changing circumstances

Complex Characters and Theme

In the most compelling dramas, complex characters change or grow as the result of their responses to internal or external conflicts. In portraying such journeys of transformation, a playwright tries to bring insight to aspects of the human condition—and ultimately reveals a message about life that audiences can understand and appreciate. That message is the **theme.**

Character Development In any work of literature, a writer uses the tools of character development, or **characterization,** to create characters and reveal their personality traits.

In **direct characterization,** a writer directly states a character's traits. A playwright might use stage directions, a chorus, a narrator, or another character to convey information that tells what a character is like.

Example: Direct Characterization

RAFAEL. Yo! Mauricio! Where you going, man? Get back here! *[turns to face audience]* I hate to say it, but you just can't trust Mauricio. He is the most unreliable man you will ever meet. Whenever you need him, he just disappears.

In **indirect characterization,** a writer shows what a character is like in any of these ways:

- Descriptions of a character's physical appearance;
- The character's own words;
- The character's actions and behavior;
- Other characters' reactions to the character.

An actor brings a character to life on the stage or in a movie by using his or her voice, facial expressions, and gestures, as well as the pitch, pacing, and phrasing of his or her speech. Actors work under the guidance of the director, the interpreter and manager of the creative aspects of a dramatic or film production. Costumes, sets, and props also help emphasize elements of a character's personality.

Reading Drama

Actors speak the words in a script and breathe life into them. When you read a drama, make the play come alive by using textual clues to understand characters' motivations, feelings, actions, and thoughts. As you read, picture details of the performance.

To read a play effectively, look at dialogue, stage directions, punctuation, and word choice. In these elements, you will find clues about a character's emotions, relationships, social class, education, and environment.

Example: Characterization in Drama

Stage Directions Suggesting Attitude: *[Yuki lifts her cup and sips loudly, eyes glaring.]*

Punctuation Showing Emotion: STANLEY. I don't buy your act. Not for one minute!

Dialogue Suggesting Social/Economic Class: JASON. I have a social engagement this afternoon. I don't have time to deal with this. Where's my butler? *[Calls out]* Edward, get in here!

Word Choice Revealing Traits or Qualities: MANUELITO. Lucy is a ridiculous creature. She's insufferable!

Dramatic Speeches Through monologues, soliloquies, and asides, playwrights provide critical clues to characters' motivations and actions. These dramatic speeches help propel the plot because they explain why characters do what they do. In addition, these speeches may express ideas that are key to the play's theme. For example, in a monologue or soliloquy, a character can explain what he or she thinks and feels. The audience learns about the character's conflicts and even his or her secrets.

Analyzing all the details a playwright provides through a complex character's words and actions will lead you to fully appreciate a drama and understand its deeper meaning.

Preparing to Read *The Tragedy of Julius Caesar*

William Shakespeare wrote masterpieces of drama and poetry during an extraordinary era in English history.

▲ Elizabeth I was crowned at the age of 25. This painting by Italian artist Federico Zuccaro is one of hundreds of portraits made of the queen during her reign.

Historical Background: Elizabethan England

A Golden Age Queen Elizabeth I came to the throne following a tumultuous period in English history. During the reign of her father, King Henry VIII, thousands of people had been executed. Warfare had been frequent, and the royal treasury was drained. The brief reigns of Elizabeth's half-brother Edward and half-sister Mary were equally stormy. Elizabeth, by contrast, proved to be a strong and successful ruler, frugal with money and popular with her people. Her long reign (1558–1603) is often seen as a golden age in English history. The relative stability that Elizabeth created allowed commerce and culture to thrive.

The Renaissance Elizabeth ruled toward the end of a flowering of European learning known as the Renaissance **(ren′ ə sans′)**. The Renaissance began in Florence and other Italian city-states around 1350, and then spread throughout Europe. The word "renaissance" means "rebirth," and the era saw renewed interest in the arts and sciences that hearkened back to ancient Greece and Rome. The cultural pursuit of art and learning had diminished in Western Europe after the fall of the Roman Empire. Influenced by the achievements of the ancients, Renaissance writers and architects created new forms and designs that emphasized individual human expression. Painters and sculptors studied ancient Greek and Roman art to explore a new focus on the human form. Philosophers and religious reformers challenged old ideas, as did scientists who strove to unlock the hidden secrets of the natural world. With new knowledge of the skies, navigators sailed the globe, expanding trade and exploring distant lands.

Sixteenth-Century English Monarchs

King Henry VIII ruled from **1509 to 1547**

King Edward VI ruled from **1547 to 1553**

Queen Mary ruled from **1553 to 1558**

Queen Elizabeth I ruled from **1558 to 1603**

The Great Chain of Being

In *Shakespeare Alive,* Joseph Papp, founder of the New York Shakespeare Festival, and his co-author Elizabeth Kirkland explain how Shakespeare and his audience viewed nature and society:

In the heavenly kingdom . . . several levels of archangels and angels spread downwards from God's throne, and each level knew its place. . . . The universe was a hierarchy too, and each planet and star was assigned to a specific position... The animal world was another very stratified society in which each species had its king: the eagle was the king of birds; the whale was the king of fish; and the lion, of course, was king of beasts.

The Great Chain of Being, stretching from the lowliest creature in the natural world all the way up to God, connected these worlds to each other, and the hierarchy of one was mirrored in the others. . . . Since all living things were linked by the Great Chain of Being, violations of order in society were thought to set off violent disturbances in the heavens or the world of nature. . . .In *Julius Caesar* [Act I, Scene iii], strange and terrible goings-on are reported in Rome as the conspirators hatch an assassination plot against the emperor. . .

The English Renaissance Elizabeth I encouraged commercial enterprise and the efforts of English navigators, such as Sir Walter Raleigh, who tried to establish a colony in Virginia, and Sir Francis Drake, who sailed around the globe. Profiting particularly from the wool trade, a strong merchant class developed in England, narrowing the gap between rich and poor. London, with nearly 200,000 people, became Europe's largest city. It was a bustling if dirty cultural and political capital that attracted newcomers from overseas as well as from the English countryside. In 1588, the English army defeated the Spanish Armada, a fleet of warships sent by King Philip II of Spain to invade England. The victory contributed to Elizabeth's legend as well as to the country's sense of national pride. It also set England firmly on the path to becoming ruler of the seas.

Elizabeth's reign was not only remarkable for its commercial and military successes. Indeed, her court was a center for musicians and artists, both Continental and native born. The philosopher Sir Francis Bacon, who pioneered the informal essay as a literary form, became an unofficial member of the queen's group of advisers. Sir Philip Sidney, a popular courtier and diplomat, wrote a series of love sonnets that were much imitated. The poet Edmund Spenser wrote an adventure-packed epic called *The Faerie Queene* that he dedicated to Queen Elizabeth. The greatest Elizabethan literature, however, was written for the stage. The greatest of these voices were the playwrights Christopher Marlowe, Ben Jonson, and—greatest of them all—William Shakespeare.

A *sonnet,* from the Italian for "little song," is a fourteen-line poem originally developed in Italy. Sidney's sonnets ushered in a sonnet-writing craze: Edmund Spenser, William Shakespeare, and just about every other Elizabethan poet produced a *sonnet sequence,* or series.

The Concern for Stability Elizabeth's father, King Henry VIII, had married six times. He divorced three of his wives and executed two others, including Elizabeth's mother, Anne Boleyn. Queen Mary, Elizabeth's half-sister, infuriated the nation by wedding Phillip II of Spain, who abandoned her soon afterward. Perhaps because of these examples, or perhaps because she worried about sharing power, Elizabeth I never married. By the late 1590s, when Shakespeare wrote *The Tragedy of Julius Caesar,* she was quite advanced in years, and many were concerned about the nation's stability after her death. That concern is echoed in several of Shakespeare's plays, including *Julius Caesar*.

Theater in Elizabethan England

London theaters drew crowds that are large even by today's standards.

▲ This image from the late sixteenth century shows the Globe theater as the audience arrives for a performance.

During the Elizabethan era, the religious plays of the Middle Ages gave way to English tragedies and comedies modeled on those of ancient Greece and Rome. Scholars at Oxford and Cambridge universities studied and translated the ancient plays into English. The first great Elizabethan playwrights attended those universities, which is why they are sometimes called the University Wits. The most prominent of the Wits, Christopher Marlowe, pioneered the use of blank verse in drama. (For more on blank verse, see p. 568.)

For a time, Elizabethan acting companies still traveled the countryside as their medieval counterparts had done. They performed at festivals, inns, and castles. Gradually, however, the better acting companies acquired noble patrons, or sponsors, and began staging private performances in their patrons' homes. They also gave performances at court, where elaborate masques—productions featuring singing and dancing—were especially popular.

From the Theatre to the Globe England's first public theater opened in 1576. Known simply as the Theatre, it was built by the actor James Burbage, whose company would later attract the young William Shakespeare. Since the performance of plays was banned in London proper, Burbage built the Theatre just outside the city walls. When its lease expired, Richard Burbage, who took charge of the company after his father's death, decided to move operations to Southwark **(suth′ ərk)**, just south across the River Thames **(temz)** from London. He built a new theater, called the Globe, which opened in 1599. Shakespeare's first play to be performed there was probably *The Tragedy of Julius Caesar.*

Theater Structure England's first theaters were two- to three-story structures with a central space open to the sky. The open space was surrounded by enclosed seating in two or three tiers, or galleries, that faced inward. On the ground floor, a stage projected into an area called the pit. Audience members called groundlings paid a small fee to stand in the pit and watch the play. Wealthier audience members, including aristocrats, occupied the more expensive sheltered gallery seats. Since artificial light was not used, performances generally took place in the afternoon. Audiences were boisterous, cheering and booing loudly. Most theaters could hold up to 3,000 people and drew the largest crowds on holidays.

Theater Stagecraft The portion of the building behind the stage was used to mount the production. This area included dressing rooms, storage rooms, and waiting areas from which actors could enter and exit the stage. The second-level gallery directly above the stage served as a performance space. There was no scenery; instead, settings were communicated through dialogue. Special effects were very simple—smoke might accompany a battle scene, for example. Actors playing members of the nobility or royalty wore elegant clothes. These were not really costumes as we think of them today, but simply the same types of clothing worn by high-ranking Elizabethans. Since acting was not considered proper for women, female roles were played by boys of about eleven or twelve, before their voices changed. Given the constraints of the era's stagecraft, the productions were unrealistic by modern standards. However, they were also fast-paced, colorful, and highly entertaining.

The upper stage could be used for particular scenes, or to stage a scene with actors on two levels. It was also the seating area for musicians, an important part of many productions. Several of Shakespeare's plays, particularly the comedies, contain songs.

The Blackfriars In 1609, Shakespeare's company, the King's Men, began staging plays at an indoor theater called the Blackfriars. They still used the Globe during the summer months. The Blackfriars was one of the first English theaters to include artificial lighting, which enabled nighttime performances. Designed to appeal to wealthy patrons only, the Blackfriars did not have inexpensive seats or a space set aside for groundlings. Indoor theaters of this sort, attracting a fashionable crowd, would become the norm in centuries to come.

▼ Shakespeare's Globe, a reconstruction of the original theater, was completed in 1997 near the site of the original building. The modern convenience of artificial lighting allows for nighttime performances, such as the one shown in the photo.

Meet the Author

William Shakespeare (1564–1616)

Unlike other famed writers of his time, William Shakespeare was neither a lofty aristocrat nor a university scholar. Nevertheless, he is widely regarded as the greatest writer in the English language.

"What's Past Is Prologue" Shakespeare was born in Stratford-upon-Avon, a market town on the Avon River about seventy-five miles northwest of London. His father, John, was a successful glove maker who served for a time as town mayor. His mother, born Mary Arden, was the daughter of a wealthy farmer who owned the land on which John Shakespeare's father lived. Although the records have been lost, it is believed that Shakespeare attended the Stratford Grammar School, where he would have studied logic, history, Latin grammar, some Greek, and works by the Roman poets Ovid, Horace, and Virgil and Roman playwrights Plautus and Terence. When he left school, he would thus have had a solid foundation in classical literature.

"All the World's a Stage" In 1582, when he was eighteen, Shakespeare married a woman named Anne Hathaway, who was twenty-six. The couple had a daughter, Susanna, in 1583 and twins, Judith and Hamnet, two years later. No one knows what Shakespeare did for the next several years, but in the early 1590s his name began to appear in the world of the London theater. Working first as an actor, Shakespeare soon began writing plays. By 1594, he was part owner and principal playwright of the Lord Chamberlain's Men, the acting company run by the Burbages. As the leading actor in most of Shakespeare's plays, Richard Burbage was also becoming famous. Soon he decided to move the company to the new theater district in Southwark. There, Burbage oversaw the construction of the Globe theater, which was larger than the company's old home in London. With bigger audiences, profits increased for Burbage, Shakespeare, and all the other co-owners.

The Lord Chamberlain's Men was named for its sponsors, first Henry Carey, Lord Hunsdon, and then his son George. Both men served in the high government post of Lord Chamberlain. After Queen Elizabeth I died in 1603, her successor, James I, became the company's patron. In his honor, the company changed its name to the King's Men.

"Parting Is Such Sweet Sorrow" In 1609, the King's Men began to perform year-round, using the Globe theater in summer and the Blackfriars during the colder months. Profits increased even more, and about a year later Shakespeare was able to retire. He returned to his childhood home of Stratford, where he bought the second-largest house in town, invested in land, and continued to write. Shakespeare died in 1616, leaving the bulk of his estate to his elder daughter, Susanna, and a smaller sum to Judith. (Hamnet had died in 1596.)

Shakespeare's Influence

Nearly four hundred years after his death, William Shakespeare remains the most influential writer in the English language. His characters are known by name around the world. Filmmakers, painters, novelists, and composers reuse his plots, and phrases he coined still slip into daily conversation. You have probably quoted Shakespeare without even knowing it. Here are just a few examples of expressions made famous in his plays.

All the world's a stage. *(As You Like It)*
Brave new world *(The Tempest)*
Brevity is the soul of wit. *(Hamlet)*
Come full circle *(King Lear)*
Dish fit for the gods *(Julius Caesar)*
A foregone conclusion *(Othello)*
It was Greek to me. *(Julius Caesar)*
Lend me your ears. *(Julius Caesar)*
Loved not wisely, but too well *(Othello)*
More sinned against than sinning *(King Lear)*
Neither a borrower nor a lender be. *(Hamlet)*
Parting is such sweet sorrow. *(Romeo and Juliet)*
Strange bedfellows *(The Tempest)*
Throw cold water on it. *(The Merry Wives of Windsor)*
Too much of a good thing *(As You Like It)*
What's past is prologue. *(The Tempest)*

The Authorship Question

Because the documentary evidence of Shakespeare's life is slim and his roots fairly humble, some have questioned whether he really wrote the plays with which he is credited. Shakespeare scholars believe that the surviving texts of the plays were edited and that a few late plays even had co-authors, but nearly all dismiss the notion that Shakespeare did not write them. Nevertheless, the theories persist. Several suggest that Will Shakespeare, actor and Burbage business partner, served as a front for some high-born person (the Earl of Oxford, the Countess of Pembroke, and so on). Some theories center around philosopher and essayist Sir Francis Bacon as the true author—ignoring the fact that Bacon's writing style is completely different from Shakespeare's. The most interesting theories surround the playwright Christopher Marlowe, who was killed in a tavern brawl in 1593. According to these theories, Marlowe used Shakespeare as a front after faking his own death to escape retribution for blasphemous writings or his career as a government spy.

Background for the Play

A Noble Roman

William Shakespeare may be the most famous person ever to write in England, but Julius Caesar, Roman general and statesman, was one of the first ever to write about it. In his account of his military exploits in Gaul (modern-day France and Belgium), Caesar describes the island of Britain and its inhabitants. Caesar invaded the island twice, in 55 and 54 B.C., but he did not remain there long. About a century later, however, the Romans returned to make the area of Britain that we now call England an outpost of their empire. The land remained in Roman hands until about A.D. 400, when the empire was collapsing and Roman troops were called home to defend their capital. As part of English history, Julius Caesar and ancient Rome were of particular interest to English writers and audiences.

Rome in Caesar's Day Since about 509 B.C., Rome had been a republic, a society ruled by a democratically elected government. Two public officials called consuls shared governing authority with the Senate and the Assemblies. Members of the Senate were high-born Romans called patricians, while members of the Assemblies were low-born Romans called plebeians (plē bē′ ənz). By the era of Julius Caesar (100–44 B.C.), Rome controlled a great empire through military expansion. However, the popularity of military leaders threatened the balance of power, and civil war became common. When a general named Pompey tried to make himself sole consul, another popular general, Julius Caesar, defeated him. As Shakespeare's play opens, all of Rome wonders whether Caesar will appoint himself emperor, thus ending the republic.

From the name Caesar come the German word *kaiser* and the Russian word *czar*, both meaning "emperor." From Julius Caesar's first name comes *July*, our word for the month named in Julius Caesar's honor.

Plutarch, Shakespeare's Source

Shakespeare's source for *The Tragedy of Julius Caesar* was *The Lives of the Noble Grecians and Romans,* Sir Thomas North's 1579 English translation of a book by the Greek philosopher Plutarch (**plōō´ tärk´**). Written late in the first century, Plutarch's *Lives* included literary sketches of Julius Caesar, Marcus Brutus, and Marcus Antonius (Mark Antony), who had lived just over a century earlier. Plutarch researched his information carefully, although he focused less on historical facts than on the personalities of his subjects. Shakespeare based his plot on the events Plutarch describes, but he condensed the timeline and added dramatic elements. For example, Plutarch writes that Antonius gave a funeral oration that stirred the common people to compassion and rage; Shakespeare did not know what Mark Antony actually said, but he gives us the speech as he imagined it.

The Play Through the Centuries

Often cited as Shakespeare's first great tragedy, *The Tragedy of Julius Caesar* has been drawing crowds ever since its premiere at the Globe Theatre in 1599. In 1916, to commemorate the three-hundredth anniversary of Shakespeare's death, a famous outdoor production was staged in the Hollywood hills, starring Douglas Fairbanks, Sr., and Tyrone Power. Students from area high schools reenacted the battle scenes. Just before World War II, Orson Welles produced a controversial adaptation that likened Caesar to Italian dictator Benito Mussolini. In 2005, a production starring Denzel Washington was mounted on Broadway. Ironically, this play about assassination is also one of the few in which Abraham Lincoln's assassin, John Wilkes Booth, performed. In an 1864 production, Booth played the role of Mark Antony.

Building Knowledge

To what extent does experience determine what we perceive?

Explore the Big Question as you read *The Tragedy of Julius Caesar,* Act I. Take notes on how both the nobility and the common people perceive Caesar.

CLOSE READING FOCUS

Key Ideas and Details: **Use Text Aids**

Because they were written in the sixteenth and seventeenth centuries, Shakespeare's plays contain unfamiliar language and references. When reading Shakespearean drama, **use text aids**.

- Review the list of dramatis personae (the cast of characters).
- Read the background information provided (pp. 536–543).
- As you read the play, consult the notes, called **glosses,** beside the text. These notes define words and explain references.

Craft and Structure: **Shakespeare's Tragedies**

Shakespeare's tragedies are dramatic works that portray a reversal of fortune, from good to bad, experienced by a noble character. Shakespeare's tragedies also have these distinctive features:

- They are sometimes based on historical figures.
- The main character displays a **tragic flaw,** a quality that contributes to his or her downfall.
- The drama emphasizes the tragic hero's internal conflict. In an **external conflict,** a character struggles against an outside force, such as another character, fate, nature, or society. In an **internal conflict**, a character battles with his or her opposing emotions.
- Commoners often provide **comic relief** in humorous scenes that serve as a break from the intense emotions of the play.

Shakespeare's plays are structured in five acts. In his tragedies, the **crisis**—the turning point that determines how the play will end—occurs in Act III. The **climax,** or point of greatest emotional intensity, often occurs in Act V, when the **catastrophe,** or disaster, befalls the hero.

Vocabulary

You will encounter the following words in this selection. Which are adjectives? Explain how you know.

replication	**servile**	**spare**
infirmity	**portentous**	**prodigious**

Common Core State Standards

Reading Literature

1. Cite strong and thorough textual evidence to support analysis of what the text says explicitly as well as inferences drawn from the text.

3. Analyze how complex characters develop over the course of a text, interact with other characters, and advance the plot or develop the theme.

5. Analyze how an author's choices concerning how to structure a text, order events within it, and manipulate time create such effects as mystery, tension, or surprise.

10. Read and comprehend literature, including stories, dramas, and poems, independently and proficiently.

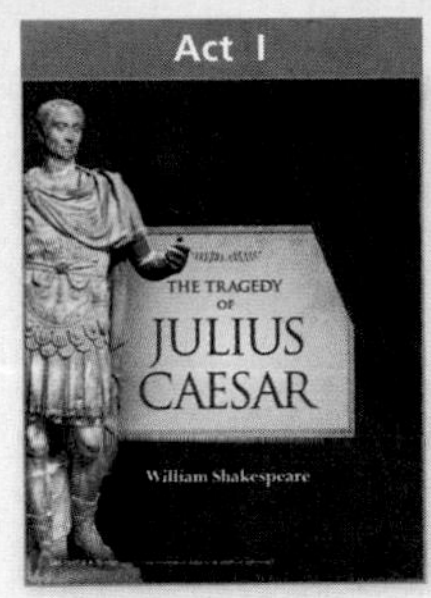

CLOSE READING MODEL

The passage below is from *The Tragedy of Julius Caesar,* Act I. The annotations to the right of the passage show ways in which you can use close reading strategies and text aids to analyze Shakespearean tragedy.

from *The Tragedy of Julius Caesar,* Act I

CHARACTERS

MARCUS BRUTUS, CASSIUS, CASCA[1] → Conspirators Against Julius Caesar

Casca. … I saw Mark Antony offer him a crown—yet 'twas not a crown neither, 'twas one of these coronets—and, as I told you, he put it by once; but for all that, to my thinking, he would fain have had it.[2] Then he offered it to him again; then he put it by again; but to my thinking, he was very loath to lay his fingers off it. And then he offered it the third time. He put it the third time by; and still as he refused it, the rabblement hooted, and clapped their chopt hands, and threw up their sweaty nightcaps, and uttered such a deal of stinking breath because Caesar refused the crown,[3] that it had, almost, choked Caesar; for he swounded and fell down at it. And for mine own part, I durst not laugh, for fear of opening my lips and receiving the bad air.

Cassius. But, soft, I pray you; what, did Caesar swound?

Casca. He fell down in the market place, and foamed at mouth, and was speechless.

Brutus. 'Tis very like he hath the falling-sickness.

Use Text Aids

1 The list of characters identifies Brutus, Cassius, and Casca as being among the conspirators against Julius Caesar, Rome's famous leader. This information will help you understand that the dialogue the three men share is secretive and that their tone is sinister.

Shakespeare's Tragedies

2 Casca notes that Julius Caesar was tempted by Marc Antony's offer of a crown, yet he refused to accept it. This hints at an internal conflict Caesar may be experiencing—a desire for power and a reluctance to assume that power.

Shakespeare's Tragedies

3 In Shakespeare's plays, common people often appear as supporting characters. In this scene Casca, one of the noble conspirators, reveals his distaste for the commoners, describing them as "rabblement" (rabble) that have "chopt (chapped) hands," "sweaty nightcaps," and "stinking breath." Despite Casca's disdain for the common people, their adoration of Caesar and his affection for them is part of the play's central conflict.

THE TRAGEDY OF JULIUS CAESAR

William Shakespeare

CHARACTERS

JULIUS CAESAR	
OCTAVIUS CAESAR, MARCUS ANTONIUS, M. AEMILIUS LEPIDUS	Triumvirs* After the Death of Julius Caesar
CICERO, PUBLIUS, POPILIUS LENA	Senators
MARCUS BRUTUS, CASSIUS, CASCA, TREBONIUS, LIGARIUS, DECIUS BRUTUS, METELLUS CIMBER, CINNA	Conspirators Against Julius Caesar
FLAVIUS, MARULLUS	Tribunes
ARTEMIDORUS OF CNIDOS	Teacher of Rhetoric
CINNA, ANOTHER POET	Poets
LUCILIUS, TITINIUS, MESSALA, YOUNG CATO, VOLUMNIUS	Friends to Brutus and Cassius
VARRO, CLITUS, CLAUDIUS, STRATO, LUCIUS, DARDANIUS	Servants to Brutus
PINDARUS	Servant to Cassius
CALPURNIA	Wife of Caesar
PORTIA	Wife of Brutus
SOOTHSAYER	
SENATORS, CITIZENS, GUARDS, ATTENDANTS, AND SO ON	

Scene: During most of the play, at Rome; afterward near Sardis, and near Philippi.

***Triumvirs** (trī um′ virz) *n.* in ancient Rome, a group of three leaders who shared power equally.

ACT I

Scene i. Rome. A street.

[*Enter* FLAVIUS, MARULLUS, *and certain* COMMONERS[1] *over the stage.*]

FLAVIUS. Hence! Home, you idle creatures, get you home!
Is this a holiday? What, know you not,
Being mechanical,[2] you ought not walk
Upon a laboring day without the sign
Of your profession?[3] Speak, what trade art thou?

CARPENTER. Why, sir, a carpenter.

MARULLUS. Where is thy leather apron and thy rule?
What dost thou with thy best apparel on?
You, sir, what trade are you?

COBBLER. Truly, sir, in respect of a fine workman,[4] I am but, as you would say, a cobbler.[5]

1. COMMONERS (kam′ ən ərz) *n.* people not of the nobility or upper classes.
2. **mechanical** of the working class.
3. **sign/Of your profession** work clothes and tools.
4. **in respect of a fine workman** in relation to a skilled worker.
5. **cobbler** (a pun) "mender of shoes" or "a clumsy, bungling worker."

Comprehension
What fact about the commoners attracts Flavius' attention?

6. **knave** (nāv) *n.* tricky rascal; rogue.
7. **be not out . . . if you be out** be not angry . . . if you have worn-out shoes.
8. **mend you** (a pun) "mend your shoes" or "improve your disposition."

Use Text Aids
Explain how glosses 7 and 8 help you to understand Marullus' reaction in lines 19–20.

9. **awl** (ôl) *n.* small, pointed tool for making holes in leather.
10. **withal** (wi*th* ôl′) *adv.* nevertheless (also a pun on "with awl").
11. **neat's leather** leather made from the hides of cattle.
12. **triumph** (trī′ əmf) *n.* procession celebrating the return of a victorious general.
13. **tributaries** (trib′ yo͞o ter′ ēz) *n.* captives.
14. **Pompey** (päm′ pē) a Roman general and triumvir defeated by Caesar in 48 B.C. and later murdered.
15. **Tiber** (tī′ bər) river that flows through Rome.
16. **concave shores** hollowed-out banks; overhanging banks.
17. **cull out** pick out; select.

Vocabulary ▶
replication (rep′ li kā′ shən) *n.* duplicate; reproduction

Critical Viewing ▶
Judging from this Roman painting, how might the characters be dressed? Explain.

MARULLUS. But what trade art thou? Answer me directly.

COBBLER. A trade, sir, that, I hope, I may use with a safe conscience, which is indeed, sir, a mender of bad soles.

FLAVIUS. What trade, thou knave?[6] Thou naughty knave, what trade?

COBBLER. Nay, I beseech you, sir, be not out with me: yet, if you be out,[7] sir, I can mend you.[8]

MARULLUS. What mean'st thou by that? Mend me, thou saucy fellow?

COBBLER. Why, sir, cobble you.

FLAVIUS. Thou art a cobbler, art thou?

COBBLER. Truly, sir, all that I live by is with the awl:[9] I meddle with no tradesman's matters, nor women's matters; but withal,[10] I am indeed, sir, a surgeon to old shoes: when they are in great danger, I recover them. As proper men as ever trod upon neat's leather[11] have gone upon my handiwork.

FLAVIUS. But wherefore art not in thy shop today?
Why dost thou lead these men about the streets?

COBBLER. Truly, sir, to wear out their shoes, to get myself into more work. But indeed, sir, we make holiday to see Caesar and to rejoice in his triumph.[12]

MARULLUS. Wherefore rejoice? What conquest brings he home?
What tributaries[13] follow him to Rome,
To grace in captive bonds his chariot wheels?
You blocks, you stones, you worse than senseless things!
O you hard hearts, you cruel men of Rome,
Knew you not Pompey?[14] Many a time and oft
Have you climbed up to walls and battlements,
To tow'rs and windows, yea, to chimney tops,
Your infants in your arms, and there have sat
The livelong day, with patient expectation,
To see great Pompey pass the streets of Rome.
And when you saw his chariot but appear,
Have you not made an universal shout,
That Tiber[15] trembled underneath her banks
To hear the **replication** of your sounds
Made in her concave shores?[16]
And do you now put on your best attire?
And do you now cull out[17] a holiday?

And do you now strew flowers in his way
That comes in triumph over Pompey's blood?[18]
Be gone!
Run to your houses, fall upon your knees,
Pray to the gods to intermit the plague[19]
That needs must light on this ingratitude.

FLAVIUS. Go, go, good countrymen, and, for this fault,
Assemble all the poor men of your sort;
Draw them to Tiber banks and weep your tears
Into the channel, till the lowest stream
Do kiss the most exalted shores of all.[20]

[*All the commoners exit.*]

18. **Pompey's blood** Pompey's sons, whom Caesar has just defeated.
19. **intermit the plague** (plāg) stop the calamity or trouble.
20. **the most exalted shores of all** the highest banks.

Comprehension
What does Marullus think about the people celebrating in the streets?

21. **whe'r their basest mettle** whether the most inferior material of which they are made.

22. **Disrobe the images . . . decked with ceremonies** strip the statues . . . covered with decorations.

23. **feast of Lupercal** (lo͞o´ pər kal) ancient Roman festival celebrated on February 15.

24. **vulgar** (vul´ gər) *n.* common people.

25. **pitch** upward flight of a hawk.

Vocabulary ▶
servile (sur´ vəl) *adj.* slavelike; humbly submissive to authority

See, whe'r their basest mettle[21] be not moved,
They vanish tongue-tied in their guiltiness.
Go you down that way toward the Capitol;
This way will I. Disrobe the images,
If you do find them decked with ceremonies.[22]

MARULLUS. May we do so?
You know it is the feast of Lupercal.[23]

FLAVIUS. It is no matter; let no images
Be hung with Caesar's trophies. I'll about
And drive away the vulgar[24] from the streets;
So do you too, where you perceive them thick.
These growing feathers plucked from Caesar's wing
Will make him fly an ordinary pitch,[25]
Who else would soar above the view of men
And keep us all in **servile** fearfulness. [*Exit*]

▼ Critical Viewing
What do the actors' poses in this movie still imply about the relationship between Caesar (left) and Antony (middle)?

Scene ii. A public place.

[*Enter* CAESAR, ANTONY (*for the course*),[1] CALPURNIA, PORTIA, DECIUS, CICERO, BRUTUS, CASSIUS, CASCA, *a* SOOTHSAYER; *after them,* MARULLUS *and* FLAVIUS.]

CAESAR. Calpurnia!

CASCA. Peace, ho! Caesar speaks.

CAESAR. Calpurnia!

CALPURNIA. Here, my lord.

CAESAR. Stand you directly in Antonius' way
When he doth run his course. Antonius!

ANTONY. Caesar, my lord?

CAESAR. Forget not in your speed, Antonius,
To touch Calpurnia; for our elders say
The barren, touchèd in this holy chase,
Shake off their sterile curse.[2]

ANTONY. I shall remember:
When Caesar says "Do this," it is performed.

CAESAR. Set on, and leave no ceremony out.

SOOTHSAYER. Caesar!

CAESAR. Ha! Who calls?

CASCA. Bid every noise be still; peace yet again!

CAESAR. Who is it in the press[3] that calls on me?
I hear a tongue, shriller than all the music,
Cry "Caesar." Speak; Caesar is turned to hear.

SOOTHSAYER. Beware the ides of March.[4]

CAESAR. What man is that?

BRUTUS. A soothsayer bids you beware the ides of March.

CAESAR. Set him before me; let me see his face.

CASSIUS. Fellow, come from the throng; look upon Caesar.

CAESAR. What say'st thou to me now? Speak once again.

SOOTHSAYER. Beware the ides of March.

CAESAR. He is a dreamer, let us leave him. Pass.

[*A trumpet sounds. Exit all but* BRUTUS *and* CASSIUS.]

1. **for the course** ready for the foot race that was part of the Lupercal festivities.

Use Text Aids
What information about the relationship between Caesar and Calpurnia do you find in the "Characters" list, on page 547?

Shakespeare's Tragedies
What is Caesar's rank?

2. **barren . . . sterile curse** It was believed that women who were unable to bear children (such as Calpurnia), if touched by a runner during this race, would then be able to bear children.

3. **press** *n.* crowd.

4. **ides of March** in the ancient Roman calendar, March 15.

Comprehension
How does Caesar respond to the soothsayer's warning?

5. **order of the course** the race.

6. **gamesome** (gām′ səm) *adj.* having a liking for sports.

7. **quick spirit** lively disposition.

8. **wont** (wōnt) *adj.* accustomed.

9. **bear . . . hand** treat too harshly and too like a stranger.

10. **if I . . . upon myself** if I have been less open, it is because I am troubled with myself.

11. **passions** *n.* feelings; emotions.

12. **of some difference** in conflict.

13. **Conceptions . . . myself** thoughts that concern only me.

14. **soil** *n.* blemish.

15. **By means . . . buried** because of which I have kept to myself.

16. **cogitations** (käj ə tā′ shənz) *n.* thoughts.

17. **'Tis just** it is true.

18. **lamented** (lə men′ təd) *v.* regretted.

19. **turn . . . shadow** reflect your hidden noble qualities so you could see their image.

20. **the best respect** the best reputation.

21. **this age's yoke** the tyranny of Caesar.

Cassius. Will you go see the order of the course?[5]

Brutus. Not I.

Cassius. I pray you do.

Brutus. I am not gamesome:[6] I do lack some part
Of that quick spirit[7] that is in Antony.
Let me not hinder, Cassius, your desires;
I'll leave you.

Cassius. Brutus, I do observe you now of late;
I have not from your eyes that gentleness
And show of love as I was wont[8] to have;
You bear too stubborn and too strange a hand[9]
Over your friend that loves you.

Brutus. Cassius,
Be not deceived: if I have veiled my look,
I turn the trouble of my countenance
Merely upon myself.[10] Vexèd I am
Of late with passions[11] of some difference,[12]
Conceptions only proper to myself,[13]
Which give some soil,[14] perhaps, to my behaviors;
But let not therefore my good friends be grieved
(Among which number, Cassius, be you one)
Nor construe any further my neglect
Than that poor Brutus, with himself at war,
Forgets the shows of love to other men.

Cassius. Then, Brutus, I have much mistook your passion;
By means whereof this breast of mine hath buried[15]
Thoughts of great value, worthy cogitations.[16]
Tell me, good Brutus, can you see your face?

Brutus. No, Cassius; for the eye sees not itself
But by reflection, by some other things.

Cassius. 'Tis just.[17]
And it is very much lamented,[18] Brutus,
That you have no such mirrors as will turn
Your hidden worthiness into your eye,
That you might see your shadow.[19] I have heard
Where many of the best respect[20] in Rome
(Except immortal Caesar), speaking of Brutus,
And groaning underneath this age's yoke,[21]
Have wished that noble Brutus had his eyes.

Brutus. Into what dangers would you lead me, Cassius,
That you would have me seek into myself
For that which is not in me?

Cassius. Therefore, good Brutus, be prepared to hear;
And since you know you cannot see yourself
So well as by reflection, I, your glass
Will modestly discover to yourself
That of yourself which you yet know not of.[22]
And be not jealous on[23] me, gentle Brutus:
Were I a common laughter,[24] or did use
To stale with ordinary oaths my love
To every new protester;[25] if you know
That I do fawn on men and hug them hard,
And after scandal[26] them; or if you know
That I profess myself in banqueting
To all the rout,[27] then hold me dangerous.
[*Flourish of trumpets and shout*]

22. **your glass . . . know not of** your mirror will make known to you without exaggeration the qualities you have of which you are unaware.
23. **be not jealous on** do not be suspicious of.
24. **common laughter** object of ridicule.
25. **To stale . . . new protester** to cheapen my friendship by avowing it to anyone who promises to be my friend.
26. **scandal** *v.* slander; gossip about.
27. **profess myself . . . rout** declare my friendship to the common crowd.

Comprehension
According to Cassius, what does Brutus not realize about himself?

◀ Critical Viewing
What does the expression of this actor in the role of Cassius convey about Cassius' intelligence? Explain.

Shakespeare's Tragedies
What internal conflict in Brutus do lines 79–82 reveal?

Brutus. What means this shouting? I do fear the people
Choose Caesar for their king.

Cassius. Ay, do you fear it?
Then must I think you would not have it so.

Brutus. I would not, Cassius, yet I love him well.
But wherefore do you hold me here so long?
What is it that you would impart to me?
If it be aught toward the general good,[28]
Set honor in one eye and death i' th' other,
And I will look on both indifferently;[29]
For let the gods so speed[30] me, as I love
The name of honor more than I fear death.

Cassius. I know that virtue to be in you, Brutus,
As well as I do know your outward favor.[31]
Well, honor is the subject of my story.
I cannot tell what you and other men
Think of this life, but for my single self,
I had as lief not be,[32] as live to be
In awe of such a thing as I myself.[33]
I was born free as Caesar; so were you:
We both have fed as well, and we can both
Endure the winter's cold as well as he:
For once, upon a raw and gusty day,
The troubled Tiber chafing with[34] her shores,

28. **aught . . . good** anything to do with the public welfare.
29. **indifferently** (in dif′ ər ənt lē) *adv.* without preference; impartially.
30. **speed** *v.* give good fortune to.
31. **favor** *n.* face; appearance.
32. **as lief not be** just as soon not exist.
33. **such a thing as I myself** another human being (Caesar).
34. **chafing with** raging against.

LITERATURE IN CONTEXT

History Connection
Roman Society

Brutus and Cassius fear that the common people will support Caesar in his bid to become emperor. Their fear reflects tensions in Roman society of the time.

- Poor *plebeians* (commoners), including farmers who could no longer compete with wealthy landowners, flooded Rome.
- They created a restless mass of unemployed poor.
- Some leaders took their side and won power with their support.
- Other leaders took the side of the *patricians* (aristocrats) and the wealthy plebeians.
- The conflict between rich and poor led to civil unrest, including riots and assassinations.

Connect to the Literature

Which scenes in Act I best reflect the division in Roman society? Explain.

Caesar said to me "Darest thou, Cassius, now
Leap in with me into this angry flood,
And swim to yonder point?" Upon the word,
Accout'red[35] as I was, I plungèd in
And bade him follow: so indeed he did.
The torrent roared, and we did buffet[36] it
With lusty sinews,[37] throwing it aside
And stemming it with hearts of controversy.[38]
But ere we could arrive the point proposed,
Caesar cried "Help me, Cassius, or I sink!"
I, as Aeneas,[39] our great ancestor,
Did from the flames of Troy upon his shoulder
The old Anchises bear, so from the waves of Tiber
Did I the tired Caesar. And this man
Is now become a god, and Cassius is
A wretched creature, and must bend his body
If Caesar carelessly but nod on him.
He had a fever when he was in Spain,
And when the fit was on him, I did mark
How he did shake: 'tis true, this god did shake.
His coward lips did from their color fly,[40]
And that same eye whose bend[41] doth awe the world
did lose his[42] luster: I did hear him groan;
Ay, and that tongue of his, that bade the Romans
Mark him and write his speeches in their books,
Alas, it cried, "Give me some drink, Titinius,"
As a sick girl. Ye gods! It doth amaze me,
A man of such a feeble temper[43] should
So get the start of[44] the majestic world,
And bear the palm[45] alone. [*Shout. Flourish of trumpets*]

Brutus. Another general shout?
I do believe that these applauses are
For some new honors that are heaped on Caesar.

Cassius. Why, man, he doth bestride the narrow world
Like a Colossus,[46] and we petty men
Walk under his huge legs and peep about
To find ourselves dishonorable[47] graves.
Men at some time are masters of their fates:
The fault, dear Brutus, is not in our stars,[48]
But in ourselves, that we are underlings.[49]
Brutus and Caesar: what should be in that "Caesar"?
Why should that name be sounded[50] more than yours?
Write them together, yours is as fair a name;

35. Accout'red (ə ko͞o′ trəd) *v.* dressed in armor.
36. buffet (buf′ it) *v.* struggle against.
37. lusty sinews (sin′ yo͞oz) strong muscles.
38. stemming it . . . controversy making progress against it with our intense rivalry.
39. Aeneas (i nē′ əs) Trojan hero of the poet Virgil's epic poem *Aeneid,* who carried his old father, Anchises, from the burning city of Troy and later founded Rome.
40. His coward lips . . . fly color fled from his lips, which were like cowardly soldiers fleeing from a battle.
41. bend *n.* glance.
42. his *pron.* its.
43. feeble temper weak physical constitution.
44. get the start of outdistance.
45. palm *n.* leaf of a palm tree carried or worn as a symbol of victory; victor's prize.
46. Colossus (kə läs′ əs) *n.* gigantic ancient statue of Apollo, a Greek and Roman god, that was set at the entrance to the harbor of Rhodes, ships would sail under its legs.
47. dishonorable (dis än′ ər ə bəl) *adj.* shameful (because they will not be free men).
48. stars *n.* destinies. The stars were thought to control people's lives.
49. underlings *n.* inferior people.
50. sounded *v.* spoken or announced by trumpets.

Comprehension
What has Cassius done to help Caesar in the past?

51. **conjure** (kän′ jər) *v.* summon a spirit by a magic spell.
52. **start** *v.* raise.
53. **great flood** in Greek mythology, a flood that drowned everyone except Deucalion and his wife Pyrrha, who were saved by the god Zeus because of their virtue.
54. **But it was famed with** without the age being made famous by.
55. **Brutus** Lucius Junius Brutus had helped expel the last king of Rome and had helped found the republic in 509 B.C.
56. **brooked** *v.* put up with.

Use Text Aids
How do the Background feature on page 542 and note 55 help you understand Cassius' appeal to Brutus?

57. **nothing jealous** not at all doubting.
58. **work me to** persuade me of.
59. **aim** *n.* idea.
60. **meet** *adj.* fit; suitable.
61. **chew upon** think about.

Shakespeare's Tragedies
What tragic flaw in Brutus' character might lines 172–175 reveal?

62. **train** *n.* attendants.

63. **chidden train** scolded attendants.

Sound them, it doth become the mouth as well;
Weigh them, it is as heavy; conjure[51] with 'em,
"Brutus" will start[52] a spirit as soon as "Caesar."
Now, in the names of all the gods at once,
Upon what meat doth this our Caesar feed,
That he is grown so great? Age, thou art shamed!
Rome, thou hast lost the breed of noble bloods!
When went there by an age, since the great flood,[53]
But it was famed with[54] more than with one man?
When could they say (till now) that talked of Rome,
That her wide walks encompassed but one man?
Now is it Rome indeed, and room enough,
When there is in it but one only man.
O, you and I have heard our fathers say,
There was a Brutus[55] once that would have brooked[56]
Th' eternal devil to keep his state in Rome
As easily as a king.

BRUTUS. That you do love me, I am nothing jealous;[57]
What you would work me to,[58] I have some aim;[59]
How I have thought of this, and of these times,
I shall recount hereafter. For this present,
I would not so (with love I might entreat you)
Be any further moved. What you have said
I will consider; what you have to say
I will with patience hear, and find a time
Both meet[60] to hear and answer such high things.
Till then, my noble friend, chew upon[61] this:
Brutus had rather be a villager
Than to repute himself a son of Rome
Under these hard conditions as this time
Is like to lay upon us.

CASSIUS. I am glad
That my weak words have struck but thus much show
Of fire from Brutus.

[*Enter* CAESAR *and his* TRAIN.][62]

BRUTUS. The games are done, and Caesar is returning.

CASSIUS. As they pass by, pluck Casca by the sleeve,
And he will (after his sour fashion) tell you
What hath proceeded worthy note today.

BRUTUS. I will do so. But look you, Cassius,
The angry spot doth glow on Caesar's brow,
And all the rest look like a chidden train:[63]

Calpurnia's cheek is pale, and Cicero
Looks with such ferret[64] and such fiery eyes
As we have seen him in the Capitol,
Being crossed in conference[65] by some senators.

Cassius. Casca will tell us what the matter is.

Caesar. Antonius.

Antony. Caesar?

Caesar. Let me have men about me that are fat,
Sleek-headed men, and such as sleep a-nights.
Yond Cassius has a lean and hungry look;
He thinks too much: such men are dangerous.

Antony. Fear him not, Caesar, he's not dangerous;
He is a noble Roman, and well given.[66]

Caesar. Would he were fatter! But I fear him not.
Yet if my name were liable to fear,
I do not know the man I should avoid
So soon as that **spare** Cassius. He reads much,
He is a great observer, and he looks
quite through the deeds of men.[67] He loves no plays,
As thou dost, Antony; he hears no music;
Seldom he smiles, and smiles in such a sort[68]
As if he mocked himself, and scorned his spirit
That could be moved to smile at anything.
Such men as he be never at heart's ease
Whiles they behold a greater than themselves,
And therefore are they very dangerous.
I rather tell thee what is to be feared
Than what I fear; for always I am Caesar.
Come on my right hand, for this ear is deaf,
And tell me truly what thou think'st of him.

[*A trumpet sounds.* Caesar *and his* Train *exit.*]

Casca. You pulled me by the cloak; would you speak with me?

Brutus. Ay, Casca; tell us what hath chanced[69] today,
That Caesar looks so sad.

Casca. Why, you were with him, were you not?

Brutus. I should not then ask Casca what had chanced.

Casca. Why, there was a crown offered him; and being offered him, he put it by[70] with the back of his hand, thus; and then the people fell a-shouting.

64. ferret (fer′ it) *adj.* ferret-like; characteristic of a ferret, a small weasel-like animal.

65. crossed in conference opposed in debate.

66. well given well disposed.

67. looks . . . deeds of men sees through people's actions to their motives.

◀ Vocabulary
spare (sper) *adj.* lean; thin

68. sort way.

69. hath chanced has happened.

70. put it by pushed it away.

Comprehension
Why does Cassius compare Brutus and Caesar?

Use Text Aids
According to the Literature in Context feature on page 554, why might the common people support Caesar?

Brutus. What was the second noise for?

Casca. Why, for that too.

Cassius. They shouted thrice; what was the last cry for?

Casca. Why, for that too.

Brutus. Was the crown offered him thrice?

Casca. Ay, marry,[71] was't, and he put it by thrice, every time gentler than other; and at every putting-by mine honest neighbors shouted.

Cassius. Who offered him the crown?

Casca. Why, Antony.

Brutus. Tell us the manner of it, gentle Casca.

Casca. I can as well be hanged as tell the manner of it: it was mere foolery; I did not mark it. I saw Mark Antony offer him a crown—yet 'twas not a crown neither, 'twas one of these coronets[72]—and, as I told you, he put it by once; but for all that, to my thinking, he would fain[73] have had it. Then he offered it to him again; then he put it by again; but to my thinking, he was very loath to lay his fingers off it. And then he offered it the third time. He put it the third time by; and still[74] as he refused it, the rabblement[75] hooted, and clapped their chopt[76] hands, and threw up their sweaty nightcaps,[77] and uttered such a deal of stinking breath because Caesar refused the crown, that it had, almost, choked Caesar; for he swounded[78] and fell down at it. And for mine own part, I durst not laugh, for fear of opening my lips and receiving the bad air.

Cassius. But, soft,[79] I pray you; what, did Caesar swound?

Casca. He fell down in the market place, and foamed at mouth, and was speechless.

Brutus. 'Tis very like he hath the falling-sickness.[80]

Cassius. No, Caesar hath it not; but you, and I,
And honest Casca, we have the falling-sickness.[81]

Casca. I know not what you mean by that, but I am sure Caesar fell down. If the tag-rag people[82] did not clap him and hiss him, according as he pleased and displeased them, as they use[83] to do the players in the theater, I am no true man.

71. marry *interjection* truly.

72. coronets (kôr′ ə nets′) *n.* ornamental bands used as crowns.

73. fain (fān) *adv.* gladly.

74. still *adv.* every time.

75. rabblement (rab′ əl mənt) *n.* mob.

76. chopt (chäpt) *adj.* chapped.

77. nightcaps *n.* workers' caps.

78. swounded *v.* swooned; fainted.

79. soft *adv.* slowly.

80. falling-sickness *n.* epilepsy.

81. we have the falling-sickness We are losing power and falling in status under Caesar's rule.

82. tag-rag people the rabble; lower-class people.

83. use *v.* are accustomed.

Brutus. What said he when he came unto himself?

Casca. Marry, before he fell down, when he perceived the common herd was glad he refused the crown, he plucked me ope his doublet[84] and offered them his throat to cut. An I had been a man of any occupation,[85] if I would not have taken him at a word, I would I might go to hell among the rogues. And so he fell. When he came to himself again, he said, if he had done or said anything amiss, he desired their worships to think it was his **infirmity**.[86] Three or four wenches,[87] where I stood, cried "Alas, good soul!" and forgave him with all their hearts; but there's no heed to be taken of them; if Caesar had stabbed their mothers, they would have done no less.

Brutus. And after that, he came thus sad away?

Casca. Ay.

Cassius. Did Cicero say anything?

Casca. Ay, he spoke Greek.

Cassius. To what effect?

Casca. Nay, an I tell you that, I'll ne'er look you i' th' face again. But those that understood him smiled at one another and shook their heads; but for mine own part, it was Greek to me. I could tell you more news too: Marullus and Flavius, for pulling scarfs off Caesar's images, are put to silence.[88] Fare you well. There was more foolery yet, if I could remember it.

Cassius. Will you sup with me tonight, Casca?

Casca. No, I am promised forth.[89]

Cassius. Will you dine with me tomorrow?

Casca. Ay, if I be alive, and your mind hold,[90] and your dinner worth the eating.

Cassius. Good; I will expect you.

Casca. Do so. Farewell, both. [*Exit*]

Brutus. What a blunt[91] fellow is this grown to be!
He was quick mettle[92] when he went to school.

Cassius. So is he now in execution[93]
Of any bold or noble enterprise,
However he puts on this tardy form.[94]

84. doublet (dub′ lit) *n.* close-fitting jacket.

85. An I . . . occupation if I had been a workingman (or a man of action).

86. infirmity *n.* Caesar's illness is epilepsy.

87. wenches (wench′ əz) *n.* young women.

◀ **Vocabulary**
infirmity (in fʉr′ mə tē) *n.* weakness; physical defect

88. for pulling . . . silence For taking decorations off statues of Caesar, they have been silenced (by being forbidden to take part in public affairs, exiled, or perhaps even executed).

89. am promised forth have a previous engagement.

90. hold *v.* does not change.

91. blunt *adj.* dull; not sharp.

92. quick mettle of a lively disposition.

93. execution *n.* carrying out; doing.

94. tardy form sluggish appearance.

Comprehension
How does Caesar respond when he is offered the crown?

This rudeness is a sauce to his good wit,[95]
Which gives men stomach to disgest[96] his words
With better appetite.

BRUTUS. And so it is. For this time I will leave you.
Tomorrow, if you please to speak with me,
I will come home to you; or if you will,
Come home to me, and I will wait for you.

CASSIUS. I will do so. Till then, think of the world.[97]

[*Exit* BRUTUS.]

Well, Brutus, thou art noble; yet I see
Thy honorable mettle may be wrought
From that it is disposed;[98] therefore it is meet
That noble minds keep ever with their likes;
For who so firm that cannot be seduced?

95. **wit** *n.* intelligence.
96. **disgest** *v.* digest.
97. **the world** present state of affairs.
98. **wrought . . . is disposed** shaped (like iron) in a way different from its usual form.

▼ Critical Viewing
How does this idyllic scene of Rome contrast with the events taking place in the play?

Caesar doth bear me hard,[99] but he loves Brutus.
If I were Brutus now, and he were Cassius,
He should not humor me.[100] I will this night,
In several hands,[101] in at his windows throw,
As if they came from several citizens,
Writings, all tending to the great opinion[102]
That Rome holds of his name; wherein obscurely
Caesar's ambition shall be glancèd at.[103]
And after this, let Caesar seat him sure;[104]
For we will shake him, or worse days endure. [*Exit*]

99. bear me hard dislike me.
100. humor me win me over.
101. several hands different handwritings.
102. tending to the great opinion pointing out the great respect.
103. glancèd at hinted at.
104. seat him sure establish himself securely.

Scene iii. A street.

[*Thunder and lightning. Enter from opposite sides,* CASCA and CICERO.]

CICERO. Good even, Casca; brought you Caesar home?
Why are you breathless? And why stare you so?

CASCA. Are not you moved, when all the sway of earth[1]
Shakes like a thing unfirm? O Cicero,
I have seen tempests, when the scolding winds
Have rived[2] the knotty oaks, and I have seen
Th' ambitious ocean swell and rage and foam,
To be exalted with[3] the threat'ning clouds;
But never till tonight, never till now,
Did I go through a tempest dropping fire.
Either there is a civil strife in heaven,
Or else the world, too saucy[4] with the gods,
Incenses[5] them to send destruction.

CICERO. Why, saw you anything more wonderful?

CASCA. A common slave—you know him well by sight—
Held up his left hand, which did flame and burn
Like twenty torches joined, and yet his hand,
Not sensible of[6] fire, remained unscorched.
Besides—I ha' not since put up my sword—
Against[7] the Capitol I met a lion,
Who glazed[8] upon me and went surly by
Without annoying me. And there were drawn
Upon a heap[9] a hundred ghastly[10] women,
Transformèd with their fear, who swore they saw
Men, all in fire, walk up and down the streets.
And yesterday the bird of night[11] did sit
Even at noonday upon the market place,
Hooting and shrieking. When these prodigies[12]
Do so conjointly meet,[13] let not men say,
"These are their reasons, they are natural,"

1. all the sway of earth the stable order of Earth.
2. Have rived have split.
3. exalted with lifted up to.
4. saucy *adj.* rude; impudent.
5. Incenses *v.* enrages.

Use Text Aids
According to the information on page 537, why would Shakespeare's audience have connected these unnatural events with the political situation in the play?

6. sensible of sensitive to.
7. Against *prep.* opposite or near.
8. glazed *v.* stared.
9. were drawn . . . heap huddled together.
10. ghastly (gast′ lē) *adj.* ghostlike; pale.
11. bird of night owl.
12. prodigies (präd′ ə jēz) *n.* extraordinary happenings.
13. conjointly meet occur at the same time and place.

Comprehension
After his conversation with Brutus, what does Cassius say he will do?

Vocabulary ▶
portentous (pôr ten′ təs) *adj.* ominous; giving signs of evil to come

14. **portentous (pôr ten′ təs) . . . upon** bad omens for the country they point to.
15. **strange-disposèd** abnormal.
16. **construe . . . fashion** explain in their own way.
17. **Clean from the purpose** different from the real meaning.

For I believe they are **portentous** things
Unto the climate that they point upon.[14]

CICERO. Indeed, it is a strange-disposèd[15] time:
But men may construe things after their fashion,[16]
Clean from the purpose[17] of the things themselves.
Comes Caesar to the Capitol tomorrow?

CASCA. He doth; for he did bid Antonius
Send word to you he would be there tomorrow.

CICERO. Good night then, Casca; this disturbèd sky
Is not to walk in.

CASCA. Farewell, Cicero. [*Exit* CICERO.]

[*Enter* CASSIUS.]

CASSIUS. Who's there?

CASCA. A Roman.

CASSIUS. Casca, by your voice.

CASCA. Your ear is good. Cassius, what night is this?

CASSIUS. A very pleasing night to honest men.

CASCA. Who ever knew the heavens menace so?

CASSIUS. Those that have known the earth so full of faults.
For my part, I have walked about the streets,
Submitting me unto the perilous night,
And thus unbracèd,[18] Casca, as you see,
Have bared my bosom to the thunder-stone;[19]
And when the cross[20] blue lightning seemed to open
The breast of heaven, I did present myself
Even in the aim and very flash of it.

CASCA. But wherefore did you so much tempt the heavens?
It is the part[21] of men to fear and tremble
When the most mighty gods by tokens send
Such dreadful heralds to astonish[22] us.

CASSIUS. You are dull, Casca, and those sparks of life
That should be in a Roman you do want,[23]
Or else you use not. You look pale, and gaze,
And put on fear, and cast yourself in wonder,[24]
To see the strange impatience of the heavens;
But if you would consider the true cause
Why all these fires, why all these gliding ghosts,
Why birds and beasts from quality and kind,[25]
Why old men, fools, and children calculate,[26]

18. **unbracèd** *adj.* with jacket open.
19. **thunder-stone** *n.* thunderbolt.
20. **cross** *adj.* zigzag.
21. **part** *n.* role.
22. **by tokens . . . to astonish** by portentous signs send such awful announcements to frighten and stun.
23. **want** *v.* lack.
24. **put on . . . in wonder** show fear and are amazed.
25. **from quality and kind** acting contrary to their nature.
26. **calculate** *v.* make predictions.

Why all these things change from their ordinance,[27]
Their natures and preformèd faculties,
To monstrous quality,[28] why, you shall find
That heaven hath infused them with these spirits[29]
To make them instruments of fear and warning
Unto some monstrous state.[30]
Now could I, Casca, name to thee a man
Most like this dreadful night,
That thunders, lightens, opens graves, and roars
As doth the lion in the Capitol;
A man no mightier than thyself, or me,
In personal action, yet **prodigious** grown
And fearful,[31] as these strange eruptions are.

Casca. 'Tis Caesar that you mean, is it not, Cassius?

Cassius. Let it be who it is; for Romans now
Have thews[32] and limbs like to their ancestors;
But, woe the while![33] Our fathers' minds are dead,
And we are governed with our mothers' spirits;
Our yoke and sufferance[34] show us womanish.

Casca. Indeed, they say the senators tomorrow
Mean to establish Caesar as a king;
And he shall wear his crown by sea and land,
In every place save here in Italy.

Cassius. I know where I will wear this dagger then;
Cassius from bondage will deliver[35] Cassius.
Therein,[36] ye gods, you make the weak most strong;
Therein, ye gods, you tyrants do defeat.
Nor stony tower, nor walls of beaten brass,
Nor airless dungeon, nor strong links of iron,
Can be retentive to[37] the strength of spirit;
But life, being weary of these worldly bars,
Never lacks power to dismiss itself.
If I know this, know all the world besides,
That part of tyranny that I do bear
I can shake off at pleasure. [*Thunder still*]

Casca. So can I;
So every bondman in his own hand bears
The power to cancel his captivity.

Cassius. And why should Caesar be a tyrant then?
Poor man, I know he would not be a wolf
But that he sees the Romans are but sheep;
He were no lion, were not Romans hinds.[38]

27. ordinance (ôrd′ 'n əns) *n.* regular behavior.
28. preformèd . . . quality established function to unnatural behavior.
29. infused . . . spirits filled them with supernatural powers.
30. monstrous state abnormal condition of government.

◀ **Vocabulary**
prodigious (prō dij′ əs) *adj.* of great size or power

31. fearful *adj.* causing fear.
32. thews (*th*yo͞oz) *n.* muscles or sinews; strength.
33. woe the while alas for the times.
34. yoke and sufferance slavery and meek acceptance of it.
35. will deliver will set free.
36. Therein (*th*er in′) *adv.* in that way (that is, by giving the weak the power to end their own lives).

Shakespeare's Tragedies
What main conflict has Shakespeare established in Act I?

37. be retentive to confine.
38. hinds (hīndz) *n.* female deer; peasants; servants.

Comprehension
What connection does Cassius make between the night's strange events and Caesar's rise to power?

39. offal (ôf´ əl) *n.* refuse; waste.

40. base matter inferior or low material; foundation materials.

41. speak this . . . answer must be made say this before a willing servant of Caesar's; then I know I will have to answer for my words.

42. fleering tell-tale sneering tattletale.

43. factious (fak´ shəs) *adj.* active in forming a faction or a political party.

44. redress (ri dres´) **of all these griefs** setting right all these grievances.

45. undergo (un´ dər gō´) *v.* undertake.

46. consequence (kän´ sə kwens´) *n.* importance.

47. by this by this time.

48. Pompey's porch portico of Pompey's Theater.

49. complexion of the element condition of the sky; weather.

50. In favor's like in appearance is like.

Those that with haste will make a mighty fire
Begin it with weak straws. What trash is Rome,
What rubbish and what offal,[39] when it serves
For the base matter[40] to illuminate
So vile a thing as Caesar! But, O grief,
Where hast thou led me? I, perhaps, speak this
Before a willing bondman; then I know
My answer must be made.[41] But I am armed,
And dangers are to me indifferent.

CASCA. You speak to Casca, and to such a man
That is no fleering tell-tale.[42] Hold, my hand.
Be factious[43] for redress of all these griefs,[44]
And I will set this foot of mine as far
As who goes farthest. [*They clasp hands.*]

CASSIUS. There's a bargain made.
Now know you, Casca, I have moved already
Some certain of the noblest-minded Romans
To undergo[45] with me an enterprise
Of honorable dangerous consequence;[46]
And I do know, by this[47] they stay for me
In Pompey's porch;[48] for now, this fearful night,
There is no stir or walking in the streets,
And the complexion of the element[49]
In favor's like[50] the work we have in hand,
Most bloody, fiery, and most terrible.

[*Enter* CINNA.]

51. close *adv.* hidden.

52. gait (gāt) *n.* style of walking.

53. incorporate (in kôr´ pə rit) / **To our attempts** part of our efforts.

54. stayed for waited for.

55. on't (ônt) *contraction* of *on it.*

56. praetor's (prē´ tərz) **chair** Roman magistrate's (or judge's) chair.

CASCA. Stand close[51] awhile, for here comes one in haste.

CASSIUS. 'Tis Cinna; I do know him by his gait;[52]
He is a friend. Cinna, where haste you so?

CINNA. To find out you. Who's that? Metellus Cimber?

CASSIUS. No, it is Casca, one incorporate
To our attempts.[53] Am I not stayed for,[54] Cinna?

CINNA. I am glad on't.[55] What a fearful night is this!
There's two or three of us have seen strange sights.

CASSIUS. Am I not stayed for? Tell me.

CINNA. Yes, you are.
O Cassius, if you could
But win the noble Brutus to our party—

CASSIUS. Be you content. Good Cinna, take this paper,
And look you lay it in the praetor's chair,[56]

Use Text Aids
Why might you need to consult glosses 56 and 57 to understand Cassius' plan?

▲ **Critical Viewing**
Which details in this relief sculpture indicate the respect and awe with which Romans regarded their leaders?

57. **Where . . . find it** where only Brutus (as the chief magistrate) will find it.
58. **old Brutus'** Junius Brutus, the founder of the Roman Republic.
59. **Repair** *v.* go.
60. **hie** (hī) *v.* hurry.

Where Brutus may but find it;[57] and throw this
In at his window: set this up with wax
Upon old Brutus'[58] statue. All this done,
Repair[59] to Pompey's porch, where you shall find us.
Is Decius Brutus and Trebonius there?

CINNA. All but Metellus Cimber, and he's gone
To seek you at your house. Well, I will hie,[60]
And so bestow these papers as you bade me.

CASSIUS. That done, repair to Pompey's Theater. [*Exit* CINNA.]
Come, Casca, you and I will yet ere day
See Brutus at his house; three parts of him
Is ours already, and the man entire
Upon the next encounter yields him ours.

CASCA. O, he sits high in all the people's hearts;
And that which would appear offense[61] in us,
His countenance,[62] like richest alchemy,[63]
Will change to virtue and to worthiness.

CASSIUS. Him, and his worth, and our great need of him,
You have right well conceited.[64] Let us go,
For it is after midnight, and ere day
We will awake him and be sure of him. [*Exit*]

61. **offense** (ə fens′) *n.* crime.
62. **countenance** (koun′ tə nəns) *n.* support.
63. **alchemy** (al′ kə mē) *n.* an early form of chemistry in which the goal was to change metals of little value into gold.
64. **conceited** (kən sēt′ id) *v.* understood.

Language Study

Vocabulary The italicized words in each numbered item appear in *The Tragedy of Julius Caesar,* Act I. Replace the italicized word in each sentence with an antonym. Then, explain which sentence makes better sense.

1. The fine-art collector was eager to spend a huge sum to buy the *replication*.
2. The long-distance runner was extremely strong and *spare*.
3. His *infirmity* was caused by an injury, not an illness.
4. In a scary movie, an unlocked door is often *portentous*.
5. The baby has a *prodigious* appetite because she is growing so quickly.

WORD STUDY

The **Latin suffix *-ile*** means "capable of" or "having the quality of." In the play, a character is worried that he will become **servile**, or take on the qualities of a slave, if Caesar becomes king.

Word Study

Part A Explain how the **Latin suffix *-ile*** contributes to the meanings of these words: *fragile, mobile,* and *projectile*. Consult a dictionary if necessary.

Part B Use the context of the sentences and what you know about the Latin suffix *-ile* to explain your answer to each question.

1. Do water, ice, and steam have the same *tactile* qualities?
2. If a person's behavior is *infantile*, is he or she acting like an adult?

Close Reading Activities

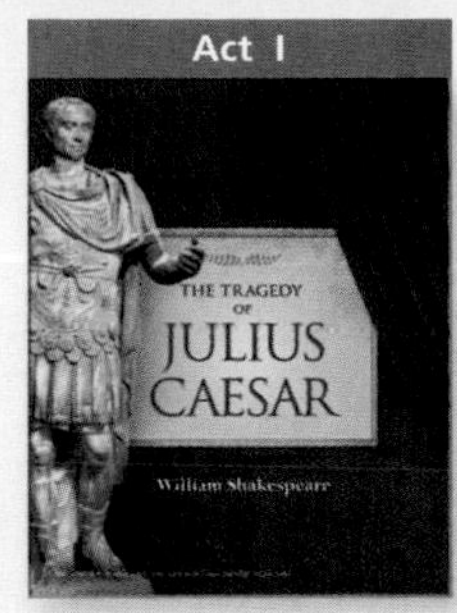

Literary Analysis

Key Ideas and Details

1. **(a)** At the opening of the play, how do common Romans such as the Cobbler react to Caesar's return? **(b) Infer:** What do noble Romans such as Flavius and Cassius fear or resent about Caesar's success? Support your answer with details from the play.
2. **(a)** What warning does the soothsayer give Caesar? **(b) Infer:** What does Caesar's reaction show about his character? Explain, citing details from the play.
3. **Use Text Aids** The text aids that precede the play include a background section on ancient Rome. Using a chart like the one shown, identify two passages in Act I that are clarified by this background information. Explain your choices.
4. **Use Text Aids** In Scene ii, how do glosses 73 and 74 help readers understand what happened in the marketplace? Explain.

	Passage 1	Passage 2
Historical Information		
Connection to Passage		

Craft and Structure

5. **Shakespeare's Tragedies (a)** What is Cassius planning to do with the help of Cinna, Casca, and other noble Romans? Support your answer with details from the text. **(b)** Why is it important to them to win Brutus' support? Explain.
6. **Shakespeare's Tragedies** Given what you have read so far, explain what tragic flaw in Brutus' character might lead him to disaster. Cite details from the text that support your analysis.

Integration of Knowledge and Ideas

7. **Interpret:** Identify two passages in Act I that show two different perspectives about Julius Caesar's victorious return from war. Explain your choices.
8. **Analyze:** Why is it important for Cassius and his co-conspirators to win Brutus' support for their plan against Caesar? Explain. In your explanation, cite examples and details from the drama.

9. THE BIG ? **To what extent does experience determine what we perceive? (a)** Analyze Brutus' values as expressed in the speech in Scene ii, lines 82–89. **(b)** Then, analyze Cassius' speech appealing to those values in lines 135–161 of Scene ii. **(c)** How do these speeches help you understand how each character perceives Caesar? Explain.

ACADEMIC VOCABULARY

As you write and speak about *The Tragedy of Julius Caesar,* use the words related to experience and perceptions that you explored on page 517 of this book.

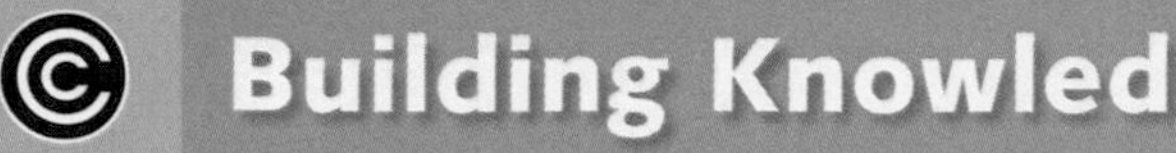

Building Knowledge

To what extent does experience determine what we perceive?

Explore the Big Question as you read *The Tragedy of Julius Caesar,* Act II. Note how characters' past experiences with Caesar affect their perceptions.

CLOSE READING FOCUS

Key Ideas and Details: **Paraphrase**

Paraphrasing a text means restating it in your own words.

- Look for punctuation that shows where sentences end.
- For each sentence, identify the subject and verb. Note that Shakespeare often uses **inversion,** syntax in which the usual word order of a sentence is reversed. If necessary, reorder the subject and verb so they follow customary sequence.
- Add helping verbs as needed to complete the meaning.
  Original: O conspiracy, / Sham'st thou to show thy dang'rous brow by night, / When evils are most free?
  Paraphrase: O conspiracy, are you ashamed to show your dangerous face at night, when it is easiest to be evil?

Craft and Structure: **Blank Verse**

The Tragedy of Julius Caesar is written in **blank verse**, a poetic form characterized by unrhymed lines of iambic pentameter.

- An **iamb** is a *foot* (unit of rhythm) in which an unstressed syllable is followed by a stressed syllable: da-DUH.
- **Pentameter** is a rhythmic pattern in which each line has five feet.
- In **iambic pentameter,** the typical line has five iambs, or five stressed syllables each preceded by an unstressed syllable:
  And THERE | fore THINK | him AS | a SER | pent's EGG

Shakespeare's noble characters speak in iambic pentameter. Lower-born characters speak in prose. Sometimes, Shakespeare breaks the rhythmic pattern in a line to add contrast or emphasis.

Vocabulary

The following words appear in the text that follows. Which ones are nouns? Explain how you know.

augmented	entreated	insurrection
resolution	wrathfully	imminent

Common Core State Standards

Reading Literature

1. Cite strong and thorough textual evidence to support analysis of what the text says explicitly as well as inferences drawn from the text.

2. Determine a theme or central idea of a text and analyze in detail its development over the course of the text, including how it emerges and is shaped and refined by specific details; provide an objective summary of the text.

5. Analyze how an author's choices concerning how to structure a text, order events within it, and manipulate time create such effects as mystery, tension, or surprise.

CLOSE READING MODEL

The passages below are from *The Tragedy of Julius Caesar,* Act II. The annotations to the right of the passages show ways in which you can use close reading skills to paraphrase text and to appreciate blank verse.

from *The Tragedy of Julius Caesar,* Act II

Lucius. Sir, March is wasted fifteen days.[1]

[*Knock within*]

Brutus. 'Tis good. Go to the gate; somebody knocks.

[*Exit* Lucius.]

Since Cassius first did whet me against Caesar,
I have not slept.[2]
Between the acting of a dreadful thing
And the first motion, all the interim is
Like a phantasma, or a hideous dream.[3]
The genius and the mortal instruments
Are then in council, and the state of a man,
Like to a little kingdom, suffers then
The nature of an insurrection.

....

Brutus. No, not an oath. If not the face of men,
The sufferance of our souls, the time's abuse—
If these be motives weak, break off betimes,
And every man hence to his idle bed.[4]
So let high-sighted tyranny range on
Till each man drop by lottery.

Blank Verse

1 Because this line has eight syllables, not ten, it is not iambic pentameter. Lower-born characters such as the servant Lucius generally do not speak in blank verse.

Blank Verse

2 Brutus, an aristocrat, usually speaks in blank verse. However, the line "I have not slept" is not blank verse. Shakespeare uses this short line to emphasize that Brutus is truly troubled.

Paraphrase

3 "The acting of" means actually doing something, and "the first motion" is the initial idea. A paraphrase could read: "The time between imagining a dreadful act and committing it seems like a terrible dream."

Paraphrase

4 Adding a subject to the first part of this sentence and a verb to the second part will help with paraphrasing. The paraphrase would read: "If these reasons are not justified, then let us quit right now and go back to our beds."

REVIEW AND ANTICIPATE

In Act I, as Caesar returns victorious from war, the common people are calling for him to be crowned emperor. Fearful of Caesar's ambitions and unwilling to surrender their own power, Cassius and others conspire against Caesar. Cassius attempts to win the support of Brutus, a highly respected Roman. Although Brutus is a friend of Caesar's, he worries about Caesar's ambition. In the meantime, Caesar receives a warning to "beware the ides of March." Act II opens on the evening before that fateful day. As you read, note how Caesar's own pride leads him to ignore danger. Note also the contrasts that emerge between Brutus and the conspirators.

◀ Critical Viewing
What details in this painting of Caesar and his wife foreshadow tragedy?

ACT II

Scene i. Rome.

[*Enter* BRUTUS *in his orchard.*]

BRUTUS. What, Lucius, ho!
I cannot, by the progress of the stars,
Give guess how near to day. Lucius, I say!
I would it were my fault to sleep so soundly.
When, Lucius, when? Awake, I say! What, Lucius!

[*Enter* LUCIUS.]

LUCIUS. Called you, my lord?

BRUTUS. Get me a taper in my study, Lucius.
When it is lighted, come and call me here.

LUCIUS. I will, my lord. [*Exit*]

BRUTUS. It must be by his death; and for my part,
I know no personal cause to spurn at[1] him,
But for the general.[2] He would be crowned.
How that might change his nature, there's the question.
It is the bright day that brings forth the adder,[3]
And that craves[4] wary walking. Crown him that,
And then I grant we put a sting in him
That at his will he may do danger with.
Th' abuse of greatness is when it disjoins
Remorse from power;[5] and, to speak truth of Caesar,
I have not known when his affections swayed[6]
More than his reason. But 'tis a common proof[7]
That lowliness[8] is young ambition's ladder,
Whereto the climber upward turns his face;
But when he once attains the upmost round,
He then unto the ladder turns his back,
Looks in the clouds, scorning the base degrees[9]
By which he did ascend. So Caesar may;
Then lest he may, prevent.[10] And, since the quarrel
Will bear no color for the thing he is,[11]
Fashion it[12] thus: that what he is, **augmented**
Would run to these and these extremities;[13]
And therefore think him as a serpent's egg
Which hatched, would as his kind grow mischievous,
And kill him in the shell.

[*Enter* LUCIUS.]

Blank Verse
Explain which character, Brutus or Lucius, speaks in blank verse and why.

1. **spurn at** kick against; rebel against.
2. **the general** the public good.
3. **adder** (ad´ ər) *n.* poisonous snake.
4. **craves** *v.* requires.
5. **disjoins . . . power** separates mercy from power.
6. **affections swayed** emotions ruled.
7. **proof** *n.* experience.
8. **lowliness** (lō´ lē nəs) *n.* humility.
9. **base degrees** low steps or people in lower positions.
10. **lest . . . prevent** in case he may, we must stop him.
11. **the quarrel . . . the thing he is** our complaint cannot be justified in terms of what he now is.
12. **Fashion it** state the case.
13. **extremities** (ek strem´ ə tēz) *n.* extremes (of tyranny).

◄ **Vocabulary**
augmented (ôg ment´ id) *adj.* made greater; enhanced

Comprehension
What does Brutus fear may happen if Caesar is crowned?

LUCIUS. The taper burneth in your closet,[14] sir.
Searching the window for a flint,[15] I found
This paper thus sealed up, and I am sure
It did not lie there when I went to bed. [*Gives him the letter*]

BRUTUS. Get you to bed again; it is not day.
Is not tomorrow, boy, the ides of March?

LUCIUS. I know not, sir.

BRUTUS. Look in the calendar and bring me word.

LUCIUS. I will, sir. [*Exit*]

BRUTUS. The exhalations[16] whizzing in the air
Give so much light that I may read by them.
[*Opens the letter and reads*]

"Brutus, thou sleep'st; awake, and see thyself.
Shall Rome, &c.[17] Speak, strike, redress.
Brutus, thou sleep'st; awake."

Such instigations[18] have been often dropped
Where I have took them up.
"Shall Rome, &c." Thus must I piece it out:[19]
Shall Rome stand under one man's awe?[20] What, Rome?
My ancestors did from the streets of Rome
The Tarquin[21] drive, when he was called a king.

14. closet *n.* study; small, private room for reading, meditation, and so on.

15. flint *n.* hard stone which, when struck with steel, makes sparks.

16. exhalations (eks′ hə lā′ shənz) *n.* meteors.

17. &c. et cetera (et set′ ər ə); Latin for "and so forth."

18. instigations (in′ stə gā ′ shənz) *n.* urgings, incitements, or spurs to act.

19. piece it out figure out the meaning.

20. under one man's awe in fearful reverence of one man.

21. Tarquin (tär′ kwin) king of Rome driven out by Lucius Junius Brutus, Brutus' ancestor.

LITERATURE IN CONTEXT

Language Connection

Archaic Word Forms

Shakespeare uses some word forms that are now archaic, or out of date. For modern readers, these words give his work a tone that is both more formal and more poetic than contemporary English. These archaic forms include the following:

thou *pron.* subjective case of a pronoun meaning "you" (the form used with family, friends, or the young)

thee *pron.* you (objective case of *thou*)

thy *pron.* your (possessive case of *thou*)

burneth *v.* third-person singular present tense of *burn*

'tis *contraction* it is

doth *v.* third-person singular present tense of *do*

dost *v.* second-person singular present tense of *do* (used with *thou*)

sham'st *v.* second-person singular present tense of *shame* (used with *thou*)

Connect to the Literature

What does this archaic language add to your experience of the play? What challenges does it pose?

"Speak, strike, redress." Am I **entreated**
To speak and strike? O Rome, I make thee promise,
If the redress will follow, thou receivest
Thy full petition at the hand of[22] Brutus!

[*Enter* LUCIUS.]

LUCIUS. Sir, March is wasted fifteen days. [*Knock within*]

BRUTUS. 'Tis good. Go to the gate; somebody knocks.
[*Exit* LUCIUS.]

Since Cassius first did whet[23] me against Caesar,
I have not slept.
Between the acting of a dreadful thing
And the first motion,[24] all the interim is
Like a phantasma,[25] or a hideous dream.
The genius and the mortal instruments[26]
Are then in council, and the state of a man,
Like to a little kingdom, suffers then
The nature of an **insurrection**.

[*Enter* LUCIUS.]

LUCIUS. Sir, 'tis your brother[27] Cassius at the door,
Who doth desire to see you.

BRUTUS. Is he alone?

LUCIUS. No, sir, there are moe[28] with him.

BRUTUS. Do you know them?

LUCIUS. No, sir; their hats are plucked about their ears,
And half their faces buried in their cloaks,
That by no means I may discover them
By any mark of favor.[29]

BRUTUS. Let 'em enter. [*Exit* LUCIUS.]
They are the faction. O conspiracy,
Sham'st thou to show thy dang'rous brow by night,
When evils are most free? O, then by day
Where wilt thou find a cavern dark enough
To mask thy monstrous visage? Seek none, conspiracy;
Hide it in smiles and affability:
For if thou path, thy native semblance on,[30]
Not Erebus[31] itself were dim enough
To hide thee from prevention.[32]

[*Enter the conspirators,* CASSIUS, CASCA, DECIUS, CINNA, METELLUS CIMBER, *and* TREBONIUS.]

◀ Vocabulary

entreated (en trēt´ id) *v.* begged; pleaded

insurrection (in´ sə rek´ shən) *n.* rebellion

22. **Thy full . . . hand of** all you ask from.
23. **whet** (hwet) *v.* sharpen; incite.
24. **motion** *n.* idea; suggestion.
25. **all the interim . . . a phantasma** (fan taz´ mə) all the time between seems like a hallucination.
26. **mortal instruments** bodily powers.
27. **brother** *n.* brother-in-law. (Cassius was married to Brutus' sister.)
28. **moe** *n.* more.
29. **discover . . . favor** identify them by any sign of their appearance.

Blank Verse

Which interjection does Shakespeare use to maintain iambic pentameter in lines 77 and 79?

30. **path . . . semblance on** walk looking as you normally do.
31. **Erebus** (er´ ə bəs) in Greek mythology, a dark region under the earth through which the dead pass on their way to Hades, the afterworld.
32. **prevention** *n.* being discovered and stopped.

Comprehension

What is Brutus' state of mind?

Cassius. I think we are too bold upon[33] your rest.
Good morrow, Brutus; do we trouble you?

Brutus. I have been up this hour, awake all night.
Know I these men that come along with you?

Cassius. Yes, every man of them; and no man here
But honors you; and every one doth wish
You had but that opinion of yourself
Which every noble Roman bears of you.
This is Trebonius.

Brutus. He is welcome hither.

Cassius. This, Decius Brutus.

Brutus. He is welcome too.

Cassius. This, Casca; this, Cinna; and this, Metellus Cimber.

Brutus. They are all welcome.
What watchful cares do interpose themselves
Betwixt your eyes and night?[34]

Cassius. Shall I entreat a word?[35] [*They whisper.*]

Decius. Here lies the east; doth not the day break here?

Casca. No.

Cinna. O, pardon, sir, it doth; and yon gray lines
That fret[36] the clouds are messengers of day.

Casca. You shall confess that you are both deceived.
Here, as I point my sword, the sun arises,
Which is a great way growing on[37] the south,
Weighing[38] the youthful season of the year.
Some two months hence, up higher toward the north
He first presents his fire; and the high[39] east
Stands as the Capitol, directly here.

Brutus. Give me your hands all over, one by one.

Cassius. And let us swear our **resolution.**

Brutus. No, not an oath. If not the face of men,
The sufferance of our souls, the time's abuse[40]—
If these be motives weak, break off betimes,[41]
And every man hence to his idle bed.
So let high-sighted[42] tyranny range on
Till each man drop by lottery.[43] But if these
(As I am sure they do) bear fire enough
To kindle cowards and to steel with valor

33. upon *adv.* in interfering with.

Paraphrase
Paraphrase Cassius' words in lines 90–93.

34. watchful . . . night worries keep you from sleep.
35. entreat (in trēt′) **a word** ask for a chance to speak with you.
36. fret (fret) *v.* decorate with a pattern.
37. growing on tending toward.
38. Weighing *v.* considering.
39. high *adj.* due.

Vocabulary ▶
resolution (rez′ ə lo͞o′ shən) *n.* strong determination; a plan or decision

40. the face . . . time's abuse the sadness on men's faces, the patient endurance of our souls, the present abuses (that is, Caesar's abuses of power).
41. betimes (bē tīmz′) *adv.* quickly.
42. high-sighted *adj.* arrogant (a reference to a hawk about to swoop down on prey).
43. by lottery by chance or in his turn.

The melting spirits of women, then, countrymen,
What need we any spur but our own cause
To prick us to redress?[44] What other bond
Than secret Romans, that have spoke the word,
And will not palter?[45] And what other oath
Than honesty to honesty[46] engaged
That this shall be, or we will fall for it?
Swear priests and cowards and men cautelous,[47]
Old feeble carrions[48] and such suffering souls
That welcome wrongs; unto bad causes swear
Such creatures as men doubt; but do not stain
The even[49] virtue of our enterprise,
Nor th' insuppressive mettle[50] of our spirits,
To think that or our cause or[51] our performance
Did need an oath; when every drop of blood
That every Roman bears, and nobly bears,
Is guilty of a several bastardy[52]
If he do break the smallest particle
Of any promise that hath passed from him.

Cassius. But what of Cicero? Shall we sound him?[53]
I think he will stand very strong with us.

Casca. Let us not leave him out.

Cinna. No, by no means.

Metellus. O, let us have him, for his silver hairs
Will purchase us a good opinion,
And buy men's voices to commend our deeds.
It shall be said his judgment ruled our hands;
Our youths and wildness shall no whit[54] appear,
But all be buried in his gravity.

Brutus. O, name him not! Let us not break with him;[55]
For he will never follow anything
That other men begin.

Cassius. Then leave him out.

Casca. Indeed, he is not fit.

Decius. Shall no man else be touched but only Caesar?

Cassius. Decius, well urged. I think it is not meet
Mark Antony, so well beloved of Caesar,
Should outlive Caesar; we shall find of[56] him
A shrewd contriver;[57] and you know, his means,
If he improve[58] them, may well stretch so far

44. prick us to redress goad or spur us on to correct these evils.
45. palter (pôl′ tər) *v.* talk insincerely.
46. honesty personal honor.
47. cautelous (kôt′ ə ləs) *adj.* deceitful.
48. carrions (kar′ ē ənz) *n.* men who are nearly corpses.
49. even *adj.* constant.
50. insuppressive mettle uncrushable courage.
51. or . . . or either our cause or.
52. guilty . . . bastardy is no true Roman.

53. sound him find out his opinion.

Spiral Review
CHARACTER What is Metellus' motivation for including Cicero in the plot against Caesar?

54. no whit (hwit) not the least bit.
55. break with him confide in him.

56. of *prep.* in.
57. contriver (kən trīv′ ər) *n.* schemer.
58. improve *v.* increase.

Comprehension
Why does Brutus think the conspirators should not swear an oath?

59. **annoy** *n.* harm.
60. **Like . . . envy afterwards** as if we were killing in anger with hatred afterward.
61. **come by Caesar's spirit** get hold of the principles of tyranny for which Caesar stands.
62. **gentle** *adj.* honorable; noble.

Vocabulary ▶
wrathfully (rath´ fəl lē) *adv.* with intense anger

As to annoy[59] us all; which to prevent,
Let Antony and Caesar fall together.

Brutus. Our course will seem too bloody, Caius Cassius,
To cut the head off and then hack the limbs,
Like wrath in death and envy afterwards;[60]
For Antony is but a limb of Caesar.
Let's be sacrificers, but not butchers, Caius.
We all stand up against the spirit of Caesar,
And in the spirit of men there is no blood.
O, that we then could come by Caesar's spirit,[61]
And not dismember Caesar! But, alas,
Caesar must bleed for it. And, gentle[62] friends,
Let's kill him boldly, but not **wrathfully**;
Let's carve him as a dish fit for the gods,
Not hew him as a carcass fit for hounds.

Critical Viewing ▶ What details of this image emphasize the differences between Brutus, on the right, and the other conspirators?

And let our hearts, as subtle masters do,
Stir up their servants[63] to an act of rage,
And after seem to chide 'em.[64] This shall make
Our purpose necessary, and not envious;
Which so appearing to the common eyes,
We shall be called purgers,[65] not murderers.
And for Mark Antony, think not of him;
For he can do no more than Caesar's arm
When Caesar's head is off.

Cassius. Yet I fear him;
For in the ingrafted[66] love he bears to Caesar—

Brutus. Alas, good Cassius, do not think of him.
If he love Caesar, all that he can do
Is to himself—take thought[67] and die for Caesar.
And that were much he should,[68] for he is given
To sports, to wildness, and much company.

Trebonius. There is no fear in him; let him not die,
For he will live and laugh at this hereafter.

[*Clock strikes.*]

Brutus. Peace! Count the clock.

Cassius. The clock hath stricken three.

Trebonius. 'Tis time to part.

Cassius. But it is doubtful yet
Whether Caesar will come forth today or no;
For he is superstitious grown of late,
Quite from the main[69] opinion he held once
Of fantasy, of dreams, and ceremonies.[70]
It may be these apparent prodigies,[71]
The unaccustomed terror of this night,
And the persuasion of his augurers[72]
May hold him from the Capitol today.

Decius. Never fear that. If he be so resolved,
I can o'ersway him;[73] for he loves to hear
That unicorns may be betrayed with trees,[74]
And bears with glasses,[75] elephants with holes,[76]
Lions with toils,[77] and men with flatterers;
But when I tell him he hates flatterers
He says he does, being then most flatterèd.
Let me work;
For I can give his humor the true bent,[78]
And I will bring him to the Capitol.

63. **their servants** that is, the hands or the passions.
64. **chide 'em** scold them.
65. **purgers** (purj´ ərz) *n.* healers.
66. **ingrafted** (in graft´ id) *adj.* deeply rooted.
67. **take thought** become melancholy.
68. **that were much he should** It is unlikely he would do that.
69. **Quite from the main** quite changed from the strong.
70. **ceremonies** *n.* omens.
71. **apparent prodigies** obvious omens of disaster.
72. **augurers** (ô´ gər ərz) *n.* augurs; officials who interpreted omens to decide if they were favorable or unfavorable for an undertaking.
73. **I can o'ersway him** I can change his mind.
74. **unicorns . . . trees** reference to the belief that standing in front of a tree as a unicorn charges and then stepping aside at the last moment causes the unicorn to bury its horn in the tree and so allows it to be caught.
75. **glasses** *n.* mirrors.
76. **holes** *n.* pitfalls.
77. **toils** *n.* nets; snares.
78. **give his humor the true bent** bend his feelings in the right direction.

Comprehension
According to Brutus, why should Antony not be killed?

79. **uttermost** *adj.* latest.
80. **doth bear Caesar hard** has a grudge against Caesar.
81. **rated** *v.* berated; scolded forcefully.

Cassius. Nay, we will all of us be there to fetch him.

Brutus. By the eighth hour; is that the uttermost?[79]

Cinna. Be that the uttermost, and fail not then.

Metellus. Caius Ligarius doth bear Caesar hard,[80]
Who rated[81] him for speaking well of Pompey.
I wonder none of you have thought of him.

Brutus. Now, good Metellus, go along by him.
He loves me well, and I have given him reasons;
Send him but hither, and I'll fashion[82] him.

82. **fashion** *v.* mold.
83. **put on** show.
84. **bear it** carry it off.
85. **formal constancy** consistent dignity.

Cassius. The morning comes upon 's; we'll leave you, Brutus.
And, friends, disperse yourselves; but all remember
What you have said, and show yourselves true Romans.

Brutus. Good gentlemen, look fresh and merrily.
Let not our looks put on[83] our purposes,
But bear it[84] as our Roman actors do,
With untired spirits and formal constancy.[85]
And so good morrow to you every one. [*Exit all but* Brutus.]
Boy! Lucius! Fast asleep? It is no matter;
Enjoy the honey-heavy dew of slumber.
Thou hast no figures nor no fantasies
Which busy care draws in the brains of men;
Therefore thou sleep'st so sound.

Paraphrase
Paraphrase Brutus' speech in lines 229–233 and explain which punctuation mark helps you identify the conclusion he draws.

[*Enter* Portia.]

Portia. Brutus, my lord.

Brutus. Portia, what mean you? Wherefore rise you now?
It is not for your health thus to commit
Your weak condition to the raw cold morning.

Portia. Nor for yours neither. Y'have ungently, Brutus,
Stole from my bed; and yesternight at supper
You suddenly arose and walked about,
Musing and sighing, with your arms across;
And when I asked you what the matter was,
You stared upon me with ungentle looks.
I urged you further; then you scratched your head,
And too impatiently stamped with your foot.
Yet I insisted, yet you answered not,
But with an angry wafter[86] of your hand
Gave sign for me to leave you. So I did,
Fearing to strengthen that impatience
Which seemed too much enkindled, and withal

Blank Verse
How does shifting the accent to the first and fourth syllables in line 240 add dramatic energy to this speech?

86. **wafter** (wäf′ tər) *n.* wave.

Hoping it was but an effect of humor,
Which sometime hath his[87] hour with every man.
It will not let you eat, nor talk, nor sleep,
And could it work so much upon your shape
As it hath much prevailed on your condition,[88]
I should not know you[89] Brutus. Dear my lord,
Make me acquainted with your cause of grief.

BRUTUS. I am not well in health, and that is all.

PORTIA. Brutus is wise and, were he not in health,
He would embrace the means to come by it.

BRUTUS. Why, so I do. Good Portia, go to bed.

PORTIA. Is Brutus sick, and is it physical[90]
To walk unbracèd and suck up the humors[91]
Of the dank morning? What, is Brutus sick,
And will he steal out of his wholesome bed,
To dare the vile contagion of the night,
And tempt the rheumy and unpurgèd air[92]
To add unto his sickness? No, my Brutus:
You have some sick offense[93] within your mind,
Which by the right and virtue of my place
I ought to know of; and upon my knees
I charm[94] you, by my once commended[95] beauty,
By all your vows of love, and that great vow[96]
Which did incorporate and make us one,
That you unfold to me, your self, your half,
Why you are heavy,[97] and what men tonight
Have had resort to you; for here have been
Some six or seven, who did hide their faces
Even from darkness.

BRUTUS. Kneel not, gentle Portia.

PORTIA. I should not need, if you were gentle Brutus.
Within the bond of marriage, tell me, Brutus,
Is it excepted[98] I should know no secrets
That appertain[99] to you? Am I your self
But, as it were, in sort or limitation,[100]
To keep with you at meals, comfort your bed,
And talk to you sometimes? Dwell I but in the suburbs[101]
Of your good pleasure? If it be no more,
Portia is Brutus' harlot, not his wife.

87. **his** *pron.* its.
88. **condition** *n.* disposition; mood.
89. **I should not know you** I would not recognize you as.
90. **physical** *adj.* healthy.
91. **walk unbracèd . . . humors** walk with jacket unfastened and take in the dampness.
92. **tempt . . . air** risk exposing yourself to the night air, which is likely to cause rheumatism and has not been purified by the sun.
93. **sick offense** harmful sickness.
94. **charm** *v.* beg.
95. **commended** *adj.* praised.
96. **great vow** marriage vow.
97. **heavy** *adj.* sorrowful.
98. **excepted** *v.* made an exception that.
99. **appertain** (ap′ ər tān′) *v.* belong.
100. **in sort or limitation** in a limited way (legal terms).
101. **suburbs** *n.* outskirts.

Comprehension
What does Portia ask of Brutus?

▲ Critical Viewing

What do the pose and expressions of Brutus and Portia in this film still reveal about their feelings?

Brutus. You are my true and honorable wife,
As dear to me as are the ruddy drops[102]
That visit my sad heart.

Portia. If this were true, then should I know this secret.
I grant I am a woman; but withal[103]
A woman that Lord Brutus took to wife.
I grant I am a woman; but withal
A woman well reputed, Cato's daughter.[104]
Think you I am no stronger than my sex,
Being so fathered and so husbanded?
Tell me your counsels,[105] I will not disclose 'em.
I have made strong proof of my constancy,
Giving myself a voluntary wound
Here in the thigh; can I bear that with patience,
And not my husband's secrets?

102. ruddy drops blood.

103. withal (wi*th* ôl′) *adv.* nevertheless.

104. Cato's daughter Marcus Porcius (pôr′ shəs) Cato (Cato the Younger; 95–46 B.C.) supported Pompey in his quarrel with Caesar and killed himself rather than allow himself to be captured by Caesar.

105. counsels *n.* secrets.

BRUTUS. O ye gods,
Render[106] me worthy of this noble wife! [*Knock*]
Hark, hark! One knocks. Portia, go in a while,
And by and by thy bosom shall partake
The secrets of my heart.
All my engagements[107] I will construe to thee,
All the charactery of my sad brows.[108]
Leave me with haste. [*Exit* PORTIA.]

[*Enter* LUCIUS *and* CAIUS LIGARIUS.]

Lucius, who's that knocks?

LUCIUS. Here is a sick man that would speak with you.

BRUTUS. Caius Ligarius, that Metellus spake of.
Boy, stand aside. Caius Ligarius! How?

CAIUS. Vouchsafe good morrow from a feeble tongue.

BRUTUS. O, what a time have you chose out,[109] brave Caius,
To wear a kerchief![110] Would you were not sick!

CAIUS. I am not sick, if Brutus have in hand
Any exploit worthy the name of honor.

BRUTUS. Such an exploit have I in hand, Ligarius,
Had you a healthful ear to hear of it.

CAIUS. By all the gods that Romans bow before,
I here discard my sickness! Soul of Rome,
Brave son, derived from honorable loins,[111]
Thou, like an exorcist,[112] hast conjured up
My mortifièd spirit.[113] Now bid me run,
And I will strive with things impossible.
Yea, get the better of them. What's to do?

BRUTUS. A piece of work that will make sick men whole.

CAIUS. But are not some whole that we must make sick?

BRUTUS. That must we also. What it is, my Caius,
I shall unfold[114] to thee, as we are going
To whom it must be done.

CAIUS. Set on[115] your foot,
And with a heart new-fired I follow you,
To do I know not what; but it sufficeth[116]
That Brutus leads me on. [*Thunder*]

BRUTUS. Follow me, then. [*Exit*]

106. Render (ren´ dər) *v.* make.

Blank Verse

By breaking the pattern of iambic pentameter, which words are emphasized in lines 307 and 308?

107. engagements *n.* commitments.

108. All the charactery of my sad brows all that is written on my sad face.

109. chose out picked out.

110. To wear a kerchief Caius wears a scarf to protect himself from drafts because he is sick.

111. derived from honorable loins descended from Lucius (lo͞o´ shē əs) Junius Brutus, founder of the Roman Republic.

112. exorcist (ek´ sôr sist) *n.* one who calls up spirits.

113. mortifièd (môrt´ ə fī ed) *adj.* deadened.

114. unfold *v.* disclose.

115. Set on advance.

116. sufficeth (sə fīs´ *eth*) *v.* is enough.

Comprehension

Why does Portia feel that Brutus should confide in her?

Scene ii. Caesar's house.

Paraphrase
Paraphrase Caesar's remarks in lines 1–3, rearranging the subject and verb in line 2.

[*Thunder and lightning. Enter* JULIUS CAESAR *in his nightgown.*]

CAESAR. Nor heaven nor earth have been at peace tonight:
Thrice hath Calpurnia in her sleep cried out,
"Help, ho! They murder Caesar!" Who's within?

[*Enter a* SERVANT.]

SERVANT. My lord?

CAESAR. Go bid the priests do present[1] sacrifice,
And bring me their opinions of success.

SERVANT. I will, my lord. [*Exit*]

[*Enter* CALPURNIA.]

CALPURNIA. What mean you, Caesar? Think you to walk forth?
You shall not stir out of your house today.

CAESAR. Caesar shall forth. The things that threatened me
Ne'er looked but on my back; when they shall see
The face of Caesar, they are vanishèd.

1. **present** *adj.* immediate.

LITERATURE IN CONTEXT

Culture Connection

Roman Augurs

In Scene ii, Caesar orders his "priests," or augurs (ô′ gərz), to make a sacrifice to determine whether he should go to the Senate.

- In ancient Rome, augurs were officials who examined signs to determine whether the gods would grant success to a particular venture or plan.
- After receiving a negative judgment from the augurs, a Roman leader might postpone an attack or cancel a meeting.
- By the first century A.D., there were sixteen official augurs.

▲ Another class of priest, the *haruspices* (hə rus′ pə sēs′), examined the patterns in the innards of a sacrificed animal.

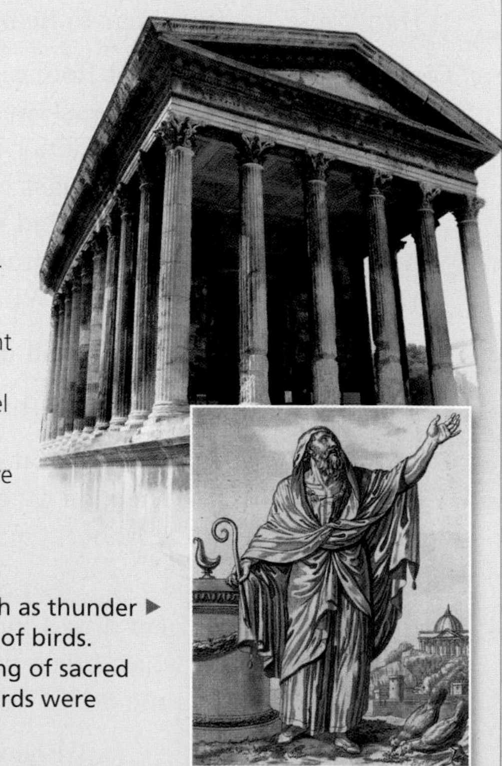

Augurs watched for signs such as thunder and lightning and the flights of birds. They also observed the pecking of sacred chickens. Omens related to birds were called auspices. ▶

Connect to the Literature What does Caesar's own interpretation of his augurs' omen show about the straightforwardness of augury?

Calpurnia. Caesar, I never stood on ceremonies,[2]
Yet now they fright me. There is one within,
Besides the things that we have heard and seen,
Recounts most horrid sights seen by the watch.[3]
A lioness hath whelpèd[4] in the streets,
And graves have yawned, and yielded up their dead;
Fierce fiery warriors fought upon the clouds
In ranks and squadrons and right form of war,[5]
Which drizzled blood upon the Capitol;
The noise of battle hurtled[6] in the air,
Horses did neigh and dying men did groan,
And ghosts did shriek and squeal about the street.
O Caesar, these things are beyond all use,[7]
And I do fear them.

Caesar. What can be avoided
Whose end is purposed[8] by the mighty gods?
Yet Caesar shall go forth; for these predictions
Are to the world in general as to Caesar.[9]

Calpurnia. When beggars die, there are no comets seen;
The heavens themselves blaze forth[10] the death of princes.

Caesar. Cowards die many times before their deaths;
The valiant never taste of death but once.
Of all the wonders that I yet have heard,
It seems to me most strange that men should fear,
Seeing that death, a necessary end,
Will come when it will come.

[*Enter a* Servant.]

What say the augurers?

Servant. They would not have you to stir forth today.
Plucking the entrails of an offering forth,[11]
They could not find a heart within the beast.

Caesar. The gods do this in shame of[12] cowardice:
Caesar should be a beast without a heart
If he should stay at home today for fear.
No, Caesar shall not; Danger knows full well
That Caesar is more dangerous than he.
We are two lions littered[13] in one day,
And I the elder and more terrible,
And Caesar shall go forth.

Calpurnia. Alas, my lord,
Your wisdom is consumed in confidence.[14]

2. **stood on ceremonies** paid attention to omens.
3. **Recounts . . . watch** tells about the awful sights seen by the watchman.
4. **whelpèd** *v.* given birth.
5. **right form of war** proper military formation of war.
6. **hurtled** (hurt´ əld) *v.* clashed.
7. **beyond all use** contrary to all experience.
8. **is purposed** is intended.
9. **for these . . . as to Caesar** because these predictions apply to the rest of the world as much as they apply to Caesar.
10. **blaze forth** proclaim with meteors and comets.
11. **Plucking . . . forth** pulling out the insides of a sacrificed animal (which were then "read" by augurs).
12. **in shame of** in order to shame.
13. **littered** *v.* born.
14. **confidence** *n.* overconfidence.

Paraphrase
Paraphrase the ideas in lines 32–33.

Comprehension
Why does Calpurnia urge Caesar to stay home?

Do not go forth today. Call it my fear
That keeps you in the house and not your own.
We'll send Mark Antony to the Senate House,
And he shall say you are not well today.
Let me, upon my knee, prevail in this.

CAESAR. Mark Antony shall say I am not well,
And for thy humor,[15] I will stay at home.

15. **humor** *n.* whim.

[*Enter* DECIUS.]

Here's Decius Brutus, he shall tell them so.

DECIUS. Caesar, all hail! Good morrow, worthy Caesar;
I come to fetch you to the Senate House.

CAESAR. And you are come in very happy time[16]
To bear my greeting to the senators,
And tell them that I will not come today.
Cannot, is false; and that I dare not, falser:
I will not come today. Tell them so, Decius.

16. **in very happy time** at just the right moment.

CALPURNIA. Say he is sick.

LITERATURE IN CONTEXT

History Connection

The Roman Senate

Caesar is preparing to meet the Senate, the oldest Roman political institution. By this time, the Senate had evolved into the most powerful part of the Roman government:

- Before Caesar's rise to power, the Senate was made up of 500 to 600 members.
- The Senate met in the Curia in the Roman Forum (see page 596).
- Senators were appointed for life. Originally, all were from the *patrician*, or aristocratic, class.
- The Senate shaped policy through advice it issued to various officials, its powers to appoint officials, and its power to negotiate with foreign countries.
- After Caesar won his victory over Pompey, he eliminated his enemies in the Senate and packed it with supporters, including men of lower rank and people from outlying provinces.

Connect to the Literature How does this information help explain the motives of the conspirators, many of whom are senators?

Caesar. Shall Caesar send a lie?
Have I in conquest stretched mine arm so far
To be afeard to tell graybeards[17] the truth?
Decius, go tell them Caesar will not come.

Decius. Most mighty Caesar, let me know some cause,
Lest I be laughed at when I tell them so.

Caesar. The cause is in my will: I will not come.
That is enough to satisfy the Senate.
But for your private satisfaction,
Because I love you, I will let you know.
Calpurnia here, my wife, stays me at home.
She dreamt tonight she saw my statue,
Which, like a fountain with an hundred spouts,
Did run pure blood, and many lusty Romans
Came smiling and did bathe their hands in it.
And these does she apply for[18] warnings and portents
And evils **imminent**, and on her knee
Hath begged that I will stay at home today.

Decius. This dream is all amiss interpreted;
It was a vision fair and fortunate:
Your statue spouting blood in many pipes,
In which so many smiling Romans bathed,
Signifies that from you great Rome shall suck
Reviving blood, and that great men shall press
For tinctures, stains, relics, and cognizance.[19]
This by Calpurnia's dream is signified.

Caesar. And this way have you well expounded[20] it.

Decius. I have, when you have heard what I can say;
And know it now, the Senate have concluded
To give this day a crown to mighty Caesar.
If you shall send them word you will not come,
Their minds may change. Besides, it were a mock
Apt to be rendered,[21] for someone to say
"Break up the Senate till another time,
When Caesar's wife shall meet with better dreams."
If Caesar hide himself, shall they not whisper
"Lo, Caesar is afraid"?
Pardon me, Caesar, for my dear dear love
To your proceeding[22] bids me tell you this,
And reason to my love is liable.[23]

17. **afeard to tell graybeards** afraid to tell old men (the senators).
18. **apply for** consider to be.

◀ Vocabulary
imminent (im´ ə nənt) *adj.* about to happen

19. **shall press . . . cognizance** Decius interprets Calpurnia's dream with a double meaning. To Caesar he suggests that people will beg for badges to show they are Caesar's servants; to the audience, that people will seek remembrances of his death.
20. **expounded** (eks pound´ id) *v.* interpreted; explained.
21. **mock . . . rendered** jeering comment likely to be made.
22. **proceeding** *n.* advancing in your career.
23. **reason . . . liable** my judgment about what I should or should not say is not as strong as my affection for you is.

Comprehension
What does Decius say about the dream?

Caesar. How foolish do your fears seem now, Calpurnia!
I am ashamèd I did yield to them.
Give me my robe,[24] for I will go.

24. **robe** *n.* toga.

[*Enter* Brutus, Ligarius, Metellus Cimber, Casca, Trebonius, Cinna, *and* Publius.]

And look where Publius is come to fetch me.

Publius. Good morrow, Caesar.

Caesar. Welcome, Publius.
What, Brutus, are you stirred so early too?
Good morrow, Casca. Caius Ligarius.
Caesar was ne'er so much your enemy[25]
As that same ague[26] which hath made you lean.
What is't o'clock?

Brutus. Caesar, 'tis strucken eight.

Caesar. I thank you for your pains and courtesy.

25. **Caius Ligarius . . . your enemy** Caesar had recently pardoned Ligarius for supporting Pompey during the civil war.
26. **ague** (ā´ gyōō) *n.* fever.
27. **revels** (rev´ əlz) *v.* makes merry.

[*Enter* Antony.]

See! Antony, that revels[27] long a-nights,
Is notwithstanding up. Good morrow, Antony.

Antony. So to most noble Caesar.

Caesar. Bid them prepare[28] within.
I am to blame to be thus waited for.
Now, Cinna; now, Metellus; what Trebonius,
I have an hour's talk in store for you;
Remember that you call on me today;
Be near me, that I may remember you.

28. **prepare** *v.* set out refreshments.

Paraphrase
Paraphrase lines 124–125.

Trebonius. Caesar, I will [*aside*] and so near will I be,
That your best friends shall wish I had been further.

Caesar. Good friends, go in and taste some wine with me,
And we (like friends) will straightway go together.

Brutus. [*Aside*] That every like is not the same,[29] O Caesar,
The heart of Brutus earns[30] to think upon. [*Exit*]

29. **That every like . . . the same** that is, that everyone who seems like a friend may actually be an enemy.
30. **earns** *v.* sorrows.

Scene iii. A street near the Capitol, close to Brutus' house.

[*Enter* Artemidorus, *reading a paper.*]

Artemidorus. "Caesar, beware of Brutus; take heed of Cassius;
come not near Casca; have an eye to Cinna; trust not
Trebonius; mark well Metellus Cimber; Decius Brutus loves

thee not; thou hast wronged Caius Ligarius. There is but one mind in all these men, and it is bent against Caesar. If thou beest not immortal, look about you: security gives way to conspiracy.[1] The mighty gods defend thee!

Thy lover,[2] ARTEMIDORUS."

Here will I stand till Caesar pass along,
And as a suitor[3] will I give him this.
My heart laments that virtue cannot live
Out of the teeth of emulation.[4]
If thou read this, O Caesar, thou mayest live;
If not, the Fates with traitors do contrive.[5] [*Exit*]

1. **security . . . conspiracy** overconfident carelessness allows the conspiracy to proceed.
2. **lover** *n.* devoted friend.
3. **suitor** (so͞ot´ ər) *n.* person who requests, petitions, or entreats.
4. **Out of the teeth of emulation** beyond the reach of envy.
5. **contrive** *v.* conspire.

Scene iv. Another part of the street.

[*Enter* PORTIA *and* LUCIUS.]

PORTIA. I prithee,[1] boy, run to the Senate House;
Stay not to answer me, but get thee gone.
Why dost thou stay?

LUCIUS. To know my errand, madam.

PORTIA. I would have had thee there and here again
Ere I can tell thee what thou shouldst do there.

1. **prithee** (prith´ ē) "pray thee"; ask you please.

Comprehension
What does Artemidorus plan to do?

◀ Critical Viewing
When might Caesar have participated in an event like the one depicted on this cup? Explain.

O constancy,[2] be strong upon my side;
Set a huge mountain 'tween my heart and tongue!
I have a man's mind, but a woman's might.[3]
How hard it is for women to keep counsel![4]
Art thou here yet?

LUCIUS. Madam, what should I do?
Run to the Capitol, and nothing else?
And so return to you, and nothing else?

PORTIA. Yes, bring me word, boy, if thy lord look well,
For he went sickly forth; and take good note
What Caesar doth, what suitors press to him.
Hark, boy, what noise is that?

LUCIUS. I hear none, madam.

PORTIA. Prithee, listen well.
I heard a bustling rumor like a fray,[5]
And the wind brings it from the Capitol.

LUCIUS. Sooth,[6] madam, I hear nothing.

[*Enter the* SOOTHSAYER.]

PORTIA. Come hither, fellow. Which way hast thou been?

SOOTHSAYER. At mine own house, good lady.

PORTIA. What is't o'clock?

SOOTHSAYER. About the ninth hour, lady.

PORTIA. Is Caesar yet gone to the Capitol?

SOOTHSAYER. Madam, not yet; I go to take my stand,
To see him pass on the Capitol.

PORTIA. Thou hast some suit[7] to Caesar, hast thou not?

SOOTHSAYER. That I have, lady; if it will please Caesar
To be so good to Caesar as to hear me,
I shall beseech him to befriend himself.

PORTIA. Why, know'st thou any harm's intended towards him?

SOOTHSAYER. None that I know will be, much that I fear may
chance.
Good morrow to you. Here the street is narrow;
The throng that follows Caesar at the heels,
Of senators, of praetors,[8] common suitors,

2. **constancy** (kän′ stən sē) *n.* firmness of mind or purpose; resoluteness.
3. **might** *n.* strength.
4. **keep counsel** keep secrets.

Blank Verse
Why might Shakespeare present Lucius' lines in blank verse in this scene?

5. **fray** (frā) *n.* fight; brawl.
6. **Sooth** (so͞o*th*) *interjection* truly.

7. **suit** (so͞ot) *n.* petition.
8. **praetors** (prē′ tərz) *n.* Roman officials of the rank below consul.

Comprehension
What does Portia ask of Lucius?

◄ Critical Viewing
Judging from its ruins, how might the Forum in Rome have compared to a modern city center?

9. **void** (void) *adj.* empty.

10. **speed** *v.* make successful.

11. **enterprise** (en′ tər prīz′) *n.* undertaking; project.

12. **command me** give my kind regard.

Will crowd a feeble man almost to death.
I'll get me to a place more void,[9] and there
Speak to great Caesar as he comes along.

[*Exit*]

Portia. I must go in. Ay me, how weak a thing
The heart of woman is! O Brutus,
The heavens speed[10] thee in thine enterprise![11]
Sure, the boy heard me—Brutus hath a suit
That Caesar will not grant—O, I grow faint.
Run, Lucius, and commend me[12] to my lord;
Say I am merry; come to me again,
And bring me word what he doth say to thee.

[*Exit separately*]

Language Study

Vocabulary The italicized word in each item below appears in *The Tragedy of Julius Caesar,* Act II. For each item, determine whether or not the words are synonyms, or words of similar meanings. Explain your reasoning.

1. *augmented*, angered
2. *insurrection*, revolt
3. *resolution*, glory
4. *wrathfully*, furiously
5. *imminent*, enduring

WORD STUDY

The **Latin prefix *en-*** means "in," "into," or "within." In the play, a character wonders if he is being **entreated**, or asked in earnest, to act for the good of his country.

Word Study

Part A Explain how the **Latin prefix *en-*** contributes to the meanings of *endanger, encircle,* and *enlighten*. Consult a dictionary if necessary.

Part B Use the context of the sentences and what you know about the Latin prefix *en-* to explain your answer to each question.

1. Are children safe if a new toy *endangers* them?
2. If critics are *enthralled* by a movie, will they give it bad reviews?

Close Reading Activities

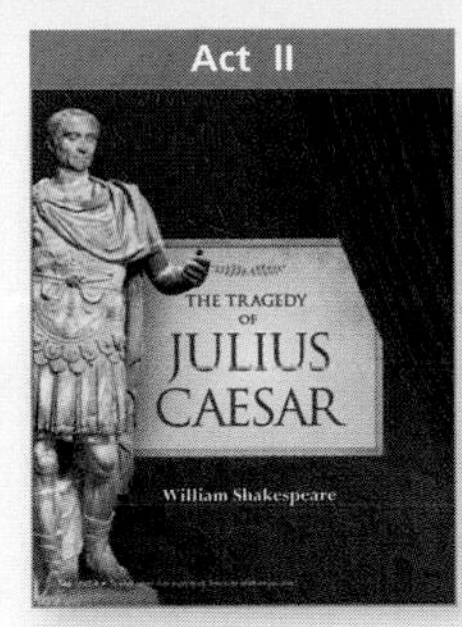

Literary Analysis

Key Ideas and Details

1. **(a)** In Act II, Scene i, what coming event disturbs Brutus? Cite details from the text that provide this information. **(b) Interpret:** In Scene i, lines 32–34, what point does Brutus make in comparing Caesar to a serpent's egg? Explain.
2. **(a)** What does the writer of the letter that Lucius finds urge Brutus to do? **(b) Infer:** Why do you think the writer leaves gaps in the letter? **(c) Infer:** What inferences can you draw from the way Brutus fills in these gaps? Explain, citing details from the text that support your inferences.
3. **Paraphrase** Paraphrase Brutus' two questions in line 234 of Scene i.
4. **Paraphrase (a)** List four words in Portia's final speech in Scene iv that are no longer used or no longer used in the same sense. For each, give a modern word that means the same thing. **(b)** Paraphrase the speech.

Craft and Structure

5. **Blank Verse (a)** Copy lines 42–43 of Scene ii and mark them to indicate the stressed (′) and unstressed (˘) syllables. **(b)** Which line of blank verse illustrates perfect iambic pentameter? **(c)** Explain how the rhythm of the other line reinforces the importance of certain words.
6. **Blank Verse** Create a chart like the one shown to examine the dialogue of Flavius, the Cobbler, Brutus, and Portia in Acts I and II. Select a passage of dialogue for each character. Indicate whether the character typically speaks in blank verse or prose, and identify each as either an aristocrat or a commoner. Complete one chart for each character.

Character
Example Dialogue
Blank Verse or Prose?
Aristocrat or Commoner?

Integration of Knowledge and Ideas

7. **(a) Analyze:** Why does Brutus decide to join the conspirators? **(b) Evaluate:** Are Brutus' reasons for joining the conspiracy convincing or flawed? Explain.

8. THE BIG ? **To what extent does experience determine what we perceive?** Calpurnia and Decius Brutus have different interpretations of Calpurnia's dream. **(a)** What is Calpurnia's perception of her dream? What information contributes to her point of view? **(b)** What is Decius Brutus' interpretation of her dream? What information underlies his explanation?

ACADEMIC VOCABULARY

As you write and speak about *The Tragedy of Julius Caesar*, use the words related to experience and perceptions that you explored on page 517 of this book.

Building Knowledge

To what extent does experience determine what we perceive?

Explore the Big Question as you read *The Tragedy of Julius Caesar,* Act III. Take notes on how the characters' experiences shape their perceptions and actions.

CLOSE READING FOCUS

Key Ideas and Details: **Analyze Imagery**

Writers often use **imagery**, language that appeals to the senses, to make abstract ideas vivid and concrete. In Act III, Shakespeare uses many images that focus on words and the body, including the following:

- Wounds that speak
- Burying Caesar's body rather than speaking praise of him
- "Plucking" a poet's name out of his heart

In each case, a reference to words (speech, praise, names) is coupled with an image of a person's physical body (a corpse, wounds, the heart). In this way, Shakespeare links physical violence in Rome with disrespect for laws—the words that bind society. As you read Act III, look for examples of such imagery.

Craft and Structure: **Dramatic Speeches**

Many plays feature specialized forms of dialogue called **dramatic speeches**.

- **Soliloquy:** a long speech in which a character, usually alone on stage, reveals private thoughts and feelings. While the character may address the audience directly, the convention is that the audience is simply overhearing the character talking or thinking out loud.
- **Aside:** a remark a character makes, usually to the audience, that is not heard by other characters on stage
- **Monologue:** a long speech by one character usually heard by the other characters

Each type of dramatic speech serves multiple purposes. For example, a monologue may reveal the play's theme or advance the plot.

Vocabulary

The words below are key to understanding the selection. Decide whether you know each word well, know it a little bit, or do not know it at all. After you read, see how your knowledge of each word has increased.

confounded	**spectacle**	**prophesy**
strife	**discourse**	**interred**

Common Core State Standards

Reading Literature

1. Cite strong and thorough textual evidence to support analysis of what the text says explicitly as well as inferences drawn from the text.

3. Analyze how complex characters develop over the course of a text, interact with other characters, and advance the plot or develop the theme.

4. Determine the meaning of words and phrases as they are used in the text, including figurative and connotative meanings; analyze the cumulative impact of word choices on meaning and tone.

Act III

THE TRAGEDY OF JULIUS CAESAR

William Shakespeare

CLOSE READING MODEL

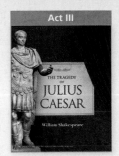

The passages below are from *The Tragedy of Julius Caesar*, Act III. The annotations to the right of the passages show ways in which you can use close reading skills to analyze imagery and dramatic speeches.

from *The Tragedy of Julius Caesar,* Act III

ANTONY. ...Gentlemen all—alas, what shall I say?
My credit now stands on such slippery ground
That one of two bad ways you must conceit me,
Either a coward or a flatterer.
That I did love thee, Caesar, O, 'tis true!
If then thy spirit look upon us now,
Shall it not grieve thee dearer than thy death
To see thy Antony making his peace,
Shaking the bloody fingers of thy foes,[1]
Most noble, in the presence of thy corse?
Had I as many eyes as thou hast wounds,
Weeping as fast as they stream forth thy blood,
It would become me better than to close
In terms of friendship with thine enemies.[2]

....

ANTONY. O pardon me, thou bleeding piece of earth,
That I am meek and gentle with these butchers!
Thou art the ruins of the noblest man
That ever livèd in the tide of times.
Woe to the hand that shed this costly blood![3]
Over thy wounds now do I prophesy
(Which like dumb mouths do ope their ruby lips
To beg the voice and utterance of my tongue),
A curse shall light upon the limbs of men;[4]
Domestic fury and fierce civil strife
Shall cumber all the parts of Italy....

Dramatic Speeches

1 In this monologue, Antony addresses the conspirators directly, and then—as the conspirators look on—delivers an emotional outpouring of grief over Caesar.

Analyze Imagery

2 Shakespeare likens Caesar's wounds to eyes streaming tears. This bold imagery links Caesar's dead body to the extraordinary grief that Antony actually feels and believes he should express.

Dramatic Speeches

3 Later in the same scene, Antony is left alone on stage to deliver this soliloquy. Out of earshot of the other characters, he reveals critical information: He will have revenge on the "butchers."

Analyze Imagery

4 Shakespeare compares Caesar's open stab wounds to mouths that beg Antony to speak. This graphic, disturbing image links the physicality of Caesar's dead body to an abstract idea—the need for justice.

REVIEW AND ANTICIPATE

Having ignored the warnings of the soothsayer in Act I and those of his wife, Calpurnia, in Act II, Caesar proceeds to the Capitol on the ides of March. Decius has told him that the Senate is ready to confer a crown upon him. Caesar is accompanied by the conspirators, led by Cassius and Brutus, as well as by his friend Mark Antony. Meanwhile, Artemidorus plans to reveal the conspiracy to Caesar. As Act III unfolds, Caesar approaches the Capitol, and events take a fateful, irreversible turn.

Act III

Scene i. Rome. Before the Capitol.

[*Flourish of trumpets. Enter* CAESAR, BRUTUS, CASSIUS, CASCA, DECIUS, METELLUS CIMBER, TREBONIUS, CINNA, ANTONY, LEPIDUS, ARTEMIDORUS, PUBLIUS, POPILIUS, *and the* SOOTHSAYER.]

CAESAR. The ides of March are come.

SOOTHSAYER. Ay, Caesar, but not gone.

ARTEMIDORUS. Hail, Caesar! Read this schedule.[1]

DECIUS. Trebonius doth desire you to o'er-read,
At your best leisure, this his humble suit.[2]

ARTEMIDORUS. O Caesar, read mine first; for mine's a suit
That touches[3] Caesar nearer. Read it, great Caesar.

CAESAR. What touches us ourself shall be last served.

ARTEMIDORUS. Delay not, Caesar; read it instantly.

CAESAR. What, is the fellow mad?

PUBLIUS. Sirrah, give place.[4]

CASSIUS. What, urge you your petitions in the street?
Come to the Capitol.

[CAESAR *goes to the Capitol, the rest following.*]

POPILIUS. I wish your enterprise today may thrive.

CASSIUS. What enterprise, Popilius?

POPILIUS. Fare you well.

[*Advances to* CAESAR]

BRUTUS. What said Popilius Lena?

CASSIUS. He wished today our enterprise might thrive.
I fear our purpose is discoverèd.

BRUTUS. Look how he makes to[5] Caesar; mark him.

CASSIUS. Casca, be sudden,[6] for we fear prevention.
Brutus, what shall be done? If this be known,
Cassius or Caesar never shall turn back,[7]
For I will slay myself.

1. **schedule** (ske´ jo͞ol) *n.* paper.
2. **suit** *n.* petition; plea.
3. **touches** *v.* concerns.

Dramatic Speeches
How does the dialogue between Artemidorus and Caesar create suspense?

4. **give place** get out of the way.

5. **makes to** approaches.
6. **be sudden** be quick.
7. **Cassius . . . back** either Cassius or Caesar will not return alive.

Comprehension
What does Artemidorus want Caesar to do?

8. **constant** *adj.* firm; calm.
9. **change** *v.* that is, change the expression on his face.
10. **presently prefer his suit** immediately present his petition.
11. **addressed** *adj.* ready.
12. **second** *v.* support.
13. **amiss . . . redress** wrong that Caesar and his Senate must correct.
14. **puissant** (pyo͞o ′ i sənt) *adj.* powerful.

Brutus. Cassius, be constant.[8]
Popilius Lena speaks not of our purposes;
For look, he smiles, and Caesar doth not change.[9]

Cassius. Trebonius knows his time; for look you, Brutus,
He draws Mark Antony out of the way.

[*Exit* Antony *and* Trebonius.]

Decius. Where is Metellus Cimber? Let him go
And presently prefer his suit[10] to Caesar.

Brutus. He is addressed.[11] Press near and second[12] him.

Cinna. Casca, you are the first that rears your hand.

Caesar. Are we all ready? What is now amiss
That Caesar and his Senate must redress?[13]

Metellus. Most high, most mighty, and most puissant[14] Caesar,
Metellus Cimber throws before thy seat
An humble heart. [*Kneeling*]

LITERATURE IN CONTEXT

History Connection

The Roman Forum

Caesar receives petitioners at the Senate House in the Roman Forum. Consisting of a plaza, or open space lined with buildings, the Forum (shown here) was the center of government and commercial activity in ancient Rome.

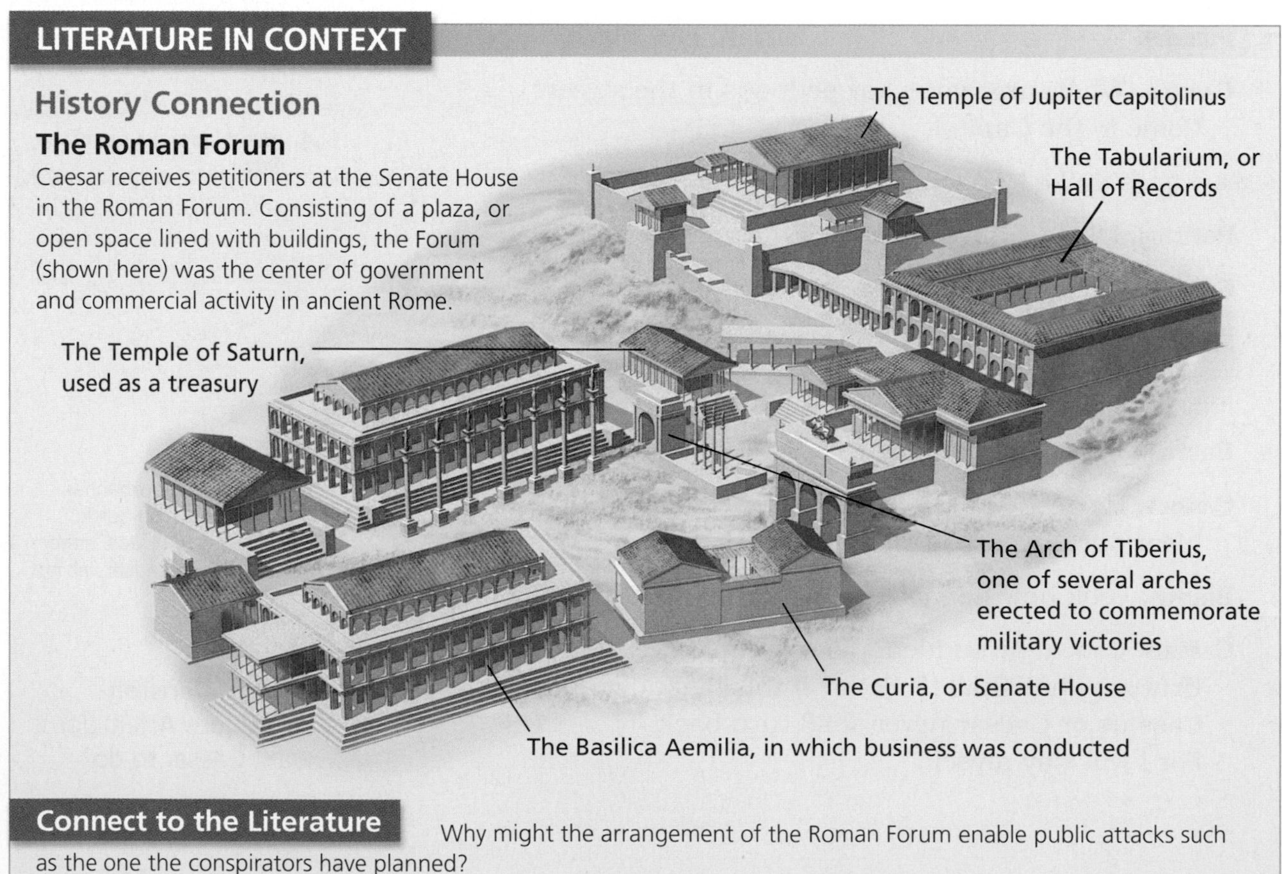

Connect to the Literature Why might the arrangement of the Roman Forum enable public attacks such as the one the conspirators have planned?

CAESAR. I must prevent thee, Cimber.
These couchings and these lowly courtesies[15]
Might fire the blood of ordinary men,
And turn preordinance and first decree
Into the law of children.[16] Be not fond[17]
To think that Caesar bears such rebel blood
That will be thawed from the true quality[18]
With that which melteth fools—I mean sweet words,
Low-crookèd curtsies, and base spaniel fawning.[19]
Thy brother by decree is banishèd.
If thou dost bend and pray and fawn for him,
I spurn[20] thee like a cur out of my way.
Know, Caesar doth not wrong, nor without cause
Will he be satisfied.

METELLUS. Is there no voice more worthy than my own,
To sound more sweetly in great Caesar's ear
For the repealing[21] of my banished brother?

BRUTUS. I kiss thy hand, but not in flattery, Caesar,
Desiring thee that Publius Cimber may
Have an immediate freedom of repeal.[22]

CAESAR. What, Brutus?

15. **couchings . . . courtesies** low bowings and humble gestures of reverence.
16. **And turn . . . law of children** and change what has already been decided as children might change their minds.
17. **fond** *adj.* foolish (enough).
18. **rebel . . . quality** unstable disposition that will lose its firmness.
19. **base spaniel fawning** low doglike cringing.
20. **spurn** *v.* kick disdainfully.
21. **repealing** *n.* recalling; ending the banishment.
22. **freedom of repeal** permission to be recalled.

Comprehension
What worries Cassius?

▼ Critical Viewing
Judging from these ruins of the Roman Forum, how large might the crowds around the Senate have been on the ides of March? Explain.

Cassius. Pardon, Caesar; Caesar, pardon!
As low as to thy foot doth Cassius fall
To beg enfranchisement[23] for Publius Cimber.

Caesar. I could be well moved, if I were as you;
If I could pray to move,[24] prayers would move me;
But I am constant as the Northern Star,
Of whose true-fixed and resting[25] quality
There is no fellow[26] in the firmament.[27]
The skies are painted with unnumb'red sparks,
They are all fire and every one doth shine;
But there's but one in all doth hold his[28] place.
So in the world; 'tis furnished well with men,
And men are flesh and blood, and apprehensive;[29]
Yet in the number I do know but one
That unassailable holds on his rank,[30]
Unshaked of motion;[31] and that I am he,

23. **enfranchisement** (en fran′ chīz mənt) *n.* freedom.
24. **pray to move** beg others to change their minds.
25. **resting** *adj.* immovable.
26. **fellow** *n.* equal.
27. **firmament** (fur′ mə mənt) *n.* sky.
28. **his** *pron.* its.
29. **apprehensive** (ap′ rə hen′ siv) *adj.* able to understand.
30. **one/That unassailable . . . rank** one who, unattackable, maintains his position.
31. **Unshaked of motion** unmoved by his own or others' impulses.

▼ Critical Viewing
Which details in this picture suggest Caesar's ignorance?

Let me a little show it, even in this—
That I was constant[32] Cimber should be banished,
And constant do remain to keep him so.

CINNA. O Caesar—

CAESAR. Hence! Wilt thou lift up Olympus?[33]

DECIUS. Great Caesar—

CAESAR. Doth not Brutus bootless[34] kneel?

CASCA. Speak hands for me! [*They stab* CAESAR.]

CAESAR. *Et tu, Brutè?*[35] Then fall, Caesar. [*Dies*]

CINNA. Liberty! Freedom! Tyranny is dead!
Run hence, proclaim, cry it about the streets.

CASSIUS. Some to the common pulpits,[36] and cry out
"Liberty, freedom, and enfranchisement!"

BRUTUS. People, and senators, be not affrighted.
Fly not; stand still; ambition's debt is paid.[37]

CASCA. Go to the pulpit, Brutus.

DECIUS. And Cassius too.

BRUTUS. Where's Publius?[38]

CINNA. Here, quite **confounded** with this mutiny.[39]

METELLUS. Stand fast together, lest some friend of Caesar's
Should chance—

BRUTUS. Talk not of standing. Publius, good cheer;
There is no harm intended to your person,
Nor to no Roman else. So tell them, Publius.

CASSIUS. And leave us, Publius, lest that the people
Rushing on us should do your age some mischief.

BRUTUS. Do so; and let no man abide[40] this deed
But we the doers.

[*Enter* TREBONIUS.]

CASSIUS. Where is Antony?

TREBONIUS. Fled to his house amazed.[41]
Men, wives, and children stare, cry out and run,
As[42] it were doomsday.

BRUTUS. Fates, we will know your pleasures.

---

32. constant *adj.* determined.

33. Olympus (ō lim′ pəs) *n.* mountain in Greece on which the Greek gods were said to live.

34. bootless (bo͞ot′ lis) *adv.* uselessly.

Analyze Imagery
In what way does line 76 combine ideas of words with images of violence?

35. Et tu, Brutè? Latin for "And you, too, Brutus?"

36. pulpits (pul′ pits) *n.* speakers' platforms.

37. ambition's . . . paid ambition received what it deserved.

38. Publius (po͞ob′ lē əs) an elderly senator.

◀ Vocabulary
confounded (kən foun′ did) *adj.* made to feel confused

39. mutiny (myo͞ot′ 'n ē) *n.* revolt against authority, such as a rebellion of soldiers against their officers.

40. let no man abide let no man take responsibility for.

41. amazed *adj.* astounded.

42. As *conj.* as if.

Comprehension
What do the conspirators do to Caesar?

That we shall die, we know; 'tis but the time,
And drawing days out, that men stand upon.[43]

Casca. Why, he that cuts off twenty years of life
Cuts off so many years of fearing death.

Brutus. Grant that, and then is death a benefit.
So are we Caesar's friends, that have abridged
His time of fearing death. Stoop, Romans, stoop,
And let us bathe our hands in Caesar's blood
Up to the elbows, and besmear our swords.
Then walk we forth, even to the market place,[44]
And waving our red weapons o'er our heads,
Let's all cry "Peace, freedom, and liberty!"

Cassius. Stoop then, and wash. How many ages hence
Shall this our lofty scene be acted over
In states unborn and accents yet unknown!

Brutus. How many times shall Caesar bleed in sport,[45]
That now on Pompey's basis lies along[46]
No worthier than the dust!

Cassius. So oft as that shall be,
So often shall the knot[47] of us be called
The men that gave their country liberty.

Decius. What, shall we forth?

Cassius. Ay, every man away.
Brutus shall lead, and we will grace his heels[48]
With the most boldest and best hearts of Rome.

[*Enter a* Servant.]

Brutus. Soft,[49] who comes here? A friend of Antony's.

Servant. Thus, Brutus, did my master bid me kneel;
Thus did Mark Antony bid me fall down;
And, being prostrate, thus he bade me say:
Brutus is noble, wise, valiant, and honest;
Caesar was mighty, bold, royal,[50] and loving.
Say I love Brutus and I honor him;
Say I feared Caesar, honored him, and loved him.
If Brutus will vouchsafe that Antony
May safely come to him and be resolved[51]
How Caesar hath deserved to lie in death,
Mark Antony shall not love Caesar dead
So well as Brutus living; but will follow
The fortunes and affairs of noble Brutus

43. 'tis but the time . . . upon It is only the time of death and the length of life that people care about.

Analyze Imagery
Find an example of an image linking blood and words in lines 103–110.

44. market place the open area of the Roman Forum, the center of government, business, and public life in ancient Rome.

45. in sport for amusement; the deed will be acted out in plays.

46. on Pompey's basis lies along by the pedestal of Pompey's statue lies stretched out.

47. knot *n.* group.

48. grace his heels do honor to his heels; follow him.

49. Soft *interjection* wait

50. royal *adj.* showing noble generosity.

51. be resolved have it explained.

Thorough the hazards of this untrod state[52]
With all true faith. So says my master Antony.

Brutus. Thy master is a wise and valiant Roman;
I never thought him worse.
Tell him, so[53] please him come unto this place,
He shall be satisfied and, by my honor,
Depart untouched.

Servant. I'll fetch him presently.[54]

[*Exit* Servant]

Brutus. I know that we shall have him well to friend.[55]

Cassius. I wish we may. But yet have I a mind
That fears him much; and my misgiving still
Falls shrewdly to the purpose.[56]

[*Enter* Antony.]

Brutus. But here comes Antony. Welcome, Mark Antony.

Antony. O mighty Caesar! Dost thou lie so low?
Are all thy conquests, glories, triumphs, spoils,
Shrunk to this little measure? Fare thee well.
I know not, gentlemen, what you intend,
Who else must be let blood,[57] who else is rank.[58]
If I myself, there is no hour so fit
As Caesar's death's hour, nor no instrument
Of half that worth as those your swords, made rich
With the most noble blood of all this world.
I do beseech ye, if you bear me hard,[59]
Now, whilst your purpled hands[60] do reek and smoke,
Fulfill your pleasure. Live[61] a thousand years,
I shall not find myself so apt[62] to die;
No place will please me so, no mean of death,[63]
As here by Caesar, and by you cut off,
The choice and master spirits of this age.

Brutus. O Antony, beg not your death of us!
Though now we must appear bloody and cruel,
As by our hands and this our present act
You see we do, yet see you but our hands
And this the bleeding business they have done.
Our hearts you see not; they are pitiful;[64]
And pity to the general wrong of Rome—
As fire drives out fire, so pity pity[65]—
Hath done this deed on Caesar. For your part,
To you our swords have leaden[66] points, Mark Antony:

52. **Thorough . . . state** through the dangers of this new state of affairs.

53. **so** *conj.* if it should.

54. **presently** *adv.* immediately.

55. **to friend** as a friend.

56. **my misgiving . . . to the purpose** my doubts always turn out to be justified.

Dramatic Speeches
What is Antony's purpose in delivering this monologue?

57. **be let blood** (a pun) "be bled for medical purposes" or "be killed."

58. **rank** (a pun) "too powerful" or "swollen with disease and therefore in need of bloodletting."

59. **bear me hard** have a grudge against me.

60. **purpled hands** bloody hands.

61. **Live** if I live.

62. **apt** *adj.* ready.

63. **mean of death** way of dying.

64. **pitiful** *adj.* full of pity or compassion.

65. **pity pity** pity for Rome drove out pity for Caesar.

66. **leaden** *adj.* dull; blunt.

Comprehension
What does Antony ask of the conspirators?

Our arms in strength of malice, and our hearts
Of brothers' temper,[67] do receive you in
With all kind love, good thoughts, and reverence.

67. **Our arms . . . / Of brothers' temper** our arms strengthened with the desire to do harm and our hearts filled with brotherly feelings.

Cassius. Your voice[68] shall be as strong as any man's
In the disposing of new dignities.[69]

68. **voice** *n.* vote.

69. **dignities** *n.* offices.

Brutus. Only be patient till we have appeased
The multitude, beside themselves with fear,
And then we will deliver[70] you the cause
Why I, that did love Caesar when I struck him,
Have thus proceeded.

70. **deliver** *v.* tell to.

Antony. I doubt not of your wisdom.
Let each man render me his bloody hand.
First, Marcus Brutus, will I shake with you;
Next, Caius Cassius, do I take your hand;
Now, Decius Brutus, yours; now yours, Metellus;
Yours, Cinna; and, my valiant Casca, yours;
Though last, not least in love, yours, good Trebonius.
Gentlemen all—alas, what shall I say?
My credit[71] now stands on such slippery ground
That one of two bad ways you must conceit[72] me,
Either a coward or a flatterer.
That I did love thee, Caesar, O, 'tis true!
If then thy spirit look upon us now,
Shall it not grieve thee dearer[73] than thy death
To see thy Antony making his peace,
Shaking the bloody fingers of thy foes,
Most noble, in the presence of thy corse?[74]
Had I as many eyes as thou hast wounds,
Weeping as fast as they stream forth thy blood,
It would become me better than to close[75]
In terms of friendship with thine enemies.
Pardon me, Julius! Here wast thou bayed,[76] brave hart;[77]
Here didst thou fall, and here thy hunters stand,
Signed in thy spoil[78] and crimsoned in thy Lethe.[79]
O world, thou wast the forest to this hart;
And this indeed, O world, the heart of thee.
How like a deer, stroken[80] by many princes.
Dost thou here lie!

Cassius. Mark Antony—

Dramatic Speeches

In this monologue, what image of his state of mind does Antony create for the conspirators?

71. **credit** *n.* reputation.

72. **conceit** (kən sēt′) *v.* think of.

73. **dearer** *adv.* more deeply.

74. **corse** *n.* corpse.

75. **close** (clōz) *v.* reach an agreement.

76. **bayed** *v.* cornered.

77. **hart** (härt) *n.* deer.

Analyze Imagery

What images of the body does Antony use to contrast his real grief with his words of friendship?

78. **Signed in thy spoil** marked by signs of your slaughter.

79. **Lethe** (lē′ *thē*) river in Hades, the mythological Greek underworld inhabited by the dead; here, a river of blood.

80. **stroken** *v.* struck down.

ANTONY. Pardon me, Caius Cassius.
The enemies of Caesar shall say this;
Then, in a friend, it is cold modesty.[81]

CASSIUS. I blame you not for praising Caesar so;
But what compact[82] mean you to have with us?
Will you be pricked[83] in number of our friends,
Or shall we on,[84] and not depend on you?

ANTONY. Therefore I took your hands, but was indeed
Swayed from the point by looking down on Caesar.
Friends am I with you all, and love you all,
Upon this hope, that you shall give me reasons
Why, and wherein, Caesar was dangerous.

BRUTUS. Or else were this a savage **spectacle**.
Our reasons are so full of good regard[85]
That were you, Antony, the son of Caesar,
You should be satisfied.

ANTONY. That's all I seek;
And am moreover suitor that I may
Produce[86] his body to the market place,
And in the pulpit, as becomes a friend,
Speak in the order[87] of his funeral.

BRUTUS. You shall, Mark Antony.

CASSIUS. Brutus, a word with you.
[*Aside to* BRUTUS] You know not what you do; do not consent
That Antony speak in his funeral.
Know you how much the people may be moved
By that which he will utter?

BRUTUS. By your pardon:
I will myself into the pulpit first,
And show the reason of our Caesar's death.
What Antony shall speak, I will protest[88]
He speaks by leave and by permission,
And that we are contented Caesar shall
Have all true rites and lawful ceremonies.
It shall advantage more than do us wrong.[89]

CASSIUS. I know not what may fall;[90] I like it not.

BRUTUS. Mark Antony, here, take you Caesar's body.
You shall not in your funeral speech blame us,
But speak all good you can devise of Caesar,

81. **cold modesty** calm, moderate speech.
82. **compact** (käm´ pakt) *n.* agreement.
83. **pricked** *v.* marked down; included.
84. **on** proceed.

◀ **Vocabulary**
spectacle (spek´ tə kəl) *n.* strange or remarkable sight

85. **so full of good regard** so carefully considered.
86. **Produce** *v.* bring forth.
87. **order** *n.* course of the ceremonies.

Dramatic Speeches
Why does Cassius wish to prevent others from hearing what he says in this aside to Brutus?

88. **protest** *v.* declare.
89. **advantage . . . wrong** benefit us more than hurt us.
90. **what may fall** what may happen.

Comprehension
What rules must Antony follow in delivering his funeral speech for Caesar?

And say you do't by our permission;
Else shall you not have any hand at all
About his funeral. And you shall speak
In the same pulpit whereto I am going,
After my speech is ended.

Antony. Be it so;
I do desire no more.

Brutus. Prepare the body then, and follow us.

[*Exit all but* Antony.]

Antony. O pardon me, thou bleeding piece of earth,
That I am meek and gentle with these butchers!
Thou art the ruins of the noblest man
That ever livèd in the tide of times.[91]
Woe to the hand that shed this costly blood!
Over thy wounds now do I **prophesy**
(Which like dumb mouths do ope their ruby lips
To beg the voice and utterance of my tongue),
A curse shall light upon the limbs of men;
Domestic fury and fierce civil **strife**
Shall cumber[92] all the parts of Italy;
Blood and destruction shall be so in use,[93]
And dreadful objects so familiar,
That mothers shall but smile when they behold
Their infants quartered with the hands of war,
All pity choked with custom of fell deeds;[94]
And Caesar's spirit, ranging[95] for revenge,
With Atè[96] by his side come hot from hell,
Shall in these confines[97] with a monarch's voice
Cry "Havoc,"[98] and let slip[99] the dogs of war,
That this foul deed shall smell above the earth
With carrion[100] men, groaning for burial.

[*Enter* Octavius' Servant.]

You serve Octavius Caesar, do you not?

Servant. I do, Mark Antony.

Antony. Caesar did write for him to come to Rome.

Servant. He did receive his letters and is coming,
And bid me say to you by word of mouth—
O Caesar! [*Seeing the body*]

Dramatic Speeches What does Antony's soliloquy in lines 254–275 reveal to the audience that other characters do not know?

91. tide of times course of all history.

92. cumber (kum´ bər) *v.* distress; burden.

Analyze Imagery Identify two ways in which lines 259–262 combine ideas of words and bodies.

Vocabulary ▶
prophesy (präf´ ə sī´) *v.* predict what will happen

strife (strīf) *n.* struggle; conflict

93. in use customary.

94. custom of fell deeds being used to cruel acts.

95. ranging *adj.* roaming like a wild beast in search of prey.

96. Atè (ā´ tē) Greek goddess personifying criminal folly or reckless ambition in people.

97. confines (kän´ fīnz) *n.* boundaries.

98. Havoc Latin for "no quarter," a signal for general slaughter.

99. let slip release from a leash.

100. carrion (kar´ ē ən) *adj.* dead and rotting.

▲ Critical Viewing
Which scene in the play might this image depict? Explain.

ANTONY. Thy heart is big;[101] get thee apart and weep.
Passion, I see, is catching, for mine eyes,
Seeing those beads of sorrow stand in thine,
Began to water. Is thy master coming?

SERVANT. He lies tonight within seven leagues[102] of Rome.

ANTONY. Post[103] back with speed, and tell him what hath
chanced.[104]
Here is a mourning Rome, a dangerous Rome,
No Rome of safety for Octavius yet.
Hie hence and tell him so. Yet stay awhile;
Thou shalt not back till I have borne this corse
Into the market place; there shall I try[105]
In my oration[106] how the people take
The cruel issue[107] of these bloody men;
According to the which, thou shalt **discourse**
To young Octavius of the state of things.
Lend me your hand. [*Exit*]

101. big *adj.* swollen with grief.
102. leagues (lēgz) *n.* units of measure, each equivalent in Roman times to about a mile and a half.
103. Post *v.* hasten.
104. hath chanced has happened.
105. try *v.* test.
106. oration (ō rā´ shən) *n.* formal public speech.
107. cruel issue outcome of the cruelty.

◀ Vocabulary
discourse (dis´ kôrs´) *v.* speak on a topic formally and at length

Comprehension
What is Antony's real response to Caesar's death?

Scene ii. The Forum

[*Enter* Brutus *and goes into the pulpit, and* Cassius, *with the* Plebeians.[1]]

Plebeians. We will be satisfied![2] Let us be satisfied!

Brutus. Then follow me, and give me audience, friends.
Cassius, go you into the other street
And part the numbers.[3]
Those that will hear me speak, let 'em stay here;
Those that will follow Cassius, go with him;
And public reasons shall be renderèd
Of Caesar's death.

First Plebeian. I will hear Brutus speak.

Second Plebeian. I will hear Cassius, and compare their reasons,
When severally[4] we hear them renderèd.

[*Exit* Cassius, *with some of the* Plebeians.]

Third Plebeian. The noble Brutus is ascended. Silence!

Brutus. Be patient till the last.
Romans, countrymen, and lovers,[5] hear me for my cause, and be silent, that you may hear. Believe me for mine honor, and have respect to mine honor, that you may believe. Censure[6] me in your wisdom, and awake your senses,[7] that you may the better judge. If there be any in this assembly, any dear friend of Caesar's, to him I say that Brutus' love to Caesar was no less than his. If then that friend demand why Brutus rose against Caesar, this is my answer: Not that I loved Caesar less, but that I loved Rome more. Had you rather Caesar were living, and die all slaves, than that Caesar were dead, to live all free men? As Caesar loved me, I weep for him; as he was fortunate, I rejoice at it; as he was valiant, I honor him; but, as he was ambitious, I slew him. There is tears, for his love; joy, for his fortune; honor, for his valor; and death, for his ambition. Who is here so base,[8] that would be a bondman?[9] If any, speak; for him have I offended. Who is here so rude,[10] that would not be a Roman? If any, speak; for him have I offended. Who is here so vile,[11] that will not love his country? If any, speak; for him have I offended. I pause for a reply.

All. None, Brutus, none!

1. **Plebeians** (plē bē´ ənz) *n.* commoners; members of the lower class.
2. **be satisfied** get an explanation.
3. **part the numbers** divide the crowd.
4. **severally** (sev´ ər əl ē) *adv.* separately.
5. **lovers** *n.* dear friends.
6. **Censure** (sen´ shər) *v.* judge.
7. **senses** *n.* powers of reason.

Dramatic Speeches
What is Brutus' purpose in delivering this monologue?

8. **base** *adj.* low.
9. **bondman** *n.* slave.
10. **rude** *adj.* uncivilized.
11. **vile** (vīl) *adj.* mean; low-born; of low character.

Brutus. Then none have I offended. I have done no more to Caesar than you shall do to Brutus. The question of his death is enrolled in the Capitol;[12] his glory not extenuated,[13] wherein he was worthy, nor his offenses enforced,[14] for which he suffered death.

12. **The question . . . in the Capitol** The issues that led to his death are on record in the Capitol.

13. **extenuated** (ek sten´ yo͞o āt´ id) *adj.* undervalued; made less of.

14. **enforced** (en fôrs'd´) *adj.* exaggerated.

[*Enter* Mark Antony, *with* Caesar's *body.*]

Here comes his body, mourned by Mark Antony, who, though he had no hand in his death, shall receive the benefit of his dying, a place in the commonwealth, as which of you shall not? With this I depart, that, as I slew my best lover for the good of Rome, I have the same dagger for myself, when it shall please my country to need my death.

Dramatic Speeches
In this monologue, how does Brutus emphasize his sincerity?

All. Live, Brutus! Live, live!

First Plebeian. Bring him with triumph home unto his house.

Second Plebeian. Give him a statue with his ancestors.

Third Plebeian. Let him be Caesar.

Fourth Plebeian. Caesar's better parts[15]
Shall be crowned in Brutus.

15. **parts** *n.* qualities.

First Plebeian. We'll bring him to his house with shouts and clamors.

Brutus. My countrymen—

Second Plebeian. Peace! Silence! Brutus speaks.

First Plebeian. Peace, ho!

Brutus. Good countrymen, let me depart alone,
And, for my sake, stay here with Antony.
Do grace to Caesar's corpse, and grace his speech
Tending to Caesar's glories,[16] which Mark Antony
By our permission, is allowed to make.
I do entreat you, not a man depart,
Save I alone, till Antony have spoke. [*Exit*]

16. **Do grace . . . glories** Show respect for Caesar's body and for the speech telling of Caesar's achievements.

17. **beholding** *adj.* indebted.

First Plebeian. Stay, ho! And let us hear Mark Antony.

Third Plebeian. Let him go up into the public chair;
We'll hear him. Noble Antony, go up.

Antony. For Brutus' sake, I am beholding[17] to you.

Fourth Plebeian. What does he say of Brutus?

Comprehension
What reason for killing Caesar does Brutus offer to the plebeians?

Third Plebeian. He says, for Brutus' sake,
He finds himself beholding to us all.

Fourth Plebeian. 'Twere best he speak no harm of Brutus here!

First Plebeian. This Caesar was a tyrant.

Third Plebeian. Nay, that's certain.
We are blest that Rome is rid of him.

Second Plebeian. Peace! Let us hear what Antony can say.

Antony. You gentle Romans—

All. Peace, ho! Let us hear him.

Antony. Friends, Romans, countrymen, lend me your ears;
I come to bury Caesar, not to praise him.
The evil that men do lives after them,
The good is oft **interrèd** with their bones;
So let it be with Caesar. The noble Brutus
Hath told you Caesar was ambitious.
If it were so, it was a grievous fault,
And grievously hath Caesar answered[18] it.
Here, under leave of Brutus and the rest
(For Brutus is an honorable man,
So are they all, all honorable men),
Come I to speak in Caesar's funeral.
He was my friend, faithful and just to me;
But Brutus says he was ambitious,
And Brutus is an honorable man.
He hath brought many captives home to Rome,
Whose ransoms did the general coffers[19] fill;
Did this in Caesar seem ambitious?
When that the poor have cried, Caesar hath wept;
Ambition should be made of sterner stuff.
Yet Brutus says he was ambitious;
And Brutus is an honorable man.
You all did see that on the Lupercal
I thrice presented him a kingly crown,
Which he did thrice refuse. Was this ambition?
Yet Brutus says he was ambitious;
And sure he is an honorable man.
I speak not to disprove what Brutus spoke,
But here I am to speak what I do know.
You all did love him once, not without cause;
What cause withholds you then to mourn for him?

◀ Critical Viewing
What does this film still of Antony addressing the plebeians suggest about the power of his words? Explain.

Dramatic Speeches
How is Antony's monologue both similar to and different from Brutus' in lines 12–34?

◀ Vocabulary
interred (in turd′) *v.* buried (said of a dead body)

18. **answered** *v.* paid the penalty for.

19. **general coffers** public treasury.

Dramatic Speeches
Contrast Antony's stated purpose in this monologue with the probable effect of lines 92–100 on his audience.

Comprehension
How does Antony describe Brutus' character?

Analyze Imagery
In lines 106–108, which images link Antony's heart and inability to continue speaking?

O judgment, thou art fled to brutish beasts,
And men have lost their reason! Bear with me;
My heart is in the coffin there with Caesar,
And I must pause till it come back to me.

FIRST PLEBEIAN. Methinks there is much reason in his sayings.

SECOND PLEBEIAN. If thou consider rightly of the matter,
Caesar has had great wrong.

THIRD PLEBEIAN. Has he, masters?
I fear there will a worse come in his place.

FOURTH PLEBEIAN. Marked ye his words? He would not take the crown,
Therefore 'tis certain he was not ambitious.

FIRST PLEBEIAN. If it be found so, some will dear abide it.[20]

SECOND PLEBEIAN. Poor soul, his eyes are red as fire with weeping.

THIRD PLEBEIAN. There's not a nobler man in Rome than Antony.

FOURTH PLEBEIAN. Now mark him, he begins again to speak.

ANTONY. But yesterday the word of Caesar might
Have stood against the world; now lies he there,
And none so poor to[21] do him reverence.
O masters! If I were disposed to stir
Your hearts and minds to mutiny and rage,
I should do Brutus wrong and Cassius wrong,
Who, you all know, are honorable men.
I will not do them wrong; I rather choose
To wrong the dead, to wrong myself and you,
Than I will wrong such honorable men.
But here's a parchment with the seal of Caesar;
I found it in his closet; 'tis his will.
Let but the commons[22] hear this testament,
Which, pardon me, I do not mean to read,
And they would go and kiss dead Caesar's wounds,
And dip their napkins[23] in his sacred blood;
Yea, beg a hair of him for memory,
And dying, mention it within their wills,
Bequeathing it as a rich legacy
Unto their issue.[24]

FOURTH PLEBEIAN. We'll hear the will; read it, Mark Antony.

ALL. The will, the will! We will hear Caesar's will!

20. dear abide it pay dearly for it.

21. so poor to low enough in rank to.

22. commons *n.* plebeians; commoners.

23. napkins *n.* handkerchiefs.

24. issue *n.* children; offspring.

Antony. Have patience, gentle friends, I must not read it.
It is not meet[25] you know how Caesar loved you.
You are not wood, you are not stones, but men;
And being men, hearing the will of Caesar,
It will inflame you, it will make you mad.
'Tis good you know not that you are his heirs;
For if you should, O, what would come of it?

Fourth Plebeian. Read the will! We'll hear it, Antony!
You shall read us the will, Caesar's will!

Antony. Will you be patient? Will you stay awhile?
I have o'ershot myself[26] to tell you of it.
I fear I wrong the honorable men
Whose daggers have stabbed Caesar; I do fear it.

Fourth Plebeian. They were traitors. Honorable men!

All. The will! The testament!

Second Plebeian. They were villains, murderers! The will!
Read the will!

Antony. You will compel me then to read the will?
Then make a ring about the corpse of Caesar,
And let me show you him that made the will.
Shall I descend? And will you give me leave?

All. Come down.

Second Plebeian. Descend. [Antony *comes down.*]

Third Plebeian. You shall have leave.

Fourth Plebeian. A ring! Stand round.

First Plebeian. Stand from the hearse,[27] stand from the body!

Second Plebeian. Room for Antony, most noble Antony!

Antony. Nay, press not so upon me; stand far[28] off.

All. Stand back! Room! Bear back.

Antony. If you have tears, prepare to shed them now.
You all do know this mantle;[29] I remember
The first time ever Caesar put it on:
'Twas on a summer's evening, in his tent,
That day he overcame the Nervii.[30]
Look, in this place ran Cassius' dagger through;
See what a rent[31] the envious[32] Casca made;
Through this the well-belovèd Brutus stabbed,
And as he plucked his cursèd steel away,

25. **meet** *adj.* fitting; suitable.

Spiral Review
CHARACTER What is Antony's real motivation for telling the crowd they should not read Caesar's testament?

26. **o'ershot myself** gone further than I meant to.

Analyze Imagery
In what way does the action on stage connect Caesar's body and the words in his will?

27. **hearse** (hʉrs) *n.* coffin
28. **far** *adv.* farther.
29. **mantle** (man′ təl) *n.* cloak; toga.
30. **Nervii** (nʉr′ vē ī) *n.* warlike European tribe conquered by Caesar in 57 B.C.
31. **rent** *n.* hole; tear; rip.
32. **envious** (en′ vē əs) *adj.* spiteful.

Comprehension
What effect does Antony's speech have on the crowd?

▲ **Critical Viewing** Compare this image with the one on page 608. Which details here suggest Antony's intensifying emotions?

Mark how the blood of Caesar followed it,
As[33] rushing out of doors, to be resolved[34]
If Brutus so unkindly[35] knocked, or no;
For Brutus, as you know, was Caesar's angel.
Judge, O you gods, how dearly Caesar loved him!
This was the most unkindest cut of all;
For when the noble Caesar saw him stab,
Ingratitude, more strong than traitors' arms,
Quite vanquished him. Then burst his mighty heart;
And, in his mantle muffling up his face,
Even at the base of Pompey's statue
(Which all the while ran blood) great Caesar fell.
O, what a fall was there, my countrymen!
Then I, and you, and all of us fell down,
Whilst bloody treason flourished[36] over us.
O, now you weep, and I perceive you feel
The dint[37] of pity; these are gracious drops.
Kind souls, what[38] weep you when you but behold
Our Caesar's vesture[39] wounded? Look you here,
Here is himself, marred as you see with[40] traitors.

First Plebeian. O piteous spectacle!

Second Plebeian. O noble Caesar!

33. **As** *conj.* as if.
34. **to be resolved** to learn for certain.
35. **unkindly** *adv.* cruelly; also, unnaturally.
36. **flourished** (flʉr´ ish ’d) *v.* swaggered; waved a sword in triumph.
37. **dint** *n.* stroke; blow.
38. **what** *adv.* why.
39. **vesture** (ves´ chər) *n.* clothing.
40. **with** *prep.* by.

THIRD PLEBEIAN. O woeful day!

FOURTH PLEBEIAN. O traitors, villains!

FIRST PLEBEIAN. O most bloody sight!

SECOND PLEBEIAN. We will be revenged.

ALL. Revenge! About![41] Seek! Burn! Fire! Kill! Slay!
Let not a traitor live!

ANTONY. Stay, countrymen.

FIRST PLEBEIAN. Peace there! Hear the noble Antony.

SECOND PLEBEIAN. We'll hear him, we'll follow him, we'll die
with him!

ANTONY. Good friends, sweet friends, let me not stir you up
To such a sudden flood of mutiny.
They that have done this deed are honorable.
What private griefs[42] they have, alas, I know not,
That made them do it. They are wise and honorable,
And will, no doubt, with reasons answer you.
I come not, friends, to steal away your hearts;
I am no orator, as Brutus is;
But (as you know me all) a plain blunt man
That love my friend, and that they know full well
That gave me public leave to speak[43] of him.
For I have neither writ, nor words, nor worth,
Action, or utterance,[44] nor the power of speech
To stir men's blood; I only speak right on.[45]
I tell you that which you yourselves do know,
Show you sweet Caesar's wounds, poor poor dumb mouths,
And bid them speak for me. But were I Brutus,
And Brutus Antony, there were an Antony
Would ruffle up your spirits, and put a tongue
In every wound of Caesar's that should move
The stones of Rome to rise and mutiny.

ALL. We'll mutiny.

FIRST PLEBEIAN. We'll burn the house of Brutus.

THIRD PLEBEIAN. Away, then! Come, seek the conspirators.

ANTONY. Yet hear me, countrymen. Yet hear me speak.

ALL. Peace, ho! Hear Antony, most noble Antony!

ANTONY. Why, friends, you go to do you know not what: Wherein
hath Caesar thus deserved your loves?

41. About let's go.

42. private griefs personal grievances.

43. public leave to speak permission to speak in public.

44. neither writ . . . utterance (ut´ ər əns) neither a written speech, nor fluency, nor reputation, nor gestures, nor style of speaking.

45. right on directly.

Analyze Imagery
Which images in Antony's speech combine ideas of words, the body, and violence?

Comprehension
How does the crowd feel toward the conspirators after Antony's speech?

Alas, you know not; I must tell you then:
You have forgot the will I told you of.

All. Most true, the will! Let's stay and hear the will.

Antony. Here is the will, and under Caesar's seal.
To every Roman citizen he gives,
To every several[46] man, seventy-five drachmas.

Second Plebeian. Most noble Caesar! We'll revenge his death!

Third Plebeian. O royal[47] Caesar!

Antony. Hear me with patience.

All. Peace, ho!

Antony. Moreover, he hath left you all his walks,
His private arbors, and new-planted orchards,[48]
On this side Tiber; he hath left them you,
And to your heirs forever: common pleasures,[49]
To walk abroad and recreate yourselves.
Here was a Caesar! When comes such another?

First Plebeian. Never, never! Come, away, away!
We'll burn his body in the holy place,
And with the brands[50] fire the traitors' houses.
Take up the body.

Second Plebeian. Go fetch fire.

Third Plebeian. Pluck down benches.

Fourth Plebeian. Pluck down forms, windows,[51] anything!

[*Exit* Plebeians *with the body.*]

Antony. Now let it work:[52] Mischief, thou art afoot,
Take thou what course thou wilt.

[*Enter* Servant.]

How now, fellow?

Servant. Sir, Octavius is already come to Rome.

Antony. Where is he?

Servant. He and Lepidus are at Caesar's house.

Antony. And thither[53] will I straight to visit him;
He comes upon a wish.[54] Fortune is merry,
And in this mood will give us anything.

Servant. I heard him say, Brutus and Cassius
Are rid[55] like madmen through the gates of Rome.

46. **several** *adj.* individual.
47. **royal** *adj.* showing noble generosity.
48. **walks . . . orchards** parks, his private stands of trees, and newly planted gardens.
49. **common pleasures** public places of recreation.

Analyze Imagery
Moved by news of Caesar's words, what action does the crowd take involving Caesar's body?

50. **brands** *n.* torches.
51. **forms, windows** benches and shutters.
52. **work** *v.* spread and expand, as yeast does; follow through to a conclusion.

53. **thither** *adv.* there.
54. **upon a wish** as I wished.
55. **Are rid** have ridden.

Antony. Belike[56] they had some notice of the people,[57]
How I had moved them. Bring me to Octavius. [*Exit*]

56. **Belike** *adv.* probably.
57. **notice of the people** word about the mood of the people.

Scene iii. A street.

[*Enter* Cinna the Poet, *and after him the* Plebeians.]

Cinna. I dreamt tonight[1] that I did feast with Caesar,
And things unluckily charge my fantasy.[2]
I have no will to wander forth of doors,[3]
Yet something leads me forth.

Dramatic Speeches To whom is Cinna's speech addressed?

First Plebeian. What is your name?

Second Plebeian. Whither are you going?

Third Plebeian. Where do you dwell?

Fourth Plebeian. Are you a married man or a bachelor?

Second Plebeian. Answer every man directly.[4]

First Plebeian. Ay, and briefly.

Fourth Plebeian. Ay, and wisely.

Third Plebeian. Ay, and truly, you were best.

Cinna. What is my name? Whither am I going? Where do I dwell? Am I a married man or a bachelor? Then, to answer every man directly and briefly, wisely and truly: wisely I say, I am a bachelor.

Second Plebeian. That's as much as to say, they are fools that marry; you'll bear me a bang[5] for that, I fear. Proceed directly.

1. **tonight** *adv.* last night.
2. **things . . . fantasy** the events that have happened give an unlucky meaning to my dream.
3. **forth of doors** outdoors.
4. **directly** *adv.* in a straightforward manner.
5. **bear me a bang** get a blow from me.

Comprehension What has Caesar left the citizens of Rome in his will?

Extispicium relief (inspection of entrails) from the Forum of Trajan, Rome. Louvre, Paris, France.

Cinna. Directly, I am going to Caesar's funeral.

First Plebeian. As a friend or an enemy?

Cinna. As a friend.

Second Plebeian. That matter is answered directly.

Fourth Plebeian. For your dwelling, briefly.

Cinna. Briefly, I dwell by the Capitol.

Third Plebeian. Your name, sir, truly.

Cinna. Truly, my name is Cinna.

First Plebeian. Tear him to pieces! He's a conspirator.

Cinna. I am Cinna the poet! I am Cinna the poet!

Fourth Plebeian. Tear him for his bad verses! Tear him for his bad verses!

Cinna. I am not Cinna the conspirator.

Fourth Plebeian. It is no matter, his name's Cinna; pluck but his name out of his heart, and turn him going.[6]

Third Plebeian. Tear him, tear him! [*They attack him.*]
Come, brands, ho! Firebrands![7] To Brutus', to Cassius'!
Burn all! Some to Decius' house, and some to
Casca's; some to Ligarius'! Away, go!

[*Exit all the* Plebeians *with* Cinna.]

Analyze Imagery
How does a confusion about Cinna's name place his body in danger?

6. **turn him going** send him on his way.
7. **Firebrands** *n.* burning pieces of wood; also, people who stir up others to revolt.

Language Study

Vocabulary The italicized words in each item below appear in Act III. Choose a word from the items that follow to complete each analogy.

1. vague : definite :: *confounded* : **(a)** certain, **(b)** lost, **(c)** unclear
2. remember : past :: *prophesy* : **(a)** sky, **(b)** present, **(c)** future
3. tuxedo : T-shirt :: *discourse* : **(a)** jeans, **(b)** lecture, **(c)** chat
4. stored : attic :: *interred* : **(a)** museum, **(b)** cemetery, **(c)** exit
5. merriment : laughter :: *strife* : **(a)** yelling, **(b)** singing, **(c)** blushing

WORD STUDY
The **Latin root *-spect-*** means "to look at" or "behold." In the play, a character refers to the **spectacle**, or astonishing sight, of Caesar's death and wonders how others will view it.

Word Study

Part A Explain how the **Latin root *-spect-*** contributes to the meanings of the words *perspective, spectator,* and *spectrum*. Consult a dictionary if necessary.

Part B Use the context of the sentences and what you know about the Latin root *-spect-* to explain your answer to each question.

1. Why is it usually important to *inspect* a car before buying it?
2. If you *speculate* about how to build a bookcase, are you actively building it?

Close Reading Activities

Literary Analysis

Key Ideas and Details

1. **(a)** What famous Latin words does Caesar say in Scene i, line 77, when he sees Brutus among the assassins? **(b) Interpret:** What emotions do these words convey? Explain your answer.
2. **(a)** How does Antony respond to the conspirators after the assassination? **(b) Analyze:** What are the motives for his actions?
3. **Analyze Imagery (a)** Identify three examples of imagery in Act III related to the human body and words. **(b)** Explain how each image links words with the human body and the meaning each image suggests.
4. **Analyze Imagery (a)** In Caesar's monologue in Scene i, lines 35–43, with what traits is blood linked? **(b)** In lines 164–172 of that same scene, with what does Brutus link Caesar's blood? Explain your answers.

Craft and Structure

5. **Dramatic Speeches** Using a chart like the one shown, analyze the following passages from Act III: Scene i, lines 183–210; Scene i, lines 254–275; and, Scene ii, lines 261–262. **(a)** Identify each speech as an aside, a soliloquy, or a monologue. **(b)** Explain who hears each speech. **(c)** Paraphrase each speech.
6. **Dramatic Speeches** Contrast the thoughts and feelings Antony expresses in his dialogue with other characters in Scene i, lines 218–222 with the thoughts and feelings he shares in Scene i, lines 254–275.
7. **Dramatic Speeches (a)** Contrast the style and purpose of Antony's and Brutus' funeral speeches. **(b)** What does each speech reveal about the speaker? **(c)** What happens as a result of each speech? Cite evidence from the text in your answers.

Lines:
Type of Speech
Who hears it?
Paraphrase

Integration of Knowledge and Ideas

8. **Make a Judgment:** Is Caesar responsible for his own death? Explain, supporting your response with evidence from the text.

9. THE BIG ? **To what extent does experience determine what we perceive?** The crowd's perception of Caesar's death changes based on the different accounts given. **(a) Summarize:** Explain how Brutus justifies the assassination in his speech to the crowd. **(b) Analyze:** Explain how Antony turns the crowd against the conspirators. Support your response with details from the text.

ACADEMIC VOCABULARY

As you write and speak about *The Tragedy of Julius Caesar*, use the words related to experience and perceptions that you explored on page 517 of this book.

Building Knowledge

To what extent does experience determine what we perceive?

Explore the Big Question as you read *The Tragedy of Julius Caesar*, Act IV. Note how the characters' earlier experiences continue to shape their perceptions and decisions.

CLOSE READING FOCUS

Key Ideas and Details: **Read Between the Lines**

When reading Shakespearean drama, combine clues in the text with your own knowledge to **read between the lines,** or make inferences about what the playwright suggests but does not directly say.

- Begin with text evidence. For example, early in Act IV, Antony describes Lepidus as "meet to be sent on errands." Antony has been deciding which of his rivals will share power. By reading between the lines, the reader understands that Antony feels Lepidus is competent to run errands but not to do much else.
- Follow indirect references. When Lucilius reports on Cassius, Brutus says, "Thou has described / A hot friend cooling." "A hot friend" refers to Cassius, whom Brutus worries is no longer his ally.
- Think about the larger ideas even small details suggest.

Craft and Structure: **External and Internal Conflict**

Conflict, a struggle between opposing forces, creates drama.

- In an **external conflict,** a character struggles with an outside force, such as another character, nature, or society.
- In an **internal conflict,** a character struggles with his or her own opposing beliefs, desires, or values.

In *The Tragedy of Julius Caesar,* characters face both types of conflict. These varied, interlinking conflicts drive the plot and form the structure of the play.

Vocabulary

You will encounter the following words in this act of the play. Decide whether you know the word well, know it a little bit, or do not know it at all. After you read, see how your knowledge of each word has increased.

legacies	**condemned**	**chastisement**
rash	**mirth**	**presume**

Common Core State Standards

Reading Literature

1. Cite strong and thorough textual evidence to support inferences drawn from the text.

5. Analyze how an author's choices concerning how to structure a text, order events within it, and manipulate time create such effects as mystery, tension, or surprise.

Language

4.d. Verify the preliminary determination of the meaning of a word or phrase.

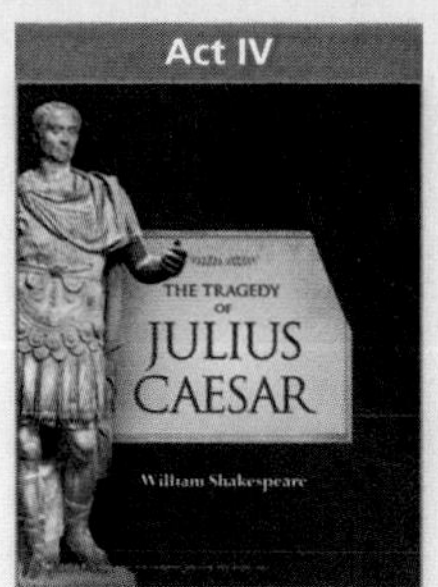

CLOSE READING MODEL

The passages below are from *The Tragedy of Julius Caesar*, Act IV. The annotations to the right of the passages show ways in which you can use close reading skills to read between the lines and analyze conflict.

from *The Tragedy of Julius Caesar,* Act IV

Brutus. Let me tell you, Cassius, you yourself
Are much condemned to have an itching palm,
To sell and mart your offices for gold
To undeservers.
Cassius. I an itching palm?
You know that you are Brutus that speaks this,
Or, by the gods, this speech were else your last.[1]
Brutus. The name of Cassius honors this corruption,
And chastisement doth therefore hide his head.

....

Brutus. No man bears sorrow better. Portia is dead.
Cassius. Ha? Portia?
Brutus. She is dead.
Cassius. How scaped I killing when I crossed you so?
O insupportable and touching loss!
Upon what sickness?
Brutus. Impatient of my absence,
And grief that young Octavius with Mark Antony
Have made themselves so strong—for with her death
That tidings came—with this she fell distract,
And (her attendants absent) swallowed fire.[2]
Cassius. And died so?
Brutus. Even so.
Cassius. O ye immortal gods!
[*Enter* Lucius, *with wine and tapers.*]
Brutus. Speak no more of her. Give me a bowl of wine.[3]
In this I bury all unkindness, Cassius. [*Drinks*]

External Conflict

1 An external conflict develops between Brutus and Cassius when Brutus accuses his co-conspirator of using his position to take bribes. Infuriated by the charge, Cassius makes threats against Brutus' life.

Read Between the Lines

2 Brutus' wife Portia has killed herself over the news that Antony's army, intent on avenging Caesar's death, has grown strong. Reading between the lines, you can infer that Brutus and Cassius are in real danger.

Internal Conflict

3 Throughout this scene Brutus admits to feeling grief over Portia's death but struggles to repress his emotions. His sorrow is in conflict with his philosophical beliefs, and he asks Cassius not to speak of Portia.

REVIEW AND ANTICIPATE

In Act III, after the conspirators assassinate Caesar, Brutus and Antony both speak at his funeral. Brutus explains that Caesar's death was necessary to keep Romans free. Antony, however, convinces the crowd that Caesar was a great man, whereas Brutus is a traitor. The crowd rushes off to find and destroy the conspirators.

As Act IV opens, Antony and his allies, Octavius and Lepidus, are deciding which of their political rivals are to be killed. Meanwhile, conflict is brewing between their enemies, Cassius and Brutus.

▶ **Critical Viewing**
Which of the qualities that Antony has shown in the play are portrayed in this sculpture of him?

Act IV

Scene i. A house in Rome.

[*Enter* Antony, Octavius, *and* Lepidus.]

Antony. These many then shall die; their names are pricked.[1]

Octavius. Your brother too must die; consent you, Lepidus?

Lepidus. I do consent—

Octavius. Prick him down, Antony.

Lepidus. Upon condition Publius shall not live,
Who is your sister's son, Mark Antony.

Antony. He shall not live; look, with a spot I damn him.[2]
But, Lepidus, go you to Caesar's house;
Fetch the will hither, and we shall determine
How to cut off some charge in **legacies**.[3]

Lepidus. What, shall I find you here?

Octavius. Or[4] here or at the Capitol. [*Exit* Lepidus.]

Antony. This is a slight unmeritable[5] man,
Meet[6] to be sent on errands; is it fit,
The threefold world[7] divided, he should stand
One of the three to share it?

Octavius. So you thought him,
And took his voice[8] who should be pricked to die
In our black sentence and proscription.[9]

Antony. Octavius, I have seen more days[10] than you;
And though we lay these honors on this man,
To ease ourselves of divers sland'rous loads,[11]
He shall but bear them as the ass bears gold,
To groan and sweat under the business,
Either led or driven, as we point the way;
And having brought our treasure where we will,
Then take we down his load, and turn him off,
(Like to the empty ass) to shake his ears
And graze in commons.[12]

Octavius. You may do your will;
But he's a tried and valiant soldier.

Antony. So is my horse, Octavius, and for that
I do appoint him store of provender.[13]

1. **pricked** *v.* checked off.
2. **with a spot . . . him** with a mark on the tablet, I condemn him.
3. **cut off some charge in legacies** save costs by changing the amount of gifts left in the will.

◀ **Vocabulary**
legacies (leg´ ə sēz) *n.* money, property, or position left in a will to someone

4. **Or** *conj.* either.
5. **slight unmeritable** insignificant and without merit.
6. **Meet** *adj.* suitable.
7. **threefold world** three areas of the Roman Empire—Europe, Asia, and Africa.
8. **voice** *n.* vote; opinion.
9. **black . . . proscription** list of those sentenced to death or exile.
10. **have seen more days** am older.
11. **divers sland'rous loads** various burdens of blame.
12. **in commons** on public pasture.
13. **appoint . . . provender** give him a supply of food.

Comprehension
What is the conflict between Antony and Octavius?

It is a creature that I teach to fight,
To wind,[14] to stop, to run directly on,
His corporal motion governed by my spirit.[15]
And, in some taste,[16] is Lepidus but so.
He must be taught, and trained, and bid go forth.
A barren-spirited[17] fellow; one that feeds
On objects, arts, and imitations,[18]
Which, out of use and staled[19] by other men,
Begin his fashion.[20] Do not talk of him
But as a property.[21] And now, Octavius,
Listen great things. Brutus and Cassius
Are levying powers;[22] we must straight make head.[23]
Therefore let our alliance be combined,
Our best friends made,[24] our means stretched;[25]
And let us presently[26] go sit in council
How covert matters may be best disclosed,
And open perils surest answerèd.[27]

Octavius. Let us do so; for we are at the stake,
And bayed about with many enemies;[28]
And some that smile have in their hearts, I fear,
Millions of mischiefs.[29] [*Exit*]

Scene ii. Camp near Sardis.

[*Drum. Enter* Brutus, Lucilius, Lucius, *and the* Army. Titinius *and* Pindarus *meet them.*]

Brutus. Stand ho!

Lucilius. Give the word, ho! and stand.

Brutus. What now, Lucilius, is Cassius near?

Lucilius. He is at hand, and Pindarus is come
To do you salutation[1] from his master.

Brutus. He greets me well. Your master, Pindarus,
In his own change, or by ill officers,
Hath given me some worthy cause to wish
Things done undone;[2] but if he be at hand,
I shall be satisfied.[3]

Pindarus. I do not doubt
But that my noble master will appear
Such as he is, full of regard[4] and honor.

Brutus. He is not doubted. A word, Lucilius,
How he received you; let me be resolved.[5]

14. **wind** (wīnd) *v.* turn.
15. **His . . . spirit** his bodily movements governed by my mind.
16. **taste** *n.* degree; measure.
17. **barren-spirited** without ideas of his own.
18. **feeds / On objects, arts, and imitations** enjoys curiosities, clever ways, and fashions.
19. **staled** *v.* cheapened.
20. **Begin his fashion** he begins to use. (He is hopelessly behind the times.)
21. **property** *n.* tool; object.
22. **levying powers** enlisting troops.
23. **straight make head** quickly gather soldiers.
24. **best friends made** closest allies chosen.
25. **stretched** *adj.* used to full advantage.
26. **presently** *adv.* immediately.
27. **How . . . answerèd** how hidden dangers may be discovered and known dangers met.
28. **at the stake . . . enemies** surrounded by enemies like a bear tied to a stake and set upon by many dogs. (Bear-baiting was a popular amusement in Elizabethan England.)
29. **mischiefs** *n.* plans to injure us.

1. **To do you salutation** to bring you greetings.
2. **In his own . . . done undone** Whether his actions are due to a change in his feelings toward me or to bad advice from subordinates, he has made me wish we did not do what we did.
3. **be satisfied** obtain an explanation.
4. **full of regard** worthy of respect.
5. **resolved** *adj.* fully informed.

Lucilius. With courtesy and with respect enough,
But not with such familiar instances,[6]
Nor with such free and friendly conference[7]
As he hath used of old.

Brutus. Thou hast described
A hot friend cooling. Ever note, Lucilius,
When love begins to sicken and decay
It useth an enforcèd ceremony.[8]
There are no tricks in plain and simple faith;
But hollow[9] men, like horses hot at hand,[10]
Make gallant show and promise of their mettle;[11]

[*Low march within*]

But when they should endure the bloody spur,
They fall their crests, and like deceitful jades
Sink in the trial.[12] Comes his army on?

6. **familiar instances** marks of friendship.
7. **conference** *n.* conversation.
8. **enforcèd ceremony** forced formality.
9. **hollow** *adj.* insincere.
10. **hot at hand** full of spirit when reined in.
11. **mettle** *n.* spirit; high character; courage.
12. **They fall . . . the trial** They drop their necks, and like worn-out, worthless horses, fail the test.

Comprehension
What is Brutus' present attitude toward Cassius?

▼ Critical Viewing
Which details in this film still reflect the fact that Antony (far right) dominates over both Lepidus and Octavius?

Lucilius. They mean this night in Sardis to be quartered;[13]
The greater part, the horse in general,[14]
Are come with Cassius.

[*Enter* Cassius *and his Powers.*[15]]

Brutus. Hark! He is arrived.
March gently[16] on to meet him.

Cassius. Stand, ho!

Brutus. Stand, ho! Speak the word along.

First Soldier. Stand!

Second Soldier. Stand!

Third Soldier. Stand!

Cassius. Most noble brother, you have done me wrong.

Brutus. Judge me, you gods! Wrong I mine enemies?
And if not so, how should I wrong a brother?

Cassius. Brutus, this sober form[17] of yours hides wrongs;
And when you do them—

Brutus. Cassius, be content.[18]
Speak your griefs softly; I do know you well.
Before the eyes of both our armies here
(Which should perceive nothing but love from us)
Let us not wrangle. Bid them move away;
Then in my tent, Cassius, enlarge[19] your griefs,
And I will give you audience.

Cassius. Pindarus,
Bid our commanders lead their charges[20] off
A little from this ground.

Brutus. Lucilius, do you the like, and let no man
Come to our tent till we have done our conference.
Let Lucius and Titinius guard our door.

[*Exit all but* Brutus *and* Cassius]

Scene iii. Brutus' tent.

Cassius. That you have wronged me doth appear in this:
You have **condemned** and noted[1] Lucius Pella
For taking bribes here of the Sardians;
Wherein my letters, praying on his side,[2]
Because I knew the man, was slighted off.[3]

Brutus. You wronged yourself to write in such a case.

13. **quartered** *v.* provided with places to stay.
14. **horse in general** cavalry.
15. ***Powers*** *n.* forces; troops.
16. **gently** *adv.* slowly.
17. **sober form** serious manner.
18. **be content** be patient.

Read Between the Lines
Brutus and Cassius are standing near their troops. Why does Brutus suggest meeting in his tent?

19. **enlarge** *v.* freely express.
20. **charges** *n.* troops.

Vocabulary ▶
condemned (kən demd′) *v.* declared to be guilty of wrongdoings

1. **noted** *v.* publicly denounced.
2. **praying on his side** pleading on his behalf.
3. **slighted off** disregarded.

Cassius. In such a time as this it is not meet
That every nice offense should bear his comment.[4]

Brutus. Let me tell you, Cassius, you yourself
Are much condemned to have an itching palm,[5]
To sell and mart[6] your offices for gold
To undeservers.

Cassius. I an itching palm?
You know that you are Brutus that speaks this,
Or, by the gods, this speech were else your last.

Brutus. The name of Cassius honors[7] this corruption,
And **chastisement** doth therefore hide his head.

Cassius. Chastisement!

Brutus. Remember March, the ides of March remember.
Did not great Julius bleed for justice' sake?
What villain touched his body, that did stab,
And not[8] for justice? What, shall one of us,
That struck the foremost man of all this world
But for supporting robbers,[9] shall we now
Contaminate our fingers with base bribes,
And sell the mighty space of our large honors[10]
For so much trash[11] as may be graspèd thus?
I had rather be a dog, and bay[12] the moon,
Than such a Roman.

Cassius. Brutus, bait[13] not me;
I'll not endure it. You forget yourself
To hedge me in.[14] I am a soldier, I,
Older in practice, abler than yourself
To make conditions.[15]

Brutus. Go to! You are not, Cassius.

Cassius. I am.

Brutus. I say you are not.

Cassius. Urge[16] me no more, I shall forget myself;
Have mind upon your health;[17] tempt me no farther.

Brutus. Away, slight[18] man!

Cassius. Is't possible?

Brutus. Hear me, for I will speak.
Must I give way and room to your **rash** choler?[19]
Shall I be frighted when a madman stares?

4. **every . . . comment** every petty fault should receive his criticism.
5. **condemned . . . palm** accused of having a hand eager to accept bribes.
6. **mart** *v.* trade.
7. **honors** *v.* gives respectability to.

◀ **Vocabulary**

chastisement (chas´ tiz mənt) *n.* severe criticism; punishment

rash (rash) *adj.* given to acting without thinking; impulsive

Read Between the Lines

When Brutus asks who stabbed Caesar "not for justice," what is he suggesting about Cassius?

8. **And not** except.
9. **But . . . robbers** Here Brutus says, for the first time, that Caesar's officials were also involved in taking bribes and that this was a motive in his assassination.
10. **honors** *n.* reputations.
11. **trash** *n.* that is, money.
12. **bay** *v.* howl at.
13. **bait** harass (as a bear tied to a stake is harassed by dogs).
14. **hedge me in** restrict my actions.
15. **make conditions** manage affairs.
16. **Urge** *v.* drive onward.
17. **health** *n.* safety.
18. **slight** *adj.* insignificant.
19. **choler** (käl´ ər) *n.* anger.

Comprehension

Of what does Brutus accuse Cassius?

20. **choleric** (käl′ ə rik) *adj.* quick-tempered.
21. **bondmen** *n.* slaves.
22. **budge** *v.* flinch away from you.
23. **observe you** show reverence toward you.
24. **crouch** *v.* bow.
25. **testy humor** irritability.
26. **digest . . . spleen** eat the poison of your spleen. (The spleen was thought to be the source of anger.)

Vocabulary ▶
mirth (murth) *n.* joyfulness; merriment

27. **waspish** *adj.* bad-tempered.
28. **vaunting** (vônt′ iŋ) *n.* boasting.
29. **learn of** hear about; learn from.
30. **durst** *v.* dared.
31. **moved** *v.* angered.

Vocabulary ▶
presume (prē zoom′) *v.* rely too much on; take advantage of

32. **drachmas** (drak′ məz) *n.* silver coins of ancient Greece.
33. **indirection** *n.* irregular methods.

CASSIUS. O ye gods, ye gods! Must I endure all this?

BRUTUS. All this? Ay, more: fret till your proud heart break.
Go show your slaves how choleric[20] you are,
And make your bondmen[21] tremble. Must I budge?[22]
Must I observe you?[23] Must I stand and crouch[24]
Under your testy humor?[25] By the gods,
You shall digest the venom of your spleen,[26]
Though it do split you; for, from this day forth,
I'll use you for my **mirth**, yea, for my laughter,
When you are waspish.[27]

CASSIUS. Is it come to this?

BRUTUS. You say you are a better soldier:
Let it appear so; make your vaunting[28] true,
And it shall please me well. For mine own part,
I shall be glad to learn of[29] noble men.

CASSIUS. You wrong me every way; you wrong me, Brutus;
I said, an elder soldier, not a better.
Did I say, better?

BRUTUS. If you did, I care not.

CASSIUS. When Caesar lived, he durst[30] not thus have
moved[31] me.

BRUTUS. Peace, peace, you durst not so have tempted him.

CASSIUS. I durst not?

BRUTUS. No.

CASSIUS. What? Durst not tempt him?

BRUTUS. For your life you durst not.

CASSIUS. Do not **presume** too much upon my love;
I may do that I shall be sorry for.

BRUTUS. You have done that you should be sorry for.
There is no terror, Cassius, in your threats;
For I am armed so strong in honesty
That they pass by me as the idle wind,
Which I respect not. I did send to you
For certain sums of gold, which you denied me;
For I can raise no money by vile means.
By heaven, I had rather coin my heart
And drop my blood for drachmas[32] than to wring
From the hard hands of peasants their vile trash
By any indirection.[33] I did send

◀ **Critical Viewing**
What does this ancient Roman sculpture suggest about the Roman attitude toward war?

To you for gold to pay my legions,[34]
Which you denied me. Was that done like Cassius?
Should I have answered Caius Cassius so?
When Marcus Brutus grows so covetous[35]
To lock such rascal counters[36] from his friends,
Be ready, gods, with all your thunderbolts,
Dash him to pieces!

Cassius. I denied you not.

Brutus. You did.

Cassius. I did not. He was but a fool
That brought my answer back. Brutus hath rived[37] my heart.

34. legions *n.* Roman military divisions of several thousand soldiers.
35. covetous (kuv′ ət əs) *adj.* greedy.
36. rascal counters worthless coins.
37. rived (rīvd) *v.* broken.

Comprehension
What is the second accusation Brutus makes against Cassius?

A friend should bear his friend's infirmities;
But Brutus makes mine greater than they are.

Brutus. I do not, till you practice them on me.

Cassius. You love me not.

Brutus. I do not like your faults.

Cassius. A friendly eye could never see such faults.

Brutus. A flatterer's would not, though they do appear
As huge as high Olympus.

Cassius. Come, Antony, and young Octavius, come,
Revenge yourselves alone[38] on Cassius,
For Cassius is aweary of the world:
Hated by one he loves; braved[39] by his brother;
Checked like a bondman;[40] all his faults observed,
Set in a notebook, learned and conned by rote[41]
To cast into my teeth. O, I could weep
My spirit from mine eyes! There is my dagger,

38. alone *adv.* only.

39. braved *adj.* defied; challenged.

40. Checked like a bondman scolded like a slave.

41. conned by rote memorized.

▼ Critical Viewing

In this film still, do Brutus and Cassius look as if they will be able to settle their conflict? Explain.

And here my naked breast; within, a heart
Dearer than Pluto's mine,[42] richer than gold;
If that thou be'st a Roman, take it forth.
I, that denied thee gold, will give my heart.
Strike as thou didst at Caesar; for I know,
When thou didst hate him worst, thou lovedst him better
Than ever thou lovedst Cassius.

BRUTUS. Sheathe your dagger.
Be angry when you will, it shall have scope.[43]
Do what you will, dishonor shall be humor.[44]
O Cassius, you are yokèd[45] with a lamb
That carries anger as the flint[46] bears fire,
Who, much enforcèd,[47] shows a hasty spark,
And straight[48] is cold again.

CASSIUS. Hath Cassius lived
To be but mirth and laughter to his Brutus
When grief and blood ill-tempered vexeth him?

BRUTUS. When I spoke that, I was ill-tempered too.

CASSIUS. Do you confess so much? Give me your hand.

BRUTUS. And my heart too.

CASSIUS. O Brutus!

BRUTUS. What's the matter?

CASSIUS. Have not you love enough to bear with me
When that rash humor[49] which my mother gave me
Makes me forgetful?

BRUTUS. Yes, Cassius, and from henceforth,
When you are overearnest with your Brutus,
He'll think your mother chides, and leave you so.[50]

[*Enter a* POET, *followed by* LUCILIUS, TITINIUS, *and* LUCIUS.]

POET. Let me go in to see the generals;
There is some grudge between 'em; 'tis not meet
They be alone.

LUCILIUS. You shall not come to them.

POET. Nothing but death shall stay me.

CASSIUS. How now? What's the matter?

POET. For shame, you generals! What do you mean?
Love, and be friends, as two such men should be;
For I have seen more years, I'm sure, than ye.

42. **Pluto's mine** all the riches in the Earth.
43. **scope** *n.* free play.
44. **dishonor . . . humor** I will consider any insults to be just the effect of your irritable disposition.
45. **yokèd** *adj.* in partnership.
46. **flint** *n.* hard mineral that, when struck by steel, makes sparks.
47. **enforcèd** *adj.* provoked.
48. **straight** *adv.* immediately.

Read Between the Lines

In this situation, what does Cassius' use of the phrase "his Brutus" suggest?

49. **humor** *n.* temperament.
50. **your mother . . . so** it is just your inherited disposition and let it go at that.

Comprehension

What happens in the quarrel between Cassius and Brutus?

51. **cynic** *n.* rude fellow.
52. **Saucy** *adj.* rude; insolent.
53. **I'll know . . . time** I'll accept his eccentricity when he chooses a proper time to exhibit it.
54. **jigging** *adj.* rhyming.
55. **Companion** *n.* fellow (used to show contempt).

Conflict
How does the arrival of the poet help end the conflict between Cassius and Brutus?

CASSIUS. Ha, ha! How vilely doth this cynic[51] rhyme!

BRUTUS. Get you hence, sirrah! Saucy[52] fellow, hence!

CASSIUS. Bear with him, Brutus, 'tis his fashion.

BRUTUS. I'll know his humor when he knows his time.[53]
What should the wars do with these jigging[54] fools?
Companion,[55] hence!

CASSIUS. Away, away, be gone! [*Exit* POET.]

BRUTUS. Lucilius and Titinius, bid the commanders
Prepare to lodge their companies tonight.

CASSIUS. And come yourselves, and bring Messala with you
Immediately to us. [*Exit* LUCILIUS *and* TITINIUS.]

BRUTUS. Lucius, a bowl of wine. [*Exit* LUCIUS.]

CASSIUS. I did not think you could have been so angry.

BRUTUS. O Cassius, I am sick of many griefs.

CASSIUS. Of your philosophy you make no use,
If you give place to accidental evils.[56]

56. **Of your philosophy . . . evils** As a Stoic, Brutus believed that chance misfortunes should not disturb his peace of mind.

BRUTUS. No man bears sorrow better. Portia is dead.

CASSIUS. Ha? Portia?

BRUTUS. She is dead.

LITERATURE IN CONTEXT

Humanities Connection

Stoicism

Brutus follows a philosophy called Stoicism (stō´ i siz´ əm), a school of thought established by the ancient Greek thinker Zeno sometime after 312 B.C. Stoicism stresses the following ideas:

- The universe is ruled by unchanging natural laws.
- A wise person lives a virtuous life, using reason to understand natural laws and to act accordingly.
- A wise person is not ruled by his or her emotions.
- Using reason, a wise person distinguishes between what is truly in his or her power and what is not.
- A wise person does not allow events that he or she does not control—even the loss of a loved one—to affect him or her.

Connect to the Literature

How do Brutus' Stoic beliefs affect his actions in Act IV?

Cassius. How scaped I killing when I crossed you so?[57]
O insupportable and touching[58] loss!
Upon[59] what sickness?

Brutus. Impatient of my absence,
And grief that young Octavius with Mark Antony
Have made themselves so strong—for with her death
That tidings[60] came—with this she fell distract,[61]
And (her attendants absent) swallowed fire.

Cassius. And died so?

Brutus. Even so.

Cassius. O ye immortal gods!

[*Enter* Lucius, *with wine and tapers.*]

Brutus. Speak no more of her. Give me a bowl of wine.
In this I bury all unkindness, Cassius. [*Drinks*]

Cassius. My heart is thirsty for that noble pledge.
Fill, Lucius, till the wine o'erswell the cup;
I cannot drink too much of Brutus' love.

[*Drinks. Exit* Lucius.]

[*Enter* Titinius *and* Messala.]

Brutus. Come in, Titinius! Welcome, good Messala.
Now sit we close about this taper here,
And call in question[62] our necessities.

Cassius. Portia, art thou gone?

Brutus. No more, I pray you.
Messala, I have here receivèd letters
That young Octavius and Mark Antony
Come down upon us with a mighty power,[63]
Bending their expedition toward Philippi.[64]

Messala. Myself have letters of the selfsame tenure.[65]

Brutus. With what addition?

Messala. That by proscription and bills of outlawry[66]
Octavius, Antony, and Lepidus
Have put to death an hundred senators.

Brutus. Therein our letters do not well agree.
Mine speak of seventy senators that died
By their proscriptions, Cicero being one.

Cassius. Cicero one?

57. **How scaped . . . you so?** How did I escape being killed when I opposed you so?
58. **touching** *adj.* deeply wounding.
59. **Upon** *prep.* as a result of.

Conflict
With what internal conflict has Brutus been struggling?

60. **with . . . tidings came** That is, Brutus received two messages at the same time: news of Portia's death and news of Octavius and Antony's success.
61. **fell distract** became distraught.
62. **call in question** examine.
63. **power** *n.* army.
64. **Bending . . . Philippi** (fi lip´ ī) directing their rapid march toward Philippi, a city in Macedonia.
65. **selfsame tenure** same message.
66. **proscription . . . outlawry** proclamation of death sentences and lists of those condemned.

Comprehension
What has happened to Brutus' wife, Portia?

Read Between the Lines

In this situation, why might Messala ask Brutus about news of Portia?

67. **aught** (ôt) *n.* anything at all.

68. **have . . . art** have as much Stoicism in theory.

69. **to our work alive** Let us go about the work we have to do as living men.

70. **presently** *adv.* immediately.

71. **offense** *n.* harm.

72. **of force** of necessity.

73. **Do stand . . . affection** support us only out of fear of force.

74. **grudged us contribution** given us aid and supplies grudgingly.

75. **shall make . . . up** will add more to their numbers.

76. **new-added** reinforced.

Messala. Cicero is dead,
And by that order of proscription.
Had you your letters from your wife, my lord?

Brutus. No, Messala.

Messala. Nor nothing in your letters writ of her?

Brutus. Nothing, Messala.

Messala. That methinks is strange.

Brutus. Why ask you? Hear you aught[67] of her in yours?

Messala. No, my lord.

Brutus. Now as you are a Roman, tell me true.

Messala. Then like a Roman bear the truth I tell,
For certain she is dead, and by strange manner.

Brutus. Why, farewell, Portia. We must die, Messala.
With meditating that she must die once,
I have the patience to endure it now.

Messala. Even so great men great losses should endure.

Cassius. I have as much of this in art[68] as you,
But yet my nature could not bear it so.

Brutus. Well, to our work alive.[69] What do you think
Of marching to Philippi presently?[70]

Cassius. I do not think it good.

Brutus. Your reason?

Cassius. This it is:
'Tis better that the enemy seek us;
So shall he waste his means, weary his soldiers,
Doing himself offense,[71] whilst we, lying still,
Are full of rest, defense, and nimbleness.

Brutus. Good reasons must of force[72] give place to better.
The people 'twixt Philippi and this ground
Do stand but in a forced affection;[73]
For they have grudged us contribution.[74]
The enemy, marching along by them,
By them shall make a fuller number up,[75]
Come on refreshed, new-added[76] and encouraged;
From which advantage shall we cut him off
If at Philippi we do face him there,
These people at our back.

Cassius. Hear me, good brother.

Brutus. Under your pardon.[77] You must note beside
That we have tried the utmost of our friends,
Our legions are brimful, our cause is ripe.
The enemy increaseth every day;
We, at the height, are ready to decline.
There is a tide in the affairs of men
Which, taken at the flood, leads on to fortune;
Omitted,[78] all the voyage of their life
Is bound[79] in shallows and in miseries.
On such a full sea are we now afloat,
And we must take the current when it serves,
Or lose our ventures.[80]

Cassius. Then, with your will,[81] go on;
We'll along ourselves and meet them at Philippi.

Brutus. The deep of night is crept upon our talk,
And nature must obey necessity,
Which we will niggard with a little rest.[82]
There is no more to say?

Cassius. No more. Good night.
Early tomorrow will we rise and hence.[83]

[*Enter* Lucius.]

Brutus. Lucius, my gown.[84] [*Exit* Lucius.]
Farewell, good Messala.
Good night, Titinius. Noble, noble Cassius,
Good night, and good repose.

Cassius. O my dear brother,
This was an ill beginning of the night.
Never come[85] such division 'tween our souls!
Let it not, Brutus.

[*Enter* Lucius, *with the gown.*]

Brutus. Everything is well.

Cassius. Good night, my lord.

Brutus. Good night, good brother.

Titinius, Messala. Good night, Lord Brutus.

Brutus. Farewell, every one.

[*Exit*]

Give me the gown. Where is thy instrument?[86]

77. **Under your pardon** excuse me.

Read Between the Lines
What does Brutus' speech indicate about the chances that he and Cassius will lose the war?

78. **Omitted** *adj.* neglected.
79. **bound** *adj.* confined.
80. **ventures** *n.* things put at risk in hope of profit—as a merchant risks goods in sending them by sea.
81. **with your will** as you wish.
82. **niggard . . . rest** satisfy stingily with a short sleep.

83. **hence** leave.

84. **gown** *n.* dressing gown; robe.

85. **Never come** may there never again come.

86. **instrument** *n.* lute (probably), a small stringed instrument related to the guitar.

Comprehension
What do Brutus and Cassius plan to do?

87. **knave** (nāv) *n.* servant.
88. **o'erwatched** *adj.* weary with too much watchfulness.
89. **raise** *v.* wake.
90. **watch your pleasure** stay alert for your command.
91. **otherwise bethink me** change my mind.
92. **touch . . . a strain or two?** play a melody or two on your instrument.
93. **an't** if it.
94. **young bloods** young bodies.
95. **murd'rous** *adj.* deathlike.
96. **mace** (mās) *n.* staff of office (an allusion to the practice of tapping a person on the shoulder with a mace when arresting him).

Lucius. Here in the tent.

Brutus. What, thou speak'st drowsily?
Poor knave,[87] I blame thee not; thou art o'erwatched.[88]
Call Claudius and some other of my men;
I'll have them sleep on cushions in my tent.

Lucius. Varro and Claudius!

[*Enter* Varro *and* Claudius.]

Varro. Calls my lord?

Brutus. I pray you, sirs, lie in my tent and sleep.
It may be I shall raise[89] you by and by
On business to my brother Cassius.

Varro. So please you, we will stand and watch your pleasure.[90]

Brutus. I will not have it so; lie down, good sirs;
It may be I shall otherwise bethink me.[91]

[Varro *and* Claudius *lie down.*]

Look. Lucius, here's the book I sought for so;
I put it in the pocket of my gown.

Lucius. I was sure your lordship did not give it me.

Brutus. Bear with me, good boy, I am much forgetful.
Canst thou hold up thy heavy eyes awhile,
And touch thy instrument a strain or two?[92]

Lucius. Ay, my lord, an't[93] please you.

Brutus. It does, my boy.
I trouble thee too much, but thou art willing.

Lucius. It is my duty, sir.

Brutus. I should not urge thy duty past thy might;
I know young bloods[94] look for a time of rest.

Lucius. I have slept, my lord, already.

Brutus. It was well done, and thou shalt sleep again;
I will not hold thee long. If I do live,
I will be good to thee.

[*Music, and a song*]

This is a sleepy tune. O murd'rous[95] slumber!
Layest thou thy leaden mace[96] upon my boy,
That plays thee music? Gentle knave, good night;
I will not do thee so much wrong to wake thee.
If thou dost nod, thou break'st thy instrument;

I'll take it from thee; and, good boy, good night.
Let me see, let me see; is not the leaf[97] turned down
Where I left reading? Here it is, I think.

[*Enter the Ghost of* CAESAR.]

How ill this taper burns. Ha! Who comes here?
I think it is the weakness of mine eyes
That shapes this monstrous apparition.[98]
It comes upon[99] me. Art thou anything?
Art thou some god, some angel, or some devil,
That mak'st my blood cold, and my hair to stare?[100]
Speak to me what thou art.

GHOST. Thy evil spirit, Brutus.

BRUTUS. Why com'st thou?

GHOST. To tell thee thou shalt see me at Philippi.

BRUTUS. Well; then I shall see thee again?

GHOST. Ay, at Philippi.

BRUTUS. Why, I will see thee at Philippi then.

[*Exit* GHOST.]

Now I have taken heart thou vanishest.
Ill spirit, I would hold more talk with thee.
Boy! Lucius! Varro! Claudius! Sirs, awake!
Claudius!

LUCIUS. The strings, my lord, are false.[101]

BRUTUS. He thinks he still is at his instrument.
Lucius, awake!

LUCIUS. My lord?

BRUTUS. Didst thou dream, Lucius, that thou so criedst out?

LUCIUS. My lord, I do not know that I did cry.

BRUTUS. Yes, that thou didst. Didst thou see anything?

LUCIUS. Nothing, my lord.

BRUTUS. Sleep again, Lucius. Sirrah Claudius!
[*To* VARRO] Fellow thou, awake!

VARRO. My lord?

CLAUDIUS. My lord?

BRUTUS. Why did you so cry out, sirs, in your sleep?

97. leaf *n.* page.
98. monstrous apparition ominous ghost.
99. upon *prep.* toward.
100. stare *n.* stand on end.

Read Between the Lines
Brutus is planning to march to battle at Philippi. In this situation, what might the ghost's warning mean?

101. false *adj.* out of tune.

Conflict
What internal conflict might the ghost's warning create for Brutus?

Comprehension
What frightens Brutus as he prepares to read a book?

102. **commend me** carry my greetings.
103. **set on . . . before** advance his troops early, before me.

BOTH. Did we, my lord?

BRUTUS. Ay. Saw you anything?

VARRO. No, my lord, I saw nothing.

CLAUDIUS. Nor I, my lord.

BRUTUS. Go and commend me[102] to my brother
Cassius;
Bid him set on his pow'rs betimes before,[103]
And we will follow.

BOTH. It shall be done, my lord. [*Exit*]

◀ **Critical Viewing**
What does this ancient Roman coin suggest about how war was fought at the time?

Language Study

Vocabulary The words below appear in *The Tragedy of Julius Caesar,* Act IV. For each word, write a definition in your own words. Then, write a brief paragraph in which you use the words correctly.

legacies **chastisement** **mirth** **rash** **condemned**

WORD STUDY
The **Latin root *-sum-*** means "to take" or "to use." In the play, Cassius tells Brutus not to **presume** upon his friendship, or take for granted his good will.

Word Study

Part A Explain how the **Latin root *-sum-*** contributes to the meanings of these words: *consume, resume,* and *sumptuous.* Consult a dictionary if necessary.

Part B Use the context of the sentences and what you know about the Latin root *-sum-* to explain your answer to each question.

1. If Rafael *assumes* the role of class president, has he stepped down from the position?
2. Does her *presumptuous* remark reveal her modesty?

Close Reading Activities

Literary Analysis

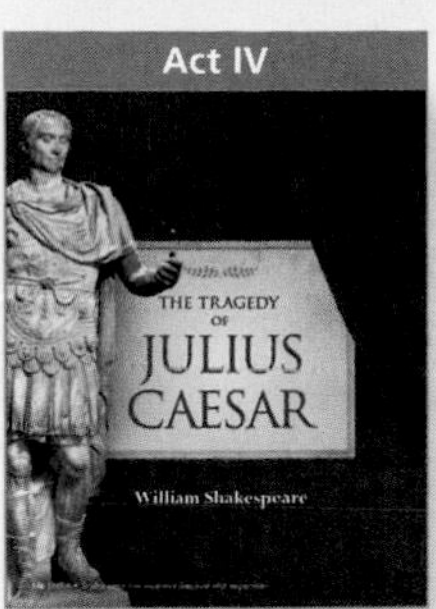

Key Ideas and Details

1. **(a)** In Scene i, what opinion of Lepidus does Antony express? **(b) Infer:** Why is Octavius surprised to hear this opinion? Explain. **(c) Compare and Contrast:** In what way is Antony's behavior toward Lepidus similar to his manipulation of the crowd at Caesar's funeral in Act III? Explain.
2. **(a)** What are two accusations Brutus makes against Cassius in Scene iii? **(b) Compare and Contrast:** What differences in their characters does their argument emphasize? Explain, citing textual details for support.
3. **(a)** In Scene iii, lines 200–220, what does Brutus say about Antony's army compared with his own? **(b) Interpret:** In Brutus' opinion, why should the fight begin immediately? **(c) Analyze:** What deeper awareness does Brutus seem to have? Explain.
4. **Read Between the Lines (a)** To whom is Brutus referring as "a brother" in Scene ii, lines 38–39? **(b)** What does he mean in these lines?
5. **Read Between the Lines (a)** What does Cassius say in Scene iii, lines 92–98? **(b)** What situation does he describe? **(c)** Explain the unspoken significance of his words.

Craft and Structure

6. **Conflict (a)** Using a diagram like the one shown, identify two external conflicts shown or referred to in Act IV. **(b)** Describe two internal conflicts Brutus experiences in Act IV.
7. **Conflict (a)** Explain the connection Brutus makes in Scene iii, lines 18–28 between his reasons for joining the conspirators and his conflict with Cassius. **(b)** Do you think Brutus will feel an internal conflict over his decision to join the conspirators? Explain, citing evidence from the text that helped you form your response.

External Conflict 1
Between:
Caused by
External Conflict 2
Between:
Caused by
Internal Conflict 1
Caused by
Internal Conflict 2
Caused by

Integration of Knowledge and Ideas

8. **Make a Judgment (a)** Which character in Act IV do you think would make the best leader for Rome? Explain and support your judgment with details from the text. **(b)** Share your ideas in a small group discussion. As a group, come to an agreement about which character would make the best leader and present your choices and reasons to the class.

9. THE BIG ? **To what extent does experience determine what we perceive? (a)** How do Brutus' past actions contribute to the appearance of Caesar's ghost? **(b)** What does Caesar's ghost represent? Explain, citing details from the play to support your response.

ACADEMIC VOCABULARY

As you write and speak about *The Tragedy of Julius Caesar*, use the words related to experience and perceptions that you explored on page 517 of this book.

Building Knowledge

To what extent does experience determine what we perceive?

Explore the Big Question as you read *The Tragedy of Julius Caesar*, Act V. Consider how characters' perceptions lead to a tragic end.

CLOSE READING FOCUS

Key Ideas and Details: **Compare and Contrast Characters**

Shakespeare often emphasizes the important qualities of one character by presenting a **foil,** another character with strongly contrasting qualities. When reading Shakespearean drama, you can often gain understanding by **comparing and contrasting characters.** Look for similarities and differences in the characters' personalities, situations, behaviors, and attitudes.

Craft and Structure: **Tragic Heroes**

In ancient Greek drama, **tragic heroes** are characters of noble birth who suffer a catastrophe. The hero's choices leading to the catastrophe may reflect a personal shortcoming, such as excessive pride, called a **tragic flaw.** While Shakespeare incorporates these traditional elements, he develops them in new ways.

- He adds complexity to his heroes, who often suffer hesitation or doubt.
- He presents a character's inner turmoil directly through devices like the soliloquy, a speech in which a character thinks aloud.
- He focuses on the choices characters make rather than on fate.
- He addresses the difference between the reasons for an action and its outcome. For example, Brutus acts for reasons of honor, but in a world full of dishonor, the results are disastrous.

Vocabulary

The words below are key to understanding the text that follows. Copy the words into your notebook. For each word, write a sentence with context clues that suggest the meaning of the word.

fawned	**presage**	**demeanor**
misconstrued	**meditates**	**disconsolate**

Common Core State Standards

Reading Literature

1. Cite strong and thorough textual evidence to support analysis of what the text says explicitly as well as inferences drawn from the text.

3. Analyze how complex characters develop over the course of a text, interact with other characters, and advance the plot or develop the theme.

7. Analyze the representation of a subject or a key scene in two different artistic mediums, including what is emphasized or absent in each treatment.

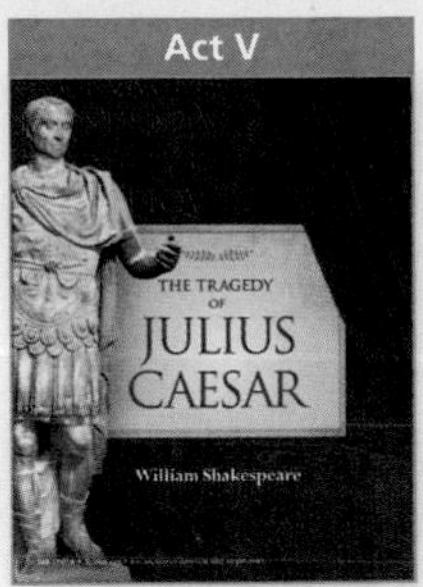

CLOSE READING MODEL

The passage below is from Shakespeare's *The Tragedy of Julius Caesar*, Act V. The annotations to the right of the passage show ways in which you can use close reading skills to compare and contrast characters and analyze tragic heroes.

from *The Tragedy of Julius Caesar*, Act V

Clitus. What ill request did Brutus make to thee?

Dardanius. To kill him, Clitus. Look, he meditates.

Clitus. Now is that noble vessel full of grief,
That it runs over even at his eyes.[1]

Brutus. Come hither, good Volumnius; list a word.

Volumnius. What says my lord?

Brutus. Why this, Volumnius:
The ghost of Caesar hath appeared to me
Two several times by night; at Sardis once,
And this last night here in Philippi fields.
I know my hour is come.[2]

Volumnius. Not so, my lord.

Brutus. Nay, I am sure it is, Volumnius.
Thou seest the world, Volumnius, how it goes;
Our enemies have beat us to the pit.
[Low calls to arms]
It is more worthy to leap in ourselves
Than tarry till they push us.[3] Good Volumnius,
Thou know'st that we two went to school together;
Even for that our love of old, I prithee
Hold thou my sword-hilts whilst I run on it.

Volumnius. That's not an office for a friend, my lord.
[Call to arms still]

Clitus. Fly, fly, my lord, there is no tarrying here.

Compare and Contrast Characters

1 In this scene, Brutus asks his companions to help him end his life. The companions discuss Brutus, telling the audience that he is weeping: His grief "runs over even at his eyes." The companions' sympathetic but more distant emotions serve to emphasize the depth of Brutus' despair.

Tragic Heroes

2 Literally haunted by his guilt and shame, Brutus sits in judgment of his own actions. He recognizes that by acting against Caesar, he has fallen into dishonor. Although Brutus is not the play's title character, a reader could argue that he is its true tragic hero—the noble figure who experiences a catastrophic downfall.

Tragic Heroes

3 After a stainless life, Brutus says he would rather die than wait until others exact their revenge for Caesar's death. However, notice that in his disgrace and shame, the noble Brutus still seeks a "worthy" path.

REVIEW AND ANTICIPATE

By the end of Act IV, Cassius and Brutus have patched up their quarrel. Brutus persuades Cassius to agree to his strategy—taking the battle to the enemy. He reasons that they should march to the city of Philippi and attack before Octavius and Antony swell their forces with new recruits. The act ends ominously as Brutus is visited by Caesar's ghost. Before disappearing, the ghost tells Brutus that they will meet again at Philippi. As Act V opens, the two armies are poised for battle on the plains of Philippi. Nothing less than the future of Rome is at stake.

▶ **Critical Viewing**
Does Brutus' personality, as suggested by this statue, fit with his personality in the story? Explain.

ACT V

Scene i. The plains of Philippi.

[*Enter* OCTAVIUS, ANTONY, *and their Army.*]

OCTAVIUS. Now, Antony, our hopes are answerèd;
You said the enemy would not come down,
But keep the hills and upper regions.
It proves not so; their battles[1] are at hand;
They mean to warn[2] us at Philippi here,
Answering before we do demand of them.[3]

ANTONY. Tut, I am in their bosoms,[4] and I know
Wherefore[5] they do it. They could be content
To visit other places, and come down
With fearful bravery,[6] thinking by this face[7]
To fasten in our thoughts[8] that they have courage;
But 'tis not so.

[*Enter a* MESSENGER.]

MESSENGER. Prepare you, generals,
The enemy comes on in gallant show;
Their bloody sign[9] of battle is hung out,
And something to be done immediately.

ANTONY. Octavius, lead your battle softly[10] on
Upon the left hand of the even[11] field.

OCTAVIUS. Upon the right hand I; keep thou the left.

ANTONY. Why do you cross me in this exigent?[12]

OCTAVIUS. I do not cross you; but I will do so. [*March*]

[*Drum. Enter* BRUTUS, CASSIUS, *and their Army;* LUCILIUS, TITINIUS, MESSALA, *and others.*]

BRUTUS. They stand, and would have parley.[13]

CASSIUS. Stand fast, Titinius, we must out and talk.

OCTAVIUS. Mark Antony, shall we give sign of battle?

ANTONY. No, Caesar, we will answer on their charge.[14]
Make forth;[15] the generals would have some words.

OCTAVIUS. Stir not until the signal.

BRUTUS. Words before blows; is it so, countrymen?

OCTAVIUS. Not that we love words better, as you do.

1. **battles** *n.* armies.
2. **warn** *v.* challenge.
3. **Answering . . . of them** appearing in opposition to us before we challenge them.
4. **am in their bosoms** know what they are thinking.
5. **Wherefore** *conj.* why.
6. **fearful bravery** show of magnificence and pretend courage concealing fear.
7. **face** *n.* appearance.
8. **fasten in our thoughts** convince us.

Compare and Contrast Characters
What contrast between Octavius and Antony is suggested by their opening speeches?

9. **bloody sign** red flag.
10. **softly** *adv.* slowly.
11. **even** *adj.* level.
12. **exigent** *n.* critical situation.
13. **parley** *n.* conference between enemies.
14. **answer on their charge** meet them when they attack.
15. **Make forth** go forward.

Comprehension
What news does the messenger bring Octavius and Antony?

Brutus. Good words are better than bad strokes, Octavius.

Antony. In your bad strokes, Brutus, you give good words;
Witness the hole you made in Caesar's heart,
Crying "Long live! Hail, Caesar!"

Cassius. Antony,
The posture[16] of your blows are yet unknown;
But for your words, they rob the Hybla bees,[17]
And leave them honeyless.

Antony. Not stingless too.

Brutus. O, yes, and soundless too;
For you have stol'n their buzzing, Antony,
And very wisely threat before you sting.

Antony. Villains! You did not so, when your vile daggers
Hacked one another in the sides of Caesar.
You showed your teeth[18] like apes, and **fawned** like hounds,
And bowed like bondmen,[19] kissing Caesar's feet;
Whilst damnèd Casca, like a cur,[20] behind
Struck Caesar on the neck. O you flatterers!

Cassius. Flatterers! Now, Brutus, thank yourself;
This tongue had not offended so today,
If Cassius might have ruled.[21]

Octavius. Come, come, the cause.[22] If arguing make us sweat,
The proof[23] of it will turn to redder drops.
Look,
I draw a sword against conspirators.
When think you that the sword goes up[24] again?
Never, till Caesar's three and thirty wounds
Be well avenged; or till another Caesar
Have added slaughter to the sword of traitors.[25]

Brutus. Caesar, thou canst not die by traitors' hands,
Unless thou bring'st them with thee.

Octavius. So I hope.
I was not born to die on Brutus' sword.

Brutus. O, if thou wert the noblest of thy strain,[26]
Young man, thou couldst not die more honorable.

Cassius. A peevish[27] schoolboy, worthless[28] of such honor,
Joined with a masker and a reveler.[29]

Antony. Old Cassius still!

Octavius. Come, Antony; away!

16. **posture** *n.* quality.
17. **Hybla bees** bees from the town of Hybla in Sicily, noted for their sweet honey.

Vocabulary ▶
fawned (fônd) *v.* flattered; acted with excessive concern for the wishes and moods of another, as a servant might

18. **showed your teeth** grinned.
19. **bondmen** *n.* slaves.
20. **cur** *n.* dog.
21. **If Cassius might have ruled** if Cassius had had his way when he urged that Antony be killed.

Tragic Heroes
Which of Brutus' earlier decisions would Cassius call tragic?

22. **cause** *n.* business at hand.
23. **proof** *n.* test.
24. **goes up** goes into its scabbard.
25. **till another Caesar . . . traitors** until I, another Caesar, have also been killed by you.
26. **noblest of thy strain** best of your family.
27. **peevish** silly.
28. **worthless** *adj.* unworthy.
29. **a masker and a reveler** one who attends masquerades and parties; Antony.

Defiance, traitors, hurl we in your teeth.
If you dare fight today, come to the field;
If not, when you have stomachs.[30]

[*Exit* OCTAVIUS, ANTONY, *and Army.*]

CASSIUS. Why, now blow wind, swell billow, and swim bark![31]
The storm is up, and all is on the hazard.[32]

BRUTUS. Ho, Lucilius, hark, a word with you.

[LUCILIUS *and* MESSALA *stand forth.*]

LUCILIUS. My lord?

[BRUTUS *and* LUCILIUS *converse apart.*]

CASSIUS. Messala.

MESSALA. What says my general?

CASSIUS. Messala,
This is my birthday; as this very day
Was Cassius born. Give me thy hand, Messala:
Be thou my witness that against my will
(As Pompey was)[33] am I compelled to set[34]
Upon one battle all our liberties.
You know that I held Epicurus strong,[35]
And his opinion; now I change my mind.
And partly credit things that do **presage**.
Coming from Sardis, on our former ensign[36]
Two mighty eagles fell,[37] and there they perched,
Gorging and feeding from our Soldiers' hands,
Who to Philippi here consorted[38] us.
This morning are they fled away and gone,
And in their steads do ravens, crows, and kites[39]
Fly o'er our heads and downward look on us
As we were sickly prey; their shadows seem
A canopy most fatal,[40] under which
Our army lies, ready to give up the ghost.

MESSALA. Believe not so.

CASSIUS. I but believe it partly,
For I am fresh of spirit and resolved
To meet all perils very constantly.[41]

BRUTUS. Even so, Lucilius.

CASSIUS. Now, most noble Brutus,
The gods today stand friendly, that we may,
Lovers[42] in peace, lead on our days to age!

30. **stomachs** appetites for battle.
31. **bark** ship.
32. **on the hazard** at stake.
33. **As Pompey was** Against his own judgment, Pompey was urged to do battle against Caesar. The battle resulted in Pompey's defeat and murder.
34. **set** stake.
35. **held Epicurus strong** believed in Epicurus' philosophy that the gods do not interest themselves in human affairs and that omens are merely superstitions.

◀ **Vocabulary**
presage (prē sāj´) *v.* give a warning sign about a future event

36. **former ensign** (en´ sīn´) standard-bearer (soldier carrying a flag) farthest in front.
37. **fell** swooped down.
38. **consorted** *v.* accompanied.
39. **ravens, crows, and kites** scavenger birds, said to gather before a battle.
40. **A canopy most fatal** a rooflike covering foretelling death.
41. **very constantly** most resolutely.
42. **Lovers** *n.* true friends.

Comprehension
What is Cassius' complaint about the battle they are about to fight?

43. **rests still incertain** always remain uncertain.
44. **reason . . . befall** reason about the worst that may happen.
45. **that philosophy** here, Stoicism.
46. **Cato** Marcus Porcius Cato (Cato the Younger) supported Pompey in his quarrel with Caesar and killed himself after Pompey's defeat.
47. **so to prevent . . . life** thus to anticipate the natural end of life.
48. **stay the providence** await the ordained fate.

Compare and Contrast Characters
Contrast the outlook Brutus expresses here with Cassius' misgivings in lines 70–88.

49. **in triumph** as a captive in the victor's procession.
50. **Thorough** *prep.* through.

Tragic Heroes
What details of Brutus' preoccupation with honor, expressed here, reflect his decision to join the conspirators?

But since the affairs of men rests still incertain,[43]
Let's reason with the worst that may befall.[44]
If we do lose this battle, then is this
The very last time we shall speak together.
What are you then determinèd to do?

Brutus. Even by the rule of that philosophy[45]
By which I did blame Cato[46] for the death
Which he did give himself; I know not how,
But I do find it cowardly and vile,
For fear of what might fall, so to prevent
The time of life,[47] arming myself with patience
To stay the providence[48] of some high powers
That govern us below.

Cassius. Then, if we lose this battle,
You are contented to be led in triumph[49]
Thorough[50] the streets of Rome?

Brutus. No, Cassius, no; think not, thou noble Roman,
That ever Brutus will go bound to Rome;
He bears too great a mind. But this same day
Must end that work the ides of March begun;
And whether we shall meet again I know not.
Therefore our everlasting farewell take.
Forever, and forever, farewell, Cassius!
If we do meet again, why, we shall smile;
If not, why then this parting was well made.

Cassius. Forever, and forever, farewell, Brutus!
If we do meet again, we'll smile indeed;
If not, 'tis true this parting was well made.

Brutus. Why then, lead on. O, that a man might know
The end of this day's business ere it come!
But it sufficeth that the day will end,
And then the end is known. Come, ho! Away! [*Exit*]

1. **bills** written orders.
2. **other side** wing of the army commanded by Cassius.
3. **cold demeanor** (di mēn′ ər) lack of spirit in their conduct.

Scene ii. The field of battle.

[*Call to arms sounds. Enter* Brutus *and* Messala.]

Brutus. Ride, ride, Messala, ride, and give these bills[1]
Unto the legions on the other side.[2]

[*Loud call to arms*]

Let them set on at once; for I perceive
But cold **demeanor**[3] in Octavius' wing,

Vocabulary ▶
demeanor (di mēn′ ər) *n.* way of conducting oneself; behavior

LITERATURE IN CONTEXT

History Connection

Roman Triumphs

Brutus and Cassius reflect on the humiliation they will experience if they are defeated and brought in triumph to Rome. A *triumph,* held to celebrate a general's victory, included these events:

- Temples were decorated and sacrifices were held.
- The victorious general and his troops marched through the city to the Capitol, preceded by the Roman Senators and trumpeters.
- The triumphant general, dressed in a royal purple toga and holding a laurel branch, rode in a golden chariot drawn by four white horses.
- On display were the spoils of war, including carts full of treasure, and exotic animals.
- Captive enemy leaders—and even their children—were marched in front of the general.
- The people of Rome gathered to view and cheer the spectacle.

Connect to the Literature Why would Cassius and Brutus wish to escape at any cost being led as prisoners in a triumph?

And sudden push gives them the overthrow,[4]
Ride, ride, Messala! Let them all come down.[5] [*Exit*]

4. **sudden push . . . overthrow** sudden attack will defeat them.
5. **Let . . . down** attack all at once.

Scene iii. The field of battle.

[*Calls to arms sound. Enter* Cassius *and* Titinius.]

Cassius. O, look, Titinius, look, the villains[1] fly!
Myself have to mine own turned enemy.[2]
This ensign here of mine was turning back;
I slew the coward, and did take it[3] from him.

Titinius. O Cassius, Brutus gave the word too early,
Who, having some advantage on Octavius,
Took it too eagerly; his Soldiers fell to spoil,[4]
Whilst we by Antony are all enclosed.

[*Enter* Pindarus.]

Pindarus. Fly further off, my lord, fly further off!
Mark Antony is in your tents, my lord.
Fly, therefore, noble Cassius, fly far off!

1. **villains** here, cowards among his own men.
2. **Myself . . . enemy** I have become an enemy to my own Soldiers.
3. **it** here, the ensign's banner.
4. **fell to spoil** began to loot.

Comprehension
How well is the battle going for Cassius and his forces?

CASSIUS. This hill is far enough. Look, look, Titinius!
Are those my tents where I perceive the fire?

TITINIUS. They are, my lord.

CASSIUS. Titinius, if thou lovest me,
Mount thou my horse and hide[5] thy spurs in him
Till he have brought thee up to yonder troops
And here again, that I may rest assured
Whether yond troops are friend or enemy.

TITINIUS. I will be here again even with a thought.[6] [*Exit*]

CASSIUS. Go, Pindarus, get higher on that hill;
My sight was ever thick.[7] Regard[8] Titinius,
And tell me what thou not'st about the field.

[*Exit* PINDARUS.]

This day I breathèd first. Time is come round,
And where I did begin, there shall I end.
My life is run his compass.[9] Sirrah, what news?

PINDARUS. [*Above*] O my lord!

CASSIUS. What news?

PINDARUS. [*Above*] Titinius is enclosèd round about
With horsemen that make to him on the spur;[10]
Yet he spurs on. Now they are almost on him.
Now, Titinius! Now some light.[11] O, he lights too!
He's ta'en![12][*Shout*] And, hark! They shout for joy.

CASSIUS. Come down; behold no more.
O, coward that I am, to live so long,
To see my best friend ta'en before my face!

[*Enter* PINDARUS.]

Come hither, sirrah.
In Parthia did I take thee prisoner;
And then I swore thee, saving of thy life,[13]
That whatsoever I did bid thee do,
Thou shouldst attempt it. Come now, keep thine oath.
Now be a freeman, and with this good sword,
That ran through Caesar's bowels, search[14] this bosom.
Stand not[15] to answer. Here, take thou the hilts,
And when my face is covered, as 'tis now,
Guide thou the sword—Caesar, thou art revenged,
Even with the sword that killed thee. [*Dies*]

5. **hide** sink.

6. **even with a thought** as quick as a thought.
7. **thick** dim.
8. **Regard** observe.

9. **his compass** its full course.

10. **make . . . spur** ride toward him at top speed.
11. **light** dismount from their horses.
12. **ta'en** taken; captured.

13. **swore thee . . . thy life** made you promise when I spared your life.
14. **search** penetrate.
15. **Stand not** do not wait.

Tragic Heroes
What heroic qualities does Cassius show?

▲ Critical Viewing
Can you tell whether the horseman in this picture is the friend or enemy of the foot soldiers? Explain what your answer suggests about the conclusions Cassius draws in battle.

Pindarus. So, I am free; yet would not so have been,
Durst[16] I have done my will. O Cassius!
Far from this country Pindarus shall run,
Where never Roman shall take note of him. [*Exit*]

[*Enter* Titinius *and* Messala.]

Messala. It is but change,[17] Titinius; for Octavius
Is overthrown by noble Brutus' power,
As Cassius' legions are by Antony.

Titinius. These tidings[18] will well comfort Cassius.

Messala. Where did you leave him?

16. **Durst** if I had dared.

17. **change** an exchange.
18. **these tidings** *n.* this news.

Comprehension
What does Cassius think has happened to Titinius?

Vocabulary ▶
disconsolate (dis kän′ sə lit) *adj.* so unhappy that nothing brings comfort

19. dews *n.* in Shakespeare's day, dew was considered harmful to the health
20. Mistrust . . . success fear that I would not succeed.

Tragic Heroes
According to Messala, what flaw doomed Cassius?

21. Melancholy's child one of gloomy temperament.
22. Why dost . . . are not? Why do you fill the receptive imagination of men with false ideas?
23. conceived *v.* created.
24. mother . . . thee Cassius (in this case), who conceived the error.
25. envenomèd poisoned.
26. Hie *v.* hurry.
27. brave *adj.* noble.

Vocabulary ▶
misconstrued (mis′ kən strood′) *v.* misinterpreted

28. hold thee wait a moment.
29. apace *adv.* quickly.
30. regarded *v.* honored.
31. By your leave with your permission.
32. part *n.* role; duty.

TITINIUS. All **disconsolate**,
With Pindarus his bondman, on this hill.

MESSALA. Is not that he that lies upon the ground?

TITINIUS. He lies not like the living. O my heart!

MESSALA. Is not that he?

TITINIUS. No, this was he, Messala,
But Cassius is no more. O setting sun,
As in thy red rays thou dost sink to night,
So in his red blood Cassius' day is set.
The sun of Rome is set. Our day is gone;
Clouds, dews,[19] and dangers come; our deeds are done!
Mistrust of my success[20] hath done this deed.

MESSALA. Mistrust of good success hath done this deed.
O hateful Error, Melancholy's child,[21]
Why dost thou show to the apt thoughts of men
The things that are not?[22] O Error, soon conceived,[23]
Thou never com'st unto a happy birth,
But kill'st the mother that engend'red thee![24]

TITINIUS. What, Pindarus! Where art thou, Pindarus?

MESSALA. Seek him, Titinius, whilst I go to meet
The noble Brutus, thrusting this report
Into his ears. I may say "thrusting" it;
For piercing steel and darts envenomèd[25]
Shall be as welcome to the ears of Brutus
As tidings of this sight.

TITINIUS. Hie[26] you, Messala,
And I will seek for Pindarus the while. [*Exit* MESSALA.]
Why didst thou send me forth, brave[27] Cassius?
Did I not meet thy friends, and did not they
Put on my brows this wreath of victory,
And bid me give it thee? Didst thou not hear their shouts?
Alas, thou hast **misconstrued** everything!
But hold thee,[28] take this garland on thy brow;
Thy Brutus bid me give it thee, and I
Will do his bidding. Brutus, come apace,[29]
And see how I regarded[30] Caius Cassius.
By your leave,[31] gods. This is a Roman's part:[32]
Come, Cassius' sword, and find Titinius' heart. [*Dies*]

[*Call to arms sounds. Enter* BRUTUS, MESSALA, YOUNG CATO, STRATO, VOLUMNIUS, *and* LUCILIUS.]

BRUTUS. Where, where, Messala, doth his body lie?

MESSALA. Lo, yonder, and Titinius mourning it.

BRUTUS. Titinius' face is upward.

CATO. He is slain.

BRUTUS. O Julius Caesar, thou art mighty yet!
Thy spirit walks abroad, and turns our swords
In our own proper entrails.[33] [*Low calls to arms*]

CATO. Brave Titinius!
Look, whe'r[34] he have not crowned dead Cassius.

BRUTUS. Are yet two Romans living such as these?
The last of all the Romans, fare thee well!
It is impossible that ever Rome
Should breed thy fellow.[35] Friends, I owe moe[36] tears
To this dead man than you shall see me pay.
I shall find time, Cassius; I shall find time.
Come, therefore, and to Thasos[37] send his body;
His funerals shall not be in our camp,
Lest it discomfort us.[38] Lucilius, come,
And come, young Cato; let us to the field.
Labeo and Flavius set our battles[39] on.
'Tis three o'clock; and, Romans, yet ere night
We shall try fortune in a second fight. [*Exit*]

Scene iv. The field of battle.

[*Call to arms sounds. Enter* BRUTUS, MESSALA, YOUNG CATO, LUCILIUS, *and* FLAVIUS.]

BRUTUS. Yet, countrymen, O, yet hold up your heads!

[*Exit, with followers*]

CATO. What bastard[1] doth not? Who will go with me?
I will proclaim my name about the field.
I am the son of Marcus Cato,[2] ho!
A foe to tyrants, and my country's friend.
I am the son of Marcus Cato, ho!

[*Enter* SOLDIERS *and fight.*]

LUCILIUS. And I am Brutus, Marcus Brutus, I;
Brutus, my country's friend; know me for Brutus![3]

[YOUNG CATO *falls.*]

O young and noble Cato, art thou down?

33. **own proper entrails** very own inner organs.

34. **whe'r** whether.

Tragic Heroes
What noble or heroic qualities does Brutus display in his reactions to Cassius' death?

35. **fellow** equal.
36. **moe** *n.* more.
37. **Thasos** an island not far from Philippi.

38. **discomfort us** discourage our Soldiers.
39. **battles** armies.

1. **bastard** person who is not a true Roman.
2. **Marcus Cato** Brutus' wife's father.
3. **And I am Brutus** Lucilius impersonates Brutus in order to protect him and confuse the enemy.

Comprehension
What error has led to Cassius' and Titinius' deaths?

Why, now thou diest as bravely as Titinius,
And mayst be honored, being Cato's son.

First Soldier. Yield, or thou diest.

Lucilius. Only I yield to die.[4]
There is so much that thou wilt kill me straight;[5]
Kill Brutus, and be honored in his death.

4. **Only . . . die** I will surrender only to die.
5. **much . . . straight** much honor in it that you will kill me immediately.

First Soldier. We must not. A noble prisoner!

[*Enter* Antony.]

Second Soldier. Room, ho! Tell Antony, Brutus is ta'en.

First Soldier. I'll tell thee news. Here comes the general.
Brutus is ta'en, Brutus is ta'en, my lord.

Antony. Where is he?

Lucilius. Safe, Antony; Brutus is safe enough.
I dare assure thee that no enemy
Shall ever take alive the noble Brutus.
The gods defend him from so great a shame!
When you do find him, or alive or dead,
He will be found like Brutus, like himself.[6]

Antony. This is not Brutus, friend, but, I assure you,
A prize no less in worth. Keep this man safe;
Give him all kindness. I had rather have
Such men my friends than enemies. Go on,
And see whe'r Brutus be alive or dead,
And bring us word unto[7] Octavius' tent
How everything is chanced.[8] [*Exit*]

6. **like himself** behaving in a noble way.
7. **unto** in.
8. **How everything is chanced** how everything has turned out; what has happened.

Scene v. The field of battle.

[*Enter* Brutus, Dardanius, Clitus, Strato, *and* Volumnius.]

Brutus. Come, poor remains[1] of friends, rest on this rock.

Clitus. Statilius showed the torchlight,[2] but, my lord,
He came not back; he is or ta'en or slain.

Brutus. Sit thee down, Clitus. Slaying is the word;
It is a deed in fashion. Hark thee, Clitus. [*Whispers*]

Clitus. What, I, my lord? No, not for all the world!

Brutus. Peace then, no words.

Clitus. I'll rather kill myself.

Brutus. Hark thee, Dardanius. [*Whispers*]

1. **poor remains** pitiful survivors.
2. **showed the torchlight** signaled with a torch.

DARDANIUS. Shall I do such a deed?

CLITUS. O Dardanius!

DARDANIUS. O Clitus!

CLITUS. What ill request did Brutus make to thee?

DARDANIUS. To kill him, Clitus. Look, he **meditates**.

CLITUS. Now is that noble vessel[3] full of grief,
That it runs over even at his eyes.

BRUTUS. Come hither, good Volumnius; list[4] a word.

VOLUMNIUS. What says my lord?

BRUTUS. Why, this, Volumnius:
The ghost of Caesar hath appeared to me
Two several[5] times by night; at Sardis once,
And this last night here in Philippi fields.
I know my hour is come.

VOLUMNIUS. Not so, my lord.

BRUTUS. Nay, I am sure it is, Volumnius.
Thou seest the world, Volumnius, how it goes;
Our enemies have beat us to the pit.[6]

[*Low calls to arms*]

It is more worthy to leap in ourselves
Than tarry till they push us.[7] Good Volumnius,
Thou know'st that we two went to school together;
Even for that our love of old, I prithee[8]
Hold thou my sword-hilts whilst I run on it.

VOLUMNIUS. That's not an office[9] for a friend, my lord.

[*Call to arms still*[10]]

CLITUS. Fly, fly, my lord, there is no tarrying here.

BRUTUS. Farewell to you; and you; and you, Volumnius.
Strato, thou hast been all this while asleep;
Farewell to thee too, Strato. Countrymen,
My heart doth joy that yet in all my life
I found no man but he was true to me.
I shall have glory by this losing day
More than Octavius and Mark Antony
By this vile conquest shall attain unto.[11]
So fare you well at once, for Brutus' tongue
Hath almost ended his life's history.

◄ **Vocabulary**
meditates (med′ ə tāts′)
v. thinks deeply

3. **vessel** container of liquid; here, a metaphor for Brutus.
4. **list** hear.

5. **several** separate.

Tragic Heroes
Why does this scene of Brutus weeping add complexity or depth to his character?

6. **pit** trap or grave.
7. **tarry . . . us** wait until they kill us.
8. **prithee** (pri*th*′ ē) *interjection* ask you, please; "pray thee."
9. **office** task.
10. **still** continuing.

Tragic Heroes
What tragic flaw in Brutus is revealed in lines 33–35?

11. **By this . . . unto** by this evil victory shall gain. (Brutus sees the victory of Octavius and Antony as causing the downfall of Roman freedom.)

Comprehension
What does Brutus ask of his servants?

12. **this hour** time of death.

13. **respect** reputation.
14. **smatch** smack or taste.

Compare and Contrast Characters
What do the differences in the way in which Brutus and Cassius meet death show about their characters?

15. **man** servant.
16. **Brutus only overcame himself** only Brutus, no one else, defeated Brutus.
17. **no man else hath honor** no other man gains honor.
18. **Lucilius' saying** See Act V, Scene iv, lines 21–22.
19. **entertain them** take them into my service.
20. **bestow** spend.
21. **prefer** recommend.

22. **save** except.
23. **that** what.

Night hangs upon mine eyes; my bones would rest,
That have but labored to attain this hour.[12]

[Call to arms sounds. Cry within, "Fly, fly, fly!"]

CLITUS. Fly, my lord, fly!

BRUTUS. Hence! I will follow.

[Exit CLITUS, DARDANIUS, *and* VOLUMNIUS.*]*

I prithee, Strato, stay thou by thy lord,
Thou art a fellow of a good respect.[13]
Thy life hath had some smatch[14] of honor in it;
Hold then my sword, and turn away thy face,
While I do run upon it. Wilt thou, Strato?

STRATO. Give me your hand first. Fare you well, my lord.

BRUTUS. Farewell, good Strato—Caesar, now be still;
I killed not thee with half so good a will.
[Dies]

[Call to arms sounds. Retreat sounds. Enter ANTONY, OCTAVIUS, MESSALA, LUCILIUS, *and the Army.]*

OCTAVIUS. What man is that?

MESSALA. My master's man.[15] Strato, where is thy master?

STRATO. Free from the bondage you are in, Messala;
The conquerors can but make a fire of him
For Brutus only overcame himself,[16]
And no man else hath honor[17] by his death.

LUCILIUS. So Brutus should be found. I thank thee, Brutus,
That thou hast proved Lucilius' saying[18] true.

OCTAVIUS. All that served Brutus, I will entertain them.[19]
Fellow, wilt thou bestow[20] thy time with me?

STRATO. Ay, if Messala will prefer[21] me to you.

OCTAVIUS. Do so, good Messala.

MESSALA. How died my master, Strato?

STRATO. I held the sword, and he did run on it.

MESSALA. Octavius, then take him to follow thee,
That did the latest service to my master.

ANTONY. This was the noblest Roman of them all.
All the conspirators save[22] only he
Did that[23] they did in envy of great Caesar;

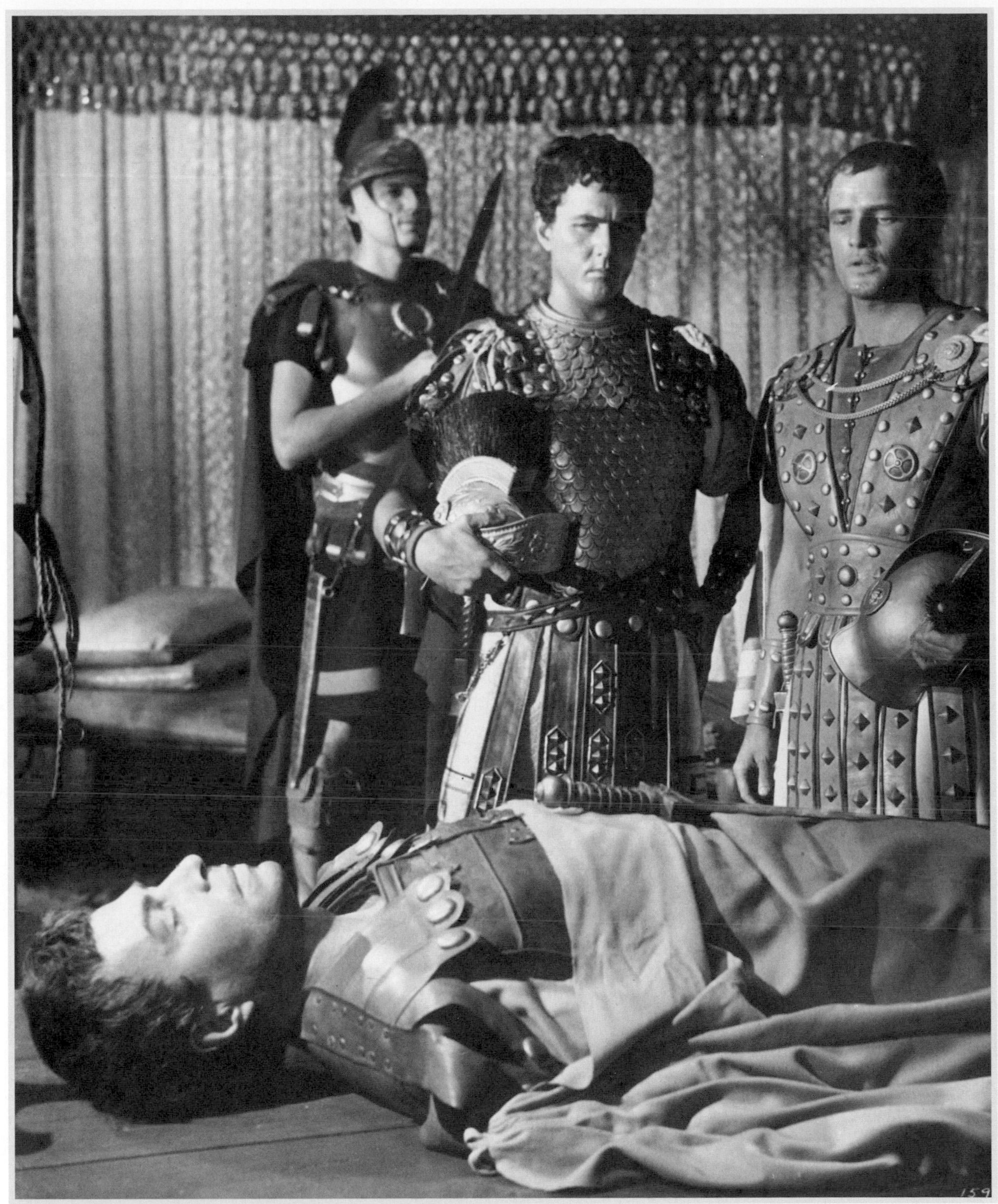

▲ Critical Viewing
Which details in this film still suggest the respect that Octavius and Antony have for Brutus, even in defeat?

24. **only in a general honest thought** with only public-minded motives.
25. **made one of them** became one of the conspirators.
26. **gentle** noble.
27. **So mixed** well balanced.
28. **virtue** excellence.
29. **use** treat.
30. **ordered honorably** treated with honor.
31. **field** army.
32. **part** share.

He, only in a general honest thought[24]
And common good to all, made one of them.[25]
His life was gentle,[26] and the elements
So mixed[27] in him that Nature might stand up
And say to all the world, "This was a man!"

Octavius. According to his virtue,[28] let us use[29] him
With all respect and rites of burial.
Within my tent his bones tonight shall lie,
Most like a soldier ordered honorably.[30]
So call the field[31] to rest, and let's away
To part[32] the glories of this happy day. [*Exit all.*]

Language Study

Vocabulary The words listed below appear in *The Tragedy of Julius Caesar*, Act V. Use one word from the list to write a complete sentence about each numbered item that follows.

fawned **presage** **demeanor** **disconsolate** **meditates**

1. being too eager to please
2. losing a friend
3. watching the sun set
4. hearing distant thunder
5. making a good impression

WORD STUDY

The **Latin root *-stru-*** means "pile up" or "build." In the play, a scene on the battlefield is **misconstrued**. It's meaning is built up or interpreted incorrectly.

Word Study

Part A Explain how the **Latin root *-stru-*** contributes to the meanings of the words *construction, instruct,* and *structural*. Consult a dictionary if necessary.

Part B Use the context of the sentences and what you know about the Latin root *-stru-* to explain your answer to each question.

1. If someone *obstructs* a doorway, is he or she allowing you to pass through it?
2. If a mathematician breaks a challenging code, has he or she *construed* its meaning?

Close Reading Activities

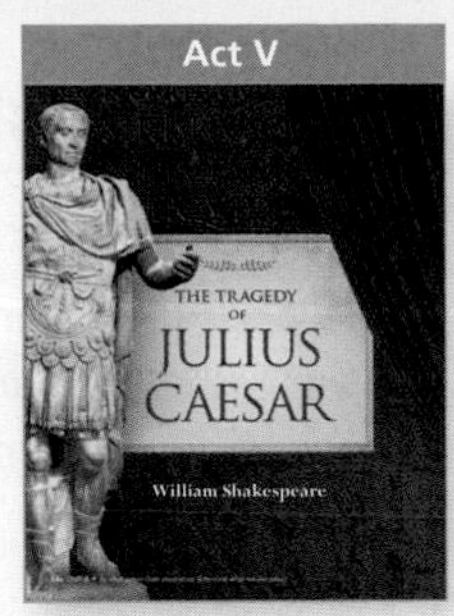

Literary Analysis

Key Ideas and Details

1. **(a)** In Act V, Scene i, lines 100–118, what action does Brutus say he will refuse to take and what situation will he not permit? **(b) Interpret:** What explanation does Brutus give for his position? Explain. **(c) Draw Conclusions:** What do Brutus' statements suggest about his beliefs and values? Explain.
2. **(a)** What does Cassius believe has happened to Titinius when Titinius rides to his tents? **(b) Analyze Cause and Effect:** What does Cassius' interpretation of events lead him to do? **(c) Connect:** How is this reaction similar to Cassius' reaction in Act I when there are signs that Caesar would become king? Explain.
3. **Compare and Contrast Characters (a)** Compare and contrast Cassius and Brutus. **(b)** Find an example from the text to show that Shakespeare sets Cassius and Brutus as foils for each other. **(c)** What do the differences between the two men emphasize about Brutus' character? Explain, citing details from the play that support your response.

Craft and Structure

4. **Tragic Heroes (a)** Using a chart like the one shown, identify details in the play that show how both Brutus and Caesar display the qualities of traditional tragic heroes. **(b)** Based on your analysis, state which character you believe is the true tragic hero of this play. Explain your position, supporting your answer with details from the text.

Noble Birth
Suffers Catastrophe
Tragic Flaw

5. **Tragic Heroes (a)** What does Brutus mean when he says, "My heart doth joy that yet in all my life / I found no man but he was true to me"? **(b)** Do these lines express a positive attitude or a blindness about human nature? Explain. Support your explanation with details from the drama.

Integration of Knowledge and Ideas

6. **(a)** Throughout most of the play, how does Antony feel about Brutus? **(b) Make Inferences:** Which lines help you infer that Antony's attitude toward Brutus changes at the end of the play? Explain your choices.

7. THE BIG ? **To what extent does experience determine what we perceive? (a)** Give two examples of situations in which Brutus expects others to act honorably and they fail to do so. **(b)** What is the outcome of each situation? **(c)** What do these situations suggest about Brutus' view of himself and the world?

ACADEMIC VOCABULARY

As you write and speak about *The Tragedy of Julius Caesar*, use the words related to experience and perceptions that you explored on page 517 of this book.

Acts I–V

THE TRAGEDY OF JULIUS CAESAR

William Shakespeare

Conventions: Absolute Phrases

An **absolute phrase** is a group of words that modifies an entire sentence. It consists of a noun or pronoun and its modifiers. An absolute phrase usually acts as a comment on the main clause.

Examples

- *The sky finally clearing,* the players returned to the field.
- *Her goal within reach,* Anna worked even harder.

The modifiers in an absolute phrase often include a participle. In the absolute phrase in the first example above, for instance, the participle *clearing* modifies the noun *sky*.

Sometimes, the participle *being* is omitted as understood. This is the case in the second example above. That same sentence, revised to include the participle *being,* reads as follows: *Her goal being within reach,* Anna worked even harder.

Some absolute phrases use infinitives or infinitive phrases rather than participles:

Example: The players left the field, *many to shower after a long, hot game.*

Practice A

Identify the absolute phrase in each sentence.

1. His power growing, Caesar was bound to become too ambitious.
2. His dislike of tyrants strong, Brutus thinks that all Romans should be equal.
3. His ambition soaring, Cassius will be happy when Caesar is dead and no longer rules Rome.
4. The people lending their ears, Antony praises Brutus for being noble.
5. Rome seeming in jeopardy, Brutus joins the conspiracy.

Reading Application Find an example of an absolute phrase in the first two acts of *The Tragedy of Julius Caesar.*

Practice B

Complete each sentence by adding an absolute phrase.

1. Brutus joined the group of conspirators.
2. Caesar was deeply saddened to see that Brutus had betrayed him.
3. Antony mourned Caesar's death.
4. Brutus knew there was no turning back.
5. Cassius had persuaded Brutus to join the conspiracy.

Writing Application Write a brief paragraph about the battle between the conspirators and Antony's forces. In your paragraph, use two absolute phrases.

Writing to Sources

Argument Imagine that you are a journalist at the time of Caesar's murder. Write an **editorial,** a brief persuasive essay that presents and defends a position, to express your thoughts on Rome's future. Use a formal style, and include a clear thesis statement with sufficient evidence to support your position.

- Jot down notes on the major events and issues in the play.
- List consequences Rome faces because of the battle between the conspirators and Antony's allies.
- Mark each consequence as desirable or undesirable, and add a note explaining why.
- Anticipate your reader's concerns, biases, or opposing viewpoints, and address them directly. For each position you take, add a sentence that deflects a counterargument—a position someone might take against it.
- Include a concluding sentence that summarizes your overall thesis.

Explanatory Text An **obituary** is a notice that someone has died. In addition to details about the death, an obituary often reports on the life and values of its subject. Write an obituary for a character who dies in *The Tragedy of Julius Caesar*.

- Review the play for details about the character's life and personality.
- Choose an effective organization. For example, open with the circumstances of the character's death and provide a brief background of the character's life.
- Use details from the text to construct a unified picture of the character's life.

Explanatory Text Following Caesar's assassination, both Mark Antony and Brutus address the people of Rome. In an **essay,** compare and contrast their two speeches. Consider the following:

- How are the two speeches similar? How are they different?
- What are the strengths and weaknesses of each speech?
- Which speech is more powerful or effective? Why?

Support your claims with strong evidence, citing specific details from the text.

Grammar Application Include absolute phrases as you write your editorial, obituary, and essay.

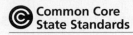

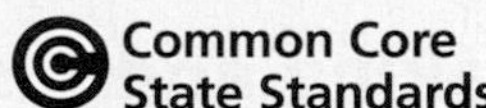

Common Core State Standards

Writing

1. Write arguments to support claims in an analysis of substantive topics or texts, using valid reasoning and relevant and sufficient evidence.

1.a. Introduce precise claim(s), distinguish the claim(s) from alternate or opposing claims, and create an organization that establishes clear relationships among claim(s), counterclaims, reasons, and evidence.

1.b. Develop claim(s) and counterclaims fairly, supplying evidence for each while pointing out the strengths and limitations of both in a manner that anticipates the audience's knowledge level and concerns.

1.e. Provide a concluding statement or section that follows from and supports the argument presented.

4. Produce clear and coherent writing in which the development, organization, and style are appropriate to task, purpose, and audience.

Language

1. Demonstrate command of the conventions of standard English grammar and usage when writing or speaking.

1.b. Use various types of phrases and clauses to convey specific meanings and add variety and interest to writing or presentations.

Speaking and Listening

Presentation of Ideas With a partner, give a **dramatic reading** of Cassius' discussion with Brutus in lines 132–177 of Act I, Scene ii. Review Act I for hints about the personality of each man. Let your knowledge of the character guide your tone of voice and attitude. Follow these suggestions:

- Make notes about how you want to pronounce certain lines. For example, you may want to display contempt, surprise, suspicion, or concern.
- Remember to project your voice strongly if you want to say a line loudly. Lower your voice if you want to convey a softer, quieter tone.
- Practice your parts and present your reading to the class.

Lead the class in a discussion to compare and contrast the experience of reading the scene silently to oneself with the experience of hearing it performed with different voices for the different roles.

Comprehension and Collaboration With a small group of students, hold a **group screening** of a filmed production of *Julius Caesar*. Afterward, discuss the production, starting with these questions:

- How effective was each actor in a major role?
- How effective was the staging of the action?
- In what ways did the production surprise you, given your reading of the play and the way you "saw" the play in your mind as you read?
- Identify and discuss the influence of the director on the production, using questions like these to guide you: How appropriate was the actors' performance style? Were the costumes effective? Did you agree with the director's overall interpretation of the story?
- During the discussion, listen closely to fully understand and evaluate your classmates' ideas.

Have two members of the group serve as note takers. Afterward, review the discussion notes, and analyze differences in members' responses. Quantify the information by identifying the percentages of students who shared certain reactions. Make a chart in which you present the reactions of the class as a whole to the film.

Research and Technology

Build and Present Knowledge Research the lives that married aristocratic women like Calpurnia and Portia led in ancient Rome. Then, write a **women's history report.** Follow these guidelines:

- Locate and evaluate information from primary and secondary sources.
- Find information about the roles some Roman women played in political affairs.
- Compare Calpurnia and Portia with the historical figures you learn about through research.

In your report, identify whether Shakespeare's presentation of women's roles in *Julius Caesar* accurately reflects the customs of ancient Rome.

Build and Present Knowledge Create an advertising poster for a performance of *Julius Caesar* as it would have been performed in Elizabethan England. Include an illustration and text that capture the essence of the performance. Conduct research to find information about the following:

- The design of the Elizabethan theater
- The costumes, scenery, and staging
- The use of special effects

Include information to attract spectators' interest in the play, such as enticing details about the plot. Create an aesthetically pleasing design for your poster and present information clearly and legibly.

Build and Present Knowledge Conduct research on the philosophy of Stoicism, which Brutus practices. Gather information about the history of the philosophy, its most important practitioners, and the ideas it promotes. Produce a **multimedia presentation** of your findings. Use these research strategies to prepare:

- Paraphrase the information you find in your research sources.
- Find appropriate visuals and music to accompany the information.
- Organize the information you will use from most to least important. Locate your strongest ideas and evidence at the top of the list. Add interesting but less significant details at the bottom.
- Include full citation information for every source you use, including those you paraphrase.

In your presentation, explain how Brutus' behavior and attitudes reflect or do not reflect the ideas of Stoicism.

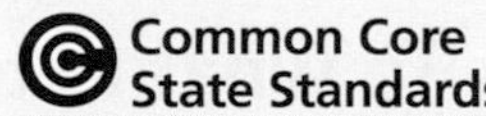

Reading Literature

7. Analyze the representation of a subject or a key scene in two different artistic mediums, including what is emphasized or absent in each treatment.

Speaking and Listening

1. Initiate and participate effectively in a range of collaborative discussions.

1.c. Propel conversations by posing and responding to questions that relate the current discussion to broader themes or larger ideas; actively incorporate others into the discussion; and clarify, verify, or challenge ideas and conclusions.

1.d. Respond thoughtfully to diverse perspectives, summarize points of agreement and disagreement, and, when warranted, qualify or justify their own views and understanding and make new connections in light of the evidence and reasoning presented.

4. Present information, findings, and supporting evidence clearly, concisely, and logically such that listeners can follow the line of reasoning.

Writing

4. Produce clear and coherent writing in which the development, organization, and style are appropriate to task, purpose, and audience.

6. Use technology, including the Internet, to produce, publish, and update individual or shared writing products, taking advantage of technology's capacity to link to other information and to display information flexibly and dynamically.

7. Conduct short as well as more sustained research projects to answer a question or solve a problem; narrow or broaden the inquiry when appropriate; synthesize multiple sources on the subject, demonstrating understanding of the subject under investigation.

Comparing Texts

To what extent does experience determine what we perceive?

Explore the Big Question as you read the excerpt from *A Raisin in the Sun.* Take notes about the experiences that shape the two characters' different perspectives. Then, compare and contrast Walter and Mama's motivations with those that propel the characters in *The Tragedy of Julius Caesar*.

READING TO COMPARE CHARACTERS' MOTIVATIONS

Playwrights Lorraine Hansberry and William Shakespeare portray complex characters who struggle with conflicting ideals, aspirations, and desires. As you read each drama, notice details in characters' dialogue, actions, and reactions that suggest what they want and show how their desires shape their decisions. After you have read the play and the excerpt, compare the motivations that drive the characters.

from *A Raisin in the Sun*

Lorraine Hansberry (1930–1965)
An important voice of the civil rights era, Lorraine Hansberry grew up in Chicago. "Both of my parents were strong-minded, civic-minded, exceptionally race-minded people who made enormous sacrifices on behalf of the struggle for civil rights throughout their lifetimes," she once recalled.

When Hansberry was about eight years old, her parents tried to move to a white neighborhood. Property owners in the neighborhood blocked African American families from purchasing homes there. Hansberry's father fought the restrictions all the way to the U.S. Supreme Court, where he eventually won his case. Years later, Hansberry used that experience as the basis for her award-winning play *A Raisin in the Sun,* which opened on Broadway in 1959.

Comparing Characters' Motivations

A **character's motivation** is the reason he or she adopts certain opinions or takes certain actions. Characters are motivated by their passions, convictions, ideas, and even illusions. Characters' motivations almost always lie at the heart of a story's action, propelling the plot and providing clues to the deeper meaning, or **theme.** To develop your own understanding of character's motivations, consider the following questions as you read:

- What goals or desires does a character state directly, either to other characters or in a dramatic speech, such as a soliloquy or a monologue?
- What personality traits and goals does the dialogue reveal?
- How does the character feel about and behave toward other characters?
- What is the character's family and social background? Do social status or aspirations contribute to the character's desires?
- Are there any striking similarities or differences between this character and others? If so, what are they?

A character can also have more than one motivation. Sometimes, these different motivations cause internal conflicts. For example, a character's closeness to her family may clash with her desire to travel the world. Both William Shakespeare's *The Tragedy of Julius Caesar* and Lorraine Hansberry's *A Raisin in the Sun* feature characters with multiple motivations, such as personal ambition and a desire for dignity.

Compare the ideas of dignity that motivate Walter and Mama in *A Raisin in the Sun* with those that motivate Cassius, Brutus, and Caesar in *Julius Caesar.* Use a diagram like the one shown to gather evidence from the text to support your understanding of the characters' motivations.

Character	Challenge to Character's Dignity	Character's Response	What Character Finds Essential

Common Core State Standards

Reading Literature
3. Analyze how complex characters (e.g., those with multiple or conflicting motivations) develop over the course of a text, interact with other characters, and advance the plot or develop the theme.

Writing
2. Write explanatory texts to examine and convey complex ideas, concepts, and information clearly and accurately through the effective selection, organization, and analysis of content.

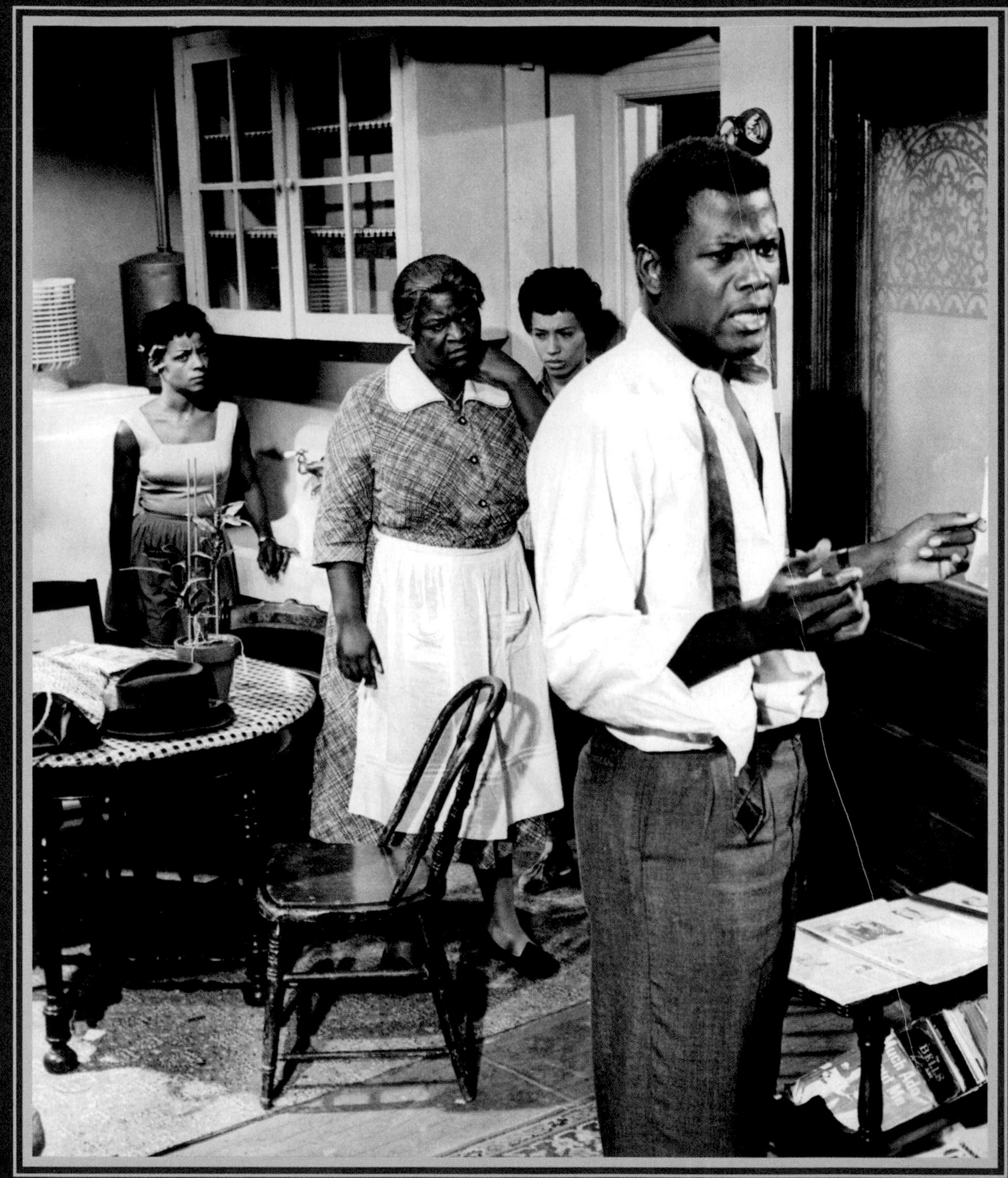

from A Raisin in the Sun

Lorraine Hansberry

from Act 1, Scene II

Background The Youngers are an African American family living in Chicago some time after World War II. During this period, African Americans faced a shortage of economic opportunities and were deprived of many civil rights. Walter Younger, his wife Ruth, and their son Travis live with Walter's mother and his younger sister, Beneatha. Walter's father has passed away. When the family learns that Walter's mother is to receive a check from the father's insurance, Walter pleads with his mother to give him money to invest in a store he wants to open with friends. She wants instead to purchase a new home and to pay for Beneatha's education.

Walter. (*Picks up the check*) Do you know what this money means to me? Do you know what this money can do for us? (*Puts it back*) Mama—Mama—I want so many things . . .

Mama. Yes, son—

Walter. I want so many things that they are driving me kind of crazy . . . Mama—look at me.

Mama. I'm looking at you. You a good-looking boy. You got a job, a nice wife, a fine boy and—

Walter. A job. (*Looks at her*) Mama, a job? I open and close car doors all day long. I drive a man around in his limousine and I say, "Yes, sir; no, sir; very good, sir; shall I take the Drive, sir?" Mama, that ain't no kind of job . . . that ain't nothing at all. (*Very quietly*) Mama, I don't know if I can make you understand.

Mama. Understand what, baby?

Walter. (*Quietly*) Sometimes it's like I can see the future stretched out in front of me—just plain as day. The future, Mama. Hanging over there at the edge of my days. Just waiting for me—a big, **looming** blank space—full of nothing. Just waiting for me. But it don't have to be. (*Pause. Kneeling beside her chair*) Mama—sometimes when I'm downtown and I pass them cool, quiet-looking restaurants where them white boys are sitting back and talking 'bout things . . . sitting there turning deals worth millions of dollars . . . sometimes I see guys don't look much older than me—

◀ Critical Viewing
This photograph is from the 1961 film production of *A Raisin in the Sun*. How does this image suggest that Walter's conflict will play a key role in the story?

Character Motivation
Explain what type of life Walter seems to desire.

◀ Vocabulary
looming (lo͞om′ iŋ) *adj.* appearing unclearly but in a threatening form; threatening to occur

Comprehension
What good things does Mama see in Walter's life?

MAMA. Son—how come you talk so much 'bout money?

WALTER. (*With immense passion*) Because it is life, Mama!

MAMA. (*Quietly*) Oh—(*Very quietly*) So now it's life. Money is life. Once upon a time freedom used to be life—now it's money. I guess the world really do change . . .

WALTER. No—it was always money, Mama. We just didn't know about it.

MAMA. No . . . something has changed. (*She looks at him*) You something new, boy. In my time we was worried about not being lynched and getting to the North if we could and how to stay alive and still have a pinch of **dignity** too . . . Now here come you and Beneatha—talking 'bout things we ain't never even thought about hardly, me and your daddy. You ain't satisfied or proud of nothing we done. I mean that you had a home; that we kept you out of trouble till you was grown; that you don't have to ride to work on the back of nobody's streetcar—You my children—but how different we done become.

Vocabulary ▶
dignity (dig′ nə tē) *n.* quality of deserving respect and honor; self-respect

WALTER. (*A long beat. He pats her hand and gets up*) You just don't understand, Mama, you just don't understand.

Critical Thinking

1. **Key Ideas and Details: (a)** What does Walter do for a living? **(b) Infer:** How does this job make him feel about the future? Support your answer with a quotation from the selection.
2. **Key Ideas and Details:** When Walter says "money is life," what does he mean? Explain your answer, citing details from the excerpt that support your interpretation.
3. **Key Ideas and Details: (a)** What is Mama's reaction to Walter's complaints? **(b) Compare and Contrast:** Compare Mama's goals in life with Walter's.
4. **Integration of Knowledge and Ideas: (a)** In what ways do Mama's past experiences affect her perceptions of freedom and dignity? **(b)** How do Walter's past experiences influence his view of what it means to be free and have dignity? Explain your answer. ***[Connect to the Big Question: To what extent does experience determine what we perceive?]***

Comparing Characters' Motivations

1. **Integration of Knowledge and Ideas (a)** Using a chart like the one shown, analyze Walter's motivation in the scene from *A Raisin in the Sun*. **(b)** Complete a similar chart about Cassius' motivation in *The Tragedy of Julius Caesar,* Act I, Scene ii, lines 90–161. **(c)** What comparisons can you identify?

Social Background	Personality	Feelings	Values	Goals

2. **Integration of Knowledge and Ideas (a)** What ideals motivate Brutus' speech in Act II, Scene i, lines 114–140? **(b)** Compare these ideals to those described by Walter's mother. **(c)** What is one difference between Brutus' goal in joining the conspiracy and Walter's dream of having a business?
3. **Integration of Knowledge and Ideas (a)** Summarize Caesar's ideas about dignity, as expressed in *Julius Caesar,* Act III, Scene i, lines 58–73. **(b)** Is his notion of dignity more like that of Walter or of Mama, or is it different from both? Explain.

Timed Writing

Explanatory Text: Essay

These dramas were written more than 300 years apart, but they address similar themes. Write a brief essay in which you compare the ideas of dignity that motivate characters in *The Tragedy of Julius Caesar* with those that motivate Walter and his mother in *A Raisin in the Sun.* **(30 minutes)**

5-Minute Planner

1. Read the prompt carefully and completely.
2. Gather your ideas by jotting down answers to these questions:
   - What are each character's beliefs, goals, and personality traits?
   - Which statements reveal each character's view of dignity?
   - What do each character's interactions with others show about his or her motivations?
   - In what ways do a specific character's motivations affect the plots and hint at the themes of each work?
3. Reread the prompt, and then draft your essay.

USE ACADEMIC VOCABULARY

As you write, use academic language, including the following words or their related forms:

character
conduct
integrity
motive

For more information about academic vocabulary, see page xlvi.

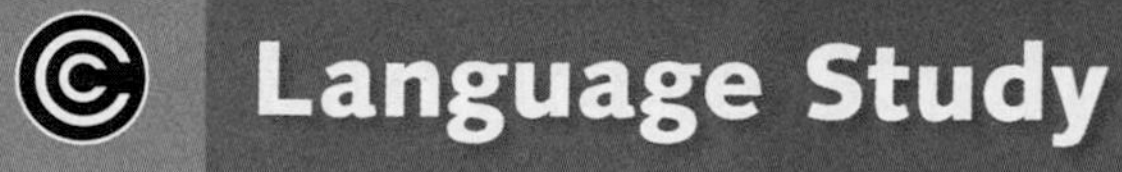

Language Study

Connotation and Denotation

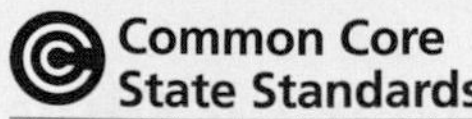

Common Core State Standards

Language

4.c. Consult general and specialized reference materials, both print and digital, to find the pronunciation of a word or determine or clarify its precise meaning, its part of speech, or its etymology.

5.b. Analyze nuances in the meaning of words with similar denotations.

A word's **denotation** is its dictionary meaning, independent of other associations that the word may have. Synonyms have nearly identical denotations. A word's **connotations** are the ideas or emotions associated with the word in addition to its dictionary meaning. Often, words have positive, negative, or neutral connotations, which can affect how people respond to them in both writing and speech.

For example, the denotations of the words *illustrious, famous,* and *notorious* are nearly identical—they all describe someone who is well known. However, the connotations of *illustrious* are positive, involving ideas about admiration and achievement. By contrast, *notorious* suggests someone who is well known for something bad. *Famous* has a more neutral connotation. Therefore, while many people might want to be famous or illustrious, few would choose to become notorious. This chart shows other words that illustrate differences in the connotations of words.

Positive →	Neutral →	Negative
prudent	timid	cowardly
self-confident	proud	arrogant
thrifty	economical	miserly

Dictionaries can give clues to connotations. The entry for *miserly*, for instance, might read, "greedy and stingy" to suggest the negative connotations of the word. Some dictionaries will also give example phrases or sentences that show how the word is used and that suggest its connotations.

Practice A

Choose the word that has the more negative connotation in each item.

1. My parents lived in that (shack, house) for twenty years.
2. Christy's uncle has always lived a/an (reckless, adventurous) life.
3. As she looked his way, the (smile, smirk) on Jarod's face disappeared.
4. When I stumbled against the stranger, he (gazed, glared) at me.
5. The two families had been (feuding, quarreling) for years.
6. The football player turned and (stomped, walked) off the field.

Practice B

Using the words listed below, complete a chart like the one shown. Fill out each numbered item in the chart with the correct synonym, identified as either *positive, neutral,* or *negative*. One word from the list will correctly fit each blank space. Use a dictionary or thesaurus if necessary.

zealot	overwrought	skinny
strategy	new	pushy
persistent	humorous	drudgery
concerned	slender	newfangled
visionary	save	employment
scheme	aggressive	stubborn

Positive →	Neutral →	Negative
1. persevering	______	______
2. ______	nervous	______
3. up-to-date	______	______
4. ______	dreamer	______
5. ______	store	hoard
6. ______	thin	______
7. hilarious	______	ridiculous
8. assertive	______	______
9. ______	work	______
10. ______	plan	______

Activity Make a note card like the one shown below for each of the following words: *bossy, daring, glamorous,* and *scrawny*. Look up each word in a dictionary and write its denotation. Then, write its connotation. Finally, use the word in an original sentence that shows its connotative meaning.

Word:

Denotation:

Connotation:

Sentence:

Comprehension and Collaboration

Using neutral connotations, write an ad about a product. Then, trade ads with a classmate and rewrite each other's ads, using words with negative connotations. Trade ads with a third classmate. Rewrite the ad using positive connotations. Together, review your ads and talk about the changes in meaning.

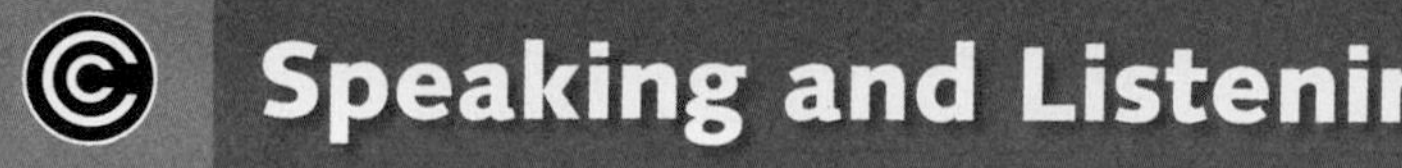

Speaking and Listening

Comparing Media Coverage

Common Core State Standards

Reading Informational Text
7. Analyze various accounts of a subject told in different mediums, determining which details are emphasized in each account.

Speaking and Listening
3. Evaluate a speaker's point of view, reasoning, and use of evidence and rhetoric, identifying any fallacious reasoning or exaggerated or distorted evidence.
4. Present information, findings, and supporting evidence clearly, concisely, and logically such that listeners can follow the line of reasoning and the organization, development, substance, and style are appropriate to purpose, audience, and task.

In today's world, the rising number of news media sources presents a challenge: In order to fully understand issues and events, readers and viewers must analyze how information is presented, who is presenting it, and how the form of the presentation affects the content. The following techniques will help you assess and compare the presentation of events in different forms of media.

Learn the Skills

Choose two different reports of the same event. Consider print, television, and Web sources.

Evaluate each report separately.

- **Determine purpose.** Is the report attempting to inform, persuade, or entertain? Is the presentation appropriate to the purpose?
- **Consider background.** Does the reporter have an agenda—a particular viewpoint or opinion to support? Knowing the background of the person or group structuring the information allows you to actively listen for *propaganda,* or one-sided and false information, and *bias,* or a prejudiced view of an issue.
- **Recognize facts and opinions.** Are the items presented as facts verifiable? Are facts accompanied by music or images that add an emotional dimension? Does the reporter add comments that are not facts of the story?
- **Actively listen and watch.** Is the language factual and objective or emotional and subjective? Is the pacing of speech designed to elicit an emotional response from the audience?

Compare the reports. After you evaluate the reports separately, compare them.

- **Focus on emphasis.** Note the facts that each report highlights. Which points are omitted from one but not the other? Which report contains more opinions? Compare the details that each reporter chooses to emphasize.
- **Analyze the techniques.** Compare the techniques each presentation uses to convey information. Note the use of music, pictures, and colors that might evoke emotional responses from the audience. Compare how each report uses language and pacing to convey a specific tone or attitude.
- **Evaluate the reports.** After you have compared the two reports, write a statement explaining which one is more factual and objective.

Practice the Skills

Presentation of Knowledge and Ideas Use what you have learned in this workshop to complete the following activity.

ACTIVITY: **Compare Coverage of the Same Event**

Evaluate the same event as presented in two different mediums, such as in print, on a Web-based source, or on radio or television. Work with a partner to present a brief report in which you compare the treatments in both examples of coverage. Include a summary of the story as it is presented in the two reports and structure your presentation so it is logical and easy to follow. In addition, answer the following questions in your report:

- What event is being covered?
- Does one version of the story include information that the other omits?
- Is one version of the story more or less detailed than the other?
- What role, if any, do the presenter's perceptions, biases, or opinions seem to play in shaping the report?
- How do formality and tone differ between the two treatments?

Use a Presentation Checklist like the one shown below to analyze classmates' presentations.

Presentation Checklist

Presentation Content

Does the presentation meet all the requirements of the activity? Check all that apply.

- ❑ accurately summarizes the content of both reports
- ❑ uses relevant and appropriate examples to compare the coverage in both mediums
- ❑ analyzes the presentation of any biases
- ❑ notes differences in formality and tone between the mediums
- ❑ presents ideas clearly and in a logical order

Presentation Delivery

Did the speaker deliver the information in an effective manner? Check all that apply.

- ❑ presented information in a logical, easy-to-follow sequence
- ❑ spoke clearly and at an appropriate pace
- ❑ maintained eye contact with the audience
- ❑ provided clear answers to audience questions

Writing Process

Write a Narrative

Autobiographical Narrative

Defining the Form An **autobiographical narrative** tells a story from the writer's own life. It can be as simple as a remembrance of a weekend vacation or as complex as the entire story of the writer's childhood. You might use elements of autobiographical narratives in journals, eyewitness accounts, and reflective essays.

Assignment Write an autobiographical narrative about an event in your life that changed you or helped you grow. Include these elements:

- ✓ a *clear sequence of events* involving you, the writer
- ✓ a *plot* or smooth progression of events centered on a *problem or conflict*
- ✓ *vivid descriptions* of people, places, and events
- ✓ effective use of narrative techniques including *dialogue* and *plot devices,* such as flashback and foreshadowing
- ✓ a *conclusion* that provides an *insight* you gained as a result of this experience
- ✓ error-free grammar, including *correct use of adverbs and adverb clauses*

To preview the criteria on which your autobiographical narrative may be judged, see the rubric on page 677.

Common Core State Standards

Writing

3. Write narratives to develop real or imagined experiences or events using effective technique, well-chosen details, and well-structured event sequences.

3.a. Engage and orient the reader by setting out a problem, situation, or observation, establishing one or multiple point(s) of view, and introducing a narrator and/or characters; create a smooth progression of experiences or events.

3.d. Use precise words and phrases, telling details, and sensory language to convey a vivid picture of the experiences, events, setting, and/or characters.

5. Develop and strengthen writing as needed by planning, revising, editing, rewriting, or trying a new approach, focusing on addressing what is most significant for a specific purpose and audience.

FOCUS ON RESEARCH

When you write an autobiographical narrative, you might perform research to

- learn how family members, friends, or others who participated in the events perceived and felt about what happened.
- read about other people who have had similar experiences.
- study the writing styles of authors who have written about their own lives.

Incorporate direct quotes smoothly into your story, noting who spoke and under what circumstances. If you use quotations from books or other print material, cite them accurately.

READING-WRITING CONNECTION

To get a feel for autobiographical narratives, read the excerpt from *Swimming to Antarctica* by Lynne Cox on page 130.

Prewriting/Planning Strategies

Ask yourself questions. Your narrative should focus on an event from your life in which you learned something important, saw something new, or faced a new challenge. To narrow in on possibilities, ask yourself questions such as the following:

- What event truly surprised me? Why?
- What conversations have I had that I remember vividly? Why?
- What is my favorite place? Why is it my favorite?
- What journey, no matter how brief in duration or short in distance, was important to me? Why?

Write down answers to your questions. Then, select an experience that is meaningful to you, interesting to readers, and not uncomfortable for you to share. (For more strategies to help you choose and focus your topic, see page 673.)

Create character and setting cards. Once you have chosen an event to share, prepare to focus your narrative by identifying the main conflict or insight you want to explain. Write an index card for each important character or setting.

- For characters, include facts like name, age, and appearance. Also note personality, habits, and the person's role in your story.
- For settings, jot down precise physical details and sensory details, such as sights and sounds, to use in your descriptions.

Characters

Name/Age

Appearance

Personality

Habits

Settings

House/Outdoor Area

Furniture/Landscape

Weather/Climate

Other Details

Gather sensory details. Create a list of words and phrases that describe your experience and appeal to the senses of sight, hearing, touch, taste, and smell. Include words that form clear, vivid pictures of the setting, people, and events and that you may include in your narrative. Identify a strong image that captures a key part of your central insight. Use a chart like the one shown to record sensory details.

	Detail	Detail
Sight:	snowy trails through dark trees	
Hearing:	lonesome sound of birds in woods	
Smell:	scent of pines	
Touch:	the velvety feel of wet snow falling on my face	
Taste:	the warm, rich taste of double hot chocolate	

Drafting Strategies

Common Core State Standards

Writing

3.a. Engage and orient the reader by setting out a problem, situation, or observation, establishing one or multiple point(s) of view, and introducing a narrator and/or characters; create a smooth progression of experiences or events.

3.b. Use narrative techniques, such as dialogue, pacing, description, reflection, and multiple plot lines, to develop experiences, events, and/or characters.

3.c. Use a variety of techniques to sequence events so that they build on one another to create a coherent whole.

3.e. Provide a conclusion that follows from and reflects on what is experienced, observed, or resolved over the course of the narrative.

Make a plot diagram. In your narrative, do not simply describe a series of loosely related events. Instead, introduce a conflict, problem, or situation. Then, sequence events so they build in intensity and finally resolve. Use a plot diagram like the one shown to structure your story. Include exposition to introduce the characters, setting, and conflict. Show how events in the rising action build to a climax, or point of highest tension, and how events in the falling action then lead to the resolution. Provide a conclusion in which you express insights about the events or reflect on what you learned from these experiences.

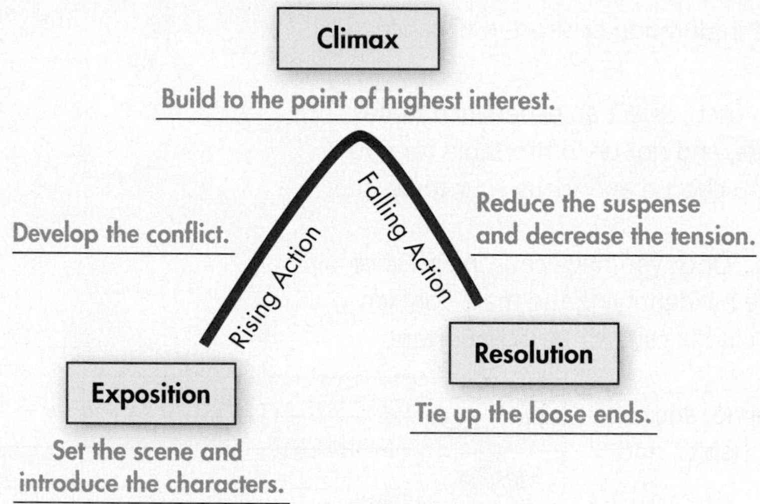

Use dialogue. *Dialogue*—the conversations between or among people in a narrative—can add interest to your writing. Use dialogue to advance the plot and show what characters are like. You might also create *interior monologues,* statements that reveal your exact thoughts at the time.

Narration	Dialogue
She told me not to go into the cave without a flashlight.	"Don't go into that cave without a flashlight," she warned me.

Use plot devices. Plot devices, including flashback and foreshadowing, can add interest to the straightforward sequence of a story. In a *flashback,* a writer describes something that happened prior to the time of the story. This earlier event can provide important background information or otherwise help readers understand an aspect of the narrative. A flashback can take the form of a memory, a dream, or a simple account of past events.

Foreshadowing is the use of textual clues that hint at events to come later in a narrative. As you draft, use foreshadowing by including telling details, conversations among characters, or descriptions that relate to something significant that will happen later.

Finding an Effective Idea

Finding the right **idea** for your autobiographical narrative is the most important task. When searching for the right idea, remember that an autobiographical narrative should tell a story from your life that is both true and important. The story you relate should have influenced your beliefs, way of thinking, or future behavior. In addition, your narrative should include a lively description of the series of events that make up the story as well as a reflection on the broader meaning of those events in your life.

Thinking About the Past Think about events or experiences from your past, and ask yourself why you find them memorable. You might look in journals, scrapbooks, or photo albums to refresh your memories. Choose an event from your early childhood that you still find vivid, or decide on a more recent event. You might also consider writing about people, such as family members, friends, or neighbors, who have played a key role in your life. Important relationships often provide ideas for stories that are truly significant. Regardless of the time of your life in which the story occurred, it should have made a lasting impression on you.

Considering the Significance The event you choose should be one that was meaningful to you or taught you an important lesson. It should also hold the reader's interest. For example, if you describe the experience of being lost in the woods and later finding your way home, you might discuss the values of self-reliance or of overcoming fear. To make the story come alive for readers, include striking descriptions, such as images of the setting as the day went on, or the ways in which you were confused by the landscape.

Refining Your Idea As you consider events from your past, jot them down in a chart like the one shown below. Also, include the lessons you learned from each event. Then, choose the event that has had the most significance or most enduring impact on your life.

How Old Was I?	What Happened/Where?	What Did I Learn?

Revising Strategies

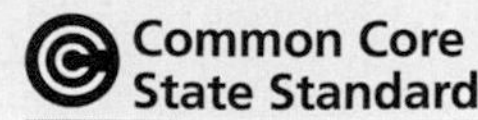

Writing

3.d. Use precise words and phrases, telling details, and sensory language to convey a vivid picture of the experiences, events, setting, and/or characters.

3.e. Provide a conclusion that follows from and reflects on what is experienced, observed, or resolved over the course of the narrative.

5. Develop and strengthen writing as needed by planning, revising, editing, rewriting, or trying a new approach, focusing on addressing what is most significant for a specific purpose and audience.

Language

1.b. Use various types of phrases and clauses to convey specific meanings and add variety and interest to writing or presentations.

Revise to clarify insight. Review your draft to make sure that you have clearly communicated the importance of the event you narrate. Underline sentences that show your reader what you learned. If necessary, add more of these sentences to better explain your insights.

Check your conclusion. Provide a satisfying ending to your narrative—one that follows from and reflects on the importance of the events you narrate.

Revise to use active voice. In the passive voice, the action of a sentence is done to the subject. In the active voice, the subject of the sentence performs the action. Active voice is almost always livelier, more precise, and more engaging than the passive voice. Review your draft and make sure you have used active voice whenever possible.

Passive Voice: The deadline was met by Krista and Rachel.

Active Voice: Krista and Rachel met their deadline.

Add sensory details. Sensory details are words that appeal to the five senses: sight, smell, taste, touch, and hearing. Carefully chosen sensory details can bring your writing to life and enable readers to experience what you are describing.

Without Sensory Details: The pie smelled good.

With Sensory Details: The freshly baked pie filled the house with the warm aroma of apples, butter, nutmeg, and cinnamon.

Using sensory language in this way allows readers to more fully understand what you are describing and engage with your experiences.

Vary sentence length. Add interest to your narrative by including both long and short sentences. If you find a series of short, choppy sentences, combine some of them. Adding a short, energetic sentence to a passage of longer sentences can emphasize an important moment.

Short, Choppy Sentences	Varied Sentences
I was lying in the hammock. I was in the front yard. I was nearly asleep. The wind rustled in the trees. Cicadas were buzzing. Everything was peaceful. Then, Savion pulled up in his red car.	I was lying in the hammock in the front yard, nearly asleep. Wind rustled in the trees, cicadas were buzzing, and the whole world seemed peaceful. Then, Savion pulled up in his red car.

Combining short sentences improves the fluidity of the paragraph. Keeping a short sentence adds emphasis to the moment.

Revising to Combine Sentences Using Adverb Clauses

Avoid choppy writing by combining some sentences using adverb, or adverbial, clauses.

Two sentences: She had sent the letter. The mail was delayed.

Combined: Although the mail was delayed, she had sent the letter.

Identifying Adverb Clauses A clause is a group of words with a subject and a verb. An *independent clause* can stand alone as a complete sentence, but a *dependent clause* cannot stand alone. An **adverb clause** is a dependent clause that begins with a subordinating conjunction and tells *where, when, in what way, to what extent, under what condition,* or *why.*

When: *Before I got on the plane,* I was afraid of flying.

Condition: Dave will carry the box *if you will open the door.*

Why: I gave her my number *so that she could call me later.*

In what way: The child swam *as if she had been born in the water.*

Combining Sentences When using adverb clauses to combine two shorter sentences, follow these steps:

1. Identify the relationship between the ideas in the sentences.
2. Select a subordinating conjunction that clarifies that relationship, and use it to turn information in one sentence into an adverb clause. Put the adverb clause at the beginning or end of the combined sentence.
3. When an adverb clause begins a sentence, use a comma to separate it from the rest of the sentence.

Subordinating Conjunctions			
after	although	as	as if
as long as	because	before	even though
if	since	so that	than
though	unless	until	when
whenever	where	wherever	while

Grammar in Your Writing

Review the introduction and conclusion of your narrative, and highlight any short sentences. Look for a relationship between the ideas in the sentences that could be clarified with an adverb clause, and combine them using an appropriate subordinating conjunction.

STUDENT MODEL: **Alexandria Symonds, Royersford, PA**

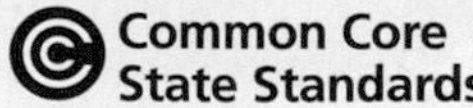

Language
2. Demonstrate command of the conventions of standard English capitalization, punctuation, and spelling when writing.

The Collision, or Hardly Extreme

Some people are simply not meant for extreme athletics, I thought to myself as I slowly regained consciousness. I am one of those people. I will never compete in the X Games; I should just stick to my orderly world where "sports" include Scrabble. I would have continued in this thought pattern, but a feeling like someone stabbing me in the eye with a dozen dull forks grabbed my attention instead.

Alexandria's thoughts provide an intriguing beginning for the narrative.

I was bored that Saturday afternoon in May of 1998–so bored, in fact, that it seemed like a bright and creative idea to see if my old girly purple bike could be used for off-roading. The "off-road" in question was to be our front and back yards (the latter of which happened, incidentally, to back up to the North Carolina woods). I planned a fairly straightforward circuit around the house, complicated only slightly by the fact that our house sat on a hill.

Specific details about Alexandria's state of mind and her bicycle add color and interest to the tale.

It is prophesied that if the earth ever loses its gravitational pull, the moon will abandon its orbit and spin, instead, in a straight line into infinity. Something similar happened to me after a couple of laps around the house. I had reached a speed so high that I concentrated solely on pedaling to maintain it—forgetting, as it were, to turn at a pivotal point in the round. The difference, however, between the moon and me is that while the moon could spin into infinity unobstructed, there was a forest in my way.

Alexandria's sense of humor gives a spark to the narrative.

I realized a split second too late that I hadn't made the turn and knew there was no use trying to do it now. In retrospect, I could have jumped off the bike, but logical thoughts rarely occur when one is hurtling toward a giant oak tree at 25 miles per hour. Instead, I stopped pedaling, closed my eyes, and braced myself for the impact.

I never actually felt it. When I opened my eyes, I was crumpled on the grass in a position I'm sure humans were never intended to take. My bike was tangled in my limbs, and a searing pain in my left eye was the only thing I could feel. After a bit of reflection about my "extreme" lack of foresight, I decided the best response was to scream as loudly as I could.

Key details create a vivid picture and also keep the story moving.

The events immediately following my ill-fated rendezvous with the tree are a blur; but I know that somehow I made it to the hospital, where I endured what seemed like endless tests and injections. I would be okay, but my recovery was a painful process. While the rest of me suffered only surface cuts and deep bruises, my left eye was swollen shut for a week. It was distended for months afterwards, and I still have some puffy scar tissue that causes my left eye to close more than the right when I smile.

Still, every time I get photos developed and notice this phenomenon, it serves as a reminder that I was simply not meant for any kind of physical activity more "extreme" than skipping.

Details here echo the beginning of the narrative and bring the story full circle.

Editing and Proofreading

Check your draft for errors in spelling, grammar, capitalization, and punctuation.

Focus on punctuating dialogue. Check that you have punctuated dialogue correctly. Quotation marks should surround a character's exact words or thoughts. As you edit, make sure that there is a closing quotation mark for every opening quotation mark.

Spiral Review
Earlier in this unit, you learned about **absolute phrases** (p. 656). Review your writing to make sure you have used absolute phrases correctly.

Publishing and Presenting

Consider one of the following ways to share your writing:

Illustrate your narrative. Use photographs or drawings to illustrate people, places, or events in your narrative. Assemble a clean, legible copy of your narrative, choosing an appropriate title and cover.

Deliver a narrative presentation. Rehearse reading your narrative aloud. Using a copy as a reading script, underline words that you will emphasize. Note places where you will vary your reading rate.

Reflecting on Your Writing

Writer's Journal Jot down your answer to this question:

How did writing about your experiences help you to better understand them?

Rubric for Self-Assessment

Find evidence in your writing to address each category. Then, use the rating scale to grade your work.

Criteria	Rating Scale
Purpose/Focus Clearly presents a narrative that develops real experiences and events; engages and orients the reader by setting out a problem, situation, or observation	*not very .... very* 1 2 3 4
Organization Creates a smooth progression of experiences or events; sequences events so they build to create a coherent whole; presents a strong conclusion that follows from and reflects on events in the narrative	1 2 3 4
Development of Ideas/Elaboration Establishes one or more clear points of view; clearly introduces a narrator and characters; effectively uses narrative techniques, such as dialogue, pacing, description, reflection, and multiple plot lines	1 2 3 4
Language Uses precise words and phrases, telling details, and sensory language to convey a vivid picture of experiences, events, settings, and characters	1 2 3 4
Conventions: Demonstrates command of the conventions of standard English in writing	1 2 3 4

Assessment: Skills

SELECTED RESPONSE

RL.9-10.1, RL.9-10.2, RL.9-10.3, RL.9-10.5; W.9-10.2, W.9-10.10; L.9-10.4.a
[For full standards wording, see the chart in the front of this book.]

I. Reading Literature

Directions: *Read the excerpt from* Tibet Through the Red Box *by David Henry Hwang. Then, answer each question that follows.*

from Act II

ALENKA. *(O.S.)* Peter, we received another letter—from your Father! *Lights reveal* ALENKA *and* PETER, *in bed. She holds the same letter that the* JINGLE-BELL BOY *pinched from* VLADIMIR.

ALENKA. All covered with a strange postmark, and these odd little stamps, and characters that can only be Chinese or maybe Japanese or—Peter, he's still alive! *(pause)* I had to run down to the post office to sign for it, and on the way home, of course, I couldn't wait to read it. He is having the most amazing adventures. In a land so strange—lamas, castles, even an abominable snowman! Here—read it.

PETER. I read the last one.

ALENKA. What is wrong with you?

PETER. Every time we get a letter, it's like we have a big party. If he really cares about us, how come he's not home yet?

ALENKA. You are so brave, Peter. The hardest thing of all is not knowing. Where he is, or whether he's even still—whether he's all right. You don't know how strong you are.

PETER. Does Father know?

ALENKA. Oh, I bet he does. And when he returns you'll be all better, running around like your old self.

PETER. How can I get better unless he comes home? *(pause)* How much money does Father make?

ALENKA. Why are you—? Enough to survive, like everyone else.

PETER. How come, all of a sudden, we can afford paints?

ALENKA. I make it a priority, what kind of—?

PETER. Is Father a traitor?

ALENKA. Who says such a—?

PETER. It doesn't matter.

ALENKA. Do your friends talk like that? The <u>delinquents</u>?

PETER. Mother, they're not—

ALENKA. He was sent away by the Russians. But he had no choice!

PETER. You said he did.

ALENKA. I never said any such—

PETER. Before he left.

ALENKA. Who are you? The secret police? You tell your friends, your Father loves his country, he's a man of peace. Then send them to me—and I'll cuff them on their pointed heads!

1. **Part A** Based on the passage, what is Peter's **internal conflict?**
   - **A.** He wants to read the letter, but it is written in a foreign language.
   - **B.** He is brave, but he knows it is better to act scared.
   - **C.** He does not know if he should trust that his father is not a traitor.
   - **D.** His mother does not like his friends.

2. How are the characters developed in the excerpt?
   - **A.** through dialogue
   - **B.** through asides
   - **C.** through a monologue
   - **D.** through soliloquies

3. **Part A** What do Alenka's words reveal about her feelings for her husband?
   - **A.** She does not believe what he writes to her.
   - **B.** She is angry with him for leaving.
   - **C.** She wants him to send more money home.
   - **D.** She loves and misses him very much.

   Part B Which lines from the excerpt most clearly reveal Alenka's feelings for her husband?
   - **A.** "He is having the most amazing adventures. In a land so strange—lamas, castles, even an abominable snowman!"
   - **B.** "Oh, I bet he does. And when he returns you'll be all better, running around like your old self."
   - **C.** "The hardest thing of all is not knowing. Where he is, or whether he's even still—whether he's all right."
   - **D.** "Why are you—? Enough to survive, like everyone else."

4. Based on the excerpt, which of the following statements about the play's **climax** is most likely true?
   - **A.** The climax occurs in Act 1 and this excerpt from Act II contains falling action.
   - **B.** The climax will be an emotional moment involving Peter and his father.
   - **C.** The climax will include comic relief provided by Peter's friends.
   - **D.** There will not be a climax.

5. What can a reader infer is Alenka's main **motivation** for showing Peter the letter?
   - **A.** to make Peter angry that his father has not come home
   - **B.** to brag to Peter about his father's accomplishments
   - **C.** to convince Peter that his father is a traitor
   - **D.** to show Peter that his father is still alive

6. **Part A** By reading between the lines, what do you learn about the state of Peter's health?
   - **A.** Peter is suffering from a lingering illness.
   - **B.** Peter is healthy and active.
   - **C.** Peter has a slight cold.
   - **D.** Peter has broken his leg.

   Part B Which line or lines from the excerpt most clearly suggest the state of Peter's health?
   - **A.** "Peter, we received another letter—from your Father!"
   - **B.** "What is wrong with you?"
   - **C.** "And when he returns you'll be all better, running around like your old self."
   - **D.** "Who are you? The secret police?"

7. Which word is closest in meaning to the underlined word *delinquents* as it is used in the passage?
   - **A.** humanitarians
   - **B.** troublemakers
   - **C.** adventurers
   - **D.** geniuses

Timed Writing

8. Write a brief essay in which you compare the characters of Peter and Alenka based on what you have learned in the excerpt. Discuss similarities and differences in the characters' personalities, attitudes, and behaviors, citing evidence from the text.

GO ON

II. Reading Informational Text

RI.9-10.2, RI.9-10.4, RI.9-10.5; L.9-10.1, L.9-10.1.b, L.9-10.3, L.9-10.4.a

[For full standards wording, see the chart in the front of this book.]

Directions: *Read the text below from a museum placard. Then, answer each question that follows.*

Welcome to the Exhibit on the Origins of World Theater!

This **exhibit** presents the costumes, sets, staging, and music of some of the world's greatest drama from Asian and Western cultures. The **art of drama** ranges from kabuki theater in Japan to the English plays of Shakespeare; from Javanese puppet plays to modern social drama. The exhibit is displayed in two main halls.

Hall One

Asian Drama Asian drama has its origins in Hindu India. Sanskrit drama, dating back to the eighth century B.C.E., influenced theater in Burma, Thailand, Java, Bali, Japan, and China. Asian theater is intensely visual and musical. It began as a sacred art form which, with royal patronage, grew more popular over time. The actors used stylized gestures, expressions, and vocal techniques that evolved into formalized traditions of high sophistication. To learn more, visit Hall One.

Hall Two

Western Drama The chronology of Western drama begins in ancient Greece. It originated as community ritual meant to celebrate myth and affirm the moral beliefs of the time. These ritualistic aspects were deemphasized with Roman theater, which developed the concept of individual characters more fully. Drama performed as religious ritual resurfaced in the Middle Ages with mystery plays, which were meant to impart spiritual values to the audience. Over the centuries, Western drama became increasingly realistic. During the Renaissance, it reached what many believe are its greatest heights. To learn more, visit Hall Two.

1. According to the placard, what was the purpose of drama in ancient Greece?

A. to celebrate myth and affirm moral beliefs
B. to entertain the rich
C. to compete with Roman theater
D. to record historical events

2. Which of these exhibits would you most likely see in Hall One?

A. a display about a mystery play
B. a video of an actor delivering a soliloquy
C. costumes worn by kabuki actors
D. an image of a Roman amphitheater

3. Part A What is the best definition of the underlined word *chronology* as it is used in the placard?

A. the study of the Greek god Chronos
B. the sequence of events in time
C. the study of time itself
D. the examination of word origins

Part B Which context clues from the placard best help the reader understand the meaning of *chronology?*

A. "affirm...beliefs"
B. "community...celebrate"
C. "Western drama...Greece"
D. "begins...originated"

III. Writing and Language Conventions

Directions: *Read the passage. Then, answer each question that follows.*

(1) At age ten, I attended my first live theater performance. (2) I followed my mom into the theater. (3) I agreed to watch the performance even though it did not interest me. (4) As we took our seats, I noticed no one was eating popcorn or candy. (5) This was not the movies or even TV! (6) The houselights dimmed. (7) The stage lights brightened at the same time. (8) Everyone became perfectly silent. (9) I was astonished as the characters began to speak. (10) I could have reached out and touched them. (11) I could see and almost feel the texture of their clothing, smell the faintly dusty odor of the stage. (12) The audience clapped at the end of each act. (13) I could feel the sadness ripple through the audience when the hero died! (14) Applauding in unison, the play ended, everyone stood. (15) I felt exhilarated, my smile a mile wide. (16) It was a unique experience. (17) To this day, I still love live theater.

1. Identify the **adverbial clause** in sentence 3.

A. agreed to watch
B. I agreed to watch the performance
C. it did not interest me
D. even though it did not interest me

2. Which revision to sentence 2 includes an **absolute phrase?**

A. My feet were dragging into the theater, and I followed my mom.
B. I followed my mom by dragging my feet into the theater.
C. I followed my mom into the theater, my feet dragging.
D. Following my mom with my feet dragging, I went into the theater.

3. Which of the following sentences *best* uses an **adverbial clause** to combine sentence 6 with sentence 7?

A. The houselights dimmed when the stage lights brightened.
B. The houselights dimmed that the stage lights brightened.
C. The houselights dimmed, and the stage lights brightened.
D. The houselights dimmed unless the stage lights brightened.

4. Which sentence contains an **absolute phrase?**

A. sentence 10
B. sentence 11
C. sentence 13
D. sentence 15

5. Which revision to sentence 14 includes an **absolute phrase?**

A. As the play ended, everyone stood, applauding in unison.
B. The play ended, everyone standing and applauding in unison.
C. The play ended with people applauding in unison, and everyone stood.
D. Standing and applauding in unison at the end, the people really enjoyed the play.

CONSTRUCTED RESPONSE

Common Core State Standards

RL.9-10.2, RL.9-10.3, RL.9-10.4, RL.9-10.5; W.9-10.7, W.9-10.8; SL.9-10.1, SL.9-10.4, SL.9-10.6; L.9-10.1, L.9-10.5

[For full standards wording, see the chart in the front of this book.]

Directions: *Follow the instructions to complete the tasks below as required by your teacher.*

As you work on each task, incorporate both general academic vocabulary and literary terms you learned in Parts 1 and 2 of this unit.

Writing

TASK 1 Literature [RL.9-10.3; W.9-10.9.a]

Analyze Character Development

Write an essay in which you analyze the development of a character portrayed in a play in Part 2 of this unit.

- Select a character with multiple or conflicting motivations from a play in Part 2 of this unit. You might select an antagonist, a protagonist, or a tragic hero.
- Explain which work and character you chose to analyze.
- Analyze the development of this character over the course of the text. Cite details that describe the character at the play's beginning. Then, trace the critical points at which the character changes. Explain how the character develops from the beginning to the end of the drama.
- Support your analysis with evidence from the texts, using direct quotations when appropriate.
- Provide a concluding statement that follows from and summarizes your analysis.

TASK 2 Literature [RL.9-10.2; W.9-10.9.a]

Analyze Theme

Write an essay in which you analyze the development of the theme in a play from Part 2 of this unit.

- State which play you chose and briefly summarize the story.
- State your interpretation of the theme and analyze how it develops over the course of the play.
- Cite relevant details from the play, including plot events and specific dialogue, that support your interpretation of the theme.
- Establish and maintain a formal tone throughout your essay.

TASK 3 Literature [RL.9-10.4; L.9-10.1, L.9-10.5]

Analyze Word Choice in a Dramatic Speech

Write an essay in which you analyze word choice in a dramatic speech.

Part 1

- Choose a major dramatic speech, such as a soliloquy or a monologue, from a play in Part 2 of this unit.
- Take notes as you review the speech. Use your notes to write a summary of the speech. Your summary should answer the following questions:

  Why is the character speaking?

  To whom is the character speaking?

  What is the character saying?

  Why is this speech important?

Part 2

- Write an essay in which you analyze the word choices employed in the speech. Consider the use of figurative language and imagery that adds to the meaning of the speech. Also consider significant connotative word choices that contribute to the development of the characters or theme.
- Use precise language, including literary and academic terms, to convey your ideas.
- Correctly use the conventions of standard English grammar and usage.

Speaking and Listening

TASK 4 **Literature [RL.9-10.5; SL.9-10.4, SL.9-10.6]**

Compare Characters

Write and deliver a presentation in which you analyze and compare two characters from a play that appears in Part 2 of this unit.

- Choose two key characters from a play in Part 2 of this unit and compare their functions in the story. For example, you might choose a protagonist and an antagonist or two supporting characters who play different roles.
- Discuss the ways in which the characters interact with each other.
- Examine the motivations of each character, or the reasons for his or her actions. Provide evidence from the text to support your ideas.
- Analyze the ways in which each character advances the play's plot or contributes to the development of the theme.
- Throughout your presentation, support your ideas with details from the text.
- Use formal English during your presentation.

TASK 5 **Literature [RL.9-10.3; SL.9-10.1]**

Analyze Conflicts

Conduct a small group discussion focusing on conflict, both internal and external, in a play from Part 2 of this unit. Analyze the connections between the types of conflict and the way in which all conflict drives the plot.

- Choose a play from Part 2 of this unit and identify the conflicts within it. Determine whether each conflict is internal or external.
- Analyze the effect that each conflict has on the development of the drama's plot. Note details from the play that support your ideas.
- Prepare a list of questions for discussion. Design the questions to be interesting. Be sure you have also formulated possible answers to the questions in advance.
- As the leader of the discussion, initiate the conversation and keep it going. Actively incorporate all group members into the discussion.
- Respond thoughtfully to diverse perspectives, referring to the text to support your positions.
- At the conclusion of the discussion, summarize the main ideas the discussion yielded, including points of agreement and disagreement.

Research

TASK 6 **Literature [RL.9-10.2; W.9-10.7, W.9-10.8]**

To what extent does experience determine what we perceive?

In Part 2 of this unit, you have read texts that explore the relationships between our experiences and our perceptions. Now you will conduct a short research project on a world leader and the experiences that have shaped his or her perceptions. Choose a contemporary or historical world leader who intrigues you, and learn about that person's life story. Use the texts you have read in this unit as well as your research to reflect upon and write about this unit's Big Question. Review the following guidelines before you begin your research:

- Focus your research on the life of one world leader.
- Gather information from at least two reliable sources. Your sources may be print or digital.
- Take notes as you investigate the relationship between the leader's life experiences and his or her perceptions.
- Cite your sources.

When you have completed your research, write a brief essay in response to the Big Question. Discuss how your initial ideas have changed or been reinforced. Support your response with examples from at least one of the texts you have read in Part 2 of this unit and from your research.

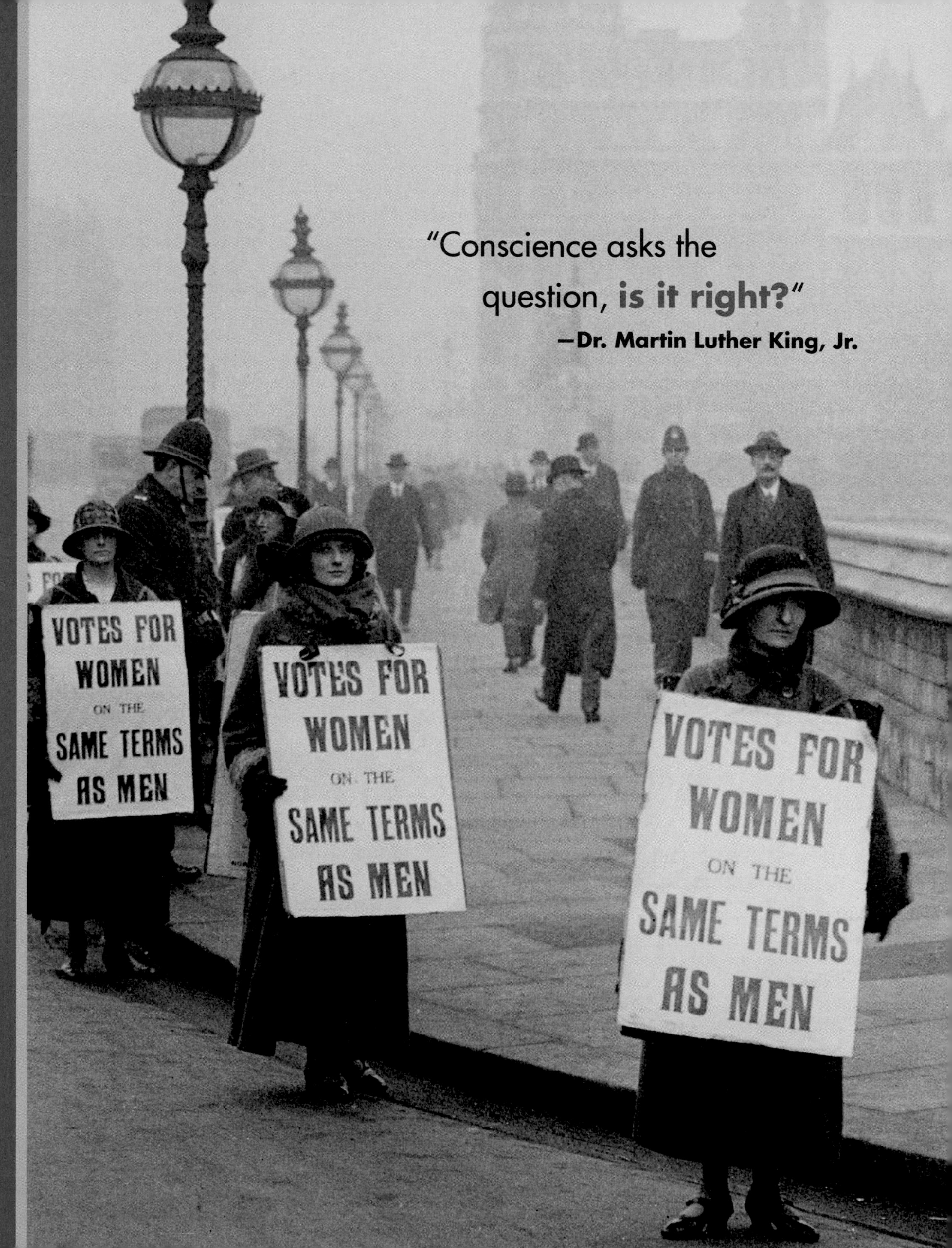

"Conscience asks the question, **is it right?**"

—Dr. Martin Luther King, Jr.

PART 3

TEXT SET DEVELOPING INSIGHT

CONSCIENTIOUS OBJECTIONS

The readings in this section explore the concept of conscientious objection, or resistance to injustice. The term "conscientious objector" refers to someone who, for reasons of belief or morality, refuses to serve in the military. However, the term can also refer to people in other areas of life who stand up for what they perceive to be right. As you read these selections, consider the factors that encourage some people to speak out against injustice while others remain silent. Then, think about how issues of conscience relate to the Big Question for this unit: **To what extent does experience determine what we perceive?**

◀ CRITICAL VIEWING What are the women in this photograph protesting? What personal risks or sacrifice do you think their protest required?

CLOSE READING TOOL

Use the **Close Reading Tool** to practice the strategies you learn in this unit.

READINGS IN PART 3

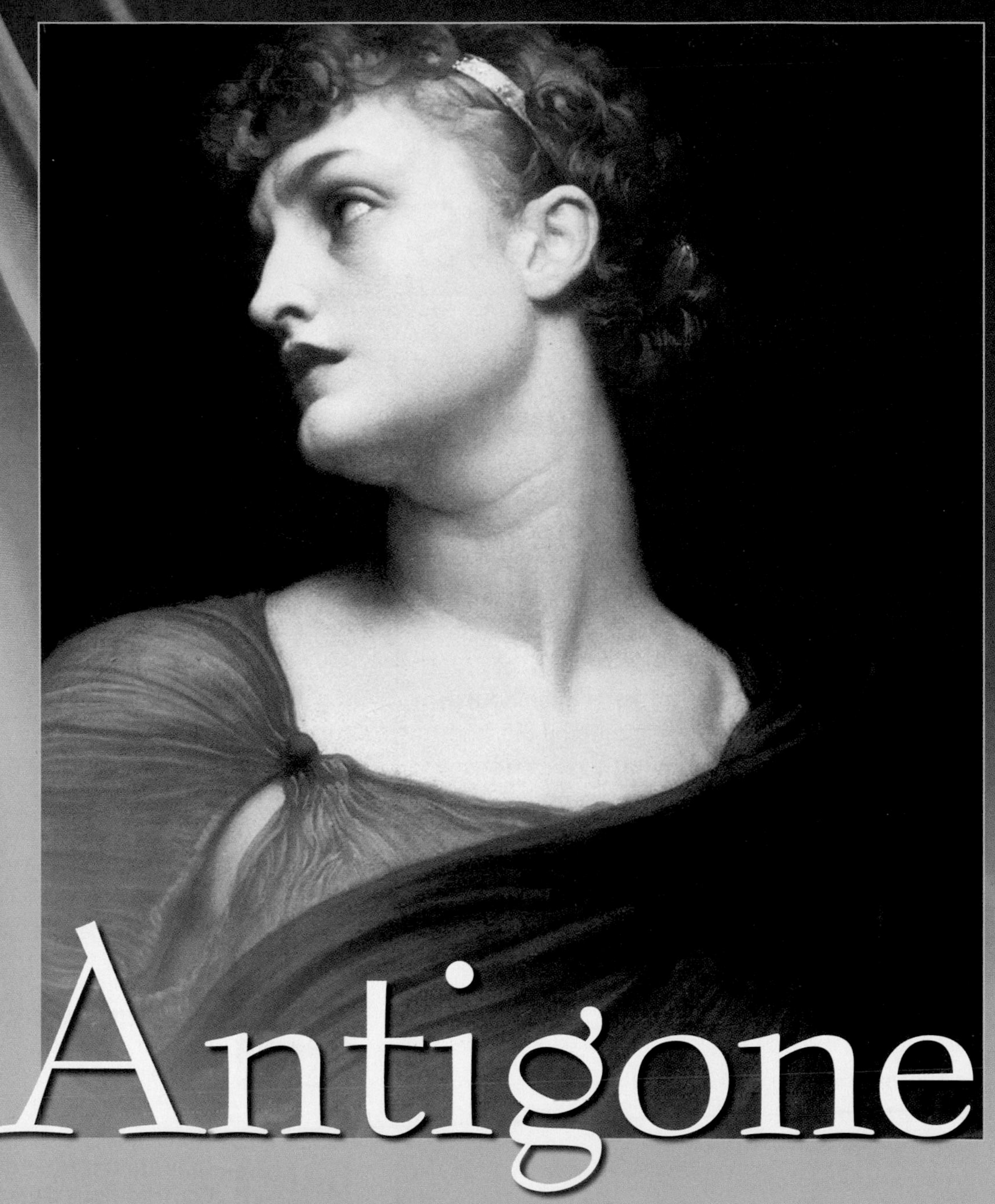

Antigone

SOPHOCLES

translated by **Dudley Fitts** and **Robert Fitzgerald**

PERSONS REPRESENTED

ANTIGONE (an tig′ ə nē′), daughter of Oedipus, former King of Thebes

ISMENE (is mē′ nē), another daughter of Oedipus

EURYDICE (yo͞o rid′ i sē′), wife of Creon

CREON (krē′ än′), King of Thebes, uncle of Antigone and Ismene

HAIMON (hī′ mən), Creon's son, engaged to Antigone

TEIRESIAS (tī rē′ sē əs), a blind prophet

A SENTRY

A MESSENGER

CHORUS

CHORAGOS (kō rā′ gəs), leader of the chorus

A BOY who leads Teiresias

GUARDS

SERVANTS

PROLOGUE–SCENE 2

Scene. *Before the palace of CREON, King of Thebes. A central double door, and two lateral doors. A platform extends the length of the facade, and from this platform three steps lead down into the "orchestra," or chorus-ground.*

Time. *Dawn of the day after the repulse of the Argive*[1] *army from the assault on Thebes.*

1. **Argive** (är′ gīv′) from Argos, the capital of a section of ancient Greece.

PROLOGUE

[ANTIGONE *and* ISMENE *enter from the central door of the Palace.*]

ANTIGONE. Ismene, dear sister,
You would think that we had already suffered enough
For the curse on Oedipus:[2]
I cannot imagine any grief
That you and I have not gone through. And now—
Have they told you of the new decree of our King Creon?

2. **curse on Oedipus** reference to the fate of Oedipus, who was doomed by a decree of the gods to kill his father and marry his mother while ignorant of their true identities.

ISMENE. I have heard nothing: I know
That two sisters lost two brothers, a double death
In a single hour; and I know that the Argive army
Fled in the night; but beyond this, nothing.

ANTIGONE. I thought so. And that is why I wanted you
To come out here with me. There is something we must do.

ISMENE. Why do you speak so strangely?

ANTIGONE. Listen, Ismene:
Creon buried our brother Eteocles
With military honors, gave him a soldier's funeral,
And it was right that he should; but Polyneices,
Who fought as bravely and died as miserably,—
They say that Creon has sworn
No one shall bury him, no one mourn for him,
But his body must lie in the fields, a sweet treasure
For carrion birds[3] to find as they search for food.
That is what they say, and our good Creon is coming here
To announce it publicly; and the penalty—
Stoning to death in the public square!
There it is,
And now you can prove what you are:
A true sister, or a traitor to your family.

3. carrion (kar′ ē ən) **birds** scavenger birds, such as vultures.

ISMENE. Antigone, you are mad! What could I possibly do?

ANTIGONE. You must decide whether you will help me or not.

ISMENE. I do not understand you. Help you in what?

ANTIGONE. Ismene, I am going to bury him. Will you come?

ISMENE. Bury him! You have just said the new law forbids it.

ANTIGONE. He is my brother. And he is your brother, too.

ISMENE. But think of the danger! Think what Creon will do!

ANTIGONE. Creon is not strong enough to stand in my way.

ISMENE. Ah sister!
Oedipus died, everyone hating him
For what his own search brought to light, his eyes
Ripped out by his own hand; and Iocaste died,
His mother and wife at once: she twisted the cords
That strangled her life; and our two brothers died,
Each killed by the other's sword. And we are left:
But oh, Antigone,
Think how much more terrible than these
Our own death would be if we should go against
Creon
And do what he has forbidden! We are only women,
We cannot fight with men, Antigone!

The law is strong, we must give in to the law
In this thing, and in worse. I beg the Dead
To forgive me, but I am helpless: I must yield
To those in authority. And I think it is dangerous business
To be always meddling.

ANTIGONE. If that is what you think,
I should not want you, even if you asked to come.
You have made your choice, you can be what you want to be.
But I will bury him; and if I must die,
I say that this crime is holy: I shall lie down
With him in death, and I shall be as dear
To him as he to me.
It is the dead,
Not the living, who make the longest demands;
We die for ever . . .
You may do as you like,
Since apparently the laws of the gods mean nothing to you.

ISMENE. They mean a great deal to me; but I have no strength
To break laws that were made for the public good.

ANTIGONE. That must be your excuse, I suppose. But as for me,
I will bury the brother I love.

ISMENE. Antigone,
I am so afraid for you!

ANTIGONE. You need not be:
You have yourself to consider, after all.

ISMENE. But no one must hear of this, you must tell no one!
I will keep it a secret, I promise!

ANTIGONE. Oh tell it! Tell everyone!
Think how they'll hate you when it all comes out
If they learn that you knew about it all the time!

ISMENE. So fiery! You should be cold with fear.

ANTIGONE. Perhaps. But I am doing only what I must.

ISMENE. But can you do it? I say that you cannot.

ANTIGONE. Very well: when my strength gives out, I shall do no more.

ISMENE. Impossible things should not be tried at all.

ANTIGONE. Go away, Ismene:
I shall be hating you soon, and the dead will too,
For your words are hateful. Leave me my foolish plan:
I am not afraid of the danger; if it means death,
It will not be the worst of deaths—death without honor.

ISMENE. Go then, if you feel that you must.
You are unwise,
But a loyal friend indeed to those who love you.

[*Exit into the Palace.* ANTIGONE *goes off, left. Enter the* CHORUS.]

PARODOS

CHORUS. [STROPHE 1]
Now the long blade of the sun, lying
Level east to west, touches with glory
Thebes of the Seven Gates.[4] Open, unlidded
Eye of golden day! O marching light
Across the eddy and rush of Dirce's stream,[5]
Striking the white shields of the enemy
Thrown headlong backward from the blaze of morning!

4. **Seven Gates** The city of Thebes was defended by walls containing seven entrances.
5. **Dirce's** (dʉr´ sēz) **stream** small river near Thebes into which the body of Dirce, one of the city's early queens, was thrown after her murder.

CHORAGOS. Polyneices their commander
Roused them with windy phrases,
He the wild eagle screaming
Insults above our land,
His wings their shields of snow,
His crest their marshalled helms.

CHORUS. [ANTISTROPHE 1]
Against our seven gates in a yawning ring
The famished spears came onward in the night;
But before his jaws were **sated** with our blood,
Or pinefire took the garland of our towers,
He was thrown back; and as he turned, great Thebes—
No tender victim for his noisy power—
Rose like a dragon behind him, shouting war.

sated ▶ (sāt´ əd) *adj.* satisfied; provided with more than enough

CHORAGOS. For God hates utterly
The bray of bragging tongues;
And when he beheld their smiling,

Their swagger of golden helms,
The frown of his thunder blasted
Their first man from our walls.

CHORUS. [STROPHE 2]
We heard his shout of triumph high in the air
Turn to a scream; far out in a flaming arc
He fell with his windy torch, and the earth struck him.
And others storming in fury no less than his
Found shock of death in the dusty joy of battle.

CHORAGOS. Seven captains at seven gates
Yielded their clanging arms to the god
That bends the battle-line and breaks it.
These two only, brothers in blood,
Face to face in matchless rage,
Mirroring each the other's death,
Clashed in long combat.

CHORUS. [ANTISTROPHE 2]
But now in the beautiful morning of victory
Let Thebes of the many chariots sing for joy!
With hearts for dancing we'll take leave of war:
Our temples shall be sweet with hymns of praise,
And the long night shall echo with our chorus.

SCENE 1

CHORAGOS. But now at last our new King is coming:
Creon of Thebes, Menoikeus'[6] son.
In this auspicious dawn of his reign
What are the new complexities
That shifting Fate has woven for him?
What is his counsel? Why has he summoned
The old men to hear him?

[*Enter* CREON *from the Palace, center. He addresses the* CHORUS *from the top step.*]

CREON. Gentlemen: I have the honor to inform you that our Ship of State, which recent storms have threatened to destroy, has come safely to harbor at last, guided by the merciful wisdom of Heaven. I have summoned you here this morning because I know that I can depend upon you: your devotion to King Laïos was absolute; you never hesitated in

6. **Monoikeus'** (me noi′ kē us əz)

your duty to our late ruler Oedipus; and when Oedipus died, your loyalty was transferred to his children. Unfortunately, as you know, his two sons, the princes Eteocles and Polyneices, have killed each other in battle; and I, as the next in blood, have suceeded to the full power of the throne.

I am aware, of course, that no Ruler can expect complete loyalty from his subjects until he has been tested in office. Nevertheless, I say to you at the very outset that I have nothing but contempt for the kind of Governor who is afraid, for whatever reason, to follow the course that he knows is best for the State; and as for the man who sets private friendship above the public welfare,—I have no use for him, cither. I call God to witness that if I saw my country headed for ruin, I should not be afraid to speak out plainly; and I need hardly remind you that I would never have any dealings with an enemy of the people. No one values friendship more highly than I; but we must remember that friends made at the risk of wrecking our Ship are not real friends at all.

These are my principles, at any rate, and that is why I have made the following decision concerning the sons of Oedipus: Eteocles, who died as a man should die, fighting for his country, is to be buried with full military honors, with all the ceremony that is usual when the greatest heroes die; but his brother Polyneices, who broke his exile to come back with fire and sword against his native city and the shrines of his fathers' gods, whose one idea was to spill the blood of his blood and sell his own people into slavery—Polyneices, I say, is to have no burial: no man is to touch him or say the least prayer for him; he shall lie on the plain, unburied; and the birds and the scavenging dogs can do with him whatever they like.

This is my command, and you can see the wisdom behind it. As long as I am King, no traitor is going to be honored with the loyal man. But whoever shows by word and deed that he is on the side of the State,—he shall have my respect while he is living, and my reverence when he is dead.

CHORAGOS. If that is your will, Creon son of Menoikeus,
You have the right to enforce it: we are yours.

CREON. That is my will. Take care that you do your part.

CHORAGOS. We are old men: let the younger ones carry it out.

CREON. I do not mean that: the sentries have been appointed.

CHORAGOS. Then what is it that you would have us do?

CREON. You will give no support to whoever breaks this law.

CHORAGOS. Only a crazy man is in love with death!

CREON. And death it is; yet money talks, and the wisest
Have sometimes been known to count a few coins too many.

[*Enter sentry from left.*]

SENTRY. I'll not say that I'm out of breath from running, King, because every time I stopped to think about what I have to tell you, I felt like going back. And all the time a voice kept saying, "You fool, don't you know you're walking straight into trouble?"; and then another voice: "Yes, but if you let somebody else get the news to Creon first, it will be even worse than that for you!" But good sense won out, at least I hope it was good sense, and here I am with a story that makes no sense at all; but I'll tell it anyhow, because, as they say, what's going to happen's going to happen, and—

CREON. Come to the point. What have you to say?

SENTRY. I did not do it. I did not see who did it. You must not punish me for what someone else has done.

CREON. A comprehensive defense! More effective, perhaps,
If I knew its purpose. Come: what is it?

SENTRY. A dreadful thing . . . I don't know how to put it—

CREON. Out with it!

SENTRY. Well, then;
The dead man—
Polyneices—

[*Pause. The* SENTRY *is overcome, fumbles for words.* CREON *waits impassively.*]

out there—
someone,—
New dust on the slimy flesh!

[*Pause. No sign from* CREON.]

Someone has given it burial that way, and
Gone . . .

[*Long pause.* CREON *finally speaks with deadly control.*]

CREON. And the man who dared do this?

SENTRY. I swear I
Do not know! You must believe me!
Listen:
The ground was dry, not a sign of digging, no,
Not a wheeltrack in the dust, no trace of anyone.
It was when they relieved us this morning: and one of them,
The corporal, pointed to it.
There it was,
The strangest—
Look:
The body, just mounded over with light dust: you see?
Not buried really, but as if they'd covered it
Just enough for the ghost's peace. And no sign
Of dogs or any wild animal that had been there.

And then what a scene there was! Every man of us
Accusing the other: we all proved the other man did it,
We all had proof that we could not have done it.
We were ready to take hot iron in our hands,
Walk through fire, swear by all the gods,
It was not I!
I do not know who it was, but it was not I!

[CREON'S *rage has been mounting steadily, but the* SENTRY *is too intent upon his story to notice it.*]

And then, when this came to nothing, someone said
A thing that silenced us and made us stare
Down at the ground: you had to be told the news,
And one of us had to do it! We threw the dice,
And the bad luck fell to me. So here I am,
No happier to be here than you are to have me:
Nobody likes the man who brings bad news.

CHORAGOS. I have been wondering, King: can it be that the gods have done this?

CREON. [*Furiously*] *Stop!*
Must you doddering wrecks
Go out of your heads entirely? "The gods!"
Intolerable!
The gods favor this corpse? Why? How had he served them?
Tried to loot their temples, burn their images,
Yes, and the whole State, and its laws with it!
Is it your senile opinion that the gods love to honor bad men?
A pious thought!—

No, from the very beginning
There have been those who have whispered together,
Stiff-necked anarchists, putting their heads together,
Scheming against me in alleys. These are the men,
And they have bribed my own guard to do this thing.

Money! [*Sententiously*]
There's nothing in the world so demoralizing as money.
Down go your cities,
Homes gone, men gone, honest hearts corrupted,
Crookedness of all kinds, and all for money!
[*To* SENTRY] But you—!
I swear by God and by the throne of God,
The man who has done this thing shall pay for it!
Find that man, bring him here to me, or your death
Will be the least of your problems: I'll string you up
Alive, and there will be certain ways to make you
Discover your employer before you die;
And the process may teach you a lesson you seem to have missed:
The dearest profit is sometimes all too dear:
That depends on the source. Do you understand me?
A fortune won is often misfortune.

SENTRY. King, may I speak?

CREON. Your very voice distresses me.

SENTRY. Are you sure that it is my voice, and not your conscience?

CREON. By God, he wants to analyze me now!

SENTRY. It is not what I say, but what has been done, that hurts you.

CREON. You talk too much.

SENTRY. Maybe; but I've done nothing.

CREON. Sold your soul for some silver: that's all you've done.

SENTRY. How dreadful it is when the right judge judges wrong!

CREON. Your figures of speech
May entertain you now; but unless you bring me the man,
You will get little profit from them in the end.

[*Exit* CREON *into the Palace.*]

SENTRY. "Bring me the man"—!
I'd like nothing better than bringing him the man!
But bring him or not, you have seen the last of me here.
At any rate, I am safe!

[*Exit* SENTRY.]

ODE I

CHORUS. [STROPHE 1]

Numberless are the world's wonders, but none
More wonderful than man; the stormgray sea
Yields to his prows, the huge crests bear him high;
Earth, holy and inexhaustible, is graven
With shining furrows where his plows have gone
Year after year, the timeless labor of stallions.

[ANTISTROPHE 1]

The lightboned birds and beasts that cling to cover,
The lithe fish lighting their reaches of dim water,
All are taken, tamed in the net of his mind;
The lion on the hill, the wild horse windy-maned,
Resign to him; and his blunt yoke has broken
The sultry shoulders of the mountain bull.

[STROPHE 2]

Words also, and thought as rapid as air,
He fashions to his good use; statecraft is his,
And his the skill that **deflects** the arrows of snow,
The spears of winter rain: from every wind
He has made himself secure—from all but one:
In the late wind of death he cannot stand.

deflects ▶
(dē flekts´) *v.* turns or makes go to one side

[ANTISTROPHE 2]

O clear intelligence, force beyond all measure!
O fate of man, working both good and evil!
When the laws are kept, how proudly his city stands!
When the laws are broken, what of his city then?
Never may the anarchic man find rest at my hearth,
Never be it said that my thoughts are his thoughts.

SCENE 2

[*Re-enter* SENTRY *leading* ANTIGONE.]

CHORAGOS. What does this mean? Surely this captive woman
Is the Princess, Antigone. Why should she be taken?

SENTRY. Here is the one who did it! We caught her
In the very act of burying him.—Where is Creon?

CHORAGOS. Just coming from the house.

[*Enter* CREON, *center.*]

CREON. What has happened?
Why have you come back so soon?

SENTRY. [*Expansively*] O King,
A man should never be too sure of anything:
I would have sworn
That you'd not see me here again: your anger
Frightened me so, and the things you threatened me with;
But how could I tell then
That I'd be able to solve the case so soon?

No dice-throwing this time: I was only too glad to come!
Here is this woman. She is the guilty one:
We found her trying to bury him.
Take her, then; question her; judge her as you will.
I am through with the whole thing now, and glad of it.

CREON. But this is Antigone! Why have you brought her here?

SENTRY. She was burying him, I tell you!

CREON. [*Severely*] Is this the truth?

SENTRY. I saw her with my own eyes. Can I say more?

CREON. The details: come, tell me quickly!

SENTRY. It was like this:
After those terrible threats of yours, King,
We went back and brushed the dust away from the body.
The flesh was soft by now, and stinking,
So we sat on a hill to windward and kept guard.
No napping this time! We kept each other awake.
But nothing happened until the white round sun

Whirled in the center of the round sky over us:
Then, suddenly,
A storm of dust roared up from the earth, and the sky
Went out, the plain vanished with all its trees
In the stinging dark. We closed our eyes and endured it.
The whirlwind lasted a long time, but it passed;
And then we looked, and there was Antigone!
I have seen
A mother bird come back to a stripped nest, heard
Her crying bitterly a broken note or two
For the young ones stolen. Just so, when this girl
Found the bare corpse, and all her love's work wasted,
She wept, and cried on heaven to damn the hands
That had done this thing.
And then she brought more dust
And sprinkled wine three times for her brother's ghost.

We ran and took her at once. She was not afraid,
Not even when we charged her with what she had done.
She denied nothing.
And this was a comfort to me,
And some uneasiness: for it is a good thing
To escape from death, but it is no great pleasure
To bring death to a friend.
Yet I always say
There is nothing so comfortable as your own safe skin!

CREON. [*Slowly, dangerously*] And you, Antigone,

You with your head hanging,—do you confess this thing?

ANTIGONE. I do. I deny nothing.

CREON. [*To* SENTRY] You may go.

[*Exit* SENTRY.]

[*To* ANTIGONE] Tell me, tell me briefly:
Had you heard my proclamation touching this matter?

ANTIGONE. It was public. Could I help hearing it?

CREON. And yet you dared defy the law.

ANTIGONE. I dared.
It was not God's proclamation. That final Justice
That rules the world below makes no such laws.

Your edict, King, was strong,
But all your strength is weakness itself against

The immortal unrecorded laws of God.
They are not merely now: they were, and shall be,
Operative forever, beyond man utterly.

I knew I must die, even without your decree:
I am only mortal. And if I must die
Now, before it is my time to die,
Surely this is no hardship: can anyone
Living, as I live, with evil all about me,
Think Death less than a friend? This death of mine
Is of no importance; but if I had left my brother
Lying in death unburied, I should have suffered.
Now I do not.
You smile at me. Ah Creon,
Think me a fool, if you like; but it may well be
That a fool convicts me of folly.

CHORAGOS. Like father, like daughter: both headstrong, deaf to reason!
She has never learned to yield.

CREON. She has much to learn.
The inflexible heart breaks first, the toughest iron
Cracks first, and the wildest horses bend their necks
At the pull of the smallest curb.
Pride? In a slave?
This girl is guilty of a double insolence,
Breaking the given laws and boasting of it.
Who is the man here,
She or I, if this crime goes unpunished?
Sister's child, or more than sister's child,
Or closer yet in blood—she and her sister
Win bitter death for this!
[*To* SERVANTS] Go, some of you,
Arrest Ismene. I accuse her equally.
Bring her: you will find her sniffling in the house there.

Antigone Pouring a Libation over the Corpse of Her Brother Polynices (1870); William Henry Rinehart ▶

Her mind's a traitor: crimes kept in the dark
Cry for light, and the guardian brain shudders;
But how much worse than this
Is **brazen** boasting of barefaced anarchy!

brazen ▶
(brā′ zən) *adj.*
shameless; bold

ANTIGONE. Creon, what more do you want than my death?

CREON. Nothing.
That gives me everything.

ANTIGONE. Then I beg you: kill me.
This talking is a great weariness: your words
Are distasteful to me, and I am sure that mine
Seem so to you. And yet they should not seem so:
I should have praise and honor for what I have done.
All these men here would praise me
Were their lips not frozen shut with fear of you.
[*Bitterly*]
Ah the good fortune of kings,
Licensed to say and do whatever they please!

CREON. You are alone here in that opinion.

ANTIGONE. No, they are with me. But they keep their tongues in leash.

CREON. Maybe. But you are guilty, and they are not.

ANTIGONE. There is no guilt in reverence for the dead.

CREON. But Eteocles—was he not your brother too?

ANTIGONE. My brother too.

CREON. And you insult his memory?

ANTIGONE. [*Softly*] The dead man would not say that I insult it.

CREON. He would: for you honor a traitor as much as him.

ANTIGONE. His own brother, traitor or not, and equal in blood.

CREON. He made war on his country. Eteocles defended it.

ANTIGONE. Nevertheless, there are honors due all the dead.

CREON. But not the same for the wicked as for the just.

ANTIGONE. Ah Creon, Creon,
Which of us can say what the gods hold wicked?

CREON. An enemy is an enemy, even dead.

ANTIGONE. It is my nature to join in love, not hate.

CREON. [*Finally losing patience*] Go join them, then; if you must have your love,
Find it in hell!

CHORAGOS. But see, Ismene comes:

[*Enter* ISMENE, *guarded.*]

Those tears are sisterly, the cloud
That shadows her eyes rains down gentle sorrow.

CREON. You too, Ismene,
Snake in my ordered house, sucking my blood
Stealthily—and all the time I never knew
That these two sisters were aiming at my throne!
Ismene,

Do you confess your share in this crime, or deny it?
Answer me.

ISMENE. Yes, if she will let me say so. I am guilty.

ANTIGONE. [*Coldly*] No, Ismene. You have no right to say so.
You would not help me, and I will not have you help me.

ISMENE. But now I know what you meant; and I am here
To join you, to take my share of punishment.

ANTIGONE. The dead man and the gods who rule the dead
Know whose act this was. Words are not friends.

ISMENE. Do you refuse me, Antigone? I want to die with you:

I too have a duty that I must discharge to the dead.

ANTIGONE. You shall not lessen my death by sharing it.

ISMENE. What do I care for life when you are dead?

ANTIGONE. Ask Creon. You're always hanging on his opinions.

ISMENE. You are laughing at me. Why, Antigone?

ANTIGONE. It's a joyless laughter, Ismene.

ISMENE. But can I do nothing?

ANTIGONE. Yes. Save yourself. I shall not envy you.
There are those who will praise you; I shall have honor, too.

ISMENE. But we are equally guilty!

ANTIGONE. No more, Ismene.
You are alive, but I belong to Death.

CREON. [*To the* CHORUS] Gentlemen, I beg you to observe these girls:
One has just now lost her mind; the other,
It seems, has never had a mind at all.

ISMENE. Grief teaches the steadiest minds to waver, King.

CREON. Yours certainly did, when you assumed guilt with the guilty!

ISMENE. But how could I go on living without her?

CREON. You are.
She is already dead.

ISMENE. But your own son's bride!

CREON. There are places enough for him to push his plow.
I want no wicked women for my sons!

ISMENE. O dearest Haimon, how your father wrongs you!

CREON. I've had enough of your childish talk of marriage!

CHORAGOS. Do you really intend to steal this girl from your son?

CREON. No; Death will do that for me.

CHORAGOS. Then she must die?

CREON. [*Ironically*] You dazzle me.
—But enough of this talk!
[*To* GUARDS] You, there, take them away and guard them well:
For they are but women, and even brave men run
When they see Death coming.

[*Exit* ISMENE, ANTIGONE, *and* GUARDS.]

ODE II

CHORUS. [STROPHE 1]

Fortunate is the man who has never tasted God's vengeance!
Where once the anger of heaven has struck, that house is shaken
For ever: damnation rises behind each child
Like a wave cresting out of the black northeast,
When the long darkness under sea roars up
And bursts drumming death upon the windwhipped sand.

[ANTISTROPHE 1]

I have seen this gathering sorrow from time long past
Loom upon Oedipus' children: generation from generation
Takes the compulsive rage of the enemy god.
So lately this last flower of Oedipus' line
Drank the sunlight! but now a passionate word
And a handful of dust have closed up all its beauty.

[STROPHE 2]

What mortal arrogance
Transcends the wrath of Zeus?[7]
Sleep cannot lull him, nor the effortless long months
Of the timeless gods: but he is young for ever,
And his house is the shining day of high Olympos.[8]
    All that is and shall be,
    And all the past, is his.
No pride on earth is free of the curse of heaven.

[ANTISTROPHE 2]

  The straying dreams of men
  May bring them ghosts of joy:
But as they drowse, the waking embers burn them;
Or they walk with fixed eyes, as blind men walk.
But the ancient wisdom speaks for our own time:
  Fate works most for woe
  With Folly's fairest show.
Man's little pleasure is the spring of sorrow.

7. **Zeus** (zo͞os) King of all Greek gods, he was believed to throw lightning bolts when angry.

8. **Olympos** (ō lim′ pəs) mountain in Greece where the gods were believed to live in ease and splendor (also spelled "Olympus").

Close Reading Activities

READ

Comprehension

Reread all or part of the text to help you answer the following questions.

1. What does Creon forbid anyone to do with Polyneices' body?
2. What does Antigone ask Ismene to do?
3. What does the sentry tell Creon has happened to Polyneices' body?
4. Why does the sentry bring Antigone to Creon?
5. To what punishment does Creon sentence Antigone?

Research: Clarify Details This play may include references that are unfamiliar to you. Choose at least one unfamiliar detail, and briefly research it. Then, explain how the information you learned from research sheds light on an aspect of the play.

Summarize Write an objective summary of this part of the play. Remember that an objective summary is free from opinion and evaluation.

Language Study

Selection Vocabulary The following lines appear in this part of the play. Define each boldface word. Then, use the word in a sentence of your own.

- But before his jaws were **sated** with our blood, / Or pinefire took the garland of our towers, / He was thrown back …
- And his the skill that **deflects** the arrows of snow, / The spears of winter rain …
- But how much more than this / Is **brazen** boasting of barefaced anarchy!

Diction and Style Study the following lines from the play, which appear below. Then, answer the questions that follow.

> I have seen this gathering sorrow from time long past / Loom upon Oedipus' children: generation from generation / Takes the compulsive rage of the enemy god.

1. **(a)** What does *gathering* mean in these lines? **(b)** What is another meaning for *gathering*?
2. **(a)** What does *loom* mean in these lines? **(b)** What other meaning can *loom* have? **(c) Interpret:** How do the multiple meanings of *loom* contribute to the overall meaning of this passage?

Conventions Read this excerpt from a speech by Ismene. Identify two absolute phrases and explain your choices. Then, explain how the use of these phrases helps Ismene structure her argument.

> Oedipus died, everyone hating him / For what his own search brought to light, his eyes / Ripped out by his own hand; and Iocaste died, / His mother and wife at once: she twisted the cords / That strangled her life; and our two brothers died, / Each killed by the other's sword.

Academic Vocabulary

The following words appear in blue in the instructions and questions on the facing page. Copy the words into your notebook. For each word, find a related word or words built on the same root (e.g., *oppose: opposing, opposition*).

contradiction **principles** **practical**

Literary Analysis

Reread the identified passages. Then, respond to the questions that follow.

Focus Passage 1 *(pp. 689–690)*

Antigone. If that is what you think …
Ismene. … friend indeed to those who love you.

Key Ideas and Details

1. **(a)** What decision does Antigone insist she will act upon? **(b) Summarize:** How does Antigone justify her decision? Explain.
2. **(a)** How does Ismene respond to Antigone's request? **(b) Analyze:** With what arguments does Ismene defend her position? Explain.

Craft and Structure

3. **(a)** Which phrase in line 58 expresses a seeming **contradiction**, or paradox? **(b) Interpret:** Explain the truth Antigone expresses in this paradox. **(c) Evaluate:** In what way does this paradoxical statement capture Antigone's argument and point of view?
4. **Define:** Both sisters refer to having "strength." Do they use the word to mean the same thing? Explain, citing textual evidence.

Integration of Knowledge and Ideas

5. **Evaluate:** How would you describe the values that define each sister's conscience? Support your answer with details from the play.

Focus Passage 2 *(pp. 691–692)*

Choragos. But now at last our new King is …
Creon. …do with him whatever they like.

Key Ideas and Details

1. **(a)** How does the Choragos refer to the members of the Chorus? **(b) Infer:** Why might such a group of citizens possess the authority to be heard by the king? Explain.
2. **(a)** What **principles** of governance, or rule, does Creon outline? **(b) Analyze:** How does Creon say he will act on these principles in regard to his nephews?

Craft and Structure

3. **(a)** How does Creon refer to the State in his opening statement? **(b) Infer:** What is meant by "recent storms?" **(c) Analyze:** What does this metaphor, as developed in the passage, suggest about the State and its challenges?
4. **(a) Distinguish:** What background information does Creon provide at the beginning of this speech? **(b) Interpret:** What **practical** purpose does this speech serve for readers and viewers? Explain.

Integration of Knowledge and Ideas

5. **Synthesize:** How would you describe the values that guide Creon's conscience? Explain.

Protagonist and Antagonist

The **protagonist** is the main character in a literary work. The **antagonist** is a character in conflict with the protagonist. Reread this part of the play, and take notes on ways in which the author uses the structure of a protagonist and an antagonist to express conflicting values of conscience.

1. **(a)** Who is the protagonist? **(b)** Which values motivate the protagonist?
2. **(a)** Who is the antagonist? **(b)** Which values drive the antagonist? **(c)** How do the values of the antagonist affect the actions of the protagonist?
3. **Conscientious Objections:** How does the Chorus respond to the conflict between protagonist and antagonist at the close of this part of the play?

Common Core State Standards

RL.9-10.1, RL.9-10.2, RL.9-10.3, RL.9-10.4, RL.9-10.5, RL.9-10.6; L.9-10.3, L.9-10.4, L.9-10.4.a, L.9-10.6

[For full standards wording, see the chart in the front of this book.]

SCENES 3–5

SCENE 3

CHORAGOS. But here is Haimon, King, the last of all your sons.
Is it grief for Antigone that brings him here,
And bitterness at being robbed of his bride?

[*Enter* HAIMON.]

CREON. We shall soon see, and no need of diviners.[1]
—Son,
You have heard my final judgment on that girl:
Have you come here hating me, or have you come
With **deference** and with love, whatever I do?

HAIMON. I am your son, father. You are my guide.
You make things clear for me, and I obey you.
No marriage means more to me than your continuing wisdom.

CREON. Good. That is the way to behave: subordinate
Everything else, my son, to your father's will.
This is what a man prays for, that he may get
Sons attentive and dutiful in his house,
Each one hating his father's enemies,
Honoring his father's friends. But if his sons
Fail him, if they turn out unprofitably,
What has he fathered but trouble for himself
And amusement for the malicious?
So you are right
Not to lose your head over this woman.
Your pleasure with her would soon grow cold, Haimon,
And then you'd have a hellcat in bed and elsewhere.
Let her find her husband in Hell!
Of all the people in this city, only she
Has had **contempt** for my law and broken it.

1. **diviners** (də vīn′ ərz) *n.* those who claim to forecast the future.

deference ▶ (def′ ər əns) *n.* a yielding to the ideas, wishes, and so on of another

contempt ▶ (kən tempt′) *n.* scorn; the attitude of someone who looks down on something or someone else

Do you want me to show myself weak before the people?
Or to break my sworn word? No, and I will not.
The woman dies.
I suppose she'll plead "family ties." Well, let her.
If I permit my own family to rebel,
How shall I earn the world's obedience?
Show me the man who keeps his house in hand,
He's fit for public authority.
                                        I'll have no dealings
With law-breakers, critics of the government:
Whoever is chosen to govern should be obeyed—
Must be obeyed, in all things, great and small,
Just and unjust! O Haimon,
The man who knows how to obey, and that man only,
Knows how to give commands when the time comes.
You can depend on him, no matter how fast
The spears come: he's a good soldier, he'll stick it out.

Anarchy, anarchy! Show me a greater evil!
This is why cities tumble and the great houses rain down,
This is what scatters armies!

No, no: good lives are made so by discipline.
We keep the laws then, and the lawmakers,

And no woman shall seduce us. If we must lose,
Let's lose to a man, at least! Is a woman stronger than we?

CHORAGOS. Unless time has rusted my wits,
What you say, King, is said with point and dignity.

HAIMON. [*Boyishly earnest*] Father:
Reason is God's crowning gift to man, and you are right
To warn me against losing mine. I cannot say—
I hope that I shall never want to say!—that you
Have reasoned badly. Yet there are other men
Who can reason, too; and their opinions might be helpful.
You are not in a position to know everything
That people say or do, or what they feel:
Your temper terrifies them—everyone
Will tell you only what you like to hear.
But I, at any rate, can listen; and I have heard them
Muttering and whispering in the dark about this girl.
They say no woman has ever, so unreasonably,
Died so shameful a death for a generous act:

"She covered her brother's body. Is this indecent?
She kept him from dogs and vultures. Is this a crime?
Death?—She should have all the honor that we can give her!"

This is the way they talk out there in the city.

You must believe me:
Nothing is closer to me than your happiness.
What could be closer? Must not any son
Value his father's fortune as his father does his?
I beg you, do not be unchangeable:
Do not believe that you alone can be right.
The man who thinks that,
The man who maintains that only he has the power
To reason correctly, the gift to speak, the soul—
A man like that, when you know him, turns out empty.

It is not reason never to yield to reason!

In flood time you can see how some trees bend,
And because they bend, even their twigs are safe,
While stubborn trees are torn up, roots and all.
And the same thing happens in sailing:
Make your sheet fast, never slacken,—and over you go,
Head over heels and under: and there's your voyage.
Forget you are angry! Let yourself be moved!
I know I am young; but please let me say this:
The ideal condition
Would be, I admit, that men should be right by instinct;
But since we are all too likely to go astray,
The reasonable thing is to learn from those who can teach.

CHORAGOS. You will do well to listen to him, King,
If what he says is sensible. And you, Haimon,
Must listen to your father.—Both speak well.

CREON. You consider it right for a man of my years and experience
To go to school to a boy?

HAIMON. It is not right
If I am wrong. But if I am young, and right,
What does my age matter?

CREON. You think it right to stand up for an anarchist?

HAIMON. Not at all. I pay no respect to criminals.

CREON. Then she is not a criminal?

Haimon. The City would deny it, to a man.

Creon. And the City proposes to teach me how to rule?

Haimon. Ah. Who is it that's talking like a boy now?

Creon. My voice is the one voice giving orders in this City!

Haimon. It is no City if it takes orders from one voice.

Creon. The State is the King!

Haimon. Yes, if the State is a desert.

[*Pause*]

Creon. This boy, it seems, has sold out to a woman.

Haimon. If you are a woman: my concern is only for you.

Creon. So? Your "concern"! In a public brawl with your father!

Haimon. How about you, in a public brawl with justice?

Creon. With justice, when all that I do is within my rights?

Haimon. You have no right to trample on God's right.

Creon. [*Completely out of control*] Fool, adolescent fool! Taken in by a woman!

Haimon. You'll never see me taken in by anything vile.

Creon. Every word you say is for her!

Haimon. [*Quietly, darkly*] And for you. And for me. And for the gods under the earth.

Creon. You'll never marry her while she lives.

Haimon. Then she must die.—But her death will cause another.

Creon. Another? Have you lost your senses? Is this an open threat?

Haimon. There is no threat in speaking to emptiness.

Creon. I swear you'll regret this superior tone of yours!

You are the empty one!

HAIMON. If you were not my father,
I'd say you were perverse.

CREON. You girlstruck fool, don't play at words with me!

HAIMON. I am sorry. You prefer silence.

CREON. Now, by God—!
I swear, by all the gods in heaven above us,
You'll watch it, I swear you shall!
[*To the* SERVANTS] Bring her out!
Bring the woman out! Let her die before his eyes!
Here, this instant, with her bridegroom beside her!

HAIMON. Not here, no; she will not die here, King.
And you will never see my face again.
Go on raving as long as you've a friend to endure you.

[*Exit* HAIMON.]

CHORAGOS. Gone, gone.
Creon, a young man in a rage is dangerous!

CREON. Let him do, or dream to do, more than a man can.
He shall not save these girls from death.

CHORAGOS. These girls?
You have sentenced them both?

CREON. No, you are right.
I will not kill the one whose hands are clean.

CHORAGOS. But Antigone?

CREON. [*Somberly*] I will carry her far away
Out there in the wilderness, and lock her
Living in a vault of stone. She shall have food,
As the custom is, to absolve the State of her death.
And there let her pray to the gods of hell:
They are her only gods:
Perhaps they will show her an escape from death,
Or she may learn,
though late,
That **piety** shown the dead is pity in vain.

[*Exit* CREON.]

piety ▶
(pī´ ə tē) *n.* loyalty and devotion to family, the divine, or some other object of respect

ODE III

CHORUS. Love, unconquerable [STROPHE 1]
Waster of rich men, keeper
Of warm lights and all-night vigil
In the soft face of a girl:
Sea-wanderer, forest-visitor!
Even the pure Immortals cannot escape you,
And mortal man, in his one day's dusk,
Trembles before your glory.
Surely you swerve upon ruin [ANTISTROPHE]
The just man's consenting heart,
As here you have made bright anger
Strike between father and son—
And none has conquered but Love!
A girl's glance working the will of heaven:

Pleasure to her alone who mocks us,
Merciless Aphrodite.[2]

SCENE 4

CHORAGOS. [*As* ANTIGONE *enters guarded*] But I can no longer stand in awe of this,
Nor, seeing what I see, keep back my tears.
Here is Antigone, passing to that chamber
Where all find sleep at last.

ANTIGONE. Look upon me, friends, and pity me [STROPHE 1]
Turning back at the night's edge to say
Good-by to the sun that shines for me no longer;
Now sleepy Death
Summons me down to Acheron,[3] that cold shore:
There is no bridesong there, nor any music.

CHORUS. Yet not unpraised, not without a kind of honor,
You walk at last into the underworld;
Untouched by sickness, broken by no sword.
What woman has ever found your way to death?

ANTIGONE [ANTISTROPHE 1]
How often I have heard the story of Niobe,[4]
Tantalos'[5] wretched daughter, how the stone
Clung fast about her, ivy-close: and they say
The rain falls endlessly
And sifting soft snow; her tears are never done.

2. **Aphrodite** (af′ rə dīt′ ē) goddess of beauty and love who is sometimes vengeful in her retaliation for offenses.

3. **Acheron** (ak′ ər än′) In Greek mythology, river in the underworld over which the dead are ferried.

4. **Niobe** (nī′ ō bē′) a queen of Thebes who was turned to stone while weeping for her slain children. Her seven sons and seven daughters were killed by Artemis and Apollo, the divine twins of Leto, after Leto complained that Niobe insulted her by bragging of maternal superiority. It was Zeus who turned the bereaved Niobe to stone, but her lament continued and her tears created a stream.

5. **Tantalos'** (tan′ tə lus əz) Niobe's father, who was condemned to eternal frustration in the underworld because he revealed the secrets of the gods.

I feel the loneliness of her death in mine.

CHORUS. But she was born of heaven, and you
Are woman, woman-born. If her death is yours,
A mortal woman's, is this not for you
Glory in our world and in the world beyond?

ANTIGONE. [STROPHE 2]
You laugh at me. Ah, friends, friends,
Can you not wait until I am dead? O Thebes,
O men many-charioted, in love with Fortune,
Dear springs of Dirce, sacred Theban grove,
Be witnesses for me, denied all pity,
Unjustly judged! and think a word of love
For her whose path turns
Under dark earth, where there are no more tears.

CHORUS. You have passed beyond human daring and come at last
Into a place of stone where Justice sits.
I cannot tell
What shape of your father's guilt appears in this.

ANTIGONE. [ANTISTROPHE 2]
You have touched it at last: that bridal bed
Unspeakable, horror of son and mother mingling:
Their crime, infection of all our family!
O Oedipus, father and brother!
Your marriage strikes from the grave to murder mine.
I have been a stranger here in my own land:
All my life
The blasphemy of my birth has followed me.

CHORUS. Reverence is a virtue, but strength
Lives in established law: that must prevail.
You have made your choice,
Your death is the doing of your conscious hand.

ANTIGONE. [EPODE]
Then let me go, since all your words are bitter,
And the very light of the sun is cold to me.
Lead me to my vigil, where I must have
Neither love nor lamentation: no song, but silence.

[CREON *interrupts impatiently.*]

CREON. If dirges and planned lamentations could put off death,
Men would be singing forever.

[*To the* SERVANTS] Take her, go!
You know your orders: take her to the vault
And leave her alone there. And if she lives or dies,
That's her affair, not ours: our hands are clean.

ANTIGONE. O tomb, vaulted bride-bed in eternal rock,
Soon I shall be with my own again
Where Persephone[6] welcomes the thin ghosts underground:
And I shall see my father again, and you, mother,
And dearest Polyneices—
dearest indeed
To me, since it was my hand
That washed him clean and poured the ritual wine:
And my reward is death before my time!

And yet, as men's hearts know, I have done no wrong,
I have not sinned before God. Or if I have,
I shall know the truth in death. But if the guilt
Lies upon Creon who judged me, then, I pray,
May his punishment equal my own.

CHORAGOS. O passionate heart,
Unyielding, tormented still by the same winds!

CREON. Her guards shall have good cause to regret their delaying.

ANTIGONE. Ah! That voice is like the voice of death!

CREON. I can give you no reason to think you are mistaken.

ANTIGONE. Thebes, and you my fathers' gods,
And rulers of Thebes, you see me now, the last
Unhappy daughter of a line of kings,
Your kings, led away to death. You will remember
What things I suffer, and at what men's hands,
Because I would not transgress the laws of heaven.

[*To the* GUARDS, *simply*]

Come: let us wait no longer

[*Exit* ANTIGONE, *left, guarded.*]

6. Persephone (pər sef´ ə nē) queen of the underworld.

ODE IV

CHORUS. [STROPHE 1]

All Danae's beauty[7] was locked away
In a brazen cell where the sunlight could not come:
A small room, still as any grave, enclosed her.
Yet she was a princess too,
And Zeus in a rain of gold poured love upon her.
O child, child,
No power in wealth or war
Or tough sea-blackened ships
Can prevail against untiring Destiny!

[ANTISTROPHE 1]

And Dryas' son[8] also, that furious king,
Bore the god's prisoning anger for his pride:
Sealed up by Dionysos[9] in deaf stone,
His madness died among echoes.
So at the last he learned what dreadful power

His tongue had mocked:
For he had profaned the revels,
And fired the wrath of the nine
Implacable Sisters[10] that love the sound of the flute.

[STROPHE 2]

And old men tell a half-remembered tale
Of horror done where a dark ledge splits the sea
And a double surf beats on the gray shores:
How a king's new woman, sick
With hatred for the queen he had imprisoned,
Ripped out his two sons' eyes with her bloody hands
While grinning Ares[11] watched the shuttle plunge
Four times: four blind wounds crying for revenge,

[ANTISTROPHE 2]

Crying, tears and blood mingled.—Piteously born,
Those sons whose mother was of heavenly birth!
Her father was the god of the North Wind
And she was cradled by gales,
She raced with young colts on the glittering hills
And walked untrammeled in the open light:
But in her marriage deathless Fate found means
To build a tomb like yours for all her joy.

7. **Danae's** (dan′ ā ēz′) **beauty** Danae was imprisoned when it was foretold that she would mother a son who would kill her father, King Acrisios. Her beauty attracted Zeus, who visited her in the form of a shower of gold. Perseus was born of the union, and Danae was exiled with the child. Years later, as prophesied, the boy did kill Acrisios, whom he failed to recognize as his grandfather.

8. **Dryas'** (drī′ us əz) **son** Lycorgos (lī kur′ gəs), whose opposition to the worship of Dionysos was severely punished by the gods. He drove the followers of Dionysos from Thrace and was driven insane. Lycorgos recovered from his madness while imprisoned in a cave, but he was later blinded by Zeus as additional punishment.

9. **Dionysos** (dī′ ə nī′ səs) god of wine, in whose honor the Greek plays were performed.

10. **nine / Implacable Sisters** nine Muses, or goddesses, of science and literature. *Implacable* (im plak′ ə bəl) means "unforgiving."

11. **Ares** (er′ ēz′) god of war.

SCENE 5

[*Enter blind* TEIRESIAS, *led by a boy. The opening speeches of* TEIRESIAS *should be in singsong contrast to the realistic lines of* CREON.]

TEIRESIAS. This is the way the blind man comes, Princes,
Princes, Lock-step, two heads lit by the eyes of one.

CREON. What new thing have you to tell us, old Teiresias?

TEIRESIAS. I have much to tell you: listen to the prophet, Creon.

CREON. I am not aware that I have ever failed to listen.

TEIRESIAS. Then you have done wisely, King, and ruled well.

CREON. I admit my debt to you.[12] But what have you to say?

TEIRESIAS. This, Creon: you stand once more on the edge of fate.

CREON. What do you mean? Your words are a kind of dread.

TEIRESIAS. Listen, Creon:
I was sitting in my chair of augury,[13] at the place
Where the birds gather about me. They were all a-chatter,
As is their habit, when suddenly I heard
A strange note in their jangling, a scream, a
Whirring fury; I knew that they were fighting,
Tearing each other, dying
In a whirlwind of wings clashing. And I was afraid.
I began the rites of burnt-offering at the altar,
But Hephaistos[14] failed me: instead of bright flame,
There was only the sputtering slime of the fat thigh-flesh
Melting: the entrails dissolved in gray smoke,
The bare bone burst from the welter. And no blaze!

This was a sign from heaven. My boy described it,
Seeing for me as I see for others.

I tell you, Creon, you yourself have brought
This new calamity upon us. Our hearths and altars
Are stained with the corruption of dogs and carrion birds
That glut themselves on the corpse of Oedipus' son.
The gods are deaf when we pray to them, their fire
Recoils from our offering, their birds of omen
Have no cry of comfort, for they are gorged
With the thick blood of the dead.

12. **my debt to you** Creon is admitting that he would not have acquired the throne if Teiresias had not moved the former king, Oedipus, to undertake an investigation that led eventually to his own downfall.

13. **chair of augury** the seat near the temple from which Teiresias would deliver his predictions about the future. Augury is the practice of reading the future from omens, such as the flight of birds.

14. **Hephaistos** (hē fes´ təs) god of fire and the forge, who would be invoked, as he was by Teiresias, for aid in the starting of ceremonial fires.

O my son,
These are no trifles! Think: all men make mistakes,
But a good man yields when he knows his course is wrong,
And repairs the evil. The only crime is pride.

Give in to the dead man, then: do not fight with a corpse—
What glory is it to kill a man who is dead?
Think, I beg you:
It is for your own good that I speak as I do.
You should be able to yield for your own good.

CREON. It seems that prophets have made me their especial province.
All my life long
I have been a kind of butt for the dull arrows
Of doddering fortunetellers!

No, Teiresias:

If your birds—if the great eagles of God himself
Should carry him stinking bit by bit to heaven,
I would not yield. I am not afraid of pollution:
No man can defile the gods.

Do what you will,

Go into business, make money, speculate
In India gold or that synthetic gold from Sardis,[15]
Get rich otherwise than by my consent to bury him.

Teiresias, it is a sorry thing when a wise man
Sells his wisdom, lets out his words for hire!

TEIRESIAS. Ah Creon! Is there no man left in the world—

CREON. To do what?—Come, let's have the aphorism![16]

TEIRESIAS. No man who knows that wisdom outweighs any wealth?

15. **Sardis** (sär′ dis) capital of ancient Lydia, which produced the first coins made from an alloy of gold and silver.

16. **aphorism** (af′ ə riz′ əm) *n.* brief saying. Creon is taunting the prophet and suggesting that the old man relies on profound-sounding expressions to make an impression.

CREON. As surely as bribes are baser than any baseness.

TEIRESIAS. You are sick, Creon! You are deathly sick!

CREON. As you say: it is not my place to challenge a prophet.

TEIRESIAS. Yet you have said my prophecy is for sale.

CREON. The generation of prophets has always loved gold.

TEIRESIAS. The generation of kings has always loved brass.

CREON. You forget yourself! You are speaking to your King.

TEIRESIAS. I know it. You are a king because of me.

CREON. You have a certain skill; but you have sold out.

TEIRESIAS. King, you will drive me to words that—

CREON. Say them, say them!
Only remember: I will not pay you for them.

TEIRESIAS. No, you will find them too costly.

CREON. No doubt. Speak:
Whatever you say, you will not change my will.

TEIRESIAS. Then take this, and take it to heart!
The time is not far off when you shall pay back
Corpse for corpse, flesh of your own flesh.
You have thrust the child of this world into living night,
You have kept from the gods below the child that is theirs:

The one in a grave before her death, the other,
Dead, denied the grave. This is your crime:
And the Furies[17] and the dark gods of Hell
Are swift with terrible punishment for you.

Do you want to buy me now, Creon?

Not many days,
And your house will be full of men and women weeping,
And curses will be hurled at you from far
Cities grieving for sons unburied, left to rot
Before the walls of Thebes.

These are my arrows, Creon: they are all for you.

[*To* BOY] But come, child: lead me home.
Let him waste his fine anger upon younger men.

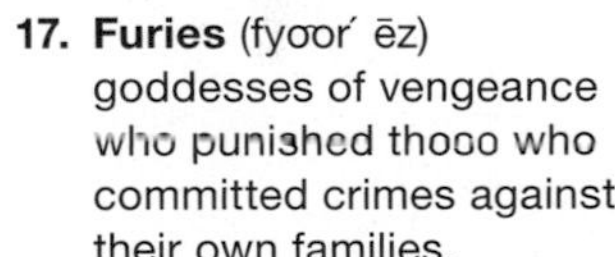
17. Furies (fyoor′ ēz) goddesses of vengeance who punished those who committed crimes against their own families.

Maybe he will learn at last
To control a wiser tongue in a better head.

[*Exit* TEIRESIAS.]

CHORAGOS. The old man has gone, King, but his words
Remain to plague us. I am old, too,
But I cannot remember that he was ever false.

CREON. That is true. . . . It troubles me.
Oh it is hard to give in! but it is worse
To risk everything for stubborn pride.

CHORAGOS. Creon: take my advice.

CREON. What shall I do?

CHORAGOS. Go quickly: free Antigone from her vault
And build a tomb for the body of Polyneices.

CREON. You would have me do this?

CHORAGOS. Creon, yes!
And it must be done at once: God moves
Swiftly to cancel the folly of stubborn men.

CREON. It is hard to deny the heart! But I
Will do it: I will not fight with destiny.

CHORAGOS. You must go yourself, you cannot leave it to others.

CREON. I will go.
—Bring axes, servants:
Come with me to the tomb. I buried her, I
Will set her free.
Oh quickly!
My mind misgives—
The laws of the gods are mighty, and a man must serve them
To the last day of his life!

[*Exit* CREON.]

PÆAN

CHORAGOS.
God of many names [STROPHE 1]

CHORUS. O Iacchos[18]
son
of Kadmeian Semele[19]
O born of the Thunder!
Guardian of the West
Regent
of Eleusis' plain[20]
O Prince of maenad Thebes[21]
and the Dragon Field by rippling Ismenos:[22]

CHORAGOS. [ANTISTROPHE 1]
God of many names

CHORUS.
the flame of torches
flares on our hills
the nymphs of Iacchos
dance at the spring of Castalia:[23]
from the vine-close mountain
come ah come in ivy:
Evohe evohe![24] sings through the streets of Thebes

CHORAGOS. [STROPHE 2]
God of many names

CHORUS. Iacchos of Thebes
heavenly Child
of Semele bride of the Thunderer!
The shadow of plague is upon us:
come
with clement[25] feet
oh come from Parnasos[26]
down the long slopes
across the lamenting water

CHORAGOS. [ANTISTROPHE 2]
Io[27] Fire! Chorister of the throbbing stars!
O purest among the voices of the night!
Thou son of God, blaze for us!

CHORUS. Come with choric rapture of circling Maenads
Who cry *Io Iacche!*[28]
God of many names!

18. **Iacchos** (ē´ ə kəs) one of several alternate names for Dionysos.
19. **Kadmeian Semele** (sem´ ə lē´) Semele was a mortal and the mother of Dionysos. She was the daughter of Thebes' founder, Kadmos.
20. **Eleusis'** (e lo͞o´ sis əz) **plain** Located north of Athens, this plain was a site of worship for Dionysos and Demeter.
21. **maenad** (mē´ nad´) **Thebes** The city is here compared to a maenad, one of Dionysos' female worshipers. Such a follower would be thought of as uncontrolled or disturbed.
22. **Dragon Field . . . Ismenos** (is mē´ nəs) The Dragon Field was located by the banks of Ismenos, a river near Thebes. Kadmos created warriors by sowing in the Dragon Field the teeth of the dragon he killed there.
23. **Castalia** (kas tā´ lē ə) location of a site sacred to Apollo.
24. **Evohe** (ē vō´ ē) triumphant shout of affirmation.
25. **clement** kind; favorable
26. **Parnasos** (pär nas´ əs) mountain that was sacred to both Dionysos and Apollo, located in central Greece.
27. **Io** (ē´ ō´) Greek word for "behold" or "hail."
28. **Io Iacche** (ē´ ō´ ē´ ə ke) cry of celebration used by Dionysian worshipers.

EXODUS

[*Enter* MESSENGER, *left.*]

29. **Kadmos** (kad′ məs) founder of the city of Thebes, whose daughter, Semele, gave birth to Dionysos.

30. **Amphion's** (am fī′ ənz) **citadel** Amphion was a king of Thebes credited with erecting the walls of the fortress, or citadel, by using a magic lyre.

MESSENGER. Men of the line of Kadmos,[29] you who live
Near Amphion's citadel:[30]
I cannot say
Of any condition of human life "This is fixed,
This is clearly good, or bad." Fate raises up,
And Fate casts down the happy and unhappy alike:
No man can foretell his Fate.
Take the case of Creon:
Creon was happy once, as I count happiness:
Victorious in battle, sole governor of the land,
Fortunate father of children nobly born.
And now it has all gone from him! Who can say
That a man is still alive when his life's joy fails?
He is a walking dead man. Grant him rich,
Let him live like a king in his great house:
If his pleasure is gone, I would not give
So much as the shadow of smoke for all he owns.

CHORAGOS. Your words hint at sorrow: what is your news for us?

MESSENGER. They are dead. The living are guilty of their death.

CHORAGOS. Who is guilty? Who is dead? Speak!

MESSENGER. Haimon.
Haimon is dead; and the hand that killed him
Is his own hand.

CHORAGOS. His father's? or his own?

MESSENGER. His own, driven mad by the murder his father had done.

CHORAGOS. Teiresias, Teiresias, how clearly you saw it all!

MESSENGER. This is my news: you must draw what conclusions you can from it.

CHORAGOS. But look: Eurydice, our Queen:
Has she overheard us?

[*Enter* EURYDICE *from the Palace, center.*]

31. **Pallas'** (pal′ us əz) Pallas Athena, the goddess of wisdom.

EURYDICE. I have heard something, friends:
As I was unlocking the gate of Pallas'[31] shrine,
For I needed her help today, I heard a voice

Telling of some new sorrow. And I fainted
There at the temple with all my maidens about me.
But speak again: whatever it is, I can bear it:
Grief and I are no strangers.

MESSENGER. Dearest Lady,
I will tell you plainly all that I have seen.
I shall not try to comfort you: what is the use,
Since comfort could lie only in what is not true?
The truth is always best.
I went with Creon
To the outer plain where Polyneices was lying,
No friend to pity him, his body shredded by dogs.
We made our prayers in that place to Hecate[32]
And Pluto,[33] that they would be merciful. And we bathed
The corpse with holy water, and we brought
Fresh-broken branches to burn what was left of it,
And upon the urn we heaped up a towering barrow
Of the earth of his own land.
When we were done, we ran
To the vault where Antigone lay on her couch of stone.
One of the servants had gone ahead,
And while he was yet far off he heard a voice
Grieving within the chamber, and he came back
And told Creon. And as the King went closer,
The air was full of wailing, the words lost,
And he begged us to make all haste. "Am I a prophet?"
He said, weeping, "And must I walk this road,
The saddest of all that I have gone before?
My son's voice calls me on. Oh quickly, quickly!
Look through the crevice there, and tell me
If it is Haimon, or some deception of the gods!"

We obeyed; and in the cavern's farthest corner
We saw her lying:
She had made a noose of her fine linen veil
And hanged herself. Haimon lay beside her,
His arms about her waist, lamenting her,
His love lost underground, crying out
That his father had stolen her away from him.

When Creon saw him the tears rushed to his eyes
And he called to him: "What have you done, child? Speak
to me.
What are you thinking that makes your eyes so strange?
O my son, my son, I come to you on my knees!"

32. Hecate (hek´ ə tē) a goddess of the underworld, the resting place of dead souls in Greek mythology.

33. Pluto (plo͞ot´ō) chief god of the underworld, who ruled the souls of the dead in Greek mythology.

But Haimon spat in his face. He said not a word,
Staring—
                    And suddenly drew his sword
And lunged. Creon shrank back, the blade missed; and the boy,
Desperate against himself, drove it half its length
Into his own side, and fell. And as he died
He gathered Antigone close in his arms again,
Choking, his blood bright red on her white cheek.
And now he lies dead with the dead, and she is his
At last, his bride in the houses of the dead.

[*Exit* EURYDICE *into the Palace.*]

CHORAGOS. She has left us without a word. What can this mean?

MESSENGER. It troubles me, too; yet she knows what is best,
Her grief is too great for public lamentation,
And doubtless she has gone to her chamber to weep
For her dead son, leading her maidens in his dirge.

CHORAGOS. It may be so: but I fear this deep silence.

[*Pause*]

MESSENGER. I will see what she is doing. I will go in.

[*Exit* MESSENGER *into the Palace.*]

[*Enter* CREON *with attendants, bearing* HAIMON'S *body.*]

CHORAGOS. But here is the King himself: oh look at him,
Bearing his own damnation in his arms.

CREON. Nothing you say can touch me any more.
My own blind heart has brought me
From darkness to final darkness. Here you see
The father murdering, the murdered son—
And all my civic wisdom!

Haimon my son, so young, so young to die,
I was the fool, not you; and you died for me.

CHORAGOS. That is the truth; but you were late in learning it.

CREON. This truth is hard to bear. Surely a god
Has crushed me beneath the hugest weight of heaven,
And driven me headlong a barbaric way
To trample out the thing I held most dear.

The pains that men will take to come to pain!

[*Enter* MESSENGER *from the Palace.*]

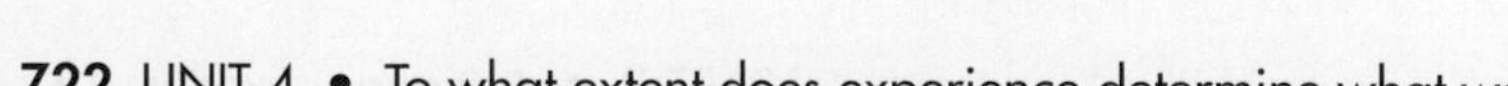

MESSENGER. The burden you carry in your hands is heavy,
But it is not all: you will find more in your house.

CREON. What burden worse than this shall I find there?

MESSENGER. The Queen is dead.

CREON. O port of death, deaf world,
Is there no pity for me? And you, Angel of evil,
I was dead, and your words are death again.
Is it true, boy? Can it be true?
Is my wife dead? Has death bred death?

MESSENGER. You can see for yourself.

[*The doors are opened, and the body of* EURYDICE *is disclosed within.*]

CREON. Oh pity!
All true, all true, and more than I can bear!
O my wife, my son!

MESSENGER. She stood before the altar, and her heart
Welcomed the knife her own hand guided,
And a great cry burst from her lips for Megareus[34] dead,
And for Haimon dead, her sons; and her last breath
Was a curse for their father, the murderer of her sons.
And she fell, and the dark flowed in through her closing eyes.

34. Megareus (mə gaˊ rē əs) oldest son of Creon and Eurydice, who was killed in the civil war by Argive forces invading Thebes.

CREON. O God, I am sick with fear.
Are there no swords here? Has no one a blow for me?

MESSENGER. Her curse is upon you for the deaths of both.

CREON. It is right that it should be. I alone am guilty.
I know it, and I say it. Lead me in,
Quickly, friends.
I have neither life nor substance. Lead me in.

CHORAGOS. You are right, if there can be right in so much wrong.
The briefest way is best in a world of sorrow.

CREON. Let it come,
Let death come quickly, and be kind to me.
I would not ever see the sun again.

CHORAGOS. All that will come when it will; but we, meanwhile,
Have much to do. Leave the future to itself.

CREON. All my heart was in that prayer!

CHORAGOS. Then do not pray any more: the sky is deaf.

CREON. Lead me away. I have been rash and foolish.
I have killed my son and my wife.
I look for comfort; my comfort lies here dead.
Whatever my hands have touched has come to nothing.
Fate has brought all my pride to a thought of dust.

[*As* CREON *is being led into the house, the* CHORAGOS *advances and speaks directly to the audience.*]

CHORAGOS. There is no happiness where there is no wisdom;
No wisdom but in submission to the gods.
Big words are always punished,
And proud men in old age learn to be wise.

The earliest Greek dramas were likely performed in the Agora, or marketplace, in Athens. Later, the Theater of Dionysus (shown here in an artist's rendering) was built on the slope of the Acropolis, the upper part of the city where other important buildings also stood.

ABOUT THE AUTHOR

SOPHOCLES (496–406 B.C.)

Sophocles (**säf´ ə klēz**) was one of three Classical Athenian playwrights who together created the basic theatrical conventions of Greek tragedy, the foundation of drama in Western civilization. The other two were Aeschylus (**es´ ki ləs**, c. 525–456 B.C.) and Euripides (**yōō rip´ ə dēz**), 480–406 B.C.). Before these three great dramatists, Greek theater had consisted of static recitations performed by a chorus and a single actor. Aeschylus added a second actor, creating the possibility of true dialogue. When Sophocles added a third actor, complex relationships among characters emerged in Greek drama.

Sophocles grew up in a prosperous family in Colonus, near Athens. At sixteen, he was one of the young men chosen to perform in a choral ode celebrating the Athenian victory over the Persians at Salamis, the event that marks the beginning of Athens' Golden Age. Throughout his long life, he remained a leading figure in Greek culture. Admired for his good looks and athleticism, he was also a talented musician and a frequent contributor to Athenian public life. He served for a time as city treasurer and also as a military leader in the conflict with Samos, an island that revolted against Athens in 441 B.C.

It was in theater, however, that Sophocles truly shone. He wrote more than 120 plays, seven of which have survived. Among the most celebrated are *Oedipus Rex,* the tragedy the philosopher Aristotle considered the best example of the form, and *Antigone*, the story of Oedipus' daughter. Sophocles is known for strong female characters and for his insight into human nature. In addition to his introduction of a third actor to drama, he also initiated the practice of using painted scenery.

Sophocles died two years before Athens surrendered to Sparta in the Peloponnesian War, the event that marks the end of the Athenian Golden Age. His works are considered among the most significant in Greek drama, and are still widely studied and performed today.

Close Reading Activities

READ

Comprehension

Reread all or part of the text to help you answer the following questions.

1. What does Haimon tell Creon about the people's reaction to Antigone's sentence?
2. How does Creon decide to punish Antigone?
3. What does Teiresias tell Creon, and what does Creon decide to do as a result?
4. What does Creon discover at the tomb?
5. What happens at the palace before Creon returns?

Research: Clarify Details This part of the play may include references that are unfamiliar to you. Choose at least one unfamiliar detail, and briefly research it. Then, explain how the information you learned from research sheds light on an aspect of the play.

Summarize Write an objective summary of this part of the play. Remember that an objective summary is free from opinion and evaluation.

Language Study

Selection Vocabulary The following lines appear in this part of the play. Define each boldface word, and state whether it has positive or negative connotations. Then, provide another word with similar denotation but different connotations. Explain your choices.

- Have you come here hating me, or have you come / With **deference** and with love, whatever I do?
- Or she may learn, / though late, / That **piety** shown the dead is pity in vain.
- Of all the people in this city, only she / Has had **contempt** for my law and broken it.

Diction and Style Study these lines from the play. Then, answer the questions that follow.

> **Choragos.** The old man has gone, King, but his words / Remain to plague us. I am old, too, / But I cannot remember that he was ever false.

1. **(a)** What does *plague* mean in these lines? **(b)** What is another meaning of *plague*?
2. **(a)** What does *false* mean in these lines? **(b)** What other meanings can *false* have? **(c)** How might all these meanings contribute to what the Choragos is trying to tell Creon? Explain.

Conventions Read this excerpt from a speech by Teiresias. Identify the adverb clause. Then, explain which verb the clause modifies and what the clause explains about the verb. Finally, explain what the clause contributes to the meaning of the passage.

> I was sitting in my chair of augury, at the place / Where the birds gather about me. They were all a-chatter, / As is their habit, when suddenly I heard / A strange note in their jangling, a scream, a / Whirring fury....

Academic Vocabulary

The following words appear in blue in the instructions and questions on the facing page.

initial **respective** **illustrate**

Categorize the words by deciding whether you know each one well, know it a little bit, or do not know it at all. Then, use a print or online dictionary to look up the definitions of the words you are unsure of or do not know at all.

Literary Analysis

Reread the identified passages. Then, respond to the questions that follow.

Focus Passage 1 *(pp. 707–708)*

Haimon. [*Boyishly earnest*] Father: / Reason is God's … to learn from those who can teach.

Key Ideas and Details

1. **(a) Interpret:** Why does Haimon feel that he must inform his father about public feeling in Thebes? **(b) Infer:** Which details in the text suggest that Haimon shares these feelings? Explain, citing specific details from the focus passage to support your answer.
2. **Infer:** What insights into the nature of Creon's leadership does Haimon's speech provide? Explain.

Craft and Structure

3. **(a)** What information about Haimon's character does the stage direction provide? **(b) Interpret:** Which details in Haimon's speech develop that characterization? Explain.
4. **(a)** What two analogies, or comparisons, does Haimon introduce in lines 83–88? **(b) Analyze:** Explain how these analogies clarify Haimon's criticism of Creon's actions and beliefs.

Integration of Knowledge and Ideas

5. **Compare and Contrast:** How do Haimon's values compare with those that drive Creon's actions? Cite textual details to support your answer.

Focus Passage 2 *(p. 718)*

Choragos. The old man has gone, King, but …
Creon. … To the last day of his life!

Key Ideas and Details

1. **(a)** What does the Choragos recall about Teiresias? **(b) Analyze Cause and Effect:** How does this recollection change Creon's mind? Explain, citing details from the text.
2. **(a)** What tools and aid does Creon call for at the end of the focus passage? **(b) Deduce:** What do these details suggest about the physical difficulty of the task he has to accomplish? Explain.

Craft and Structure

3. **Analyze:** This passage includes many short lines, including lines 102, 106, 113, and 116. What mood, or feeling, does this pattern of short lines suggest? Explain.
4. **(a)** What does the Choragos advise Creon to do? **(b) Analyze:** How does the playwright use dialogue to show Creon's **initial** resistance to this advice followed by his eager anxiety? Explain.

Integration of Knowledge and Ideas

5. **Interpret:** How does this passage show Creon's new understanding that his power as a ruler is, or should be, limited? Explain.

Tragic Flaw

A **tragic flaw** is the personal weakness that causes the downfall of a tragic hero. Reread this part of the play, and note which qualities in Antigone and Creon could be viewed as their **respective** tragic flaws.

1. **(a)** What trait in Antigone could be considered her tragic flaw? **(b)** What is Creon's tragic flaw? **(c)** To what extent does each character's flaw lead to his or her downfall? Explain.
2. **Conscientious Objections:** What do the tragic flaws of Antigone and Creon **illustrate** about the exercise of conscience? Explain.

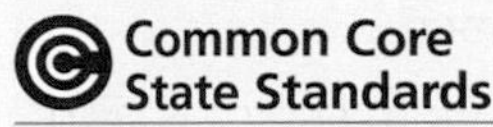

RL.9-10.1, RL.9-10.2, RL.9-10.3, RL.9-10.4, RL.9-10.5, RL.9-10.6; L.9-10.1.b, L.9-10.3, L.9-10.4, L.9-10.6
[For full standards wording, see the chart in the front of this book.]

DISCUSS

From Text to Topic **Small Group Discussion**

Discuss the following passage from Scene 3 with a small group of classmates. Take notes during the discussion. Contribute your own ideas, and support them with examples from the text.

> **Creon.** … How shall I earn the world's obedience? / Show me the man who keeps his house in hand, / He's fit for public authority. / I'll have no dealings / With law-breakers, critics of the government: / Whoever is chosen to govern should be obeyed—/Must be obeyed, in all things, great and small.

QUESTIONS FOR DISCUSSION

1. What type of father, uncle, and king does Creon present himself to be?
2. Is the type of obedience Creon requires a show of his strength or of his weakness?
3. Why might Creon's attitude stir rebellion where a more flexible position might not?

WRITE

Writing to Sources **Informative Text**

Some tragedies include a supporting character who serves as a *foil*—a character that presents opposing traits—for the tragic hero. The audience gains insight into the hero through comparisons to the foil.

Assignment

Write a **compare-and-contrast essay** in which you analyze Antigone and Ismene. Explain the values that motivate each sister to act as she does. Then, consider whether Ismene serves as a foil to Antigone, and explain your position.

Prewriting and Planning Reread the play, looking for details that show how Antigone and Ismene express different values through their statements and actions.

- **Character Trait List:** In a chart, list the qualities, beliefs, and values each character displays. Use one column for Antigone and the other for Ismene. Then, compare the two columns and identify similarities and differences.
- **Belief-Action-Consequences Diagram:** For each character, create a diagram that identifies a value or belief, an action that expresses it, and the consequences of that action. Compare the results.

Drafting Explain your analysis of the characters, and support your points with details and examples from the text. Draw a clear conclusion about whether Ismene serves as a foil for Antigone.

Revising Make sure that your word choice is vivid and expresses your ideas accurately. Replace vague words and phrases with vivid, precise choices.

Editing and Proofreading Check that you have spelled characters' names correctly and referred to elements of Greek drama accurately. Reread your draft, and make any necessary corrections.

CONVENTIONS

As you compare and contrast characters, use parallelism. Identify similar ideas within a sentence or passage and use the same grammatical patterns to express them.

Antigone
SOPHOCLES

RESEARCH

Research **Investigate the Topic**

Ethics in Ancient Greece Ancient Greek had no equivalent word for our term *sin,* which means "an offense against God, religion, or good morals." Instead, the Greeks had the terms *hamartia* (hä´ mär tē´ ə), meaning "error," and *hubris* (hyōō´ bris), or *hybris,* often translated as "excessive pride" or "arrogance." Hamartia and hubris often play critical roles in ancient Greek dramas and the myths upon which the plays were based.

Assignment

Conduct research to learn about *hamartia* and *hubris* and how these ethical concepts were expressed in ancient Greek tragedies. Consult online or print references such as general encyclopedias, classical dictionaries, and histories of Greek drama and thought. Share your findings in an **annotated bibliography**—a list of sources that includes brief annotations, or paragraphs, about the content and quality of each source.

PREPARATION FOR ESSAY

You may use the knowledge you gain during this research assignment to support your claims in an essay you will write at the end of this section.

Gather Sources Locate print and electronic sources you might want to recommend to other researchers. Include ancient Greek sources, such as Aristotle's *Poetics,* as well as modern discussions and interpretations of those sources. Use a variety of sources to ensure that you present your readers with a strong list of choices.

Take Notes Take notes on each source. Label each page or set of notes with the title and author of the source. Review the source and draft an initial summary of your findings. As you read through sources, note the page numbers or locations of key information. This will save time later if you need to retrace your steps to confirm details.

Synthesize Multiple Sources Assemble data about each source, organize it into bibliography form, and write the annotations. Use the citation format your teacher prefers—usually either MLA (Modern Language Association) or APA (American Psychological Association) style. Provide objective information, including the type of source and the content it presents. Then, write your annotations, including your observations about the clarity and thoroughness of the writing. Conclude by explaining why a researcher would or would not find each source useful.

Organize and Present Ideas Share your bibliography with a small group and discuss what you learned about the ancient Greek concepts of hamartia and hubris. In particular, discuss the significance of those concepts in Sophocles' play *Antigone.*

Common Core State Standards

W.9-10.2a–b, W.9-10.2d, W.9-10.2f, W.9-10.4, W.9-10.5, W.9-10.7, W.9-10.8, W.9-10.9a; SL.9-10.1, SL.9-10.4; L.9-10.1.a, L.9-10.2, L.9-10.3a

[For full standards wording, see the chart in the front of this book.]

Conscientious Objector

Edna St. Vincent Millay

I shall die, but that is all that I shall do for Death.

I hear him leading his horse out of the stall; I hear the
clatter on the barn-floor.
He is in haste; he has business in Cuba, business in the
Balkans, many calls to make this morning.
But I will not hold the bridle while he cinches the girth.
And he may mount by himself: I will not give him a leg up.

Though he **flick** my shoulders with his whip, I will not tell
him which way the fox ran.
With his hoof on my breast, I will not tell him where the
black boy hides in the swamp.
I shall die, but that is all that I shall do for Death; I am not
on his pay-roll.

I will not tell him the whereabouts of my friends nor of my
enemies either.
Though he promise me much, I will not map him the route to
any man's door.

Am I a spy in the land of the living, that I should **deliver** men
to Death?
Brother, the password and the plans of our city are safe with
me; never through me
Shall you be **overcome**.

◀ **flick**
(flik) *v.* touch or hit lightly

◀ **deliver**
(di livˊər) *v.* surrender someone or something; hand over

◀ **overcome**
(ōˊvər kumˊ) *v.* master or prevail over

ABOUT THE AUTHOR

Edna St. Vincent Millay (1892–1950)

Edna St. Vincent Millay was not yet in college when she first won fame as a poet. In 1912 her prize-winning lyric "Renascence" was published, bringing her to the attention of a benefactor who enabled the young poet to attend Vassar College. After graduation in 1917, Millay moved to New York City, where she acted in plays and pursued her writing career. Living in the artistic neighborhood of Greenwich Village, Millay became a kind of literary "flapper," celebrating the new freedom enjoyed by young women in the Roaring Twenties. In 1923, Millay's fourth collection of poems, *The Harp Weaver,* was awarded the Pulitzer Prize. Today, Millay is widely regarded as one of the twentieth century's most skillful writers of sonnets.

Close Reading Activities

READ

Comprehension

Reread all or part of the text to help you answer the following questions.

1. What is the speaker willing to do for Death?
2. Cite two ways in which the speaker refuses to help Death.
3. Cite three things the speaker will not tell Death.
4. What is safe with the speaker?

Research: Clarify Details This poem may include references that are unfamiliar to you. Choose at least one unfamiliar detail, and briefly research it. Then, explain how the information you learned from research sheds light on an aspect of the poem.

Summarize Write an objective summary of the poem, one that is free from opinion and evaluation.

Language Study

Selection Vocabulary The phrases at right appear in the poem. Create a word map or graphic that identifies at least one synonym and one antonym for each boldface word. Then, use the word in a sentence of your own.

- Though he **flick** my shoulders with his whip
- that I should **deliver** men to Death
- Shall you be **overcome**

Literary Analysis

Reread the identified passage. Then, respond to the questions that follow.

Focus Passage *(p. 730)*
I hear him leading … his pay-roll.

Key Ideas and Details

1. **(a)** Where does Death have "business"?
   (b) Deduce: What do these details suggest about events in these places during the time period in which Millay was writing? Explain.
2. **Infer:** What social ill does the speaker's reference to the "black boy" hiding in the swamp **implicitly** criticize? Explain.

Craft and Structure

3. **(a)** Identify how the poet uses capitalization to transform the idea of death into a character.
   (b) Distinguish: Cite at least four other details that present death as a person rather than a force of nature. **(c) Analyze:** How does this use of personification suggest that Death is the leader of an evil or corrupt organization? Cite details from the poem to support your answer.

Integration of Knowledge and Ideas

4. **Evaluate:** Does this poem convey an **absolute,** unbending stance in favor of conscientious objection? Explain.

The Speaker in Poetry

A **speaker** is the imaginary voice that says the words of a poem. Reread the poem and take notes on how the poet uses the speaker to create a study of conscience.

1. Is the speaker in this poem a person, or is it a state of mind? Explain, citing details from the poem to support your response.
2. **Conscientious Objections: (a)** At what point in the poem does the speaker address someone directly? **(b)** How does that direct address create a bond between the reader and the speaker? Explain.

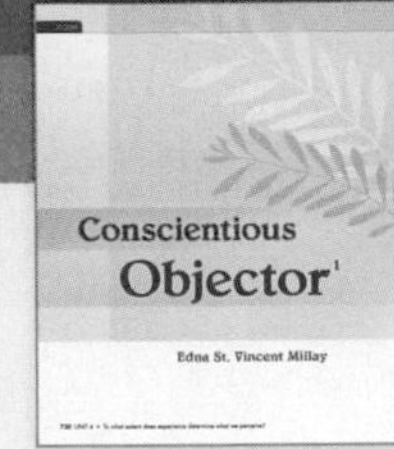

DISCUSS • RESEARCH • WRITE

From Text to Topic **Partner Discussion**

Discuss the following passage with a classmate. Listen closely and build on each other's ideas, supporting them with examples from the text.

> I will not tell him the whereabouts of my friends nor of my enemies either. / Though he promise me much, I will not map him the route to any man's door.

QUESTIONS FOR DISCUSSION

1. Why does the speaker make no distinction between betraying friends or enemies?
2. What rewards could Death promise someone?
3. Given those rewards, how does the speaker's refusal to cooperate emphasize his or her nobility?

Research **Investigate the Topic**

Conscientious Objection in U.S. History The speaker in "Conscientious Objector" refuses to serve Death in any capacity. Throughout history, conscientious objectors have refused to participate in warfare based on their religious or ethical beliefs.

Assignment

Conduct research on the influence of a notable conscientious objector in American history, and identify ways in which this person's actions do or do not **resonate** with the speaker in Millay's poem. Consult reliable and authoritative print or online resources. Take clear notes and carefully identify your sources. Share your findings in a **research report.**

PREPARATION FOR ESSAY

You may use the results of this research in an essay you will write at the end of this section.

Writing to Sources **Narrative**

Standing as a conscientious objector can take courage, especially if the moral stance runs counter to popular opinion.

Assignment

Write a **reflective essay** in which you describe a time when you or someone you know asserted a position in the face of others' disapproval. The event might have centered on a political difference, a social issue, or another controversy. Follow these steps:

- Describe the situation, including positions on both sides of the argument.
- Explain how you or the person you are describing arrived at a decision to take a stand.
- Reflect on what the experience taught you about the costs and the benefits of following one's conscience.
- Draw a meaningful connection between the experience you describe and the message of the poem "Conscientious Objector."

ACADEMIC VOCABULARY

Academic terms appear in blue on these pages. If these words are not familiar to you, use a dictionary to find their definitions. Then, use them as you speak and write about the text.

Common Core State Standards

RL.9-10.1, RL.9-10.2, RL.9-10.4; W.9-10.2, W.9-10.3, W.9-10.4, W.9-10.7; SL.9-10.1; L.9-10.4, L.9-10.5.a, L.9-10.6

[For full standards wording, see the chart in the front of this book.]

SPEECH

from

Nobel Lecture

Alexander Solzhenitsyn

translated by F.D. Reeve

I am, however, encouraged by a keen sense of WORLD LITERATURE as the one great heart that beats for the cares and misfortunes of our world, even though each corner sees and experiences them in a different way.

In past times, also, besides age-old national literatures there existed a concept of world literature as the link between the summits of national literatures and as the aggregate of reciprocal literary influences. But there was a time lag: readers and writers came to know foreign writers only belatedly, sometimes centuries later, so that mutual influences were delayed and the network of national literary high points was visible not to contemporaries but to later generations.

Today, between writers of one country and the readers and writers of another, there is an almost instantaneous **reciprocity**, as I myself know. My books, unpublished, alas, in my own country, despite hasty and often bad translations have quickly found a responsive world readership. Critical analysis of them has been undertaken by such leading Western writers as Heinrich Böll.[1] During all these recent years, when both my work and my freedom did not collapse, when against the laws of gravity they held on seemingly in thin air, seemingly ON NOTHING, on the invisible, mute surface tension of sympathetic people, with warm gratitude I learned, to my complete surprise, of the support of the world's writing fraternity. On my fiftieth birthday I was astounded to receive greetings from well-known European writers. No pressure put on me now passed unnoticed. During the dangerous weeks when I was being expelled from the Writers' Union,[2] THE PROTECTIVE WALL put forward by prominent writers of the world saved me from worse persecution, and Norwegian writers and artists hospitably prepared shelter for me in the event that I was exiled from my country. Finally, my being nominated for a Nobel Prize was originated not in the land where I live and write but by François Mauriac[3] and his colleagues. Afterward, national writers' organizations expressed unanimous support for me.

◄ **reciprocity** (res´ ə präs´ ə tē) *n.* relations of exchange; interdependence

As I have understood it and experienced it myself, world literature is no longer an abstraction or a generalized concept invented by literary critics, but a common body and common spirit, a living, heartfelt unity reflecting the growing spiritual unity of mankind. State borders still turn crimson, heated red-hot by electric fences and machine-gun fire; some ministries of internal affairs still suppose that literature is "an internal affair" of the countries under their jurisdiction; and newspaper headlines still herald, "They have no right to interfere in our internal affairs!" Meanwhile, no

1. **Heinrich** (hīn´ riH) **Böll** (böl) (1917–1985) German novelist and winner of the Nobel Prize in Literature.
2. **Writers' Union** official Soviet writers' organization, which enforced government policies on literature and gave privileges to writers. In addition to being expelled from this union, Solzhenitsyn was forbidden to live in Moscow.
3. **François** (frän swá´) **Mauriac** (mô´ rē ak´) (1885–1970) French novelist and essayist.

such thing as INTERNAL AFFAIRS remains on our crowded Earth. Mankind's salvation lies exclusively in everyone's making everything his business, in the people of the East being anything but indifferent to what is thought in the West, and in the people of the West being anything but indifferent to what happens in the East. Literature, one of the most sensitive and responsive tools of human existence, has been the first to pick up, adopt, and assimilate this sense of the growing unity of mankind. I therefore confidently turn to the world literature of the present, to hundreds of friends whom I have not met face to face and perhaps never will see.

My friends! Let us try to be helpful, if we are worth anything. In our own countries, torn by differences among parties, movements, castes, and groups, who for ages past has been not the dividing but the uniting force? This, essentially, is the position of writers, spokesmen of a national language, of the chief tie binding the nation, the very soil which the people inhabit, and, in fortunate circumstances, the nation's spirit too.

I think that world literature has the power in these frightening times to help mankind see itself accurately despite what is advocated by partisans and by parties. It has the power to transmit the condensed experience of one region to another, so that different scales of values are combined, and so that one people accurately and concisely knows the true history of another with a power of recognition and acute awareness as if it had lived through that history itself—and could thus be spared repeating old mistakes. At the same time, perhaps we ourselves may succeed in developing our own WORLDWIDE VIEW, like any man, with the center of the eye seeing what is nearby but the periphery of vision taking in what is happening in the rest of the world. We will make correlations and maintain worldwide standards.

Who, if not writers, are to condemn their own unsuccessful governments (in some states this is the easiest way to make a living; everyone who is not too lazy does it) as well as society itself, whether for its cowardly humiliation or for its self-satisfied weakness, or the lightheaded escapades of the young, or the youthful pirates brandishing knives?

We will be told: What can literature do against the pitiless onslaught of naked violence? Let us not forget that violence does not and cannot flourish by itself; it is inevitably intertwined with LYING. Between them there is the closest, the most profound and natural bond: nothing screens violence except lies, and the only way lies can hold out is by violence. Whoever has once announced violence as his METHOD must **inexorably** choose lying as his PRINCIPLE. At birth, violence behaves openly and even proudly. But as soon as it becomes

inexorably ▶
(in eks´ ə rə blē)
adv. without the possibility of being delayed or stopped

stronger and firmly established, it senses the thinning of the air around it and cannot go on without befogging itself in lies, coating itself with lying's sugary oratory. It does not always or necessarily go straight for the gullet; usually it demands of its victims only allegiance to the lie, only complicity in the lie.

◀ **oratory** (ôr′ ə tôr′ ē) *n.* act of public speaking; strategies used in such speaking

The simple act of an ordinary courageous man is not to take part, not to support lies! Let *that* come into the world and even reign over it, but not through me. Writers and artists can do more: they can VANQUISH LIES! In the struggle against lies, art has always won and always will. Conspicuously, incontestably for everyone. Lies can stand up against much in the world, but not against art.

Once lies have been dispelled, the repulsive nakedness of violence will be exposed—and hollow violence will collapse.

Writers and artists can do more: they can VANQUISH LIES!

That, my friends, is why I think we can help the world in its red-hot hour: not by the nay-saying of having no armaments,[4] not by abandoning oneself to the carefree life, but by going into battle!

In Russian, proverbs about TRUTH are favorites. They persistently express the considerable, bitter, grim experience of the people, often astonishingly:

ONE WORD OF TRUTH OUTWEIGHS THE WORLD.

On such a seemingly fantastic violation of the law of the conservation of mass and energy are based both my own activities and my appeal to the writers of the whole world.

---

4. **the nay-saying of having no armaments** Solzhenitsyn is referring to the idea that nations should limit the number or kind of weapons that they hold ready for war.

ABOUT THE AUTHOR

Alexander Solzhenitsyn (1918–2008)

Alexander Solzhenitsyn was born in the mountainous Caucasus region of southern Russia between the Black Sea and the Caspian Sea. He fought for the Soviet Union during World War II but was sent to a prison camp in 1945 for writing letters that were critical of Soviet leader Joseph Stalin. The author spent the next 11 years in prison camps, labor camps, and forced exile.

In Solzhenitsyn's first novel, *One Day in the Life of Ivan Denisovich* (1962), the author describes a typical day in the life of an inmate in a gulag, a Russian prison camp. Published in Russia during a brief relaxation of official censorship policies, the novel made Solzhenitsyn a celebrity overnight. The political climate in the Soviet Union soon changed, however, and Solzhenitsyn was denied official publication for his succeeding books. Nevertheless, his writings continued to circulate secretly in Russia and when published abroad increased his international reputation. In 1970, Solzhenitsyn was awarded the Nobel Prize in Literature.

Close Reading Activities

READ

Comprehension

Reread all or part of the text to help you answer the following questions.

1. In Solzhenitsyn's view, how has world literature today changed from what it was in the past?
2. State at least two ways in which Solzhenitsyn feels European writers helped him.
3. According to the author, what responsibility do writers hold toward their own societies?

Research: Clarify Details This speech may include references that are unfamiliar to you. Choose at least one unfamiliar detail and briefly research it. Then, explain how the information you learned from research sheds light on an aspect of the speech.

Summarize Write an objective summary of the speech. Remember that an objective summary is free from opinion and evaluation.

Language Study

Selection Vocabulary The phrases at right appear in "Nobel Lecture." Define each boldfaced word. Then, identify another word that shares the same root but has a different suffix.

- an almost instantaneous **reciprocity**
- must **inexorably** choose lying
- lying's sugary **oratory**

Literary Analysis

Reread the identified passage. Then, respond to the questions that follow.

Focus Passage *(pp. 736–737)*
We will be told ... complicity in the lie.

Key Ideas and Details

1. **(a)** According to the author, how does government violence behave "at birth"? **(b)** What happens as violence "becomes stronger"? Explain.

Craft and Structure

2. **(a) Define:** What is the difference between "method" and "principle"? **(b) Analyze:** How is violence a method and lying a principle?
3. **(a) Define:** What does Solzhenitsyn mean by "sugary oratory"? **(b) Connect:** Why might oratory in defense of violence be "sugary"? Explain.
4. **Interpret:** What is the author suggesting about the ways in which leaders of oppressive governments justify their **policies**? Explain.

Integration of Knowledge and Ideas

5. **Interpret:** According to the author, how does literature refuse "complicity in the lie"?

Rhetorical Devices

Rhetorical devices are word patterns that emphasize ideas and stir emotion. Reread the speech and note the author's use of rhetorical devices.

1. **(a)** Cite at least two examples of Solzhenitsyn's use of exclamation—an urgent message punctuated with an exclamation point. **(b)** For each example, explain both the content of the statement and the emotion it conveys.
2. **Conscientious Objections: (a)** What Russian proverb about truth does Solzhenitsyn quote? **(b)** How does this quote support the author's beliefs about the importance of literature?

DISCUSS • RESEARCH • WRITE

From Text to Topic **Panel Discussion**

Conduct a panel discussion about the following passage. Prepare for the discussion by reading the passage closely and taking notes. During the discussion, contribute your ideas, and support them with examples.

> The simple act of an ordinary courageous man is not to take part, not to support lies! Let *that* come into the world and even reign over it, but not through me. Writers and artists can do more: they can VANQUISH LIES! In the struggle against lies, art has always won and always will.

QUESTIONS FOR DISCUSSION

1. What is Solzhenitsyn saying about the power of ordinary people against an oppressive government?
2. In his view, what power do artists and writers have against a corrupt state?

Research **Investigate the Topic**

International PEN Founded in London in 1921, International PEN is a world organization of writers dedicated to promoting freedom of expression.

Assignment
Conduct research about the goals and activities of International PEN. Locate news stories and articles about the group's endeavors, and consult writings that are both laudatory and critical. Take clear notes and carefully record your sources. Share your findings in a **blog post** for the class.

PREPARATION FOR ESSAY

You may use the results of this research in an essay you will write at the end of this section.

Writing to Sources **Informative Text**

In his speech, Nobel **laureate** Alexander Solzhenitsyn celebrates the power of literature to unite the world and create **awareness** of our shared concerns.

Assignment
Write a **reflective essay** in which you discuss how your exposure to a work of world art, literature, or film gave you insight into the history and values of a different culture. Follow these steps:

- Clearly identify the work of art, literature, or film, and explain what it shows you about the culture from which it came.
- Relate your experience of seeing the art, reading the work, or watching the film to ideas Solzhenitsyn expresses in this speech.
- Use vivid, precise language to convey your experiences and insights.

ACADEMIC VOCABULARY

Academic terms appear in blue on these pages. Use a dictionary to find their definitions. Then, use them as you speak and write about the text.

Common Core State Standards

RI.9-10.1, RI.9-10.2, RI.9-10.4, RI.9-10.5, RI.9-10.6; W.9-10.2, W.9-10.2.d, W.9-10.4, W.9-10.6, W.9-10.7; SL.9-10.1; L.9-10.4.b, L.9-10.6

[For full standards wording, see the chart in the front of this book.]

SHORT STORY

THE CENSORS

Luisa Valenzuela

translated by David Unger

Poor Juan! One day they caught him with his guard down before he could even realize that what he had taken as a stroke of luck was really one of fate's dirty tricks. These things happen the minute you're careless, as one often is. Juancito let happiness—a feeling you can't trust—get the better of him when he received from a confidential source Mariana's new address in Paris and knew that she hadn't forgotten him. Without thinking twice, he sat down at his table and wrote her a letter. *The* letter that now keeps his mind off his job during the day and won't let him sleep at night (what had he scrawled, what had he put on that sheet of paper he sent to Mariana?).

Juan knows there won't be a problem with the letter's contents, that it's **irreproachable**, harmless. But what about the rest? He knows that they examine, sniff, feel, and read between the lines of each and every letter, and check its tiniest comma and most accidental stain. He knows that all letters pass from hand to hand and go through all sorts of tests in the huge censorship offices and that, in the end, very few continue on their way. Usually it takes months, even years, if there aren't any snags; all this time the freedom, maybe even the life, of both sender and receiver is in jeopardy. And that's why Juan's so troubled: thinking that something might happen to Mariana because of his letters. Of all people, Mariana, who must finally feel safe there where she always dreamt she'd live. But he knows that the *Censor's Secret Command* operates all over the world and cashes in on the discount in air fares; there's nothing to stop them from going as far as that hidden Paris neighborhood, kidnapping Mariana, and returning to their cozy homes, certain of having fulfilled their noble mission.

◀ **irreproachable** (ir′ i prō′ chə bəl) *adj.* above criticism

Well, you've got to beat them to the punch, do what everyone tries to do: sabotage the machinery, throw sand in its gears, get to the bottom of the problem so as to stop it.

This was Juan's sound plan when he, like many others, applied for a censor's job—not because he had a calling or needed a job: no, he applied simply to intercept his own letter, a consoling albeit unoriginal idea. He was hired immediately, for each day more and more censors are needed and no one would bother to check on his references.

ulterior ▶ (ul tir′ ē ər) *adj.* further; beyond what is openly stated or implied

Ulterior motives couldn't be overlooked by the *Censorship Division*, but they needn't be too strict with those who applied. They knew how hard it would be for the poor guys to find the letter they wanted and even if they did, what's a letter or two when the new censor would snap up so many others? That's how Juan managed to join the *Post Office's Censorship Division*, with a certain goal in mind.

staidness ▶ (stād′ nəs) *n.* state of being settled; calm

The building had a festive air on the outside that contrasted with its inner **staidness**. Little by little, Juan was absorbed by his job, and he felt at peace since he was doing everything he could to get his letter for Mariana. He didn't even worry when, in his first month, he was sent to *Section K* where envelopes are very carefully screened for explosives.

It's true that on the third day, a fellow worker had his right hand blown off by a letter, but the division chief claimed it was sheer negligence on the victim's part. Juan and the other employees were allowed to go back to their work, though feeling less secure. After work, one of them tried to organize a strike to demand higher wages for unhealthy work, but Juan didn't join in; after thinking it over, he reported the man to his superiors and thus got promoted.

You don't form a habit by doing something once, he told himself as he left his boss's office. And when he was transferred to *Section F*, where letters are carefully checked for poison dust, he felt he had climbed a rung in the ladder.

By working hard, he quickly reached *Section E* where the job became more interesting, for he could now read and analyze the letters' contents. Here he could even hope to get hold of his letter, which, judging by the time that had elapsed, had gone through the other sections and was probably floating around in this one.

Soon his work became so absorbing that his noble mission blurred in his mind. Day after day he crossed out whole paragraphs in red ink, pitilessly chucking many letters into the censored basket. These were horrible days when he was shocked by the subtle and conniving ways employed by people to pass on subversive messages; his instincts were so sharp that he found behind a simple "the weather's unsettled" or "prices continue to soar" the wavering hand of someone secretly scheming to overthrow the Government.

His zeal brought him swift promotion. We don't know if this made him happy. Very few letters reached him in *Section B*—only a handful passed the other hurdles—so he read them over and over again, passed them under a magnifying glass, searched for microprint with an electronic microscope, and tuned his sense of smell so that he was beat by the time he made it home. He'd barely manage to warm up his soup, eat some fruit, and fall into bed, satisfied with having done his duty. Only his darling mother worried, but she couldn't get him back on the right track. She'd say, though it wasn't always true: Lola called, she's at the bar with the girls, they miss you, they're waiting for you. Or else she'd leave a bottle of red wine on the table. But Juan wouldn't overdo it: any distraction could make him lose his edge and the perfect censor had to be alert, keen, attentive, and sharp to nab cheats. He had a truly patriotic task, both self-denying and uplifting.

His basket for censored letters became the best fed as well as the most cunning basket in the whole *Censorship Division.* He was about to congratulate himself for having finally discovered his true mission, when his letter to Mariana reached his hands. Naturally, he censored it without regret. And just as naturally, he couldn't stop them from executing him the following morning, another victim of his devotion to his work.

ABOUT THE AUTHOR

Luisa Valenzuela (b. 1938)

Born in Buenos Aires, Luisa Valenzuela first pursued a career as a painter, but she soon discovered her true gift was for writing. Like many other contemporary Latin American writers, Valenzuela takes an experimental approach to literary style and language. In an interview, she observed, "I feel that words possess power, they are charged with power which we have diluted and filed away so as to render words harmless.... One of the few duties of a writer is the restoration of the true meaning of words."

Close Reading Activities

READ

Comprehension

Reread all or part of the text to help you answer the following questions.

1. Why does Juan take a job as a censor?
2. Why is the Censorship Division not that careful about who they hire?
3. What is the result of Juan's zeal on the job?
4. What does Juan do when he finds his letter to Mariana?

Research: Clarify Details This short story may include references that are unfamiliar to you. Choose at least one unfamiliar detail, and briefly research it. Then, explain how the information you learned from research sheds light on an aspect of the short story.

Summarize Write an objective summary of the story. Remember that an objective summary is free from opinion and evaluation.

Language Study

Selection Vocabulary The following sentences appear in "The Censors." Define each boldface word, and explain the context clues that reveal its meaning.

- Juan knows there won't be a problem with the letter's contents, that it's **irreproachable,** harmless.
- **Ulterior** motives couldn't be overlooked by the *Censorship Division,* but they needn't be too strict with those who applied.
- The building had a festive air on the outside that contrasted with its inner **staidness.**

Literary Analysis

Reread the identified passage. Then, respond to the questions that follow.

Focus Passage *(p. 741)*

Juan knows ... so as to stop it.

Key Ideas and Details

1. Why does Juan fear for Mariana's safety even in "that hidden Paris neighborhood"?

Craft and Structure

2. **(a) Distinguish:** Identify four idiomatic expressions in the last paragraph of the focus passage and explain what each one means. **(b) Interpret:** What do these idioms convey about Juan's intentions? Explain.
3. **(a)** How does the *Censor's Secret Command* afford its global travels? **(b) Analyze:** What purpose does this detail serve in the paragraph? Explain.

Integration of Knowledge and Ideas

4. **(a) Connect:** What happens to Juan at the end of the story? **(b) Interpret:** Explain how the story's ending emphasizes the absurdity of the entire **premise** of censorship.

Tone

The **tone** of a literary work is the writer's attitude toward the subject or audience. Tone is created primarily through diction, or word choice. Reread the story, and take notes about the author's tone.

1. **(a)** Describe the author's tone in this story. **(b)** Cite three examples of diction that support your description.
2. How does the tone of the story contrast with the seriousness of its subject? Explain.
3. **Conscientious Objections:** Is this story an expression of protest? Explain, citing textual details.

DISCUSS • RESEARCH • WRITE

From Text to Topic **Small Group Discussion**

Discuss the following passage with a small group of classmates. Take notes during the discussion. Contribute your own ideas, and support them with examples from the text.

> But Juan wouldn't overdo it: any distraction could make him lose his edge, and the perfect censor had to be alert, keen, attentive, and sharp to nab cheats. He had a truly patriotic task, both self-denying and uplifting.

QUESTIONS FOR DISCUSSION

1. How does Juan's ambition to be a perfect censor demonstrate the changes in his character?
2. What does this passage suggest about the ways in which someone might come to accept ideas they had previously **reviled**?

Research **Investigate the Topic**

Dystopias and Utopias In this story, Luisa Valenzuela presents a glimpse of a dystopia, a dreadful society. The opposite of a dystopia is a utopia, an ideal society.

Assignment

Conduct research to find out about the contrasting literary traditions of utopia and dystopia, including the histories of the words themselves. Consult reliable print and electronic sources. Take careful notes and capture complete source information so that you can write accurate citations later. Share your findings in a **research summary.**

PREPARATION FOR ESSAY

You may use the results of this research in an essay you will write at the end of this section.

Writing to Sources **Argument**

"The Censors" might be described as a "dystopian fable," a morality story set in a dreadful society. Such stories may serve as cautionary tales—painting a picture of what can happen if the ideals that **regulate** a democratic society are lost.

Assignment

Write a **position paper** in which you discuss the value of contemplating a dystopia in literature, film, or visual art. Consider whether the artful presentation of a dystopia invites people to reflect on the strengths and possible weaknesses of their own society. Follow these steps:

- Introduce the topic and provide a clear statement of your position.
- Support your arguments with evidence from "The Censors" as well as other dystopian works with which you may be familiar.
- Provide clear transitions that help readers follow your line of reasoning.

ACADEMIC VOCABULARY

Academic terms appear in blue on these pages. If these words are not familiar to you, use a dictionary to find their definitions. Then, use them as you speak and write about the text.

Common Core State Standards

RL.9-10.1, RL.9-10.2, RL.9-10.4, RL.9-10.6; W.9-10.1, W.9-10.4, W.9-10.7, W.9-10.9; SL.9-10.1; L.9-10.4, L.9-10.6

[For full standards wording, see the chart in the front of this book.]

Culture of Shock

Stephen Reicher
and **S. Alexander Haslam**

In 1961 Stanley Milgram embarked on a research program that would change psychology forever. Fueled by a desire to understand how ordinary Germans had managed to participate in the horrors of the Holocaust, Milgram decided to investigate when and why people obey authority. To do so, he developed an ingenious experimental **paradigm** that revealed the surprising degree to which ordinary individuals are willing to inflict pain on others.

paradigm ▶ (par´ ə dīm´) *n.* model; example

Half a century later Milgram's obedience studies still resonate. They showed that it does not take a disturbed personality to harm others. Healthy, well-adjusted people are willing to administer lethal electric shocks to another person when told to do so by an authority figure. Milgram's findings convulsed the world of psychology and horrified the world at large. His work also left pressing questions about the nature of conformity unanswered. Ethical concerns have prompted psychologists to spend decades struggling to design equally powerful experiments without inflicting distress on the participants.

Researchers have now begun developing tools that allow them to probe deeper into his experimental setup. This work is pointing the way to new understandings of when and why people obey—and of the atrocities conformity can enable.

Obedience to Authority

When he began this project, Milgram had another goal in mind. He intended to assess whether some nationalities are more willing than others to conform to the wishes of an authority figure. His plan was to start studying obedience in the U.S. and then to travel to Europe to look for differences in behavior among populations there.

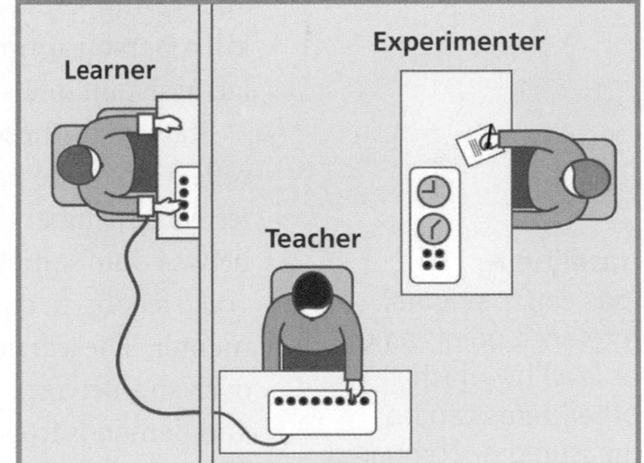

The topic of conformity was not new, and indeed Milgram had been heavily influenced by psychologist Solomon Asch, with whom he had studied in 1959 at the Institute for Advanced Study in Princeton, N.J. Asch had shown that when asked to make public judgments about the length of a line, people were often willing to bend to the views of their peers even when doing so meant defying the evidence of their own eyes.

Milgram suspected that Asch's results held hidden potential that might be revealed if he studied behaviors of greater social significance than simply judging lines. So Milgram designed an experiment in which participants—most of whom were men living near Yale University's psychology department, where the study was conducted—were told to act as a "teacher" assisting an experimenter in a study of memory. Their task was to administer a memory test to a learner, who in reality was an actor employed by Milgram. When this learner supplied an incorrect answer, the participant was to give him an electric shock. The ostensible goal was to investigate the impact of punishment on learning: Would the shocks improve the learners' performance or not?

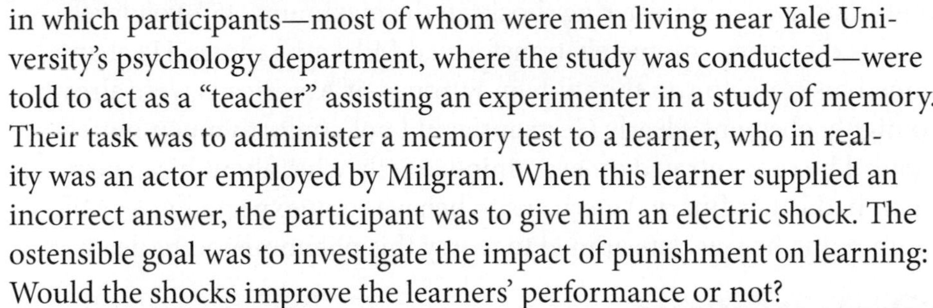

To administer the shocks, the teacher had in front of him a shock generator with 30 switches on its front panel. The buttons were arranged in ascending order from 15 volts, labeled with the words "slight shock," all the way up to 450 volts, ominously labeled "XXX." After each error the teacher had to depress the next switch to the right, increasing the jolt by 15 volts. Milgram was interested in seeing how far they would go. Would they administer a "strong shock" of 135 volts? What about an "intense shock" of 225 volts? Perhaps they would instead stop at 375 volts: "danger: severe shock." Surely, Milgram thought, very few subjects would go all the way—although people from some countries might go further than residents of other nations. In particular, he posited that Germans might be willing to deliver bigger shocks than Americans typically would.

Milgram was taken aback by what he found next. His initial pilot studies[1] with Yale students showed that people regularly followed the experimenter's instructions. Indeed, the vast majority continued pressing switches all the way to the highest voltage—well beyond the point at which the shocks would prove lethal.

Of course, the shock generator was not real, so the learners never really suffered. But the participants did not know this, so by all appearances Milgram's subjects seemed willing to deliver shocks sufficient to kill a person simply because they were asked to do so by a gray-coated lab assistant in a science experiment.

Startled by these findings, at first Milgram dismissed the results as a reflection of the particular nature of "Yalies." Only when he reran the studies with members of the broader American public did he begin to realize he was onto something big. In what became known as the **baseline**, or voice feedback, condition, the teacher sits in the same room as the experimenter. The learner is in another room, and communication occurs only over an intercom. As the shock levels increase, the learner expresses pain and demands to be released from the study. At 150 volts he cries out, "Experimenter, get me out of here! I won't be in the experiment any more! I refuse to go on!" Despite these pleas, 26 of the 40 participants, or 65 percent, continued administering shocks to the maximum, 450-volt level.

baseline ▶ (bās′ līn) *n.* original reference point, amount, or level by which other items can be measured or compared

This discovery completely transformed Milgram's career. He abandoned his plans to run the study in Europe—if Americans were already so highly obedient, clearly Germans could not conform much more. Instead he concentrated on examining exactly what about his experiment had led ordinary Americans to behave so unexpectedly. As Milgram put it, he was determined to worry this phenomenon to death.

Science of Defiance

Popular accounts of Milgram's work most often mention only the baseline study, with its 65 percent compliance. In fact, he conducted a very large number of studies. In his book from 1974, *Obedience to Authority,* Milgram describes 18 variants. He also conducted many studies to develop the paradigm that were never published. In one pilot experiment

1. **pilot studies** *n.* small experiments done in the early stages of full-scale research projects to help clarify or correct the overall project design.

Milgram, Arendt, and the Holocaust

While Milgram was conducting his studies at Yale University, the young German philosopher Hannah Arendt was sitting in a Jerusalem courtroom watching the trial of Adolf Eichmann. Eichmann, a key bureaucrat of the Holocaust, had arranged for Jews to be deported to the death camps. Everyone expected a person who had done such horrific things to look like a monster. But when he entered, people saw a slightly hunched, balding, and altogether nondescript character.

Arendt argued that this ordinariness was what made Eichmann truly frightening. He demonstrated that even the blandest functionary possesses the ability to do unspeakable things. She coined the phrase "the banality of evil," which, she argued, arises when people stop thinking about the consequences of their actions and instead concentrate on the details of the performance itself. She wrote that "Eichmann . . . never realized what he was doing."

Milgram is clear about his debt to Arendt. He wrote that "Arendt's conception of the banality of evil comes closer to the truth than one might dare imagine." Indeed, a combination of historical, philosophical, and psychological evidence supporting Arendt's idea made it a dominant view in academia, politics, and popular culture alike.

In recent years, however, historians have cast doubts on Arendt's account of Eichmann, just as psychologists have begun questioning Milgram's notion of the "agentic state." In a recent biography of Eichmann, historian David Cesarani concludes that his protagonist not only knew what he was doing but even celebrated the slaughter of Jews. More generally, even though "ordinary people" may have helped perpetrate the Holocaust, the claim that they were simply onlookers with no awareness of their actions is hard to sustain.

the learner provided no feedback to the participants—and almost every teacher went all the way to 450 volts. Another variant, in which participants helped in the study but did not actually depress the lever to deliver the shock, produced similar results.

When the subjects sat in the same room as the learner and watched as he was shocked, however, the percentage of obedient teachers went down to 40. It fell further when the participant had to press the learner's hand onto an electric plate to deliver the shock. And it went below 20 percent when two other "participants"—actually actors—refused to comply. Moreover, in three conditions nobody went up to 450 volts: when the learner demanded that shocks be delivered, when the authority was the victim of shocks, or when two authorities argued and gave conflicting instructions.

In short, Milgram's range of experiments revealed that seemingly small details could trigger a complete reversal of behavior—in other words, these studies are about both obedience and *dis*obedience. Instead of only asking why people obey, we need to ask when they obey and also when they do not.

In his various papers describing the studies, Milgram provides a rich and diverse set of explanations for his findings. He describes how the participants are presented with the experiments' worthy purpose to advance understanding, a goal the participants respect. He notes how a subject is often torn between the demands of the experimenter and the victim, with the one urging him to go on and the other pleading him to stop. He also expressed interest in the way other factors, such as the physical distance between the parties involved, might influence whom the participant listens to.

In the public eye, however, one theory has come to dominate: the idea that participants in the experiment enter into what Milgram terms

Experimenting with Ethics

In a biography of Milgram, psychologist Thomas Blass of the University of Maryland described the furor that ensued after the *New York Times* ran an article on Milgram's studies in 1963. An editorial in the *St. Louis Post-Dispatch* described the studies as "open-eyed torture." The famous psychoanalyst Bruno Bettelheim called Milgram's work "vile" and "in line with the human experiments of the Nazis." He was even attacked in *The Dogs of Pavlov,* a 1973 play by Welsh poet Dannie Abse. One character, Kurt, describes the setup of the obedience studies as . . . "fraudulent" and a "cheat."

Milgram responded robustly, claiming that "no one who took part in the obedience study suffered damage, and most subjects found the experience to be instructive and enriching." The data he collected from a questionnaire completed after each experiment are nuanced, however. Of the 656 participants in the studies, 84 percent said they were glad to have taken part, 15 percent were neutral, and a mere 1 percent were sorry. More than half admitted to some level of discomfort during the studies, but only about one third admitted to having felt troubled by them since—in this latter group, only 7 percent agreed that they had been "bothered by it quite a bit." Although Milgram was probably right in saying that most people were fine, it is equally probable that a minority suffered to some degree.

Still, the fact that Milgram collected these data demonstrates that he was attuned to the ethical issues and aware of their importance.

an "agentic state" in which they cede authority to the person in charge. He developed this idea partly from Hannah Arendt's famous analysis of Adolf Eichmann, a perpetrator of the Nazi Holocaust. As Milgram put it, "the ordinary person who shocked the victim did so out of a sense of obligation—a conception of his duties as a subject—and not from any peculiarly aggressive tendencies." In the face of authority, humans focus narrowly on doing as they are told and forget about the consequences of their actions. Their concern is to be a good follower, not a good person.

Milgram was a brilliant experimentalist, but many psychologists are profoundly skeptical of the idea of the agentic state. For one thing, the hypothesis cannot explain why the levels of conformity varied so greatly across different versions of the study. More broadly, this analysis focuses only on participants' obligations to the experimenter, although at several points in the studies they were also attuned to the fate of the learner.

When you examine the grainy footage of the experiments, you can see that the participants agonize visibly over how to behave. As Milgram recognized early on, the dilemma comes from their recognition of their duties to both the experimenter and the learner. They argue with the experimenter. They reflect the learner's concerns back to him. They search for reassurance and justification.

In fact, in designing the studies, Milgram anticipated this process. To make it somewhat more controlled, he devised four verbal prods, which the experimenter would use if the participant expressed doubts. A simple "please continue" was followed by "the experiment requires that you continue" and then "it is absolutely essential that you continue." The most extreme prompt was "you have no other choice, you *must* go on."

As psychologist Jerry Burger of Santa Clara University has observed, of these four instructions only the last is a direct order. In *Obedience,* Milgram gives an example of one reaction to this prod:

> Experimenter: You have no other choice, sir, you must go on.
> Subject: If this were Russia maybe, but not in America.
> *(The experiment is terminated.)*

In a recent partial replication of Milgram's study, Burger found that every time this prompt was used, his subjects refused to go on. This point is critically important because it tells us that individuals are not narrowly focused on being good followers. Instead they are more focused on doing the right thing.

The irony here is hard to miss. Milgram's findings are often portrayed as showing that human beings mindlessly carry out even the most extreme orders. What the shock experiments actually show is that we stop following when we start getting ordered around. In short, whatever it is that people do when they carry out the experimenter's bidding, they are not simply obeying orders.

Morality and Leadership

The fact that we could so easily be led to act in such extreme ways makes it all the more important to explore when and why this happens. But at the same time, it raises acute ethical issues that in fact render the necessary research unacceptable. As much as we wish to help society understand human atrocity, and thus prevent it, we also must not distress the participants in our studies who afterward will have to confront their own actions.

Obedient people are not mindless zombies after all.

For a long time, researchers conducted secondary analyses of Milgram's data, studied historical events, and designed experiments with less extreme behaviors, such as having subjects be negative about job applicants or squash bugs. No matter how clever the design, none of these studies investigated how humans can inflict extreme harm on one another as directly as Milgram's did, nor did they have the same impact or social relevance.

Recently this stalemate has begun to shake loose. Mel Slater, a computer scientist at University College London, has developed a virtual-reality **simulation** of the obedience paradigm. He has shown that people behave much the same way in this environment as they do in real contexts, and he has suggested that his simulation can serve as a new venue[2] for carrying out obedience experiments. Moreover, Burger has argued persuasively that those who obey the experimenter's instructions at 150 volts are most likely to carry on obeying right up to XXX. By stopping the trials at this level, then, we can address the same issues that Milgram did without actually asking people to inflict extreme harm on others—and having those individuals suffer later from the knowledge that they are willing to do so.

simulation ▶ (sim´ yo͞o lā´ shən) *n.* duplication or reproduction of certain characteristics or conditions from an original source; model or representation

The key issue remains: how to define the circumstances that enable people to inflict pain on others. Milgram himself suggested that group formation and identification might play a role in determining whether we side more with authority or its victims. Other studies closely related to Milgram's have flagged these same processes—notably Philip Zimbardo's prison experiment at Stanford University in 1971. Evidence suggests that we enact an authority figure's wishes only when we identify with

2. **venue** (ven´yo͞o´) *n.* site or situation where something takes place.

that person and his or her goals. In essence, obedience is a consequence of effective leadership. Followers do not lose their moral compass so much as choose particular authorities to guide them through the ethical dilemmas of everyday life. Obedient people are not mindless zombies after all.

This radical reinterpretation of Milgram's studies clearly requires more data to support it, as well as further debate. Sadly, the need for this debate is no less pressing today than it was in 1961. With the recent government-led massacres in Libya and Syria and the shadows of Abu Ghraib and Guantánamo Bay[3] hanging over us, we need more than ever to understand how people can be led to harm others—and how we can stop them.

---

3. **Abu Ghraib** (ä bo͞o′ greb′) . . . **Guantánamo** (gwän tä′nə mō′) **Bay** sites of U.S. detention centers where controversial interrogations involving torture of suspected terrorists were allegedly conducted. Abu Ghraib is in Iraq, and Guantánamo Bay is in Cuba.

ABOUT THE AUTHORS

Stephen Reicher and **S. Alexander Haslam**

Steve Reicher is professor of social psychology at the University of St. Andrews in Scotland. Alex Haslam is professor of psychology at the University of Queensland in Australia. Both are well known researchers in the area of crowd psychology. Reicher and Haslam collaborated on the award-winning BBC Prison Study, which explored the social and psychological consequences of putting people in groups of unequal power. The goal of the study was to determine when people will accept inequality and when they will challenge it. Findings from the study were broadcast by the BBC in 2002 and have since been published in leading scientific journals and textbooks.

Close Reading Activities

READ

Comprehension

Reread all or part of the text to help you answer the following questions.

1. What was Milgram's initial goal for his series of experiments?
2. Why did the results of Milgram's experiments horrify the public?
3. In Milgram's experiments, what factors tended to reverse participants' willingness to obey?

Research: Clarify Details This article may include references that are unfamiliar to you. Choose at least one unfamiliar detail and briefly research it. Then, explain how the information you learned from research sheds light on an aspect of the article.

Summarize Write an objective summary of the article. Remember that an objective summary is free from opinion and evaluation.

Language Study

Selection Vocabulary: Psychology The phrases at right appear in the article. State the scientific meaning of each boldfaced word. Then, identify a meaning for each word in a nonscientific context.

- an ingenious experimental **paradigm**
- In what became known as the **baseline**
- a virtual-reality **simulation** of the obedience paradigm

Literary Analysis

Reread the identified passage. Then, respond to the questions that follow.

Focus Passage *(pp. 747–748)*

To administer the shocks … in a science experiment.

Key Ideas and Details

1. What were Milgram's subjects supposed to do if "learners" made mistakes?
2. **Infer:** How were "teachers" in the experiments meant to comprehend the label "XXX"? Explain.

Craft and Structure

3. **(a) Distinguish:** Which sentences in the passage paraphrase Milgram's thoughts? **(b) Interpret:** What information do these paraphrases provide? **(c) Analyze:** Why do you think the authors chose to put the reader inside Milgram's thought process? Explain.

Integration of Knowledge and Ideas

4. **Connect:** How does the description of the scientist at the end of the passage relate to the idea from the sidebar of the "blandest **functionary**" and the "**banality** of evil"? Explain.

Expository Structure

The **structure** of a work refers to the way in which information is ordered. Reread the article and note how the authors structure information.

1. **(a)** What information is presented in the first three paragraphs? **(b)** What is the purpose of this section?
2. Explain how the authors group and order the following types of information: description of the main experiments; complexity of the findings; questions raised by the experiments; current investigations into Milgram's results.

DISCUSS • RESEARCH • WRITE

From Text to Topic **Panel Discussion**

Conduct a panel discussion about the following passage. Prepare by reading the passage closely and taking notes. During the discussion, evaluate the arguments classmates present, contribute your ideas, and support them with examples.

> In short, Milgram's range of experiments revealed that seemingly small details could trigger a complete reversal of behavior—in other words, these studies are about both obedience and *dis*obedience. Instead of only asking why people obey, we need to ask when they obey and also when they do not.

QUESTIONS FOR DISCUSSION

1. What complex view of human nature does this passage suggest?
2. How are ideas about obedience and disobedience related to conscientious objection?

Research **Investigate the Topic**

The Ethics of Research According to the authors, one of the responses of researchers to Milgram's study has been a decades-long struggle "to design equally powerful experiments without inflicting distress on the participants."

Assignment

Conduct research to learn about ethical standards for designing and conducting psychological research. Consult print and digital sources, including publications from professional organizations. Take clear notes, and carefully record your sources. Write an **annotated outline** of your findings and share them in a small group discussion.

PREPARATION FOR ESSAY

You may use the results of this research in an essay you will write at the end of this section.

Writing to Sources **Informative Text**

In their conclusion to this article, the authors state: "Evidence suggests that we enact an authority figure's wishes only when we identify with that person and his or her goals."

Assignment

Write an **editorial** in which you argue for the need to elect responsible, ethical leaders based on recent reinterpretations of the Milgram experiments. Develop a set of **criteria** for what makes a leader responsible and ethical, and suggest how voters might use such criteria to evaluate candidates for office.

- Incorporate details and evidence from "Culture of Shock."
- Organize related ideas in clear sections, and present them in a logical order.

ACADEMIC VOCABULARY

Academic terms appear in blue on these pages. If these words are not familiar to you, use a dictionary to find their definitions. Then, use them as you speak and write about the text.

Common Core State Standards

RI.9-10.1, RI.9-10.2, RI.9-10.4, RI.9-10.5; W.9-10.2, W.9-10.4, W.9-10.7, W.9-10.9; SL.9-10.1, SL.9-10.1.a, SL.9-10.3; L.9-10.3, L.9-10.4, L.9-10.6

[For full standards wording, see the chart in the front of this book.]

from

Army Regulation 600-43: Conscientious Objection

Department of the Army

1–5. Policy

a. Personnel who qualify as conscientious objectors under this regulation will be classified as such, consistent with the effectiveness and efficiency of the Army. However, requests by personnel for qualification as a conscientious objector after entering military service will not be favorably considered when these requests are—

(1) Based on a claim of conscientious objection that existed and satisfied the requirements for classification as a conscientious objector according to section 6(j) of the Military Selective Service Act, as amended (50 USC, App 456(j)), and other provisions of law when such a claim was not presented before dispatch of the notice of induction, enlistment, or appointment. Claims based on conscientious objection growing out of experiences before entering military service, however, which did not become fixed until after the person's entry into the service, will be considered.

(2) Based solely on conscientious objection claimed and denied on their merits by the Selective Service System before induction when application under this regulation is based on substantially the same grounds, or supported by substantially the same evidence, as the request that was denied under the Selective Service System.…

(3) Based solely upon policy, **pragmatism**, or **expediency**. Applicants who are otherwise eligible for conscientious objector status may not be denied that status simply because of their views on the nation's domestic or foreign policies.

pragmatism ▶ (prag′mə tiz′əm) *n.* attitude or outlook addressing actual practices, not theory or speculation; practicality

expediency ▶ (ek spē′dē ən sē) *n.* quality of being appropriate or suited to a particular goal

(4) Based on objection to a certain war.

(5) Based upon insincerity.

(a) The most important consideration is not whether applicants are sincere in wanting to be designated as a conscientious objector, but whether their asserted convictions are sincerely held. Sincerity is determined by an impartial evaluation of each person's thinking and living in totality, past and present. The conduct of persons, in particular their outward manifestation of the beliefs asserted, will be carefully examined and given substantial weight in evaluating their application.

(b) Relevant factors that should be considered in determining a person's claim of conscientious objection include training in the home and church; general **demeanor** and pattern of conduct; participation in religious

demeanor ▶ (di mēn′ər) *n.* outward behavior

activities; whether ethical or moral convictions were gained through training, study, contemplation, or other activity comparable in rigor and dedication to the processes by which traditional religious convictions are formulated; credibility of persons supporting the claim.

(c) Applicants may have sought release from the Army through several means simultaneously, or in rapid succession (medical or hardship discharge, and so forth). They may have some major commitments during the time their beliefs were developing that are inconsistent with their claim. They may have applied for conscientious objector status shortly after becoming aware of the prospect of undesirable or hazardous duty or having been rejected for a special program. The timing of their application alone, however, is never enough to furnish a basis in fact to support a disapproval. These examples serve merely as indicators that further inquiry as to the person's sincerity is warranted. Recommendations for disapproval should be supported by additional evidence beyond these indicators.

b. Care must be exercised not to deny the existence of beliefs simply because those beliefs are incompatible with one's own. Church membership or adherence to certain theological tenets[1] are not required to warrant separation or assignment to noncombatant training and service. Mere affiliation with a church or other group that advocates conscientious objection as a tenet of its creed does not necessarily determine a person's position or belief. Conversely, affiliation with a church group that does not teach conscientious objection does not necessarily rule out adherence to conscientious objection beliefs. Applicants may be or may have been a member of a church, religious organization, or religious sect; and the claim of conscientious objection may be related to such membership. If so, inquiry may be made as to their membership, the teaching of their church, religious organization or sect, as well as their religious activity. However, the fact that these persons may disagree with, or not subscribe to, some of the tenets of their church does not necessarily discredit their claim. The personal convictions of each person will dominate so long as they derive from the person's moral, ethical, or religious beliefs. The task is to decide whether the beliefs professed are sincerely held and whether they govern the claimant's actions in word and deed.

---

1. **tenets** (ten′its) *n.* principles; doctrines; beliefs

Close Reading Activities

READ

Comprehension

Reread all or part of the text to help you answer the following questions.

1. What is the purpose of this document?
2. Can someone qualify as a conscientious objector because he or she objects to a particular war?
3. Does membership in a church that objects to war automatically qualify someone as a conscientious objector?

Research: Clarify Details This document may include references that are unfamiliar to you. Choose at least one unfamiliar detail, and briefly research it. Then, explain how the information you learned from research sheds light on the text.

Summarize Write an objective summary of the text. Remember that an objective summary is free from opinion and evaluation.

Language Study

Selection Vocabulary The phrases at right appear in Army Regulation 600-43. Define each boldface word. Then, use the word in a sentence of your own.

- (3) Based solely upon policy, **pragmatism,** or **expediency.**
- general **demeanor** and pattern of conduct

Literary Analysis

Reread the identified passage. Then, respond to the questions that follow.

Focus Passage *(pp. 756–757)*

(a) The most important ... supporting the claim.

Key Ideas and Details

1. **Compare and Contrast:** Between what two types of sincerity does the statement distinguish?
2. **Generalize:** How does the U.S. Army consider an applicant's religious views when determining conscientious objector status?

Craft and Structure

3. **(a) Distinguish:** Which parallel grammatical structure appears in the first sentence? **(b) Interpret:** To what fact does this parallel structure call attention? Explain.
4. **(a) Define:** What does the phrase "outward **manifestation** of the beliefs asserted" mean? **(b) Connect:** Which details in paragraph *(b)* relate to that idea? Explain.

Integration of Knowledge and Ideas

5. **Evaluate:** Are the U.S. Army's standards for determining the sincerity of conscientious objector applicants fair? Explain your position.

Technical Terms

Technical terms are words that have particular meanings within a profession. Reread the document, and note its use of technical terms.

1. **(a)** What do the words *induction, enlistment,* and *appointment* mean in a military context? **(b)** What does the term *classification* mean in this context?
2. Why would technical terminology be particularly important in a document like this one that explains a law or official process? Explain.

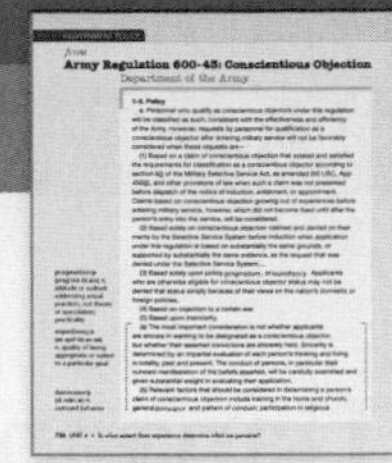

DISCUSS • RESEARCH • WRITE

From Text to Topic Group Discussion

Discuss the following passage with a group of classmates. Build on one another's ideas and support them with details from the text. Summarize your discussion to share with the class as a whole.

> Mere affiliation with a church or other group that advocates conscientious objection as a tenet of its creed does not necessarily determine a person's position or belief. Conversely, affiliation with a church group that does not teach conscientious objection does not necessarily rule out adherence to conscientious objection beliefs.

QUESTIONS FOR DISCUSSION

1. Which two religious positions on war are contrasted in this passage?
2. What does the passage indicate about the importance of religious **affiliation** in judging applicants for conscientious objector status?

Research Investigate the Topic

Conscientious Objection Around the World The United States military provides service people with the right to claim conscientious objection and defines strict **criteria** for qualification. Other countries also define positions on conscientious objection.

Assignment
Conduct research to learn how another country views conscientious objection to war. Research the policy of one other nation, and compare its positions to those of the United States. Consult reliable sources, including both print and online materials. Carefully organize your notes and source information. Share your findings in an **informal presentation.**

PREPARATION FOR ESSAY

You may use the results of this research in an essay you will write at the end of this section.

Writing to Sources Informative Text

One key concept addressed in the policy statement is that of sincerity.

Assignment
Write a **definition essay** in which you examine the concept of sincerity and propose a definition of this quality. Consider how sincerity might be expressed through a person's views about war. Follow these steps:

- Create an effective organization, using transitions to signal the movement from general concepts to specifics.
- Draw evidence from the U.S. Army policy statement about the personal convictions or beliefs that relate to sincerity.
- In your conclusion, summarize your ideas and offer an insight about how someone demonstrates sincerity.

ACADEMIC VOCABULARY

Academic terms appear in blue on these pages. Use a dictionary to find their definitions. Then, use them as you speak and write about the text.

Common Core State Standards

RI.9-10.1, RI.9-10.2, RI.9-10.4, RI.9-10.5; W.9-10.2, W.9-10.2.c, W.9-10.2.f, W.9-10.4, W.9-10.7; SL.9-10.1, SL.9-10.4; L.9-10.4, L.9-10.6
[For full standards wording, see the chart in the front of this book.]

Tiananmen Square "Tank Man," Beijing, China, 1989

ABOUT THE PHOTOGRAPH

In the spring of 1989, a series of pro-democracy demonstrations led by students occurred in various Chinese cities. During the night of June 3, the government ordered the military to disperse protesters assembled in Beijing's central Tiananmen Square. Tanks and heavily armed troops moved into the area, attacking those who tried to block their way. An unknown number of demonstrators were killed or wounded. By June 5, the military had already taken complete control when Jeff Widener of the Associated Press photographed a lone protester temporarily halting a column of tanks. Shortly after this photograph was taken, the man was escorted away from the tanks. It is unknown what became of the "Tank Man."

READ • RESEARCH • WRITE

Common Core State Standards

W.9-10.1, W.9-10.7
[For full standards wording, see the chart in the front of this book.]

Comprehension

Look at the photograph closely. Then, answer the following questions.

1. What type of environment does the photo depict? Explain.
2. What are the tanks doing, and what is the man doing?

Critical Analysis

Key Ideas and Details

1. **(a)** How is the man dressed? **(b)** What does he appear to be carrying? **(c) Infer:** Does the man seem to have prepared to take this action, or does it appear to have been an impulse? Explain your reasoning.

Craft and Structure

2. Where in relation to the scene in the street does the photographer seem to have been standing when he took this photograph? Explain.
3. **Interpret:** How does a sense of **scale**—the size of the space compared to the people and objects within it—contribute to the power of the photo?

Integration of Knowledge and Ideas

4. **Interpret:** What quality does the man's **isolation** give to his protest?
5. **(a) Deduce:** What can viewers gather about the man's character based on this image? **(b) Generalize:** What does this photograph express about the **integrity** of conscience? Explain.

ACADEMIC VOCABULARY

Academic terms appear in blue on these pages. If these words are not familiar to you, use a dictionary to find their definitions. Then, use them as you speak and write about the text.

Research **Investigate the Topic**

The Goddess of Liberty The "Tank Man" incident occurred during a series of Chinese pro-democracy demonstrations in the spring of 1989. Another iconic image from these demonstrations is a statue known as the Goddess of Democracy.

PREPARATION FOR ESSAY

You may use the results of this research in an essay you will write at the end of this section.

Assignment

Conduct research to learn about the "Goddess of Democracy." Provide details on how and where it was built and what it came to represent during the spring of 1989. Share your findings in a **visual presentation.**

Writing to Sources **Argument**

Write a brief **argumentative essay** in which you state and defend a position about the importance of images, such as photographs, in creating public awareness of injustice. Cite the "Tank Man" photograph as an example.

Speaking and Listening: Group Discussion

Conscientious Objections and Experience The texts in this section vary in genre, length, style, and perspective. All of them, however, comment in some way on the role of experience in shaping a person's moral perception, or conscience. This link between experience and conscience is fundamentally related to the Big Question addressed in this unit: **To what extent does experience determine what we perceive?**

▲ Refer to the selections you read in Part 3 as you complete the activities on this assessment.

Assignment

Conduct discussions. With a small group of classmates, conduct a discussion about the connection between conscience and experience. Refer to the texts in this section, other texts you have read, and your personal experience and knowledge to support your ideas. Begin your discussion by addressing the following questions:

- How are experience, perception, and conscience related?
- Which types of experiences shape a person's conscience?
- Is conscience one of the most important human qualities? Are any other qualities equally or more important than conscience?
- Under what circumstances might the exercise of conscience be negative or destructive?

Summarize and present your ideas. After you have fully explored the topic, summarize your discussion and present your findings to the class as a whole.

Criteria for Success

✓ **Organizes the group effectively**
Appoint a group leader and a timekeeper. The group leader should open the discussion with a question and present follow-up questions. The timekeeper should make sure the discussion takes no longer than 20 minutes.

✓ **Maintains discussion focus**
As a group, stay on topic and avoid straying into other subject areas.

✓ **Involves all participants equally and fully**
All group members should take turns speaking and contributing ideas equally and fully.

✓ **Follows the rules for collegial discussion**
All group members should share ideas in a respectful manner and use language appropriate to an academic setting. All participants should listen to one another carefully, build on one another's ideas, and support viewpoints with strong reasoning and evidence.

USE NEW VOCABULARY

As you speak and share ideas, work to use the vocabulary words you have learned in this unit. The more you use new words, the more you will "own" them.

Writing: **Narrative**

Common Core State Standards

W.9-10.3a–e, W.9-10.4; SL.9-10.1.a–d, SL.9-10.4, SL.9-10.6

[For full standards wording, see the chart in the front of this book.]

Conscientious Objections and Experience A shared experience is one that most people in a community have known. The community might be as small as a family or as large as an entire nation. Some shared experiences contribute to the formation and exercise of conscience.

> **Assignment**
> Write an **autobiographical narrative,** or true story about your own life, in which you describe how a shared experience shaped your conscience or how an act of conscience gave you a new perspective. Relate this experience to the texts that you have read and the research you have conducted in this section.

Criteria for Success

Purpose/Focus

✓ **Connects specific incidents with larger ideas**
Make meaningful connections between your experiences and the texts you have read in this section.

✓ **Clearly conveys the significance of the story**
Provide a conclusion in which you summarize and reflect on what you have experienced.

Organization

✓ **Sequences events logically**
Structure your narrative so that readers can easily follow the sequence of events and make connections to important ideas.

Development of Ideas/Elaboration

✓ **Supports insights**
Include both personal examples and details from the texts you have read in this section.

✓ **Uses narrative techniques effectively**
Include storytelling elements that add interest. Consider using interior monologues, or passages that reveal what a person is thinking.

Language

✓ **Uses descriptive language effectively**
Use sensory details and images that help readers visualize events.

Conventions

✓ **Does not have errors**
Check your narrative to eliminate errors in grammar, spelling, and punctuation.

WRITE TO EXPLORE

The writers whose work you have explored in this section care deeply about their topics. By writing your own narrative, you too can strengthen your ideas about conscience and experience.

Writing to Sources: **Argument**

Conscientious Objections and Experience The related readings in this section present a range of ideas about experience, perception, and conscience. They raise questions, such as the following, about how experience leads to individual acts of conscience and how individual actions can affect society as a whole.

- How might a person's perceptions and experiences contribute to his or her conscience?
- What relationship exists between the health of a society and the ethical or moral standing of its individual members?
- How might social conflict that arises from individual expressions of conscience serve a greater good?

Focus on the question that intrigues you the most, and then complete the following assignment.

Assignment

Write an **essay** in which you state and defend a claim about the relationship between perception, individual conscience, and the good of society. Build evidence for your claim by analyzing the presentation of perception, conscience, and society in two or more texts from this section. Clearly present, develop, and support your ideas with examples and details from the texts.

INCORPORATE RESEARCH

Strengthen your position by drawing on facts, quotations, and data you gathered while conducting research related to the readings in this section. Make sure to cite your sources correctly.

Prewriting and Planning

Choose texts. Review the texts in this section to determine which ones you will cite in your essay. Select two or more that will provide the strongest supporting material.

Gather details and craft a working thesis, or claim. Use a chart like the one shown to develop your ideas. Though you may refine or change your position as you write, the working version will establish a clear direction.

Focus Question: What relationship exists between the health of a society and the ethical or moral standing of its individual members?

Text	Passage	Notes
"Conscientious Objector"	With his hoof on my breast, I will not tell him where the black boy hides in the swamp.	The speaker's refusal to help Death makes society better.
"Culture of Shock"	What the shock experiments actually show is that we stop following when we start getting ordered around.	The Milgram experiments did not just document blind obedience and conformity.
Example Claim: Each individual's willingness to challenge injustice contributes to the overall well-being of a society.		

Prepare counterarguments. Anticipate counterclaims or differing positions and plan your response, including the evidence you will use to support your ideas.

Drafting

Structure your ideas and evidence. Present your ideas in a logical sequence. Use transitional words and phrases to clarify the relationships among your ideas and support each one with specific pieces of evidence.

Address counterclaims. Strong argumentation takes differing ideas into account and addresses them directly. As you order your ideas, build in sections in which you explain opposing opinions or differing interpretations. Then, write a reasoned, well-supported response to those counterclaims.

Frame and connect ideas. Write an introduction that will engage your reader from the outset. Then, write a strong conclusion that ends your essay with a clear, memorable statement. Use words, phrases, and clauses to link the major sections of your essay, and clarify the relationships between your positions and reasons, the evidence you cite, and your discussion of counterclaims.

Revising and Editing

Review content. Make sure that your claim is clearly stated and that you have supported it with strong evidence from the texts. To do so, underline the main ideas in your paper and check that you have supported each one sufficiently. Add more proof as needed.

Review style. Make sure you have not used inappropriately informal diction. Check that you have found the most precise and vivid way to communicate your ideas.

W.9-10.5; L.9-10.3.a

[For full standards wording, see the chart in the front of this book.]

CITING VISUAL SOURCES

Information from visual sources such as photographs can enhance your argument. See the Citing Sources pages in the Introductory Unit of this textbook for guidance on citing visual sources.

Self-Evaluation Rubric

Use the following criteria to evaluate the effectiveness of your essay.

Criteria	Rating Scale
PURPOSE/FOCUS Introduces a precise claim and distinguishes the claim from (implied) alternate or opposing claims; provides a concluding section that follows from and supports the argument presented	*not very* .... *very* 1 2 3 4
ORGANIZATION Establishes a logical organization; uses words, phrases, and clauses to link the major sections of the text, create cohesion, and clarify relationships among claims, reasons, and evidence, and between claims and counterclaims	1 2 3 4
DEVELOPMENT OF IDEAS/ELABORATION Develops the claim and counterclaims fairly, supplying evidence for each while pointing out the strengths and limitations of both	1 2 3 4
LANGUAGE Establishes and maintains a formal style and an objective tone	1 2 3 4
CONVENTIONS Attends to the norms and conventions of the discipline	1 2 3 4

Independent Reading

Titles for Extended Reading

In this unit, you have read texts in a variety of genres. Continue to read on your own. Select works that you enjoy, but challenge yourself to explore new authors and works of increasing depth and complexity. The titles suggested below will help you get started.

INFORMATIONAL TEXT

Black, Blue & Gray: African Americans in the Civil War
by Jim Haskins
Simon & Schuster, 1998

EXEMPLAR TEXT

In this engaging **nonfiction** book, Haskins describes the contributions of black soldiers—178,000 fighting for the North—during the Civil War. The book brings the story of these men to life with photographs, as well as authentic letters and diary entries.

Today's Nonfiction
Prentice Hall Library

This collection of **autobiographical narratives** brings together different styles and cultures. From Ernesto Galarza's story of learning English in school to Joan Didion's description of her visit to Pearl Harbor, each real-life story in this collection vividly captures a moment as unique as it is universal.

Democracy in America
Alexis de Tocqueville

In 1831, Frenchman Alexis de Tocqueville traveled throughout the United States for nearly a year. He was supposed to report on America's prisons but wound up writing with both precision and admiration about American society in general. The resulting two-volume work has become a classic of **political science**.

A Testament of Hope: The Essential Writings and Speeches of Martin Luther King, Jr.
Martin Luther King, Jr.

EXEMPLAR TEXT

This collection of Dr. Martin Luther King's famous **speeches** and other writings demonstrates King's hopes for America's future as a country that would one day honor and respect all citizens regardless of race, religion, or background. King's message and rhetoric is widely considered among the most stirring in American history.

LITERATURE

Sophocles: The Theban Plays
by Sophocles

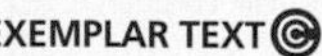

EXEMPLAR TEXT

In this book of three ancient Greek **plays**—*Oedipus the King, Oedipus at Colonus, and Antigone*—Sophocles tells the stories of the ill-fated characters Oedipus and his daughter Antigone. Oedipus becomes the victim of a tragic prophecy, whereas Antigone suffers the consequences of taking a principled stand.

A Raisin in the Sun
by Lorraine Hansberry
Vintage Books, 1994

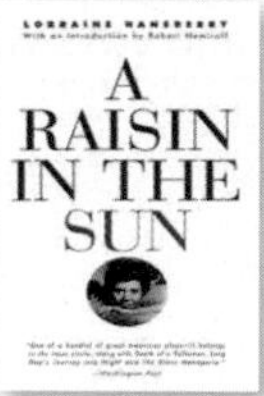

What would you do if you received a check for $10,000? This is the challenge the African American Younger family must confront. In Hansberry's **play,** family members clash over their perceptions of success and what this $10,000 should mean for them.

To Kill a Mockingbird
by Harper Lee

EXEMPLAR TEXT

In this classic **novel,** Harper Lee tells a story of racial prejudice in a fictional Alabama town during the Great Depression. The narrator is eight-year-old Scout Finch, a young girl whose father defends an innocent man in a trial that raises questions about race and justice in America.

ONLINE TEXT SET

REFLECTIVE ESSAY
from **In Commemoration: One Million Volumes** Rudolfo A. Anaya

EXPOSITORY ESSAY
Artful Research Susan Vreeland

NOVEL EXCERPT
from **Fahrenheit 451**
Ray Bradbury

Preparing to Read Complex Texts

Reading Literature/ Informational Text
10. By the end of Grade 10, read and comprehend literature, including stories, dramas, poems, and literary nonfiction at the high end of the grades 9–10 text complexity band independently and proficiently.

Attentive Reading As you read literature on your own, bring your imagination and questions to the text. The questions shown below and others that you ask as you read will help you learn and enjoy literature even more.

When reading drama, ask yourself...

Comprehension: **Key Ideas and Details**

- Who is the main character? What struggles does this character face?
- What other characters are important? How do these characters relate to the main character?
- Is there more than one conflict? If so, how do they connect?
- What is the setting of the play? Does the setting cause conflicts or affect the characters' actions? Why or why not?
- Is there more than one setting? If so, do the settings create different moods or conflicts?
- Are the characters, setting, and events believable? Why or why not?

Text Analysis: **Craft and Structure**

- How is the play structured? How many acts does it have? What events unfold in each act?
- Are there multiple plots—a main plot and a subplot? If so, how do the different plots relate to each other?
- Does the dialogue sound authentic and believable? Why or why not?
- What do the stage directions tell me about the characters and situations? In what other ways do I learn about the characters?
- At what point in the play do I feel the most concern for the characters? Why?

Connections: **Integration of Ideas**

- What theme or insight do I think the play conveys? Is that theme or insight important and true?
- What do I find most interesting, unusual, or powerful about this play?
- In what ways is the play similar to or different from others I have read or seen?
- What actors would I choose to play the roles in this play?
- If I were directing this play, how might I stage it?
- After reading this play, do I want to read others by this playwright? Why or why not?

© UNIT 5

THE BIG ? Can anyone be a hero?

UNIT PATHWAY

PART 1
SETTING EXPECTATIONS

- INTRODUCING THE BIG QUESTION
- CLOSE READING WORKSHOP

PART 2
TEXT ANALYSIS
GUIDED EXPLORATION

TIMELESS VOICES

PART 3
TEXT SET
DEVELOPING INSIGHT

THE ARTHURIAN LEGEND

PART 4
DEMONSTRATING INDEPENDENCE

- INDEPENDENT READING
- ONLINE TEXT SET

CLOSE READING TOOL

Use this tool to practice the close reading strategies you learn.

STUDENT eTEXT

Bring learning to life with audio, video, and interactive tools.

ONLINE WRITER'S NOTEBOOK

Easily capture notes and complete assignments online.

Find all Digital Resources at **pearsonrealize.com**

Introducing the Big Question

Can anyone be a hero?

In certain types of literature and many areas of popular culture, heroes are anything but ordinary people. They may be legendary knights who go on dangerous quests and never waiver in their loyalty or bravery. They may be noble figures with super powers that separate them even more from the vast population of regular people. However, in real life, heroes may not be so different from everyone else. Perhaps the hero is simply the person who, when the moment counts, makes a selfless decision. Perhaps the hero is the one child who stands up to a bully, or the neighbor who performs a small, even unnoticed, act of kindness. Is heroism possible for everyone? Can anyone be a hero?

Exploring the Big Question

Collaboration: Group Discussion Start thinking about the Big Question by making a list of people you have known, heard about, or read about who can be considered heroes. Describe one specific example of each of the following types of heroes:

- a legendary or mythical person who performs great deeds
- someone who helps others on a daily basis
- a person who makes a personal sacrifice in order to help others
- a courageous individual with a dangerous job
- a character in literature or a real person whose determination leads to great accomplishments

Share your responses with a partner. Discuss the traits that the hero in each example demonstrates. Then, decide which attributes you think truly define a hero.

As you talk, you may discover you have very different perspectives about heroism and heroes. Work to understand one another's ideas by posing meaningful questions and answering thoughtfully. Pause periodically to summarize ways in which you agree and disagree. Consider whether your partner's ideas help you to see the topic in new ways. Finally, gather your ideas into a brief report and share it with the class.

Connecting to the Literature Each reading in this unit will give you additional insight into the Big Question. After you read each selection, consider what it illustrates about the nature of heroism.

Vocabulary

Acquire and Use Academic Vocabulary The term "academic vocabulary" refers to words you typically encounter in scholarly and literary texts and in technical and business writing. It is the language that helps to express complex ideas. Review the definitions of these academic vocabulary words.

character (kar´ ik tər) *n.* moral strength or discipline

conduct (kän´dukt´) *n.* way in which a person behaves

inherent (in hir´ ənt) *adj.* existing in something or someone as permanent and inseparable

integrity (in teg´ rə tē) *n.* state of being of sound moral principle; uprightness

principles (prin´ sə pəls) *n.* rules for right conduct

resolute (rez´ ə lo͞ot´) *adj.* committed, determined, or firm

responsibility (ri spon´ sə bil´ ə tē) *n.* obligation or duty

Use these words as you complete Big Question activities in this unit that involve reading, writing, speaking, and listening.

Gather Vocabulary Knowledge Additional words related to heroism are listed below. Categorize the words by deciding whether you know each one well, know it a little bit, or do not know it at all.

attributes	**honor**	**sacrifice**
courage	**legendary**	**selflessness**
determination	**persevere**	

Then, complete the following steps:

1. Work with a partner to write each word on one side of an index card, with its definition on the other side.
2. Verify each definition by looking the word up in a print or online dictionary and revising its meaning as needed.
3. Place the cards in a pile with the words facing up.
4. Take turns drawing a word card. Pronounce the word on the front of the card, and use it in a true-or-false statement about heroes or heroism. For example, *Mario was commended for his* selflessness *when he helped his grandfather to safety*. Invite your partner to explain whether the statement is true or false.

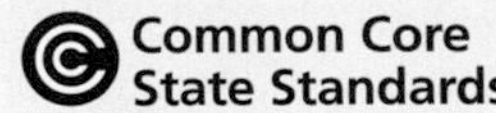
Common Core State Standards

Speaking and Listening

1. Initiate and participate effectively in a range of collaborative discussions with diverse partners on grades 9–10 topics, texts, and issues, building on others' ideas and expressing their own clearly and persuasively.

1.c. Propel conversations by posing and responding to questions that relate the current discussion to broader themes or larger ideas; actively incorporate others into the discussion; and clarify, verify, or challenge ideas and conclusions.

1.d. Respond thoughtfully to diverse perspectives, summarize points of agreement and disagreement, and, when warranted, qualify or justify their own views and understanding and make new connections in light of the evidence and reasoning presented.

Language

6. Acquire and use accurately general academic and domain-specific words and phrases, sufficient for reading, writing, speaking, and listening at the college and career readiness level; demonstrate independence in gathering vocabulary knowledge when considering a word or phrase important to comprehension or expression.

Close Reading Workshop

In this workshop, you will learn an approach to reading that will deepen your understanding of literature and will help you better appreciate the author's craft. The workshop includes models for the close reading, discussion, research, and writing activities you will complete as you study literature in this unit. After you have reviewed the strategies and models, practice your skills with the Independent Practice selection.

Common Core State Standards

RL.9-10.1, RL.9-10.2, RL.9-10.3, RL.9-10.4, RL.9-10.5, RL.9-10.6; W.9-10.7, W.9-10.9.a; SL.9-10.1

[For full standards wording, see the chart in the front of this book.]

CLOSE READING: WORLD LITERATURE

In Part 2 of this unit, you will focus on works of literature from different cultures. Use these strategies as you read the texts:

Comprehension: Key Ideas and Details

- Read first for basic meaning.
- Use context clues to help you determine the meanings of unfamiliar words. Consult a dictionary, if necessary.
- Identify unfamiliar details, such as place names or cultural references, that you might need to clarify through research.
- Distinguish between what a character or the narrator states directly and what readers must infer.

Ask yourself questions such as these:

- Who are the main characters? What conflicts do they face?
- How do the characters interact? How do their interactions reveal their personality traits?
- What is the setting? Does the setting contribute to the conflict?

Text Analysis: Craft and Structure

- Consider how the genre of the work shapes both the story and the readers' expectations.
- Identify specific details that reflect the work's cultural context.
- Take note of archetypes—character types, plot patterns, and images that are common to literature across time and culture.
- Consider the mood of the story and note how events build in intensity.

Ask yourself questions such as these:

- What view of human nature and society does the work express?
- Do characters display multiple, complex traits or are they flat and one-dimensional? Do characters change?
- What emotions or ambitions motivate characters? Do these ambitions seem universal or culturally specific?

Connections: Integration of Knowledge and Ideas

- Look for connections among key ideas. Note causes and effects, and comparisons and contrasts.
- Notice details, such as social order or customs, that are culturally specific and others, such as individuals' emotions, that seem universal.

Ask yourself questions such as these:

- What does the main character learn? Does that lesson suggest a deeper insight about life?
- Does this story remind me of others I have read? If so, in what ways is it similar and different?
- Does this story have a moral or teach a lesson? If so, what is it?

Read

As you read this excerpt from a novel, take note of the annotations that model ways to closely read the text.

In his novel *Things Fall Apart,* Nigerian author Chinua (chin yōō ä) Achebe (ä chā bā) depicts the impact of British colonization on traditional Ibo tribal culture. This excerpt is from Chapter 1 of the novel.

Reading Model

from *Things Fall Apart* by Chinua Achebe

Okonkwo was well known throughout the nine villages and even beyond. His fame rested on solid personal achievements. As a young man of eighteen he had brought honor to his village by throwing Amalinze the Cat. Amalinze was the great wrestler who for seven years was unbeaten, from Umuofia to Mbaino. He was called the Cat because his back would never touch the earth. It was this man that Okonkwo threw in a fight[1] which the old men agreed was one of the fiercest since the founder of their town engaged a spirit of the wild for seven days and seven nights.[2]

The drums beat and the flutes sang and the spectators held their breath. Amalinze was a wily craftsman, but Okonkwo was as slippery as a fish in water. Every nerve and every muscle stood out on their arms, on their backs and their thighs, and one almost heard them stretching to breaking point. In the end Okonkwo threw the Cat.

That was many years ago, twenty years or more, and during this time Okonkwo's fame had grown like a bush-fire in the *harmattan*.[3] He was tall and huge, and his bushy eyebrows and wide nose gave him a very severe look. He breathed heavily, and it was said that, when he slept, his wives and children in their houses could hear him breathe. When he walked, his heels hardly touched the ground and he seemed to walk on springs, as if he was going to pounce on somebody. And he did pounce on people quite often. He had a slight stammer and whenever he was angry and could not get his words out quickly enough, he would use his fists. He had no patience with unsuccessful men.[4] He had had no patience with his father.

Unoka, for that was his father's name, had died ten years ago. In his day he was lazy and improvident and was quite incapable of thinking about tomorrow. If any money came his way, and it seldom did, he immediately bought gourds of palm-wine, called round his neighbors and made merry.[5] He always said that whenever he saw a dead man's mouth he saw the folly of not eating what one had in one's lifetime. Unoka was, of course, a debtor, and he owed every neighbor some money, from a few cowries to quite substantial amounts.

Key Ideas and Details

1 Okonkwo is an archetypal hero—one whose traits mirror those of heroes in stories across time and culture. His extended community of "nine villages" admires Okonkwo for his physical strength and athleticism.

Craft and Structure

2 The elders compare Okonkwo's battle to one of local legend. The founding of a village by a hero is an archetypal plot pattern, as is the concept of a battle that lasts for many days.

Key Ideas and Details

3 You might research the noun *harmattan* to learn that it refers to a hot, dry wind that blows on the northwest Atlantic coast of Africa. This detail adds to the authenticity of the setting.

Key Ideas and Details

4 Okonkwo's actions and attitudes show what kind of man he is—aggressive, impatient, and proud.

Craft and Structure

5 Note the dramatic contrast that Achebe presents between the aggressive son, Okonkwo, and his passive father. In Ibo culture, the father was considered a failure because he lacked strength and aggression.

He was tall but very thin and had a slight stoop. He wore a haggard and mournful look except when he was drinking or playing on his flute. He was very good on his flute, and his happiest moments were the two or three moons after the harvest when the village musicians brought down their instruments, hung above the fireplace. Unoka would play with them, his face beaming with blessedness and peace. Sometimes another village would ask Unoka's band and their dancing *egwugwu* to come and stay with them and teach them their tunes. They would go to such hosts for as long as three or four markets, making music and feasting. Unoka loved the good fare and the good fellowship, and he loved this season of the year, when the rains had stopped and the sun rose every morning with dazzling beauty. [6] And it was not too hot either, because the cold and dry harmattan wind was blowing down from the north. Some years the harmattan was very severe and a dense haze hung on the atmosphere. Old men and children would then sit round log fires, warming their bodies. Unoka loved it all, and he loved the first kites[7] that returned with the dry season, and the children who sang songs of welcome to them. He would remember his own childhood, how he had often wandered around looking for a kite sailing leisurely against the blue sky. As soon as he found one he would sing with his whole being, welcoming it back from its long, long journey, and asking it if it had brought home any lengths of cloth.

That was years ago, when he was young. Unoka, the grown-up, was a failure. He was poor and his wife and children had barely enough to eat. People laughed at him because he was a loafer, and they swore never to lend him any more money because he never paid back. But Unoka was such a man that he always succeeded in borrowing more, and piling up his debts.[8]

One day a neighbor called Okoye came in to see him. He was reclining on a mud bed in his hut playing on the flute. He immediately rose and shook hands with Okoye, who then unrolled the goatskin which he carried under his arm, and sat down. Unoka went into an inner room and soon returned with a small wooden disc containing a kola nut, some alligator pepper and a lump of white chalk.

"I have kola," he announced when he sat down, and passed the disc over to his guest.

Integration of Knowledge and Ideas

6 Achebe presents Ibo society in all its complexity, countering European stereotypes of Africans as "primitive." The details about Ibo customs, fellowship, and appreciation of food and beauty reveal a rich and sophisticated cultural heritage.

Key Ideas and Details

7 You might consult an encyclopedia to learn that a kite is a bird of prey found throughout the warm regions of the world. The African version ranges from Nigeria to Somalia.

Craft and Structure

8 This direct statement cements Achebe's contrast of father and son. The strong son is considered a hero; the passive, musical father is considered a failure.

"Thank you. He who brings kola brings life. But I think you ought to break it," replied Okoye, passing back the disc.

"No, it is for you, I think," and they argued like this for a few moments before Unoka accepted the honor of breaking the kola. Okoye, meanwhile, took the lump of chalk, drew some lines on the floor, and then painted his big toe.

As he broke the kola, Unoka prayed to their ancestors for life and health, and for protection against their enemies.[9] When they had eaten they talked about many things: about the heavy rains which were drowning the yams, about the next ancestral feast and about the impending war with the village of Mbaino. Unoka was never happy when it came to wars. He was in fact a coward and could not bear the sight of blood. And so he changed the subject and talked about music, and his face beamed. He could hear in his mind's ear the blood-stirring and intricate rhythms of the *ekwe* and the *udu* and the *ogene*, and he could hear his own flute weaving in and out of them, decorating them with a colorful and plaintive tune. The total effect was gay and brisk, but if one picked out the flute as it went up and down and then broke up into short snatches, one saw that there was sorrow and grief there.[10]

Okoye was also a musician. He played on the *ogene*. But he was not a failure like Unoka. He had a large barn full of yams and he had three wives. And now he was going to take the Idemili title, the third highest in the land.[11] It was a very expensive ceremony and he was gathering all his resources together. That was in fact the reason why he had come to see Unoka. He cleared his throat and began:

"Thank you for the kola. You may have heard of the title I intend to take shortly."

Having spoken plainly so far, Okoye said the next half a dozen sentences in proverbs. Among the Ibo the art of conversation is regarded very highly, and proverbs are the palm-oil with which words are eaten. Okoye was a great talker and he spoke for a long time, skirting round the subject and then hitting it finally. In short, he was asking Unoka to return the two hundred cowries he had borrowed from him more than two years before. As soon as Unoka understood what his friend was driving at, he burst out laughing. He laughed loud and long and his voice rang out clear as the *ogene*, and tears stood in his eyes. His visitor was amazed, and sat speechless....

Craft and Structure

9 These details suggest that spiritual devotion to ancestors is an important part of Ibo culture and may play a role in the story's events.

Craft and Structure

10 Unoko's thoughts about music hint at the author's point of view: There is beauty and joy as well as sorrow in Ibo culture and in life.

Integration of Knowledge and Ideas

11 Here, Achebe begins to set up yet another contrast: Okoye is wealthy and successful, while Unoka is a failure. These contrasts, as well as those introduced earlier between Okonkwo and his father, introduce themes of status and ambition. Through descriptions of Ibo culture, Achebe also introduces the theme of tradition. The author will develop these thematic strands throughout the novel.

Discuss

Sharing your own ideas and listening to the ideas of others can deepen your understanding of a text and help you look at a topic in a whole new way. As you participate in collaborative discussions, work to have a genuine exchange in which classmates build upon one another's ideas. Support your points with evidence and ask meaningful questions.

Discussion Model

Student 1: It's interesting that in traditional Ibo culture, "success" has to do with physical strength, ambition, competition, and power. It's like today's professional athletes or popular politicians or even successful businesspeople. This story may take place in a different culture, but I think those ideas of physical strength and success are universal.

Student 2: But I thought Achebe seemed most sympathetic toward Unoka, the "weak" one. I think that Unoka has the best qualities for leadership. He wants to avoid war, he enjoys culture, and he shows respect for others and for tradition.

Student 3: That's true, so maybe that connection to tradition is important in this story. I wonder how the Ibo values and beliefs might have changed when Britain colonized that part of Africa. There must be information about how British rules, laws, and traditions affected the Ibo people.

Research

Targeted research can clarify unfamiliar details and shed light on various aspects of a text. Consider questions that arise in your mind as you read, and use those questions as the basis for research.

Research Model

Questions: *How did Ibo culture change under British rule?*

Key Words for Internet Search: Ibo AND Nigeria AND country AND history AND study

Result: *A Country Study: Nigeria,* Federal Research Division, Library of Congress

What I Learned: The Ibo people settled in Africa in what is now Nigeria as early as the eighth century. These deep cultural roots were weakened by Britain's presence in the region, which began in 1861. The British introduced the English language and Christianity to the Ibo, who believed in and respected ancestral spirits. After several years of British control, however, some Ibo people began to fight for their independence, which they finally earned in 1960.

Write

Writing about a text will deepen your understanding of it and will also allow you to share your ideas more formally with others. The following model essay analyzes Achebe's portrayals of characters and cites evidence to support the main ideas.

Writing Model: Informative Text

Achebe's Characters: A Collision of Values

In this excerpt from the novel *Things Fall Apart,* Chinua Achebe presents two archetypal characters—Okonkwo and his father, Unoka—who have widely different beliefs and traits. He then introduces a third character, Okoye, who holds a more balanced value system.

The writer introduces a specific claim in the first paragraph.

Okonkwo represents traditional masculinity in both appearance and his ambitious pursuit of status. He is huge and physically fit, with bushy eyebrows and "a very severe look." As a young man, he gained fame as a fierce fighter, triumphing over a wrestler who had been unbeaten for seven years. As an adult, Okonkwo is revered as a hero and widely feared. Unable to speak clearly due to a stammer, he reacts with his fists when angry. He is an aggressive and intolerant man.

The writer supports the claim by citing specific details about Okonkwo's traits and actions.

Okonkwo is particularly irritated with Unoka, his own father. Unoka is the complete opposite of his son. He is thin and often wears a "haggard and mournful look." He is considered a failure because he does not appreciate money, status, or ambition. He lives in the moment, and he finds his greatest joys in music and culture. Okonkwo and others in the village see Unoka as a coward because he hates war and prays for life, health, and for protection against his people's enemies. He openly laughs when his friend Okoye, who pretends to call on Unoka for a friendly visit, reveals that he has come primarily to collect a debt.

Next, the writer cites evidence regarding Unoka, directly contrasting him with Okonkwo.

Okoye is a blend between the two archetypes. Like Unoka, he enjoys music and is a man of culture. He shows respect for Unoka and the traditions of their village. However, Okoye is also similar to Okonkwo in that Okoye is successful and ambitious. Okoye combines and builds on the strengths of both Unoka and Okonkwo without developing their weaknesses. He also adds an important leadership skill: he is an eloquent speaker.

The writer presents evidence about Okoye, then compares and contrasts him to the two previous archetypes.

What will happen to these characters and their value systems once the British become a dominant force in their region in 1914? Achebe's title—*Things Fall Apart*—provides a strong clue that the British arrival will not bring happy times. Unoka does not have his people's respect, and Okonkwo's aggressive nature is not conducive to diplomacy. Of the three characters, Okoye may be the best candidate to guide his people through a period of drastic change. Already respected by his people for his wealth and success, he is a man of culture with a politician's talent for smooth, persuasive speech.

Based on research, the writer concludes by relating the characters to the conflict the Ibo will face. Then, based on textual evidence, the writer explains why Okoye would be the best leader during this difficult time.

As you read the following short story, apply the close reading strategies you have learned. You may need to read the story multiple times to fully understand the sequence of events, appreciate the development of characters, and analyze the deeper meaning or theme.

Meet the Author

Award-winning author **Anita Desai** was born in 1937 in India to a German mother and an Indian father. As a child, she learned to speak German, Hindi, and English, and she published her first story at the age of nine. Today, Desai writes novels and short stories in English and is widely regarded as one of India's foremost writers.

Vocabulary ▶
arid (arʹ id) *adj.* completely dry; lifeless

CLOSE READING TOOL

Read and respond to this selection online using the **Close Reading Tool.**

Games at Twilight

by Anita Desai

It was still too hot to play outdoors. They had had their tea, they had been washed and had their hair brushed, and after the long day of confinement in the house that was not cool but at least a protection from the sun, the children strained to get out. Their faces were red and bloated with the effort, but their mother would not open the door, everything was still curtained and shuttered in a way that stifled the children, made them feel that their lungs were stuffed with cotton wool and their noses with dust and if they didn't burst out into the light and see the sun and feel the air, they would choke.

"Please, Ma, please," they begged. "We'll play in the veranda and porch—we won't go a step out of the porch."

"You will, I know you will, and then—"

"No—we won't, we won't," they wailed so horrendously that she actually let down the bolt of the front door so that they burst out like seeds from a crackling, over-ripe pod into the veranda, with such wild, maniacal yells that she retreated to her bath and the shower of talcum powder and the fresh sari[1] that were to help her face the summer evening.

They faced the afternoon. It was too hot. Too bright. The white walls of the veranda glared stridently in the sun. The bougainvillea hung about it, purple and magenta, in livid balloons. The garden outside was like a tray made of beaten brass, flattened out on the red gravel and the stony soil in all shades of metal—aluminum, tin, copper and brass. No life stirred at this **arid** time of day—the birds still drooped, like dead fruit, in the papery tents of the trees; some squirrels lay limp on the wet earth under the garden tap. The outdoor dog lay stretched as if dead on the veranda mat, his paws and ears and tail

1. **sari** (säʹ rē) *n.* a long piece of cloth wrapped around the body, with one end forming a skirt and the other end draped over one shoulder; the traditional garment of Indian women.

all reaching out like dying travelers in search of water. He rolled his eyes at the children—two white marbles rolling in the purple sockets, begging for sympathy—and attempted to lift his tail in a wag but could not. It only twitched and lay still.

Then, perhaps roused by the shrieks of the children, a band of parrots suddenly fell out of the eucalyptus tree, tumbled frantically in the still, sizzling air, then sorted themselves out into battle formation and streaked away across the white sky.

The children, too, felt released. They too began tumbling, shoving, pushing against each other, frantic to start. Start what? Start their business. The business of the children's day which is—play.

"Let's play hide-and-seek."

"Who'll be It?"

"You be It."

"Why should I? You be—"

"You're the eldest—"

"That doesn't mean—"

The shoves became harder. Some kicked out. The motherly Mira **intervened**. She pulled the boys roughly apart. There was a tearing sound of cloth but it was lost in the heavy panting and angry grumbling and no one paid attention to the small sleeve hanging loosely off a shoulder.

◀ **Vocabulary**
intervened (in′ tər vēnd′) *v.* came between

"Make a circle, make a circle!" she shouted, firmly pulling and pushing till a kind of vague circle was formed. "Now clap!" she roared and, clapping, they all chanted in melancholy unison: "Dip, dip, dip—my blue ship—" and every now and then one or the other saw he was safe by the way his hands fell at the crucial moment—palm on palm, or back of hand on palm—and dropped out of the circle with a yell and a jump of relief and jubilation.

Raghu was It. He started to protest, to cry "You cheated—Mira cheated—Anu cheated—" but it was too late, the others had all already streaked away. There was no one to hear when he called out, "Only in the veranda—the porch—Ma said—Ma *said* to stay in the porch!" No one had stopped to listen, all he saw were their brown legs flashing through the dusty shrubs, scrambling up brick walls, leaping over compost heaps and hedges, and then the porch stood empty in the purple shade of the bougainvillea and the garden was as empty as before; even the limp squirrels had whisked away, leaving everything gleaming, brassy and bare.

Only small Manu suddenly reappeared, as if he had dropped out of an invisible cloud or from a bird's claws, and stood for a moment in the center of the yellow lawn, chewing his finger and near to tears as he heard Raghu shouting, with his head pressed against the veranda wall, "Eighty-three, eighty-five, eighty-nine, ninety . . ." and then made off in a panic, half of him wanting to fly north, the other half counseling south. Raghu turned just in time to see the flash of his white shorts and the uncertain skittering of his red sandals, and charged after him with such a bloodcurdling yell that Manu stumbled over the hosepipe, fell into its rubber coils and lay there weeping, "I won't be It—you have to find them all—all—All!"

"I know I have to, idiot," Raghu said, superciliously[2] kicking him with his toe. "You're dead," he said with satisfaction, licking the beads of perspiration off his upper lip, and then stalked off in search of worthier prey, whistling spiritedly so that the hiders should hear and tremble.

Ravi heard the whistling and picked his nose in a panic, trying to find comfort by burrowing the finger deep—deep into that soft tunnel. He felt himself too exposed, sitting on an upturned flower pot behind the garage. Where could he burrow? He could run around the garage if he heard Raghu come—around and around and around—but he hadn't much faith in his short legs when matched against Raghu's long, hefty, hairy footballer legs. Ravi had a frightening glimpse of them as Raghu combed the hedge of crotons and hibiscus, trampling delicate ferns underfoot as he did so. Ravi looked about him desperately, swallowing a small ball of snot in his fear.

The garage was locked with a great heavy lock to which the driver had the key in his room, hanging from a nail on the wall under his work-shirt. Ravi had peeped in and seen him still sprawling on his string-cot in his vest and striped underpants, the hair on his chest and the hair in his nose shaking with the vibrations of his phlegm-obstructed snores. Ravi had wished he were tall enough, big enough to reach the key on the nail, but it was impossible, beyond his reach for years to come. He had sidled away and sat **dejectedly** on the flower pot. That at least was cut to his own size.

Vocabulary ▶ dejectedly (dē jek′ tid lē) *adv.* in a depressed way

But next to the garage was another shed with a big green door. Also locked. No one even knew who had the key to the lock. That shed wasn't opened more than once a year when Ma turned out all the old broken bits of furniture and rolls of matting and leaking buckets, and the white ant hills were broken and swept away and Flit sprayed into the spider webs and rat holes so that the whole operation was like the looting of a poor, ruined and conquered city. The green leaves of the door sagged. They were nearly off their rusty hinges. The hinges were large and made a small gap between the door and the walls—only just large enough for rats, dogs, and, possibly, Ravi to slip through.

Ravi had never cared to enter such a dark and depressing mortuary of **defunct** household goods seething with such unspeakable and alarming animal life but, as Raghu's whistling grew angrier and sharper and his crashing and storming in the hedge wilder, Ravi suddenly slipped off the flower pot and through the crack and was gone. He chuckled aloud with astonishment at his own temerity[3] so that Raghu came out of the hedge, stood silent with his hands on his hips, listening, and finally shouted "I

Vocabulary ▶ defunct (dē fuŋkt′) *adj.* no longer in use or existence

---

2. **superciliously** (so͞o′ pər sil′ ē əs lē) *adv.* haughtily; in a manner expressing pride in oneself and scorn for the other person.
3. **temerity** (tə mer′ ə tē) *n.* recklessness; foolish boldness.

heard you! I'm coming! *Got* you—" and came charging round the garage only to find the upturned flower pot, the yellow dust, the crawling of white ants in a mud-hill against the closed shed door—nothing. Snarling, he bent to pick up a stick and went off, whacking it against the garage and shed walls as if to beat out his prey.

Ravi shook, then shivered with delight, with self-congratulation. Also with fear. It was dark, spooky in the shed. It had a muffled smell, as of graves. Ravi had once got locked into the linen cupboard and sat there weeping for half an hour before he was rescued. But at least that had been a familiar place, and even smelled pleasantly of starch, laundry and, reassuringly, of his mother. But the shed smelled of rats, ant hills, dust and spider webs. Also of less definable, less recognizable horrors. And it was dark. Except for the white-hot cracks along the door, there was no light. The roof was very low. Although Ravi was small, he felt as if he could reach up and touch it with his finger tips. But he didn't stretch. He hunched himself into a ball so as not to bump into anything, touch or feel anything. What might there not be to touch him and feel him as he stood there, trying to see in the dark? Something cold, or slimy—like a snake. Snakes! He leapt up as Raghu whacked the wall with his stick—then quickly realizing what it was, felt almost relieved to hear Raghu, hear his stick. It made him feel protected.

But Raghu soon moved away. There wasn't a sound once his footsteps had gone around the garage and disappeared. Ravi stood frozen inside the shed. Then he shivered all over. Something had tickled the back of his neck. It took him a while to pick up the courage to lift his hand and explore. It was an insect—perhaps a spider—exploring *him*. He squashed it and wondered how many more creatures were watching him, waiting to reach out and touch him, the stranger.

There was nothing now. After standing in that position—his hand still on his neck, feeling the wet splodge of the squashed spider gradually dry—for minutes, hours, his legs began to tremble with the effort, the inaction. By now he could see enough in the dark to make out the large solid shapes of old wardrobes, broken buckets and bedsteads piled on top of each other around him. He recognized an old bathtub—patches of enamel glimmered at him and at last he lowered himself onto its edge.

He contemplated slipping out of the shed and into the fray. He wondered if it would not be better to be captured by Raghu and be returned to the milling crowd as long as he could be in the sun, the light, the free spaces of the garden and the familiarity of his brothers, sisters and cousins. It would be evening soon. Their games would become legitimate. The parents would sit out on the lawn on cane basket chairs and watch them as they tore around the garden or gathered in knots to share a loot of mulberries or black, teeth-splitting *jamun* from the garden trees. The gardener would fix the hosepipe to the water tap and water would fall lavishly through the air to the ground, soaking the dry yellow grass and the red gravel and arousing the sweet, the intoxicating scent of water on dry earth—that loveliest scent in the world. Ravi sniffed for a whiff of it. He half-rose from the bathtub, then heard the despairing scream of one of the girls as Raghu bore down upon her. There was the sound of a crash, and of rolling about in the bushes, the shrubs, then screams and accusing sobs of, "I touched the den—" "You did not—" "I did—" "You liar, you did not" and then a fading away and silence again.

Ravi sat back on the harsh edge of the tub, deciding to hold out a bit longer. What fun if they were all found and caught—he alone left unconquered! He had never known that sensation. Nothing more wonderful had ever happened to him than being taken out by an uncle and bought a whole slab of chocolate all to himself, or being flung into the soda-man's pony cart and driven up to the gate by the friendly driver with the red beard and pointed ears. To defeat Raghu—that hirsute,[4] hoarse-voiced football champion—and to be the winner in a circle of older, bigger, luckier children—that would be thrilling beyond imagination. He hugged his knees together and smiled to himself almost shyly at the thought of so much victory, such laurels.[5]

There he sat smiling, knocking his heels against the bathtub, now and then getting up and going to the door to put his ear to the broad crack and listening for sounds of the game, the pursuer and the pursued, and then returning to his seat with the dogged determination of the true winner, a breaker of records, a champion.

Vocabulary ▶
dogged (dôg´ id) *adj.* stubborn

It grew darker in the shed as the light at the door grew softer, fuzzier, turned to a kind of crumbling yellow pollen that turned to yellow fur, blue fur, gray fur. Evening. Twilight. The sound of water gushing, falling. The scent of earth receiving water, slaking its thirst in great gulps and releasing that green scent of freshness, coolness. Through the crack Ravi saw the long purple shadows of the shed and the garage lying still across the yard. Beyond that, the white walls of the house. The bougainvillea had lost its lividity, hung in dark bundles that quaked and twittered and seethed with masses of homing sparrows. The lawn was shut off from his view. Could he hear the children's voices? It seemed to him that he could. It seemed to him that he could hear them chanting, singing, laughing. But what about the game? What had happened? Could it be over? How could it when he was still not found?

---

4. **hirsute** (hur´ so͞ot´) *adj.* hairy.
5. **laurels** (lôr´ əlz) *n.* leaves of the laurel tree; worn in a crown as an ancient symbol of victory in a contest.

It then occurred to him that he could have slipped out long ago, dashed across the yard to the veranda and touched the "den." It was necessary to do that to win. He had forgotten. He had only remembered the part of hiding and trying to **elude** the seeker. He had done that so successfully, his success had occupied him so wholly that he had quite forgotten that success had to be clinched by that final dash to victory and the ringing cry of "Den!"

◀ **Vocabulary**
elude (ē lo͞od′) *v.* escape or avoid

With a whimper he burst through the crack, fell on his knees, got up and stumbled on stiff, benumbed legs across the shadowy yard, crying heartily by the time he reached the veranda so that when he flung himself at the white pillar and bawled, "Den! Den! Den!" his voice broke with rage and pity at the disgrace of it all and he felt himself flooded with tears and misery.

Out on the lawn, the children stopped chanting. They all turned to stare at him in amazement. Their faces were pale and triangular in the dusk. The trees and bushes around them stood inky and sepulchral,[6] spilling long shadows across them. They stared, wondering at his reappearance, his passion, his wild animal howling. Their mother rose from her basket chair and came toward him, worried, annoyed, saying, "Stop it, stop it, Ravi. Don't be a baby. Have you hurt yourself?" Seeing him attended to, the children went back to clasping their hands and chanting "The grass is green, the rose is red. . . . "

But Ravi would not let them. He tore himself out of his mother's grasp and pounded across the lawn into their midst, charging at them with his head lowered so that they scattered in surprise. "I won, I won, I won," he bawled, shaking his head so that the big tears flew. "Raghu didn't find me. I won, I won—"

It took them a minute to grasp what he was saying, even who he was. They had quite forgotten him. Raghu had found all the others long ago. There had been a fight about who was to be It next. It had been so fierce that their mother had emerged from her bath and made them change to another game. Then they had played another and another. Broken mulberries from the tree and eaten them. Helped the driver wash the car when their father returned from work. Helped the gardener water the beds till he roared at them and swore he would complain to their parents. The parents had come out, taken up their positions on the cane chairs. They had begun to play again, sing and chant. All this time no one had remembered Ravi. Having disappeared from the scene, he had disappeared from their minds. Clean.

"Don't be a fool," Raghu said roughly, pushing him aside, and even Mira said, "Stop howling, Ravi. If you want to play, you can stand at the end of the line," and she put him there very firmly.

---

6. sepulchral (sə pul′ krəl) *adj.* of the tomb; gloomy.

The game proceeded. Two pairs of arms reached up and met in an arc. The children trooped under it again and again in a lugubrious[7] circle, ducking their heads and intoning

"The grass is green,
The rose is red;
Remember me
When I am dead, dead, dead, dead . . ."

And the arc of thin arms trembled in the twilight, and the heads were bowed so sadly, and their feet tramped to that melancholy refrain so mournfully, so helplessly, that Ravi could not bear it. He would not follow them, he would not be included in this funereal game. He had wanted victory and triumph—not a funeral. But he had been forgotten, left out and he would not join them now. The ignominy[8] of being forgotten—how could he face it? He felt his heart go heavy and ache inside him unbearably. He lay down full length on the damp grass, crushing his face into it, no longer crying, silenced by a terrible sense of his insignificance.

---

7. **lugubrious** (lə go͞o´ brē əs) *adj.* very sad, especially in an exaggerated or ridiculous way.
8. **ignominy** (ig´ nə min´ ē) *n.* shame and dishonor.

Close Reading Activities

Read

Comprehension: **Key Ideas and Details**

1. **(a)** How does Ravi think it would feel to be "the winner in a circle of older, bigger, luckier children"? **(b) Draw Conclusions:** What do his feelings show about his view of the other children? Explain.
2. **(a) Infer:** Why do the other children stop searching for Ravi? **(b) Draw Conclusions:** What do the other children think of Ravi? Give details from the story to support your answer.
3. **(a)** What mistake causes Ravi to lose the game? **(b) Interpret:** What lesson does he learn at the end of the story? Support your answer with details from the text.
4. **Summarize:** Write a brief, objective summary of the story. Cite story details in your writing.

Text Analysis: **Craft and Structure**

5. **(a) Distinguish:** Identify a suspenseful moment in the story. **(b) Analyze:** How does the author's portrayal of both Ravi's situation and his internal struggles contribute to that suspenseful moment? Use story details to explain.
6. **(a) Interpret:** What archetypal characters or plot patterns, if any, do you find in this story? Explain. **(b) Analyze:** How might the story be different if it were told through Raghu's eyes? Explain.
7. **(a) Interpret:** How important is the setting—time, place, and conditions—to the plot of this story? Explain. **(b) Draw Conclusions:** Which aspects of the setting most affect Ravi's conflicts? Explain.
8. **(a) Interpret:** Are Ravi's conflicts settled at the end of the story? Explain. **(b) Synthesize:** Describe an alternative ending for the story. Then, explain how this alternative ending would express a different message or theme than does the original version. Cite story details in your response.

Connections: **Integration of Knowledge and Ideas**

Discuss

Conduct a **small group discussion** about the cause-and-effect chain that moves the plot forward the moment Ravi enters the shed. For example, discuss how the lock on the shed door is a major link in the chain.

Research

This story is set in India during the 1940s, specifically during the hot season. Briefly research the climate of South Asia. Find facts about the following seasonal weather patterns:

a. the names of the seasons and how they progress

b. the duration of the hot season

c. the average daytime temperatures during the various seasons

Take notes as you perform your research. Then, write a brief **explanation** of how the climate of the setting affects the plot of this story.

Write

Most games are fair, but sometimes they favor some people over others. Write an **essay** in which you analyze the game and the players in this story. Explain whether you feel the game in the story is "fair" or should be played by specific rules. Cite details from the story to support your analysis and conclusions.

THE BIG ? Can anyone be a hero?

As Ravi hides during the game, he imagines himself as a "true winner, a breaker of records, a champion." Did he become the hero he created in his mind? Why or why not? Explain your answer.

"I will tell you
something about
stories...They are
all we have...
to fight off illness
and death."
—Leslie Marmon Silko

PART 2

TEXT ANALYSIS GUIDED EXPLORATION

TIMELESS VOICES

Every culture in every age has its stories of both heroes and fools. Some survive the centuries because they capture universal truths, showing what it means to be human regardless of one's culture or the era in which one lives. As you read the timeless works in this section, consider what each suggests about the qualities that make ordinary people heroic and the faults that make heroes human. Then, think about the answers these selections suggest to the Big Question for this unit: **Can anyone be a hero?**

◀ CRITICAL VIEWING What types of characters and stories do you think this ancient Greek vase depicts? Which details in this image support your perceptions?

READINGS IN PART 2

CLOSE READING TOOL

Use the **Close Reading Tool** to practice the strategies you learn in this unit.

Focus on Craft and Structure

Elements of the Oral Tradition

In the **oral tradition**, storytellers pass along stories by word of mouth, preserving shared **cultural values**.

Long before the invention of writing and books, singers and storytellers recited the tales and lore of their cultures. Passed from one generation to the next, the poems and stories they told are referred to as the **oral tradition.** Through the oral tradition, the stories of different cultures have been preserved through the ages.

The oral tradition is a treasure trove of tragic, exciting, and funny stories. In their day, these stories also served as a powerful tool for education. By giving memorable, moving examples of heroes and monsters, of deeds both good and bad, the oral tradition helped a culture answer questions such as "What should I be like?" and "What should I do?"

Like other literature, stories from the oral tradition express **themes**—insights about life and human nature. One important source of these themes is the **cultural experience** of the storytellers—their core values and concerns. At the same time, these stories express **universal themes,** or truths about life that are meaningful to people of all times and all places. Examples of universal themes include the virtues of courage and the dangers of greed.

In telling their tales, traditional storytellers often used **archetypes**—characters, situations, images, or symbols that recur in the narratives of all cultures. The chart below gives examples of some archetypes.

Storytellers in the oral tradition explore **universal themes**—insights into life that recur throughout world literature. Often, they develop these themes using **archetypes.** The use of archetypal patterns probably made stories easier to remember and retell.

Examples of Archetypal Characters

- The **wise and virtuous ruler,** whose reign brings in a golden age, or time of peace and prosperity
- The **dreamer** or **transgressor,** a character who imagines new possibilities and defies danger to bring an important gift to society
- The **hero,** an unpromising youth who triumphs over stronger forces through cleverness or virtue and blossoms into a wise, strong, and courageous leader

Examples of Archetypal Patterns

- The struggle between the **protagonist,** or main character, and the **antagonist,** a person or force that opposes the protagonist
- A series of tests that a character must pass
- A quest or task that a character must complete
- Characters, events, or objects that come in threes
- A fair and just end that rewards good or punishes evil

Forms and Characteristics of the Oral Tradition

Generations of storytellers in the oral tradition developed narrative forms following the same basic patterns. These forms are found in nearly every culture, and include myths, folk tales, legends, fairy tales, and epics.

Traditional stories in these forms do not express an individual author's **point of view,** or attitudes and beliefs about the world. (Indeed, historians have no way of identifying the original authors of most folk literature.) Instead, stories in these forms tend to express the shared **values,** or model behaviors and attitudes, cherished by the society from which they originated.

Despite that fact, individual storytellers did leave their marks on these tales. As the tales were retold and passed down, the storytellers sometimes changed narrative details, resulting in different versions of the same basic story. For example, stories about King Arthur have been retold throughout the ages, through various forms—poetry, song, and novel—and set in different places and time periods.

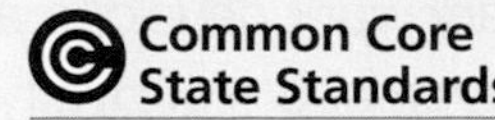

Reading Literature

2. Determine a theme or central idea of a text and analyze in detail its development over the course of the text, including how it emerges and is shaped and refined by specific details; provide an objective summary of the text.

6. Analyze a particular point of view or cultural experience reflected in a work of literature from outside the United States, drawing on a wide reading of world literature.

Narrative Forms in the Oral Tradition

Form	Characteristics
Myths	• Explain the actions of gods and their interactions with humans • May explain the causes of natural phenomena or the origins of cultural traditions
Folk Tales	• Deal with heroic acts, adventures, magic, or romance; often concern the relationship between mortals and gods • Focus on human or animal heroes
Legends	• Are folk tales about larger-than-life heroes and events from the past • Often are based on historical fact, with factual details becoming exaggerated and fictionalized over time
Fairy Tales	• Are similar to folk tales but generally involve royal characters • Include magic or supernatural elements
Epics	• Are long narrative poems that use elevated language and extended, elaborate comparisons of unlike subjects called epic similes • Combine features of myths and legends • Describe the adventures of larger-than-life **epic heroes,** who are important to the history of their cultures • Often tell of the heroes' journeys or quests, on which the heroes are helped or hindered by gods and other supernatural creatures • Often begin with the poet's mention of the subject and a plea to a divine being for inspiration and guidance in the telling of the tale

Analyzing Theme

A literary work develops a **theme**, or central message or insight, which may be **universal** or **culturally specific**.

The **theme** of a work is the insight it conveys into life or human nature. To develop a theme, a story combines narrative elements, such as characters, setting, and plot, in ways that express an underlying meaning. Usually, the theme of a story is not directly stated, although a character may make statements that suggest it. Instead, the theme is usually implied, or indirectly expressed, by the arrangement of story elements.

Literary Elements The following literary elements often contribute to the development of theme:

- Characters—the people, animals, or creatures that take part in the action
- Setting—the time and place of a story
- Plot—the sequence of events in a story
- Conflict—the struggle between opposing forces that drives the plot
- Archetypes—patterns of story elements that recur across cultures and often have strong associations

Theme and Point of View An author's **point of view,** or perspective, consists of the author's thoughts and attitude about a topic. Point of view is often closely tied to theme. For example, if an author believes that society is too preoccupied with money, the author might convey themes about the dangers of losing touch with the natural world.

To recognize an author's point of view, focus on the way the author describes settings, situations, characters, and characters' actions. Pay close attention to the author's **diction,** or word choice, which can indicate positive or negative attitudes.

Development of Theme To understand how narrative elements can be used to develop a theme, consider the story outlined in the following example.

Story Element	Development of Theme
Characters: One brother is selfish. The other is generous.	This contrast between characters encourages you to focus on ideas of selfishness and generosity.
Conflict: The selfish brother is robbed, but none of his friends will help him because he is mean-spirited.	Selfishness is connected to a bad outcome—it deprives a person of the help of others. This connection refines the theme.
Plot: The kind brother lends the selfish brother the money he needs.	The contrast between selfishness and generosity is reinforced.
Character's Insight: The selfish brother thanks the kind brother and begs his forgiveness.	This insight further develops the idea that it is better to be generous than selfish.
Theme: It is better to be generous than selfish.	

While the example story does not state its theme directly, an alert reader will find the theme developed through the patterns and associations the story creates using literary elements.

Theme and Cultural Experience Point of view and theme are influenced by the author's **cultural experiences**—the events, beliefs, and values that shape the culture in which the author lives. Those cultural experiences may be reflected in the values and beliefs characters hold as well as in the practices and customs they follow.

In works from the oral tradition, readers often do not distinguish the teller's point of view from that of the culture as a whole. A work is taken to "speak for" its entire culture.

Universal and Culturally Specific Themes

While a given cultural experience may shape a work in important ways, the work may still convey a **universal theme**—an insight into life that recurs in the literature of various times and places. At the same time, a work may express themes that are **culturally specific;** they reflect the particular circumstances and beliefs of the author's culture. Consider the example of "Pandora's Box," a Greek myth. The work conveys both universal and culturally specific themes.

Pandora's Box	Universal Themes	Culturally Specific Themes
When Zeus created Pandora, he bestowed many wonderful gifts on her, including a box that he told her never to open. However, among her other gifts was curiosity, which caused Pandora to open the box. When she did, all the previously unknown evils and horrors of the world escaped.	• Unbridled curiosity can lead to trouble. • We must follow the rules or deal with he consequences.	• It is risky for mortals to ignore the gods. • The gods know what is best for mortals.

Shifting Points of View As stories were passed down through the oral tradition, story details changed as the point of view of the authors changed. Consider, for example, how a changing view of the world affected retellings of the traditional fairy tale "Snow White."

Example: Snow White Because the Queen is jealous of her stepdaughter, the beautiful Snow White, she plots to kill her.
German Version: "Little Snow White"—retold by the Brothers Grimm in 1812, based on original Old World tales **Point of View:** Reflects the cruel, chaotic, and violent medieval view of the world **Details:** The Queen asks a huntsman to take Snow White into the woods, kill her, and bring back her liver and lungs, which are to be served for dinner. In the end, the Queen dances herself to death at Snow White's wedding in a pair of burning-hot iron shoes.
English Version: "Snow Drop"—retold by Edgar Taylor in 1823 **Point of View:** Reflects a softer, kinder view of the world **Details:** The Queen asks a huntsman to take Snow Drop away but does not request proof of the girl's death. Snow Drop dies from eating a poisoned apple, but revives when the chunk of apple falls from her mouth. In the end, the Queen dies after choking with anger at Snow Drop's wedding.

Theme and Point of View in Nonfiction

Like works in the oral tradition, modern fiction expresses themes. In addition, some literary nonfiction may be said to have themes. For example, a writer may tell true stories of friendship that illustrate the central idea, or theme, that our friends know us better than we know ourselves. Literary nonfiction may also present an author's point of view explicitly, as when the writer argues a position, or implicitly, as when a true story suggests an author's beliefs and attitudes.

Building Knowledge

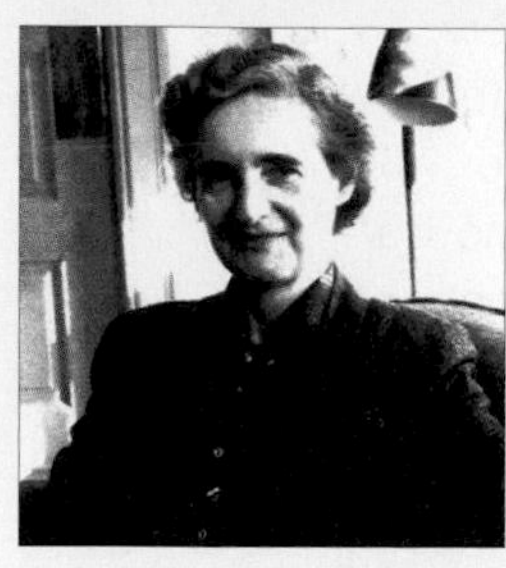

Meet the Author

Author and educator **Olivia E. Coolidge** (1908–2006) wrote twenty-seven books, mainly biographies and historical fiction, during a distinguished career. She received numerous awards for her work, including the prestigious Newbery Honor for children's literature.

Can anyone be a hero?

Explore the Big Question as you read this myth. Note details that challenge the reader about the qualities that make someone heroic.

CLOSE READING FOCUS

Key Ideas and Details: **Analyzing Cultural Context**

The cultural context of a literary work is the set of values, beliefs, traditions, and experiences that define the society in which it is set. To understand a myth, **analyze cultural context,** or determine how the story reflects the perspectives of those who told it. Before you read, generate questions, such as the following, about the cultural context.

- Where did the myth-tellers live? How did their surroundings affect their customs and beliefs?
- How did the myth-tellers obtain food, water, and shelter? How did these activities affect their values?
- What personal qualities did the myth-tellers admire?

Craft and Structure: **Myths**

Myths are stories from the oral tradition: Before being written down, they were retold from one generation to the next. All myths reflect the beliefs and values of their cultures of origin.

- Some myths explain how the world was made or how a natural feature or custom came to be.
- Myths feature heroes who embody personal qualities the culture admired. Myths also feature fantastic or supernatural characters who may be helpful, harmful, or both.
- Some myths tell of a quest for knowledge or an important object. Other myths tell of a transgression, or the violation of a rule.

Vocabulary

The words below are critical to understanding the text that follows. Which is an adjective? Explain how you know.

toil	**heedless**	**inhabit**
counsel	**disembarked**	**endure**

Common Core State Standards

Reading Literature

1. Cite strong and thorough textual evidence to support analysis of what the text says explicitly as well as inferences drawn from the text.

6. Analyze a particular point of view or cultural experience reflected in a work of literature from outside the United States.

7. Analyze the representation of a subject or a key scene in two different artistic mediums.

CLOSE READING MODEL

The passage below is from Olivia Coolidge's retelling of "Prometheus and the First People." The annotations to the right of the passage show ways in which you can use close reading skills to analyze cultural context and the elements of myths.

from "Prometheus and the First People"

Before this time fire was a divine thing and belonged only to the gods. It was one of their greatest treasures, and Zeus would never have given Prometheus permission to use it in the creation of man.[1] Therefore when Prometheus stole it, Zeus was furious indeed. He chained Prometheus to a great, lofty rock, where the sun scorched him by day and the cruel frost tortured him by night. Not content with that, he sent an eagle to tear him, so that, though he could not die, he lived in agony.[2] For many centuries Prometheus hung in torment, but he was wiser than Zeus, and by reason of a secret he had, he forced Zeus in later ages to set him free. By then, also, Zeus had learned that there is more in ruling than power and cruelty. Thus, the two at last were friends.[3]

Myths

1 This myth explains the origins of fire on Earth. Prometheus stole this divine property—"one of their greatest treasures"—from the gods and gave it to humanity. Prometheus' theft was a transgression, a violation of a divine rule. However, it also advances the development of humanity.

Analyze Cultural Context

2 Zeus' grueling punishment of Prometheus both reflects the extreme nature of the crime and shows that the Greeks viewed the gods as somewhat exaggerated versions of people. Zeus exhibits the human qualities of both possessiveness (over fire itself) and extreme anger.

Analyze Cultural Context

3 Prometheus' wisdom ultimately sets him free and restores his friendship with Zeus. This suggests that the Greeks valued reason, wisdom, and intelligence. The fact that Zeus grows in understanding is another clue that the Greeks saw the gods as imperfect, prone to error but also capable of change.

Prometheus and the First People

Olivia E. Coolidge

Humanity's Beginnings

The Greeks have several stories about how man came to be. One declares that he was created in the age of Kronos,[1] or Saturn, who ruled before Zeus [zo͞os]. At that time, the legend says, there was no sorrow, **toil**, sickness, or age. Men lived their lives in plenty and died as though they went to sleep. They tilled[2] no ground, built no cities, killed no living thing, and among them war was unknown. The earth brought forth strawberries, cherries, and ears of wheat for them. Even on the bramble bushes grew berries good to eat. Milk and sweet nectar flowed in rivers for men to drink, and honey dripped from hollow trees. Men lived in caves and thickets, needing little shelter, for the season was always spring.

Another legend declares that Zeus conceived of animals first and he entrusted their creation to Prometheus [prō mē´ thē əs] and Epimetheus [ep ə mē´ thē əs], his brother. First, Epimetheus undertook to order all things, but he was a **heedless** person and soon got into trouble. Finally he was forced to appeal to Prometheus.

"What have you done?" asked Prometheus.

"Down on the earth," answered his brother, "there is a green, grassy clearing, ringed by tall oak trees and shaded by steep slopes from all but the midday sun. There I sat and the animals came to me, while I gave to each the gifts which should be his from this time forward. Air I gave to the birds, seas to the fishes, land to four-footed creatures and the creeping insects, and to some, like the moles, I gave burrows beneath the earth."

"That was well done," answered Prometheus. "What else did you do?"

"Strength," said Epimetheus, "I gave to lions and tigers, and the fierce animals of the woods. Size I gave to others like the great whales of the sea. The deer I made swift and timid, and the insects I made tiny that they might escape from sight. I gave warm fur to the great bears and the little squirrels, keen eyes and sharp talons[3] to the birds of prey, tusks to the elephant, hide to the wild boar, sweet songs and bright feathers to the birds. To each I gave some special excellence, that whether large or small, kind or terrible, each might live in his own place, find food, escape enemies, and enjoy the wide world which is his to **inhabit**."

"All this is very good," said his brother, Prometheus. "You have done well. Wherein lies your trouble?"

1. **Kronos** (krō´ nəs) son of the sky and the earth; father of Zeus.
2. **tilled** *v.* cultivated; plowed or hoed.
3. **talons** (tal´ ənz) *n.* claws (of birds of prey).

◀ Analyze Representations
Compare and contrast this painting of Prometheus with his portrayal in the myth.

◀ Vocabulary
toil (toil) *n.* hard, tiring work

heedless (hēd´ lis) *adj.* careless; thoughtless

inhabit (in hab´ it) *v.* live in

Myths
Which details show you that this myth will explain the origins of something?

Analyze Cultural Context
What question does this paragraph suggest to you about the region where the Greeks lived?

Comprehension
What task does Zeus give to Prometheus and his brother?

LITERATURE IN CONTEXT

Culture Connection

The Twelve Olympian Gods
The ancient Greeks worshiped a family of gods said to have their home on Mount Olympus:
Zeus (zo͞os) ruler of the gods
Hera (hir´ ə) queen of the gods; goddess of marriage
Aphrodite (af´ rə dīt´ ē) goddess of love and beauty
Apollo (ə päl´ ō) god of music, poetry, and light
Ares (er´ ēz´) god of war
Artemis (är´ tə mis) goddess of the moon, wild animals, and hunting
Athene (ə thē´ nē) goddess of wisdom
Demeter (di mēt´ ər) goddess of grain and agriculture
Hephaestus (hē fes´ təs) god of fire; blacksmith of the gods
Hermes (hʉr´ mēz´) messenger of the gods; god of business, science, and speech
Hestia (hes´ tē ə) goddess of the hearth
Poseidon (pō sī´ dən) god of earthquakes, the sea, and horses

Connect to the Literature

According to this myth, what is the relationship between the gods and humans like?

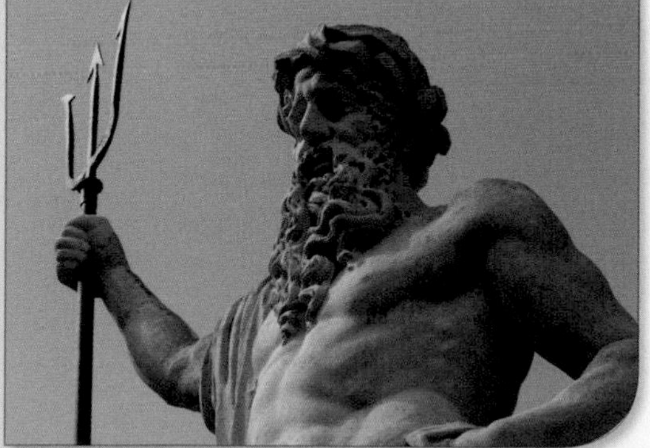

"Because I did not think it out beforehand," said the heedless brother sadly, "I did not count how many animals there were to be before I started giving. Now when I have given all, there comes one last animal for whom I have neither skill nor shape, nor any place to dwell in. Everything has been given already."

"What is this animal," said Prometheus, "who has been forgotten?"

"His name," said Epimetheus, "is Man."

Thus it was that the future of man was left to Prometheus, who was forced to make man different from all other creatures. Therefore he gave him the shape of the gods themselves and the privilege of walking upright as they do. He gave him no special home, but made him ruler over the whole earth, and over the sea and air. Finally, he gave him no special strength or swiftness, but stole a spark from heaven and lighted a heavenly fire within his mind which should teach him to understand, to count, to speak, to remember. Man learned from it how to build cities, tame animals, raise crops, build boats, and do all the things that animals cannot. Prometheus also kindled fire on earth that man might smelt[4] metals and make tools. In fact, from this heavenly fire of Prometheus all man's greatness comes.

Before this time fire was a divine thing and belonged only to the gods. It was one of their greatest treasures, and Zeus would never have given Prometheus permission to use it in the creation of man. Therefore when Prometheus stole it, Zeus was furious indeed. He chained Prometheus to a great, lofty rock, where the sun scorched him by day and the cruel frost tortured him by night. Not content with that, he sent an eagle to tear him, so that, though he could not die, he lived in agony. For many centuries Prometheus hung in torment, but he was wiser than Zeus, and by reason of a secret he had, he forced Zeus in later ages to set him free. By then, also, Zeus had learned that there is more in ruling than power and cruelty. Thus, the two at last were friends. ●

4. **smelt** *v.* purify metal by melting it.

The Coming of Evil

After the punishment of Prometheus, Zeus planned to take his revenge on man. He could not recall the gift of fire, since it had been given by one of the immortals,[5] but he was not content that man should possess this treasure in peace and become perhaps as great as were the gods themselves. He therefore took **counsel** with the other gods, and together they made for man a woman. All the gods gave gifts to this new creation. Aphrodite [af′ rə dīt′ ē] gave her fresh beauty like the spring itself. The goddess Athene [ə thē′ nē] dressed her and put on her a garland of flowers and green leaves. She had also a golden diadem[6] beautifully decorated with figures of animals. In her heart Hermes [hur′ mēz′] put cunning, deceit, and curiosity. She was named Pandora [pan dôr′ ə], which means All-Gifted, since each of the gods had given her something. The last gift was a chest in which there was supposed to be great treasure, but which Pandora was instructed never to open. Then Hermes, the Messenger, took the girl and brought her to Epimetheus.

Epimetheus had been warned by his brother to receive no gifts from Zeus, but he was a heedless person, as ever, and Pandora was very lovely. He accepted her, therefore, and for a while they lived together in happiness, for Pandora besides her beauty had been given both wit and charm. Eventually, however, her curiosity got the better of her, and she determined to see for herself what treasure it was that the gods had given her. One day when she was alone, she went over to the corner where her chest lay and cautiously lifted the lid for a peep. The lid flew up out of her hands and knocked her aside, while before her frightened eyes dreadful, shadowy shapes flew out of the box in an endless stream. There were hunger, disease, war, greed, anger, jealousy, toil, and all the griefs and hardships to which man from that day has been subject. Each was terrible in appearance, and as it passed, Pandora saw something of the misery that her thoughtless action had brought on her descendants. At last the stream slackened,[7] and Pandora, who had been paralyzed with fear and horror, found strength to shut her box. The only thing left in it now, however, was the one good gift the gods had put in among so many evil ones. This was hope, and since that time the hope that is in man's heart is the only thing which has made him able to bear the sorrows that Pandora brought upon him.

◀ **Vocabulary**
counsel (koun′ səl) *n.* advice; discussion

Spiral Review
UNIVERSAL THEMES
What ideas about human nature do Pandora's actions represent? Explain.

Comprehension
Why does Zeus punish Prometheus?

5. **immortals** (im môrt′ ′lz) *n.* those who do not die.
6. **diadem** (dī′ ə dem′) *n.* crown.
7. **slackened** (slak′ ənd) *v.* diminished; became less active.

▲ Analyze Representations
Which details in this painting echo details in the text of the myth? What details in the myth are not represented in the painting?

The Great Flood

When evil first came among mankind, people became very wicked. War, robbery, treachery, and murder prevailed throughout the world. Even the worship of the gods, the laws of truth and honor, reverence[8] for parents and brotherly love were neglected.

Finally, Zeus determined to destroy the race of men altogether, and the other gods agreed. All the winds were therefore shut up in a cave except the South Wind, the wet one. He raced over the earth with water streaming from his beard and long, white hair. Clouds gathered around his head, and dew dripped from his wings and the ends of his garments. With him went Iris, the rainbow goddess,

8. **reverence** (rev´ ə rəns) *n.* feeling or display of great respect.

while below Poseidon [pō sī´ dən] smote the earth with his trident until it shook and gaped open, so that the waters of the sea rushed up over the land.

Fields and farmhouses were buried. Fish swam in the tops of the trees. Sea beasts were quietly feeding where flocks and herds had grazed before. On the surface of the water, boars, stags, lions, and tigers struggled desperately to keep afloat. Wolves swam in the midst of flocks of sheep, but the sheep were not frightened by them, and the wolves never thought of their natural prey. Each fought for his own life and forgot the others. Over them wheeled countless birds, winging far and wide in the hope of finding something to rest upon. Eventually they too fell into the water and were drowned.

All over the water were men in small boats or makeshift rafts. Some even had oars which they tried to use, but the waters were fierce and stormy, and there was nowhere to go. In time all were drowned, until at last there was no one left but an old man and his wife, Deucalion [dōō kāl´ ē ən] and Pyrrha [pir´ ə]. These two people had lived in truth and justice, unlike the rest of mankind. They had been warned of the coming of the flood and had built a boat and stocked it. For nine days and nights they floated until Zeus took pity on them and they came to the top of Mount Parnassus, the sacred home of the Muses.[9] There they found land and **disembarked** to wait while the gods recalled the water they had unloosed.

◀ **Vocabulary**
disembarked (dis´ im bärkt´) *v.* left a ship to go ashore

When the waters fell, Deucalion and Pyrrha looked over the land, despairing. Mud and sea slime covered the earth; all living things had been swept away. Slowly and sadly they made their way down the mountain until they came to a temple where there had been an oracle.[10] Black seaweed dripped from the pillars now, and the mud was over all. Nevertheless the two knelt down and kissed the temple steps while Deucalion prayed to the goddess to tell them what they should do. All men were dead but themselves, and they were old. It was impossible that they should have children to people the earth again. Out of the temple a great voice was heard speaking strange words.

"Depart," it said, "with veiled heads and loosened robes, and throw behind you as you go the bones of your mother."

Pyrrha was in despair when she heard this saying. "The bones of our mother!" she cried. "How can we tell now where they lie? Even

Comprehension
Why does Zeus punish man?

9. **Muses** (myōōz´ əz) *n.* nine goddesses who rule over literature and the arts and sciences.
10. **oracle** (ôr´ ə kəl) *n.* person who, when consulted on a matter, is said to reveal the will of the gods.

Myth
What fact of life is explained by the myth of Deucalion and Pyrrha?

if we knew, we could never do such a dreadful thing as to disturb their resting place and scatter them over the earth like an armful of stones."

"Stones!" said Deucalion quickly. "That must be what the goddess means. After all Earth is our mother, and the other thing is too horrible for us to suppose that a goddess would ever command it."

Accordingly both picked up armfuls of stones, and as they went away from the temple with faces veiled, they cast the stones behind them. From each of those Deucalion cast sprang up a man, and from Pyrrha's stones sprang women. Thus the earth was repeopled, and in the course of time it brought forth again animals from itself, and all was as before. Only from that time men have been less sensitive and have found it easier to **endure** toil, and sorrow, and pain, since now they are descended from stones.

Vocabulary ▶
endure (en door′)
v. hold up under pain or hardship

Language Study

Vocabulary The italicized words in each item appear in "Prometheus and the First People." Copy each of the following word pairs. Write *S* for synonyms or *A* for antonyms. Explain each of your choices.

1. *toil,* work
2. *heedless,* cautious
3. *counsel,* recommendation
4. *disembarked,* boarded
5. *inhabit,* abandon

WORD STUDY
The **Latin root *-dur-*** means "hard" or "to last." In the story of the great flood, humans learn to **endure** pain and sorrow, or to last through hardship and suffering without quitting.

Word Study

Part A Explain how the **Latin root *-dur-*** contributes to the meanings of the words *duration, duress,* and *obdurate*. Consult a dictionary if necessary.

Part B Use the context of the sentences and what you know about the Latin root *-dur-* to explain your answer to each question.

1. Will a *durable* pair of shoes usually fall apart quickly?
2. Does training for a marathon usually help to build up one's *endurance*?

Close Reading Activities

Literary Analysis

Key Ideas and Details

1. **(a)** What problem does Epimetheus face when it is humanity's turn to receive a gift? **(b) Compare and Contrast:** Contrast the gifts Prometheus gives to humanity with those Epimetheus gives to the animals. **(c) Evaluate:** Which gifts are most valuable? Support your answers with details from the myth.
2. **(a)** Which of Prometheus' actions enrages Zeus? **(b)** Why does this action anger him? Cite details from the myth in your answer.
3. **Analyze Cause and Effect:** What changes does Pandora bring to the world by opening the box? Explain.
4. **Analyze Cultural Context (a)** Write down two questions you might ask to analyze the cultural context of a myth. **(b)** What answers do these three myths provide to each question? Explain, supporting your answer with details from the text.

Craft and Structure

5. **Myths** Use a chart like the one shown to identify the characteristics of myths that appear in "Prometheus and the First People." Support your choices with textual evidence.
6. **Myths (a)** What do these three myths suggest about the value the ancient Greeks placed on the human power to reason? Explain with references to the text. **(b)** In what way does the story of Pandora show that the gift of intelligence may also be a curse? Explain. **(c)** Working from your previous answers, draw a conclusion about how ancient Greeks perceived human nature. Explain your reasoning, citing details and examples from the text.
7. **Myths (a)** Why does Zeus save Deucalion and Pyrrha? **(b)** Which passage in the story reveals his thinking? **(c)** Draw a conclusion about ancient Greek values from this story. Support your conclusion with details from the text.

Origins the Story Explains
Exceptional or Fantastic Characters
Quest for Something of Value
Transgression

Integration of Knowledge and Ideas

8. THE BIG ? **Can anyone be a hero? (a)** Which characters in these three myths make heroic efforts during trying circumstances? **(b)** Are all of these characters typical heroes? **(c)** What view of heroism do these myths promote? Explain, citing details from the text to support your answers.

ACADEMIC VOCABULARY

As you write and speak about "Prometheus and the First People," use the words related to heroism that you explored on page 771 of this book.

Conventions: Independent and Dependent Clauses

A **clause** is a group of words that has both a subject and a verb. An **independent clause** can stand by itself as a sentence. A **dependent,** or **subordinate, clause** has a subject and a verb, but it cannot stand alone as a complete sentence.

There are three types of dependent clauses:

- An **adverb** (or **adverbial**) **clause** acts as an adverb in a sentence. It begins with a subordinating conjunction, such as *if, when, because, although, unless, before, after, while,* or *since.*
  Example: *When they left,* Jo was sad. (modifies *sad*)
- A **relative clause** acts as an adjective in a sentence. It usually begins with a relative pronoun, such as *who, whom, whose, which,* or *that.*
  Example: The boy *who came late* is Al. (modifies *boy*)
- A **noun clause** acts as a noun in a sentence. It usually begins with a word such as *what, whatever, when, whenever, where, how,* or *why.*
  Example: *Whatever she does* is perfect. (subject of *is*)

Practice A

Identify the clause in each item. Then, state whether it is an adverb clause, a relative clause, or a noun clause.

1. When the flood waters rose, the gods helped the man and woman to survive.
2. Why all the other creatures perished is a story to be told in the legends.
3. Epimetheus, who gave gifts to the animals, was a heedless person.
4. Pandora opened the box, which loosened all the evils of the world.

Reading Application Identify an adverb clause, a noun clause, and a relative clause in the myth "Prometheus and the First People."

Practice B

Complete each sentence by adding the type of clause named in parentheses.

1. (Noun clause) was the gift of fire.
2. Deucalion and Pyrrha (relative clause) survived the terrible flood.
3. The land was repopulated (adverb clause).
4. Pandora was curious about (noun clause).

Writing Application Write a paragraph about Prometheus' adventures in "Prometheus and the First People." Your paragraph should include at least one noun clause, one relative clause, and one adverb clause. After you have completed your paragraph, go back and label the three types of clauses you used.

Writing to Sources

Narrative With a small group, write a contemporary **myth.** You may write about the origin of some aspect of human life, such as how gossip or forgiveness entered the world, or you may describe the origin of a modern convenience, such as television or cars. Follow these steps:

- Agree on a topic that group members find interesting.
- Make a plan for writing that addresses your purpose, identifies characters and a logical sequence of events, and sets a time frame for completion.
- Mirror the types of incidents, language, and issues expressed in "Prometheus and the First People" but recast them with concerns and details that reflect the modern world.
- One member of the group should write the first paragraph. Then, with your planned sequence in mind, each group member should write a paragraph that logically follows from the one before. Writers should develop the action with dialogue, pacing, and description.
- Review the story as it progresses, and make any revisions necessary to clarify the sequence of events or add interest.

Share your myth with the class.

Grammar Application As you write your myth, vary your sentences by using different types of dependent clauses.

Speaking and Listening

Presentation of Ideas Locate another Greek myth that shows the relationship between the gods and humanity. Present your own **retelling** of the myth to the class. Apply these guidelines to make sure your retelling is interesting and effective:

- Engage your audience with an exciting introduction to the story.
- Present the sequence of events in a logical order.
- Accurately and vividly describe important scenes, actions, and characters, using sensory details whenever possible.
- Vary the pitch and tone of your voice to reflect the action and mood.
- End with a conclusion that helps listeners understand the story's meaning.

Have classmates summarize your retelling. Then, lead a discussion about how your retelling compares to the original story.

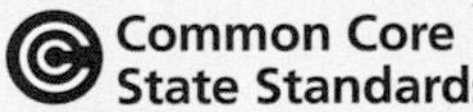

Writing

3. Write narratives to develop real or imagined experiences or events using effective technique, well-chosen details, and well-structured event sequences.

3.a. Engage and orient the reader by setting out a problem, situation, or observation, establishing one or multiple point(s) of view, and introducing a narrator and/or characters; create a smooth progression of experiences or events.

3.b. Use narrative techniques to develop experiences, events, and/or characters.

Speaking and Listening

6. Adapt speech to a variety of contexts and tasks, demonstrating command of formal English when indicated or appropriate.

Language

1.b. Use various types of phrases and clauses to convey specific meanings and add variety and interest to writing or presentations.

Building Knowledge

Can anyone be a hero?

Explore the Big Question as you read the excerpt from *Sundiata: An Epic of Old Mali*. Take notes on qualities that make Mari Djata an unlikely hero.

Meet the Retellers

Sundiata (known as Mari Djata as a child) was a hero who united the Malinke people of Mali in West Africa. Sundiata's achievements were celebrated over the centuries by West African oral historians known as griots (grē′ ōz). The twentieth-century griot **Mamadou Kouyaté** (mä′ mä do͞o ko͞o ya′ tā) continued this tradition. The scholar **D. T. Niane** (nī′ yan) wrote an account of Sundiata based on Kouyaté's retellings.

CLOSE READING FOCUS

Key Ideas and Details: **Analyze Cultural Context**

When you **analyze cultural context**, you determine ways in which a text reflects the ideals, values, and customs of the historical period and the culture in which it was composed. As you read a text, you can acquire information about the culture in these ways:

- Read text features, such as footnotes, and apply the information to better understand the culture.
- Draw conclusions about cultural practices from details in the selection.

Craft and Structure: **Epic and Epic Hero**

An **epic** is a long narrative poem about the deeds of heroes. The typical **epic hero** is a warrior, and his character may be based on a historic or legendary figure. In some epics, the hero strives to win immortality through great deeds, especially in combat. The typical epic hero has the following characteristics:

- He has a high position in society and is often a natural leader.
- He has the virtues of a warrior, such as strength, courage, and perseverance.
- He behaves ethically—fighting evil and striving for justice.
- He may receive special blessings from the gods or suffer from special burdens.

An epic reflects the culture that created it, celebrating that culture's achievements and reinforcing its ideals.

Vocabulary

The words below are key to understanding the text that follows. Identify which words you know well, which you know a little, and which you do not know at all. After you read, see how your knowledge of each word has increased.

fathom	**innuendo**	**estranged**
derisively	**affront**	**efface**

Common Core State Standards

Reading Literature

1. Cite strong and thorough textual evidence to support analysis of what the text says explicitly as well as inferences drawn from the text.

6. Analyze a particular point of view or cultural experience reflected in a work of literature from outside the United States.

CLOSE READING MODEL

The passages below are from *Sundiata: An Epic of Old Mali.* The annotations to the right of the passages show ways in which you can use close reading skills to analyze cultural context and understand epics.

from *Sundiata: An Epic of Old Mali*

The king's first wife was the first to rejoice at Sogolon Djata's infirmity. Her own son, Dankaran Touman, was already eleven. He was a fine and lively boy, who spent the day running about the village with those of his own age. He had even begun his initiation in the bush. The king had had a bow made for him and he used to go behind the town to practice archery with his companions.[1]

....

As men have short memories, Sogolon's son was spoken of with nothing but irony and scorn. People had seen one-eyed kings, one-armed kings, and lame kings, but a stiff-legged king had never been heard tell of. No matter how great the destiny promised for Mari Djata might be, the throne could not be given to someone who had no power in his legs;[2] if the jinn loved him, let them begin by giving him the use of his legs.[3] Such were the remarks that Sogolon heard every day. The queen mother, Sassouma Bérété, was the source of all this gossip.

Analyze Cultural Context

1 The reference to an "initiation" offers a glimpse of how boys are treated in the culture of the epic. Likewise, the idea that boys "practice archery" suggests that hunting, strength, and physical skills are important in this culture.

Epic and Epic Hero

2 Epic heroes are sometimes fated to suffer from special burdens. In this case, Mari Djata has the burden of a physical impairment—he cannot walk properly. His community so values physical strength and skill they are unable to perceive his capabilities as a leader because of this infirmity.

Analyze Cultural Context

3 The "jinn" are supernatural beings who the Malinke believe influence human affairs. This reference provides a window into the beliefs held by people in the culture of the epic. It also indicates that Mari Djata is marked for favor by supernatural beings—a trait common to epic heroes.

FROM

SUNDIATA

AN EPIC OF OLD MALI

D. T. NIANE

Critical Viewing ▶ Contrast this depiction of Mari (or Sogolon) Djata with the child described in the opening paragraphs.

CHARACTERS IN SUNDIATA

Balla Fasséké (bä´ lä fä sä´ kä): Griot and counselor of Sundiata

Boukari (bo͞o kä´ rē): Son of the king and Namandjé, one of his wives; also called Manding (män´ diŋ) Boukari

Dankaran Touman (dän´ kä rän to͞o´ män): Son of the king and his first wife, Sassouma, who is also called Sassouma Bérété

Djamarou (jä mä´ ro͞o): Daughter of Sogolon and the king; sister of Sundiata and Kolonkan

Farakourou (fä rä ko͞o´ ro͞o): Master of the forges

Gnankouman Doua (nän ko͞o´ män do͞o´ ə): The king's griot; also called, simply, Doua

Kolonkan (kō lōn´ kən): Sundiata's eldest sister

Namandjé (nä män´ jē): One of the king's wives

Naré Maghan (nä´ rā mäg´ hän): Sundiata's father; the king of Mali before Sundiata

Nounfaïri (no͞on´ fä ē´ rē): Soothsayer and smith; father of Farakourou

Sassouma Bérété (sä so͞o´ mä be´ re te): The king's first wife

Sogolon (sô gô lōn´): Sundiata's mother; also called Sogolon Kedjou (kā´ jo͞o)

Sundiata (so͞on dyä´ tä): Legendary king of Mali; referred to as Djata (dyä´ tä) and Sogolon Djata ("son of Sogolon"), and Mari (mä´ rē) Djata.

CHILDHOOD

God has his mysteries which none can **fathom**. You, perhaps, will be a king. You can do nothing about it. You, on the other hand, will be unlucky, but you can do nothing about that either. Each man finds his way already marked out for him and he can change nothing of it.

◀ **Vocabulary**
fathom (fa*th*´ əm) *v.* understand thoroughly

Sogolon's son had a slow and difficult childhood. At the age of three he still crawled along on all-fours while children of the same age were already walking. He had nothing of the great beauty of his father Naré Maghan. He had a head so big that he seemed unable to support it; he also had large eyes which would open wide whenever anyone entered his mother's house. He was taciturn[1] and used to spend the whole day just sitting in the middle of the house. Whenever his mother went out he would crawl on all-fours to rummage about in the calabashes[2] in search of food, for he was very greedy.

Comprehension
Why is Mari (or Sogolon) Djata's childhood difficult?

1. **taciturn** (tas´ ə tʉrn´) *adj.* almost always silent; not liking to talk.
2. **calabashes** (kal´ ə bash´ əz) *n.* dried, hollow shells of gourds (squashlike fruits), used as bowls, cups, and so on.

Analyze Cultural Context
What detail does the background information in footnote 2 help you understand?

Malicious tongues began to blab. What three-year-old has not yet taken his first steps? What three-year-old is not the despair of his parents through his whims and shifts of mood? What three-year-old is not the joy of his circle through his backwardness in talking? Sogolon Djata (for it was thus that they called him, prefixing his mother's name to his), Sogolon Djata, then, was very different from others of his own age. He spoke little and his severe face never relaxed into a smile. You would have thought that he was already thinking, and what amused children of his age bored him. Often Sogolon would make some of them come to him to keep him company. These children were already walking and she hoped that Djata, seeing his companions walking, would be tempted to do likewise. But nothing came of it. Besides, Sogolon Djata would brain the poor little things with his already strong arms and none of them would come near him any more.

Epic and Epic Hero
In what two ways is Mari (or Sogolon) Djata set apart from other children?

The king's first wife was the first to rejoice at Sogolon Djata's infirmity. Her own son, Dankaran Touman, was already eleven. He was a fine and lively boy, who spent the day running about the village with those of his own age. He had even begun his initiation in the bush.[3] The king had had a bow made for him and he used to go behind the town to practice archery with his companions. Sassouma was quite happy and snapped her fingers at Sogolon, whose child was still crawling on the ground. Whenever the latter happened to pass by her house, she would say, "Come, my son, walk, jump, leap about. The jinn didn't promise you anything out of the ordinary,[4] but I prefer a son who walks on his two legs to a lion that crawls on the ground." She spoke thus whenever Sogolon went by her door. The **innuendo** would go straight home and then she would burst into laughter, that diabolical laughter which a jealous woman knows how to use so well.

Vocabulary ▶
innuendo (in′ yo͞o en′ dō) *n.* indirect insult or accusation; insinuation

estranged (e strānjd′) *adj.* kept apart; in the condition of having had affection turn into indifference or hostility

Her son's infirmity weighed heavily upon Sogolon Kedjou; she had resorted to all her talent as a sorceress to give strength to her son's legs, but the rarest herbs had been useless. The king himself lost hope.

How impatient man is! Naré Maghan became imperceptibly **estranged** but Gnankouman Doua never ceased reminding him of the hunter's words. Sogolon became pregnant again. The king hoped for a son, but it was a daughter called Kolonkan. She

3. **initiation in the bush** education in tribal lore given to twelve-year-old West African boys so they can become full members of the tribe.
4. **The jinn . . . ordinary** Jinn are supernatural beings said to influence human affairs. They promised that the son of Sogolon would make Mali a great empire.

resembled her mother and had nothing of her father's beauty. The disheartened king debarred Sogolon from his house and she lived in semi-disgrace for a while. Naré Maghan married the daughter of one of his allies, the king of the Kamaras. She was called Namandjé and her beauty was legendary. A year later she brought a boy into the world. When the king consulted soothsayers[5] on the destiny of this son he received the reply that Namandjé's child would be the right hand of some mighty king. The king gave the newly-born the name of Boukari. He was to be called Manding Boukari or Manding Bory later on.

Naré Maghan was very perplexed. Could it be that the stiff-jointed son of Sogolon was the one the hunter soothsayer had foretold?

"The Almighty has his mysteries," Gnankouman Doua would say and, taking up the hunter's words, added, "The silk-cotton tree emerges from a tiny seed."

One day Naré Maghan came along to the house of Nounfaïri, the blacksmith seer of Niani. He was an old, blind man. He received the king in the anteroom which served as his workshop. To the king's question he replied, "When the seed germinates growth is not always easy; great trees grow slowly but they plunge their roots deep into the ground."

"But has the seed really germinated?" said the king.

"Of course," replied the blind seer. "Only the growth is not as quick as you would like it; how impatient man is."

This interview and Doua's confidence gave the king some assurance. To the great displeasure of Sassouma Bérété the king restored Sogolon to favor and soon another daughter was born to her. She was given the name of Djamarou.

However, all Niani talked of nothing else but the stiff-legged son of Sogolon. He was now seven and he still crawled to get about. In spite of all the king's affection, Sogolon was in despair. Naré Maghan aged and he felt his time coming to an end. Dankaran Touman, the son of Sassouma Bérété, was now a fine youth.

One day Naré Maghan made Mari Djata come to him and he spoke to the child as one speaks to an adult. "Mari Djata, I am growing old and soon I shall be no more among you, but before death takes me off I am going to give you the present each king gives his successor. In Mali every prince has his own griot. Doua's father was my father's griot, Doua is mine and the son of Doua, Balla Fasséké here, will be your griot. Be inseparable friends from

WHAT THREE-YEAR-OLD HAS NOT YET TAKEN HIS FIRST STEPS?

Spiral Review
ARCHETYPES What transformation common to heroic characters is foreshadowed in the exchange between the king and the seer? Explain your answer.

Comprehension
What advice does the blind seer give to the king?

---

5. **soothsayers** (so͞oth′ sā′ ərz) *n.* people who profess to foretell the future.

this day forward. From his mouth you will hear the history of your ancestors, you will learn the art of governing Mali according to the principles which our ancestors have bequeathed to us. I have served my term and done my duty too. I have done everything which a king of Mali ought to do. I am handing an enlarged kingdom over to you and I leave you sure allies. May your destiny be accomplished, but never forget that Niani is your capital and Mali the cradle of your ancestors."

The child, as if he had understood the whole meaning of the king's words, beckoned Balla Fasséké to approach. He made room for him on the hide he was sitting on and then said, "Balla, you will be my griot."

"Yes, son of Sogolon, if it pleases God," replied Balla Fasséké.

The king and Doua exchanged glances that radiated confidence.

◀ **Critical Viewing**
What relationship in the epic might this picture illustrate? Explain.

THE LION'S AWAKENING

A short while after this interview between Naré Maghan and his son the king died.

Sogolon's son was no more than seven years old. The council of elders met in the king's palace. It was no use Doua's defending the king's will which reserved the throne for Mari Djata, for the council took no account of Naré Maghan's wish. With the help of Sassouma Bérété's intrigues, Dankaran Touman was proclaimed king and a regency council[6] was formed in which the queen mother was all-powerful. A short time after, Doua died.

As men have short memories, Sogolon's son was spoken of with nothing but irony and scorn. People had seen one-eyed kings, one-armed kings, and lame kings, but a stiff-legged king had never been heard tell of. No matter how great the destiny promised for Mari Djata might be, the throne could not be given to someone who had no power in his legs; if the jinn loved him, let them begin by giving him the use of his legs. Such were the remarks that Sogolon heard every day. The queen mother, Sassouma Bérété, was the source of all this gossip.

Analyze Cultural Context
What do the details here indicate about the way in which West African society was ruled?

Having become all-powerful, Sassouma Bérété persecuted Sogolon because the late Naré Maghan had preferred her. She banished Sogolon and her son to a back yard of the palace. Mari

Comprehension
After the king's death, who takes power in the kingdom?

6. **regency** (rē′ jən sē) **council** group that rules instead of the king or queen when the king or queen is still a child or is otherwise incapable of ruling.

Epic and Epic Hero
In what way is the honor of Mari Djata's family threatened?

Djata's mother now occupied an old hut which had served as a lumber-room of Sassouma's.

The wicked queen mother allowed free passage to all those inquisitive people who wanted to see the child that still crawled at the age of seven. Nearly all the inhabitants of Niani filed into the palace and the poor Sogolon wept to see herself thus given over to public ridicule. Mari Djata took on a ferocious look in front of the crowd of sightseers. Sogolon found a little consolation only in the love of her eldest daughter, Kolonkan. She was four and she could walk. She seemed to understand all her mother's miseries and already she helped her with the housework. Sometimes, when Sogolon was attending to the chores, it was she who stayed beside her sister Djamarou, quite small as yet.

Sogolon Kedjou and her children lived on the queen mother's leftovers, but she kept a little garden in the open ground behind the village. It was there that she passed her brightest moments looking after her onions and gnougous.[7] One day she happened to be short of condiments and went to the queen mother to beg a little baobab leaf.[8]

"Look you," said the malicious Sassouma, "I have a calabash full. Help yourself, you poor woman. As for me, my son knew how to walk at seven and it was he who went and picked these baobab leaves. Take them then, since your son is unequal to mine." Then she laughed **derisively** with that fierce laughter which cuts through your flesh and penetrates right to the bone.

Vocabulary ▶
derisively (di rī′siv lē) *adv.* in a mocking and ridiculing manner

affront (ə frunt′) *n.* open insult

Sogolon Kedjou was dumbfounded. She had never imagined that hate could be so strong in a human being. With a lump in her throat she left Sassouma's. Outside her hut Mari Djata, sitting on his useless legs, was blandly eating out of a calabash. Unable to contain herself any longer, Sogolon burst into sobs and seizing a piece of wood, hit her son.

"Oh son of misfortune, will you never walk? Through your fault I have just suffered the greatest **affront** of my life! What have I done, God, for you to punish me in this way?"

Mari Djata seized the piece of wood and, looking at his mother, said, "Mother, what's the matter?"

"Shut up, nothing can ever wash me clean of this insult."

"But what then?"

"Sassouma has just humiliated me over a matter of a baobab leaf. At your age her own son could walk and used to bring his mother baobab leaves."

---

7. **gnougous** (no͞o′ go͞oz′) *n.* root vegetables.
8. **baobab** (bā′ ō bab′) **leaf** The baobab is a thick-trunked tree; its leaves are used to flavor foods.

"Cheer up, Mother, cheer up."

"No. It's too much. I can't."

"Very well then, I am going to walk today," said Mari Djata. "Go and tell my father's smiths to make me the heaviest possible iron rod. Mother, do you want just the leaves of the baobab or would you rather I brought you the whole tree?"

▼ Critical Viewing
Why might Mari Djata have difficulty gathering leaves from a baobab tree like this one?

"Ah, my son, to wipe out this insult I want the tree and its roots at my feet outside my hut."

Balla Fasséké, who was present, ran to the master smith, Farakourou, to order an iron rod.

Sogolon had sat down in front of her hut. She was weeping softly and holding her head between her two hands. Mari Djata went calmly back to his calabash of rice and began eating again as if nothing had happened. From time to time he looked up discreetly at his mother who was murmuring in a low voice, "I want the whole tree, in front of my hut, the whole tree."

All of a sudden a voice burst into laughter behind the hut. It was the wicked Sassouma telling one of her serving women about the scene of humiliation and she was laughing loudly so that Sogolon could hear. Sogolon fled into the hut and hid her face under the blankets so as not to have before her eyes this heedless boy, who was more preoccupied with eating than with anything else. With her head buried in the bedclothes Sogolon wept and her body shook violently. Her daughter, Sogolon Djamarou, had come and sat down beside her and she said, "Mother, Mother, don't cry. Why are you crying?"

Mari Djata had finished eating and, dragging himself along on his legs, he came and sat under the wall of the hut for the sun was scorching. What was he thinking about? He alone knew.

The royal forges were situated outside the walls and over a hundred smiths worked there. The bows, spears, arrows and shields of Niani's warriors came from there. When Balla Fasséké came to order the iron rod, Farakourou said to him, "The great day has arrived then?"

"Yes. Today is a day like any other, but it will see what no other day has seen."

Comprehension
What incident provokes Mari Djata to order an iron bar?

Analyze Cultural Context
What do these details suggest about the role of blacksmiths and warriors in West African culture?

Vocabulary ▶
efface (ə fās′) *v.* rub or blot out

The master of the forges, Farakourou, was the son of the old Nounfaïri, and he was a soothsayer like his father. In his workshops there was an enormous iron bar wrought by his father, Nounfaïri. Everybody wondered what this bar was destined to be used for. Farakourou called six of his apprentices and told them to carry the iron bar to Sogolon's house.

When the smiths put the gigantic iron bar down in front of the hut the noise was so frightening that Sogolon, who was lying down, jumped up with a start. Then Balla Fasséké, son of Gnankouman Doua, spoke.

"Here is the great day, Mari Djata. I am speaking to you, Maghan, son of Sogolon. The waters of the Niger can **efface** the stain from the body, but they cannot wipe out an insult. Arise, young lion, roar, and may the bush know that from henceforth it has a master."

The apprentice smiths were still there, Sogolon had come out and everyone was watching Mari Djata. He crept on all-fours and came to the iron bar. Supporting himself on his knees and one hand, with the other hand he picked up the iron bar without any effort and stood it up vertically. Now he was resting on nothing but his knees and held the bar with both his hands. A deathly silence had gripped all those present. Sogolon Djata closed his eyes, held tight, the muscles in his arms tensed. With a violent jerk he threw his weight on to it and his knees left the ground. Sogolon Kedjou was all eyes and watched her son's legs which were trembling as though from an electric shock. Djata was sweating and the sweat ran from his brow. In a great effort he straightened up and was on his feet at one go—but the great bar of iron was twisted and had taken the form of a bow!

Then Balla Fasséké sang out the "Hymn to the Bow," striking up with his powerful voice:

"Take your bow, Simbon,
Take your bow and let us go.
Take your bow, Sogolon Djata."

When Sogolon saw her son standing she stood dumb for a moment, then suddenly she sang these words of thanks to God, who had given her son the use of his legs:

"Oh day, what a beautiful day,
Oh day, day of joy;
Allah[9] Almighty, you never created a finer day.
So my son is going to walk!"

Epic and Epic Hero
What qualities of an epic hero does Mari Djata display here?

Comprehension
What causes both Mari Djata's mother and his griot to sing?

9. **Allah** (al´ ə) Muslim name for God.

LITERATURE IN CONTEXT

Culture Connection

Griot: The Mind of the People

In West Africa, the griot (pronounced "gree-oh") was the storyteller and historian of the village. The griot memorized the births, deaths, marriages, hunts, and wars of the people and its ancestors. Sometimes speaking or singing for days, the griot recited these events as stories, often to musical accompaniment. To the Mandinka, the griot was the "mind" of the people, an oral library of history and culture.

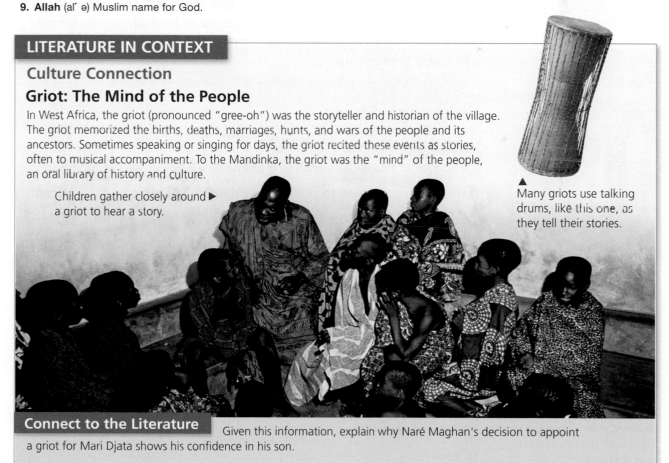

Children gather closely around ▶ a griot to hear a story.

▲ Many griots use talking drums, like this one, as they tell their stories.

Connect to the Literature Given this information, explain why Naré Maghan's decision to appoint a griot for Mari Djata shows his confidence in his son.

Standing in the position of a soldier at ease, Sogolon Djata, supported by his enormous rod, was sweating great beads of sweat. Balla Fasséké's song had alerted the whole palace and people came running from all over to see what had happened, and each stood bewildered before Sogolon's son. The queen mother had rushed there and when she saw Mari Djata standing up she trembled from head to foot. After recovering his breath Sogolon's son dropped the bar and the crowd stood to one side. His first steps were those of a giant. Balla Fasséké fell into step and pointing his finger at Djata, he cried:

Analyze Cultural Context
What do the images in the griot's song indicate about the region in which the Malinke live?

"Room, room, make room!
The lion has walked;
Hide antelopes,
Get out of his way."

Behind Niani there was a young baobab tree and it was there that the children of the town came to pick leaves for their mothers. With all his might the son of Sogolon tore up the tree and put it on his shoulders and went back to his mother. He threw the tree in front of the hut and said, "Mother, here are some baobab leaves for you. From henceforth it will be outside your hut that the women of Niani will come to stock up."

Language Study

Vocabulary The words listed below appear in the selection. Use one word from the list in a sentence about each of the situations noted in the numbered items.

fathom **innuendo** **estranged** **efface** **affront**

1. ceasing to socialize with a group of friends
2. confusion about a friend's buying a python as a pet
3. an exchange of snide remarks
4. an effort to harm someone's reputation
5. attempt to wipe away graffiti

WORD STUDY
The **Latin suffix *-ive*** means "belonging to" or "quality of." In this story, a character chuckles **derisively**, or in a manner filled with derision (scorn and ridicule).

Word Study

Part A Explain how the **Latin suffix *-ive*** contributes to the meanings of the words *elusive, persuasive,* and *restorative*. Consult a dictionary if necessary.

Part B Use the context of the sentences and what you know about the Latin suffix *-ive* to explain your answer to each question.

1. Is someone who is *combative* usually the peacemaker?
2. If a plant is *native* to North America, did it come from overseas?

Close Reading Activities

Literary Analysis

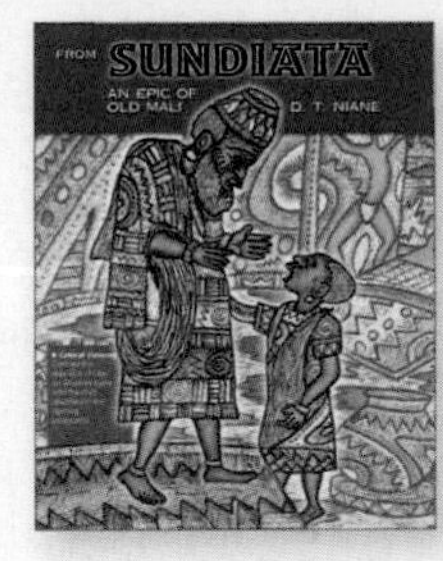

Key Ideas and Details

1. **(a)** What is Mari Djata's main physical difficulty? **(b) Connect:** How does this problem affect the way people treat his mother? Support your answer with examples from the epic.
2. **(a)** What does the king wish for Mari Djata's future? **(b) Analyze Cause and Effect:** How do the soothsayers' predictions help prompt the king's wishes? Support your answer with details from the epic.
3. **Analyze Cultural Context (a)** After the king's death, where does Sassouma Bérété force Sogolon and Mari Djata to live? **(b)** What does this detail reveal about Malinke culture and laws? Explain. **(c)** Why does Sassouma Bérété treat Mari Djata and Sogolon as she does? Cite details from the text to support your response.
4. **Analyze Cultural Context (a)** List two things that you learned about West African culture from the footnotes. **(b)** Explain how information about the cultural context in which *Sundiata* was written helps you to better understand the characters and conflicts it portrays.

Craft and Structure

5. **Epic and Epic Hero** Using a chart like the one shown, cite examples from the text that show Mari Djata possesses the qualities of an epic hero.
6. **Epic and Epic Hero (a)** What does the soothsayer mean when he tells the king "great trees grow slowly"? Explain. **(b)** Why do you think Mari Djata is later compared to a lion? Support your answer with details from the text.

Noble Birth
Warrior Virtues
Acts Honorably
Chosen by the Gods or Fate

Integration of Knowledge and Ideas

7. **Interpret:** Why do you think Mari Djata did not respond to the crowds that tormented him over the years? Does this suggest a weakness or a strength in his character? Explain, citing details from the text.

8. THE BIG ? **Can anyone be a hero? (a)** In what ways is Mari Djata an unlikely hero? **(b)** What event finally prompts him to transcend his own problems? **(c)** Why would his actions be considered heroic? **(d)** What does this epic suggest about the ways in which people assess or judge others and the deeper qualities that allow someone to realize his or her potential? Cite details from the text in your responses.

ACADEMIC VOCABULARY

As you write and speak about the excerpt from *Sundiata,* use the words related to heroism that you explored on page 771 of this book.

Close Reading Activities Continued

Conventions: Sentence Types

A **clause** is a group of words with a subject and a verb. An **independent clause** is a clause that can stand on its own as a sentence. A **dependent,** or **subordinate, clause** has a subject and verb but cannot stand alone as a complete sentence. Clauses form different types of sentences.

- A **simple sentence** consists of a single independent clause.
- A **compound sentence** contains two or more independent clauses linked by a semicolon or a coordinating conjunction, such as *and, but, or, for, nor, so,* or *yet*.
- A **complex sentence** contains one independent clause and one or more dependent clauses.
- A **compound-complex sentence** contains at least one dependent clause and at least two independent clauses.

In the following chart, subjects are underlined once and verbs are underlined twice.

Simple Sentence	Compound Sentence	Complex Sentence	Compound-Complex Sentence
The hero of an epic accomplishes great feats.	Sassouma insults Sogolon, and Sogolon goes back to her hut and cries.	Although Sundiata endured a hard childhood, he later became a king.	The boy would hit the other children who visited him, and then they would no longer approach him.

Practice A

Identify each sentence as simple, compound, complex, or compound-complex.

1. Although he was born to a king, Mari Djata had a difficult childhood.
2. Sogolon's enemies treated her son badly.
3. When the king was about to die, he called Mari Djata to him, and he spoke to the child as if he were an adult.
4. The king named Mari Djata as his successor, but the council of elders did not comply.

Reading Application In the excerpt from *Sundiata: An Epic of Old Mali,* find one example of each type of sentence: simple, compound, complex, and compound-complex.

Practice B

Use each clause below to create the type of sentence indicated in parentheses. Add other clauses where necessary.

1. the boy could only crawl (complex)
2. when the king restored Sogolon to favor (compound-complex)
3. the wicked queen mother moved them to an old hut (compound)
4. the boy became a hero (simple)

Writing Application Write a simple sentence about an image used to illustrate the epic. Add a dependent clause to make it a complex sentence. Then, add another independent clause to make it a compound-complex sentence.

Writing to Sources

Informative Text In *Sundiata: An Epic of Old Mali,* Mari Djata performs heroic feats after enduring a diffcult childhood. Write a **news story** about the events that occur as a result of Sogolon's humiliation by Sassouma.

- Take notes in which you identify the main characters and key events and establish a clear sequence.
- Develop your story with facts and details that fully answer the following questions: *Who was involved in the incident? What happened? Where did it happen? When did it happen? How did it happen?* and *Why did it happen?*
- Include believable quotations from participants and onlookers.
- Add a headline to engage readers' attention, as well as subheads and illustrations.

After you finish your draft, design and produce your story. Choose readable headline and text fonts. Then, publish your story on a class blog or Web site.

Grammar Application As you draft use varied sentence types to add interest and fluidity to your writing.

Speaking and Listening

Comprehension and Collaboration With classmates, present an improvised dialogue about one of the following situations:

- A queen of Mali, her son, and a sage discuss an insult a rival queen delivered to the queen.
- A West African king and a sage discuss the king's wishes for his children and for the empire.

Apply what you have learned about West African culture, and be sure that characters speak in a manner suited to their positions.

- As your group brainstorms for ideas, have one group member take notes. Then, use the notes to draft your dialogue.
- Take ten minutes to prepare and ten minutes for the presentation.
- When presenting, make eye contact with the audience and vary your speaking volume to emphasize key words.

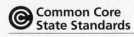

Writing

2. Write informative/explanatory texts to examine and convey complex ideas, concepts, and information clearly and accurately through the effective selection, organization, and analysis of content.

2.b. Develop the topic with well-chosen, relevant, and sufficient facts, extended definitions, concrete details, quotations, or other information and examples appropriate to the audience's knowledge of the topic.

6. Use technology to produce, publish, and update individual or shared writing products.

Speaking and Listening

1. Initiate and participate effectively in a range of collaborative discussions with diverse partners on grades 9–10 topics, texts, and issues, building on others' ideas and expressing their own clearly and persuasively.

Language

1.b. Use various types of phrases and clauses to convey specific meanings and add variety and interest to writing or presentations.

3. Apply knowledge of language to understand how language functions in different contexts, to make effective choices for meaning or style, and to comprehend more fully when reading or listening.

Can anyone be a hero?

Explore the Big Question as you read "Damon and Pythias." Take notes on what the story suggests about friendship and heroism.

Meet the Reteller

William F. Russell (b. 1945), a reteller of this and many other myths and legends, is also the author of a widely read newspaper column on education.

CLOSE READING FOCUS

Key Ideas and Details: **Analyze Worldviews**

A **worldview** consists of the values and beliefs held by a culture in which a story is set. A worldview includes the culture's understanding of human nature, the natural world, society, art, and religion. In a traditional story, like the ancient Greek legend of Damon and Pythias, the worldview forms a foundation for the story. To better understand this ancient tale, analyze the worldview it presents.

- Identify details that indicate characters' beliefs and values.
- Notice references to supernatural figures and consider what they suggest about the culture's beliefs.
- Analyze portrayals of leaders and characters in other social roles.

Craft and Structure: **Legends and Legendary Heroes**

Legends are stories about the past that have been handed down for generations. Because they are shared over time, legends gradually change, becoming more fiction than fact. Nevertheless, the connection of a legend to a people's history remains powerful. Legends share these additional characteristics:

- They focus on the adventures of **legendary heroes,** or characters who are human yet "larger than life." Some legendary heroes are based on real people but their characters become exaggerated and fictionalized as their stories are retold.
- They address ideals of right and wrong.
- They express feelings of national pride and reflect a culture's values.

Vocabulary

The words below are critical to understanding the text that follows. Copy the words into your notebook. Which word is a synonym for *peacefulness*?

composure	**dire**	**evade**
impediments	**serenity**	**tyrant**

Common Core State Standards

Reading Literature

1. Cite strong and thorough textual evidence to support analysis of what the text says explicitly as well as inferences drawn from the text.

6. Analyze a particular point of view or cultural experience reflected in a work of literature from outside the United States, drawing on a wide reading of world literature.

CLOSE READING MODEL

The passage below is from the legend of Damon and Pythias. The annotations to the right of the passage show ways in which you can use close reading skills to compare worldviews and analyze legends.

from "Damon and Pythias"

Damon and Pythias were two noble young men who lived on the island of Sicily in a city called Syracuse. They were such close companions and were so devoted to each other that all the people of the city admired them as the highest examples of true friendship.[1] Each trusted the other so completely that nobody could ever have persuaded one that the other had been unfaithful or dishonest,[2] even if that had been the case.

Now it happened that Syracuse was, at that time, ruled by a famous tyrant named Dionysius, who had gained the throne for himself through treachery, and who from then on flaunted his power by behaving cruelly to his own subjects[3] and to all strangers and enemies who were so unfortunate as to fall into his clutches. This tyrant, Dionysius, was so unjustly cruel that once, when he awoke from a restless sleep during which he dreamt that a certain man in the town had attempted to kill him, he immediately had that man put to death.[4]

Legends and Legendary Heroes

1 "All the people of the city admired" Damon and Pythias, who represent the highest possible ideal of friendship. The two are exemplary figures, perfect in their loyalty and devotion to one another.

Analyze Worldviews

2 Trust, faithfulness and honesty—the traits everyone admires in Damon and Pythias—reflect the importance of these values to the ancient Greeks.

Analyze Worldviews

3 The ancient Greeks believed in legitimate government. That someone like Dionysius would seize power by treachery and then act so cruelly offended the ancient Greeks, just as it would offend people in most countries today.

Legends and Legendary Heroes

4 The tyrant Dionysius is larger than life but in a negative way. His extraordinary cruelty and abuse of power provides a foil, or clear opposite, to the legendary goodness of Damon and Pythias.

DAMON *and* PYTHIAS

retold by **William F. Russell, Ed.D.**

Damon [dā′ mən] and Pythias [pith′ ē əs] were two noble young men who lived on the island of Sicily in a city called Syracuse. They were such close companions and were so devoted to each other that all the people of the city admired them as the highest examples of true friendship. Each trusted the other so completely that nobody could ever have persuaded one that the other had been unfaithful or dishonest, even if that had been the case.

Vocabulary ▶
tyrant (tī′ rənt) *n.* cruel, oppressive ruler; despot

Now it happened that Syracuse was, at that time, ruled by a famous **tyrant** named Dionysius [dī ə nis′ ē əs],[1] who had gained the throne for himself through treachery, and who from then on flaunted his power by behaving cruelly to his own subjects and to all strangers and enemies who were so unfortunate as to fall into his clutches. This tyrant, Dionysius, was so unjustly cruel that once, when he awoke from a restless sleep during which he dreamt that a certain man in the town had attempted to kill him, he immediately had that man put to death.

It happened that Pythias had, quite unjustly, been accused by Dionysius of trying to overthrow him, and for this supposed crime of treason Pythias was sentenced by the king to die. Try as he might, Pythias could not prove his innocence to the king's satisfaction, and so, all hope now lost, the noble youth asked only for a few days' freedom so that he could settle his business affairs and see to it that his relatives would be cared for after he was executed. Dionysius, the hardhearted tyrant, however, would not believe Pythias' promise to return and would not allow him to leave unless he left behind him a hostage, someone who would be put to death in his place if he should fail to return within the stated time.

Vocabulary ▶
dire (dīr) *adj.* extremely serious; urgent

Pythias immediately thought of his friend Damon, and he unhesitatingly sent for him in this hour of **dire** necessity, never thinking for a moment that his trusty companion would refuse his request. Nor did he, for Damon hastened straightaway to the palace—much to the amazement of King Dionysius—and gladly

1. **Dionysius** Dionysius the Elder (ca. 430 B.C.E.–367 B.C.E.), ruler of ancient Syracuse.

offered to be held hostage for his friend, in spite of the dangerous condition that had been attached to this favor. Therefore, Pythias was permitted to settle his earthly affairs before departing to the Land of the Shades,[2] while Damon remained behind in the dungeon, the captive of the tyrant Dionysius.

After Pythias had been released, Dionysius asked Damon if he did not feel afraid, for Pythias might very well take advantage of the opportunity he had been given and simply not return at all, and then he, Damon, would be executed in his place. But Damon replied at once with a willing smile: "There is no need for me to feel afraid, O King, since I have perfect faith in the word of my true friend, and I know that he will certainly return before the appointed time—unless, of course, he dies or is held captive by some evil force. Even so, even should the noble Pythias be captured and held against his will, it would be an honor for me to die in his place."

Such devotion and perfect faith as this was unheard of to the friendless tyrant; still, though he could not help admiring the true nobility of his captive, he nevertheless determined that Damon should certainly be put to death should Pythias not return by the appointed time.

And, as the Fates would have it, by a strange turn of events, Pythias *was* detained far longer in his task than he had imagined. Though he never for a single minute intended to **evade** the sentence of death to which he had been so unjustly committed, Pythias met with several accidents and unavoidable delays. Now his time was running out and he had yet to overcome the many **impediments** that had been placed in his path. At last he succeeded in clearing away all the hindrances, and he sped back the many miles to the palace of the king, his heart almost bursting with grief and fear that he might arrive too late.

Meanwhile, when the last day of the allotted time arrived, Dionysius commanded that the place of execution should be readied at once, since he was still ruthlessly determined that if one of his victims escaped him, the other should not. And so, entering the chamber in which Damon was confined, he began to utter words of sarcastic pity for the "foolish faith," as he termed it, that the young man of Syracuse had in his friend.

In reply, however, Damon merely smiled, since, in spite of the fact that the eleventh hour had already arrived, he still believed that his lifelong companion would not fail him. Even when, a short time later, he was actually led out to the site of his execution, his **serenity** remained the same.

▲ Critical Viewing
As he appears on this coin, does Dionysius seem to have the characteristics of the man in the legend? Explain.

Analyze Worldviews
What does this reference to "the Fates" suggest about the ancient Greeks' view of life on earth?

◄ Vocabulary
evade (ē vād´) *v.* escape; get away

impediments (im ped´ ə mənts) *n.* obstructions; obstacles

serenity (sə ren´ ə tē) *n.* state of calm or peace

Comprehension
What does Damon agree to do for his friend Pythias?

2. **Land of the Shades** in Greek mythology, place where people go when they die.

Vocabulary ▶
composure (kəm pō′ zhər) *n.* calmness of mind or manner; tranquility

Great excitement stirred the crowd that had gathered to witness the execution, for all the people had heard of the bargain that had been struck between the two friends. There was much sobbing and cries of sympathy were heard all around as the captive was brought out, though he himself somehow retained complete **composure** even at this moment of darkest danger.

Presently the excitement grew more intense still as a swift runner could be seen approaching the palace courtyard at an astonishing speed, and wild shrieks of relief and joy went up as Pythias, breathless and exhausted, rushed headlong through the crowd and flung himself into the arms of his beloved friend, sobbing with relief that he had, by the grace of the gods, arrived in time to save Damon's life.

This final exhibition of devoted love and faithfulness was more than even the stony heart of Dionysius, the tyrant, could resist. As the throng of spectators melted into tears at the companions' embrace, the king approached the pair and declared that Pythias was hereby pardoned and his death sentence canceled. In addition, he begged the pair to allow him to become their friend, to try to be as much a friend to them both as they had shown each other to be.

Legends and Legendary Heroes
How might Dionysius' change of heart help build national pride among the people of Syracuse?

Thus did the two friends of Syracuse, by the faithful love they bore to each other, conquer the hard heart of a tyrant king, and in the annals of true friendship there are no more honored names than those of Damon and Pythias—for no person can do more than be willing to lay down his life for the sake of his friend.

Language Study

Vocabulary The italicized words in each item below appear in "Damon and Pythias." Using your knowledge of these words, explain why each statement is usually true or usually false.

1. If the consequences of an action are *dire,* most people hesitate to do it.
2. Nervous and flustered people usually show great *composure*.
3. No one can be faulted for trying to *evade* the laws of the land.
4. A gently flowing brook in a forest can foster a mood of *serenity*.
5. A runner's speed will be improved if she faces *impediments*.

WORD STUDY

The **Latin suffix *-ant*** means "something that performs the action." In this story, the ruler Dionysius is a **tyrant.** He performs acts of tyranny—arbitrary, unjust, and cruel rule—among his subjects.

Word Study

Part A Explain how the **Latin suffix *-ant*** contributes to the meanings of the words *servant, occupant,* and *consultant*. Consult a dictionary if necessary.

Part B Use the context of the sentences and what you know about the Latin suffix *-ant* to explain your answer to each question.

1. If you sprayed *retardant* on a fire, what would probably happen?
2. Would an *applicant* for a job be interested in being employed?

Close Reading Activities

Literary Analysis

Key Ideas and Details

1. **(a)** What does Damon risk for Pythias? **(b) Interpret:** What does his decision show you about their friendship? **(c) Analyze:** Why is Damon patient and unafraid as he waits for Pythias, even as time runs out? Explain, citing details from the story.
2. **Analyze Worldviews (a)** Of what crime is Pythias accused and how is his guilt determined? **(b)** What view of government do these details give? Explain.
3. **Analyze Worldviews** How does the ending of the story suggest that the Greeks valued a well-ordered state in which justice prevails? Explain, citing details from the story.

Craft and Structure

4. **Legends and Legendary Heroes** Use a chart like the one shown to identify the features of legends that are present in the tale of "Damon and Pythias." Cite specific examples from the text.

Life Story of Legendary Hero
Concern With Right and Wrong
Reflections of National Pride

5. **Legends and Legendary Heroes (a)** The heroes of legends are often described as "larger than life." In what ways do Damon and Pythias meet this description? **(b)** Would you describe Dionysius as "larger than life"? Explain.
6. **(a) Compare and Contrast:** Compare and contrast Dionysius' behavior at the beginning and end of the story. **(b) Evaluate:** Do you find this portrayal of a tyrant realistic? Use story details to support your position.

Integration of Knowledge and Ideas

7. **Connect:** What is the relationship between loyalty and power in "Damon and Pythias"? Cite story details in your response.
8. **Analyze:** A moral dilemma is a situation in which any potential choice of action conflicts with a character's sense of right and wrong. Do Damon and Pythias face moral dilemmas, or are their choices always clear? Explain, citing details from the story.
9. THE BIG ? **Can anyone be a hero? (a)** Who do you think is more heroic—Damon or Pythias? Explain. **(b)** Does Dionysius' decision to spare both men make him a hero, as well? Why or why not?

ACADEMIC VOCABULARY

As you write and speak about "Damon and Pythias," use the words related to heroism that you explored on page 771 of this text.

Close Reading Activities Continued

Conventions: Fixing Common Usage Problems

Many students misuse certain words when making comparisons.

Identifying Usage Problems With *like, as,* and *as if* When it is not used as a verb (I *like* baseball), the word *like* is a preposition meaning "similar to" or "such as." The word *like* should not be used in place of *as*, *as if*, or *as though*, which are conjunctions that introduce clauses.

Incorrect: The sand felt *like* it was a warm slipper. (before a clause)
Correct: The sand felt *like* a warm slipper. (before a noun)
Correct: The sand felt as *if* it were a warm slipper. (before a clause)

Prepositional Phrase vs. Clause

A **prepositional phrase** includes a preposition and a noun or pronoun. It has no subject or verb.

Examples: *like* a feather *like* a snoring elephant

A **clause** has a subject and a verb.

S V
Example: My friend looked [as if *she* had overslept.]
clause

Identifying Usage Problems With *among* and *between* Use *between* to compare two things. Use *among* to compare three or more things.

Incorrect: The cloud hovered *among* the horizon and infinity.
Correct: The cloud hovered *between* the horizon and infinity.

Incorrect: The sunlight danced *between* the many clouds.
Correct: The sunlight danced *among* the many clouds.

Practice A

Explain why each sentence is correct or incorrect.

1. Dionysius acted like he was a dictator.
2. Damon behaved like a true friend.
3. The Greeks honored the friends as if they were heroes.
4. Others have written stories like this legend.
5. This story portrays friendship like it was the most important thing in the world.

Reading Application In the selection, find and explain an example showing the correct use of *as* or *like*.

Practice B

Explain why each sentence is correct or incorrect.

1. A strong friendship developed among Damon and Pythias.
2. The two friends did not let the ruler's cruelty come between them.
3. The legend of the two friends was told between the Greeks.

Writing Application Write a paragraph about "Damon and Pythias." Use *like* to begin a phrase and *as* or *as if* to begin a clause. In addition, use the prepositions *between* and *among* correctly at least once each.

Writing to Sources

Informative Text In the world of the legend, the heroic friendship of the two young nobles and the startling and unprecedented pardon offered by Dionysius are important news stories. Write a brief **script** for a documentary film about these events. To do so, follow these tips:

- Provide the facts, including *who* is involved, *what* happened, and *where, when, why,* and *how* it happened.
- Outline the various perspectives you will offer. For example, you might open with a scholar who introduces the story, cut to a witness who saw the pardon, and conclude with a discussion among commentators.
- As you draft, clearly identify each speaker and describe the visuals you would incorporate.
- Revise, making sure the tone of your report is objective.

Grammar Application Edit your script to avoid common usage problems in both spoken dialogue and any text you display.

Research and Technology

Build and Present Knowledge Over the centuries, the legend of Damon and Pythias has inspired visual artists, writers, and musicians. Research another interpretation of this tale in music, literature, or popular culture. Then, fill out a two-column **"influences" chart** that reflects the choices the writer, composer, or other artist made to represent this ancient Greek legend. Follow these steps to complete your chart:

- Review the representations of the legend you find, observing the choices made to interpret the story in a striking or memorable way. Choose one version to analyze more fully.
- Compare similarities and differences between the version of the story you have chosen and the retelling of the legend by William Russell in this book.
- In one column, note details that show how William Russell interprets the legend.
- In the other column, note details that tell how the other version differs from or complements the legend as it appears in your textbook.

Present your findings to the class.

Common Core State Standards

Reading Literature

7. Analyze the representation of a subject or a key scene in two different artistic mediums, including what is emphasized or absent in each treatment.

Writing

2. Write informative/explanatory texts to examine and convey complex ideas, concepts, and information clearly and accurately through the effective selection, organization, and an analysis of content.

2.b. Develop the topic with well-chosen, relevant, and sufficient facts, extended definitions, concrete details, quotations, or other information and examples appropriate to the audience's knowledge of the topic.

Language

1. Demonstrate command of the conventions of standard English grammar and usage when writing or speaking.

Building Knowledge

Meet the Author

Miguel de Cervantes (1547–1616) Born near Madrid, Spain, Miguel de Cervantes (mē gel′ də sər vän tēz) joined the army as a young man. While returning to Spain from war, he was captured by pirates, who enslaved him for five years. Even after his release Cervantes' troubles were not over: Financial problems eventually led to fines and imprisonment. However, the author's luck changed with the publication of his novel *Don Quixote* (dän′ kē hōt′ ē). The book eased his debts and won him fame. Today, Cervantes is widely regarded as Spain's greatest writer.

Common Core State Standards

Reading Literature

1. Cite strong and thorough textual evidence to support analysis of what the text says explicitly as well as inferences drawn from the text.

6. Analyze a particular point of view or cultural experience reflected in a work of literature from outside the United States, drawing on a wide reading of world literature.

Can anyone be a hero?

Explore the Big Question as you read this selection. Take notes about Cervantes' rather unflattering portrait of Don Quixote at the beginning of the novel.

CLOSE READING FOCUS

Key Ideas and Details: Compare Worldviews

A serious work of literature reflects the writer's **worldview,** his or her basic concept of what the world is like. A writer's worldview defines his or her sense of human nature, social structures, art, nature, and religion. A worldview is the writer's understanding of reality.

A writer's worldview may be similar to those generally held by people in his or her own time, or may differ greatly. In parody, satire, and other works that mock or criticize, a writer may portray a commonly held worldview as an illusion and therefore open to ridicule. As you read, pay attention to Cervantes' descriptions of the stories Don Quixote enjoys and the worldview they represent. Consider the point Cervantes is making about the nature of illusion and reality.

Craft and Structure: Parody

A **parody** is a humorous work in which the author imitates the style or ideas of other works in an exaggerated or a ridiculous way. For example, the following passage parodies the style, conflict, and characters typically found in sports stories:

> John was tense as he flipped the final peanut into the air. Then, he exploded into action. In one flawless move, he snapped his head back, and the peanut dropped neatly into his mouth.

Although parodies are humorous, they often have a deeper purpose: to convey a **theme** or insight by pointing out faulty attitudes, ideals, or values. As you read a parody, look for words and sentences that exaggerate and mock ideas from other literary works.

Vocabulary

The following words are key to your understanding the selection. Copy the words into your notebook. Which is a synonym for *creativity*?

lucidity	**affable**	**ingenuity**
sonorous	**veracious**	**extolled**

CLOSE READING MODEL

The passage below is from the novel *Don Quixote* by Cervantes. The annotations to the right of the passage show ways in which you can use close reading skills to understand elements of parody and to compare worldviews.

from *Don Quixote*

You must know that the above-named gentleman [Don Quixote] devoted his leisure (which was mostly all the year round) to reading books of chivalry—and with such ardor and avidity that he almost entirely abandoned the chase and even the management of his property. To such a pitch did his eagerness and infatuation go that he sold many an acre of tillage to buy books of chivalry to read,[1] bringing home all he could find.

But there were none he liked so well as those written by the famous Feliciano de Silva, for their lucidity of style and complicated conceits were as pearls in his sight, particularly when in his reading he came upon outpourings of adulation and courtly challenges. There he often found passages like *"the reason of the unreason with which my reason is afflicted so weakens my reason that with reason I complain of your beauty"*; or again, *"the high heavens, that of your divinity divinely fortify you with the stars, render you deserving of the desert your greatness deserves."*[2]

Over this sort of folderol the poor gentleman lost his wits...[3]

Compare Worldviews

1 Don Quixote is so captivated by fantasy stories of knights and adventure that he ignores the realities of life, such as attending to his property. He even sells "tillage land," or productive farmland, to buy more books. In the narrator's judgment, Don Quixote's worldview does not reflect what is real and important.

Parody

2 Cervantes mocks the overblown writing style that was common to the books of chivalry that Don Quixote so enjoys. In Don Quixote's eyes, these passages are beautiful and inspirational, but Cervantes' parody shows them as ridiculous.

Compare Worldviews

3 *Folderol* means "foolish nonsense." With a wry sense of humor, the narrator states that Don Quixote actually goes mad from reading too many bad books. In Cervantes' worldview, good writing and clear thinking matters.

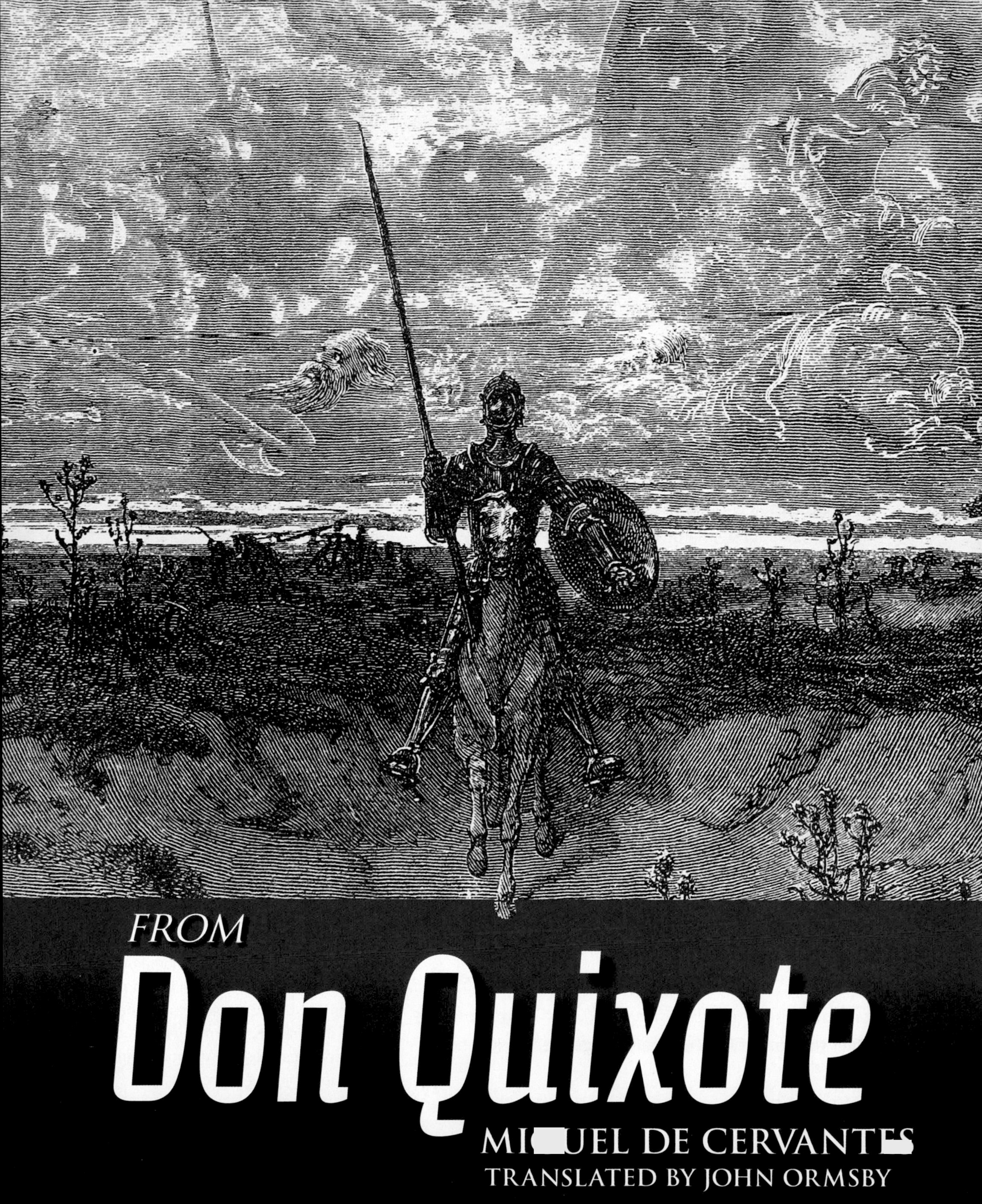

FROM

Don Quixote

MIGUEL DE CERVANTES
TRANSLATED BY JOHN ORMSBY

CHAPTER I

Which Treats of the Character and Pursuits of the Famous Gentleman Don Quixote[1] of La Mancha[2]

In a village of La Mancha, which I prefer to leave unnamed, there lived not long ago one of those gentlemen that keep a lance in the lance-rack, an old shield, a lean hack, and a greyhound for hunting. A stew of rather more beef than mutton, hash on most nights, bacon and eggs on Saturdays, lentils on Fridays, and a pigeon or so extra on Sundays consumed three quarters of his income. The rest went for a coat of fine cloth and velvet breeches and shoes to match for holidays, while on weekdays he cut a fine figure in his best homespun. He had in his house a housekeeper past forty, a niece under twenty, and a lad for the field and marketplace, who saddled the hack as well as handled the pruning knife. The age of this gentleman of ours was bordering on fifty. He was of a hardy constitution, spare, gaunt-featured, a very early riser, and fond of hunting. Some say that his surname was Quixada or Quesada (for there is no unanimity among those who write on the subject), although reasonable conjectures tend to show that he was called Quexana. But this scarcely affects our story; it will be enough not to stray a hair's breadth from the truth in telling it.

Parody
Which details in this paragraph make the formal-sounding chapter title seem ridiculous?

You must know that the above-named gentleman devoted his leisure (which was mostly all the year round) to reading books of chivalry—and with such ardor and avidity that he almost entirely abandoned the chase and even the management of his property. To such a pitch did his eagerness and infatuation go that he sold many an acre of tillage land to buy books of chivalry to read, bringing home all he could find.

But there were none he liked so well as those written by the famous Feliciano de Silva, for their **lucidity** of style and complicated conceits[3] were as pearls in his sight, particularly when in his reading he came upon outpourings of adulation[4] and courtly challenges. There he often found passages like "*the reason of the unreason with which my reason is afflicted so weakens my reason that with reason I complain of your beauty*"; or again, "*the high heavens, that of your divinity divinely fortify you with the stars, render you deserving of the desert your greatness deserves.*"

Over this sort of folderol[5] the poor gentleman lost his wits, and he used to lie awake striving to understand it and worm

◄ **Vocabulary**
lucidity (lo͞o sid′ ə tē) *n.* clarity; quality of being readily understood

Parody
What qualities of the language of heroic tales are mocked in the quotations in this paragraph?

Comprehension
To what activity does Quixada devote most of his time?

1. **Don Quixote** (dän′ kē hōt′ ē).
2. **La Mancha** province (region) in south-central Spain.
3. **conceits** (kən sēts′) *n.* elaborate comparisons or metaphors.
4. **adulation** (a′ jo͞o lā′ shən) *n.* intense or excessive praise or admiration.
5. **folderol** (fäl′ də räl′) *n.* mere nonsense.

▲ **Critical Viewing** What feelings or ideas might Don Quixote associate with this image? Explain.

out its meaning; though Aristotle[6] himself could have made out or extracted nothing, had he come back to life for that special purpose. He was rather uneasy about the wounds which Don Belianís gave and received, because it seemed to him that, however skilled the surgeons who had cured him, he must have had his face and body covered all over with seams and scars. He commended, however, the author's way of ending his book, with a promise to go on with that interminable adventure, and many a time he felt the urge to take up his pen and finish it just as its author had promised. He would no doubt have done so, and succeeded with it too, had he not been occupied with greater and more absorbing thoughts.

Many an argument did he have with the priest of his village (a learned man, and a graduate of Sigüenza[7]) as to which had been the better knight, Palmerín of England or Amadís of Gaul. Master Nicolás, the village barber, however, used to say that neither of them came up to the Knight of Phœbus, and that if there was any that could compare with *him* it was Don Galaor, the brother of Amadís of Gaul, because he had a spirit equal to every occasion, and was no wishy-washy knight or a crybaby like his brother, while in valor he was not a whit behind him.

Spiral Review
THEME What central idea about reading is expressed in this paragraph?

Compare Worldviews
Why might Don Quixote's illusion be so appealing to him?

In short, he became so absorbed in his books that he spent his nights from sunset to sunrise, and his days from dawn to dark, poring over them; and what with little sleep and much reading his brain shriveled up and he lost his wits. His imagination was stuffed with all he read in his books about enchantments, quarrels, battles, challenges, wounds, wooings, loves, agonies, and all sorts of impossible nonsense. It became so firmly planted in his mind that the whole fabric of invention and fancy he read about was true, that to him no history in the world was better substantiated. He used to say the Cid Ruy Díaz[8] was a very good knight but that he was not to be compared with the Knight of the Burning Sword who with one backstroke cut in half two fierce and monstrous giants. He thought more of Bernardo del Carpio because at Roncesvalles he slew Roland in spite of enchantments, availing himself of Hercules' trick when he strangled Antæus the son of Terra in his arms. He approved highly of the giant Morgante, because, although of the giant breed which is always arrogant and ill-mannered, he alone was **affable** and well-bred. But above all he admired Reinaldos of

Vocabulary ▶
affable (af′ ə bəl) *adj.* pleasant; friendly

6. **Aristotle** (ar′ is tät′'l) ancient Greek thinker and scientist.
7. **Sigüenza** (sē gwän′ sä) one of a group of "minor universities" granting degrees that were often laughed at by Spanish humorists.
8. **Cid Ruy Díaz** (sēd ro͞o′ ē dē′ äs) famous Spanish soldier Ruy Díaz de Vivar; called "the Cid," a derivation of the Arabic word for "lord."

Montalbán, especially when he saw him sallying forth from his castle and robbing everyone he met, and when beyond the seas he stole that image of Mohammed which, as his history says, was entirely of gold. To have a bout of kicking at that traitor of a Ganelon he would have given his housekeeper, and his niece into the bargain.

In a word, his wits being quite gone, he hit upon the strangest notion that every madman in this world hit upon. He fancied it was right and requisite, no less for his own greater renown than in the service of his country, that he should make a knight-errant of himself, roaming the world over in full armor and on horseback in quest of adventures. He would put into practice all that he had read of as being the usual practices of knights-errant: righting every kind of wrong, and exposing himself to peril and danger from which he would emerge to reap eternal fame and glory. Already the poor man saw himself crowned by the might of his arm Emperor of Trebizond[9] at least. And so, carried away by the intense enjoyment he found in these pleasant fancies, he began at once to put his scheme into execution.

The first thing he did was to clean up some armor that had belonged to his ancestors and had for ages been lying forgotten in a corner, covered with rust and mildew. He scoured and polished it as best he could, but the one great defect he saw in it was that it had no closed helmet, nothing but a simple morion.[10] This deficiency, however, his **ingenuity** made good, for he contrived a kind of half-helmet of

▲ Critical Viewing
In this illustration, what elements convey Don Quixote's condition?

◀ Vocabulary
ingenuity (in′ jə no͞o′ ə tē) *n.* cleverness

Comprehension
What effect does Don Quixote's reading have on his mind?

9. **Trebizond** (treb′ i zänd′) in medieval times, a Greek empire off the southeast coast of the Black Sea.
10. **morion** (mōr′ ē än′) *n.* old-fashioned soldier's helmet with a brim, covering the top part of the head.

Compare Worldviews How does the narrator's view of the helmet differ from Don Quixote's?

pasteboard which, fitted on to the morion, looked like a whole one. It is true that, in order to see if it was strong and fit to withstand a cut, he drew his sword and gave it a couple of slashes, the first of which undid in an instant what had taken him a week to do. The ease with which he had knocked it to pieces disconcerted him somewhat, and to guard against the danger he set to work again, fixing bars of iron on the inside until he was satisfied with its strength. Then, not caring to try any more experiments with it, he accepted and commissioned it as a helmet of the most perfect construction.

He next proceeded to inspect his nag, which, with its cracked hoofs and more blemishes than the steed of Gonela, that "*tantum pellis et ossa fuit,*"[11] surpassed in his eyes the Bucephalus of Alexander or the Babieca of the Cid.[12] Four days were spent in thinking what name to give him, because (as he said to himself) it was not right that a horse belonging to a knight so famous, and one with such merits of its own, should be without some distinctive name. He strove to find something that would indicate what it had been before belonging to a knight-errant, and what it had now become. It was only reasonable that it should be given a new name to match the new career adopted by its master, and that the name should be a distinguished and full-sounding one, befitting the new order and calling it was about to follow. And so, after having composed, struck out, rejected, added to, unmade, and remade a multitude of names out of his memory and fancy, he decided upon calling it Rocinante. To his thinking this was a lofty, **sonorous** name that nevertheless indicated what the hack's[13] status had been before it became what now it was, the first and foremost of all the hacks in the world.

Parody How does the contrast between the "lofty, sonorous name" and the horse's actual qualities add to the parody?

Having got a name for his horse so much to his taste, he was anxious to get one for himself, and he spent eight days more pondering over this point. At last he made up his mind to call himself Don Quixote—which, as stated above, led the authors of this **veracious** history to infer that his name quite assuredly must have been Quixada, and not Quesada as others would have it. It occurred to him, however, that the valiant Amadís was not content to call himself Amadís and nothing more but added the name of his kingdom and country to make it famous and called himself Amadís of Gaul. So he, like a good knight, resolved to add on the name of his own region and style himself Don Quixote of La Mancha. He believed that this accurately described his origin and country, and

Vocabulary ▶

sonorous (sän´ ər əs) *adj.* having a rich or impressive sound

veracious (və rā´ shəs) *adj.* truthful; honest

11. ***"tantum pellis et ossa fuit"*** (tän´ tum pel´ is et äs´ ə fo͞o´ it) "creature made of skin and bones" (Latin).
12. **Bucephalus** (byo͞o sef´ ə ləs) **of Alexander or the Babieca** (bäb ē ā´ kä) **of the Cid** Bucephalus was Alexander the Great's war horse; Babieca was the Cid's war horse.
13. **hack's** A hack is an old, worn-out horse.

that he did it honor by taking its name for his own.

So then, his armor being furbished, his morion turned into a helmet, his hack christened, and he himself confirmed, he came to the conclusion that nothing more was needed now but to look for a lady to be in love with, for a knight-errant without love was like a tree without leaves or fruit, or a body without a soul.

Don Quixote, **Pablo Picasso**. Bridgeman Art Library, London/New York. @ 2004 Estate of Pabllo Picasso/Artists Rights Society, (ARS), New York.

"If, for my sins, or by my good fortune," he said to himself, "I come across some giant hereabouts, a common occurrence with knights-errant, and knock him to the ground in one onslaught, or cleave him asunder at the waist, or, in short, vanquish and subdue him, will it not be well to have someone I may send him to as a present, that he may come in and fall on his knees before my sweet lady, and in a humble, submissive voice say, 'I am the giant Caraculiambro, lord of the island of Malindrania, vanquished in single combat by the never sufficiently **extolled** knight Don Quixote of La Mancha, who has commanded me to present myself before your grace, that your highness may dispose of me at your pleasure'?"

Oh, how our good gentleman enjoyed the delivery of this speech, especially when he had thought of someone to call his lady! There was, so the story goes, in a village near his own a very good-looking farm-girl with whom he had been at one time in love, though, so far as is known, she never knew it nor gave a thought to the matter. Her name was Aldonza Lorenzo, and upon her he thought fit to confer the title of Lady of his Thoughts. Searching for a name not too remote from her own, yet which would aim at and bring to mind that of a princess and great lady, he decided upon calling her Dulcinea del Toboso, since she was a native of El Toboso. To his way of thinking, the name was musical, uncommon, and significant, like all those he had bestowed upon himself and his belongings.

▲ **Critical Viewing**
In this painting, how does the physical contrast between Sancho Panza and Don Quixote reflect different views of the world?

◀ **Vocabulary**
extolled (ek stōld′) *adj.* praised

Comprehension
What three steps has Don Quixote taken to transform himself into a knight?

CHAPTER VIII

Of the Good Fortune Which the Valiant Don Quixote Had in the Terrible and Undreamed-of Adventure of the Windmills, With Other Occurrences Worthy to Be Fitly Recorded

At this point they came in sight of thirty or forty windmills that are on that plain.

"Fortune," said Don Quixote to his squire, as soon as he had seen them, "is arranging matters for us better than we could have hoped. Look there, friend Sancho Panza,[14] where thirty or more monstrous giants rise up, all of whom I mean to engage in battle and slay, and with whose spoils we shall begin to make our fortunes. For this is righteous warfare, and it is God's good service to sweep so evil a breed from off the face of the earth."

"What giants?" said Sancho Panza.

"Those you see there," answered his master, "with the long arms, and some have them nearly two leagues[15] long."

Compare Worldviews
What different ideas about the windmills do Sancho Panza and Don Quixote have?

"Look, your worship," said Sancho. "What we see there are not giants but windmills, and what seem to be their arms are the vanes that turned by the wind make the millstone go."

"It is easy to see," replied Don Quixote, "that you are not used to this business of adventures. Those are giants, and if you are afraid, away with you out of here and betake yourself to prayer, while I engage them in fierce and unequal combat."

So saying, he gave the spur to his steed Rocinante, heedless of the cries his squire Sancho sent after him, warning him that most certainly they were windmills and not giants he was going to attack. He, however, was so positive they were giants that he neither heard the cries of Sancho, nor perceived, near as he was, what they were.

"Fly not, cowards and vile beings," he shouted, "for a single knight attacks you."

A slight breeze at this moment sprang up, and the great vanes began to move.

"Though ye flourish more arms than the giant Briareus, ye have to reckon with me!" exclaimed Don Quixote, when he saw this.

So saying, he commended himself with all his heart to his lady Dulcinea, imploring her to support him in such a peril. With lance braced and covered by his shield, he charged at Rocinante's fullest gallop and attacked the first mill that stood in front of him. But as he drove his lance-point into the sail, the wind whirled it around with

14. Sancho Panza a simple countryman whom Don Quixote takes as his squire. In contrast to Don Quixote, Panza is practical and has common sense.

15. leagues (lēgz) *n.* A league is a distance of about three miles in English-speaking countries.

such force that it shivered the lance to pieces. It swept away with it horse and rider, and they were sent rolling over the plain, in sad condition indeed.

Sancho hastened to his assistance as fast as the animal could go. When he came up he found Don Quixote unable to move, with such an impact had Rocinante fallen with him.

"God bless me!" said Sancho. "Did I not tell your worship to watch what you were doing, because they were only windmills? No one could have made any mistake about it unless he had something of the same kind in his head."

"Silence, friend Sancho," replied Don Quixote. "The fortunes of war more than any other are liable to frequent fluctuations. Moreover I think, and it is the truth, that that same sage Frestón who carried off my study and books, has turned these giants into mills in order to rob me of the glory of vanquishing them, such is the enmity he bears me. But in the end his wicked arts will avail but little against my good sword."

"God's will be done," said Sancho Panza, and helping him to rise got him up again on Rocinante, whose shoulder was half dislocated. Then, discussing the adventure, they followed the road to Puerto Lápice, for there, said Don Quixote, they could not fail to find adventures in abundance and variety, as it was a well-traveled thoroughfare. For all that, he was much grieved at the loss of his lance, and said so to his squire.

"I remember having read," he added, "how a Spanish knight, Diego Pérez de Vargas by name, having broken his sword in battle, tore from an oak a ponderous bough or branch. With it he did such things that day, and pounded so many Moors, that he got the surname of Machuca, and he and his descendants from that day forth were called Vargas y Machuca. I mention this because from the first oak I see I mean to tear such a branch, large and stout. I am determined and resolved to do such deeds with it that you may deem yourself very fortunate in being found worthy to see them and be an eyewitness of things that will scarcely be believed."

"Be that as God wills," said Sancho, "I believe it all as your worship says it. But straighten yourself a little, for you seem to be leaning to one side, maybe from the shaking you got when you fell."

▲ Critical Viewing
Which details in this painting capture the humor of Don Quixote's "battle" with the windmills?

Parody
How does the contrast between Don Quixote's ridiculous defeat and these brave words contribute to the humor in this parody?

Comprehension
Which "enemy" does Don Quixote decide to battle?

"That is the truth," said Don Quixote, "and if I make no complaint of the pain it is because knights-errant are not permitted to complain of any wound, even though their bowels be coming out through it."

"If so," said Sancho, "I have nothing to say. But God knows I would rather your worship complained when anything ailed you. For my part, I confess I must complain however small the ache may be, unless this rule about not complaining applies to the squires of knights-errant also."

Don Quixote could not help laughing at his squire's simplicity, and assured him he might complain whenever and however he chose, just as he liked. So far he had never read of anything to the contrary in the order of knighthood.

Sancho reminded him it was dinner time, to which his master answered that he wanted nothing himself just then, but that Sancho might eat when he had a mind. With this permission Sancho settled himself as comfortably as he could on his beast, and taking out of the saddlebags what he had stowed away in them, he jogged along behind his master munching slowly. From time to time he took a pull at the wineskin with all the enjoyment that the thirstiest tavernkeeper in Málaga might have envied. And while he went on in this way, between gulps, he never gave a thought to any of the promises his master had made him, nor did he rate it as hardship but rather as recreation going in quest of adventures, however dangerous they might be.

Compare Worldviews What contrasting views of bodily comfort do Don Quixote and Sancho Panza have?

Language Study

Vocabulary Replace the italicized word in each numbered sentence with an antonym from the list of words shown in blue. Explain which version of the sentence makes better sense.

lucidity **affable** **ingenuity** **sonorous** **veracious**

1. The *vagueness* of his idea convinced other scientists to accept it.
2. The speaker's *squeaky* voice soothed his listeners.
3. Everyone liked her because of her *unpleasant* personality.
4. Her clear and original science project showcased her *inability*.
5. She was *dishonest* to a fault and always said what she meant.

WORD STUDY

The **Latin prefix *ex-*** means "up" or "out." In this selection, a character thinks his accomplishments have not been adequately **extolled**, or praised highly enough.

Word Study

Part A Explain how the **Latin prefix *ex-*** contributes to the meanings of these words: *excel, exalt,* and *expansion*. Consult a dictionary if necessary.

Part B Use the context of the sentences and what you know about the Latin prefix *ex-* to explain your answer to each question.

1. If you *excavate* a hole, are you filling it in?
2. If a store charges *exorbitant* prices, are its prices normal?

Literary Analysis

Key Ideas and Details

1. **(a)** What does Don Quixote spend most of his time doing before he becomes a knight? **(b) Analyze Cause and Effect:** In what way does this activity bring about his decision? Explain.
2. **(a)** Why does Don Quixote attack the windmills? **(b) Connect:** How does he explain his failure to conquer them? **(c) Hypothesize:** What would happen to his dreams of knightly adventure if he admitted the truth about the windmills? Use details from the text to support your answer.
3. **Infer:** Why do you think Sancho agrees to go adventuring with Don Quixote? Cite details from the text to support your response.
4. **Compare Worldviews (a)** Compare and contrast Don Quixote's responses with Sancho Panza's in two situations. **(b)** In what way do these contrasts emphasize the fact that Don Quixote's beliefs are illusions? Explain.

Craft and Structure

5. **Parody** In what way is Don Quixote's adventure with the windmills a parody of an episode from a romance or legend? Explain, citing specific details from the text.
6. **Parody** Using a chart like the one shown, note examples of specific ways in which Don Quixote is a parody of a heroic knight. Then, explain how his deeds and appearance both reflect and contrast with the traditional character of a knight.
7. **Parody (a)** In *Don Quixote,* what attitudes, values, and beliefs does Cervantes criticize through parody? **(b)** Based on your reading of the parody, what values and beliefs do you think Cervantes respects? Cite details from the text that support your responses.

Legendary Knight
1. wears shining armor
2. rides a great steed
3. pledges love to a lady
4. conquers giants
5. other: ____________ ____________
Don Quixote
1.
2.
3.
4.
5.

Integration of Knowledge and Ideas

8. **Interpret:** Why does Don Quixote insist on calling Aldonza by the name of Dulcinea del Toboso? Explain, citing details from the text to support your response.

9. THE BIG ? **Can anyone be a hero? (a)** Do you think that Don Quixote displays heroic qualities in a genuine way? Explain why or why not. **(b)** If a person takes heroic action, does it matter if their motivations are muddled or what the results are? Explain your position, using Don Quixote as an example.

ACADEMIC VOCABULARY

As you write and speak about *Don Quixote*, use the words related to heroism that you explored on page 771 of this textbook.

Conventions: Semicolons, Colons, and Ellipsis Points

Semicolons, colons, and **ellipses** are three types of punctuation that suggest pauses in a sentence.

Use a **semicolon** to join independent clauses that are not already joined by a coordinating conjunction (*and, but, or, nor, for, so,* and *yet*). You may also use semicolons to separate items in a series when one or more of the items already contains a comma.

Example: Don Quixote devised a plan; he was confident of success.

A **colon** directs the reader's attention to the text that follows it. Use a colon to introduce a list, a quotation, or an example.

Example: The list contained only a few items: milk, soap, and eggs.

The three spaced periods that form an **ellipsis** represent a gap or a pause within a sentence. Ellipsis points may also show that text has been omitted from a passage.

Example: Don Quixote loved a farm girl named Aldonza, although he insisted on calling her Dulcinea … he liked that name better.

Practice A

Copy each of the following sentences, adding semicolons, colons, or ellipsis points where necessary.

1. Sancho Panza was content to follow his master he did not care if his master was strange.
2. Don Quixote believed in knightly virtues chivalry, honesty, and courage.
3. "Sir," Sancho said hesitantly. "I'm very tired can we please stop and eat?"

Reading Application Find an example of a semicolon in the excerpt from *Don Quixote*. Explain the function the punctuation serves.

Practice B

Rewrite the following sentences, correcting any errors by inserting or deleting semicolons, colons, or ellipsis points. If no corrections are necessary, write "correct."

1. Don Quixote collected the necessary items; armor, a helmet, his sword, and a horse.
2. They decided to: fight a great foe . . . windmills.
3. Don Quixote conquers the windmills; although Sancho does not help him.

Writing Application Write three sentences about the illustration on page 833. Use a semicolon, a colon, or ellipsis points in each sentence.

Writing to Sources

Narrative Write a **parody** of a heroic tale in which Don Quixote is transplanted to the twenty-first century. In your parody, have him take on a twenty-first-century challenge. Follow these tips:

- Choose a modern situation that Don Quixote might misunderstand. Outline the sequence of events you will relate in your parody.
- Choose your story's narrator and decide the attitude he or she will hold toward the characters and events.
- Clearly depict both the reality of what is happening and the illusions in characters' minds. Write interior monologues expressing the characters' feelings and opinions. Use dialogue to depict interactions among the characters.
- Add details in longer sentences to slow the story's pace and introduce characters or settings. Use short sentences and punchy language to speed the pace and add excitement.
- Exaggerate details and descriptions of characters' actions and reactions to convey the humor of the events.

Grammar Application Make sure you have properly used semicolons, colons, and ellipsis points in your parody.

Research and Technology

Build and Present Knowledge Working with a group, write and design a **biographical brochure** of Miguel de Cervantes. Brainstorm several research questions to guide your research. Then, use biographical dictionaries, the Internet, the library, and other reliable sources to find answers to your questions. Once you have gathered your information, write and design the brochure, following these tips:

- Identify key details and events from the author's life, including information about his literary works and achievements.
- Make meaningful connections between the information you learn from research and the excerpt from *Don Quixote*.
- Use publishing software to design and publish your document.
- Apply design principles when setting margins, tabs, spacing, or columns. Select a clear readable font.
- Incorporate drawings and graphics into your finished work.

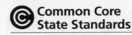

Common Core State Standards

Writing

3.b. Use narrative techniques, such as dialogue, pacing, description, reflection, and multiple plot lines, to develop experiences, events, and/or characters.

3.c. Use a variety of techniques to sequence events so that they build on one another to create a coherent whole.

3.d. Use precise words and phrases, telling details, and sensory language to convey a vivid picture of the experiences, events, setting, and/or characters.

7. Conduct short as well as more sustained research projects to answer a question or solve a problem; narrow or broaden the inquiry when appropriate; synthesize multiple sources on the subject, demonstrating understanding of the subject under investigation.

Language

2. Demonstrate command of the conventions of standard English capitalization, punctuation, and spelling when writing.

2.a. Use a semicolon to link two or more closely related independent clauses.

2.b. Use a colon to introduce a list or quotation.

Comparing Texts

Can anyone be a hero?

Explore the Big Question as you read these texts. Take notes on the ways in which each story presents heroic figures.

READING TO COMPARE ARCHETYPAL NARRATIVE PATTERNS

These two stories—one a myth and the other a fairy tale—are classic examples of archetypal narratives. As you read each text, notice how it exhibits certain patterns or types of events. Then, compare those archetypal elements.

MYTH

Cupid

There once lived a king and queen who had three daughters. The two elder daughters were beautiful, but the youngest daughter, Psyche,[1] was the loveliest maiden in the whole world. The fame of her beauty was so great that strangers from neighboring countries came in crowds to admire her, paying her the homage which is only due Venus[2] herself. In fact, Venus found her altars deserted, as men turned their devotion to the exquisite young girl. People sang her praises as she walked the streets, and strewed chaplets and flowers before her.

This adulation infuriated Venus. Shaking her silken locks in indignation, she exclaimed, "Am I then to be eclipsed by a mortal girl? In vain did that royal shepherd whose judgment was approved by Jupiter himself give me the palm of beauty over my illustrious rivals, Minerva and Juno.[3] I will give this Psyche cause to repent of so unlawful a beauty."

She complained to her son, Cupid, and led him to the land where Psyche lived, so that he could see for himself the insults the girl unconsciously heaped upon his mother. "My dear son," said Venus, "punish that beauty. Give thy mother a revenge as sweet as her injuries are great. Infuse into the bosom of that haughty girl a passion for some low, mean, unworthy being, so that she may reap a shame as great as her present joy and triumph."

1. **Psyche** a beautiful princess in Roman mythology.
2. **Venus** the Roman goddess of love and beauty.
3. **royal shepherd. . . Minerva and Juno** in Greek and Roman mythology, Paris, a prince who lived as a shepherd, was called to judge who was most beautiful of three goddesses: Juno, queen of the gods; Minerva, goddess of wisdom; or Venus, goddess of love.

FAIRY TALE

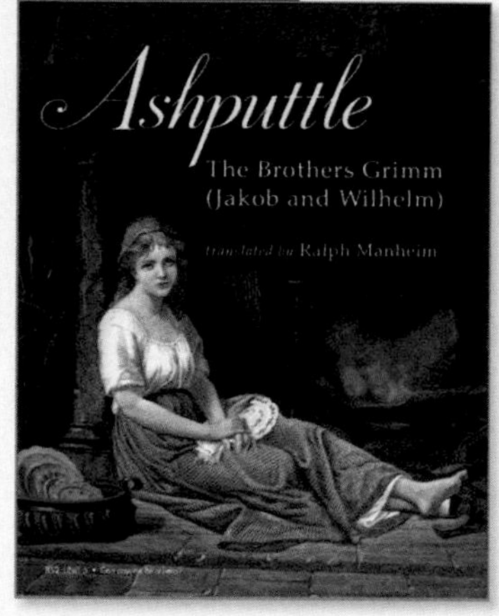

"Cupid and Psyche"

Lucius Apuleius (ca. A.D. 124–170)
Sally Benson (1897–1972)

Although the tale of Cupid and Psyche goes back to Greek mythology, the best-known version is in the *Metamorphoses* by the ancient Roman writer Lucius Apuleius. Sally Benson, who reworked the original version for modern readers, won fame with her own short stories. Her collection *Meet Me in St. Louis,* based on her Missouri childhood, was adapted as a movie musical.

"Ashputtle"

Jakob Grimm (1785–1863)
Wilhelm Grimm (1786–1859)

Born in the German state of Hesse, Jakob and Wilhelm Grimm grew up in poverty after their father died. Although both studied law, they were most interested in language and literature. The brothers began collecting tales that people told in Hesse and neighboring places. Today, the Brothers Grimm are most remembered for the fairy tales they preserved, including "Rumpelstiltskin" and "Snow White."

Comparing Archetypal Narrative Patterns

Archetypal narrative patterns are storytelling structures found in the literature of cultures from throughout the world. These patterns often appear in stories from the oral tradition, such as folk tales, fairy tales, legends, and myths. Like familiar routines, these patterns make stories easier to remember and retell. Common archetypal narrative patterns include the following types of events, characters, and thematic elements:

- a series of tests, often seemingly impossible, that a character must pass
- an arduous quest or task a character must perform
- characters, events, or objects that come in threes
- secondary characters, who are often supernatural figures and guide, comfort, or help the hero or heroine
- a greedy, cruel, or jealous relative—often a parent or stepparent—who behaves unfairly
- an ideal romantic match and unworthy rivals
- a hero or heroine, often of noble birth, whose true, elevated identity is hidden or secret
- a hero who triumphs over stronger forces through cleverness or virtue
- a just end that rewards good and punishes evil

These narrative patterns may seem very familiar to you, and not just from stories you have read. Although they originate in folk literature, archetypal structures continue to shape modern narratives in all genres. Movies, television shows, and video games are often built on such archetypes. Some psychological theories hold that the existence of archetypal patterns in literature from every era and culture shows essential truths about how human beings experience life, understand ourselves, and process information.

As you read this myth and fairy tale, use a chart like the one shown to analyze the archetypal narrative pattern each one follows.

Story Detail	Archetypal Pattern
three sisters	characters that come in threes
help from the birds	

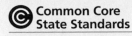

Common Core State Standards

Reading Literature

2. Determine a theme or central idea of a text and analyze in detail its development over the course of the text, including how it emerges and is shaped and refined by specific details; provide an objective summary of the text.

5. Analyze how an author's choices concerning how to structure a text, order events within it, and manipulate time create such effects as mystery, tension, or surprise.

Writing

2. Write informative/explanatory texts to examine and convey complex ideas, concepts, and information clearly and accurately through the effective selection, organization, and analysis of content.

2.c. Use appropriate and varied transitions to link the major sections of the text, create cohesion, and clarify the relationships among complex ideas and concepts.

10. Write routinely over extended time frames and shorter time frames for a range of tasks, purposes, and audiences.

Cupid

There once lived a king and queen who had three daughters. The two elder daughters were beautiful, but the youngest daughter, Psyche,[1] was the loveliest maiden in the whole world. The fame of her beauty was so great that strangers from neighboring countries came in crowds to admire her, paying her the homage which is only due Venus[2] herself. In fact, Venus found her altars deserted, as men turned their devotion to the exquisite young girl. People sang her praises as she walked the streets, and strewed chaplets and flowers before her.

This **adulation** infuriated Venus. Shaking her silken locks in indignation, she exclaimed, "Am I then to be eclipsed by a mortal girl? In vain did that royal shepherd whose judgment was approved by Jupiter himself give me the palm of beauty over my illustrious rivals, Minerva and Juno.[3] I will give this Psyche cause to repent of so unlawful a beauty."

She complained to her son, Cupid, and led him to the land where Psyche lived, so that he could see for himself the insults the girl unconsciously heaped upon his mother. "My dear son," said Venus, "punish that beauty. Give thy mother a revenge as sweet as her injuries are great. Infuse into the bosom of that haughty girl a passion for some low, mean, unworthy being, so that she may reap a shame as great as her present joy and triumph."

1. **Psyche** (sī´ kē) a beautiful princess in Roman mythology.
2. **Venus** (vē´ nəs) the Roman goddess of love and beauty.
3. **royal shepherd. . . Minerva** (mi nur´ və) **and Juno** (jo͞o´ nō) In Greek and Roman mythology, Paris, a prince who lived as a shepherd, was called to judge who was most beautiful of three goddesses: Juno, queen of the gods; Minerva, goddess of wisdom; or Venus, goddess of love.

Now, there were two fountains in Venus' garden, one of sweet waters, the other of bitter. Cupid filled two amber vases, one from each fountain and, suspending them from the top of his quiver, hastened to Psyche's chamber, where she lay asleep. He shed a few drops from the bitter fountain over her lips, though she looked so beautiful in her sleep that he was filled with pity. Then he touched her side with the point of his arrow. At the touch, she awoke and opened her eyes on Cupid, who was so startled by their blue enchantment that he wounded himself with his own arrow. He hovered over her, invisible, and to repair the damage he had done, he poured the water from the sweet fountain over her silken ringlets.

Psyche, thus frowned upon by Venus, derived no benefit from all her charms. All eyes were still cast eagerly upon her and every mouth spoke her praise, but neither king, royal youth, or common man presented himself to demand her hand in marriage. Her two elder sisters were married to royal princes, but Psyche, in her lonely apartment, wept over her beauty, sick of the flattery it aroused, while love was denied her.

Her parents, afraid that they had unwittingly incurred the anger of the gods, consulted the oracle of Apollo,[4] and received this answer: "The girl is destined for the bride of no mortal lover. Her future husband awaits her on the top of the mountain. He is a monster whom neither the gods nor men can resist."

This dreadful decree of the oracle filled all the people with dismay, and her parents abandoned themselves to grief. But Psyche said, "Why, my dear parents, do you now lament me? You should rather have grieved when the people showered undeserved honors upon me and with one voice called me 'Venus.' I now perceive I am a victim to that name. I submit. Lead me to that rock to which my unhappy fate has destined me."

She dressed herself in gorgeous robes, and her beauty was so dazzling that people turned away as it was more than they could bear. Then, followed by wailing and lamenting crowds, she and her parents ascended the mountain. On the summit, her father and mother left her alone, and returned home in tears.

◀ Critical Viewing
For some artists, Psyche is a symbol of the human soul striving after wisdom. Which details in this painting support this interpretation?

Archetypal Narrative Patterns
Which archetypal pattern does the fact that there are three sisters illustrate?

◀ Vocabulary
adulation (a´ jo͞o lā´ shən) *n.* excessive praise

Comprehesion
Why is Venus angry with Psyche?

4. **oracle** (ôr´ ə kəl) **of Apollo** (ə päl´ ō) Apollo was the Greek and Roman god of light, music, and medicine. An oracle was a person who revealed the will of the gods in answer to people's questions.

▲ **Critical Viewing**
Which details of this painting suggest Cupid's love for Psyche?

While Psyche stood on the ridge of the mountain, panting with fear and sobbing aloud, the gentle Zephyrus[5] raised her from the earth and bore her with an easy motion into a flowery dale. There she lay down on a grassy bank and fell asleep. She awoke refreshed, and saw near by a pleasant grove of tall and stately trees. She entered it, and discovered a fountain sending forth clear and crystal waters, and near it stood a magnificent palace that was too stupendous to have been the work of mortal hands. Drawn by admiration and wonder, she walked through the huge doors. Inside, golden pillars supported the vaulted roof, and the walls were hung with delightful paintings. She wandered through the empty rooms marveling at what she saw, when suddenly a voice addressed her. "Sovereign lady," it said, "all that you see is yours. We whose voices you hear are your servants and shall obey all your commands with the utmost care and diligence. Retire, therefore, to your chamber and repose on your bed of down, and when you see fit, repair to the bath. Supper awaits you in the adjoining alcove when it pleases you to take your seat there."

Psyche listened with amazement, and, going to her room, she lay down and rested. Then, after a refreshing bath, she went to the alcove, where a table wheeled itself into the room without any visible aid. It was covered with the finest delicacies and the most wonderful wines. There even was music from invisible performers.

She had not yet seen her destined husband. He came only in the hours of darkness and fled before dawn, but his accents were full of love and inspired a like passion in her. She often begged him to stay and let her behold him, but he would not consent. On the contrary, he charged her to make no attempt to see him, for it was his pleasure, for the best of reasons, to remain concealed. "Why should you wish to behold me?" he asked. "Have you any doubt of my love? If you saw me, perhaps you would fear me, perhaps adore me. But all I ask of you is to love me. I would rather have you love me as an equal than adore me as a god."

Archetypal Narrative Patterns
What test does Cupid set for Psyche?

This reasoning satisfied Psyche for a time and she lived quite happily alone in the huge palace. But at length she thought of her

5. **Zephyrus** (zef′ ə rəs) in Greek mythology, god of the west wind.

parents who were in ignorance of her fate, and of her sisters with whom she wished to share the delights of her new home. These thoughts preyed on her mind and made her think of her splendid mansion as a prison. When her husband came one night, she told him of her distress, and at last drew from him an unwilling consent that her sisters should be brought to see her.

So, calling Zephyrus, she told him of her husband's command, and he soon brought them across the mountain down to their sister's valley. They embraced her, and Psyche's eyes filled with tears of joy. "Come," she said, "enter my house and refresh yourselves." Taking them by their hands, she led them into her golden palace and committed them to the care of her numerous train[6] of attendant voices, to refresh themselves in her baths and at her table, and to show them all her treasures. The sight of all these splendid things filled her sisters with envy, and they resented the thought that she possessed such splendor which far exceeded anything they owned.

They asked her numberless questions, and begged her to tell them what sort of person her husband was. Psyche replied that he was a beautiful youth who generally spent the daytime in hunting upon the mountains. The sisters, not satisfied with this reply, soon made her confess that she had never seen him. They then proceeded to fill her bosom with dire suspicions. "Call to mind," they said, "the Pythian oracle[7] that declared that you were destined to marry a direful and tremendous monster. The inhabitants of this valley say that your husband is a terrible and monstrous serpent, who nourishes you for a while with dainties that he may by and by devour you. Take our advice. Provide yourself with a lamp and a sharp knife. Put them in concealment so that your husband may not discover them, and when he is sound asleep, slip out of bed, bring forth your lamp and see for yourself whether what they say is true or not. If it is, hesitate not to cut off the monster's head, and thereby recover your liberty."

Spiral Review
ARCHETYPAL CHARACTERS How are the sisters similar to other antagonists found in literature?

Psyche resisted these persuasions as well as she could, but they did not fail to have their effect on her mind, and when her sisters were gone, their words and her own curiosity were too strong for her to resist. She prepared her lamp and a sharp knife, and hid them out of sight of her husband. When he had fallen into his first sleep, she silently arose, and uncovering her lamp beheld him. He lay there, the most beautiful and charming of the gods, with his golden ringlets wandering over his snowy neck and crimson cheek. On his shoulders were two dewy wings, whiter than snow, with shining feathers.

Comprehension
What do Psyche's sisters persuade her to do?

---

6. **train** (trān) *n.* group of followers, such as servants.
7. **Pythian** (pith′ ē ən) **oracle** oracle of Apollo, called Pythian after Python, the monstrous snake that Apollo killed.

As she leaned over with the lamp to have a closer view of his face, a drop of burning oil fell on his shoulder, and made him wince with pain. He opened his eyes and fixed them full upon her. Then, without saying a word, he spread his white wings and flew out of the window. Psyche cried out and tried to follow him, falling from the window to the ground. Cupid, beholding her as she lay in the dust, stopped his flight for an instant and said, "O foolish Psyche! Is it thus you repay my love? After having disobeyed my mother's commands and made you my wife, will you think me a monster and cut off my head? But go. Return to your sisters whose advice you seem to think better than mine. I inflict no other punishment on you than to leave you forever. Love cannot dwell with suspicion."

He soared into the air, leaving poor Psyche prostrate on the ground.

Archetypal Narrative Patterns
In what other stories have you encountered a mysterious building like the palace?

When she recovered some degree of composure, she looked around her. The palace and gardens had vanished, and she found herself in an open field not far from the city where her sisters dwelt. She went to them and told them the whole story of her misfortune, at which, pretending to grieve, they inwardly rejoiced. "For now," they said, "he will perhaps choose one of us." With this idea, without saying a word of her intentions, each of them rose early the next morning and ascended the mountain and, having reached the top, called upon Zephyrus to receive her and bear her to his lord. Then, leaping into space, and not being sustained by Zephyrus, they fell down the precipice and were dashed to pieces.

Psyche, meanwhile, wandered day and night, without food or rest, in search of her husband. One day, seeing a lofty mountain in the distance, she sighed and said to herself, "Perhaps my love, my lord, inhabits there."

On the mountain top was a temple and she no sooner entered it than she saw heaps of corn, some in loose ears and some in sheaves,[8] with mingled ears of barley. Scattered about lay sickles and rakes, and all the instruments of harvest, without order, as if thrown carelessly out of the weary reapers' hands in the sultry hours of the day.

Psyche put an end to this unseemly confusion by separating and sorting everything to its proper place and kind, believing that she ought to neglect none of the gods, but endeavor by her piety to engage them all in her behalf. The holy Ceres,[9] whose temple it was, finding her so religiously employed, spoke to her, "O Psyche, truly worthy of our pity, though I cannot shield you from the frowns of Venus, yet I can teach you how to best allay her displeasure. Go then, and voluntarily surrender yourself to her, and try by modesty and submission to win her forgiveness, and perhaps her favor will restore you to the husband you have lost."

Vocabulary ▶
allay (a lā´) *v.* relieve; lessen; calm

8. **sheaves** (shēvz) *n.* bundles of stalks of grain.
9. **Ceres** (sir´ ēz´) Roman goddess of farming.

Psyche obeyed the commands of Ceres and journeyed to the temple of Venus. Venus received her in a fury of anger. "Most undutiful and faithless of servants," she said, "do you at last remember that you really have a mistress? Or have you come to see your sick husband, yet laid up with the wound given him by his loving wife? You are so ill-favored and disagreeable that the only way you can merit your lover must be by dint of industry and diligence. I will make trial of your housewifery."

She ordered Psyche to be led to the storehouse of her temple, where a great quantity of wheat, barley, millet, beans and lentils, which was used as food for her pigeons, lay scattered about the floors. Then Venus said, "Take and separate all these grains into their proper parcels, and see that you get it done before evening."

Psyche, in consternation over the enormous task, sat stupid and silent. While she sat despairing, Cupid stirred up the little ant, a native of the fields, to take compassion on her. The leader of the ant-hill, followed by whole hosts of his six-legged subjects, went to work and sorted each grain to its parcel. And when all was done, the ants vanished out of sight.

At twilight, Venus returned from the banquet of the gods, crowned with roses. Seeing the task done, she exclaimed, "This is no work of yours, wicked one, but his, whom to your own and his misfortune you have enticed." So saying, she threw her a piece of black bread for her supper and went away.

Next morning Venus ordered Psyche to be called and said to her, "Behold yonder grove which stretches along the margin of the water. There you will find sheep feeding without a shepherd, with gold-shining fleeces on their backs. Go, fetch me a sample of that precious wool from every one of their fleeces."

Psyche obediently went to the river side, prepared to do her best to execute the command. But the river god inspired the reeds with harmonious murmurs, which seemed to say, "O maiden, severely tried, tempt not the dangerous flood, nor venture among formidable rams on the other side, for as long as they are under the influence of the rising sun they burn with a cruel rage to destroy mortals with their sharp horns or rude teeth. But when the noontide sun has driven the cattle to the shade, and the serene spirit of the flood has lulled them to rest, you may then cross in safety, and you will find the woolly gold sticking to the bushes and the trunks of the trees."

She followed the compassionate river god's instructions and soon returned to Venus with her arms full of the golden fleece. Venus, in a rage, cried, "I know very well it is by none of your own doings that you have succeeded in this task. And I am not satisfied yet that you have any capacity to make yourself useful. But I have another task for you. Here, take this box, and go your way to the infernal shade

Comprehension
What does Cupid do after Psyche exposes his identity?

Archetypal Narrative Patterns
Identify an archetypal pattern developed here.

and give this box to Proserpina[10] and say, 'My mistress, Venus, desires you to send her a little of your beauty, for in tending her sick son, she has lost some of her own.' Be not too long on your errand, for I must paint myself with it to appear at the circle of gods and goddesses this evening."

Psyche was now sure that her destruction was at hand, being obliged to go with her own feet down to the deathly regions of Erebus.[11] So as not to delay, she went to the highest tower prepared to hurl herself headlong from it down to the shades below. But a voice from the tower said to her, "Why, poor unlucky girl, dost thou design to put an end to thy days in so dreadful a manner? And what cowardice makes thee sink under this last danger who hast been so miraculously supported in all thy former perils?"

Then the voice told her how she might reach the realms of Pluto[12] by way of a certain cave, and how to avoid the perils of the road, how to pass by Cerberus,[13] the three-headed dog, and prevail on Charon,[14] the ferryman, to take her across the black river and bring her back again. And the voice added, "When Proserpina has given you the box filled with her beauty, of all things this is chiefly to be observed by you, that you never once open or look into the box, nor allow your curiosity to pry into the treasure of the beauty of the goddesses."

Psyche, encouraged by this advice, obeyed in all things, and traveled to the kingdom of Pluto. She was admitted to the palace of Proserpina, and without accepting the delicate seat or delicious banquet that was offered her, but content with coarse bread for her food, she delivered her message from Venus. Presently the box was returned to her, shut, and filled with the precious commodity. She returned the way she came, happy to see the light of day once more.

Having got so far successfully through her dangerous task, a desire seized her to examine the contents of the box. "What," she said to herself, "shall I, the carrier of this divine beauty, not take the least bit to put on my cheeks to appear to more advantage in the eyes of my beloved husband!" She carefully opened the box, and found nothing there of any beauty at all, but an infernal and truly Stygian[15] sleep, which, being set free from its prison, took possession of her. She fell down in the road, unconscious, without sense or motion.

---

10. **infernal shade . . . Proserpina** (prō sur´ pi nə) In Greek and Roman mythology, the dead inhabit an "infernal shade," or dark region under the earth. Proserpina, daughter of Ceres, is the wife of Pluto, the god who rules this region.
11. **Erebus** (er´ ə bəs) in Greek mythology, the place under the earth through which the dead pass before entering the underworld.
12. **Pluto** (plo͞ot´ ō) Roman god of the underworld.
13. **Cerberus** (sur´ bər əs) in Greek and Roman mythology, the three-headed dog guarding the entrance to the underworld.
14. **Charon** (ker´ ən) in Greek mythology, the ferryman who carried the dead over the river Styx into the underworld.
15. **Stygian** (stij´ ē ən) *adj.* of the river Styx, a mythological river crossed by the dead on their way to the underworld.

Cupid had recovered from his wound and was no longer able to bear the absence of his beloved Psyche. He slipped through the smallest crack in the window of his chamber and flew to the spot where Psyche lay. He gathered up the sleep from her body and closed it again in the box. Then he waked Psyche with a light touch from one of his arrows.

"Again," he said, "hast thou almost perished by the same curiosity. But now perform exactly the task imposed on you by my mother, and I will take care of the rest."

Swift as lightning, he left the earth and penetrated the heights of heaven. Here he presented himself before Jupiter with his supplication. The god lent a favoring ear, and pleaded the cause of the lovers so earnestly with Venus that he won her consent. Then he sent Mercury to bring Psyche up to the heavenly assemblage, and when she arrived, he handed her a cup of ambrosia[16] and said, "Drink this, Psyche, and be immortal. Nor shall Cupid ever break away from the knot in which he is tied, but these nuptials[17] shall be perpetual."

Psyche became at last united to Cupid forever.

---

16. **ambrosia** (am brō´ zhə) *n.* food of the gods.
17. **nuptials** (nup´ shəlz) *n.* wedding.

Critical Thinking

1. **Key Ideas and Details: (a)** What reason does Venus give for sending Cupid to Psyche? **(b) Compare and Contrast:** Compare her plan with its actual outcome.
2. **Key Ideas and Details: (a)** What tasks does Venus require Psyche to perform? **(b) Connect:** In the third task, in what way does Psyche repeat her earlier mistake with Cupid?
3. **Key Ideas and Details: (a)** What does Cupid mean when he says, "Love cannot dwell with suspicion"? **(b) Draw Conclusions:** What lesson does the story suggest about love? Explain.
4. **Integration of Knowledge and Ideas:** Do you think that Psyche could be considered a hero? If your answer is *yes*, explain in what way you think she is heroic. If your answer is *no*, what do you think she could have done differently that would have made her a hero? ***[Connect to the Big Question: Can anyone be a hero?]***

Ashputtle

The Brothers Grimm (Jakob and Wilhelm)

translated by Ralph Manheim

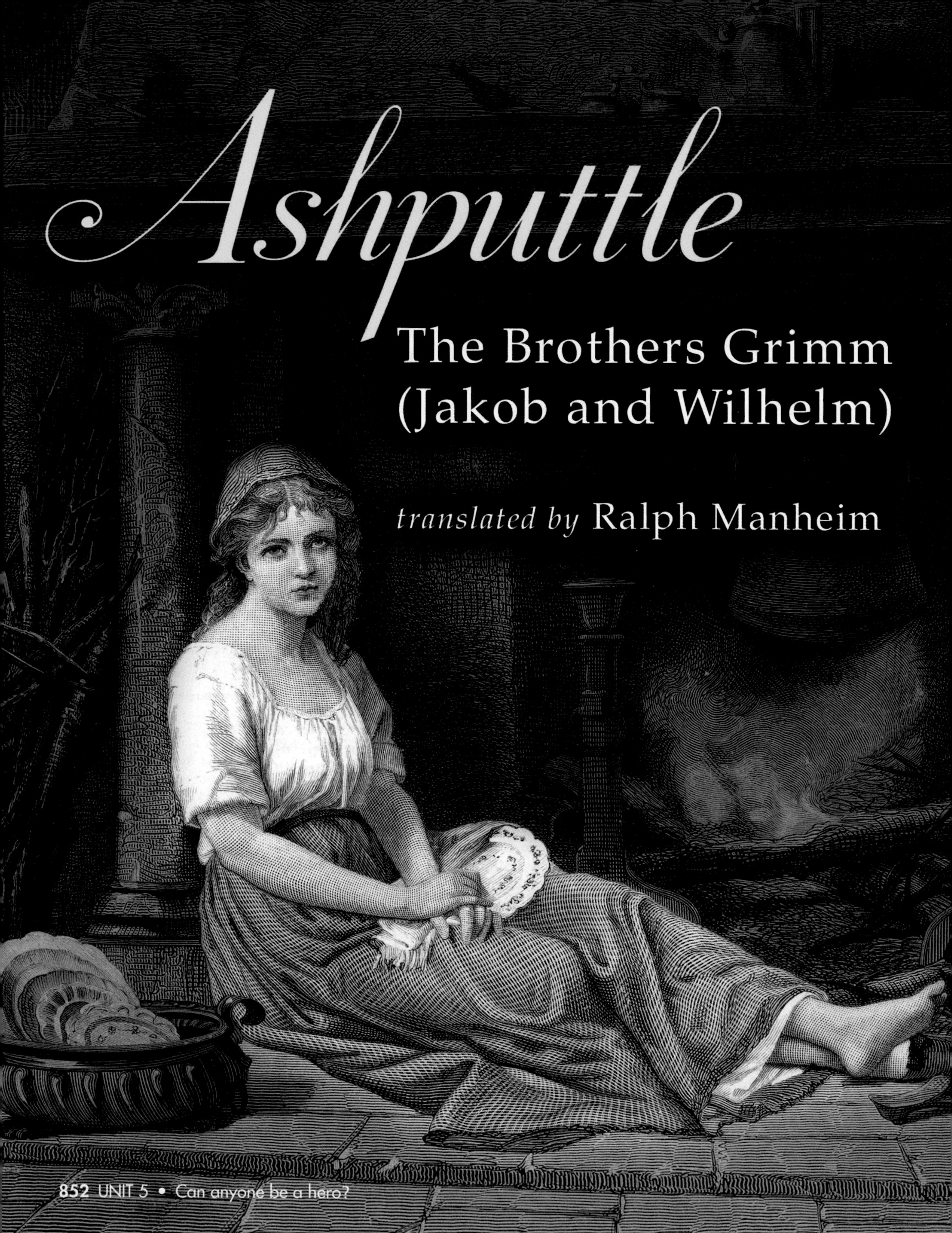

A rich man's wife fell sick and, feeling that her end was near, she called her only daughter to her bedside and said: "Dear child, be good and say your prayers; God will help you, and I shall look down on you from heaven and always be with you." With that she closed her eyes and died. Every day the little girl went out to her mother's grave and wept, and she went on being good and saying her prayers. When winter came, the snow spread a white cloth over the grave, and when spring took it off, the man remarried.

His new wife brought two daughters into the house. Their faces were beautiful and lily-white, but their hearts were ugly and black. That was the beginning of a bad time for the poor stepchild. "Why should this silly goose sit in the parlor[1] with us?" they said. "People who want to eat bread must earn it. Get into the kitchen where you belong!" They took away her fine clothes and gave her an old gray dress and wooden shoes to wear. "Look at the haughty princess in her finery!" they cried and, laughing, led her to the kitchen. From then on she had to do all the work, getting up before daybreak, carrying water, lighting fires, cooking and washing. In addition the sisters did everything they could to **plague** her. They **jeered** at her and poured peas and lentils[2] into the ashes, so that she had to sit there picking them out. At night, when she was tired out with work, she had no bed to sleep in but had to lie in the ashes by the hearth. And they took to calling her Ashputtle because she always looked dusty and dirty.

One day when her father was going to the fair, he asked his two stepdaughters what he should bring them. "Beautiful dresses," said one. "Diamonds and pearls," said the other. "And you, Ashputtle. What would you like?" "Father," she said, "break off the first branch that brushes against your hat on your way home, and bring it to me." So he bought beautiful dresses, diamonds and pearls for his two stepdaughters, and on the way home, as he was riding through a copse,[3] a hazel branch brushed against him and knocked off his hat. So he broke off the branch and took it home with him. When he got home, he gave the stepdaughters what they had asked for, and gave Ashputtle the branch. After thanking him, she went to her mother's grave and planted the hazel sprig over it and cried so hard that her tears fell on the sprig and watered it. It grew and became a beautiful tree. Three times a day Ashputtle went and sat under it and wept and prayed. Each time a little white bird came and perched on the tree, and when Ashputtle made a wish the little bird threw down what she had wished for.

Now it so happened that the king arranged for a celebration. It was to go on for three days and all the beautiful girls in the

◀ Critical Viewing
Based on this illustration, predict what Ashputtle's personality will be like in the story.

◀ Vocabulary
plague (plāg) *v.* pester; harass; torment

jeered (jird) *v.* made fun of

Archetypal Narrative Patterns
What other stories do you know that feature a heroine faced with cruel relatives?

Comprehension
Describe the way that Ashputtle's stepsisters treat her.

1. **parlor** (pär′ lər) *n.* room set aside for entertaining guests; living room.
2. **lentils** (lent′ 'lz) *n.* pea-like, edible seeds of the lentil, a plant in the pea family.
3. **copse** (käps) *n.* group of small trees growing thickly together.

kingdom were invited, in order that his son might choose a bride. When the two stepsisters heard they had been asked, they were delighted. They called Ashputtle and said: "Comb our hair, brush our shoes, and fasten our buckles. We're going to the wedding at the king's palace." Ashputtle obeyed, but she wept, for she too would have liked to go dancing, and she begged her stepmother to let her go. "You little sloven!"[4] said the stepmother. "How can you go to a wedding when you're all dusty and dirty? How can you go dancing when you have neither dress nor shoes?" But when Ashputtle begged and begged, the stepmother finally said: "Here, I've dumped a bowlful of lentils in the ashes. If you can pick them out in two hours, you may go." The girl went out the back door to the garden and cried out: "O tame little doves, O turtledoves, and all the birds under heaven, come and help me put

Archetypal Narrative Patterns
What task does Ashputtle's stepmother set for her?

the good ones in the pot,
the bad ones in your crop."[5]

Two little white doves came flying through the kitchen window, and then came the turtledoves, and finally all the birds under heaven came flapping and fluttering and settled down by the ashes. The doves nodded their little heads and started in, peck peck peck peck, and all the others started in, peck peck peck peck, and they sorted out all the good lentils and put them in the bowl. Hardly an hour had passed before they finished and flew away. Then the girl brought the bowl to her stepmother, and she was happy, for she thought she'd be allowed to go to the wedding. But the stepmother said: "No, Ashputtle. You have nothing to wear and you don't know how to dance; the people would only laugh at you." When Ashputtle began to cry, the stepmother said: "If you can pick two bowlfuls of lentils out of the ashes in an hour, you may come." And she thought: "She'll never be able to do it." When she had dumped the two bowlfuls of lentils in the ashes, Ashputtle went out the back door to the garden and cried out: "O tame little doves, O turtledoves, and all the birds under heaven, come and help me put

the good ones in the pot,
the bad ones in your crop."

Archetypal Narrative Patterns
What does the fact that the birds help Ashputtle suggest about her character?

Then two little white doves came flying through the kitchen window, and then came the turtledoves, and finally all the birds under heaven came flapping and fluttering and settled down by the ashes. The doves nodded their little heads and started in, peck peck peck peck, and all the others started in, peck peck peck peck, and they sorted out all the good lentils and put them in the bowls.

4. **sloven** (sluv′ ən) *n.* dirty or untidy person.
5. **crop** (kräp) *n.* part of a bird's throat in which it stores food.

Before half an hour had passed, they had finished and they all flew away. Then the girl brought the bowls to her stepmother, and she was happy, for she thought she'd be allowed to go to the wedding. But her stepmother said: "It's no use. You can't come, because you have nothing to wear and you don't know how to dance. We'd only be ashamed of you." Then she turned her back and hurried away with her two proud daughters.

When they had all gone out, Ashputtle went to her mother's grave. She stood under the hazel tree and cried:

"Shake your branches, little tree,
Throw gold and silver down on me."

▲ **Critical Viewing**
Name another fairy tale that this picture might illustrate. Explain.

Whereupon the bird tossed down a gold and silver dress and slippers embroidered with silk and silver. Ashputtle slipped into the dress as fast as she could and went to the wedding. Her sisters and stepmother didn't recognize her. She was so beautiful in her golden dress that they thought she must be the daughter of some foreign king. They never dreamed it could be Ashputtle, for they thought she was sitting at home in her filthy rags, picking lentils out of the ashes. The king's son came up to her, took her by the hand and danced with her. He wouldn't dance with anyone else and he never let go her hand. When someone else asked for a dance, he said: "She is my partner."

She danced until evening, and then she wanted to go home. The king's son said: "I'll go with you, I'll see you home," for he wanted to find out whom the beautiful girl belonged to. But she got away from him and slipped into the dovecote.[6] The king's son waited until her father arrived, and told him the strange girl had slipped into the dovecote. The old man thought: "Could it be Ashputtle?" and he sent for an ax and a pick and broke into the dovecote, but there was no one inside. When they went indoors, Ashputtle was lying in the ashes in her filthy clothes and a dim oil lamp was burning on the chimney piece, for Ashputtle had slipped out the back end of the dovecote and run to the hazel tree. There she had taken off her fine clothes and put them on the grave, and the bird had taken them away. Then she had put her gray dress on again, crept into the kitchen and lain down in the ashes.

Next day when the festivities started in again and her parents and stepsisters had gone, Ashputtle went to the hazel tree and said:

Comprehension
How does it come about that Ashputtle is able to attend the wedding?

6. **dovecote** (duv′ kōt′) *n.* small house with compartments for nesting birds.

"Shake your branches, little tree,
Throw gold and silver down on me."

Spiral Review
UNIVERSAL THEME
What universal theme is suggested by Ashputtle's daring return to the wedding?

Whereupon the bird threw down a dress that was even more dazzling than the first one. And when she appeared at the wedding, everyone marveled at her beauty. The king's son was waiting for her. He took her by the hand and danced with no one but her. When others came and asked her for a dance, he said: "She is my partner." When evening came, she said she was going home. The king's son followed her, wishing to see which house she went into, but she ran away and disappeared into the garden behind the house, where there was a big beautiful tree with the most wonderful pears growing on it. She climbed among the branches as nimbly as a squirrel and the king's son didn't know what had become of her. He waited until her father arrived and said to him: "The strange girl has got away from me and I think she has climbed up in the pear tree." Her father thought: "Could it be Ashputtle?" He sent for an ax and chopped the tree down, but there was no one in it. When they went into the kitchen, Ashputtle was lying there in the ashes as usual, for she had jumped down on the other side of the tree, brought her fine clothes back to the bird in the hazel tree, and put on her filthy gray dress.

He took her by the hand and danced with no one but her.

On the third day, after her parents and sisters had gone, Ashputtle went back to her mother's grave and said to the tree:

"Shake your branches, little tree,
Throw gold and silver down on me."

Whereupon the bird threw down a dress that was more radiant than either of the others, and the slippers were all gold. When she appeared at the wedding, the people were too amazed to speak. The king's son danced with no one but her, and when someone else asked her for a dance, he said: "She is my partner."

When evening came, Ashputtle wanted to go home, and the king's son said he'd go with her, but she slipped away so quickly that he couldn't follow. But he had thought up a trick. He had arranged to have the whole staircase brushed with pitch,[7] and as she was running down it the pitch pulled her left slipper off. The king's son picked it up, and it was tiny and delicate and all gold. Next morning he went to the father and said: "No girl shall be my wife but the one this golden shoe fits." The sisters were overjoyed,

7. **pitch** (pich) *n.* sticky substance used for waterproofing.

for they had beautiful feet. The eldest took the shoe to her room to try it on and her mother went with her. But the shoe was too small and she couldn't get her big toe in. So her mother handed her a knife and said: "Cut your toe off. Once you're queen you won't have to walk any more." The girl cut her toe off, forced her foot into the shoe, gritted her teeth against the pain, and went out to the king's son. He accepted her as his bride-to-be, lifted her up on his horse, and rode away with her. But they had to pass the grave. The two doves were sitting in the hazel tree and they cried out:

"Roocoo, roocoo,
There's blood in the shoe.
The foot's too long, the foot's too wide,
That's not the proper bride."

He looked down at her foot and saw the blood spurting. At that he turned his horse around and took the false bride home again. "No," he said, "this isn't the right girl; let her sister try the shoe on." The sister went to her room and managed to get her toes into the shoe, but her heel was too big. So her mother handed her a knife and said: "Cut off a chunk of your heel. Once you're queen you won't have to walk any more." The girl cut off a chunk of her heel, forced her foot into the shoe, gritted her teeth against the pain, and went out to the king's son. He accepted her as his bride-to-be, lifted her up on his horse, and rode away with her. As they passed the hazel tree, the two doves were sitting there, and they cried out:

"Roocoo, roocoo,
There's blood in the shoe.
The foot's too long, the foot's too wide,
That's not the proper bride."

He looked down at her foot and saw that blood was spurting from her shoe and staining her white stocking all red. He turned his horse around and took the false bride home again. "This isn't the right girl, either," he said. "Haven't you got another daughter?" "No," said the man, "there's only a puny little kitchen drudge[8] that my dead wife left me. She couldn't possibly be the bride." "Send her up," said the king's son, but the mother said: "Oh no, she's much too dirty to be seen." But he insisted and they had to call her. First she washed her face and hands, and when they were clean, she went upstairs and curtseyed to the king's son. He handed her the golden slipper and sat down on a footstool, took her foot out of her heavy wooden shoe, and put it into the slipper. It fitted perfectly.

Archetypal Narrative Patterns
How does the number of dances Ashputtle attends reflect an archetypal narrative element?

Comprehension
How does the prince propose to find the woman he wishes to marry?

8. **drudge** (druj) *n.* person whose job consists of hard, unpleasant work.

And when she stood up and the king's son looked into her face, he recognized the beautiful girl he had danced with and cried out: "This is my true bride!" The stepmother and the two sisters went pale with fear and rage. But he lifted Ashputtle up on his horse and rode away with her. As they passed the hazel tree, the two white doves called out:

"Roocoo, roocoo,
No blood in the shoe.
Her foot is neither long nor wide,
This one is the proper bride."

Then they flew down and alighted on Ashputtle's shoulders, one on the right and one on the left, and there they sat.

On the day of Ashputtle's wedding, the two stepsisters came and tried to ingratiate themselves and share in her happiness. On the way to church the elder was on the right side of the bridal couple and the younger on the left. The doves came along and pecked out one of the elder sister's eyes and one of the younger sister's eyes. Afterward, on the way out, the elder was on the left side and the younger on the right, and the doves pecked out both the remaining eyes. So both sisters were punished with blindness to the end of their days for being so wicked and false.

Archetypal Narrative Patterns
Which events show that evil is punished in the story?

Critical Thinking

1. **Key Ideas and Details: (a)** What does Ashputtle do with her father's gift? **(b) Infer:** What do her actions suggest about her character? **(c) Contrast:** Contrast Ashputtle with her stepmother and stepsisters.
2. **Key Ideas and Details: (a)** What type of help does Ashputtle receive? **(b) Connect:** What lesson about life is suggested by the fact that a person like Ashputtle receives this help? Explain, citing story details.
3. **Key Ideas and Details: (a)** In what way do the schemes of the stepmother and stepsisters lead to their punishment? Explain. **(b) Connect:** In what way do these events support the lesson of "Ashputtle"? Cite story details in your response.
4. **Integration of Knowledge and Ideas:** Do you think that Ashputtle is a hero? If your answer is *yes,* explain in what way you think she is heroic. If your answer is *no,* what do you think she could have done differently that would have made her a hero? ***[Connect to the Big Question: Can anyone be a hero?]***

Writing to Sources 

Comparing Archetypal Narrative Patterns

1. Craft and Structure Identify the archetypal characters in "Cupid and Psyche" and "Ashputtle."

Heroine	Powerful Older Woman	Ideal Lover	Rivals for Love	Supernatural Assistant

2. Craft and Structure Compare the tasks that Psyche must perform with the tasks that Ashputtle must perform. Consider each of these structural elements: **(a)** the number of tasks; **(b)** who assigns the task and why; **(c)** the difficulty of the task; and **(d)** the methods or means the character uses to complete the task.

3. Integration of Knowledge and Ideas What **archetypal narrative patterns** do the stories of Psyche and Ashputtle display? Explain, supporting your answer by drawing on the comparisons you made in response to question 2.

 Timed Writing

Explanatory Text: Essay

In an essay, compare and contrast the characters of Psyche and Ashputtle in these two tales. Decide whether each heroine is simply an archetypal figure or has a unique personality, as well. **(40 minutes)**

5-Minute Planner

1. Read the prompt carefully and completely.
2. Use these questions to help you analyze the characters:
   - What is the same and what is different about each character's situation in life?
   - How does each character respond to her situation? What qualities do these responses reveal?
   - How does each character react to the forces that help or hinder her?
3. As you draft your essay, remember to include transitions to connect your ideas and clarify meaning. Words and phrases like *by contrast, on the other hand,* and *alternatively* show contrast, while *similarly, likewise,* and *in addition to* suggest similarities.

USE ACADEMIC VOCABULARY

As you write, use academic language, including the following words or their related forms:

character
context
meaning
principles

For more information about academic vocabulary, see page xlvi.

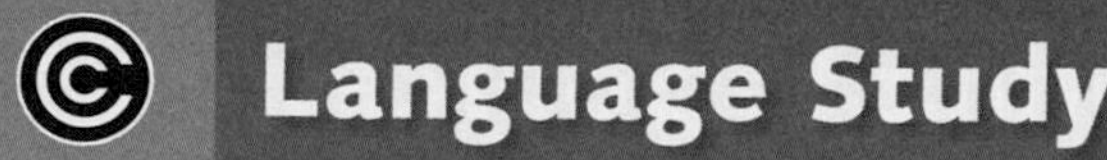

Language Study

Idioms, Jargon, and Technical Terms

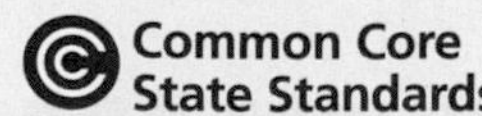

Language
4.d. Verify the preliminary determination of the meaning of a word or phrase.
5. Demonstrate understanding of figurative language, word relationships, and nuances in word meanings.

Idioms are common expressions that are characteristic of a region, community, or class of people. A type of figurative language, they cannot be understood literally. Some idioms originated in activities where they have literal meanings. Over time, those expressions moved into general use, at which point their literal meanings faded but their figurative meanings remained. For example, the idiom "the cut of one's jib," which means "one's general appearance," comes from sailing, where it literally refers to the shape of a small sail.

Idiom	Meaning
It *beats me.*	I don't know.
Let's *call it a day.*	Let's stop working for today.
Amy should *brush up on* her Spanish.	Amy should refresh her knowledge of Spanish.
The thief tried to *cover her tracks.*	The thief tried to hide what she had done.

Technical terms are words used by people in specific fields to describe their activities. The words themselves may be familiar, but they have specialized meanings in a particular profession. Examples from the field of theater include *stage left, curtain time, fly space,* and *apron*. Technical terms help those with knowledge of the field communicate effectively.

Jargon, like technical terminology, is the specialized language used in a specific field. However, when jargon is used with people outside the field, it results in confusion. Try to figure out what this publishing jargon means: *When you get the proof, stet the correx.* It means that the corrections should not be made on a page printout. In most writing, jargon should be avoided.

Practice A

Identify the jargon in each sentence. Then, rewrite the sentence using more understandable language. Use a dictionary if necessary.

1. Bringing up that topic will have a negative impact on our relationship.
2. The real estate agent flipped the property.
3. The business owner said it was necessary to downsize.
4. Occasioned by an increase in the number of the involuntarily undomiciled, the city council opened new shelter units.
5. We will hold the decision in abeyance until we have heard from all members of the council.

Practice B

Identify the idiom in each sentence and write a definition for each one. If you are unsure of the meaning of the idiom, check the definition in a dictionary.

1. Let's fan out and try to find Sarah's lost earring.
2. I think you had better be quiet, if you catch my drift.
3. The sound of nails on a chalkboard drove her up the wall.
4. I'll go on record in support of the new proposal.
5. George left no stone unturned as he searched for his car keys.
6. Jordan's little sister is a pain in the neck.
7. They were taken to the principal's office and given the third degree.
8. Your mother started tearing her hair out when you didn't answer your cell phone.
9. Three hundred people in the box factory got the axe.
10. The district will break ground on the new high school tomorrow.

Comprehension and Collaboration

Working with one or two classmates, research a profession and the jargon typically used in that field. For example, you might interview a sports coach to learn jargon associated with gymnastics or swimming. Compile a glossary and share your findings with classmates.

Activity Prepare five note cards like the one shown below for each of the following words: *case, strike, term, pitch,* and *pin.* Write the word on a card. Look the word up in a dictionary and write down its main meaning. Then, identify the field or profession in which the word is used technically and write the technical meaning on the card.

Word:
Definition:
Field:
Technical Definition:

Speaking and Listening

Delivering a Multimedia Presentation

Common Core State Standards

Speaking and Listening

2. Integrate multiple sources of information presented in diverse media or formats, evaluating the credibility and accuracy of each source.

5. Make strategic use of digital media in presentations to enhance understanding of findings, reasoning, and evidence and to add interest.

Transform a research report into a **multimedia presentation** by adding sounds and visuals that create drama and interest for an audience. A successful multimedia presentation offers clear ideas and information about a topic using a variety of supporting media such as images, music, charts, graphs, or video clips.

Learn the Skills

Use the following strategies to complete the activity on page 863.

Prepare the Content Consider your topic, audience, and available media and equipment when choosing which media to use.

- Decide which parts of your research report can be enhanced with the use of visuals or sounds.
- Choose media that suit your topic. For example, you might play music of a time period appropriate to your report as a soundtrack.
- Choose media that suit your audience. For example, you might choose certain music for an audience of classmates but other music if the audience is your parents.
- Use media that will help your audience understand the presentation. For example, if your research paper is about Gothic architecture, use images to show examples of Gothic-style buildings.
- Make sure any media and technology you choose is used ethically. Consult copyright notices and cite your sources to avoid plagiarism.
- Verify that all visual images can be seen by the entire audience. If you are presenting pictures on paper, enlarge small images. If you are presenting images on a screen, make sure the resolution, or clarity, works with larger dimensions.

Prepare Your Delivery To smoothly integrate words, sounds, and images into your presentation, you must practice it.

- Double-check your equipment to make sure that everything is in working condition and properly connected.
- Have a backup plan in case your equipment fails. Prepare copies of illustrations or graphic organizers to hand out.
- Do not read your research report word for word. Instead, talk to your audience, articulating your ideas with energy. To make sure you stay on track, refer to your notes each time you shift to a new idea.

Practice the Skills

Presentation of Knowledge and Ideas Use what you have learned in this workshop to perform the following task.

ACTIVITY: **Produce a Multimedia Presentation**

Use the steps shown to prepare and deliver a multimedia presentation of a research paper you have already written.

- Identify the most important ideas in your report.
- Consider creative ways to define, illustrate, or summarize those ideas with media, such as images or sounds.
- Research sources of graphics and other images that can help explain challenging concepts.
- Incorporate sounds and images that convey your point of view on your subject and that appeal to your target audience.
- Write an outline of your presentation that explains how you will integrate text, visuals, and sounds effectively.
- Preview the Presentation Checklist shown below to anticipate how your audience will evaluate your presentation.
- Record your work or present it to the class in person.

Use the Presentation Checklist to analyze your classmates' use of visual and sound techniques in their multimedia presentations.

Presentation Checklist

Rate each statement on a scale of 1 (strongly disagree) to 5 (strongly agree). Explain your ratings.

Content

- The presentation conveys a clear message. Rating:________
- The presenter supports main ideas with appropriate details. Rating:________

Use of Visual Techniques

- The visuals help explain concepts. Rating:________
- The visuals convey the presenter's thesis. Rating:________
- The visual techniques appeal to me. Rating:________

Use of Sound Techniques

- The sounds support the presentation's purpose. Rating:________
- The sounds convey the presenter's thesis. Rating:________
- The sounds appeal to me. Rating:________

Comprehension and Collaboration Take notes as you listen to your classmates' multimedia presentations. Analyze how speakers convey their ideas using visual and sound techniques. Based on this analysis, discuss which techniques were most successful.

Writing Process

Write an Informative Text

Comparison-and-Contrast Essay

Defining the Form A **comparison-and-contrast essay** explores the similarities and differences between or among two or more topics, thus bringing the topics into clearer focus. You might use elements of the comparison-and-contrast essay in profiles of historical figures, reviews of literature or performances, or descriptive essays.

Assignment Write a comparison-and-contrast essay about two literary characters, two concepts, or two events. Include these elements:

✓ an introduction that describes your topic and a clear *thesis statement* that expresses your purpose and main idea

✓ a clear and logical *organizational pattern* that allows you to effectively explain the comparisons and contrasts between your chosen subjects

✓ *supporting evidence,* including facts, details, and examples that illustrate the similarities and differences between the two subjects

✓ *transitions* that show clear relationships between ideas

✓ Thoughtful *use of language* that establishes an academic, objective *tone* suitable for your audience and purpose

✓ error-free grammar and *varied sentence structures*

To preview the criteria on which your comparison-and-contrast essay may be judged, see the rubric on page 871.

Common Core State Standards

Writing

2.a. Introduce a topic; organize complex ideas, concepts, and information to make important connections and distinctions; include formatting, graphics, and multimedia when useful to aiding comprehension.

2.b. Develop the topic with well-chosen, relevant, and sufficient facts, extended definitions, concrete details, quotations, or other information and examples appropriate to the audience's knowledge of the topic.

5. Develop and strengthen writing as needed by planning, revising, editing, rewriting, or trying a new approach, focusing on addressing what is most significant for a specific purpose and audience.

FOCUS ON RESEARCH

When you write comparison-and-contrast essays, you might perform research to

- learn more about the similarities and differences between your chosen subjects;
- locate data in the form of facts and statistics to support your ideas;
- find examples to illustrate comparisons and contrasts.

Be sure to note all resources you use in your research, and to accurately credit those sources in your final draft. Refer to the Research Workshop in the Introductory Unit for more information on how to properly cite materials.

READING-WRITING CONNECTION

To get a feel for comparison-and-contrast essays, read "Understanding Stonehenge: Two Explanations," by Rossella Lorenzi on page 490.

Prewriting/Planning Strategies

Your comparison-and-contrast essay should explore subjects that share traits but are significantly different. Use these strategies to find a topic:

List related topics. Think of a broad subject area, such as music, sports, or fictional characters. Then, list specific items. For example, you might list favorite athletes or unusual places. Look for similarities—and differences—between two or more items on your list. Choose one set as your subject.

Fill in a sentence frame. Find at least three ways to complete a sentence frame. Then, choose your best idea to explore in your essay.

Sample Sentence Frame

I often confuse ______ and ______ because they are both ______.
However, they are also different because of ______ and ______.

Consider your purpose. The comparisons and contrasts you explore should fulfill a larger purpose or idea, such as one of the following:

- **To persuade**—You believe one of your subjects is better than the other and you want to convince your readers to share your opinion.
- **To reflect**—Both subjects are meaningful to you, but in different ways, and you want to explore why this is the case.
- **To describe**—The similarities and differences in your subjects are very striking and you want to portray them.

Evaluate your topic. Be sure your topics offer enough interesting similarities and differences. To evaluate your topic choices, use a Venn diagram like the one shown.

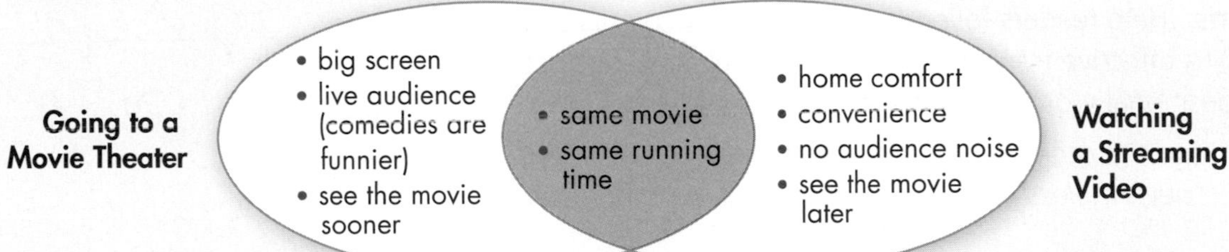

Conduct research. Consider conducting research to further explore your analysis. For example, after creating a Venn diagram, a writer might read movie industry journals to find the average time between a movie's release into theaters and its release as streaming video.

Formulate a thesis statement. Write a *thesis statement* that incorporates a sense of your larger purpose. You will include this thesis statement in your introduction.

Drafting Strategies

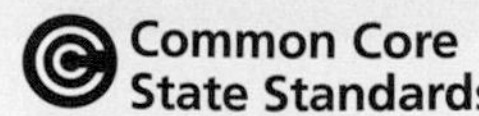

Writing

2.a. Introduce a topic; organize complex ideas, concepts, and information to make important connections and distinctions.

2.b. Develop the topic with well-chosen, relevant, and sufficient facts, extended definitions, concrete details, quotations, or other information and examples appropriate to the audience's knowledge of the topic.

2.c. Use appropriate and varied transitions to link the major sections of the text, create cohesion, and clarify the relationships among complex ideas and concepts.

2.d. Use precise language and domain-specific vocabulary to manage the complexity of the topic.

2.f. Provide a concluding statement or section that follows from and supports the information or explanation presented.

Choose an organization. Most comparison-and-contrast essays are organized in one of two ways. In **subject-by-subject organization,** you analyze all of the features of one subject and then all the features of the second subject. In **point-by-point organization,** you discuss one point about both subjects and then move on to a second point. Select an organizational structure that best suits your subjects.

Types of Organization

Subject-by-Subject	Point-by-Point
Subject A • Point 1 • Point 2 Subject B • Point 1 • Point 2	Point A • Subject 1 • Subject 2 Point B • Subject 1 • Subject 2

Use your thesis statement and purpose. Include your thesis in your introduction. Check that the ideas you include in each body paragraph connect directly to your thesis statement and purpose. Restate or reevaluate your thesis statement in a strong and memorable concluding section.

Support opinions. Using a wide variety of evidence can make your ideas more convincing and add interest to your essay.

- **Examples:** Illustrations help clarify similarities and differences.
- **Facts:** Evidence helps readers understand each subject.
- **Quotations:** The exact words of experts add authority.

Use transitions. Help readers follow the logic of your comparisons and contrasts by using effective transitions to show the relationships between ideas. These transitional words and phrases are especially useful:

similarly	*on the other hand*	*conversely*	*however*
although	*nevertheless*	*in contrast*	*whereas*

Model: Using Transitions to Clarify Connections

If you have to choose one sport in which to participate, the three most popular are basketball, soccer, and volleyball. All are fast-moving sports that require being in good physical condition, a commitment of time and energy, and an ability to think and react quickly.

Despite the similarities in the physical demands they make, each sport has its own special requirements.

The writer uses a transitional phrase to signal a shift from comparison to contrast.

Choosing Strong, Effective Words

Word choice refers to the specific words or figures of speech that a writer uses to convey ideas to the reader. In a comparison-and-contrast essay, strong word choices help distinguish the two topics and clarify their similarities and differences with precision. The right words will help readers better understand your ideas and visualize your examples.

Describing Your Subjects In order for readers to understand the two subjects of your essay, provide detailed information about both. If you are comparing physical objects, use vivid descriptive words to show what they look like or how they function. If you are comparing ideas, use concrete examples that will make concepts tangible and clear.

Subject	Descriptive Words and Concrete Examples
maple tree	Maple trees display a brilliant array of foliage during the autumn. Vivid shades of red, orange, and gold color the landscape as the season cools.
courage	Many of the "firsts" of childhood require courage—the first day of school, the first time you ride a bike, the first time you leave home.

Clarifying Similarities and Differences Strong word choices should highlight the degree to which your subjects are similar and different.

Weak Word Choice: A sparrow's beak is <u>small</u> when compared to that of a toucan's.

Precise Word Choice: A sparrow's beak is <u>diminutive</u> when compared to that of a toucan's.

Even though the words *small* and *diminutive* have similar denotations, *diminutive* is a stronger adjective. It emphasizes just how much the two beaks differ in size, and allows the reader to visualize the contrast.

Using Authentic Words As you experiment with diction, choose words that extend your vocabulary but still feel true to your personality. Review your essay, circling words or phrases that seem inauthentic. Consider revising your essay with words that are more natural yet still precise.

Forced: *Father always sported a fedora of unobtrusive green.*

Genuine: *Dad always wore a hat that was a modest, faded green.*

Revising Strategies

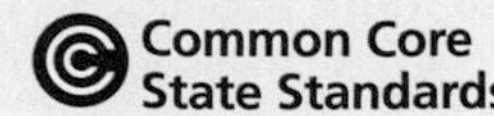

Writing

2.d. Use precise language and domain-specific vocabulary to manage the complexity of the topic.

Language

1. Demonstrate command of the conventions of standard English grammar and usage when writing or speaking.

3. Apply knowledge of language to understand how language functions in different contexts, to make effective choices for meaning or style, and to comprehend more fully when reading or listening.

Revise to balance your organization. An effective comparison-and-contrast essay provides a thorough analysis of each subject being compared. Follow these steps to check the balance of your coverage:

- Use a highlighting tool to identify the points at which you discuss each subject you are comparing and contrasting.
- Then, review your highlighted draft to determine whether you have addressed each subject equally and provided sufficient information to make your comparisons and contrasts clear. Add details to support any under-developed subjects.

Model: Revising to Create Balance

Basketball requires the ability to turn, pivot, start, and stop suddenly. It also requires the ability to instantaneously read and react to the opponents' moves. Soccer requires the ability to predict the ball's movement, be aware of the location of team members, and quickly intervene in plays. Volleyball also requires quick reflexes. ^ *Players must be prepared to make snap judgments about whether a ball is going out of bounds or requires a return.*

The writer adds information about her third topic to create a better balance.

Revise for precision. When you compare and contrast, you discuss subjects that share many traits. To clearly distinguish one from the other, use words that are specific and precise.

Vague: The effects used in the first *Star Wars* movies were *good*, but today's computerized images *are also good*.

Specific: The effects used in the first *Star Wars* movies were *convincing*, but today's computerized images *are truly lifelike*.

Peer Review

Ask a partner to read your essay and evaluate how well you have presented details about your subjects of comparison. Discuss whether or not you need to provide additional support for either subject. Consider developing an idea further or adding details to provide more thorough comparisons and contrasts.

Revising to Vary Sentence Patterns

To make your writing more fluid and engaging, vary your style by beginning some sentences with prepositional phrases.

Identifying Prepositional Phrases A preposition and its object—the accompanying noun or pronoun—is called a prepositional phrase. Some prepositional phrases act as adjectives and some act as adverbs.

Preposition		Noun/Pronoun		Prepositional Phrase
of	+	moon	=	of the silvery moon
of		mall		at the local mall

Many prepositions express spatial or time-order relationships, which make them useful tools when writing a description.

Time: after the game; before dinner; at two o'clock; for a day

Space: under the table; near the river; in school; in my hand

Varying Sentences With Prepositional Phrases In these examples, subjects are italicized, verbs are underlined, and prepositional phrases appear in parentheses:

Repeated subject-verb pattern: *She* <u>wakes</u> up early. *She* <u>makes</u> breakfast. *She* <u>makes</u> lunch (after that).

Revision: *She* <u>wakes</u> up early. *She* <u>makes</u> breakfast. (After that), *she* <u>makes</u> lunch.

Follow these steps to vary your sentences in your own writing.

1. Read your draft aloud. Listen for overuse of the subject-verb sentence pattern.
2. Identify sentences that contain a prepositional phrase.
3. Rewrite the sentence, starting with the prepositional phrase. Be sure the phrase is close to the word it modifies.
4. If the prepositional phrase contains four or more words, set it off from the words that follow with a comma.

Grammar in Your Writing

Reread the first two paragraphs of your comparison-and-contrast essay, looking for overuse of the subject-verb sentence pattern. Rewrite some sentences by beginning them with prepositional phrases.

STUDENT MODEL: **Amanda Goodman, Glen Rock, NJ**

You've Got Mail

Personal communications have gone through a major evolution in modern times. The letter gave way to the telephone call, and now they have both been overwhelmed in popularity by e-mail. While the three modes of communication have a lot in common, there are differences that let each stand out on its own.

In her introduction, Amanda identifies the subjects she will compare.

Letters, phone calls, and e-mail are similar because they all involve personal communication. They allow people to share ideas and feelings with other people. Communicators do not have to be face to face; they can be across the world and get the same points across. Letter writers, phone callers, and e-mailers are generally not limited by time either. They can create and share their communications round the clock.

In this paragraph, Amanda discusses the similarities that the three formats share.

Despite their similarities, letters, phone calls, and e-mail communicate differently. Letters require some effort and make recipients especially happy when received. They can be saved, to be reread (often over and over) at a later time. Unlike a letter, e-mail is usually more spontaneous and less likely to be reread. Phone call messages quickly fade. Of all three modes, letters take the longest time between the sender and the receiver. If time is important, letters are probably the worst format to use.

E-mail often requires less effort than a letter. It is more convenient than "snail mail," though. You never have to move away from your computer. Plus, you can edit without cross-outs. Once you send an e-mail, it is delivered instantly. This speed has its disadvantages. Because people often write e-mails in haste, they do not stop to think carefully about what they want to say—or correct grammar or spelling mistakes—before they click an e-mail on its way.

In the third, fourth, and fifth paragraphs, Amanda addresses the unique qualities of each form.

A phone call is extremely personal, and it shows that you have set aside time for the other person. You are able to hear the tone of voice and expression of the other person. Phone calls may be expensive, temporary, and time-sensitive—unlike a letter or an e-mail, which a recipient can read when he or she has the time. Another problem with the phone is that once you say something, you cannot take it back, in contrast to the way you can edit writing.

Transitions help clarify the contrasts between subjects.

There is a time and a place for all three types of communication. People are often so busy that they have time only for e-mail, but maybe people should set aside some time to write a letter or call a friend.

Editing and Proofreading

Review your draft to correct errors in grammar, spelling, and punctuation.

Focus on transitional words. Double-check the meanings of the transitional words you have used, and make sure they are punctuated correctly. If you start a sentence with a coordinating conjunction, such as *however* or *nevertheless,* follow it with a comma.

Spiral Review
Earlier in this unit, you learned about **semicolons, colons, and ellipsis points** (p. 840). Check your essay to be sure that you have used these punctuation marks correctly.

Publishing and Presenting

Consider one of the following ways to share your writing:

Present a shared reading. With a partner, deliver an oral presentation of your essay. First, present to a small group. Read the paragraphs that discuss one subject, while your partner reads the paragraphs that discuss the other subject. Ask for listeners' comments to improve your presentation before sharing it with another group.

Create a class book. Compile a collection of comparison-and-contrast essays. Devise a title that reflects the content of the collection and place the finished book in your classroom or school library.

Reflecting on Your Writing

Writer's Journal Jot down your answers to this question:
How did comparing and contrasting your subjects help you better understand them?

Self-Evaluation Rubric

Use the following criteria to evaluate the effectiveness of your essay.

Criteria	Rating Scale
Purpose/Focus Introduces a specific topic; provides a concluding section that follows from and supports the information or explanation presented	*not very* .... *very* 1 2 3 4
Organization Organizes complex ideas, concepts, and information to make important connections and distinctions; uses appropriate and varied transitions to link the major sections, create cohesion, and clarify relationships among ideas	1 2 3 4
Development of Ideas/Elaboration Develops the topic with well-chosen, relevant and sufficient facts, extended definitions, concrete details, quotations or other information and examples appropriate to the audience's knowledge of the topic	1 2 3 4
Language Uses precise language and domain-specific vocabulary to manage the complexity of the topic; establishes and maintains a formal style and objective tone	1 2 3 4
Conventions: Attends to the norms and conventions of the discipline	1 2 3 4

SELECTED RESPONSE

RL.9-10.1, RL.9-10.2, RL.9-10.3, RL.9-10.5; W.9-10.10; L.9-10.4.a
[For full standards wording, see the chart in the front of this book.]

I. Reading Literature

Directions: *Read the excerpt from the Native American (Blackfeet) story "The Orphan Boy and the Elk Dog." Then, answer each question that follows.*

He grew up into a fine young hunter, tall and good-looking in the quilled buckskin outfit the chief's wife made for him. He helped his grandfather in everything and became a staff for Good Running to lean on. But he was lonely, for most people in the camp could not forget that Long Arrow had once been an outcast. "Grandfather," he said one day, "I want to do something to make you proud and show people that you were wise to adopt me. What can I do?"

Good Running answered, "Someday you will be a chief and do great things."

"But what's a great thing I could do now, Grandfather?"

The chief thought for a long time. "Maybe I shouldn't tell you this," he said. "I love you and don't want to lose you. But on winter nights, men talk of powerful spirit people living at the bottom of a faraway lake. Down in that lake the spirit people keep mystery animals who do their work for them. These animals are larger than a great elk, but they carry the burdens of the spirit people like dogs. So they're called Pono-Kamita—Elk Dogs. They are said to be swift, strong, gentle, and beautiful beyond imagination. Every fourth generation, one of our young warriors has gone to find these spirit folk and bring back an Elk Dog for us. But none of our brave young men has ever returned."

"Grandfather, I'm not afraid. I'll go and find the Elk Dog."

"Grandson, first learn to be a man. Learn the right prayers and ceremonies. Be brave. Be generous and open-handed. Pity the old and the fatherless, and let the holy men of the tribe find a medicine for you which will protect you on your dangerous journey. We will begin by purifying you in the sweat bath."

So Long Arrow was purified with the white steam of the sweat lodge. He was taught how to use the pipe, and how to pray to the Great Mystery Power. The tribe's holy men gave him a medicine and made for him a shield with designs on it to ward off danger.

Then one morning, without telling anybody, Good Running loaded his best travois dog with all the things Long Arrow would need for traveling.

1. **Part A** "The Orphan Boy and the Elk Dog" is most clearly an example of which type of story?

   A. fairy tale
   B. contemporary short story
   C. parody
   D. myth

   Part B Which statement is true of the story and helps to define its type?

   A. The story is based on historical facts.
   B. The story expresses the values of a culture.
   C. The story mimics other stories in a comic way.
   D. The story expresses a theme.

2. Which answer choice reveals the most about the **cultural context** of this selection?

   A. "He grew into a fine young hunter, tall and good-looking in the quilled buckskin outfit the chief's wife made for him."
   B. "'They are said to be swift, strong, gentle, and beautiful beyond imagination.'"
   C. "'But none of our brave young men has ever returned.'"
   D. "'Grandfather, I'm not afraid. I'll go and find the Elk Dog.'"

3. **Part A** Judging from this excerpt, which **narrative pattern** will the story most likely follow?

   A. A hero desires power and uses others to get it.
   B. A protagonist struggles with an antagonist, and the protagonist triumphs.
   C. A character must complete a challenging quest.
   D. A protagonist foolishly wastes a gift.

   Part B Which story detail most clearly suggests that narrative pattern?

   A. "'Grandfather, I'm not afraid. I'll go and find the Elk Dog.'"
   B. "So Long Arrow was purified by the white steam of the sweat lodge."
   C. "He helped his grandfather in everything."
   D. "'Learn the right prayers and ceremonies.'"

4. Which of the following details reveal character traits that are important to Long Arrow's grandfather?

   A. "'But what's a great thing I could do now, Grandfather?'"
   B. "'Be brave. Be generous and open-handed. Pity the old and the fatherless... '"
   C. "He was taught how to use the pipe, and how to pray to the Great Mystery Power."
   D. "'These animals are larger than a great elk, but they carry the burdens of the spirit people like dogs.'"

5. What supernatural qualities do Elk Dogs have?

   A. They are kept by and do work for the spirit people.
   B. They are swift and gentle.
   C. They can carry much heavier loads than dogs can.
   D. They are brave and generous.

6. Which answer choice accurately lists qualities typical of an **epic hero?**

   A. strong warrior; fights for good; embodies society's values
   B. dreamer; has magical abilities; avoids conflicts
   C. pretender; behaves foolishly; lacks courage
   D. villain; causes trouble; embodies society's fears

7. Based on context clues, what can you infer is the best definition of the underlined word *travois?*

   A. work
   B. sight
   C. sled
   D. guard

Timed Writing

8. In a paragraph, identify one **universal theme** suggested by this excerpt. Explain which details in the excerpt support your response.

GO ON

II. Reading Informational Text

Directions: *Read the passage. Then, answer each question that follows.*

Common Core State Standards

RI.9–10.1, RI.9-10.2, RI.9-10.5; L.9-10.1.b, L.9-10.2.a, L.9-10.2.b, L.9-10.3

[For full standards wording, see the chart in the front of this book.]

The Fire Makers

The use and production of fire is one of humanity's most distinctive traits. As long as 1.5 million years ago, one of our earliest ancestors—*Homo erectus*—may have been using fire. U.S. and South African researchers have found evidence of burnt bones in South Africa. Using a method called "electron spin resonance," the scientists have determined that the bones had been heated to high temperatures, leading them to believe that the bones were burnt in a hearth fire. According to Dr. Anne Skinner, "These bones could have been burnt in a forest fire or brush fire, but that's generally a low temperature flame. These had been heated to a very high temperature."

There is little evidence to tell us exactly when humans learned this skill. Scientists have determined that prehistoric people commonly used caves as shelters and have found the remains of communal campfires. These sites include bones of extinct animals such as cave bears and saber-toothed tigers, indicating these sites are very old. *Using* fire, however, is not *making* fire, and whether the fires were created or were "stolen" from natural brush fires remains uncertain. Because carrying fire can be hazardous and fires can easily go out, though, it seems likely that nomadic hunter-gatherers must have learned to make fires themselves, as they did not remain in one place. Additionally, being without fire in Ice Age Europe would almost certainly have meant death; people would have had to know how to create their own fires to survive.

1. Part A Which claim is presented in the first paragraph?

A. *Homo erectus* made fire.
B. *Homo erectus* used fire.
C. *Homo erectus* "stole" brush fires.
D. *Homo erectus* was one of humanity's most distinctive ancestors.

Part B Which evidence supports the claim presented in the first paragraph?

A. The use of fire is one of humanity's distinctive traits.
B. Scientists use electron spin resonance to gather information.
C. Scientists have found evidence of forest and brush fires.
D. Scientists have found animal bones that had been burned at very high temperatures.

2. Part A Which claim in the passage is introduced with a counterclaim?

A. Fire originated in South Africa.
B. Ancient hunter-gatherers could actually make fire.
C. *Homo erectus* used fire.
D. European Ice Age hunters never used fire.

Part B Which statement from the passage is a counterclaim?

A. "...indicating that these sites are very old."
B. "Scientists...have found the remains of communal campfires."
C. "'These had been heated to a very high temperature.'"
D. "*Using* fire, however, is not *making* fire..."

III. Writing and Language Conventions

Directions: *Read the passage. Then, answer each question that follows.*

Guidelines for Volunteer Counselors

(1) All children will be pre-registered. (2) When they arrive at the facility, escort them directly to Room 12B. (3) First, make sure that each child has a name tag. (4) Check tags against the master list. (5) Once you organize the children, bring them to the buses. (6) Provide activities for them on the long bus ride. (7) When you arrive at the site park, rangers will have lighted the campfire. (8) Adult counselors will be present to conduct activities singing songs, learning rhymes, and playing games. (9) Children, like puppies, often wander off, so make sure that they do not get lost between the trees in the forest. (10) At the end of the event, help children reboard the bus check name tags against the list. (11) You arrive at the facility. (12) Each parent should sign his or her child out of camp.

1. Which of these sentences contains a **dependent clause?**

A. sentence 7
B. sentence 1
C. sentence 4
D. sentence 11

2. What sort of **clause** is "When they arrive at the facility" in sentence 2?

A. independent clause
B. noun clause
C. relative clause
D. adverbial clause

3. Which revision corrects the **usage problem** in sentence 9?

A. Change *between* to *among*.
B. Change *like* to *as*.
C. Change *like* to *as if*.
D. The sentence is correct as is.

4. Where should a **colon** be added in sentence 8?

A. after *counselors*
B. after *activities*
C. after *rhymes*
D. The sentence should not include a colon.

5. In what way should the **punctuation** in sentence 10 be revised?

A. Add a comma after the word *bus*.
B. Add a semicolon after the word *bus*.
C. Add ellipses points after the word *bus*.
D. The sentence is correct as is.

6. Which revision combines sentences 11 and 12 into a single **complex sentence?**

A. After you arrive at the facility, each parent should sign his or her child out of camp.
B. Arrive back at the facility and make sure that each parent signs his or her child out of camp.
C. Make sure that each parent signs his or her child out of camp, but you can only do that after you arrive at the facility.
D. Arriving at the facility, each parent should sign his or her child out of camp.

CONSTRUCTED RESPONSE

Directions: *Follow the instructions to complete the tasks below as required by your teacher.*

As you work on each task, incorporate both general academic vocabulary and literary terms you learned in Parts 1 and 2 of this unit.

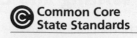

RL.9-10.2, RL.9-10.3, RL.9-10.5, RL.9-10.6; W.9-10.7, W.9-10.9.a; SL.9-10.4; L.9-10.1, L.9-10.2
[For full standards wording, see the chart in the front of this book.]

Writing

TASK 1 Literature [RL.9-10.5; W.9-10.9.a]

Analyze Archetypal Narrative Patterns

Write an essay in which you compare the use of archetypal narrative patterns in two works from Part 2 of this unit.

- Select two works from Part 2 of this unit that contain similar archetypal narrative structures, such as quests, patterns of threes, tests or trials, transgressions, or endings in which good is rewarded and evil is punished. Identify the narrative structures you will compare, and provide enough information about each pattern so that readers can easily understand your points.
- Evaluate the function of the archetypal narrative structures in each work. For example, you might compare how the narrative structures affect the reader and help to convey meaning.
- Make inferences about the cultures in which the stories originated based on the particular way in which archetypal patterns are used.
- Support your ideas with details from the texts.
- Correctly apply the conventions of standard English grammar and usage in your writing.

TASK 2 Literature [RL.9-10.2; W.9-10.9.a]

Analyze Theme

Write an essay in which you trace the development of a universal theme through culturally specific details.

- Select a work from Part 2 of this unit that offers both a strong cultural context and a universal theme. State the universal theme.
- Trace the development of the universal theme through specific cultural details. Refer to story elements that describe the time, place, social structure, beliefs, conflicts, and lifestyle.
- Draw a conclusion about whether or not the cultural context of the work alters the theme in any way.
- Use a variety of sentence structures in your writing. Throughout your essay, apply the conventions of standard English grammar and usage.

TASK 3 Literature [RL.9-10.6; W.9-10.9.a]

Analyze Cultural Context

Write an essay in which you analyze how cultural experience is reflected in a work of world literature from Part 2 of this unit.

Part 1

- Review and evaluate a story from Part 2 of this unit that represents the ideas and values of a culture other than your own.
- As you are reviewing the story, make notes on specific details that reveal the work's cultural context, and analyze what you can infer about the culture from these details. Remember that cultural context includes customs, beliefs, attitudes, values, and traditions, as well as time and place.

Part 2

- Write an essay explaining the ways in which the culture is reflected in the story. You might include characters, plot, conflict, setting, or theme in your explanation.
- Provide a conclusion that follows from and supports your points.

Speaking and Listening

TASK 4 Literature [RL.9-10.3; SL.9-10.4]

Compare Heroic Characters

Prepare and deliver an oral presentation in which you compare two heroes and their significance.

- Select two heroes from works in Part 2 of this unit.
- Describe each hero, using details from the text. Include physical attributes, personality traits, and motivations, as well as strengths and weaknesses. If the character can be considered a legendary or an epic hero, explain why.
- Describe the conflicts that each hero faces and explain how he or she responds. Determine whether the hero changes over the course of the work and, if so, in what ways.
- Make inferences about what each hero's qualities reveal about the culture from which his or her story arose.
- In your conclusion, present a generalization about the relationship between heroes and the cultures that create them.
- Present your ideas and evidence clearly, logically, and concisely so that listeners can follow your reasoning.

TASK 5 Literature [RL.9-10.5; SL.9-10.4]

Analyze Plot

Prepare and deliver a speech in which you compare myth, epic, and legend—genres that have their roots in the oral tradition.

- Define myth, epic, and legend. To provide examples and evidence, focus on one example of each genre from Part 2 of this unit.
- Discuss similarities among the genres, including any ways in which a sense of the oral tradition is evident in each of the examples you have chosen.
- Explain any significant differences among the genres.
- Examine ways in which each genre communicates cultural information.
- Draw a conclusion about the lasting power of myth, legend, and epic.
- Speak expressively, establish eye contact, and use appropriate volume as you present your speech.

Research

TASK 6 Literature [W.9-10.7]

Can anyone be a hero?

In Part 2 of this unit, you have read literature about heroes. Now you will conduct a short research project on someone you consider to be a hero. Use the literature you have read in Part 2 of this unit and your research to reflect on and write about this unit's Big Question. Review the following guidelines before you begin your research:

- Focus your research on one hero.
- Gather information from at least two reliable sources. Your sources may be print or digital.
- Take notes as you find information about the hero you chose.
- Cite your sources.

When you have completed your research, write a brief essay in response to the Big Question. Discuss how your initial ideas about heroes have changed or been reinforced. Support your response with an example from the literature you have read and the research you have conducted.

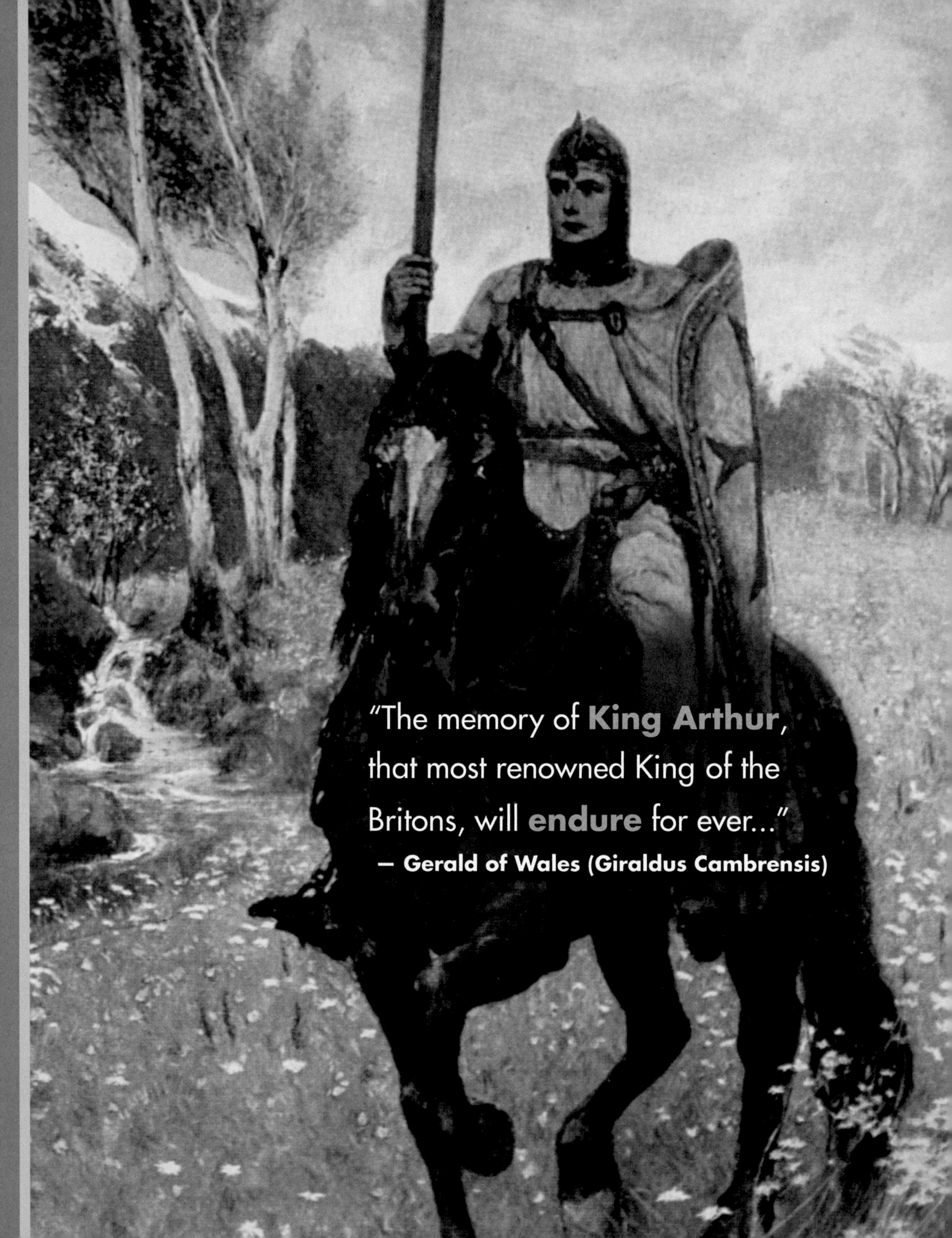
"The memory of King Arthur,
that most renowned King of the
Britons, will endure for ever..."
– Gerald of Wales (Giraldus Cambrensis)

PART 3

TEXT SET DEVELOPING INSIGHT

THE ARTHURIAN LEGEND

The tales of King Arthur and his Knights of the Round Table have captured readers' imaginations for centuries. One of the great characters in British literature, Arthur has come to be the model for the noble hero. The readings in this section explore the Arthurian legend and examine all that it has come to mean—chivalrous knighthood, bravery, heroism, and benevolent rule. As you read each selection, think about how it portrays King Arthur as both a character and a symbol. Then, consider the answer each selection suggests to the Big Question for this unit: **Can anyone be a hero?**

◀ CRITICAL VIEWING What image of knighthood does this painting convey? Which details in the painting suggest those qualities?

CLOSE READING TOOL

Use the **Close Reading Tool** to practice the strategies you learn in this unit.

READINGS IN PART 3

Arthur Becomes King of Britain

from

The Once and Future King

T. H. White

King Pellinore arrived for the important weekend in a high state of flurry.

"I say," he exclaimed, "do you know? Have you heard? Is it a secret, what?"

"Is what a secret, what?" they asked him.

"Why, the King," cried his majesty. "You know, about the King?"

"What's the matter with the King?" inquired Sir Ector. "You don't say he's comin' down to hunt with those darned hounds of his or anythin' like that?"

"He's dead," cried King Pellinore tragically. "He's dead, poor fellah, and can't hunt any more."

Sir Grummore stood up respectfully and took off his cap of maintenance.

"The King is dead," he said. "Long live the King."

Everybody else felt they ought to stand up too, and the boys' nurse burst into tears.

"There, there," she sobbed. "His loyal highness dead and gone, and him such a respectful gentleman. Many's the illuminated picture I've cut out of him, from the Illustrated Missals,[1] aye, and stuck up over the mantel. From the time when he was in swaddling bands,[2] right through them world towers till he was a-visiting the dispersed areas as the world's Prince Charming, there wasn't a picture of 'im but I had it out, aye, and give 'im a last thought o' nights."

"Compose yourself, Nannie," said Sir Ector.

"It is solemn, isn't it?" said King Pellinore, "what? Uther the Conqueror, 1066 to 1216."

---

1. **Missals** (mis′ əlz) *n.* books produced by the Roman Catholic Church for solemn religious purposes.
2. **swaddling** (swäd′ 'liŋ) **bands** in former times, long, narrow bands of cloth wrapped around a newborn baby.

"A solemn moment," said Sir Grummore. "The King is dead. Long live the King."

"We ought to pull down the curtains," said Kay, who was always a stickler for good form, "or half-mast[3] the banners."

"That's right," said Sir Ector. "Somebody go and tell the sergeant-at-arms."

It was obviously the Wart's[4] duty to execute this command, for he was now the junior nobleman present, so he ran out cheerfully to find the sergeant. Soon those who were left in the solar[5] could hear a voice crying out, "Nah then, one-two, special mourning fer 'is lite majesty, lower awai on the command Two!" and then the flapping of all the standards, banners, pennons, pennoncells, banderolls, guidons, streamers and cognizances[6] which made gay the snowy turrets of the Forest Sauvage.

"How did you hear?" asked Sir Ector.

"I was pricking through the purlieus[7] of the forest after that Beast, you know, when I met with a solemn friar of orders gray, and he told me. It's the very latest news."

"Poor old Pendragon," said Sir Ector.

"The King is dead," said Sir Grummore solemnly. "Long live the King."

"It is all very well for you to keep on mentioning that, my dear Grummore," exclaimed King Pellinore petulantly, "but who is this King, what, that is to live so long, what, accordin' to you?"

"Well, his heir," said Sir Grummore, rather taken aback.

"Our blessed monarch," said the Nurse tearfully, "never had no hair. Anybody that studied the loyal family knowed that."

"Good gracious!" exclaimed Sir Ector. "But he must have had a next-of-kin?"

"That's just it," cried King Pellinore in high excitement. "That's the excitin' part of it, what? No hair and no next of skin, and who's to succeed to the throne? That's what my friar was so excited about, what, and why he was asking who could succeed to what, what? What?"

"Do you mean to tell me," exclaimed Sir Grummore indignantly, "that there ain't no King of Gramarye?"

"Not a scrap of one," cried King Pellinore, feeling important. "And there have been signs and wonders of no mean might."

---

3. **half-mast** *v.* lower a flag halfway down a pole as a sign of mourning.
4. **the Wart's** In this novel, Arthur's childhood nickname is the Wart.
5. **solar** (sō´ lər) *n.* sun room.
6. **standards . . . cognizances** (käg´ nə zən´ səz) banners or flags.
7. **purlieus** (purl´ yo͞oz´) *n.* outlying part of a forest, in which forest laws were not enforced.

"I think it's a scandal," said Sir Grummore. "God knows what the dear old country is comin' to. Due to these lollards and communists, no doubt."

"What sort of signs and wonders?" asked Sir Ector.

"Well, there has appeared a sort of sword in a stone, what, in a sort of a church. Not in the church, if you see what I mean, and not in the stone, but that sort of thing, what, like you might say."

"I don't know what the Church is coming to," said Sir Grummore.

"It's in an anvil,"[8] explained the King.

"The Church?"

"No, the sword."

"But I thought you said the sword was in the stone?"

"No," said King Pellinore. "The stone is outside the church."

"Look here, Pellinore," said Sir Ector. "You have a bit of a rest, old boy, and start again. Here, drink up this horn of mead[9] and take it easy."

"The sword," said King Pellinore, "is stuck through an anvil which stands on a stone. It goes right through the anvil and into the stone. The anvil is stuck to the stone. The stone stands outside a church. Give me some more mead."

"I don't think that's much of a wonder," remarked Sir Grummore. "What I wonder at is that they should allow such things to happen. But you can't tell nowadays, what with all these Saxon agitators."[10]

"My dear fellah," cried Pellinore, getting excited again, "it's not where the stone is, what, that I'm trying to tell you, but what is written on it, what, where it is."

"What?"

"Why, on its pommel."[11]

8. **anvil** (an′ vəl) *n.* iron or steel block on which a blacksmith rests metal to hammer it into shape.
9. **mead** (mēd) *n.* drink made of fermented honey and water.
10. **Saxon** (sak′ sən) **agitators** (aj′ i tāt′ ərz) The Saxons were a Germanic people who conquered parts of England during the early centuries of the Middle Ages. Agitators are people who stir up trouble.
11. **pommel** (päm′ əl) *n.* knob at the end of the hilt of some swords.

"Come on, Pellinore," said Sir Ector. "You just sit quite still with your face to the wall for a minute, and then tell us what you are talkin' about. Take it easy, old boy. No need for hurryin'. You sit still and look at the wall, there's a good chap, and talk as slow as you can."

"There are words written on this sword in this stone outside this church," cried King Pellinore piteously, "and these words are as follows. Oh, do try to listen to me, you two, instead of interruptin' all the time about nothin', for it makes a man's head go ever so."

"What are these words?" asked Kay.

"These words say this," said King Pellinore, "so far as I can understand from that old friar of orders gray."

"Go on, do," said Kay, for the King had come to a halt.

"Go on," said Sir Ector, "what do these words on this sword in this anvil in this stone outside this church, say?"

"Some red propaganda, no doubt," remarked Sir Grummore.

King Pellinore closed his eyes tight, extended his arms in both directions, and announced in capital letters, "Whoso Pulleth Out This Sword of this Stone and Anvil, is Rightwise King Born of All England."

"Who said that?" asked Sir Grummore.

"But the sword said it, like I tell you."

skeptically ▶ (skep′ ti kəl lē) *adv.* with doubt; questioningly

"Talkative weapon," remarked Sir Grummore **skeptically**.

"It was written on it," cried the King angrily. "Written on it in letters of gold."

"Why didn't you pull it out then?" asked Sir Grummore.

"But I tell you that I wasn't there. All this that I am telling you was told to me by that friar I was telling you of, like I tell you."

"Has this sword with this inscription been pulled out?" inquired Sir Ector.

"No," whispered King Pellinore dramatically. "That's where the whole excitement comes in. They can't pull this sword out at all, although they have all been tryin' like fun, and so they have had to proclaim a tournament all over England, for New Year's Day, so that the man who comes to the tournament and pulls out the sword can be King of all England forever, what, I say?"

"Oh, father," cried Kay. "The man who pulls the sword out of the stone will be the King of England. Can't we go to the tournament, father, and have a shot?"

"Couldn't think of it," said Sir Ector.

"Long way to London," said Sir Grummore, shaking his head.

"My father went there once," said King Pellinore.

Kay said, "Oh, surely we could go? When I am knighted I shall have to go to a tournament somewhere, and this one happens at just the right date. All the best people will be there, and we should see the famous knights and great kings. It does not matter about the sword, of course, but think of the tournament, probably the greatest there has ever been in Gramarye, and all the things we should see and do. Dear father, let me go to this tourney, if you love me, so that I may bear away the prize of all, in my maiden fight."

"But, Kay," said Sir Ector, "I have never been to London."

"All the more reason to go. I believe that anybody who does not go for a tournament like this will be proving that he has no noble blood in his veins. Think what people will say about us, if we do not go and have a shot at that sword. They will say that Sir Ector's family was too vulgar and knew it had no chance."

"We all know the family has no chance," said Sir Ector, "that is, for the sword."

"Lot of people in London," remarked Sir Grummore, with a wild **surmise**. "So they say."

◀ **surmise** (sər mīz′) *n.* guess; idea based on evidence that is not conclusive

He took a deep breath and goggled at his host with eyes like marbles.

"And shops," added King Pellinore suddenly, also beginning to breathe heavily.

"Dang it!" cried Sir Ector, bumping his horn mug on the table so that it spilled. "Let's all go to London, then, and see the new King!"

They rose up as one man.

"Why shouldn't I be as good a man as my father?" exclaimed King Pellinore.

"Dash it all," cried Sir Grummore. "After all, it is the capital!"

"Hurray!" shouted Kay.

"Lord have mercy," said the nurse.

At this moment the Wart came in with Merlyn, and everybody was too excited to notice that, if he had not been grown up now, he would have been on the verge of tears.

"Oh, Wart," cried Kay, forgetting for the moment that he was only addressing his squire, and slipping back into the familiarity of their boyhood. "What do you think? We are all going to London for a great tournament on New Year's Day!"

"Are we?"

"Yes, and you will carry my shield and spears for the jousts, and I shall win the palm[12] of everybody and be a great knight!"

"Whoso Pulleth Out This Sword of this Stone and Anvil, is Rightwise King Born of All England."

12. **win the palm** be the winner. A palm leaf is a symbol of victory.

"Well, I am glad we are going," said the Wart, "for Merlyn is leaving us too."

"Oh, we shan't need Merlyn."

"He is leaving us," repeated the Wart.

"Leavin' us?" asked Sir Ector. "I thought it was we that were leavin'?"

"He is going away from the Forest Sauvage."

Sir Ector said, "Come now, Merlyn, what's all this about? I don't understand all this a bit."

"I have come to say Goodbye, Sir Ector," said the old magician. "Tomorrow my pupil Kay will be knighted, and the next week my other pupil will go away as his squire. I have outlived my usefulness here, and it is time to go."

"Now, now, don't say that," said Sir Ector. "I think you're a jolly useful chap whatever happens. You just stay and teach me, or be the librarian or something. Don't you leave an old man alone, after the children have flown."

"We shall all meet again," said Merlyn. "There is no cause to be sad."

"Don't go," said Kay.

"I must go," replied their tutor. "We have had a good time while we were young, but it is in the nature of Time to fly. There are many things in other parts of the kingdom which I ought to be attending to just now, and it is a specially busy time for me. Come, Archimedes,[13] say Goodbye to the company."

"Goodbye," said Archimedes tenderly to the Wart.

"Goodbye," said the Wart without looking up at all.

"But you can't go," cried Sir Ector, "not without a month's notice."

"Can't I?" replied Merlyn, taking up the position always used by philosophers who propose to dematerialize. He stood on his toes, while Archimedes held tight to his shoulder—began to spin on them slowly like a top—spun faster and faster till he was only a blur of grayish light—and in a few seconds there was no one there at all.

"Goodbye, Wart," cried two faint voices outside the solar window.

"Goodbye," said the Wart for the last time—and the poor fellow went quickly out of the room.

The knighting took place in a whirl of preparations. Kay's sumptuous bath had to be set up in the box room, between two towel-horses and an old box of selected games which contained a wornout straw dart-board—it was called fléchette in those days—because all the other rooms were full of packing. The nurse spent the whole time constructing new warm pants for everybody, on the

13. Archimedes (är′ kə mē′ dēz′) Merlyn's owl, who is able to talk.

principle that the climate of any place outside the Forest Sauvage must be treacherous to the extreme, and, as for the sergeant, he polished all the armor till it was quite brittle and sharpened the swords till they were almost worn away.

At last it was time to set out.

Perhaps, if you happen not to have lived in the Old England of the twelfth century, or whenever it was, and in a remote castle on the borders of the Marches at that, you will find it difficult to imagine the wonders of their journey.

The road, or track, ran most of the time along the high ridges of the hills or downs, and they could look down on either side of them upon the **desolate** marshes where the snowy reeds sighed, and the ice crackled, and the duck in the red sunsets quacked loud on the winter air. The whole country was like that. Perhaps there would be a moory marsh on one side of the ridge, and a forest of a hundred thousand acres on the other, with all the great branches weighted in white. They could sometimes see a wisp of smoke among the trees, or a huddle of buildings far out among the impassable reeds, and twice they came to quite respectable towns which had several inns to boast of, but on the whole it was an England without civilization. The better roads were cleared of cover for a bow-shot on either side of them, lest the traveler should be slain by hidden thieves.

◀ **desolate** (des´ ə lit) *adj.* empty; solitary

They slept where they could, sometimes in the hut of some cottager who was prepared to welcome them, sometimes in the castle of a brother knight who invited them to refresh themselves, sometimes in the firelight and fleas of a dirty little hovel with a bush tied to a pole outside it—this was the signboard used at that time by inns—and once or twice on the open ground, all huddled together for warmth between their grazing chargers. Wherever they went and wherever they slept, the east wind whistled in the reeds, and the geese went over high in the starlight, honking at the stars.

London was full to the brim. If Sir Ector had not been lucky enough to own a little land in Pie Street, on which there stood a respectable inn, they would have been hard put to it to find a lodging. But he did own it, and as a matter of fact drew most of his dividends from that source, so they were able to get three beds between the five of them. They thought themselves fortunate.

On the first day of the tournament, Sir Kay managed to get them on the way to the lists at least an hour before the jousts could possibly begin. He had lain awake all night, imagining how he was going to beat the best barons in England, and he had not been able to eat his breakfast. Now he rode at the front of the cavalcade, with pale cheeks, and Wart wished there was something he could do to calm him down.

For country people, who only knew the dismantled tilting ground[14] of Sir Ector's castle, the scene which met their eyes was ravishing. It was a huge green pit in the earth, about as big as the arena at a football match. It lay ten feet lower than the surrounding country, with sloping banks, and the snow had been swept off it. It had been kept warm with straw, which had been cleared off that morning, and now the close-worn grass sparkled green in the white landscape. Round the arena there was a world of color so dazzling and moving and twinkling as to make one blink one's eyes. The wooden grandstands were painted in scarlet and white. The silk pavilions of famous people, pitched on every side, were azure and green and saffron and checkered. The pennons and pennoncells which floated everywhere in the sharp wind were flapping with every color of the rainbow, as they strained and slapped at their flagpoles, and the barrier down the middle of the arena itself was done in chessboard squares of black and white. Most of the combatants and their friends had not yet arrived, but one could see from those few who had come how the very people would turn the scene into a bank of flowers, and how the armor would flash, and the scalloped sleeves of the heralds jig in the wind, as they raised their brazen trumpets to their lips to shake the fleecy clouds of winter with joyances[15] and fanfares.

"Good heavens!" cried Sir Kay. "I have left my sword at home."

"Can't joust without a sword," said Sir Grummore. "Quite irregular."

"Better go and fetch it," said Sir Ector. "You have time."

"My squire will do," said Sir Kay. "What an awful mistake to make! Here, squire, ride hard back to the inn and fetch my sword. You shall have a shilling[16] if you fetch it in time."

The Wart went as pale as Sir Kay was, and looked as if he were going to strike him. Then he said, "It shall be done, master," and turned his ambling palfrey[17] against the stream of newcomers. He began to push his way toward their hostelry[18] as best he might.

"To offer me money!" cried the Wart to himself. "To look down at this beastly little donkey-affair off his great charger and to call me Squire! Oh, Merlyn, give me patience with the brute, and stop me from throwing his filthy shilling in his face."

When he got to the inn it was closed. Everybody had thronged to see the famous tournament, and the entire household had followed after the mob. Those were lawless days and it was not safe to leave your house—or even to go to sleep in it—unless you were certain that

---

14. **tilting ground** ground on which a joust takes place.
15. **joyances** (joi′ əns iz) *n.* old word meaning "rejoicing."
16. **shilling** (shil′ iŋ) *n.* British silver coin.
17. **palfrey** (pôl′ frē) *n.* old term for a saddle horse, especially one for women.
18. **hostelry** (häs′ təl rē) *n.* inn.

it was impregnable.[19] The wooden shutters bolted over the downstairs windows were two inches thick, and the doors were double-barred.

"Now what do I do," asked the Wart, "to earn my shilling?"

He looked ruefully at the blind little inn, and began to laugh.

"Poor Kay," he said. "All that shilling stuff was only because he was scared and miserable, and now he has good cause to be. Well, he shall have a sword of some sort if I have to break into the Tower of London.

"How does one get hold of a sword?" he continued. "Where can I steal one? Could I waylay some knight, even if I am mounted on an ambling pad, and take his weapons by force? There must be some swordsmith or armorer in a great town like this, whose shop would be still open."

He turned his mount and cantered off along the street. There was a quiet churchyard at the end of it, with a kind of square in front of the church door. In the middle of the square there was a heavy stone with an anvil on it, and a fine new sword was stuck through the anvil.

"Well," said the Wart, "I suppose it is some sort of war memorial, but it will have to do. I am sure nobody would grudge Kay a war memorial, if they knew his desperate straits."

He tied his reins round a post of the lych gate,[20] strode up the gravel path, and took hold of the sword.

"Come, sword," he said. "I must cry your mercy and take you for a better cause.

"This is extraordinary," said the Wart. "I feel strange when I have hold of this sword, and I notice everything much more clearly. Look at the beautiful gargoyles[21] of the church, and of the monastery which it belongs to. See how splendidly all the famous banners in the aisle are waving. How nobly that yew[22] holds up the red flakes of its timbers to worship God. How clean the snow is. I can smell something like fetherfew and sweet briar—and is it music that I hear?"

It was music, whether of pan-pipes or of recorders, and the light in the churchyard was so clear, without being dazzling, that one could have picked a pin out twenty yards away.

"There is something in this place," said the Wart. "There are people. Oh, people, what do you want?"

> "Well," said the Wart, "I suppose it is some sort of war memorial, but it will have to do."

19. **impregnable** (im preg´ nə bəl) *adj.* not capable of being captured or entered by force.
20. **lych** (lich) **gate** roofed gate at the entrance to a churchyard.
21. **gargoyles** (gär´ goilz´) *n.* grotesque sculptures of animals or fantastic creatures decorating a building.
22. **yew** (yo͞o) *n.* type of evergreen tree with red cones.

Nobody answered him, but the music was loud and the light beautiful.

"People," cried the Wart, "I must take this sword. It is not for me, but for Kay. I will bring it back."

There was still no answer, and Wart turned back to the anvil. He saw the golden letters, which he did not read, and the jewels on the pommel, flashing in the lovely light.

"Come, sword," said the Wart.

He took hold of the handles with both hands, and strained against the stone. There was a melodious consort[23] on the recorders, but nothing moved.

The Wart let go of the handles, when they were beginning to bite into the palms of his hands, and stepped back, seeing stars.

"It is well fixed," he said.

He took hold of it again and pulled with all his might. The music played more strongly, and the light all about the churchyard glowed like amethysts; but the sword still stuck.

"Oh, Merlyn," cried the Wart, "help me to get this weapon."

There was a kind of rushing noise, and a long chord played along with it. All round the churchyard there were hundreds of old friends. They rose over the church wall all together, like the Punch-and-Judy[24] ghosts of remembered days, and there were badgers and nightingales and vulgar crows and hares and wild geese and falcons and fishes and dogs and dainty unicorns and solitary wasps and corkindrills and hedgehogs and griffins and the thousand other animals he had met. They loomed round the church wall, the lovers and helpers of the Wart, and they all spoke solemnly in turn. Some of them had come from the banners in the church, where they were painted in heraldry, some from the waters and the sky and the fields about—but all, down to the smallest shrew mouse, had come to help on account of love. Wart felt his power grow.

"Put your back into it," said a Luce (or pike) off one of the heraldic banners, "as you once did when I was going to snap you up. Remember that power springs from the nape of the neck."

"What about those forearms," asked a Badger gravely, "that are held together by a chest? Come along, my dear embryo,[25] and find your tool."

A Merlin sitting at the top of the yew tree cried out, "Now then, Captain Wart, what is the first law of the foot? I thought I once heard something about never letting go."

---

23. consort (kän′ sôrt′) *n.* piece of music composed for a small group.

24. Punch-and-Judy puppets of the quarrelsome Punch and his wife, Judy, who fight constantly in a comical way.

25. embryo (em′ brē ō′) *n.* anything in an early stage of development.

"Don't work like a stalling woodpecker," urged a Tawny Owl affectionately. "Keep up a steady effort, my duck, and you will have it yet."

A White-Front said. "Now, Wart, if you were once able to fly the great North Sea, surely you can coordinate a few little wing-muscles here and there? Fold your powers together, with the spirit of your mind, and it will come out like butter. Come along, Homo sapiens,[26] for all we humble friends of yours are waiting here to cheer."

The Wart walked up to the great sword for the third time. He put out his right hand softly and drew it out as gently as from a scabbard.

There was a lot of cheering, a noise like a hurdy-gurdy[27] which went on and on. In the middle of this noise, after a long time, he saw Kay and gave him the sword. The people at the tournament were making a frightful row.

"But this is not my sword," said Sir Kay.

"It was the only one I could get," said the Wart. "The inn was locked."

"It is a nice-looking sword. Where did you get it?"

"I found it stuck in a stone, outside a church."

Sir Kay had been watching the tilting nervously, waiting for his turn. He had not paid much attention to his squire.

"That is a funny place to find one," he said.

"Yes, it was stuck through an anvil."

"What?" cried Sir Kay, suddenly rounding upon him. "Did you just say this sword was stuck in a stone?"

"It was," said the Wart. "It was a sort of war memorial."

Sir Kay stared at him for several seconds in amazement, opened his mouth, shut it again, licked his lips, then turned his back and plunged through the crowd. He was looking for Sir Ector, and the Wart followed after him.

---

26. Homo sapiens (hō´ mō sā´ pē enz´) scientific name for human beings.

27. hurdy-gurdy (hur´ dē gur´ dē) *n.* musical instrument played by turning a crank.

"Father," cried Sir Kay, "come here a moment."

"Yes, my boy," said Sir Ector. "Splendid falls these professional chaps do manage. Why, what's the matter, Kay? You look as white as a sheet."

"Do you remember that sword which the King of England would pull out?"

"Yes."

"Well, here it is. I have it. It is in my hand. I pulled it out."

Sir Ector did not say anything silly. He looked at Kay and he looked at the Wart. Then he stared at Kay again, long and lovingly, and said, "We will go back to the church."

"Now then, Kay," he said, when they were at the church door. He looked at his firstborn kindly, but straight between the eyes. "Here is the stone, and you have the sword. It will make you the King of England. You are my son that I am proud of, and always will be, whatever you do. Will you promise me that you took it out by your own might?"

Kay looked at his father. He also looked at the Wart and at the sword.

Then he handed the sword to the Wart quite quietly.

He said, "I am a liar. Wart pulled it out."

As far as the Wart was concerned, there was a time after this in which Sir Ector kept telling him to put the sword back into the stone—which he did—and in which Sir Ector and Kay then vainly tried to take it out. The Wart took it out for them, and stuck it back again once or twice. After this, there was another time which was more painful.

He saw that his dear guardian was looking quite old and powerless, and that he was kneeling down with difficulty on a gouty[28] knee.

"Sir," said Sir Ector, without looking up, although he was speaking to his own boy.

"Please do not do this, father," said the Wart, kneeling down also. "Let me help you up, Sir Ector, because you are making me unhappy."

"Nay, nay, my lord," said Sir Ector, with some very feeble old tears. "I was never your father nor of your blood, but I wote[29] well ye are of an higher blood than I wend[30] ye were."

"Plenty of people have told me you are not my father," said the Wart, "but it does not matter a bit."

---

28. gouty (gout´ ē) *adj.* having gout, a disease causing swelling and severe pain in the joints.
29. wote (wōt) *v.* old word meaning "know."
30. wend (wend) *v.* thought (past tense of ween, an old word meaning "think").

"Sir," said Sir Ector humbly, "will ye be my good and gracious lord when ye are King?"

"Don't!" said the Wart.

"Sir," said Sir Ector, "I will ask no more of you but that you will make my son, your foster-brother, Sir Kay, seneschal[31] of all your lands?"

Kay was kneeling down too, and it was more than the Wart could bear.

"Oh, do stop," he cried. "Of course he can be seneschal, if I have got to be this King, and, oh, father, don't kneel down like that, because it breaks my heart. Please get up, Sir Ector, and don't make everything so horrible. Oh, dear, oh, dear, I wish I had never seen that filthy sword at all."

And the Wart also burst into tears.

---

31. seneschal (sen′ ə shəl) *n.* steward, or manager, in the house of a medieval noble.

ABOUT THE AUTHOR

T. H. White (1906–1964)

Terence Hanbury White was born in Bombay (now Mumbai) when India was still a British colony. He returned to England for his education, later attending Queens College, Cambridge, where he received first-class honors in English. After graduation, White went to work as a teacher. Following the critical success of his memoir *England Have My Bones* (1936), the thirty-year-old White left teaching to become a full-time writer. His best known work, *The Once and Future King*, is a cycle of four novels largely based on *Le Morte d'Arthur*, the prose version of the Arthurian legends written by Sir Thomas Malory around 1470. The first novel, *The Sword in the Stone*, was published in 1938 and the final novel was published in 1958. White's version of the legends has inspired movies, as well as the musical *Camelot*. White also wrote poetry, short stories, detective and fantasy fiction, historical novels, and social history. He died in 1964. His headstone reads, "T. H. White, 1906–1964, Author Who from a Troubled Heart Delighted Others Loving and Praising This Life." A conclusion to *The Once and Future King* was found among White's papers after his death. This fifth novel was published in 1977 as *The Book of Merlyn*.

Close Reading Activities

READ

Comprehension

Reread all or part of the text to help you answer the following questions.

1. What has happened to the king?
2. What will the sword in the stone reveal?
3. Why do Sir Ector, Kay, and the Wart go to London?
4. Who pulls the sword out of the stone?
5. What does that action reveal about the Wart's true identity?

Research: Clarify Details This text may include references that are unfamiliar to you. Choose at least one unfamiliar detail and briefly research it. Then, explain how the information you learned from research sheds light on an aspect of the text.

Summarize Write an objective summary of the text. Remember that an objective summary is free from opinion and evaluation.

Language Study

Selection Vocabulary The following sentences appear in the selection. Define each boldfaced word. Then, use it in a sentence of your own.

- "Talkative weapon," remarked Sir Grummore **skeptically.**
- "Lot of people in London," remarked Sir Grummore, with a wild **surmise.**
- The road, or track, ran most of the time along the high ridges of the hills or downs, and they could look down on either side of them upon the **desolate** marshes…

Diction and Style Study the passage from the novel that appears below. Then, answer the questions that follow.

> "Nay, nay, my lord," said Sir Ector, with some very feeble old tears. "I was never your father nor of your blood, but I wote well ye are of an higher blood than I wend ye were."

1. **(a)** Identify the words that are forms of the Middle English verbs *witen,* which means "know," and *wenen,* which means "suppose." Explain your choices. **(b)** What does Sir Ector mean by "blood"? Explain.
2. Why do you think the author chose to weave archaic terms into Sir Ector's dialogue? Explain.

Conventions Read this passage from the selection in which Sir Kay anticipates the fun of participating in a real tournament. Identify the dependent and independent clauses. Then, explain how the use of clauses adds to the excited flow of Sir Kay's speech.

> When I am knighted I shall have to go to a tournament somewhere, and this one happens at just the right date. All the best people will be there, and we should see the famous knights and great kings. It does not matter about the sword, of course, but think of the tournament, probably the greatest there has ever been in Gramarye, and all the things we should see and do.

Academic Vocabulary

The following words appear in blue in the instructions and questions on the facing page.

implicit **alternative** **complexity**

Categorize the words by deciding whether you know each one well, know it a little bit, or do not know it at all. Then, use a print or online dictionary to look up the definitions of the words you are unsure of or do not know at all.

Literary Analysis

Reread the identified passages. Then, respond to the questions that follow.

Focus Passage 1 *(pp. 881–882)*
"There, there," she sobbed … Forest Sauvage."

Key Ideas and Details

1. **Interpret:** What information about the King does the reader learn from the nurse and from King Pellinore's dialogue?
2. What do Kay, Sir Ector, and the Wart do in honor of the king's death?

Craft and Structure

3. **(a) Interpret:** An anachronism is a detail that does not belong in the time period of a setting. In what ways is the nurse's description of cutting pictures from missals anachronistic? Explain. **(b) Connect:** To what type of modern person and behavior is the author likening the nurse? **(c) Analyze:** What is the effect of this **implicit** comparison? Explain.
4. **(a)** Cite an example of dialogue from the passage in which the speaker has a strong accent. **(b) Deduce:** How does the author indicate that accent? Explain. **(c) Analyze:** Explain how this detail adds to the portrayal of the Forest Sauvage and its inhabitants.

Integration of Knowledge and Ideas

5. **Synthesize:** How does the author create a humorous tone about a topic that is normally serious? Cite examples from the text.

Focus Passage 2 *(p. 888)*
For country people … You have time."

Key Ideas and Details

1. What setting does this passage describe?
2. **(a)** What has Kay forgotten? **(b) Infer:** What does this mistake suggest about his character? Explain.

Craft and Structure

3. **(a) Distinguish:** What **alternative** words does the author use to identify the colors red, blue, and yellow? **(b) Interpret:** How does this word choice add a sense of luxury and **complexity** to the description? Explain.
4. **(a) Analyze:** In what ways does the description of the setting highlight the differences between Sir Ector and his party and the king's court? Explain, citing specific details that support your response. **(b) Connect:** How does Kay's exclamation add to that portrayal? Explain.

Integration of Knowledge and Ideas

5. **Synthesize:** In what ways does this passage both reflect and undermine the noble qualities of the Arthurian legend and its characters?

Dialogue

Dialogue refers to characters' spoken words and the conversations they share. Reread the selection, and take notes on how the author uses dialogue to develop characters and advance the plot of the story.

1. **(a)** Identify two examples of Sir Grummore's dialogue in the excerpt. **(b)** What does each example suggest about his character? Explain.
2. What character trait does the Wart's dialogue at the end of the selection reveal? Explain, citing details that support your answer.
3. **The Arthurian Legend:** How does the dialogue help to establish a specific tone, or attitude, toward Arthurian legend and medieval tradition? Explain, citing details from the selection to support your ideas.

RL.9-10.1, RL.9-10.3, RL.9-10.4, RL.9-10.6; L.9-10.1.b, L.9-10.4, L.9-10.5, L.9-10.6
[For full standards wording, see the chart in the front of this book.]

DISCUSS • RESEARCH • WRITE

From Text to Topic **Panel Discussion**

Conduct a panel discussion about the following passage. Prepare for the discussion by reading the passage closely and taking notes. During the discussion, contribute your ideas, and support them with examples.

"Oh, Merlyn," cried the Wart ... as gently as from a scabbard. *(p. 890–891)*

QUESTIONS FOR DISCUSSION:

1. How does the use of modern language highlight the legendary nature of the events themselves?
2. How does this passage emphasize the idea that Arthur's royalty is authentic, recognized by nature itself?

WRITE

Writing to Sources **Explanatory Text**

Assignment

Write a work of **literary criticism** in which you analyze the humor in "Arthur Becomes King of Britain." Discuss how T. H. White combines a modern sensibility with the heroic style of traditional tales.

Prewriting and Planning Reread the text, looking for examples of humor and the literary techniques that White uses to achieve it. In particular, consider his uses of dialogue and description, as well as details that emphasize contrasts between medieval realities and a modern way of seeing the world. Record your notes in a list or an outline. Use the examples to build your thesis, or central idea.

Drafting Select an organizational structure. An effective critical essay can be organized into three parts:

- **Introduction:** Present the thesis.
- **Body:** Introduce evidence from the text to support the thesis. To present information from the text, use direct quotations, paraphrases, or summaries.
- **Conclusion:** Summarize the evidence and evaluate the author's style.

In your draft, refer to the effects of specific literary techniques, such as description and dialogue. Be sure to use literary terms correctly.

Revising Reread your essay, making sure that you have recorded any direct quotations from the text exactly as they appear in the original, word for word.

Editing and Proofreading In some cases, a direct quotation from the text will include dialogue, which will therefore already have double quotation marks. Make sure to use single quotation marks to punctuate a quotation within a quotation.

Punctuating a Quotation Within a Quotation: "'Lot of people in London,' remarked Sir Grummore, with a wild surmise. 'So they say.'"

CONVENTIONS

Make sure all direct quotations are enclosed in quotation marks. Precede a direct quotation in your essay with a comma or a colon, unless the quotation begins a sentence.

RESEARCH

Research **Investigate the Topic**

Knighthood in Medieval Tradition T. H. White's characters and much of his plot revolve around the medieval institution of knighthood. Kay is about to be knighted, and the tournament that the characters attend features jousting and other games with knights. Knighthood established a social hierarchy and provided entertainment during the Middle Ages.

> **Assignment**
> Conduct research about Medieval knighthood. Consult a variety of sources about the role of knights in the society, the equipment they used, and their portrayals in art and literature. Organize your findings into an **illustrated dictionary with quotations** of five key terms related to knighthood.

PREPARATION FOR ESSAY
You may use the knowledge you gain during this research assignment to support your claims in the essay you will write at the end of this section.

Gather Sources Locate authoritative print and electronic sources. Secondary sources, such as historical analyses and informational Web sites, provide details and insight into the roles knights played in Europe during the Middle Ages. You may also use primary sources, such as journals or firsthand accounts, but you will likely need to use modern translations. Consult expert sources and reliable institutions for authentic images of knights, ladies, armor, and other objects that were part of knightly culture. Document your sources for citation.

Take Notes Take notes on each source. Follow these steps to apply an organized note-taking strategy.

- Use the Bookmark feature on your Web browser to file electronic sources in appropriate folders.
- Copy and paste direct quotations so you do not introduce errors from typing. Be sure to credit all direct quotations accurately.
- Record all citation information as you research so you can easily locate sources and create a Works Cited list.

Synthesize Multiple Sources Assemble data and images from your sources and organize them into a cohesive presentation. Write brief, clear definitions and match images and quotations precisely to the definitions. Provide a Works Cited list of the sources you used. For additional guidance in citing sources, see the Citing Sources pages in the Introductory Unit of this textbook.

Organize and Present Ideas Design your dictionary so that images show up clearly. Make sure definitions are clear, precise, and accurate.

Common Core State Standards

W.9–10.2.a–b, W.9–10.2.d, W.9–10.2.f, W.9–10.4, W.9–10.5, W.9–10.8, W.9–10.9; SL.9–10.1.a, SL.9–10.3; L.9–10.2, L.9–10.2.b, L.9–10.3.a
[For full standards wording, see the chart in the front of this book.]

Morte d'Arthur

Alfred, Lord Tennyson

The Epic

At Francis Allen's on the Christmas eve—
The game of forfeits[1] done—the girls all kissed
Beneath the sacred bush and passed away—
The parson Holmes, the poet Everard Hall,
The host, and I sat round the wassail-bowl,[2]
Then halfway ebbed; and there we held a talk,
How all the old honor had from Christmas gone,
Or gone or dwindled down to some odd games
In some odd nooks like this; till I, tired out
With cutting eights[3] that day upon the pond,
Where, three times slipping from the outer edge,
I bumped the ice into three several stars,
Fell in a doze; and half-awake I heard

---

1. **forfeits** (fôr´ fits) *n.* game in which something is taken away as a penalty for making a mistake.
2. **wassail-bowl** (wäs´ əl bōl´) *n.* punch bowl.
3. **cutting eights** ice-skating in such a way that the skates cut figure eights in the ice.

The parson taking wide and wider sweeps,
Now harping on the church commissioners,
Now hawking at geology and schism;[4]
Until I woke, and found him settled down
Upon the general decay of faith
Right through the world: "at home was little left,
And none abroad; there was no anchor, none,
To hold by." Francis, laughing, clapped his hand
On Everard's shoulder, with "I hold by him."
"And I," quoth Everard, "by the wassail-bowl."
"Why yes," I said, "we knew your gift that way
At college; but another which you had—
I mean of verse (for so we held it then)—
What came of that?" "You know," said Frank, "he burnt
His epic, his King Arthur, some twelve books"—
And then to me demanding why: "O, sir,
He thought that nothing new was said, or else
Something so said 'twas nothing—that a truth
Looks freshest in the fashion of the day;
God knows; he has a mint of reasons; ask.
It pleased *me* well enough." "Nay, nay," said Hall,
"Why take the style of those heroic times?
For nature brings not back the mastodon,
Nor we those times; and why should any man
Remodel models? these twelve books of mine
Were faint Homeric echoes,[5] nothing-worth,
Mere chaff and draff, much better burnt." "But I,"
Said Francis, "picked the eleventh from this hearth,
And have it; keep a thing, its use will come.
I hoard it as a sugarplum for Holmes."
He laughed, and I, though sleepy, like a horse
That hears the corn-bin open, pricked my ears;
For I remembered Everard's college fame
When we were freshmen. Then at my request
He brought it; and the poet, little urged,
But with some prelude of disparagement,
Read, mouthing out his hollow o's and a's,
Deep-chested music, and to this result.

---

4. **schism** (siz′ əm) *n.* division within an organization, especially a church, because of a difference of opinion.
5. **Homeric** (hō mer′ ik) **echoes** imitations of the Greek poet Homer (of the eighth century B.C.E.).

Morte d'Arthur

So all day long the noise of battle rolled
Among the mountains by the winter sea,
Until King Arthur's table, man by man,
Had fallen in Lyonnesse[6] about their lord,
King Arthur; then, because his wound was deep,
The bold Sir Bedivere uplifted him,
Sir Bedivere, the last of all his knights,
And **bore** him to a chapel nigh the field,
A broken chancel[7] with a broken cross,
That stood on a dark strait of barren land.
On one side lay the ocean, and on one
Lay a great water, and the moon was full.
Then spake King Arthur to Sir Bedivere:
"The sequel of today unsolders[8] all
The goodliest fellowship of famous knights
Whereof this world holds record. Such a sleep
They sleep—the men I loved. I think that we
Shall never more, at any future time,
Delight our souls with talk of knightly deeds,
Walking about the gardens and the halls
Of Camelot, as in the days that were.
I perish by this people which I made—
Though Merlin[9] sware that I should come again
To rule once more—but let what will be be,
I am so deeply smitten through the helm
That without help I cannot last till morn.
Thou therefore take my brand Excalibur,
Which was my pride; for thou rememberest how
In those old days, one summer noon, an arm
Rose up from out the bosom of the lake,
Clothed in white samite,[10] mystic, wonderful,
Holding the sword—and how I rowed across
And took it, and have worn it, like a king;
And, wheresoever I am sung or told
In aftertime, this also shall be known.
But now delay not; take Excalibur,
And fling him far into the middle mere;[11]

bore ▶
(bôr) *v.* carried

6. **Lyonnesse** (lī´ ə nes´) *n.* legendary country off the southwestern coast of England, supposed to have sunk beneath the sea.
7. **chancel** (chan´ səl) *n.* part of a church around the altar.
8. **unsolders** (un säd´ ərz) *v.* separates.
9. **Merlin** sorcerer who advised King Arthur.
10. **samite** (sam´ īt) *n.* heavy silk fabric worn in the Middle Ages.
11. **mere** (mir) *n.* old or poetic word for "lake."

Watch what thou seest, and lightly[12] bring me word."
To him replied the bold Sir Bedivere:
"It is not meet,[13] Sir King, to leave thee thus,
Aidless, alone, and smitten through the helm.
A little thing may harm a wounded man.
Yet I thy hest will all perform at full,[14]
Watch what I see, and lightly bring thee word."
So saying, from the ruined shrine he stepped
And in the moon athwart the place of tombs,
Where lay the mighty bones of ancient men,
Old knights, and over them the sea wind sang
Shrill, chill, with flakes of foam. He, stepping down
By zigzag paths and juts of pointed rock,
Came on the shining levels of the lake.
There drew he forth the brand Excalibur,
And o'er him, drawing it, the winter moon,
Brightening the skirts of a long cloud, ran forth
And sparkled keen with frost against the hilt;
For all the haft twinkled with diamond sparks,
Myriads of topaz-lights, and jacinth-work[15]
Of subtlest jewelry. He gazed so long
That both his eyes were dazzled, as he stood,
This way and that dividing the swift mind,
In act to throw; but at the last it seemed
Better to leave Excalibur concealed
There in the many-knotted water flags,[16]
That whistled stiff and dry about the marge.[17]
So strode he back slow to the wounded king.
Then spake King Arthur to Sir Bedivere:
"Hast thou performed my mission which I gave?
What is it thou hast seen, or what hast heard?"
And answer made the bold Sir Bedivere:
"I heard the ripple washing in the reeds,
And the wild water lapping on the crag."
To whom replied King Arthur, faint and pale:
"Thou hast betrayed thy nature and thy name,
Not rendering[18] true answer, as beseemed
Thy fealty,[19] nor like a noble knight;

---

12. **lightly** *adv.* old or poetic word for "quickly."
13. **meet** *adj.* old or poetic word for "proper."
14. **I thy hest will all perform at full** I will carry out your order completely.
15. **topaz-lights, and jacinth-work** yellow and reddish-orange jewels.
16. **water flags** marsh plants.
17. **marge** (märj) *n.* margin; edge.
18. **rendering** (ren´ dər iŋ) *v.* giving.
19. **beseemed** (bē sēm´ əd) / **Thy fealty** (fē´ əl tē) was suitable to the loyalty you owe your lord.

For surer sign had followed, either hand,
Or voice, or else a motion of the mere.
This is a shameful thing for men to lie.
Yet now, I charge thee, quickly go again
As thou art lief and dear, and do the thing
I bade thee, watch, and lightly bring me word."
Then went Sir Bedivere the second time
Across the ridge, and paced beside the mere,
Counting the dewy pebbles, fixed in thought;
But when he saw the wonder of the hilt,
How curiously and strangely chased,[20] he smote
His palms together, and he cried aloud:
"And if indeed I cast the brand away;
Surely a precious thing, one worthy note,
Should thus be lost forever from the earth,
Which might have pleased the eyes of many men.
What good should follow this, if this were done?
What harm, undone? deep harm to disobey,
Seeing obedience is the bond of rule.
Were it well to obey then, if a king demand
An act unprofitable, against himself?
The king is sick, and knows not what he does.
What record, or what relic of my lord
Should be to aftertime, but empty breath
And rumors of a doubt? But were this kept,
Stored in some treasure-house of mighty kings,
Some one might show it at a joust of arms,
Saying, 'King Arthur's sword, Excalibur,
Wrought by the lonely maiden of the lake;
Nine years she wrought it, sitting in the deeps
Upon the hidden bases of the hills.'
So might some old man speak in the aftertime
To all the people, winning reverence;
But now much honor and much fame were lost."
So spake he, clouded with his own conceit,
And hid Excalibur the second time,
And so strode back slow to the wounded king.
Then spoke King Arthur, breathing heavily:
"What is it thou hast seen, or what hast heard?"
And answer made the bold Sir Bedivere:
"I heard the water lapping on the crag,
And the long ripple washing in the reeds."
To whom replied King Arthur, much in wrath:

20. chased *adj.* decorated by engraving or embossing.

"Ah, miserable and unkind, untrue,
Unknightly, traitor-hearted! Woe is me!
Authority forgets a dying king,
Laid widowed of the power in his eye
That bowed the will. I see thee what thou art,
For thou, the latest-left of all my knights,
In whom should meet the offices[21] of all,
Thou wouldst betray me for the precious hilt;
Either from lust of gold, or like a girl
Valuing the giddy pleasure of the eyes.
Yet, for a man may fail in duty twice,
And the third time may prosper, get thee hence;
But, if thou spare to fling Excalibur,
I will arise and slay thee with my hands."
   Then quickly rose Sir Bedivere, and ran,
And, leaping down the ridges lightly, plunged
Among the bulrush beds,[22] and clutched the sword,
And strongly wheeled and threw it. The great brand
Made lightnings in the splendor of the moon,
And flashing round and round, and whirled in an arch,
Shot like a streamer of the northern morn,[23]
Seen where the moving isles of winter shock[24]
By night, with noises of the northern sea.
So flashed and fell the brand Excalibur;
But ere he dipped the surface, rose an arm
Clothed in white samite, mystic, wonderful,
And caught him by the hilt, and **brandished** him
Three times, and drew him under in the mere.
And lightly went the other to the king.
   Then spoke King Arthur, drawing thicker breath:
"Now see I by thine eyes that this is done.
Speak out; what is it thou hast heard, or seen?"
   And answer made the bold Sir Bedivere:
"Sir King, I closed mine eyelids, lest the gems
Should blind my purpose, for I never saw,
Nor shall see, here or elsewhere, till I die,
Not though I live three lives of mortal men,
So great a miracle as yonder hilt.
Then with both hands I flung him, wheeling him;
But when I looked again, behold an arm,
Clothed in white samite, mystic, wonderful,
That caught him by the hilt, and brandished him

◀ **brandished** (bran´ disht) *v.* showed, waved, or shook in a threatening or triumphant manner

21. offices *n.* duties.
22. bulrush (bool´ rush´) **beds** growth of marsh plants.
23. a streamer of the northern morn northern lights; the aurora borealis.
24. the moving isles of winter shock icebergs crash.

Three times, and drew him under in the mere."
And answer made King Arthur, breathing hard:
"My end draws nigh; 'tis time that I were gone.
Make broad thy shoulders to receive my weight,
And bear me to the margin; yet I fear
My wound hath taken cold, and I shall die."
So saying, from the pavement he half rose,
Slowly, with pain, reclining on his arm,
And looking wistfully with wide blue eyes
As in a picture. Him Sir Bedivere
Remorsefully regarded through his tears,
And would have spoken, but he found not words,
Then took with care, and kneeling on one knee,
O'er both his shoulders drew the **languid** hands,
And rising bore him through the place of tombs.
But, as he walked, King Arthur panted hard,
Like one that feels a nightmare on his bed
When all the house is mute. So sighed the king,
Muttering and murmuring at his ear, "Quick, quick!
I fear it is too late, and I shall die."
But the other swiftly strode from ridge to ridge,
Clothed with his breath, and looking, as he walked,
Larger than human on the frozen hills.
He heard the deep behind him, and a cry
Before. His own thought drove him like a goad.[25]
Dry clashed his harness[26] in the icy caves
And barren chasms, and all to left and right
The bare black cliff clanged round him, as he based
His feet on juts of slippery crag that rang
Sharp-smitten with the dint of armèd heels—
And on a sudden, lo! the level lake,
And the long glories of the winter moon.
Then saw they how there hove a dusky barge,
Dark as a funeral scarf from stem to stern,
Beneath them; and descending they were ware
That all the decks were dense with stately forms
Black-stoled, black-hooded, like a dream—by these
Three queens with crowns of gold—and from them rose
A cry that shivered to the tingling stars,
And, as it were one voice, an agony
Of lamentation, like a wind that shrills
All night in a waste land, where no one comes,
Or hath come, since the making of the world.

languid ▶ (laŋ´ gwid) *adj.* without energy

25. goad (gōd) *n.* sharp-pointed stick used to drive oxen.
26. harness (här´ nis) *n.* armor.

Then murmured Arthur, "Place me in the barge,"
And to the barge they came. There those three queens
Put forth their hands, and took the king, and wept.
But she that rose the tallest of them all
And fairest laid his head upon her lap,
And loosed the shattered casque, and chafed his hands,
And called him by his name, complaining loud,
And dropping bitter tears against his brow
Striped with dark blood; for all his face was white
And colorless, and like the withered moon
Smote by the fresh beam of the springing east;
And all his greaves and cuisses dashed with drops
Of onset; and the light and lustrous curls—
That made his forehead like a rising sun
High from the dais-throne—were parched with dust;
Or, clotted into points and hanging loose,
Mixed with the knightly growth that fringed his lips.
So like a shattered column lay the king;
Not like that Arthur who, with lance in rest,
From spur to plume a star of tournament,
Shot through the lists at Camelot, and charged
Before the eyes of ladies and of kings.
Then loudly cried the bold Sir Bedivere:
"Ah! my Lord Arthur, whither shall I go?
Where shall I hide my forehead and my eyes?
For now I see the true old times are dead,
When every morning brought a noble chance,
And every chance brought out a noble knight.
Such times have been not since the light that led
The holy Elders with the gift of myrrh.[27]
But now the whole ROUND TABLE is dissolved
Which was an image of the mighty world;
And I, the last, go forth companionless,
And the days darken round me, and the years,
Among new men, strange faces, other minds."
And slowly answered Arthur from the barge:
"The old order changeth, yielding place to new,
And God fulfills himself in many ways,
Lest one good custom should corrupt the world.
Comfort thyself: what comfort is in me?
I have lived my life, and that which I have done
May He within himself make pure! but thou,

---

27. the light . . . of myrrh (mur) star that guided the three kings ("the holy Elders") with their gifts of myrrh (a gum from plants, used to make incense and perfume), to Bethlehem at the birth of Jesus.

If thou shouldst never see my face again,
Pray for my soul. More things are wrought by prayer
Than this world dreams of. Wherefore, let thy voice
Rise like a fountain for me night and day.
For what are men better than sheep or goats
That nourish a blind life within the brain,
If, knowing God, they lift not hands of prayer
Both for themselves and those who call them friend?
For so the whole round earth is every way
Bound by gold chains about the feet of God.
But now farewell. I am going a long way
With these thou seest—if indeed I go—
For all my mind is clouded with a doubt—
To the island-valley of Avilion;[28]
Where falls not hail, or rain, or any snow,
Nor ever wind blows loudly, but it lies
Deep-meadowed, happy, fair with orchard lawns
And bowery[29] hollows crowned with summer sea,
Where I will heal me of my grievous wound."
So said he, and the barge with oar and sail
Moved from the brink, like some full-breasted swan
that, fluting a wild carol ere her death,
Ruffles her pure cold plume, takes the flood
With swarthy webs. Long stood Sir Bedivere
Revolving many memories, till the hull
Looked one black dot against the verge of dawn,
And on the mere the wailing died away.

Here ended Hall, and our last light, that long
Had winked and threatened darkness, flared and fell;
At which the parson, sent to sleep with sound,
And waked with silence, grunted "Good!" but we
Sat rapt: it was the tone with which he read—
Perhaps some modern touches here and there
Redeemed it from the charge of nothingness—
Or else we loved the man, and prized his work;
I know not; but we sitting, as I said,
The cock crew loud, as at that time of year
The lusty bird takes every hour for dawn.
Then Francis, muttering, like a man ill-used,
"There now—that's nothing!" drew a little back,
And drove his heel into the smoldered log,

---

28. island-valley of Avilion According to ancient British myth, heroes were taken after death to the island paradise of Avalon, called "Avilion" here.

29. bowery (bou´ ər ē) *adj.* enclosed by overhanging boughs of trees or by vines.

That sent a blast of sparkles up the flue.
And so to bed, where yet in sleep I seemed
To sail with Arthur under looming shores,
Point after point; till on to dawn, when dreams
Begin to feel the truth and stir of day,
To me, methought, who waited with the crowd,
There came a bark that, blowing forward, bore
King Arthur; like a modern gentleman
Of stateliest port;[30] and all the people cried,
"Arthur is come again: he cannot die."
Then those that stood upon the hills behind
Repeated—"Come again, and thrice as fair";
And, further inland, voices echoed—"Come
With all good things, and war shall be no more."
At this a hundred bells began to peal,
That with the sound I woke, and heard indeed
The clear church bells ring in the Christmas morn.

---

30. Of stateliest port who carried himself in a most majestic or dignified manner.

ABOUT THE AUTHOR

Alfred, Lord Tennyson (1809–1892)

Alfred, Lord Tennyson was born in a rural town in Lincolnshire, an English county bordering the North Sea. The region's landscape, with its dunes and marshes, was a strong influence on his poetry. The fourth of twelve children, Tennyson was a sensitive child who had the run of the large library of his father, a clergyman who supervised his son's education and predicted a brilliant future for him as a poet. Despite this encouragement, however, Tennyson's home life was embittered by his family's poverty and his father's ill health. As a teenager, Tennyson attended Cambridge University, where he met Arthur Henry Hallam, who became his closest friend. In 1830, with Hallam's encouragement, Tennyson published *Poems, Chiefly Lyrical*. Three years later, Hallam suddenly died, leaving Tennyson devastated. During this period of grief, he probably began drafting his poem "Morte d'Arthur" which was finally published in 1842. Throughout his life, Tennyson had been fascinated by the Arthurian legend. Over the next forty years, he produced a cycle of twelve poems in which he retold the story of the rise and fall of King Arthur and the Knights of the Round Table. The first four poems, collected as *Idylls of the King*, appeared in 1859. The final poem in the cycle was published in 1885. Tennyson was immensely popular during his lifetime and was appointed poet laureate of England in 1850.

Close Reading Activities

READ

Comprehension

Reread all or part of the text to help you answer the following questions.

1. Why does Everard read his poem aloud?
2. In Everard's poem, what does King Arthur ask Sir Bedivere to do?
3. What happens when Sir Bedivere finally obeys King Arthur's instructions?

Research: Clarify Details Choose at least one unfamiliar detail from this poem, and briefly research it. Then, explain how the information you learned helps you better understand the poem.

Summarize Write an objective summary of the poem, one that is free from opinion and evaluation.

Language Study

Selection Vocabulary The following passages appear in the poem. Define each boldface word. Then, explain the context clues that clarify its meaning.

- The bold Sir Bedivere uplifted him / … And **bore** him to a chapel nigh the field…
- So flashed and fell the brand Excalibur; / But ere he dipped the surface, rose an arm / … And caught him by the hilt, and **brandished** him…
- Then took with care, and kneeling on one knee, / O'er both his shoulders drew the **languid** hands…

Literary Analysis

Reread the identified passage. Then, respond to the questions that follow.

Focus Passage *(p. 900)*
So all day long … cannot last till morn.

Key Ideas and Details

1. What has happened to Arthur and most of his men?

Craft and Structure

2. **(a) Distinguish:** Cite details in lines 59–63 that relate to ruin or desolation. **(b) Compare and Contrast:** How do these images compare to Arthur's memories in lines 70 and 71? Explain.
3. **Analyze:** How do details in the passage connect Arthur's physical body to the broken fellowship of knights and to the land itself? Explain.

Integration of Knowledge and Ideas

4. **Synthesize:** Explain how Arthur's statement, "I perish by these people which I made" is a reference to his status as a legendary figure.

Frame Story

A **frame story** is a story that brackets—or frames—another story. This device creates a story-within-a-story narrative structure.

1. **(a)** What question about "bringing back heroic times" does Hall ask in the frame story? **(b)** After listening to the poem and going to sleep, how does the narrator's dreaming vision answer Hall's question? Support your answer with details from the poem.
2. **The Arthurian Legend:** How do both the frame story and the interior poem suggest the importance of King Arthur in British culture? Use details from the poem in your answer.

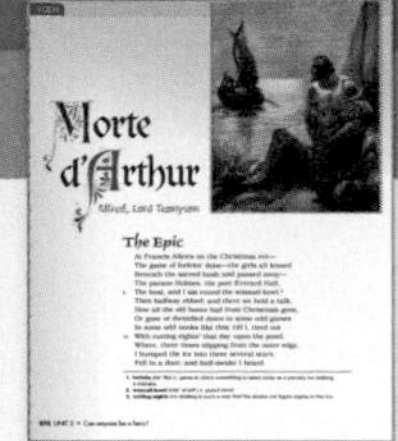

DISCUSS • RESEARCH • WRITE

From Text to Topic **Debate**

Debate the ideas expressed in the following passage with your classmates. Take notes during the debate. Address opposing views first and then contribute your own ideas, supporting them with examples from the text.

> Why take the style of those heroic times? / For nature brings not back the mastodon, / Nor we those times; and why should any man / Remodel models?…

QUESTIONS FOR DISCUSSION

1. Is Everard's observation ironic in the context of Tennyson's poem?
2. Do you agree with Everard, or is there a benefit to revisiting ideas from the past and "remodeling" them for the present?

Research **Investigate the Topic**

Versions of Arthur Tennyson's version of King Arthur's death is an **adaptation** of its presentation in Sir Thomas Malory's story, written during the late fifteenth century. Malory's and Tennyson's versions are not the only **renditions** of this tale.

Assignment

Conduct research to identify two other versions of King Arthur's death and to analyze their similarities and differences. Consult both traditional and contemporary stories based on his character. Organize your notes carefully to make sure you refer to and cite the correct version of the story. Share your findings in an **informal speech** for the class.

PREPARATION FOR ESSAY

You may use the results of this research in an essay you will write at the end of this section.

Writing to Sources **Informative Text**

Tennyson provides readers with an account of King Arthur's final moments and his reflections on life and humanity through his conversation with Sir Bedivere. In addition, the narrator of the frame story expresses nineteenth-century ideas about these topics.

Assignment

Write an **analytical essay** in which you discuss the beliefs the main characters express in both the frame story and the interior poem. Follow these steps:

- Identify repeated ideas or themes in the poem and use them to **establish** a point of analysis.
- State your topic and central idea in an introductory paragraph.
- Develop your topic and support your reasoning with well-chosen, relevant, and sufficient evidence from the text.
- Conclude with a section that follows from and restates your central idea and most important pieces of evidence.

ACADEMIC VOCABULARY

Academic terms appear in blue on these pages. If these words are not familiar to you, use a dictionary to find their definitions. Then, use them as you speak and write about the text.

Common Core State Standards

RL.9-10.1, RL.9-10.2, RL.9-10.3, RL.9-10.4, RL.9-10.5, RL.9-10.6, RL.9-10.7; W.9-10.2, W.9-10.4, W.9-10.7, W.9-10.9.a; SL.9-10.1, SL.9-10.4; L.9-10.4, L.9-10.6

[For full standards wording, see the chart in the front of this book.]

from A Connecticut Yankee in King Arthur's Court

Mark Twain

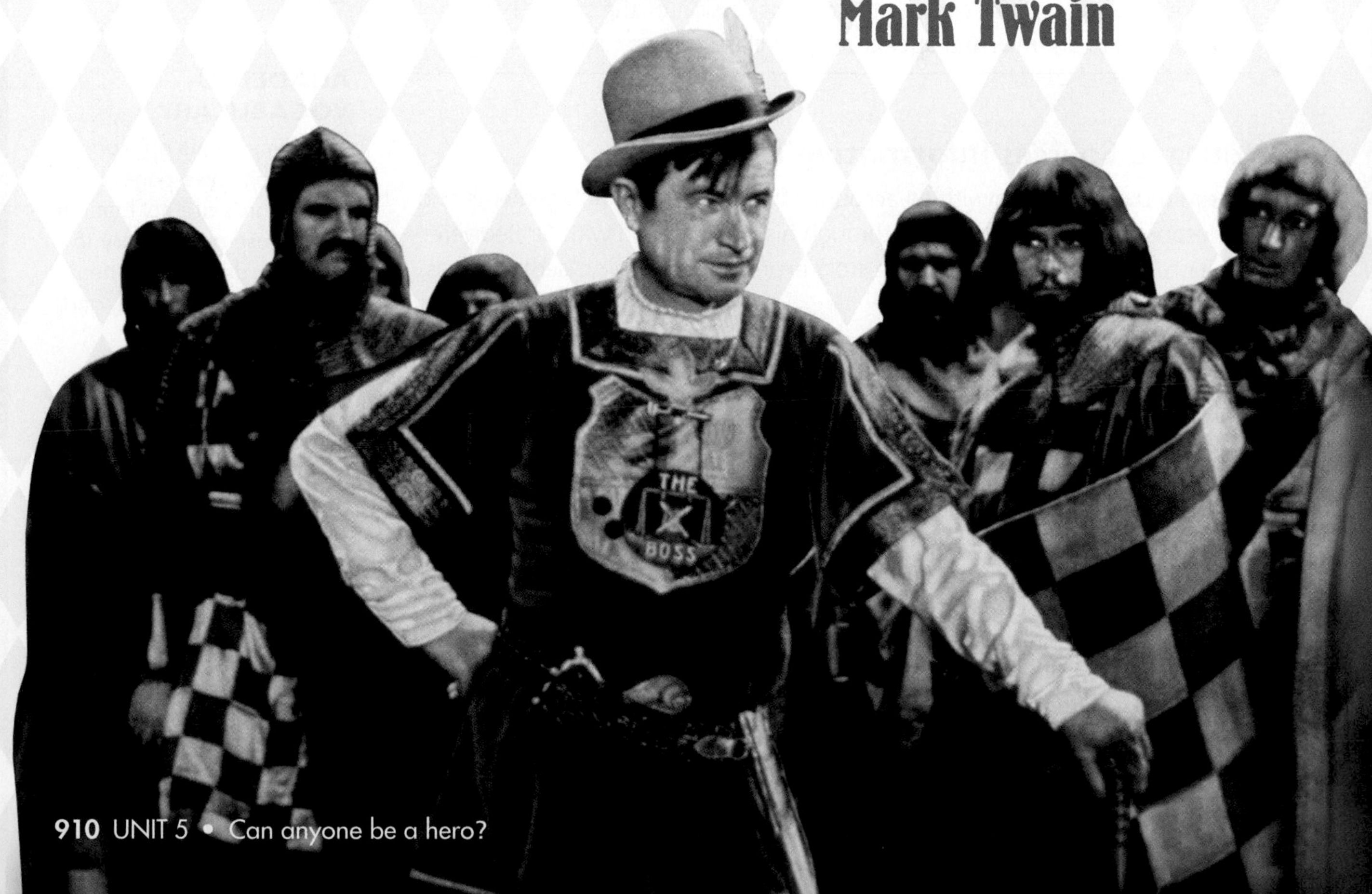

The main character in this comic novel is the practical Hank Morgan, a manager of an arms factory in Connecticut in 1879. One day, in a fight with an employee named Hercules, he is knocked unconscious. Awakening in a strange place, he finds himself the prisoner of a knight in armor, Sir Kay. On their way to King Arthur's court, Hank meets Clarence, a friendly young page. Hank is unsure of where he is, and he is astonished when Clarence tells him that it is June 19 in the year 528.

Chapter V - An Inspiration

I was so tired that even my fears were not able to keep me awake long.

When I next came to myself, I seemed to have been asleep a very long time. My first thought was, "Well, what an astonishing dream I've had! I reckon I've waked only just in time to keep from being hanged or drowned or burned or something. . . . I'll nap again till the whistle blows, and then I'll go down to the arms factory and have it out with Hercules."

But just then I heard the harsh music of rusty chains and bolts, a light flashed in my eyes, and that butterfly,[1] Clarence, stood before me! I gasped with surprise; my breath almost got away from me.

1. **butterfly** *n.* sociable, lighthearted person.

◀ Will Rogers portrays Hank Morgan in the 1931 film version of *A Connecticut Yankee in King Arthur's Court.*

"What!" I said, "you here yet? Go along with the rest of the dream! scatter!"

But he only laughed, in his light-hearted way, and fell to making fun of my sorry plight.

"All right," I said resignedly, "let the dream go on; I'm in no hurry."

"Prithee[2] what dream?"

"What dream? Why, the dream that I am in Arthur's court—a person who never existed; and that I am talking to you, who are nothing but a work of the imagination."

"Oh, la, indeed! and is it a dream that you're to be burned to-morrow? Ho-Ho—answer me that!"

The shock that went through me was distressing. I now began to reason that my situation was in the last degree serious, dream or no dream; for I knew by past experience of the lifelike intensity of dreams, that to be burned to death, even in a dream, would be very far from being a jest, and was a thing to be avoided, by any means, fair or foul, that I could contrive. So I said beseechingly:

"Ah, Clarence, good boy, only friend I've got—for you *are* my friend, aren't you?—don't fail me; help me to devise some way of escaping from this place!"

"Now do but hear thyself! Escape? Why, man, the corridors are in guard and keep of men-at-arms."

"No doubt, no doubt. But how many, Clarence? Not many, I hope?"

"Full a score.[3] One may not hope to escape." After a pause—hesitatingly: "and there be other reasons—and weightier."

"Other ones? What are they?"

"Well, they say—oh, but I daren't, indeed and indeed, I daren't!"

"Why, poor lad, what is the matter? Why do you blench? Why do you tremble so?"

"Oh, in sooth, there is need! I do want to tell you, but—"

"Come, come, be brave, be a man—speak out, there's a good lad!"

He hesitated, pulled one way by desire, the other way by fear; then he stole to the door and peeped out, listening; and finally crept close to me and put his mouth to my ear and told me his fearful news in a whisper, and with all the cowering apprehension of one who was venturing upon awful ground and speaking of things whose very mention might be freighted with death.

"Merlin, in his malice, has woven a spell about this dungeon, and there bides not the man in these kingdoms that would be desperate enough to essay to cross its lines with you! Now God pity me, I have told it! Ah, be kind to me, be merciful to a poor boy who means thee well; for an thou betray me I am lost!"

---

2. Prithee (pri*th'* ē) interjection; old term for "please."

3. a score twenty.

I laughed the only really refreshing laugh I had had for some time; and shouted:

"Merlin has wrought a spell! *Merlin*, forsooth! That cheap old humbug,[4] that maundering old ass? Bosh, pure bosh, the silliest bosh in the world! Why, it does seem to me that of all the childish, idiotic, chuckleheaded, chicken-livered superstitions that ev—oh, [curse] Merlin!"

But Clarence had slumped to his knees before I had half finished, and he was like to go out of his mind with fright.

"Oh, beware! These are awful words! Any moment these walls may crumble upon us if you say such things. Oh, call them back before it is too late!"

Now this strange exhibition gave me a good idea and set me to thinking. If everybody about here was so honestly and sincerely afraid of Merlin's pretended magic as Clarence was, certainly a superior man like me ought to be shrewd enough to contrive some way to take advantage of such a state of things. I went on thinking, and worked out a plan. Then I said:

"Get up. Pull yourself together; look me in the eye. Do you know why I laughed?"

"No—but for our blessed Lady's sake, do it no more."

"Well, I'll tell you why I laughed. Because I'm a magician myself."

"Thou!" The boy recoiled a step, and caught his breath, for the thing hit him rather sudden; but the aspect which he took on was very, very respectful. I took quick note of that; it indicated that a humbug didn't need to have a reputation in this asylum; people stood ready to take him at his word, without that. I resumed.

"I've known Merlin seven hundred years, and he—"

"Seven hun—"

"Don't interrupt me. He has died and come alive again thirteen times, and traveled under a new name every time: Smith, Jones, Robinson, Jackson, Peters, Haskins, Merlin—a new alias every time he turns up. I knew him in Egypt three hundred years ago; I knew him in India five hundred years ago—he is always blethering around in my way, everywhere I go; he makes me tired. He don't amount to shucks, as a magician; knows some of the old common tricks, but has never got beyond the rudiments, and never will. He is well enough for the provinces[5]—one-night stands and that sort of thing,

"What dream? Why, the dream that I am in Arthur's court—a person who never existed . . ."

4. **humbug** *n.* con artist; impostor; one who misrepresents himself or herself in order to take advantage of others.
5. **for the provinces** (präv′ ins iz) for unsophisticated audiences in places far from a big city.

Frank Albertson as Clarence and Will Rogers as Hank Morgan in the 1931 film version of *A Connecticut Yankee in King Arthur's Court*

you know—but dear me, *he* oughtn't to set up for an expert—anyway not where there's a real artist. Now look here, Clarence, I am going to stand your friend, right along, and in return you must be mine. I want you to do me a favor. I want you to get word to the king that I am a magician myself—and the Supreme Grand High-yu-Muckamuck and head of the tribe, at that; and I want him to be made to understand that I am just quietly arranging a little **calamity** here that will make the fur fly in these realms if Sir Kay's project is carried out and any harm comes to me. Will you get that to the king for me?"

calamity ▶
(kə lam′ ə tē) *n.* terrible misfortune; disaster

The poor boy was in such a state that he could hardly answer me. It was pitiful to see a creature so terrified, so unnerved, so demoralized. But he promised everything; and on my side he made me promise over and over again that I would remain his friend, and never turn against him or cast any enchantments upon him. Then he worked his way out, staying himself with his hand along the wall, like a sick person.

Presently this thought occurred to me: how heedless I have been! When the boy gets calm, he will wonder why a great magician like me should have begged a boy like him to help me get out of this place; he will put this and that together, and will see that I am a humbug.

I worried over that heedless blunder for an hour, and called myself a great many hard names, meantime. But finally it occurred to me all of a sudden that these animals didn't reason; that *they* never put this and that together; that all their talk showed that they didn't know a discrepancy when they saw it. I was at rest, then.

But as soon as one is at rest, in this world, off he goes on something else to worry about. It occurred to me that I had made another blunder: I had sent the boy off to alarm his betters with a threat—I intending to invent a calamity at my leisure; now the people who are the readiest and eagerest and willingest to swallow miracles are the very ones who are hungriest to see you perform them; suppose I should be called on for a sample? Suppose I should be asked to name my calamity? Yes, I had made a blunder; I ought to have invented my calamity first. "What shall I do? what can I say, to gain a little time?" I was in trouble again; in the deepest kind of trouble: . . . "There's a footstep!—they're coming. If I had only just a moment to think. . . . Good, I've got it. I'm all right."

You see, it was the eclipse. It came into my mind, in the nick of time, how Columbus, or Cortez, or one of those people, played an eclipse as a saving trump once, on some savages, and I saw my chance. I could play it myself, now; and it wouldn't be any plagiarism, either, because I should get it in nearly a thousand years ahead of those parties.

Clarence came in, subdued, distressed, and said:

"I hasted the message to our liege the king, and straightway he had me to his presence. He was frighted even to the marrow, and was minded to give order for your instant enlargement,[6] and that you be clothed in fine raiment and lodged as befitted one so great; but then came Merlin and spoiled all; for he persuaded the king that you are mad, and know not whereof you speak; and said your threat is but foolishness and idle vaporing. They disputed long, but in the end, Merlin, scoffing, said, 'Wherefore hath he not *named* his brave calamity? Verily it is because he cannot.' This thrust did in a most sudden sort close the king's mouth, and he could offer naught to turn the argument; and so, reluctant, and full loth to do you the discourtesy, he yet prayeth you to consider his perplexed case, as noting how the matter stands, and name the calamity—if so be you have determined the nature of it and the time of its coming. Oh, prithee delay not; to delay at such a time were to double and treble the perils that already compass thee about. Oh, be thou wise—name the calamity!"

I allowed silence to accumulate while I got my impressiveness together, and then said:

---

6. enlargement *n.* old term for "release."

"How long have I been shut up in this hole?"

"Ye were shut up when yesterday was well spent. It is nine of the morning now."

"No! Then I have slept well, sure enough. Nine in the morning now! And yet it is the very complexion of midnight, to a shade. This is the 20th, then?"

"The 20th—yes."

"And I am to be burned alive to-morrow." The boy shuddered.

"At what hour?"

"At high noon."

"Now then, I will tell you what to say." I paused, and stood over that cowering lad a whole minute in awful silence; then, in a voice deep, measured, charged with doom, I began, and rose by dramatically graded stages to my colossal climax, which I delivered in as sublime and noble a way as ever I did such a thing in my life: "Go back and tell the king that at that hour I will smother the whole world in the dead blackness of midnight; I will blot out the sun, and he shall never shine again; the fruits of the earth shall rot for lack of light and warmth, and the peoples of the earth shall famish and die, to the last man!"

I had to carry the boy out myself, he sunk into such a collapse. I handed him over to the soldiers, and went back.

Chapter VI - The Eclipse

In the stillness and the darkness, realization soon began to supplement knowledge. The mere knowledge of a fact is pale; but when you come to *realize* your fact, it takes on color. It is all the difference between hearing of a man being stabbed to the heart, and seeing it done. In the stillness and the darkness, the knowledge that I was in deadly danger took to itself deeper and deeper meaning all the time; a something which was realization crept inch by inch through my veins and turned me cold.

But it is a blessed provision of nature that at times like these, as soon as a man's mercury[7] has got down to a certain point there comes a revulsion, and he rallies. Hope springs up, and cheerfulness along with it, and then he is in good shape to do something for himself, if anything can be done. When my rally came, it came with a bound. I said to myself that my eclipse would be sure to save me, and make me the greatest man in the kingdom besides; and straightway my mercury went up to the top of the tube, and my solicitudes all vanished. I was as happy a man as there was in the

7. **mercury** referring to the liquid metal used in a thermometer; the mercury rises and falls in the thermometer with the temperature.

world. I was even impatient for tomorrow to come, I so wanted to gather in that great triumph and be the center of all of the nation's wonder and reverence. Besides, in a business way it would be the making of me; I knew that.

Meantime there was one thing which had got pushed into the background of my mind. That was the half-conviction that when the nature of my proposed calamity should be reported to those superstitious people, it would have such an effect that they would want to compromise. So, by and by when I heard footsteps coming, that thought was recalled to me, and I said to myself, "As sure as anything, it's the compromise. Well, if it is good, all right, I will accept; but if it isn't, I mean to stand my ground and play my hand for all it is worth."

The door opened, and some men-at-arms appeared. The leader said:

"The stake is ready. Come!"

The stake! The strength went out of me, and I almost fell down. It is hard to get one's breath at such a time, such lumps come into one's throat, and such gaspings; but as soon as I could speak, I said:

"But this is a mistake—the execution is tomorrow."

"Order changed; been set forward a day. Haste thee!"

I was lost. There was no help for me. I was dazed, stupefied; I had no command over myself; I only wandered purposelessly about, like one out of his mind; so the soldiers took hold of me, and pulled me along with them, out of the cell and along the maze of underground corridors, and finally into the fierce glare of daylight and the upper world. As we stepped into the vast inclosed court of the castle I got a shock; for the first thing I saw was the stake, standing in the center, and near it the piled fagots[8] and a monk. On all four sides of the court the seated **multitudes** rose rank above rank, forming sloping terraces that were rich with color. The king and the queen sat in their thrones, the most **conspicuous** figures there, of course.

◄ **multitudes** (mul´ tə to͞odz´) *n.* crowds; large numbers of people

conspicuous (kən spik´ yo͞o əs) *adj.* easy to see

To note all this, occupied but a second. The next second Clarence had slipped from some place of concealment and was pouring news into my ear, his eyes beaming with triumph and gladness. He said:

"'Tis through *me* the change was wrought! And main hard have I worked to do it, too. But when I revealed to them the calamity in store, and saw how mighty was the terror it did engender, then saw I also that this was the time to strike! Wherefore I diligently pretended, unto this and that and the other one, that your power against the sun could not reach its full until the morrow; and so if any would save the sun and the world, you must be slain today, while your

8. **fagots** (fag´ əts) *n.* bundles of sticks used as fuel.

enchantments are but in the weaving and lack potency. Odsbodikins, it was but a dull lie, a most indifferent invention, but you should have seen them seize it and swallow it, in the frenzy of their fright, as it were salvation sent from heaven; and all the while was I laughing in my sleeve the one moment, to see them so cheaply deceived, and glorifying God the next, that He was content to let the meanest[9] of His creatures be His instrument to the saving of thy life. Ah, how happy has the matter sped! You will not need to do the sun a *real* hurt—ah, forget not that, on your soul forget it not! Only make a little darkness—only the littlest little darkness, mind, and cease with that. It will be sufficient. They will see that I spoke falsely—being ignorant, as they will fancy—and with the falling of the first shadow of that darkness you shall see them go mad with fear; and they will set you free and make you great! Go to thy triumph, now! But remember—ah, good friend, I implore thee remember my supplication, and do the blessed sun no hurt. For *my* sake, thy true friend."

I choked out some words through my grief and misery; as much as to say I would spare the sun; for which the lad's eyes paid me back with such deep and loving gratitude that I had not the heart to tell him his good-hearted foolishness had ruined me and sent me to my death.

As the soldiers assisted me across the court the stillness was so profound that if I had been blindfold I should have supposed I was in a solitude instead of walled in by four thousand people. There was not a movement perceptible in those masses of humanity; they were as rigid as stone images, and as pale; and dread sat upon every countenance. This hush continued while I was being chained to the stake; it still continued while the fagots were carefully and tediously piled about my ankles, my knees, my thighs, my body. Then there was a pause, and a deeper hush, if possible, and a man knelt down at my feet with a blazing torch; the multitude strained forward, gazing, and parting slightly from their seats without knowing it; the monk raised his hands above my head, and his eyes toward the blue sky, and began some words in Latin; in this attitude he droned on and on, a little while, and then stopped. I waited two or three moments; then looked up; he was standing there petrified. With a common impulse the multitude rose slowly up and stared into the sky. I followed their eyes; as sure as guns, there was my eclipse beginning! The life went boiling through my veins; I was a new man! The rim of black spread slowly into the sun's disk, my heart beat higher and higher, and still the assemblage and the priest stared into the sky, motionless. I knew that this gaze would be turned upon

---

9. meanest *adj.* lowest; least significant.

me, next. When it was, I was ready. I was in one of the most grand attitudes I ever struck, with my arm stretched up pointing to the sun. It was a noble effect. You could see the shudder sweep the mass like a wave. Two shouts rang out, one close upon the heels of the other:

"Apply the torch!"

"I forbid it!"

The one was from Merlin, the other from the king. Merlin started from his place—to apply the torch himself, I judged. I said:

"Stay where you are. If any man moves—even the king—before I give him leave, I will blast him with thunder, I will consume him with lightnings!"

The multitude sank meekly into their seats, and I was just expecting they would. Merlin hesitated a moment or two, and I was on pins and needles that little while. Then he sat down, and I took a good breath; for I knew I was master of the situation now. The king said:

"Be merciful, fair sir, and essay no further in this perilous matter, lest disaster follow. It was reported to us that your powers could not attain unto their full strength until the morrow; but—"

"Your Majesty thinks the report may have been a lie? It *was* a lie."

That made an immense effect; up went appealing hands everywhere, and the king was assailed with a storm of supplications that I might be bought off at any price, and the calamity stayed.

The king was eager to comply. He said:

"Name any terms, reverend sir, even to the halving of my kingdom; but banish this calamity, spare the sun!"

> "Name any terms, reverend sir, even to the halving of my kingdom; but banish this calamity, spare the sun!"

My fortune was made, I would have taken him up in a minute, but I couldn't stop an eclipse; the thing was out of the question. So I asked time to consider. The king said:

"How long—ah, how long, good sir? Be merciful; look, it groweth darker, moment by moment. Prithee how long?"

"Not long. Half an hour—maybe an hour."

There were a thousand pathetic protests, but I couldn't shorten up any, for I couldn't remember how long a total eclipse lasts. I was in a puzzled condition, anyway, and wanted to think. Something was wrong about that eclipse, and the fact was very unsettling. If this wasn't the one I was after, how was I to tell whether this was the sixth century, or nothing but a dream? Dear me, if I could only prove it was the latter! Here was a glad new hope. If the boy was right about the date, and this was surely the 20th, it *wasn't* the sixth century. I reached for the monk's sleeve, in considerable excitement, and asked him what day of the month it was.

Hang him, he said it was the *twenty-first!* It made me turn cold to hear him. I begged him not to make any mistake about it; but he was sure; he knew it was the 21st. So, that feather-headed boy had botched things again! The time of the day was right for the eclipse; I had seen that for myself, in the beginning, by the dial[10] that was near by. Yes, I *was* in King Arthur's court, and I might as well make the most of it I could.

The darkness was steadily growing, the people becoming more and more distressed. I now said:

"I have reflected, Sir King. For a lesson, I will let this darkness proceed, and spread night in the world; but whether I blot out the sun for good, or restore it shall rest with you. These are the terms, to wit: You shall remain king over all your dominions, and receive all the glories and honors that belong to the kingship; but you shall appoint me your perpetual minister and executive, and give me for my services one per cent. of such actual increase of revenue[11] over and above its present amount as I may succeed in creating for the state. If I can't live on that, I sha'n't ask anybody to give me a lift. Is it satisfactory?"

There was a prodigious roar of applause, and out of the midst of it the king's voice rose, saying:

"Away with his bonds, and set him free! and do him homage, high and low, rich and poor, for he is become the king's right hand, is clothed with power and authority, and his seat is upon the highest step of the throne! Now sweep away this creeping night, and bring the light and cheer again, that all the world may bless thee."

But I said:

"That a common man should be shamed before the world, is nothing; but it were dishonor to the *king* if any that saw his minister naked should not also see him delivered from his shame. If I might ask that my clothes be brought again—"

"They are not meet," the king broke in. "Fetch raiment of another sort; clothe him like a prince!"

My idea worked. I wanted to keep things as they were till the eclipse was total, otherwise they would be trying again to get me to dismiss the darkness, and of course I couldn't do it. Sending for the clothes gained some delay, but not enough. So I had to make another excuse. I said it would be but natural if the king should change his mind and repent to some extent of what he had done under excitement; therefore I would let the darkness grow awhile, and if at the end of a reasonable time the king had kept his mind the

---

10. dial *n.* sundial, or device used to measure time by the position of the sun in the sky.

11. revenue (rev´ ə no͞o´) *n.* money taken in by a government in the form of taxes, fees, and penalties.

same, the darkness should be dismissed. Neither the king nor anybody else was satisfied with that arrangement, but I had to stick to my point.

It grew darker and darker and blacker and blacker, while I struggled with those awkward sixth-century clothes. It got to be pitch-dark, at last, and the multitude groaned with horror to feel the cold uncanny night breezes fan through the place and see the stars come out and twinkle in the sky. At last the eclipse was total, and I was very glad of it, but everybody else was in misery; which was quite natural. I said:

"The king, by his silence, still stands to the terms." Then I lifted up my hand—stood just so a moment—then I said, with the most awful solemnity: "Let the enchantment dissolve and pass harmless away!"

There was no response, for a moment, in that deep darkness and that graveyard hush. But when the silver rim of the sun pushed itself out, a moment or two later, the assemblage broke loose with a vast shout and came pouring down like a deluge to smother me with blessings and gratitude.

And Clarence was not the last of the wash, to be sure.

ABOUT THE AUTHOR

Mark Twain (1835–1910)

Samuel Clemens, who would later win fame as Mark Twain, grew up in the small Mississippi River town of Hannibal, Missouri. When Clemens was around twelve years old, his father died unexpectedly, and Clemens had to leave school in order to work. He learned the printing trade and at the age of fifteen began writing as a journalist. Clemens later found work as a steamboat pilot on the Mississippi. He took his famous pen name from a riverboat cry, "Mark twain!" which indicated that the water was deep enough for a safe passage. When riverboat traffic on the Mississippi River was halted by the Civil War, Clemens headed west, hunting for silver in Nevada and gold in California while writing accounts of his travels. His first writings signed "Mark Twain" were published during this period. In 1870, Twain married Olivia Langdon and began to raise a family. Settling in Hartford, Connecticut, he wrote his popular boyhood novels *The Adventures of Tom Sawyer* (1876) and *The Adventures of Huckleberry Finn* (1884) as well as a series of other bestsellers. Twain died at his home in Connecticut at the age of seventy-four.

Close Reading Activities

READ

Comprehension

Reread all or part of the text to help you answer the following questions.

1. Where is Hank Morgan when he wakes up?
2. What fate is planned for Hank?
3. What kind of person does Hank pretend to be?
4. What "calamity" does Hank pretend to create?

Research: Clarify Details This novel excerpt may include references that are unfamiliar to you. Choose at least one unfamiliar detail, and briefly research it. Then, explain how the information you learned from research sheds light on an aspect of the text.

Summarize Write an objective summary of the text, one that is free from opinion and evaluation.

Language Study

Selection Vocabulary The following passages appear in the selection. Identify two synonyms for each boldface word. Then, use the word in a sentence of your own.

- I am just quietly arranging a little **calamity** here…
- On all four sides of the court the seated **multitudes** rose rank above rank…
- The king and the queen sat in their thrones, the most **conspicuous** figures there, of course.

Literary Analysis

Reread the identified passage. Then, respond to the questions that follow.

Focus Passage *(pp. 916–917)*

In the stillness … I knew that.

Key Ideas and Details

1. What does Hank realize with growing intensity?
2. **Interpret:** Why does Hank feel the eclipse will be "the making" of him? **(c) Infer:** What does this expectation reveal about his character and motivations?

Craft and Structure

3. **(a) Distinguish:** Cite sensory details related to sight, hearing, vision, and touch that the narrator uses to explain how "knowledge" differs from "realization." **(b) Analyze:** According to Hank, what does realization feel like? **(c) Compare and Contrast:** What does hope feel like to Hank? Explain, citing details from the text.

Integration of Knowledge and Ideas

4. **Synthesize:** How do Hank's observations reflect a modern **sensibility** and **viewpoint**? Explain.

Parody

A **parody** is a humorous piece of writing that mocks the characteristics of a literary genre, work, or style. Reread the excerpt, and take notes on ways in which the author parodies Arthurian legend.

1. **(a)** What main personality traits do Merlin and King Arthur display? **(b)** How do Twain's characters differ from their **counterparts** in traditional Arthurian legends?
2. How is Hank a parody of a heroic figure? Explain.
3. **The Arthurian Legend:** Does this parody criticize or does it uphold traditional heroic ideals, such as those presented in the King Arthur tales? Explain.

DISCUSS • RESEARCH • WRITE

From Text to Topic Small Group Discussion

Discuss the following passage with a small group of classmates. Take notes during the discussion. Contribute your own ideas and support them with examples from the text.

> "...These are the terms, to wit: You shall remain king over all your dominions, and receive all the glories and honors that belong to the kingship; but you shall appoint me your perpetual minister and executive, and give me for my services one per cent. of such actual increase of revenue over and above its present amount as I may succeed in creating for the state. If I can't live on that, I sha'n't ask anybody to give me a lift. Is it satisfactory?"

QUESTIONS FOR DISCUSSION

1. What two types of language does Hank combine in this speech? What effect does it have?
2. What aspects of traditional heroic figures and ideals does this passage parody?

Research Investigate the Topic

Medieval Astronomy In this episode from Twain's novel, Hank Morgan is able to take advantage of medieval ignorance about the causes of eclipses.

Assignment
Conduct research to learn how people of the Middle Ages viewed the heavens and what they understood about the relationships among Earth, the moon, and the sun. Identify your sources for citation. Share your findings in a **multimedia presentation.**

PREPARATION FOR ESSAY

You may use the results of this research in an essay you will write at the end of this section.

Writing to Sources Narrative

In Twain's novel, Hank Morgan travels back in time to King Arthur's court. He uses his knowledge of history and science to secure a high place in society.

Assignment
Write a **fictional narrative** in which you adapt the story of the eclipse and Hank's planned execution, retelling it from the point of view of a different character, such as King Arthur, Clarence, or Merlin. Follow these steps:

- Consider how your narrator perceives the events described in Twain's story, and introduce the characters and conflict from that point of view.
- Use a variety of narrative techniques such as dialogue, reflection, and characterization to develop your story and new point of view.
- Use precise words, phrases, and details to convey a vivid picture of events.
- Provide a resolution that ends the narrative in a satisfying way.

ACADEMIC VOCABULARY

Academic terms appear in blue on these pages. Use a dictionary to find their definitions. Then, use them as you speak and write about the text.

Common Core State Standards

RL.9-10.1, RL.9-10.2, RL.9-10.3, RL.9-10.4; W.9-10.3, W.9-10.4, W.9-10.6, W.9-10.7; SL.9-10.1, SL.9-10.2; L.9-10.4, L.9-10.6

[For full standards wording, see the chart in the front of this book.]

from Youth and Chivalry

from A Distant Mirror: The Calamitous 14th Century

Barbara W. Tuchman

More than a code of manners in war and love, chivalry was a moral system, governing the whole of noble life. That it was about four parts in five **illusion** made it no less governing for all that. It developed at the same time as the great crusades of the 12th century as a code intended to fuse the religious and **martial** spirits and somehow bring the fighting man into accord with Christian theory. Since a knight's usual activities were as much at odds with Christian theory as a merchant's, a moral gloss was needed that would allow the Church to tolerate the warriors in good conscience and the warriors to pursue their own values in spiritual comfort. With the help of Benedictine thinkers, a code evolved that put the knight's sword arm in the service, theoretically, of justice, right, piety, the Church, the widow, the orphan, and the oppressed. Knighthood was received in the name of the Trinity after a ceremony of purification, confession, communion. A saint's relic was usually embedded in the hilt of the knight's sword so that upon clasping it

◀ **illusion**
(i lo͞o′zhən) *n.* belief not supported by facts

◀ **martial**
(mär′shəl) *adj.* warlike

as he took his oath, he caused the vow to be registered in Heaven. Chivalry's famous celebrator Ramon Lull, a contemporary of St. Louis, could now state as his thesis that "God and chivalry are in concord."

But, like business enterprise, chivalry could not be contained by the Church, and bursting through the pious veils, it developed its own principles. Prowess, that combination of courage, strength, and skill that made a chevalier *preux*, was the prime essential. Honor and loyalty, together with courtesy—meaning the kind of behavior that has since come to be called "chivalrous"—were the ideals, and so-called courtly love the presiding genius.[1] Designed to make the knight more polite and to lift the tone of society, courtly love required its disciple to be in a chronically amorous condition, on the theory that he would thus be rendered more courteous, gay, and gallant, and society in consequence more joyous. Largesse[2] was the necessary accompaniment. An open-handed generosity in gifts and hospitality was the mark of a gentleman and had its practical value in attracting other knights to fight under the banner and bounty of the *grand seigneur*. Over-celebrated by troubadours[3] and chroniclers who depended on its flow, largesse led to reckless extravagance and careless bankruptcies.

stamina ▶ (stam′ə nə) *n.* resistance to fatigue or hardship; endurance

Prowess was not mere talk, for the function of physical violence required real **stamina**. To fight on horseback or foot wearing 55 pounds of plate armor, to crash in collision with an opponent at full gallop while holding horizontal an eighteen-foot lance half the length of an average telephone pole, to give and receive blows with sword or battle-ax that could cleave a skull or slice off a limb at a stroke, to spend half of life in the saddle through all weathers and for days at a time, was not a weakling's work. Hardship and fear were part of it. "Knights who are at the wars ... are forever swallowing their fear," wrote the companion and biographer of Don Pero Niño, the "Unconquered Knight" of the late 14th century. "They expose themselves to every peril; they give up their bodies to the adventure of life in death. Moldy bread or biscuit, meat cooked or uncooked; today enough to eat and tomorrow nothing, little or no wine, water from a pond or a butt,[4] bad quarters, the shelter of a tent or branches, a bad bed, poor sleep with their armor still on their backs, burdened with iron, the enemy an arrow-shot off. 'Ware! Who goes there? To arms! To arms!' With the first drowsiness, an alarm; at dawn, the trumpet. 'To horse! To horse! Muster! Muster!' As lookouts,

1. **genius** (jēn′yəs; jē′nē əs) *n.* essential spirit.
2. **largesse** (lär jes′) *n.* generous giving by a patron.
3. **troubadours** (tro͞o′ bə dôrz′) *n.* medieval minstrels.
4. **butt** (but) *n.* large barrel.

as sentinels, keeping watch by day and by night, fighting without cover, as foragers, as scouts, guard after guard, duty after duty. 'Here they come! Here! They are so many—No, not as many as that—This way—that—Come this side—Press them there—News! News! They come back hurt, they have prisoners—no, they bring none back. Let us go! Let us go! Give no ground! On!' Such is their calling."

Horrid wounds were part of the calling. In one combat Don Pero Niño was struck by an arrow that "knit together his gorget[5] and his neck," but he fought on against the enemy on the bridge. "Several lance stumps were still in his shield and it was that which hindered him most." A bolt from a crossbow "pierced his nostrils most painfully whereat he was dazed, but his daze lasted but a little time." He pressed forward, receiving many sword blows on head and shoulders which "sometimes hit the bolt embedded in his nose making him suffer great pain." When weariness on both sides brought the battle to an end, Pero Niño's shield "was tattered and all in pieces; his sword blade was toothed like a saw and dyed with blood ... his armor was broken in several places by lance-heads of which some had entered the flesh and drawn blood, although the coat was of great strength." Prowess was not easily bought.

Loyalty, meaning the pledged word, was chivalry's fulcrum.[6] The extreme emphasis given to it derived from the time when a pledge between lord and vassal[7] was the only form of government. A knight who broke his oath was charged with "treason" for betraying the order of knighthood. The concept of loyalty did not preclude treachery or the most egregious trickery as long as no knightly oath was broken. When a party of armed knights gained entrance to a walled town by declaring themselves allies and then proceeded to slaughter the defenders, chivalry was evidently not violated, no oath having been made to the burghers.[8]

Chivalry was regarded as a universal order of all Christian knights, a trans-national class moved by a single ideal, much as Marxism later regarded all workers of the world. It was a military guild in which all knights were theoretically brothers....

Fighting filled the noble's need of something to do, a way to exert himself. It was his substitute for work. His leisure time was spent chiefly in hunting, otherwise in games of chess, backgammon, and dice, in songs, dances, pageants, and other entertainments. Long winter evenings were occupied listening to the recital of interminable

---

5. **gorget** (gôr′jit) *n.* piece of armor protecting the throat.
6. **fulcrum** (fulˊkrəm) *n.* support for a lever; figuratively, something that exerts a key influence.
7. **vassal** (vasˊəl) *n.* under the medieval system of feudalism, a tenant who received land in exchange for a pledge of service to a lord.
8. **burghers** (burˊgərzˊ) *n.* townspeople.

verse epics. The sword offered the workless noble an activity with a purpose, one that could bring him honor, status, and, if he was lucky, gain. If no real conflict was at hand, he sought tournaments, the most exciting, expensive, ruinous, and delightful activity of the noble class, and paradoxically the most harmful to his true military function. Fighting in tournaments concentrated his skills and absorbed his interest in an increasingly formalized clash, leaving little thought for the tactics and strategy of real battle.

> ...the tournament was the peak of nobility's pride and delight in its own valor and beauty.

Originating in France and referred to by others as "French combat" (*conflictus Gallicus*), tournaments started without rules or lists[9] as an agreed-upon clash of opposing units. Though justified as training exercises, the impulse was the love of fighting. Becoming more regulated and mannered, they took two forms: jousts by individuals, and melees by groups of up to forty on a side, either *à plaisance* with blunted weapons or *à outrance* with no restraints, in which case participants might be severely wounded and not infrequently killed. Tournaments proliferated as the noble's primary occupation dwindled. Under the extended rule of monarchy, he had less need to protect his own fief,[10] while a class of professional ministers was gradually taking his place around the crown. The less he had to do, the more energy he spent in tournaments artificially re-enacting his role.

A tournament might last as long as a week and on great occasions two. Opening day was spent matching and seeding the players, followed by days set apart for jousts, for melees, for a rest day before the final tourney, all interspersed with feasting and parties.... About a hundred knights usually participated, each accompanied by two mounted squires, an armorer, and six servants in livery. The knight had of course to equip himself with painted and gilded armor and crested helmet costing from 25 to 50 livres, with a war-horse costing from 25 to 100 livres in addition to his traveling palfrey, and with banners and trappings and fine clothes. Though the expense could easily bankrupt him, he might also come away richer, for the loser in combat had to pay a ransom and the winner was awarded his opponent's horse and armor, which he could sell back to him or to anyone. Gain was not recognized by chivalry, but it was present at tournaments.

---

9. **lists** (lists) *n.* fenced-off areas for medieval jousts.
10. **fief** (fēf) *n.* under feudalism, land held by a vassal.

Because of their extravagance, violence, and vainglory, tournaments were continually being denounced by popes and kings, from whom they drained money. . . . Although St. Louis condemned tournaments and Philip the Fair[11] prohibited them during his wars, nothing could stop them permanently or dim the enthusiasm for them.

With brilliantly dressed spectators in the stands, flags and ribbons fluttering, the music of trumpets, the parade of combatants making their draped horses prance and champ on golden bridles, the glitter of harness and shields, the throwing of ladies' scarves and sleeves to their favorites, the bow of the heralds to the presiding prince who proclaimed the rules, the cry of poursuivants announcing their champions, the tournament was the peak of nobility's pride and delight in its own valor and beauty.

---

11. **St. Louis . . . Philip the Fair** Louis IX (1214–1270), king of France, was declared a saint by the Catholic Church soon after his death. Philip IV (1268–1314), king of France, also called Philip the Fair, was the grandson of Louis IX.

ABOUT THE AUTHOR

Barbara W. Tuchman (1912–1989)

Pulitzer Prize-winning historian Barbara Tuchman was born in New York City to a wealthy family. As a correspondent for *The Nation* magazine, she reported on the Spanish Civil War. After she married in 1940, she took a leave from writing until her three children were older. She returned to writing in the late 1950s, receiving critical recognition for *The Zimmerman Telegram* (1958), a detailed study of a crucial episode during World War I. Tuchman won her first Pulitzer Prize for *The Guns of August* (1962), an account of the beginning of the World War I. She received a second Pulitzer for *Stilwell and the American Experience in China* (1970). At this point, Tuchman's scholarship took a dramatic change in direction. For the next seven years, she researched and wrote *A Distant Mirror: The Calamitous 14th Century* (1978), a study of life in medieval France from which this excerpt is taken. A trademark of Tuchman's style as a writer is her use of arresting historical detail. She has said that to infuse her accounts of the past with suspense, she sought to present events from the point of view of those who lived through them and had no idea what the outcome would be.

Close Reading Activities

READ

Comprehension

Reread all or part of the text to help you answer the following questions.

1. According to Tuchman, why was the code of chivalry developed?
2. Which quality was essential for a knight to possess?
3. What did knights spend much of their time doing?

Research: Clarify Details This text may include references that are unfamiliar to you. Choose at least one unfamiliar detail and briefly research it. Then, explain how the information you learned from research sheds light on an aspect of the text.

Summarize Write an objective summary of the text, one that is free from opinion and evaluation.

Language Study

Selection Vocabulary The following passages appear in "Youth and Chivalry." Define each boldfaced word. Then, write a paragraph in which you use all three words in a logical way.

- That it was about four parts in five **illusion** made it no less governing for all that.
- It developed at the same time as the great crusades of the 12th century as a code intended to fuse the religious and **martial** spirits…
- …for the function of physical violence required real **stamina.**

Literary Analysis

Reread the identified passage. Then, respond to the questions that follow.

Focus Passage *(pp. 926–927)*
Prowess was not … Such is their calling."

Key Ideas and Details

1. **Analyze:** What central idea **unifies** this paragraph?

Craft and Structure

2. **(a) Summarize:** What information about the knight's existence is provided in the quotation about Don Pero Niño? Explain. **(b) Analyze:** How does the style of that quotation paint a clear picture of a knight's life? Cite uses of repetition, exclamations, dialogue, and sensory details in your response.

Integration of Knowledge and Ideas

3. **Synthesize:** What evidence does this passage provide about the **integrity** with which medieval knights followed the code of chivalry? Cite details from the text in your response.

Exposition

Exposition is writing or speech that explains a process or presents information. Reread the excerpt and take notes on ways in which the author uses exposition.

1. **(a)** What is the purpose of the first sentence of the selection? **(b)** How does the structure of the sentence support this purpose? Explain.
2. **(a)** What contradiction does the author introduce in the second sentence? **(b)** What insight about chivalry does this contradiction reveal? **(c)** What is the purpose of the remainder of the first paragraph?
3. **The Arthurian Legend:** What view of chivalry and knighthood does the author's exposition present?

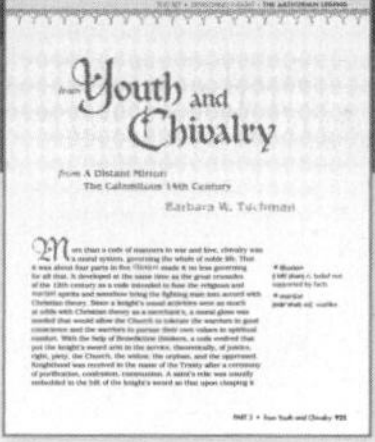

DISCUSS • RESEARCH • WRITE

From Text to Topic **Partner Discussion**

Discuss the following passage with a partner. Take notes during the discussion. Contribute your own ideas and support them with examples from the text.

> But, like business enterprise, chivalry could not be contained by the Church, and bursting through the pious veils, it developed its own principles. Prowess, that combination of courage, strength, and skill that made a chevalier *preux*, was the prime essential. Honor and loyalty, together with courtesy—meaning the kind of behavior that has since come to be called "chivalrous"—were the ideals, and so-called courtly love the presiding genius.

QUESTIONS FOR DISCUSSION

1. What qualities were considered chivalrous during the Middle Ages? Are those same qualities still seen as chivalrous today?
2. Do you think many knights actually possessed all these qualities?

Research **Investigate the Topic**

King Arthur and the Code of Chivalry Barbara Tuchman describes the uncomfortable and often violent realities of medieval knighthood.

Assignment

Conduct research to learn more about both the code of chivalry and the King Arthur tales. Consider whether the Arthurian legends present idealized or realistic versions of knights. Organize your notes and identify all sources. Share your findings in an **informal presentation.**

PREPARATION FOR ESSAY

You may use the results of this research in an essay you will write at the end of this section.

Writing to Sources **Argument**

In "Youth and Chivalry," Barbara W. Tuchman discusses how the code of chivalry was adopted by the Church to **interject** moral values into warfare.

Assignment

Write a **persuasive essay** in which you express and defend a position on the ethics of the knight's code of chivalry. Follow these steps:

- Define the knight's code of chivalry as you interpret it. Cite evidence from "Youth and Chivalry" to support your definition. If you do not agree with Barbara Tuchman's definition, present evidence to support your perspective.
- Clearly present and support your position about the ethics of the knight's chivalric code as you have defined it.
- Write a strong conclusion in which you restate or summarize the key points of your essay.

ACADEMIC VOCABULARY

Academic terms appear in blue on these pages. If these words are not familiar to you, use a dictionary to find their definitions. Then, use them as you speak and write about the text.

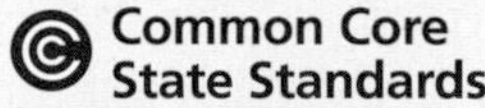

Common Core State Standards

RI.9–10.1, RI.9–10.2, RI.9-10.6, RI.9–10.8; W.9–10.1.a–b, W.9-10.1.e, W.9-10.4, W.9-10.7, W.9–10.8, W.9-10.9; SL.9-10.1, SL.9-10.4; L.9-10.4, L.9-10.6

[For full standards wording, see the chart in the front of this book.]

from The Birth of Britain

Winston S. Churchill

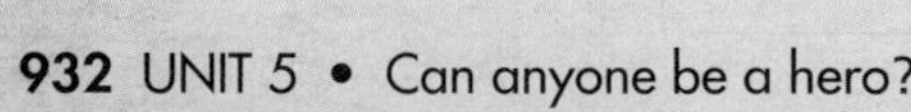

There looms, large, uncertain, dim but glittering, the legend of King Arthur and the Knights of the Round Table. Somewhere in the Island a great captain gathered the forces of Roman Britain and fought the barbarian invaders to the death. Around him, around his name and his deeds, shine all that romance and poetry can bestow.

Twelve battles, all located in scenes untraceable, with foes unknown, except that they were heathen, are punctiliously set forth in the Latin of Nennius.[1] Other authorities say, "No Arthur; at least, no proof of any Arthur." It was only when Geoffrey of Monmouth[2] six hundred years later was praising the splendors of feudalism and martial aristocracy that chivalry, honor, the Christian faith, knights in steel and ladies bewitching, are enshrined in a glorious circle lit by victory. Later this would have been retold and embellished by the genius of Mallory, Spenser, and Tennyson. True or false, they have gained an immortal hold upon the thoughts of men. It is difficult to believe it was all an invention of a Welsh writer. If it was, he must have been a marvelous inventor.

King Arthur and the Knights of the Round Table; from "Roman de la Table Ronde," 1488.

Modern research has not accepted the annihilation of Arthur. Timidly but resolutely the latest and best-informed writers unite to proclaim his reality. They cannot tell when in this dark period he lived, or where he held sway and fought his battles. They are ready to believe however that there was a great British warrior, who kept the light of civilization burning against all the storms that beat, and

1. **Nennius** (nen′ē əs) (flourished c. A.D. 800) Welsh historian whose Latin chronicle *Historia Brittonum* (*History of the Britons*) provides the earliest known reference to King Arthur.
2. **Geoffrey** (jef′rē) **of Monmouth** (died 1155) English bishop whose Latin chronicle, *Historia regum Britanniae* (*History of the Kings of Britain*), introduced the Arthurian legend into European literature.

that behind his sword there sheltered a faithful following of which the memory did not fail. All four groups of the Celtic tribes which dwelt in the tilted uplands of Britain cheered themselves with the Arthurian legend, and each claimed their own region as the scene of his exploits. From Cornwall to Cumberland a search for Arthur's realm or sphere has been pursued.

contradicted ▶ (kän′trə dik′ təd) *v.* denied; opposed verbally

The reserve of modern assertions is sometimes pushed to extremes, in which the fear of being **contradicted** leads the writer to strip himself of almost all sense and meaning. One specimen of this method will suffice.

> It is reasonably certain that a petty chieftain named Arthur did exist, probably in South Wales. It is possible that he may have held some military command uniting the tribal forces of the Celtic or highland zone or part of it against raiders and invaders (not all of them necessarily Teutonic). It is also possible that he may have engaged in all or some of the battles attributed to him; on the other hand, this attribution may belong to a later date.

exterminated ▶ (ek stur′mə nāt′əd) *v.* destroyed completely; wiped out

This is not much to show after so much toil and learning. None the less, to have established a basis of fact for the story of Arthur is a service which should be respected. In this account we prefer to believe that the story with which Geoffrey delighted the fiction-loving Europe of the twelfth century is not all fancy. If we could see exactly what happened we should find ourselves in the presence of a theme as well founded, as inspired, and as inalienable from the inheritance of mankind as the *Odyssey* or the Old Testament. It is all true, or it ought to be; and more and better besides. And wherever men are fighting against barbarism, tyranny, and massacre, for freedom, law, and honor, let them remember that the fame of their deeds, even though they themselves be **exterminated**, may perhaps be celebrated as long as the world rolls round. Let us then declare that King Arthur and his noble knights, guarding the Sacred Flame of Christianity and the theme of a world order, sustained by valor, physical strength, and good horses and armor, slaughtered innumerable hosts of foul barbarians and set decent folk an example for all time.

We are told he was a Dux Bellorum.[3] What could be more natural or more necessary than that a commander-in-chief should be accepted—a new Count of Britain, such as the Britons had appealed to Aetius[4] to give them fifty years before? Once Arthur is recognized as the commander of a mobile field army, moving from one part of the country to another and uniting with local forces in

3. **Dux Bellorum** (duks be lôr′ əm), Roman title for a provincial military commander; from Latin meaning "leader of wars." *Dux* is the Latin root of the English word *duke*.
4. **Aetius** (ā ē′ shē ə) (died A.D. 454) Roman general and statesman.

each district, the disputes about the scenes of his actions explain themselves. Moreover the fourth century witnessed the rise of cavalry to the dominant position in the battlefield. The day of infantry had passed for a time, and the day of the legion had passed forever. The Saxon invaders were infantry, fighting with sword and spear, and having little armor. Against such an enemy a small force of ordinary Roman cavalry might well prove **invincible**. If a chief like Arthur had gathered a band of mail-clad cavalry he could have moved freely about Britain, everywhere heading the local resistance to the invader and gaining repeated victories. The memory of Arthur carried with it the hope that a deliverer would return one day. The legend lived upon the increasing tribulations of the age. Arthur has been described as the last of the Romans. He understood Roman ideas, and used them for the good of the British people. "The heritage of Rome," Professor Collingwood says, "lives on in many shapes, but of the men who created that heritage Arthur was the last, and the story of Roman Britain ends with him."

◀ **invincible** (in vin´sə bəl) *adj.* incapable of being defeated; unbeatable

ABOUT THE AUTHOR

Winston S. Churchill

(1874–1965)

As the son of a British father and an American mother, Winston Churchill was well suited for one of his key roles as Britain's prime minister during World War II—forging an alliance with U.S. president Franklin D. Roosevelt. After a mediocre career at school, Churchill entered the army, where he achieved success and fame both as a soldier and as a writer. He next followed his father's example and entered politics, winning election to Parliament as a Conservative in 1900, but switching to the Liberal party four years later. Throughout the next three decades, Churchill's political career would continue to be erratic, culminating in his finding himself out of office in the 1930s and mistrusted by politicians on all sides. During the same period, however, he enjoyed great success as a writer of history and biography. The rise of Adolf Hitler and the Nazis in Germany gave Churchill a new political focus. He opposed the British government's efforts to appease Germany and urged preparation for the war he was sure was coming. Following the German invasion of Poland and the beginning of World War II, Churchill rejoined the government, becoming prime minister in May 1940. His powerful wartime speeches helped rally the resolve of the British people to fight against what seemed to be an invincible German military. After leaving office, Churchill focused on writing historical works. He was awarded the Nobel Prize in Literature in 1953 "for his mastery of historical and biographical description as well as for brilliant oratory in defending exalted human values."

Close Reading Activities

READ

Comprehension

Reread all or part of the text to help you answer the following questions.

1. What question does Churchill explore in this text?
2. What do Geoffrey of Monmouth, Mallory, Spenser, and Tennyson have in common?
3. What stance do modern researchers take on the question of King Arthur's existence?

Research: Clarify Details This text may include references that are unfamiliar to you. Choose at least one unfamiliar detail, and briefly research it. Then, explain how the information you learned from research sheds light on an aspect of the text.

Summarize Write an objective summary of the selection. Remember that an objective summary is free from opinion and evaluation.

Language Study

Selection Vocabulary The following phrases appear in the selection. For each boldface word, create a word map in which you list at least one synonym and one antonym.

- the fear of being **contradicted**
- even though they themselves be **exterminated**
- might well prove **invincible**

Literary Analysis

Reread the identified passage. Then, respond to the questions that follow.

Focus Passage *(p. 934)*

This is not much … for all time.

Key Ideas and Details

1. **Interpret:** How does Churchill evaluate scholars' success in proving the existence of a historical Arthur? Explain.

Craft and Structure

2. What attitude toward the Arthurian legend is restated in the phrases, "we prefer to believe…," and "It is all true, or it ought to be."
3. **(a) Infer:** In the final sentence of the focus passage, what does Churchill suggest about the portrayal of good and evil in the Arthur legend? Explain. **(b) Analyze:** How does this sentence support the idea that the British people *choose* to believe in Arthur? Explain.

Integration of Knowledge and Ideas

4. **Synthesize:** Why might a society choose to believe in the historical reality of a figure who was not, in fact, real? Cite details from the selection in your response.

Connotation

The **connotation** of a word is the set of emotional associations it carries. Reread the selection and note how connotations help to convey precise meanings and attitudes.

1. **(a)** What connotation does *barbarian* have? **(b)** Why do you think Churchill repeats this word?
2. **The Arthurian Legend: (a)** What is another way to say "Modern research has not accepted the annihilation of Arthur"? **(b)** How do the connotations of *annihilation* affect Churchill's tone?

DISCUSS • RESEARCH • WRITE

From Text to Topic **Panel Discussion**

Conduct a panel discussion about the following passage. Prepare for the discussion by reading the passage closely and taking notes. During the discussion, contribute your ideas, and support them with examples.

> The Saxon invaders were infantry, fighting with sword and spear, and having little armor. Against such an enemy a small force of ordinary Roman cavalry might well prove invincible. If a chief like Arthur had gathered a band of mail-clad cavalry he could have moved freely about Britain, everywhere leading the local resistance to the invader and gaining repeated victories.

QUESTIONS FOR DISCUSSION

1. How did Arthur's troops differ from the invading Saxons?
2. Why might Arthur have been able to organize **resistance** to the Saxon invaders?

Research **Investigate the Topic**

Arthur as the Last Roman In this history, Winston Churchill presents Arthur as the last defender of civilized Britain during the period of the Anglo-Saxon invasions in the fifth century.

Assignment
Conduct research on the history of Britain in the period when Arthur might have lived. Take clear notes and carefully identify your sources so that you can easily access the information later. Share your findings in a **short research report.**

PREPARATION FOR ESSAY

You may use the results of this research in an essay you will write at the end of this section.

Writing to Sources **Argument**

In this excerpt from *The Birth of Britain,* Winston Churchill claims that the question of whether King Arthur really existed is not as important as the basic, **enduring** values that the Arthurian legend **embodies**.

Assignment
Write a **response to literature** in which you analyze Churchill's claim and explain whether you agree or disagree with him. Follow these steps:

- Explain Churchill's argument and identify the key pieces of evidence he uses to support it.
- State whether you agree or disagree with Churchill's position entirely, or agree with some aspects but not with others.
- Take into account other points of view, and explain how they may be interesting but are not convincing.
- Organize your ideas logically, and cite evidence from the text to support them.
- Write a strong conclusion in which you restate your central idea.

ACADEMIC VOCABULARY

Academic terms appear in blue on these pages. Consult a dictionary to find their definitions. Then, use them as you speak and write about the text.

Common Core State Standards

RI.9-10.1, RI.9-10.2, RI.9-10.3, RI.9-10.4, RI.9-10.5, RI.9-10.6, RI.9-10.8; W.9-10.1, W.9-10.1.a, W.9-10.4, W.9-10.9.b; SL.9-10.1.a; L.9-10.4.d, L.9-10.5, L.9-10.6

[For full standards wording, see the chart in the front of this book.]

MAGAZINE ARTICLE

from

A Pilgrim's Search for Relics of the Once and Future King

Caroline Alexander

▲ A modern day view of the coast of Cornwall with the ruins of Tintagel castle, King Arthur's supposed birthplace, in the background

Hidden in a thicket, I drew my coat around me and peered into the darkness. It was Christmas Eve. The night was clear and still and without moonlight. I had positioned myself beside a muddy bridle path[1] that winds down a hill between the trees and was quietly awaiting the thunder of hoofbeats. The hill behind me is known as Cadbury Castle, for centuries regarded as the most likely site of King Arthur's Camelot. According to legend, on Christmas Eve the ghosts of Arthur and his knights gallop out of the castle's fallen gates on silver-footed horses.

1. **bridle** (brīd′'l) **path** *n.* trail suitable for horseback riding.

Cadbury Castle is in Somerset just outside the village of South Cadbury, in southwest England. In daylight, the open grassy summit is brilliant green, rising above an encircling band of forest. From the top, you can look down on flocks grazing the clipped pasturage at the base of the hill. Northward lies the whole width of Glastonbury plain. The first recorded identification of Cadbury Castle as Camelot was made by the antiquarian John Leland in 1542. But it wasn't until the 1960s that parts of the hill's many layers of former settlements were finally excavated, revealing that it had been occupied off and on since at least early Neolithic times. More important, ruins from the Arthurian period were well represented, with evidence of former ramparts, a fortified gate-tower and a sizable timber structure thought to have been a great hall.

I had expected to share my vigil on Christmas Eve with any number of other faithful (or **gullible**) pilgrims. But when I trudged across the frosty fields to my thicket, I was very much alone. The whirring wings of a disturbed wood pigeon made the only sound I heard all night. At last I reluctantly gave up my post and trudged back down through the fields. The once and future king had failed to appear.

◀ **gullible**
(gul′ ə bəl) *adj.*
easily tricked; too easily convinced

How to account for the spell that Camelot has cast over the world's imagination? In scores of languages and shaped to all sorts of storytelling genres, from medieval epic to modern musical, tales of Arthur and his knights have been enthralling people for more than a thousand years. On plot alone, the legend is hard to resist: the undistinguished boy, Arthur, pulling the sword from the stone to become king of England; his marriage to beautiful Guinevere; the brotherhood of the chivalrous Round Table knights; the quest for that elusive object, the Holy Grail; the disastrous passion between Lancelot and the queen; evil Mordred's treachery; the ultimate destruction of Arthur's realm; the banishment of loyalty, piety and righteousness from the land.

But the emotional pull of Camelot is greater than its captivating storybook romance. Arthur's loss of his Round Table, though set in the worldly realm of kings and counselors, jousting tourneys, swashbuckling knights and bewitching ladies, is a replay of mankind's fall from grace in the Garden of Eden. It ends in treason and civil war, with brother against brother, father against son. It has become part of the geography of our collective imagination. Today, that "fleeting wisp of glory called Camelot" stirs an overwhelming sense of loss—a **nostalgic** yearning for a better-ordered and more-spiritual age that we long to believe once existed.

◀ **nostalgic**
(näs tal′ jik) *adj.*
feeling a longing for something long ago or far away

A Magic World of Profound Melancholy

I have spent years more or less in thrall to the Camelot story. Walt Disney's film *The Sword in the Stone* set me on the path, imparting beyond the comedy and magic a sense of something grave and wondrously tragic. Based on T. H. White's *The Once and Future King*, it opened up Arthur's whole life and world, a medieval land full of hawking and archery and imagined fighting described in whimsical detail yet marked by overwhelming melancholy. Later, Thomas Malory's unwieldy but masterful epic poem *Le Morte d'Arthur* worked for me at a more profound level of regret and grown-up loss, its archaic language evoking images of armored footsteps receding down deserted flinty halls. But it was through Tennyson's epic *Idylls of the King* that all the "Arthurian" emotions—loyalty and loss and the impotent regret of wisdom learned too late—became entirely personal.

Like many pilgrims, then, I had come to England hoping to find something that might allow me to believe that Camelot was "real." And indeed, the West Country of England is shaped by Arthurian associations. At Tintagel, where Arthur supposedly was conceived, a ruined castle still clings to the dark, sea-beaten cliffs guarding the Cornish coast. A few miles inland, on the willow-fringed banks of the unprepossessing river Camel, is Slaughter Bridge, a village so nondescript that I drove right through it before realizing it is supposed to be the site of the Battle of Camlann, where Arthur and Mordred meet in mortal combat.

From here, so the story goes, the grievously wounded king was carried inland by faithful Sir Bedivere to the heart of brooding Bodmin Moor. One evening I walked the moor toward a pond called Dozmary Pool, near whose waters Arthur's wounded body was laid and into which he thrice commanded the reluctant Bedivere to hurl his sword, Excalibur. Reflecting an evening of vivid sunset, the pool's shallow waters turned blood red. Perhaps it was after seeing such an apocalyptic sight that Tennyson described an astonishing arm: "Clothed in white samite, mystic, wonderful," rising from the water to catch, to thrice brandish and finally sink forever beneath its surface with the world's most famous sword.

Arthur, an old soldier after all, never really dies but fades away...

A hundred miles or so west from Dozmary Pool in the town of Amesbury, I visited a pretty cruciform[2] church where the repentant Guinevere is said to have retreated to the spacious grounds of an early abbey, now a ruin. A pub and some shops have claimed a good deal of the old abbey land, but behind the church is a gently flowing river where a black swan stretched its neck among a crowd of ducks.

---

2. **cruciform** (kro͞o′sə fôrm′) *adj.* cross-shaped; here, with its ground plan in the shape of a cross.

Arthur, an old soldier after all, never really dies but fades away—to the enchanted Isle of Avalon, which, since the late 12th century, has been associated with Glastonbury. The extraordinary hill, known as Glastonbury Tor, that juts abruptly from the plain just outside the modern town was formerly surrounded by marsh and may once have had the appearance of a misty, enchanted island. In 1191, the grave of Arthur and his queen was "discovered" in Glastonbury Abbey—a find that launched a **lucrative** pilgrimage industry and enabled the canny monks to rebuild their abbey, which had burned to the ground in 1184.

◀ **lucrative**
(lo͞o′ krə tiv) *adj.* producing wealth; profitable

In each of these places I caught a glimpse of the kind of romantic "truth" I was seeking. Amesbury was the most evocative, perhaps because it was so easy to imagine the grieving queen pacing the riverbank on a winter's morning, or perhaps because for me the end of Camelot, especially in *Idylls of the King*, has always been most irrevocably signaled by the final parting between Arthur and Guinevere. In the end, however, all these towns and castles failed me. In part this was due to modern realities, such as the King Arthur tourist shops dominating Tintagel, that kept crowding my vision. In larger part, though, it was because I knew before I arrived that the few historical facts known about Arthur cannot be squared with any of these places.

ABOUT THE AUTHOR

Caroline Alexander (b. 1956)

Caroline Alexander was born in Florida in 1956, the daughter of a professor of art history. As a journalist, Alexander has written for *Smithsonian*, *The New Yorker, National Geographic,* and other magazines. In her books, Alexander has often combined literary detective work with travel writing. In *The Way to Xanadu* (1994), for example, Alexander describes her journeys to spots around the globe in search of the actual places that may have inspired the exotic imagery of Samuel Taylor Coleridge's famous poem "Kubla Khan." She is also drawn to the examination and reinterpretation of heroic legend, as in her recent book *The War That Killed Achilles: The True Story of Homer's Iliad* (2009). About her own career as a writer, Alexander has said, "I believe in the classical ideal of a combination of the active and contemplative life; hence the union in my own life of travel writing and classical scholarship."

Close Reading Activities

READ

Comprehension

Reread all or part of the text to help you answer the following questions.

1. What place does the author visit on Christmas Eve?
2. Name two other sites the author visits.
3. Why does she make this pilgrimage?
4. What versions of the Arthur tales does the author mention?

Research: Clarify Details This article may include references that are unfamiliar to you. Choose at least one unfamiliar detail and briefly research it. Then, explain how the information you learned from research sheds light on an aspect of the article.

Summarize Write an objective summary of the article, one that is free from opinion and evaluation.

Language Study

Selection Vocabulary The phrases at right appear in the article. Define each boldfaced word. Then, use each word in a sentence of your own.

- other faithful (or **gullible**) pilgrims
- overwhelming sense of loss—a **nostalgic** yearning
- a find that launched a **lucrative** pilgrimage industry

Literary Analysis

Reread the identified passage. Then, respond to the questions that follow.

Focus Passage *(p. 940)*
Like many pilgrims ... most famous sword.

Key Ideas and Details

1. **Analyze:** Why do you think the author encloses the word *real* in quotation marks? Explain.

Craft and Structure

2. **(a) Distinguish:** What phrase does the author use to describe the image of the sunset over Dozmary Pool? **(b) Interpret:** Why might such an image be "apocalyptic"? **(c) Analyze:** What is the author suggesting about the power of the Arthurian story through these images and word choices? Explain.

Integration of Knowledge and Ideas

3. **Synthesize:** In what ways does the author's description of Slaughter Bridge **highlight** the differences between her imagination, the drama of the legends, and reality? Explain.

Tone

Tone is the writer's attitude toward his or her subject and can often be described by a single adjective, such as formal, serious, playful, gentle, or bitter. Reread the selection, and take notes on the author's tone.

1. What tone does Alexander create by referring to herself as a pilgrim on a pilgrimage? Explain.
2. **(a)** What does the parenthetical phrase "or gullible" in the third paragraph suggest about the author's attitude? **(b)** Does she **maintain** a similar tone throughout the work? Support your answer with textual details.

DISCUSS • RESEARCH • WRITE

From Text to Topic **Partner Discussion**

Discuss the following passage with a classmate. Listen closely and build on one another's ideas, supporting them with examples from the text.

> Arthur's loss of his Round Table … is a replay of mankind's fall from grace in the Garden of Eden.… It has become part of the geography of our collective imagination. Today, that "fleeting wisp of glory called Camelot" stirs an overwhelming sense of loss—a nostalgic yearning for a better-ordered and more-spiritual age that we long to believe once existed.

QUESTIONS FOR DISCUSSION

1. How is Arthur's fall like "mankind's fall from grace"?
2. What might cause the "sense of loss" **associated** with Camelot?

Research **Investigate the Topic**

Visiting "Camelot" Caroline Alexander relates her experiences visiting the present-day site of what may have been Camelot, King Arthur's legendary castle.

Assignment

Conduct research about tourism at settings associated with the Arthurian legend (such as Glastonbury). Take clear notes and carefully identify your sources so that you can easily access the information later. Share your findings in a **travel article or blog post.**

PREPARATION FOR ESSAY

You may use the results of this research in an essay you will write at the end of this section.

Writing to Sources **Narrative**

In this article, Caroline Alexander describes how she was inspired by the tales of King Arthur as she grew up. That inspiration grew even deeper as Alexander became an adult and gained greater insights into the tales and their meanings.

Assignment

Write a **reflective essay** in which you describe how a text—whether a story, a film, a TV show, a graphic novel, or a comic book—inspired you as a child and still inspires you today. Consider how maturity has given you greater insight into the text and its meaning to you.

- Introduce the text and describe why you loved it as a child and why you still find it powerful today.
- Use details and sensory language to paint a vivid word picture of your experiences.
- Consider how your experiences are similar to or different from Caroline Alexander's, citing details from her article to support your comparisons.

ACADEMIC VOCABULARY

Academic terms appear in blue on these pages. Consult a dictionary to find their definitions. Then, use them as you speak and write about the text.

Common Core State Standards

RI.9-10.1, RI.9-10.2, RI.9-10.3, RI.9-10.4, RI.9-10.5; W.9-10.3, W.9-10.3.d, W.9-10.4, W.9-10.7, W.9-10.9; SL.9-10.1; L.9-10.4, L.9-10.5, L.9-10.6

[For full standards wording, see the chart in the front of this book.]

Cartoon from *The New Yorker*

Despite some initial reservations, the knights were often grateful for Guinevere's presence at the Round Table.

Close Reading Activities 

READ • DISCUSS • WRITE

Comprehension

Look at the cartoon again and reread the caption and speech bubble to help you answer the following questions.

1. Who are the people gathered around the table and what are they doing?

2. How does the text in the caption relate to the text in the speech bubble?

Critical Analysis

Key Ideas and Details

1. (a) Infer: Why are all the men at the table covering their ears?
(b) Analyze: Why does the caption say that the knights are grateful for Guinevere's presence?

2. Distinguish: How does Guinevere's remark to Arthur **signal** the **privileged** relationship she has with the king? Explain.

Craft and Structure

3. (a) Analyze: Which details indicate that the scene is happening in the Medieval period? **(b) Compare and Contrast:** How do the medieval details of the cartoon contrast with the characters' actions?

4. (a) What is taking place in the background of the cartoon?
(b) Analyze: How does this detail add humor?

Integration of Knowledge and Ideas

5. Synthesize: Even though this cartoon is funny, it also conveys a serious message about power and authority. What is that message? Explain.

Speaking and Listening

Discuss the cartoon and its message with classmates. You may want to use the following discussion questions to focus your conversation.

1. In what ways does this cartoon make King Arthur and his Round Table more **relatable** for a modern audience?

2. Would the cartoon still be funny to someone who has no knowledge of King Arthur's legend?

Writing to Sources **Narrative**

Write a **short story** in which you describe what occurs at this meeting after King Arthur takes Guinevere's suggestion. Combine details from the cartoon with your understanding of Arthurian characters to write believable dialogue.

Common Core State Standards

RL.9-10.7, RI.9-10.7; W.9-10.3; SL.9-10.1

[For full standards wording, see the chart in the front of this book.]

ACADEMIC VOCABULARY

Academic terms appear in blue on these pages. If these words are not familiar to you, use a dictionary to find their definitions. Then, use them as you speak and write about the text.

Assessment: Synthesis

Speaking and Listening: Group Discussion

The Arthurian Legend The texts in this section vary in genre, length, style, and perspective. All of them, however, comment in some way on the heroic values and ideals of the Arthurian legends. These values and ideals are related to the Big Question addressed in this unit: **Can anyone be a hero?**

▲ Refer to the selections you read in Part 3 as you complete the activities on this assessment.

Assignment

Conduct discussions. With a small group of classmates, conduct a discussion about the tales of King Arthur and the image of heroism they convey. Refer to the texts in this section, other texts you have read, and your personal experience and knowledge to support your ideas. Begin your discussion by addressing the following questions:

- How do the legends of King Arthur embody the ideals and values of knighthood?
- Is the image of the knight portrayed in the tales of King Arthur idealized, realistic, or both?
- What makes King Arthur a hero?
- Does the code of chivalry also function as a set of rules for any hero?

Summarize and present your ideas. After you have fully explored the topic, summarize your discussion and present your findings to the class as a whole.

Criteria for Success

✓ **Organizes the group effectively**
Appoint a group leader and a timekeeper. The group leader should present the discussion questions. The timekeeper should make sure the discussion takes no longer than 20 minutes.

✓ **Maintains focus of discussion**
As a group, stay on topic and avoid straying into other subject areas.

✓ **Involves all participants equally and fully**
No one person should monopolize the conversation. Rather, everyone should take turns speaking and contributing ideas.

✓ **Follows the rules for collegial discussion**
As each group member speaks, others should listen carefully. Build on one another's ideas and support viewpoints and opinions with sound reasoning and evidence. Express disagreement respectfully.

USE NEW VOCABULARY
As you speak and share ideas, work to use the vocabulary words you have learned in this unit. The more you use new words, the more you will "own" them.

Writing: Narrative

The Arthurian Legend The background of the Arthurian legends is rich and complex. It combines the history of Rome and Britain, the medieval ideals of chivalry, and the values of later writers, such as Tennyson, who reinterpreted the earlier tradition.

Common Core State Standards

W.9-10.3a–e, W.9-10.4, W.9-10.9; SL.9-10.1.a–d, SL.9–10.3, SL.9-10.4, SL.9–10.6

[For full standards wording, see the chart in the front of this book.]

Assignment

Write a **fictional narrative** about a hero in King Arthur's court. You might choose King Arthur, Sir Bedivere, or another legendary figure to feature in your story. Alternatively, you might create your own fictional hero to place in Arthur's time period and locale. Be sure to base your story on the reading and research you have completed in this section. Focus your plot line on a specific conflict that confronts and then motivates your hero.

WRITE TO EXPLORE

As you write your story, you may generate new ideas about the characters, settings, or events. Allow for this and use your discoveries to help form your narrative.

Criteria for Success

Purpose/Focus

✓ **Connects specific incidents with larger ideas**

Incorporate knowledge you have gained from the texts in this section and your research to establish the setting, develop the conflict and the characters, and express themes about heroism.

✓ **Clearly conveys the significance of the story**

Provide a resolution to the story in which you reflect on what characters learned or how they changed over the course of the story.

Organization

✓ **Sequences events effectively**

Structure your story so that the conflict leads to a climax and is then resolved. Make sure events build logically toward that moment of greatest tension.

Development of Ideas/Elaboration

✓ **Supports insights**

Weave in details suggested by the texts you have read in this section to add realism to your narrative.

✓ **Uses narrative techniques effectively**

Use narrative techniques, such as dialogue, description, and multiple plot lines to develop events and characters.

Language

✓ **Uses description effectively**

Use descriptive details to paint word pictures that help readers visualize settings and characters.

Conventions

✓ **Does not have errors**

Check your narrative to eliminate errors in grammar, spelling, and punctuation.

Writing to Sources: **Informative Text**

The Arthurian Legend The related readings in this section focus on the heroes of Arthurian legend. They raise questions, such as the following:

- What ideals and values are expressed in the Arthurian legends?
- How have scholars, poets, and fiction writers of later centuries modified the Arthurian legends? What do those changes reveal about differences in attitudes between later writers and those who first told the Arthur stories?
- What relevance do the values and ideals of the Arthurian legends have today?
- Why are the Arthurian legends still so captivating for so many people?

Focus on the question that intrigues you the most, and then complete the following assignment.

Assignment

Write an **essay** in which you analyze the portrayal of heroism in Arthurian legends and consider why the stories have had such enduring power. Make important connections and distinctions using at least two of the texts you have read in this section. Clearly present, develop, and support your ideas with examples and details from the texts.

INCORPORATE RESEARCH

Strengthen your analysis by drawing on facts, quotations, and data you gathered while conducting research related to the readings in this section. Make sure to cite your sources correctly.

Prewriting and Planning

Choose texts. Review the texts in the section to determine which ones you will cite in your essay. Select at least two that will provide strong material to support your analysis.

Gather details and develop your central idea. Use a chart like the one shown to gather and interpret details from the texts. Though you may refine or change your ideas as you write, the working version will establish a clear direction.

Focus Question: What relevance do the values and ideals of the Arthurian legends have today?

Text	Passage	Notes
"Morte d'Arthur"	Not like that Arthur who, with lance in rest, / From spur to plume a star of tournament, / Shot through the lists at Camelot.... (lines 273–275)	Physical strength and skills were medieval values that Arthur embodied.
from *The Birth of Britain*	Let us then declare that King Arthur and his noble knights ... set decent folk an example for all time.	Arthur and his knights provide a heroic ideal for people today.
Example Central Idea: The Arthurian legends embody ideals of nobility and honor and provide a model of heroism that still matters.		

Drafting

Sequence your ideas and evidence. Present your ideas in a logical sequence. Lead your readers through your thought process by using accurate transitional words and expressions that convey precise relationships among ideas.

Develop your topic. Include well-chosen, relevant, and sufficient facts, concrete details, quotations, or other information and examples to develop your topic. Be sure to use textual support and include applicable information from the research you conducted throughout this part.

Frame and connect ideas. Write an introduction that will grab the reader's attention. Consider beginning with a compelling quotation or a detail. State a clear thesis or central idea and develop it with related or subordinate ideas in your body paragraphs. Then, write a strong conclusion that restates your central idea. Throughout your essay, make sure to define or explain any terms or concepts that may be unfamiliar to your readers.

Revising and Editing

Review content. Make sure that your central and related ideas are clearly stated and that you have supported them with clear evidence from the texts. Underline main ideas in your paper and check that each one is supported with strong and sufficient evidence. Add more proof as needed.

Review style. Check that you have found the clearest, simplest way to communicate your ideas. Omit unnecessary words.

W.9-10.2.a–f, W.9-10.4, W.9-10.5, W.9-10.9.a; L.9-10.3.a

[For full standards wording, see the chart in the front of this book.]

WORKS CITED

Follow accepted conventions to cite all sources you use in your essay. See the Citing Sources pages in the Introductory Unit of this textbook for additional guidance.

Self-Evaluation Rubric

Use the following criteria to evaluate the effectiveness of your essay.

Criteria	Rating Scale			
	not very	....		*very*
PURPOSE/FOCUS Introduces a specific topic; provides a concluding section that follows from and supports the information or explanation presented.	1	2	3	4
ORGANIZATION Organizes complex ideas, concepts, and information to make important connections and distinctions; uses appropriate and varied transitions to link the major sections, create cohesion, and clarify relationships among ideas	1	2	3	4
DEVELOPMENT OF IDEAS/ELABORATION Develops the topic with well-chosen, relevant and sufficient facts, extended definitions, concrete details, quotations, or other information and examples appropriate to the audience's knowledge of the topic	1	2	3	4
LANGUAGE Uses precise language and domain-specific vocabulary to manage the complexity of the topic; establishes and maintains a formal style and objective tone	1	2	3	4
CONVENTIONS Attends to the norms and conventions of the discipline	1	2	3	4

Independent Reading

Titles for Extended Reading

In this unit, you have read texts in a variety of genres. Continue to explore thematic connections in literature. Select works that you enjoy, but challenge yourself to explore new writers and works of increasing depth and complexity. The titles suggested below will help you get started.

INFORMATIONAL TEXT

Early Irish Myths and Sagas
Translated by Jeffrey Gantz

Capturing a mystical world of battle and beauty, these ancient **myths** and **sagas** provide a glimpse into the mind and soul of Celtic culture. First written down around the eighth century, these tales are far older, having been transmitted orally from generation to generation centuries before that time.

Son of the Morning Star: Custer and the Little Bighorn
by Evan S. Connell
EXEMPLAR TEXT

This **nonfiction** book gives a compelling and comprehensive history of the Battle of the Little Bighorn, focusing on Custer, who was a commander of the U.S. 7th Cavalry Regiment, and Crazy Horse and others, who led the combined forces of the Lakota Sioux and Northern Cheyenne nations.

A Sacred Union of Citizens: George Washington's Farewell Address and the American Character
by Matthew Spalding and Patrick J. Garrity
Rowman and Littlefield, 1998
EXEMPLAR TEXT

This **nonfiction** book, part biography and part history, tells the story of Washington's life and his efforts to establish the new republic. It includes the full text of his farewell speech, still quoted today by historians and politicians to warn against entangling America's foreign policy goals with the ambitions of other nations.

Bury My Heart at Wounded Knee
by Dee Brown
EXEMPLAR TEXT

In this work of **historical nonfiction**, Dee Brown explores the conflicts between nineteenth-century American settlers and native peoples. The author includes firsthand accounts by Native Americans, who reveal the hardships they faced in trying to maintain their culture and way of life.

LITERATURE

Candide
by Voltaire
EXEMPLAR TEXT

In this **novel** and political satire, the agreeable Candide is expelled from his home after kissing the baron's daughter and spends his life trying to reunite with her. Along the way, Voltaire pokes fun at nearly every important figure and institution of his era. While the novel was initially banned due to its sharp religious and political satire, Voltaire arranged for it to be published secretly. It quickly became an underground hit that was read eagerly throughout Europe.

The Once and Future King
by T. H. White
Ace, 1987

Escape into the legendary world of Camelot, where chivalry defines the age. This **novel** describes in vivid detail the rise of King Arthur, the valiant knights of his Round Table, his idealistic kingdom, and its eventual collapse.

The Metamorphosis
by Franz Kafka
EXEMPLAR TEXT

As this **novella** begins, Gregor Samsa wakes up to discover that he has been transformed into a giant insect. Gregor has to work through feelings of fear and alienation, as well as more practical matters—such as how to turn over—in this darkly comic story.

ONLINE TEXT SET

EXPOSITORY NONFICTION
Making History With Vitamin C
Penny Le Couteur; Jay Burreson

SHORT STORY
The Masque of the Red Death
Edgar Allan Poe

SCIENCE JOURNALISM
Black Water Turns the Tide on Florida Coral NASA News

Preparing to Read Complex Texts

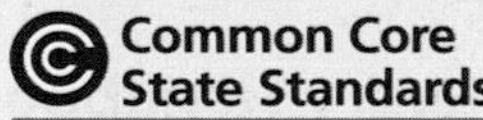

Reading Literature/ Informational Text
10. By the end of Grade 10, read and comprehend literature, including stories, dramas, poems, and literary nonfiction at the high end of the grades 9–10 text complexity band independently and proficiently.

Attentive Reading As you read literature on your own, bring your imagination and questions to the text. The questions shown below and others that you ask as you read will help you learn and enjoy literature even more.

When reading world literature, ask yourself...

Comprehension: **Key Ideas and Details**

- Who are the main characters in this text, and what conflicts or struggles do they face?
- From what culture does this text come? What elements of the culture do I see in the text? For example, do I notice beliefs, foods, traditions, or settings that have particular meaning for the people of this culture?
- Do any aspects of this text seem familiar to me? For example, do any characters, settings, or events in the plot remind me of those in other stories I have read?

Text Analysis: **Craft and Structure**

- What type of text is this? For example, is it an epic, a myth, a tale, or a legend? How does the genre affect my expectations of the text?
- Is this text a retelling by a modern author? If so, does the author change the text for modern readers?
- What do I notice about the language, including descriptions and dialogue? Does the language reflect values or customs related to the cultural or historical context of the text?
- Does the text include symbols? If so, do they have special meanings in the original culture of the text? Do they also have universal meanings?
- Does the text include patterns of events or repetitions of statements or images? If so, which ones? What is the effect?

Connections: **Integration of Ideas**

- How does this text round out the picture of the culture I might get from a nonfiction source, such as an encyclopedia entry?
- Does this text express universal ideas or values—those that are common to people in many different cultures and time periods?
- If I were researching this culture for a report, would I include passages from this text? If so, what would those passages show?

Resources

Literary Terms

ACT See ***Drama.***

ALLEGORY An ***allegory*** is a story or tale with two or more levels of meaning—a literal level and one or more symbolic levels. The events, setting, and characters in an allegory are symbols for ideas and qualities.

ALLITERATION ***Alliteration*** is the repetition of initial consonant sounds. Writers use alliteration to give emphasis to words, to imitate sounds, and to create musical effects. In the following line from Theodore Roethke's "The Waking", there is alliteration of the *f* sound:

> I *f*eel my *f*ate in what I cannot *f*ear.

ALLUSION An ***allusion*** is a reference to a well-known person, place, event, literary work, or work of art. The title of the story "By the Waters of Babylon" (p. 456) is an allusion to the Bible's Psalm 137, in which the Hebrew people lament their exile in Babylon. It begins, "By the rivers of Babylon, there we sat down, yea, we wept. . . ."

ANALOGY An ***analogy*** makes a comparison between two or more things that are similar in some ways but otherwise unalike.

ANECDOTE An anecdote is a brief story told to entertain or to make a point. In the excerpt from "The Way to Rainy Mountain" (p. 480), N. Scott Momaday tells anecdotes about his grandmother to reveal her character and provide a glimpse into a vanishing way of life.

See also ***Narrative.***

ANTAGONIST An ***antagonist*** is a character or force in conflict with a main character, or protagonist.

ANTICLIMAX Some stories end in an ***anticlimax.*** Like a climax, an *anticlimax* is the turning point in a story. However, an anticlimax is always a letdown. It is the point at which you learn that the story will not turn out in a way that truly resolves the problem or satisfies the reader.

ARCHETYPE An ***archetype*** is a type of character, detail, image, or situation that appears in literature throughout history. Some critics believe that archetypes reveal deep truths about human experience.

ARGUMENT See ***Persuasion.***

ASIDE An ***aside*** is a short speech delivered by a character in a play in order to express his or her thoughts and feelings. Traditionally, the aside is directed to the audience and is presumed not to be heard by the other characters.

ASSONANCE ***Assonance*** is the repetition of vowel sounds followed by different consonants in two or more stressed syllables. Assonance is found in this phrase from Elizabeth Bishop's "The Fish" (p. 364): "frayed and wavering."

ATMOSPHERE See ***Mood.***

AUTOBIOGRAPHICAL ESSAY See ***Essay.***

AUTOBIOGRAPHY An ***autobiography*** is a form of nonfiction in which a writer tells his or her own life story. An autobiography may tell about the person's whole life or only a part of it. An example of an autobiography is Erik Weihenmayer's *Touch the Top of the World* (p. 192).

See also ***Biography*** and ***Nonfiction.***

BALLAD A ***ballad*** is a songlike poem that tells a story, often one dealing with adventure and romance. Most ballads are written in four- to six-line stanzas and have regular rhythms and rhyme schemes. A ballad often features a *refrain*—a regularly repeated line or group of lines.

See also ***Oral Tradition.***

BIOGRAPHY A ***biography*** is a form of nonfiction in which a writer tells the life story of another person. Biographies have been written about many famous people, historical and contemporary, but they can also be written about "ordinary" people.

See also ***Autobiography*** and ***Nonfiction.***

BLANK VERSE ***Blank verse*** is poetry written in unrhymed iambic pentameter lines. This verse form was widely used by William Shakespeare.

CHARACTER A ***character*** is a person or an animal who takes part in the action of a literary work. The main character, or protagonist, is the most important character in a story. In Chinua Achebe's story "Civil Peace" (p. 54), Jonathan Iwegbu is the protagonist. This character often changes in some important way as a result of the story's events.

Characters are sometimes classified as round or flat, dynamic or static. A ***round character*** shows many different traits—faults as well as virtues. A *flat character* shows only one trait. A *dynamic character* develops and grows during the course of the story; a ***static character*** does not change.

See also ***Characterization*** and ***Motivation.***

CHARACTERIZATION ***Characterization*** is the act of creating and developing a character. In direct characterization, the author directly states a character's traits. For example, in "The Masque of the Red Death", Poe directly characterizes Prince Prospero: "But the Prince Prospero was happy and dauntless and sagacious."

In indirect characterization, an author gives clues about a character by describing what a character looks like, does, and says, as well as how other characters react to him or her. It is up to the reader to draw conclusions about the character based on this indirect information.

The most effective indirect characterizations usually result from showing characters acting or speaking.

See also ***Character.***

CLIMAX The ***climax*** of a story, novel, or play is the high point of interest or suspense. The events that make up the rising action lead up to the climax. The events that make up the falling action follow the climax.

See also ***Conflict, Plot,*** and ***Anticlimax.***

COMEDY A ***comedy*** is a literary work, especially a play, that has a happy ending. Comedies often show ordinary characters in conflict with society. These conflicts are introduced through misunderstandings, deceptions, and concealed identities. When the conflict is resolved, the result is the correction of moral faults or social wrongs. Types of comedy include *romantic comedy,* which involves problems among lovers, and the *comedy of manners,* which satirically challenges the social customs of a sophisticated society. Comedy is often contrasted with tragedy, in which the protagonist meets an unfortunate end.

COMIC RELIEF ***Comic relief*** is a technique that is used to interrupt a serious part of a literary work by introducing a humorous character or situation.

CONFLICT A ***conflict*** is a struggle between opposing forces. Characters in conflict form the basis of stories, novels, and plays.

There are two kinds of conflict: external and internal. In an *external conflict,* the main character struggles against an outside force. This force may be another character, as in "Civil Peace" (p. 54), in which Jonathan Iwegbu struggles with the leader of the thieves. The outside force could also be the standards or expectations of a group, such as the oppression and censorship that Juan struggles against in "The Censors" (p. 740). The outside force may be nature itself, as when Erik Weihenmayer struggles to climb Mt. Everest in *Touch the Top of the World* (p. 192).

An *internal conflict* involves a character in conflict with himself or herself. In *Julius Caesar* (p. 546), Brutus experiences an internal conflict when trying to decide whether to assassinate Caesar.

See also ***Plot.***

CONNOTATION The ***connotation*** of a word is the set of ideas associated with it in addition to its explicit meaning.

See also ***Denotation.***

CONSONANCE ***Consonance*** is the repetition of final consonant sounds in stressed syllables with different vowel sounds, as in *hat* and *sit*.

CONTEMPORARY INTERPRETATION A ***contemporary interpretation*** is a literary work of today that responds to and sheds new light on a well-known, earlier work of literature. Such an interpretation may refer to any aspect of the older work, including plot, characters, settings, imagery, language, and theme. T. H. White's *The Once and Future King* (p. 880) provides a modern version of the legend of King Arthur.

COUPLET A ***couplet*** is a pair of rhyming lines, usually of the same length and meter. In the following couplet from Sonnet 29 by William Shakespeare, the speaker comforts himself with the thought of his love:

> For thy sweet love remember'd such wealth brings
> That then I scorn to change my state with kings.

See also ***Stanza.***

DENOTATION The ***denotation*** of a word is its dictionary meaning, independent of other associations that the word may have. The denotation of the word *lake*, for example, is "an inland body of water." "Vacation spot" and "place where the fishing is good" are connotations of the word *lake*.

See also ***Connotation.***

DESCRIPTION A ***description*** is a portrait in words of a person, place, or object. Descriptive writing uses sensory details, those that appeal to the senses: sight, hearing, taste, smell, and touch. Description can be found in all types of writing. Anita Desai's "Games at Twilight" (p. 778) has vivid descriptive passages.

DESCRIPTIVE ESSAY See ***Essay.***

DIALECT ***Dialect*** is a special form of a language, spoken by people in a particular region or group. It may involve changes to the pronunciation, vocabulary, and sentence structure of the standard form of the language. Rudyard Kipling's "Danny Deever" is a poem written in the Cockney dialect of English, used by working-class Londoners.

DIALOGUE A ***dialogue*** is a conversation between characters that may reveal their traits and advance the action of a narrative. In fiction or nonfiction, quotation marks indicate a speaker's exact words, and a new paragraph usually indicates a change of speaker. Following is an exchange between two characters in "The Monkey's Paw" (p. 24):

> "*What's that?*" cried the old woman, starting up.
> "A rat," said the old man in shaking tones—"a rat. It passed me on the stairs."

Quotation marks are not used in *script,* the printed copy of a play. Instead, the dialogue follows the name of the speaker, as in this example from *Julius Caesar* (p. 546):

> **PORTIA.** Is Caesar yet gone to the Capitol?

DICTION ***Diction*** refers to an author's choice of words, especially with regard to range of vocabulary, use of slang and colloquial language, and level of formality. This sentence from "The Masque of the Red Death" is an example of formal diction containing many words derived from Latin: "This was an extensive and magnificent structure, the creation of the prince's own eccentric yet august taste."

See also ***Connotation*** and ***Denotation.***

DIRECT CHARACTERIZATION
See ***Characterization.***

DRAMA A ***drama*** is a story written to be performed by actors. The script of a drama is made up of ***dialogue***—the words the actors say—and ***stage directions,*** which are descriptions of how and where action happens.

The drama's ***setting*** is the time and place in which the action occurs. It is indicated by one or more sets, including furniture and backdrops, that suggest interior or exterior scenes. *Props* are objects, such as a sword or a cup of tea, that are used onstage.

At the beginning of most plays, a brief ***exposition*** gives the audience some background information about the characters and the situation. Just as in a story or novel, the plot of a drama is built around characters in conflict.

Dramas are divided into large units called *acts,* which are divided into smaller units called *scenes.* A long play may include many sets that change with the scenes, or it may indicate a change of scene with lighting. *Julius Caesar* (p. 546) is a play in five acts.

See also ***Dialogue, Genre, Stage Directions,*** and ***Tragedy.***

DRAMATIC IRONY See ***Irony.***

DRAMATIC MONOLOGUE A ***dramatic monologue*** is a poem in which a character reveals himself or herself by speaking to a silent listener or thinking aloud.

DRAMATIC POETRY ***Dramatic poetry*** is poetry that utilizes the techniques of drama. The dialogue between the bride and the bridegroom at the end of "The Bridegroom" (p. 368) is an example.

END RHYME See ***Rhyme.***

EPIC An ***epic*** is a long narrative poem about the deeds of gods or heroes. *Sundiata: An Epic of Old Mali* (p. 806) and the *Ramayana* are examples of the genre.

An epic is elevated in style and usually follows certain patterns. In Greek epics and in the epics modeled after them, the poet begins by announcing the subject and asking a Muse—one of the nine goddesses of the arts, literature, and sciences—to help.

An *epic hero* is the larger-than-life central character in an epic. Through behavior and deeds, the epic hero displays qualities that are valued by the society in which the epic originated.

See also ***Epic Simile*** and ***Narrative Poem.***

EPIC SIMILE An ***epic simile,*** also called ***Homeric simile,*** is an elaborate comparison of unlike subjects. In this example from the *Odyssey,* Homer compares the bodies of men killed by Odysseus to a fisherman's catch heaped up on the shore:

> Think of a catch that fishermen haul in to a
> half-moon bay
> in a fine-meshed net from the whitecaps of the sea:
> how all are poured out on the sand, in throes
> for the salt sea,
> twitching their cold lives away in Helios' fiery air:
> so lay the suitors heaped on one another.

See also ***Figurative Language*** and ***Simile.***

EPIPHANY An ***epiphany*** is a character's sudden flash of insight into a conflict or situation. At the end of the poem "The Fish" (p. 364), the speaker has an epiphany that causes her to release the fish.

ESSAY An ***essay*** is a short nonfiction work about a particular subject. While classification is difficult, five types of essays are sometimes identified.

A *descriptive essay* seeks to convey an impression about a person, place, or object.

An *expository essay* gives information, discusses ideas, or explains a process. In "The Spider and the Wasp", Alexander Petrunkevitch compares and contrasts the two creatures mentioned in the title.

A *narrative essay* tells a true story. In "The Dog That Bit People" (p. 257), James Thurber tells the story of a troublesome pet. An *autobiographical essay* is a narrative essay in which the writer tells a story from his or her own life.

A *persuasive essay* tries to convince readers to do something or to accept the writer's point of view. In "Keep Memory Alive" (p. 234), Elie Wiesel argues the importance of speaking out against evil.

See also ***Description, Exposition, Genre, Narration, Nonfiction,*** and ***Persuasion.***

EXPOSITION ***Exposition*** is writing or speech that explains a process or presents information. In the plot of a story or drama, the exposition is the part of the work that introduces the characters, the setting, and the basic situation.

See also ***Plot.***

EXPOSITORY ESSAY See ***Essay.***

EXTENDED METAPHOR In an ***extended metaphor,*** as in regular metaphor, a writer speaks or writes of a subject as though it were something else. An extended metaphor sustains the comparison for several lines or for an entire poem. In *Julius Caesar* (p. 546), Brutus uses an extended metaphor in Act II, Scene i, lines 21–27, when he speaks of "ambition's ladder."

See also ***Figurative Language*** and ***Metaphor.***

FALLING ACTION See ***Plot.***

FANTASY A ***fantasy*** is a work of highly imaginative writing that contains elements not found in real life. Examples of fantasy include stories that involve supernatural elements, such as fairy tales, and stories that deal with imaginary places and creatures.

See also ***Science Fiction.***

FICTION ***Fiction*** is prose writing that tells about imaginary characters and events. The term is usually used for novels and short stories, but it also applies to dramas and narrative poetry. Some writers rely on their imaginations alone to create their works of fiction. Others base their fiction on actual events and people, to which they add invented characters, dialogue, and plot situations.

See also ***Genre, Narrative,*** and ***Nonfiction.***

FIGURATIVE LANGUAGE ***Figurative language*** is writing or speech not meant to be interpreted literally. It is often used to create vivid impressions by setting up comparisons between dissimilar things.

Some frequently used figures of speech are ***metaphors, similes,*** and ***personifications.***

See also ***Literal Language.***

FLASHBACK A ***flashback*** is a means by which authors present material that occurred earlier than the present time of the narrative. Authors may include this material in the form of a characters' memories, dreams, or accounts of past events, or they may simply shift their narrative back to the earlier time.

FOIL A ***foil*** is a character who provides a contrast to another character. In *Julius Caesar* (p. 546), the impetuous and resentful Cassius is a foil for the cooler and more rational Brutus.

FOOT See ***Meter.***

FORESHADOWING ***Foreshadowing*** is the use in a literary work of clues that suggest events that have yet to occur. This technique helps to create suspense, keeping readers wondering about what will happen next.

FREE VERSE ***Free verse*** is poetry not written in a regular pattern of meter or rhyme. Cornelius Eady's "The Poetic Interpretation of the Twist" (p. 349) is an example.

GENRE A ***genre*** is a category or form of literature. Literature is commonly divided into three major types of writing: poetry, prose, and drama. For each type, there are several distinct genres, as follows:

1. Poetry: Lyric Poetry, Concrete Poetry, Dramatic Poetry, Narrative Poetry, and Epic Poetry
2. Prose: Fiction (Novels and Short Stories) and Nonfiction (Biography, Autobiography, Letters, Essays, and Reports)
3. Drama: Serious Drama and Tragedy, Comic Drama, Melodrama, and Farce

See also ***Drama, Poetry,*** and ***Prose.***

HAIKU The ***haiku*** is a three-line verse form. The first and third lines of a haiku each have five syllables. The second line has seven syllables. A haiku seeks to convey a single vivid emotion by means of images from nature.

HOMERIC SIMILE See ***Epic Simile.***

HYPERBOLE A ***hyperbole*** is a deliberate exaggeration or overstatement. In Mark Twain's "The Notorious Jumping Frog of Calaveras County," the claim that Jim Smiley would follow a bug as far as Mexico to win a bet is a hyperbole. As this example shows, hyperboles are often used for comic effect.

IAMB See ***Meter.***

IDIOM An ***idiom*** or ***idiomatic expression*** is an expression that is characteristic of a language, region, community or class of people. Idiomatic expressions mean something more than or different from the meaning of the words making them up. Following is an example of an idiom from T. H. White's *The Once and Future King* (p. 880): "Think what people will say about us, if we do not go and *have a shot* at that sword."

See also ***Dialect.***

IMAGE An ***image*** is a word or phrase that appeals to one or more of the five senses—sight, hearing, touch, taste, or smell. Writers use images to re-create sensory experiences in words.

See also ***Description.***

IMAGERY ***Imagery*** is the descriptive or figurative language used in literature to create word pictures for the reader. These pictures, or images, are created by details of sight, sound, taste, touch, smell, or movement.

INDIRECT CHARACTERIZATION
See ***Characterization.***

INTERNAL RHYME See ***Rhyme.***

IRONY ***Irony*** is the general term for literary techniques that portray differences between appearance and reality, or expectation and result. In *verbal irony,* words are used to suggest the opposite of what is meant. In *dramatic irony,* there is a contradiction between what a character thinks and what the reader or audience knows to be true. In *irony of situation,* an event occurs that directly contradicts the expectations of the characters, the reader, or the audience.

LITERAL LANGUAGE ***Literal language*** uses words in their ordinary senses. It is the opposite of ***figurative language.*** If you tell someone standing on a diving board to jump in, you speak literally. If you tell someone on the street to "go jump in a lake," you are speaking figuratively.

See also ***Figurative Language.***

LYRIC POEM A ***lyric poem*** is a poem written in highly musical language that expresses the thoughts, observations, and feelings of a single speaker.

MAIN CHARACTER See ***Character.***

METAPHOR A ***metaphor*** is a figure of speech in which one thing is spoken of as though it were something else. Unlike a simile, which compares two things using *like* or *as,* a metaphor implies a comparison between them. In "A Tree Telling of Orpheus" (p. 446), the speaker is a tree and describes music as if it were water: "my roots felt music moisten them."

See also ***Extended Metaphor*** and ***Figurative Language.***

METER The ***meter*** of a poem is its rhythmical pattern. This pattern is determined by the number and arrangements of stressed syllables, or beats, in each line. To describe the meter of a poem, you must scan its lines. Scanning involves marking the stressed and unstressed syllables, as shown with the following two lines from *Julius Caesar* (p. 546):

> Wĕ bóth hăve féd ăs wéll, ăñd wé căn bóth
> Eñdúre thĕ wíntĕr's cóld ăs wéll ăs hé . . .

As you can see, each stressed syllable is marked with a slanted line (´) and each unstressed syllable with a horseshoe symbol (˘). The stressed and unstressed syllables are then divided by vertical lines (|) into groups called *feet.* The following types of feet are common in English poetry:

1. *Iamb:* a foot with one unstressed syllable followed by a stressed syllable, as in the word "again"
2. *Trochee:* a foot with one stressed syllable followed by an unstressed syllable, as in the word "wonder"
3. *Anapest:* a foot with two unstressed syllables followed by one strong stress, as in the phrase "on the beach"
4. *Dactyl:* a foot with one strong stress followed by two unstressed syllables, as in the word "wonderful"
5. *Spondee:* a foot with two strong stresses, as in the word "spacewalk"

Depending on the type of foot that is most common in them, lines of poetry are described as *iambic, trochaic, anapestic,* and so forth.

Lines are also described in terms of the number of feet that occur in them, as follows:

1. *Monometer:* verse written in one-foot lines
   All things
   Must pass
   Away.
2. *Dimeter:* verse written in two-foot lines
   Thomas | Jefferson
   What do | you say
   Under the | gravestone
   Hidden | away?
   —Rosemary and Stephen Vincent Benét,
   "Thomas Jefferson, 1743–1826"
3. *Trimeter:* verse written in three-foot lines
   I know | not whom | I meet
   I know | not where | I go.
4. *Tetrameter:* verse written in four-foot lines
5. *Pentameter:* verse written in five-foot lines
6. *Hexameter:* verse written in six-foot lines
7. *Heptameter:* verse written in seven-foot lines

Blank verse, used by Shakespeare in *Julius Caesar* (p. 546), is poetry written in unrhymed iambic pentameter.

Free verse, used by Cornelius Eady in "The Poetic Interpretation of the Twist" (p. 349), is poetry that does not follow a regular pattern of meter and rhyme.

MONOLOGUE A ***monologue*** in a play is a long speech by one character that, unlike a *soliloquy,* is addressed to another character or characters. An example from Shakespeare's *Julius Caesar* (p. 546) is the famous speech by Antony to the Roman people in Act III, Scene ii. It begins, "Friends, Romans, countrymen, lend me your ears. . . ." (line 74).

See also ***Soliloquy.***

MOOD ***Mood,*** or ***atmosphere,*** is the feeling created in the reader by a literary work or passage. The mood is often suggested by descriptive details. Often the mood can be described in a single word, such as lighthearted, frightening, or despairing. Notice how this passage from Edgar Allan Poe's "The Masque of the Red Death" contributes to an eerie, fearful mood:

> And now was acknowledged the presence of the Red Death. He had come like a thief in the night. And one by one dropped the revelers in the blood-bedewed halls of their revel, and died each in the despairing posture of his fall.

See also ***Tone.***

MORAL A ***moral*** is a lesson taught by a literary work, especially a fable—many fables, for example, have a stated moral at the end. It is customary, however, to discuss contemporary works in terms of the themes they explore, rather than a moral that they teach.

MOTIVATION ***Motivation*** is a reason that explains or partially explains why a character thinks, feels, acts, or behaves in a certain way. Motivation results from a combination of the character's personality and the situation he or she must deal with. In *Antigone* (p. 686), the protagonist is motivated by loyalty to her dead brother and reverence for the laws of the gods.

See also ***Character*** and ***Characterization.***

MYTH A ***myth*** is a *fictional* tale that describes the actions of gods and heroes or explains the causes of natural phenomena. Unlike legends, myths emphasize supernatural rather than historical elements. Many cultures have collections of myths, and the most familiar in the Western world are those of the ancient Greeks and Romans. "Prometheus and the First People"(p. 794) is a retelling of a famous ancient Greek myth.

See also ***Oral Tradition.***

NARRATION ***Narration*** is writing that tells a story. The act of telling a story in speech is also called narration. Novels and short stories are fictional narratives. Nonfiction works—such as news stories, biographies, and autobiographies—are also narratives. A narrative poem tells a story in verse.

See also ***Anecdote, Essay, Narrative Poem, Nonfiction, Novel,*** and ***Short Story.***

NARRATIVE A ***narrative*** is a story told in fiction, nonfiction, poetry, or drama.

See also ***Narration.***

NARRATIVE ESSAY See ***Essay.***

NARRATIVE POEM A ***narrative poem*** is one that tells a story. Alexander Pushkin's "The Bridegroom" (p. 368) is a narrative poem that tells how Natasha, a merchant's daughter, outwits a thief and murderer.

See also ***Dramatic Poetry, Epic,*** and ***Narration.***

NARRATOR A ***narrator*** is a speaker or character who tells a story. The writer's choice of narrator determines the story's *point of view,* or the perspective from which the story is told. By using a consistent point of view, a writer controls the amount and type of information revealed to the reader.

When a character in the story tells the story, that character is a *first-person narrator.* This narrator may be a major character, a minor character, or just a witness. Readers see only what this character sees, hear only what he or she hears, and so on. Stephen Vincent Benét's "By the Waters of Babylon" (p. 456) is told by a first-person narrator. Viewing unfolding events from this character's perspective, the reader shares in his discoveries and feels more suspense than another point of view would provide.

When a voice outside the story narrates, the story has a *third-person narrator.* An *omniscient,* or all-knowing, third-person narrator can tell readers what any character thinks and feels. For example, in "The Monkey's Paw" (p. 24), we know the thoughts of the father, the wife, and the son. A *limited third-person narrator* sees the world through one character's eyes and reveals only that character's thoughts. In Jack Finney's "Contents of the Dead Man's Pocket" (p. 110), the narrator reveals only Tom's thoughts and feelings.

See also ***Speaker.***

NONFICTION ***Nonfiction*** is prose writing that presents and explains ideas or that tells about real people, places, ideas, or events. To be classified as nonfiction, a work must be true. Dorothy West's "The Sun Parlor" (p. 222) is a true account of events related to a particular room in a house.

See also ***Autobiography, Biography,*** and ***Essay.***

NOVEL A ***novel*** is a long work of fiction. It has a plot that explores characters in conflict. A novel may also have one or more subplots, or minor stories, and several themes.

OCTAVE See ***Stanza.***

ONOMATOPOEIA ***Onomatopoeia*** is the use of words that imitate sounds. *Whirr, thud, sizzle,* and *hiss* are typical examples. Writers can deliberately choose words that contribute to a desired sound effect.

ORAL TRADITION The ***oral tradition*** is the retelling of songs, stories, and poems passed orally, or by spoken word, from generation to generation. Many folk songs, ballads, fairy tales, legends, and myths originated in the oral tradition.

See also ***Myth.***

OXYMORON An ***oxymoron*** is a combination of words that contradict each other. Examples are "deafening silence," "honest thief," "wise fool," and "bittersweet." This device is effective when the apparent contradiction reveals a deeper truth.

PARADOX A ***paradox*** is a statement that seems contradictory but that actually may express a deeper truth. Because a paradox is surprising, it catches the reader's attention.

PARALLELISM See ***Rhetorical Devices.***

PERSONIFICATION ***Personification*** is a type of figurative language in which a nonhuman subject is given human characteristics. Denise Levertov personifies a tree in her poem "A Tree Telling of Orpheus" (p. 446). In fact, the tree is the speaker in this poem: "I listened, and language came into my roots . . ."

See also ***Figurative Language.***

PERSUASION ***Persuasion*** is writing or speech that attempts to convince the reader to adopt a particular opinion or course of action.

An *argument* is a logical way of presenting a belief, conclusion, or stance. A good argument is supported with reasoning and evidence.

PERSUASIVE ESSAY See ***Essay.***

PLOT ***Plot*** is the sequence of events in a literary work. In most novels, dramas, short stories, and narrative poems, the plot involves both characters and a central conflict. The plot usually begins with an ***exposition*** that introduces the setting, the characters, and the basic situation. This is followed by the *inciting incident,* which introduces the central conflict. The conflict then increases during the *development* until it reaches a high point of interest or suspense, the ***climax.*** All the events leading up to the climax make up the *rising action.* The climax is followed by the *falling action,* which leads to the *denouement,* or *resolution,* in which the conflict is resolved and in which a general insight may be conveyed.

POETRY ***Poetry*** is one of the three major types of literature, the others being prose and drama. Most poems make use of highly concise, musical, and emotionally charged language. Many also make use of imagery, figurative language, and special devices of sound such as rhyme. Poems are often divided into lines and stanzas and often

STYLE ***Style*** refers to an author's unique way of writing. Elements determining style include diction; tone; characteristic use of figurative language, dialect, or rhythmic devices; and typical grammatical structures and patterns.

See also ***Diction*** and ***Tone.***

SURPRISE ENDING A ***surprise ending*** is a conclusion that violates the expectations of the reader but in a way that is both logical and believable.

O. Henry's "One Thousand Dollars" and Saki's "The Open Window" (p. 85) have surprise endings. Both authors were masters of this form.

SYMBOL A ***symbol*** is a character, place, thing or event that stands for something else, often an abstract idea. For example, a flag is a piece of cloth, but it also represents the idea of a country. Writers sometimes use conventional symbols like flags. Frequently, however, they create symbols of their own through emphasis or repetition. In "The Garden of Stubborn Cats", for example, the cats come to symbolize nature's stubborn resistance to human development.

THEME A ***theme*** is a central message or insight into life revealed through a literary work.

The theme of a literary work may be stated directly or implied. When the theme of a work is implied, readers think about what the work suggests about people or life.

Archetypal themes are those that occur in folklore and literature across the world and throughout history. The hero who makes civilization possible, the theme of "Prometheus and the First People" (p. 794), is an example of an archetypal theme.

TONE The ***tone*** of a literary work is the writer's attitude toward his or her audience and subject. The tone can often be described by a single adjective, such as *formal* or *informal, serious* or *playful, bitter* or *ironic*. When Valenzuela discusses the fate of Juan in "The Censors" (p. 740), she uses an ironic tone: ". . . another victim of his devotion to his work."

See also ***Mood.***

TRAGEDY A ***tragedy*** is a work of literature, especially a play, that tells of a catastrophe, a disaster or great misfortune, for the main character. In ancient Greek drama, the main character was always a significant person—a king or a hero—and the cause of the tragedy was often a tragic flaw, or weakness, in his or her character. In modern drama, the main character can be an ordinary person, and the cause of the tragedy can be some evil in society itself. Tragedy not only arouses fear and pity in the audience, but also, in some cases, conveys a sense of the grandeur and nobility of the human spirit.

Shakespeare's *Julius Caesar* (p. 546) is a tragedy. Brutus suffers from the tragic flaw of blindness to reality and people's motives. His noble-mindedness is almost a form of arrogance. This flaw ultimately leads to his death.

See also ***Drama.***

UNDERSTATEMENT An ***understatement*** is a figure of speech in which the stated meaning is purposely less than (or "under") what is really meant. It is the opposite of ***hyperbole,*** which is a deliberate exaggeration.

UNIVERSAL THEME A ***universal theme*** is a message about life that can be understood by most cultures. Many folk tales and examples of classic literature address universal themes such as the importance of courage, the effects of honesty, or the danger of greed.

VERBAL IRONY See ***Irony.***

VILLANELLE A ***villanelle*** is a nineteen-line lyric poem written in five three-line stanzas and ending in a four-line stanza. It uses two rhymes and repeats two refrain lines that appear initially in the first and third lines of the first stanza. These lines then appear alternately as the third line of subsequent three-line stanzas and, finally, as the last two lines of the poem. Theodore Roethke's "The Waking" is a villanelle.

VOICE ***Voice*** is a writer's distinctive "sound" or way of "speaking" on the page. It is related to such elements as word choice, sentence structure, and tone. It is similar to an individual's speech style and can be described in the same way—fast, slow, blunt, meandering, breathless, and so on.

Voice resembles ***style,*** an author's typical way of writing, but style usually refers to a quality that can be found throughout an author's body of work, while an author's voice may sometimes vary from work to work.

See also ***Style.***

Tips for Discussing Literature

As you read and study literature, discussion with other readers can help you understand, enjoy, and develop interpretations of what you read. Use the following tips to practice good speaking and listening skills while participating in group discussions of literature.

• Understand the purpose of your discussion

When you discuss literature, your purpose is to broaden your understanding and appreciation of a work by testing your own ideas and hearing the ideas of others. Stay focused on the literature you are discussing and keep your comments relevant to that literature. Starting with one focus question will help to keep your discussion on track.

• Communicate effectively

Effective communication requires thinking before speaking. Plan the points that you want to make and decide how you will express them. Organize these points in logical order and cite details from the work to support your ideas. Jot down informal notes to help keep your ideas focused.

Remember to speak clearly, pronouncing words slowly and carefully so that others can understand your points. Also, keep in mind that some literature touches readers deeply—be aware of the possibility of counterproductive emotional responses and work to control them. Negative emotional responses can also be conveyed through body language, so work to demonstrate respect in your demeanor as well as in your words.

• Encourage everyone to participate

While some people are comfortable participating in discussions, others are less eager to speak up in groups. However, everyone should work to contribute thoughts and ideas. To encourage the entire group's participation, try the following strategies:

- If you enjoy speaking, avoid monopolizing the conversation. After sharing your ideas, encourage others to share theirs.
- Try different roles. For example, have everyone take turns being the facilitator or host of the discussion.
- Use a prop, such as a book or gavel. Pass the prop around the group, allowing whomever is holding the prop to have the floor.

• Make relevant contributions

Especially when responding to a short story, a poem, or a novel, avoid simply summarizing the plot. Instead, consider *what* you think might happen next, *why* events take place as they do, or *how* a writer provokes a response in you. Let your ideas inspire deeper thought or discussion about the literature.

• Consider other ideas and interpretations

A work of literature can generate a wide variety of responses in different readers—and that can make your discussions exciting. Be open to the idea that many interpretations can be valid. To support your own ideas, point to the events, descriptions, characters, or other literary elements in the work that produced your interpretation. To consider someone else's ideas, decide whether details in the work support the interpretation he or she presents. Be sure to convey your criticism of the ideas of others in a respectful and supportive manner.

- **Ask questions and extend the contributions of others**

Get in the habit of asking questions to help you clarify your understanding of another reader's ideas. You can also use questions to call attention to possible areas of confusion, to points that are open to debate, or to errors.

In addition, offer elaboration of the points that others make by providing examples and illustrations. To move a discussion forward, pause occasionally to summarize and evaluate tentative conclusions reached by the group members. Then, continue the discussion with a fresh understanding of the material and ideas you have already covered.

- **Manage differing opinions and views**

Each participant brings his or her own personality, experiences, ideas, cultural background, likes and dislikes to the experience of reading, making disagreement almost inevitable. As differences arise, be sensitive to each individual's point of view. Do not personalize disagreements, but keep them focused on the literature or ideas under discussion.

When you meet with a group to discuss literature, use a chart like the one shown to analyze the discussion.

Work Being Discussed:	
Focus Question:	
Your Response:	Another Student's Response:
Supporting Evidence:	Supporting Evidence:
One New Idea That You Considered About the Work During the Discussion:	

Literary Criticism

Criticism is writing that explores the meaning and techniques of literary works, usually in order to evaluate them. Writing criticism can help you think through your experience of a work of literature and can also help others deepen their own understanding. All literary criticism shares similar goals:

- ***Making Connections*** within or between works, or between a work of literature and its context
- ***Making Distinctions*** or showing differences between elements of a single work or aspects of two or more works
- ***Achieving Insights*** that were not apparent from a superficial reading
- ***Making a Judgment*** about the quality or value of a literary work

Critics use various ***theories of literary criticism*** to understand, appreciate, and evaluate literature. Some theories focus on the context of the work while others focus on the work itself. Sometimes critics combine one or more theories. These charts show a few examples of the many theories of criticism:

Focus on Contexts	
Human Experience	**Mythic Criticism** Explores universal situations, characters, and symbols called archetypes as they appear in a literary work
Culture and History	**Historical Criticism** Analyzes how circumstances or ideas of an era influence a work
Author's Life	**Biographical Criticism** Explains how the author's life sheds light on the work

Focus on the Work Itself
Formal Criticism Shows how the work reflects characteristics of the genre, or literary type, to which it belongs

Examples of Literary Theories in Action

- ***Mythic Criticism:*** discussing how the Greek myth "Prometheus and the First People," p. 794, reveals Prometheus as an archetypal character
- ***Historical Criticism:*** showing how William Shakespeare was influenced by Elizabethan concepts of nature and politics in *Julius Caesar*, p. 546
- ***Biographical Criticism:*** showing how James Thurber's family relationships influenced the theme of "The Dog That Bit People," p. 257
- ***Formal Criticism:*** analyzing how "Contents of the Dead Man's Pocket," p. 110, combines short-story elements like plot, suspense, setting, character, and theme

Literary Movements

Our literary heritage has been shaped by a number of ***literary movements,*** directions in literature characterized by shared assumptions, beliefs, and practices. This chart shows, in chronological order, some important literary movements. While these movements developed at particular historical moments, all of them may still influence individual writers working today.

Movement	Beliefs and Practices	Examples
Classicism Europe during the Renaissance (c. 1300–1650)	• Looks to classical literature of ancient Greece and Rome as models • Values logic, clarity, balance, and restraint • Prefers "ordered" nature of parks and gardens	the clarity and restraint of Robert Frost's verse ("Mowing," p. 438)
Romanticism Europe during the late 1700s and the early 1800s	• Rebels against Classicism • Values imagination and emotion • Focuses on everyday life	the celebration of the natural world in Rachel Carson's writings ("The Marginal World")
Realism Europe and America from the mid-1800s to the 1890s	• Rebels against Romanticism's search for the ideal • Focuses on everyday life	the faithful rendering of Russian life in Anton Chekhov's fiction ("A Problem," p. 66)
Naturalism Europe and America during the late 1800s and early 1900s	• Assumes people cannot choose their fate but are shaped by psychological and social forces • Views society as a competitive jungle	the indifference to human life that characters show in Guy de Maupassant's fiction ("Two Friends")
Modernism Worldwide between 1890 and 1945	• In response to WWI, questions human reason • Focuses on studies of the unconscious and the art of primitive peoples • Experiments with language and form	the experiments with free verse in Carl Sandburg's poetry ("Jazz Fantasia," p. 407)
Post-Modernism Worldwide after 1945; still prevalent today	• Believes works of art comment on themselves • Finds inspiration in information technology	the self-consciousness about tradition in John Phillip Santos's nonfiction (from *Places Left Unfinished at the Time of Creation*)

Tips for Improving Reading Fluency

When you were younger, you learned to read. Then, you read to expand your experiences or for pure enjoyment. Now, you are expected to read to learn. As you progress in school, you are given more and more material to read. The tips on these pages will help you improve your reading fluency, or your ability to read easily, smoothly, and expressively.

Keeping Your Concentration

One common problem that readers face is the loss of concentration. When you are reading an assignment, you might find yourself rereading the same sentence several times without really understanding it. The first step in changing this behavior is to notice that you do it. Becoming an active, aware reader will help you get the most from your assignments. Practice using these strategies:

- Cover what you have already read with a note card as you go along. Then, you will not be able to reread without noticing that you are doing it.
- Set a purpose for reading beyond just completing the assignment. Then, read actively by pausing to ask yourself questions about the material as you read.
- Use the Reading Strategy instruction and notes that appear with each selection in this textbook.
- Stop reading after a specified period of time (for example, 5 minutes) and summarize what you have read. To help you with this strategy, use the Reading Check questions that appear with each selection in this textbook. Reread to find any answers you do not know.

Reading Phrases

Fluent readers read phrases rather than individual words. Reading this way will speed up your reading and improve your comprehension. Here are some useful ideas:

- Experts recommend rereading as a strategy to increase fluency. Choose a passage of text that is neither too hard nor too easy. Read the same passage aloud several times until you can read it smoothly. When you can read the passage fluently, pick another passage and keep practicing.
- Read aloud into a tape recorder. Then, listen to the recording, noting your accuracy, pacing, and expression. You can also read aloud and share feedback with a partner.
- Use the *Prentice Hall Listening to Literature* audiotapes or CDs to hear the selections read aloud. Read along silently in your textbook, noticing how the reader uses his or her voice and emphasizes certain words and phrases.

Understanding Key Vocabulary

If you do not understand some of the words in an assignment, you may miss out on important concepts. Therefore, it is helpful to keep a dictionary nearby when you are reading. Follow these steps:

- Before you begin reading, scan the text for unfamiliar words or terms. Find out what those words mean before you begin reading.
- Use context—the surrounding words, phrases, and sentences—to help you determine the meanings of unfamiliar words.
- If you are unable to understand the meaning through context, refer to the dictionary.

Paying Attention to Punctuation

When you read, pay attention to punctuation. Commas, periods, exclamation points, semicolons, and colons tell you when to pause or stop. They also indicate relationships between groups of words. When you recognize these relationships, you will read with greater understanding and expression. Look at the chart below.

Punctuation Mark	Meaning
comma	brief pause
period	pause at the end of a thought
exclamation point	pause that indicates emphasis
semicolon	pause between related but distinct thoughts
colon	pause before giving explanation or examples

Using the Reading Fluency Checklist

Use the checklist below each time you read a selection in this textbook. In your Language Arts journal or notebook, note which skills you need to work on and chart your progress each week.

Reading Fluency Checklist
☐ Preview the text to check for difficult or unfamiliar words.
☐ Practice reading aloud.
☐ Read according to punctuation.
☐ Break down long sentences into the subject and its meaning.
☐ Read groups of words for meaning rather than reading single words.
☐ Read with expression (change your tone of voice to add meaning to the word).

Reading is a skill that can be improved with practice. The key to improving your fluency is to read. The more you read, the better your reading will become.

Types of Writing

Good writing can be a powerful tool used for many purposes. Writing can allow you to defend something you believe in or show how much you know about a subject. Writing can also help you share what you have experienced, imagined, thought, and felt. The three main types of writing are argument, informative/explanatory, and narrative.

Argument

When you think of the word *argument,* you might think of a disagreement between two people, but an argument is more than that. An argument is a logical way of presenting a belief, conclusion, or stance. A good argument is supported with reasoning and evidence.

Argument writing can be used for many purposes, such as to change a reader's point of view or opinion or to bring about an action or a response from a reader.

There are three main purposes for writing a formal argument:

- to change the reader's mind
- to convince the reader to accept what is written
- to motivate the reader to take action, based on what is written

The following are some types of argument writing:

Advertisements An advertisement is a planned communication meant to be seen, heard, or read. It attempts to persuade an audience to buy a product or service, accept an idea, or support a cause. Advertisements may appear in printed or broadcast form.

Several common types of advertisements are public-service announcements, billboards, merchandise ads, service ads, and political campaign literature.

Persuasive Essay A persuasive essay presents a position on an issue, urges readers to accept that position, and may encourage a specific action. An effective persuasive essay

- Explores an issue of importance to the writer
- Addresses an issue that is arguable
- Uses facts, examples, statistics, or personal experiences to support a position
- Tries to influence the audience through appeals to the readers' knowledge, experiences, or emotions
- Uses clear organization to present a logical argument

Forms of persuasion include editorials, position papers, persuasive speeches, grant proposals, advertisements, and debates.

Informative/Explanatory

Informative/explanatory writing should rely on facts to inform or explain. Informative/explanatory writing serves some closely related purposes: to increase readers' knowledge of a subject, to help readers better understand a procedure or process, or to provide readers with an enhanced comprehension of a concept. It should also feature a clear introduction, body, and conclusion. The following are some examples of informative/explanatory writing:

Cause-and-Effect Essay A cause-and-effect essay examines the relationship between events, explaining how one event or situation causes another. A successful cause-and-effect essay includes

- A discussion of a cause, event, or condition that produces a specific result
- An explanation of an effect, outcome, or result
- Evidence and examples to support the relationship between cause and effect
- A logical organization that makes the explanation clear

Comparison-and-Contrast Essay A comparison-and-contrast essay analyzes the similarities and differences between or among two or more things. An effective comparison-and-contrast essay

- Identifies a purpose for comparison and contrast
- Identifies similarities and differences between or among two or more things, people, places, or ideas
- Gives factual details about the subjects
- Uses an organizational plan suited to the topic and purpose

Descriptive Writing Descriptive writing creates a vivid picture of a person, place, thing, or event. Most descriptive writing includes

- Sensory details—sights, sounds, smells, tastes, and physical sensations
- Vivid, precise language
- Figurative language or comparisons
- Adjectives and adverbs that paint a word picture
- An organization suited to the subject

Types of descriptive writing include descriptions of ideas, observations, travel brochures, physical descriptions, functional descriptions, remembrances, and character sketches.

Problem-and-Solution Essay A problem-and-solution essay describes a problem and offers one or more solutions to it. It describes a clear set of steps to achieve a result. An effective problem-and-solution essay includes

- A clear statement of the problem, with its causes and effects summarized for the reader
- The most important aspects of the problem
- A proposal of at least one realistic solution
- Facts, statistics, data, or expert testimony to support the solution
- A clear organization that makes the relationship between problem and solution obvious

Research Writing Research writing is based on information gathered from outside sources. A research paper—a focused study of a topic—helps writers explore and connect ideas, make discoveries, and share their findings with an audience. An effective research paper

- Focuses on a specific, narrow topic, which is usually summarized in a thesis statement
- Presents relevant information from a wide variety of sources
- Uses a clear organization that includes an introduction, body, and conclusion
- Includes a bibliography or works-cited list that identifies the sources from which the information was drawn

Other types of writing that depend on accurate and insightful research include multimedia presentations, statistical reports, annotated bibliographies, and experiment journals.

Workplace Writing Workplace writing is probably the format you will use most after you finish school. In general, workplace writing is fact-based and meant to communicate specific information in a structured format. Effective workplace writing

- Communicates information concisely
- Includes details that provide necessary information and anticipate potential questions
- Is error-free and neatly presented

Common types of workplace writing include business letters, memorandums, résumés, forms, and applications.

Narrative

Narrative writing conveys experience, either real or imaginary, and uses time to provide structure. It can be used to inform, instruct, persuade, or entertain. Whenever writers tell a story, they are using narrative writing. Most types of narrative writing share certain elements, such as characters, a setting, a sequence of events, and, often, a theme. The following are some types of narration:

Autobiographical Writing Autobiographical writing tells a true story about an important period, experience, or relationship in the writer's life. Effective autobiographical writing includes

- A series of events that involve the writer as the main character
- Details, thoughts, feelings, and insights from the writer's perspective
- A conflict or an event that affects the writer
- A logical organization that tells the story clearly
- Insights that the writer gained from the experience

Types of autobiographical writing include autobiographical sketches, personal narratives, reflective essays, eyewitness accounts, and memoirs.

Short Story A short story is a brief, creative narrative. Most short stories include

- Details that establish the setting in time and place
- A main character who undergoes a change or learns something during the course of the story
- A conflict or a problem to be introduced, developed, and resolved
- A plot, the series of events that make up the action of the story
- A theme or message about life

Types of short stories include realistic stories, fantasies, historical narratives, mysteries, thrillers, science-fiction stories, and adventure stories.

Writing Friendly Letters

A friendly letter is an informal letter to a friend, a family member, or anyone with whom the writer wants to communicate in a personal way. Most friendly letters are made up of five parts:

- ✔ the heading
- ✔ the salutation, or greeting
- ✔ the body
- ✔ the closing
- ✔ the signature

The purpose of a friendly letter is often one of the following:

- ✔ to share personal news and feelings
- ✔ to send or to answer an invitation
- ✔ to express thanks

Model Friendly Letter

In this friendly letter, Betsy thanks her grandparents for a birthday present and gives them some news about her life.

11 Old Farm Road
Topsham, Maine 04011

April 14, 20—

Dear Grandma and Grandpa,

Thank you for the sweater you sent me for my birthday. It fits perfectly, and I love the color. I wore my new sweater to the carnival at school last weekend and got lots of compliments.

The weather here has been cool but sunny. Mom thinks that "real" spring will never come. I can't wait until it's warm enough to go swimming.

School is going fairly well. I really like my Social Studies class. We are learning about the U.S. Constitution, and I think it's very interesting. Maybe I will be a lawyer when I grow up.

When are you coming out to visit us? We haven't seen you since Thanksgiving. You can stay in my room when you come. I'll be happy to sleep on the couch. (The TV is in that room!!)

Well, thanks again and hope all is well with you.

Love,

Betsy

The **heading** includes the writer's address and the date on which he or she wrote the letter.

The **body** is the main part of the letter and contains the basic message.

Some common **closings** for personal letters include "Best wishes," "Love," "Sincerely," and "Yours truly."

Writing Business Letters

Formatting Business Letters

Business letters follow one of several acceptable formats. In **block format,** each part of the letter begins at the left margin. A double space is used between paragraphs. In **modified block format,** some parts of the letter are indented to the center of the page. No matter which format is used, all letters in business format have a heading, an inside address, a salutation, or greeting, a body, a closing, and a signature. These parts are shown and annotated on the model business letter below, formatted in modified block style.

Model Business Letter

In this letter, Yolanda Dodson uses modified block format to request information.

Students for a Cleaner Planet
c/o Memorial High School
333 Veteran's Drive
Denver, CO 80211

January 25, 20—

Steven Wilson, Director
Resource Recovery Really Works
300 Oak Street
Denver, CO 80216

Dear Mr. Wilson:

Memorial High School would like to start a branch of your successful recycling program. We share your commitment to reclaiming as much reusable material as we can. Because your program has been successful in other neighborhoods, we're sure that it can work in our community. Our school includes grades 9–12 and has about 800 students.

Would you send us some information about your community recycling program? For example, we need to know what materials can be recycled and how we can implement the program.

At least fifty students have already expressed an interest in getting involved, so I know we'll have the people power to make the program work. Please help us get started.

Thank you in advance for your time and consideration.

Sincerely,

Yolanda Dodson

Yolanda Dodson

The **heading** shows the writer's address and organization (if any), and the date.

The **inside address** indicates where the letter will be sent.

A **salutation** is punctuated by a colon. When the specific addressee is not known, use a general greeting such as "To whom it may concern:"

The **body** of the letter states the writer's purpose.

The **closing** "Sincerely" is common, but "Yours truly" or "Respectfully yours" are also acceptable. To end the letter, the writer types her name and provides a **signature.**

Writing a Résumé

Writing a Résumé

A résumé summarizes your educational background, work experiences, relevant skills, and other employment qualifications. It also tells potential employers how to contact you. An effective résumé presents the applicant's name, address, and phone number. It follows an accepted résumé organization, using labels and headings to guide readers.

A résumé should outline the applicant's educational background, life experiences, and related qualifications using precise and active language.

Model Résumé

With this résumé, James, a college student, hopes to find a full-time job.

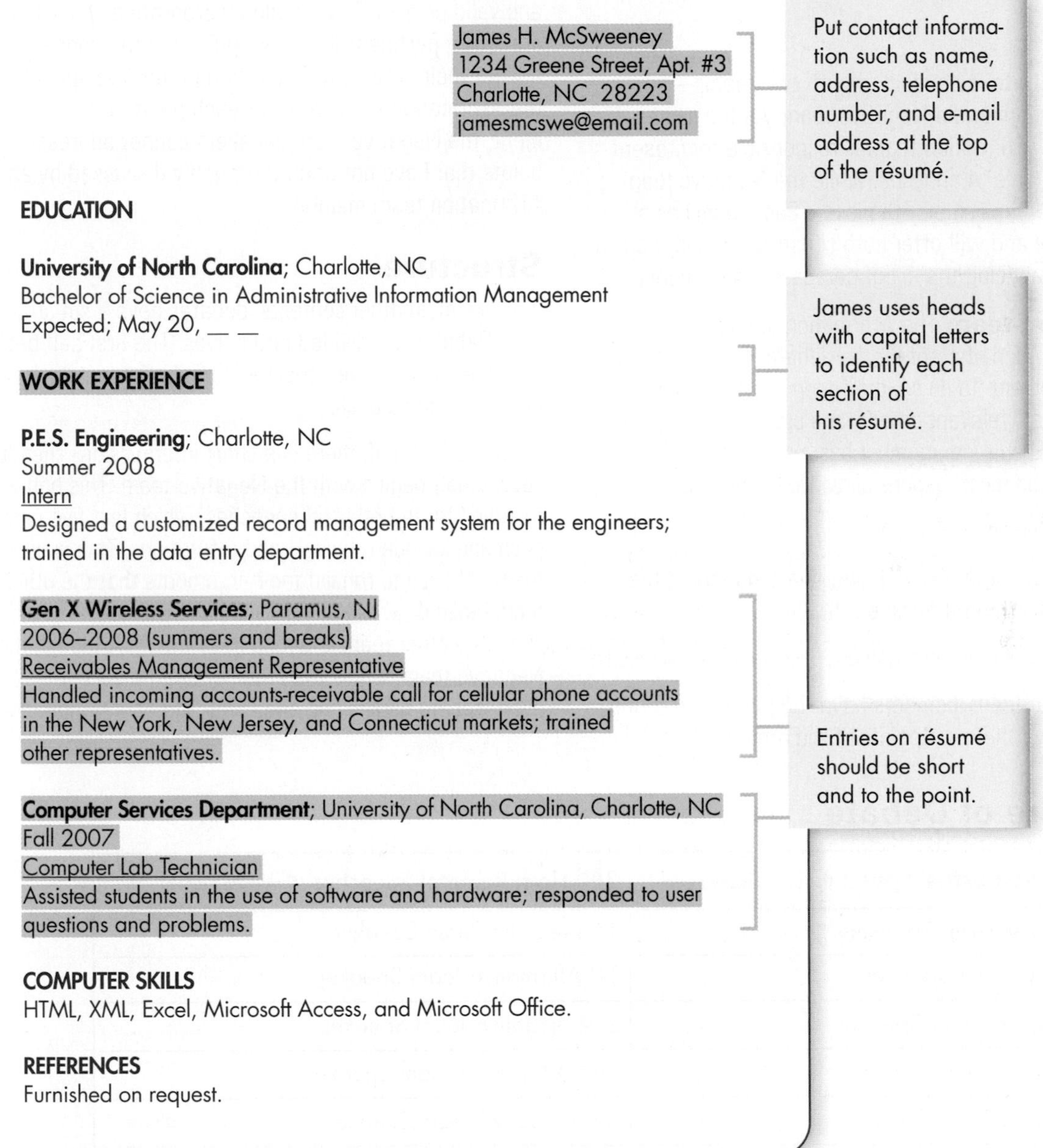
James H. McSweeney
1234 Greene Street, Apt. #3
Charlotte, NC 28223
jamesmcswe@email.com

EDUCATION

University of North Carolina; Charlotte, NC
Bachelor of Science in Administrative Information Management
Expected; May 20, __ __

WORK EXPERIENCE

P.E.S. Engineering; Charlotte, NC
Summer 2008
Intern
Designed a customized record management system for the engineers; trained in the data entry department.

Gen X Wireless Services; Paramus, NJ
2006–2008 (summers and breaks)
Receivables Management Representative
Handled incoming accounts-receivable call for cellular phone accounts in the New York, New Jersey, and Connecticut markets; trained other representatives.

Computer Services Department; University of North Carolina, Charlotte, NC
Fall 2007
Computer Lab Technician
Assisted students in the use of software and hardware; responded to user questions and problems.

COMPUTER SKILLS
HTML, XML, Excel, Microsoft Access, and Microsoft Office.

REFERENCES
Furnished on request.

Put contact information such as name, address, telephone number, and e-mail address at the top of the résumé.

James uses heads with capital letters to identify each section of his résumé.

Entries on résumé should be short and to the point.

Rules of Debate

A **debate** is a structured contest based on a formal discussion of opinion. In essence, it is a battle of intellect and verbal skill. The goal is mastering the art of persuasion. Who can best express, argue, and support opinions on a given topic? Who can best refute an argument, showing that the opponent's points are invalid? Which team, in the end, can convince the judges that their argument is the most sound?

Teams

A **formal debate** is conducted with two teams—an Affirmation team and a Negative team. As the names suggest, the Affirmation team is responsible for presenting the "pro" side of an issue, while the Negative team presents the "con" side of the issue. Each team has a main purpose and will offer both constructive and rebuttal speeches, practicing the art of persuasion and debate.

Affirmation team The Affirmation team as a whole carries the burden of proof for the debate. They must prove there is a problem. To do so, they need to cite credible sources, include relevant details, and present and support valid points. Each team member has a specific job. The first speaker has the most responsibility. He or she must

- define the issue or problem
- introduce the team line—a one-line summary of the team's position on the issue
- identify the point of the argument each speaker will discuss

The remaining team members have the job of presenting and supporting the main points of the argument.

Negative team Though the Negative team does not carry the burden of proof, the team must show that there is no problem or that the Affirmation team's solutions are invalid. Though their purpose is to rebut an argument, the rebuttal technique calls for a formation of their own argument. They must argue against the Affirmation team. To construct their argument, they must use—like the Affirmation team—credible sources, relevant details, and valid points. They should incorporate any available statistics, pertinent facts, or applicable testimonies to bolster their argument. Even though the first speaker of the Affirmation team lays out each point of the argument, the Negative team speakers cannot address points that have not been thoroughly discussed by an Affirmation team member.

Structure

Just like most other contests, debates have a set structure. Debates are divided into halves. The first half begins with the constructive speeches from both teams, which last ten minutes each.

After the first half, there is a short intermission. Then, the second half begins with the Negative team. This half is reserved for the rebuttal speeches, which last five minutes each and include rebuttals and refutations. This is each team's chance to rebuild their arguments that the other team broke down (rebuttal), and put forth evidence to show the other team is wrong (refutation). Although the Negative team begins the argument in the second half, every debate begins and ends with the Affirmation team.

Structure of Debate

1st Half: Constructive Speeches (10 minutes each)	2nd Half: Rebuttal Speeches (5 minutes each)
1st Affirmative Team Speaker	1st Negative Team Speaker
1st Negative Team Speaker	1st Affirmative Team Speaker
2nd Affirmative Team Speaker	2nd Negative Team Speaker
2nd Negative Team Speaker	2nd Affirmative Team Speaker
3rd Affirmative Team Speaker	3rd Negative Team Speaker
3rd Negative Team Speaker	3rd Affirmative Team Speaker

Speeches—Content, Organization, and Delivery

Debate speeches are the result of practicing the art of persuasion. To be effective, speakers must include pertinent content, use clear and logical organization, and have a powerful delivery. These combined elements make a strong speech.

Content Debates often focus on concrete issues that can be proved or disproved. The basis for a debate speech is its content. The Affirmation team should first determine their position. They should be sure to include any facts and/or statistics that concretely support the argument. Speech writers should cite specific instances and occurrences that solidify their position. Writers might also include testimonies or ideas from professionals. Finally, the Affirmation team needs to propose possible solutions to the problem or issue and examine the costs and effects of those solutions.

Though the Negative team does not have to state a position—their position is automatically the opposing position—they still need to include facts, statistics, testimony, and descriptions of specific instances or occurrences to make their counterpoints. They need to analyze the Affirmation team's proposed solutions and explain why they will not work. In essence, the Negative team must construct an argument around the Affirmation team's argument.

Organization Debate speeches are organized like other speeches and essays. They should have an introduction, transitions, body, and conclusion. The speeches should have clear main points and supporting details for those points. Because a debate is a structured discussion, there will be a specific order of points and the speakers who present them must be identified. Speakers can use note cards to help them stick to the planned organization, but they should only use brief notes, never reading directly from the cards.

Delivery The manner in which a speech is delivered can make or break the argument. The impression the speaker makes on the audience, including the judges, is key. To make a good impression, the speaker must present the material with confidence. He or she can portray confidence by forming a connection with the audience through eye contact, glancing away only briefly to consult notes. A speaker should focus on his or her voice, varying the tone, volume, and pace appropriately. Body movements should not include fidgeting or nervous movement. They should only be used if they are deliberate and help express or underscore a point. Finally, speakers should be concise, focusing on vivid and clear word choice and using words that emphasize the point.

Scoring

Debates are scored much like other contests. Each side is judged on the content and delivery of their speeches. Judges contemplate different elements of content and delivery in order to determine the number of points to give each team. They might ask themselves the questions in the chart below in order to determine the score.

Finally, judges look at the observation of debate etiquette. Speakers are expected to be mature and respectful of their opponents. Speakers should never attack an opponent, but instead should attack the argument. Judges will deduct points for personal attacks.

Scoring Criteria

Content	Delivery
Were arguments convincing?	Were speakers able to speak extemporaneously?
Were arguments supported with credible, valid and relevant reasons?	Were body movements deliberate and effective?
Were refutations and rebuttals effective?	Did speakers make a connection with the audience?
Were speakers confident and knowledgeable?	Did speakers stay within their time limits?

Parts of Speech

Nouns A **noun** is the name of a person, place, or thing. A **common noun** names any one of a class of people, places, or things. A **proper noun** names a specific person, place, or thing.

Common Noun	***Proper Noun***
city	Washington, D.C.

Pronouns A **pronoun** is a word that stands for a noun or for a word that takes the place of a noun.

A **personal pronoun** refers to (1) the person speaking, (2) the person spoken to, or (3) the person, place, or thing spoken about.

	Singular	***Plural***
First Person	I, me, my, mine	we, us, our, ours
Second Person	you, your, yours	you, your, yours
Third Person	he, him, his, she, her, hers, it, its	they, them, their, theirs

Antecedents are nouns (or words that take the place of nouns) for which pronouns stand. In the following sentence, the pronoun *it* stands for the noun *Florida*.

Florida is popular because it has a warm climate.

A **reflexive pronoun** ends in *-self* or *-selves* and adds information to a sentence by pointing back to a noun or a pronoun earlier in the sentence.

"If you were honest folk *yourselves* you wouldn't let a thief go free."

— Leo Tolstoy

An **intensive pronoun** ends in *-self* or *-selves* and simply adds emphasis to a noun or a pronoun in the same sentence.

After a time, I *myself* was allowed to go into the dead houses and search for metal.

— Stephen Vincent Benét, p. 456

A **demonstrative pronoun** directs attention to a specific person, place, or thing.

this these that those

These are the juiciest pears I have ever tasted.

A **relative pronoun** begins a subordinate clause and connects it to another idea in the sentence.

The poet *who* wrote "Fear" is Gabriela Mistral.

An **interrogative pronoun** is used to begin a question. The five interrogative pronouns are *what, which, who, whom,* and *whose*.

An **indefinite pronoun** refers to a person, place, or thing, often without specifying which one.

all anyone each everyone few one someone

And then, for a moment, *all* is still, . . .

— Edgar Allan Poe

Verbs A **verb** is a word that expresses time while showing an action, a condition, or the fact that something exists.

An **action verb** indicates the action of someone or something. An action verb is **transitive** if it directs action toward someone or something named in the same sentence.

He *dusted* his hands, muttering.

— Jack Finney, p. 110

An action verb is **intransitive** if it does not direct action toward something or someone named in the same sentence.

I *smiled* and looked up at the crew . . .

— Lynne Cox, p. 130

A **linking verb** is a verb that connects the subject of a sentence with a noun or a pronoun that renames or describes the subject. The noun, pronoun, or phrase acting as a noun that renames the subject is called a **predicate nominative.**

Romance at short notice was her specialty.

— Saki, p. 85

A **helping verb** is a verb that can be added to another verb to make a verb phrase.

Nor *did* I suspect that these experiences could be part of a novel's meaning.

Adjectives An **adjective** describes a noun or a pronoun or gives a noun or a pronoun a more specific meaning. Adjectives answer these questions:

What kind?	*blue* lamp, *large* tree
Which one?	*this* table, *those* books
How many?	*five* stars, *several* buses
How much?	*less* money, *enough* votes

The articles *the, a,* and *an* are adjectives. *An* is used before a word beginning with a vowel sound.

A noun may sometimes be used as an adjective.

diamond necklace *summer* vacation

Adverbs An **adverb** modifies a verb, an adjective, or another adverb. Adverbs answer the questions *where, when, in what way,* or *to what extent*.

He could stand *there*. (modifies verb *stand*)

He was *blissfully* happy. (modifies adjective *happy*)

It ended *too* soon. (modifies adverb *soon*)

Prepositions A **preposition** relates a noun or a pronoun that appears with it to another word in the sentence.

before the end *near* me *inside* our fence

Conjunctions A **conjunction** connects words or groups of words.

A **coordinating conjunction** connects similar kinds or groups of words.

mother *and* father   simple *yet* stylish

Correlative conjunctions are used in pairs to connect similar words or groups of words.

both Sue *and* Meg   *neither* he *nor* I

A **subordinating conjunction** connects two complete ideas by placing one idea below the other in rank or importance.

You would know him *if* you saw him.

Sentences, Phrases, and Clauses

Sentences A **sentence** is a group of words with a subject and a predicate. Together, these parts express a complete thought.

A **fragment** is a group of words that does not express a complete thought.

The Four Structures of Sentences There are two kinds of clauses: independent and subordinate. An independent clause can stand by itself as a sentence; a subordinate clause cannot. These can be used to form four basic sentence structures: *simple, compound, complex,* and *compound-complex.*

A **simple sentence** consists of a single independent clause.

A **compound sentence** consists of two or more independent clauses.

The clauses in a compound sentence can be joined by a comma and a coordinating conjunction *(and, but, for, nor, or, so, yet)* or by a semicolon (;).

A **complex sentence** consists of one independent clause and one or more subordinate clauses.

The independent clause in a complex sentence is often called the *main clause* to distinguish it from the subordinate clause or clauses.

A **compound-complex sentence** consists of two or more independent clauses and one or more subordinate clauses.

Phrases A **phrase** is a group of words, without a subject and a verb, that functions in a sentence as one part of speech.

A **prepositional phrase** is a group of words that includes a preposition and a noun or a pronoun that is the object of the preposition.

outside my window   below the counter

An **adjective phrase** is a prepositional phrase that modifies a noun or a pronoun by telling *what kind* or *which one.*

The wooden gates *of that lane* stood open.

An **adverb phrase** is a prepositional phrase that modifies a verb, an adjective, or an adverb by pointing out *where, when, in what way,* or *to what extent.*

On a sudden impulse, he got to his feet. . . .

— Jack Finney, p. 110

An **appositive phrase** is a noun or a pronoun with modifiers, placed next to a noun or a pronoun to identify it or add information and details.

M. Morissot, watchmaker by trade but local militiaman for the time being, stopped short. . . .

— Guy de Maupassant

A **participial phrase** is a participle with its modifiers or complements. The entire phrase acts as an adjective.

Choosing such a tide, I hoped for a glimpse of the pool.

— Rachel Carson

A **gerund** is a form of a verb that is used as a noun. It ends in *-ing.* A **gerund phrase** is a gerund with modifiers or a complement, all acting together as a noun.

. . . *moving along the ledge* was quite as easy as he had thought it would be.

— Jack Finney, p. 110

An **infinitive** is the form of a verb using to. It acts as a noun, adjective, or adverb. An **infinitive phrase** is an infinitive with modifiers, complements, or a subject, all acting together as a single part of speech.

To be dead, and never again behold my city!

—My City, p. 386

Clauses A **clause** is a group of words with a subject and a verb.

An **independent clause** has a subject and a verb and can stand by itself as a complete sentence.

A **subordinate clause** has a subject and a verb but cannot stand by itself as a complete sentence; it can only be part of a sentence.

An **adjective clause** is a subordinate clause that modifies a noun or a pronoun by telling *what kind* or *which one.*

The people *who read the book* loved it.

An **adverb clause** modifies a verb, an adjective, an adverb, or a verbal by telling *where, when, in what way, to what extent, under what condition,* or *why.*

They read it as soon *as it was published.*

A **noun clause** is a subordinate clause that acts as a noun.

Whoever reads it is overcome with joy.

Parallelism **Parallelism** is the placement of equal ideas in words, phrases, or clauses of similar type.

Parallel Words: The camp has excellent facilities for *riding, hiking,* and *swimming.*

Parallel Phrases: Jennings had gone to the country *to rest, to think,* and *to catch a few fish.*

Parallel Clauses: A news story should tell *what happened, when it happened,* and *who was involved.*

Verb Usage

The Four Principal Parts of Verbs A verb has four **principal parts:** the *present,* the *present participle,* the *past,* and the *past participle.*

Regular verbs form the past and past participle by adding *-ed* to the present form.

Present: walk

Present Participle: (am) walking

Past: walked

Past Participle: (have) walked

The past and past participle of an **irregular verb** are not formed by adding *-ed* or *-d* to the present form. Irregular verbs form the past and past participle by changing form. Whenever you are in doubt about the principal parts of an irregular verb, use a dictionary to check them.

Present: go

Present Participle: (am) going

Past: went

Past Participle: (have) gone

Pronoun Usage

Pronoun Case The **case** of a pronoun is the form it takes to show its use in a sentence. There are three pronoun cases: *nominative, objective,* and *possessive.*

The **nominative case** is used to rename the subject of the sentence. The nominative case pronouns are *I, you, he, she, it, we, you, they.*

As the subject: *She* is brave

Renaming the subject: The leader is *she.*

The **objective case** is used as the direct object, indirect object, or object of the preposition. The objective case pronouns are *me, you, him, her, it, us, you, them.*

As a direct object: Tom called me.

As an indirect object: My friend gave *me* advice.

As an object of preposition: The coach gave pointers to *me.*

The **possessive case** is used to show ownership. The possessive pronouns are *my, your, his, her, its, our, their, mine, yours, his, hers, its, ours, theirs.*

Agreement

Subject and Verb Agreement To make a subject and verb agree, make sure that both are singular or both are plural.

Many *storms are* the cause of beach erosion.

In the case of a plural and a singular subject joined by *or* or *nor,* choose the form of the verb that agrees with the closer of the two.

Either the *cats* or the *dog is* hungry.

Neither *Angie* nor *her sisters were* present.

Pronoun-Antecedent Agreement Pronouns must agree with their antecedents in number and gender. Use singular pronouns with singular antecedents and plural pronouns with plural antecedents. Many errors in pronoun-antecedent agreement occur when a plural pronoun is used to refer to a singular antecedent for which the gender is not specified.

Incorrect: Everyone did their best.

Correct: Everyone did his or her best.

The following indefinite pronouns are singular: *anybody, anyone, each, either, everybody, everyone, neither, nobody, no one, one, somebody, someone.*

The following indefinite pronouns are plural: *both, few, many, several.*

The following indefinite pronouns may be either singular or plural: *all, any, most, none, some.* Treat these pronouns as singular when the antecedent is singular.

All of the gold is gone, and we do not know who took *it.*

Treat these pronouns as plural when the antecedent is plural.

Most of my friends are going, and *they* will have a good time.

Using Modifiers

Degrees of Comparison Most adjectives and adverbs have three different forms to show degrees of comparison—the *positive,* the *comparative,* the *superlative.*

Use *-er* or *more* to form the comparative degree and *-est* or *most* to form the superlative degree of most one- and two-syllable modifiers.

Use *more* and *most* to form the comparative and superlative degrees of all modifiers with three or more syllables.

The irregular comparative and superlative forms of certain adjectives and adverbs must be memorized.

The form of some irregular modifiers differs only in the positive degree. The modifiers *bad, badly,* and *ill,* for example, all have the same basic form in the comparative and superlative degrees (*worse, worst*).

Capitalization and Punctuation

Capitalization Capitalize the first word of a sentence and also the first word in a quotation if the quotation is a complete sentence.

"No matter," he concluded, "I'll go toward the rising sun." — Leo Tolstoy

Capitalize all proper nouns and adjectives.

W. W. Jacobs Flanders Fields African writers

Capitalize a person's title when it is followed by the person's name or when it is used in direct address.

Reverend Tallboys Mrs. Prothero "Hello, Major."

Capitalize titles showing family relationships when they refer to a specific person and are used with a name or as a name.

Aunt Mae Let's ask Grandmother. *but* his father

Capitalize the first word and all other key words in the titles of books, periodicals, poems, stories, plays, paintings, and other works of art.

Lord of the Flies "Spring and All"

End Marks Use a **period** to end a declarative sentence, an imperative sentence, an indirect question, and most abbreviations.

The class will meet at noon.

Use a **question mark** to end a direct question, an incomplete question, or a statement that is intended as a question.

Did you prepare your assignment?

Use an **exclamation mark** after a statement showing strong emotion, an urgent imperative sentence, or an interjection expressing strong emotion.

Wait until you hear the news!

Commas Use a **comma** before the coordinating conjunction to separate two independent clauses in a compound sentence.

His arms had begun to tremble from the steady strain of clinging to this narrow perch, and he did not know what to do now. . . . — Jack Finney, p. 110

Use commas to separate three or more words, phrases, or clauses in a series.

. . . he produced about fifteen hundred *drawings, prints, pastels,* and *oil paintings* with ballet themes.
— Richard Mühlberger

Use commas to separate adjectives of equal rank. Do not use commas to separate adjectives that must stay in a specific order.

With *pink, dimpled* knees, Henri, not yet a year old, sprawls on the lap of his nurse. . . .
[In Degas's painting], the *creamy white* tones of the passengers stand out.
— Richard Mühlberger

Use a comma after an introductory word, phrase, or clause.

When Marian Anderson again returned to America, she was a seasoned artist.
— Langston Hughes

Use commas to set off parenthetical and nonessential expressions.

Now, *yes, now,* it was about to set!
— Leo Tolstoy

Use commas with places, dates, and titles.

Poe was raised in Richmond, Virginia.
August 4, 2026
Alfred, Lord Tennyson

Use a comma to indicate the words left out of an elliptical sentence, to set off a direct quotation, and to prevent a sentence from being misunderstood.

Vincent Canby writes for *The New York Times*; Roger Ebert, for the *Chicago Sun Times*.

Semicolons Use a **semicolon** to join independent clauses that are not already joined by a conjunction.

They could find no buffalo; they had to hang an old hide from the sacred tree.
— N. Scott Momaday, p. 480

Use a semicolon to join independent clauses separated by either a conjunctive adverb or a transitional expression.

James Thurber wrote many books; moreover, he was a cartoonist and a journalist.

Use semicolons to avoid confusion when independent clauses or items in a series already contain commas.

Thurber is remembered for his character Walter Mitty; for his cartoons, many of which illustrated his books; and for his terrifically funny essays.

Colons Use a **colon** in order to introduce a list of items following an independent clause.

The authors we are reading include a number of poets: Robert Frost, Octavio Paz, and Emily Dickinson.

Use a colon to introduce a formal quotation.

The next day Howard Taubman wrote enthusiastically in *The New York Times*: "Marian Anderson has returned to her native land one of the great singers of our time. . . ."
— Langston Hughes

Quotation Marks A **direct quotation** represents a person's exact speech or thoughts and is enclosed in quotation marks.

"Clara, my mind is made up."

An **indirect quotation** is a restatement or paraphrase of what a person said or thought and does not require quotation marks.

The cops suggested that it might be a good idea to tie the dog up, but mother said that it mortified him to be tied up. . . . — James Thurber, p. 257

Always place a comma or a period inside the final quotation mark.

"Eh, you're a stranger," she said. "I thought so." — Josephina Niggli, p. 40

Place a question mark or an exclamation mark inside the final quotation mark if the end mark is part of the quotation; if it is not part of the quotation, place it outside the final quotation mark.

He asked, "Which poetry do you like best?"

Have you ever read the poem "Africa"?

Use single quotation marks for a quotation within a quotation.

Use quotation marks around the titles of short written works, episodes in a series, songs, and titles of works mentioned as parts of a collection.

"Making a Fist" "These Are Days"

Underline or italicize titles of longer works, such as plays, movies, or novels.

Dashes Use **dashes** to indicate an abrupt change of thought, a dramatic interrupting idea, or a summary statement.

It made her so mad to see Muggs lying there, oblivious of the mice—they came running up to her—that she slapped him and he slashed at her, but didn't make it. — James Thurber, p. 257

Parentheses Use **parentheses** to set off asides and explanations only when the material is not essential or when it consists of one or more sentences.

When I finished (What a lot of facts I found out!), I turned in my report.

Hyphens Use a **hyphen** with certain numbers, after certain prefixes, with two or more words used as one word, and with a compound modifier coming before a noun.

fifty-two greenish-blue water

Apostrophes Add an **apostrophe** and s to show the possessive case of most singular nouns.

Prospero's castle the playwright's craft

Add an apostrophe to show the possessive case of plural nouns ending in *-s* and *-es*.

the sailors' ships the babies' mothers

Add an apostrophe and *-s* to show the possessive case of plural nouns that do not end in *-s* or *-es*.

the children's games the people's friend

Use an apostrophe in a contraction to indicate the position of the missing letter or letters.

I *didn't* love any one of you more than any other. — William Melvin Kelley

Glossary of Common Usage

among, between: *Among* is usually used with three or more items. *Between* is generally used with only two items.

Among the poems we read this year, Eve Merriam's "Metaphor" was my favorite.

"Like the Sun" tells of the conflict *between* telling the truth and telling white lies.

around: In formal writing, *around* should not be used to mean *approximately* or *about*. These usages are allowable, however, in informal writing or in colloquial dialogue.

Romeo and Juliet had its first performance in *approximately* 1595.

Shakespeare was *about* thirty when he wrote it.

as, because, like, as to: The word *as* has several meanings and can function as several parts of speech. To avoid confusion, use *because* rather than *as* when you want to indicate cause and effect.

Because Cyril was interested in African American poetry, he wrote his report on Langston Hughes.

Do not use the preposition *like* to introduce a clause that requires the conjunction *as*.

James Thurber conversed as he wrote—wittily.

The use of *as to* for *about* is awkward and should be avoided.

Rosa has a theory *about* Edgar Allan Poe's style.

beside, besides: *Beside* is a preposition meaning "at the side of" or "close to." Do not confuse *beside* with *besides*, which means "in addition to." *Besides* can be a preposition or an adverb.

As the men cross the lawn and approach the open window, a brown spaniel trots *beside* them.

There are many other Indian oral epics *besides* the *Ramayana*.

can, may: The verb *can* generally refers to the ability to do something. The verb *may* generally refers to permission to do something.

Dylan Thomas describes his childhood Christmases so vividly that most readers can visualize the scenes.

Creon's edict states that no one may bury Polyneices.

different from, different than: The preferred usage is *different from*.

The structure and rhyme scheme of a Shakespearean sonnet are *different from* the organization of a Petrarchan sonnet.

farther, further: Use *farther* when you refer to distance. Use *further* when you mean "to a greater degree" or "additional."

The *farther* the ants travel, the more ominous and destructive they seem.

The storm in Act I of *The Tragedy of Julius Caesar* *further* hints at the ominous deeds to come.

fewer, less: Use *fewer* for things that can be counted. Use *less* for amounts or quantities that cannot be counted.

Poetry often uses *fewer* words than prose to convey ideas and images.

It takes *less* time to perform a Greek tragedy than to perform a Shakespearean play.

good, well: Use the adjective *good* after linking verbs such as *feel, look, smell, taste,* and *seem.* Use *well* whenever you need an adverb or as an adjective describing health.

Caesar remarks that Cassius does not look *good*; on the contrary, his appearance is "lean."

Twain wrote especially *well* when he described eccentric characters.

hopefully: Do not attach this adverb to a sentence loosely, as in "*Hopefully,* the rain will stop by noon." Rewrite the sentence so that *hopefully* modifies a specific verb. Other possible ways of revising such sentences include using the adjective *hopeful* or a phrase such as *everyone hopes that.*

Dr. Martin Luther King, Jr., wrote and spoke *hopefully* about his dream of racial harmony.

Mr. White was *hopeful* that the monkey's paw would bring him good fortune.

Everyone hopes that the class production of *Antigone* will be a big success.

its, it's: Do not confuse the possessive pronoun its with the contraction *it's,* used in place of "it is" or "it has."

In *its* very first lines, "The Stolen Child" establishes an eerie mood.

In "The Street of the Cañon," Pepe Gonzalez knows that *it's* dangerous to attend the party.

just, only: When you use *just* as an adverb meaning "no more than," be sure you place it directly before the word it logically modifies. Likewise, be sure you place *only* before the word it logically modifies.

Just one wish changed the Whites' lives forever.

A short story can usually develop *only* a few characters, whereas a novel can include many.

kind of, sort of: In formal writing, you should not use these colloquial expressions. Instead, use a word such as *rather* or *somewhat.*

Poe portrays Prince Prospero as *rather* arrogant.

The tone of the biography is *somewhat* harsh.

lay, lie: Do not confuse these verbs. *Lay* is a transitive verb meaning "to set or put something down." Its principal parts are *lay, laying, laid, laid. Lie* is an intransitive verb meaning "to recline." Its principal parts are *lie, lying, lay, lain.*

They laid the monkey's paw on the table for a while before anyone dared to pick it up.

La Belle Dame sans Merci enchants the knight as he *lies* in her "elfin grot."

leave, let: Be careful not to confuse these verbs. *Leave* means "to go away" or "to allow to remain." *Let* means "to permit."

Threatening Antigone not to disobey his orders, Creon angrily *leaves* the stage.

Creon did not want to *let* Antigone bury her brother.

raise, rise: *Raise* is a transitive verb that usually takes a direct object. *Rise* is an intransitive verb and never takes a direct object.

In his speech, Antony unexpectedly *raises* the subject of Caesar's will.

When the Cabuliwallah comes to call, Mini *rises* from her chair and runs to greet him.

set, sit: Do not confuse these verbs. *Set* is a transitive verb meaning "to put (something) in a certain place." Its principal parts are *set, setting, set, set. Sit* is an intransitive verb meaning "to be seated." Its principal parts are *sit, sitting, sat, sat.*

Antigone's conduct *sets* a high standard for us.

Jerry's mother *sits* in her beach chair while Jerry swims in the ocean.

so, so that: Be careful not to use the coordinating conjunction *so* when your context requires *so that. So* means "accordingly" or "with the result that" and expresses a cause-and-effect relationship. *So that* expresses purpose—what someone intends to achieve.

He wanted to do well on the test, *so* he read *The Tragedy of Julius Caesar* again.

Antony uses eloquent rhetoric to stir up the people *so that* they will rebel.

than, then: The conjunction *than* is used to connect the two parts of a comparison. Do not confuse *than* with the adverb *then,* which usually refers to time.

I enjoyed "The Marginal World" more *than* "Flood."

Marian Anderson gave a triumphant singing recital in New York that evening, and she *then* embarked on a coast-to-coast American tour.

that, which, who: Use the relative pronoun *that* to refer to things. Use *which* only for things and *who* only for people.

The poem *that* Cheryl liked the most was "The street."

Haiku, *which* consists of only seventeen syllables, is often built around one or two vivid images.

The assassin *who* strikes Caesar first is Casca.

unique: Because *unique* means "one of a kind," you should not use it carelessly to mean "interesting" or "unusual." Avoid such illogical expressions as "most unique," "very unique," and "extremely unique."

Emily Dickinson's bold experiments with form make her *unique* in the history of nineteenth-century American poetry.

when, where: Do not directly follow a linking verb with *when* or *where*. Be careful not to use *where* when your context requires *that*.

Faulty: The exposition is *when* an author provides the reader with important background information.
Revised: In the exposition, an author provides the reader with important background information.
Faulty: Madras, India, is *where* R. K. Narayan was born.
Revised: R. K. Narayan was born in Madras, India.
Faulty: We read *where* the prizes were worth hundreds of dollars.
Revised: We read *that* the prizes were worth hundreds of dollars.

Glossary

PRONUNCIATION KEY

Symbol	Sample Words	Symbol	Sample Words
a	at, tap, mat	oi	oil, toy, royal
ā	ate, rain, break	ou	out, now, sour
ä	car, father, heart	u	mud, ton, trouble
ch	chew, nature, such	ʉ	her, sir, word
e	end, feather, said	’l	cattle, paddle, cuddle
ē	sea, steam, piece	’n	sudden, hidden, sweeten
ə	ago, pencil, lemon	ŋ	ring, anger, pink
i	it, stick, gym	sh	shell, mission, fish
ī	nice, lie, sky	th	thin, nothing, both
ō	no, oat, low	*th*	then, mother, smooth
ô	all, law, taught	zh	vision, treasure, seizure
oo	look, would, pull	yoo	cure, furious
o͞o	boot, drew, tune	yo͞o	cute, few, use

Academic vocabulary appears in blue type.

A

absolute (ab´ sə lo͞ot´) *adj.* free from restriction or limitation; complete

abstract (ab strakt´) *adj.* unrelated to a material object; not concrete

accessible (ak ses´ ə bəl) *adj.* easy to approach or enter

accomplices (ə käm´ plis iz) *n.* people who help another person commit a crime

account (ə kount´) *n.* report, description, or story

adamant (ad´ ə mənt) *adj.* not giving in; unyielding; firm

adapt (ə dapt´) *v.* change or adjust

adaptation (ad´ əp tā´ shən) *n.* modification; in literature, a version of another work, often rendered in a different genre

adulation (a´ jo͞o la´ shən) *n.* high or excessive praise; intense admiration

adversity (ad vʉr´ sə tē) *n.* state of hardship or misfortune

affable (af´ə bəl) *adj.* pleasant; friendly

affiliation (ə fil´ ē ā´ shən) *n.* membership within an organization; connection; association

affront (ə frunt´) *n.* open insult

align (ə līn´) *v.* arrange in a straight line; bring into agreement

allay (a lā´) *v.* relieve; lessen; calm

alternative (ôl tʉr´ nə tiv) *adj.* reflecting other choices

ambient (am´ bē ənt) *adj.* surrounding; on all sides

amenable (ə mē´ nə bəl) *adj.* responsive; open

amiably (ā´mē ə blē) *adv.* in a friendly way

analyses (ə nal´ ə sēz) *n.* detailed examinations

anguish (aŋ´ gwish) *n.* extreme suffering, as from grief or pain

anticipate (an tis´ ə pāt´) *v.* look forward to

apathy (ap´ ə thē) *n.* lack of interest or emotion

application (ap´ li kā´ shən) *n.* act of putting something to use

apprehension (ap´ rē hen´ shən) *n.* anxious feeling; fear; anxiety

arduously (är´ jo͞o əs lē) *adv.* with great difficulty; laboriously

arid (ar´ id) *adj.* completely dry; lifeless

articulate (är tik´ yo͞o lāt´) *v.* say clearly

aspects (as´ pekts´) *n.* component parts or qualities; elements

assertion (ə sʉr´ shən) *n.* positive statement; declaration

associated (ə sō´ shē āt´ id) *v.* joined together; connected

attributed (ə trib´ yo͞ot id) *v.* considered as a characteristic or quality of a person, place, or thing

attributes (a´ trə byo͞ots´) *n.* characteristics of a person or thing

audaciously (ô dā´ shəs lē) *adv.* in a bold manner

auditory (ô´ də tôr´ ē) *adj.* related to hearing or the organs of hearing

augmented (ôg ment´ id) *adj.* made greater; enhanced

auroras (ə rōr´ əz) *n.* patterns of light arranged in streams or arcs

awareness (ə wer´ nis) *n.* realization or consciousness of something

B

background (bak´ ground´) 1. *n.* all of a person's education, training, and experience; 2. *n.* factors that contribute to present circumstances or to the qualities of a person, place, or thing

banality (bə nal´ ə tē) *n.* condition of being stale or tired; lacking in innovation or freshness

baseline (bās´ līn) *n.* original reference point, amount, or level by which other items can be measured or compared

bias (bī´ əs) *n.* prejudice; preference for one thing, person, or group, often in a way considered unfair

bore (bôr) *v.* carried

brandished (bran´ disht) *v.* showed, waved, or shook in a threatening or triumphant manner

brazen (brā´ zən) *adj.* shameless; bold

buffer (buf´ ər) *v.* lessen a shock; cushion

C

cajoling (kə jōl´ iŋ) *n.* action of coaxing with flattery

calamity (kə lam´ ə tē) *n.* terrible misfortune; disaster

candid (kan´ did) *adj.* honest; direct

captures (kap´ chərz) *v.* describes well

change (chānj) *v.* become different; transform

character (kar´ ik tər) *n.* moral strength; self-discipline

chastisement (chas´ tiz mənt) *n.* severe criticism; punishment

choleric (käl´ ər ik) *adj.* quick tempered; inclined to anger

clenching (klench´ iŋ) *v.* closing, holding tightly

commemorates (kə mem´ ə rāts´) *v.* honors a memory

commencement (kə məns´ mənt) *n.* ceremony marking school graduation and conferring of degrees

commiserate (kə miz´ ər āt´) *v.* sympathize with; show sorrow for

complex (käm´ pleks) *n.* assemblage of units, such as houses or other buildings, that together form a single section or group

complexities (kəm pleks´ ə tēz) *n.* qualities that suggest complexity and depth; intricacies

complexity (kəm pleks´ ə tē) *n.* richness; depth

comprehend (käm´ prē hend´) *v.* grasp mentally; understand

compromise (käm´ prə mīz´) *n.* agreement in which both sides give something up

concession (kən sesh´ ən) *n.* acceptance; yielding to an opposing point of view or demand

concrete (kän´ krēt´) *adj.* something that can be observed through the senses; specific; tangible

condemned (kən demd´) *v.* declared to be guilty of wrongdoing; convicted

conduct (kän´ dukt´) *n.* way in which a person acts; behavior

configuration (kən fig´ yə rā´ shən) *n.* arrangement of parts; pattern

confirm (kən fʉrm´) *v.* establish the truth or correctness of something

confounded (kən found´ id) *adj.* made to feel confused

confrontation (kän´ frən tā´ shən) *n.* clashing of forces or ideas

confusion (kən fyo͞o´ zhən) *n.* state of disorder or distraction; lack of clarity or understanding

conjured (kän´ jərd) *v.* performed tricks in which things seem to appear, disappear, or change as if by magic

connection (kə nek´ shən) *n.* causal or logical relation or sequence

conspicuous (kən spik´ yo͞o əs) *adj.* easy to see

constricting (kən strikt´ iŋ) *adj.* preventing freedom of movement; limiting

contemporary (kən tem´ pə rer´ ē) *adj.* of present or recent times

contempt (kən tempt´) *n.* scorn; attitude of someone who looks down on something or someone else

contested (kən test´ əd) *v.* tried to disprove or invalidate something; disputed

context (kän´ tekst´) 1. *n.* circumstances that form the setting of an event; 2. *n.* situation in which something is found

contradicted (kän´ trə dikt´ əd) *v.* made a statement that disproved or opposed another statement

contradiction (kän´ trə dik´ shən) *n.* statement that directly opposes another

contrived (kən trīvd´) *adj.* created from a plan; not happening naturally

convalesce (kän´ və ləs´) *v.* regain strength and health; heal

converge (kən vʉrj´) *v.* meet at a specific point; come together

convey (kən vā´) *v.* communicate, express, or make known

convoluted (kän´ və lo͞ot´ əd) *adj.* twisted in a complicated way; distorted

counsel (koun´ səl) *n.* advice; discussion

countenance (kount´ 'n əns) 1. *n.* face; 2. *n.* look of a face, showing a person's nature

counterparts (kount´ ər pärts´) *n.* person or thing that corresponds to or closely resembles another

courage (kʉr´ ij) *n.* quality that allows someone to face rather than withdraw from difficulty, pain, or danger

credulity (krə dōō´ lə tē) *n.* tendency to believe too readily

criteria (krī tir´ ē ə) *n.* standards or rules by which something can be measured or judged

curdled (kʉrd´ 'ld) *v.* spoiled or soured

customary (kus´ tə mer´ ē) *adj.* following common practices; usual; habitual

D

debate (dē bāt´) *v.* argue or discuss

deference (def´ ər əns) *n.* respectful yielding to the ideas, wishes, and so on of another

deflects (dē flekts´) *v.* turns or makes go to one side

defunct (dē fuŋkt´) *adj.* no longer in use or existence

dejectedly (dē jek´ tid lē) *adv.* in a depressed way

deliver (di liv´ ər) *v.* surrender someone or something; hand over

delusion (di lōō´ zhən) *n.* false belief that is held despite evidence to the contrary

demeanor (di mēn´ ər) *n.* way of conducting oneself; outward behavior

demise (dē mīz´) *n.* state of ceasing to exist; death

derisively (di rī´ siv lē) *adv.* in a mocking and ridiculing manner

derive (di rīv´) *v.* come to an understanding by reasoning; deduce or infer

derived (di rīvd´) *v.* reached an understanding by reasoning

desolate (des´ ə lit) *adj.* empty; barren

destitute (des´ tə tōōt´) *adj.* lacking the basic necessities of life; poverty-stricken

determination (di tʉr´ mi nā´ shən) *n.* firmness of purpose

detestable (dē tes´ tə bəl) *adj.* deserving of hate or scorn; offensive

detractors (dē trak´ tərz) *n.* those who discredit someone's accomplishments

dexterous (deks´ tər əs) *adj.* having or showing mental or physical skill

differentiate (dif´ ər en´ shē āt´) *v.* distinguish between

dignity (dig´ nə tē) *n.* quality of deserving respect and honor; self-respect

dilemma (di lem´ ə) *n.* difficult choice or situation

diligence (dil´ ə jəns) *n.* constant, careful effort

dire (dīr) *adj.* extremely serious; urgent

discern (di sʉrn´) *v.* tell the difference between two or more things; perceive

disconsolate (dis kän´ sə lit) *adj.* so unhappy that nothing brings comfort; miserable

discourse (dis´ kors) 1. *v.* speak (on a topic) formally and at length; 2. *n.* ongoing communication of ideas and information

disdain (dis dān´) *n.* disgust for something or someone; scorn

disembarked (dis´ im bärkt´) *v.* left a ship to go ashore

disreputable (dis rep´ yōō tə bəl) *adj.* not respectable; having or deserving a bad reputation

dissent (di sent´) *n.* refusal to accept a common belief or opinion; disagreement

distinct (di stiŋkt´) *adj.* clearly different; separate

distortion (di stôr´ shən) *n.* anything that shows something in an untrue way

dogged (dôg´ id) *adj.* stubborn

E

ebony (eb´ ə nē) *adj.* black

edifying (ed´ i fī´ iŋ) *adj.* instructive; morally or intellectually improving

efface (ə fās´) *v.* rub or blot out

elements (el´ ə mənts) *n.* components, parts, or qualities

elude (ē lōōd´) *v.* avoid; escape by quickness or cleverness

embodied (em bäd´ ēd) *v.* gave form to; made concrete

embodies (em bäd´ ēz) *v.* gives bodily form to; incarnates

emigrants (em´ i grənts) *n.* people who leave their country or region to settle elsewhere

emotion (i mō´ shən) *n.* state of feeling, such as love

empathy (em´ pə thē) *n.* state of sharing in another person's feelings

emphatic (em fat´ ik) *adj.* expressed, felt, or done with emphasis

empirical (em pir´ i kəl) *adj.* based on observation or experience

encroaching (en krōch´ iŋ) *adj.* intruding on, especially in a gradual way

endeavored (en dev´ ərd) *v.* tried to achieve a set goal

endure (en door´) *v.* hold up under pain or hardship

enduring (en door´ iŋ) *adj.* continuing for a long time; permanent

enlighten (en līt´ 'n) *v.* make clear through knowledge

entirety (en tī´ rə tē) *n.* completeness; wholeness

entreated (en trēt´ id) *v.* begged; pleaded with

episode (ep´ ə sōd´) *n.* event that is complete in itself but that forms part of a larger event

equilibrium (ē´ kwi lib´ rē əm) *n.* state of balance

establish (ə stab´ lish) *v.* order, ordain, or enact

estranged (e strānjd´) *adj.* kept apart; in the state of having had affection turn into indifference or hostility

eternal (ē tʉr´ nəl) *adj.* without beginning or end; everlasting

evade (ē vād´) *v.* escape; get away

evaluate (ē val´ yōō āt´) *v.* determine the worth or quality of something

evolve (ē välv´, -vôlv´) *v.* develop through gradual changes

excavation (eks´ kə vā´ shən) *n.* unearthing or digging up of something buried, such as an artifact

exorbitant (eg zôr′ bi tənt) *adj.* excessive

expectations (ek′ spek tā′ shənz) *n.* things looked forward to; feelings about how something should be or what should happen

expediency (ek spē′ dē ən sē) *n.* quality of being appropriate or suited to a particular goal

explanation (eks′ plə nā′ shən) *n.* clarifying statement

exploit (eks′ ploit′) *v.* take advantage of

expound (ek spound′) *v.* explain in detail

exterminated (ek stur′ mə nāt′ əd) *v.* destroyed completely; wiped out

extolled (ek stōld′) *adj.* praised

extricating (eks′ tri kāt′ iŋ) *v.* setting free; removing from a difficult situation

exuberance (eg zo͞o′ bər əns) *n.* good health and high spirits

F

factors (fak′ tərz) *n.* circumstances or conditions that bring about a result

falteringly (fôl′ tər iŋ lē) *adv.* spoken hesitatingly or with a wavering voice

fathom (fa*th*′ əm) *v.* understand thoroughly

fawned (fônd) *v.* flattered; acted with excessive concern for the wishes and moods of another, as a servant might

felled (feld) *v.* cut or knocked down

findings (fīn′ diŋz) *n.* conclusions reached after a consideration of facts or data

flaxen (flak′ sən) *adj.* light yellow

flick (flik) *v.* touch or hit lightly

flourishes (flur′ ish əs) *v.* grows vigorously; thrives

focal (fō′ kəl) *adj.* at the center of activity or attention

foreboding (fôr bōd′ iŋ) *n.* feeling that something bad will happen; premonition

functionary (fuŋk′ shə ner′ ē) *n.* person who performs a certain task; an official

fundamentally (fun′ də ment′ ə lē) *adv.* with regard to basic or central factors

furtively (fur′ tiv lē) *adj.* secretively; sneakily; stealthily

G

gauge (gāj) *v.* measure or determine size, amount, capacity or extent

gradients (grā′ dē ənts) *n.* series of gradual changes that go across a unit in a single direction

grave (grāv) *adj.* very serious and worrying

growth (grōth) *n.* process of developing

gullible (gul′ ə bəl) *adj.* easily tricked; too easily convinced

H

haphazardly (hap′ haz′ ərd lē) *adv.* in an unplanned or a disorganized way

harbor (här′ bər) *v.* house or shelter; be the place where something belongs

haste (hāst) *n.* quickness of motion; rapidity

haunches (hänch′ əz) *n.* hind pair of legs on a four-legged animal

heedless (hēd′ lis) *adj.* careless; thoughtless

hierarchy (hī′ ər är′ kē) *n.* group of people or things arranged in order of rank, grade, or class

highlight (hī′ līt′) *v.* give prominence to; emphasize

history (his′ tə rē) *n.* account of what has happened

honor (än′ ər) *n.* strong sense of right and wrong

hypocrisy (hi päk′ rə sē) *n.* act of saying one thing but doing another; pretense

I

idealistic (ī′ dē ə lis′ tik) *adj.* representing things as they should be rather than how they are

identity (ī den′ tə tē) *n.* condition of being oneself and not another

ignorance (ig′ nə rəns) *n.* lack of knowledge or education

illusion (i lo͞o′ zhən) *n.* belief not supported by facts; false sense of reality

illustrate (il′ ə strāt′) *v.* make clear; explain

imminent (im′ ə nənt) *adj.* about to happen

impediments (im ped′ ə mənts) *n.* obstructions; obstacles

impending (im pend′ iŋ) *adj.* about to happen

imperiously (im pir′ ē əs lē) *adv.* arrogantly

impervious (im pur′ vē əs) *adj.* not affected by (used with *to*)

impetuosity (im pech′ o͞o äs′ i tē) *n.* quality of acting suddenly, with great force and little thought; rashness

implicit (im plis′ it) *adj.* implied; suggested but not stated directly

implicitly (im plis′ it lē) *adv.* in a manner that suggests but does not directly state or reveal

impression (im presh′ ən) *n.* effect produced on the mind

improbable (im präb′ ə bəl) *adj.* not likely to happen or be true

inaudibly (in ôd′ ə blē) *adv.* in a way that cannot be heard

incessant (in ses′ ənt) *adj.* not stopping; constant

incredulity (in′ krə do͞o′ lə tē) *n.* unwillingness to believe

indigenous (in dij′ ə nəs) *adj.* existing or produced naturally in a region or country; native to a specific place

indignant (in dig′ nənt) *adj.* feeling anger, especially at injustice

indignation (in′ dig nā′ shən) *n.* anger that is a reaction to injustice or meanness

individual (in′ də vij′ o͞o əl) *adj.* relating to a single person or thing

inexorably (in eks′ ə rə blē) *adv.* without the possibility of being delayed or stopped

infirmity (in fur′ mə tē) *n.* weakness; physical defect

influence (in′ flo͞o əns) *n.* power of people to affect others

ingenuity (in′ jə no͞o′ ə tē) *n.* cleverness; creativity

ingratiating (in grā′ shē āt′ iŋ) *adj.* acting in a way intended to win someone's favor

inhabit (in hab′ it) *v.* live in

inherent (in hir′ ənt) *adj.* existing in someone or something as permanent and inseparable; inborn

initial (i nish′ əl) *adj.* first; at the beginning

innuendo (in′ yo͞o en′ dō) *n.* indirect statement, insult, or accusation; insinuation

insight (in′ sīt′) *n.* clear idea of the nature of things

instilled (in stild′) *v.* introduced or taught an idea, feeling, or principle little by little

insurrection (in′ sə rek′ shən) *n.* rebellion

integrity (in teg′ rə tē) *n.* quality or state of being of sound moral principle; uprightness

interact (in′ tər akt′) *v.* relate to one another; affect another

interject (in′ tər jekt′) *v.* throw in between; interrupt with

interminable (in tur′ mi nə bəl) *adj.* endless or seemingly endless

interpretation (in tur′ prə tā′ shən) *n.* someone's perception or explanation of the meaning of something

interred (in turd′) *v.* buried (said of a dead body)

intervened (in′ tər vēnd′) *v.* came between conflicting people or groups

intricate (in′ tri kit) *adj.* having many parts; complex

inverted (in vurt′ id) *adj.* in the opposite or reverse position

invincible (in vin′ sə bəl) *adj.* incapable of being defeated; unbeatable

irascible (i ras′ ə bəl) *adj.* irritable

irreproachable (ir′ i prō′ chə bəl) *adj.* above criticism

isolation (ī′ sə lā′ shən) *n.* state of aloneness or separation from others

J

jauntiness (jônt′ ē nəs) *n.* carefree, easy attitude

jeered (jird) *v.* made fun of; mocked; taunted

juxtaposes (juks′ tə pōz′ iz) *v.* places side by side or close together

K

keenest (kēn′ ist) *adj.* sharpest; most cutting

knowledge (näl′ ij) *n.* awareness and understanding of information

L

lamentation (lam′ ən tā′ shən) *n.* act of crying out in grief; wailing

language (laŋ′ gwij) 1. *n.* system used for expressing or communicating; 2. *n.* word choice

languid (laŋ′ gwid) *adj.* without energy

laureate (lôr′ ē it) *n.* person on whom honor or distinction is conferred

lavished (lav′ isht) *v.* gave with extreme generosity

lease (lēs) *n.* contract by which something is rented for a specified period of time; rental

legacies (leg′ ə sēz) *n.* money, property, or position left in a will to someone

legendary (lej′ ən der′ ē) *adj.* extraordinary; memorable

lofty (lôf′ tē) *adj.* elevated in rank or character; noble

looming (lo͞om′ iŋ) 1. *adj.* appearing unclearly but in a threatening form; 2. *adj.* threatening to occur

lucidity (lo͞o sid′ ə tē) *n.* quality of being clear; readily understood

lucrative (lo͞o′ krə tiv) *adj.* producing wealth; profitable

M

maintain (mān tān′) *v.* keep or keep up; continue with

maligned (mə līnd′) *adj.* spoken ill of

manifest (man′ ə fest′) *v.* make clear; show plainly; reveal

manifestation (man′ ə fes tā′ shən) *n.* something made clear or evident, or shown plainly

manipulate (mə nip′ yo͞o lāt′) *v.* control by use of influence, often in an unfair way

manipulated (mə nip′ yo͞o lāt′ id) *v.* managed or controlled through clever moves

marginal (mär′ jə nəl) *adj.* borderline; between good enough and not good enough

martial (mär′ shəl) *adj.* warlike

meaning (mē′ niŋ) *n.* ideas that are indicated or expressed; significance

meditates (med′ ə tāts′) *v.* thinks deeply

melancholy (mel′ ən käl′ ē) *adj.* sad; depressed

mirth (murth) *n.* joyfulness; merriment

misconstrued (mis′ kən stro͞od′) *v.* misinterpreted

misinterpret (mis′ in tur′ prit) *v.* understand incorrectly

modified (mäd′ ə fīd′) *v.* changed; altered partially

momentous (mō men′ təs) *adj.* important; of great significance

monotonously (mə nät′ ′n əs lē) *adv.* in a dull, unvarying way

motive (mōt′ iv) *n.* incentive; reason a person takes a particular action

multitudes (mul′ tə to͞odz) *n.* crowds; large number of people

N

negotiate (ni gō′ shē āt′) *v.* bargain with the hope of reaching an agreement

neural (no͝or′ əl) *adj.* related to nerves or the nervous system

nevertheless (nev´ ər *thə* les´) *adv.* in spite of that; however

nomadic (nō mad´ ik) *adj.* moving from place to place; without a permanent home

nonchalantly (nän´ shə länt´ lē) *adv.* casually; indifferently

nostalgic (näs tal´ jik) *adj.* feeling a longing for something long ago or far away

O

obliterated (ə blit´ ər āt´ id) *adj.* destroyed; wiped out

oblivious (ə bliv´ ē əs) *adj.* unaware

opined (ō pīnd´) *v.* stated an opinion

oppose (ə pōz´) *v.* set against; disagree with

oppressive (ə pres´ iv) *adj.* causing great discomfort; distressing

oratory (ôr´ ə tôr´ ē) *n.* public speaking; strategies used in such speaking

ornate (ôr nāt´) *adj.* heavily ornamented or adorned, sometimes to excess

overall (ō´ vər ôl´) *adj.* in general

overcome (ō´ vər kum´) *v.* master or prevail over

P

pallor (pal´ ər) *n.* lack of color; unnatural paleness

paradigm (par´ ə dīm´) *n.* model; example

parameters (pə ram´ ət ərz) *n.* boundaries or limits

pastiche (pas tēsh´) *n.* artistic work made up of parts taken from different sources

perpetually (pər pech´ o͞o əl ē) *adv.* continuing forever; constantly

persevere (pur´ sə vir´) *v.* continue despite difficulty; persist

perspective (pər´ spek´ tiv) 1. *n.* how one sees things; viewpoint. 2. *n.* spatial relationships of objects within a scene as viewed from a particular distance, location, or angle

phenomena (fə näm´ ə nə) *n.* events, circumstances, or experiences that are apparent to the senses and can be scientifically described

physiological (fiz´ ē ə läj´ i kəl) *adj.* relating to the branch of biology that deals with the vital processes of living organisms

piety (pī´ ə tē) *n.* loyalty and devotion to family, the divine, or some other object of respect

plague (plāg) *v.* pester; harass; torment

plane (plān) *n.* flat, two-dimensional surface

plausibility (plô´ zə bil´ i tē) *n.* believability; seeming truth

poignant (poin´ yənt) *adj.* emotionally affecting; touching; moving

policies (päl´ ə sēz) *n.* principles, plans, or rules as pursued by a government or organization

portentous (pôr ten´ təs) *adj.* ominous; giving signs of evil to come

practical (prak´ ti kəl) *adj.* usable; workable; useful and sensible

pragmatism (prag´ mə tiz´ əm) *n.* attitude or outlook addressing actual practices, not theory or speculation; practicality

precision (prē sizh´ ən) *n.* exactness; accuracy

premise (prem´ is) *n.* statement or idea that serves as the basis for an argument

presage (prē säj´) *v.* give a warning sign about a future event

presume (prē zo͞om´) *v.* rely too much on; take advantage of

presumptuous (prē zump´ cho͞o əs) *adj.* overstepping appropriate bounds; too bold

pretense (prē tens´) *n.* a pretending; a false show of something

primacy (prī´ mə sē) *n.* state of being first in time, order, rank, etc.

primary (prī´ mer´ ē) *adj.* first; that from which others are derived; basic

principles (prin´ sə pəls) *n.* rules for right conduct; truths, laws, doctrines, or motivating forces upon which others are based

privileged (priv´ lijd) *adj.* not subject to the rules; special

prodigious (prō dij´ əs) *adj.* of great size or power

progress (präg´ res) *n.* development; improvement

prone (prōn) *adj.* lying or leaning face downward

prophesy (präf´ ə sī´) *v.* predict what will happen

provocative (prə väk´ ə tiv) *adj.* exciting; stimulating

purified (pyoor´ ə fīd´) *v.* rid of impurities or pollution; made pure

Q

quench (kwench) *v.* satisfy; fulfill the needs or desires of something

question (kwes´ chən) *v.* express uncertainty about; ask

R

radical (rad´ i kəl) *adj.* drastic; complete; extreme

rash (rash) *adj.* too hasty in speech or action; reckless

reality (rē al´ ə tē) *n.* quality of being true to life

realizations (rē´ ə li zā´ shənz) 1. *n.* concepts or truths suddenly understood upon an experience or event; 2. *n.* things made real; things made fully understood

reciprocity (res´ ə präs´ ə tē) *n.* relations of exchange; interdependence

reconciliation (rek´ ən sil´ ē ā´ shən) *n.* restoration of friendship and harmony

recurrent (ri kur´ ənt) *adj.* happening again and again

reflect (ri flekt´) *v.* think seriously about something

regarded (ri gärd´ əd) *adj.* taken into account as; considered

regulate (reg´ yə lāt´) *v.* control or direct according to a rule or principle

rejoiced (ri joist´) *v.* showed happiness

rejuvenation (ri jo͞o´ və nā´ shən) *n.* state of becoming new, youthful, or energetic again; revitalization

relatable (ri lāt´ ə bəl) *adj.* familiar; recognizable

reminiscent (rem´ ə nis´ ənt) *adj.* tending to remind; suggesting

renditions (ren dish´ ənz) *n.* performances or interpretations

replication (rep´ li kā´ shən) *n.* duplicate; reproduction

represent (rep´ ri zent´) *v.* present a likeness or image of

resistance (ri zis´ təns) *n.* act of opposing or withstanding

resolute (rez´ ə lo͞ot´) *adj.* showing a fixed purpose

resolution (rez´ ə lo͞o´ shən) *n.* strong determination; a plan or decision

resolve (ri zälv´, -zôlv) *v.* reach a conclusion or decision

resonate (rez´ ə nāt´) *v.* resound or echo; be in sympathy with

respective (ri spek´ tiv) *adj.* as relates separately to two or more people or things

respond (ri spänd´) *v.* answer

responsibility (ri spon´ sə bil´ ə tē) *n.* state of being answerable or accountable; obligation

reveling (rev´ əl iŋ) *v.* taking great pleasure or delight

reverence (rev´ ə rəns) *n.* respect or honor that is shown

reviews (ri vyo͞oz´) 1. *v.* surveys in thought, speech, or writing; 2. *v.* gives an evaluation of

reviled (ri vīld´) *v.* spoke poorly or harshly of

revise (ri vīz´) *v.* reconsider; modify

S

sacrifice (sak´ rə fīs´) *v.* give up

sated (sāt´ əd) *adj.* satisfied; provided with more than enough

scale (skāl) 1. *n.* proportion that a painting or sketch bears relative to the real object or scene; 2. *n.* proportion

scrutinized (skro͞ot´ 'n īzd) *v.* examined carefully

secular (sek´ yə lər) *adj.* of worldly, as opposed to religious, matters

self-expression (self ek spresh´ən) *n.* assertion or sharing of one's personality or emotions

selflessness (self´ lis nes) *n.* being devoted to others' interests rather than one's own

sensibility (sen´ sə bil´ ə tē) *n.* intellectual, moral, or artistic values and perceptions

serenity (sə ren´ ə tē) *n.* state of calm or peace

servile (sʉr´ vīl) *adj.* slavelike; humbly submissive to authority

signal (sig´ nəl) *v.* indicate; make known

simulation (sim´ yo͞o lā´ shən) *n.* duplication or reproduction of certain characteristics or conditions from an original source; model or representation

skeptically (skep´ ti kəl lē) *adv.* with doubt; questioningly

slight (slīt) *v.* treat with disrespect or indifference

social (sō shəl) *adj.* of or related to human society or organization

sonorous (sä´ nôr əs) *adj.* having a rich or impressive sound

spare (sper) *adj.* lean; thin

sparse (spärs) *adj.* thinly spread; not plentiful

spectacle (spek´ tə kəl) *n.* strange or remarkable sight

staidness (stād´ nəs) *n.* state of being settled; calm

stamina (stam´ ə nə) *n.* resistance to fatigue or hardship; endurance

stance (stans) *n.* way one stands, especially the placement of the feet

stark (stärk) *adj.* rigorous, harsh; severe

stereotype (ster´ ē ə tīp´) *n.* overly broad and often incorrect notion of a group

strife (strīf) *n.* struggle; conflict

struggle (strug´ əl) *v.* make great effort; face difficulty

subdued (səb do͞od´) *adj.* quiet; lacking energy

subjective (səb jek´ tiv) *adj.* personal; based on or influenced by a person's feelings or point of view

subordinate (sə bôrd´ 'n it) *adj.* below another in importance or rank

subtle (sut´ 'l) *adj.* fine; delicate

subversion (səb vʉr´ zhən) *n.* activity meant to overthrow something established; rebellion

successive (sək ses´ iv) *adj.* following one after another in sequence

succinct (sək siŋkt´) *adj.* clearly and briefly stated

succumb (sə kum´) *v.* yield to

sullen (sul´ ən) *adj.* gloomy and showing resentment

sumptuous (sump´ cho͞o əs) *adj.* lavish

surmise (sər mīz´) *n.* guess; idea based on evidence that is not conclusive

surpass (sər pas´) *v.* go beyond in degree; exceed

T

temperate (tem´ pər it) *adj.* mild; kept within limits

tempering (tem´ pər iŋ) *n.* changing to make more suitable, usually by mixing with something

tenacious (tə nā´ shəs) *adj.* persistent in seeking a goal

tentative (ten´ tə tiv) *adj.* hesitant; not confident

tenuous (ten´ yo͞o əs) *adj.* flimsy; not strong

theorize (thē´ ə rīz´) *v.* speculate

threshold (thresh´ ōld´) 1. *n.* bottom of a doorway; 2. *n.* entrance or a point of beginning

toil (toil) *n.* hard, tiring work

trajectory (trə jek´ tə rē) *n.* curve or surface that follows a particular path

transcends (tran sendz´) *v.* goes beyond the limits of; exceeds

transformative (trans fôrm´ ə tiv) *adj.* capable of changing something to another shape, structure, or character

tremulous (trem´ yo͞o ləs) *adj.* trembling; quivering; timid; fearful

tumult (to͞o´ mult) *n.* noisy commotion

tyrant (tī´ rənt) *n.* cruel, oppressive ruler; despot

U

ulterior (ul tir´ ē ər) *adj.* hidden; beyond what is openly stated or implied

understanding (un´ dər stan´ diŋ) *n.* power to recognize and comprehend

unifies (yo͞o´ nə fiz´) *v.* combines into one

unify (yo͞o´ nə fi´) *v.* combine into one

universal (yo͞o´ nə vʉr´ səl) *adj.* existing in all things

unorthodox (un ôr´ thə däks´) *adj.* not typical; breaking with tradition

urban (ʉr´ bən) *adj.* relating to, or characteristic of, a city

V

vagaries (vā´ gər ēz) *n.* erratic or unpredictable actions; whims

vantage (van´ tij) *n.* position or place from which to see

venerable (ven´ ər ə bəl) *adj.* worthy of respect because of age or character

veracious (və rā´ shəs) *adj.* truthful; honest

verbal (vʉr´ bəl) *adj.* of, relating to, or consisting of words

viewpoint (vyo͞o´ point´) *n.* attitude from which situations are considered and judged

vigorously (vig´ ər əs lē) *adv.* with full vital strength

W

wither (wi*th*´ ər) *v.* dry up; shrivel from loss of moisture

worldview (wʉrld´ vyo͞o´) *n.* comprehensive personal philosophy of the world and of human life

wrathfully (rath´ fəl lē) *adv.* with intense anger

writhe (rī*th*) *v.* make twisting or turning movements as from pain

Spanish Glossary

El vocabulario académico aparece en **azul**.

A

absolute / absoluto *adj.* libre de restricción o limitación; completo

abstract / abstracto *adj.* no relacionado a un objeto material; no concreto

accessible / accesible *adj.* de fácil acceso o entrada

accomplices / cómplices *s.* personas que ayudan a otros a cometer un crimen

account / recuento *s.* reporte, descripción o historia

adamant / obstinado *adj.* que no cede; inflexible; firme

adapt / adaptar *v.* cambiar o ajustar

adaptation / adaptación *s.* modificación; en la literatura, una versión de otra obra, con frecuencia representada en otro género

adulation / adulación *s.* grandes o excesivos elogios; intensa admiración

adversity / adversidad *s.* estado de dificultad o infortunio

affable / afable *adj.* agradable; amistoso

affiliation / afiliación *s.* membresía dentro de una organización; conexión; asociación

affront / afrenta *s.* insulto abierto

align / alinear *v.* organizar en línea recta; poner de acuerdo

allay / aliviar *v.* mitigar; reducir; calmar

alternative / alternativo *adj.* que refleja otras opciones

ambient / ambiente *adj.* que rodea un cuerpo; en todos los lados

amenable / receptivo *adj.* sensible; abierto

amiably / amigablemente *adv.* de manera jovial y amistosa

analyses / análisis *s.* exámenes detallados

anguish / angustia *s.* sufrimiento extremo, como de pena o dolor

anticipate / anticipar *v.* aguardar con interés

apathy / apatía *s.* falta de interés o sentimiento

application / aplicación *s.* el acto de poner algo en uso

apprehension / aprensión *s.* sentimiento ansioso; temor

arduously / arduamente *adv.* con gran dificultad; laboriosamente

arid/árido *adj.* completamente seco; sin vida

articulate / articular *v.* decir claramente

aspects / aspectos *s.* partes componentes o cualidades; elementos

assertion / afirmación *s.* declaración positiva

associated / asoció *v.* unió; conectó

attributed / atribuyó *v.* consideró como una característica o cualidad de una persona, un lugar o una cosa

attributes / atributos *s.* características de una persona o cosa

audaciously / audazmente *adv.* de manera intrépida

auditory / auditivo *adj.* relacionado con la audición o los órganos de la audición

augmented / aumentado *adj.* hecho más grande; realzado

auroras / auroras *s.* fenómeno atmosférico que consiste en tiras o arcos de luz

awareness / conciencia *s.* conocimiento; entendimiento de algo

B

background / antecedentes *s.* condiciones que rodean o preceden a algo

banality / banalidad *s.* condición de superficial o de no tener importancia

baseline / punto de referencia *s.* cantidad, base o nivel original con el cual otros artículos pueden ser medidos o comparados

bias / prejuicio *s.* parcialidad; renuencia a considerar puntos de vista alternativos

bore / portó *v.* cargó

brandished / blandió *v.* mostró, esgrimió o batió de manera amenazante o triunfante

brazen / descarado *adj.* sin vergüenza; audaz

buffer / amortiguar *v.* aminorar un golpe; suavizar

C

cajoling / lisonjeo *s.* persuasión de alguien con lisonjas

calamity / calamidad *s.* desgracia terrible; desastre

candid / candoroso *adj.* franco; directo

captures / capta *v.* describe bien

change / cambiar *v.* convertirse en algo distinto; transformar

character / temperamento *s.* fortaleza moral; autodisciplina

chastisement / castigo *s.* crítica severa; corrección

choleric / colérico *adj.* malgeniado; irascible

clenching / apretando *v.* cerrando; agarrando firmemente

commemorates / conmemora *v.* honra la memoria de

commencement / ceremonia de graduación *s.* ceremonia en la que se gradúan estudiantes y se otorgan títulos, especialmente en las universidades

commiserate / compadecer *v.* apiadarse de; tener lástima por

complex / complejo *s.* conjunto de unidades, tales como casas u otros edificios, que juntos conforman una sección o grupo

complexities / complejidades *s.* algo intrincado; complicaciones

complexity / complejidad *s.* sofisticación; profundidad; dificultad

comprehend / comprender *v.* captar mentalmente; entender

compromise / acuerdo *s.* convenio donde ambas partes ceden algo

concession / concesión *s.* abandono de una posición u opinión a favor de una contraria

concrete / concreto *adj.* algo que puede ser observado a través de los sentidos; específico; tangible

condemned / condenado *v.* que ha sido declarado culpable de fechorías; sentenciado por un juez

conduct / conducta *s.* la forma de actuar de una persona; comportamiento

configuration / configuración *s.* disposición de partes; patrón

confirm / confirmar *v.* establecer la verdad o precisión de algo

confounded / aturdido *adj.* que se siente confundido

confrontation / confrontación *s.* choque de fuerzas o ideas

confusion / confusión *s.* estado de desorden o distracción; falta de claridad o entendimiento

conjured / invocó *v.* llamó como por acto de magia

connection / conexión *s.* relación entre cosas

conspicuous / conspicuo *adj.* fácil de ver

constricting / restrictivo *adj.* que impide la libertad de movimiento; limitante

contemporary / contemporáneo *adj.* del presente o tiempos recientes

contempt / desprecio *s.* desdén; la actitud de alguien que menosprecia a algo o a alguien

contested / disputó *v.* que intentó refutar o invalidar algo; impugnó

context / contexto 1. *s.* circunstancias que forman el marco de un evento; 2. *s.* situación en la que se encuentra algo

contradicted / contradijo *v.* hizo una declaración que refutó o se opuso a otra declaración previa

contradiction / contradicción *s.* declaración que se opone directamente a otra

contrived / forzado *adj.* artificial; que no ocurre naturalmente

convalesce / convalecer *v.* recuperar fuerza y salud

converge / converger *v.* unirse en un punto específico

convey / transmitir *v.* comunicar o dar a conocer

convoluted / intrincado *adj.* retorcido de manera complicada

counsel / consejo *s.* orientación; discusión

countenance / semblante *s.* rostro; la expresión de una cara que muestra la naturaleza de una persona

counterparts / equivalente *s.* persona o cosa que corresponde a o se parece a otra

courage / valor *s.* cualidad que permite que alguien enfrente una dificultad o peligro

credulity / credulidad *s.* tendencia a creer con demasiada facilidad

criteria / criterios *s.* estándares o reglas por las cuales algo puede ser medido o juzgado

curdled / cuajó *v.* se agrió o se dañó

customary / habitual *adj.* prácticas comunes; lo usual

D

debate / debatir *v.* argumentar o discutir

deference / deferencia *s.* el ceder respetuosamente a las ideas, deseos, etc. de otra persona

deflects / desvía *v.* hace que algo dé vuelta o doble hacia un lado

defunct / difunto *adj.* que ya no está en uso o existencia; muerto

dejectedly / abatidamente *adv.* de forma desalentada o deprimida

deliver / entregar *v.* dar algo a alguien; hacer entrega de algo

delusion / ilusión *s.* creencia errónea que se mantiene a pesar de haber evidencia en contra

demeanor / comportamiento *s.* manera de comportarse; conducta

demise / muerte *s.* el acto de dejar de existir; fallecimiento

derisively / burlonamente *adv.* de manera irónica y ridiculizante

derive / derivar *v.* deducir; inferir

derived / derivó *v.* comprendió mediante razonamiento

desolate / desolado *adj.* vacío; solitario

destitute / indigente *adj.* carente de las necesidades básicas de la vida; de gran pobreza

determination / determinación *s.* firmeza de propósito

detestable / detestable *adj.* que merece odio o desprecio; ofensivo

detractors / detractores *s.* aquellos que desacreditan los logros de una persona

dexterous / diestro *adj.* que tiene o muestra destreza mental o física

differentiate / diferenciar *v.* distinguir entre

dignity / dignidad *s.* cualidad de merecer respeto y honor; respeto de sí mismo

dilemma / dilema *s.* situación o decisión difícil

diligence / diligencia *s.* esfuerzo constante y esmerado

dire / abrumador *adj.* sumamente serio; urgente

discern / discernir *v.* distinguir la diferencia entre dos o más cosas; percibir

disconsolate / desconsolado *adj.* tan infeliz que nada le reconforta; miserable

discourse / disertar 1. *v.* hablar (sobre un tema) formal y detalladamente; 2. *s.* comunicación contínua de ideas e información

disdain / desdeño *s.* disgusto por alguien o algo; desprecio

disembarked / desembarcó *v.* abandonó un buque para ir a tierra

disreputable / desacreditado *adj.* no respetable; que tiene o merece mala reputación

dissent / desacuerdo *s.* renuencia a aceptar una creencia u opinión común; desavenencia

distinct / distinto *adj.* claramente diferente; separado

distortion / distorsión *s.* cualquier cosa que muestra algo de manera engañosa

dogged / obstinado *adj.* terco

E

ebony / ébano *adj.* de color negro

edifying / edificante *adj.* educativo; que permite que la persona mejore moral o intelectualmente

efface / tachar *v.* borrar o suprimir

elements / elementos *s.* componentes; partes o cualidades

elude / eludir *v.* evitar; escapar con celeridad o astucia

embodied / materializó *v.* dio forma a; concretó

embodies / encarna *v.* da forma corporal; representa

emigrants / emigrantes *s.* personas que abandonan su país o región para establecerse en otro lugar

emotion / emoción *s.* sentimiento fuerte, como el amor

empathy / empatía *s.* acto de compartir los sentimientos de otra persona

emphatic / enfático *adj.* expresado, sentido o hecho con énfasis

empirical / empírico *adj.* basado en la observación o experiencia

encroaching / invadiendo *adj.* cometiendo una intrusión, especialmente de manera gradual

endeavored / se esforzó por *v.* trató de alcanzar una meta fijada

endure / soportar *v.* aguantar con dolor o penuria

enduring / duradero *adj.* que continúa por un largo tiempo; permanente

enlighten / ilustrar *v.* aclarar algo mediante el conocimiento

entirety / totalidad *s.* plenitud; por completo

entreated / suplicó *v.* imploró; rogó

episode / episodio *s.* evento que es completo en sí mismo pero que forma parte de un evento más grande

equilibrium / equilibrio *s.* estado de balance

establish / establecer *v.* fundar; crear; ordenar

estranged / apartado *adj.* que se mantiene separado; que está en una condición en la que el afecto se torna en indiferencia u hostilidad

eternal / eterno *adj.* sin principio ni fin; perpetuo

evade / evadir *v.* huir de; escapar

evaluate / evaluar *v.* determinar el valor de algo

evolve / evolucionar *v.* desarrollarse a través de cambios graduales

excavation / excavación *s.* perforación para desenterrar algo, como por ejemplo un artefacto

exorbitant / exorbitante *adj.* más allá de lo razonable; excesivo

expectations / expectativas *s.* cosas que se esperan; sentimientos acerca de cómo debe ser algo o cómo debe pasar algo

expediency / conveniencia *s.* cualidad de ser apropiado o adecuado para un logro particular

explanation / explicación *s.* declaración aclaratoria

exploit /explotar *v.* tomar ventaja de algo o alguien

expound / enunciar *v.* explicar en detalle

exterminated / exterminado *v.* destruido completamente; eliminado

extolled / elogió *adj.* halagó

extricating / liberando *v.* desenredando; sacando de una situación difícil

exuberance / exuberancia *s.* buena salud; vivacidad

F

factors / factores *s.* circunstancias o condiciones que llevan a un resultado

falteringly / de manera titubeante *adv.* dicho con titubeo o con voz trémula

fathom / desentrañar *v.* comprender a fondo

fawned / aduló *v.* lisonjeó; actuó con preocupación excesiva por los deseos y antojos de otro, como lo haría un sirviente

felled / derribó *v.* cortó o tumbó

findings / hallazgos *s.* conclusiones alcanzadas luego de considerar hechos o datos

flaxen / rubio *adj.* amarillo claro

flick / golpear ligeramente *v.* tocar suavemente

flourishes / florece *v.* que crece vigorosamente; que prospera

focal / focal *adj.* en el centro de actividad o atención

foreboding / presentimiento *s.* una sensación de que algo malo ocurrirá; premonición

functionary / funcionario *s.* persona que realiza una determinada labor; un oficial

fundamentally / fundamentalmente *adv.* que se relaciona con factores básicos o centrales

furtively / furtivamente *adv.* ocultamente; secretamente; sigilosamente

G

gauge / aforar *v.* medir el tamaño, cantidad, alcance o capacidad de algo

gradients / gradientes *s.* serie de cambios graduales que atraviesan una unidad en una sola dirección

grave / grave *adj.* que requiere de consideración seria; importante e inquietante

growth / crecimiento *s.* proceso de desarrollarse

gullible / crédulo *adj.* fácil de engañar; fácil de convencer

H

haphazardly / al azar *adv.* de manera no planeada o desorganizada

harbor / alberguer *v.* amparar; refugiar

haste / apuro *s.* rapidez de movimiento; prisa

haunches / ancas *s.* mitades laterales de la parte trasera de un animal de cuatro patas

heedless / desatento *adj.* descuidado; imprudente

hierarchy / jerarquía *s.* grupo de personas o cosas organizadas por rango, grado o clase

highlight / destacar *v.* darle prominencia a algo; enfatizar

history / historia *s.* relato de lo que ha pasado

honor / honor *s.* fuerte sentido del bien y del mal

hypocrisy / hipocresía *s.* acto de fingir ser o sentir lo que uno no es o siente

I

idealistic / idealista *adj.* que representa las cosas como deberían ser en lugar de como son en realidad

identity / identidad *s.* cualidades de una persona que representan lo que es

ignorance / ignorancia *s.* falta de conocimiento o educación

illusion / ilusión *s.* creencia no sustentada por hechos; falso sentido de la realidad

illustrate / ilustrar *v.* aclarar; explicar

imminent / inminente *adj.* a punto de suceder

impediments / impedimentos *s.* cosas que retrasan a alguien o a algo, o que obstaculizan; barreras

impending / inminente *adj.* a punto de suceder

imperiously / imperiosamente *adv.* arrogantemente

impervious / impenetrable *adj.* que no lo afecta algo

impetuosity / impetuosidad *s.* calidad de actuar repentinamente, con gran fuerza y poca consideración; temeridad

implicit / implícito *adj.* inferido en lugar de ser expresado directamente

implicitly / implícitamente *adv.* en una manera que sugiere algo en lugar de expresarlo directamente

impression / impresión *s.* efecto que se produce sobre la mente

improbable / improbable *adj.* que no es factible que suceda o sea verdad

inaudibly / inaudiblemente *adv.* de forma que no se pueda oír

incessant / incesante *adj.* que no se detiene; constante

incredulity / incredulidad *s.* renuencia a creer

indigenous / autóctono *adj.* que existe o es producido naturalmente en una región o en un país; nativo de un lugar específico

indignant / indignado *adj.* que siente ira, especialmente por una injusticia

indignation / indignación *s.* ira en reacción a la injusticia o mezquindad

individual / individual *adj.* relativo a una sola persona o cosa

inexorably / inexorablemente *adv.* sin la posibilidad de que lo atrasen o detengan; inalterablemente

infirmity / enfermedad *s.* debilidad; defecto físico

influence / influencia *s.* poder de algunas personas de afectar a los demás

ingenuity / ingenio *s.* inventiva; creatividad

ingratiating / congraciado *adj.* que actúa de cierta manera para ganarse el favor de alguien

inhabit / habitar *v.* residir en

inherent / inherente *adj.* que existe en alguien o en algo de manera permanente o inseparable; innato

initial / inicial *adj.* primero

innuendo / alusión *s.* insulto o acusación indirecta; insinuación

insight / discernimiento *s.* idea clara de la naturaleza de las cosas

instilled / inculcado *v.* instruyó poco a poco de ideas, sentimientos o principios

insurrection / insurrección *s.* rebelión

integrity / integridad *s.* cualidad o estado de tener sólidos principios morales; rectitud

interact / interactuar *v.* relacionarse entre sí; afectar el uno al otro

interject / interrumpir *v.* interponer

interminable / interminable *adj.* sin fin o que da la impresión de que no tiene fin

interpretation / interpretación *s.* explicación del significado de algo

interred / sepultó *v.* enterró (dícese de un cuerpo)

intervened / intermedió *v.* se interpuso entre personas en conflicto procurando reconciliarlas

intricate / intrincado *adj.* que tiene muchas partes; complejo

inverted / invertido *adj.* en posición contraria o reversa

invincible / invencible *adj.* incapaz de ser derrotado; imbatible

irascible / irascible *adj.* irritable

irreproachable / irreprochable *adj.* por encima de la crítica

isolation / aislamiento *s.* condición de estar solo o aislado de los demás

J

jauntiness / garbo *s.* actitud libre y desenvuelta

jeered / burló *v.* escarneció; mofó; ridiculizó

juxtaposes / yuxtapone *v.* ubica lado a lado o juntos

K

keenest / más agudo *adj.* el más penetrante; cortante

knowledge / conocimiento *s.* conciencia y comprensión de información

L

lamentation / lamento *s.* acto de vociferar con aflicción; gemido; llanto

language / lenguaje 1. *s.* sistema usado para expresarse o comunicar; 2. *s.* selección de palabras

languid / lánguido *adj.* falto de energía

laureate / laureado *s.* persona a la cual se le confiere honor o distinción

lavished / derrochó *v.* dio con extrema generosidad

lease / arrendamiento *s.* contrato mediante el cual algo es alquilado por un plazo determinado de tiempo; alquiler

legacies / legados *s.* dinero, propiedades o posición que se deja a alguien en un testamento

legendary / legendario *adj.* extraordinario; memorable

lofty / eminente *adj.* elevado en rango o temperamento; noble

looming / que aparece 1. *adj.* que se asoma en forma vaga, indistinta, pero amenazante; 2. *adj.* que amenaza con ocurrir

lucidity / lucidez *s.* cualidad de ser fácilmente entendido

lucrative / lucrativo *adj.* que produce riqueza; rentable

M

maintain / mantener *v.* conservar o continuar haciendo algo; seguir

maligned / difamado *adj.* que se habló mal de

manifest / manifestar *v.* aclarar; mostrar; revelar

manifestation / manifestación *s.* algo claro o evidente o mostrado directamente; aparición

manipulate / manipular *v.* controlar mediante el uso de influencia, a menudo de forma injusta

manipulated / manipuló *v.* que manejó o controló mediante jugadas astutas

marginal / marginal *adj.* que está al margen; cerca del borde

martial / marcial *adj.* relativo a la guerra

meaning / significado *s.* ideas indicadas o expresadas; el sentido de algo

meditates / medita *v.* que piensa profundamente

melancholy / melancólico *adj.* triste; deprimido

mirth / regocijo *s.* alegría; júbilo

misconstrued / malinterpretó *v.* entendió mal

misinterpret / malinterpretar *v.* no entender correctamente

modified / modificó *v.* cambió; alteró ligeramente

momentous / trascendental *adj.* grave; de gran importancia

monotonously / monótonamente *adv.* de forma aburrida e invariable

motive / motivo *s.* lo que causa que una persona actúe de cierta manera

multitudes / multitudes *s.* gran cantidad de personas o cosas

N

negotiate / negociar *v.* pactar con la esperanza de llegar a un acuerdo

neural / neural *adj.* relacionado con los nervios o el sistema nervioso

nevertheless / sin embargo *adv.* a pesar de eso; no obstante

nomadic / nómada *adj.* que se traslada de un lugar a otro; sin hogar permanente

nonchalantly / indiferentemente *adv.* casualmente; imperturbablemente

nostalgic / nostálgico *adj.* que añora algo que pasó hace mucho tiempo o que está muy lejos

O

obliterated / arrasado *adj.* destruido; eliminado

oblivious / distraído *adj.* absorto

opined / opinó *v.* presentó una opinión

oppose / oponer *v.* ponerse en contra; estar en desacuerdo con

oppressive / opresivo *adj.* que causa gran incomodidad; angustiante

oratory / oratoria *s.* acto de hablar en público; estrategias usadas en disertaciones

ornate / ornamentado *adj.* adornado en exceso; decorado

overall / en general *adj.* en total

overcome / vencer *v.* conquistar o prevalecer sobre

P

pallor / palor *s.* carencia de color; palidez poco natural

paradigm / paradigma *s.* modelo; ejemplo

parameters / parámetros *s.* límites

pastiche / pastiche *s.* trabajo artístico realizado con partes tomadas de distintas procedencias

perpetually / perpetuamente *adv.* que continua para siempre; constantemente

persevere / perseverar *v.* continuar a pesar de dificultades u obstáculos; persistir

perspective / perspectiva 1. *s.* como uno ve las cosas; punto de vista; 2. *s* relación espacial de los objetos dentro de una escena, vistos desde una cierta distancia, posición o ángulo

phenomena / fenómenos *s.* eventos, circunstancias o experiencias que son aparentes a los sentidos y que pueden ser descritos científicamente

physiological / fisiológico *adj.* con relación a la rama de la biología que trata sobre los procesos vitales de los organismos vivos

piety / piedad *s.* lealtad y devoción hacia la familia, lo divino o algún otro objeto de respeto

plague / importunar *v.* molestar; fastidiar; atormentar

plane / plano *s.* superficie plana bidimensional

plausibility / admisibilidad *s.* credibilidad; verdad aparente

poignant / conmovedor *adj.* que afecta emocionalmente; que conmueve; desgarrador

policies / políticas *s.* principios, planes o reglas que son seguidos por un gobierno o una organización

portentous / portentoso *adj.* ominoso; que da señales de cosas nefastas por venir

practical / práctico *adj.* de fácil uso; útil y sensible

pragmatism / pragmatismo *s.* actitud que considera las consecuencias reales e inmediatas, que no se basa en teoría ni especulación; funcionalidad

precision / precisión *s.* exactitud

premise / premisa *s.* declaración o idea que sirve como base en un argumento

presage /presagio *v.* dar una señal que advierte sobre un suceso en el futuro

presume / presumir *v.* depender demasiado de; abusar de

presumptuous / descarado *adj.* que traspasa los límites de lo correcto; demasiado imprudente

pretense / pretensión *s.* jactancia; simulación fingida de algo

primacy / primacía *s.* estado de ser el primero en tiempo, orden, rango, etc.

primary / primario *adj.* primero; aquello de lo cual otros se derivan; básico

principles / principios *s.* verdades, leyes, doctrinas o fuerzas motivacionales en las cuales se basan otras

privileged / privilegiado *adj.* no sujeto a las reglas; especial

prodigious / prodigioso *adj.* de gran tamaño o poder

progress / progreso *s.* desarrollo; mejoras

prone / boca abajo *adj.* acostado de cara a la superficie

prophesy/ profetizar *v. predecir* algo que pasará en el futuro

provocative / provocativo *adj.* excitante; estimulante

purified / purificó *v.* libró de impurezas o contaminación; hizo puro

Q

quench / aplacar *v.* satisfacer; llenar las necesidades o deseos de algo

question / preguntar *v.* expresar incertidumbre sobre algo; formular una pregunta

R

radical / radical *adj.* drástico; completo; extremo

rash / imprudente *adj.* demasiado apresurado en el dicho o en el hecho; precipitado

reality / realidad *s.* calidad de ser conforme a la verdad

realizations / entendimientos 1. *s.* cosas que se comprenden o penetran de repente; 2. *s.* cosas que son completamente entendidas

reciprocity / reciprocidad *s.* relaciones de intercambio; interdependencia

reconciliation / reconciliación *s.* reestablecimiento de la amistad y la armonía

recurrent / recurrente *adj.* que sucede una y otra vez

reflect / reflexionar *v.* pensar seriamente sobre algo

regarded / considerado *adj.* tomado en cuenta como

regulate / regular *v.* controlar o dirigir de acuerdo a una norma o principio

rejoiced / regocijó *v.* mostró alegría

rejuvenation / rejuvenecimiento *s.* acto de renovar, de hacer joven o energético una vez más; revitalización

relatable / fácil de relacionarse *adj.* familiar; reconocible

reminiscent / evocativo *adj.* que tiende a recordar; que sugiere

renditions / interpretaciones *s.* presentaciones o ejecuciones

replication / réplica *s.* duplicado; reproducción

represent / representar *v.* presentar una semblanza o una imagen de algo

resistance / resistencia *s.* acto de oponerse o de soportar algo

resolute / resuelto *adj.* que muestra un propósito fijo

resolution / resolución *s.* fuerte determinación; plan o decisión firme

resolve / resolver *v.* llegar a una conclusión o decisión

resonate / resonar *v.* prolongar un sonido que va disminuyendo; acoger positivamente un mensaje

respective / respectivo *adj.* que se aplica separadamente a dos o más personas o cosas

respond / responder *v.* contestar

responsibility / responsabilidad *s.* condición o estado de tener que responder ante alguien o algo; obligación de rendir cuentas por el éxito o el fracaso

reveling / deleitarse *v.* disfrutar; celebrar

reverence / reverencia *s.* sentimiento y muestra de profundo respeto, amor o admiración

reviews / critica 1. *v.* examina cuidadosamente para dar una evaluación; 2. *v.* evalúa

reviled / injurió *v.* habló mal o con dureza de otro

revise / revisar *v.* reconsiderar; modificar

S

sacrifice / sacrificar *v.* ceder o renunciar a algo

sated / saciado *adj.* satisfecho; provisto con más que suficiente

scale / escala 1. *s.* proporción de una pintura o bosquejo frente al objeto o escenario real; 2. *s.* proporción

scrutinized / escudriñó *v.* examinó detenidamente

secular / seglar *adj.* relativo a asuntos mundanos, en comparación con religiosos

self-expression / expresión del carácter propio *s.* afirmación de la personalidad o las emociones propias, o acto de compartirlas con otros

selflessness / desprendimiento *s.* devoción por los intereses de los demás por encima de los propios

sensibility / sensibilidad *s.* valores y percepciones intelectuales, morales o artísticas

serenity / serenidad *s.* estado de calma o paz

servile / servil *adj.* semejante a un esclavo; humildemente sumiso a la autoridad

signal / señalar *v.* indicar; dar a conocer

simulation / simulación *s.* duplicación o reproducción de ciertas características o condiciones a partir de un modelo original; representación

skeptically / escépticamente *adv.* con duda; interrogativamente

slight / desairar *v.* tratar irrespetuosamente o con indiferencia

social / social *adj.* de o relacionado con la sociedad humana u organización de personas

sonorous / sonoro *adj.* que tiene un sonido intenso o impresionante

spare / frugal *adj.* enjuto; descarnado

sparse / escaso *adj.* esparcido; no abundante

spectacle / espectáculo *s.* evento extraño o extraordinario

staidness / sobriedad *s.* estado de estar tranquilo; sosegado

stamina / aguante *s.* resistencia a la fatiga

stance / postura *s.* la forma en que uno se para, especialmente en cuanto a la colocación de los pies

stark / desolado *adj.* desierto; severo

stereotype / estereotipo *s.* noción de un grupo que es demasiado amplia y a menudo incorrecta

strife / refriega *s.* lucha; conflicto

struggle / luchar *v.* hacer un gran esfuerzo; enfrentar dificultades

subdued / alicaído *adj.* quieto; que le falta energía

subjective / subjetivo *adj.* basado en o influenciado por los sentimientos o punto de vista de una persona

subordinate / subordinado *adj.* inferior a otro en importancia o rango

subtle / sutil *adj.* fino; delicado

subversion / subversión *s.* actividad con intención de derrocar algo establecido; rebelión

successive / sucesivo *adj.* siguiendo uno al otro en secuencia

succinct / sucinto *adj.* expresado clara y brevemente

succumb / sucumbir *v.* ceder ante

sullen / taciturno *adj.* malhumorado y que muestra resentimiento

sumptuous / suntuoso *adj.* costoso; espléndido

surmise / suposición *s.* conjetura; idea basada en evidencia que no es concluyente

surpass / sobrepasar *v.* ir más allá; exceder

T

temperate / temperado *adj.* moderado; que se mantiene dentro de los límites

tempering / temperación *s.* acto de cambiar para hacer más apto, generalmente al mezclarlo con otra cosa

tenacious / tenaz *adj.* persistente hasta alcanzar un logro

tentative / tentativo *adj.* vacilante; incierto

tenuous / tenue *adj.* sin fuerza

theorize / teorizar *v.* especular

threshold / umbral *s.* la parte inferior de un portal; entrada o punto de inicio

toil / labor *s.* trabajo arduo y cansado

trajectory / trayectoria *s.* curva o superficie que sigue un camino particular

transcends / trasciende *v.* que va más allá de los límites de; excede

transformative / transformativo *adj.* capaz de cambiar algo a otra forma, estructura o carácter

tremulous / trémulo *adj.* tembloroso; que se estremece

tumult / tumulto *s.* conmoción ruidosa

tyrant / tirano *s.* dictador cruel y opresivo; déspota

U

ulterior / ulterior *adj.* escondido; mas allá de lo que está declarado abiertamente

understanding / entendimiento *s.* poder de comprender y discernir

unifies / unifica *v.* hace de muchas cosas una

unify / unificar *v.* combinar en uno solo

universal / universal *adj.* que existe en todas las cosas

unorthodox / no ortodoxo *adj.* atípico; que rompe con la tradición

urban / urbano *adj.* de la ciudad o relativo a ella

V

vagaries / caprichos *s.* acciones erráticas o impredecibles; antojos

vantage / punto de observación *n.* posición o lugar desde el cual se puede ver

venerable / venerable *adj.* digno de respeto debido a edad o posición

veracious / veraz *adj.* verdadero; honesto

verbal / verbal *adj.* relativo a las palabras

viewpoint / punto de vista *s.* actitud desde la cual se juzgan y consideran situaciones

vigorously / vigorosamente *adv.* con fuerza vital y total

W

wither / marchitarse *v.* secarse; encogerse por falta de humedad

worldview / visión del mundo *s.* filosofía personal sobre el mundo y la vida humana

wrathfully / coléricamente *adv.* con intenso enojo

writhe / retorcerse *v.* hacer movimientos y contorsiones como cuando se siente algún dolor

Index of Skills

Literary Analysis

Comprehension Skills

Writing

Applications

Process

Rubrics for Self-Assessment

Speaking and Listening

Activities

Strategies

Research

Activities

Strategies

Language Conventions

Vocabulary

Assessment

Index of Authors and Titles

The following authors and titles appear in the print and online versions of Pearson Literature.

Additional Selections: Author and Title Index

The following authors and titles appear in the Online Literature Library.

Acknowledgments

Grateful acknowledgment is made to the following for copyrighted material:

Caroline Alexander "A Pilgrim's Search for Relics of the Once and Future King," by Caroline Alexander. © February, 1996, *Smithsonian Magazine,* Volume 26, Number 11, pp. 33–41. Reprinted with permission from the author.

American Psychological Association (APA) "Grit: Perseverance and Passion for Long Term Goals." *Journal of Personality and Social Psychology,* 2007, Vol. 92, No. 6, 1087–1101. The American Psychological Association

Atlanta-Fulton Public Library System "Atlanta-Fulton Public Library System: Library Cards / AFPLS Logo" from Atlanta-Fulton Public Library System One Margaret Mitchell Square Atlanta GA 30303. Copyright © 2006 Atlanta-Fulton Public Library System. All Rights Reserved. Used by permission.

The Bancroft Library, Admin Offices From "Desert Exile: The Uprooting of a Japanese-American Family" pp. 69–78 by Yoshiko Uchida. Copyright © 1982 by University of Washington Press: Seattle. Courtesy of the Bancroft Library, University of California, Berkeley. Used by permission.

James Berardinelli "The Joy Luck Club: A Film Review" by James Berardinelli from *www.reelviews.net*. Copyright © 1993 by James Berardinelli. Used by permission.

Susan Bergholz Literary Services From "In Commemoration: One Million Volumes" by Rudolfo A. Anaya from *A Million Stars*. Copyright © 1995 by Rudolfo Anaya. First published as "In Commemoration: One Million Volumes" in A Mill Stars; Millionth Acquisition for U. of NM General Library, U. of NM Press, 1982. "Tepeyac" by Sandra Cisneros from *Woman Hollering Creek*. Copyright © 1991 by Sandra Cisneros. Published by Vintage Books, a division of Random House, Inc., New York and originally in hardcover by Random House, Inc. Used by permission of Susan Bergholz Literary Services, New York, NY and Lamy, NM. All rights reserved.

Borders Classics "Metamorphoses" by Ovid, translated by A.S. Kline from Daphne. Ann Arbor: Borders Classics, 2004 (AD 8).

Brandt & Hochman Literary Agents, Inc. "By the Waters of Babylon" by Stephen Vincent Benét from *The Selected Works of Stephen Vincent Benet*. Copyright © 1937 by Stephen Vincent Benet Copyright renewed © 1965 by Thomas C. Benet, Stephanic Mahin and Rachel B. Lewis. Used by permission of Brandt & Hochman Literary Agents, Inc.

Brooks Permissions "The Bean Eaters" by Gwendolyn Brooks from *Blacks*. Copyright © 1991 by Gwendolyn Brooks, published by Third World Press, Chicago. Used by Consent of Brooks Permissions.

Curtis Brown Ltd. "The Leader in the Mirror" by Pat Mora from *Teaching Tolerance*. Copyright © 1994 by Pat Mora. First published in *Teaching Tolerance*, published by Southern Poverty Law Center. Used by permission of Curtis Brown, Ltd.

California State University, Fullerton "California State University, Fullerton Catalog: Music" from *http://www.fullerton.edu/catalog*. Used by permission.

Charlotte County Board of County Commissioners "Charlotte-Glades Library System: About the Library / CGLS Logo" from *http://www.charlottecountyfl.com/Library*. Used by permission.

Chicago Tribune "Mothers and daughters: A dazzling first novel illuminations two generations of Chinese-American life" by Michael Dorris from *Chicago Tribune, March 12 1989*.

Estate of Sir Winston Churchill "The Lost Island" in *The Birth of Britain,* by Winston S. Churchill. © 1956. Sterling Publishing Company. Reproduced with permission of Curtis Brown, London on behalf of the Estate of Sir Winston Churchill.

City of Boca Raton "The City of Boca Raton Volunteer Application & Volunteer Service Agreement" from *http://www.ci.boca-raton.fl.us*.

City of Fort Lauderdale "City of Fort Lauderdale Paramedic/Firefighter Examination Process" from *http://ci.ftlaud.fl.us/*. Used by permission.

City of Perry Fire Department "City of Perry Firefighter Application/ Perry, GA Fire Dept. Seal" from *www.perry-ga.gov*. Used by permission.

Don Congdon Associates, Inc. "Contents of the Dead Man's Pockets" by Jack Finney from Collier's, 1950. Copyright © 1956 by Crowell Publishing, renewed 1984 by Jack Finney. "There Will Come Soft Rains" by Ray Bradbury Copyright © 1950 by Crowell Collier Publishing Company, renewed 1977 by Ray Bradbury. Used by permission.

Crown Publishers, a division of Random House, Inc. "Damon and Pythias" by William F. Russell, Ed.D. from *Classic Myths to Read Aloud*. Copyright © 1988 by William F. Russell. Copyright © 1989 by William F. Russell. Used by permission of Crown Publishers, a division of Random House, Inc.

Del Ray Books Excerpt from *Fahrenheit 451* by Ray Bradbury from Del Ray Books. Copyright © 1953 by Ray Bradbury. Copyright renewed © 1981 by Ray Bradbury. All rights reserved.

Dial Books for Young Readers, a division of Penguin Young Readers Group "Cupid and Psyche" by Sally Benson from *Stories of the Gods and Heroes*. Copyright © 1940 by Sally Benson. Copyright © renewed 1968 by Sally Benson. All rights reserved. Used by permission.

Discovery News "Understanding Stonehenge: Two Explanations," by Rossella Lorenzi. © 2012. Discovery News.

DK Publishing "Seeing Things" in *How the Brain Works,* by John McCrone. © 2002. DK Publishing.

Doubleday, a division of Random House, Inc. "The Sun Parlor" by Dorothy West from *The Richer, The Poorer*. Copyright © 1995 by Dorothy West. "The Waking" by Theodore Roethke from *The Collected Poems of Theodore Roethke*. Copyright © 1953 by Theodore Roethke. Used by permission of Doubleday, a division of Random House, Inc.

Doubleday, a division of Random House, Inc. and Emma Sweeney Agency, LLC "Civil Peace" by Chinua Achebe from *Girls at War and Other Stories*. Copyright © 1972, 1973 by Chinua Achebe. Used by permission of Doubleday, a division of Random House, Inc. and Emma Sweeney Agency.

Cornelius Eady "The Empty Dance Shoes" and "The Poetic Interpretation of the Twist" by Cornelius Eady from *Victims of the Latest Dance Craze: Poems by Cornelius Eady*. Copyright © 1985 by Cornelius Eady. All rights reserved. Used by permission.

Eastman & Eastman o/b/o Billy Joel "Hold Fast Your Dreams–and Trust Your Mistakes" by Billy Joel from *Hold Fast Your Dreams: Twenty Commencement Speeches*. Copyright © 1996 by Carrie Boyko and Kimberly Colen. All rights reserved. Used by permission.

Farrar, Straus & Giroux "The Fish" by Elizabeth Bishop from *The Complete Poems 1927–1979.* Copyright © 1979, 1983 by Alice Helen Methfessel. From "Nobel Lecture" by Alexander Solzhenitsyn translated by F.D. Reeve. Translation copyright © 1972 by Farrar, Straus & Giroux, LLC. Copyright © 1972 by the Nobel Foundation. Used by permission of Farrar, Straus and Giroux, LLC. "Early Autumn" by Langston Hughes from *Langston Hughes Short Stories.*

Dr. Renee Friedman "Archaeology's Interactive Dig - Narmer's Temple: Week 1" by Renee Friedman from *http://www.archaeology.org* Copyright © 2003 Archaeological Institute of America. Used by permission.

Sanford J. Greenburger Associates "The Threads of Time" by C.J. Cherryh from *The Collected Short Fiction of C.J. Cherryh.* First Printing, February 2004. All rights reserved. Used by permission.

Grove/Atlantic, Inc. "Science Fiction and the Future," from *Dancing at the Edge of the World,* © 1989 by Ursula K. Le Guin. Used by permission of Grove/Atlantic, Inc. Any third-party use of this material, outside of this publication is prohibited. "Tanka: The Clustering Clouds" from *Anthology of Japanese Literature* by Minamoto no Toshiyori, translated by Donald Keene. Copyright © 1965 by Grove Atlantic, Inc. Used by permission.

Hachette Book Group USA "The Statue that Didn't Look Right" in *Blink: The Power of Thinking Without Thinking,* by Malcolm Gladwell. © 2005. Hachette Book Group USA.

Harcourt, Inc. "The Garden of Stubborn Cats" by Italo Calvino from *Marcovaldo of the Seasons in the City,* copyright © 1963 by Giulio Einaudi editore s.p.a., Torino. English translation by William Weaver copyright © 1983 by Harcourt, Inc. and Martin Secker & Warburg, Ltd. "How to React to Familiar Faces" from *How to Travel with a Salmon & Other Essays* by Umberto Eco, copyright © Gruppo Editoriale Fabbri, Bompiani, Sonzogno, Etas S.p.A., English translation by William Weaver copyright © 1994 by Harcourt, Inc. "Jazz Fantasia" by Carl Sandburg from *Smoke and Steel.* Copyright © 1920 by Harcourt, Inc. and renewed 1948 by Carl Sandburg. "Antigone" by Sophocles from *Sophocles: The Oedipus Cycle, An English Version.* The Oedipus Cycle: An English Version by Dudley Fitts and Robert Fitzgerald, copyright © 1939 by Harcourt Inc., and renewed 1967 by Dudley Fitts and Robert Fitzgerald. This material may not be reproduced in any form or by any means without the prior written permission of the publisher.
CAUTION: All rights, including professional, amateur, motion picture, recitation, lecturing, performance, public reading, radio broadcasting, and television are strictly reserved. Inquiries of all rights should be addressed to Harcourt, Inc., Permissions Dept., Orlando, FL 32887. Used by permission of the publisher.

Harper's Magazine "The Leap" by Louise Erdrich from *Harper's Magazine.* Copyright © 1990 by Harper's Magazine Foundation. Used from the March issue by special permission.

Harvard Observatory "Classifying the Stars" by Annie J. Cannon from *The University of Stars.* Cambridge, Mass.: Harvard Observatory, 1926.

Harvard University Press "Tell all the Truth but tell it slant (#1129)", "The Wind-tapped like a tired man (#436)" by Emily Dickinson from *The Poems of Emily Dickinson,* Thomas H. Johnson, ed., Cambridge, Mass.: The Belknap Press of Harvard University Press, Copyright © 1951, 1955, 1979, 1983 by the President and Fellows of Harvard College. Used by permission of the publishers and the Trustees of Amherst College. Copyright © 1951, 1955, byt the President and Fellows of Harvard College. © Copyright 1914, 1914, 1918, 1919, 1924, 1929, 1930, 1932, 1935, 1937, 1942 by Martha Dickinson Bianchi.

Hispanic Society of America "The Guitar" by Federico García Lorca from *Translations From Hispanic Poets.* Copyright 1938 by The Hispanic Society of America. Used with permission of the Hispanic Society of America.

The Barbara Hogenson Agency, Inc. "The Dog That Bit People" by James Thurber from *My Life and Hard Times.* Copyright © 1933, 1961 by James Thurber. Used by arrangement with Rosemary Thurber and The Barbara Hogenson Agency. All rights reserved.

Houghton Mifflin Company, Inc. "The Marginal World" from *The Edge of the Sea* by Rachel Carson. Copyright © 1955 by Rachel L. Carson, renewed 1983 by Roger Christie. "Prometheus and the First People" (originally titled "The Creation of Man" and "The Coming of Evil") from *Greek Myths* by Olivia E. Coolidge. Copyright © 1949 by Olivia E. Coolidge; copyright renewed © 1977 by Olivia E. Coolidge. Adapted by permission of Houghton Mifflin Company. Text © 1949 by Olivia E. Coolidge. Used by permission of Houghton Mifflin Co. All rights reserved.

David Henry Hwang From "Tibet Through the Red Box" from Act II by David Henry Hwang. Used by permission.

The Jazz Society of Pensacola "The Jazz Society of Pensacola, March 2007 Newsletter" by Andrew R. Metzger from *http://www.jazzpensacola.com.* Copyright © 2001 Jazz Society of Pensacola. Used by permission.

Johnson & Alcock Ltd., London "The Bridegroom" by Alexander Pushkin from *The Bronze Horseman and Other Poems,* Secker & Warburg, 1982. Translation © D.M. Thomas. Used by permission of Johnson and Alcock Ltd., London.

Johnson Outdoors Inc. "Compass Directions and Warranty" by Staff from *www.silvacompass.com* Copyright 2002 Johnson Outdoors Inc. All rights reserved. Used by permission.

Alfred A. Knopf, Inc. From "Swimming to Antarctica: Tales of a Long-Distance Swimmer" by Lynne Cox. Copyright © 2004 by Lynne Cox. "The Weary Blues" by Langston Hughes from *Selected Poems of Langston Hughes,* copyright © 1994 by The Estate of Langston Hughes. Copyright © 1926 Alfred A. Knopf, Inc., Renewed 1954 Estate of Langston Hughes. Used by permission of Alfred A. Knopf, a division of Random House, Inc. All rights reserved. "Youth and Chivalry" in *A Distant Mirror: The Calamitous 14th Century.* Barbara W. Tuchman © 1978. Alfred A. Knopf.

Little, Brown & Company, Inc. "Theseus" from *Mythology* by Edith Hamilton. Copyright © 1942 by Edith Hamilton. Copyright © renewed 1969 by Dorian Fielding Reid and Doris Fielding Reid. By permission of Little, Brown, and Co., Inc.

Liveright Publishing Corporation "Reapers" by Jean Toomer from *Cane.* Copyright 1923 by Boni & Liveright, renewed 1951 by Jean Toomer. Used by permission of Liveright Publishing Corporation.

Los Angeles Public Library "Los Angeles Public Library: Borrower Services" from *http://www.lapl.org.* Used by permission of the City of Los Angeles.

The Jennifer Lyons Literary Agency, LLC "Fear" by Gabriela Mistral from *Selected Poems of Gabriela Mistral,* translated by Doris Dana. Copyright 1961, 1964, 1970, 1971 by Doris Dana. Used by permission.

Marco Mielcarek "Voices from the Wall: Ich bin ein Berliner" by Marco Mielcarek. Used by permission.

Edna St. Vincent Millay Society "Conscientious Objector" by Edna St. Vincent Millay from *Collected Poems.* Copyright © 1934, 1962 by Edna St. Vincent Millay and Norma Millay Ellis. All rights reserved. Copyright © 1917, 1921, 1923, 1928, 1931, 1933, 1934, 1936, 1937, 1938, 1939, 1940, 1941, 1950 by Edna St. Vincent Millay. Copyright ©

1945, 1946, 1947, 1951, 1952, 1953, 1954, 1956 by Norma Millay Ellis. Used by permission of Elizabeth Barnett, literary executor.

Navarre Scott Momaday From "The Way to Rainy Mountain" by N. Scott Momaday. Copyright © 1969 by The University of New Mexico Press. Used by permission.

William Morris Agency "A Visit to Grandmother" by William Melvin Kelley from *Dances on the Shore*. Copyright © 1964, 1992 by William Melvin Kelley. Used by permission of William Morris Agency, LLC on behalf of the author.

National Aeronautics and Space Administration "Black Water Turns the Tide on Florida Coral" from *http://www.nasa.gov*

National Science Teachers Assocation Publications "An Interview with Firefighter Denise Dierich" by Megan Sullivan from *http://newsite.nsta.org* Copyright © 2003 NSTA. Used by permission.

Navajivan Trust From *Defending Nonviolent Resistance* by Mohandas K. Gandhi. Used by permission.

New American Library, a division of Penguin "An Enemy of the People" by Henrik Ibsen from *The Complete Major Prose Plays of Henrik Ibsen* translated by Rolf Fjelde, copyright © 1965, 1970, 1978 by Rolf Fjelde. Used by permission of Dutton Signet, a division of Penguin Group (USA) Inc.

New Directions Publishing Corporation "Do Not Go Gentle into That Good Night" by Dylan Thomas from *The Poems of Dylan Thomas*. Copyright © 1952 by Dylan Thomas. "Spring and All" by William Carlos Williams from *Collected Poems, 1909–1939, Volume I*. Copyright © 1938 by New Directions Publishing Corp. "A Tree Telling of Orpheus" by Denise Levertov from *Poems, 1968–1972*. Copyright © 1965, 1966, 1967,1968, 1969, 1970, 1971 by Denise Levertov Goodman. Copyright © 1970, 1971, 1972, 1987 by Denise Levertov. Used by permission of New Directions Publishing Corp. "I Am Offering This Poem" by Jimmy Santiago Baca from *Immigrants in Our Own Land & Selected Early Poems*. Copyright © 1979 by Jimmy Santiago Baca. Reprinted by permission of New Directions Publishing Corporation.

The New York Times "Mr. Gorbachev's Role" by Staff from *The New York Times (Late Edition)* November 10, 1999. Copyright © 1999 by The New York Times Inc. All rights reserved. Used by permission and protected by the Copyright Laws of The United States. The printing, copying, redistribution, or retransmission of the Material without express written permission is prohibited.

The New York Times Agency "Feel the City's Pulse? It's Be-bop, Man!" by Ann Douglas from *The New York Times August 28, 1998*. Copyright © 1998 by the New York Times. All rights reserved. Used by permission and protected by the Copyright Laws of The United States. The printing, copying, redistribution, or retransmission of the Material without express written permission is prohibited.

North Point Press, div of Farrar, Straus & Giroux "All" by Bei Dao translated by Donald Finkel and Xueliang Chen from *A Splintered Mirror: Chinese Poetry From the Democracy Movement*. Translation copyright © 1991 by Donald Finkel. Used by permission of North Point Press, a division of Farrar, Straus and Giroux, LLC. "Also All" by Shu Ting, translated by Donald Finkel and Jinsheng Yi from *A Splintered Mirror: Chinese Poetry From the Democracy Movement*. Translation copyright © 1991 by Donald Finkel.

Norwegian Nobel Institute Keep Memory Alive" by Elie Wiesel from *Elie Wiesel's Nobel Prize Acceptance Speech*. Used with permission from the Norwegian Nobel Institute. Copyright © 1986 by the Nobel Foundation.

Naomi Shihab Nye "Making a Fist" by Naomi Shihab Nye from *Hugging the Jukebox*. Copyright © 1982 by Dutton: New York. Used by permission of the author, Naomi Shihab Nye.

Harold Ober Associates, Inc. From *Marian Anderson: Famous Concert Singer* by Langston Hughes. Copyright © 1954 by Langston Hughes. Renewed 1982 by George Houston Bass. Used by permission of Harold Ober Associates Incorporated.

Oxford University Press, UK "How Much Land Does a Man Need?" by Leo Tolstoy translated by Louise and Aylmer Maude from *The Raid and Other Stories*. Edited by Maude, Louise & Aylmer. Copyright © 1935 Oxford University Press. Used with permission of Oxford University Press.

Pantheon Books, a div of Random House Inc. "The Orphan Boy and the Elk Dog" by Blackfoot from *American Indian Myths and Legends* by Richard Erdoes and Alfonso Ortiz. Copyright © 1984 by Richard Erdoes and Alfonso Ortiz. Used by permission.

Pearson Education "Tides" by Staff from *Prentice Hall Science Explorer: Earth Science*. Copyright © 2001 by Pearson Education, Inc., publishing as Pearson Prentice Hall. All rights reserved. Used by permission.

Pearson Education Ltd. From "Sundiata: An Epic of Old Mali: Childhood, The Lion's Awakening" by D.T. Niane translated by G.D. Pickett from *Sundiata: An Epic of Old Mali*. Copyright © Longman Group Limited 1965, used by permission of Pearson Education Limited. Copyright © Presence Africaine 1960 (original French version: Soundjata, ou L'Epopee Mandingue) © Longman Group Ltd. (English Version) 1965.

Penguin Group (USA) Inc. "Everest" from *Touch the Top of the World: A Blind Man's Journey to Climb Farther than the Eye Can See* by Erik Weihenmayer. Copyright © 2002 by Erik Weihenmayer. All rights reserved.

Penguin Putnam, Inc From "Places Left Unfinished at the Time of Creation" by John Phillip Santos. Copyright © 1999 by John Philip Santos. All rights reserved. Used by permission.

Psychology Today The Winning Edge: Passion and perseverance may be more important to success than mere talent, by Peter Doskoch. ©2005. *Psychology Today*.

G.P. Putnam's Sons, a division of Penguin "Arthur Becomes King" Part I, Chapter XXII from *The Once and Future King* by T.H. White. Copyright © 1938, 1939, 1940, © 1958 by T. H. White, renewed.

Random House, Inc. From "A Raisin in the Sun, Act I, Scene ii" by Lorraine Hansberry from *A Raisin in the Sun*. Copyright © 1984 by Robert Nemiroff, an an unpublished work. Copyright © 1959, 1966, 1984 by Robert Nemiroff. All rights reserved. "Occupation: Conductorette" from *I Know Why the Caged Bird Sings* by Maya Angelou. Copyright © 1969 by Maya Angelou. All rights reserved. Used by permission. "A Quilt of a Country" by Anna Quindlen from *Loud and Clear*. Copyright © 2004 by Anna Quindlen. All rights reserved. Excerpt(s) from "Youth and Chivalry" in A DISTANT MIRROR: THE CALAMITOUS 14TH CENTURY by Barbara W. Tuchman, copyright © 1978 by Barbara W. Tuchman. Used by permission of Alfred A. Knopf, an imprint of the Knopf Doubleday Publishing Group, a division of Random House LLC. All rights reserved.

Random House Children's Books "Ashputtle" by Jakob and Wilhelm Grimm translated by Ralph Manheim from *Grimm's Tales for Young and Old: The Complete Stories*, copyright © 1977 by Ralph Manheim. Translation copyright © 1977 by Ralph Manheim. All rights reserved. Used by permission of Random House Children's Books, a division of Random House, Inc.

Marian Reiner, Literary Agent "Metaphor" by Eve Merriam from *It Doesn't Always Have to Rhyme.* Copyright © 1964, 1970, 1973, 1986 by Eve Merriam. Used by permission of Marian Reiner.

Rogers, Coleridge and White, Ltd. "Games at Twilight" by Anita Desai from *Games at Twilight and Other Stories.* Copyright © 1978 by Anita Desai. Used by permission of the author c/o Rogers, Coleridge & White Ltd., 20 Powis Mews, London W11 1JN.

Heyden White Rostow "The American Idea" by Theodore H. White from *The New York Times Magazine, July 6, 1986.* Copyright © 1986 by Theodore H. White. Copyright © 1986 by The New York Times Company. All rights reserved. Used by permission.

St. Martin's Press "Circumference: Eratosthenos and the Ancient Quest to Measure the Globe" by Nicholas Nicastro from *The Astrolabe.* St. Martin's Press, 2008.

Scientific American Culture of Shock: Fifty years after Stanley Milgram conducted his series of stunning experiments, psychologists are revisiting his findings on the nature of obedience, by Stephen Reicher and Alexander Haslam. © 2011, *Scientific American.* Reprinted with permission of Scientific American. "The Spider and the Wasp" by Alexander Petrunkevitch from *Scientific American, August, 1952.* Copyright © 1952 by Scientific American, Inc. Used by permission.

The Sheep Meadow Press "Pride" by Dahlia Ravikovitch translated by Chana Bloch and Ariel Bloch from *The Window.* Copyright © 1987 by Chana Bloch. All rights reserved. Used by permission.

Signet Classic *A Doll's House* by Henrik Ibsen from Act I. New York: Signet Classics, 2006. (1879)

Elyse Sommer "A Curtain Up Review: Antigone As Acted and Played by the Three Fates on the Way to Becoming the Three Graces". Review by Elyse Sommer in www.curtainup.com, the online theater magazine. Copyright 2004, Elyse Sommer. Used by permission.

Sonoma County "The County of Sonoma Volunteer Application" from *http://www.sonoma-county.org.* Used by permission.

Talkin' Broadway "Antigone (Theatre Review)" by Matthew Murray from www.talkinbroadway.com. Used by permission.

Jeremy P. Tarcher/Putnam "Making History with Vitamin C (originally titled: Ascorbic Acid)" by Penny Le Couteur and Jay Burreson from *Napoleon's Buttons: How 17 Molecules Changed History.* Copyright © 2003 by Micron Geological Ltd. and Jay Burreson. All rights reserved.

Taylor and Francis Group, LLC "How To Look at Nothing" in *How To Use Your Eyes,* by James Elkins. © 2000. Routledge Publishing, Inc. Reproduced by permission of Taylor and Francis Group, LLC, a division of Informa plc.

Anthony Thwaite "Tanka: "Was it that I went to sleep"" by Ono no Komachi translated and co-edited by Geoffrey Bownas and Anthony Thwaite from *The Penguin Book of Japanese Verse.* "When I went to visit" by Ki no Tsurayuki translated by Bownas & Thwaite from *The Penguin Book of Japanese Verse.* "One cannot ask loneliness" by Priest Jakuren translated by Bownas & Thwaite from *The Penguin Book of Japanese Verse.* Penguin Books copyright © 1964, revised edition 1998. Translation copyright © Geoffrey Bownas and Anthony Thwaite, 1964, 1998. Used by permission.

UCLA Office of Media Relations "Strong Earth Tides Can Trigger Earthquakes" from *http://www.newsroom.ucla.edu/.* Courtesy of UCLA. Used by permission.

David Unger "The Censors" by Luisa Valenzuela translated by Hortense Carpentier from *Open Door: Stories.* Copyright © translation by David Unger. Used by permission.

United States Army Central Army Regulation 600-43: Conscientious Objection. United States Army Central.

University of North Carolina Press The Street of the Canon" by Josefina Niggli from *Mexican Village.* Copyright © 1945 by the University of North Carolina Press, renewed 1972 by Josefina Niggli. Used by permission of the publisher.

U.S. News & World Report Will All the Blue Men End Up in Timbuktu?" by Stefan Lovgren from *US News and World Report, December 7, 1998.* Copyright © 1998 U.S. News & World Report, L.P. All rights reserved. Used by permission.

Viking Penguin, Inc. *Collapse: How Societies Choose to Fail or Succeed,* by Jared Diamond. © 2011. Viking Penguin, Inc. "Like the Sun" by R.K. Narayan, from *Under the Banyan Tree.* Copyright © 1985 by R. K. Narayan. "My City" by James Weldon Johnson from *Saint Peter Relates an Incident.* Copyright © 1935 by James Weldon John, © renewed 1963 by Grace Nail Johnson. All rights reserved. From "What Makes a Degas a Degas?" by Richard Muhlberger. Published by The Metropolitan Museum of Art, New York, and Viking, a Division of Penguin Putnam Books for Young Readers, copyright © 1993 by The Metropolitan Museum of Art. "What Makes a Degas a Degas?" is a registered trademark of The Metropolitan Museum of Art. All rights reserved.

Susan Vreeland "Artful Research" by Susan Vreeland from *The Writer, January 2002.* Copyright © 2001. "Magdalena Looking" by Susan Vreeland from *Girl in Hacinth Blue.* Copyright © 1999 by Susan Vreeland. Available in hardback: MacAdam-Cage; paperback: Penguin. Used with permission.

W. W. Norton & Company, Inc. "Don Quixote", excerpt from *Don Quixote: A Norton Critical Edition: The Ormbsby Translation, Revised,* by Miguel de Cervantes, edited by Joseph Jones and Kenneth Douglas. Copyright © 1981 by W.W. Norton & Company, Inc. Used by permission of W.W. Norton & Company, Inc.

Walker Publishing Company "Imaginary Lines" by Dava Sobel from *Longitude: The True Story of a Lone Genius Who Solved the Greatest Scientific Problem of His Time.* Copyright © Dava Sobel, 1995. All rights reserved. Used by permission.

Wallace Literary Agency, Inc. "Rama's Initiation" from *The Ramayana* by R.K. Narayan. Published by Penguin Books. Copyright © 1972 by R.K. Narayanan. Used by permission of the Wallace Literary Agency, Inc.

Wesleyan University Press "Glory" by Yusef Komunyakaa from *Magic City* (Wesleyan University Press, 1992) Copyright © 1992 by Yusef Komunyakaa and used by permission of Wesleyan University Press.

John Wiley & Sons, Inc. "The Shape of the World" in *Life by the Numbers* by Keith Devilin. © 1999. Used by permission of John Wiley & Sons, Inc.

WNYC, American Public Media and Dubner Productions "The Upside of Quitting" by Stephen J. Dubner. Freakonomics Radio transcript courtesy of WNYC, American Public Media and Dubner Productions. Used by permission.

World Vision Magazine "Thank Heaven for Little Girls" by Rich Stearns from *World Vision Magazine,* Spring 2007. Used by permission.

The Wylie Agency, Inc. "The Garden of Stubborn Cats" by Italo Calvino from *Marcovaldo or the Seasons in the City.* Copyright © 1963 by Guilio Einaudi editore s.p.a., used with the permission of the Wylie Agency Inc. English translation copyright © 1983 by Harcourt Brace Jovanovich, Inc. and Martin Secker & Warburg Limited.

Credits

Photos Credits

Photo locators denoted as follows: Top (T), Center (C), Bottom (B), Left (L), Right (R), Background (Bkgd)

Cover Tom Asz/Shutterstock

000 Digital Vision/Photodisc/Getty Images; 9 Ulf Andersen/Getty Images; 16 andreiuc88/Shutterstock; 22 © Bettmann/CORBIS; 24 (C) © Sebastian Derungs/Reuters/Corbis, (Bkgd) © Alen MacWeeney/CORBIS; 25 pio3/Shutterstock; 26 Frederick Ayer III / Photo Researchers, Inc.; 29 pamelajane/iStockphoto; 33 NathanJamesCox/iStockphoto; 40(C)Dance in Tehuantepec (Danza en Tehuantepec) (c) 2013 Museum Associates/ LACMA. Licensed by Art Resource, NY, (Bkgd) MaraZe/Shutterstock; 43(B)© Images/Corbis, (Bkgd) MaraZe/Shutterstock; 45 (C) John Newcomb / SuperStock; (Bkgd) MaraZe/Shutterstock; 47 Bridgeman Art Library; 52 Axel Seidemann/AP Images; 54 © Jane Hahn/Corbis; 56 Liba Taylor/Corbis; 57 © William Campbell/Sygma/Corbis; 59 Corel Professional Photos CD-ROM™; 64 Bettmann/Corbis; 66 (Bkgd) Annmarie Young/Shutterstock, (Bkgd) Photosani/Shutterstock, (C) Portrait of a Youth, 1959 (oil on board) Surovtsev, Andrei (b.1931)/ Private Collection/The Bridgeman Art Library.; 68 Lebrecht Music & Arts; 71 (Bkgd) Katrina Brown/Shutterstock, (Bkgd) Annmarie Young/ Shutterstock, (C) Candelabra, 2003 (oil on canvas), Ireland, William (Contemporary Artist) / Private Collection / The Bridgeman Art Library; 73 Emperor Franz Joseph At A Ball In Vienna In 1900, To Salute The Start Of A New Century, Gause, Wilhelm(1853-1916 German)Museum der Stadt, Vienna/ Photo, © SuperStock, Inc.; 78 (L) Associated Press, (R)The Granger Collection, NYC — All rights reserved; 80 Transia_art/ Shutterstock; 81 Transia_art/Shutterstock; 83 (L) Scott Griessel/ Creatista/Fotolia, (R) Transia_art/Shutterstock; 84 Transia_art/ Shutterstock; 85 Through a Window, 1922, Farmer, Walter (1887-1947) / Private Collection / The Bridgeman Art Library; 108 worradirek/ Shutterstock; 110 © RG Images/Stock4B/Corbis; 113 LuckyPix/Corbis; 116 Johannes Mann/Corbis; 123 ©robynmac/Fotolia; 124 Kim Komenich//Time Life Pictures/Getty Images; 125 ixer/Shutterstock; 130 © Patrik Giardino/Corbis Outline; 138 Keren Su/Getty Images; 139 Associated Press; 142 Can Balgioglu/Shutterstock; 146 Andreas Feininger/Time & Life Pictures/Getty Images; 147 Getty Images/ Stringer; 150 (R) Judy Eddy/WENN/Newscom, (L) Tish Wells/MCT/Getty Images; 151 Kae Deezign/Shutterstock; 154 Christian Sinibaldi/eyevine/ Redux; 158 Andre Kosters/EPA Photo Lusa/Newscom; 160 (T) Charles Rex Arbogast/AP Images, (L) Lebrecht Music and Arts Photo Library/ Alamy; 168 Lukiyanova Natalia/frenta/Shutterstock; 171 (T) MarcelClemens/Shutterstock, (B) DanTuffs/Getty Images; 174 SSPL/ National Media Museum / Art Resource, NY; 180 © Classic Image / Alamy; 182 Alberto Ruggieri/Illustration Works/Getty Images; 192 Prentice Hall; 200 Mandy Pritty/Photodisc/Getty Images; 206 Newscom; 208 (Bkgd) Attitude/Shutterstock, (C) © Mike Agliolo/CORBIS; 210 Les Stone / Corbis; 213 As for Resolution' (oil on canvas), Brooks, Robin / Private Collection/ The Bridgeman Art Library; 214 Portrait of George III (1738–1820) in his Coronation Robes, c.1760 (oil on canvas), Ramsay, Allan (1713-84) / Private Collection / The Bridgeman Art Library; 215 The Worshipful Company of Clockmakers' Collection, UK / The Bridgeman Art Library; 220 Alison Shaw / AP Photo; 221 © Pam Ingalls/Corbis; 222 © Pam Ingalls/Corbis; 225 © Colin Bootman/ Bridgeman Art Library/ Getty Images; 227 © Pam Ingalls/Corbis; 229 © Pam Ingalls/Corbis; 230 © Pam Ingalls/Corbis; 232 © Everett Collection Inc./Alamy; 234 (C) Bettman/Corbis, (Bkgd) naten/Shutterstock; 235 Corbis; 236 Alain Nogues/ CORBIS SYGMA; 240 Carl Mydans/Time Life Pictures/Getty Images; 242 (C) Petrov Stanislav/Shutterstock, (Bkgd)RoyStudio.eu/ Shutterstock,(CL) Natykach Nataliia/Shutterstock; 243 RoyStudio.eu/ Shutterstock; 244 (L)© SuperStock, Inc.,(Bkgd) RoyStudio.eu/ Shutterstock; 245 (R) Collection of the New-York Historical Society, USA, / The Bridgeman Art Library International,(L)Private Collection, Peter Newark American Pictures / The Bridgeman Art Library International, (Bkgd) RoyStudio.eu/Shutterstock; 250 (L) Courtesy of the Library of Congress, (R)Bettman/Corbis; 252, 253, 254 istockphoto; 253 John A. Anderson/Shutterstock; 257 My Life and Hard Times Copyright ©1933 by James Thurber. Copyright © renewed 1961 by James Thurber. Reprinted by arrangement with Rosemary A. Thurber and The Barbara Hogenson Agency.; 260 My Life and Hard Times Copyright ©1933 by James Thurber. Copyright © renewed 1961 by James Thurber. Reprinted by arrangement with Rosemary A. Thurber and The Barbara Hogenson Agency.; 282 Jon Bower Hong Kong/Alamy; 284 Andy Warhol Foundation/Photo ©The Gallery Collection, Corbis/Joerg Aners ©Andy Warhol Foundation for the Visual Arts/Art Resource,NY; 287 BALTEL/SIPA/Newscom; 292(C)Tomas Abad/Alamy, (Bkgd) ©Kayros Studio/Fotolia; 293 ©Kayros Studio/Fotolia; 295 Archivart/Alamy; 299 Peter Horree/Alamy; 301 Prentice Hall; 304 Rodolfo Arpia/Alamy; 307 Rodolfo Arpia/Alamy; 307 Nimatallah/Art Resource, NY; 309 ZUMA Press, Inc./Alamy; 312 Alex Staroseltsev/Shutterstock; 315 The New York Public Library/Art Resource, NY; 316 Alfonso de Tomas/ Shutterstock; 317 Michael Schmeling/Alamy; 320 Sopotnicki/ Shutterstock; 320 © Brocreative/Fotolia; 321 doc-stock/Alamy; 323 Lightspring/Shutterstock; 324 (Bkgd) Sopotnicki/Shutterstock, (C)©Brocreative/Fotolia; 325 ©Brocreative/Fotolia; 328 ADA_photo/ Shutterstock; 334 Car Reflections, 1970 (acrylic on masonite) by Estes, Richard (b.1936); 121.9x76.2 cm; Indianapolis Museum of Art, USA; Purchased with funds from the Penrod Society and the National Endowment for the Arts/Bridgeman Art Library, © Richard Estes, courtesy Marlborough Gallery, New York; 342 ©Images/Corbis; 346 Album/ Art Resource, NY; 349 Prentice Hall; 354 ©Burstein Collection/Corbis; 362 (TC) AP/Wide World Photos, (BC) Art Resource, NY;(B)The Granger Collection, NYC — All rights reserved,(T) Newscom; 363 Butterfly Hunter/Shutterstock; 364 © Olga Rutko/Fotolia; 366 Album/Art Resource, NY; 368 Before the Wedding, 1890 (oil on canvas), Makovsky, Konstantin Egorovich (1839-1915) / Museum of Art, Serpukhov, Russia / The Bridgeman Art Library; 382 (TC) National Museum and Gallery of Wales, Cardiff/Bridgeman Art Library, (C) The Granger Collection, New York, (T) Nat'l Portrait Gallery London/SuperStock, (B)V&A Images, London/Art Resource, NY, (BC)©Asian Art & Archaeology, Inc./Corbis; 383 (Bkgd)istockphoto, (R)Georgios Kollidas/Fotolia, 384 Rijksmuseum Kroller-Muller, Otterlo, Netherlands / The Bridgeman Art Library; 386 © Patti Mollica / SuperStock; 388 Bibliotheque Nationale, Paris, France/ The Bridgeman Art Library394 Time Life Pictures/Getty Images; 394 (C) Everett Collection Inc/Alamy, (T) Dan Porges; 395 Bridgeman Art Library; 396 Grischa Georgiew/Shutterstock; 396 Grischa Georgiew/ Shutterstock; 398 Alfred Eisenstaedt/Pix Inc./Time & Life Pictures/Getty Images; 399 © Michael A. Keller/Corbis; 406 (T)The Granger Collection, New York, (TC)Bettmann/Corbis,(B) The Granger Collection, New York, (BC) Everett Collection Inc/Alamy; 408 Smithsonian American Art Museum, Washington, DC / Art Resource, NY; 410 Patti Mollica/ Superstock; 412 3LH-Fine Art/SuperStock; 416 (B)Dorothy Alexander,(C) Alberto Paredes/Alamy; 418 (T) L. Caryle/WENN/Newscom,(C) Getty Images, Inc.,(TL) CBW/Alamy, (TR) L. Caryle/WENN/Newscom; 422 © xiaoliangge/Fotolia; 423 Bridgeman Art Library; 444 Luis Davilla/ Photodisc/Getty Images; 446 Corel Corporation; 451 AP Photo/New Directions, The Luce Studio; 462 (Bkgd) Irina_QQQ/Shutterstock,(L) wongwean/Shutterstock,(CL) Iakov Filimonov/Shutterstock; 467 Pirie MacDonald/Corbis; 470 Collection of the Nevada Museum of Art, purchased with partial funding from City of Reno Arts and Culture Commission.;476Donald Sawvel/Shutterstock; 480 WorldPhotos/Alamy; 483 Corbis; 484 PhotoXite/Shutterstock; 487 Chris Felver/Getty Images; 487 ivanovskyy/Shutterstock; 490 ©Skyscan/Corbis; 496 Ivan Vdovin/ Alamy; 500 © Macduff Everton/Corbis; 503 Tom Johnson/Newscom;

514 ©Marc Dozier/Hemis/Corbis; 523 Bettmann/CORBIS; 530 Mlenny Photography/Getty Images; 536(BR)©V&A Images/Alamy Images, (BCL) ©Mary Evans Picture Library/Alamy Images, (CR) ©Classic Images/ Alamy Images, (BCR) ©Lebrecht Music and Arts Photo Library/Alamy Images,(BCL)Scala/Ministero per I Beni e le Attivita Culturali/Art Resource, NY; 537 ©Mary Evans Picture Library/The Image Works; 538 ©Mary Evans Picture Library/The Image Works; 539 ©Jeremy Hoare PCL/Superstock; 540 ©Steve Vidler/SuperStock; 542 Erich Lessing/Art Resource, NY; 544 © RMN-Grand Palais/Art Resource,NY; 546 (L)© Bettmann/CORBIS, (Bkgd) Georgios Kollidas/Shutterstock; 549 Painting from the Villa Boscoreale (fresco), Roman, (1st century BC)/Museo Archeologico Nazionale, Naples, Italy, Giraudon/Bridgeman Art Library; 550 Picture Post/Stringer/Getty Images; 553 © Sunset Boulevard/Corbis; 560 Scala/Art Resource; 565 Nimatallah/Art Resource, NY; 570 (B) Death of Julius Caesar (100-44 BC) (oil on canvas) by Vincenzo Camuccini (1773–1844). Museo e Gallerie Nazionali di Capodimonte, Naples, Italy/The Bridgeman Art Library, (T)fabiomax/ Fotolia; 576 Everett Collection, Inc.; 580 Hulton Archive/Getty Images; 582 (CR) © Doug Pearson/JAI/Corbis, (BR)Mary Evans Picture Library/ Alamy, (L)© RMN-Grand Palais/Art Resource, NY; 585 Gianni Dagli Orti/ Art Resource, NY586 Reunion de Musees Nationaux/Art Resource, NY; 587 (c) RMN-Grand Pailais/Art Resource, NY; 588 Archive Timothy McCarthy/Art Resource, NY; 594 (B)©RMN-Grand Palais/Art Resource, NY, (R) Georgios Kollidas/Shutterstock; 596 Pearson Education, Inc.; 597 © Doug Pearson/JAI/Corbis; 598 The Kobal Collection at Art Resource, NY; 605 © John Springer Collection/CORBIS; 608 © Bettmann/CORBIS; 612 AF archive/Alamy; 615 Alinari/Art Resource, NY;620 (BL)© Bettmann/CORBIS, (R) Georgios Kollidas/Shutterstock, (Bkgd) fabio-max/Fotolia; 623 Hulton Archive/Stringer/Getty Images; 627 Dagli Orti/ The Art Archive at Art Resource, NY0630 Erich Lessing/Art Resource, NY;630 Erich Lessing/Art Resource, NY; 634 fabiomax/Fotolia; 636 Reunion de Musees Nationaux/Art Resource, NY; 640 (BR)Museo Nzaionale del Bargello, Florence,Italy/Alinari/The Bridgeman Art Library,(R) Georgios Kollidas/Shutterstock, (Bkgd) fabiomax/Fotolia; 645 New Walk Museum, Leicester City Museum Service. UK/The Bridgeman Art Library; 647 Hulton Archive/Stringer/Getty Images; 653 Hulton Archive/Stringer/Getty Images; 660 (C) © Bettmann/CORBIS,(L) Everett Collection Inc.; 684 ©Bettmann/Corbis; 692 Erich Lessing/Art Resource, NY; 699 The Metropolitan Museum of Art/Art Resource, NY; 719 Mary Evans Picture Library/Alamy; 724 Classic Image/Alamy; 737 © de Keerle-Le Segretain/Sygma/Corbis; 738 Ollf Lindeborg/AFP/ GettyImages; 740 Smithsonian American Art Museum, Washington, DC/Art Resource, NY; 742 Everett Collection Inc.; 743 Javier Moreno/ picture-alliance / dpa/Newscom; 757 United States Army; 760 © Bettmann/Corbis; 768 Fine Art Images/SuperStock/Getty Images; 778 Colin McPherson/CORBIS; 786 ©Araldo de Luca/Corbis; 792 Courtesy, Houghton Mifflin Company; 794 Art Resource, NY; 794 Ela Kwasniewski/ Shutterstock; 796 dragunov/Shutterstock; 797 Pandora, Oil on canvas, Private Collection/Photo: The Bridgeman Art Library; 800 Nimatallah/Art Resource, NY; 806 David Wisniewski/ Houghton Mifflin Company; 0810 John Lei/ Omni-Photo Communications, Inc.; 813 Pierre-Yves Babelon/ Shutterstock; 814 The Granger Collection; 815 Getty Images; 822 Niday Picture Library/Alamy; 823 bpk, Berlin (Muenzkabinett, Staaliche Museen)/Art Resource, NY; 828 The Granger Collection, New York83 Nicku/Shutterstock; 832 Bridgeman Art Library; 833 Nicku/ Shutterstock; 835 Don Quixote, Pablo Picasso, Bridgeman Art Library, London/New York, ©2004Estate of Pablo Picasso/Artists Rights Society (ARS), New York/ Photo: The Bridgeman Art Library, NY; 837 Nicku/ Shutterstock; 838 Nicku/Shutterstock; 842 (L) Sir Edward Burne-Jones/ The Bridgeman Art Library,(R)Bettman/ Corbis; 844 Sir Edward Burne-Jones/The Bridgeman Art Library; 846 Sir Edward Burne-Jones/ The Bridgeman Art Library; 852 Bettman/Corbis; 855 Charles Perrault/ Bridgeman Art Library; 878 ©Stapleton Collection/Corbis; 880 Arletta Cwalina/Alamy; 883 Arletta Cwalina/Alamy; 891 The Granger Collection; 898 (Border) Vector/ Shutterstock, (R)Hilary Morgan/Alamy; 903 InterfotoAlamy; 907 Bettmann/ Corbis; 910 ©20th Century Fox Film Corp. All rights reserved/Everett Collection.; 914 Everett Collection Inc.; 921 (B)Library of Congress, (T) Steve Bloom Images/Alamy; 924 Superstock; 929 Erich Hartmann/Magnum Photos; 933 Ancient Art & Architecture Collection Ltd/Alamy; 935 David Cole/Alamy; 938 SuperStock/Alamy; 941 Janette Beckman/Getty Images; 944 J.B. Handelsman/The New Yorker Collection/cartoonbank.

Staff Credits

Dori Amtmann, Tricia Battipede, Rachel Beckman, Nancy Bolsover, Laura Brancky, Odette Calderon, Pam Carey, Kelly Casanova, Geoff Cassar, Jessica Cohn, Sarah Cunningham. Anthony DeSacia, Kim Doster, Irene Ehrmann, Andy Ekedahl, Sandy Engleman, Samantha Fahy, Janet Fauser, Amy Fleming, Pam Gallo, Mark Gangi, Nicole Gee, Susan Graef, Leslie Griffin, Elaine Goldman, Brian Hawkes, Steve Hernacki, Martha Heller, Amanda House, Rick Hickox, Patricia Isaza, Etta Jacobs, Blair Jones, Jim Kelly, Nathan Kinney, Sarah Kraus, Gregory Lynch, Nancy Mace, Jim McPherson, Charles Morris, Pa Moua, Elizabeth Nielsen, Kim Ortell, Kathleen Pagliaro, Jennie Rakos, Sheila Ramsay, Karen Randazzo, Julianne Regnier, Christopher Richardson, Melissa Schreiner, Hillary Schwei, Jeff Shagawat, Susan Sheehan, Charlene Smith, DeAnn Smith, Sheila Smith, Cynthia Summers, Morgan Taylor, Brian Thomas, Lucia Tirondola, Karen Tully, Merle Uuesoo, Kristen Varina, Jackie Westbrook, Jessica White